ENCYCLOPEDIA OF CONTEMPORARY LATIN AMERICAN AND CARIBBEAN CULTURES

ENCYCLOPEDIA OF CONTEMPORARY LATIN AMERICAN AND CARIBBEAN CULTURES

Volume 1: A–D

Edited by
Daniel Balderston, Mike Gonzalez
and Ana M. López

London and New York

First published 2000
by Routledge
11 New Fetter Lane, London EC4P 4EE

Simultaneously published in the USA and Canada
by Routledge
29 West 35th Street, New York, NY 10001

Routledge is an imprint of the Taylor & Francis Group

© 2000 Routledge

Typeset in Baskerville by Taylor & Francis Books Ltd
Printed and bound in Great Britain by TJ International Ltd,
Padstow, Cornwall

British Library Cataloguing in Publication Data
A catalogue record for this book is available from the British Library

Library of Congress Cataloging in Publication Data
Encyclopedia of contemporary Latin American and Caribbean cultures/
edited by Daniel Balderston, Mike Gonzalez and Ana M. López.
p. cm
Includes bibliographical references and index.
1. Latin America–Encyclopedias. 2. Caribbean Area–Encyclopedias.
I. Balderston, Daniel, 1952- II. Gonzalez, Mike. III. López, Ana M.
F1406 .E515 2000
972.9'003–dc21   00–032303

ISBN 0–415–13188–X (set)
ISBN 0415–22971–5 (vol 1)
ISBN 0415–22972–3 (vol 2)
ISBN 0415–22973–1 (vol 3)

Contents

Editorial team

List of contributors

Gerard Aching
New York University, USA

Rosanne Adderley
University of Virginia, USA

Gonzalo Aguilar
University of Buenos Aires, Argentina

Funso Aiyejina
Trinidad

Pablo Alabarces
Argentina

María Alba Bovisio
Argentina

Jill E. Albada-Jelgersma
USA

Elizabeth Allen
University of Glasgow, UK

Diego Alonso
Reed College, USA

Daniel Altamiranda
Arizona State University, USA

Teresa Alvarenga
Venezuela

Gaston Alzate
Arizona State University, USA

Adriana Amante
Universidad de Buenos Aires, Argentina

Danny J. Anderson
University of Kansas, USA

Pablo Javier Ansolabehere
Argentina

Raul Antelo
Universida de Federal de Santa Catarina, Brazil

Pauline Antrobus
UK

David Appleby
USA

María Pilar Aquino
Mexico, USA

Joseph Arbena
Clemson University, USA

Eduardo Archetti
University of Oslo, Norway

Arturo Arias
University of Redlands, USA

Guillermo Arisó
Argentina

Charles Arthur
UK

Jon Askeland
University of Nergen, Norway

Daniel Balderston
University of Iowa, USA

Fernando Balseca
Universidad Andina Simón Bolívar, Ecuador

María José Somerlate Barbosa
University of Iowa, USA

Isabel Barbuzza
University of Iowa, USA

Efraín Barradas
University of Massachussetts, USA

Cristina L. Barros
Mexico

Paul Bary
Tulane University, USA

Isabel Bastos
University of Maryland, USA

Janette Becerra
University of Puerto Rico

Catherine L. Benamou
Duke University, USA

Diego Bentivegna
Argentina

José Bernardi
Arizona State University, USA

Leopoldo Bernucci
University of Colorado, USA

Trish Bethany
Grenada

Esperanza Bielsa
University of Glasgow, UK

Kenneth Bilby
USA

Rudi Bleys
Belgium

Álvaro Félix Bolaños
University of Florida, USA

Mary Boley
Goldsmiths College, UK

Libertad Borda
Argentina

Karen Bracken
Tulane University, USA

César Braga-Pinto
Rutgers University, USA

Luis Britto García
Universidad Central de Venezuela

Aart G. Broek
Curaçao

Stephen Brown
University of Toronto, Canada

James Buckwalter-Arias
Whitman College, USA

Marcos Buenrostro
Mexico

Michael Burnett
University of Surrey, Roehampton, UK

Magdalena Cajías de la Vega
Bolivia

Erik Camayd-Freixas
Florida International University, USA

María Marta Camisassa
Universidade Federal de Viçosa, Brazil

Wilfredo Cancio Isla
USA

Luis E. Cárcamo-Huechante;
Cornell University, USA

Miguel A Cardinale
USA

Susana Carro-Ripalda
UK

Violeta Casal

Nel Casimiri
Netherlands Antilles

Beatriz Castillo
Argentina

Rafael Castillo Zapata
Universidad Central de Venezuela

Sara Castro-Klaren
Johns Hopkins University, USA

Horacio Cerutti Guldberg
UNAM, Mexico

Silvia Chaves
USA

Sergio Chefjec
Venezuela

Santiago Colás
University of Michigan, USA

Roberto Conduru
Universidade do Estado do Rio de Janeiro, Brazil

Eduardo Contreras Soto
CENIDIM, Mexico

Scott A. Cooper
Hanover College, USA

Beatriz Cortez
Arizona State University, USA

Tania Costa Tribe
University College London, UK

Sandra Courtman
UK

Linda J. Craft
North Park University, USA

Lourdes Cruz González Franco
Mexico

Tessa Cubitt
University of Portsmouth, UK

Linda A. Curcio-Nagy
University of Nevada, USA

Celia Langdeau Cussen
Chile

Sofia da Silva Telles
Brazil

Leslie H. Damasceno
Duke University, USA

Maria Julia Daroqui
Spain

J. Michael Dash
University of the West Indies, Jamaica

Silvana Daszuk
Argentina

Darién Davis
Middlebury College, USA

Sophia de la Calle
USA

Sergio de la Mora
University of California at Davis, USA

J.M. de la Vega Rodríguez
Bolivia

Catherine Den Tandt
University of Montreal, Canada

Eduardo Di Mauro
Instituto Latinoamericano del Títere

Mark Dinneen
University of Southampton, UK

Ruth Dominguez
USA

Christopher Dunn
Tulane University, USA

Pat Dunn
University of the West Indies

Thomas Edsall
Tulane University, USA

Jorge Elbaum
Argentina

Maria Elva Echenique
USA

Sarah Chon England
USA

Juan Armando Epple
University of Oregon, USA

Luis L. Esparza Serra
El Colegio de Michoacan, Mexico

Cynthia Estep
USA

José Antonio Evora
USA

Héctor D. Fernández L'Hoeste
Georgia State University, USA

Alvaro Fernández-Bravo
Universidad de San Andrés, Argentina

Cristina Ferreira-Pinto
University of Texas at Austin, USA

Nuala Finnegan
National University of Ireland, Cork

Edward F. Fischer
Vanderbilt University, USA

Evelyn Fishburn
University of North London, UK

Enrique Foffani
Argentina

Jacinto Fombona
USA

Aníbal Ford
Argentina

Merlin H. Forster
Brigham Young University, USA

David William Foster
Arizona State University, USA

Joe Foweraker
University of Essex, UK

Jean Franco
Columbia University, USA

Valerie Fraser
University of Essex, UK

Juan Carlos Gamboa
USA

Sandra Garabano
Gettysburg College, USA

Magdalena García Pinto
University of Missouri, USA

Florencia Garramuño
Universidad de San Andrés, Argentina

Sandra Gasparini
Universidad de Buenos Aires, Argentina

Alan Gilbert
University College London, UK

Gabriel Giorgi
New York University, USA

Norah Giraldi Dei Cas
Université de Lille, France

Margo Glantz
UNAM, Mexico

John Gledson
University of Liverpool, UK

Florinda F. Goldberg
Hebrew University of Jerusalem, Israel

Ilene S. Goldman
USA

Brian Gollnick
University of Iowa, USA

Mike Gonzalez
University of Glasgow, UK

Laura Graham
University of Iowa, USA

Andrew Graham-Yooll
Argentina

Duncan Green
UK

Alex Greene
University of California, Davis, USA

Guillermo Gregorio
USA

Alejandro Grimson
Argentina

Mihai Grünfeld
Vassar College, USA

Lucía Guerra
University of California, USA

Eduardo Guízar-Alvarez
University of Iowa, USA

Luis Gusman
Argentina

Bret Gustafson
Harvard University, USA

Donna J. Guy
University of Arizona, USA

Oscar Hahn
University of Iowa, USA

Jorge Halperin
Argentina

E. Brooke Harlowe
College of St. Catherine, USA

Olivia Harris
Goldsmiths College, UK

Regina Harrison
University of Maryland, USA

John Harvey
Tulane University, USA

Milton Hatoum
Universidade Nacional de Amazonas, Brazil

Joy E. Hayes
University of Iowa, USA

Ben A. Heller
Hofstra University, USA

Theordore A. Henken
Tulane University, USA

James Higgins
University of Liverpool, UK

Jonathan D. Hill
Southern Illinois University, USA

Servando Z. Hinojosa
Tulane University, USA

Norman S. Holland
Hampshire College, USA

Lennox Honeychurch
University of Oxford, UK

Amanda Hopkinson
Cardiff University, UK

Harry Howard
Tulane University, USA

Cristina Iglesia
University of Buenos Aires, Argentina

Veronica Jaffé
Venezuela

Clara Alicia Jalif de Bertranou
Argentina

Louis James
University of Kent at Canterbury, UK

Pablo Jamilis
Argentina

Alejandra Jaramillo
Tulane University, USA

Keith Jardim
Trinidad

Randal Johnson
University of California at Los Angeles, USA

Bridget Jones
UK

Amy Kaminsky
University of Minnesota, USA

Liam Kane
University of Glasgow, UK

Cristóbal Kay
Institute of Social Studies, The Hague, The Netherlands

Diana Kay
The Open University, The Netherlands

John King
University of Warwick, UK

Gwen Kirkpatrick
University of California, USA

Thomas Klingler
Tulane University, USA

John Kraniauskas
Birbeck College, UK

Pablo Kreimer
Universidad de Quilmes, Argentina

Alejandra Laera
University of Buenos Aires, Argentina

David Lehmann
Cambridge University, UK

Lorraine Leu
King's College London, UK

Thomas A. Lewis
University of Iowa, USA

Tracy K. Lewis
State University of New York at Oswego, USA

Lazaro Lima
Dickinson College, USA

Daniel Link
Universidad de Buenos Aires, Argentina

Sita Dickson Littlewood
UK

Fernanda Longo Elia
Argentina

Maria Angelica Guímaráes Lopes
University of South Carolina, USA

Ana M. López
Tulane University, USA

Tomas López-Pumarejo
Canada/USA

Esteban E. Loustaunau
Ohio State University, USA

George Lovell
Queens University, Canada

Donna Lybecker

Roberto Madero
Richard Stockton College of New Jersey, USA

Marco Maggi
USA

Anne Malena
University of Alberta, Canada

Anupama Mande
Yale University, USA

Monica Mansour
Mexico

Celina Manzoni
Universidad de Buenos Aires, Argentina

Gerald Martin
University of Pittsburgh, USA

Victor Martínez Escamilla
Universidad Autónoma Metropolitana, Mexico

Stella Martini
Argentina

Tony Mason
De Montfort University, UK

Judith Maxwell
Tulane University, USA

David Maybury-Lewis
Harvard University, USA

Nora Mazziotti
Universidad de Buenos Aires, Argentina

José Antonio Mazzotti
Temple University, USA

Michael McClintock
Human Rights Watch, USA

Richard V. McGehee
Concordia University at Austin, USA

Ximena Medinaceli
Bolivia

Marit Melhuus
University of Oslo, Norway

Anupama Mende

Teresa Méndez-Faith
Saint Anselm College, USA

Carlos Mesa
Bolivia

Francesca Miller
USA

Carlos Monsiváis
Mexico

Graciela Montaldo
Universidad Simón Bolivar, Venezuela

Winston Moore
Bolivia

Samuel Morales

Pamela Mordecai
Canada

Nancy Morris
Temple University, USA

Luiz Mott
University of Bahia, Brazil

Stephen Mumme
Colorado State University, USA

Julie Murphy Erfani
Arizona State University West, USA

Graciela Musachi
Argentina

Edith Negrín
Colegio de Mo-Murcia

University of Iowa, USA

Rita K. Noonan
University of Iowa, USA

Philip O'Brien
University of Glasgow, UK

Hugh O'Shaughnessy
UK

Rafael Olea Franco
Colegio de M Paulo, Brazil

Juan Carlos Orihuela
Bolivia

Eliana Ortega
Chile

Alicia Ortega
Universidad Andina Simón Bolívar, Ecuador

Roberto Carlos Ortiz
Tulane University, USA

David Oubiña
Universidad de Buenos Aires, Argentina

Carola Oyarzún
Pontificia Universidad Católica de Chile

Alfonso Padilla
University of Helsinki, Finland

Jussi Pakkasvirta
University of Helsinki, Finland

Diana Paladino
Universidad de Buenos Aires, Argentina

Carlos Paolillo
Instituto Universitario de Danza, Venezuela

Roger L. Parks
University of Iowa, USA

Betsy Partyka
Ohio University, USA

John Patton
Tulane University, USA

Marcial Hector Pavon
Argentina

Rodrigo Peiretti
Argentina

Marta Peixoto
New York University, USA

Juan Pellicer
University of Oslo, Norway

Rosalina Perales
Universidad de Puerto Rico

Amalia Pereira
University of Iowa, USA

Luis Pérez Oramas
Venezuela

Gabriel Pérez-Barreiro, USA
Americas Society, USA

John D. Perivolaris
University of Manchester, UK

Charles A. Perrone
University of Florida, USA

Derek Petrey
Ohio State University, USA

Marina Pianca
University of California at Riverside, USA

Zuzana M. Pick
Carlton University, Canada

Jouni Pirttijärvi
University of Helsinki, Finland

Laura Podalsky
Ohio State University, USA

Brian H. Pollitt
University of Glasgow, UK

Marianna Pool Westgaard
Colegio de México, Mexico

Julio Premat
Université de Lille, France

Antonio Prieto-Stambaugh
El Colegio de Michoacán, Mexico

Shalini Puri
University of Pittsburgh, USA

Susan Canty Quinlan
University of Georgia, USA

Juan Carlos Quintero Herencia
Puerto Rico

José Quiroga
George Washington University, USA

Fernando Rabossi
Argentina

Cecilia Rabossi
Brazil

Karen Ranucci
USA

Ivan Reyna
University of California, USA

Barbara D. Riess
Arizona State University, USA

Marcie D. Rinka
Tulane University, USA

Alicia Ríos
Universidad Simón Bolívar, Venezuela

June Roberts
USA

J. Timmons Roberts
Tulane University, USA

Ian Robertson
The University of the West Indies

Humberto E. Robles
Northwestern University, USA

Mercedes Robles
Loyola University of Chicago, USA

Ileana Rodríguez
Ohio State University, USA

María Cristina Rodríguez
University of Puerto Rico

María Elena Rodríguez Castro
University of Puerto Rico

Paula Rodríguez Marino
Argentina

Grínor Rojo
Universidad de Chile, Chile

Jorge Romero León
Universidad de Venezuela, Venezuela

Fernando J. Rosenberg
Johns Hopkins University, USA

Beatriz Rossells
Bolivia

Carlos Rosso Orozco
Bolivia

Victoria Ruétalo
Tulane University, USA

César Salas
Arizona State University, USA

Josefa Salmón
University of California, USA

Frank Salomon
University of Wisconsin, USA

Eduardo Santa Cruz
Hanover College, USA

Vivaldo Santos
Georgetown University, USA

Oscar D. Sarmiento
SUNY at Potsdam, USA

Elaine Savory
USA

Julio Schvartzman
University of Buenos Aires, Argentina

Jorge Schwartz
Universidade de São Paulo, Brazil

T.M. Scruggs
University of Iowa, USA

Ana Seoane

Maaria Seppänen
University of Helsinki, Finland

Nicolau Sevcenko
Universidade de São Paulo, Brazil

Peggy Sharpe
University of Mississippi, USA

Maureen Shea
Tulane University, USA

Peter Lloyd Sherlock
University of East Anglia, UK

Amelia Simpson
USA

Laura Siri
Argentina

Elzbieta Sklodowska
Washington University, USA

Saúl Sosnowski
University of Maryland, USA

Cynthia Steele
University of Washington, USA

Maarten Steenmeijer
University of Nijmegen, Holland

Camilla Stevens
Rutgers University, USA

Ann Marie Stock
College of William and Mary, USA

Joseph Straubhaar
Brigham Young University, USA

Hernan G.H. Taboada
UNAM, Mexico

Julie Thompson
University of California at Los Angeles, USA

Dolores Tierney
Tulane University, USA

Claudia Torre
Universidad de Buenos Aires, Argentina

Carlos Alberto Torres
University of California at Los Angeles, USA

Víctor Federico Torres
Universidad de Puerto Rico

Patricia Torres San Martín
Universidad de Guadalajara, Mexico

Mary Jane Treacy
Simmons College, USA

David Treece
King's College London, UK

Liliana Trevizán
SUNY at Potsdam, USA

Mark Ungar
Brooklyn College, USA

Vicky Unruh
University of Kansas, USA

Nicasio Urbina
Tulane University, USA

USP Group – University of São Paulo Group
Carlos Augusto Calil

Carlos Adriano

Alfredo Manevy

Eduardo Morettin

Manoel Rangel

Leandro Saraiva

Fernando Valerio-Holguín
Colorado State University, USA

Raúl Vallejo
Universidad Andina Simón Bolívar, Ecuador

Mirta Varela
Argentina

Tito Vasconcelos
UNAM, Mexico

Antonio Carlos Vaz
USA

Adam Versényi
University of North Carolina, USA

Douglas W. Vick
University of Stirling, UK

María Dora Villa Gómez
Bolivia

Christopher von Nagy
Tulane University, USA

Elina Vuola
University of Helsinki, Finland

Berta Waldmann
Universidade Estadual de Campinas, Brazil

Carol J. Wallace
Central College, USA

Anne Walmsley
UK

Peter Watt
University of Iowa, USA

Eric Weil
Argentina

Liliana Weinberg
UNAM, Mexico

Irene Wherritt
University of Iowa, USA

Neil Lancelot Whitehead
University of Wisconsin–Madison, USA

Gay Wilentz
East Carolina University, USA

Raymond L. Williams
University of Colorado, USA

Sergio Wolf
Argentina

David Wood
University of Sheffield, UK

Simon Wright
Oxford University Press, UK

Ismail Xavier
Universidade de Sâo Paulo, Brazil

George Yudice
New York University, USA

Juan Zevallos-Aguilar
Temple University, USA

Marc Zimmerman
University of Illinois at Chicago, USA

Liliana Zuccotti
University of Buenos Aires, Argentina

Fernanda A. Zullo
Whitman College, USA

Introduction

Culture is concerned with networks and connections – what Raymond Williams called 'structures of feeling'. Despite the existence of innumerable histories of Latin American and Caribbean art, literature and music, for example, their development is not and cannot be seen in isolation from one another, or indeed from any of the multiple behaviours and practices through which human beings apprehend, make sense of, organize, and represent the world. Every cultural act – and by that we understand everything from making a painting to building a house, or speaking about either activity – is an event which relates to other practices, whether previous or contemporary, and in turn shapes and frames every successive such act. So at whatever point we enter that complex of relations, we will encounter or at least become aware of the presence of other objects, acts and relationships. This whole is what we call culture.

This work is in our view the first serious attempt to trace those interconnections in the cultures of Latin America and the Caribbean without being captive to artificial internal divisions and exclusions, which often obscure those networks. Thus, we can quite happily acknowledge the different forms, genres, movements, spaces and institutions in which cultural activity takes place without an impulse to placing them in a hierarchical relation to one another and thus give differential weight to the many manifestations of that activity of understanding and representing the world. Therefore, without apology we include within the cultural sphere, which we have set out to map in these volumes, the whole range of 'structures of feeling' and material practices that constitute the contemporary culture of the many countries of Latin America and the Caribbean. This embraces 'the arts' – literary, visual and performative – but also forms of social organization; expressions of collective experience, ritual, religious or political; mass culture, both as patterns of consumption and forms of resistance; material culture, including food, drink, sport, and the other rituals of daily life; and of course the historical frame in which all of this takes place.

Our cultural mapping of this complicated and contradictory region has to accomplish two things at the same time: on the one hand, tracing lines of connection that link events and structures that co-exist at any one time, and on the other, understanding their relationships through time and their particular and shared histories. So the ambitious task we have set ourselves is to attempt to locate important cultural events, sites and moments, while at the same time seeing them as parts of a whole series of different constellations. So, any single cultural act can belong within a class of such acts – writing, performing, organizing, making, for example – while occurring within a space – national, urban or rural, interior or exterior, limited or open – which will equally give the act its meaning. It will also be bounded by the social origins and location of its participants, shaped by gender, race, class, sexuality and ethnicity, and as such also participate in their desires, hopes and aspirations. These in turn will give entirely legitimate descriptive terms like 'utopian', 'realist', 'adaptive', 'cooperative' or indeed 'revolutionary' a specific reference in time and space, as well as a disciplinary function that has to do with ordering and representing.

The format of this work is alphabetical, which of course highlights the accidental ordering of the material that follows. However, the 'keywords' that are the titles of our entries function as nodes in a network: points that are not only significant in themselves, but also as connectors and sites of tension or contradiction. Like the vast networks that the Venezuelan artist Gego builds, invading the sanitized spaces of museums and galleries, and involving the spectator in a sometimes uncomfortable journey through asymmetrical and unexpected spaces, a journey into culture should be full of surprises and unpredictable twists and turns.

A simply linear reading betrays that complexity, though we certainly invite our readers to seek out narratives that run through the text. In a way, the decade entries that open this work (because they do not fit comfortably in the alphabetical list) provide a sort of temporal narrative frame. In the same sense, the country entries offer another story locating the same series of events in space; other plots arise out of generic entries which look at cultural acts in terms of their internal laws and classifications (fields, disciplines, genres, movements). A quite different journey would be taken if the reader jumped through the work following the cross-references ('see alsos' and boldface keywords) in pursuit of connections that have more to do with the particular than the general. For example, the several possible interpretations of any single act, the impact of one event upon other activities or actors, the multiple webs that any individual or work can find themselves simultaneously entangled in, can in turn generate from the same starting point a series of quite different meanings. The authors neither could nor would wish to limit or exclusively define any one set of such meanings as true or false, or more or less significant – because after all the reader too is involved in his or her own frameworks. So what might appear to be simply a publisher's device – the system of cross-referencing – is in fact an invitation to multiple explorations, not unlike the routes that Julio Cortázar set out as possible ways through his experimental novel *Rayuela* (Hopscotch), published in 1963.

What we have argued so far is in a way a broad and universal materialist definition of culture as rooted in representations and practices. Within that general frame, there is a specificity about the cultures of Latin America and the Caribbean – and please note that we use cultures in the plural – which multiply and diversify the possible cultural

encounters that can occur. (One might think of the Uruguayan writer Isidore Ducasse, Count Lautréamont, so dear to the surrealists, who spoke of the chance encounter of a sewing machine and an umbrella on an operating table.) The linguistic dimension leads to consideration of contact, cultural overlay, bi- and multilingualism, which are as much the consequence of a brutal but in some ways unresolved historical confrontation between civilizations and cultures as the result of a differential contemporary relationship, economic, social and ideological, reflected in hierarchies and tensions in language. One need only think of the linguistic map of the Caribbean, for instance, with supposed English islands where French creoles are spoken, where there are continuing debates among the specialists about the precise origins of some of the languages (Papiamentu is the most famous example), not to mention their destinations. It is worth saying that Papiamentu was a language that was entirely spoken, yet within the recent past it has developed a literature which will both ensure its survival and almost certainly sever it from its own history. Looking to what is usually described as Spanish America, with reference both to its colonial history and to its dominant linguistic parameters, what looks like unity conceals a series of internal linguistic and cultural circuits in which other languages prevail, though they are in their turn subordinate to the national or official language. Thus, in the Andean region Quechua and Aymara have maintained their existence through time and yet have not broken out of the siege of a Spanish-speaking world: this paradox informed the life's work of one of Latin America's key writers and thinkers about culture, José María Arguedas. In Paraguay the fact that Guaraní is the dominant spoken language forces writers and intellectuals to negotiate an almost impossible path between orality and literacy, the spoken and the written, as yet unreconciled (and here the key figure is Augusto Roa Bastos). Portugal's legacy in Brazil, now by far the largest Portuguese-speaking country in the world, has been challenged and transformed by the confrontation with equally historically charged languages of African origin, as well as the extraordinary importance in the colonial period of Tupi; as a result, Brazilian Portuguese has been claimed as a new and different language by lexicographers, writers, and social theorists, yet it is the site of a dynamic and aggressive cultural encounter expressed through the metaphor of anthropophagy, languages cannibalizing one another. That constant fusion and rejection is expressed with great power in the song lyrics of Caetano Veloso and the counterpoint and polyphony of Villa-Lobos's compositions, particularly the Bachianas Brasileiras, as well as in Mário de Andrade's great novel or 'rhapsody' *Macunaíma* (1928).

The attempt to understand these networks and relationships in the particular context of Latin America and the Caribbean has produced a range of important new cultural models that seek to both acknowledge and explain that encounter and its effects. García Canclini's concept of hybridity, for example, suggests that the cultural forms and expressions produced by that encounter are distinct from their origin, and constitute a different way of understanding modernity. These 'hybrid cultures', as he calls them, respond to the circumstance of uneven development and cultural overlay, and the possibility of improvisation and acts of imagination, that imply the constitution of new agents and new actors. Fernando Ortiz's much earlier model of 'transculturation', taken up later by Angel Rama and Mary Louise Pratt, also implied negotiation, improvisation, and strategies for survival. Even seemingly pessimistic models like cultural dependency, which assumed that economic subordination would automatically imply cultural dominance, have provided the opportunity for contestation: Quino's Mafalda is an answer to Schultz's Peanuts, just as Diego Rivera was called to paint a mural in the Rockefeller Center (even if in the end that mural was erased by its disgruntled sponsor).

A significant proportion of what follows concerns what can broadly be described as popular culture, but even the category contains different cultural practices, meanings, relationships. The Puerto Rican dentist turned television astrologer, Walter Mercado, delights in what cultural theorists have termed kitsch and camp. But what do these terms mean? Are they a form of mimicry or parody? Are they terms that police the cultural field? That paradox is probably more immediately and persistently present in popular culture than in the so-called 'higher arts' (or Culture with a capital C), in part at least because popular culture engages directly with ideological representation on the one hand and the pressing necessities of material life on the other. There is a range of representations whose effect is in some way or another to reconcile its consumer with reality, either by declaring it closed to all change or by mobilizing active support. This after all is the role of an increasingly powerful television and print media, which must find ways of 'disappearing' the manifest contradictions of a modernity in which the latest in electronic technology can coexist in a single space with craft survivals of uncertain age. One hugely successful way of doing that has been to draw enormous and loyal transnational publics into a world of fictional reconciliation and resolution: the hero or heroine of the Latin American telenovela is usually reconciled with the world in the end. But the other face of popular culture is that it is also a locus of resistance: the craft tradition, for example, became an instrument of struggle and contestation when the patchwork artists used the most domestic of forms, *arpillera*, to comment on public events. When Fernando Birri, the Argentine film-maker, talked about an 'imperfect cinema' he was laying down a challenge to the sophisticated production values of a Hollywood which provided counterfeit worlds in perfect technicolour; the raw, unfinished nature of his films refused closure while the society from which they emerged was still so riven with unresolved contradictions.

This way of looking at the cultural field is destabilizing but also liberating. We propose to include the whole 'canon' of high culture, but to locate it not in an ivory tower or what the modernistas called a *reino interior*, an inner realm, but in constant traffic with the noise and confusion of modern life. Thus, Borges, Guimarães Rosa, Lispector, Lezama Lima – that is, the intellectuals considered emblematic of 'high culture' – are here shown in an active, and sometimes conflictive, relationship with other forms of cultural activity. 'Our' Borges works in journalism, talks about tango, translates and promotes crime fiction, and writes dense texts that call into question some of the most powerful universal explanations, but without faith in their replacement by other more plausible alternatives. 'Our' García Márquez finds in magical realism a route back to the reality of a Colombia torn apart then and now by La Violencia, and directly engages as a journalist with the day to day realities of the region. Yet he locates his responses within an oral tradition which links the response to immediate events with the accumulated experience of a historical community. 'Our' Caetano Veloso uses popular music as a means of bringing poetry and cultural critique to 'the people', as his colleague and friend Gilberto Gil has done with regard to local politics and racial struggle.

When Borges, in his essay on the Argentine writer and the Western tradition, defined that relationship in terms of connection or lineage but also distance and irreverence, he provided a model for creativity that others have found exciting. An inscription by the clock tower at the centre of the University of São Paulo campus, built in the 1960s or 1970s, reads: NO UNIVERSO DA CULTURA O CENTRO ESTA EM TODA PARTE (in the universe of culture the centre is everywhere), a phrase that echoes Borges's collection of examples of this very image, and locates that centre in Latin America, not in some distant place.

Circumstantially, Borges is witness to the moment from which this encyclopedia begins. 1920 is not so much a precise date as a conjuncture, a historical moment at which Latin America and the Caribbean confront modernity and the paralysis of an old order whose focus was in Europe. As its cultural icons began to lose their power to define and contain the world, a new force seemed both to offer progress, prosperity and change, and to threaten the destruction of an older Latin America which for all its contradictions and repressions represented some kind of continuity with the past. For that reason, that time seems an appropriate moment at which to ask how Latin America can begin to explain itself to itself in these new and sometimes frightening circumstances.

We are concluding these lines, and the several years of this dizzying and exciting project, on the eve of a new millennium. Contemplating the cultural landscape, whole regions have disappeared or been transformed beyond recognition by a combination of natural disaster, economic change, social conflict, globalization, and many other factors. And yet, it is valid to ask whether this represents an achievement and an enrichment of the lives of the millions who inhabit the place, or whether the outcome is a net loss for the majority and minority populations of the continent. What has happened to that spirit of innovation and imagination, that delight in improvisation, that impulse to freedom, in a continent where suddenly the new proliferation of religion seems to suggest uncertainty in the face of future? But in contrast, it is still obviously the case that people continue to imagine futures that they then seek by every means at their disposal to construct in reality. The Brazilian landless people's movement, the Movimento Sem Terra, is an inspiring example. So, it seems that it is not only poets and artists who dream. There is no frontier that can contain a truly liberating understanding.

In João Guimarães Rosa's great novel *Grande Sertão: Veredas*, near the end, a model of understanding the world, of teaching and learning, is proposed: 'Mestre não e quem ensina, mas quem de repente aprende' (the teacher is not the one who teaches, but the one who suddenly understands). Unforeseen connections are the ones that we have delighted in during the compilation of this work, and which we invite you to discover for yourselves.

DANIEL BALDERSTON
MIKE GONZALEZ
ANA M. LÓPEZ

How to use this encyclopedia

The framework of this Encyclopedia is an idea of culture and cultural studies whose underlying assumption is the connectedness of all forms of cultural expression. For the user, then, this will mean that there is a narrative to be followed through the book, whatever the point of entry. You may begin by consulting the entry on 'samba', for example; but the system of cross references, marked in bold in each entry, and the 'See alsos' that follow some entries, should take you into a constellation of related fields and issues – in this case through 'black cultures' or 'Carnival' to 'Brazil' via the 'Estado Novo' or 'Cinema Novo' towards 'bossa nova' and 'samba-reggae'. These routes will build a complex cultural narrative across themes, fields, time-frames and countries.

The entries are listed alphabetically but also, at the start of the book, listed by field and by country – from Literature and the Visual Arts to Music and Cinema. There are also a number of entries which explore cultural concepts and categories – like 'Time' or 'Meat' or 'Exile' – and others that provide brief biographies of significant figures with date and place of birth and death. We have tried, wherever possible, to give some sense of individuals and their achievement or significance rather than listing titles and dates.

The time-frame that we have interpreted as 'contemporary' embraces most of the twentieth century (with a tiny incursion into the twenty-first) with a starting point around 1920. This is not entirely arbitrary, since we would argue that that general time-frame acknowledges the beginning of a process of cultural decolonization which continued across a broken terrain through the century.

A note on spelling, names and order

The overall organization of the text is alphabetical. Surnames in the Hispanic world are often double. But there is a different usage in Spanish America and in Brazil; in the case of Spanish names, entries are arranged using the first name; in the case of Brazil, it is the final surname that is used and under which the individual is listed. For English, French and Dutch names the normal usage applies – following the Portuguese or English pattern.

Where appropriate, entries contain references to specific works like books, films or paintings. We have given the title in its original language in every case and followed it with the translation of title into English in brackets. In some cases, particularly in cinema, works have been published or released with a different title in English; where that is the case we give the name under which the film, say, was released. Otherwise the translations are literal.

Bibliographies and further reading

Items of 400 words or more normally carry a short bibliography. It is an indicative list, with no pretension to exhaustiveness; its purpose is to give the interested reader a starting point for further research or reading. Translations of titles are not normally given in the 'Further reading' section, but wherever possible there will be readings in English as well as the source language.

Finally

Cultures are complex interrelationships, cultural

practice is diverse and creative. In some way, what is involved here is an attempt to make sense of the world, or to reshape. That activity is not restricted to the grand, self-conscious interventions in the world; a popular tune or a national dish may tell as complex a story as a literary work. Our starting point has been that all these diverse manifestations have value and significance – and that they deserve to coexist in the book as they do in the world.

Acknowledgements

The editors are grateful to the many graduate assistants who have worked on this project, including Vicky Ruétalo, James Buckwalter-Arias, Fernanda Zullo, Elizabeth Smith, Scott Cooper, Eduardo Santa Cruz, Marcie Rinka, Alejandra Jaramillo and Dolores Tierney at Tulane, Peter Watt at the University of Glasgow and the University of Iowa, Eduardo Guizar Alvarez, Stephanie Vague, David Gilbert, Aminta Pérez, Alfredo Alonso Estenoz, Jesús Jambrina and Carol Wallace at the University of Iowa. They are also grateful for the generous support of their institutions, Tulane University, the University of Iowa, and the University of Glasgow. At Routledge, Fiona Cairns signed us up and kept us in shape, while Lia Zografou, Seth Denbo, Matthew Gale, Stephanie Rogers, Denise Rea and Tarquin Acevedo were vital during the more than five years of the development of the project. Thanks too to Jean Franco and Sylvia Molloy, who had the good sense to say that they had other things to do and pointed to us as being perhaps just nutty enough to take this on. And to our hundreds of contributors around the world: we are grateful for the education you have given us.

Thematic entry list

Antigua

Antigua
Bird, Vere C.
Kincaid, Jamaica
Prince, Ralph
Richards, Viv
Romeo-Mark, Althea

Architecture

Acosta, Wladimiro
Alvarez, Augusto H.
Alvarez, Mario Roberto
Ambasz, Emilio
architecture in Latin America
art nouveau
Artigas, João Batista Vilanova
Aterro do Flamengo
Avenida 9 de julio
Avenida de Mayo
Avenida Paulista
Avenida President Getulio Vargas
Banco de Londres
Barragán, Luis
Basilica of Guadalupe
Bauhaus architecture
beaux arts
Belmopan
Bernardes, Sergio
Biblioteca Nacional (Argentina)
Bo Bardi, Lina
Boca, La
Bologna, Francisco
botanical gardens
Brasília
Bratke, Oswaldo Arthur
Bullrich, Francisco
Bustillo, Alejandro
Candela, Félix
cemeteries
Centro Cultural Banco do Brasil
Centro Cultural Recoleta

Chacarita, La
Ciudad Darío
Ciudad Satélite
Ciudad Universitaria
Colón Cemetery
Congress Building (Chile)
Copacabana
Copan
Costa, Lucio
De Groote, Cristian
déco art and architecture
Dieste, Eladio
Duhart, Emilio
Espacio Escultórico
Florida
Fresnedo Siri, Román
Gasparini, Graziano
González de León, Teodoro
Hardoy, Jorge Enrique
historic centres
Insurgentes Avenue
International Style
Klotz, Mathías
Laird, Colin
Lazo, Carlos
Legorreta, Ricardo
Lima, Attilio Correia
López Rangel, Rafael
Machu Picchu
Maia, Éolo
Malecón, El
María Lionza Monument
Marx, Roberto Burle
Mindlin, Henrique
Ministerio de Educaçáo e Saúde
(MES)
Monumento a la Revolución
Moral, Enrique del
Moreira, Jorge Machado
Museu de Arte de São Paulo
Museu de Arte Moderno
national styles

Niemeyer (Soares Filho), Oscar
Nunes, Luiz
Palacio Nacional, Managua
Pampulha
Pani, Mario
Paysée Reyes, Mario
Pelourinho
Petrobrás building
Piña, Plácido
planned cities
Plaza de la Revolución
Plaza de las Tres Culturas
Plaza de Mayo
Polyforum
Praça da Sé
Prebisch, Alberto
Proyecto PREVI
Puerto Madero
Quintana, Antonio
railroad stations
Ramblas, Las
Ramírez Vázquez, Pedro
Recinos, Efrain
Recoleta, La
Reidy, Affonso Eduardo
Roberto family
Roca, Miguel Angel
Rocha, Paulo Mendes da
Salmona, Rogelio
Samper Gnecco, Germán
Santiago Airport, International
Terminal
SEPRA
squares
Testa, Clorindo
Tlatelolco
Torre Latinoamericana
UNAM
Valdés, Héctor
Varadero
Vargas Salguero, Ramón
Vasconcellos, Maria Josefina

Cinema

Colombia

Costa Rica

Geography

St Lucia
Suriname
Trinidad and Tobago
tropics
Uruguay
Venezuela
Virgin Islands, British
Virgin Islands, USA
volcanoes
West Indies
Windward Islands

Cuba

Abakua Society
Acevedo, Myriam
Acosta, Agustín
Acosta, Angel León
Alberto, Eliseo
Alhambra Theatre
Almendros, Néstor
Alonso, Alicia
Alonso, Fernando
Alvarez Guedes, Guillermo
Alvarez, Adalberto
Alvarez, Santiago
Anales del Caribe
Anunciación, La
Ardevol, Jose
Arenas, Reinaldo
Arias, Constantino
Arrom, José Juan
Arrufat, Antón
asere
Bacallao, Juana
Ballagas, Emilio
Ballet Nacional de Cuba
Baquero, Gastón
Barnet, Miguel
Batista y Zaldivar, Fulgencio
Bedia, José
Benítez Rojo, Antonio
Bergnes, Gustavo Arcos
Bermúdez, Cundo
Biografia de un cimarrón
Blanco, Juan
Blanco, Roberto
Bodeguita del medio
Bofill, Ricardo
Bohemia
Bola de Nieve
bolita
Brouwer, Leo
Burke, Elena
Cabrera Infante, Guillermo
Cabrera, Lydia
Cachao

Caignet, Félix B.
Caimán Barbudo, El
Caliban
Campaneris, Bert
Capablanca, José Raúl
Carpentier, Alejo
Carreño, Mario
Carrillo, Isolina
Carteles
Casa de las Américas
Casey, Calvert
Castro Ruz, Fidel
CDR
Céspedes, Carlos Manuel de
Chapotín, Félix
Chaves, Ricardo
Chibas, Eduardo
Ciclón
Cienfuegos, Camilo
Cine Cubano
cine imperfecto
cine móvil
CMQ-TV
Colón Cemetery
Combinado del Este
Contrapunteo cubano del tabaco y
   del azúcar
Corales
Corrales, Raúl
Corrieri, Sergio
Cortazar, Octavio
Cruz, Celia
CTC
Cuba
Cuentos fríos
Cuni, Miguelito
D'Rivera, Paquito
David, Juan
De cierta manera
derecho de nacer, El
Desnoes, Edmundo
Diario de la Marina
Díaz Rodríguez, Jesús
Díaz Torres, Daniel
Díaz, Rolando
Diego, Eliseo
Diez, Barbarito
Dihigo, Martín
Duque, Adolfo D.
Eiriz, Antonia
Electra Garrigó
Elpidio Valdés
Enríquez, Carlos
Escuela de Tres Mundos
Estévez, Abilio
Estorino, Abelardo

expresión americana, La
Federación de Mujeres Cubanas
feeling
Feijóo, Samuel
Fernández Retamar, Roberto
Fernández, Pablo Armando
Ferrer, Pedro Luis
Figuerola, Enrique
Florit, Eugenio
Formell, Juan
Fornes, Rosita
Fornet, Ambrosio
Franqui, Carlos
Fresa y chocolate
Gaceta de Cuba, La
Garay, Sindo
García Canturla, Alejandro
García Espinosa, Julio
García Joya, Mario
García Marruz, Fina
García, Victor Manuel
Gattorno, Antonio
Giral, Sergio
Gitana Tropical
Gómez, Manuel Octavio
Gómez, Sara
González, Celina
Gramatges, Harold
Granma
Grau San Martín, Ramón
Grupo de Renovación Musical
Grupo Escambray
Grupo Minorista
guanguancó
Guantanamera
Guantánamo
guaracha
guayabera
Guerra Sánchez, Ramiro
Guevara, Alfredo
Guevara, Ernesto (Che)
Guillén, Nicolás
Guillot, Olga
Guiteras, Antonio
Gutiérrez Alea, Tomás
Havana film festival
ICAIC
ICRT
Ingenio, El
Irakere
Isidrón, Chanito
Isla 70
isla de la Juventud
Isla que se repite, La
Jiménez Leal, Orlando
jinetera

Cultural institutions/ phenomena

Abakua Society
agitprop
Alhambra Theatre
Americas Society
Americas Watch
AMIA
Archivos
asere
beauty pageants
Best Village Competition
Biblioteca Ayacucho
black cultures
black movements
Bodeguita del medio
CARIFESTA
Caribbean Artists Movement
Casa de América
Casa de las Américas
Casa de Rui Barbosa
Casa de Teatro
CELCIRP
censorship
Centraal Historisch Archief van de
  Nederlandse Antillen
Centro Cultural Borges
Centro Nacional de las Artes
CLACSO
CONAC
CONAIE
CONICET
Consejo Nacional para la Cultura y
  las Artes
Conselho Nacional da Pesquisa
CPC
Créolité
Crusoob
Cultural imperialism
cultural nationalism
DIP
Feria del Libro, La
FLACSO
Fondo Nacional de las Artes
FUNARTE
gay and lesbian cultures
Hogar Obrero, El
Ibero-Amerikanisches Archiv
Ile Aiye
INAH
Indigenismo
indigenous cultures
indigenous movements
Institute of Jamaica
Instituto Caro y Cuervo

Instituto de Cultura
  Puertorriqueña
Instituto Di Tella
Instituto Internacional de
  Literatura Iberoamericana
Instituto Nacional de Bellas Artes
Latin American Studies
  Association (LASA)
Lecumberri
libraries
Maison de l'Amérique Latine
Memorial de América Latina
Mexicanidad, Movimiento de la
modernism, Brazilian
modernismo, Spanish American
Movimento Armorial
Nobel Prizes
Organization of American States
Palabras a los intelectuales
palo de mayo
Pan American Union
piñata
postmodernism
pulque and pulquerías
repentistas
SERMAC
Sociedad de Estudios Afrocubanos
Solentiname
Taller de Historia Oral Andina
UNEAC
UNESCO
Wie eegie sanie
women's movements

Curaçao

See Netherlands Antilles and
  Aruba

Decades

1920s, the
1930s, the
1940s, the
1950s, the
1960s, the
1970s, the
1980s, the
1990s, the

Dominica

Allfrey, Phyllis Shand
Charles, Dame Mary Eugenia
Dominica
jing ping
Rhys, Jean
Wide Sargasso Sea

Dominican Republic

Alcántara Almánzar, José
bachata
Balaguer, Joaquín
Bido, Cándido
Bobadilla, José Antonio
Bosch, Juan
Caamaño Deñó, Francisco Alberto
Cabral, Manuel del
Casa de Teatro
Cassá, Roberto
Castro, Tomás
Céspedes, Diógenes
Chahín, Plinio
Chapuseaux, Manuel
Convite
Días, Luis
Disla, Reynaldo
Dominican Republic
Domínguez, Franklin
Faro a Colón
Fernández Spencer, Antonio
Fortunato, René
García Romero, Rafael
García, Juan Francisco
Grupo Convite
Guerra, Juan Luis
Henríquez Ureña, Camila
Henríquez Ureña, Maximiliano
Henríquez Ureña, Pedro
Hernández Núñez, Angela
Javier, Adrián
Jesús, Dionisio de
Lora, Silvano
Marichal, Juan
Mármol, José
Mateo, Andrés L.
Meléndez, Agliberto
merengue
Mir, Pedro
Moya Pons, Frank
Muñiz, Angel
Nacional, El
Olivorismo
Oviedo, Ramon
Peix, Pedro
Pellerano, Soucy de (Jesusa Castillo)
Peña Gómez, José Francisco
Pérez, Guillo
Piantini, Carlos
Piña, Plácido
Poesía Sorprendida
Prats Ramírez, Ivelisse
Radio Televisión Dominicana
Raful, Tony

Romero, Oscar
Salarrué

Fashion and design

BKF furniture
clothing and dress
guayabera
Herrera, Carolina
kitsch
Mazza, Valeria
Meiling
Organización Cisneros
panama hat
Pitanguy, Ivo
Renta, Oscar de la
Rojas, Efrén
Sánchez, Angel

Food and drink

acarajá
bananas
beans
beer
cacao
cachaca
callaloo
carurú
ceviche
chewing gum
cigars
coffee
corn and corncakes
dendé oil
doubles
eating out
fast food
feijoada
food and drink
llapingacho
maize
manioc
meat in Argentina
mescal
Mexican cookery
mezcal
moqueca
nacatamal
pepperpot
potato
restaurants
roti
rum
sancocho
Scannone, Armando
sugar

tequila and mescal
tereré
tobacco
vatapá
Villapol, Nitza
yerba mate

French Antilles

French Antilles

French Guyana

Damas, Léon Gontrand
French Guyana
Wailing roots

Guadeloupe

Condé, Maryse
Glissant, Gabriel
Guadeloupe
Lara, Christian
Maldoror, Sarah
Perse, Saint-John
Pineau, Gisele
Schwarz-Bart, Simone
Warner-Vieyra, Myriam

Guatemala

Ak'abal, Humberto
Arango, Luis Alfredo
Arbenz, Jacobo
Arce Leal, Manuel José
Arévalo Martínez, Rafael
Arias, Arturo
Asturias, Miguel Angel
Behrhorst, Carroll
Cardoza y Aragón, Luis
Carrera, Margarita
Castillo, Otto René
CEDIM
Cojti, Demetrio
Cruz Martínez, Rogelia
Foppa, Alaíde
Galich, Franz
Galich, Manuel
Gaspar Ilóm
González, Otto Raul
Guatemala
Illescas, Carlos
Liano, Dante
Martínez Peláez, Severo
Mayan Revitalization Movement
Menchú Tum, Rigoberta
Mérida, Carlos
Monterroso, Augusto
Morales, Mario Roberto

Morales Santos, Francisco
Música Grande
Obregón Morales, Roberto
Payeras, Mario
Perera, Victor
Recinos Avila, Adrián
Recinos, Efraín
Ríos Montt, Efraín
Rodas, Ana María
Señor Presidente, El
Solórzano, Carlos
Ubico, Jorge
URNG

Guyana

Agard, John
Allsop, Richard
Bascom, Harold
Best, Lloyd
Burnham, Forbes
Cameron, Norman Eustace
Carew, Jan
Carter, Martin (Wylde)
Cuffy (Kofi) Statue
Dabydeen, Cyril
Dabydeen, David
Dathorne, Oscar
Gilkes, Michael
Gilroy, Beryl
Goodison, Lorna Gaye
Guyana
Guyana Chronicle
Harris, Wilson
Heath, Roy
Hopkinson, Slade
Jagan, Cheddi
Kempadoo, Peter
Kyk-Over-Al
Matthews, Marc
McAndrew, Wordsworth
McDonald, Ian
McWatt, Mark
Melville, Pauline
Mittelholzer, Edgar Austin
Monar, Rooplall
Narain, Harry
Nichols, Grace
Palace of the Peacock
pepperpot
Pilgrim, Frank
Richmond, Angus
Rodney, Walter
Roopnaraine, Rupert
Seymour, A.J.
Shinebourne, Janice
Smith, Michael Garfield

Walrond, Eric
Williams, Aubrey
Williams, Denis
Williams, N D

Haiti

Alexis, Jacques Stephen
Antonin, Arnold
Aristide, Jean-Bertrand
Bellegarde, Dantès
Benoit, Rigaud
Bigaud, Wilson
Brierre, Jean Fernand
Brouard, Carl
Castor, Suzy
Charlemagne, Emmanuel
Compère Général Soleil
Depestre, René
Duvalier, Francois
Duvalier, Jean Claude
Gouverneurs de la rosée
Haiti
Haitian creole
Hyppolite, Hector
indigenisme
Labuchin, Rassoul
Laferriere, Dany
Laleau, León
Lemoine, Bob
Liautaud, Georges
méringue
noirisme
Obin, Philome
Paul, Evans
Peck, Raoul
Pierre-Charles, Gérard
Price-Mars, Jean
Roumain, Jacques
Roumer, Emile
sequin art and voodoo flags
Thoby-Marcelin, Phillipe
Tontons Macoutes
Vodun
Vodun flags

Honduras

Acosta, Oscar
Honduras
punta rock
Reyes, Candelario
Sosa, Roberto
Suárez, Clementina
Teatro de la Basura
Teatro La Fragua
Valle, Rafael Heliodoro

Intellectual life

Achugar, Hugo
Aguirre Beltrán, Gonzalo
Ainsa, Fernando
Alleyne, Mervyn C.
Allsop, Richard
Anderson Imbert, Enrique
Antelo, Raúl
anthropology
Arce de Vázquez, Margot
archaeology
Ardao, Arturo
Arrigucci Jr, Davi
Arrom, José Juan
Asociación Amigos del Arte
Barrán, José Pedro
Barrenechea, Ana María
Barrow, Dame Nita
Bartra, Roger
Bellegarde, Dantès
Benacerraf, Baruj
Benítez Rojo, Antonio
Benítez, Jaime
Bernal, Ignacio
Best, Lloyd
Bianchi, Soledad
biology
Bishop, Pat
Black Jacobins, The
Blanco Fombona, Rufino
Blest Riffo, Clotario
Block de Behar, Lisa
Bosi, Alfredo
Botana, Natalio
Botana, Natalio
Boulton, Alfredo
Briceño Guerrero, José Manuel
Brunner, José Joaquín
Buarque de Holanda, Sérgio
Bunge family
Caliban
Cámara Cascudo, Luis de
Candido, Antonio
Capitalism and Slavery
Cardoso, Fernando Henrique
Carneiro, Édison de Souza
Casa de la Cultura Ecuatoriana
Caso, Alfonso
Casa grande e senzala
Caso, Antonio
Cassá, Roberto
Castañeda, Jorge G.
Castro Leiva, Luis
CELARG
Cerutti Guldberg, Horacio

Céspedes, Diógenes
chemistry
Contrapunteo cubano del tabaco y
   del azúcar
Cordova, Arnaldo
Cornejo Polar, Antonio
Costa, João Cruz
Coutinho, Afrânio
Crespo, Luis Alberto
criollismo
Cueva, Agustín
Del buen salvaje al buen
   revolucionario
dependency theory
Di Tella, Guido
Diaz Quiñones, Arcadio
Díez de Medina, Fernando
Discours Antillais, Le
Domíngues Caballero, Diego
Donoso Pareja, Miguel
Ecker, Enrique Eduardo
Enigma of Arrival, The
Escudero, Gonzalo
Eulálio, Alexandre
existentialism
Fals Borda, Orlando
Fanon, Frantz
Feijóo, Samuel
Fernandes, Florestan
Fernández Retamar, Roberto
Ferrer, Horacio
Fierro, Enrique
Fletcher, Lea
Flores Galindo, Alberto
Flores, Angel
Floria, Carlos Alberto
Fornet, Ambrosio
Franceschi, Gustavo
Francovich, Guillermo
Franqui, Carlos
Freire, Paulo
Freyre, Gilberto
Friedemann, Nina S. de
Gaos, José
García Calderón, Ventura
García Canclini, Néstor
García, Germán Leopoldo
Garibay, Angel
Garvey, Marcus Mosiah
Gerchunoff, Alberto
Gesta Bárbara
Glusberg, Jorge
Gomes, Paulo Emílio Salles
Goveia, Elsa Vesta
Guerra Sánchez, Ramiro
Guevara, Alfredo

antipoetry
Antología de la literatura fantástica
Apando, El
arielismo
Astillero, El
autobiography
avant garde in Latin America
Banana Bottom
beso de la mujer araña, El
best-sellers
Biografía de un cimarrón
biography
Boom
Boquitas pintadas
Cahier d'un retour au pays natal
Canto General
Chasqui
children's literature
Cien años de soledad
ciudad y los perros, La
comics
Compère Général Soleil
concrete poetry
Cóndores no entierras todos los
　días
Contemporáneos
costumbrismo
crime fiction
crónica
Cuentos fríos
cultural theory
dub poetry
Electra Garrigó
En el corazón de junio
Entenado, El
essay
estridentismo
Expresión americana, La
fantastic literature
Ficciones
folheto
gay male literature
Gouverneurs de la rosée
Grande sertão: veredas
Grupo de Barranquilla
Grupo de Guayaquil
Grupo minerista
Guaracha del Macho Camacho
Guayaquil Group
Hasta no verte Jesus mío
Hijo de hombre
Hortensias, Las
House for Mr. Biswas, A
In the Castle of My Skin
indigenisme
indigenous literature

Inkarri
Insularismo
Jewish writing
Lau, Hazel
Laurel
lesbian literature
Lézarde, La
literary criticism
Literary histories
literatura de cordel
literature
llano en llamos, El
Los que se van
Macunaíma
magical realism
manifestos
marginal poets
Mimeograph poets
modernism, Brazilian
modernism, Spanish American
Morte e vida severina
mundonovismo
Mutabaraka
negrismo
neo-baroque
Noche de los Asesinos, La
noche de Tlatelolco, la
Noigandres Group
novel
obsceno pájaro de la noche, El
Omeros
Onda, La
Palace of the Peacock
Paradiso
pasos perdidos, Los
Peau noire, masques blancs
Pedro Páramo
Piedra de Sol
Plural
Poesía Sorprendida
poetry
postboom
prison writing
Rayuela
real maravilloso, lo
regionalismo
reino de este mundo, El
Respiración artificial
Rights of Passage
ríos profundos, Los
science fiction
señor Presidente, El
short story
siglo de las Luces, El
Techo de la Ballena, El
Testimonio

Tráfico
translation in Latin America
translations of Latin American
　literature
travel writing
verdeamarelismo
Vida breve, La
vorágine, La
Watunna
Wide Sargasso Sea
women's writing
workshop poety
Yo el Supremo

Martinique

béguine (biguine)
Cahier d'un retour au pays natal
Capécia, Mayotte
Césaire, Aimé
Chamoiseau, Patrick
Confiant, Raphael
Créolité
Discours Antillais, Le
Fanon, Frantz
Glissant, Edouard
Images Caraïbes
Kassav'
Lézarde, La
Malavoi
Maran, René
Martinique
Palcy, Euzhan
Peau noire, masques blancs
Placoly, Vincent
Rameau, Will
Rue Cases-Nègres, La
SERMAC
Stellio
Zobel, Joseph
zouk

Media

A esta hora se improvisa
ABC Color
Agachados, Los
Alarma
All Jamaica Library
Amauta
Americas
Amigos del Libro, Los
Anales del Caribe
Angélica
Antilliaanse Cahiers
Arca
Asir, Revista

Mexico

rumba
Salinas, Horacio
salsa
samba
samba schools
samba-reggae
Sandoval, Arturo
Santa Cruz Wilson, Domingo
Santamaría, Mongo
Santoro, Cláudio
Santos, Daniel
Saquito, Nico
Sas, Andrés
Schidlowsky, Leon
Sepultura
Serenata Guayanesa
Siboney
Silva, Orlando
Silvestre, Sonia
Simó, Manuel
Simone, Mercedes
Sivuca
ska
Smetak, Walter
soca
Soda Stereo
SODRE
Solís, Javier
Solo pueblo, Un
son
son huasteca
son jarocho music
song festivals
sonido 13
Sonora Matancera, La
Sosa, Julio
Sosa, Mercedes
Spinetta, Luis Alberto
steelband
Stellio
sucusucu
Sui Géneris
Sumo
tango
Tanguito
Tata Guines
Teles, Sílvia
Third World
Timbalada
Titãs
Todos tus muertos
Toña la Negra
Toquinho
Tosar, Héctor
Tosh, Peter
Toto la Momposina

tres
Tres, Los
trio elétrico
Trío los Panchos
Trío Matamoros
Troilo, Aníbal
Tropicália
trova tradicional
trova Yucateca
Uakti
Urrutia Blondel, Jose
Valcárcel, Edgar
Valcárcel, Teodoro
Valdés, Merceditas
vallenato
Van Van, Los
Vandre, Geraldo
Vargas, Chavela
Vargas, Pedro
Vargas, Wilfrido
Velásquez, Consuelo
Veloso, Caetano Emaunel Viana
    Teles
Ventura, Johnny B.
Vera, Ana María
Víctor Víctor
vidalita
Viglietti, Daniel
Villa-Lobos, Heitor
Villalpando, Alberto
Villamil Cordovez, Jorge
Vinay, Ramón
Violadores, Los
Virus
Vives, Carlos
volcanto
Wailing roots
Walsh, Maria Elena
waltz
Widmer, Ernst
Williams, Alberto
Wisnik, José Miguel
yaraví
Yordano
Yupanqui, Atahualpa
Zafiros, Los
zamba
Zapato Tres
Zé Tom
Zitarrosa, Alfredo
zouk

Netherlands Antilles and Aruba

Abath, Ciro

Anemaet, Jo
Antilliaanse Cahiers
Aruba
Bacilio, Gilbert
Blinder, Oda
Boskaljon, Rudolf Frederik Willen
Capricorne, José Maria
Carrilho, Nelson
Centraal Historisch Archief van de
    Nederlandse Antillen
Dania, Winfred
Debrot, Nicolaas
Ecker, Enrique Eduardo
Ecury, Nydia Maria Enrica
Engels, Christiaan Joseph
    Hendrikus
Engels-Boskaljon, Lucila, Lucila
Fray, Manuel Antonio
Girigorie, Jean
Haseth, Carel P. de
Henriquez, May
Houwen, Ria
Isle, Ludwig de l'
Juliana, Elis
Kirindongo, Yubi
Kroon, Willem E.
Kuiperi, Stan
Lauffer, Minerva
Lauffer, Pierre A.
Lebacs, Diane
Leeuwen, Willem Christaan
    Jacobus van
López, Elvis
Marchena, Pedro Pablo Medardo
    de
Martina, Harold
Martinus (Arion), Frank E.
Marugg, Silvio Alberto
Melaan, C.
Nepomuceno, Max
Netherlands Antilles and Aruba
Ocalia, Hipolito
Palm, Jules Ph. De
Papiamentu
Parabirsingh, Sam
Pool, Johan Joseph (John) de
Richardson, Roland
Sekou, Lasana M.
Simadán
Simon, Nel
Sling, Norva
Stoep, de
Zanolino, Philippe

Nicaragua

Aguilar, Rosario

Porras Barrenechea, Raúl
Portal, Magda
Portugal, Ana María
Proyecto PREVI
Revista de Crítica Literaria
 Latinoamericana
Reyes, Lucha
Ribeyro, Julio Ramón
ríos profundos, Los
Sabogal, José
Salazar Bondy, Augusto
Sánchez Cerro, Luis
Sánchez, Luis Alberto
Sas, Andrés
Scorza, Manuel
Sendero Luminoso
Siete ensayos
Sologuren, Javier
Szyszlo, Fernando de
TAFOS
Tsuchiya, Tilsa
Valcárcel Vizcarra, Luis Eduardo
Valcárcel, Edgar
Valcárcel, Teodoro
Vallejo, César
Varela, Blanca
Vargas Llosa, Mario
Vargas, Virginia
Velasco Alvarado, Juan
Villa El Salvador
Westphalen, Emilio Adolfo
Yzaga, Jaime

Politics and history

abertura
Adams, Grantley
Albizu Campos, Pedro
Allende, Salvador
Alsogaray, María Julia
AMNLAE
anarchism
APRA
Aranha, Osvaldo
Arbenz, Jacobo
ARENA
Arias, Oscar
Aristide, Jean-Bertrand
Balaguer, Joaquín
Batista y Zaldívar, Fulgencio
Belaúnde Terry, Fernando
Bergnes, Gustavo Arcos
Betancourt, Rómulo
Bird, Vere C.
Bishop, Maurice
Blanco, Hugo
Blyden, Edward

Bofill, Ricardo
Bogotazo, El
Bolivian Revolution
Bonafini, Hebe de
Borge Martínez, Tomás
Bouterse, Desi
Burnham, Forbes
Bustamante, Sir William Alexander
Butler, Uriah
Caamaño Deñó, Francisco Alberto
Cárdenas, Cuauhtémoc
Cárdenas, Lázaro
Castello Branco, Humberto de
 Alencar
Castro Ruz, Fidel
Cayetano Carpio, Salvador
Chaco War
Chamorro, Violeta Barrios de
Charles, Eugenia
Chibas, Eduardo
Christian Democracy
CIA
Cienfuegos, Camilo
Cold War, impact of
Collor, Fernando
Columbian quincentenary
communist parties
Condarco Morales, Ramiro
contras
Cordobazo
coronelismo
Cristero revolt
Cruz Martínez, Rogelia
D'Abuisson, Roberto
decolonization and independence
democracy
Duvalier, Francois
Duvalier, Jean Claude
Echeverría Alvarez, Luis
esquerda festiva
Estado Novo
Estigarribia, José Félix
Fagoth, Stedman
fascism in Latin America
Figueras Ferrer, José
Finot, Enrique
Firmenich, Mario
FMLN
foco
Fonseca, Carlos
Frei Montalva, Eduardo
Frei Ruiz Tagle, Eduardo
Frente Amplio
FSLN
Fujimori, Alberto
Gómez Hurtado, Álvaro

Gómez, Juan Vicente
Gairy, Eric M.
Gaitan, Jorge Eliécer
García, Alan
Gaspar Ilóm
Gisbert, Teresa
González Casanova, Pablo
Goulart, João
Grau San Martín, Ramón
Grove, Marmaduke
Gueiller Tejada, Lidia
guerrillas
Guevara Arce, Walter
Guevara, Ernesto (Che)
Guiteras, Antonio
Guzmán, Abimael
Harnecker, Marta
Haya de la Torre, Víctor Raúl
human rights
Integralismo
Inter American Court of Human
 Rights
Jagan, Cheddi
Jagger, Bianca
Juruna, Mario
Justo, Agustín P.
Justo, Juan Baustista
Kubitschek, Juscelino
López Rega, José
Lampião and Maria Bonita
Lechín Oquendo, Juan
Lombardo Toledano, Vicente
Lula
Mármol, Miguel
Méndez Fleitas, Epifanio
M-19
Machado y Morales, Gerardo
Madres de Plaza de Mayo
Manley, Norman Washington
Marcial
Marcos, Subcomandante
Marighela, Carlos
Martí, Farabundo
Marxism in Latin America
Mella, Julio Antonio
Mendoza Leiton, Gunar
Menem, Carlos Saúl
MISURASATA
Montoneros
Movimiento Negro Unificado
Movimiento Revolucionario Tupac
 Amaru
MST
Muñoz Marín, Luis
NACLA
Neves, Tancredo

Rodríguez Julia, Edgardo
Rodríguez, Tito
Rodríguez, Walter
Romero, Marta
San Juan Star
Sánchez, Luis Rafael
Santos Febres, Mayra
Santos, Daniel
Schomburg, Arthur
Soto Vélez, Clemente
Soto, Pedro Juan
Spanish in Puerto Rico
Texera, Diego de la
Umpierre, Luz María
Vega, Ana Lydia
Vientós Gastón, Nilita
Vocero, El
Zona de carga y descarga
Zurinaga, Marcos

Religion

Alves, Rubem
Aquino, María Pilar
Arns, Paulo Evaristo
Baptists
Boff, Leonardo
Bonfim
Cámara, Dom Helder
Candomblé
Casaldáliga, Pedro
Catholicism
CELAM
Céspedes, Carlos Manuel de
Christian Base Organizations
Christmas
CNBB
D'Escoto, Miguel
Didi
Dussel, Enrique
Espiritismo
feminist liberation theology
García Herreros, Padre Rafael
Gebara, Ivone
Gutiérrez, Gustavo
Hernández, José Gregorio
Hinduism
Holy Week
Hurtado, Padre Alberto
Islam
Ixtapalapa Crucifixion
Judaism
Kumina
liberation theology
López Trujillo, Cardinal
Macumba
Mãe Menininha

Mãe, Stella
Martín-Baró, Ignacio
Medellín Conference
Méndez Arceo, Sergio
missionaries
Mita
Molina, Uriel
Mormonism
myalism
Namuncurá, Ceferino
New Age
Obando y Bravo, Miguel
Obeah
Olivorismo
Opus Dei
orishás
orishas (Trinidad)
Orixás
Ortega Alamino, Jaime
Parrilla, Antulio
Pentecostals
pilgrimages
popular religion
Proaño, Leonidas
Protestantism
Rastafarianism
religion and politics
ritual calendars
Rivera Pagán, Luis
Romero, Oscar
Sabina, María
saints' days
San José, Maria de
Santería
Santo Daime
shango
Sobrino, Jon
syncretism
Tamez, Elsa
Torres, Camilo
Trinidad Shouters
Umbanda
Verger, Pierre
Virgins, miraculous
Vodun
yage

Society

ageing and senior citizens
AIDS
altitude sickness
Amerindians in the Caribbean
Andean culture
Aridjis, Homero
Barrios de Chungara, Domitila
Behrhorst, Carroll

Bobbitt, Lorena
boto
Brumana, Herminia
buses
CAFRA
campesino
capital punishment
Caribs
cartel
CDR
Chagas' disease
charro
childhood
cholera
cholo
city
class
COB
CODEFF
cofradía
Cojti, Demetrio
compadrazgo and comadrazgo
Comunidad Homosexual
   Argentina
CONAIE
concheros
Condori Mamani, Gregorio
Constitutions
corruption
creole
Crespi, Carlos
criollo
cross-dressing
CTC
cultural survival
Day of the Dead
death squads
dengue fever
disappeared, the
domestic labor
domestic violence
dreadlocks
East Indians
encuentros feministas
environmental issues
EPS
Escobar Gaviria, Pablo
ethnicity
evil eye
exile
fairs and markets
family
Federación de Mujeres Cubanas
femininity
feminism
fiesta

Sport and leisure

Chalbaud, Román
Chester, Ilan
Chocrón, Isaac
Ciudad Universitaria
CONAC
Concepción, David
Crespo, Luis Alberto
Cruz-Diez, Carlos
culebrón
D'Léon, Oscar
Danzahoy
de la Parra, Teresa
Del buen salvaje al buen
    revolucionario
Díaz Solís, Gustavo
Díaz, Simón
Elite
Ferrer, Lupita
Figueredo, Ignacio
Frometa, Billo
Gallegos, Rómulo
Garmendia, Salvador
Gasparini, Graziano
Gego
Gerbasi, Vicente
Giménez, Carlos
Gómez, Juan Vicente
Gramcko, Ida
Henríquez, Graciela
Hernández, Carlos 'Morocho'
Hernández, José Gregorio
Herrera Luque, Francisco
Herrera, Carolina
Holguín, Grishka
Hoogesteijn, Solveig
Imber, Sofia
Izaguirre, Boris
Lanz, Rigoberto
Lerner, Elisa
Liscano, Juan
María Lionza Monument
Marisol
Márquez Rodríguez, Alexis
Mata Gil, Milagros
Mayz Vallenilla, Ernesto
Méndez, Lucía
Meneses, Guillermo
Moliendo café
Monte Avila
Montejo, Eugenio
Morillo, Lila
Nacional, El
Narvaez, Francisco
Nebreda, Vicente
Nueva Sociedad
Núñez, Enrique Bernardo

Organización Cisneros
Orta, Carlos
Otero Silva, Miguel
Otero, Alejandro
Ottolina, Renny
Palacios, María Fernanda
Palomares, Ramón
Pantin, Yolanda
Pérez Alfonzo, Juan Pablo
Pérez Jiménez, Marcos
Pérez, Carlos Andrés
Perna, Claudio
Petkoff, Teodoro Malec
Picón Salas, Mariano
Plaza, Juan Bautista
Pocaterra, José Rafael
Polidor, Gustavo
Primera, Ali
Quintero, Ednodio
Quinteto Contrapunto
Rajatabla
Ramos Sucre, José Antonio
Rebolledo, Carlos
Reverón, Armando
Revista Nacional de Cultura
Rial, José Antonio
Rivas, Bárbaro
Rodríguez, José Luis
Rodríguez, Zhandra
Rojas Guardia, Armando
Rojas, Efrén
Romero, Aldemaro
Romero, Denzil
Sáez, Irene
Sambrano Urbaneta, Oscar
San José, Maria de
Sánchez Peláez, Juan
Sánchez, Angel
Sánchez, Juan Félix
Sanoja, Sonia
Santana, Rodolfo
Sardio
Scannone, Armando
Serenata Guayanesa
Soto, Jesús
Sucre, Guillermo
Teatro Teresa Carreño
Techo de la Ballena, El
Terán, Ana Enriqueta
Terragno, Rodolfo
theatre festivals
Torres, Ana Teresa
Torres, Fina
Tráfico
Trayectodanza
Trejo, Oswaldo

Uslar Pietri, Arturo
Venevisión
Venezuela
Villanueva, Carlos Raúl
Watunna
Yanomami
Yordano
Zapata, Pedro León
Zapato Tres
Zona Franca

Virgin Islands

Virgin Islands, British
Virgin Islands, USA

Visual arts

Abath, Ciro
Acosta, Angel León
Afro-Latin American arts
Aizenberg, Roberto
Alcántara, Pedro
Alladdin, Mohammed Pharouk
Alonso, Carlos
Alvarez Bravo, Lola
Alvarez Bravo, Manuel
Amaral, Tarsila do
Anemaet, Jo
Antúnez, Nemesio
Anunciación, La
Apurimak
Arden Quin, Carmelo
Arias, Constantino
art history
art periodicals, contemporary
Arte Madí
Assis Chateaubriand
ASTC
Atl, Dr
Atteck, Sybil
Badi, Líbero
Balmes, José
Bardi, Pietro Maria
Barradas, Rafael
Bay, Juan
Bayón, Damián
Bedia, José
Beltrán García, Alberto
Benedit, Luis
Benmayor, Samy
Benoit, Rigaud
Bermúdez, Cundo
Berni, Antonio
Bido, Cándido
Bienal de São Paulo
Bigaud, Wilson

Writers

Dávila Andrade, César
Díaz Solís, Gustavo
Dabydeen, Cyril
Dabydeen, David
Dalton, Roque
Damas, Léon Gontrand
Dathorne, Oscar
D'Costa, Jean
de Boissiere, Ralph A.C.
De Greiff, León
de la Parra, Teresa
Debroise, Olivier
Debrot, Nicolaas
Del Paso, Fernando
Del Río, Ana María
Delgado, Susy
Denis Molina, Carlos
Depestre, René
Desnoes, Edmundo
D'Halmar, Augusto
Di Benedetto, Antonio
Diego, Eliseo
Diez, Barbarito
Disla, Reynaldo
Dobru, R.
Donoso, José
Dorfman, Ariel
Drayton, Geoffrey
Drummond de Andrade, Carlos
Duncan, Quince
Ecury, Nydia Maria Enrica
Edgell, Zee
Edwards Bello, Joaquín
Edwards, Jorge
Egüez, Iván
Eguren, José María
Elizondo, Salvador
Ellis, Zoila
Eltit, Diamela
Emar, Juan
Engels, Christiaan Joseph
  Hendrikus
Escoffrey, Gloria Blanche
Espínola, Francisco
Espínola, Lourdes
Espinet, Ramabai
Espinosa, Germán
Esquivel, Laura
Estupiñán Bass, Nelson
Fallas, Carlos Luis
Fariña, Soledad
Ferland, Barbara
Fernández Spencer, Antonio
Fernández, Macedonio
Fernández, Pablo Armando
Ferré, Rosario

Ferrer, Renée
Figueroa, John
Filloy, Juan
Florit, Eugenio
Fonseca, Rubem
Forde, A.N.
Fray, Manuel Antonio
French, Stanley
Fuentes, Carlos
Fuguet, Alberto
Futoransky, Luisa
Gálvez, Manuel
Gómez, Ana Ilce
Güiraldes, Ricardo
Gabeira, Fernando
Gaitán Durán, Jorge
Galeano, Eduardo Hughes
Galich, Franz
Galich, Manuel
Gallegos Lara, Joaquín
Gallegos, Rómulo
Galvão, Patricia
García Marquez, Gabriel
García Marruz, Fina
García Ponce, Juan
García Romero, Rafael
Gardea, Jesús
Garmendia, Salvador
Garro, Elena
Gayoso, Milia
Gelman, Juan
Gerbasi, Vicente
Giardinelli, Mempo
Gil Gilbert, Enrique
Gilkes, Michael
Gilroy, Beryl
Girondo, Oliverio
Girri, Alberto
Gladwell, Joyce
Glantz, Margo
Glissant, Edouard
Gonzalez, Anson
González de Alba, Luis
González Tuñón, Raúl
González, José Luis
González, Otto Raul
Goodison, Lorna
Gorodischer, Angélica
Gorostiza, José
Gramcko, Ida
Guardia, Gloria
Guebel, Daniel
Guedes, Lino
Guerra, Lucía
Guido, Beatriz
Guillén, Nicolás

Gusman, Luis
Gutiérrez, Miguel
Guy, Rosa
Guzmán, Augusto
Guzmán, Martín Luis
Hahn, Oscar
Hamilton, Judith
Harris, Claire
Harris, Wilson
Haseth, Carel P. de
Hatoum, Milton
Hearne, John
Heath, Roy
Helman, Albert
Hendricks, Arthur Lemiére
Henriquez, May
Heraud, Javier
Herbert, Cecil
Hercules, Frank E.M.
Hernández Núñez, Angela
Hernández, Felisberto
Hernández, Juan José
Herrera Luque, Francisco
Herrera, Darío
Hidalgo, Alberto
Hill, Errolk
Hippolyte, Kendel
Hodge, Merle
Holst, Gilda
Hopkinson, Slade
Hosein, Clyde
Huerta, Efraín
Huidobro, Vicente
Hutchinson, Lionel
Hyatt, Charles
Ibáñez, Roberto
Ibáñez, Sara de
Ibarbourou, Juana de
Icaza, Jorge
Illescas, Carlos
Ingram, Kenneth
Izaguirre, Boris
Jackman, Oliver
Jara, Cronwell
Jaramillo Agudelo, Darío
Jaramillo Levi, Enrique
Javier, Adrián
Jekyll, Walter
Jesús, Dionisio de
John, Errol
Jones, Marion
Juarroz, Roberto
Juliana, Elis
Kamenszain, Tamara
Karlik, Sara
Keens Douglas, Paul

Decades

1920s, the

The decade of the 1920s in most of Latin America was a period of economic growth, political stabilization and renewed optimism. It was characterized by a steadily rising population, **urbanization**, industrialization, an ever closer integration into the international economy, rise in political tension, ideological strife, labour radicalism and an increased economic and military intervention by the USA. This gave rise to many nationalist movements that had an important role in ideologically shaping the continent. It was the first great formative phase in the development of national art galleries and the era of the symphony orchestra, while architecture, painting, music and the arts in general came to parallel their European counterparts in the search for self-identification.

Most countries throughout the continent pursued an outward-directed growth strategy. Foreign investment resumed after the First World War on a massive scale and now came chiefly from the USA, whose stake rose to $5.4 billion in 1929 as against $1.6 billion in 1914. New capital flowed into the continent, developing new industries like the Venezuelan petroleum industry, controlled mainly by US, British and Dutch interests. The first half of this century was characterized by a steadily rising population in Latin America, from roughly 60 million in 1900 to 155 million at mid-century. The urban proportion had reached about 40 per cent, though there were great differences between countries. In urban settings there was a steady expansion of white-collar and professional groups. These middle sectors were the chief beneficiaries of the expansion of educational facilities, which they strongly supported and used as means of upward mobility. Urban workers, for their part, had access to primary education but rarely secondary, whereas in most rural areas Latin Americans did not receive any education. The growth of an urban middle class that was asking for a share in power, the example of Soviet and Mexican revolutions, and the spread of Marxist (see **Marxism in Latin America**) and socialist (see **socialism**) thought made for a more precarious position for the oligarchy who, in order to maintain their political hold, had to share power with other groups. The middle sectors – mostly middle class and sometimes urban workers – were being co-opted and gained a meaningful share through their participation in the power and benefits. The rural population, who still represented the vast majority on the continent, were largely ignored.

Latin America witnessed the spread of imported ideologies in the 1920s, both on the left and right. While some political organizations were influenced by fascism (see **fascism in Latin America**) – widespread in Europe at this time – in most Latin American countries membership in fascist organizations was numerically insignificant. The European anarcho-syndicalism that had provided a model for many of Latin America's earliest radical cadres declined sharply in importance after the First World War. Socialist parties appeared throughout the continent in many forms, some independent, some directly under the influence of the Soviet Union and some advocating land reform following the Mexican Revolution model. Eventually, many of these parties were drawn under the umbrella of the Soviet Union and transformed into **communist parties**, as was the case of the Socialist Party of Peru.

The Mexican Revolution of 1910 was a source of inspiration for revolutionary, oppositional or social change-orientated groups for many years to come. It was an example of the challenges to existing regimes brought about by the expanding middle sectors, working class and peasants. Miners, urban workers, and peasants saw an opportunity to express their own grievances, as formulated in the new Constitution of 1917. Some of the outcomes of the revolution were the recognition of the working class's rights to unionize and strike, minimum wages, the eight-hour working day and universal voting rights (however, not for women – the first country to adopt women's suffrage, though it still required literacy to vote, was Ecuador in 1929). The influence of the Church was curtailed, especially in education and political activities, the land and the subsoil were declared property of the State and, finally, there was significant land distribution to the working peasants through the **agrarian reform**, whose most successful exponent was President Lázaro **Cárdenas** (1934–40). The Mexican Revolution was an inspiration for reform or revolutionary minded groups throughout the continent. Víctor Raúl **Haya de la Torre**, founder of the **APRA** (Alianza Popular Revolucionaria Americana) was heavily influenced by it. Haya founded APRA in 1924 while in exile in Mexico. Its programme combined economic nationalism with Latin American solidarity, called for incorporation of the Indians into the mainstream of national life and had a strong anti-imperialist – specifically anti-USA – stance.

The growing importance of foreign investments and the US intervention in the Caribbean, Central America and Mexico (occupation of the Dominican Republic (1916), invasion of Haiti (1915), several interventions in Cuba between 1917 and 1919, multiple interventions in Nicaragua, landing of marines in Panama, El Salvador, Costa Rica, Guatemala and Honduras, and several interventions during the Mexican Revolution) provoked a nationalist backlash and reinforced the cultural nationalism already strong among groups of intellectuals. The leading anti-imperialist spokesmen tended to be left-wing parties, labour unions

and intellectuals. While Haya de la Torre's APRA took one of the strongest stances against Western imperialism, the main anti-imperialist ideas had been present among intellectuals since the beginning of the century, as seen for example in José Martí's warning against future US interventions in his essay, 'Nuestra América'. Augusto César **Sandino**'s successful resistance to the presence of the US army in Nicaragua between 1912–32 was a model hailed with much enthusiasm throughout Latin America. Anti-colonialist thinking of poets like Luis **Palés Matos**, Nicolás **Guillén** or Oswald de **Andrade** was often expressed and discussed in avant-garde journals like *Revista de avance* (1927–30) of Cuba or *Revista de antropofagia* (1928–9) of Brazil. The 1917 Mexican Constitution that declared the subsoil resources exclusive property of the nation was also a good example of nationalism. It resulted in serious labour unrest and eventual nationalization of the petroleum industry in Mexico. Similarly the United Fruit Company of Boston was hit by a violent strike in late 1928 in the Colombian banana zone. A further escalation of economic nationalism came with the world economic Depression of 1929.

The deep changes that the Soviet Revolution brought about created a real interest in Marxist and socialist ideology throughout Latin America. Many intellectuals travelled to the Soviet Union to see these changes for themselves and learn from them. They brought back a renewed enthusiasm for the revolution and social change, which was spoken of and envisioned as a real possibility by both the socialist and communist parties in the 1920s and 1930s. Many essays and vanguard literary texts of the time speak of revolution and social changes, as for example Magda Portal y Serafín Delmar's book of short stories, *El derecho de matar* (The Right to Kill) (1926). The Peruvian José Carlos **Mariátegui**, one of the most prominent Latin American thinkers, upon his return from Europe, founded the Peruvian Socialist Party (1928). His *Siete ensayos* (Seven Interpretive Essays on Peruvian Reality) (1928) analyses from a Marxist position the social, economic and cultural problems of Peru, explaining that the dismal living conditions of the indigenous people is a direct result of the semi-feudal land tenure system that has not changed substantially since colonial times.

Mariátegui is one of the most important representatives of the *indigenista* movement in Latin America and his journal, ***Amauta***, published the best exponents of *indigenismo* in poetry, prose, essay and arts – they included Jorge **Icaza**, Luis **Valcárcel** and others.

There were several literary movements that co-existed during the 1920s. *Postmodernismo* was in direct reaction to the refinement and excess rhetoric of the *modernista* (see ***modernismo, Spanish American***) movement and expressed emotions in a simple, direct, almost prosaic manner. Four women stood out as the best representatives of *postmodernismo*: Delmira Agustini (1886–1914) and Juana de **Ibarbourou**, whose erotic images in poetry represented a rebellion against the patriarchal society they lived in; Alfonsina **Storni**, who expressed her frustration and demanded a more just place for women in her society; and, finally, love in its various manifestations, maternal longing and social protest were the subject matter of Gabriela **Mistral**'s work. The avant-garde (see **avant-garde in Latin America**) movement of the 1920s that closely followed and at one time co-existed with the *postmodernistas* represented a significant cultural development that gave voice to a relatively unified and distinctly Latin American art, even as it was part of a larger international movement. In realist prose the most outstanding narrative writings were the so-called regionalist novels (see ***regionalismo***), interested in describing different rural areas and the inhabitants of Latin America. The best-known novels of this time were: *Don Segundo Sombra* (1926) by Ricardo **Güiraldes**, which idealized the Argentine **gaucho** and the ***pampa***; *La vorágine* (The Vortex) (1924) by the Colombian José Eustacio **Rivera**, described survival in the tropical forest and the rubber exploitation in the Amazonian region; and *Doña Bárbara* (1919) by Rómulo **Gallegos**, which replayed the well-known nineteenth-century theme of civilization against barbarism in showing the influence of nature over the inhabitants in the Venezuelan plains.

Parallel with the *indigenista* movement mentioned above, Latin America in the 1920s was witness to an interest in the emancipation of its black population. ***Negrismo*** as a literary movement had as a first impulse the European avant-garde's interest in so called primitive cultures. However, in Latin America this movement was also based on writings of the Cuban anthropologist, Fernando **Ortiz**, and expressed the desire for emancipation of an important sector of a racially mixed population, especially from the Caribbean area but also present in many other nations like Brazil, Peru and Colombia. Some of its better-known writers were the Puerto Rican Luis Palés Matos, the Cuban Nicolás Guillén and the Dominican Manuel de **Cabral**. In painting, the Brazilian Tarsila do **Amaral** and the Uruguayan Pedro **Figari** were among many others depicting the African character of Latin American society.

An important ideological influence with repercussions for education throughout the continent was the University Reform movement. It started at the University of Córdoba in Argentina in 1918, ignited in most major universities in the 1920s and resulted in the creation of numerous popular universities. Some of the main demands made public in the 'Manifiesto de la juventud Argentina de Córdoba a los hombres libres de América', of 1918, were political autonomy for the University, student representation, an end of the tenure system and elective courses.

The 1920s represent a pinnacle of the voyage towards self-discovery in arts while integrating modernist European techniques. José **Vasconcelos**, Minister of Education in Mexico, gave impetus to the muralist movement (see **muralism**) – unleashing a vast programme of cultural renovation with the explicit purpose of reconciling fine art with popular arts and crafts. Diego **Rivera** synthesizes in his socially committed murals Renaissance fresco techniques, pre-Colombian art, the styles and images of Mexican contemporary popular culture, and Soviet-style socialist realism. Together with painters like David Alfaro **Siqueiros** and José Clemente **Orozco** they decorated the walls of the Ministry of Education, Chapingo Agricultural School, the National Palace and other places. Siqueiros's 'Manifesto to the plastic artists of America' (Barcelona, 1921) expressed the essence of the muralists' project by calling for a 'public art, a monumental and heroic art, a human art...pre-Columbian in inspiration and workerist in orientation'. Muralism had an important influence in the political art of this century throughout the world. In the Andean region nativism was led by José **Sabogal**, who became Peru's militant indigenist and aesthetic nationalist, and led this movement for the next thirty years. Rufino **Tamayo**'s paintings, while deeply rooted in the indigenism that underpinned the muralist movement, searched for forms that could communicate his Mexican experience and engage simultaneously with universal currents. The quasi-geometrical indigenous stylizations of Guatemalan Carlos **Mérida** move entirely beyond folklore.

A fusion of vernacular with the avant-garde styles was represented by Cuban Amelia **Peláez** and Venezuelan Armando **Reverón** while Uruguayan Pedro Figari is characterized by a unique personal post-impressionist mode. Uruguayan Joaquín **Torres García**'s trajectory spanned cubism, fauvism and neo-*plasticismo* in a journey towards geometrical aesthetics. Emilio **Pettoruti** of Argentina effectively introduced the constructivist method of geometrical abstraction into Latin America. Finally, the 1920s in Brazil presented a colourful tapestry of regionalism, nationalism and cosmopolitanism all under the banner of *modernismo*. The most outstanding painters are expressionist Lasar **Segall**, Anita **Malfatti**, Tarsila do Amaral, Emiliano di **Cavalcanti** and Cândido **Portinari**, the great vehicle of artistic nationalism during the 1920 and 1930s.

In music the Brazilian Heitor **Villa-Lobos** dominated the scene. His vast work combined formal innovation with primitive content, and synthesized Portuguese, African and Indian musical traditions. The Mexican Carlos **Chávez** was the other great name in twentieth-century Latin American music. While he wrote piano arrangements of popular revolutionary songs like Adelita and La cucaracha (The Roach), he tried not to recreate pre-Colombian musical patterns or techniques as such but to connote them, thus making the past communicate with the present. The 1920s were also the era of symphony orchestras. Innumerable nationalist works were premièred by, among others, Chávez and Silvestre **Revueltas**, whose music drew mainly on contemporary folk and popular music. *Afrocubanismo*, an intricate fusion of native folk elements with sophisticated cosmopolitan orchestration and a mixture of native

and European instruments, characterized the music of Cuban Amadeo **Roldán** developed in *Obertura sobre temas cubanos* (Overture on Cuban Themes) (1925) and *Motivos de son* (1930) based on Guillén's poems. Alejandro **García Caturla** maintained identification with black culture through the adaptation of the conga, **son**, comparsa and **rumba** in his *Tres danzas Cubanas* (Three Cuban Dances) (1928).

Starting in the 1920s, the rapid spread of the new medium of **radio** and the record industry was exemplary of the emerging mass culture. The popularization of the Argentine **tango** and the Mexican **corrido**, the foundation of the first **samba** school in Rio de Janeiro or the spread of Cuban music in Latin America, due mainly to the US recording industry, are examples of this massification process. The arrival of electricity in most urban centres witnessed not only the advent of the radio, but also of the silent film. By the 1920s, Argentina and Brazil had become Hollywood's third and fourth largest film markets after Britain and Australia. In Chile eighty feature films were supposed to have been made between 1916 and 1931, and films were also made in Colombia and Peru. In Brazil there was a considerable regional production of films. In Recife thirteen films were made in the course of eight years. Indigenous themes were frequent. In Bolivia *Corazón aymara* (Aymara Heart) (1925), by Pedro Sambarino and *La profecia del lago* (The Prophecy of the Lake) (1925) by José María Velasco Maidana (1901–89) dealt with indigenous themes, while in Argentina *Nobleza gaucha* (Gaucho Noblesse) (1915) by Eduardo Martínez de la Pera, or the extraordinarily successful *El último malón* (The Last Indian Uprising) (1918) by Alcides Greca, explored the valorization of the gaucho and the national tradition. Melodramas, films exalting patriotic historical themes, aspects of the life of the nascent middle class or films re-enacting contemporary crimes were also common. In Mexico *El hombre sin patria* (The Man without a Country) (1922) by Miguel Contreras Torres addressed the theme of Mexican workers in the USA. Mário **Peixoto**'s *Limite* (The Boundary) (1929) is a landmark of the Brazilian avant-garde hailed as a work of genius by Eisenstein. José Agustín **Ferreyra** was the most innovative and prolific of the Argentine **silent-**

film directors, painting bitter-sweet portraits of the immigrant neighbourhoods of Buenos Aires's south side and producing more than twenty films in the decade, ending in 1927. *La muchacha del arrabal* (The Girl from the Outskirts of Town) (1922) is the tale of a young painter who frequents south-side cafés and becomes the lover of a fallen young woman, drawn to the city in search of fame as a tango singer but becoming a prostitute instead. This film shows how in Argentine popular culture the history of the tango and the cinema are closely intertwined. By the end of the decade the cinemas were full of tango orchestras accompanying silent films (see **tango melodramas**). *La muchacha del arrabal*'s title song was also recorded a year after the film's release by the country's most famous tango singer, Carlos **Gardel**. In the 1920s and 1930s he was highly popular as an interpreter of the melancholy ballads of the tango in night-clubs, and in several motion pictures like the early *Luces de Buenos Aires* (Lights of Buenos Aires) (1931) filmed in Paris.

Further reading

Barnard, T. and Rist, P. (1996) *South American Cinema. A Critical Filmography 1915–1994*, New York/London: Garland.

Béhague, G. (1979) *Music in Latin America: An Introduction*, New Jersey: Prentice Hall.

Bethell, L. (1995) *The Cambridge History of Latin America*, vol. X, Cambridge: Cambridge University Press.

Castedo, L. (1969) *A History of Latin American Art and Architecture from Precolombian Times to the Present*, New York: Praeger.

Catlin, S.L. and Grieder, T. (1966) *Art of Latin America since Independence*, New Haven: Yale University.

Chanan, M. (1996) 'Cinema in Latin America', in G. Nowell-Smith (ed.) *The Oxford History of World Cinema*, Oxford: Oxford University Press, pp. 427–35.

Franco, J. (1973) *Spanish American Literature since Independence*, Cambridge: Cambridge University Press.

—— (1969) *An Introduction to Spanish American Literature*, Cambridge: Cambridge University Press.

Skidmore, T. and Smith, P.H. (1992) *Modern Latin America*, fourth edn, New York/Oxford: Oxford University Press.

MIHAI GRUNFELD

1930s, the

The 1930s were structured around conflict and confrontation along three vectors. First, the artistic avant-garde and cultural modernization introduced their cosmopolitan, urban values; on the other side, (literary and musical) regionalism (see *regionalismo*), in defending the representativity, originality and anti-centralism of its propositions, attacked the premises of the avant-garde, with their tendency to unify everything. Between these two positions, however, the socialist orientation (which was dominant in the narrative and the plastic arts) agreed with the avant-garde with respect to their shared urban and internationalist framework, which translated into techniques of fragmentation, tension and confrontation, while at the same time it offered a critique of avant-garde formalism on the basis of Stalinist collectivist schema.

Yet the socialist aesthetic project also extended the mimetic principles of realism that had nourished the regionalist proposal, while at the same time recriminating the latter for its short-sighted nationalism. As in every peripheral region, in Latin America the avant-garde connoted nationalism, so it should come as no surprise that its institutionalization should have culminated in the formation of a relatively autonomous lay field that was pregnant with potentially explosive conflicts. It was neither in avant-garde poetry nor in regionalist or socialist realist short stories where this conflict of values found its characteristic register, but in the essay. The problem of the national as a verbal artefact, an organization of representations and belief systems, was explored in the seminal works of the decade: Paulo **Prado**'s *Retrato do Brasil* (Portrait of Brazil) (1928), Sérgio **Buarque de Holanda**'s *Raizes do Brasil* (Roots of Brazil) (1936), Ezequiel **Martínez Estrada**'s *Radiografía de la pampa* (X-ray of the *Pampa*) or Eduardo **Mallea**'s *Historia de una pasión argentina* (History of an Argentine Passion)

(1937). Some of **Discépolo**'s tangos, like *Yira yira* (1930) or *Cambalache* (1935) could also be included here. And the same phenomenon embraces Ortega y Gasset's global diagnostic essays like *El tema de nuestro tiempo* (The Theme of our Time) and *La rebelión de las masas* (The Rebellion of the Masses) or Keyserling's *South American Meditations*, as well as the work of the intellectual travellers, whether those in flight from war like Stefan Zweig and Witold Gombrowicz, adventurers in the absolute like Antonin Artaud or Henri Michaux or the professional of difference like Lévi-Strauss or Alfred Métraux. In all of them there arises a need to discover a regime of legibility for a problematic society, which at one moment is transformed in adapting to what is new (on the Atlantic side of the Southern Cone one-fifth of the population are European immigrants), yet at another reconstructs meanings through violent traditionalist actions. This urgency and possibility of signification is discussed in the essays of Antonio **Candido**, who identified the period equally with the oligarchic historicism of Gilberto **Freyre** on the one hand and on the other the historical realism of Caio Prado Jr, who went beyond the *enfants terribles* of the 1920s but at the same time showed that in Brazil, more than anywhere else, the conflict between avant-garde and regionalists laid down the most extreme options: the politicization of art or the aestheticization of hierarchy, the abstraction of private life or the abstraction of the State. It is no accident that by 1936 questionnaires were circulating concerning the exhaustion of modern art, and that in their replies writers like Murilo Mendes should distance themselves from the modernist rupture and develop consistent positions of cultural hybridity or retroactive reconstruction closer to the modernism of Baudelaire. Neither is it a mere coincidence that a politician like Getúlio **Vargas**, forger of conciliatory politics and ambiguous alliances, should have had recourse to a historiographical operation *après coup*, whereby he argued that the artistic rupture represented by the Semana de Arte Moderna (see **Modern Art Week**) in 1922 corresponded to the politics of compromise of the **Estado Novo**, thus legitimating the revolutionary movement of 1930. The confusion between avant-garde and modernity mixes up the residual

aspects of tradition and presents them as replacement values in the face of the emerging unknown.

It would be wrong to identify the essay with a simple preponderance of programmatic writing. In fact the free, open and flexible character of the historical imagination adapted better than any other discourse to a particular kind of work of sophisticated abstraction of evolutionary historicism, giving shape to a concept of time at once discontinuous and diasporic. A certain disillusioned pessimism, not only with regard to scientific aspirations but also with the promises of capitalism, leads to a return to the vitalist postulates of post-literature (Nietzsche, Bergson) now enriched with the diagnosis of the cultural malaise provided by psychoanalysis. In this intersection of perspectives complementary to the analysis, the abstraction of languages denies the dichotomy between matter and consciousness or between subject and object. As a self-generated universal or as a pure difference between examples, not only textual but cultural, which are dynamized or destabilized in terms of interactive canonical effects in a constant permutation of actors and processes, the modern essay abstracts discourses. The task, based on the architecture of memory, precisely coincides with the modern concept of fiction that is being elaborated concomitantly. **Borges**'s *Historia universal de la infamia* (Universal History of Infamy) (1935) or *Historia de la eternidad* (History of Eternity) (1936), or **Onetti**'s *El pozo* (The Well) (1939) serve to illustrate this concept of fiction as a phantasmagorical essay. If the interventions of Mallea or Martínez Estrada still aspired to *interpret* the national in its time of crisis (which meant translating what was double into a transcendental unity), the fictions of Borges and Onetti, by contrast, implied the inversion and reorganization of the place and the effects of the concept of literature, a textual rupture that, as a theoretical point of departure, shows the crisis in the act as well as the violent inversion of cultural legibility that it brings with it. They demonstrate not just the crisis of the national, but the crisis of the story and the history of these concepts as unitary concepts. They put on trial a space and a consistency of writing that exposes the 'literary' (pretend) character of this 'history' of a 'national' 'consciousness', and in revealing their actually contradictory character, define fiction no longer as a specific language, oscillating between rupture and permanence, but as the irreversible destruction of all literary language. This destruction of discourses is a transition without end: the hybridities of *Espantapájaros* (Scarecrow) (1932) by Oliverio **Girondo**, simple first steps in the post-Utopian experience of *En la masmédula*; the possibility of suspending developments in logic and understanding language as an incessant difference, whether in the quotations from Mário de **Andrade**'s *Contos de Belazarte* (Belazarte's Stories) (1933) or Miguel Angel **Asturias**'s *Leyendas de Guatemala* (Legends of Guatemala) (1930), or in the transculturation of Alejo **Carpentier**'s *Ecue-Yambo-O* (1931) or *Muerte de Narciso* (Death of Narcissus) (1937) by **Lezama Lima**. All the essays on time and eternity that we can find in the first steps of Octavio **Paz** or Carlos **Pellicer**, in César **Vallejo**'s *Poemas humanos* (Human Poems) (1939), Murilo Mendes's *A poesía em pánico* (Poetry in a Panic) (1938) or Leopoldo **Marechal**'s *Descenso y ascenso del alma por la belleza* (Descent and Ascent of the Soul into Beauty) (1933) – attempt to write the experience of the extreme. None of these options, however, could have happened without the presence of the avant-garde, as Beatriz **Sarlo** suggests in an observation regarding Borges that is equally apposite here:

> [T]he linguistic imagination leapt backwards and sideways with a freedom that only the avant-garde could have produced towards the gauchesque, towards the old *criollo* traditions, towards the inflections of plain and trivial oral language. Cultural nationalism was thus given a new formal and aesthetic definition by the avant-garde of the 1920s. And the literary imagination. free at last from *modernismo*, redefined the space of Latin American literature in the 1930s.

Further reading

Campos, H. de (1979) 'Seraphim a great nonbook', in Osvaldo de Andrade (ed.) *Seraphim Grosse Pointe*, Austin: Texas University Press.

Franco, J. (1970) *The Modern Culture of Latin America: Society and the Artist*, London: Pall Mall.

Halperin, D. (1969) *Historia contemporánea de América Latina*, Madrid: Alianza Editorial.

Sarlo, B. (1993) *Jorge Luis Borges*, London: Verso.

Skidmore, T. (1967) *Politics in Brazil 1930–1964: An Experiment in Democracy*, New York: Oxford University Press.

RAUL ANTELO

1940s, the

The decade opened in Latin America with the arrival of numerous refugees from the Spanish Civil War (see **Spanish Civil War, impact of**), particularly to Mexico and Argentina, some of whom (Luis **Buñuel**, Paul Casals, José **Gaos** and the founders of the publishing houses **Sudamericana** and **Losada**) were to make significant contributions to the cultural scene of their new countries. International solidarity with the embattled Spanish republic, in which many Latin American intellectuals were active, also contributed to anti-fascist activities directed not only at fascism in Germany, Italy, Spain and Portugal but also at fascist tendencies in the armed forces and governments of several Latin American countries, notably Argentina and Brazil. The entry of the United States into the Second World War at the end of 1941 had a dramatic impact on the entire Latin American and Caribbean region, with strong pressure by the USA on pro-Axis elements in the Argentine military, the entry of Brazil and several other countries into the late stages of the war on the Allied side, the growth of US bases in Trinidad, Puerto Rico and elsewhere, and some skirmishes around the Vichy-held outposts on the French Caribbean islands of Martinique and Guadeloupe. The government of Franklin D. Roosevelt conceived the Good Neighbour Policy as a way of increasing cooperation between the USA and Latin America during the war, an effort led by Nelson Rockefeller (with a network of collaborators throughout the continent, including María Rosa **Oliver** in Argentina). This facet of US policy had a strong impact, particularly on the representation of Latin America in Hollywood cinema; this was the heyday of Carmen **Miranda**, Lupe **Vélez** and others, and of significant cooperation between the

US and Mexican film industries (e.g. the John Huston film *The Fugitive* (1947), photographed by Gabriel **Figueroa**). The Rockefeller-led effort, which aimed to soften and improve the image of Latin America in US media, was also part of an effort to heighten US penetration into the Latin American mass communications market. After the war, in 1948, the Pan American Union (founded in 1910) was renamed the **Organization of American States** (OAS), still headquartered in Washington, where it would play a significant role in Cold War politics in the western hemisphere.

Juan Domingo **Perón** began his rise to power with the consolidation of a small group of army officers in the early 1940s, becoming labour minister and vice president, then *de facto* president, then elected president in 1946. The most dramatic political event of the decade, the rise of **Peronism** transformed the political landscape with its anti-imperialist (but also anti-Communist) threads, **populism**, **cultural nationalism**, and with the mass mobilization of newly unionized workers; it also gave women the vote for the first time in Argentina and promulgated a new constitution. An important event of a different kind was the election of Getulio **Vargas** as president of Brazil in 1945; Vargas had led the fascistic **Estado Novo** in the 1930s, but in the wake of the Second World War and the defeat of fascism in Europe, he repackaged himself as a democrat. The most dramatic event of the end of the decade, the civil war in Colombia known as La **Violencia**, began with the assassination of Jorge Eliécer Gaitán in Bogotá in 1948; there were similar conflicts on a smaller scale in Peru, Costa Rica, Guatemala and elsewhere, culminating in the abolition of the army in Costa Rica (1949) and, with the election of Arévalo in 1948, the beginning of the conflict in Guatemala that would culminate in the 1954 CIA-led *coup*. Although many countries adopted democratic facades in the period, partly to satisfy the USA, this did not imply real change in political and economic structures: where even mild challenges were made or limited modernizations attempted, the response was immediate and violent.

The 1940s were a period of significant cultural ferment, particularly with the growth of urban culture industries: film studios that were intended to rival Hollywood in Argentina (**Argentina Sono Film**), Brazil (**Vera Cruz Studios**) and Mexico (**Churubusco Studios**) were set up. The period is known as the 'Golden Age' of Mexican cinema, with a series of remarkable films by Emilio 'El Indio' **Fernández** and others, starring such names as María **Félix**, Pedro **Armendáriz**, Jorge **Negrete** and Pedro **Infante**, with music by Agustín **Lara** and other great composers of the **bolero**. The **tango** evolved into its 'big band' period (**Troilo** and others), while the bolero and the **rumba** captured audiences throughout the region, and also in the USA and Europe. Music, like the cinema, became increasingly industrial in this period, with a similar star system and heavy advertising, ties to the cinema and **radio**, and a striking international nature, transcending the national music scenes that had characterized earlier periods (except for the occasional exception like Carlos **Gardel**, who had become a star all over Spanish-speaking Latin America before he died in 1937 while on tour in Colombia); radio, tours and film roles made stars all over Latin America of such singers as Libertad **Lamarque**, Carmen Miranda (though in her case there was significant backlash to her 'tropicalization' of stereotypes of Latin America), Javier **Solís**, Jorge Negrete and **Toña la Negra**.

In literature, Jorge Luis **Borges** (with Adolfo **Bioy Casares** and others) promoted the exploration of the fantastic (see **fantastic literature**), as well as of science fiction and **crime fiction**, to open up alternatives to the rural cycle of works, many influenced by *mundonovismo* and *indigenismo*, which dominated fictional production (and the lists of publishers like **Losada** in Buenos Aires). The *Antología de la literatura fantástica* (1940) would be remarkably influential, opening up space for the emerging narrative works of such authors as Juan **Rulfo**, Julio **Cortázar** and José **Donoso**, all of whom began publishing in this decade. Alejo **Carpentier**, in the famous 1949 preface to *El reino de este mundo*, proposed that instead of looking to fantasy (or to the collage approach advocated by Parisian surrealism) the Latin American writer could find what he termed *lo real maravilloso* (the marvellous real) in the geography, history and hybrid cultures of Latin America. The decade is also marked by the emergence of a tradition of urban fiction: works by **Onetti** (*Tierra de nadie*) (1941), **Marechal** (*Adán Buenosayres*) (1948), **Sabato** (*El túnel*) (1948). Though Ciro **Alegría**'s *El mundo es ancho y ajeno* won a New York literary prize in 1941, it marked the end of the old rural/*indigenista* novel: the future lay largely with experimental urban fiction and with 'magic realist' explorations of indigenous cultures and the popular (see **magical realism**).

Gabriela **Mistral** became the first Latin American writer to win a Nobel Prize for Literature (1943). During the decade **Neruda** was working feverishly on the poems that would become the book-length ***Canto general*** (1950), while also being heavily involved in Chilean politics and forced to escape in a dramatic journey across the Andes (narrated in his long poem, which also includes accounts of Latin American geography, history, political persecution, everyday lives, and impassioned calls for action against Latin American rightist dictators and US imperialism). In a similar vein, the *negrista* (see ***negrismo***) and **négritude** groups that had emerged in the previous decade continued their work, though **Césaire** changed direction to some extent by participating in French politics, leading to criticism from more radical nationalist and revolutionary sectors in the French Caribbean. But the decade also saw the emergence of very different poetic voices: José **Lezama Lima** (and his magazine ***Orígenes***), Silvina **Ocampo** and Juan Rodolfo **Wilcock** in Argentina, and the Spanish and **Guarani** poetry of Augusto **Roa Bastos** in Paraguay.

New developments in the performing arts included the introduction of the theatre of the absurd in Virgilio **Piñera**'s ***Electra Garrigó*** (1948) and the founding of two of the most celebrated dance companies of the next decades, the Ballet Alicia Alonso (later **Ballet Nacional de Cuba**) and the Ballet Nacional de México (later **Ballet Folklórico de México**).

In 1940, the Cuban anthropologist Fernando **Ortiz** proposed the idea of transculturation (see **cultural theory**) as a model for cultural change (an idea endorsed by Malinowski in his foreword to Ortiz's book ***Contrapunteo cubano del tabaco y del azúcar*** (Cuban Counterpoint)). Gilberto **Freyre** in Brazil, Samuel **Ramos** in Mexico, José María **Arguedas** in Peru, Aimé **Césaire** in

Martinique and Ezequiel **Martínez Estrada** in Argentina had similar concerns with the definition and evolution of culture in the region, and with the cultural importance of **race**, conflicts between the rural and the urban, and the relation between élite and popular culture. These debates contributed to the growing professionalization of **anthropology** and other social sciences as a field in universities throughout the region, with publication of such major works as Eric **Williams**'s ***Capitalism and Slavery*** (1943), Gilberto **Freyre**'s *Interpretação do Brasil* (Interpretation of Brazil) (1945), Luis da **Câmara Cascudo**'s *Antologia do folclore brasileiro* (Anthology of Brazilian Folklore) (1943), and the foundation of the **Casa de la Cultura Ecuatoriana** by Benjamín Carrión and others. The study of literature was also professionalized in such works as Pedro **Henríquez Ureña**'s *Las corrientes literarias en la América Hispánica* (Literary Currents in Hispanic America) (1949), Antonio Cândido's work on Sílvio Romero (1945) and Arturo **Torres-Ríoseco**'s new history of Latin American literature (1945), among the first to endeavour to link the histories of the national literatures into a continental whole. The University College of the West Indies (later **University of the West Indies**) was founded (leading to the group of a local – black – intelligentsia that was to be important in **decolonization and independence**). The decade also saw the founding of groups for the advancement of science and other academic research.

In the visual arts and architecture, the decade was marked by numerous declarations of artistic modernity. The Madí (see **Arte Madí**), Independientes and Nuevas Realidades groups in Argentina promoted several varieties of modern art including abstraction, while emerging artists elsewhere included **Matta** in Chile, **Otero** in Venezuela, **Szyszlo** in Peru, and the architects **Niemeyer** in Brazil, **Villanueva** in Venezuela, Alberto **Prebisch** in Argentina and **Barragán** in Mexico. Modern art museums were founded in Rio de Janeiro and São Paulo in 1948. Monuments of modern architecture of the period include Villanueva's El Silencio complex in Caracas, Niemeyer and others' designs for **Pampulha** in Belo Horizonte, and the plans by Le Corbusier and his Latin American disciples for dramatic redesign of the urban fabric in Rio de Janeiro, Buenos Aires and elsewhere. These currents linked modernization with the emerging **International Style** in architecture. **Muralism** by the Mexican artists **Rivera**, **Siqueiros** and **Orozco**, the Brazilian **Portinari** and others continued, but in retrospect the decade was of interest for the emergence of the feminist works (influenced to some extent by surrealism) of Frida **Kahlo**, Leonora **Carrington** and Remedios **Varo**, the bold new work of Matta, Otero, Rufino **Tamayo** and Carlos **Mérida**, and emergence of constructivist groups such as the **Taller Torres García** in Uruguay and the Arturo group in Argentina.

The emergence of 'internationalist' currents in Latin American music, in the works of **Ardevol** in Cuba, Juan Carlos **Paz** in Argentina and **Koellreutter** in Brazil, among others, led to an international recognition of modern **art music** from the region for piano, string quartets and other small groups, as well as for orchestra. The first scholarly works on Latin American music were published in 1945 by Gilbert Chase (*A Guide to the Music of Latin America*) and Nicholas Slonimsky (*Music of Latin America*). Mário de Andrade left his *Dicionário da música brasileira* (Dictionary of Brazilian Music) unfinished at the time of his death in 1945 (though he had published *Música do Brasil* [The Music of Brazil] in 1941), but Carpentier's book *La música en Cuba* (Music in Cuba) (1946) and Oneyda Alvarenga's *Música popular brasileira* (Brazilian Popular Music) (1947) evince similar interests in the intersection of popular culture, the professionalized study of music, and the definition of national identity. Meanwhile, in the world of popular music, a new, rather more international, sense of Latin American identity was being forged, particularly in the great popular phenomenon of the decade, the **bolero**.

The 1940s saw the emergence of an institutional framework for Latin American and unity (through the OAS, despite the tutelage in that institution of the USA), the development of a variety of associations, institutions, congresses that began to bring Latin American intellectuals and political figures together on a regular basis, the first important histories of Latin American literature, and international recognition of Latin American and Caribbean contributions to world culture (the Nobel Prize to Mistral, the bolero, rumba and mambo crazes, Carmen Miranda, etc.). At the same time, the decade was marked by powerful nationalist tendencies in Argentina and elsewhere. Emblematic of the decade are the founding by Jesús Silva Herzog of the magazine *Cuadernos Americanos* in Mexico, the creation of the **Fondo de Cultura Económica** in Mexico (important for its promotion of Latin American classics in its Biblioteca Americana, begun in 1947), and the emergence of other media enterprises of increasingly great influence over the coming decades in the worlds of cinema, music, publishing and radio. The controlled modernization that marked the end of the decade was under the tutelage of the USA and of the emergent world economic institutions (the World Bank and International Monetary Fund, both started at the Bretton Woods Conference in 1948); the Cold War, with cultural arms like the Congress for Cultural Freedom, was positioning the region within the US sphere of influence.

Further reading

Arciniegas, G. (ed.) (1944) *The Green Continent: A Comprehensive View of Latin America by its Leading Writers*, New York: Alfred A. Knopf.

Gunther, J. (1942) *Inside Latin America*, London: Hamish Hamilton.

Novo, S. (1994) *La vida en el período presidencial de Manuel Avila Camacho*, Mexico City: Consejo Nacional de Cultura.

—— (1994) *La vida en el período presidencial de Miguel Alemán*, Mexico City: Consejo Nacional de Cultura.

Potash, R. (1969) *The Army and Politics in Argentina*, Stanford: Stanford University Press.

Prebisch, R. (1950) *The Economic Development of Latin America and Its Principal Problems*, Lake Success, NY: United Nations, Department of Economic Affairs.

Wood, B. (1961) *The Making of the Good Neighbor Policy*, New York: Columbia University Press.

DANIEL BALDERSTON

1950s, the

A turbulent yet profoundly determining decade in Latin America and elsewhere, the achievements of which have often been overshadowed by the far more radical 1960s (see **1960s, the**). Throughout this contradictory decade, Latin America manifested heightened prosperity and cultural effervescence but also growing inequality and new forms of critical and revolutionary awareness. According to **Halperin Donghi**, these post-war years constitute a well-defined period 'marked by hopes for industrialization in the larger nations and the high prestige of liberal democracy everywhere'. Yet, as a corollary of industrialization and import substitution (see **import substitution industrialization**), **internal migration** from rural areas to the major cities increased exponentially, changing the face of the cities with shanty towns (see **shanty towns and slums**) that housed the migrants, who often became a new class of urban marginals. An additional incongruity resulted from the increasingly evident contradiction between the rhetoric of national sovereignty and increasing neo-colonial economic dependency and political authoritarianism throughout the region.

The political ethos of frustrated revolutions of the 1950s is framed by the assassination of the popular leader, Carlos Eliécer Gaitán, in Bogotá in 1948, an event that unleashed fourteen years of political violence (La **Violencia**), and, at the other end, the Cuban Revolution of 1959 (see **revolutions**), which brought Fidel **Castro** to power. In between, politically radical movements clamouring for social justice erupted throughout the continent and were also, sooner or later, silenced. In 1951, liberal Guatemalan president, Jacobo **Arbenz**, initiated ground-breaking land reforms (aimed at United Fruit's huge banana plantations (see **bananas**)) and other progressive measures despite protests from the military, the oligarchy and the USA; in 1954 his government was toppled in a USA-backed military *coup* led by CIA-trained troops under the command of Colonel Carlos Castillo Armas. For the next thirty years, military officers controlled Guatemala. In Bolivia in 1952, an armed revolution led by groups of workers and peasants brought Víctor **Paz Estenssoro** to power; his government nationalized the tin mines and other industries, initiated agrarian reforms, and conferred voting rights on all citizens, including the previously disenfranchised indigenous population. Yet by 1957, under great economic pressures, Bolivia was forced to accept a USA-drafted 'stabilization' plan that led to the reversal of many of the nationalizations, opening up, for example, Bolivia's rich petroleum resources to US interests (culminating in a military *coup* in 1965). While in 1955 Argentina Juan **Perón** was deposed by a military *coup*, in 1954 Brazil Getulio **Vargas**, elected president in 1951 (after his **Estado Novo** had been toppled by a *coup* in 1945) was threatened by another *coup* and chose to commit suicide, an ingenious, albeit fatal, political ploy, which enabled the election of Juscelino **Kubitschek** in 1956 and the onset of the Brazilian developmentalist 'economic miracle'.

The Cold War had a dramatic impact on political and cultural relations between the USA and Latin America. With the hardening of the Soviet Bloc and the so-called 'free world', US policy-makers made loyalty to an anti-communist position a requirement for foreign aid, in areas as diverse as assistance with trade union (see **trade unions**) organizing (a programme organized through the AFL-CIO and the Department of Labour) and cultural relations. The Congress for Cultural Freedom, funded through the CIA (as became publicly clear in the 1960s when the *New York Times* ran a series of stories on the topic), was set up to build a network of anti-communist **intellectuals** throughout the world. (A famous publication that came out of this campaign was the book, *The God That Failed* (1950), with writings by former communists including Arthur Koestler and Ignazio Silone.) The Congress's Latin American operations were led in the 1950s by the Colombian intellectual, Germán **Arciniegas**. (The Congress's activities in the following decade included the funding of the controversial magazine, ***Mundo nuevo***.) The Soviet Union, meanwhile, organized its own international networks – the World Student Federation, the International Congress of Trade Unions – each of which mirrored the US versions. The hardening of positions was perhaps more visible after the Cuban Revolution of 1959 (see **revolutions**), but there were attempts made by both sides throughout the decade to sign up allies and to build networks.

The 1950s witnessed the triumph of internationalism in the arts, marked by a general acceptance of the phenomenal as a legitimate area of interest, both as subject matter and medium, limited only by the unity of the work and its expressive organization. **Constructivism** was the first stage, and it thrived especially in Argentina under the influence of Uruguayan master, **Torres García**, but also in Brazil. It was particularly influential in architecture and architectural planning, leading to the creation of **Brasília** (inaugurated in 1960) and university complexes in Caracas (Carlos Raúl **Villanueva**'s Central University of Venezuela) and Mexico, the gardens of Burle **Marx** in Rio de Janeiro and **Vázquez**'s museums in Mexico City. Although apparently contradictory, a tradition of freewheeling abstraction in painting also emerged in the 1950s that was basically expressionist, esoteric and identifiably individual, directly influenced by the work of Kandinsky and surrealism (see **surrealism in Latin American art**). This contradiction was also apparent in the rhetoric of the two camps: the former spoke of artistic invention in rational, scientific and technological terms; for the latter, artistic creation, albeit bound up with technology, was above all spiritual. Important exponents of this latter abstract (or, as it was often called, informalist) tendency were, among others, **Testa** in Argentina, de **Szyszlo** in Peru and **Mabe** in Brazil. Informalism was also the matrix for the important work of the Argentine neo-figurist school, especially Macciá, de la **Vega**, **Noé** and **Seguí**, whose large canvasses often depicted the barbaric instincts beneath modern civilization.

Of great significance for the arts was the resurrection of the tradition of the Paris salons in a new guise: the international biennial exhibition. Especially in São Paulo (**Bienale de São Paulo**, since 1951), Mexico City (1956) and Buenos Aires, the large biennials began to set international standards of judgement. Furthermore, the tradition of patronage was also reinvented through the establishment of important new museums and art galleries in all major cities, many heirs of renewed cultural nationalist sentiment, others directly financed by large corporations and their founda-

tions: the **Instituto Di Tella** in Buenos Aires, International Petroleum in Colombia, General Electric in Montevideo.

Art music thrived in the 1950s, as many composers who had begun in the 1940s reached artistic maturity. A crucial figure was **Ginastera**; while his Pampeana no. 2 (1954) was a symphonic pastoral, his Quartet no. 2 (1958) initiated his important neo-expressionist phase. In Mexico, Carlos **Chávez** retired as director of the Instituto Nacional de Bellas Artes in 1953 (and had resigned as director of the Mexico City symphony orchestra in 1948). His compositions from the period include *Prometeo* (Prometheus) (1956), a cantata and the opera, *Los visitantes* (The Visitors) (1953–6). Although Rodolfo **Halffter**'s music typically followed a melodic tonal tradition, with his 1953 *Tres hojas de álbum* for piano (Three Album Pages) (1953) he became the first Mexican composer to employ serialism. In Cuba, Jose **Ardévol** (part of the **Grupo de Renovación Musical**) composed *Música* (1957) for chamber orchestra and his *Third String Quartet* (1958), while Argeliers **León**'s work demonstrated the influence of Afro-Cuban music in *Akorín: cantos negros para piano* (1956), Danzón no. 3 (1957), also for piano, and *Cuatro danzas cubanas* (Four Cuban Dances) (1959) for string orchestra. Other avant-garde composers were Roque Cordero in Panama, who produced serialist compositions such as his second symphony (1956) and Leon **Schidlowsky** in Chile and his avant-garde treatment of polyrhythmic elements, and dodecaphony in works like *Nacimiento* (Birth) (1956). José Vicente Asuar was also developing there the first experiments in electronic music.

The increasing significance of nationalism, either as social criticism or analysis, was very evident in literature. In some sense, it might be argued that this stood in opposition to many visual arts and contemporary composers exploring modern idioms – though in many cases, in music at least, they pursued the two in parallel – Chávez and Ginastera are cases in point. Some writers explored facets of their national reality in a basically realist mode, though with surreal or mythic elements that both pointed ahead to the new novels of the 1960s and distinguished them from the cruder didacticism of the realism of the 1930s: **Asturias**'s *Hombres de maíz* (Men of Maize)

(1949), **Rulfo**'s *El llano en llamas* (The Burning Plain) (1953) and *Pedro Páramo* (1955), João Guimarães **Rosa**'s *Grande sertão: veredas* (The Devil to Pay in the Backlands) (1956), José María **Arguedas**'s *Los ríos profundos* (Deep Rivers) (1958), and Jorge **Amado**'s *Gabriela, cravo e canela* (Gabriela, Clove and Cinnamon) (1958). The writers of the **Boom** were already beginning to write by the end of the decade – Carlos **Fuentes**'s *La región más transparente* (Where the Air is Clear) (1958) marked a definitive transition for the novel into urban space, for example. Meanwhile, Pablo **Neruda** in Chile proved that poetry need not be concerned only with beautiful things or anguished passions in his monumental *Canto general* (General Song) (1950) – though paradoxically his most successful poems of the decade were the books of *Odas elementales*, which sought to develop a simpler poetry of everyday experience. Although best known for his poetry, Octavio **Paz** in Mexico published his vastly influential interpretation of the Mexican character, *El laberinto de la soledad* (The Labyrinth of Solitude) in 1950. Women writers also established their own voice in this decade, notably, Rosario **Castellanos** with *Balún Canán* (The Nine Guardians) (1957) and Clarice **Lispector** with *Laços de família* (Family Ties) (1960).

The cultural debates of the 1950s paralleled the discussions evolving towards the definition of dependency (see **dependency theory**) later in the decade. Here the economic predecessors, the ECLA school, were posing the central issue of national independence and autonomous development. Against that background, the proliferation of works analysing the 'national psyche', of which Paz's had been a precursor, reflected an urgent need to identify the 'obstacles to progress' – economic, political and, in the widest sense, cultural. Gilberto **Freyre**, Celso **Furtado**, Afrânio **Coutinho**, Fernando **Ortiz**, Cintio **Vitier**, Augusto **Salazar Bondy**, Sérgio **Buarque de Holanda**, Angel **Flores** and Fernando **Alegría** all contributed to the discussion.

Cultural nationalism and radical politics had a great impact upon the cinema. Under pressure from increasingly cosmopolitan and university-educated middle classes, and given the bankruptcy of most efforts at industrial film-making (such as **Vera Cruz Studios** in Brazil), a different

conception of the cinema began to emerge from newly created **cine clubs**, **cinemateques** and **film magazines**, and reinvigorated film criticism practices (see **film criticism and scholarship**). Rather than an industrial commodity, the cinema began to be conceived of as an art form with potentially far-reaching aesthetic and social aspirations. As early as 1950, at opposite ends of the continent, two film-makers seemed to be pointing in new *auteurist* directions: Leopoldo **Torre Nilsson** in Argentina and Luis **Buñuel**, who had managed to carve a niche for himself within the insular and commercialized Mexican industry. By mid-decade, the spirit of renovation and change was visible at the **SODRE**-sponsored documentary (see **documentary**) and experimental film festival in Montevideo (1954); in the work of Fernando **Birri** at the **Escuela de Cine Documental de Santa Fe** of the University of the Litoral in Santa Fe, Argentina; and in Nelson Pereira dos **Santos**'s *Rio quarenta graus* (Rio, 40 degrees) (1955) in Brazil. This somewhat frenzied search for new practical and aesthetic approaches to the cinema would result in the 'new' cinemas of the 1960s – the **Generación del 60** in Argentina, **Cinema Novo** in Brazil, the **ICAIC** cinema in Cuba – and the **New Latin American Cinema**.

Perhaps the decade's most significant development in the dramatic arts was the inauguration of two avant-garde theatrical companies: the **Arena Theatre Group** in São Paulo in 1953 and Teatro El **Galpón** in Uruguay in 1949. A 'circle' theatre, with audiences surrounding a stage set in the centre, Arena became an emblem for politicized theatre in Brazil, though not without internal contradictions. While Gianfrancesco **Guarnieri** produced extraordinarily powerful realist plays like *Eles não usam black-tie* (They Don't Wear Black Tie), Augusto **Boal** adhered to a more Brechtian (see **Brechtian theatre**) line that became very influential in the 1960s. Arena was also the first professional theatre company to feature an Afro-Brazilian actor, Milton **Goncalves**, in non-black roles. Montevideo's El Galpón, housed in an abandoned warehouse, was founded by Atahualpa del **Cioppo** and others, and was committed to engaging with the community artistically and politically. Resolutely non-dogmatic, the company combined Brecht's social engagement with a

Stanislavskian emotional realism, and its resonant productions combined clear ideological content with coherent characterizations.

Although not yet a significant competitor for the cinema, the introduction of **television** was also emblematic of the decade and would have profound repercussions in the 1960s. Introduced in Mexico, Brazil and Cuba in 1950, throughout the decade the medium began to thrive, freely borrowing and mixing stars and programming formats from radio and the cinema, and developed its own unique and significant genres, especially the *telenovela* (see **telenovelas**) (Mexico broadcast its first *telenovela* in 1957). Television also became an important ally of popular music, as performers flocked to the new medium to popularize their songs and rhythms. Of particular significance in the 1950s were 'new' Caribbean rhythms like the **mambo**, **calypso** and new versions of the **cha cha cha** and **rumba**. Cuba reaffirmed its status as a musical leader, catapulting Celia **Cruz**, **Pérez Prado** and others into stardom and contributing greatly to the *risqué* appeal of the Mexican cinema's *Cabaretera* genre (see **Cabaretera films**). The 1950s was the decade of Latin American rhythms, when, even in the typically insular USA, a Cuban band leader was the co-star of the most popular television programme (Desi Arnaz in *I Love Lucy*).

In the arena of sports, many had reason to celebrate national achievements. The decade began with Brazil hosting the football **World Cup** in 1950 and inaugurating in Rio de Janeiro the specially built Maracanã stadium, to date the largest in the world, seating 220,000. The clear favourite, Brazil, lost to Uruguay. Uruguay celebrated while Brazil mourned: composer Ary **Barroso**, who was doing a national radio commentary, swore off broadcasting forever and the defeat was dubbed 'the worst tragedy in Brazil's history'. But the 1950s ended with a stunning Brazilian victory in the 1958 cup in Sweden (the first time that a country playing outside its own continent won) and the consecration of **Pelé**, since then the world's most famous football player, and **Garrincha**. In other sports, too, Latin Americans were winning world attention – the great Argentine racing driver Juan **Fangio** was one.

Fidel **Castro**'s successful take-over of Cuba in 1959 was both a resounding finale to the 1950s and the beginning of a radically different decade. This was the first revolutionary movement to come to power based upon guerrilla warfare (see **guerrillas**) to develop a broad base of popular support, and its achievements – and failures – reverberated throughout all spheres of Latin American life in the 1960s.

Further reading

Burton, J. and Ruffinelli, J. (eds) (1999) 'Revisioning film in the fifties', special issue of *Nuevo Texto Crítico* 21–2.

Cometta Manzoni, A. (1960) *El indio en la novela de América*, Buenos Aires: Ed Futuro.

Franco, J. (1967) *The Modern Culture of Latin America*, New York: Praeger.

Furtado, Celso (1962) *Dialética do desenvolvimento*, Rio de Janeiro: Fondo de Cultura.

—— (1959) *A formação economica do Brasil*, Rio de Janeiro: Fondo de Cultura.

Gerassi, John (1963) *The Great Fear*, New York: Macmillan.

Halperin Donghi, T. (1993) *The Contemporary History of Latin America*, Durham: Duke University Press.

Lieuwen, Edwin (1961) *Arms and Politics in Latin America*, New York: Praeger.

Wolf, Eric (1959) *Sons of the Shaking Earth*, Chicago: University of Chicago Press.

ANA M. LÓPEZ

1960s, the

The 1960s was a period of change and redirection in Latin America as much as in Europe and the USA. The decade was framed by two major political events – the Cuban Revolution of 1959 and the election of Salvador **Allende** to the Chilean Presidency at the end of 1970. But in a sense these were manifestations of more complex transformations – cultural, economic, social as well as political – which also echoed global changes at each of these levels.

The late 1950s (see **1950s, the**) witnessed important economic changes in Latin America; in the wake of the economic growth that was the regional echo of the Second World War, those industrial goods that were once imported from the West now began to be produced within the region – the result was the **import substitution industrialization** that brought new industries and production centres to the major cities. They attracted provincial migrants of every class, as agriculture began to cede its central place as the motor of the economy in countries like Argentina, Mexico and Brazil. The cities grew overnight, an expansion described in novels like Carlos **Fuentes**'s *La región más transparente* (Where the Air is Clear) (1958). **Urbanization** now came to mean not the planned growth symbolized by **Brasília** and some of the other planned cities like **Belmopan** in Belize or the more radical plans of Miguel Angel Roca in Córdoba, Argentina, but a much more chaotic explosion of shanty towns (see **shanty towns and slums**) around the major cities where the new migrant labourers lived. Some of them worked on the new building projects designed to absorb the new middle classes, many of whom found work in an expanding State sector that was directing, or at least attempting to direct, the process of economic development. Yet the workers continued to live (and sometimes die, like the protagonist of Chico **Buarque**'s song, Construçâo (Construction Site)) in the new, sprawling, urban slums around the major capitals of the region.

Modernity came, then, as a complete package – and not as the outcome of a process of organic growth across the society as a whole. The result was a co-existence of rural poverty and under-development compared and combined with the appearances of modernity. This paradox was, in some senses, the result of policies evolved elsewhere, and in response to the Cuban Revolution. The first reaction in Latin America to the overthrow of the Batista dictatorship was a sort of awakening; after a decade of Cold War politics and directed growth based on Western models, a more radical proposal now appeared on the agenda. It found its theoretical expression in **dependency theory**, whose more radical voices, like André Gunder **Frank**, asserted that underdevelopment was the result of an unequal global *relationship* in which the weaker countries nourished growth in the developed world at their own expense. The political version of that insight was a search for

forms of struggle that could break the cycle of dependency. Nationalism – the rapid construction of a Nation State capable of accumulation and economic command – was at the core of each of the variety of solutions that debated the future throughout the decade.

The reaction of the US government to the Cuban events was to impose an economic embargo on Cuba in January 1960, which continued until the end of the millennium. This naked aggression against Cuba elicited dire warnings from commentators in both the Americas as the governments of Latin America reacted warily to the implications of Cuba. The policy of aggression and control from the north was to continue throughout the decade, but in a more subtle form than the simple support for repressive dictatorships characteristic of earlier times. The Punta del Este meeting in 1961 produced a regional security agreement (TIAR) which drew Latin American and North American governments into a close military alliance whose purpose was to isolate Cuba militarily. The carrot accompanying the stick was enshrined in the **Alliance for Progress**, conceived by President Kennedy, whose objective was to evolve programmes of development that could occur in concert with Western interests and in controlled circumstances, ensuring that the Cuban example would not reproduce itself across the continent. The new reformism would have as its vehicle the Christian Democratic parties (see **Christian Democracy**), which began to receive significant financial support throughout the region, just as they had in Europe through the post-Second World War Marshall Plan. The Bay of Pigs invasion of Cuba in 1961 left little room for doubt as to what was really involved in this double policy, and the reaction of Fidel **Castro** – a declaration of the revolution's Marxist ideology and a new *rapprochement* with Russia – seemed to confirm the worst conservative nightmares. Cuba, they believed, was now demonstrably a stalking-horse for Moscow.

The contradiction was that Cold War ideology sat uneasily with the democratic discourse of modernization and democracy. Educational provision (see **education**) increased at an extraordinary pace as a new generation demanded access to modernity, and a new urban milieu imposed both social and cultural change. The reality of city life became the central subject matter of the new writing encapsulated in the term, the **Boom**. Naturalistic descriptions of rural circumstance gave way to a more complex narrative capable of exploring the multiple and contradictory nature of the new Latin American city – **Cortázar**'s *Rayuela* (1963) was an influential example, as was the work of Fuentes, **Vargas Llosa**, Salvador **Garmendia**, David **Viñas** among others. Outstanding among them, Gabriel **García Márquez**, from Colombia, addressed the encounter between the *hojarasca* (leaf storm) of modernity and the pre-modern structures of feeling embedded in myth and story. The encounter produced a literary form (**magical realism**) and the acknowledged masterpiece of the genre, *Cien años de soledad* (One Hundred Years of Solitude) (1967).

At the same time, a new kind of writing – oral history or *testimonio* – controversially marked a route back from ethnography into narrative, fictional or realist. Miguel **Barnet**'s recording of the memoirs of Esteban Montejo in Cuba (*Biografía de un cimarrón* (Autobiography of a Runaway Slave) (1963)) was a key work in this respect, as was Elena **Poniatowska**'s fictionalized account of the life of Jesusa Palancares (*Hasta no verte Jesús mío* (Until I See You My Lord) (1969)).

It was this young, educated, urban sector who provided the readership for the Boom generation; and it was they who most enthusiastically identified with the Cuban Revolution and its political methods. In several senses, it was Ernesto 'Che' **Guevara** more than any other individual who came to represent the generation. Guevara's *Guerrilla Warfare* (1962) generalized the Cuban experience into a method of political organization and struggle that was adopted by a generation of young revolutionaries, for whom the success of the Cuban Revolution was the only evidence they needed that revolution was now a possibility. The Sandinistas (see **Sandinista Revolution**) were created in Nicaragua in 1961; a year earlier Yon Sosa and Luis Turcios Lima created the Guatemalan guerrilla organizations. In the Dominican Republic, Juan **Bosch** took up the banner of national self-determination. In Peru, dissident sections from **APRA** and other smaller organizations launched a major assault in 1965. In Paraguay a similar group was betrayed and all its

members murdered before they could cross the Argentine border. In the rather different conditions of Uruguay, an urban-based guerrilla group, the **Tupamaros**, was built by Raúl **Sendic**. In reality the guerrilla experience was neither very long nor particularly successful; but its symbolic significance arose from another aspect of the Guevara myth – the ideology of the revolutionary will, where external conditions could be overcome by the devotion and sincerity of individual revolutionaries. It was an idea that corresponded well enough to the aspirations of a new generation impatient for change yet not historically connected to earlier traditions of organized mass struggle or trade union organization. Many of the new radicals, indeed, emerged as dissidents from populist or Christian Democratic organizations.

Key moments in the decade expressed the confrontation between the old and new forces with dramatic clarity. The failed guerrilla war of 1965 in Peru was followed in 1968 by the new military reformers under **Velasco Alvarado**. But the indigenous rising led by Hugo **Blanco** in the La Convención region of southern Peru, though eventually crushed, left a legacy that would echo through subsequent decades. Omar **Torrijos** in Panama represented a similar strategy of guided reform-from-above. In Brazil the revolutionary transfer of power advocated by the urban guerrilla movement led by Carlos **Marighela** failed to materialize and the subsequent authoritarian governments, particularly after 1968, produced an '**economic miracle**' that was achieved in conditions of repression and terror. In Mexico the growth of a mainly student movement in 1968, which challenged the absence of democracy and the **PRI**'s monopoly of power was crushed when a public rally in **Tlatelolco** square was encircled and attacked by troops and irregulars leaving hundreds dead. Ironically, the Olympic Games of that year in Mexico (see **1968 Olympic Games, Mexico**), which began just three days later, is probably best remembered for the act of defiance by three black American athletes who raised a black glove from the podium in a salute to black power.

Yet if 1968 marked a peak of revolutionary fervour, it was a turning point in Cuba's relations with the rest of the region. Events coincided: the death of Guevara in October 1967 in Bolivia, the defeat of the left in Brazil, the rise of what came to be called military reformism in Peru and Panama combined with the defeat of guerrilla strategies in Peru, Bolivia and Venezuela (though the outstanding leader of the Venezuelan guerrillas, Douglas Bravo, disagreed vehemently), and the emergence of an extremely critical oppositional current within the Roman Catholic Church (see **liberation theology**). For Fidel Castro, these circumstances were proof of the inadequacy of a strategy of guerrilla warfare. By the end of the decade, Cuba had entered fully into the Soviet orbit and had begun to situate itself at the core of a 'Third-World' bloc that could and did include regimes of a distinctly non-revolutionary stripe.

Yet the combination of modernization, urban expansion, the growth in student numbers and the end of the Cold War produced an ideological space, filled largely by nationalism and other revolutionary currents too (**Trotskyism**, communism, Maoism), which had a profound cultural impact. On the one hand the growth of the mass media; on the other the opening of new sites in every field where experiment and innovation, in both form and content, coincided with a great debate about culture as an active tool of social transformation. In Brazil, the **Tropicália** movement, taking its name from an installation by Oiticica, burgeoned in 1968–9 with an extraordinary album that used irony and aesthetic experiment to comment on a country about to enter a period of military authoritarianism – its key figures, the musicians Caetano **Veloso** and Chico **Buarque**, were exiled as a result. In Chile, the *nueva canción* grew out of the work of Violeta **Parra** and drew in a new generation of musicians who would for the most part become directly and deeply involved with the presidential campaign of Salvador Allende in 1970. But the new music of Cuba, particularly the songs of the *nueva trova* (including Silvio **Rodríguez** and Pablo **Milanés**), created a new idiom – at once lyrical and overtly political – which found a resonance with the younger generation. The result was the work of *cantautores* (see *cantautor*) like Daniel **Viglietti** in Uruguay and Roy **Brown** in Puerto Rico among many others. Cinema too was undergoing significant transformations in this period. Brazilian

Cinema Novo began in the late 1950s to address the profound crisis of Brazilian society in adventurous ways, introducing mythic and poetic elements into an exploration of a contradictory universe of thought and action. In Bolivia, by contrast, the Ukamau Group (see **Grupo Ukamau**) produced powerful dramatic statements to correspond to the urgent task of social change, particularly when the short-lived government of Juan José Torres attempted to carry through some of its promises. That sense of urgency and 'contingency' characterized the powerful current of 'newsreel' cinema (see **newsreels**) in Cuba identified with Santiago **Alvarez**; this was closer to the documentary impulse linked to the work of Fernando **Birri** in Argentina and to the different schools of 'militant' or activist cinema that arose at different points through the decade everywhere in Latin America (see **New Latin American Cinema**). The many exciting new developments in theatre were particularly concentrated in Colombia (with the work of Enrique **Buenaventura** and others) and Chile (through the **Teatro de la Universidad de Chile**). Although theatre was confronted with the demand that it too commit its work to the achievement of social change, there was a powerful argument that aesthetic transformations should also be part of that process. In other words, that an artistic revolution should accompany cultural and political transformation; that was the position of other avant-garde directors like **Jodorowsky**, working both in Chile and in Mexico. Thus the emergence of performance art alongside experimental and avant-garde theatre, the co-existence of Cinema Novo and guerrilla film units, and the growth of an interventionist art of posters (see **poster art**) (particularly in Cuba, Chile and Puerto Rico), murals (in Chile), graphics (see **graphic art**) and folk art (in Haiti for example) with exciting innovation in areas of **kinetic art**, sculpture (see **sculpture, contemporary Latin American**) and abstract expression, notably in Venezuela and Brazil.

By the end of the decade Cuba, despite the continuing assertions to the contrary coming from Washington, was no longer in the business of fomenting revolution in Latin America; the election of Allende and the emergence of reformism from above in several countries, seemed to suggest a possibility of directed change without major social upheaval. The subsequent decade would soon give the lie to that. But the enormous cultural transformations that occurred through the decade of the 1960s could not be so easily undone. The new awareness of indigenous America could not simply be wiped away, nor the debate about the obligations of art and artists so easily denied.

Further reading

Debray, R. (1967) *Revolution in the Revolution*, Harmondsworth: Penguin.

Franco, J. (1967) *The Modern Culture of Latin America*, London: Pall Mall.

Fuentes, C. (1969) *La nueva novela latinoamericana*, Mexico City: Joaquín Mortiz.

García Márquez, G. (1967) *Cien años de soledad*, Buenos Aires: Sudamericana.

Gerassi, J. (1965) *The Great Fear in Latin America*, New York: Collier.

Gheerbrandt, A. (1970) *La iglesia rebelde de América Latina*, Mexico: Siglo XXI.

Gott, R. (1970) *Guerrilla Warfare in Latin America*, Harmondsworth: Penguin.

Guevara, E. (1961) *Guerrilla Warfare*, New York: Monthly Review.

Teran, O. (1991) *Nuestros años sesenta*, Buenos Aires: Puntosur.

MIKE GONZALEZ

1970s, the

Latin American politics in the decade of the 1970s are marked most obviously by the often violent reaction of the military and the ruling elites to the popular and revolutionary movements of the previous decade, and by the response of national governments to specific local effects of the rapidly changing world economy. The military overthrew democratically elected governments in Chile (1973), Argentina (1976), and Uruguay (1973), and political repression under the military government in Brazil (imposed in 1964) was to become more severe, particularly between 1968 and 1972. The 'disappearance' (see **disappeared, the**) and torture (**torture and disappearance, reports**

of) of fellow citizens by the military and/or paramilitary in the **Southern Cone** placed human rights at the centre of political struggle in the region, and there was a concomitant creation of **exile** cultures in Europe and the Americas by those citizens who were forced to flee their countries. In the northern Andean countries, there was also little advance or deepening of democratic practice. Taking Peru and Colombia as examples: the military held power in Peru (1968–80), though during the **Velasco** period (1968–75), it was a corporatist regime with a project of nationalization and **agrarian reform**; and while Colombia still operated under the pattern of alternation of political parties established in the 1950s, it continued to face a heritage of violence and social upheaval, with armed struggle ongoing in the countryside, to which the various elected governments had an inadequate response. In Mexico, while President **Echeverría** (1970–6) sought to ameliorate in small part the political and social effects of the violence used against the protest movement of 1968 (culminating in the massacre in **Tlatelolco**) and the financial crises of the early 1970s, his successor, President López Portillo (1976–82), openly embraced policies that served international investors. In Cuba, a socialist country that embraced popular and revolutionary movements, the decade, which opened with the failure to meet the announced goal of a ten-million-tonne sugar harvest and closed with the Mariel boatlift (1979), witnessed a variety of decisions that allowed the government to abandon the alternative political-economic experiments of the first decade of the revolution and adopt more conservative, institutional practices along the lines of its ally, the Soviet Union. In Nicaragua, to the contrary, at the end of the decade, the Sandinistas (see **Sandinista Revolution**) came to power (1979) after a long period of struggle against the Somoza dictatorship (see **Somoza dynasty**).

In literary production, the decade witnessed the transition from the **Boom** to the **post-Boom**. Angel **Rama** periodized the Boom in relation to the exuberant, albeit late, recognition of the New Latin American Narrative by European and US critics, a recognition paralleled by publishing and marketing campaigns outside the region, particularly around the **novel** and **magical realism** in the 1960s, together with new editorial efforts in Latin America. Jean Franco has examined the Boom in relation to a literary engagement with mass culture and image culture, an engagement that often reworked the writer's traditional role as a public intellectual (see **intellectuals**) and national voice, recasting the writer as an international celebrity:

> ... the totalizing project by which the novelist constructed the 'alternative reality' seems to have become impossible by the late 1960s. The effect of the spread of mass culture in Latin America was thus not only the attempt of the more entrenched avant-garde writers to produce the unconsumable text but also the confrontation of authors of the boom with the irresistible glamour of the superstar and the predominance of the image. (pp. 166–7)

Though in retrospect the periodization of the post-Boom easily elides with that of **postmodernism**, Franco's argument instead highlights the changing role of the intellectual. Thus, while it is generally accepted that the Utopian political projects of the previous decade gave way before the dire political realities and continuing social injustice of the 1970s, the writer as well as artists and intellectuals in general were confronted with the necessity of redefining the nature of politically committed art. On the one hand, the literature of the decade confirms the continuing anti-imperialist stance of those on the left. On the other, it reveals the writer no longer to be a significant mediator between classes within the nation state, nor the paradigmatic critical voice of a national culture. With dictatorships undermining free expression and economics tending to value a transnational consumerism, writers had to question for whom and to whom they spoke. Not surprisingly, the decade also witnessed the publication of texts by women writers and a new concern with excluded or suppressed voices and cultures. A telling juxtaposition for literature and the intellectual sector in Latin America takes place in Cuba at the beginning of the decade: *Caliban* (1971) by Roberto **Fernández Retamar** belongs to the same year as the **Padilla** case (1971), the first being a text that speaks back to empire from the position of the oppressed, and the second a case of the imprison-

ment of a writer that revealed the authoritarian fissures in a critical cultural project. Politically committed poetry was honoured internationally during the decade: Pablo **Neruda** was awarded the Nobel Prize for Literature (see **Nobel Prizes**) in 1971 (Neruda died shortly after the Chilean *coup* in 1973). Important social analyses of the early decade included Eduardo **Galeano**'s *Las venas abiertas de América Latina* (The Open Veins of Latin America) and Ariel **Dorfman** and Armando Mattelart's *Para leer el Pato Donald* (**How to Read Donald Duck**). In 1972, Gabriel **García Márquez** and, in 1977, Carlos **Fuentes** were awarded the Premio Internacional Rómulo Gallegos. In 1974, the Montevideo weekly, *Marcha*, was closed down by the military government; its editor then founded the **Biblioteca Ayacucho** in Caracas. By mid-decade, the incorporation of mass culture into literature found mature expression in Manuel **Puig**'s *El beso de la mujer araña* (Kiss of the Spider Woman) (1976), and, by the decade's end, the literary responses to State violence, most of which would be published in the 1980s, could already be glimpsed in *testimonios* (see **testimonio**) and in journalism, with such texts as Rodolfo **Walsh**'s 'Open Letter' denouncing the Argentine military.

In the arts, there was also a movement away from the revolutionary politics of 1968 towards a consideration of the impact of social divisions and social struggle on individuals and communities. Marta **Traba** saw this decade as a period in which the graphic arts (see **graphic art**) flourished, in particular drawing and printmaking, which were celebrated in various biennials and recurrent exhibitions (among them, San Juan, 1970; Cali, 1970; Maracaibo, 1977 to 1981). Traba noted as well a growing interest in the late 1960s in objects (sculptural, **ceramics**, etc.), textiles and primitive paintings, and, both in the case of textiles and primitive paintings, there was often an attempt to incorporate folk art and pre-Columbian culture. With respect to the avant-garde in the 1970s, Traba wrote that it 'was characterized by "anti-art" manifestations and by an aggressive attitude which was immediately neutralized in art centres by the power of the media and establishment institutions'. The place and meaning of art made the cultural industry itself a site of contestation.

The greatest change within popular music was the success of the Afro-Cuban **son**, reworked in the Puerto Rican communities of New York and dubbed **salsa**. Growing to encompass various styles under this rubric, salsa became the dance music of choice in urban areas from Puerto Rico and the Dominican Republic to Venezuela, even rivalling the **cumbia** in its native Colombia. Rubén **Blades** and Willie **Colón** came to represent a different, more articulate and socially conscious salsa – though it never lost the dance beat. A very different music expanded into an international arena, as exiled Chilean musicians carried the Andean sound of the *nueva canción* into protest meetings and rallies against the Chilean military. Together with Mercedes **Sosa**, Alfredo **Zitarrosa** and Daniel **Viglietti** from the Southern Cone, as well as others throughout the continent, all of these musicians brought music to the forefront as a vehicle for communicating a message denouncing injustice and calling for social change.

Commercial cinema in the decade was contested by both independent and political cinema. In two Southern Cone countries, **New Latin American Cinema** was transmuted into a cinema of exile as film-makers fled arrest or death, such as Miguel **Littín** and Patricio **Guzmán** in Chile, and Fernando **Solanas** in Argentina. Littín's *La tierra prometida* (The Promised Land), filmed under the **Popular Unity** government, was completed in exile and footage for the third part of Guzmán's documentary, *La batalla de Chile* (The Battle of Chile), was smuggled out of the country and edited in Cuba. After the Argentine *coup*, Solanas completed post-production in Paris on *Los hijos de Fierro* (1978), a lyrical, if Peronist (see **Peronism**), adaptation of the José Hernández poem, *Martín Fierro* (1872–9). In Argentina, the brief return to democracy and Peronist culture from 1973–6 produced important populist films such as *La Patagonia rebelde* (Rebellion in Patagonia) (1974) directed by Héctor **Olivera**, but after the military *coup* only entertainment films could be produced until the early 1980s, when veiled political references could be included (in *Tiempo de revancha* (Time of Revenge) in 1981, for example).

In Brazil, the decade was to bring to a conclusion the political and aesthetic projects of **Cinema Novo**. Ismail Xavier has written:

In the 1970s, the Cinema Novo generation itself moved toward a more decisive incorporation of market values, keeping the national question on the agenda and continuing its debate with the remnants of Marginal Cinema, who were excluded from the new state-based system of production; in the 1980s, a new generation made its own proposals and took Cinema Novo's '**aesthetics of hunger**' and national style as the tradition to be denied. (p. 263)

Indeed, Nelson Pereira dos **Santos**'s *Como era gostoso o meu francés* (How Tasty was My Little Frenchman) (1971) opens the decade with cannibalist film, but the films to follow had to face, in one way or another, different demands for historical contextualization (among them a government plan to give financial support to historical films).

Literary adaptations such as *São Bernardo* (1993), **Dona Flor e seus dois maridos** (Dona Flor and Her Two Husbands) (1976) and *Tenda dos milagros* (Tent of Miracles) (1977) provided a way for film-makers to discuss national culture and politics, as did historical films such as those by Carlos **Diegues**, which dealt with slave culture. Film-makers' relations with the State organization, **Embrafilme**, were often debated; but particularly after its reorganization in 1975, Embrafilme was the major source for film funding.

In Mexico, early in the decade the continuing efforts to create an art cinema (such as envisioned by the *Nuevo Cine* generation of the 1960s) were apparent in the work of directors such as Arturo **Ripstein**, who returned to commercial film-making with *El castillo de la pureza* (The Castle of Purity) (1972), and Paul **Leduc**, whose independent 16 mm *Reed: México insurgente* (Reed: Insurgent Mexico) (1971) undercut a heroic view of the Mexican Revolution (see **revolutions**). During the Echeverría *sexenio* (six-year presidency), the State established its own production companies and, in 1975, a second film school (Centro de Capacitación Cinematográfica) was created, but traditional views still held regarding aesthetics and less experimentation took place than might have been hoped. Marcela **Fernández Violante**, who released *De todos modos Juan te llamas* (In Any Case Your Name is Juan) in 1976, is the one woman to maintain prominence as a director, though other feminist film-maker's short works were becoming known. Jaime Humberto **Hermosillo** (who was to gain international recognition for directing Mexico's first explicitly gay film in 1984) and Felipe **Cazals** are the other two directors who are considered to have created a significant body of work in the decade. Cazals's *Canoa* (1975), which recreated the murder of university employees in a rural town and examined the social divisions that produced such violence, is considered key to an understanding of Mexican film's trajectories in the decade.

In Cuba, cinema continued to be one of the most vital areas of expression of the revolution, with **ICAIC** sponsoring both fiction and documentary production, and promoting **animation**, including the first feature-length animation film, *Elpidio Valdés* (1979), by Juan **Padrón**. Notable for the decade are the treatments of the history of race relations in films directed by Sergio **Giral**, Sara **Gómez** and Tomás **Gutiérrez Alea**. The Family Code of 1974 found its on screen dramatization in Pastor **Vega**'s *Retrato de Teresa* (Portrait of Teresa) (1975), a cinematic polemic on gender hierarchies that provoked widespread discussion. In 1979, the first **Festival Internacional del Nuevo Cine Latinoamericano** was inaugurated and it was to become the principal site of exchange for Latin American film-makers in the next decade.

Further reading

Franco, J. (1999) *Critical Passions: Selected Essays*, Durham/London: Duke University Press.

King, J. (1990) *Magical Reels: A History of Cinema in Latin America*, London/New York: Verso.

Miller, N. (1999) *In the Shadow of the State: Intellectuals and the Quest for National Identity in Twentieth-Century Spanish America*, London/New York: Verso.

Rama, A. (ed.) (1981) *Más allá del boom: Literatura y mercado*, Mexico: Marcha Editores.

Skidmore, T.E. and Smith, P.H. (1997) *Modern Latin America*, fourth edn. New York/Oxford: Oxford University Press.

Traba, M. (1994) *Art of Latin America, 1900–1980*, Baltimore: The Johns Hopkins University Press and the Inter-American Development Bank.

KATHLEEN NEWMAN

1980s, the

Perhaps we may best understand the 1980s as the beginning of the end of the period of revolution and counter-revolution whose symbolic, and in some ways substantive, beginning we may conveniently mark with the triumph of the Cuban Revolution (see **revolutions**) on 1 January 1959. Economically, most of the region began the decade with massive foreign debt and ended it with the flurry of privatizations, cuts in government expenditures and regional free-trade agreements that comprise the turn toward what has come to be called **neoliberalism**. Politically, the counter-revolutionary military dictatorships that governed in most of the region began to give way to parliamentary democracies. These, in turn, were faced with the task of reconstructing the tattered remnants of civil society while negotiating the conflicting demands of existing military elites and the long oppressed millions who emerged on the political scene in the novel form of **new social movements**. Culturally, the region's scene became a confusing one, at least for those comfortable with conventional, but now challenged, distinctions between 'politics' and 'culture', or between 'high' and 'low' or 'traditional' and 'modern' culture.

In 1979, the Sandinista National Liberation Front (**FSLN**), a guerrilla-led revolutionary movement born in the early 1960s and partly inspired by the Cuban example, took power in Managua, Nicaragua and established the region's second socialist regime. The battle between revolutionaries and counter-revolutionaries, which had seemed decided in much of South America with the triumph of USA-supported military regimes throughout the 1970s, seemed, with the victory of the Sandinistas (and the fierce civil wars in El Salvador and Guatemala), to regain full force. By the end of the decade, however, the Sandinistas had lost power in Nicaragua. In the rest of the region, ten years of continuous and destructive civil war was now reaching an end through a series of negotiated peace deals. At the same time, those countries (a majority in the region) that had suffered under counter-revolutionary military dictatorships in 1980 were now shakily working their way towards political stability under democracies of one sort or another. In this way, the decade witnessed a gradual moderation of the extreme, winner-take-all atmosphere of armed revolution and counter-revolution, which had scarred the region for thirty years, leaving millions hungry, tortured, imprisoned, exiled, disappeared or dead.

Between 1950 and 1980, both per capita income and life expectancy grew in Latin America. But by 1990, most of the region's economies were smaller than they had been in 1980 and most of its inhabitants poorer. The revolutionary era had, in part, been fuelled by the generalization of heightened expectations that often comes with economic growth, particularly in an area like Latin America, with great disparity in the distribution of income. Faced with the instability that accompanied armed revolution and counter-revolution in the region, domestic and foreign business interests began to insist upon social order and political stability as a condition for continued investment in the region. At this point, between the mid-1960s and the mid-1970s, the military took over in a number of countries. It was in this context that foreign dollars once again flowed into the region, most significantly in the form of loans. However, most of the military regimes (with the much publicized exception of Chile) were unable to transform these loans into self-sustaining economic growth. On the contrary, by August 1982, the **debt crisis** grew gravely concrete when Mexico threatened to default. Widespread unemployment and worsening poverty among an increasing proportion of the region's population – not to mention outrage against these regimes' brutal violations of human rights – sparked further instability and eventually brought down the military regimes. The civilian governments that replaced them were confronted with massive external debt. International lending institutions, such as the World Bank and the International Monetary Fund, insisted on a variety of so-called 'austerity' measures as a condition for further investment in the region. Thus, already

fragile civilian regimes were forced into a series of unpopular (not to say anti-popular) domestic economic policies including rolling back government expenditures on health, education and welfare, the privatization of government-owned industries and the reduction of protective tariffs on inter-State trade. In sum, the 1980s saw an economic crisis, driven by massive external debt, give way slowly to the reconstruction of national economies along lines quite similar to those operating in the late nineteenth-century, liberalist Latin America: privately (and often foreign) owned and operated enterprises orientated towards the export of primary goods, hence the name **neoliberalism**.

Politically, the decade was a treacherous and challenging one. Military governments, of various ideological stripes and forms of organization, were the rule at the outset of the decade. But the social order they promised came at too high a cost, both economically and in terms of human rights and political freedoms, for most Latin Americans. Accordingly, these regimes began to give way to domestic and foreign pressure by the middle of the decade. The civilian regimes that followed in their wake were faced, not only with the substantial economic problems described above, but with a populace demoralized and polarized by the experience of military rule. Exiting military elites resented insinuations of criminality and threatened civilian regimes with new *coups*, while human-rights activists and ordinary citizens demanded justice for those lost to military repression. These activists, in addition, were only one of the host of political actors, known collectively as 'new social movements' mobilized during the 1980s, which, in the absence of now-decimated traditional left organizations, demanded satisfaction of particular needs such as sanitation or electricity, education, health care or ecological responsibility. In this way, the outcome of a decade and a half of military counter-revolution was to force a shift in progressive politics from vanguardist revolutionary activity aimed at the seizure of political power to grassroots, needs-based social movements, often local or regional in scope, aiming their demands equally at social, political and cultural institutions.

The economic tendency of the 1980s was towards growing privatization, a withdrawal of

State funding for economic undertakings. At the same time, the political tendency was toward a parliamentary system that, in its very weakness and narrowness, provoked more radically democratic alternative political expressions. Both of these changes, in turn, provoked new crises and new expressions in culture and the arts; crises and expressions that, in some cases, reverberated back into the political and economic spheres. Indeed, the fading of certain boundaries – such as those separating political and artistic or cultural activity, those separating elite 'high' cultural forms and 'low', 'popular' or 'mass' culture, those separating 'national' from 'international' expressions, or those separating 'modern' from 'traditional' cultural forms – may be the definitive hallmark of this period of Latin American cultural history.

While these changes left no area of Latin American cultural production – from film to journalism to television to the textile production of highland Guatemala – unaffected, it may be easier to visualize the changes by focusing upon an example of their effects in the realm of literature. Ironically, it was the very cultural crisis of the 1970s and 1980s that shook Latin American writing out of the complacency that had followed the dizzying '**Boom**' success of the 1960s and early 1970s. As powerfully concrete historical forces swept over them, a number of different kinds of individuals became writers, or, better yet, chroniclers, replacing the entrancing, mythical sweep of the 1960s novel with the no less creative, but definitely more localized, and arguably more lucid, accounts of recent history. These took a number of forms, depending on the history and culture of the local situation in which they were produced and on the personal history and inclination of the writer, ranging from *testimonio* (first-person autobiographical, or testimonial, narrative), to historical romance novels, to mixes of journalism and fiction, to elaborate literary historical reflections. In sum, they represent well the tendency to blur boundaries that is characteristic of culture in the 1980s.

The testimonial narrative, of which the best known in English is probably *Yo, Rigoberta* **Menchú** (I Rigoberta Menchú: An Indian Woman in Guatemala) (1983), usually involves a common individual – certainly not a writer or intellectual in any conventional sense of those terms – telling their

life story to a sympathetic interlocutor. There are many different forms that this relationship can take, and different ways of understanding the issues of authorship that arise. What is crucial about the *testimonio*, in this context, is, first, that its boundaries between culture (narrative) and politics (the narrator's, usually harrowing, encounters with recent history) are quite concretely blurred, and, second, that individuals from the general population – often women, often of colour – suddenly found themselves speaking in a forum usually reserved for educated, white, male, professional writers or intellectuals. In addition, the case of Rigoberta Menchú illustrates a third blurring of boundaries in her creative mixing of traditional and modern, native and foreign, cultural resources.

While testimonial narrative often aspires to set the historical record straight, to correct official accounts of a given political or social process, or to assert for the first time an alternative account of historical events, historical fictions – of the various sorts enumerated above – remain more unsettled about the possibility of historical truth given the manipulation of culture that was part and parcel of dictatorship and civilian regime alike in the 1980s. By imagining fantastic happenings alongside real historical events, or, vice-versa, by situating real historical figures or events in the context of a fictional narrative, novelists like Isabel **Allende** (*La casa de los espíritus* (The House of the Spirits) (1985)), Tomás Eloy **Martínez** (*La novela de Perón* (The Peron Novel) (1985) and Ricardo **Piglia** (*Respiración artificial* (Artificial Respiration) (1980)), among many others, challenged conventional assumptions about truth and fiction, and about the role of storytelling in historical processes. In *La casa de los espíritus* Isabel Allende, niece of the late Chilean President Salvador **Allende**, adapts the 'magical realist' styles and generational structure (see **magical realism**) made famous by Gabriel **García Márquez** to depict the slide of a nation – much like her own Chile – into brutal dictatorship with its ravaging effects on daily life and family relationships. Allende's novel, which received critical acclaim, successfully blurred the boundary between high literature and popular fiction by also becoming a best-seller in Latin America and the USA, as well as through its adaptation to film. Argentine expatriate journalist Tomás Eloy Martínez took a slightly different approach to address Argentine history in *La novela de Perón*, a story first published in serial form in Argentina. Martínez invents a journalist charged with piecing together, from the stories of various figures, 'the truth' of General Juan **Perón**, whose real historical return to Argentina, after nearly two decades in exile, on 20 June 1973 forms the centre around which the different perspectives revolve. In this way, Martínez provides not only a gripping (and popular) novel, but a virtual encyclopedia of conflicting perspectives on Argentine history. In his challenging novel, *Respiración artificial*, the Argentine novelist Ricardo Piglia eluded censors in his native Argentina by, in effect, encoding a history of that country's descent into military dictatorship within a series of letters and tales embedded within tales, all ostensibly orientated towards solving a seemingly trivial family mystery. All these writers, like Rigoberta Menchú, struggled to reassert the value of narrative, and of independent cultural production more generally, as well as to pluralize a hitherto exclusive domain, during a period in which official channels of cultural production were closed.

One result of the transition to democracy, spurred in part by the reports on torture and disappearance written soon after the demise of the military regimes in Argentina, Chile and Uruguay, was the emergence in every medium of works that interrogated that painful and immediate past – from within or from the **exile** into which many artists had been cast. Thus, for example, *La historia oficial* and *Sur* addressed these issues in Argentina. In Chile itself, the repressive silence of the 1970s gave way in the early 1980s and, in the face of economic crisis, to new social fractures that produced strikes and protests on the one hand, and new forms of cultural resistance on the other – among them the work of the performance group Las **Yeguas del Apocalipsis** and the punk-style music of Los **Prisioneros**. Jesusa **Rodríguez** in Mexico was exploring similar areas. In Argentina, Charly **García** and **rock nacional** provided a focus for collective discontent in the early 1980s, and continued to do so even after the restoration of democracy in 1984.

The transition, however, did not lead to a restoration of the pre-existing situation. In the global market of the mid- to late 1980s, there was no possibility of recovering the projects for State-led growth and protectionism that had inspired Salvador Allende's project among others. In the market in general, and in the field of culture in particular, the tendency towards privatization and commercialization was impossible to resist. The mass media, for example, were now dominated by commercial conglomerates like **Globo**, **Televisa** and **Venevisión**; State film enterprises like **Embrafilme** or **Chile Films** folded during the decade, and with them the subsidized documentary realism of the previous period. The new film-makers, like María **Novaro**, **Hermosillo** or **Ripstein** in Mexico, offered idiosyncratic and intensely individual works, though ones that challenged in searching ways sexual and social stereotypes and conventions. Globalization, in its turn, brought both a reaffirmation of national cultures and traditions, in particular in the cultural expressions of indigenous peoples, and a kind of parody of the national in performers like Mexico's Astrid **Hadad** and Juan Gabriel. It was Néstor **García Canclini** who produced the theoretical expression of this contradictory dynamic in his notion of hybrid cultures (see **hybridity**) in which the modern and the traditional exchanged and negotiated new cultural spaces. And that process of contradictory insertion into a globalizing world would become more urgent and more problematic as the fall of the Berlin Wall in 1989 led to a deep and searching reconsideration of the revolutionary projects of previous years.

Further reading

Beverley, J., Oriedo, J. and Arouna, M. (1995) *The Postmodern Debate in Latin America*, Durham: Duke University Press.

Colas, S. (1994) *Postmodernity in Latin America*, Durham: Duke University Press.

Garcià Canclini, N. (1995) Hybrid Cultures: *Strategies for Leaving and Entering Modernity*, Minneapolis: University of Minnesota Press.

Petras, J. and Morlty, M. (1992) *Latin America in the Time of Cholera*, New York: Routledge.

SANTIAGO COLÁS

1990s, the

The final decade of the twentieth century was dramatic and contradictory. One of its defining events was, oddly enough, the commemoration of the first voyage of a Genoese sailor 500 years earlier: the **Columbian quincentenary** commemorations of 1992 revealed the extent to which indigenous peoples (see **indigenous movements**) in the hemisphere did not accept the confident narrative of European expansion, and the political force of their movements (which included **CONAIE** in Ecuador and the **Mayan Revitalization Movement** in Guatemala) on their national stages. The decade ends with somewhat more muted preparations for commemorations of Cabral's accidental voyage to Brazil in 1500; but the new millennium begins with the powerful intervention of CONAIE in bringing about the downfall of a president in Ecuador.

The Nobel Peace Prize (see **Nobel Prizes**) awarded in 1992 to Rigoberta **Menchú Tum** was symbolically a recognition of centuries of indigenous resistance. Two years later, on 1 January 1994, the entry of Mexico into a North American common market with the USA and Canada was complicated by another act of indigenous resistance when a heretofore unknown movement, the Zapatista National Liberation Army, or EZLN (see **Zapatistas**), took control of several cities and towns in the southern Mexican state of Chiapas. The Zapatista spokesman, the astute Subcomandante Marcos (see **Subcomandante Marcos**), has proved himself a master of the media, using the Internet as well as the printed and spoken word to reach millions (even publishing a book for children).

In the economic sphere, the decade was notable for the similar directions that were imposed on the economies of the Latin American and Caribbean countries, thanks in large measure to the policies of the World Bank and the International Monetary Fund (IMF). **Structural adjustment** and privatization were watchwords, with privatization reaching directly into the lives of ordinary households as government social security and pension funds were privatized (most fully in Chile), as well as telecommunications, transportation and, even in some countries, the post office. These policies had unintended consequences: crises of domestic production and of exports, serious environmental damage (most notably in **Amazonia**, Chiapas and Central America), and the chaotic advance of what one economist, Hernando **De Soto**, optimistically termed 'el otro sendero' (the other path, in reference to the **Sendero Luminoso** or Shining Path guerrilla movement), but which is more widely termed the informal economy. The casualization of labour, the rise of *maquiladoras* and *zonas francas* (duty-free zones), and the cutback in public-sector social services made the decade a period of crisis for many middle class as well as poor people. Argentina and Brazil, and later Ecuador, joined Panama in trying to stabilize their economies by pegging their currency to the dollar (and contemplating using the dollar as national currency); curiously, Cuba, with its dual economy based on a national currency in which salaries are paid and a few basic services bought, but in which the US dollar is the preferred means of exchange, was the country where the currency crisis was most dramatic.

In the aftermath of civil war and military dictatorship, the Central American countries and the **Southern Cone** struggled towards peace and justice, though the desire for justice was often frustrated. The **disappeared** and other victims of repression in the previous two decades would not in fact disappear: their memory is seared in consciousness, their outlines painted on sidewalks and walls, their relatives still demanding justice. The event that proved that there was no forgetting was the unexpected arrest in London, at the behest of a Spanish judge, of the former Chilean dictator, Augusto **Pinochet**, in November 1998. Though many in Chile had argued that the transition to democracy and the neoliberal economy (see **neoliberalism**) had made further discussion of events of the 1970s counter-productive, once those discussions began they were far-reaching. In a similar development, in 1998 and 1999 several leaders of the Argentine juntas of the 1970s were arrested for the stealing of children from disappeared families, dramatized in the 1986 film, *La historia oficial* (The Official Story), a crime that they had unwisely not pushed to have included in the amnesties they had demanded as part of the so-called transition to democracy. Issues of **human rights** were pushed to the forefront by these developments in many countries as the world celebrated the fiftieth anniversary of the UN Declaration of Human Rights (1948).

Simultaneously, the decade was marked by the rise of new *caudillo* figures, most often espousing right-wing populist (see **populism**) projects. Three important figures were Alberto **Fujimori** in Peru, Carlos Saúl **Menem** in Argentina and Hugo Chávez in Venezuela, all of whom succeeded in changing their countries' **Constitutions** in the direction of greater power for the executive branch of government. (Some other Constitutions were changed in this period in the direction of recognition of indigenous and minority communities, and greater participation in democracy, for example in Colombia – but that was largely not the case of the *caudillos*' new Constitutions, which did not come out of a popular process of negotiation.) The crisis on the left was exemplified by the 1990 electoral loss of the Sandinistas (see **Sandinista Revolution**) in Nicaragua and the subsequent revelations of their stealing from the public purse (see *piñata*), and by the final defeat of Sendero Luminoso and the capture of Abimael **Guzmán** in Peru. Alternatively, signs of robust democracy and the force of popular will were shown by the impeachment of Fernando **Collor** in Brazil and that of Abdala Bucaram in Ecuador. In a curious development, several notable dependency theorists (see **dependency theory**) of the 1960s and 1970s occupied positions of power in the 1990s: Fernando Henrique **Cardoso** became president of Brazil (defeating **Lula** and the **PT**), and José Joaquín **Brunner** occupied several posts as government minister in Chile under the neoliberal Concertación governments.

The decade was notable for the strength of **new social movements**, including the Movimiento sem Terra and other movements of landless peasant, indigenous movements (including CONAIE and the Mapuche (see **Mapuches**) movements in Chile), the new public voice acquired by leaders of gay and lesbian movements (the **Grupo Gay da Bahia**, the Movimiento Homosexual de Lima, **MHOL**, and others), **black movements**, new feminisms, etc. Many of these movements founded small presses or acquired access to newspapers like *La Jornada* and *Página 12*, while **Radio Tierra** in Chile and Tito **Vasconcelos** in

his long-running radio programme in Mexico City reached audiences that were not addressed by the mainstream media.

In religion, the most important developments were the rise of evangelical movements, making **Protestantism** a significant force in the region for the first time, and the attack on **liberation theology** that issued from the Vatican of the Polish anti-communist Pope John Paul II. The liberation theologian, Leonardo **Boff** of Brazil, was literally silenced for a year, but eloquent voices from the movement like Gustavo Gutiérrez of Peru and Bishop Samuel Ruiz of Chiapas, and the poet/priest/politican, Ernesto **Cardenal**, found it harder to have a voice within the Roman Catholic Church (see **Catholicism**). (The death of retired archbishop, Helder **Cámara**, in 1999 closed an important chapter in the history of the Brazilian Catholic church.) At the same time that evangelical movements found success in their missionary (see **missionaries**) activities, there was a resurgence of folk religions based on indigenous and African-based systems of belief, and the rise of a great variety of **New Age** religions.

Guerrilla war (see **guerrillas**) was revived in several countries, most notably in the case of the FARC in Colombia, but in an ambiguous co-dependency with drug traffic (see **drugs in Latin America**). Violence related to drug traffic and corruption erupted in Mexico, resulting in the assassinations of the bishop of Guadalajara and of **PRI** presidential candidate, Luis Donaldo Colosio, while demands for human rights and social justice apparently led to the assassination of the archbishop of Guatemala City.

Cuba spent the whole of the 1990s in what was quaintly termed a *'período especial en tiempos de paz'* (special period in times of peace), with little food, electricity, gasoline or transportation, and the spectacular rise of an 'informal economy' based on prostitution (see *jinetera*), **tourism**-related services and (officially sanctioned?) drug traffic. This 'special period' has been notable for the ingenuity of popular humour – jokes and stories – that circulated ever more widely (at the time of the Pope's visit to the island in 1998, for instance) and for other powerful critical voices that emerged in the cultural sphere. Tomás **Gutiérrez Alea**'s final film, *Guantanamera* (1996), was a notable product of the special period, as was the music of Pedro Luis **Ferrer**.

The decade will also be remembered for a terrible series of natural disasters: floods and mudslides provoked by El **Niño**, **hurricanes**, volcanic eruptions (see **volcanoes**) and earthquakes. The **cholera** epidemic that hit Peru and many countries along the Pacific coast of South and Central America, the spread of **Chagas' disease** beyond the rural areas where it had been located, the rise of new strains of tuberculosis and **malaria** that were resistant to the existing medications and the dramatic spread of dengue (see **dengue fever**) confirmed that some of the old challenges to **public health** were far from being under control. And **AIDS** has continued to spread across the region, the new therapies beyond the abilities of many patients to pay for, though AIDS organisations have been forceful in making their case for full treatment of affected populations and protection of human rights.

If in post-*piñata* Nicaragua one of the most famous Sandinista politicians, Sergio **Ramírez**, has announced his return to literature, there is some question what literature he and others will find – or create. The 1990s has been a decade of market consolidation by the great multinational publishers, most notably Berthelsmann of Germany, which now controls Planeta, Alfaguara, Seix Barral and many of the other major publishing houses in the Spanish world. In the new publishing world dominated by media empires (that often reach into newspapers, radio, television and cinema), the best seller (see **best-sellers**) phenomenon has come to dominate the marketing of books. The **Planeta Chilena** generation is perhaps most unhappily exemplified by the pop novelist, Luis **Sepúlveda**, who actually has the nerve in one of his novels to explain that in the southern hemisphere the seasons of the year are the reverse of those in the north, an explanation that suggests that he is uncertain where his reading public is (or perhaps certain that it is not in Chile). Isabel **Allende** and Paulo **Coelho**, both New Age writers in their different ways, have been the most significant best-selling authors to emerge from the region. Another media phenomenon is the Peruvian gay novelist, Jaime **Bayly**, whose day work is as a television talk show host.

This was a decade of deaths and funerals: Octavio **Paz**, Claudio **Arrau**, Atahualpa **Yupanqui**, Roberto **Goyeneche**, Astor **Piazzola**, Alfredo **Zitarrosa**, **Cazuza**, Caio Fernando **Abreu**, **Henfil**. And it ended with the massive – and mindless – celebrations in Buenos Aires and elsewhere of the centenary of the birth of Jorge Luis **Borges**, who died in 1986. His birthday was marked at the opera house, the **Teatro Colón**, with a heavy-metal concert – an unexpected event to be sure.

The theatre world was transformed in the 1990s by the rise of **performance art**: figures like Astrid **Hadad**, Tito **Vasconcelos**, Liliana **Felipe** and Jesusa **Rodríguez** combined political humour, camp, musical theatre and improvisation. The 1990s fashion for androgyny had perhaps been anticipated by Ney **Matogrosso** in Brazil, but his successor, Edson Cordeiro, went farther than Ney had. Pedro **Lemebel** used performance art, journalism and writing to invent a forceful voice as a gay activist and AIDS survivor in neoliberal Chile.

Paradoxically, while suffering under the economic constraints of globalization, the cinema thrived, especially in the latter half of the decade, which witnessed the revitalization of industries, like the Brazilian, which had been decimated by the sudden withdrawal of State support (with the closing of **Embrafilme** during the Collor presidency). Of great impact in the late 1990s was the great international reception accorded to Walter Salles Jr's *Central do Brasil* (Central Station) (1998), with an Oscar nomination for best actress for Fernanda **Montenegro**. At no time in the history of Latin American film-making have international **film distribution** and **co-productions** been as important. For some national cinemas, like the Cuban film institute (**ICAIC**), co-productions have become essential for survival: Cuba's most notable films of the decade, Tomás Gutiérrez Alea's (with Juan Carlos **Tabio**) *Fresa y chocolate* (Strawberry and Chocolate) (1993) and *Guantanamera* (1997), were both co-productions, and reached the widest audience of Cuban film history as a result of being picked up by a powerful US distributor. Although the Mexican industry has sustained reasonable levels of production, filmmakers there also increasingly look north. 'Real' success there (and elsewhere) is measured not in terms of domestic box-office receipts, **Arieles** or **Corales**, but in terms of international market penetration, such as that of María **Novaro**'s *Danzón* (1991), which can also often serve as an entry into Hollywood for the film-makers, as witnessed by Alfonso **Arau**'s *Como agua para chocolate* (Like Water for Chocolate) (1991) and Guillermo **del Toro**'s *Cronos* (1992). Although thematically the films of the 1990s have been extraordinarily diverse, there has been a trend toward a gritty, shocking, and almost semi-documentary realism used to depict hostile urban environments in which the young have few options. Victor **Gaviria**'s *Rodrigo D: no futuro* (Rodrigo D: No Future) (1990) from Colombia was an early example; the latest was the brilliant *Pizza, birra y faso* (Pizza, Beer and Smokes) (1997), an opera prima from two young Argentine film-makers, Bruno Stagnaro and Adrián Caetano. On the opposite aesthetic register, others have opted for extreme stylization, often used to revitalize old genres. Some notable examples were Gustavo **Mosquera**'s *Moebius* (1996, Argentina), a successful example of fantastic cinema without monsters or expensive special effects, and Francisco Athié's stylized thriller about the labyrinthine Mexican power structure, *Fibra óptica* (Fibre Optic) (1998). Other notable films include Patricio **Guzmán**'s *Chile, la memoria obstinada* (Chile, Obstinate Memory) (1997), Eduardo Mignogna's *Sol de otoño* (Autumn Sun) (1998) and Ricardo Larraín's *La frontera* (The Frontier) (1991). The Guzmán film, like Leonardo **Favio**'s *Gatica el mono* (1993) and Gabriel Retes's *El bulto* (1991), works with repressed memory, particularly memory of political violence.

Eugenio **Dittborn** in Chile (and, in a different register, Juan **Dávila**, a Chilean in Australia, famous for his image of Simón Bolívar in drag) also work with memory in their powerful artwork. Nahum **Zenil**, one of the most notable painters of contemporary Mexico, is openly gay in his subject matter, which works with elements of personal history, popular religion, the art of Frida **Kahlo** and of popular *retablo* artists and national symbols (see *retablos* **and** *ex votos*). Sculpture embraced elements of theatre and kineticism in the kind of transformation of public space exemplified by

Gyula Kosice. More generally, the city changes its face and its culture as globalization rendered it international. For the glass and steel monuments of the banking boom of the 1980s still co-exist with street sellers and shanty towns. Jesús **Martin Barbero** and Néstor **García Canclini** (with an excess of reverence for a modish postmodernism) have examined the contradictions that this process engenders, on the one hand sweeping aside the alternative national project – dead in the ruins of the Berlin Wall and the dynamics of global consumption – but on the other producing forms of local resistance that sometimes assimilated and parodied the very forms of consumption themselves – the rise of rap (see **rap music**) in particular and youth cultures in general may be a sign of a new culture from below. And in a similar sense, the curiosity of the internationalization of some aspects of Latin American culture and tradition – the ubiquity of Andean headwear and Mexican blankets, the enormous popularity of Mexican food and Cuban music – is counterbalanced in contradictory and mysterious ways by the Latin Americanization of aspects of the culture of the north.

Some of the most striking music of the decade is fusion music: ***chicha* music** in Peru, **samba-reggae** in Brazil, **chutney** in Trinidad and Guyana, **dancehall** in Jamaica and London, **rapso** in the English-speaking Caribbean, and the **maroon music** of the forests of the Guyanas are musics that have emerged as part of – but also in resistance to – the globalisation of culture. Kenneth Bilby in a fascinating paper on maroon musics at the **Latin American Studies Association** meetings in Guadalajara in 1997 defined the impulse as 'Act Globally, Think Locally' (inverting the well-known slogan). Contemporary musical groups like **Café Tacuba** in Mexico and Karnak in Brazil are certainly products of 'world music'. But the 'world music' phenomenon has been strongly criticized by one of Latin American music's leading intellectuals, Caetano **Veloso**, who sees it as a marketing device contrived by the ignorant. Besides the work of artists like these, an interesting phenomenon has been a sort of nostalgia industry – the marketing of elderly Cuban musicians as the *Buena Vista Social Club*, the recordings of old boleros (see **bolero**) by **Luis**

Miguel and of old tangos by Daniel **Barenboim**, the revitalization of **salsa** in younger musicians like Ricky **Martin**, Marc Anthony and India, and of **merengue** by Juan Luis **Guerra**. An important feature of recent years has been the remastering in digital form of old recordings – tangos, **son**, **choro** and chorinho, boleros, **béguine**, early Latin **jazz** – which has been part of the 'fusion' process in that many of these musical recordings are themselves products of fusion (tango and jazz in Oscar **Alemán**, for instance).

Gayatri Spivak asked in a famous article 'Can the subaltern speak?' and answered her own question in the negative. David Stoll has raised the same question in his work on the *testimonio* of Rigoberta **Menchú Tum**. By foregrounding the problem of truth in *testimonio*, Stoll has revived reflections on the problem of authorship in the genre and the question of its authenticity. Menchú, to her credit, has responded to Stoll by continuing to speak and to write. More broadly, the initial impetus behind the search for an authentic popular voice remains a powerful one – though the perception of oral culture as a repository of authentic and unchanged values has been made problematic by the discussions of **hybridity**, which reveal the spaces for selection and partial and opportunistic recuperation of elements of a dominant culture, and a great skill among many of the most marginal in learning the techniques of survival in the hostile city. The Brazilian MST and the Zapatistas are shining examples.

With the coming of a new millennium – in January 2000 by popular acclaim, but in January 2001 by decree of Fidel **Castro** – the old question 'What is to be done?' is still with us. Past days of public-service broadcasting, democratic education, the protection of collective rights by sympathetic populist governments are clearly memories now – the progressives of yesterday are in many cases today the perplexed administrators of structural adjustment. The optimistically labelled 'national bourgeoisie' of past debates are now collaborators in a multinational private enterprise culture. And yet with persistent skill and ingenuity, traditions of struggle are merged with methods of the new millennium; resistance continues, but the sense of connectedness, of an overarching purpose shared and collectively pursued has yet to be rediscovered for a new age.

Castro's Cuba is no longer a model – though it may have been a heroic emblem once; whatever happens across the Florida Strait, the future is under construction in the most surprising and unexpected places.

Further reading

Castañeda, J. (1993) *Utopia Unarmed*, New York: Alfred A. Knopf.

Dore, E. (ed.) (1997) *Gender Politics in Latin America: Debates in Theory and Practice*, New York: Monthly Review Press.

Franco, J. (1999) *Critical Passions*, eds M.L. Pratt and K. Newman, Durham/London: Duke University Press.

García Canclini, N. (1989) *Culturas híbridas: cómo entrar y salir de la modernidad*, Mexico: Era.

Jonas, S. and McCaughan, E.J. (1994) *Latin America Faces the Twenty First Century: Reconstructing a Social Justice Agenda*, Boulder, CO: Westview Press.

Monsiváis, C. (1997) *Mexican Postcards*, ed. and trans. J. Kraniauskas, London: Verso.

Petras, J, and Morley, M. (1992) *Latin America in the Time of Cholera: Electoral Politics, Market Economics and Permanent Crisis*, New York/London: Routledge.

DANIEL BALDERSTON,
MIKE GONZALEZ
AND ANA M. LÓPEZ

A

A esta hora se improvisa

A popular political discussion programme, *A esta hora se improvisa* (At This Time of Day You Improvise) was shown on Chile's television channel 13, run by the Universidad Católica, between 1970 and 1973, broadcast at prime time on Sunday evenings. Moderated by Jaime Celedón, it reflected the sometimes violent political conflicts unleashed during the **Popular Unity** period. Politicians were nominated by their parties to appear alongside journalists Julio Martínez, José M. de Navasal and Tito Mundt. Participants included José Tohá of **Popular Unity**, Jaime Guzmán representing the Right and Claudio Orrego for the Christian Democrats, among others.

ELIANA ORTEGA

Abakua Society

A secret society originating in the Calabar region of Nigeria, the Abakua Society's exclusively male membership are called *ñáñigos*. Introduced into Cuba in 1836 through the city of Regla, near Havana, and later extended into Matanzas, it began as a secret organization of slaves and free blacks, as a mutual protection society and to preserve traditional religion. Its secret rituals are accompanied by the *ekue* friction drum; its ceremonials include initiation, purification, renewal and funeral rites overseen by the *ireme*, or

little devil. Any member who violates its codes is severely punished.

JOSÉ ANTONIO EVORA

Abalos, Los Hermanos

Los Hermanos Abalos are a highly regarded Argentine folk group from Santiago del Estero Province, comprising Napoleón Benjamín (*Machingo*), Adolfo Armando, Roberto Wilson, Víctor Manuel (*Vitilo*) and Marcelo Juan (*Machaco*) Abalos. Musicians, authors and composers of popular folk music, their career spans fifty years of performing and recording folk music from Santiago, Tucumán and Salta provinces that has contributed to the popularization of this genre. They are the authors of memorable classic zambas (see **zamba**) such as 'Agitando pañuelos' (Waving Handkerchiefs) and 'Nostalgias santiagueñas' (Santiago Memories). They have played an important role in disseminating this music in Argentina and throughout the world.

MAGDALENA GARCÍA PINTO

Abath, Ciro

b. 1954, Aruba

Artist

A ceramic artist, Abath was trained and formed in

the Netherlands. He is convinced that everybody is born with a language of forms determined by culture, which is handed down from generation to generation. As the Caribbean is a melting pot of various cultures, in his ceramic art he searches for his different roots. In his big abstract ceramic forms, one can often find fossil-like frogs and lizards or even pre-Columbian artefacts. Sometimes he also applies other natural materials like stones, corals or shelves to his work.

NEL CASIMIRI

ABC Color

ABC Color, 'un diario joven con fe en la patria' (a young daily with faith in our country), is an independent daily newspaper of the Paraguayan political center, founded in 1967. It was closed down by the dictatorship of Alfredo **Stroessner** in March 1984 on the ambiguous grounds that its rebellious nature 'endangered the peace of the republic and the stability of institutions'. As the daily itself put it, it was closed for defending freedom. *ABC Color* resumed publication in 1989 after the February military *coup* which overthrew Stroessner. At time of writing it had reached a circulation of 75,000.

BETSY PARTYKA

abertura

The term '*abertura*' (opening) was used in Brazil to describe the gradual relaxation of military rule and the re-establishment of civil institutions, in the latter part of the 1964–85 military period, beginning in 1978 near the end of the term of President Ernesto Geisel. The process accelerated after the inauguration of another military president, João Figueiredo, in 1979; he authorized a partial amnesty and the creation of new political parties. Nevertheless, the 'opening' to redemocratization was lukewarm: censorship was not suspended, torture and other abuses did not disappear, and elections were not fully free. The 1982 elections were marred by restrictive new rules, and the mass campaign of 1984 for direct presidential elections

was beaten back in Congress, though military rule did end in the following year.

DANIEL BALDERSTON

Abreu, Caio Fernando

b. 1948, Santiago, Rio Grande do Sul, Brazil; d. 1996, Menino, Porto Alegre, Brazil

Short-story writer and novelist

An urban writer, Abreu speaks for the generation that lived through the turmoil of the 1960s, the drug and sexual revolutions, and, in Brazil, through the political repression of the military regime. His fiction displays a poignant lyricism combined with elements of pop culture, and his characters typically deal with social and psychological alienation. In several of his stories, Abreu focuses on homosexuality and society's violent reaction to it. In *Onde andará Dulce Veiga?* (Where is Dulce Veiga?) (1989; English translation 2000, University of Texas Press), a novel in which the fast, parodic, self-mocking style reflects the chaos of contemporary urban life, Abreu discusses **AIDS**, which he later described as a metaphor for the contemporary human condition. Already a widely-acclaimed author, Abreu was the focus of national attention in 1995, when he publicly acknowledged having AIDS. In an interview with ***IstoÉ*** he brought this taboo subject to light, fostering public awareness and debate on the issues.

CRISTINA FERREIRA-PINTO

acarajá

No celebration in the Brazilian state of Bahia can be complete without *acarajá*, an Afro-Brazilian snack made from a batter of dried shrimp and skinless dried beans. The process of making *acarajá* is as important as the ingredients and it is typically produced by Bahian women dressed in billowy white cotton, lacy turbans and jangling beads and silver bracelets. The outer skins of blanched *fradinho* beans (like black-eyed peas) are painstakingly rubbed with a grinding stone and the beans are then mashed into a paste and mixed with dried shrimp and other condiments. Spoonfuls of the mixture are deep fried in hot **dendé oil** until they puff up and look like elongated dumplings. After draining, the *acarajás* are served cold and split down the centre, with a saucy paste (hot peppers, onions, ginger and more dried shrimp sautéed in *dendê*) spread along the centre. *Acarajá* is the ultimate Brazilian finger food and is, as once described by a cookery author, 'cholesterol nectar'.

ANA M. LÓPEZ

accordion and bandoneón

The accordion and bandoneón are closely related instruments of the reed organ family, with air supplied by a bellows that is operated by the player. The accordion was probably invented in Berlin in 1822 and patented in Vienna in 1829; it has piano-like keys. The bandoneón (sometimes called the button accordion) was invented by Heinrich Band, or perhaps by C. Zimmermann, in Germany in about 1850; it has buttons instead of keys. Both instruments came to the Americas with German immigrants; the accordion is used much more widely in Latin America, while the bandoneón is used exclusively in Argentina and Uruguay in the **tango**.

The accordion is an essential element of Tex-Mex and norteña music, being prominent in the Texas and northern Mexican polka (another German loan); one of the great masters of this style of accordion playing is the Texas musician Flaco Jiménez. Accordions are also important in the Brazilian northeast (where they are called *sanfonas*), particularly in **forró**, with musicians like **Sivuca** being masters of the instrument. In the Brazilian south (where it is called *gaita*), the accordion is an important part of **gaúcho culture** and is used widely in the music of Rio Grande do Sul and Santa Catarina (both of which have substantial German immigrant communities). The accordion is also played in many other areas of the region, including Colombia, Chile, Panama, and in several islands in the Caribbean including the Dominican Republic, Barbados and the Bahamas.

The bandoneón is an essential element of the tango orchestra, giving a sensuous, quirky, often mischievous air to the music. A German invention, it was exported in large quantities to Argentina in the 1920s. Since 1971, it has not been manufactured in Germany. An early master of the Argentine bandoneón style was Roberto Firpo; others included Aníbal **Troilo**, Pedro Maffia and Osvaldo Fresedo. The most famous and innovative player of the bandoneón in the second half of the twentieth century was Astor **Piazzola**. The bandoneón is also used in **chamamé** and other kinds of music in northern Argentina; a similar button accordion is used in Colombian **vallenato**.

Piazzola's bandoneón style has influenced the accordion style of Renato **Borghetti** in Brazil, as well as that of younger bandoneón players like Daniel Binelli in Argentina. All tango *aficionados* hold that it is blasphemous for tango to be played with accordion instead of bandoneón. The US-based Tango Project, which uses accordions, sounds hopelessly inauthentic to anyone acquainted with the real thing.

Further reading

Méndez, G., Peñón, A. and Peñón, J. (1988) *The Bandonion: A Tango History*, trans. T. Barnard, London, Ont.: Nightwood Editions.

Olsen, D.A. and Sheehy, D.E. (eds) (1998) *The Garland Encyclopedia of World Music: South America, Mexico, Central America, and the Caribbean*, vol. 2, New York: Garland.

DANIEL BALDERSTON

Acevedo, Myriam

b. 1930?, Güines, Cuba

Actress

Acevedo became a national icon in the 1960s with her performances in works by Sartre, Brecht and Lizárraga, and **Triana**'s *La noche de los asesinos* (Night of the Assassins), with which she successfully toured Europe in 1966. She remained in Italy, returning to the theatre in 1971; she has appeared in the *Oresteia*, *Richard III* and *Hiroshima mon amour*, directed by Cristine Cibils. She has also written and directed the autobiographical piece *Al compás del estaberio* (In Time) (1988), as well as her one-woman show about recent Cuban history, *A quien pueda interesar* (To Whom it May Concern) (1991).

WILFREDO CANCIO ISLA

Achugar, Hugo

b. 1943, Montevideo, Uruguay

Writer and critic

An accomplished poet, Achugar has received important awards for several of his books. He is also an influential critical voice, writing on a range of Latin American literature and culture topics. A disciple of Angel **Rama**, his investigations aim at interpreting literary works in their historical context. He has made an important contribution to Modernism, focusing on Uruguay in *Poesía y sociedad* (*Uruguay 1880–1911*) (Society and Poetry. Uruguay 1880–1911) (1985). Since the 1980s, he has made Uruguayan society and culture the centre of his reflections as he examines the impact of the millennium.

MAGDALENA GARCÍA PINTO

Achugar, Walter

b. 1938, Montevideo, Uruguay

Film producer and distributor

One of the key figures behind the scenes of the **New Latin American Cinema** movement, Achugar founded an independent company – Renascimiento Films – in Montevideo in the early 1960s which eventually distributed films from all over Latin America and also provided a material base for productions such as Mario **Handler**'s short films. Through Renascimiento, Achugar distributed Brazilian **Cinema Novo**, Cuban cinema, and other 'new' cinemas in Uruguay and Buenos Aires. Simultaneously, he organized the **Marcha** film festivals of 1967 and 1968 and, in 1969, created the Cinemateca del Tercer Mundo, a film society/distributor dedicated to political film-making activities. An indefatigable film promoter, Achugar began producing in Argentina with Leonardo **Favio**'s *Crónica de un niño solo* (Chronicle of a Boy Alone) (1964); later he produced Jorge **Sanjinés**'s brilliant documentary reconstruction *El coraje del pueblo* (The Courage of the People) in Bolivia in 1971. In exile after the military *coup d'état* of 1973 (which also shut down the Cinemateca), Achugar continued to promote and produce Latin American film, first in Venezuela and later in Spain, where he worked to develop a European market for Latin American film.

ANA M. LÓPEZ

Acosta, Agustín

b. 1886, Matanzas, Cuba; d. 1979, Miami, USA

Poet

Acosta was a precursor of the 1920s current of social poetry in Cuba, characterized by its nationalism in the face of US domination. A graduate in law, he was a political prisoner throughout the **Machado** regime. His volume *La Zafra* (The Harvest) (1926) included his best known and most popular poems, 'Las carretas en la noche' (Carts in the Night) and 'Mediodía en el campo' (Midday in the Country). His later volumes include *Las islas desoladas* (The Desolate Islands) (1943) and *Caminos de hierro* (Iron Roads) (1963). He left Cuba in 1973.

WILFREDO CANCIO ISLA

Acosta, Angel León

b. 1932, Havana, Cuba; d. 1963, Havana

Visual artist

Acosta's style has been described as a kind of 'primitive surrealism' – cars, palm trees, tractors and coffee makers appear to fuse in the atmosphere of his paintings, where objects and places announce their autobiographical significance. A bus conductor before entering the San Alejandro Academy, where he emerged top of his sculpture class, his paintings won several awards in Cuba in 1958 and 1959. His painting *Carruaje* (The Cart) was awarded a prize at the 1960 Mexico Bienale. However, it is the canvas called *Familia en la ventana* (Family at the Window) (1959) that marks a break with the academic tradition and the beginning of a mature period which culminates in his fantasy *Colombinas* (Colombines) and *Juguetes* (Toys) series. He travelled to Europe with a grant in 1962; he committed suicide by jumping from the boat that was taking him back to Cuba from the Netherlands.

WILFREDO CANCIO ISLA

Acosta, Delfina

b. 1956, Asunción, Paraguay

Writer

A pharmacist by profession, Acosta has been devoted to literature since she was young. Her first poems appeared in 1984 in *Poesía itinerante* (Itinerant Poetry), a collective publication. Subsequently she published two books of poetry: *Todas las voces, mujer...* (All the Voices, Woman...) (1986) and *La Cruz del Colibrí* (Hummingbird's Cross) (1993). Several of her works have received literary awards, including *Pilares de Asunción* (Pillars of Asunción) (1987) and the short story 'La fiesta en la mar' (The Party at Sea). *El viaje* (The Trip) (1995) is a collection of prize-winning short stories.

TERESA MÉNDEZ-FAITH

Acosta, Oscar

b. 1933, Tegucigalpa, Honduras

Writer

Primarily a short story writer, Acosta has also published highly praised poems and essays and edited several anthologies. His *El arca* (The Chest) (1956) renovated the short story in Honduras, following new narrative themes and techniques introduced by **Borges**. His stories of the quotidian and intimate have a clear, sober and unaffected style. His poetry is intensely lyrical and flows

naturally; rhythms are neither forced nor excessively free. Active in Hondura's cultural life and the winner of various prizes, Acosta has served as president of the Honduran PEN Club and the Press Association.

LINDA J. CRAFT

Acosta, Wladimiro

b. 1900, Odessa, Russia; d. 1967, Buenos Aires, Argentina

Architect and town planner

Influenced by Van Doesburg and Le Corbusier, Acosta was responsible among others for introducing architectural modernism into Argentina. He built only a few buildings in Buenos Aires, as well as the Santa Fe psychiatric hospital, but in his writings and lectures, published after his death as *Vivienda y ciudad* (Housing and the City) (1967), he proposed a synthesis of housing, environment and landscape: a futuristic city of 'city blocks' with ground levels left free for traffic and construction determined by the location of the sun. These ideas were incorporated into the design of **Brasília**.

GONZALO AGUILAR

Adams, Grantley

b. 1898, St Michael, Barbados; d. 1971, Bridgetown, Barbados

Politician

Adams was the first Prime Minister of Barbados and founding member of the Barbados Labour Party. In 1938 he helped establish the Progressive League that led to the formation of the Labour Party; under his leadership from the 1940s the Labour Party expanded the right to vote by reducing the income qualification and giving women the franchise. He arranged a series of constitutional changes that moved Barbados towards independence. Adams represented Barbados in the West Indian Federation from 1958 through its dissolution in 1962, and was frustrated in efforts to keep the coalition alive. Adams provided the pivotal leadership that produced Independence for Barbados on November 30, 1966.

JOHN H. PATTON

Adán, Martín

b. 1907, Lima, Peru; d. 1985, Lima

Poet and novelist

Martín Adán was the pen name of Rafael de la Fuente Benavides. He published his first poems in **Amauta**, the influential cultural and literary magazine founded by José Carlos **Mariátegui**, who remarked on the innovative format of Adán's modern sonnets as 'anti-sonnets'. Adán's *Itinerario de primavera* (Springtime Itinerary) (1928) is endowed with an anti-traditional tone that signals his affinity with the generation of writers who claimed that poets could aspire to the divine power of creation by the alchemy of the word.

Equally innovative in prose, his *Casa de cartón* (Cardboard Shack) (1928) is a vanguardist novel much admired for the linguistic experimentation that foregrounded the centrality of language. With a thin plot and undetermined characterization, it is a dynamic stylistic adventure of the first order. His major work is *Travesía de extramares* (Voyage beyond the Seas) (1950), where the poet is the explorer of the other side of life. It is a voyage into the unknown nourished by the yearning to break down boundaries, a quest powerfully reflected in its expressive system of lexical and syntactic experimentation, alluded to in the title of the collection. The volume consists of sonnets, and his strict adherence to traditional versification allowed him to confine the maximum of emotion within the most prestigious of classical forms. The nautical metaphor of the title is one of the central images of the book. He shared with other poets, like César **Moro**, the idea that poetry's reality is elsewhere, unreachable even for the poet himself. He skilfully constructed a poetic system based on the Romantic music of Frédéric Chopin and the language of French symbolist poetry, hence its subtitle *Sonetos a Chopin* (Sonnets to Chopin). His other two important works are *La mano desasida: Canto a Macchu Picchu* (The Unclutched Hand: A Song to

Macchu Picchu) (1964) and *Diario de un poeta* (Diary of a Poet) (1975).

Further reading

Bendezú, E. (1969) *La poética de Martín Adán*, Lima: Villanueva.

Higgins, J. (1982) *The Poet in Peru: Alienation and the Quest for a Super-Reality*, Liverpool: Francis Cairns.

Lauer, M. (1983) *Los exilios interiores: una introducción a Martín Adán*, Lima: Hueso Húmero.

MAGDALENA GARCÍA PINTO

Adoum, Jorge Enrique

b. 1923, Ambato, Ecuador

Writer

An influential writer, Adoum's work constitutes an itinerary of the Ecuadorean experience, from colonial times to the present. The denunciation of the poverty and social problems of his native country are constants, as are the sense of alienation and the search for identity. He frequently experiments with language and the form and nature of poetry and narrative. His writings include *Los cuadernos de la tierra* (Notebooks of the Land) (1963), *No son todos los que están* (Not All Are Here) (1979), *Entre Marx y una mujer desnuda* (Between Marx and a Naked Woman) (1976), which was made into a film by Camilo Luzuriaga in 1996, and *Ciudad sin ángel* (City without Angel) (1995).

HUMBERTO E. ROBLES

Advis, Luis

b. 1935, Iquique, Chile

Composer

Advis has composed chamber music, works and songs for popular singers, music for more than one hundred plays, films and television programmes. His chamber music is characteristically neo-romantic and nationalist (for example *Preludios*, for piano, *Suite latinoamericana* for seven instruments) while his popular pieces combine baroque elements with music from popular and folk music traditions. In 1969–70 he composed the *Cantata popular Santa María de Iquique* (referring to a famous miners' strike in Chile in 1906) for the group **Quilapayún**, one of the key works in the Chilean *nueva canción* movement. Other major works include the *Canto para una semilla* (Song for a Seed), based on a poem by Violeta **Parra** and *Los tres tiempos de América* (The Three Ages of Latin America) with texts by the composer.

ALFONSO PADILLA

aesthetics of hunger

'Aesthetics of hunger' was a term coined by Brazilian Cinema Novo film director Glauber **Rocha** to explain the relationship between the film practices of **Cinema Novo** and Brazilian socio-political reality and underdevelopment. Rocha first presented a paper titled 'An Aesthetics of Hunger' at a film festival in Genoa, Italy, in 1965; the manifesto (see **manifestos**) was later published in Portuguese in *Revista Civilizacão Brasiliera* and has been widely translated and reprinted. In 'An Aesthetics of Hunger', Rocha contrasted Cinema Novo and its 'gallery of starving people' with mainstream 'digestive cinema'. He denounced Brazil's neo-colonial oppression and called for Brazilians to take their political and cinematic destinies into their own hands. Arguing along lines reminiscent of Frantz **Fanon**, he posited violence as the authentic cultural expression of a hungry people and explained the work of the cinemanovistas as follows: 'so we make these sad, ugly, desperate films that scream; films where reason does not always prevail. In this way, a culture of hunger, mirrored unto itself, becomes aware of its real structure and can actively begin the process of qualitative social change'.

ANA M. LÓPEZ

afoxé

Afoxé is a type of Afro-Brazilian **carnival** group from Salvador, Bahia, dating from the nineteenth century. It usually features a percussion ensemble

which plays the slow, hypnotic ijexá rhythm using a variety of instruments including atabaques (hand-held drums), agogôs (double bells), and xiquerês (gourd shakers). During civic and religious festivals such as carnival, *afoxés* parade in the streets singing secularized versions of sacred **Candomblé** chants. The most famous and enduring *afoxé*, the **Filhos de Gandhi**, has thousands of revelers and has become a symbol of the Bahian carnival.

CHRISTOPHER DUNN

African influences on Latin American music

The strong and compelling presence of African rhythms and references among Latin America's black populations – in Brazil, Cuba and Ecuador particularly – do not represent a survival of pure African forms, as some might suggest. They do reflect, however, both the continuity of cultural resistance by black communities through time and the centrality of music in that resistance, given the repression of most other forms of expression – **African languages**, religions or forms of communal organization, for example.

The slaves taken from West Africa to work the plantations of Cuba and Brazil arrived continuously from the sixteenth to the nineteenth century. Some escaped (see **Zumbi dos Palmares** and **maroons**.) but most remained enslaved and oppressed on the sugar plantations. Their religion was maintained, though often hidden behind Roman Catholic iconography, and remains a powerful and living force in the late twentieth century – as **Candomblé** or **Umbanda** in Brazil, and **Santería** in Cuba. Traditional, African-based musical forms that have survived tend to be those most directly related to popular religious ritual – the ring dance and the forms of ritual dance that often invoke spirit-possession, the call-and-response form, the exclusive use of percussion and related instruments like the marimbula (the thumb piano), though the complicated syncopations appear in Afro-Cuban music but not in the Afro-Brazilian tradition. In Brazil, that African link is expressed in the continuity of **capoeira**, the martial art/dance-play originating in Angola, and the folk drama,

Bumba-meu-boi. But it is the African-derived **samba** that has come to be identified with Brazilian national music. Originally a rural folk dance, it was the urban development in Bahia and beyond that defined the samba rhythm of the twentieth century. The great samba musicians of the 1920s, like **Donga** and **Pixinguinha**, represented the moment of transition. As the new urban samba adopted new musics, the slum districts continued the traditions of collective song and dance in forms like the samba de morro, **pagode** and ultimately in the **samba-reggae** of the 1990s, which reaffirmed the experience of ethnic identity at the heart of the samba tradition.

The encounter between different African-based traditions has produced new fusions, like the works of the Brazilian ensemble, **Olodum**, who bring together Afro-Brazilian traditions and the **son** and **merengue** lineages of the Caribbean. Many elements of the original African cultures of the slaves continue to exist in the Caribbean region – in work songs and drumming traditions. Though their origins are by now largely forgotten, they pervade all the island societies of the region. **Carnival** itself denotes a secularization of ritual uses of mask and dance, while African rhythms and musical forms have merged with the frequent migrant cultures to create hybrid forms like **danzón**, **béguine**, **rumba** and others. In Cuba **Yoruba** dance and drumming traditions remained alive because they were largely permitted – so the bata drum, the basis of traditional Afro-Cuban music and the accompaniment to most popular Santería religious rituals, is the foundation of most subsequent Cuban percussion. Other traditions – from the Congo and the **Abakua**, for example – made their own particular contributions. Cuba's most famous, and most influential, musical form, the son, is the result of a meeting between African-based percussion and the plucked string instruments of Hispanic origin. Though born in the plantation region of Oriente in eastern Cuba, son spread through the island and beyond in the late 1920s and early 1930s, adding instruments and rhythmic elements as it went. Rumba, a family of rhythms of different origin – partly the consequence of Haitian migrations to Cuba in the early nineteenth century – gave world music the tumbadora, or conga drums.

The Pacific coast of Colombia has its own identifiable African-derived traditional music, with its characteristic rattles and scrapers (güiros or guachas) and the central importance of the *currulao* ensembles, accompanying festive dances with drums and marimbas (see **marimba**) in both Colombia and Ecuador's Pacific regions. The most widely diffused African-derived music from Colombia is, of course, the **cumbia**, originally performed on drums, scrapers and pipe, until its urban variants introduced guitar, bass, accordion and clarinet into cumbia dance music. In Peru, the characteristic music of the black community is the *festejo*, which uses guitar, drum-box and hand-claps to accompany elaborate dancing and improvised rhyming couplets.

The diffusion of music of African origin has meant that its presence may be detected in most of Latin America's many musics – from the Argentine **tango** to the **punta rock** of Belize.

Further reading

Behague, G. (ed.) (1994) *Music and Black Ethnicity*, Miami: North–South Center, University of Miami.

Carvalho, J.J. de (1994) *The Multiplicity of Black Identities in Brazilian Popular Music*, Brasília: Universidad de Brasília.

Cornelius, S. and Amira, J. (1992) *The Music of Santería: Traditional Rhythms of the Bata Drums*, Crown Point, IN: White Cliffs Media.

Daniel, Y. (1994) *Rumba: Dance and Social Change in Contemporary Cuba*, Bloomington: Indiana University Press.

Manuel, P. (1995) *Caribbean Currents*, Philadelphia: Temple University Press.

Ortiz, F. (1954) *Los instrumentos de la música afrocubana*, Havana: Cárdenas y Cia.

MIKE GONZALEZ

African languages

Having all but obliterated the indigenous population in parts of America, through disease, slavery and systematic extermination, Spain and Portugal turned to Africa for new hands to build their empires.

Literally hundreds of African languages were taken to Latin America during the period of European colonialism. Few have survived the rigours of enslavement and ethnic oppression, and their influence on the official European languages spoken in Latin America today has been relatively small, especially when one considers the number of African slaves exported to America. None the less, vestiges of their presence can still be noted today and their influence is arguably more weighty in terms of lexical content than in grammatical structure. A very large number of words from African languages are used in Spanish, Portuguese, French and English today.

This relative lack of change in terms of the grammar of European languages in Latin America can perhaps be explained by a policy employed by many plantation owners. These owners would deliberately buy slaves who came from several different African communities and who did not speak a common language. If the slaves could not organize themselves by means of language, then they would not pose the threat of revolt and insurrection. When a group of slaves came from the same linguistic community, plantation owners prohibited the use of their language. On many plantations, slaves would create a pidgin tongue, consisting of African words brought from home, strongly influenced by the language of their European oppressors. Very few of these languages were written down, as history in America was almost always written by the hand of the white colonial oppressor. However, some evidence can be found in contemporary Spanish and Portuguese writings – colonial authors often tried to imitate African pidgins or bozals in their works, though it is difficult to judge the linguistic accuracy and to what extent the language has been stereotyped for the entertainment of the reader.

Despite the attempts of the colonialists, evidence of Africanized speech is still predominant in many areas of Latin America. A heavy African influence can still be found in Cuba, where many **Yoruba** and Kikongo words still surface in Cuban Spanish, especially in reference to religious practices. African religions in Cuba were practised clandestinely as plantation owners prohibited them; under the guise of practising Christianity, slaves would use the names of African gods to denote Christian symbols. In Bahia and Marinho in northeastern Brazil, to this day, Yoruba is commonly employed in religious ceremonies in favour of, and alongside, Portuguese. The Palenquero dialect of Palenque de San Basilio (a town founded by a group of escaped slaves) in Colombia still retains strong evidence of African roots, while the dialect of the Chota valley in the Ecuadorian Andes, a relatively isolated black community, uses a notably more Africanized Spanish than the Afro-Ecuadorians in the coastal port of Esmereldas – who have had more contact with mestizos, and whose dialect is thus more homogenized. In the ex-Dutch, French and British colonies, many unofficial **creole languages**, incorporating elements of both African and European languages, have evolved over the course of the past few centuries, creating a *mélange* of languages that is neither completely European nor African, but distinctively American.

Further reading

Blackburn, R. (1997) *The Making of New World Slavery*, London: Verso.

Fardon, R. and Furniss, G. (eds) (1994) *African Languages, Development and the State*, London: Routledge.

Greenberg, J. (1963) *Language in the Americas*, Stanford: Stanford University Press.

Moreno Fraginals, M. (ed.) *Africa in Latin America: Essays on History, Culture and Socialization*, trans. Leonor Blum, New York: Holms & Meier.

PETER WATT

Afro-Latin American arts

The presence in Latin America of large numbers of West African slaves brought to work in plantations and mines has powerfully contributed to the establishment of distinct local identities, particularly in and around the Caribbean and in Brazil. The conditions of the trade grouped Africans of disparate origins together, preventing the direct transmission of their cultures to the Americas and forcing the creation of entirely new social structures which were rooted in African traditions linked by elements from the surrounding European culture. Many slaves escaped into remote regions, where they set up isolated rebel communities. Among these, the Saramaka of Suriname are notable for their unique cultural complex of clear African derivation. Others, however, adapted to the established social framework of European origin, infusing new vitality into its cultural and artistic life especially from the eighteenth century onwards. A good example is the Brazilian-born mulatto Antônio Francisco Lisboa, nicknamed 'Aleijadinho' (Little Cripple), who created the monumental Baroque architectural-sculptural complex of Bom Jesus dos Matozinhos (1796–99) in Minas Gerais, Brazil; or the Trinidadian painter Michel Jean Cazabon (1813–88), who produced delicate and romantic Caribbean landscapes and portraits.

A major vehicle for cultural resistance was the practice of African-derived religions, like **Santería** in Cuba, **Vodun** in Haiti and **Candomblé** in Brazil. As well as their importance as complex ritual performances, these religions required the production of often aesthetically elaborate tools, clothing, sculpture, emblems and ideograms, which in turn found their way into the iconography of much twentieth-century art and became an integral part of the identity-building process. This can be seen in the works of Manuel **Mendive** and Ana **Mendieta** (Cuba), for instance, or of Rubem Valentim and Mario **Cravo Neto** (Brazil). Secular Afro-Latin American preoccupations are also important, as in the many re-interpretations of the successful Haitian slave revolution of 1804 painted by untutored artists such as Senèque and Philomé **Obin**. In the work of the Cuban surrealist painter Wifredo **Lam**, rituals and forms of African derivation transcend local cultural and geographical frontiers to enter and revitalize the vocabulary of mainstream Western art history.

See also: primitive painting

Further reading

Lindsay, A. (ed.) (1996) *Santería Aesthetics in Contemporary Latin American Art*, Washington and London: Smithsonian Institution Press.

Price, S. and Price, R. (1980) *Afro-American Arts of the Suriname Rain Forest*, Berkeley and Los Angeles: University of California Press.

TANIA COSTA TRIBE

Agachados, Los

After *Los **supermachos**, Los Agachados* (The Crouched) is the second most popular creation of **Rius**, the controversial Mexican cartoonist and constant critic of the political apparatus. An atypical comic series, *Los Agachados* appeared in September 1968, a new genre of **comics** without developing plot or a continuing story which, as Rius acknowledged, gave him total freedom. Once again, there were stock stereotyped Mexican characters, but this time in a collage of new graphic elements like old and new engravings, press cuttings, photographs and so on. No longer within a microcosm of Mexican society, *Los agachados* approached universal and taboo themes in a more didactic and politicized language.

EDUARDO SANTA CRUZ

Agard, John

b. 1949, Guyana

Actor and writer

Author of several books for children in Guyanese vernacular, Agar started acting and writing in his teens, eventually touring the Caribbean with the All Ah We performance group. In 1977 he went to England, where he worked for the Commmonwealth Institute. His poetry includes *Shoot Me with Flowers* (1973), *Quetzy de Saviour*, a story in verse (1976), and *Man to Pan*, winner of the **Casa de las Américas** Prize (1982). In recognition of the oral sources of Caribbean poetry and story-telling, he coined the term 'poetsonian'.

KEITH JARDIM

ageing and senior citizens in Latin America

As in most other regions of the world, the elderly population of Latin America is expanding ever more quickly. Between 1960 and 2000 the proportion of residents aged sixty years or more will have grown from 5.9 to 8.6 per cent. There is, however, considerable variation between countries. As many as 13.6 per cent will be aged sixty or more in Argentina by the end of the century, whereas in Honduras the figure will only be 5.2. Population ageing reflects broader processes of economic development and social modernization which have led to sharp falls in the birth rate (reducing the proportion of younger people) and increases in life expectancy.

Most Latin American countries have long-established welfare programmes which offer retirement pensions and other services for their elderly. Even so, large numbers of elderly, particularly the poor, remain excluded from these programmes and since the early 1980s many welfare schemes have been cut back. In some countries, the shortcomings of these programmes have prompted vocal protest from elderly political groups. In Argentina, for example, pensioners organize weekly protests outside the National Congress building and their plight is now seen as a major political issue. In other countries the elderly have yet to develop as an organized interest group and their welfare problems are given scant attention by either politicians or the general public.

Although many of the region's most prominent cultural, political and historical figures have maintained high public profiles when elderly, old age remains highly stigmatized in most aspects of Latin American life, particularly in urban areas. The pace of change has left many elderly isolated and disorientated and they are widely perceived as possessing few relevant social or economic skills. Little has been done to redress widespread discrimination against the elderly in the formal labour market. Local grassroots groups and NGOs (National Government Organizations) pay much more attention to the problems of other groups, such as mothers, young children and unemployed men. Whilst most elderly live with other relatives, the needs of other family members tend to be placed before their own.

In rural districts the position of the elderly is more variable. The Vilcabamba Valley of Ecuador enjoys possibly the highest life expectancy in the world, due in part to the local climate, diet and lifestyles. Here the elderly have a relatively privileged social position and play an active role in the community. More typically, rural elderly are faced with a stark choice between abject destitution or migrating to live with younger relatives in cities.

Further reading

Lloyd-Sherlock, P. (1997) *Old Age and Urban Poverty in the Developing World. The Shanty Towns of Buenos Aires*, Basingstoke: St Martin's Press.

SEADE (1990) *O idoso na Grande São Paulo*, São Paulo: Fundaçâo Sistema Estadual de Análise de Dados.

Tout, K. (1989) *Ageing in developing countries*, Oxford: Oxford University Press.

PETER LLOYD SHERLOCK

agitprop

Derived from the early years of the Russian Revolution of 1917 and the artists associated with the German revolutionary movement of the years that followed, agitprop (agitation and propaganda) places art at the service of politics. The variety of ways in which this has been achieved is wide. In theatre, the socialist realism of the 1930s was clearly intended to mobilize audiences around a denunciation of social injustice and a broad spectrum of progressive political causes; its forms derived in one way or another from **Brechtian theatre**'s key notion of transforming the theatrical audience from passive spectators into active participants in social change. Thus, agitprop both informed and educated, and mobilized. In the 1960s this tradition was rediscovered by a new generation making political theatre, particularly in Colombia, through the work of **Teatro Experimental de Cali** and in particular its leader, Enrique **Buenaventura**, and in Mexico, where street theatre played its part in the student movement of 1968.

The early documentaries (see **documentary**) of the Latin American cinema served a similar directly political purpose, and some of the leading members of the **New Latin American Cinema** movement – like Fernando **Birri** or the makers of *La **hora de los hornos*** in Argentina, and later Santiago **Alvarez** in Cuba – saw that as its primary purpose. That tradition clearly influenced Chilean film-makers like Patricio **Guzmán** and Miguel **Littín** in the conflictive conditions of the **Popular Unity** government (1970–3), where they continued to offer highly charged political narratives rooted in contemporary events.

In art, too, the stark realism of the 1930s evoked a brutal and unjust world, and suggested action against it. This was achieved through the content of such works as well as their public and monumental form – exemplified by the work of the Mexican muralists, in particular Diego **Rivera** (see **muralism**). Literature, and particularly its more immediate forms like poetry and the polemical essay, sought an interventionist role, like Pablo **Neruda**'s more directly political work or the protest poetry of Ernesto **Cardenal** couched in the language of public utterance. A series of socialist realist novels appeared in the 1930s, like Jorge **Icaza**'s *Huasipungo* (1934) or César **Vallejo**'s *El tungsteno* (Tungsten) (1931).

Music was perhaps the most direct means of social protest and agitation, able to make immediate commentaries on social reality: what Silvio **Rodríguez** of Cuba called *canciones contingentes* (songs for the political moment); or the *nueva canción* written and sung by Víctor **Jara** in Chile to give voice to the spirit and the vision of the movement – like the *Palabras por Puerto Montt*, which protested against the suppression of a squatters' demonstration by riot police in Chile's southern city.

The poster (see **poster art**), **photography** and the cartoon are often ideal methods of response to repression or dictatorship – as in the work of Mexico's **Taller de Gráfica Popular**, for example; more unusually, the *arpilleras* or patchworks of Chile provided a means for the families of political prisoners of making known the day-to-day realities of life under the **Pinochet**

military dictatorship. Under conditions of political censorship or repression, artists must seek out new ways to express their protest, like the work of Chile's **Yeguas del Apocalipsis** or the *rock nacional* concerts in Argentina. But agitprop always rests on the assumption that it is possible to move large numbers of people into action.

Further reading

Burton, J. (ed.) (1990) *The Social Documentary in Latin America*, Pittsburgh: University of Pittsburgh Press.

Taylor, D. (1991) *Theatre of Crisis: Drama and Politics in Latin American Theatre*, Lexington: University of Kentucky Press.

MIKE GONZALEZ

agrarian reform

A literal translation of the Spanish *reforma agraria*, the more common English term, land reform, is rarely used in Latin America. Agrarian reform is a process by which the state seeks to transform a highly unequal agrarian structure or land tenure system, in which *latifundios* (see **latifundio**) (which comprised roughly five per cent of farm units) owned about four-fifths of the land, while small farms or *minifundios* (see **minifundio**) (which made up roughly four-fifths of farm units) controlled only five per cent.

The impulse behind agrarian reform is political and economic. Rural conflicts arising from exploitative landlord–peasant relations were a source of instability, especially when they fuelled peasant movements and led to land occupations or seizures of estates. US and Latin American governments, haunted by the spectre of socialism following the Cuban Revolution of 1959 (see **revolutions**), launched the Alliance for Progress in the early 1960s, which used agrarian reforms to defuse peasant uprisings and prevent more fundamental political and economic changes. Agrarian reform policies aimed to replace the inefficient *hacienda* system with a more dynamic and productive agrarian system. Large farms such as *haciendas*, *latifundios* and plantations (see **plantation**) were expropriated and the land transferred to beneficiaries under collective, cooperative or individual ownership. Beneficiaries were usually restricted to former tenants and farm workers of the expropriated estate, thereby excluding many *campesinos* (see **campesino**), especially smallholders and members of indigenous communities.

Agrarian reforms have been implemented in all Latin American countries except Argentina. In Brazil, only very limited agrarian reform has taken place. The most far-reaching agrarian reforms were the outcome of social revolutions such as in Mexico (1917), Bolivia (1952), Cuba (1959) and Nicaragua (1979). However, agrarian reforms in Chile (1964–73) and Peru (1969–75) were also quite extensive in terms of amount of land expropriated and number of *campesino* beneficiaries. Currently, landless peasants in Brazil are pushing strongly for land reform.

Agrarian reforms failed to fulfil expectations for many reasons. In some cases, the political will or power to enforce them was lacking. Mistakes in design and implementation also contributed to their unravelling. The more radical agrarian reforms encountered opposition from landlords, and in some cases an agrarian reform was partially reversed following a counter-revolution, a reactionary military *coup d'état* or the election of a government opposed to the collectivist tendency of earlier agrarian reforms. The legacy of agrarian reform is therefore complex. Certainly, the more radical agrarian reforms put an end to the *latifundia* system and the dominance of the landed oligarchy in Latin America. In general, they contributed to capitalist development through institutional changes.

Further reading

de Janvry, A. (1981) *The Agrarian Question and Reformism in Latin America*, Baltimore, MD: Johns Hopkins University Press.

Thiesenhusen, W.H. (ed.) (1989) *Searching for Agrarian Reform in Latin America*, Winchester, MA: Unwin Hyman.

CRISTÓBAL KAY

Agresti, Alejandro

b. 1961, Buenos Aires, Argentina

Film-maker

One of the most important film-makers to emerge after the return to democracy in Argentina, Agresti's career began in Holland, where he lived until 1996 and where he directed more than ten films. Despite his European base, his films remained insistently Argentine, presenting typical *porteño* characters, texts (**tango** and **Lunfardo**) and situations upon which he superimposes philosophical dilemmas. Very influenced by Roberto **Arlt**, his work typically has a literary base, although he is also a masterful visual stylist. *Buenos Aires viceversa* (1996), an Argentine–Dutch co-production, won an award at the Mar del Plata festival and marked his return home. In 1997 he directed *La cruz* (The Cross) in Argentina.

ANA M. LÓPEZ

Agrupación Nueva Música

The Agrupación Nueva Música (New Music Group), or ANM, was founded in Argentina in 1944 under the direction of Juan Carlos **Paz** and including Belgian organist Julio Perceval, Italian composer Esteban Eitler and musicologist Daniel Devoto. After leaving the Grupo Renovación, in 1937 Paz began the New Music Concerts to disseminate modern currents in contemporary music, an activity continued by the ANM. Some of the most talented young composers of the 1940s and 1950s were associated with the ANM, among them Mario Davidowsky, Francisco **Kröpfl** and Mauricio **Kagel**. Although the Group continued after the death of Paz in 1972, it became less important thereafter.

ALFONSO PADILLA

Aguilar, Rosario

b. 1938, León, Nicaragua

Novelist

Aguilar's novel *Aquel mar sin fondo ni playa* (That Sea without Depth or Beach) (1970) was the first written by a woman in Nicaragua. A member of one of León's most respected families, Aguilar's father was a university chancellor and mentor to a generation of intellectuals. In her writing she is concerned with feminine ontology, yet does not declare herself a feminist; though politically progressive, she never openly supported the Sandinistas (see **Sandinista Revolution**). Her intimate, subjective narrative concentrated on the world of women, their psychological obsessions and doubts. Her early novels were raw and unfinished, but her later work shows a greater sense of her craft.

SILVIA CHAVES AND ILEANA RODRÍGUEZ

Aguilera Malta, Demetrio

b. 1909, Guayaquil, Ecuador; d. 1982, Mexico City

Writer

A member of the **Guayaquil Group**, which also included Joaquín **Gallegos Lara** and Enrique Gil Gilbert, Aguilera Malta was co-author of *Los que se van* (Those Who Leave) (1930), which crystallized the nativist orientation of social protest literature that shaped writers of his generation. His later work *Don Goyo* (1933), *La isla virgen* (Solitary Island) (1942) and his masterpiece *Siete lunas y siete serpientes* (Seven Moons and Seven Serpents) (1970), explored legends, myth and superstitions. He also wrote historical novels and drama, which evolved from an early realism to expressionism. In 1979 he was named ambassador to Mexico.

MERCEDES M. ROBLES

aguinaldos and villancicos

A villancico or aguinaldo is any Christmas vocal–instrumental musical piece which consists of several stanzas preceded and followed by a chorus, or on some occasions composed as a solo vocal, with an accompaniment of vihuela, **guitar**, cuatro, güiro or the maracas. Carolers serenade outside the homes of friends, who invite them in for refreshments. It has been present in Latin America since the sixteenth century in multiple forms, mainly as a religious poem reflecting the joy of the shepherds or the Magi present at the Annunciation. It was also cultivated in secular form. However, it was during the seventeenth century that the villancico was revived, mainly as a religious musical piece similar to the ecclesiastic cantata, which could be performed in churches and cathedrals along with the psalms at matins.

EDUARDO GUÍZAR-ALVAREZ

Aguinis, Marcos

b. 1935, Río Cuarto, Córdoba, Argentina

Writer

A neurosurgeon and psychiatrist, Aguinis reflects in his writings a fascination with human drives and motivations. His fiction reflects his wide-ranging interests including national politics (he was Secretary of Culture in the **Alfonsín** government), international affairs (notably concerning Israel and the Palestinians), and music. His works span subjects from the Medieval Jewish philosopher Maimonides to probing analyses of authoritarianism and redemocratization. From *La cruz invertida* (The Inverted Cross) (1970), his writing gained a growing readership; *La gesta del marrano* (The Converso's Story) (1993), a novel based on the sixteenth-century trial of Francisco Maldonado da Silva, was a best-seller.

SAÚL SOSNOWSKI

Aguirre Beltrán, Gonzalo

b. 1908, Tlacotalpan, Veracruz; d. 1995, Mexico City

Ethnographer

Aguirre Beltrán's innovative fieldwork and analyses and his stewardship of government institutions left a lasting mark on studies of Mexican culture. His studies of Mexico's population of African descent, combined with his extensive work on Indian health care and religion, formed the basis for his theories regarding the different acculturation of Blacks and Indians. His 'refuge region' theory introduced the concept of internal colonialism into the study of Mexican national society. In *Zongolica* (1986), he argued presciently for the revolutionary potential of the combined influence of **liberation theology** and the evangelization of **Protestantism** in Mexico's Indian hinterlands.

CYNTHIA STEELE

Aguirre, Isidora

b. 1919, Santiago, Chile

Playwright

Aguirre's theatre, agitational and political in the manner of Brecht, addresses the plight of the dispossessed. *Población Esperanza* (A Shanty Called Hope) was first presented in Concepción in 1959; the highly successful *La pérgola de las flores* (The Pergola of the Flowers), a musical comedy with a social message, a year later. In 1969 the **Teatro de la Universidad de Chile** put on her *Los que van quedando en el camino* (The Ones that Get Left Behind), which showed the early stages of a workers' revolution. She also writes novels including the biographical *Carta a Roque Dalton* (A Letter to Roque Dalton) (1990).

ELIANA ORTEGA

Agustín, José

b. 1944, Acapulco, Mexico

Novelist

José Agustín was the Mexican literary scene's *enfant terrible* of the late 1960s and the leading novelist of '**La Onda**', a literary and countercultural movement characterized by extensive use of urban middle-class slang and an irreverent attitude toward Mexican ideology, institutions and authority. His recent works draw heavily on Jungian theory to explore the crisis in Mexican politics. His major novels include *De perfil* (In Profile, 1966), *Se está haciendo tarde (final en laguna)* (It's Getting Late (Ending in the Lake), 1973); *Ciudades desiertas* (Deserted Cities) (1982), a satirical novel about the International Writing Program of the University of Iowa; and *Cerca del fuego* (Near the Fire, 1986).

CYNTHIA STEELE

Ahunchaín, Alvaro

b. 1962, Montevideo, Uruguay

Playwright, actor and director

Ahunchaín's work, from *El séptimo domingo* (Seventh Sunday) (1981) (premiered when he was nineteen) to his adaptions of Macbeth and Don Juan, critique the growing urbanization and technologization of Latin American life. Rather than proposing a return to some non-existent Eden, it questions the cost of change and the dystopias it creates. His other plays include *Se deshace más fácil el país de un hombre que el de un pájaro* (A Man's Country is Destroyed More Easily Than a Bird's) (1991). In 1982 Ahunchaín also became one of Uruguay's youngest advertising executives.

ADAM VERSÉNYI

AIDS

The AIDS (acquired immune deficiency syndrome) epidemic has hit parts of Latin America and the Caribbean hard. Puerto Rico, Jamaica, Haiti,

Brazil and Honduras all have high rates of infection; Cuba, because of a controversial policy of quarantine of HIV-positive persons early in the epidemic, has a relatively low rate. Honduras and Haiti differ to some extent from other countries in the Americas in that the rate of heterosexual transmission is relatively high (a situation that is also the case in sub-Saharan Africa). The **public health** systems of the different countries have reacted very differently to the epidemic, usually in response to the degree of organization (or dis-organization) of the affected populations. The rate of infection diminished for a time, but the number of cases expanded greatly in 1997 (though it is still only 0.2 per cent). In the Caribbean in general, 35 per cent of those affected are women, the highest such rate for any region of the world outside of Africa.

Haiti has the highest rate of infection in the Caribbean, and became famous early in the epidemic as one of the possible vectors of the spread of the virus, though this was challenged. More than 8 per cent of the economically active population is affected. Haiti is the poorest nation in the hemisphere, and its public health system is not able to cope with this and other challenges. Moreover, the current political vacuum in the country has meant that there is little leadership in providing anti-viral medicine, legal protections or adequate care to the affected population.

A very different situation has developed in Brazil and Argentina, both countries with well-developed **gay and lesbian movements** and a long history of public sector involvement in medicine. In 1990, the Argentine congress passed a law that the state public health system would provide care to persons suffering from complications from AIDS, which was extended in 1996 to cover the 'viral cocktail'. In 1997 the Argentine government spent 54 million dollars to buy anti-viral drugs. A similar bill passed the Brazilian congress and was signed into law by Fernando Henrique **Cardoso** in 1996; the provision of the new drug cocktail has resulted in a 35 per cent reduction in AIDS-related deaths in São Paulo in one year. In Costa Rica a similar situation came about through the courts, when a patient sued the national health care system for violating his constitutional rights in not providing him with access to the health and welfare system.

Mobilization around AIDS issues has varied greatly throughout the region. Mexico, a country with a strong public sector health system, has a national council on AIDS (CONASIDA), but has so far resisted having the state provide free access to anti-viral drugs, despite marches, lobbying and a considerable degree of public debate. A monthly supplement to the newspaper *La Jornada*, 'Letra S', which focuses on sexuality, health and AIDS, has been very important in bringing the issue to the fore.

The following individuals, among others, made public their infection with the virus, and their deaths were the occasion for public recognition of the issue: Caio Fernando **Abreu**, **Cazuza** and **Henfil** of Brazil; Néstor **Perlongher** and **Copi** of Argentina; Luis **Caballero** of Colombia; Manuel **Ramos Otero** of Puerto Rico; and Severo **Sarduy** and Reinaldo **Arenas** of Cuba. (There are of course a number of others who were not as public in their declarations, and their choice is respected here.) Carlos Rodríguez Matos has gathered a significant body of poetry in Spanish (from Latin America, Spain and the USA) in his anthology *POESIdA* (Poetry/AIDS) (1995), which includes several masterpieces of black humour by Sarduy (written in the traditional décima form) on his own approaching death.

Further reading

Leiner, M. (1994) *Sexual Politics in Cuba: Machismo, Homosexuality and AIDS*, Boulder, CO: Westview Press.

Letra S Monthly supplement of *La Jornada*. Available in electronic form at http://sida.udg.mx

Rodríguez Matos, C.A. (ed.) (1995) *POESIdA: An Anthology of AIDS Poetry from the United States, Latin America and Spain*, Jackson Heights, NY: Ollantay Press.

DANIEL BALDERSTON

Ainsa, Fernando

b. 1937, Palma de Mallorca, Spain

Writer

Ainsa's fiction includes short stories and two novels

– *El testigo* (The Witness) (1964) and *Con cierto asombro* (With Some Surprise) (1968). His essays address literary criticism, the analysis of cultural movements – in *La narración y el teatro en los años 20* (Narrative and Theatre of the Twenties) (1968) and *Nuevas fronteras de la narrativa uruguaya (1960–1993)* (New Frontiers of Uruguayan Narrative) (1993) – and seminal reflections on Latin American culture in volumes like *Identidad cultural de Iberoamérica en su narrativa* (Cultural Identity of Iberoamerica in its Narrative) (1986). Ainsa is a regular contributor to journals and newspapers in Uruguay, and works for UNESCO in Paris.

CELINA MANZONI

Aira, César

b. 1949, Coronel Pringles, Argentina

Writer

A friend and disciple of Osvaldo **Lamborghini**, Aira has published more than twenty books, among them *Ema, la cautiva* (Emma, the Captive) (1981), a parody of nineteenth-century frontier literature. Concerned in general with recurrent themes like perception, childhood and the nature of 'the Argentine', his novels always display a subtle humour as well as rich and explosive descriptions. His novel *La abeja* (The Bee) (1996) is a satire of the terrors felt by the Argentine middle class.

DANIEL LINK

Aizenberg, Roberto

b. 1928, Entre Ríos, Argentina

Painter and sculptor

One of Latin America's most important surrealist painters (see **surrealism in Latin American art**), influenced by de Chirico and the Argentine surrealist Juan Batlle Planas, Roberto Aizenberg served his apprenticeship with Batlle Planas in the 1950s. In the mid-1950s and 1960s, he participated regularly in group exhibitions of young artists in Buenos Aires, Rio de Janeiro, the prestigious **Bienale de São Paulo**, Caracas and Medellín,

as well as Europe. His work earned him the prestigious *Acquarone* Award in 1961. He presented a retrospective exhibition of his work at the **Instituto Di Tella** in 1969 and received the Cassandra Foundation Award.

MAGDALENA GARCÍA PINTO

Ak'abal, Humberto

b. 1952, Totonicapán, Guatemala

Writer

Ak'abal, whose name means 'Dawn' in his native Quiché, is a prime late twentieth-century example of the re-emergence of Mayan literature in Guatemala. He was the grandson of Mayan religious leaders, and grew up poor without formal Spanish-language schooling. His first collection of poems, *El animalero* (1991), met with immediate success. Ak'abal writes in Quiché and then translates his work into an inflected Spanish. His poems are imbued with Mayan images and lore. Often they are humorous presentations of life in the country, but at times they become oppositional and political.

MARC ZIMMERMAN

Alarma

Alarma is a Mexican weekly tabloid founded in 1963 by Mario Sojo Acosta. Published by Publicaciones Llergo and targeted towards a working-class readership, it has become an icon of Mexican popular culture. Every Wednesday its thirty-two pages feature graphic and often gruesome coverage of true crime and other violent events, including stories of murder, rape and mutilation. *Alarma* has a circulation of one million, mostly in Mexico City, making it the most widely-read newspaper in the country. Until as recently as the late 1980s, *Alarma* was the only tabloid of its kind in Mexico.

JUAN CARLOS GAMBOA

Alazraki, Benito

b. 1921, Mexico City

Film-maker

Alazraki's first feature, *Raíces* (Roots) (1953), won him a Critics Prize at Cannes and an international reputation not confirmed by his subsequent work – commercial genre films like ***Tin Tan*** *y las modelos* (Tin Tan and the Models) (1959) or *Santo contra los zombies* (**Santo** versus the Zombies) (1961). In 1962 he moved to Spain where he wrote and directed more than 100 television programmes. Returning to Mexico in 1972, he worked with Channel 13 and was director general of **Conacine uno, dos** (1978–82). In 1987 he returned to the commercial cinema, producing films of decreasing merit.

PATRICIA TORRES SAN MARTÍN

Alberto, Eliseo

b. 1951, Arroyo Naranjo, Cuba

Writer

Raised and educated in revolutionary Cuba, 'Lichi' Alberto studied journalism at the University of Havana, directed the literary magazine ***El caimán barbudo***, and was on the editorial board of the magazine ***Cine cubano***. He won acclaim in Cuba as a novelist, poet and screenwriter, and gained international attention for his screenplay for *Guantanamera* (directed by Tomás **Gutiérrez Alea**) (1995). Nevertheless, he has been described as a writer of 'post-revolutionary' literature, and since the publication of his novel *Informe contra mí mismo* (Report Against Myself) (1996) he has been denied permission to return to Cuba from Mexico, where he now lives. He won the Premio Internacional Alfaguara de Novela for his novel *Caracol Beach* (1998).

JAMES BUCKWALTER-ARIAS

Albizu Campos, Pedro

b. 1891, Ponce, Puerto Rico; d. 1965, San Juan, Puerto Rico

Political activist and lawyer

President of the Puerto Rican Nationalist Party (see **Partido Nacionalista Puertorriqueño**) from 1930 to his death, Albizu Campos dedicated his entire life to the liberation of Puerto Rico. He was arrested by US authorities and accused of conspiracy against the US government, and was sentenced to ten years in a US prison. He returned to Puerto Rico in 1947 only to be arrested once more after four members of the Nationalist Party attacked the US House of Representatives. His health was destroyed while imprisoned in Atlanta, Georgia, and it is suspected that he was exposed to radiation there.

MARÍA CRISTINA RODRÍGUEZ

Alcántara, Pedro

b. 1942, Cali, Colombia

Painter

Alcántara's drawings and engravings address his concern with the reality of Colombian society. He has exhibited in various galleries in Colombia, Puerto Rico as well as the New African House Art Gallery at Amherst, Massachusetts. He studied in Italy and was awarded the Gubbio prize in Rome in 1961.

ALEJANDRA JARAMILLO

Alcántara Almánzar, José

b. 1946, Santo Domingo, Dominican Republic

Writer and artist

Sociologist and critic, Alcántara is a prolific short story writer with several published short story collections, among them *Callejón sin salida* (Blind Alley) (1975) and *La carne estremecida* (Quivering Flesh) (1989). Two of his books have received awards at the Premio Anual de Cuento (Annual Short Story Prize). As a critic, he has published articles and reviews in magazines and newspapers since the early 1970s; he is also the editor of an anthology of Dominican literature and has taught at several universities in the Dominican Republic.

FERNANDO VALERIO-HOLGUÍN

Alcoriza, Luis

b. 1921, Badajoz, Spain; d. 1992, Cuernavaca, Mexico

Film-maker

Alcoriza arrived in Mexico during the Spanish Civil War and had bit parts in films until given star billing in Miguel **Contreras Torres**' 1943 religious diptych *María Magdalena* and *Reina de reinas* (Queen of Queens). *El gran calavera* (The Great Skull) (1949) marked the beginning of his collaboration with Luis **Buñuel**. Through the 1960s and 1970s he directed some twenty films, among them *Tiburonero* (Shark Fisher) (1962), *Mecánica nacional* (National Mechanics) (1971) and *Las fuerzas vivas* (Living Forces) (1975) – a body of work that defied the worn-out formulas that dominated the Mexican film industry.

PATRICIA TORRES SAN MARTÍN

Aleandro, Norma

b. 1936, Buenos Aires, Argentina

Actress

Born into a family of actors, Norma Aleandro began with **teatro independiente** but became known in the 1960s for her work on television (*Cuatro mujeres para Adán* (Four Women for Adam)) in Fernando **Ayala**'s *La flaca* (The Thin Woman) (1968) and Leopoldo **Torre Nilsson**'s *Los siete locos* (The Seven Madmen) (1972). Upon returning from exile in Spain, she starred in *La **historia oficial*** (The Official Version) (1985) winning the Best

Actress Award at Cannes and ensuring her international reputation. She later published a book of short stories and wrote the screenplay for David Stivel's 1990 film *Los herederos* (The Heirs).

DIANA PALADINO

Alegría, Ciro

b. 1909, Sartimbanba, Huamachuco, Peru; d. 1967, Trujillo, Peru

Writer

A key figure in **indigemismo**, Ciro Alegría's 1941 novel *El mundo es ancho y ajeno* (Broad and Alien is the World) marked a turning point from the brutal social realism of earlier representations of the Indian in works like Jorge **Icaza**'s *Huasipungo* (1934) and Alegría's own *Los perros hambrientos* (The Hungry Dogs) (1938). *El mundo...*, by contrast, portrays a complex Indian community which first resists then unsuccessfully seeks integration into a wider Peruvian society. The book's vision reflected Alegría's lifelong involvement with **APRA**, whose central idea was a notion of 'community' rooted in an Indian past as represented, somewhat idealistically, by Alegra.

MIKE GONZALEZ

Alegría, Claribel

b. 1924, Managua, Nicaragua

Writer

One of the most important Central American writers of the second half of the twentieth century, Alegría is an outstanding poet and narrator, with more than twenty-five titles to her name and translations into a dozen languages. Her first publication was *Anillo de silencio* (Ring of Silence) (1948), but it was *Cenizas de Izalco* (1966) (Ashes of Izalco) (1989) that gained her international renown. Written in collaboration with her husband Darwin J. Flakoll (the translation is his), *Cenizas de Izalco* describes the 1932 genocide of the Izalco Indians. It is important because of its testimonial nature and because of its female narrator, who eventually confesses her love for a visitor from the USA, exposing the repression and unhappiness of life with her husband. In this respect, *Cenizas de Izalco* is a revolutionary narrative, contesting Latin American political, social and aesthetic paradigms.

Alegría's poetry reflects both her literary skill and her social preoccupations. From *Vía única* (Only Way) (1965), to *Y este poema río* (And This Poem-River) (1988), we see the relentless search for a simple poetic language which probes the limits of the establishment. Her poems are tender and beautiful, but always subvert somehow the tradition and canons that sustain them. *Luisa en el país de la realidad* (Luisa in Realityland) (1987) is an excellent collection of poems that presents life in a Salvadoran town through the eyes of a little girl. In this intelligent reversal of Lewis Carroll's famous work, childhood innocence clearly formulates and denounces the atrocities and cruelty of Salvadoran society.

Alegría has contributed important texts to the history of the Central American people's struggles for freedom and democracy. *No me agarran viva: La mujer salvadoreña en lucha*, (They Won't Take Me Alive: Salvadoran Women in Struggle for National Liberation) (1987) is an impressive and painful **testimonio** of women's involvement in that civil war. On the other hand, books like *Pueblo de Dios y de Mandinga* (Family Album) (1985) is about an artists' community in Sitges, on the Mediterranean coast of Spain. To these accomplishments Alegría adds a dozen and a half English translations, many in collaboration with Flakoll, which provide wider access to new and high-quality young Latin American poets and narrators. She is currently living in Nicaragua, though she continues to travel widely; she holds Salvadoran citizenship.

NICASIO URBINA

Alegría, Fernando

b. 1918, Santiago, Chile

Writer

In his first novel **Recabarren** (1938), Alegría rescues the marginalized figure of a leftist leader, modifying the traditional repertoire of national icons. His subsequent novels reveal a dissident position towards the authorized versions of history and official memory. While *El paso de los gansos* (The Goosestep) (1980) and *Coral de guerra* (War Chorale) (1979) present military dictatorship in Chile through fragmentation and a plurality of voices, *La rebelión de los placeres* (The Pleasure Rebellion) (1990) is an ironic postmodern re-elaboration of history. Alegría is also the author of critical studies on Chilean and Latin American literature, and is professor emeritus at Stanford University.

LUCÍA GUERRA

Alejandro, Marcial

b. 1955, Mexico

Composer and singer

Alejandro is a Mexican composer and singer of trova music or Canto Nuevo ('new song'), a kind of musical poetry in the manner of the ancient troubadours or balladeers, with the singer singing his own compositions. In Alejandro's case these include, but are not limited to, social protest songs. Alejandro's public career began in the 1970s with the La Nopalera group; he now appears primarily in concert as a soloist or with a small number of other trova singers, like David **Haro**, Elbio Escobedo, or Carlos Porcel Nahuel.

EDUARDO GUÍZAR-ALVAREZ

Alemán, Oscar

b. 1909, Resistencia, Chaco, Argentina; d. 1980, Buenos Aires, Argentina

Musician

Argentine guitarist and band-leader, Alemán is famous for his raffish style and mastery of all kinds of **guitar**, including the Hawaiian and the Brazilian cavaquinho. Known equally for his work in **tango** and **jazz**, Alemán's jazz work is similar to that of his friend the Belgian guitarist, Django Reinhardt. While playing in Les Loups, a band led by a Brazilian musician Gaston Bueno Lobo, Alemán travelled to Europe in 1929 to accompany the tap-dancer Harry Flemming. Alemán remained in Paris after leaving Les Loups, playing in Josephine Baker's band for a time. In 1940, back in Buenos Aires, he formed a swing band that was popular for some years. After the Second World War he returned to Europe with a jazz band. He spent two decades in obscurity before being rediscovered late in his life. His repertory includes versions of classic tangos like **La cumparsita**, a bizarre version of the Mexican folk song La cucaracha, the famous Agustín **Lara** waltz, Noche de ronda, Consuelo Velázquez's **bolero**, Bésame mucho, and the Brazilian **choro**, *Tico tico no fuba*. He also worked on the soundtracks of various films, and appeared as an actor in *Historia de una carta* (Story of a Letter), directed by Julio Porter in 1957.

DANIEL BALDERSTON

Alerce Records

Founded by Ricardo **García** in 1976, and symbolically named for a tree that withstands all storms, Alerce Records provided a channel for reviving the music and ideas of the Chilean *nueva canción* in the repressive conditions of the military dictatorship. Under the 'cultural blackout' imposed by the dictatorship, Alerce was the first record company to distribute recordings of **Quilapayún**, **Inti-Illimani**, Víctor **Jara**, and other banned musicians of *nueva canción*, and to promote the new generation of musicians who created **Canto Nuevo**. Alerce outlived the dictatorship, continuing as an outlet for new Chilean music after democracy returned to Chile.

See also: DICAP

NANCY MORRIS

Alexis, Jacques Stephen

b. 1922, Gonaives, Haiti; d. 1961, place
  unknown

Novelist and essayist

One of Haiti's major novelists, Alexis's life was tragically cut short in a political murder. Born during the US Occupation, he was the son of the Haitian diplomat and novelist Stephen Alexis. He was influenced at an early age by the Marxist politics of Jacques **Roumain** and later by surrealism (see **surrealism in Latin American art**) thanks to André Breton's visit to Haiti and Alejo **Carpentier**'s theory of *real maravilloso* (marvellous realism). He rose to prominence as one of the leaders of the student movement La Ruche, which played a leading role in the overthrow of the government in 1946. After studying neurology in Paris, he returned home where he wrote his major works, lyrical and dense novels about the Haitian masses. Like Alejo Carpentier, Alexis used history as a source of narrative. His 1955 novel, *Compère Général Soleil* (Comrade General Sun), dealt with the massacre of Haitian cane-cutters in the Dominican Republic by General **Trujillo**'s troops. *Les arbres musiciens* (The Musical Trees) (1957) documented the effects of the Catholic Church's anti-superstitious campaign to get rid of the **Vodun** religion. His later work tended to be less conventionally historical, taking greater liberties with the novel form. An interest in the marvellous is ever present in Alexis's fiction and his 1959 novel *L'espace d'un cillement* (In the Twinkling of an Eye), less constrained by recorded history, is a symbolic narrative in which a Dominican prostitute and a Cuban mechanic encounter each other in a Haitian brothel. His last published work was a book of folktales, which most fully elaborated his concept of the marvellous in the popular imagination. *Romancero aux étoiles* (Songbook to the Stars) (1960) recounts a number of tales both traditional and invented which evoke the Haitian people's creative response to their history of privation and dislocation.

Like his predecessor, Jacques Roumain, Alexis remained a dedicated Marxist for his entire life and while in Paris as a student he became a member of the French Communist Party. On his return to Haiti, he founded the Party of Popular Accord and in 1959 published his *Manifesto for Haiti's Second Independence*, a continuation of the Marxist analysis of Haitian society begun by Roumain in 1934. Alexis is best-known for his 1956 paper on the 'Marvellous Realism of the Haitians', presented at the First Congress of Black Writers in Paris.

Because of his opposition to the **Duvalier** regime, he went into exile and travelled to the Soviet Union, China and Cuba. His life came to a tragic end in 1961 at the hands of the **Tontons Macoutes** after landing clandestinely in Haiti.

Further reading

Antoine, Y. (1993) *Semiologie et personnages romanesques chez Jacques Stephen Alexis*, Montreal: Ed. Balzac.
Dash, J.M. (1975) *Jacques Stephen Alexis*, Toronto: Black Images.

J. MICHAEL DASH

Alfonsina y el mar

This famous song (**zamba**) was played for the first time in 1969 and quickly became a classic of the Argentine repertoire. Its lyrics, rich in metaphor, pay tribute to the poet Alfonsina **Storni**. Its writer, Felix **Luna**, thoroughly researched her life and work in the context of the period in which she lived, for her death left an open wound, a sharp reminder of the intolerance of her society. The music for 'Alfonsina y el mar,' by Ariel **Ramírez**, consolidated the composer's international reputation.

RODRIGO PEIRETTI

Alhambra Theatre

Opened in Havana in 1900, the Alhambra Theatre continued the nineteenth-century comic opera tradition associated with the Teatro Cervantes until its collapse in 1935. The Alhambra's repertoire was the most complete expression of Cuban popular culture, presenting *zarzuelas* (light operas), review and comedies renowned for their musical and theatrical sophistication as well as their satirical content. It was regarded as a true conservatory of national music, where a wide range of song and dance forms were preserved and interwoven; its best known composers were Federico Villoch and Francisco Robreño. Its significance was commemorated in Enrique **Pineda Barnet**'s film, *La Bella del Alhambra* (The Beauty from the Alhambra) (1989).

WILFREDO CANCIO ISLA

All Jamaica Library

Although literary pieces began to be published in the eighteenth century, literary publishing in Jamaica began in earnest with the All Jamaica Library of Thomas Henry MacDermot (Tom **Redcam**), which produced affordable books by Jamaicans about Jamaican subjects. Five numbers (four volumes) appeared between 1904 and 1909, beginning with MacDermot's novel *Becka's Backra Baby* (1904) and E.A. Dodd's *Maroon Medicine* (1905), a collection of stories; these were followed by W.A. Campbell's *Marguerite: A Story of the Earthquake* (1907). Volume 4, a long MacDermot novel called *One Brown Girl And*, was produced as a double issue (numbers IV and V) in 1909. Other than Dodd's stories and MacDermot's first novel, the works are undistinguished.

PAT DUNN AND PAMELA MORDECAI

Alladin, Mohammed Pharouk

b. 1919, Trinidad; d. 1980, Trinidad

Visual artist

Alladin's work is primarily associated with the period immediately following independence, in which he sought to convey the new power relations of the era and its implications for post-colonial identity. Many of his paintings, usually impressionist in style, like *Fishermen* (1979) and *Cane Cutters* (undated), focus on validating the culture of rural or marginal communities as a source for the elaboration of a national identity. Heavily influenced by the US civil rights movement, he was a key figure of the Trinidad Art Society, as well as poet, broadcaster and Director of Culture in the Ministry of Education.

LORRAINE LEU

Allende, Isabel

b. 1942, Lima, Peru

Writer

Isabel Allende worked as a journalist in Santiago, Chile until the 1973 military *coup d'état* that ousted and assassinated President Salvador **Allende**, her uncle. She then went into exile in Venezuela, and began writing fiction in 1981 when she was unable to find work as a journalist. After the publication of her third novel in English, she moved to the United States, where she currently resides.

Permanent **exile** and the constant changing of countries and cultures has marked many twentieth-century Latin American writers and **intellectuals**. Allende is one of these writers in exile. In her first two books, *La casa de los espíritus* (The House of the Spirits) (1982) and *De amor y sombras* (Of Love and Shadows) (1984), the context of the stories is Chile, although never mentioned in the former, but clearly suggested by historical figures. As her work brought her international acclaim and best-seller status (see **best-sellers**), her fictional settings became less anchored in a Latin American context, as is clear in her novel *Eva Luna* (1987). The collection of short stories entitled *Los cuentos de Eva Luna* (The Stories of Eva Luna) (1990), offer the fictional stories of the protagonist Eva Luna, alluded to but not included in the 1987 work. Allende uses repetition and allusion to former characters as well as the theme of writing about writing a story as recursive elements in her work. She has remarked that both Eva Luna books marked the emergence of a new woman that learned to appreciate womanhood as a force rather than a handicap in life. Since then, she has increasingly shaped her view of the world from a feminist (see **feminism**) viewpoint, a stance that she was hesitant to take at the beginning of her literary career. Her fifth novel, *El plan infinito* (The Infinite Plan) (1991), takes place in California. Her latest novel, *La hija de la fortuna* (Daughter of Fortune), appeared in 1999.

Another recent best-seller, *Paula* (1994) is named after her daughter Paula, who suffered a long illness and died at the age of twenty-eight. She wrote the book during the several months she spent in a hospital and in her hotel room in Madrid. Coincidentally, these are also the time markers that indicate the division of the book in two parts. Her vigil over her daughter's illness provided the context for reflecting on her own life trajectory, which she records in great detail. She harks back to her life in Chile, giving a colourful recollection of picturesque relatives with whom she grew up, her youth and romance with her first husband, the military *coup* against her uncle, President Salvador Allende, her difficulties under General Augusto **Pinochet**'s regime, her leaving Chile, settling in Caracas, Venezuela, and her immediate success as a world-acclaimed writer of stories whose romantic component has had an extraordinary appeal worldwide. Allende is the first Latin American woman of letters to succeed in the international literary scene on such a grand scale. She has acquired celebrity status, simultaneously providing new possibilities for other women in the literary field and bringing attention to women's literary production. Her novels have been translated into many languages.

Further reading

Guerra Cunningham, L. (ed) (1990) *Splintering Darkness: Latin American Women Writers in Search for themselves*, Pittsburgh, PA: Latin American Literary Review Press.

Hart, P. (1989) *Narrative Magic in the Fiction of Isabel Allende*, Cranbury, NJ: Associated University Presses.

MAGDALENA GARCÍA PINTO

Allende, Salvador

b. 1908, Valparaiso, Chile; d. 1973, Santiago, Chile

Politician

Elected President of Chile (1970–3), Allende was killed when the Presidential Palace (La Moneda) was bombed during the military *coup* that overthrew his government on 11 September 1973. A doctor, he supported Marmaduke **Grove**'s '100 Day Socialist Republic' in 1932, and was a founder of Chile's Socialist Party which claimed to combine **Marxism** and nationalism. Briefly Minister of

Health, he was his party's presidential candidate in 1952, 1958, 1964 and in 1970 as candidate of Unidad Popular (**Popular Unity**). He argued that the 'Chilean road to socialism' could be achieved by constitutional means. During his presidency, he faced an increasingly radicalized situation. He turned finally to the military to restore order, but instead, led by Augusto **Pinochet**, the armed forces organized a *coup* against him.

MIKE GONZALEZ

Allende Saron, Pedro Humberto

b. 1885, Santiago, Chile; d. 1959, Santiago

Composer and ethnomusicologist

Allende Saron is the most important representative of Chilean musical nationalism. Interested in Chile's indigenous music and folklore, he was the first to record Mapuche (see **Mapuches**) music. He was the first President of the Chilean National Association of Composers and the first composer to win Chile's National Arts Prize (in 1945). His style combines impressionist language with elements of traditional Chilean music. His principal works include the orchestral suite *Escenas campesinas chilenas* (Scenes from Chilean Peasant Life) (1913–14) and *Doce tonadas* (Twelve Tonadas) (1918–22) for piano.

ALFONSO PADILLA

Alleyne, Mervyn C.

b.1933, Trinidad

Sociolinguist, writer and scholar

Alleyne has defined the study of Caribbean sociolinguistics. Son of a builder and a schoolteacher, Alleyne as a child listened carefully to the cadences of his community. He has researched and written on the cultural matrix of a range of creoles and pidgins (see **creole languages**), spanning both Anglophone and Francophone Caribbean, in studies like *Comparative Afro-America* (1980). His *Roots of Jamaican Culture* (1988) focuses specifically on

Jamaica's African heritage, from traditional healing practices to the impact of the Rastafarian movement (see **Rastafarianism**). Presently, Alleyne teaches at the **University of the West Indies**, Mona, and is the president of the Society of Caribbean Linguistics.

GAY WILENTZ

Allfrey, Phyllis Shand

b. 1908, Dominica, West Indies; d. 1986, Dominica

Writer and politician

A poet and journalist as well as a leading political figure in Dominica, Allfrey settled in England in the 1930s, becoming an active member of the Labour Party. In 1953 she published *The Orchid House*, a multi-generational novel about a white creole family on a Caribbean island moving towards independence, after which she returned to Dominica. She was a founder member of the Dominica Labour Party in 1954, and later served as Minister of Labour for the Federation of the West Indies. She edited the Dominican *Star* (1965–82) and published several volumes of poetry.

LOUIS JAMES

Alliance for Progress

Every Latin American country except Cuba signed the Charter of Punta del Este on 17 August 1961 which formally established the Alliance, proposed by President Kennedy in response to the Cuban Revolution of 1959 (see **revolutions**). Its ten-year programme promised to satisfy the basic needs of the Latin American people for land, housing, employment, health and schools. The USA made long-term, low interest loans available to Latin American governments that submitted long-term development plans including tax **agrarian reform**. The radical proposals met conservative opposition north and south and very few were implemented. The Alliance did succeed, however, in isolating Cuba within Latin America.

PHILIP O'BRIEN

Allsopp, Richard

b. 1923, British Guiana

Lexicographer and writer

In 1996, Oxford University Press published Allsopp's *Dictionary of Caribbean English Usage*, a monumental work involving research in eighteen Caribbean territories from Guyana through the Bahamas and Belize. It was the culmination of a long and distinguished career in Caribbean lexicography. He earned his Ph.D. at the University of London in 1962, and lectured for many years at the **University of the West Indies**' Barbados campus. Allsopp's many awards and academic posts include the Crane Gold Medal for Education, British Guiana 1958 and a Visiting Lectureship at Howard University. He has contributed over sixty essays on **Caribbean English** usage and remains one of the most eminent scholars in his field.

KEITH JARDIM

Alma llanera

Jaropo from the *zarzuela* (comic opera) called *Alma llanera* (Soul of the Plains), composed by Pedro Elías Gutiérrez (1870–1954), with libretto by Rafael Bolívar Coronado, it was first performed on 19 September 1914. Over time this tune has become the musical emblem of Venezuelan nationhood, a kind of alternative national anthem that every inhabitant of the country knows by heart. Repeatedly performed in every medium, and learned and sung by schoolchildren, *Alma llanera* is one of those national symbols which enshrine a range of imagined collective representations composing what is more or less officially recognized as the 'Venezuelan character'.

RAFAEL CASTILLO ZAPATA

Almeida, Neville d'

b. 1941, Belo Horizonte, Brazil

Film-maker

After working as assistant to Nelson Pereira dos **Santos**, Almeida's first film as director was *O bem-aventurado* (The Fortunate Man) (1966). A member of the **Cinema Marginal** group until the mid-1970s, he broke with them to make highly commercial films like *Os sete gatinhos* (Seven Cats) (1977), set among the Rio de Janeiro middle class, and *Rio Babilónia* (1982), depicting the bourgeoisie. His *Música para sempre* (Music Forever) (1980) documented the First São Paulo **Jazz** Festival. *Matou a familia e foi o cinema* (He Killed the Family and Went to the cinema) (1990) was a remake of **Bressane**'s classic film about life on the margins.

ISMAIL XAVIER AND THE USP GROUP

Almendros, Néstor

b. 1930, Barcelona, Spain; d. 1992, New York, USA

Film-maker

One of Cuba's foremost contemporary cinematographers, Almendros emigrated to Cuba in 1948 where he wrote regular film reviews for small magazines while still a student. He was a founder member of the first Cuban cine club (later the Cinemateca de Cuba) in 1949, and contributed studies on the use of colour in film and the art documentary film in the journal, *Noticias de arte*. He made three experimental short films with Tomás **Gutiérrez Alea** between 1948 and 1950, and later studied at the Experimental Cinema Centre in Rome (1956–7). Returning to Cuba in 1959 he wrote film criticism for the magazine, ***Carteles***, and the weeklies, ***Lunes de Revolución*** and ***Bohemia***, where he made subtle criticisms of socialist film production and of the censorship that began to affect cinema production and distribution in Cuba. At the same time, he made some twenty films for **ICAIC**, the Cuban Film Institute, as lighting cameraman and as director, one of which, *Gente en la playa* (People on the Beach) (1960), was banned by ICAIC itself. That year, he resigned from ICAIC and shortly thereafter left Cuba for France, where he edited the film section of the journal, *Cuadernos* (1963–4), published in Paris. In the two decades that followed, he photographed more than fifty films, working with directors like François Truffaut, Eric Rohmer, Martin Scorsese and Alan Pakula. His work on films like *Kramer versus Kramer* (1979), *Blue Lagoon* (1980) and *Sophie's Choice* (1982) brought him international fame and confirmed his status as one of the most important innovators in the techniques and aesthetics of film lighting. In the 1980s he made advertisements for Giorgio Armani and Calvin Klein. His concerns about the situation of Cuba led him to make *Conducta impropia* (Improper Conduct) (1984) and *Nadie escuchaba* (Nobody Listened) (1987) about human rights and the lack of freedom in Cuba. For Martin Scorsese, Almendros was 'one of the great cameramen of our time, combining theoretical knowledge and artistic sensibility, political passion and great erudition'. In 1990, Almendros published *Días de una cámara* (Days of a Camera), memoirs of a professional career.

Further reading

Almendros, N. (1992) *Cinemanía: Ensayos sobre cine*, Barcelona: Seix Barral.
Chanan, M. (1985) *New Cuban Cinema*, London: BFI.

WILFREDO CANCIO ISLA

Alomia Robles, Daniel

b. 1871, Huánuco, Peru; d. 1942, Lima

Composer

One of Peru's most prolific and celebrated composers, his compositions include the now internationally recognized 'El condor pasa' (The Condor Passes), recorded by Simon and Garfunkel in 1973. Fundamentally a collector of indigenous music, Robles's collection of some 650 pieces includes a 'Himno al sol' (Hymn to the Sun) that Robles claimed to have heard sung by a 117-year-old Peruvian Indian. Of indigenous origin himself,

his work was heavily influenced by the music of the Andes and included the symphonic poem, *Resurgimiento de los Andes* (Resurgence of the Andes), first performed in 1940, and the opera, *Illa cori* (La Conquista de Quito par Huayana Capac/The Conquest of Quito by Huayana Capac), the first act of which was played at the opening ceremony of the Panama Canal in 1914.

PETER WATT

Alone

b. 1891, Santiago, Chile; d. 1979, Santiago

Writer

For half a century, Alone (Hernán Díaz Arrieta) was a polemical figure in Chilean letters. His book reviews in *El Diario Ilustrado* and **El mercurio** could determine the commercial success of a book. Although he advocated subjectivity and impressionism in literary criticism, his books offer a well-organized overview of the Chilean literary canon. *Memorialistas chilenos* (Chilean Memoir Writers) (1960) is a comprehensive study of autobiographical texts; Alone's own memoirs, entitled *Pretérito Imperfecto* (Past Imperfect) (1976), and his *Historia personal de la literatura chilena* (Personal History of Chilean Culture) (1954) offer important insights into Chilean history and culture. His film criticism has been collected as *Alone y la crítica de cine* (Alone and Cinema Criticism) (1993).

LUCÍA GUERRA

Alonso, Alicia

b. 1921, Havana, Cuba

Ballerina, choreographer and teacher

Prima Ballerina Assoluta and director of the **Ballet Nacional de Cuba**, Alonso is the top figure in classical dance in Latin America and a key figure in the history of dance.

Born Alicia Martínez, she began her dance studies in Havana's Musical Pro-Arte Society Ballet School in 1931, where she met her future husband,

Fernando **Alonso**. Later, she moved to the USA and studied with Enrico Zanfretta, Alexandra Fedórova and several eminent professors of the School of American Ballet. She made her professional début in 1938 in Broadway musical comedies, but a year later became a member of the American Ballet Caravan (now the New York City Ballet). She joined the Ballet Theater of New York upon its foundation in 1940 and, after replacing the prima ballerina of *Giselle* in a 1943 performance, became known as a supreme performer of the romantic and classic ballet repertoire. Although her eyesight was rapidly deteriorating (after surgery in 1941 she was told by experts that her dance career was over), Alonso persevered with incredible courage and ambition. Through the 1940s, she worked with outstanding choreographers like George Balanchine, Bronislava Nijinska, Jerome Robbins and Agnes de Mille, and was the prima ballerina in the début of important choreographies like de Mille's *Fall River Legend* (1948).

In 1948, her concern for developing ballet in Cuba led her to found the Alicia Alonso Ballet Company in Havana (today known as the **Ballet Nacional de Cuba**) with husband Fernando Alonso and his brother, Alberto. Through the 1950s, she divided her activities between the American Ballet Theater and her own company, which she maintained with little or no official support until 1959, when the new Cuban Revolutionary Government offered her the necessary assistance and recognized her achievements. Throughout her career Alonso has received innumerable accolades and awards. She was the first dancer from the Western hemisphere to be invited to perform in the Soviet Union and the first figure from the Americas to perform in Moscow's Bolshoi and Leningrad's Kirov theatres. For several decades, Alonso toured the world, most often with her company, but also as a solo artist.

Her work as a choreographer, especially her versions of classic ballets, are internationally famous and have been performed by important companies like the ballet companies of the Paris Opera (*Giselle, Grand pas de quatre, Sleeping Beauty*); the San Carlo in Naples (*Giselle*), the Prague Opera (*La fille mal gardée*) and the Scala in Milan (*Sleeping Beauty*). Although she has been almost totally blind since the 1970s and could only perform following

lights hidden onstage, she continued performing well into the 1980s, including a triumphant tour with her company in the USA.

Further reading

Baquero, J. (1984) *Alicia Alonso*, Havana: Editorial Letras Cubanas.

Simón, P. (1996) *Alicia Alonso, órbita de una leyenda*, Madrid: Sociedad General de Autores y Editores.

Terry, W. (1981) *Alicia and her Ballet Nacional de Cuba*, Garden City, NY: Anchor Books.

ANA M. LÓPEZ

Alonso, Carlos

b. 1929, Tunuyán, Mendoza, Argentina

Artist, illustrator and engraver

Alonso's artistic and political concerns focus on man in his historical reality from a critical realist framework. He studied with **Spilimbergo** in Tucumán, and in 1957 won an award to illustrate the second part of *Don Quixote* (the first had been illustrated by Salvador Dalí). In 1968 he illustrated Dante's *Divine Comedy*, introducing contemporary events into Dante's Inferno. In 1969 he produced the series 'The Anatomy Lesson' on the death of Che **Guevara**, based on Rembrandt's work of the same name and the photographs that appeared in the mass media. In the 1970s his work mounted a crude challenge to the structures of power.

CECILIA RABOSSI

Alonso, Fernando

b. 1919, Havana, Cuba

Ballet dancer and teacher

Despite the fact that ballet dancing for men was frowned upon in Cuba's extraordinarily *machista* culture, Fernando and his brother, Alberto Alonso, broke with the prejudices of the era and began studying ballet in Havana's Musical Pro-Arte Society Ballet School. After his marriage to the rising ballerina, Alicia **Alonso**, the trio formed a formidable union, collaborating and complementing each other's talents: Alicia took centre stage as prima ballerina, but Fernando, abandoning dance to concentrate on teaching, and Alberto, as a brilliant choreographer, did more than their share to bring the **Ballet Nacional de Cuba**, the company they founded in 1948, to international prominence. In 1967, amidst rumours of discord with Alicia, Fernando departed for the province of Camaguey, where he founded the Ballet Nacional de Camaguey, yet another brilliant company with a broad repertoire of classic and contemporary ballets, which has become an important 'feeder' of talent for the Ballet Nacional in Havana.

ANA M. LÓPEZ

Alou, Felipe

b. 1935, Haini, Dominican Republic

Baseball player

Born Felipe Rojas y Alou, he had a distinguished seventeen-year career in the US professional **baseball** leagues. A dark-skinned man, he arrived in the US in the late 1950s speaking little English, and he was at first a target of abuse for many baseball spectators. He became an outspoken defender of Latin American players, who were underpaid and stereotyped. In the 1990s Alou was one of the three best baseball field managers. His brothers Mateo and Jesús (with whom he played in 1963) and son Moisés are also major league players.

DOUGLAS W. VICK

Alsogaray, María Julia

b. 1942, Buenos Aires, Argentina

Politician

A graduate in industrial engineering, Alsogaray's political career began in the Nueva Fuerza movement founded by her father. In 1983 she returned to Buenos Aires from Uruguay to enter politics with the rightist Unión de Centro Democrático

Party, which fiercely opposed the Alfonsín government. A controversial figure, in 1989 she was asked by the **Menem** administration to oversee the privatization of several state-owned corporations. Since then, serving in various capacities, she has remained in the public eye, both admired and feared.

MAGDALENA GARCÍA PINTO

Altazor

Vicente **Huidobro**'s *Altazor* (1919–31), a meditation upon language and the subject, is one of the most radical experiments in Latin American poetry. In the preface, the poet's doppelgänger – Altazor – nostalgically recreates a fable of his own beginnings, plunging the reader into seven cantos enacting the character's supposed fall from grace. After the third canto, the hero disappears in a sea of words that perversely try to create a linguistic universe without a subject. In *Altazor*, words are troped upon themselves by means of visual games. The last canto is a random collection of vowels hurling through space, opaque remnants from the debris of words: sounds crystallized, the skin and the cloth of Altazor's broken parachute.

JOSÉ QUIROGA

Alterio, Héctor

b. 1929, Buenos Aires

Actor

A great dramatic actor who began with Teatro Nuevo (1950–68), Alterio has had a successful career in television and theatre. In 1974, while presenting Sergio **Renan**'s *La tregua* (The Truce) at the San Sebastián Film Festival, he was threatened by the right-wing terrorist organization AAA. He remained in exile in Spain, where he appeared in films such as Carlos Saura's *Criacuervos* (1975), and Jaime Chávarri's *A un dios desconocido* (To an Unknown God) (1977), which earned him the prize for Best Actor at San Sebastián. Since 1980, he has divided his time between Argentina and Spain.

DIANA PALADINO

altiplano

Altiplano (high plateau) is a term used for the inhabited areas of the high Andes, although not all of the area that is referred to in this way is actually plateau. In Bolivia and southern Peru, the Andes splits into two ranges, with the area between being plateau, lakes (the largest is Lake Titicaca) and river valleys; farther north (and south), the term is sometimes used for intermontane valleys. Highland agriculture is centred on the **potato**, while domestic animals include the llama, alpaca and cuy (guinea pig). Much of the inhabited altiplano is at an altitude (see **altitude sickness**) of about four thousand metres.

DANIEL BALDERSTON

altitude sickness

Altitude sickness is caused by lack of oxygen in the thin mountain air of areas over 3,000 metres above sea level – like the Bolivian **altiplano**, where the average altitude is around 4,000 metres. It can affect anyone, regardless of physical condition. The common symptoms are headaches, nausea and problems with sleep; its incidence and its severity have to do with altitude, physical exertion and prior acclimatization – it is wise to stage the ascent to these heights. In rare cases it can be serious and pulmonary oedema can occur, in which case medical treatment should be sought urgently. Normally, however, it passes without treatment after a few days. Precautions may be taken before travel, such as avoiding excessive exertion and overuse of alcohol or narcotics, and raising fluid intake. Diamox, a diuretic, may help symptoms but if they persist it is best to move back to a lower altitude.

MIKE GONZALEZ

Alturas de Macchu Picchu

Written after a visit to the abandoned city of Machu Picchu in 1945, the poem 'Alturas de Macchu Picchu' (Heights of Machu Picchu) is included in Pablo **Neruda**'s *Canto general* (1950). Its twelve metaphorically charged sections stage a mystical encounter between the poetic subject and the monumental Inca city of Machu Picchu. The first five parts describe a cosmological quest for truth; the fifth signals the ascent of the poet to a city which resonates with ancestral history. The final sections delve into the human and American past concealed beneath the ruins. Neruda's text appeals to a dead 'brother' who embodies the ancestors of the indigenous South America as well as the oppressed people of the present and future.

LUIS E. CÁRCAMO-HUECHANTE

Alvarez, Adalberto

b. 1948, Havana, Cuba

Musician

Alvarez is one of Cuba's most popular composers, arrangers and instrumentalists. His family was from Camagüey, but he was born in Havana where his father's group Avance Juvenil was playing. From 1966 he studied woodwind at the National School of Art, later teaching at Camagüey's Provincial School of Music. From 1978 to 1984 he led the group Son 14 in Santiago, before moving to Havana to set up Adalberto Alvarez y Su Son, one of Cuba's most popular orchestras. His many successful compositions include 'Y qué tu quieres que te den, mamí' (What do You Expect Girl?) and 'Agua que cae del cielo' (Water that Falls From the Sky).

JOSÉ ANTONIO EVORA

Alvarez Benítez, Mario Rubén

b. 1954, Potrero Yvaté, Paraguay

Writer

A poet and professor of **Guarani**, Alvarez Benítez

was twice awarded first prize by the Instituto de Cultura Hispánica del Paraguay (1977, 1979). His poems have appeared in collective volumes: ...*Y ahora la palabra* (...And Now the Word) (1979), *Poesía-Taller* (Poetry Workshop) (1982), and *Poesía Itinerante* (Itinerant Poetry) (1984). In 1992 he published *La sangre insurrecta* (The Insurgent Blood), and later translated into Guarani *Ecos de monte y de arena* (Echoes of Woodland and Sand) (1994), a book of ecological short stories by Luisa Moreno de Gabaglio, under the title *Kapi'yva*. He has worked as a radio journalist.

TERESA MÉNDEZ-FAITH

Alvarez Bravo, Lola

b. 1907, Lagos de Moreno, Jalisco, Mexico; d. 1993, Mexico City

Photographer

Born Dolores Martínez de Anda, Lola Alvarez Bravo was a pioneer of modernist photography in Mexico and a mentor to numerous younger photographers in the course of her long artistic life. Although initially overshadowed by her own teacher and husband, Manuel **Alvarez Bravo**, by the 1930s Lola had established her own photographic style and thematic repertoire, combining empathy for the working class and poor with criticism of social disparities. Paradigmatic of this theme is *El sueño de los pobres* (The Dream/Sleep of the Poor), in which a poor child sleeps soundly, ensconced in piles of *huaraches* (rope sandals). Later Alvarez Bravo recreated this shot as a photo montage, replacing the sandals with obscene mountains of gold coins. She was also one of the first modern Mexican photographers to document popular celebrations, and among the first to explore the rich spiritual life of women. For instance, in *El rapto* (The Rapture) a girl daydreams on a carousel; in *En su propia cárcel* (In Her Own Prison) a young housewife seems trapped inside her apartment by bars of afternoon shadow; and in *Visitación* (Visitation) two women from Juchitán, Oaxaca pose in a doorway in fond embrace.

CYNTHIA STEELE

Alvarez Bravo, Manuel

b. 1902, Mexico City

Photographer

As part of the avant-garde left in Mexico City during the 1920s, Alvarez Bravo replaced Tina Modotti as photographer of the murals of Diego **Rivera**, José Clemente **Orozco**, and David Alfaro **Siqueiros**, for the journal *Mexican Folkways*. He was influenced by the modernist school of photography of Modotti and Edward Weston, as well as by André Breton and the surrealist movement.

In 1932 Alvarez Bravo had his first individual shows in Mexico City and Paris, and in 1935 he exhibited in New York and Mexico City, alongside Walker Evans and Henri Cartier-Bresson. It was during this decade that he first achieved recognition as the leading photographer of Latin America and one of the world's major photographers.

During the 1950s Alvarez Bravo taught at the Academia San Carlos (fine arts academy) and in the Mexican Institute of Cinematography. He was among the founders of the Fondo Editorial de la Plástica Mexicana (Publishing Fund for the Mexican Visual Arts), and he participated in the cinematography and still photography for several films, including Luis **Buñuel**'s *Nazarín*.

Alvarez Bravo was active in the anti-fascist movement, and some of his photographs include social commentary (for instance, *Los agachados* (The Underdogs) and *Obrero en huelga asesinado* (Worker on Strike, Murdered)). The latter sparked controversy, when it was discovered recently that the slain worker in the photograph was actually killed in a brawl, rather than in response to his political activism. This has raised questions about the staging or posing of photographs, and the implications for their authenticity and reliability. These truths and fictions are the subject of a recent book of digital photographs by the leading Mexican photographer of the generation following Alvarez Bravo, Pedro **Meyer**.

Above all Alvarez Bravo's work is characterized by its lyricism, masterful composition, and communication of the intense inner life of the subjects. While his photographs often portray scenes from modern urban Mexico, their effect is not journalistic or ethnographic. Rather, they use everyday objects or scenes (a rocking horse, a lunchroom, a girl leaning on a balcony railing) as springboards for transporting both subject and viewer onto a plane of shared human transcendence.

The first complete retrospective of Alvarez Bravo's work was in 1997 at the Museum of Modern Art in New York and the Centre for Contemporary Art in Mexico City.

Further reading

Alvarez Bravo, M. (1990) *Revelaciones: The Art of Manuel Alvarez Bravo*, San Diego: Museum of Photographic Arts.

Debroise, O. (1994) *Fuga mexicana: Un recorrido por la fotografía en Mexico*, Mexico City: Consejo Nacional para la Cultura y las Artes.

Livingston, J. (1978) *Manuel Alvarez Bravo*, Boston: D.R. Godine.

Pacheco, C. (1988) *La luz de Mexico*, Guanajuato: Gobierno del Estado de Guanajuato; and Mexico City: Fondo de Cultura Económica.

CYNTHIA STEELE

Alvarez del Toro, Federico

b. 1953, Mexico City

Composer

Although born in Mexico City, Alvarez del Toro was raised in Tuxtla Gutiérrez, the capital of Chiapas, in a family of zoologists and conservationists. The musician's concern with ecology is highlighted in his chamber music piece 'Desolación – drama en un bosque' (Desolation – Drama in a Forest) (1976); 'Sinfonía de las plantas' (Symphony of the Plants) (1977); and *Gneiss*, a work for string quartet, voice, percussion instruments and tape recorder, recorded in 1982 with Ozomatli, which incorporates a natural stone **marimba** found in the caves of Chiapas.

CYNTHIA STEELE

Alvarez Gardeazábal, Gustavo

b. 1945, Tuluá, Colombia

Writer and polititian

Alvarez Gardeazábal has been one of Colombia's most productive and irreverent novelists. His early works, *La tara del papa* (The Pope's Idiocy) (1971), ***Cóndores no entierran todos los dias*** (They Don't Bury Condors Every Day) (1972), about La **Violencia**, *Dabeiba* (1973) and *El bazar de los idiotas* (The Idiots's Bazaar) (1974), were strong social critiques set in Tuluá, a small town in Western Colombia near Cali. His most virulent satire of the local oligarchy was *Los mios* (My People) (1981). He is also a journalist, and in the 1990s was actively involved in politics, serving two terms as mayor of Tuluá and as governor of Cauca department, as well as several years in prison.

RAYMOND L. WILLIAMS

Alvarez Guedes, Guillermo

b. 1927, Unión de Reyes, Cuba

Comedian

As Cuba's most famous humorist, his stage performances, in which he tells jokes and satirizes everyday life, are a solo variant of the Cuban vernacular, *costumbrista* tradition. Sixth of seven children, his older sister Eloísa was a famous actress in Cuba. Arriving as a young man in Havana, he began singing with various groups and in 1949 joined the cast of a famous series of dramatic reconstructions of famous crimes. In 1950 he took part in the first sketch broadcast by the new Cuban television service. In 1952 he joined what was to become the famous 'Casino de la alegría', though he was probably more familiar as half of the *Rita and Willy* TV series that he shared with Rita **Montaner**. He began to present his one-man shows after establishing residence in the USA and touring in Spain and Puerto Rico. It was in 1973, in Spain, that he first included 'swear words' in his show – his uninhibited performances brought success and an album, originally recorded for Cuban audiences, which became a hit across Latin

America. Since then Alvarez Guedes has recorded twenty-nine albums, CDs and cassettes under the appropriate acronym of GAG Enterprises. Although they are banned in Cuba, they circulate widely – there can be no Cuban household where Alvarez Guedes's stories are not favourite listening.

JOSÉ ANTONIO EVORA

Alvarez, Augusto H.

b. 1914, Mérida, Mexico; d. 1995,
Mexico City

Architect

The main exponent of the **International Style** in Mexico, Alvarez's rationalist approach was influenced by Le Corbusier and Mies van der Rohe. Graduating from Mexico's National University (**UNAM**) in 1939, his earliest functionalist designs were distinguished by the absence of ornamentation and high quality finishes, and his skill in working with a variety of materials including concrete, steel, prefabricated units and glass. His office buildings are outstanding, including Mexico City's **Torre Latinoamericana** (Latin American Tower) (1950–2), IBM Offices (1971–2), the Bancomer operational centre (1974–5) and the Transportación Marítima Mexicana (Mexican Maritime Transport) building (1983–4).

LOURDES CRUZ GONZÁLEZ FRANCO

Alvarez, Carlos

b. 1943, Bucaramanga, Colombia

Critic and film-maker

Alvarez was actively involved in critical film culture and, with his wife Julia Alvarez, participated in the **New Latin American Cinema**. His documentaries of the late 1960s and early 1970s were militant, urgent films of social analysis. *¿Qué es la democracia?* (What is Democracy?) (1971), a dialectical critique of the shortcomings of Colombian democracy, landed Alvarez in jail for eighteen months. Since returning to

Colombia from voluntary exile in the mid-1980s, Alvarez has concentrated on writing film history and criticism.

ILENE S. GOLDMAN

Alvarez, Jorge

b. *c.* 1930, Buenos Aires, Argentina

Publisher and editor

An active participant in the cultural modernization of the sixties, Alvarez produced the early concerts by Argentine rock artists like Manal and **Sui Géneris**, but his major contribution was the establishment of the Editorial **Jorge Alvarez**, which published the new novelists like Rodolfo **Walsh** and Manuel **Puig** whose work had been rejected by the bigger publishers for commercial reasons or because of censorship. Key **intellectuals** of the 1970s, like Josefina **Ludmer** and Ricardo **Piglia** were also associated with him. He was forced into exile by the military *coup* of 1976.

DANIEL LINK

Alvarez, Mario Roberto

b. 1913, Buenos Aires, Argentina

Architect

Alvarez's prolific work, mainly in Buenos Aires, includes the Panedile building (1969), the **Teatro San Martín** (1960), the IBM and Banco Río de la Plata buildings (both 1983), shopping centres like the Galería Jardín and the ambitious office building for Somisa Steel (1966–77), built in steel and the first in the world to be soldered entirely with that metal. His style is rationalist, rejects architectural revivals (as his remodelling of the Teatro Cervantes testified) and is influenced by Mies van der Rohe's treatment of space.

GONZALO AGUILAR

Alvarez, Santiago

b. 1919, Havana, Cuba; d. 1998, Havana

Film-maker

The most celebrated documentary maker in Cuba, almost all of his films are political propaganda, as he himself recognized. He was considered the 'official film-maker' for the Cuban government, and there is no event including Fidel **Castro** that was not recorded by Alvarez. His international reputation rests on the popularity of Cuba and Castro in the 1960s and 1970s. His films were also formal and technical achievements. *Now* (1965), a film that protests against racism in the USA, is considered to be the precursor of the music video; in *Hanoi Martes 13* (Hanoi Tuesday the 13th) and *LBJ* (1968), Alvarez showed his intense, eloquent use of photo-animation synchronized with a soundtrack that used Lena Horne's version of *Hava nagila* alongside extracts of Orff's *Catuli Carmina*, to great effect. The original director of the *Noticiero ICAIC Latinoamericano*, Alvarez said in 1989 that 'As soon as I see a photo I transform it in my imagination, because even static images have an internal movement just waiting to be discovered.'

JOSÉ ANTONIO EVORA

Alves, Carmelo Heriberto   *see*   Arden Quin, Carmelo

Alves, Francisco

b. 1898, Rio de Janeiro, Brazil; d. 1952, São Paulo, Brazil

Musician

Alves's career began in the early 1920s, with recordings of carnival hits by Sinhô and singing in popular theatre alongside established stars such as Vicente Celestino. In 1927 Alves made the first electronically produced recording in Brazil for the Odeon label, and went on to form one of Brazil's most famous singing duos, with Mário Reis, as well as a triple songwriting partnership with Ismael Silva and Noel **Rosa**. He was responsible for

launching the nationalistic variety of **samba** known as *samba-exaltação*, recording Ary **Barroso**'s 'Aquarela do Brasil' (Brazilian Watercolour) and appearing in the musical *Alô, Alô, Brasil* (1935).

DAVID TREECE

Alves, Rubem

b. 1933, Boa Esperança, Minas Gerais, Brazil

Theologian

Alves is one of the most important Protestant exponents of **liberation theology**, whose doctoral dissertation from the Princeton Theological Seminary, *A Theology of Human Hope*, was published in 1969. He is professor of philosophy at the State University of Campinas, a poet and a psychoanalyst. Within liberation theology, he has been interested in issues of language and body. He insists on a more poetic and immanent theological language as well as on a more inclusive image of human beings, having thus become one of the representatives of *teologia do corpo* (theology of the body).

ELINA VUOLA

Amado, Jorge

b. 1912, Itabuna, Bahia, Brazil

Novelist

The social conflicts, customs and rich popular culture of Amado's native Bahia have provided most of the raw material for his writing which, during a literary career of over sixty years, has passed through several distinct phases. He established himself as one of Brazil's major social realist novelists in the 1930s with works such as *Suor* (Sweat) (1934), *Mar morto* (Sea of Death) (1936) and *Capitães de areia* (Captains of the Sands) (1937). These focus on the struggle of the Bahian working classes, attempting to show how their acquisition of political consciousness and development of solidarity open the way for social change.

The communist sympathies underlying his

works resulted in Amado's arrest on several occasions during the **Estado Novo** dictatorship, and in the public burning of copies of his novels in 1937. For many critics, the high point of his documentary realism was reached with the publication in 1943 of *Terras do sem fim* (translated as The Violent Land). Amado's parents had been involved in *cacao* planting, and the violence of the land disputes that accompanied the expansion of *cacao* production in Southern Bahia provided the theme for that highly acclaimed work. By the mid-1940s Amado was fully active in the Brazilian Communist Party, which was legalised again following the collapse of the Estado Novo in 1945. That same year he was elected Federal Deputy for the Party, representing the state of São Paulo. He served until 1947 when the party was outlawed once more, and Amado went into exile.

Amado's writing during this period was shaped by the dictates of socialist realism, as proposed by the Communist Party, and culminated with the publication in 1954 of *Os subterraneos da liberdade* (The Freedom Underground), a trilogy which focused on the struggle of the Brazilian Communist Party during the dictatorship. The anti-Stalin revelations of the mid-1950s and the Soviet invasion of Hungary finally led him to leave the Communist Party in 1956 and to reject socialist realism. A new phase of his writing career was launched in 1958 with the publication of *Gabriela, cravo e canela* (Gabriela, Clove and Cinnamon), a highly popular novel of comedy and social satire, far removed from the overtly political works of previous years. This set the pattern for the narratives that followed, such as *Os pastores da noite* (Shepherds of the Night) (1964) and, in 1966, ***Dona Flor e seus dois maridos*** (Dona Flor and her Two Husbands). These works, relying considerably on humour, irony and regional colour, confirmed Amado as Brazil's best-selling novelist.

Always keenly interested in Bahian popular culture, Amado gave **Candomblé** and *literatura de cordel* a central role in his novels. The Afro-Brazilian deities central to Candomblé ritual intervene directly in the plot of his novel *A tenda dos milagres* (Tent of Miracles) (1969), which Amado has declared to be his most important work, since it

focuses on what he believes to be one of the most vital and yet frequently neglected issues in Brazilian society: that of racial prejudice and the role of black culture (see **black cultures**). *Tereza Batista cansada de guerra* (Tereza Batista, Home from the Wars) (1972) not only includes popular religion but also draws on the traditions of *literatura de cordel* as the basis for its themes, tone and structure. For Amado, popular culture provides the means for examining the continual resistance of the poor, though what results at times is exoticism.

Amado is a prolific writer who has also produced biographies, short stories, children's books and, to mark his eightieth birthday in 1992, a book of memoirs, but it is his novels, now translated into nearly forty languages, that have made him Brazil's best-known twentieth-century writer. The popularity of his work has undoubtedly been increased through the many adaptations that have been made of his novels for television soap operas and for the cinema, with wide acclaim given to such films as *Dona Flor e seus dois maridos* by Bruno **Barreto**, *A tenda dos milagres* by Nelson Pereira dos **Santos** and *Gabriela, cravo e canela* by Luiz Carlos **Barreto** and Bruno Barreto. Amado's work has thus reached new audiences in Brazil and abroad, well beyond the novel-reading public. He has become a national celebrity, and in 1986 a government decree founded the Casa de Jorge Amado Foundation in Salvador to further promote his work. However, he has also generated more controversy than any other contemporary Brazilian writer. Some argue that his writing has become increasingly dependent on the market, which has compromised both its political commitment and its quality. In his defence, others claim that his long lasting popularity testifies to his considerable skills as a narrator, and that he has never abandoned social protest but simply found more sophisticated techniques through which to express it.

Further reading:

Chamberlain, B. (1990) *Jorge Amado*, New York: Twayne.

MARK DINNEEN

Amadori, Luis César

b. 1902, Pescana, Italy; d. 1977, Buenos
Aires, Argentina

Film-maker

Known as 'the director of great hits', Amadori was
first a journalist and songwriter. After his directorial debut with Mario **Soffici** – *Puerto Nuevo*
(Another Port) (1934) – he directed forty-three
films in Argentina, four in Mexico, and fifteen in
Spain, where he lived from 1956 onwards due to
political problems after the fall of **Perón**. Influenced by Hollywood, he worked in all genres and
with the best-known actors, including Niní **Marshall**, Zully **Moreno**, and Luis **Sandrini**.
Perhaps his best-known film is ***Dios se lo pague***
(May God Reward You) (1946), the Oscar-
nominated melodrama that made Arturo de
Córdova a star.

RODRIGO PEIRETTI

Amaral, Suzana

b. 1932, São Paulo, Brazil

Film-maker

Since 1974, Amaral has been associated with
television production, as producer and director of
São Paulo's educational television channel TV
Cultura. In the early 1970s she made two shorts:
Sua Majestade Piolim (His Highness Piolim) about a
legendary popular clown, and *Semana de 22*,
concerning the considerable impact of the **Modern Art Week** events of 1922. She became famous
for her *Minha vida, nossa luta* (My Life, Our Struggle)
(1979) on the women's organization in the São
Paulo slums and for her adaptation of Clarice
Lispector's *A **hora da estrela*** (Hour of the Star)
(1985), a powerful socio-psychological study of an
immigrant from the northeast.

ISMAIL XAVIER AND THE USP GROUP

Amaral, Tarsila do

b. 1886, Capivari, Brazil; d. 1973, São
Paulo, Brazil

Painter

Tarsila do Amaral (often referred to simply as
Tarsila) is the most significant painter of the 1920s
generation of Brazilian modernists (see **Brazilian
modernism**). Like many Latin American artists
of her generation, Tarsila studied in Europe. In
Paris from 1920 to 1922, she was influenced by the
cylindrical forms and bright abstractions of Fernand Léger. In June 1922 she returned to São
Paulo, several months too late to visit the important
Semana de Arte Moderna (**Modern Art Week**)
which was the first attempt to introduce modernist
art into Brazil. Nonetheless she was to be closely
associated with the São Paulo **intellectuals** who
organized the event, and married Oswald de
Andrade, the leading theorist of the group
together with Mário de **Andrade**, an influential
poet and novelist. In 1922 she formed the 'Grupo
dos Cinco' (Group of Five) with Oswald and Mário
de Andrade, Anita **Malfatti** and Paulo Menotti
del Picchia. In late 1922 she left São Paulo for Paris
with her husband. During this stay she became
interested in industrial forms and in primitive art,
both central concerns of the Parisian avant-garde.
In 1923 she painted the important canvas *A negra*
(The Negress), which is prophetic of her interest in
using the formal language of European art to
express a distinctly Brazilian reality. In late 1923
she returned to São Paulo and in 1924 painted
EFCB (Brazilian Central Railway) in which a bright
industrial landscape is created, devoid of people yet
with a peculiar sense of animation and presence in
inanimate objects. In March 1924, Oswald de
Andrade published the important *Manifesto Pau-
Brasil* (Brazil-Wood Manifesto) which postulated a
reversal of Brazil's tradition of cultural dependency
on Europe (see **dependency theory**).

By the late 1920s Tarsila's style had become
more fantastic, showing some influence of surrealism. Her painting *Antropofagia* (Cannibalism) of
1929 is related to Oswald de Andrade's contem-

porary *Manifesto Antropófago* in which the image of the cannibal provides a metaphor for Europe's fantasized image of Latin America and also for the way in which this group of intellectuals claimed to devour European culture as the cannibals devoured Europeans. In 1931, now separated from Andrade, she travelled to the Soviet Union and was impressed by **socialist realism**. Upon her return she incorporated some of this social interest into her work, but her most significant period remains that of the 1920s and early 1930s.

Further reading

Amaral, A. (1975) *Tarsila: sua obra e seu tempo*, São Paulo: Perspectiva/USP.

Day, H. and Sturges, H. (1987) *Art of the Fantastic*, Indianapolis, IN: Indianapolis Museum of Art.

Tarsila (1969) Rio de Janeiro: Museu de Arte Moderna.

GABRIEL PEREZ-BARREIRO

Amauta

A cultural magazine edited monthly by José Carlos **Mariátegui** in Lima between 1926–30, *Amauta* (the title comes from the Quechua name given to the philosophers of the Inca State), was the leading channel of Mariátegui's socialist, anti-imperialist and indigenous ideas as well as a continentally distributed cultural magazine. In his first editorials, Mariátegui described the magazine as the starting point of a new era, during which Peruvian problems would be studied scientifically and from a socialist perspective.

Mariátegui started to publish *Amauta* during Augusto B. Leguía's dictatorship, and the magazine was repeatedly closed down for political reasons. Contributions to the magazine came from all over Latin America as well as from leading European left-wing intellectuals. *Amauta* also reproduced and translated articles, for example Leon Trotsky's article on Lenin and Sigmund Freud's introduction to psychoanalysis.

Amauta's most distinctive aspect, however, was Mariátegui's new interpretation of the role of indigenous people, which rejected the previous

idealized or paternalistic attitudes of Latin American intellectuals. That is why *Amauta* included many articles on the indigenous cultures. The magazine was striking, illustrated with *indigenista* graphics inspired by pre-Columbian art.

Amauta ceased to appear shortly after Mariátegui died in 1930. However, the magazine still maintains its symbolic continental importance, not least because its role was later glorified as a crucial part of Mariátegui's lifework by the Peruvian Editorial Amauta and by Latin American leftist **intellectuals**.

See also: indigenismo

Further reading

Amauta (1982) *Edición facsímil*, Lima: Empresa Editora Amauta S.A.

Tauro, A. (1974) *Amauta y su influencia*, Lima: Empresa Editora Amauta.

JUSSI PAKKASVIRTA

Amazonia

Amazonia embraces almost the whole of the northern half of South America: the states of Acre, Amapá, Amazonas, Pará, Rondonia, Roraima and Tocantins in Brazil; the three Guyanas (Guyana, Surinam and French Guiana); eastern and southern Venezuela (Delta Amacuro and Amazonas); south and south eastern Colombia (Caquetá and the territories of Amazonas, Guaiania, Putumayo, Uaupés and Vichada); eastern Ecuador (Napo and Pastaza), and Peru (Loreto and Madre de Dios) and the departments of La Paz and Beni in northern Bolivia.

In Brazil Amazonia refers to the river basin of the Amazon and its tributaries, the Negro, Madeira, Purus, Xingu, Tapajós and Tocantins. Geopolitical motives led the 1964 military government to define an 'Amazonia legal' (official Amazon) which could be integrated into the developmentalist economic model linked to a national security concept of the state. Its 500,631,680 hectares include the states mentioned above as well as parts of Mato Grosso, Goiás and Maranhao – 57 per cent of Brazil's territory and 65 per cent of continental Amazonia. Sparsely populated, and covered almost entirely by rainforests (see **rainforest**) comprising 31 per cent of the world's total forests, the region embraces ten different types of vegetation harbouring an estimated 80,000 plant species and some 30 million documented animal species in distinct environments – flatlands, fields and savannahs irrigated by a river system responsible for 20 per cent of the fresh water that flows into the Atlantic and providing 50 per cent of Brazil's hydroelectric potential.

Amazonia includes the majority of Indian lands recognized or in process of recognition by the Brazilian state; 160 nations have been contacted there (of 206 in the whole country), comprising 170,000 indigenous people (1 per cent of the population of the Amazon and 0.02 per cent of the Brazilian population) belonging to the Arawak, Carib, Tupi, Pano and Je linguistic families. A possible further 53 indigenous groups within Amazonia have so far avoided contact with the national state, though **FUNAI**, the government indigenous agency, has confirmed the existence of twelve such groups. At the end of 1997 there were 372 legally recognized Indian areas, covering 98,825,190 hectares of territory; thus the right of occupation of 19.74 per cent of the land in the Official Amazon belongs to the indigenous communities. Only 45,219,040 hectares, or 9.3 per cent of the territory, are included in Conservation Areas, **national parks**, Nature Conservancy Areas, Biological Reserves, Environmental Protection Zones, etc.

Although still practically intact as the twentieth century ends, Amazonia has become the object of intense interest from those seeking to exploit its natural resources as well as those who warn of its far-reaching ecological and climatic consequences for the whole planet. The notion of Amazonia as the lungs of the earth is the latest in the history of myths about the region. It has been seen as a lost world, as a green hell, as the cellar of the world, home to wild beasts and breeding ground for uncontrollable plagues. There is agreement that the Amazon forest is essential for maintaining the earth's temperature, and that its still uncharted biological diversity has a crucial role in countering the progressive deterioration of of the environment produced by demographic explosion, gas and dust emissions and the discarding of domestic and industrial waste into the air, the soil and waters of the planet. While apocalyptic visions vie with the prevailing economic pragmatism, future development projects are based on the exploitation of the region's generous natural resources. Its wood offers an alternative source to the nearly exhausted Malaysian supplies; it has iron, gold, aluminium (bauxite) and copper as well as other minerals of strategic importance for the military and aviation industries.

The second poorest region in Brazil, Amazonia's natural resources provide a variety of protein-rich food like fish, condiments (pepper) and tubers (dozens of varieties of **manioc**). The larger cities of the region – Manaus and Belén – have tried to adopt a model of urban development based on industry and services, but without the necessary urban infrastructure like sewage and basic hygiene facilities.

Amazonia's role as provider of raw materials to the rest of the world, its low living standards and lack of basic services, coexist with a rich cultural heritage. The subsistence activities of Indians, *caboclos* and extractive communities – small plots, fishing and the extraction of latex – provide little access to a money economy or consumer goods beyond what is absolutely necessary for the maintenance of life and limb. On the other hand, material scarcity coexists with a wealth of cultural habits inherited from Indian traditions and the migrations from the northeast that began in the nineteenth century; they provide a rich stock of myths to explain the origins of the world, the waters and the forest.

See also: Xingu; Yaromani; boto

Further reading

Aldine, A. and Souza, M. (1994) *Breve historia da Amazonia*, São Paulo: Marco Zero.
Meggers, B. (1971) *Amazonia, Man and Culture in a Counterfeit Paradise*, Chicago.

MILTON HATOUM

Ambasz, Emilio

b. 1943, Resistencia, Chaco, Argentina

Architect

An internationally acclaimed architect and industrial designer, Ambasz has been a critic of postmodern academicism. He is an admirer of the Mexican architect Luis **Barragán**, whose work he introduced into the United States with an influential exhibition, 'The Architecture of Luis Barragán', at New York's Museum of Modern Art in 1974. Like Barragán, Ambasz embraces the passionate, the emotional and the sensual in architecture. Often blending his buildings into the natural landscape by sinking them into the earth, he aspires to a form of man-made nature. His architecture mingles minimalism with surrealism (see **surrealism in Latin American art**), for example in his Lucille Halsell Conservatory (1985) in San Antonio, Texas. The transnational cultural impact of his art is especially evident in his award-winning design of the Vertebra chair (1974).

JULIE A. MURPHY ERFANI

America

Name of one of the five parts into which Europe divided the world. The term appears first on the 1507 *mapamundi* of Martín Waldseemüller; throughout the colonial period it was called the New World or the Indies. In 1776 the newly independent USA incorporated the name of the continent and its mythological attributes. Since then the words America and American took on an ambiguity which only Spanish speakers of Latin America have tried to correct by coining the name '*estadounidense*' for the inhabitants of the USA. English speakers refer to the hemisphere as 'The Americas', acknowledging the distinct features of its north, central and southern regions.

LUIS ESPARZA

Americas

Americas is a bimonthly official publication of the **Organization of American States**, regularly published since 1949 in Washington, DC. Articles focus on the arts, cultures, histories and ecology of member countries. The magazine includes popular articles, colourful illustrations, and book and music reviews. Issued in English and Spanish, it is indexed in *Hispanic American Periodicals Index*.

PAUL BARY

Americas Society

The Americas Society is a non-profit, non-governmental organization whose objective is to inform people in the United States of the cultures of Latin America, the Caribbean and Canada, and to foster understanding of the social, political and economic issues facing the region. Founded in 1965 by David Rockefeller and based in New York, the Society (originally called the the Center for Inter-American Relations) is funded by individual and corporate membership fees. Its staff of fifteen work on various projects, such as holding presentations by heads of state and government ministers, conducting panel discussions on current issues, and sponsoring tours and exhibits by writers, musicians and artists. It publishes the journal ***Review***.

MARK UNGAR

Americas Watch

One of five regional divisions of Human Rights Watch, an international human rights organization founded in 1978. Based in Washington, D.C. and New York, Americas Watch has a staff of nine people. It conducts missions and writes reports to expose a broad range of rights abuses throughout the Americas, including torture, arbitrary detention, summary executions, discrimination and violation of the guarantees of due process and the freedoms of association, religion and expression. To pressure governments that allow such practices, Americas Watch publicizes information, works in international fora, and supports local rights organizations throughout the hemisphere.

MARK UNGAR

Amerindians in the Caribbean

It is commonly supposed that native peoples were utterly destroyed by the European colonial occupation of the Caribbean. However, their descendants – Carib in Trinidad, Dominica and St Vincent, Garifuna (see **Garinagu**) in Belize and Taíno in the Dominican Republic and the continental USA – still stubbornly persist today (see **Caribs**).

The Carib, also known as *Island Caribs* and *Karipuna*, are descendants of the people that encountered Columbus in the fifteenth century. Through five hundred years of constant colonial repression, resulting from their perceived identity as 'cannibals', the Carib have retained their autonomy from both the colonial and national societies of the Caribbean. Of course Carib identity and culture has changed over this period, and the influx of Africans into Carib society, as a result of the establishment of plantation slavery in the region, was particularly important for understanding the situation today.

Descendants of escaped African slaves were integrated into Carib society and, following their deportation from St Vincent by the British, these 'Black Caribs' went on to become the Garifuna, or Garinagan), of modern Belize. Here, paradoxically, much of the aboriginal culture and language of the Island Caribs was retained, even as it had largely disappeared from the Antilles by the beginning of this century. Nevertheless, a growing awareness of this history has led to current attempts by the Island Caribs to revive both language use and cultural forms, especially dance and storytelling, as well as material culture. This stress on cultural origins and preservation has also led to growing links with Native American people in both North and South America.

In the case of the Taíno, these forces for cultural revival have led to the overt invention of tradition, for no such identity as 'Taíno' pre-existed the European arrival. Rather, persons from the Dominican Republic and Puerto Rico have begun claiming Native American descent from the indigenous population of the old Spanish colonies of Santo Domingo, Puerto Rico and Cuba, using the term 'Taíno' (actually invented in the nineteenth century) as a means to make manifest this heritage. Using this notion of 'Taíno' to reclaim a past that is ignored in colonial and national histories of the region has become a powerful cultural means to register the continuing presence of Amerindian people in the Caribbean, otherwise obscured by the demographic preponderance of the peoples that followed in the wake of European invasion and conquest.

Further reading

González, N. (1988) *Sojourners of the Caribbean: Ethnogenesis and Ethnohistory of the Garifuna*, Urbana, IL: University of Illinois Press.

Gullick, C. (1985) *Myths of a Minority: The Changing Traditions of the Vincentian Caribs*, Assen: Van Gorcum.

Hulme, P. and Whitehead, N.L. (eds.) (1992) *Wild Majesty: Encounters with Caribs from Columbus to the Present Day*, Oxford: Clarendon Press.

Whitehead, N.L. (ed.) (1995) *Wolves from the Sea: Readings in the Anthropology of the Native Caribbean*, Leiden: KITLV Press.

NEIL L. WHITEHEAD

AMIA

The Asociación Mutual Israelita Argentina (the Israeli-Argentine Mutual Society) was founded in 1949 to assist the Jewish community in Argentina, fusing several existing institutions born out of successive Jewish migrations beginning in the late nineteenth century. AMIA is concerned primarily with the coordination of Jewish schools and the provision of social and community assistance, for example the maintenance of Jewish cemeteries, old people's homes and so on. In June 1994 a bomb completely destroyed its offices in Pasteur Street in Buenos Aires, killing one hundred people. The bomb shocked the local community, particularly since those responsible were never identified.

See also: Judaism

PABLO KREIMER

Amigos del Libro, Los

Family-run publishers and booksellers, Los Amigos del Libro were founded in 1945 in Oruro, Bolivia, by Edith Adamson Lublin and Werner Guttentag to cater to the growing German immigrant community. The bookshop moved to Cochabamba in 1946; branches later opened throughout the country. Its first publication was Jesús Lara's indigenous novel *Surumi* (1950). In 1962 it started publishing the *Bolivian Encyclopedia* with over 30 volumes printed to date. In 1963 Guttentag began compiling the *Bolivian BioBibliography*, a comprehensive catalogue of all work published in Bolivia. Los Amigos del Libro has published some 820 titles, an achievement in a country of 8 million people with Latin America's highest illiteracy rate.

WINSTON MOORE

AMNLAE

AMNLAE (Asociación de Mujeres Nicaragüenses Luisa Amanda Espinoza, the Luisa Amanda Espinoza Association of Nicaraguan Women), the official Sandinista women's organization (see **Sandinista Revolution**), was named after the first Sandinista woman to be killed by the Somoza dictatorship (see **Somoza dynasty**). Because of its links to the **FSLN** (the Sandinistas), AMNLAE never succeeded in keeping separate the interests of the Frente and the demands of a specifically women's organization. It promoted legislation favourable to women in the fields of health and education and argued for sexual and racial equality, including equal pay and health benefits. While remaining ambivalent on questions like abortion, the FSLN did finally declare its support for women in the late 1980s. After the Sandinistas' defeat in the elections of 1990, AMNLAE was superseded by more ambitious and more specifically feminist projects.

SILVIA CHAVES AND ILEANA RODRÍGUEZ

Amorim, Enrique

b. 1900, Salto, Uruguay; d. 1960, Salto

Writer

Amorim wrote in various genres but is remembered for his novels with rural settings and his questioning of the romantic myth of the **gaucho**. His novels included *La carreta* (The Cart) (1929) and *El paisano Aguilar* (Aguilar the Countryman) (1934). In 1947 he joined the Communist Party, and left Argentina, where he had been living, for political reasons in 1950. Amorim also wrote two crime novels, *El asesino desvelado* (The Murderer Revealed) (1945), published by **Borges** and **Bioy Casares** in the *Séptimo Círculo* (Seventh Circle) series, and *Feria de farsantes* (Rogues' Fair) (1952).

GONZALO AGUILAR

Ana Carolina   *see* Teixeira Soares, Ana Carolina

Anales del Caribe

Anales del Caribe is an annual journal specializing in Caribbean issues, published by the Centro de Estudios del Caribe (Caribbean Studies Centre) of Cuba's **Casa de las Américas**. Founded in 1981 and directed since then by Emilio Jorge Rodríguez, its essays and articles have provided information about the art and literature of the Caribbean as well as addressing scientific, socio-historical, economic and religious issues. Texts are published in English and French as well as Spanish, and illustrations are provided by outstanding Caribbean artists. Writer George **Lamming** is its chief editorial adviser.

WILFREDO CANCIO ISLA

anarchism

The influence of anarchism began to fade in Latin America, as it did elsewhere, with the impact of the Russian Revolution and the creation in its wake of the Third International. The ideas of anarchism, with the stress on individual freedom and a rejection of the State, seemed increasingly inappropriate for a new propertyless industrial working class, whose power was a collective one, and in conditions in which the construction of a Workers' State was a priority for the new Soviet government. Traditional anarchism had already adapted to the new realities of collective working-class organization by developing towards anarcho-syndicalism – anarchism working in that organized context. In the period during which Latin America's **communist parties** were forming, after 1917, many anarcho-syndicalists joined the new parties, though others, in Russia and elsewhere, remained openly hostile to the Bolshevik concept of revolutionary organization and the Workers' State. Only in Spain, among agricultural workers on the one hand, and artisan-based industries on the other, did anarchism remain a mass force into the 1930s.

None the less, anarchist groups were crucially influential in the early part of the century, when the first trade unions were being built and new industries were emerging – like **mining**, railways and the beginnings of manufacturing. In Mexico at the turn of the century, for example, the influence of Ricardo Flores Magón and his newspaper *Regeneración* was extremely significant until the Mexican Revolution (1910–17). In Peru, the anarchist newspaper *La Protesta* was central in the early period of building trade unions out of the late nineteenth-century mutual associations and early artisans' guilds. Anarchism was particularly strong in Argentina, where the growth in the size of the working class between 1880 and 1930 occurred largely as a result of immigration from Southern Europe, where anarchism was still a potent force. Initially resistant to labour organization, the anarcho-syndicalist currents within anarchism came to prevail in the first decade of the twentieth century, and were present through the Federación Obrera Argentina in the building of the early trade union federations. They also benefited from the characteristic chauvinism and protectionism of the early socialist parties who seemed unwilling, in Latin America as in the USA, to admit non-native speakers into the unions. In the mass actions of the

1910s, this policy changed. In Brazil, it was the rail, textile and port workers who formed the COB – the Brazilian Confederation of Labour – in 1906, under anarcho-syndicalist influence. As elsewhere in Latin America, the realignment of the political left in response to the Russian Revolution of 1917 really marked the end of its political influence – although this was also the result of a gradual change in the nature of industry and labour as it moved progressively away from the early craft-based forms of industrial production.

The social and cultural organizations and activities that had been, as Francisco Foot Hardman has shown, one of anarchism's important contributions to working-class culture – libraries, adult education, picnics and festivals – also gradually faded from the scene in the 1930s.

Anarchism experienced a sort of renaissance in the 1980s and in the 1990s particularly, in a political and a cultural guise. In Latin America and elsewhere in the world, the politics of direct action underwent a modest rebirth as the Eastern European regimes began to fall and a political vacuum marked a renewed debate about the socialist project. At the same time punk rock and other alternative musical movements among youth produced a kind of 'cultural libertarianism' that articulated a deep distrust of all formal politics and a broad rejection of the system, particularly in relation to environmental destruction and minority oppression. These currents were particularly strong in the major urban centres of Brazil, Argentina and Mexico.

Further reading

Gomez, A. (1980) *Anarquismo y anarcosindicalismo en América Latina*, Paris/Barcelona: Ruedo Ibérico.

Hardman, F.F. (1984) *Nem patria nem patrão*, São Paulo: Brasiliense.

Munck, R., Falcón, R. and Galitelli, B. (1987) *Argentina from Anarchism to Peronism*, London: Zed Books.

Nettlau, M. (1927) *Contribución a la bibliografía anarquista de la America Latina hasta 1914*, Buenos Aires: Editorial La Protesta.

Poole, D. (ed.) (1977) *Land and Liberty: Anarchist Influences in the Mexican Revolution*, Sanday, Orkney: Cienfuegos Press.

Rama, C.M. (1990) *El anarquismo en América Latina*, Caracas: Biblioteca Ayacucho.

Spalding, H. (1977) *Organized Labour in Latin America*, New York: Harper & Row.

MIKE GONZALEZ

Andean culture

'Culture' cannot be described as a whole or even as a timeless reality. It is in a permanent flux and in the Andes, culture is constantly being negotiated and redefined among the various cultures, languages and traditions that have been in contact in the region. New identities and cultures, trying to forge a popular culture in the interplay of the autochthonous and the imposed (or imported), make up a fluid and rich cultural mosaic where Hispanic, indigenous, African and Asiatic traditions are constitutive elements. As **Mariátegui** (1927) said 'tradition always remoulds itself before our eyes, while we so frequently insist on imagining it as motionless and exhausted'.

In 1532 the Spanish Empire came upon the Tawantinsuyu, a multi-ethnic Inca empire, stretching across the Andes from the northern part of what is today Chile and Argentina to southern Colombia, from the Pacific coast to the jungles of the eastern slopes. Inca descendants and many other subjugated native peoples have survived and with them, many of the ancient practices, traditions and languages. All of them make up the modern nations colonized by the Spanish Empire. **Quechua** (**Quichua**, Kichwa) language, the administrative language of the Tawantinsuyu, was extended during the colonial period by the colonial administration and by missionaries; the Roman alphabet was used to write Quechua early and frequently in the colonial period. As far as the contemporary linguistic situation is concerned, Spanish coexists with many indigenous languages. Of the indigenous languages Quechua and **Aymara** are the major ones in terms of their number of speakers. In the Andes eight million people speak Quechua and another half a million, Aymara. Peru's Quechua is divided into multiple dialects whose number depends on the criteria used for classification. Some are mutually intelligi-

ble. The Ecuadoran case is different from the Peruvian one because it appears that during the Inca expansion Quechua was superimposed on a population that spoke various other autochthonous languages and was later used as a lingua franca in commerce. Dialectal variation of Ecuadoran Quichua is not as marked as that of Peru. This, together with indigenous mobilization, has given Quichua a higher social status, particularly in the sector of **education**.

In Bolivia, besides Spanish and Aymara, **Guarani** is spoken by approximately 80,000 Bolivian Guaranis. Most of them have a good knowledge of Spanish without having abandoned their mother tongue. The most common situation is a functional diglossia where Spanish is used for formal contexts and Guarani for community life and informal situations. Linguistic awareness is growing and language has been an important tool of empowerment in the process of ethnic and cultural revival.

In Bolivia, Peru and Ecuador **bilingual education** programmes are in place and while there have been some advances in changing prejudices of both non-indigenous and indigenous sectors towards the native languages, there is still considerable work to be done in this area. The most difficult obstacles to be overcome are the funding of those programmes, and the conviction that Spanish is the language of prestige and economic advancement.

The colonial period was contested by more than a hundred Indian rebellions in Peru and Bolivia between 1720 and 1790, some opposing tyranny and some with a messianic character. The rebellion of Tupac Amaru in 1780 left a legacy in Peru and Bolivia that lasts until today in ethnic nationalists and guerrilla groups (see **Tupamaros**).

The movement of *indigenismo* has had great importance in Andean culture. The consciousness of an 'Indian problem' and racial division was brought into sharp relief by Peru's defeat in the Pacific War (1879–83). *Indigenismo* has suffered change over time; these changes are reflected in the presentation of social issues, as well as in tendencies in the visual arts, music, literature and politics. The most prominent **creole intellectuals** of the movement in 1920s were from Cuzco and they spread the idea that the way to renew the nation was the revival of the indigenous principles, promoting the Quechua language and claiming that Cuzco was the true capital of the nation. This indigenist agenda served to promote Cuzco over Lima, considered the bastion of the Hispanic culture. Nevertheless, the language, religion and music that were brought from Spain are also key elements of Andean culture. Names associated with the *indigenistas* are Martín **Chambi**, Luis Valcárcel, Uriel García, José María **Arguedas**, Gamaliel **Churata** (Alejandro Peralta), and Manuel **Scorza**.

The trauma caused by the conquest has been the theme of various festivals across the centuries and has generated a series of myths of which the most famous is the myth of **Inkarri**. According to this myth the Inca, decapitated by the Spaniards, has started bringing together his dismembered body to restore his power and that of the Inca empire. The festival of **Inti Raymi**, celebrated in Cuzco during winter solstice on 24 June, is an imaginative recreation of an Inca festival, which attracts large numbers of participants and tourists (see **tourism**). However, the script of the Inti Raymi in present use in the festival was written in the 1952 by a group of local creole intellectuals whose Quechua was so 'pure' (or so they believed) and so stylized that it is unintelligible to contemporary Quechua speakers. In addition, the tradition of Inti Raymi was interrupted for several centuries, so the 'authenticity' of the present spectacle is open to question.

See also: Andean Music; CONAIE; Columbian quincentenary; Grupo Chasqui; Grupo Ukama; Jorge Sanjinés; Inti Raymi; language policy

Further reading

Arguedas, J.M. (1987) *Formación de una cultura indoamericana*, Mexico City: Siglo XXI.

Mannheim, B. (1991) *The Language of the Inka since the European Invasion*, Austin, TX: University of Texas.

Mariátegui, J.C. (1927) *Seven Interpretive Essays on Peruvian Reality*, Austin, TX: University of Texas Press.

Murra, J. (1980) *The Economic Organization of the Inca State*, Hartford: JAI.

MERCEDES NIÑO-MURCIA AND FRANK SALOMON

Andean music

Early accounts and surviving musical instruments offer some considerable knowledge about the pre-Columbian music of the Andean region. What is clear is that contemporary Andean music is based only in part on the indigenous musical tradition, because it incorporates a number of instruments that were brought to the New World by the Spaniards, such as the **harp**, the **guitar**, the violin and the mandolin (which evolved into the present-day **charango**, usually made with an armadillo shell). However, the indigenous tradition did influence present-day Andean music in that pentatonic and other scales are used instead of the European major and minor scales. Also, the preferred vocal style is a high-pitched nasal sound, and Andean instruments – primarily pipes and drums, such as the **quena**, the zampoña (pan pipes) and the clarín (long trumpet) – are used to carry the melody, while the imported instruments, primarily strings, are often used for background or harmony. As Turino points out, however, there is considerable local variation.

The two principal genres of traditional Andean music are the **huayno** (or wayno) and the **yaraví**. The huayno today is a hybrid form based to some extent on the Spanish ballad tradition, with some narrative elements and refrains, and is often sung in Spanish. The yaraví, a lament, sounds more indigenous and less Spanish, and is often sung in Quechua. Recent innovations in Andean music, the product of the migration of highland people to Lima and other coastal cities, include *música chicha* (see *chicha* **music**), which fuses Andean music with elements from **cumbia** and rock, including electric instruments. Andean music of the kind discussed above has also influenced **art music**, particularly in works by such composers as Daniel **Alomía Robles**, from whose 1913 *zarzuela* of the same name was derived the melody known as **El condor pasa**. Andean music has also influenced the **zamba** and **cueca** of northern Argentina and Chile, particularly works by Atahualpa **Yupanqui** and Los Chalchaleros. Musicologists who did important work on Andean music include Nicomedes Santa Cruz and José María **Arguedas**.

Andean music became known all over the continent, and indeed around the world, when it was adopted as the favoured music of the Chilean Unidad Popular (see **Popular Unity**) and of the Latin American left of the late 1960s. Groups such as **Inti-Illimani**, composed largely of non-Indian musicians, took the Andean musical tradition, adapting it freely, to rallies in stadia and to street demonstrations, as well as to huge public concerts; later, after the exile from Chile and other countries of artists and intellectuals, the Andean musical tradition found a home in *peñas* (see ***peña***) from Mexico City to Berkeley to Stockholm. Turino (1993) comments, contrasting this music with the indigenous music that it emulates: 'much native Andean music, particularly when played by larger ensembles, has a hard, driving, slightly dissonant quality that contrasts fundamentally with the sweet, more consonant sound of the urban-revivalist Andean style, well known internationally as played by bands with solo kena, zampoña, charango, guitar and drum'.

Further reading

Cohen, J. (1984) *Mountain Music of Peru*, New York: Cinema Guild. Film/video.

Stevenson, R.M. (1960) *Music in Aztec and Inca Territory*, Berkeley: University of California Press.

Turino, T. (1993) *Moving away from Silence: Music of the Peruvian Altiplano and the Experience of Urban Migration*, Chicago: University of Chicago Press.

—— (1998) 'Quechua and Aymara', *The Garland Encyclopedia of World Music: South America, Mexico, Central America and the Caribbean*, New York: Garland Press, pp. 205–24.

DANIEL BALDERSTON AND
MERCEDES NIÑO-MURCIA

Andean Pact

The 1970 Cartagena Agreement between Bolivia, Chile, Colombia, Ecuador and Peru (and later Venezuela) was designed to establish an Andean Common Market within the Latin American Free Trade Agreement. A radical proposal, it included controls over transnational companies (Decision 24), regional planning, a common external tariff and special treatment for the more backward Ecuador and Bolivia. In 1976 Chile withdrew after the implementation of **Pinochet**'s free market policies. In 1980 Bolivia also boycotted meetings. In practice, from 1982 all Pact members failed to meet policy harmonisation targets. The 1987 Modifying Protocol abandoned all the original major objectives, including Decision 24 and the customs union, effectively ending the Pact, although there are still areas of cultural cooperation among the countries.

PHILIP O'BRIEN

Anderson Imbert, Enrique

b. 1910, Córdoba, Argentina

Writer

Imbert's diversity is evidenced by his contributions to the socialist newspaper *La vanguardia* from 1931 to 1937, the novel *Vigilia* (Vigil) (1934), the collection of essays *La flecha en el aire* (The Arrow in the Air) (1937) and the fantastic (see **fantastic literature**) short stories of *El grimorio* (The Other Side of the Mirror) in 1961. He began teaching in 1940. In his canonical yet problematic *Historia de la literatura hispanoamericana* (Spanish-American Literature: A History) (1954) he categorized literature by generations and offered only impressionistic views of female writers.

FERNANDA A. ZULLO

andinismo

Recent archeological discoveries in the high Andes have confirmed that pre-Columbian peoples, including the Incas, scaled the mountains to make sacrifices to the mountain spirits. Mountain climbing for sport, called andinismo in South America to distinguish it from alpinismo (which is the Spanish term for the sport, but has to do with the Alps instead of the Andes), begins in some sense with the travels of Alexander von Humboldt in the early nineteenth century. The volcanoes of Ecuador were an early draw (Humboldt scaled Chimborazo), and volcanoes throughout the region are often scaled today by adventure tourists (see **tourism**). Technical climbers have concentrated particularly on the sheer rock surfaces of the southern Patagonian Andes (see **Patagonia**), particularly the Fitzroy and Cerro Torre area in Argentina's Parque Nacional Los Glaciares and Torres del Paine in Chile. Cerro Torre, long thought unclimbable, was first scaled by an Italian, Cesare Maestri, in 1970, who climbed it in an unorthodox manner with the aid of a portable compressor drill; the first proper ascent was by another Italian party, led by Casimiro Ferrari, in 1974. Many cities in the Andean countries have a Club Andino, a mountain climbing organization.

DANIEL BALDERSTON

Andrade, Joaquim Pedro de

b. 1932, Rio de Janeiro, Brazil; d. 1988, Rio de Janeiro

Film-maker

An iconoclastic intellectual who expressed his literary preferences and ambitions through supremely cinematic films, Andrade was one of the principal film-makers of the **Cinema Novo** movement in Brazil. After experimenting with home movies and producing two documentaries (on sociologist Gilberto **Freyre** and poet Manuel **Bandeira**), Andrade studied film-making in Paris (IDHEC – Institut des Hautes Études Cinématographiques), London, and New York (where he worked with the Maysles brothers, innovators of direct cinema). While in Paris, he completed the short *Couro de gato* (Cat Skin) (1961), one of the episodes of the **CPC**-sponsored *Cinco vezes favela* (Five Times Favela) (1962), considered one of the first Cinema Novo films. His first feature, *Garrincha, alegria do povo* (Garrincha, the People's Happiness) (1963) criticized the alienating effects of soccer upon the poor. His first fiction film, *O padre e a moça* (The Priest and the Girl) (1965) was adapted from a Carlos Drummond de **Andrade** poem, and evidenced his love for the Brazilian literary *modernismo* movement (see **Brazilian modernism**), later made manifest by his brilliant adaptation of Mário de **Andrade**'s *Macunaíma* (1969). Combining *Antropofagia* with elements of the *chanchada*, *Macunaíma* was

Cinema Novo's greatest commercial success, attracting audiences with its irreverent parody, yet delivering a hard-hitting critique of the repressive military government in power.

Following an **Embrafilme** call for educational historical films, de Andrade produced *Os Inconfidentes* (The Conspirators) (1972), a profoundly Brechtian film so faithful to the historical record that it could not be censored despite its acerbic critique of contemporary politics via the allegory of an intellectual caught in the political tensions of a dictatorship. Always struggling to find forms amenable to audiences through which to continue his ongoing dialogue with Brazilian literature, he then adapted a group of Dalton **Trevisan** stories for *Guerra conjugal* (War of the Sexes) (1974), which borrowed from and critiqued the *pornochanchada*, a project he continued in the episode *Vereda tropical* for *Contos Eróticos* (Erotic Stories) (1977). *O homen do Pau-Brasil* (Brazil Wood Man) (1981), his last film, returned to *modernismo* and had Oswald de Andrade as his protagonist. Unable to find backing for his films, he wrote two brilliant screenplays before his early death, *O imponderável Bento contra o crioulo voador* (The Inscrutable Bento Against the Flying Blackman) and an adaptation of Freyre's classic *Casa grande e senzala*.

Further reading

Benta, I. (1996) *Joaquim Pedro de Andrade*, Rio de Janeiro: Relume.

ISMAIL XAVIER AND THE USP GROUP

Andrade, Mário Raúl de Moraes

b. 1893, São Paulo, Brazil; d. 1945, São Paulo

Critic, musicologist, ethnologist, writer and cultural administrator

One of Brazil's leading writers and **intellectuals**, best known for his rhapsodic novel *Macunaíma* (1928), at the age of eighteen Mário de Andrade abandoned a course in commerce to study music and piano at the São Paulo Conservatory. By his mid-twenties he had already gained a reputation as teacher and critic of art, music and poetry. A politely devastating critique of the literary establishment, 'Mestres do Passado' (Past Masters), published in 1921 together with his first collection of poetry, *Há uma gota de sangue em cada poema* (There is a Drop of Blood in Every Poem), led fellow modernist Oswald de **Andrade** (no relation) to declare him 'my futurist poet'. Although he vigorously repudiated the title, he effectively confirmed his critical and artistic leadership of Brazil's modernist movement with his next volume, *Paulicéia Desvairada* (Hallucinated City), which appeared in the same year as São Paulo's momentous **Modern Art Week** (1922).

Andrade's theory of modernist poetics, expounded in the 'Extremely Interesting Preface' to *Paulicéia Desvairada*, was set to work in wildly extended free verse compositions that assaulted the conservative complacency of Brazil's *belle époque* bourgeoisie in a defiantly surrealist (see **surrealism in Latin American art**) and colloquial Portuguese, which evoked the painful yet tumultuous birth of a modern, European-style city in the tropics, a 'Gallicism bellowing in the deserts of America!'

This awareness of the contradiction at the heart of Brazilian modernity remained with Andrade, and by the mid-1920s, following the formal and linguistic iconoclasm of the Modern Art Week, he was leading the movement in its exploration of the wealth of rural and regional traditions which lay beyond the islands of urban development in the southeast. An extended journey through the country's north and northeast in 1927 produced the strongly folkloric poetry of *Clã do Jaboti* (Clan of the Tortoise), with its Utopian vision of an uncomplicated culture of 'indolence' and pure being among the rubbertappers of the Amazon. The clash between that 'primitive' universe and the capitalist mentality of the city was played out in his most famous work, *Macunaíma*. This extraordinarily fertile period in Andrade's career, when his ethnomusicological researches also produced a pioneering *Ensaio sobre a música brasileira* (Essay on Brazilian Music) (1928) and *Compêndio da história da música* (Compendium of Music History) (1929), can best be seen as a multidisciplinary reflection on the dialectic between diversity and identity in Brazilian culture. When he wrote, in a poem of 1929, 'There

are three hundred, three hundred and fifty of me/ But one day at last I will find myself,' he was speaking as much of a national, as of a personal dilemma.

The following year brought a political dimension to bear on this dilemma, as Getulio **Vargas** took power and the authoritarian, centralising aspirations of the new regime clashed with São Paulo's determination to defend its regional autonomy. Despite an intellectual's scepticism about organized politics, the instinctive democrat Andrade felt a visceral identification with the socialist cause against the growth of the far right, something he expressed in the anguished, surrealistic language of the poem 'O Carro da Miséria' (The Wagon of Misery) in the mid-1930s.

Paradoxically, though, the emergence of a strongly centralised state seemed to offer Andrade the opportunity to turn his ideas for democratising culture into reality in the public sphere. In 1935 he was appointed to São Paulo's Department of Culture where, as its Director from 1937, he undertook the preliminary plans to establish a Department of National Historical and Artistic Heritage. The next two years saw a series of unprecedented initiatives in the cultural life of the city, all of them due to Andrade's vision and energy: a Society of Ethnology and Folklore; a Congress for the National Language in Song; the creation of children's parks with their own folk festivals; the first mobile library, music and record libraries; and the organisation of free musical and dramatic performances at the Municipal Theatre, which opened its doors for the first time to working people.

However, in 1938, with the installation of a fully-fledged dictatorship in the shape of Vargas's **Estado Novo** and a drastic reform of the civil service, Andrade's cultural mission was cruelly cut short. Removed from his post as Municipal Director of Culture, he retreated into academic life in Rio de Janeiro and was eventually forced to cease his journalistic activities, spending the remaining years of his life hovering between illness and depression. One of his last, most outspoken public interventions, which angrily belies the general defeatism of this period, was a lecture published in 1942 under the title 'The Modernist Movement'. This was a severe critique of the avant-garde (see **avant-garde in Latin America**) generation which he had led in the 1920s, and of its failure to come down out of the ivory tower of experimentation and speculation into the real world and meet the challenge of social responsibility.

Yet Andrade's own career represented an incomparable example of the socially responsible artist–intellectual at work. It combined the painstaking dedication of the ethnographer dirtying his hands in the field, with the intellectual discipline of the library-bound researcher, the vision and initiative of the political activist with the poet's sensitivity to the language of individual experience. This grasp of the complex relationship between the particular and the general, between the detail and substance of cultural life and the larger picture, his intervention in such a range of disciplinary fields and his sober honesty in confronting the dilemmas of cultural change, make Mário de Andrade the single most enlightened commentator on his country's development, and one of the true pioneers of the art of cultural studies in Brazil.

Further reading

Andrade, M. de (1943) *Aspectos da literatura brasileira*, São Paulo: Martins.

—— (1965) *Aspectos da música brasileira*, São Paulo: Martins.

—— (1987) *Poesias completas*, São Paulo: Itatiaia.

—— (1988) *Macunaíma*, trans. R. Goodland, London: Carcanet.

Antelo, R. (1986) *Na ilha de marapatá: Mário de Andrade lê os hispano-americanos*, São Paulo: Ed. Hucitéc.

Duarte, P. (1971) *Mário de Andrade por ele mesmo*, São Paulo: Edart.

Lopez, T.P.A. (1972) *Mário de Andrade: ramais e caminho*, São Paulo: Duas Cidades.

DAVID TREECE

Andrade, Oswald de

b. 1890, São Paulo, Brazil; d. 1954, São Paulo

Writer and philosopher

Oswald de Andrade represents the Dionysian face of **Brazilian modernism**. His renovating impulse earned him his place as Brazil's most original avant-garde (see **avant-garde in Latin America**) figure. And in evoking such a figure, the critic has no alternative but to use descriptions like inventive, sarcastic, irreverent genius of corrosive, libidinous and biting humour.

Andrade was marked always by a creative will to transgress and oppose norms, be they literary, political or social. Few writers have maintained such a close connection between their life and their literary work. Fragments of his life were captured in characters like João Miramar and Serafim (a name he liked to use himself), especially in *Un homem sem profissão – sob as ordens de mamãe* (A Man with no Profession – Under Mothers' Orders) (1954), written a few years before his death, where he declared his passion and his insatiable curiosity for life and literature: 'I gather together everything, I add things up, I absorb'. His relationship with the world was, as he put it, anthropophagic; everything is devoured, to be later transformed into literary material.

Andrade's multiple personality makes him as different as it is possible to be from the salon literati. In the 1920s, he was a cosmopolitan intellectual (see **intellectuals**) responsible for the promotion of modernism (see **Brazilian modernism**). It was he who discovered new young talents like Mário de **Andrade** (no relation), while his own work developed in a variety of genres; he was poet, novelist, playwright, essayist, writer of memoirs and a polemical journalist. His life and work were devoted to breaking literary and cultural traditions. Although he adopted infinitely varied genres and forms of expression, the nation (Brazil) is a constant in all the different manifestations of his art. Titles like *Pau-Brasil* (Brazil Wood) (1925) or ***Antropofagia*** identify him immediately with Brazilian ideology. The national elements of his poetry and fiction, however, are opposed to a nineteenth-century rhetoric of nation-building tied to a Romantic exoticism of Brazilian landscape (in José de Alencar), to the opposition civilization–barbarism (Euclides da Cunha) or to the representation of customs characteristic of realism and naturalism (Aluísio de Azevedo). Andrade's Brazilian adventure was based upon an avant-garde project with European, and particularly futuristic, roots. He looked towards both Brazil and Europe.

Andrade had to distance himself in order to understand his Brazil, to rediscover his roots and to propose a new poetic style; hence the journeys to Europe and the sojourns in Paris. Just as the anthropophagists devoured their enemies (not out of hunger, but out of a ritualistic desire to assimilate the best of the other), so Oswald proposed to 'devour' techniques of composition in order to produce something new.

During his first journey to Europe in 1912, Andrade made contact with the avant-garde, with the futurism of Marinetti, the cubism of Picasso and the poetic theories of Apollinaire. These theoretical principles, together with his own extraordinary intuition, produced the new poetry of *Pau-Brasil*. 'The forest is a school', he declared in his *Manifesto Antropófago*, symbolically combining the autochthonous elements of the land with the knowledge he had gained in Europe.

These ideas were continued and developed in a far-reaching project whose theoretical foundations were laid in the *Manifesto Antropófago*. The manifesto revealed how revolutionary his principles were, how directly connected with radical social transformation. The Utopian nation proposed by Andrade would be built on an alliance of natural man and twentieth-century technology. Liberated from the tyranny of labour, man would be free to return to the exercise of his natural idleness: 'In the supertechnological world to come, when the final barriers of Patriarchy have crumbled, man will be able to indulge his innate laziness, the mother of fantasy, invention and love. He will thus finally be restored, after his long period of negativity, to the synthesis of technical change which is civilization and natural life which is culture, to his ludic instincts...

In this new society, the patriarchal, oppressive system that privileges the inherited rights of the patriarch's son would be abolished. In its place would arise the Matriarchy of Pindorama, which celebrates man's natural impulses in a classless society where all land is held in common. This was the anthropophagic culture, whose idealistic principles Andrade continued to explore and develop until the publication of *A crise da filosofia messiânica* (Crisis of Messianic Philosophy) in 1950.

Outstanding among Andrade's fiction is *Memórias sentimentais de João Miramar* (Sentimental Memoirs of João Miramar) (1924). His cinematographic prose captured the simultaneity of the real through montage and the superimposition of fragments. He emphasizes the dynamic, plastic elements of the scenes he narrates or describes. His roots in the avant-garde are evident in the interweaving of traditionally irreconcilable styles (prose, poetry, theatre, propaganda, and so on), the constant presence of humour and the satirical dimension that permeates the work, a violent critique of contemporary society. *Serafim Pont Grande*, though written in the 1920s, was not published until 1933; it represented the most radical extension of all his earlier propositions. It is a rebellious, transgressive text, realized through erotic humour and the exploration of the grotesque. The polemical character of these novels derives as much from their formal innovations as from their content. Both had to wait more than forty years for a second edition and for their recognition as major works. Together with Mário de Andrade's **Macunaíma**, these books are the most important prose works of Brazilian modernism.

Andrade's avant-garde poetry and his innovative fiction are one of the most important and challenging legacies of contemporary Brazilian culture. His ideas continue to provoke reflection and admiration. The presentation in 1967 of his play *O rei da vela* (King of the Candle) produced its own revolution; the concrete poets (see **concrete poetry**) acknowledged him as one of their principal ancestors, and the 1960s *tropicalista* movement in music and cinema returned to anthropophagy and drew on its subversiveness and its corrosive and anarchic humor directed against bourgeois values.

Further reading

Andrade, O. de (1990–96) *Obras completas de Oswald de Andrade*, São Paulo: Globo (23 vols).

—— (1979) *Seraphim Grosse Pointe*, trans. K.D. Jackson and A. Bork, Austin, TX: New Latin Quarter Editions.

Fonseca, M.A. (1990) *Oswald de Andrade: Biografia*, São Paulo: Art Editora/Secretaria do Estado da Cultura.

Jackson, K.D. (ed.) (1978) *A prosa vanguardista na literatura brasileira*, São Paulo: Ed. Perspectiva.

Nunes, B. (1979) *Oswald Canibal*, São Paulo: Perspectiva.

Schwartz, J. (ed.) (2000) *Oswald de Andrade: obra incompleta*, São Paulo: Col. Archivos.

JORGE SCHWARTZ

Anemaet, Jo

b. 1911, Philipsburg, St. Maarten

Painter

As a soldier, Jo Anemaet went to Indonesia. He came back to Curaçao after the Second World War, and has lived and worked there since then. He is an autodidact who draws and paints (oils and water colours) his surroundings, particularly the landscapes, urban houses and the people of places such as Indonesia, Aruba, Curaçao and the other islands of the Netherlands Antilles. He has had several exhibitions in the Netherlands and on Curaçao, and is still very busy painting and drawing in his atelier.

NEL CASIMIRI

Angel, Albalucía

b. 1939, Pereira, Colombia

Art critic, writer, journalist and singer

Angel's fiction is representative of the new narrative by women authors of the 1970s. Having moved to Paris in her early twenties, she published her first novel *Dos veces Alicia* (Alicia Twice Over) (1972) in Barcelona, Spain, where she met some of the writers of the **Boom**. Her second and best-known novel, *Estaba la pájara pinta sentada en el verde limón* (The Spotted Female Bird was Sitting on the Green Lemon Tree) (1982), titled after a children's rhyme, won an award in Colombia. Her third novel, *Misiá señora* (Madam Lady) (1983) is an ambitious and experimental work both in content and form.

MAGDALENA GARCÍA PINTO

Angélica

b. 1973, São Bernardo do Campo, Brazil

Media personality

Born Angélica Ksyvickis, Angélica is a Brazilian television phenomenon who followed **Xuxa** as the 'Queen of Kids'. While still a teenager she fronted her own show on **SBT**, and later on TV **Manchete**. A commercial empire developed selling products bearing her name, including the Angélica doll. In 1996 she was contracted by **Globo** to present the highly successful talent show 'Caça Talentos'. By 1997 she had 48 official fan clubs and 350 licenced products including sandals, cereals and nail varnish.

ANTONIO CARLOS MARTINS VAZ

animation

The art of filming hand-drawings via stop-motion cinematography to produce the illusion of movement, first exploited in Paris by Emile Cohl's short film *Fantasmagorias* in 1908, was soon adopted in Latin America. The earliest and most extraordinary example of animation was produced by film pioneer Federico Valle, who decided – against all the odds – to make a feature-length animated film in 1918 Argentina – as far as we know the first such effort in the history of animation. With only a vague knowledge of the techniques of animation, Valle experimented and invented the equipment to film the drawings vertically and a special motor to stop the camera after each exposure. Valle chose to tackle a political satire based on president Hipólito Yrigoyen's new, controversial government and came up with the title *El apóstol* (The Apostle). With the collaboration of political cartoonist 'El Mono' Taborda, Valle managed to film 58,000 photograms – for fifty minutes of running time – and to stun audiences both with the brilliant satire of the government and with his technical virtuosity. He followed up *El apóstol* with yet another first in the history of animation: *Una noche en el Colón* (A Night at the Colon Theatre) – the world's first animated feature using clay figurines, in 1919.

Despite these early experiments, animation

languished in Latin America in the 1920s–1960s. For example, Carlos Borcosque produced the first Chilean animated film in 1925, but with no consequent development. In the field of animation, industry quickly triumphed over innovation, and it became increasingly difficult to combat the products emerging from the USA, especially from the Walt Disney studios. This was after the coming of sound and the genre's reorientation towards children's entertainment rather than sophisticated satire.

However, with the advent of the **New Latin American Cinema**, animation began to make a reappearance on the cinematic horizon, most notably with Walter Tournier's brilliant short, *En la selva hay mucho por hacer* (There's Much to do in the Jungle) (1973), produced in collaboration with the Cinemateca del Tercer Mundo. Stemming from the premise of an illustrated letter written by a Uruguayan political prisoner to his daughter, the film attempts to explain the reasons for political imprisonment using the metaphor of jungle animals struggling for survival.

The late 1970s and 1980s were fertile years for Latin American animation, with much experimentation. Especially notable is the work of Juan **Padrón** in Cuba, whose popular comic strip character, **Elpidio Valdés** – a revolutionary in the independence struggles against Spain – was brought to the screen via **ICAIC** in 1974. Padrón also produced ICAIC's first animated feature, the popular *Vampiros en la Habana* (Vampires in Havana) (1984), a great international box-office success, and he collaborated with the Argentine cartoonist, **Quino**, in the celebrated short series, **Quinoscopios**, which at one time preceded the screening of all films in Cuba and have since been anthologized on video.

Currently, Latin American animators continue to use the cinema to combat what is perceived as the noxious influence of US cartoons aired on television. Walter Tournier's work in the series *Los Tatitos* in Uruguay has been notable, as has Cao Hamburger's work in clay-figure animation in Brazil, and the *Manuelita* cartoons, featuring an animated turtle, in Argentina. In-roads are also being made in the field of digital computer-generated animation. The Argentine company, Patagonik Film, has just announced the release in 2000 of the first Latin American digital animated feature, *Condor Crux*, a science fiction adventure directed by Juan Pablo Buscarini. As is to be expected in this era of high-tech globalization, however, the company is a partnership between a Buenos Aires media conglomerate (**El Clarín**) and Disney's film subsidiary, Buena Vista International.

ANA M. LÓPEZ

Anne Zwing

Based in Cartagena, Colombia, this band pioneered a new genre of popular **maroon music** in the late 1980s. Leader Viviano Torres and several other members hail from the famous community of Palenque de San Basilio, founded by escaped slaves whose freedom was recognized by the Spanish crown in the early eighteenth century. (Anne Zwing means 'they swing' in the Palenquero language.) Skilfully blending cosmopolitan Afro-Atlantic genres such as **reggae**, **soca**, **zouk** and soukous with local stylistic signifiers, they create compelling dance music that mediates between their specific Palenquero maroon identity and a broader Afro-Colombian identity.

KEN BILBY

Another Life

This autobiographical poem by Nobel Laureate Derek **Walcott** was written between 1965 and 1972 and published in 1973. The poem explores Walcott's childhood and early adulthood. Its focus, however, is not simply on describing his experiences with family, friends and acquaintances, but on exploring how those experiences engage questions of post-colonial Caribbean identity. Walcott vividly renders both the natural and human landscape of his boyhood Saint Lucia. Like much of his work, *Another Life* mixes meditations on the unique nature of Caribbean life with allusions to European texts. With the blossoming of Walcott's career and international acclaim in the 1980s and 1990s, *Another Life* was to some extent overshadowed by his later works, particularly the epic poem **Omeros** (1990).

ROSANNE ADDERLEY

Ansiedad

Chelique Sarabia, a singer and song writer from La Asunción in Venezuela, wrote the song 'Ansiedad' (Anxiety) in the mid-1950s, when he was just fifteen years old. A ballad in the rhythm of a slow waltz, the simple lyrics tell of the longing the singer feels for the lover from whom he is separated: 'Ansiedad de tenerte en mis brazos/musitando palabras de amor' (Longing to have you in my arms, murmuring words of love). The success of the song, which rapidly achieved popularity in Venezuela and beyond, won Sarabia several awards, and he established himself as one of Venezuela's most acclaimed popular musicians during the following decades.

MARK DINNEEN

Antelo, Raúl

b. 1951, Buenos Aires, Argentina

Literary critic

An Argentine critic and essayist now living in Brazil, Antelo was educated in Buenos Aires before moving to São Paulo and later to Florianópolis. His marginal location on the academic map is also significant for his critical work. Thinking through the production of meaning, he reads literature and art as an allegory. Thus he does not limit himself to Brazilian or Latin American texts but thinks in terms of the networks and circuits through which discourses, figures and movements intercept and modify one another. Mário de **Andrade**, Le Corbusier and Oliverio **Girondo** have each given him an opportunity to develop one of the most original critical discourses of late twentieth-century Latin America.

GRACIELA MONTALDO

Anthony, Michael

b. 1932, Mayaro, Trinidad

Writer and historian

Considered one of Trinidad's foremost historians, Anthony travelled to England in 1955, where he worked in factories and as a telegraphist. His literary career began with contributions to the magazine **Bim**. His first novel, *The Games Were Coming*, was published in 1963; his most famous, *The Year in San Fernando*, in 1965. Other writings include short collections *Cricket in the Road* (1973), *Sandra Street and Other Stories* (1973) and *The Chieftain's Carnival and Other Stories* (1993), where each story is based on significant events in Trinidad's history. Much of his work after 1975 consists of historical research into his native island.

KEITH JARDIM

anthropology

The role of national and international anthropology in modern Latin America is complex. Anthropology historically has focused on indigenous tribal and peasant peoples within the region, though African and **mestizo** groups are also an object of study. The vast majority of studies form part of an international, comparative discourse on the nature and development of humanity, though many anthropological projects have served the needs of national or local development, either through attempts to empower local communities in a culturally sensitive fashion or to facilitate national infrastructure development and education aspirations and agendas. Anthropological research is conducted by a large number of institutions, including Latin American and foreign universities, federal and state level institutes within Latin America, and museums. University- and museum-based research generally is focused on scholarly problems – everything from theories of optimal hunting behaviour, to styles of storytelling, agricultural systems and systems of health knowledge, to Native history. National anthropological programmes frequently are more applied in focus, dealing with issues of development but also attempting to serve as a means of ensuring cultural survival.

Although certainly not unimportant in previous decades, ethnohistory began to emerge as a dominant research orientation of Latin American anthropologists in the 1970s. Historical records, especially those deriving from the first centuries of Spanish presence in the Americas, have been utilized by archaeologists and anthropologists since the nineteenth century to contextualize archaeological and ethnographic information. Increasingly today, ethnographers are turning to history to understand the cultural configurations they encounter in the field. Many institutions and conventions of Native American life, once thought to be direct survivals of the pre-Hispanic period, are now understood as profoundly transformed or even newly created out of the centuries long collision of indigenous and Spanish culture and society.

The twentieth century witnessed a precipitous decline in population percentages of self-identifying indigenous peoples in Latin America, increasingly accelerated through rural outmigration, invasive development, and internationalization of cultural forms. As a consequence, many anthropologists are concerned with the cultural and social survival of native peoples throughout the Americas. Beginning with efforts to create applied anthropologies in the 1950s and 1960s, anthropologists increasingly work in concert with the communities they study, to enhance survival chances. Work on **literacy** and literary programmes, advocacy in national and international arenas, and, increasingly important, defence of ownership of genetic and other resources are ways in which anthropologists and other concerned professionals give back to the communities they study. A dramatic increase in interest in indigenous knowledge of the pharmacological properties of numerous plant, animal, and fungal species during the 1980s and 1990s has made issues of ownership crucially important.

Further reading

Emery, A.F. (1996) *The Anthropological Imagination in Latin American Literature*, Columbia: University of Missouri Press.

Hale, C.R. (1997) 'Cultural Politics of Identity in Latin America', in *Annual Review of Anthropology*, 26, Palo Alto, CA: Annual Reviews, Inc.

Smith, G.A. (1995) *Memory at the Margins: Essays in Anthropology and World History*, Victoria, BC: World History Caucus, University of Victoria.

Weil, C. (1988) *Lucha: The Struggles of Latin American Women*, Minneapolis, Minnesota: Prisma Institute.

CHRISTOPHER VON NAGY

Antigua

Antigua and neighbouring Barbuda form a small nation in the Leeward islands of the Caribbean, with an estimated population of 64, 246 (1999), of whom about 1200 live on Barbuda. Claimed by the British in 1632, Antigua gained independence from Britain in 1981 after a compromise was reached which granted relative autonomy in its internal affairs to the much smaller Barbuda. Its capital is St John. The majority of the people of Antigua and Barbuda are descendants of the enslaved Africans of the colonial era, but the population also includes the descendants of British, Spanish, French and Dutch colonists, and of Portuguese, Lebanese and Syrian immigrants. Tourism is the dominant industry, accounting for about 60 per cent of employment, with manufacturing and agriculture lagging far behind, accounting for about 14 per cent and 12 per cent of employment respectively.

CAROL J. WALLACE

Antilliaanse Cahiers

Antilliaanse Cahiers (Antillean Journals) is a literary magazine, published in the Netherlands and appearing from 1955 to 1967, and edited by Cola **Debrot**, Henk Dennert and, for the first volume, Jules de **Palm**. It was dedicated to literary writing from the Dutch Antilles, published prose and poetry in Dutch and, in its last issue, drama writing in Papiamentu. Without defending a specific poetic manifesto, it promoted prose and poetry writing in Dutch rather than in Papiamentu and attracted various up-and-coming writers, including Tip **Marugg** and Frank **Martinus** Arion.

AART G. BROEK

Antín, Manuel

b. 1926, Chaco, Argentina

Film-maker and writer

Before making his first film, Antín had already authored a considerable body of writing. *La cifra impar* (The Odd Number) (1962) was the first of a trilogy of films, completed by *Circe* (1964) and *Intimidad de los parques* (The Intimacy of Parks) (1965), based on Julio **Cortázar** short stories. He was influenced by the French New Wave, yet his staccato narratives, temporal shifts and dramatic visual compositions give his work a unique style. In the 1970s, he turned towards historical films and **gaucho** settings. He was director of the Instituto Nacional de Cinematografía (National Cinematographic Institute) from 1983 to 1989.

DIANA PALADINO

antipoetry

The term *antipoesía* (antipoetry) belongs to the Chilean poet Nicanor **Parra** – though it had been used before by earlier poets, some belonging to the Latin American avant-garde movements (see **avant-garde in Latin America**). Parra's *antipoesía* was defined above all in his poetic practice; and though critics may continue to argue over its precise meaning, two elements seem clear. First, the poetic subject – the voice of the poetry – is anti-heroic, insistent on the ordinariness of its experience ('Los vicios del mundo moderno' – The Vices of the Modern World, as one poem is entitled). Second, the language of the poetry eschews high rhetoric, elevated language and all elements of the sublime ('*nosotros conversamos/en el lenguaje de todos los días*' – we speak in everyday language). Clearly iconoclastic, many have assumed that the implied opposite, the poetry to Parra's antipoetry, was Pablo **Neruda**'s. Others have seen it as a precursor to the *poesía conversacional* (conversational

poetry) that dominated Latin American poetry of the 1960s and after.

MIKE GONZALEZ

Antología de la literatura fantástica

This polemical anthology was published in 1940 by Editorial Sudamericana. Edited by Jorge Luis **Borges**, Adolfo **Bioy Casares** and Silvina **Ocampo**, the anthology included an essay on the fantastic (see **fantastic literature**) by Bioy that made clear that the editors were arguing for the genre, but also attacking the **socialist realism** and *costumbrismo* traditions in Spanish American literature. Most of the selections were short stories translated from English (and some from German); among the few Spanish American texts included in the first edition (others were stories by **Lugones** and Peyrou) was one of Borges's first major *Ficciones*, the famous (and famously baffling) 'Tlön, Uqbar, Orbis Tertius', which appeared in the 1940 edition with a postscript dated 1947. The second edition of the anthology, published in 1965, included a significantly larger number of Spanish American texts, including **Bianco**'s great novella, *Sombras suele vestir* (Shadow Play) (1941), which had been written for the first edition but not finished in time for publication there, and stories by **Garro**, **Wilcock**, **Murena**, Ocampo and Bioy. The fact that there was much more to include was due to the influence of the anthology itself: **Cortázar**, in his essay on the fantastic, recognizes that it played a seminal role in the history of subsequent Spanish American fiction.

DANIEL BALDERSTON

Antoni, Robert

b. *c.*1955, Trinidad and Tobago

Writer

Antoni's successful first novel, *Divine Trace* (1991), won a Commonwealth Writers Prize for Best First Novel and is considered a landmark in Caribbean literature. *Blessed Is the Fruit*, his second novel, was published in 1997 to great acclaim. Senior editor of the literary journal *Conjunctions*, he is also associate director of the University of Miami's Caribbean Writers Summer Institute. He is currrently a professor at the same university, where he teaches fiction writing and **magical realism**. Antoni has lived most of his life in the Bahamas.

KEITH JARDIM

Antonin, Arnold

b. 1942, Port-au-Prince, Haiti

Film-maker

A pioneer of politically motivated cinema in Haiti in the 1970s, Antonin directed *Haiti, le chemin de la liberté* (Haiti, the Path to Freedom) (1975) a boldly anti-**Duvalier** film. In the same year he directed the documentary *Art naïf et repression en Haïti* (Naive Art and Repression in Haiti), which denounced the international pillage of Haiti's cultural heritage as well as the Duvalier dictatorship's self-serving promotion of the country's folkloric image. His *Un Tonton Macoute peut-il être poète?* (Can a **Tonton Macoute** be a Poet?) (1980) again presented the political situation as a barrier to cultural development.

CHARLES ARTHUR

Antropofagia

This cultural theory and movement was led by Brazilian Oswald de **Andrade** and dated from the publication of his *Manifesto Antropófago* (Cannibalist Manifesto) in the movement's journal, the *Revista de antropofagia*, in 1928. Four years previously, in his *Manifesto da Poesia Pau-brasil* (Brazil-Wood Poetry Manifesto), Andrade had proposed a flexible, dynamic model for Brazil's cultural development, illuminating the dialectic of forces, traditional and modern, indigenous and metropolitan, that had shaped the post-colonial condition. In part a response to the challenge of the crudely xenophobic nationalism of *verdeamarelismo* (Greenyellowism) in the intervening years, Andrade

now radicalized his earlier analysis by placing at its centre the very concept which had, in colonial discourse, most defined the Latin American 'Other' as primitive and barbaric: cannibalism.

Far from being the exclusive preserve of a peripheral, pre-modern culture, anthropophagy, argued Andrade, constituted 'The only law of the world. The masked expression of all individualisms, of all collectivisms. Of all religions. Of all peace treaties.' The cannibalist impulse to absorb 'the sacred enemy ... to transform him into a totem' was thus reclaimed as a subversive, revolutionary force immanent, not only in Brazil's history of anti-colonial struggle, but also in the metropolitan world's desire to escape its own internal contra-dictions: 'But it wasn't crusaders that came. They were fugitives from a civilization that we are eating'. The reappropriation and reinvention of **carnival** and Christianity (in the form of **Candomblé**) by black Brazilians were manifestations of the anthropophagous instinct to invert the relationship between coloniser and colonised by 'digesting' imported values and resynthesising them in an autonomous form: 'We were never cate-chized ... We gave birth to Christ in Bahia.' They therefore prefigured not only a national, but a universal revolution, echoing the world-historic act of patricide depicted in Freud's *Totem and Taboo*. Ritualistically consuming the patriarchal body-politic of Western civilization, its oppressive power would be neutralized and incorporated by the popular, indigenous and pre-industrial values of Andrade's matriarchal Utopia 'without complexes, without madness, without prostitutes and with-out penitentiaries'.

During the brief fourteen months of its ex-istence, the Cannibalist movement, and especially its journal, the *Revista de antropofagia*, provided an important pole of attraction for some of the most radically experimental artists of the decade, including Tarsila do **Amaral**, Carlos **Drummond de Andrade** and Raul Bopp. Mário de **Andrade**'s prose narrative, *Macu-naíma*, was acclaimed the cannibalist masterpiece and, although arguably more pessimistic in out-look, his work nevertheless shared a similar concern with the questions of acculturation, cultural **hybridity** and the subversive potential of so-called 'primitive' cultures. The potential repercussions of *antropofagia* were cut short by the reaction against avant-garde (see **avant-garde in Latin America**) experimentation from 1930 onwards. But Oswald de Andrade's ideas were 'rediscovered' in the mid-1960s by the Concretists and **Tropicalists**, who found their blend of nationalism and internationalism, their synthesis of the archaic and the modern, of 'high' and 'low' culture, a refreshing alternative to the mechanical populism and traditionalism that dominated contemporary cultural politics.

Further reading

Andrade, O. de (1991) ' "Cannibalist Manifesto" by Oswald de Andrade', trans. L. Bary in *Latin American Literary Review* 19(31): 35–47.
Helena, L. (1983) *Uma literatura antropofágica*, Fortaleza: Universidade Federal do Ceará.
Johnson, J.R. (1987) 'Tupy or not Tupy: Cannibalism and Nationalism in Contemporary Brazilian Literature and Culture' in J. King (ed.), *Modern Latin American Fiction: A Survey*, London: Faber & Faber, 41–59.

DAVID TREECE

Antunes, Arnaldo

b. 1960, São Paulo, Brazil

Musician and poet

Antunes is the founder of Os **Titãs** (The Titans), a seminal band of the 1980s which released seven highly acclaimed records fusing punk rock, heavy metal, funk, **reggae**, and Brazilian rhythms. After leaving the band in 1992, Antunes produced *Nome* (Name) a multi-media project featuring a sound recording, a book of poems, and a video which received several awards at international festivals. In 1995, he released his second solo recording entitled *Ninguém* (Nobody). Antunes has co-authored many songs with top Brazilian artists including Gilberto **Gil**, Marisa **Monte** and Jorge Benjor. Many of his poems and song lyrics evidence deep affinities with **concrete poetry**.

CHRISTOPHER DUNN

Antunes Filho

b. 1929, São Paulo, Brazil

Theatre director

One of the best-known directors of **experimental theatre** in Brazil, Filho (born José Antunes Filho) is justly celebrated for his bold work, mostly in São Paulo. Antunes's company, the Centro de Pesquisa Teatral (Centre for Theatrical Research), was launched with its spectacular production of **Macunaíma** in 1978, remembered for the shock of naked bodies on stage, for its brilliant choreography and for its ingenious adaptation of the Mário de **Andrade** novel. Antunes followed with adaptations of two Nelson **Rodrigues** plays (1982), a bold modern *Romeo and Juliet* (1984), *A hora e a vez de Augusto Matraga* (Augusto Matraga's Hour of Truth) (1986), based on the brilliant story by João Guimarães **Rosa**, and Luís Alberto Abreu's *Xica da Silva* (1986). Many of these productions have toured to festivals abroad, making Antunes's style widely known. Antunes has trained many of those currently prominent in Brazilian theatre including Cacá Rosset, Bia Lessa and Ulysses Cruz. His fluid style, almost choreographic in its concentration on bodies and movement, has been of decisive importance for contemporary Brazilian theatre.

DANIEL BALDERSTON

Antúnez, Nemesio

b. 1918, Santiago, Chile; d. 1993, Santiago

Painter and printmaker

Antúnez's style was always figurative, and his mastering of printmaking techniques made him the figurehead of an important tradition of high-quality printmaking in Chile. He first studied architecture in Santiago, completing his studies in New York. Between 1950 and 1953 he lived in Paris, and from 1961 to 1964 he was director of the Museo de Arte Contemporáneo of the Universidad de Chile. In the 1980s he directed the Taller 99 collective of artists in Santiago.

GABRIEL PEREZ-BARREIRO

Anunciación, La

Antonia **Eiriz**'s painting *La anunciación* (The Annunciation) is one of finest examples of Cuban expressionism. Created in 1963–4, this free inter-pretation of the Biblical theme synthesizes the artist's existential concerns about the human condition, terror and death. In the painting, the Archangel Gabriel is represented as a grotesque and aggressive figure, while the Virgin Mary appears as a humble seamstress. The work not only symbolizes the violence and horror of the human drama, it also becomes an exploration of the splits and divisions appearing at the time of its creation. It belongs to the collection of Havana's National Museum of Fine Art.

WILFREDO CANCIO ISLA

Apando, El

Photographed by Alex Phillips and scripted by José **Revueltas** and José **Agustín**, Felipe **Cazals**'s *El Apando* (Solitary) (1975) was based on Revueltas's novel of the same name, published while he was in prison for his participation in the 1968 student movement. The film tells the story of a group of common criminals who are brutalized when they try to smuggle drugs into **Lecumberri** prison. While not explicitly political, the plot has been linked to Revueltas's own prison experiences and the violent end of the 1968 movement. The film provoked public outcry over its representation of torture, which was in large part responsible for the closing of the prison.

EDITH NEGRÍN

Aparicio Montiel, Luis

b. 1934, Maracaibo, Venezuela

Baseball player

Aparicio began his career in professional baseball at the age of nineteen, playing for the Gavilanes club, in Maracaibo. His father, Luis Aparicio Ortega (1912–71), was an outstanding player, but Aparicio Junior surpassed his achievements. He made his début in the US Major Leagues in 1956, with the Chicago White Sox. No other Venezuelan player has had such success in the USA, where he played for eighteen seasons. He established a series of records, and is regarded as one of the best short stops in the history of the game. In 1984 he became the first Venezuelan to earn a place in the US Baseball Hall of Fame.

MARK DINNEEN

APRA

APRA (Alianza Popular Revolucionaria Ameri-cana (American Popular Revolutionary Alliance)) is a continental political movement against political and economic imperialism, founded by the exiled Peruvian Víctor Raúl **Haya de la Torre** in Mexico City in 1924. Its full programme was synthesized in five points: Latin American political unity, opposition to 'Yankee imperialism', nationa-lization of land and industries, internationalization of the Panama Canal and solidarity of all oppressed peoples. The aim was to organize a separate national party/branch in each Latin American country to apply Aprista doctrine in local circum-stances. By the late 1920s, the movement had branches in most Latin American countries and even in Paris and London.

In 1927, Haya severed the movement's links with communism, arguing that Marxism was too Eurocentric to be applicable in Latin America. APRA's ideology became increasingly middle class and the new Partido Aprista Peruano (Peruvian Aprista Party – PAP), founded in 1930, claimed to be a united front of manual and intellectual workers. After an Aprista revolt in northern Peru in 1932, the party was outlawed until 1945: it participated in elections under different names, but gained control of the Peruvian government in 1985. The first Aprista president was Alan **García**, who started an aggressive campaign to reduce the payment of foreign debt. Supported at first by Peruvian business elites, García was much criticized for his attempts to nationalize private banks. García also failed in his efforts to gain Latin American support for his fight against the International Monetary Fund. In 1990 APRA lost the elections, accused of bureaucracy and corruption.

After Alberto **Fujimori**'s election as president in 1990, APRA dramatically lost its political support in Peru. Between 1931 and 1990, however, it was the most significant political movement in Peru, creating a new kind of populist (see **populism**) and participatory political culture, a model for many reformist political movements in Latin America.

Further reading

Alexander, R. (1973) *Aprismo: The Ideas and Doctrines of Víctor Raúl Haya de la Torre*, Kent, OH: Kent State University Press.

Crabtree, J. (1992) *Peru Under García: An Opportunity Lost*, Pittsburgh: University of Pittsburgh Press.

Kantor, H. (1966) *The Ideology and Program of the Peruvian Aprista Movement*, Washington, DC: Savile Books.

Klaren, P. (1973) *Modernization, Dislocation and Aprismo: Origins of the Peruvian Aprista Party 1870–1932*, Austin, TX: University of Texas Press.

JUSSI PAKKASVIRTA

Apurímak

b. 1900, Abancay, Peru; d. 1985, Lima, Peru

Painter

Apurímak (real name Alejandro González Trujillo) studied at the Concha Academy in Lima (1914–17). In 1919 he entered the National School of Fine Arts (ENBA), where he studied with the painter Daniel Hernández and the Spanish sculptor Manuel Piqueras Cotoli. Piqueras particularly influenced the young painter with his concept of a 'neo-Peruvian style', combining elements of the pre-Hispanic tradition with features of Spanish art; this was in contrast to the dogmatic *indigenismo* which the painter José **Sabogal** sought to impose within the same institution.

Apurímak, who first signed his work Alexis before adopting his more enduring pseudonym, worked in his youth as a draughtsman at the Peruvian Museum of Archaeology together with the archaeologist Julio C. **Tello**, an experience which brought him into direct contact with pre-Hispanic art and influenced the orientation of his own work towards vernacular subjects. Between 1933 and 1936 he travelled widely in Peru, before going to France in 1937 where he was responsible for the decor of the Peruvian pavilion at the International Exhibition of Arts and Crafts in Paris. In 1939 he returned to Peru, becoming himself a professor at ENBA, where he taught from 1943 to 1967.

Apurímak's work passed through several different phases, as the painter himself acknowledged. His subjects were vernacular throughout, but he distanced himself from pictorial indigenism by incorporating Hispanic elements, following Piqueras's postulates; his stay in Paris also opened him to the influence of European avant-garde (see **avant-garde in Latin America**) currents like surrealism (see **surrealism in Latin American art**), post-impressionism, Cubism, fauvism, constructivism and abstraction. His work represents an attempt to go beyond a painting based solely on the external features of the landscapes and people of Peru to project the aesthetic values of the native tradition into universally applicable forms and resolutions. The result is a body of work that conserves the powerful presence of indigenous roots but subjects them to stylizations that reveal the painter's own aesthetic concerns.

Further reading

Lauer, M. (1976) *Introducción a la pintura peruana del siglo XX*, Lima: Mosca Azul.

CÉSAR SALAS

Aquino, María Pilar

b. 1956, Ixtlán del Río, Nayarit, Mexico

Theologian

Aquino is one of the most outspoken representatives of Latin American **feminist liberation theology**. Her doctoral dissertation from Salamanca, Spain, in 1991 was the first systematic analysis of feminist concerns within **liberation theology**. She is also a well-known representative of the Hispanic women's community in the USA. She is associate professor of theological and religious studies at the University of San Diego. Born a Catholic, she entered the Society of Helper Sisters at the age of eighteen, but has been a lay person since 1983. She is interested in an explicitly feminist Latin American liberation theology to serve the most marginalized people, as for example in her *Our Cry for Life: Feminist Theology from Latin America* (1993).

ELINA VUOLA

Araiz, Oscar

b. 1940, Punta Alta, Argentina

Ballet choreographer

Araiz is known particularly for his work with the Ballet Contemporáneo of the Teatro San Martín in Buenos Aires, one of the world's most famous modern-dance companies, which he directed from 1968–72 and from 1990–7. His avant-garde, eclectic style combines classical, contemporary and folkloric motifs, as witnessed in his tango-ballet renditions of such classical works as *Faust* or church cantatas. Most recently, he has been a kind of freelance choreographer, staging his works with companies throughout the world, particularly in Geneva, Paris and Rome. Outstanding among his dance creations are *La consagración de la primavera* (The Rite of Spring) (1970), *Adagietto* (1985), *Tango* (1981), *Stelle* (1989), *Numen* (Inspiration) (1991) and *Boquitas Pintadas* (Painted Lips), based on Manuel **Puig**'s novel of the same name.

EDUARDO GUÍZAR-ALVAREZ

Arango, Gonzalo

b. 1931, Andes, Colombia; d. 1976, Tocancipá, Colombia

Poet

Arango was the founder of the Colombian poetic movement *Nadaísmo*, whose anti-institutional aesthetics reflected **existentialist** influences as well as Arango's personal crisis of religious belief. In 1958, he published his first *Manifiesto nadaísta* (Nadaísta Manifesto); followed by another in 1962. His first poems appeared in two anthologies in 1963: *13 poetas nadaístas* and *De la Nada al Nadaísmo* (From Nothingness to Nadaísmo). Three more collections followed, including *Providencia* (Providence) (1972) and *Fuego en el altar* (Fire on the Altar) (1974). In his later years he distanced himself from his *nadaísta* colleagues, accusing them of a desperate nihilism.

MIGUEL A. CARDINALE

Arango, Luis Alfredo

b. 1935, Totonicapán, Guatemala

Writer

Poet, narrator, and founding member of *Nuevo Signo* (New Sign), he represented indigenous peoples realistically, and was one of the best writers of his generation (winning the **Asturias** literary prize in 1988). In Totonicapán, Arango was a rural school teacher who cultivated direct ties with oppressed Indian communities. He represented their experience and values in expressive poems and stories that exhibit a remarkable sense of humour and a balance between lyricism and epigrammatic wit. Among his books are *El amanecido: o cargando el arpa* (Up at Dawn or The Harp Corner), *Archivador de pueblos* (The People's Archivist), *Lola dormida* (Lola Asleep), *Después del tango vienen los moros* (After the Tango, the Moors) and *El volador* (The Flyer).

MARC ZIMMERMAN

Aranha, Oswaldo

b. 1894, Alegrete, Brazil; d. 1960, Rio de Janeiro

Diplomat

An important figure in national politics and the United Nations, Aranha trained as a lawyer in Paris, returning to Brazil after the First World War. In 1934 he was named Brazilian ambassador in Washington. In 1938 he returned to take up the post of Foreign Secretary. In 1947 he was head of the Brazilian delegation when Brazil occupied the presidency of the UN Security Council and later presided over the Special UN Assembly on Palestine. He became Economics Minister under **Vargas**, and in 1957 he headed the Brazilian delegation to the XII General Assembly.

ANTONIO CARLOS MARTINS VAZ

Arau Inchautegui, Alfonso

b. 1932, Mexico City

Film-maker and dancer

His feature film *Como agua para chocolate* (Like Water For Chocolate) (1991), based on the eponymous novel by his then wife Laura **Esquivel**, won him his international reputation. Arau began as a dancer with the Chapultepec Ballet. For eight years (1952–60) he worked with comedian Sergio Corona on the theatre circuit, then moved on to Cuban television (1959–64), presenting his comic-theatre programme *El show de Arau*. His first film, in 1968, was *El águila descalza* (Barefoot Eagle); six films followed, including *Mojado power* (Wetback Power) (1979) and *A Walk in the Clouds* (1994).

PATRICIA TORRES SAN MARTÍN

Araújo, Helena

b. 1934, Bogotá, Colombia

Writer

The daughter of a diplomat, Araújo spent her childhood and adolescence in Colombia and Brazil. During the late 1950s she established herself as a literary critic and journalist, contributing to the newsweekly *Semana* (Week) and other publications. In 1971 she moved to Lausanne, Switzerland, to serve as an academic, centring her research on Latin American women's writing. Her work includes short stories, a novel, *Fiesta en Teusaquillo* (A Party in Teusaquillo) (1981), and two books on literary criticism: *Signos y mensajes* (Signs and Messages), published in 1976, and *La Scherezada criolla* (The Native Scherezade), in 1989.

HÉCTOR D. FERNÁNDEZ L'HOESTE

Arbenz, Jacobo

b. 1913, Quetzalquetanango, Guatemala; d. 1971, Mexico City

Politician

In 1944, while a military officer, Arbenz participated in the overthrow of dictator Jorge **Ubico**, and became a member of the 'revolutionary triumvirate' which governed until the election of Juan José Arévalo in 1945. Arbenz himself became president in 1950, heading a progressive nationalist government whose social democratic orientation was seen by the United States as communistic. His 1952 land reform attacked the interests of the powerful United Fruit Company, which began actively plotting his overthrow. A **CIA**-backed invasion was launched from Honduras in May 1954, and in June Arbenz resigned and went into exile.

ARTURO ARIAS

Arca

Angel **Rama** convinced José Pedro Díaz and German Rama to establish the publishing house Arca in 1962 to make their work known in Uruguay. Arca's first book on President Batlle established its political orientation. Although publications increased from 1966 to 1968, Arca was restricted during the dictatorship. Alberto Oreggioni, editor-in-chief from 1967 to 1993, oversaw the publication of books in the areas of music, cinema, literature, politics and economics.

VICTORIA RUÉTALO

Arce de Vázquez, Margot

b. 1904, Caguas, Puerto Rico; d. 1990, Hato Rey, Puerto Rico

Critic

Margot Arce was instrumental in the creation and growth of modern literary criticism in Puerto Rico. She did a doctorate in Madrid, studying with Américo Castro and Tomás Navarro Tomás, and completing a dissertation on the Spanish Renaissance poet Garcilaso de la Vega, then returned to direct the department of Hispanic Studies at the University of Puerto Rico for a period of many years. Her critical work on the poetry of her friend Gabriela **Mistral** (1958) helped establish Mistral's work as worthy of serious study. Much of her criticism is focused on modern Puerto Rican writing, including studies of Tomás Blanco, Luis **Lloréns Torres** and Luis **Palés Matos**.

DANIEL BALDERSTON

Arce Leal, Manuel José

b. 1935, Guatemala City; d. 1985, Paris, France

Writer

One of the founders of the Moira poetry group and polemical journalist/poet, Arce wrote surrealist plays (see **surrealism in Latin American art**) attacking the consumerism of Guatemala's rising middle class and the 1960s extrajudicial executions. His urban, existentialist 'anti-poetry' revealed him to be a master of subjective lyricism. The Guatemalan crisis of his final years led to highly polemical poems (*Guatemala* (1982), published in Paris) and to a body of journalistic essays collected in *Diario de un escribiente* (A Scribe's Diary) (1988).

Exiled for his anti-military writings, yet dubbed the conscience of his country, Arce died of cancer.

MARC ZIMMERMAN

archaeology

Archaeology is the study of the material past, a past extending through historical time into a far less well known and far larger territory conventionally labelled the prehistoric. It is about creating narratives of the past which may include or exclude contemporary populations living within the geographic encompass of a given narrative. Archaeology is also about the universal human story and cultural processes which drive it – the conversion of itinerant gatherers and hunters into villagers, the emergence of agrarian economies, the birth of cities, kingdoms and empire. It is even about the construction of the individual. Gender, familial relations and political economy are all within the purview of modern archaeology. The urban civilizations of Mesoamerica, the Andes, and emerging knowledge since the 1980s about the complexity and density of the societies of pre-Hispanic Amazonia and Orinoqia play a central role in the global discourse on these issues. Less well known and understood regions, such as Isthmian Central America and Northern South America also play an increasingly important role.

From a modest inception in the sixteenth century, archaeology in Latin America concerned the native populations of the region and the status of their 'civilizations' from the point of view of colonial, later, *criollo* and national populations. In the twentieth century it has played an increasingly important role in the construction of national identity and histories, though its importance varies by region and ethnicity. Among Latin American Indian peoples, archaeological narratives of their histories have not been important historically. It is of primary importance to nations such as Mexico, Peru, Ecuador, and Bolivia, where national histories link directly to the pre-Hispanic civilizations of Mesoamerica and the Andes, but plays a different, less central role in the national imaginations of those Latin American countries which emphasize other aspects of the past and where the population has a less direct relationship to pre-Hispanic communities. In Brazil, Argentina, and Chile, where aboriginal populations were small and suffered catastrophic declines due to the introduction of Old World diseases, as was the case among the large riverine communities and towns of sixteenth-century Amazonia, or were devastated through nineteenth-century programmes of extermination, national archaeologies are more the study of the Indian 'other'.

Although places like Teotihuacán in Mexico, Cuzco in Peru, and Tikal in Guatemala play important roles in national imaginations, they play an equally important economic role as focal points of conventional and **ecotourism**. Many modern national archaeological programmes in Latin America are strongly focused on the conservation, reconstruction, and presentation of large pre-Hispanic sites to national and international audiences. Strong national archaeological programmes of pure research exist in several Latin American countries today, including Mexico and Peru; however, international archaeological research frequently plays a pivotal role in the exploration and interpretation of the archaeological heritage of Latin America. North American and, to a lesser extent, French, German, and Dutch archaeologists frequently dominate the field. Archaeology, which has a strong ecological component, has also made strong contributions to the study of human ecological systems since the 1970s, including detection and reconstructions of raised field systems in both lowland and highland Central and South American contexts. This research, especially research at the margin of Lake Titicaca, Bolivia, has some implications for future sustainable development.

Further reading

Arenas Vargas, I. (1995) 'The Perception of History and Archaeology in Latin America: A Theoretical Approach', in P.R. Schmidt and T.C. Patterson (eds) *Making Alternative Histories: the practice of archaeology and history in non-Western settings*, Santa Fe: School of American Research Press.

Oyuela-Cayecedo, A. (1994) *History of Latin American Archaeology*, Aldershot: Avebury.

Polotis, G. (1995) 'The Socio-Politics of the Development of Archaeology in Hispanic South America', in P.J. Ucko (ed.) *Theory in Archaeology: A World Perspective*, London: Routledge.

CHRISTOPHER VON NAGY

architecture in Latin America

The history of architecture in Latin America parallels the process of Latin America's insertion into the global system of nations; architecture can only be understood therefore in terms of its dialectical relationship with particularly complex Latin American societies. At the end of the 1920s, the intellectual elite of those countries adopted aspects of the then current European architectural ideas as a reaction against an outdated academic neo-Classicism. That academic style had taken its inspiration from the most dynamic of European nations, and was the expression of the ruling classes that emerged in the region in the nineteenth century after the collapse of Spanish colonialism. Academic neo-Classicism and eclecticism were an expression of Latin America's subordination to the rising capitalist powers of Europe. By 1930, however, they seemed sterile and empty styles, particularly to the observers of the great transformations in art and architecture that were taking place in the wake of the First World War.

With varying degrees of success, the architectural developments of the early years of the century in Europe, particularly those that had occurred under the aegis of functionalism or the **International Style**, were then applied in the Latin American context. (In Argentina, the articulation of academic eclecticism and the new style was realized through art deco, whose principal representative was Alejandro Virasoro.) Rationalism brought together ideas of democracy, social equality, creative freedom and confidence in science in a rationalistic construction project and a functional concept of design. It was not just formal changes that were proposed, but an entirely new concept of living space that paralleled a new conception of society itself. A key representative of one such current, Le Corbusier exercised a considerable influence on modern architecture and town planning in Latin America. His tour of Latin America in 1929 produced pilot plans for the cities of Buenos Aires, Montevideo, São Paulo and Río de Janeiro.

In Argentina it was Alberto **Prebisch** who first embarked on the systematic dissemination of rational ideas in architecture through the pages of the journal *Martín Fierro*, and in exemplary works like the Gran Rex cinema (1937). Other representatives of the new rationalist currents included Antonio U. **Vilar** (designer of the Hindú Club), Bartolomé M. Repetto and León Dourge; the architectural partnership of Sánchez, Lagos and de la Torre (the Kavanagh Building); Joselevich and Douillet (Comega building). The German influence (of Gropius and Hans Scharoun) is also visible in this period.

In Brazil, Gregori **Warchavchik** was the principal representative of the rationalist tendency; his 1925 *Manifesto of Functional Architecture* held clearly to Le Corbusier's positions, particularly to his concept of 'the machine for living'. At almost exactly the same time, in Mexico, the group around Luis Villagrán announced their adherence to the same principles. Unlike the Brazilians, however, the Mexican avant-garde architects rejected aesthetic concerns, deeming them antisocial. In a country which had just lived through a revolution, architects like Juan **O'Gorman** (designer of the Diego **Rivera** house) and Juan Legorreta had learned their craft in a struggle with ornamental academicism, expression of the social privilege that characterised the regime of Porfirio Díaz. The work of these architects therefore took on a severity that was closer to the work of Hannes Meyer and the Russian Constructivists. Other important figures in the Mexican architectural movement of the time included José Arnal, Enrique de la Mora y Palomar, José Creixell, Enrique Yáñez and Pedro Bustamante.

In Uruguay, Julio **Vilamajó**, with his deep understanding of landscape and context, had a considerable influence on the innovative generation of Uruguayan and Argentine architects that followed him. Adherents of rationalism in Uruguay included Mauricio Cravotto, Alberto Muñoz del Campo, Juan Aubriot and Ricardo Valabrega.

A cultural import, the Latin American functionalism and rationalism of the 1930s found support only among the progressive intelligentsia – it was firmly rejected by the majority of the bourgeoisie. The result was that, in this new context, rationalism was emptied of content by a bourgeois class that refused to accept aesthetic, political or social preferences that flew in the face of the traditional ways of life; instead it became just one more eclectic style. The acritical siting of these forms in any and every context, however, produced a glaring contradiction with the basic concepts of functionalism.

In Argentina, a critical revision of primitive rationalism was expressed in the *Voluntad y acción* (Will and Action) manifesto of 1939, published by the Austral group that included Antonio Bonet, Jorge Ferrari Hardoy and Juan Kurchan. The Austral Group proposed an architecture based on the foundations suggested by Le Corbusier but made regional and national in both a social, economic and technical sense and taking into account climate and landscape. The work of Amancio **Williams** (the Bridge house at Mar del Plata), Eduardo Sacriste, Jorge Vivanco, Horacio Caminos, Eduardo Catalano and the theoretical work of Wladimiro **Acosta** belong within the same current of thought.

In Brazil, the new direction was manifest in Río de Janeiro's **Ministério da Educacão e Saúde** building (1938–43). The project, by Oscar **Niemeyer** and Lúcio **Costa**, enjoyed Le Corbusier's collaboration. In this building, Le Corbusier's ideas are merged with regionalist elements. Other architects, too, made their contribution to a Brazilian architecture that would become world famous – they included Roberto Burle **Marx**, Rino Levi, Eduardo Affonso Reidy, Milton **Roberto** and Henrique **Mindlin**.

In the 1940s, several Latin American governments invested architectural works with a social significance; the state, as mediator between the dominant economic interests and the new emerging classes, promoted cooperation between a professional elite and various state institutions. In a period of industrialization, several states sponsored public works like the construction of housing complexes. In Argentina, the government of **Perón** incorporated into its buildings both modern architectural concepts and a pragmatic search for a form of expression at once official and popular.

The result was a series of rationalist and post-rationalist buildings: blocks of apartments, Eduardo Sacriste's Tucumán hospital (1948), Mario Roberto Alvarez's Teatro Municipal San Martín in Buenos Aires (1953), as well as academic and folkloric works.

In Brazil, from the beginning of Getulio **Vargas**'s **Estado Novo**, the government elected to develop the new architecture initiated with the Ministry of Education Building. This architecture became the image of a particular kind of populism whose spectacular culmination was the construction of **Brasília**. Designed by Lucio Costa as the seat of government during the presidency of Juscelino **Kubitschek** (1956–61), Brasília also exposes some of the limitations of certain interpretations of rationalist principles. It fails to offer an integrated, participatory experience because there are insufficient spaces devoted to social interaction. The city, conceived as the highest expression of Latin American democratic planning, proved in the end, despite Niemeyer's intentions and his outstanding buildings, to be an empty monument that could be used equally in any political context.

This was also the moment of the great Venezuelan housing projects like the 23 de enero, El Paraíso and Cerro Piloto complexes (1955–7) in Caracas, built under the direction of Carlos Raúl **Villanueva**, architect of the El Silencio complex and square (1941). These huge complexes, designed around superblocks, were the response of the Venezuelan government – whose principal task had been the administration of the income from the exploitation of local oil by foreign companies – to a growing public demand, and it was also an expression of an architectural populism. Caracas's **Ciudad Universitaria** (University City) dates from the same period; designed by Villanueva, it is a spectacular example of a combination of vernacular elements with elements of the international style, high technology structures and works of art by international celebrities like Alexander Calder, Fernand Léger, Victor Vasarely, Mateo Manaure, Hans Arp and Henri Laurens.

Mexico City's University City at **UNAM** also set out to achieve an integration of art and architecture; in this case, the formal and technical elements of an architecture based on rationalism are amalgamated in monumental form with an artistic 'Mexicanism' inspired by the attempts by the Muralists (see **muralism**) to recreate the pre-Columbian past. Outstanding in the complex is the Library building (1953) by Juan O'Gorman, Gustavo Saavedra and Juan Martínez de Velazco.

The late 1950s and early 1960s brought a change of direction in Latin American architecture; it could be seen as the second phase of a questioning of the principles of modern architecture which began in the 1930s, and as a search for new architectural models. In Argentina the anti-rationalist 'white house' movement offered a drastic critique of functionalist concepts. This reaction coincided with a new direction on the international level expressed in Nordic neo-empiricism, British 'new brutalism' and the new direction in Le Corbusier's work expressed in the chapel at Ronchamps (1950–4). To a degree romantic, the 'white houses' took their inspiration from Frank Lloyd Wright's organic theories as well as Le Corbusier's new thinking and a reinterpretation of elements of Argentine colonial architecture. This movement included Claudio Caveri, Eduardo Ellis, Miguel Ascensio and Rafael E.J. Iglesia. A different example, but one that also demonstrates the change in attitudes, was the headquarters of the **Banco de Londres** in Buenos Aires (1960–6) designed by Clorindo **Testa**, Sánchez Elia (see **SEPRA**), Peralta Ramos and Agostini. This building, made possible by a highly original and sculptural structure, presents a new conception of interior space in its relation to external spaces, particularly the street. The movement of renewal in the 1960s also embraced Juan Manuel Borthagaray, Horacio Baliero, Justo Solsona, Javier Sánchez Gómez and Francisco **Bullrich**.

In Colombia, Rogelio **Salmona** proposed a new vision of social housing in the Marulandia housing complex (1965) in Bogotá, designed together with Hernán Vieco. Based on a stepped design with a profound sense of landscape, this complex, conceived for families with middle to high incomes, used bricks on a massive scale.

In Uruguay, Nelson Bayardo brought together the 'brutalist' Le Corbusier, Vilamajó's Uruguayan tradition and **Torres García**'s constructivism. Mario **Paysée Reyes**, also a Uruguayan, worked in the same direction, while in Mexico Luis

Barragán, together with a team of younger professionals, developed forms elaborating the local and the popular. In Chile, Le Corbusier's new direction, interacting with landscape and regional elements, produced a synthesis of the highest quality. Two works are outstanding in this regard; the UN building near Santiago (1966), designed by Emilio **Duhart**, and the church of the Benedictine Monastery at Las Condes (1965), designed by Brothers Martin and Gabriel.

In Brazil it was Joaquim Guedes who marked a new direction that departed from the work of the previous generation of Niemeyer, Reidy and others – he too adopted a 'new brutalism' close to Le Corbusier's new thinking. What is most notable about Guedes's buildings is their crudeness of form, their anti-aesthetic and anti-academic attitude – in a word, their primary concern with the economic realities of building. That same concern led two Latin American engineers to produce works of great originality and technological innovation. Eladio **Dieste** in Uruguay produced a redefinition of the use of brick, while Félix **Candela** in Mexico approached reinforced concrete as a continuous organism rather than an object of abstract analysis.

The structural limitations on the models of development employed in Latin America exposed how restricted were the resources that governments could deploy for social programmes – indeed such resources seemed to be on the verge of disappearing altogether. If the policy of **import substitution industrialization** and urban growth were promoted by some governments from 1940 through 1970, it was the private sector which from the 1960s onwards became the principal engine of construction. This sector was not concerned with social housing, of course, with the accompanying proliferation of loss-making housing schemes for the very poor. Architectural renewal now took place as a result of individual and often unconnected experiments. Cuba was untypical in this respect, since the 1959 revolution was followed by a period of euphoria in both design and building which produced a range of expressions, from formal experimentation and the search for a specific identity to housing complexes which pragmatically redefined the rationalist project. Examples of the former are the Escuelas de Artes Plásticas and the Escuela de Danza Moderna

(Schools of Art and Modern Dance) (1963–5) by Ricardo Porro and the Escuela de Ballet and the Escuela de Música (Ballet and Music Schools) (1963–4) by Vittorio Garatti, all in Havana. The second current is represented by the J.A. Echeverría University Residences (1964–5) by José Fernández and associates, in Havana, and the Manicaragua housing project in Las Villas (1964) by Fernando Salinas.

From 1970 onwards, Latin American architecture showed several faces; the various US and European 'postmodernisms', so-called 'deconstructionism', 'high tech' and a variety of 'neo-'s have all had their impact in the region. Yet this diversity has also opened new possibilities for regional and national expression. In Argentina, Clorindo Testa with his highly original designs has redefined the landscape and locations of the city (the **Centro Cultural Recoleta** is an example), as has Miguel Angel **Roca**, who has worked extensively on the reformulation and recuperation of public spaces in the city ('Intervenciones' in Córdoba, Community Centres etc.). On the other hand the Manteola, Sánchez Gómez, Santos y Solsona architectural group have redefined the modernist tradition through their great spatial inventiveness (ATC and Fate buildings).

In Brazil the sculptural works of Éolo **Maia**, Jo **Vasconcellos** and Sylvio de Podestá have entered a dialogue with the redefined rationalism of Luis Paulo Conde; while in Chile, De Groote, Martinho and Browne have alternated the recuperation of certain avant-garde forms from the modern movement (constructivism, expressionism) with works structured around a perception of the surrounding landscape. In Colombia, Rogelio Salmona has worked on the syncretic re-elaboration of Maya architectural spaces, of colonial (and including Islamic) architecture, and of the modern, using geography and vegetation as structuring elements – as in the Guest House for Illustrious Visitors in Cartagena (1982). In Mexico there is a range of examples of the hybridization of different architectural styles, for example in the work of the Grupo de Diseño Urbano (Urban Design Group), Ricardo **Legorreta**, Abraham **Zabludovsky**, Teodoro **González de León**, Francisco Serrano, Aurelio Nuño and Javier Sordo Madaleno.

One effect of capitalist globalization and the internationalization of production is deterritorialization and an unprecedented penetration of local cultures by global capitalist culture. While an insistence on the local could become a reactionary celebration of pre-modern forms of exploitation on the one hand, on the other a critical appropriation of the local and some forms of syncretism may also create a new site of resistance.

Further reading

Browne, E. (1988) *Otra arquitectura en América Latina*, Mexico City: Gustavo Gili.

Fernandez Cox, C. and Toca Fernández, A. (1998) *América Latina: nueva arquitectura. Una modernidad posracionalista*, Mexico City: Gustavo Gili.

López Rangel, R. and Segre, R. (1986) *Tendencias arquitectónicas y caos urbano en América Latina*, Mexico City: Gustavo Gili.

Ramos de Dios, J. (1991) *El sistema del Art Déco: centro y periferia. Un caso de apropiación en la arquitectura latinoamericana*, Santa Fé de Bogotá: Escala.

Roca, M.A. (1995) *The Architecture of Latin America*, London: Academy.

Segre, R. (ed.) (1981) *Latin America in its Architecture*, New York and London: Holmes and Meier.

Segre, R. (1991) *América Latina. Fim de Milénio*, São Paulo: Nobel.

GUILLERMO GREGORIO

Archivos

The 'Archivos' collection is the product of a multilateral agreement between various academic organizations in Argentina, Brazil, Colombia, Spain, France, Italy, Mexico and Portugal. Directed by Amos Segala, Archivos began publishing its collection of the most representative literary works of Latin America and the Caribbean in 1984 brought together under the umbrella of **UNESCO**. It is a collection of critical, analytical editions, including the text with its variants, followed by studies of the context in which it was produced, of the reception of the work, as well as supporting documents and interpretative writings. The object of the enterprise is to associate genetic criticism

with the other current critical currents, thus providing exhaustive reference editions.

JULIO PREMAT

Arciniegas, Germán

b. 1900, Bogotá, Colombia; d. 1999, Bogotá

Essayist and historian

For his conspicous cultural contribution, Arciniegas has been called Universal Colombian. In addition, in 1989, the **Americas Society** awarded him the title Man of the Americas. A member of Los Nuevos, a group of Colombian intellectuals who were born in the first decades of this century, he advocated the modernization and sociopolitical advancement of his country. Arciniegas earned a degree in Law, and while a university student, he founded the Federación de Estudiantes de Colombia (Colombian Students Federation). As a student leader, he advocated academic freedom in the classroom and educational reform. When elected a representative in the Congress, he proposed a bill to reform the university system (see **higher education**). In 1928, he was named director of the editorial section of the newspaper *El **Tiempo***, for which he wrote a column for some seventy years (his newspaper articles are estimated to total some 15,000).

Arciniegas started his diplomatic career as vice consul in London (1929). He was also Colombian ambassador to Italy, Israel, Venezuela, and the Vatican City. Arciniegas was elected to the Congress several times, and was twice minister of education. He was a professor in Colombia and several US universities. At the Universidad de los Andes, in Bogotá, Arciniegas for several years directed the Cátedra de las Américas course in which he invited distinguished thinkers of the Americas and Europe to lecture. He was instrumental in the founding and leadership of the Latin American branch of the Congress for Cultural Freedom.

Arciniegas's thought is found in numerous articles and essays. He took a strong interest in studying the peoples and cultures of the Americas with an emphasis on the sociocultural interelationships among the American, the European, and the

African worlds. Arciniegas viewed the New World in a dynamic and progressive way that he thought created favourable conditons for freedom and democracy. In contrast, the rise of dictatorships in Latin America has been one of his major concerns. *Entre la libertad y el miedo* (The state of Latin America) (1952) discusses the historic background that made possible the rise of dictators like **Perón** and Odría. Other works include: *El estudiante de la mesa redonda* (The Student of the Round Table) (1932), *América, tierra firme* (America, Terra Firma) (1937), *Biografía del Caribe* (Biography of the Caribbean) (1945), *Colombia, itinerario de la Independencia* (Colombia, the Road to Independence) (1969), *América en Europa* (America in Europe) (1975), and *Bolívar y la Revolución* (Bolivar and the Revolution) (1984). His works for an English-speaking audience include an anthology of excerpts of Latin American classics, *The Green Continent* (1944); in the introduction Arciniegas argued: 'It is not in the light of the present but of the future that the importance of the Latin-American nations must be evaluated.'

The obituary for Arciniegas in *El tiempo* asks: 'What was Arciniegas: A politician? A diligent polemicist? A historian? A journalist? The discoverer of a literary continent?' It answered by saying that he was all of these and more.

Further reading

Arciniegas, G. (1990) *Tierra firme y otros ensayos*, Caracas: Biblioteca Ayacucho.

Cobo-Borda, J.G. (1990) *Germán Arciniegas: 90 años escribiendo: un intento de bibliografía*, Bogotá: Universidad Central/Instituto Colombiano de Estudios Latinoamericanos y del Caribe.

Cobo-Borda, J.G. (ed.) (1990) *Una visión de América: La obra de Germán Arciniegas*, Bogotá: Instituto Caro y Cuervo.

MIGUEL A. CARDINALE

Ardao, Arturo

b. 1912, Lavalleja, Uruguay

Historian

One of Latin America's most important historians

of ideas, Ardao was a university lecturer in Uruguay and in Caracas, Venezuela while in exile. Returning to Uruguay he continued his historical work, developing in particular his central notion of the Latin American historical subject in search of emancipation. His work includes important studies of Carlos **Vaz Ferreira**, Andrés Bello and José Enrique Rodó as well as *Génesis de la idea y el nombre de América Latina* (Genesis of the Idea and the Name of Latin America) (1980) and *La inteligencia latinoamericana* (The Latin American Intelligentsia) (1987).

CLARA ALICIA JALIF DE BERTRANOU

Arden Quin, Carmelo

b. 1913, Rivera, Uruguay

Painter, sculptor and poet

The early life and training of Arden Quin (real name Carmelo Heriberto Alves) is the source of much debate. At some point in the late 1930s or early 1940s he moved first to Montevideo and then to Buenos Aires. In 1944, already using the name Carmelo Arden Quin, he was, with Edgar **Bayley**, **Gyula Kosice** and Rhod Rothfuss, one of the co-editors of the single-issue magazine *Arturo*, to which he contributed a poem and a theoretical text. His first reliably documented visual works date from this period. Following the publication of *Arturo* he was involved in a number of exhibitions and events grouped under the general term of 'Arte Concreto-Invención'. In August 1946 he co-founded the movement **Arte Madí** in Buenos Aires with Kosice and Rothfuss. His early paintings use the 'structured frame' device proposed by Rothfuss in *Arturo* and show a stylistic debt to the Uruguayan Constructivist Joaquín **Torres García**, as well as an interest in primitive art. His early writings show a strong commitment to orthodox Marxist politics, despite the opposition of the Communist Party to abstract art. By 1947 Arden Quin had split from Kosice and Rothfuss and set up an alternative Madí group with his colleague Martín Blaszko. By this stage, his more radical political views were tempered by a more poetic and humorous style. In 1948 he moved to Paris, making it his permanent home. In Paris he led a French Madí group which participated in the Salon des Réalités Nouvelles through the late 1940s and early 1950s. In 1955 he returned briefly to Buenos Aires, where he played a central role in founding an association of abstract art called Arte Nuevo. In the 1960s, Arden Quin was involved in the **concrete poetry** movement and published a magazine called *Ailleurs*. In the 1990s, Arden Quin led a revival of Madí art in Europe, based in Paris.

Further reading

De Maistre, A. (1996) *Arden Quin*, Nice: Editions Demaistre.
Madí Internacional: 50 años después (1996) Zaragoza: Centro de Exposiciones y Congresos.

GABRIEL PEREZ-BARREIRO

Ardevol, Jose

b. 1911, Barcelona, Spain

Composer and conductor

Ardevol is the author of more than one hundred works, from symphonies to concertos, as well as a historical study of Cuban music, published in 1969. He took Cuban nationality in 1930. His first teacher was his father, Fernando Ardevol. In 1934 he founded the Orquesta de Cámara de La Habana (Havana Chamber Orchestra) which he directed for eighteen years. From 1938 he was professor of composition at Havana's Municipal Conservatory and leader of the Grupo de Renovación Musical, formed in 1942. In the 1970s and 1980s he headed the musical sections of the Consejo Nacional de Cultura (National Cultural Council) and the **UNEAC** (Cuban Union of Artists and Writers).

JOSÉ ANTONIO EVORA

ARENA

ARENA (Alianza Republicana Nacionalista, Nationalist Republican Alliance) is an ultra right-wing political party in El Salvador founded on 29 September 1981 by Roberto **D'Abuisson**, a former member of the Salvadoran army. ARENA's presence began to be felt after the 1982 legislative elections, but it was not until the 1988 legislative elections that ARENA won a majority in the legislature. Due to D'Abuisson's alleged connections to death squad activity (see **death squads**), he was never elected president. On 19 March 1989, however, ARENA's candidate Alfredo Cristiani was elected president while D'Abuisson remained the head of the party. The subsequent Salvadoran President Armando Calderón-Sol was also a member of ARENA.

BEATRIZ CORTEZ

Arena Theatre Group

Established in São Paulo in 1953, the Arena Theatre Group spurred on national dramaturgy and *engagé* theatre of social protest. Founded by José Renato and his colleagues from the *Escola de Arte Dramática*, Arena utilized an open theatre-in-the-round well-suited to low budget companies. In 1958, following a series of unremarkable productions, Arena staged Gianfrancesco **Guarnieri**'s extraordinarily successful *Eles não usam black-tie* (They Don't Wear Black-tie) which portrayed the existential, social, and political dilemmas of urban workers during a strike (see **strikes**). Following the right-wing military *coup* of 1964, Arena staged a series of protest musicals, most notably *Arena conta Zumbi* (Arena Tells the Story of Zumbi), directed by Augusto **Boal** about **Zumbi dos Palmares**.

CHRISTOPHER DUNN

Arenas, Reinaldo

b. 1943, Holguín, Cuba; d. 1990, New York City

Writer

The international success of Arenas's memoir *Antes que anochezca* (Before Night Falls) (1993) has renewed interest in the work of one of the most polemical Cubans of recent times. Until his death from **AIDS**, Arenas wrote novels, short stories, poems and essays. Among his narrative works, the best known are *Celestino antes del alba* (Singing from the Well) (1967), *El mundo alucinante. Una novela de aventuras* (The Ill-Fated Peregrinations of Fray Servando) (1967), *Otra vez el mar* (Once Again the Sea) (1982), and the story collections *Con los ojos cerrados* (With Closed Eyes) (1972) and *Termina el desfile* (The Parade's Over) (1981). Most of his essays, and his long poem *El central* (The Sugar Mill) (1981) document the repressive conditions under which Arenas lived in Cuba. As part of the first post-revolutionary generation, Arenas was always a contentious political liability for the regime and was tireless and unyielding in his dissidence to Fidel **Castro**.

Born in the provinces into a poor family, Arenas joined the Rebel army in 1958. He lived in Havana from 1962, where he also dedicated himself to writing. He was the finalist in the Cirilo Villaverde prize in narrative in 1965, but began to have problems with the government in 1973, in part due to his homosexuality but mostly because Arenas responded to Cuban censorship by sending his manuscripts abroad for publication. He was imprisoned in El Morro for a time, and lived in a general state of poverty and disaffection until he left Cuba clandestinely through the Mariel boatlift in 1980. His major work completed in exile was the *Pentagonía* (1967–91) – a sequence of five novels which give an account of the personal and political struggles of Cubans during the Republic and after the Revolution – *Cantando en el pozo* (Singing from the Well) (1967), *El palacio de las blanquísimas mofetas* (The Palace of the White Skunks) (1980), *Otra vez el mar* (Farewell to the Sea) (1982), *El color del verano* (The Colour of the Summer) (1991), and *El asalto* (The Assault) (1991). Arenas was a tireless innovator, like many Latin American writers in the 1960s, but his sense of experimentation went beyond the much-touted **magical realism**. Like Virgilio **Piñera**, he created a sense of the absurd that does not conceal its roots in a certain kind of despair. It is for the particular tone of anger guided by furies that Arenas will be remembered, both in Cuba and abroad, as well as for his ability to represent a defiant subjectivity besieged by networks of power.

Further reading

Exte, O. (ed.) (1992) *La escritura de la memoria*, Frankfurt: Vervuet Verlag.

Hernández-Miyares, J. and Rozencvaig, P. (eds) (1990) *Reinaldo Arenas: alucinaciones, fantasías y realidad*, Glenview, IL: Scott Foresman Montesinos.

Lugo Nayario, F. (1995) *La alucinación y los recursos literarios en las novelas de Reinaldo Arenas*, Miami: Universal.

Sánchez, R. (ed.) (1994) *Reinaldo Arenas: recuerdo y presencia*, Miami: Universal.

Soto, F. (1990) *Conversación con Reinaldo Arenas*, Madrid: Betania.

—— (1994) *Reinaldo Arenas: The 'Pentagonía'*, Gainesville, FL: University Presses of Florida.

Valero, R. (1991) *El desamparado humor de Reinaldo Arenas*, Miami: Iberian Studies Institute, University of Miami.

JOSÉ QUIROGA

Aretz de Ramón y Rivera, Isabel

b. 1913, Buenos Aires, Argentina

Musicologist

A prominent figure in Latin American musicology, Aretz studied piano and composition at the National Conservatory in Buenos Aires, instrumentation with **Villa-Lobos** and ethnomusicology with Carlos Vega, obtaining her doctorate in Musicology in Buenos Aires in 1967. She taught ethnomusicology at the Argentine School of Dance before moving to Caracas, Venezuela in 1952, where she directed the Inter-American Institute of Ethnomusicology and Folklore. She has published widely and researched the music of at least twelve countries. As a composer, her work combines elements of traditional Latin American music with modern compositional techniques.

ALFONSO PADILLA

Arévalo Martínez, Rafael

b. 1884, Guatemala City; d. 1975,
   Guatemala City

Writer

A major *modernista* (see **modernismo, Spanish
American**) poet and fiction writer, Arévalo is best
known for his psychological novels and 'psycho-
zoological tales', which caricature national figures
by mixing human and animal traits; the most
famous is 'El hombre que parecía un caballo' (The
Man Who Looked Like a Horse) about Arévalo's
friendship with Porfirio **Barba-Jacob**. His two
1914 autobiographical novels, *Una vida* (A Life) and
Manuel Aldano, highlighted the central themes of
twentieth-century Guatemalan literature: the Indian and imperialism. Arévalo's later work explores
the impact of national dictatorships – for example,
his 1939 chronicle-biography of Estrada Cabrera,
¡Ecce Pericles! (1945), and his novels *Hondura* (1947)
and *Ubico* (published posthumously in 1984).

MARC ZIMMERMAN

Argentina

Argentina is located on the Atlantic side of
southern South America. Its land mass is almost
one third of the size of Europe, extending 3,460
kilometres from north to south. Its distinct
geographical areas include the Andean region in
the west, the marshy plains of the northeast, the
rich grassland *pampas* (see **pampa**) in the heart of
the country, and the more isolated areas of
Patagonia in the south. Its population of
32,608,560 (1991 census) was 85 per cent urba-
nised and 96 per cent literate. One third of its
inhabitants live in the capital and port city of
Buenos Aires and its surrounding areas (Greater
Buenos Aires); other cities of over 500,000
inhabitants include Córdoba, Rosario, Mendoza,
La Plata, San Miguel de Tucumán and Mar del
Plata. All road and rail networks converge on the
capital. The language is Spanish with some traces
of indigenous languages in the north. Its population is mainly of recent European descent, through
mass immigration at the end of the nineteenth

century and early in the twentieth century; only 1
per cent of the population is indigenous, with small
groups of Asian and Middle Eastern origin.

Modern Argentine culture reflects this literate,
urbanized, relatively prosperous society. Since the
turn of the twentieth century a complex and
vibrant cultural field has developed, centred, like
the export economy that provided the wealth of the
nation from the late nineteenth century, on the city
of Buenos Aires. The current city is a mixture of
styles, with some colonial buildings, solid tene-
ments or conventillos that housed the turn of the
last century immigrants around the dockland area,
a few blocks from the lavish French-style town
houses of the aristocracy. The boulevards are now
traversed by a major highway, the **Avenida 9 de
Julio**, high-rise buildings abound, and the city
spreads into ever growing suburbs fringed by
shanty towns (see **shanty towns and slums**)
that house, in the main, migrants from the interior
(with some immigrants from Bolivia and Paraguay). The elegant shops and bars and *galerías* of
downtown **Florida**, the hub of intellectual and
creative life for many years, are now gradually
being replaced by shopping malls, the postmodern
site of consumer culture (see **postmodernism**).
Certain buildings and spaces have a significant
cultural charge: the obelisk designed by Alberto
Prebisch in the 1930s; the **Recoleta** cemetery
where the rich have their elaborate graves and
monuments, now fringed by art centres and some
of the finest cafés and restaurants in the city; and
the Casa Rosada, the government building, opening on to the **Plaza de Mayo**, the site of many
remarkable demonstrations, both big and small,
from the millions crowding to hear speeches from
the balcony, to the **Madres de Plaza de Mayo**,
silently protesting the disappearance (see **disappeared, the**) of their children under the military
dictatorship of 1976–83, the **Proceso**, to the
popular celebrations in support of the military
adventure of the **Malvinas** War.

Argentine history from 1943 on is dominated by
the figure of Juan Domingo **Perón** who, with his
wives Evita (see **Perón, María Eva Duarte de**)
and Isabelita, invented a powerful but ambiguous
form of populism. Alain Rouquié has argued that
Argentine politics is not explained as a conflict
between the military (see **military cultures**) and

the civilian politicians but as one of a conflict between intransigent political parties, particularly the Partido Justicialista (see **Peronism**) and the **Unión Cívica Radical**, in which the military is brought into politics by the disaffected. One of the key destabilizing elements in modern Argentina have been periodic bouts of hyperinflation (see **inflation and hyperinflation**) and capital flight, which wreck the import-substitution and export economies. Key moments of fracture in the political history of the country have been 1943–44 (the rise of Perón), 1955 (the 'Revolución Libertadora' or Liberating Revolution against Perón), 1969 (the **Cordobazo**), 1976 (the military *coup* of the Proceso), and 1989 (the hyperinflation cycles which led to the early resignation of Alfonsín and the presidency of **Menem**).

Though officially a Roman Catholic country until fairly recently (when Menem, from a Muslim family though nominally Catholic himself, had the clause removed from the Constitution), Argentina has the most important Jewish (see **Judaism**) community in Latin America (though there are powerful anti-Semitic forces behind several bombings, notably that of the Jewish centre **AMIA**), and, with Caracas and a few spots in the English-speaking Caribbean, is an important centre for **Islam** in the continent. The Catholic hierarchy, mostly very conservative, has been important in politics and society throughout the twentieth century, though **liberation theology** animated the Catholic left groups that formed the **Montoneros**. More recent conflicts around morals and individual rights have focused on feminist (see **feminism**) demands for abortion rights and legal equality, and vocal movements for gay and lesbian rights and the rights of transsexuals (see **gay and lesbian movements**).

In the social sciences, Argentina has produced important figures like Eliseo **Verón**, and Ernesto **Laclau** in political theory, historians like Tulio **Halperin Donghi**, and economists like Raúl **Prebisch** and Torcuato di Tella. **Psychology** was dominated earlier in the century by José **Ingenieros** and Enrique Pichon Riviere. Since the 1960s, Argentina has become a powerful centre of psychoanalytic practice and theory, in particular the Lacanian school, led by Oscar **Masotta** and Germán **García**. In the sciences (see **science**),

Argentines like **Leloir** and **Houssay** have been internationally prominent, though funding has not kept up with other countries, producing a **brain drain** of Argentine scientists.

The avant-garde literary groups of both the 1920s and the 1960s shared a fascination with the sprawling modernity of the city and were acutely aware that Argentina was not an autarchic space but rather a meeting place of cultures from all over the world, in particular from Europe, that could be mixed and fashioned in distinctive ways. This 'bridge between cultures' was the project of Argentina's most famous and influential literary magazine *Sur*. There has been constant renewal and development in Argentine literature; the poets of the 1920s railed against the influence of *modernismo* (see ***modernismo*, Spanish American**), while the revolutionary fictions of Jorge Luis **Borges**, Adolfo **Bioy Casares** and Silvina **Ocampo** in the 1940s overturned the flat realism of a Manuel **Gálvez**; and Julio **Cortázar** and Manuel **Puig** in the 1960s reinvented the novel form, the latter questioning the canon of high art in fictions that incorporated the language and desires of mass culture. Currently, the leading figures in the novel include Ricardo **Piglia**, Juan José **Saer** and César **Aira**. Women writers (from Silvina Ocampo and Alejandra **Pizarnik** through Tamara **Kamenszain** and Diana **Bellessi**) have found ample space to create alongside, or in opposition to, the men. Publishing houses (Emecé, **Sudamericana**, **Losada**, **Centro Editor de América Latina**) and literary magazines (***Diario de poesía**, **Punto de vista*** and many others) have flourished. Cultural critics and theorists, notably Beatriz **Sarlo**, David **Viñas**, Noé **Jitrik** and Josefina **Ludmer**, are of great importance in the country, while emigrants to other countries have included Néstor **García Canclini**, Raúl **Antelo**, Sylvia **Molloy** and Ernesto Laclau.

Music in Argentina is not confined to **tango**, though this is doubtless the popular song and dance form most deeply associated with the country. Tango was a product of the city's lowlife in the 1870s, connected with the bars and brothels around the port. It developed as a dance in Argentina and Uruguay and, from about 1917, became a successful song form. The quintessential voice of tango was Carlos **Gardel**, Latin America's first singing superstar; later developments in tango include the jazz synthesis of Astor **Piazzola**. Younger generations have also been attracted to the exponents of the *nueva canción* movement such as Mercedes **Sosa** and the singers and lyricists of **rock nacional** (Charly **García**, Fito **Páez**, Los **Fabulosos Cadillacs**). Elsewhere in the country, popular musical forms such as **milonga**, **zamba**, **chamamé** and Andean music flourish in the voices of major figures like Atahualpa **Yupanqui** and Teresa **Parodi**. The symbol of the power and prestige of Argentina's classical music tradition is the Colón opera house and concert hall. Symphony and chamber orchestras throughout Argentina and concert halls have attracted performers from all over the world. The 'nationalist' composers like Juan José **Castro** and Alberto **Ginastera** had their counterpoint in the avant-garde experimentation of Juan Carlos **Paz**, the first exponent of dodecophany in Latin America. Their influences can be traced in younger composers such as Gerardo **Gandini** and Francisco **Kröpfl** who were associated with the first school ever established for training Latin American composers, at the Di Tella Arts Centre in the 1960s.

The desire to fuse national concerns with the languages of international cultural movements can also be seen in the plastic arts. Once again, Buenos Aires has a well-developed gallery system and schools of fine art, and a number of Argentine artists (one example being Antonio **Seguí**) have found international recognition in Paris and New York. Argentine variations of all the international movements in art of the twentieth century can be charted: the surrealist, esoteric work of Alejandro **Xul Solar** in the 1920s and beyond; the expressive realism of Antonio **Berni**; the mixture of concrete art and literature in the Madí group of the 1940s (see **Arte Madí**); the kinetic artists of the 1960s such as Julio **Le Parc**; **Otra Figuración**, the pop artists (see **pop art**) and organizers of **happenings** in the same period; the move into both direct political art and also into **conceptual art** in the 1970s; and the wide range of different styles that emerged in the 1980s and 1990s, from the provocative statues of Pablo **Suárez** to the complex maps of Guillermo **Kuitca**. The most ambitious attempt to give Argentine art international prominence was represented by the work of

the Di Tella Arts Centre in the 1960s, which offered a showcase for the new and prizes for international and national art. Such an ambitious initiative could not be sustained, however, through the political turmoil of the next decade.

In the 1960s, theatre groups mixed with the painters and musicians in the Di Tella Arts Centre as part of a complex avant-garde experiment: the most innovative director of that period, now based in Paris, was Alfredo Rodríguez Arias. But most work in performing arts continued in a network of theatres that, throughout the twentieth century, catered to both mainstream and avant-garde tastes. The most popular theatrical form of the early twentieth century, reflecting the desires and frustrations of the new immigrant groups, was known as *grotesco criollo*, and the leading dramatists were **Defilippis Novoa** and Armando **Discépolo**. Independent theatre saw its origins in the 1930s, with the founding of the Teatro del Pueblo by Leónidas Barletta, which mixed European and North American playwrights with important Argentine writers such as Roberto **Arlt**. Independent theatre became a coherent movement in the 1940s and 1950s, in particular in its critical distance from **Peronism**, and produced writers in very different styles, from the critical realism of Carlos **Gorostiza** through the Brechtian experiments of Osvaldo **Dragún** to the satirical farces of Agustín **Cuzzani**.

The 1960s and early 1970s saw both a boom in experimental theatre in all forms and in political theatre (in particular the work of Ricardo **Monti**). The most significant dramatists to emerge from this period were Griselda **Gambaro** and Eduardo **Pavlovsky**. The political euphoria of the early 1970s gave way to the repression of the military dictatorship and in this period theatre played an important role in keeping cultural debate alive, through allegory and ellipsis, evading the censors. Theatre also signalled an early democratizing movement with the work of **Teatro Abierto** and **Teatro de la Libertad** offering a challenge in the early 1980s to the weakened military regime. Contemporary theatre, with figures like Rubén **Szuchmacher**, reflects an awareness of world theatre and an openness to stage plays from all over the world combined with the original work of national dramatists.

The national cinema, although dominated by the power of Hollywood production, distribution and exhibition, was nevertheless a strong force continentally through the 1930s and 1940s, and demonstrated a modest national output and a range of directorial styles. National cinema in Argentina was built on the early successes of studio-based **tango** melodramas in the 1930s and 1940s, with their own star system. By the mid-1950s, however, political and aesthetic changes in the industry were embodied in the work of the auteur Leopoldo **Torre Nilsson**, and the radical documentary film-maker, Fernando **Birri**, and, later, the young film-makers of the **Generación del 60**. These tendencies continued through the 1960s, culminating in the famous work of political cinema *La hora de los hornos* (Hour of the Furnaces) (1968) and the essay 'Hacia un tercer cine' (Towards a Third Cinema) (1969), by the Peronist film-makers Octavio Getino and Fernando **Solanas**. The moment of revolutionary euphoria was silenced by the military regime of 1976–83, which imposed severe **censorship** and confined film-makers to internal and external exile. The return to democracy heralded a very productive period for Argentine cinema with the Oscar-winning *La historia oficial* (The Official Story) (1986) and the box office successes of María Luisa **Bemberg** and Solanas, amongst others. Production continues despite the restrictions of the global market and the constant problem of cinema throughout the continent: the lack of adequate resources.

The move towards global media monopolies is a current feature of Latin American broadcasting (Argentine examples include Goar **Mestre** and the **Noble** family). Argentina pioneered the reception of **radio** in the 1920s and since the 1950s, **television** has taken over as the main broadcast medium. By 1992, there were nine million television sets in Argentina and over three million VCRs and today cable and satellite channels proliferate and state channels have been privatized. The staple fare of these channels are game shows, sport and **telenovelas**, although Argentina has not developed *telenovelas* to the extent of Brazil, Venezuela or Mexico. National media conglomerates combine ownership of radio and television channels and newspapers. There are over a dozen daily and Sunday national newspapers, as well as regional dailies. There is also a thriving glossy magazine market and specialist journals cover most aspects of economics, politics and the leisure industries.

The most thumbed pages of newspapers and magazines deal with sport, especially **football**; many talented Argentine players now appear in the European leagues. The national leagues have gone into decline, although the barras bravas, the fanatical supporters of local teams, continue their pattern of vocal support and occasional mayhem. Argentine successes in the **World Cup** are greeted by national celebration and stars such as the 'golden boy' Diego **Maradona** are national heroes, despite his conviction and bans for taking cocaine. The boxer Carlos **Monzón**, a world middleweight champion, had a similar rags-to-riches story, with a similar cloudy ending. The racing drivers Juan Manuel **Fangio** and Carlos Reuterman also figure in the pantheon of stars, alongside tennis players Gabriela **Sabattini** and Guillermo **Vilas**. **Horse racing** is a national pastime and, in élite circles, centred around the membership of the jockey club (see **jockey clubs**), Argentines produce the best **polo** players in the world and try their hands at the more quintessential British aspects of cultural influence, **cricket** and rugby.

Sarmiento observed in 1845 that the **gaucho** diet consisted almost entirely of meat (see **meat in Argentina**), something still largely true today, though heavy immigration from Italy has meant that pizza and pasta are important elements of the national cuisine. **Yerba mate**, the drink of Indians and gauchos, continues to be popular, though it is perhaps less dominant in urban spaces in Argentina than in neighbouring Uru-guay.

Argentine culture reveals, in its best manifestations, the famous Borges dictum that Argentines can handle all European themes, 'without superstition' or inferiority, with an irreverence which, in his analysis, can have, and already does have, fortunate consequences. Icons of Latin American culture as varied as Che **Guevara**, Julio Cortázar, Eva **Perón** and **Quino** have made irreverence a defining mark of the impact of Argentina in the continent and in the world.

Further reading

Guy, D.J. (1992) *Sex and Danger in Buenos Aires: Prostitution, Family and Nation in Argentina*, Lincoln: University of Nebraska.

King, J. (1985) *El Di Tella y el desarrollo cultural argentino en la década del sesenta*, Buenos Aires: Ediciones de Arte Galianone.

—— (1986) *Sur: A Study of the Argentine Literary Journal and its Role in the Development of a Culture 1931–1970*, Cambridge: Cambridge University Press.

Rock, D. (1985) *Argentina 1516–1982: From Spanish Colonization to the Malvinas War*, Berkeley: University of California Press.

Rouquié A. (1982) *Argentina hoy*, Mexico City: Siglo XIX.

Sarlo, B. (1988) *Una modernidad periférica: Buenos Aires 1920 y 1930*, Buenos Aires: Ediciones Nueva Visión.

JOHN KING

Argentina Sono Film

Since 1933 the principal Argentine film studio has been Argentina Sono Film. Headed by Angel Mentasti and his descendants, Sono came together to produce *¡Tango!* (1933) and went on to produce hundreds of films by the best directors and most revered stars in its 40,000 square metre 'dream factory' built in 1938. Typical of Sono's directors was Luis César **Amadori** and his superbly crafted star vehicles. In the 1940s Sono also produced the Noticiero Panamericano directed first by Homero **Manzi** and, later, by Raúl Alejandro Apold. In 1977 the studios were sold to a television company, but Sono reinitiated production in the mid-1980s, producing, for example, *Tangos: el exilio de Gardel* (1985).

RODRIGO PEIRETTI

Argerich, Martha

b. 1941, Buenos Aires, Argentina

Musician

Argerich is an internationally acclaimed concert pianist who gave her début performance in Buenos Aires in 1946. She studied with Nikita Magaloff and Friedrich Gulda, moving to Europe in 1955. In 1957 she won the Busoni Competition in Bolzano, going on to win the Chopin International Competition in Warsaw in 1965. Her London début was given in 1964. Argerich is particularly known for her live and recorded interpretations of Chopin, Liszt, Schumann, Prokofiev and Bartók.

SIMON WRIGHT

Arguedas, Alcides

b. 1879, La Paz, Bolivia; d. 1946, La Paz

Historian, writer and sociologist

Almost all Arguedas's writings were marked by a determinist view that physical environment and race are the prevailing factors in society. Lacking faith in the people of Bolivia, he wrote from a profoundly pessimistic perspective, particularly in *Pueblo enfermo* (A Sick People) (1909) in which he berates Bolivia for its incapacity as a nation. He was acknowledged as an *indigenista* writer after the publication of his *Raza de bronce* (Bronze Race) (1916), although recent criticism has been less convinced of his *indigenista* credentials.

MARÍA DORA VILLA GÓMEZ

Arguedas, José María

b. 1911, Andahuaylas, Peru; d. 1969, Lima, Peru

Novelist and ethnographer

Born in highland Peru, Arguedas spent his early childhood under the care of **Quechua**-speaking indigenous people. This formative encounter generated his life-long dedication to communicating Peruvian indigenous experience and shaped his literary and ethnographic achievements, including folkloric studies and compilations, Spanish translations of Quechua poetry and his own poetry (written primarily in Quechua), and the short stories and five novels comprising his most widely read work. Arguedas' suicide in 1969 has been attributed partly to despair over the continued oppression of Peruvian Indians. In style and narrative perspective, however, his novelistic expression of these concerns constitutes a fundamental move away from traditional Spanish-American **indigenismo**. While this artistic mode had often romanticized or stereotyped its subjects, Arguedas sought to represent indigenous worlds from within and to portray the shifting linguistic experience and complex, cross-cultural negotiations characterizing a multi-ethnic society. Arguedas's multifaceted work as a teacher, translator, ethnographer and literary creator constitutes a coherent and dynamic intellectual project.

Because his mother died before he was three and his father travelled the Andean *sierra* as an itinerant lawyer, Arguedas lived with Quechua servants. Joining his father as an adolescent, he witnessed Indians' treatment under *latifundismo* and attended ethnically diverse schools. From 1931–7 he studied literature at Lima's Universidad de San Marcos, while working for the post office and, well into the 1940s, as a secondary teacher. During the 1930s and 1940s, Arguedas published compilations and studies of Quechua literary, folkloric and musical materials, including the collections of indigenous music *Canto Kechwa* (1937) and the story and song anthology *Canciones y cuentos del pueblo quechua* (Song and Stories of the Quechua People) (1949). He published the story collection *Agua* (Water) in 1935 and the novel *Yawar Fiesta* in 1951. The latter presents a confrontation over **bullfighting** in a small Andean town and anticipates Arguedas's later narratives in its demonstration of cross-cultural interactions in the Andean world. These works also signal Arguedas's reluctant decision to write prose in Spanish and represent early efforts to render in Spanish the syntactical and lyrical qualities of Quechua. He would achieve this most effectively in *Los **ríos profundos*** (Deep Rivers) (1958).

Arguedas was most productive from the mid-1950s until his death in 1969. He earned a doctorate in ethnology in 1963 from San Marcos with a dissertation on *Las comunidades de España y del Perú* (The Communities of Spain and Peru) (1968). He was also a leader of national institutes and museums of culture, folklore and history; published extensively on Quechua ethnography, folklore, and

musicology; launched and collaborated in journals of Peruvian culture; and travelled to symposia to conduct research in Spanish America, Europe, and the United States.

His critically acclaimed novel *Los ríos profundos* (The Deep Rivers) appeared in 1958. In this autobiographical novel of formation, an adolescent white Peruvian boy, raised among Quechua speakers, attends a provincial, religious boarding school populated by students of varied social and ethnic backgrounds. Shaped by the myths and lyrical worldviews recalled from childhood, the boy decodes the social hierarchies and injustices in the school and town, which together form a microcosm of Peru. Discerning cultural conflicts, he focuses particularly on the diverse conceptions of language held by various groups and identifies most strongly with rebellious *chola* (*mestiza*) women and Indian serfs.

Published in 1963, *El Sexto* (The Sixth), like *Los ríos profundos*, presents a microcosmic view of Peruvian social problems, but in the more urban setting of an infamous Lima jail and through the eyes of a student political prisoner. By contrast, Arguedas's 1965 novel *Todas las sangres* (All the Bloods) creates a more panoramic narrative world that expands the struggle between two *sierra* brothers, a *hacendado* and a mine owner, to address class and ethnic conflicts between owners and workers, the Western and the indigenous, the *sierra* and the coast, and the ideologies of nationalism and capitalist modernity. Arguedas's unfinished final novel, *El zorro de arriba y el zorro de abajo* (The Fox From Above, the Fox From Below), explores the chaotic and developing coastal world of Chimbote, a town teeming with what he described as a 'human swarm' of multiple ethnic and social origins. In this most experimental of Arguedas's works, narrative portions juxtapose vanguardist images of a rapidly developing Chimbote with the non-Western, mythical worldview and expressive forms of the character who confronts it. Arguedas's personal diary entries interrupt these narrative portions to address the novel's composition and the author's suicidal thoughts.

While critics have focused on the novels, in his poetry of the 1960s (published posthumously as *Tembla-Katatay*, 1972), Arguedas realized a long-standing resolve to write in Quechua. His cultural project as a whole resists a critical privileging of the literary, as even the novels weave together narrative, poetic, ethnographic and musical motifs into a thick description of Andean experience. All of his work was shaped as well by the ardent commitment to demonstrate the creative richness of Andean verbal and musical art, and he fittingly dedicated his last novel to the poet Emilio Adolfo **Westphalen** and to his good friend, the Quechua-speaking musician and violinist Máximo **Damián Huamani**. Thus Arguedas's literary and ethnographic work constitutes a remarkable, life-long search for effective communication and reconciliation among the contentious elements that marked his own life and that shape the modern Peruvian experience of rapid cultural change.

Further reading

Arguedas, J.M. (1990) *El zorro de arriba y el zorro de abajo*, ed. E. Fell, Paris: Archivos.

Cornejo Polar, A. (1973) *Los universos narrativos de José María Arguedas*, Buenos Aires: Losada.

Lienhard, M. (1981) *Cultura popular andina y forma novelesca: Zorros y danzantes en la última novela de Arguedas*, Lima: Latinoamericana.

Rowe, W. (1996) *Ensayos arguedianos*, Lima: Sur.

Vargas Llosa, M. (1978) *José María Arguedas, entre sapos y halcones*, Madrid: Ediciones Cultura Hispánica.

VICKY UNRUH

Argüelles, Hugo

b. 1932, Veracruz, Mexico

Playwright

Argüelles is one of the most prolific and frequently staged of the contemporary Mexican playwrights, both at home and abroad. As a teacher, he has trained the recent generation of *Nueva Dramaturgia* (New Drama) playwrights. His dramas are notable for their sardonic critique of middle and upper class morality, and include some of the strongest female characters of Mexican theatre, such as the

possessive Andrea of *El cerco de la cabra dorada* (The Siege of the Golden Goat) (1991).

ANTONIO PRIETO-STAMBAUGH

Argüello, Alexis

b. 1952, Managua, Nicaragua

Boxer

The first Nicaraguan to win three world boxing titles, at featherweight (1974), junior lightweight (1978) and lightweight (1981), Argüello was beaten for the welterweight crown in one of the decade's finest bouts against Aaron Pryor in 1982. A millionaire by age thirty, Argüello received preferential treatment from the Somoza dictatorship (see **Somoza dynasty**); in return, he campaigned for Somoza in several elections. After the 1979 Sandinista (see **Sandinista Revolution**) triumph, his property was confiscated and he settled in Miami. He fought briefly with the **contras** after the death of his brother. When some of his properties were returned after the 1990 elections he returned to Managua, where he manages a gymnasium.

ESTEBAN E. LOUSTAUNAU AND
ILEANA RODRÍGUEZ

Argueta, Manlio

b. 1936, San Salvador, El Salvador

Writer

Manlio Argueta is one of the best known and most widely read Central American writers. His novel *Un día en la vida* (1980), translated as *One Day of Life* (1983), is a chronology of one day in the life of a Salvadoran family involved in the bloody struggles of the 1970s and 1980s. This novel has the urgency of the ***testimonio***, and challenges both literary genres. Argueta has published six novels, three books of poetry and numerous articles. Due to his political activities he lived in Costa Rica for twenty-one years, but is currently living in El Salvador.

NICASIO URBINA

Arias, Arturo

b. 1950, Guatemala City

Writer

A US-based Guatemalan novelist, critic and professor, Arias publishes literary, historical and theoretical studies on Central American and Guatemalan themes. In his 1979 novel, *Después de las bombas* (After the Bombs) (1990), he portrays the effect of the 1954 intervention on his generation. *Itzam Na* (1981) describes the turbulent life of teenagers educated in Guatemala City's 'best' high schools but caught up in political violence, while his epic novel *Jaguar en llamas* (Jaguar in Flames) (1989) takes four characters through the major events of Guatemalan history. These works show Arias's concern with Guatemalan history and novelistic form.

MARC ZIMMERMAN

Arias, Constantino

b. 1926, Havana, Cuba; d. 1992, Havana

Photographer

Arias's work provides an outstanding photographic record of twentieth-century Cuban history. Some critics regard him as a forerunner of Italian Neorealism. His images of the desperation of the poor and the luxury of Cuba's rich provide a clear image of the nature of social class in Cuba before 1959. His photographs record the student demonstrations and the workers' strikes launched against the dictatorship of Fulgencio **Batista**. Self-taught, he worked in the photographic agency of the Hotel Nacional (1941–59) and on the journals, *Alma Mater* and ***Bohemia*** (1960–83). His work has been exhibited in Cuba and Mexico.

WILFREDO CANCIO ISLA

Arias, Oscar

b. 1940, Heredia, Costa Rica

Politician

President of Costa Rica from 1986 to 1990, Arias devoted himself to designing a framework for peace and stability in Central America. The resulting accords, based on Arias's proposal – known as Esquipulas II (for the place where the negotiations took place) – were signed by Honduras, Guatemala, Nicaragua, El Salvador and Costa Rica in 1987. In recognition, Arias was awarded the Nobel Peace Prize in 1987 (see **Nobel Prizes**). Prior to his election as president Arias wrote two books, *Grupos de presión en Costa Rica* (Pressure Groups in Costa Rica) (1971) and *¿Quién gobierna en Costa Rica?* (Who Governs Costa Rica?) (1976). In the years since the end of his presidential term, Arias has travelled widely, giving lectures on world peace and on environmental issues; he also lectures at the foundation that bears his name and which works on these issues.

DANIEL BALDERSTON

Arias, Pepe (José Pablo)

b. 1900, Buenos Aires, Argentina; d. 1967, Buenos Aires

Actor

A brilliant comedian and incisive political commentator, Arias's acting career developed uninterrupted in many genres (**sainete**, comedy and revue) for fifty years (1916–66). In 1933 he made his debut in the first Argentine sound film, Luis Moglia Barth's *¡Tango!* Twenty-three films followed, among them *Kilómetro 111* (Mario **Soffici**, 1938), *Las seis suegras de Barba Azul* (Bluebeard's Six Mothers-in-Law) (Carlos H. **Chistensen**, 1948) and *Mercado de abasto* (Wholesale Market) (Lucas **Demare**, 1955). He was also famous for his radio monologues.

DIANA PALADINO

Aridjis, Homero

b. 1940, Michoacán, Mexico

Writer and green activist

Aridjis is a poet and narrator who has long held an important place in Mexican letters. He studied journalism and was a member of the literary workshop of Juan José **Arreola**, winning the prestigious Xavier **Villaurrutia** prize in 1964. Collaborator and contributor to a compilation of comtemporary Mexican Poetry *Poesía en movimiento* (Poetry in Motion) (1966) along with Octavio **Paz**, Alí Chumacero and José Emilio **Pacheco**, Aridjis has served the Mexican government as a cultural attaché in Holland and as ambassador to Switzerland. A recurrent concern in his creative work is the destruction of the environment. He currently leads the Grupo de los Cien, a green activist group (see **green activism**).

EDUARDO SANTA CRUZ

Arieles

This Mexican film prize has been awarded annually since 1946 to the best films, directors and performers of the year. The awards were established by the Academia Mexicana de Ciencias y Artes Cinematográficas (The Mexican Academy of Motion Picture Arts and Sciences), an organization modelled on the US Academy of Motion Pictures Arts and Sciences, which distributes the annual Oscars. The Academia considers all films exhibited in a given calendar year for its awards, not the year of production. In general, its awards have not been greatly controversial, signalling both a modicum of quality and, above all, as with the Oscars, box-office success.

ANA M. LÓPEZ

arielismo

A term derived from José Enrique Rodó's 1900 essay *Ariel*, directed at the youth of Latin America. Evoking the ethereal spirit from Shakespeare's *The Tempest*, Rodó makes a claim that Latin cultures are light and spiritual, in contrast to the materialist cultures of the Anglo-Saxon countries (which he associates with Caliban). What was subsequently called *arielismo* is usually associated with an aesthetic based on spiritualism and elitism, and, for a time, seemed to define the lofty role some **intellectuals** aspired to, hoping to be exemplars in the modernizing process in Latin America, not sullied with direct political involvement. Writers who have sometimes been associated with this tendency are Alfonso **Reyes**, Mariano **Picón Salas** and Pedro **Henríquez Ureña**. In Montevideo, a student group christened itself Ariel and published a journal with that name from 1919 to 1931; ironically, one of its leaders was Carlos Quijano, the future founder of *Marcha*, a journal that leaves behind the spiritualist legacy of Rodó. Critics of *arielismo* included Alberto **Zum Felde**, José Carlos **Mariátegui**, Luis Alberto **Sánchez**, and, most famously, Roberto **Fernández Retamar**, whose *Caliban* (1971) reread *The Tempest* through dialectical materialism, identifying the people of Latin America with Caliban and their oppressors with Ariel and Prospero.

DANIEL BALDERSTON

Aries Cinematográfica

With the Argentine national film industry in crisis after **Perón**'s fall in 1955, Fernando **Ayala** and Héctor **Olivera** founded the production company Aries in 1956. With renewed state support they made *El Jefe* (The Boss) (1958), a brilliant analysis of a charismatic leader coscripted by David **Viñas**, and embarked upon a series of quality, politically hard-hitting films. To finance the company, they undertook more commercial productions such as *Hotel alojamiento* (Apartment Hotel) (1965), a very successful sex-farce. This strategy of using the success of commercial films to sustain 'quality' productions such as Ayala's *La Patagonia rebelde* (Rebellious Patagonia) (1974) kept the company going continuously until they merged with **Argentina Sono Film** in the 1990s.

RODRIGO PEIRETTI

Aristaraín, Adolfo

b. 1943, Buenos Aires, Argentina

Film-maker

Aristaraín made his first film, *La parte del león* (The Lion's Share), in 1978. There followed two commercial films and the thriller ***Tiempo de revancha*** (Time of Revenge) (1981), an allegory about the military dictatorship. *Ultimos días de la víctima* (The Victim's Last Days) (1982), confirmed his directorial talent, but financial difficulties led him to work with Spanish television. Finally in 1991 he won international recognition with his *Un lugar en el mundo* (A Place in the World), and entered a period of fruitful co-productions with Spain that yielded *La ley de la frontera* (Border Justice) (1995) and *Martín H* (1997).

DIANA PALADINO

Aristide, Jean-Bertrand

b. 1953, Port-Salut, Haiti

Priest and politician

Born into a poor peasant family, Aristide was able to acquire a solid education in Port-au-Prince with the Catholic Salesian Order. A brilliant student, he was ordained into the priesthood in 1982. His vocation was strengthened by the many acts of violence perpetrated by the regime of Francois **Duvalier** and the **Tontons Macoutes**. Aristide became one of the strongest figures of **liberation theology** in the Caribbean. Expelled by the Salesian Order in 1988, he was elected President of Haiti in 1990 with the support of the popular movement *Lavalas* ('torrent', in creole), only to be ousted by a *coup* in 1991. During his three years in exile, he wrote *Tout homme est un homme* (An Autobiography) (1993) and later *Dignité* (Dignity) (1996), an account of his struggle to return to Haiti, which he achieved successfully in 1994 with the help of the USA and the United Nations, becoming president for one full term.

ANNE MALENA

Arlt, Roberto

b. 1900, Buenos Aires, Argentina; d. 1942, Buenos Aires

Writer

One of Spanish America's first urban novelists, Arlt (born Roberto Godofredo Christophersen Arlt) is known for his gritty but somewhat surreal portrayals of Buenos Aires, best exemplified in his 1929 novel, *Los siete locos* (The Seven Madmen), and its 1931 sequel, *Los lanzallamas* (The Flame-throwers). The memorable characters of these novels propose to found an anarchist Utopia funded by the income from prostitution. Arlt worked as a journalist for the newspapers, *El mundo* and ***Crítica***; his journalistic columns were collected in several volumes of *Aguafuertes* (Water-colours), some first collected in 1933 but others still coming to light more than a half-century after the author's death. He also wrote for the theatre and worked as an amateur inventor. Associated with members of both the Boedo and Florida groups (see **Boedo vs Florida**), Arlt – a writer whose work is open to **anarchism** and proletarian writing as well as to the avant-garde movements (see **avant-garde in Latin America**) – has been championed in recent years by Ricardo **Piglia**, often celebrated as one of the essential protagonists of Argentina's modernity.

DANIEL BALDERSTON

Armendáriz, Pedro

b. 1912, Mexico City; d. 1963, Mexico City

Actor

A cinema idol during the Mexican cinema's 'Golden Age', his career took off in the 1940s when he starred in several films by Emilio 'El Indio' **Fernández**, including ***María Candelaria*** and ***Flor silvestre*** (Wild Flower) with Dolores **Del Rio** in 1943, *La perla* (The Pearl) (1945) and *Enamorada* (Woman in Love) (1946) with María **Félix**. He made several cinema stereotypes his own – the landowner, the noble and submissive Indian, the revolutionary and the indomitable macho. His screen presence attracted directors from France (Christian Jaque), Italy (DeSantis) and the United States (John Huston, Dick Powell and Terence Young). He made 121 films.

PATRICIA TORRES SAN MARTÍN

Arns, Paulo Evaristo

b. 1921, Forquilhinha, Brazil

Priest, archbishop and cardinal

Arns is an outspoken proponent of **liberation theology** and defender of **human rights** among Latin American Roman Catholic bishops. Ordained a Franciscan priest in 1945 and Archbishop of São Paulo in 1970, he was made a cardinal in 1973. He was by the mid-1970s the most influential church spokesperson against state repression, torture and violence in Brazil. A proponent of indigenous Latin American Christian socialism, he strongly supported the work of the Christian Base Organizations (CBOs) among urban and rural poor. He has publicly defended liberation theologians like Leonardo **Boff**. His many writings include *Em Defensa dos Direitos Humanos* (In Defence of Human Rights) (1978).

ELINA VUOLA

Arrate, Marina

b. 1957, Santiago, Chile

Writer

Drawing on her experience as a psychologist and a critic, Arrate's writing constitutes an exploration of female identity, possibly the darkest area of Latin American experience. Within women's poetry and the variety of national poetic conventions, her voice stands out as a liberating project, with her themes of love and eroticism. Her works include *Este lujo de ser* (This Luxury of Being) (1986), *Máscara negra* (Black Mask) (1990), *Tatuaje* (Tattoo) (1992) and in

1996 an *Antología* which also includes *El hombre de los lobos* (The Wolf Man).

ELIANA ORTEGA

Arrau, Claudio

b. 1903, Chillán, Chile; d. 1991, Mürzzuschlag, Austria

Musician

A child prodigy, Arrau gave his first public recital at the age of five, playing Beethoven, Mozart and Chopin before an amazed Santiago audience. With a scholarship from the Chilean Congress, he studied at Stern's Conservatory under Martin Krause (one of Liszt's disciples) from 1912 to 1918, winning a number of awards. After his first recital in Berlin in 1914, he toured Europe and played with leading orchestras.

In 1924, Arrau joined the staff of Stern's Conservatory, where he taught until 1940. In 1927 his international reputation was enhanced by winning the Grand Prix International des Pianistes in Geneva. Between 1935 and 1936 he presented twelve recitals in which he played the entire keyboard works of Bach on the modern piano. After a successful tour of the USA, Arrau and his family settled in New York.

Although usually identified with Beethoven, Brahms and Chopin, his repertoire was diverse; his vast discography contains over two hundred listings ranging from Albéniz to Weber. Arrau was a true interpreter, putting his virtuoso technique at the service of the composer and adhering to every authorial indication of phrasing and dynamics. His emphasis on accuracy led him to consult original manuscripts and scholarly documents in an effort to negate personal whim or technical display. His technique relied on natural body weight; rather than pressing down on the keys, he let gravity do the work for him. Unlike players who favour fixed hand positions, he set his fingers, wrists, elbows and shoulders at various angles and heights, readjusting the levers and joints as needed.

In his long career, Arrau balanced interpretive objectivity and personal passion, though his sometimes unusually slow tempos and his attention to detail suggested a lack of spontaneity and momentum. As one of the least ostentatious of pianists, his rich-toned and thoughtful playing conveyed exceptional intellectual power and depth of feeling. He left a most valuable legacy to pianists such as Philip Lorenz, Daniel **Barenboim** and Garrick Ohlsson, who were his students.

Further reading

Arrau, C. (1967) 'A Performer Looks at Psychoanalysis', *High Fidelity* 17 (2): 50.

Horowitz, J. (1982) *Conversations with Arrau*, London: Collins.

Osborne, R. (1972) 'Keyboard Oracle: Claudio Arrau in Conversation', *Records & Recording* 16 (1): 26.

LUCÍA GUERRA

Arreola, Juan José

b. 1918, Ciudad Guzmán, Jalisco, Mexico

Writer

An outstanding writer of stories and other short fictions, Arreola is as famous for his writing as for his public appearances, particularly on television, as a witty commentator on contemporary manners. Wit and humour (often quite a savage humour) characterize his writings, published in *Confabulario* (Confabulary) (1952), *Bestiario* (Bestiary) (1958) and *Palindroma* (Palindrome) (1964). Arreola is fascinated by language – at times this produces an elegant and restrained style, at times witty word play, and at others excessive and pretentious expression. But the link between his literary work and his public performance is a preoccupation with the spoken word, its sounds and rhythms, and its curious contradictions. His epigrams and sayings have been collected in two volumes, *La palabra educación* (The Word Education) (1973) and *Inventario* (Inventory) (1976).

MIKE GONZALEZ

Arrigucci Jr, Davi

b. 1943, São João da Boa Vista, São Paulo, Brazil

Literary critic

One of the most influential critics of his generation, Arrigucci studied with Antonio **Candido**. His approach is, if anything, more 'aesthetic' than that of his Marxist friend Roberto **Schwarz**. He has written on Spanish American topics (a book on **Cortázar** and excellent essays on **Rulfo** and **Borges**), but also enjoys writing about 'minor' aspects of Brazilian literature, journalism, memoirs, short stories and so on. It is natural that Arrigucci's *Humildade, Paixão e Morte* (Humility, Passion and Death) (1990) should be on Manuel **Bandeira**, who defined himself as a 'minor' poet.

JOHN GLEDSON

Arriví, Francisco

b. 1915, San Juan, Puerto Rico

Playwright

Arriví was instrumental in developing a national theatre in Puerto Rico during the 1940s–1960s. He founded theatre groups, directed a radio programme that introduced hundreds of plays to the island, and supervised the theatre wing of the **Instituto de Cultura Puertorriqueña**. Arriví has written several major essays on Puerto Rican theatre as well as plays ranging from absurdist fantasy and farce to poetic realism. His plays employ anti-mimetic techniques to treat social themes from a psychological perspective. *Vejigantes* (Masks) (1958), his major work, is a part of a trilogy that deals with racism (see **race**) in Puerto Rico and the United States.

CAMILLA STEVENS

Arrom, José Juan

b. 1910, Holguín, Cuba

Critic

An outstanding scholar of Latin American literature, Arrom lived in the United States from an early age, graduating from Yale University. His historical and critical essays on Cuba and Latin America include *Historia de la literatura dramática cubana* (History of Cuban Drama) (1944), *El teatro en Hispanoamérica en la época colonial* (Hispanic American Theatre in the Colonial Era) (1956), *Esquema generacional de las letras hispanoamericanas* (Generational Model of Latin American Literature) (1963) and *En el fiel de América* (In the Scale of America) (1985).

WILFREDO CANCIO ISLA

Arrufat, Antón

b. 1935, Santiago de Cuba

Writer and dramatist

His first poems were published in the magazine *Ciclón*. In 1968, his play *Los siete contra tebas* (Seven Against Thebes) was awarded the **UNEAC** theatre prize, a decision which unleashed an intense public debate; Arrufat was marginalized and the work banned for fifteen years. His drama is collected in *Teatro* (1963) and *La tierra permanente* (The Permanent Earth) (1987); he has published volumes of poetry, a novel and short stories including *Mi antagonista y otras observaciones* (My Antagonist and Other Observations) (1963), as well as a personal testimony *Virgilio Piñera; entre él y yo* (Between **Piñera** and Me) (1994).

WILFREDO CANCIO ISLA

art history

It is difficult to separate the art historian from the art critic in Latin America, although in some countries the distinction has become clearer since the 1980s as art history has gained more autonomy and status within the academic community. Few art history books are published, and texts tend to appear in exhibition catalogues or in art periodicals (see **art periodicals, contemporary**).

In the 1940s in Argentina, Jorge **Romero Brest** founded a magazine and association called *Ver y Estimar*, which served as a training ground for critics like Damián Carlos **Bayón**, Jorge **Glusberg** and Marta **Traba**. Although Romero Brest's approach was then rather traditional and Eurocentric, many of his students developed general theories of art in Latin America. Bayón, for example, produced numerous books covering the history of Latin American art from the baroque to the present. Traba was very influential in the 1970s, following the publication in Colombia of *Dos décadas vulnerables* (Two Vulnerable Decades) (1973) in which she elaborated a general model for Latin American art in opposition to foreign (particularly US) cultural domination. Her views coincided with the political aspirations of many contemporary intellectuals, and she became something of an icon.

From the mid-1970s, there was a shift from the more politically aware art criticism of writers like Traba to more theoretical writing, strongly influenced by international developments like **postmodernism**, post-structuralism and cultural studies. In Chile, Nelly **Richard** provided a dense theoretical framework for the conceptual artists (see **conceptual art**) of the Grupo **CADA** from the late 1970s to the early 1980s. Relying heavily on French thinkers like Derrida or Baudrillard, Richard's theories address issues surrounding cultural marginality.

Cultural politics became the central concern of many writers from the early 1980s, among them the Cuban Gerardo Mosquera and the Uruguayan Luis **Camnitzer**, who focused on Latin America's relationship to globalisation and postmodern fragmentation. In the 1990s, there was something of a revival of interest in art history in many parts of Latin America, and many artists from the early twentieth century were 'rediscovered'. From the late 1980s, there was also an international explosion of interest in Latin American art history, and more European and US art historians began to study the art of the region.

Further reading

Ades, D. (1989) *Art in Latin America: The Modern Era*, London: Yale University Press.

Bayón, D. (ed.) (1977) *El artista latinoamericano y su identidad*, Caracas: Monte Avila.

Mosquera, G. (ed.) (1995) *Beyond the Fantastic: Contemporary Art Criticism from Latin America*, London: Institute of International Visual Arts.

GABRIEL PEREZ-BARREIRO

art music

The broad category of art music embraces a range of styles and forms – from post-impressionism through romanticism and the neo-classical expressions associated with Stravinsky to the variety of avant-garde (see **avant-garde in Latin America**) forms. What links them all, is that they originate in Europe or North America. Art music in Latin America, therefore, can be defined as that music of European origin learned by a process of formal education by Latin Americans first in European and North American institutions, and later (from the 1940s onwards) in schools and institutions within Latin America founded to propagate and develop those ideas.

Through the second decade of the twentieth century, the questioning of European artistic and cultural hegemony was sparked by the First World War and its aftermath. The collapse of European models of social progress and civilization into the muddy fields of Flanders generated a scepticism and a revulsion that extended into every area of culture too. Hastened by events like the Mexican Revolution (1910–17) and the *Reforma Universitaria*, the artists of the early 1920s turned their glance back to their own world and began to seek there the foundations of a new aesthetic. In a sense, this continued in a direction encouraged by romanticism's fascination with locality; but now, in a climate of nationalism and anti-imperialism, the search for national forms of expression assumed a new urgency.

In Mexico, with the vigorous support of José Vasconcelos's Education Ministry, Carlos **Chávez** and Silvestre **Revueltas** were active in encouraging national rhythms and forms, derived from folk and popular musics, which might correspond to similar projects in art (see **muralism**), literature and education. Andrés **Sas** and Theodoro **Valcárcel** were similarly engaged in Peru, where an increasingly influential *indigenista* movement (see **indigenismo**) sought the roots of national expression among the Andean populations, whose music had until then developed continuously but largely in isolation from the urban musics whose influences were overwhelmingly European. In Argentina, Alberto **Ginastera** came to prominence during this period, though his influence would be decisive in his country's music for several decades to come. Brazil was witness to an artistic revolution of sorts during the early 1920s, symbolized and expressed in the gathering of new expression in all the arts under the aegis of the **Modern Art Week** of 1922. Among those attending the events in São Paulo during that week was Heitor **Villa-Lobos** who, together with Camargo **Guarnieri**, continued from there on a creative musical journey which drew on the whole range of national musical traditions as well as the techniques and compositional practices of the European classical tradition – an encounter exemplified by Villa-Lobos.

While there is no clear point at which nationalism ceases to be the dominant idiom in Latin American art music, the search for an 'international style' originating in Latin America came increasingly to define the musical milieu. In Brazil, for example, Hans Joachim **Koellreutter** (who like Holzman and others had studied with Hindemith) formed the Música Viva ensemble on an explicitly anti-nationalist basis to disseminate and teach twelve-tone composition and the range of new music emerging from Europe. His pupils included César Guerra Peixe (1914–93), who worked throughout his career to create a twelve-tone music rooted in indigenous traditions. Villa-Lobos meanwhile remained prolific throughout the 1930s and 1940s, albeit with variable results; though he moved in a more neo-classical direction, he was still able to produce works of great creative originality, like his ballet *Emperor Jones* (1956).

An experimental direction was established much earlier in Argentina, largely due to the influence of Juan Carlos Paz and his **Agrupación Nueva Música**, founded in 1944, whose influences were Frabn and Webern. Younger composers like

Mauricio **Kagel** responded to the work of John Cage and Messiaen whose aleatory techniques and explorations of dissonance found several adherents. During the 1960s the opening of the music department of the **Instituto Di Tella** under Ginastera's direction provided a space for continuing experiment and education in the new music; this included a developing interest in electronic music, as young artists like Alcides **Lanza** and Francisco **Kröpfl** returned from periods of study at the influential specialised Columbia-Princeton Electronic Music Laboratory. And Ginastera's own work was evolving, particularly in the area of music theatre, as his opera **Bomarzo** was to demonstrate.

A similar range of work in Chile owed its initial impulse to the continuing work of Domingo Santa Cruz and the Instituto de Extensión Musical de la Universidad de Chile, which developed both performance and musical scholarship to a high standard exemplified by one of the country's best known composers, Juan **Orrego-Salas** (who in 1961 became director of the Latin American Music Centre at Indiana). The Taller Experimental del Sonido at Chile's Catholic University ensured the development of electronic music, while Gustavo **Becerra-Schmidt** addressed the possibility that modern music could carry a political message and Fernando **García** and Leon **Schidlowsky** respectively explored serialist and aleatory techniques.

The impact of the Di Tella extended beyond Argentina; it provided an alternative, or at least an additional centre to those in Europe and the USA for Latin American students of the new music. They included Peru's most important avant-garde composers, César Bolaños and Theodoro **Valcárcel**, both of whom evolved within the framework of electronic music.

In Mexico, the influence of Chávez certainly waned, and the star of the twelve-tone work of Rodolfo **Halffter** rose in its stead. Joaquín **Gutiérrez Heras**, under the influence of Messiaen, adopted a free atonal style while maintaining a purity and simplicity of line. Manuel **Enríquez**, Mexico's leading electronic composer, also attended the Princeton-Columbia Centre after moving towards Cage's principles of indeterminacy in the previous decade.

In Cuba, Ardevol's **Grupo de Renovación Musical**, founded in 1942, had as its explicit purpose the creation of a 'Cuban school of composers' which could hold its own in an international new musical environment. The group drew young composers like Harold **Gramatges** and Argeliers **León**, because of its rigorous preparation in technique and its neo-classical performance, but they in turn took quite different directions at a later stage – León, for example, moved towards serialism, as indeed did Ardevol himself in the late 1950s. Some of his students, like Leo **Brouwer** and Edgardo Martín would play an important role in achieving a marriage of avant-garde form and political content after the 1959 revolution.

In greater isolation, other composers enriched the experimental stream – Jacqueline Nova (1938–) and Isabel Aretz in Venezuela, Mesías Maiguaschca (1938–) in Ecuador, Alberto **Villalpando** in Bolivia and Panama's most important musical presence Roque **Cordero**, among them.

It would by the late twentieth century be entirely legitimate to claim that Latin America had finally entered a musical dialogue with Europe and the USA rather than simply listening in silence.

Further reading

Appleby D. (1983) *The Music of Brazil*, Austin: University of Texas Press.

Behague G. (1979) *Music in Latin America*, Eaglewood Cliffs, NJ: Prentice-Hall.

Carpentier, A. (1946) *La música en Cuba*, Mexico: FCE.

Perolomo Escobar J.I. (1963) *Historia de la música en Colombia*, Bogotá: Ediciones ABC.

Stevenson R. (1952) *Music in Mexico: a Historical Survey*, New York: Thomas Crowell.

MIKE GONZALEZ

art nouveau

Art nouveau expresses refined bourgeois culture marked by non-academic freedom. The sensuous lines of vegetation combine with glass and iron to embody European traits of Italian liberty, Catalan modernism and Viennese secession. In Mexico, the final era of the Porfirio Díaz regime was expressed in the Palace of Bellas Artes (1900) by Adamo Boari with an interior (1931) by Federico Mariscal. Brazilian examples include the Sorocabana Station (1907) by Victor Dubugras, the House on Rua Russel Rio by Antonio Vizzi and the Maternity of São Paulo by Carlos Eckman. In Argentina, the works of Julián García Núñez, Francisco Roca Simó, Francisco Gianotti and Mario Palenti are significant.

JOSÉ BERNARDI

art periodicals, contemporary

These are magazines and other publications, appearing at regular periods, which are crucial to the understanding of specific discussions on twentieth-century Latin American art. Contemporary art periodicals can be divided into printed matter and on-line publications; both types of publications have been extremely important in the development of recent research. These periodicals also carry information about exhibitions and reviews, and provide a vehicle for public debate on contemporary issues in Latin American art. Some periodicals are more transitory in nature, particularly the on-line publications. Regardless, on-line periodicals offer the possibility of showing extremely high-quality reproductions of artwork. On-line periodicals provide an appropriate medium to show avant-garde works that, in the past, were only available for short periods of time and with small circulations – such as **Klaxon** (São Paulo, 1922–3), **Amauta** (Lima, 1926–30) and **Martin Fierro** (Buenos Aires).

The arts in Latin America are seen in a broad intellectual spectrum and many contemporary periodicals include valuable showcases of Latin American culture, including literature, art and film. *Art Nexus: Journal for Latin American Art* has been published quarterly since 1976 in Bogotá. *El cuarto del Quenepón*, the on-line magazine for visual arts, design, web projects, new media, poetry, theatre and culture news is published in Puerto Rico. *La biblioteca según el Quenepón* (archives) offers files to download on the arts and culture of Puerto Rico

and Latin America (in Spanish with contributions partly in English). *Heterogénesis*, a periodical for the visual arts – especially in Latin America – is published in Lund, Sweden (in Spanish). *Latin Art International*, a monthly on-line magazine from Mexico, has essays and information on international art with a special focus on the contemporary art of Latin America (in English and Spanish). *Luna córneais* is a periodical on photography, published quarterly in English and Spanish, and includes a website. *Rabid Sphinx – Online Culture Magazine* is an on-line journal of cultural production, which includes contributions from Carlos Basualdo and Coco Fusco. *Señas. Combios* is an on-line magazine for culture and leisure in Spain and Latin America, and includes a section on the arts. *TRANS* is a periodical/on-line magazine for art, culture and media printed three times per year in English and Spanish. *Virtualia – Cibercultura y nuevas tecnologías* is an on-line periodical of culture and art, with articles, news, a virtual gallery, an in-box for letters to the editor and an archive of former issues (in Spanish). *Zone Zero Magazine* is an on-line virtual photo-gallery. **Review** covers Latin American literature and arts, and is published twice a year by the **Americas Society** (in Spanish, English and Portuguese). *Polyester* is a quarterly Mexican publication devoted entirely to contemporary Latin American art (in English and Spanish).

ISABEL BARBUZZA

Arte Madí

Arte Madí was an artistic movement created in Buenos Aires in 1946 by Carmelo **Arden Quin**, **Gyula Kosice** and Rhod Rothfuss. The three artists had been involved in publishing the single issue of *Arturo* magazine in 1944. Following disputes with the Asociación Arte Concreto-Invención, led by Tomás **Maldonado**, the three artists came together to form their own movement. The first use of the term 'Madí' was in a series of broadsheet declarations dated June 1946, but the first exhibition with this name was in August 1946 at the Instituto Francés de Estudios Superiores in Buenos Aires. 'Madí' is probably a nonsense word, reflecting an interest in the subversion of language and 'respectable' practices which was at the heart of the movement. Although ostensibly a constructivist movement (see **constructivism**), some of the most interesting aspects of Madí are born of its chaotic nature, which sometimes seems to place it closer to dada or futurism. There is a Madí Manifesto which was first published in the review *Arte Madí Universal* in 1947, the authorship of which has been hotly disputed by Kosice and Arden Quin. Shortly after its foundation, Arden Quin split from Kosice and Rothfuss to create his own movement with the painter Martín Blaszko, before continuing his activities in France from 1948. Kosice led the Buenos Aires movement, attracting many participants such as Juan **Bay** through his magazine *Arte Madí Universal* until 1954. Madí aspired to be a multi-media group, encompassing the visual arts, dance, music, drama and literature. Humour and fantasy were vital elements in Madí works. Stylistically it was a loose group, but all paintings were composed within irregular frames and sculptures tended to be mobile and transformable. These were all strategies of breaking down the distance between the artist and the spectator, and increasing the participation of the latter. During the 1990s, Arden Quin relaunched the movement in Europe, reviving an old battle between Kosice and Arden Quin over supremacy of the movement.

Further reading

Arte Concreto-Invención Arte Madí (1995) Basle: Galerie von Bartha.
Arte Madí Internacional: 50 años después (1996) Zaragoza: Centro de Exposiciones y Congresos.
Kosice, G. (1982) *Arte Madí*, Buenos Aires: Gaglianone.
Perazzo, N. (1980) *Vanguardias de la década del cuarenta*, Buenos Aires: Museo Sívori.
Perez-Barreiro, G. (1994) 'The Negation of all Melancholy: Arte Madí/Concreto-Invención 1944–1950', in D. Elliott (ed.) *Art from Argentina 1920–1994*, Oxford: Museum of Modern Art.
Rivera, J.B. (1976) *Madí y la vanguardia argentina*, Buenos Aires: Paidós.

GABRIEL PEREZ-BARREIRO

Artigas, João Batista Vilanova

b. 1915, Curitiba, Brazil; d. 1984, São Paulo, Brazil

Architect

A major modernist architect who learned his craft with **Niemeyer** and others, Artigas is regarded as a key figure in the 'new brutalist school' of São Paulo, where his work greatly influenced a younger generation of architects including **Mendes de Rocha** and Roy Ohtake. In 1938 he was a member of the team led by Gregori **Warchavchik**; his own earlier work, like the Rio Branco Paranhos's house, was influenced by the 'organicist' ideas of Frank Lloyd Wright. By the late 1940s, and after a period in the USA, Artigas was won over by the ideas of Le Corbusier, particularly in his use of reinforced concrete and geometric forms – but he held to Wright's notions of light and space, a combination obvious in his 1961 design for the São Paulo School of Architecture. An active communist, Artigas was marginalised and deprived of his political rights during the period of military dictatorship (1964–84).

MIKE GONZALEZ

Aruba   *see*   Netherlands Antilles and Aruba

Arvelo Larriva, Enriqueta

b. 1886, Barinitas, Venezuela; d. 1962, Barinitas

Poet

Considered today to be one of the founders of women's poetry in Venezuela and one of the country's principal avant-garde (see **avant-garde in Latin America**) poets, Enriqueta Arvelo was largely overshadowed during her lifetime by her brother Alfredo, himself a poet. Her writing is austere, erotic and spare. She spent most of her life in her native town, and wrote about love, the landscape of the Venezuelan plains (the *llanos*) and her own inner life. In 1958 she was awarded the

Municipal Poetry Prize for her volume *Mandato del Canto* (The Instruction to Sing).

JORGE ROMERO LEON

asere

Asere is a common Cuban term, meaning a friend or companion, not recognised by the Real Academia de la Lengua Española. Its origins are in the African languages brought to Cuba, but its etymology is unclear. It sits alongside other terms of similar meaning: *consorte, monina, bongo, nague* (or *nawe*), the English word 'brother' and others in Cuban slang. Anago's *Vocabulario Lucumí* (the Cuban **Yoruba** language) provides the following definitions: '*asere* – mad, crazy; *asiere* – horse, ungrateful, stupid'.

JOSÉ ANTONIO EVORA

Asir, Revista

Asir was a Uruguayan cultural journal (1948–59) founded by Washington Lockhart and linked to the 1945 Generation. From no. 14 onwards its contributors included Montevideo intellectuals like Domingo Bordoli and Líber Falco who steered it in a sort of existentialist spiritualist direction. *Asir* privileged rural writers like J.J. Morosoli and Francisco **Espínola**, but also published Felisberto **Hernández** and Carlos **Denis Molina** and in later issues introduced a new generation of young poets. Ediciones Asir, its co-operative publishing imprint, included Carlos Real de Azúa and Angel **Rama** and published, among other works, **Onetti**'s *El infierno tan temido* (A Hell So Feared) (1962) and Denis Molina's *Lloverá siempre* (It Will Always Rain) (1967).

NORAH GIRALDI DEI CAS

Asis, Jorge

b. 1946, Buenos Aires, Argentina

Writer, journalist and diplomat

The fiction of Jorge Asis belongs within a realist

current, the major representative of which is Roberto **Arlt**. He has published several highly successful novels, including *La manifestación* (The Demonstration) (1971), *Don Abdel Salim* (1972), *Flores robadas en los jardines de Quilmes* (Flowers Stolen from the Garden of Quilmes) (1980), *Carne picada* (Minced Meat) (1981), *Sandra, la trapera* (Sandra the Seller of Used Clothes) (1996); several of them have been translated into a number of languages. He has been Argentine ambassador to UNESCO and was a member of its Executive Committee between 1989 and 1994, and also served as Minister of Culture and Ambassador to Portugal.

GRACIELA MUSACHI

Asociación Amigos del Arte

This private cultural institution was founded in 1925 in Buenos Aires with Elena Sansinena de Elizalde as its president and Julio Noé as secretary. Its journal **Martín Fierro** underlined its important role in opening a cultural space for modern Argentine painters; it also provided a platform for speakers like Marinetti, Leopoldo **Lugones**, Le Corbusier, José León Pagano and Guillermo de Torre. Its spirit of openness and eclecticism allowed it to occupy a key place in the movement of cultural innovation through the 1920s.

C.M. MANZONI

Assis Chateaubriand (Bandeira de Melo), Francisco de

b. 1892, Umbuzeiros, Brazil; d. 1968, São Paulo, Brazil

Media magnate

Founder of the **Museu de Arte de São Paulo** (MASP) in 1947, this impoverished descendant of an eminent northeastern family eventually owned numerous newspapers, radio stations, magazines and television stations throughout Brazil, and acquired significant political influence. A shrewd planner, he seized the opportunity to collect art objects for sale in war-ravaged Europe, cajoling funds out of São Paulo millionaires. The Italian art critic P.M. **Bardi** and the architect Lina **Bo Bardi** (his wife), who designed the second and permanent MASP building (1968), were his principal collaborators.

M.A. GUIMARÃES LOPES

Assumpção, Itamar

b. 1950, Tietê, Brazil

Singer and composer

A key figure in the alternative music scene of São Paulo, Itamar Assumpção has created a unique fusion of **samba**, funk and **reggae** noted for complex and sophisticated vocal arrangements. With a mixture of irony and pathos, his lyrics document the urban underground of metropolitan São Paulo and its working class periphery. His first two recordings with the band Isca da polícia (Police Bait) established his vanguardist credentials. In the late 1980s, he released *Samba Midnight* and *Intercontinental!* which had greater pop appeal. In 1994, Assumpção recorded the two-volume *Bicho de Sete Cabeças* (Seven-headed Beast), featuring the all-female group As Orquídeas (The Orchids).

CHRISTOPHER DUNN

ASTC

ASTC (Asociación Sandinista de Trabajadores Culturales, the Sandinista Association of Cultural Workers) was founded shortly after the 1979 **Sandinista Revolution**. Directed by Rosario **Murillo**, poet and wife of President Daniel **Ortega**, ASTC was a government-backed union for cultural workers. Housed in a spacious modern building in Managua, it held numerous *peñas* or readings by Nicaraguan and visiting authors. The emphasis was on **popular art**, with groups of muralists working in downtown Managua around the Olaf Palme Center, and outreach work in the *casas de cultura* (cultural centres) around the country. While the poet (and Catholic priest) Ernesto

Cardenal was Minister of Culture, its emphasis shifted to widespread **literacy** programmes.

AMANDA HOPKINSON

Astillero, El

Written by the Uruguayan writer Juan Carlos **Onetti** and published in 1961, *El astillero* (The Shipyard) is part of a series of novels and stories set in an imaginary town, Santa María, in the River Plate region. The naively enthusiastic protagonist, Larsen, returns to work for Petrus, the shipyard owner. With two other employees, Galvéz and Kunz, he maintains the illusion of a functional shipyard by studying decaying plans and paying imaginary bills. The facade slowly becomes an integral part of the characters. Onetti creates a ghostly feeling of unreality while appropriating realist conventions and the interior monologues of frustrated characters.

VICTORIA RUÉTALO

astronomical observatories

Many of the most important observatories in the southern sky are located in the so-called Norte Chico in Chile near the city of La Serena. The clear desert sky, low humidity and visibility for about 280 days a year have made this a favourite area for observatories, though one of the challenges facing designers of facilities there has been **earthquakes**. The largest telescopes are at Cerro Tololo near the Elqui Valley at the Inter-American Observatory, run by the US Association of Universities for Research in Astronomy (AURA). Cerro Tololo was dedicated in 1967; the European Southern Observatory, north of La Serena at Cerro La Silla, is also building the Very Large Telescope at Paranal in the Atacama Desert, projected to be completed in 2002.

DANIEL BALDERSTON

Asturias, Miguel Angel

b. 1899, Guatemala City; d. 1974,
Madrid, Spain

Novelist

A member of the same crucial generation of writers
as Jorge Luis **Borges**, Alejo **Carpentier** and
Pablo **Neruda**, Asturias was the first Latin
American novelist to be awarded the Nobel Prize
(see **Nobel Prizes**), in 1967, and is without a
doubt the dominant literary figure of Guatemala
and the most influential novelist in the history of
Central America to date. Nevertheless, the last
twenty years have seen a decline in interest in his
work even though, curiously, *Hombres de maíz* (Men
of Maize) (1949), a novel previously neglected by
critics, is now routinely granted masterwork status.

More than that of any other Latin American
country except perhaps Peru, the history of
Guatemala has been structured and dominated
by what used to be called the 'Indian problem'. It is
not surprising, then, that Asturias's entire oeuvre is
similarly conditioned. His first major work was
Leyendas de Guatemala (Legends of Guatemala),
published in Madrid in 1930, a collection of stories
based on the heterogeneity of Guatemala's cultural
identity. These stories retain the capacity to
surprise and delight which inspired a famous
prologue by Paul Valéry when the French translation appeared in 1932. Moreover, they reveal an
incipient consciousness which historians would
later call postcolonial.

Asturias was born in Guatemala City, the elder
son of a lawyer who found it difficult to practise
effectively during the savage dictatorial regime of
Manuel Estrada Cabrera (1898–1920). His middle-
class mother was forced to open a shop to make
ends meet, and this humiliation had a radicalizing
effect upon her son. Asturias took full part in
university politics between 1917 and 1923, including the overthrow of Estrada in 1920; and like all
Guatemalans, he experienced the great earthquake
of 1917 which, he said, transformed the capital city
and Guatemalan society and became one of the
great symbols of revolution in his subsequent work.

Although radicalized by student politics, Asturias was still no revolutionary by the time he
graduated. Admittedly, he did write Guatemala's

first university thesis on the 'social problem of the
Indian' in 1923, but it owed more to nineteenth-
century race-based positivist sociology than to the
new revolutionary doctrines of the twentieth
century. His consciousness developed with extraordinary speed, however, after his arrival in Paris in
1924, at one of the great cultural moments of
Western history. Within ten years he had written
more than 400 newspaper articles, translated the
best-known Maya text *Popol Vuh* (Book of the
Council) into Spanish (from French!), published the
Leyendas de Guatemala and, above all, completed
what would become his most famous work, a
historical and stylistic point of reference for Latin
American literature as a whole, *El Señor Presidente*
(The President) (1946), about the Estrada Cabrera
era. The novel shows clearly the influence of
surrealism (see **surrealism in Latin American
art**) on Asturias's language and technique, but its
perceptions are used functionally to convey humanistic disbelief at the horrors of oppression and
injustice.

El Señor Presidente would have to wait thirteen
years for publication, from 1933, when Asturias
returned to Guatemala, until 1946, when the work
appeared in Mexico. The reason, ironically but
unsurprisingly, was the existence of another US-
backed dictatorship, that of Jorge **Ubico** (1931–
44). Asturias lay as low as possible and worked on
his most important novel, *Hombres de maíz*, which
was eventually published in Buenos Aires. A
difficult, complex and controversial work, *Hombres
de maíz* traces the long, painful and uncompleted
interaction between the Indian cultures which
occupied Central America at the time of the
sixteenth-century conquest and the Europeans who
invaded and subjugated them. The work's rele-
vance is enhanced by Asturias's prescient analysis
of how European imperialism seeks to dominate
not only other human beings but everything else,
including nature, culture and thought itself.

In the 1950s, the era of literary *engagement*,
Asturias devoted himself to political concerns
through his controversial *Trilogía bananera* (Banana
Trilogy), an interesting but not entirely successful
amalgam of **magical realism** and **socialist
realism** which documents US imperialism in
Guatemala and prophesies revolutionary victory
for the Guatemalan people. He also published

Weekend en Guatemala (1956), a collection of stories protesting the 1954 US-backed invasion of his country which sent him into exile.

In the 1960s he returned to his early interest in Guatemalan cultural syncretism, first with *Mulata de tal* (Mulata) (1963) and later with *Maladrón* (The Bad Thief) (1969). Though without the full continental resonance of his first three works, these were novels of a remarkable freshness for a writer in his sixties, and Asturias continued the trend with *Tres de cuatro soles* (Three of Four Suns), published after his death in 1974. By that time, despite the Nobel Prize, his star was in decline, but his is likely to be remembered as one of the most original Latin American voices of the twentieth century.

Further reading

Asturias, M.A. (1963) *The President*, London: Gollancz.
Brotherston, G. (1978) *The Emergence of the Latin American Novel*, Cambridge University Press.
Callan, R. (1968) *Miguel Angel Asturias*, Boston: Twayne.
Martin, G. (1989) *Journeys through the Labyrinth: Latin American Fiction in the Twentieth Century*, London: Verso.
Prieto, R. (1993) *Miguel Angel Asturias's Archeology of Return*, Cambridge: Cambridge University Press.

GERALD MARTIN

Asuar, José Vicente

b. 1933, Santiago, Chile

Composer

Asuar assembled Latin America's first electronic music laboratory at the Universidad Católica in Chile, and produced what is probably the region's first electronic composition, *Spectral Variations* (1959). A graduate in music and engineering in Chile, he pursued further studies in Germany with Balcher and Wildberger. Later, he moved on to Venezuela, creating an electronic laboratory there, and in 1970 went to the USA to work with Hiller. His compositions include *La noche* (Night) (1966), *Caleidoscopio* (Kaleidoscope) (1967) and *Formas I* and

Formas II, which marked Asuar's move into working with computers.

MIKE GONZALEZ

Ateneo Puertorriqueño

Founded in San Juan in 1876 by Manuel de Elzaburru y Vicarrondo, and conceived by the Puerto Rican writer Alejandro Tapia y Rivera, the Ateneo Puertorriqueño became an important centre for political and cultural debates at the turn of the century. It has been led at different times by key figures in Puerto Rican intellectual life. It has an important library, and sponsors annual competitions for writers, visual artists and video-makers.

JUAN CARLOS QUINTERO HERENCIA

Aterro do Flamengo

A beautiful example of modern urban planning, the levelling of the Santo Antonio hill in Rio de Janeiro allowed a coastal landfill for express highways and a public park. It returned to Le Corbusier's idea, expressed in his 1929 plans for Rio de Janeiro, of using contemporary techniques to establish a harmony between man and nature. Partially completed in 1962, it was developed by a team with a deep commitment to urban planning that included Lota Mercedes Soares (co-ordinator), Affonso Eduardo Reidy, Jorge Machado **Moreira** and Helio Mamede (architects), Bertha Leitchic (engineer), Luiz Emigdio de Mello Filho (botanist) and Roberto Burle **Marx** (landscape architect).

ROBERTO CONDURU

Atilla the Hun

b. 1892, Trinidad; d. 1962, Trinidad

Calypsonian and writer

Seven times acknowledged the Calypso King of Trinidad and often called 'the Shakespeare of **calypso**', Atilla the Hun (Raymond Quevedo) was well-known for his lyrics and was an indefatigable fighter for social reform, closely watched by the colonial police. In 1946 he was elected deputy mayor of Port of Spain. He was simultaneously President General of the Trinidad Labour Party and a member of the Carnival Improvement Committee. Ultimately he rejected opportunities of influential positions in government and business and became a full-time calypsonian.

KEITH JARDIM

Atl, Dr

b. 1875, Guadalajara, Mexico; d. 1964, Mexico City

Artist

Born Gerardo Murillo and remembered as much as a teacher and popularizer of art as an artist in his own right, Atl was profoundly affected by French impressionism. Having changed his name to 'Atl' (the Náhuatl for 'water'), he returned to Mexico from Europe in 1903 where he organized exhibitions of art and taught at the San Carlos Academy. In 1910 he countered Porfirio Díaz's centenary exhibition of European art with one of independent Mexican artists. He became Minister of Fine Arts in the post-revolutionary government of 1920, began his murals for the Church of Saints Peter and Paul, and resumed an earlier interest in painting volcanoes, particularly Paracutín.

AMANDA HOPKINSON

Atlântida

Film production company founded in Rio de Janeiro, Brazil, in 1941. For twenty years it produced successful popular films combining elements of carnival, burlesque and farce. Luis Severiano Ribeiro Jr, its principal shareholder, reduced production costs while benefitting from protective cinema laws mandating the regular exhibition of national films (see **cinema laws in Brazil**). Atlântida's profitability enabled this rare example of Brazilian studio production to survive, employing directors like **Burle** and Carlos **Manga** to produce parodies of Hollywood and *chancha-*

das, the popular musical genre of the 1940s and 1950s. With the crisis of the film industry in the late 1950s Atlântida's stars and technicians migrated to the new television industry.

ISMAIL XAVIER AND THE USP GROUP

Atteck, Sybil

b. 1911, Port-of-Spain, Trinidad; d. 1975, Port-of-Spain

Visual artist

Atteck was at the centre of the post-Second World War generation of Trinidadian artists who called themselves the Independents, all trained abroad and influenced by developments in Europe or the USA. Their themes reflected a search for a Trinidadian identity in the years before Independence, focusing on Afro-Caribbean and East Indian festivals and religious rites, rural life and the urban barrack-yard. In 1943 Atteck founded the Trinidad Art Society, whose emphasis on European notions of painting reflected the ambiguous position of colonial artists. Atteck's piece, *Moon Dancers*, an undated acrylic, is an expressionistic rendering of the Muslim festival of Hosay.

LORRAINE LEU

Atwell, Winifred

b. 1913, Tunapuna, Trinidad; d. 1983, London, England

Pianist

Atwell showed early promise as a pianist. During Second World War, she entertained army personnel stationed in Trinidad with her rendering of the new craze, boogie-woogie music. Moving to the US, she studied classical piano under Alexander Borovsky, and later at the Royal Academy of Music, London. Although Atwell supported herself through boogie-woogie gigs, a recital at London Coliseum established her as a touring concert pianist. She recorded boogie-woogie albums for Phillips, while the album *Ivory and Steel* blended Trinidadian steel pan (see **steelband**) and classical music. Her contribution to the music and culture of Trinidad was recognized by the Winifred Atwell Foundation, set up in 1993.

JILL E. ALBADA-JELGERSMA

Audiovisuales Chirripó

Audiovisuales Chirripó (Chirripó Audiovisuals) is an audiovisual collective founded in 1988 to provide an alternative vision for the people of Costa Rica, and to create a video bank for Central America. Chirripó has produced films about the environment, local culture, women, children, and social problems, including *Lo que aún tenemos* (What Is Still Left For Us), a 5-minute documentary addressing ecotourism and environmental destruction; *Imágenes de un encuentro* (When Cultures Meet, dir. Roberto Miranda, 1990), a 'music video' depicting the month-long journey of a group of Scandanavian singers through Costa Rica and Nicaragua; *Madres Niñas* (Child Mothers) (1991), an investigation of the problems facing young mothers in Central America; and *Aprendiendo juntos* (Learning Together) (1993), strategies for educating children with disabilities.

ANN MARIE STOCK

auto racing

A highly popular sport all over South America, although the poverty of the region means that the costly Formula One world championship races are only held semi-regularly in Brazil and in Argentina once a year. There is a continental Formula Three championship with over a dozen races annually, with mostly Argentine and Brazilian drivers.

There are weekly races, mostly in Argentina, for all types of vehicle from stock cars to lorries as well as rallies – one stage of the World Rally Championship is held annually in Argentina – which attract large numbers of spectators and a sizeable television audience. Many of the cars taking part are, if not locally manufactured, locally souped up for racing. Races are held on roads over long distances, or over circuits.

South American drivers have won 13 Formula

One world championships, beginning with the legendary Argentine driver Juan Manuel **Fangio** who won it a record five times (1951, and 1954–7). He was followed by Brazilians Emerson **Fittipaldi** (1972, 1974), Nelson **Piquet** (1981, 1983, 1987) and Ayrton **Senna** (1988, 1990, 1991). Brazil is the only South American Formula One presence today, largely because of the availability of sponsorhip which every driver in this class must have, while occasionally there is one Argentine participant in a less powerful car due to having lesser sponsorship.

South Americans have a reputation as fearless drivers, but the reason why they are so good is because they are schooled in all types of car and over poor roads; they often prepare their own cars for races, which makes them particularly knowledgeable about cars and engines.

While many of the stock car and similar races use brand name cars produced locally, some Formula Three cars use locally produced engines and others from abroad. There are no Formula One cars or engines produced in South America, however; on the other hand, there are some excellent mechanics and technicians well used to doing wonders with limited materials.

ERIC WEIL

autobiography

In her book *At Face Value* (1991), Sylvia **Molloy** has observed that: 'whereas there are and have been a good many autobiographies written in Spanish America, they have not always been read autobiographically: filtered through the dominant discourse of the day, they have been hailed either as history or as fiction, and rarely considered as occupying a space of their own'. She examines, among others, autobiographical works by Victoria **Ocampo**, Mariano **Picón Salas** and José **Vasconcelos**. In all of them she observes a certain uneasiness about speaking about the private or the intimate: these are very largely the public lives of famous people, recorded for their contemporaries and for posterity. When they seem to be most intimate, she observes, instead of narrating the self (the hallmark of autobiography since Rousseau), these writers take refuge in telling the stories of their families or their ancestors: autobiography shades into **biography**.

Neruda's *Confieso que he vivido: memorias* (translated simply as *Memoirs*) (1974), a work not discussed by Molloy, is a useful case in point. Assembled by Neruda (or perhaps by his heirs, since it was published posthumously) from bits of his journalism, this work contains profiles of his friends (and enemies) and of his times – life as a consul in Asia, the Spanish Civil War (see **Spanish Civil War, impact of**), exile in Mexico, his returns to Chile – but it is surprisingly lacking in self-disclosure: it is as if Neruda put on the costumes that decorate his houses in Santiago and Isla Negra and never took them off. The great set piece that is at the centre of the book, the telling of his decision to join the Chilean Communist Party in 1945 (see **communist parties**), is oddly distanced: Neruda tells of being asked by miners in the desert of northern Chile to read his poetry, and reports that his poetry has earned him the laurel crown of a worker who salutes him as a brother. He then reports: 'I entered the Chilean Communist Party on 15 July 1945'. The event is presented is an oddly flat way, as if its significance were given to him by others, not by his own decision.

The autobiographical impulse is strongly present in fictional works, including those of Felisberto **Hernández**, Ricardo **Güiraldes**, Virgilio **Piñera**, Clarice **Lispector**, José **Lezama Lima**, Molloy herself, and Ricardo **Piglia**, as well as (more fleetingly) in the works of **Borges**, **Rulfo**, **Cortázar** and **Onetti**. To some extent, elements of self-disclosure which seem relatively lacking in many of the autobiographies are more fully present in these fictions, perhaps precisely because of the ruse that this is not the whole nor nothing but the truth. Another genre that flirts with autobiography is *testimonio*, though here the life that is told is not being written by the one who experienced it (Rigoberta **Menchú**, Domitila Chungara, Esteban Montejo, Jesusa Palancares) but is being told to another who writes (Elizabeth Burges-Debray, Moemi Viezzer, Miguel **Barnet**, Elena **Poniatowska**). This is obviously rather distant from the writing of one's own life, which involves self-definition or self-construction, and the negotiation with a reader about what can be told, about what is fit to print.

Further reading

Iglesia, C. (1996) *Islas de la memoria*, Buenos Aires: Cuenca del Plata.

Molloy, S. (1991) *At Face Value: Autobiographical Writing in Spanish America*, Cambridge: Cambridge University Press.

Prieto, A. (1966) *La literatura autobiográfica argentina*, Buenos Aires: Jorge Alvarez.

Rosa, N. (1990) *El arte del olvido*, Buenos Aires: Puntosur.

DANIEL BALDERSTON

avant-garde in Latin America

Until the late 1950s, the Latin American avant-garde was perceived as derivative of the European avant-garde, without recognition of its originality of influence on subsequent literary and artistic movements. With the exception of a few major figures, such as Pablo **Neruda**, César **Vallejo**, Vicente **Huidobro** and Nicolás **Guillén**, little attention had been given to the period that Peter Bürger has called the 'historic avant-garde' (between the early 1910s and the 1940s). The emergence of the Latin American novel, the so-called '**Boom**', in the early 1950s and 1960s inspired an examination of its antecedents, and with it, an interest in understanding the Latin American avant-garde as a significant cultural development that gave voice to a relatively unified and distinctly Latin American art, also part of a larger international movement.

The international character of the Latin American avant-garde is due principally to the unprecedented flow of political ideas and aesthetic styles between different urban and regional centres and across national borders. This aesthetic and ideological cross-fertilization was made possible by the free movement of artists throughout Europe and the Americas and a steady migration towards the national capitals. Capital cities in Latin America, including Buenos Aires, Mexico City, Lima, Havana and Santiago de Chile, joined New York City and established European capitals in an international network with Paris at its centre. In addition to the formative voyage that Latin American artists ritually undertook to Europe, many avant-garde artists spent long periods there.

Notable among these were **Borges**, who lived in Switzerland and Spain, Cesár Vallejo, who spent most of his adult life in Paris, and Oliverio **Girondo**, who made annual trips to Europe. At the same time, many Europeans made their way to South America searching for inspiration for their artistic experiments. André Breton spent time among the Tarahumaras in Mexico; Blaise Cendrars lived in Brazil; and Guillermo de Torre lived in Argentina. Finally, Latin America avant-garde artists explored their own continent and made contacts with avant-garde artists from other Latin American countries and regions. Pablo Neruda, Pablo de **Rokha**, Oliverio Girondo and Carlos **Pellicer** illustrate this deliberate and conscious effort to explore Latin America and write about the cultural and aesthetic issues they encountered in their travels.

Along with increased ease of transatlantic travel, breakthroughs in communications technology contributed to the internationalism of the avant-garde movement. The telegraph, **radio**, **cinema** and flourishing print industries were seen as icons of a new era and a new and radically different spirit. New art forms emerged that sought to describe and consciously shape a new international reality, as well as challenge the traditional relationship between society, art and artist. The artist was seen as being in a formative relationship with society. Thus, in the symbolic universe of the arts, the arrival of the avant-garde represented the dissolution of ideological, political and cultural centrality, and with it the erosion of European dominance, which allowed for a more inclusive and relativistic view of cultural and historical phenomena.

The Latin American avant-garde was, however, more than an expression of the larger international movement. Vicky Unruh has pointed out that Latin American vanguardism was also 'autochthonous in its orientation, as artists interacted with European avant-garde currents in keeping with their own cultural exigencies'. The Latin American avant-garde affirmed its own distinctive identitiy, whether national, regional or continental. Nelson **Osorio** has explained this independence by defining the avant-garde as a product of specific Latin American socioeconomic conditions. He understands it as a response to the anti-oligarchic

spirit of the era and an expression of hope for political and ideological change. This is seen in the increased demand for political power by the nascent middle class, the working class, farmers, students and ethnic groups as well as a response to **socialism, communist parties, anarchism, fascism in Latin America** and union-based philosophies.

One of the main characteristics that defines the Latin American avant-garde is a desire to break with the past, both politically and aesthetically. The *modernista* aesthetic no longer adequately described the New World at the beginning of this century. The avant-garde defined itself in terms of a 'modern' sensibility, coupled with a desire to belong to 'modernity' (often, in Latin America, this was expressed as a longing) and, at times, to an almost futuristic world. The avant-garde artist can be understood as a vagabond, a wandering camera, an eye registering and commenting on the modern **city** and its technologies. The poetry of Girondo, Luis **Cardoza y Aragón**, Borges, Jorge **Carrera Andrade**, Manuel **Maples Arce** and others describes this new and changing architectural landscape of major Latin American cities together with their European counterparts.

Another important characteristic of the Latin American avant-garde was political activism and a commitment to social and political change. This was expressed in the revolutionary content of art works and in formal experimentation, both of which sought to recreate the world anew. Ideologically, art was viewed not as a mere reflection of society but as an active participant in shaping society. By changing perceptions of the world, art could also change the world itself. Whether expressed in Marxist terminology, anti-colonial ideology or populist union-based thinking, the avant-garde engaged in a fight against *modernismo* (see ***modernismo,* Spanish American**) as an aesthetic form that stood for the ideology of the oligarchic political structure in power throughout most of Latin America. The murals of Diego **Rivera**, José Clement **Orozco** and David Alfaro **Siqueiros**, members of the League of Revolutionary Writers and Artists in Mexico, evidence a search to find an art that was both national and popular. Their explicit goals were to create art for the masses and serve the ideology of revolution. Other examples of social and political commitment in the avant-garde can be found in the formal experimentation and political content of works by Neruda, Vallejo, Magda **Portal**, Alejandro Peralta (Gamaliel **Churata**) and the Afro-Caribbean poetry of Nicolás Guillén and Luis **Palés Matos**.

A third characteristic of the Latin American avant-garde is a continuous experimentation with form and content in the search for an ever-changing newness that better expresses the condition of modernity. Examples of this experimentation include destruction of the concept of beauty; harmony and unity in art through dislocation, parody and irony; elimination of a single narrator or cohesive poetic voice; hybridization of genres; interest in and the assimilation of popular or mass art (the circus, cabaret, recitals, film) as well as primitive or anonymous art; dismemberment of traditional poetic form (use of free verse, poems without stanzas, rhyme, traditional syntax or metre); the innovative use of typographical spaces on the page; the use of different physical and representational materials in montage; and the use of calligramatic and concrete poetry. Together, this experimentation reflected a general desire to destroy the concept of art as a bourgeois institution and artistic objects as possessions to be owned by individuals.

The fourth characteristic of the Latin American avant-garde is that the world it created and expressed was no longer governed by logic and reason. Formal experimentation led to descriptions of a reality understood or experienced as fragmented, discontinuous, without obvious psychic unity, and often with irrational foundations. The speaking subject was no longer a stable psychic unity but a shifting voice or point of view. The basic feeling expressed through its dislocated language was that of alienation for the world. The reader was integrated into the avant-garde text. The reader became the speaker's ally as seen in the multitude of avant-garde **manifestos** in which the voice fights against a common enemy (the old system, past literary school or poetic forms). At times the reader became the enemy attached or disregarded through an aggressive or totally cryptic language that did not concern itself with 'communicating' with the reader.

Finally, it is important to examine the Latin American avant-garde as a national phenomenon that had unique expressions in different parts of Latin America. While there was avant-garde activity throughout most of Latin America, the major vanguard centres were Buenos Aires, Mexico City, Lima, Havana and São Paulo. An examination of avant-garde activities specific to national centres illustrates the crucial importance of vanguard group activities and the journals in which art and ideas were published. Studying avant-garde at the national level also facilitates a better understanding of the relationship between individual artists, their specific socio-political contexts, and the national or regional ideological traditions within which they worked. This relationship is well illustrated by the Brazilian avant-garde, for example, notable for both its national expression in the incorporation of a non-academic 'Brazilian' language, and for its cosmopolitan tendencies. After the centennial independence celebration of the **Modern Art Week** in São Paulo in 1922, a number of distinct and diverse vanguard groups appeared, located in different urban centers such as São Paulo, Rio de Janeiro, Belo Horizonte and Cataguases in Minas Gerais. The 'Dinamista' group was led by Graça Aranha, who had a special interest in futurist elements such as movement, velocity and material and technical progress; the 'Primitivista' group was led by Oswald de **Andrade**; the 'nacionalista' group was located in São Paulo and published the journals *Verdeamarelo* (1926), *Anta* (1927) and *Bandeira* (1936); the 'Espiritualista' group was located in Rio de Janeiro; and the 'Desvairista' group was centred around the magnetic personality of Mário de **Andrade**. Also of note was the participation of three Brazilian women: cubist painter Anita **Malfatti**, whose 1917 show in São Paulo was considered scandalous; the painter Tarsila do **Amaral**, who participated in the '**Antropofagia**' group and published, along with her husband Oswald de Andrade, in its important journal *Revista de antropofagia* (São Paulo, 1928–9); and the poet Cecília **Meireles**, who was associated with the magazine *Festa*.

The Argentine avant-garde was polarized between two groups. The Boedo group was working class and socialist, and primarily wrote prose, while the Florida group (associated especially with the journal **Martín Fierro** (1924–7)) was cosmopolitan, upper class and wrote mostly poetry (see **Boedo vs Florida**). In Peru, most vanguard activity was centred on the exceptional journal **Amauta** (1926–30), edited by José Carlos **Mariátegui**; it often dealt with the issue of **indigenismo**. There were important national avant-gardes in most capitals of the continent. Two additional avant-garde journals played a critical role in the development of both a national and continental Latin American avant-garde: the Cuban **Revista de avance** (1927–30) and the Costa Rican **Repertorio Americano** (1919–59).

The 'historical' Latin American avant-garde can be understood as playing an important formative role in the remarkable experimentation of contemporary Latin American literature and art. The **Boom** narrative of the 1960s is directly indebted to the experimentation of the historical avant-garde, even through writers – among them Gabriel **García Márquez**, Julio **Cortázar**, Carlos **Fuentes** and others – have not always acknowledged their debt to prose works by Borges, Vallejo, Huidobro and María Luisa **Bombal**. Poetical avant-garde experimentation also anticipated some of the works of the Brazilian Poesia Concreta movement (see **concrete poetry**) of the 1950s and 1960s (especially the **Noigandres group**, which included the poets Augusto de **Campos**, Décio **Pignatari** and Haroldo de **Campos**), the Poema/Proceso group from Rio de Janeiro led by Wladimir Dias Pino, the Poesía para y/o Realizar of Edgardo Antonio Vigo and the Poesía Inobjetal of the Uruguayan Clemente Padín. All of these follow in the footsteps of the historical avant-garde in their experimentation with the visual aspect of poetry and notions of poetry as art, action and engagement.

Further reading

Ades, D. (1989) *Art in Latin America: The Modern Era 1820–1980*, New Haven: Yale University Press.

Espinosa, C. (ed.) (1990) *Corrosive Signs: Essays on Experimental Poetry*, trans. H. Polkinhorn, Washington, DC: Maisonneuve Press.

Grünfeld, M. (1995) *Antología de la poesía latinoamericana de vanguardia*, Madrid: Hiperión.

Holliday, T.D. and Sturges, H. (1987) *Art of the Fantastic: Latin America 1920–1987*, Indianapolis, IN: Indianapolis Museum of Art.

Osorio, N. (1988) *Manifiestos, proclamas y polémicas de las vanguardia literaria hispanoamericana*, Caracas: Ayacucho.

Schwartz, J. (1991) *Las vanguardias latinoamericanas: Textos programáticos*, Madrid: Cátedra.

Unruh, V. (1994) *Latin American Vanguards: The Art of Contentious Encounters*, Berkeley, CA: University of California Press.

MIHAI GRÜNFELD

Avenida 9 de julio

Avenida 9 de julio is an avenue running north-south through the heart of Buenos Aires, first conceived in 1889. Its first stage was opened in 1937, when its 140 metres formed the world's widest avenue. Thirty-three city blocks were demolished to allow its construction. At its intersection with Corrientes Avenue stands a 66-metre-high obelisk, designed by Alberto **Prebisch** and opened in 1936, which has come to symbolize the city. The Ministry of Public Works stands in the middle of the avenue, which today feeds a series of highways connecting the city with the wider metropolitan area.

LILIANA ZUCCOTTI

Avenida de Mayo

One kilometre long, Buenos Aires's Avenida de Mayo links the Casa Rosada, Argentina's seat of government, and the National Congress. Opened in 1894, it was designed by Torcuato de Alvear (1884), the precursor of urban modernization. The avenue's buildings vary in style, from the 'art nouveau' Hotel Chile, by French architect Jules Dubois, to the romantic-gothic Pasaje Barolo (Barolo Arcade) by Italian Mario Palanti. The Palacio Municipal and the **La Prensa** building stand there, while Latin America's first metro (opened in 1913) runs beneath it (see **subways**. Theatres like the Avenida (1908) and Buenos Aires's most popular cafés, such as Los 36 Billares and Tortoni, the oldest in the city, guarantee its continuing cultural life.

LILIANA ZUCCOTTI

Avenida Paulista

Built by the Uruguayan engineer Joaquin Eugenio de Lima and inaugurated in 1891, it is the principal avenue of São Paulo, the centre of its cultural and financial activities. Built above the city, it attracted the São Paulo élite at the turn of the century. Number 1 belonged to the Von Bullow family, owners of the Antárctica brewery; opposite lived the Weizflogs, of the Melhoramentos publishing company. The romantic image changed with urban expansion in the 1930s; in 1939 the first multistorey block appeared, a seven-floor building on the corner of Frei Caneca Street. By the 1990s, a million people used the avenue daily, which was lined with skyscrapers.

ANTONIO CARLOS MARTINS VAZ

Avenida President Getulio Vargas

First planned in the nineteenth century to facilitate access to the centre-north of Rio de Janeiro, the avenue was built in the 1940s, and involved the destruction of long-standing neighbourhoods. Dedicated to dictator Getúlio **Vargas**, it was part of an attempt to monumentalize an urban space, designed for parades supporting the regime. It combined contradictory academic and modern principles of urban planning, different scales without graduation, creating a residual space where the new and the surviving buildings were articulated. The Avenue is a hiatus, the product of an authoritarian intervention in the city, and a wound that still has not healed.

ROBERTO CONDURU

Avila, Roberto

b. 1924, Veracruz, Mexico

Baseball player and politician

A **baseball** player in the US major professional leagues in the 1950s, Roberto (Beto) Avila was the first Latin American to win a league batting award. A handsome and charismatic man, Avila was a national hero in his native Mexico, and he was elected mayor of Veracruz after he retired from baseball. Later, he became president of the Mexican baseball league.

DOUGLAS W. VICK

axé

A central concept to **Yoruba**-inspired Afro-Atlantic religions such as Brazilian **Candomblé** and Cuban **Santería**, *axé* (Portuguese spelling; also *aché* or *ashê*) is divine power incarnate or the 'power to make things happen'. The supreme avatars of axé are male and female deities representing forces of nature called *orixás*, but it is also manifest in vital fluids like blood and semen. In Brazil and Cuba, *axé* has crept into colloquial speech as an expression of agreement or solidarity. It can mean 'so be it' or 'you said it'. In the 1990s, the word provided the namesake for Brazilian 'axé music', a type of pop music from Bahia.

CHRISTOPHER DUNN

Ayahuasca   *see* Yage

Ayala (Pérez), Daniel

b. 1906, Abalá, Yucatan, Mexico; d. 1975, Veracruz, Mexico

Composer, conductor

Ayala's worldwide fame came as the result of his avant-garde style of composition, integrating

Mayan music and instruments in pentatonic modes with a vigorous, rhythmic beat. Typical of his compositions, written almost entirely in the 1930s and 1940s, are *Uchben XíCoholte* (Ancient Cemetery) (1933), for soprano and chamber orchestra; *U Kayil Chaac* (Song to the Rain) (1936), for soprano, chamber orchestra and Mayan instruments; the symphonic suite-ballet *El Hombre Maya* (Mayan man) (1940); and *Los Yaquis y los Seris* (1938, 1942), two suites for voice, chamber ensemble and indigenous percussion instruments. His career as a widely known conductor of symphonic orchestras, particularly that of Yucatan, which he founded in 1942, spanned a number of years.

EDUARDO GUÍZAR ALVAREZ

Ayala, Fernando

b. 1920, Entre Ríos, Argentina

Film-maker

Ayala began as an assistant director at the **Lumitón** studios, and in 1955 directed his first film, *Ayer fue primavera* (Spring Was Yesterday), an innovative work anticipating the narrative strategies of the **Generación del 60**. In 1956 he founded the production company **Aries Cinematográfica** (with Héctor **Olivera**), and began to specialize in socio-political parables like *El jefe* (The Chief) (1958) and *El candidato* (The Candidate) (1959). *Las locas del conventillo* (Slum Queens) and *Hotel Alojamiento* (Apartment-Hotel) (both 1965) marked a turn towards commercial cinema, but *Plata dulce* (Sweet Money) (1982) and *El arreglo* (The Arrangement) (1983) returned to his earlier social criticism.

DIANA PALADINO

Ayllón, Eva

b. 1950, Lima, Peru

Singer

Arguably one of Peru's most distinguished and accomplished female vocalists, this Afro-Peruvian's music is a *mélange* of Cuban '**feeling**' and *nueva*

trova, Argentine popular song, *nueva canción* and Caribbean rhythms. It has an enthusiastic audience in her native country as well as abroad. Working as a soloist after singing with the group Los Kipus, she shot to fame with her hits 'El embrujo' (Bewitched) in 1973 and later 'El otro sitio' (The Other Place), and has had a successful musical career ever since. She has collaborated with Chabuca **Granda** and Elena Bustamante, and has greatly influenced a new generation of Latin American musicians.

PETER WATT

Aymara

Aymara is an Amerindian language spoken by over two million people in Bolivia, southern Peru and northern Chile. Also called *jaqi* or *jaqaru* (human speech), Aymara is part of the Jaqi language family, which includes the Jaqi and Kawki languages in Peru. In Bolivia and Peru the Aymara are neighbours of **Quechua**-speaking peoples. Though Aymara and Quechua have not been shown to be linguistically related, many similarities in vocabulary and grammar exist between the two languages as a result of centuries of contact. The Aymara are one of the core populations of indigenous people in South America, and are a significant political and cultural force in the region.

In Bolivia, La Paz and the neighbouring city of El Alto are primary centres of urban Aymara speakers, where Spanish–Aymara bilingualism is prevalent. The rural, more monolingual Aymara core is centered in the high **altiplano** of the states of Oruro and Potosí, and around the shores of Lake Titicaca in Peru and Bolivia. Aymara colonists in the sub-tropical Yungas and eastern Bolivia, as well as Aymara communities in northern Chile, are highly bilingual, and in many cases the Aymara language in these areas is being gradually displaced by Spanish.

Aymara linguistic and cultural communities in many settings represent a long period of resistance to Inca, Spanish and modern state expansionism. Aymara literature and culture have always been a fundamental, if often suppressed and publicly forgotten, part of Andean history. Early colonial grammars by the Jesuit Ludovico Bertonio in the seventeenth century and texts by Guaman or Waman Poma are the first sources of written Aymara literature. In recent years, the University of Florida Aymara Project, the formation of organizations like the *Instituto Nacional de Estudios Lingüísticos*, the *Instituto de Lengua y Cultura Aymara* and the **Taller de Historia Oral Andina** are promoting Aymara recovery and expansion in various media. In addition, Aymara linguists and language activists work in bilingual education, radio broadcasts, grammatical studies and theatre. Victor Hugo Cárdenas, an Aymara intellectual and defender of Aymara–Spanish education, served as Bolivia's vice-president from 1993 to 1997. With a large population and a heritage of resistance, Aymara speakers appear to have positive prospects for maintaining their language and a range of cultural identities, despite homogenizing pressures by the 'modernizing' state and global media.

See also: Sanjinés, Jorge; Ukamau

Further reading

Albó, X. (ed.) (1988) *Raíces de América: el mundo Aymara*, Madrid: Alianza Editorial Sociedad Quinto Centenario.

BRET GUSTAFSON

Azar, Héctor

b. 1930, Atlixco, Mexico

Playwright and poet

An important innovator in Mexican theatre, Azar's first major contribution was the Teatro en Coapa, established in 1955, which promoted experimentation on the basis of classic texts. He was also the author of the El Espacio C (C Space) theory, and founder of the CADAC Theatre School. He was Director of the National Theatre Company, the Theatre Department of the Mexican Institute of Fine Arts and headed the Drama department at the Mexican National University (**UNAM**). His theatrical writings include *Olímpica* (1962) and *Los juegos del azar* (Games of Chance) (1973).

TITO VASCONCELOS

Azcárraga, Emilio *see* Televisa

Azevedo, Geraldo

b. 1945, Petrolina, Pernambuco, Brazil

Composer and musician

Geraldo Azevedo, the 'Bard of Petrolina', is best known for transforming and modernizing folk traditions of the Brazilian northeast. In 1963 he moved to Recife and founded the group Construção, with master percussionist Naná Vasconcelos. Four years later, both relocated to Rio de Janeiro and joined the Quarteto Livre which accompanied the famed protest singer Geraldo **Vandré**. Since launching his solo career in the mid-1970s, Azevedo has collaborated with fellow northeasterners Alceu Valença, Elba Ramalho, **Elomar** and Xangai. His compositions include paeans to feminine beauty and nature and well as songs expressing social and environmental concerns.

CHRISTOPHER DUNN

Azevedo, Luiz Heitor Corrêa de

b. 1905, Rio de Janeiro, Brazil; d. 1992, Paris, France

Musicologist

Widely respected as the leading Brazilian musicologist of his generation, Azevedo wrote many texts still regarded as seminal, including *A música brasileira e seus fundamentos* (Foundations of Brazilian Music) (1948), *Música e músicos do Brasil* (Music and Musicians of Brazil) (1950), and *150 anos de música no Brasil, 1800–1950* (150 Years of Music in Brazil) (1956). Azevedo worked as Librarian in the Instituto Nacional de Música (1932) and founded the pioneering *Revista brasileira de música* (1934). His employment with **UNESCO** in Paris (from 1947 until 1965) involved providing hospitality for many visiting Brazilian musicians, including **Villa-Lobos**.

SIMON WRIGHT

Azuaga, Moncho

b. 1953, Asunción, Paraguay

Writer

Co-founder (with Emilio Lugo and Ricardo de la Vega) of the journal **Cabichu'í 2**, Azuaga's literary work has been honoured in various foreign and national competitions. From his many writings, the following titles stand out: in poetry, *Bajo los vientos del sur* (Under the Southern Winds) (1986) and *Ciudad sitiada* (Besieged City) (1989); in narrative, the collection of short stories *Arto cultural y otras joglarías...* (Cultural 'arto' and other folk tools...) (1989) and the novel *Celda 12* (Cell 12) (1991), a requiem to **Stroessner**'s dictatorship; and in theatre, *En moscas cerradas* (In Closed Flies) (1976).

TERESA MÉNDEZ-FAITH

Azuela, Mariano

b. 1873, Lagos de Moreno, Jalisco, Mexico; d. 1952, Mexico City

Writer

A major novelist of the Mexican Revolution (see **revolutions**), Azuela's most famous work, *Los de abajo* (The Underdogs) (1925) had first appeared in 1915 in El Paso, Texas, in serial form. It represented the revolution as an increasingly directionless process taken over by power seekers and opportunists, echoing the disillusionment Azuela expressed in several other novels. A doctor and supporter of Francisco Madero, he joined Pancho **Villa** before withdrawing from politics. He wrote prolifically, usually in the same episodic realist style as his early work, apart from three experimental novels written, he claimed, as a challenge to critical fashions.

MIKE GONZALEZ

B

Babenco, Héctor

b. 1946, Mar del Plata, Argentina

Film-maker

A truly international figure, Babenco left home at seventeen for Europe, where he worked as a film extra and assistant to Mario Bava, Sergio Carbucco and Mario Camus. He travelled to Africa and Puerto Rico, and settled in Brazil, where he made a series of tourist documentaries for the government and began filming *O fabuloso Fittipaldi* (Fabulous **Fittipaldi**) (1972), later completed by Roberto Farías. His 1975 film, *O rei da noite* (King of the Night), anticipated many of the stylistic topics and thematic lines of his later work. Two years later he achieved his first major success with *Lúcio Flavio, o passageiro da agonia* (The Dying Passenger), an exposé of police corruption, complicity with death squads and torture. ***Pixote a lei do mais fraco*** (Pixote, Law of the Weakest) (1980) pursues similar themes. A fiction film with strong documentary elements, it is centred on a young boy placed in a correctional facility where he learns the law of the survival of the fittest, and its injustices and abuses. The international impact of the film allowed Babenco access to North American financial support for his next project, *The Kiss of the Spider Woman* (1985), adapted from the novel and play by Manuel **Puig**, *El **beso de la mujer araña***. The film depicts the relationship between a political activist and a homosexual (played by Raúl **Juliá** and William Hurt, respectively) who share a prison cell and exchange memories. The film's success further opened Hollywood doors and Babenco

embarked on *Ironweed* (1987), a twenty-three-million-dollar superproduction based on the novel by William Kennedy, who also wrote the adaptation. The theme, once again, is marginality, in this case represented by two hoboes (Jack Nicholson and Meryl Streep) who have broken with their previous life, but cannot throw off the past. Subsequent films included *The Second Killing of the Dog* (1988), *My Foolish Heart* (1990) and *At Play in the Fields of the Lord* (1991), adapted from a novel by Peter Matthiessen.

Further reading

Amar Rodriguez, V.M. (1994) *Héctor Babenco: una profuesta de lectura cinematográfica*, Madrid: Dickinson.

DIANA PALADINO

Babo, Lamartine de Azeredo

b. 1904, Rio de Janeiro, Brazil; d. 1963, Rio de Janeiro

Songwriter and lyricist

One of the most expressive representatives of Brazilian music. Although he had no formal musical training, he began composing in his teens. At the age of sixteen, Lamartine left school to work as an office-boy. In his spare time, he listened to music and created his own songs. In the 1930s, the popularity of his songs earned him the title 'King of **Carnival**'. He wrote nearly 150 songs in different styles (**samba**, marcha, **tango** and waltz), many of which remain carnival favourites.

ISABEL BARBUZZA

Baca, Susana

b. 1944, Chorrillos, Peru

Singer

The foremost figure in Afro-Peruvian music, Baca became known internationally when she represented Peru at the Seville Expo of 1992 and was featured on David Byrne's compilation, *The Soul of Black Peru* (1995). She had been performing professionally in Peru since 1970, under the auspices of the Instituto Nacional de Cultura (National Institute of Culture). Known for her versions of Chabuca **Granda** songs as well as for traditional Afro-Peruvian music, Baca is a powerful performer who has toured widely. Originally trained as a teacher, some of her albums – on the African heritage in Latin American music in general, and on the black contribution to Peruvian popular music in particular – have a didactic quality.

DANIEL BALDERSTON

Bacallao, Juana

b. 1925, Havana, Cuba

Singer

Born Nerys Martínez, Juana Bacallao had a unique stage presence and a carnivalesque abandon that made her the undisputed star of the cabarets at the Havana night spots of the 1950s – like the Riviera, the Parisien, the Caribe, the **Tropicana** and the Capri. Her career began a decade earlier, at Havana's Martí night spot, and she toured both the USA and Latin America before becoming the toast of Havana's night life. Her act embraces dance, song, drama and humour – the documentary, *Yo soy Juana Bacallao* (I am Juana Bacallao) (1989), by

Miriam Talavera bears witness to her qualities as an entertainer.

WILFREDO CANCIO ISLA

Baccino Ponce de León, Napoleón

b. 1947, Montevideo, Uruguay

Writer

Maluco (1989), his first novel, gained Baccino international acclaim and various prizes. Defying established histories, *Maluco* is a postmodern parodic reconstruction of the Magellan voyage, related by a buffoon through an extensive letter to King Charles V of Spain. Baccino's later novels *Un amor en Bangkok* (Love in Bangkok) (1994) and *Arte de perder* (The Art of Losing) (1995) are written in the same witty style. He has also published articles on Uruguayan writer Horacio **Quiroga**, cultural criticism for various newspapers and journals, and more than seventy short stories.

VICTORIA RUÉTALO

bachata

The bachata is a rhythm and dance originating from the *música de amargue* (music of bitterness) in the shanty towns (see **shanty towns and slums**) of the Dominican Republic in the early 1960s. At first, bachata was considered vulgar and low-class. There are now two types of bachata: the popular bachata and the middle-class bachata, also called tecno-bachata. In 1991, Juan Luis **Guerra** and his group 4:40 released the CD *Bachata rosa* (Bachata in Pink), which became an international success. Other bachata composers and singers include Luis Diás, Víctor **Víctor** and Sonia **Silvestre**.

FERNANDO VALERIO-HOLGUÍN

Bachianas brasileiras

A propensity for adapting existing musical forms and nomenclature to his own needs (sometimes drastically, as in the 1923 Nonet) characterized the work of Heitor **Villa-Lobos**. By extension, he was adept at coining completely new titles to identify forms of his own invention. *Bachianas brasileiras* (untranslatable in any language, and signifying both singular and plural) is his best-known neologism, the title for nine works composed between 1930 and 1945, in which Villa-Lobos attempted to evoke a broadly Brazilian ambience within a framework of forms and mannerisms redolent of Bach, paying homage both to his homeland and the composer.

The works are:

no. 1 (1930/1938) orchestra of cellos
no. 2 (1930) orchestra
no. 3 (1938) orchestra with solo piano
no. 4 (1930/1941) versions for solo piano, or orchestra
no. 5 (1938/1945) soprano with orchestra of cellos
no. 6 (1938) flute and bassoon
no. 7 (1942) orchestra
no. 8 (1944) orchestra
no. 9 (1945) versions for orchestra of voices, or string orchestra

The *Bachianas brasileiras* evolved when Villa-Lobos was intensely involved with musical education in Rio de Janeiro and premiering major works by Palestrina, Bach, and Beethoven – evolved, because the 'cycle' was in no way planned. Instead, it progressed sporadically and chaotically, and was certainly not composed in the published numerical order. *Bachianas* no. 2 adapted several existing cello and piano works. The first movement of no. 5 was hastily revised after Villa-Lobos was sued for copyright infringement; the second movement followed seven years later. *Bachianas* no. 4 was constructed from earlier piano pieces. Like Bach himself, Villa-Lobos was unafraid of re-using existing material, or raiding work by others.

To a degree, the *Bachianas* reflect the 1930s vogue for musical neoclassicism, but they also represent an important attempt to amalgamate elements of 'world music' with established classical forms some sixty years before the practice became widespread. This duality is stressed by the double titles of *Bachianas* movements, one 'Bachian', the other Brazilian: hence 'Ária (O canto da nossa terra)' in no. 2, or 'Tocata (Catira batida)' in no. 8.

While the use of baroque techniques in these works is superficial, the celebrated 'Ária (Cantilena)' of no. 5 is clearly the most often recorded and universally popular piece of art music to come from Latin America.

Further reading

Wright, S. (1992) *Villa-Lobos*, Oxford: Oxford University Press.

SIMON WRIGHT

Bacilio, Gilbert

b. 1950, Curaçao, Netherlands Antilles
Playwright and director

Inspired by Augusto **Boal**, Gilbert (Gibi) Bacilio scoffed at traditional theatre and took his group of amateur actors onto the streets of Curaçao in search of an audience. Bacilio studied philosophy in Colombia and theology in the Netherlands, but later turned to drama. Operating under the name of *Teatro Foro* (Forum Theatre) in the 1980s, Bacilio produced over a dozen plays in **Papiamentu**, which invariably invited audience participation. His work focuses on social problems such as housing, schooling, medical care and political patronage. His play *Karni òf Wesu* (Flesh or Bones) (1987), about AIDS prevention, was especially successful.

AART G. BROEK

Back to Africa movements *see* Garvey, Marcus

Badii, Líbero

b. 1916, Arezzo, Italy
Sculptor

Badii is an elegant stylizer of the feminine figure, strongly influenced by pre-Columbian sculpture; volume and geometrical forms of great purity characterize his work. Arriving in Argentina in

1927, he began to work with marble in his father's workshop while attending night school. A watershed moment in his career as a sculptor came when he travelled in South America, learning about ancient American art. In 1946 he joined the workshop of José **Fioravanti** and Carlos de la Cárcova. His work has been exhibited in Argentina, Brazil and Europe.

MAGDALENA GARCÍA PINTO

Baha Men

Bahamian band that earned international fame during the 1990s performing music which combined early Bahamian calypsos (see **calypso**) with recent influences such as US hip hop beats. They have also produced their own contemporary Bahamian music. Many of their own compositions use rhythms derived from the traditional Bahamian masquerade and music street festival known as **junkanoo**. Founded in the 1970s as 'High Voltage', for many years the group performed almost exclusively for local or tourist audiences in the Bahamas. With their revival and name change, however, they not only achieved some measure of international and commercial success but also helped to reinvigorate national interest in Bahamian music.

ROSANNE ADDERLEY

Bahamas

An archipelago of over 700 islands stretching from off the coast of Florida in the north towards the coasts of Cuba and Haiti in the south. The first landfall of Columbus in the Americas took place in the central Bahamas in October 1492, probably on the island currently known as San Salvador. The archipelago held little interest for the Spanish who concentrated their Caribbean colonization efforts mostly on Hispaniola and Cuba. During the first decades of the sixteenth century virtually the entire native Lucayan population of the Bahamas – about 20,000 people – was removed to Hispaniola as forced labour. Pirates and privateers sailed Baha-

mian waters for almost a century before Britain formally claimed the archipelago in 1624.

The first significant settlements were attempted on the island of Eleuthera in the 1640s and 1650s mostly by dissenting Puritans from Bermuda, but these never grew beyond about one hundred inhabitants. Even after the appointment of eight proprietors to administer the islands in 1663, the archipelago remained sparsely populated. Appointment of a royal governor in 1718 suppressed piracy but the majority of the inhabitants remained engaged mostly in minor subsistence agriculture, trade or maritime pursuits. In the mid-eighteenth century the population consisted of approximately 4,000 people with roughly equal numbers of whites and non-whites, with most of the non-white segment being enslaved Africans and their descendants. The arrival of American loyalists and their slaves in the 1780s after US independence nearly doubled the white population and increased the black population almost fourfold, still mostly enslaved. Loyalist arrival also brought commercial expansion and the most aggressive attempts ever seen in the colony at plantation agriculture using slave labour. However, the slave economy of the Bahamas, based on cotton, food crops and salt raking never came anywhere close to the prosperity of Caribbean sugar colonies. For more than a century after British slave emancipation in 1834 the colony remained something of an economic backwater with small-scale agriculture and fishing. Export crops such as sisal, pineapples and sea sponges enjoyed some success but not enough to radically transform the Bahamian economy.

Politically the colony, which possessed an elected legislative branch, remained dominated by a white minority, although small numbers of black and coloured people did enjoy political participation and some economic success. These economic, political and social patterns continued until the mid-twentieth century, which saw the birth of large-scale political activism and organization by the black majority and also the growth of a modern tourist industry. In 1967 the Bahamas elected its first legislature with a black majority. The victorious Progressive Liberal Party (PLP) headed by Lynden **Pindling** led the colony to independence from Great Britain in 1973.

Meanwhile, the advent of cheaper air travel after the Second World War had made large-scale tourism possible. With significant investments in advertising, infrastructure and planning first by the local Development Board and later by the Ministry of Tourism, Bahamian tourism grew from approximately 30,000 visitors in 1950 to several million tourists annually by the 1990s. **Tourism** became the country's largest employer and was responsible for approximately 70 per cent of the gross national product, with offshore banking making the second largest contribution. These economic successes and a population of just under 300,000 made the Bahamas one of the most prosperous countries of the Caribbean region at the end of the twentieth century. In contrast to earlier eras, significant numbers of the black majority population had entered the ranks of the middle and upper classes, although major income disparities between the wealthiest and the poorest remained.

Further reading

Craton, Michael and Saunders, Gail (1992 and 1998) *Islanders in the Stream: A History of the Bahamian People, Volumes One and Two*, Athens: University of Georgia Press.

ROSANNE ADDERLEY

Balaguer, Joaquín

b. 1907, Villa Bisonó, Dominican Republic

Politician and lawyer

Balaguer has dominated the political life of the Dominican Republic throughout the second half of the twentieth century. He graduated from the University of Santo Domingo in 1929 and began his political career in the following year in the group supporting the Presidential candidacy of Rafael Estrella Ureña. He occupied a number of posts during the dictatorship of Rafael **Trujillo** (1930–61), including the Vice-Presidency of the Republic from 1957 to 1960. After the resignation of Héctor B. Trujillo, he took over the Presidency, and continued to hold the post after the assassination of Trujillo on May 30th 1961, until popular pressure forced him out of office and he was obliged to seek asylum with the Papal Nuncio in January 1962.

While in exile in New York, Balaguer worked intensively to form the *Partido Reformista* (Reformist Party). On his return, he was pronounced the winner in the fraudulent Presidential elections of June 1966, held during the US military occupation; not surprisingly, ex-President Juan **Bosch** was deemed the loser. The fraud was particularly extensive in the rural areas, still occupied by 70 per cent of the population and subject to an unprecedented level of military repression.

Balaguer maintained himself in power for three consecutive terms by holding what purported to be free elections every four years. This period between 1966 and 1978 is known as the *Balaguerato* (the Balaguer years) – a regime which revived many of the forms of the Trujillo dictatorship. During this period, Balaguer opened the country to foreign investment and encouraged the growth of capitalism. The external debt grew to $700 million by 1975, and bureaucratic corruption reached unprecedented levels. According to Juan Bosch, 300 new millionaires appeared during the Balaguer years.

Just as Trujillo had done before him, Balaguer launched a campaign of counter-revolutionary terror throughout the country; thousands of young people were persecuted and imprisoned, and many were forced to abandon the country in fear of their lives. Over a thousand people were murdered in their homes or in the street, and paramilitary gangs (like the 'Banda colorá') terrorized the civilian population.

In 1978, Balaguer suffered a crushing defeat at the polls, but was again the victor in 1988 in elections characterized by fraud and large-scale vote-buying; he held power for two and a half terms. The vote-rigging that occurred in the 1994 ballot was so flagrant that Balaguer was finally forced to yield to national and international pressure and cut short his period of government to allow new elections in 1996.

Further reading

Cassá R. (1980) *Modos de producción, clases sociales y*

luchas políticas (República Dominicana siglo XX),
Santo Domingo: Alfa y Omega
—— (1986) *Historia económica y social de la república Dominicana* vol 2, Santo Domingo: Alfa y Omega.

FERNANDO VALERIO-HOLGUÍN

Ballagas, Emilio

b. 1908, Camagüey, Cuba; d. 1954,
Havana, Cuba

Poet

Associated with Cuba's major avant-garde literary journal, *Avance* (1927–30), Ballagas's first poems balanced a *modernista* aesthetic with an avant-garde vocabulary. He moved to 'pure poetry' (removed from social concerns), as represented by his first collection *Júbilo y fuga* (Jubilation and Flight) (1931) and by the celebrated *Cuaderno de poesía negra* (Black Poetry Notebook) (1934), his contribution to Afro-Cuban poetry. Ballagas's most effective poems are the elegies of *Sabor eterno* (Eternal Taste) (1938), love poems which lament the failure of a homosexual relationship. Although married with one son, Ballagas was homosexual; he was 'outed' in a 1955 essay by Virgilio **Piñera**.

BEN A. HELLER

Ballet Folklórico de México

The Ballet Folklórico de México is the most celebrated Mexican folk dance company, founded in 1952 by Amalia **Hernández**. Later, the company joined the Instituto Nacional de Bellas Artes, began to tour internationally and became a cultural ambassador for Mexico. Its performances at the Palacio de Bellas Artes (Palace of Fine Arts) in Mexico City have become a tourist attraction. Among its best-known numbers are 'Los Mayas' and 'Boda en Tehuantepec'. Each performance showcases examples of folk dances from Mexico's regions and indigenous cultures, taking considerable artistic licence in the process and mixing elements of Mexican **muralism**, sculpture and

cinema in its stylized choreography, costumes and scenery.

ANTONIO PRIETO-STAMBAUGH

ballet in Latin America

Latin America has produced many outstanding ballet artists, both dancers and choreographers. The names of Alicia **Alonso** of Cuba, the Brazilian Marcia Haydee, the Venezuelans Vicente **Nebreda** and Zhandra **Rodríguez** and the Argentines Oscar **Araiz** and Julio **Bocca**, among many others, illustrate the achievements in classical dance across the whole continent.

The Second World War years and their aftermath led many dancers and teachers to migrate to Latin America in search of a new artistic space. Earlier, some of the legendary figures of the ballet world had visited the region at the turn of the century, including Anna Pavlova and Fanny Essler. Slowly, from those beginnings, ballet began to attain high professional levels in Latin America.

In classical ballet, Cuba's leading role owes much to the Alonsos: Alicia, the renowned prima ballerina, Fernando, a rigorous ballet master and Alberto, an inventive choreographer. They laid the foundations for the so-called Cuban School of Ballet which enjoyed the highest reputation across the continent and produced one of Latin America's most important companies, the **Ballet Nacional de Cuba**, which for fifty years has produced dancers of international level.

Argentina has also made important contributions. The ballet company of Buenos Aires, housed at the **Teatro Colón**, is one of the most important of Latin America's professional institutions. The Colon's prestigious Instituto Superior has produced internationally recognised artists like Jorge **Donn** and Julio Bocca as well as Maximiliano Guerra and the rising star Paloma Herrera. Argentine ballet has had a diverse and versatile history. Not only has it developed the universal classical repertoire, it has also been open to contemporary dance currents whose highest representative has been the choreographer Oscar Araiz, whose work is also internationally known.

Venezuela has exercised its influence particularly in the neoclassical and contemporary fields. The internationally renowned choreographer Vicente Nebreda and the noted dancer Zhandra Rodríguez have occupied a leading role. The work of Nebreda, director of the Ballet Nacional del **Teatro Teresa Carreño** in Caracas, is marked by his characteristic creativity, plasticity and musicality. Rodríguez, founder of the Ballet Nuevo Mundo, has developed a powerful modern style through her company.

Other Latin American countries have established important centres of ballet within their main theatres: the Teatro Municipal in Rio de Janeiro, Brazil, the Teatro Municipal in Santiago de Chile, and the Teatro **SODRE** in Montevideo, Uruguay all have significant ballet companies. The Colombian city of Cali has an exemplary centre for ballet education and information – Incolballet – created at the initiative of the dancer and promoter Gloria Castro. Brazil, too, has sought to develop its own variation on classical dance based on its particular cultural reality, reflected in the Ballet Stagium and Ballet Corpo companies among others. Latin American ballet rests on a number of important experiences and careers. Though the ballet tradition is not widespread through the region, the variety and versatility of its interpretations point to a promising future.

Further reading

Itinerario por la danza escénica de América Latina (1994) Caracas: Conac.

CARLOS PAOLILLO

Ballet Nacional de Cuba

The Ballet Nacional de Cuba is one of the most prestigious dance companies in Latin America and the world because of the technical and artistic achievements of its dancers and the breadth and diversity of its repertoire.

The company was founded as the Ballet Alicia Alonso in 1948 by ballerina Alicia **Alonso**, her husband Fernando **Alonso**, also a dancer, and his brother, the choreographer Alberto Alonso. It was Cuba's first professional ballet company and, in its earliest years, attracted many dancers from New York's Ballet Theater through Alonso's connections. In 1950, the Alonsos annexed the Escuela Nacional de Ballet Alicia Alonso to the company, an important training ground for all subsequent generations of Cuban dancers.

From its inception, the company focused upon the romantic classics, although it also stimulated the work of innovative young choreographers seeking to develop a national dance style. In the 1950s, the company performed classics like *Giselle* and *Swan Lake*, alongside stagings of modernist works from Diaghilev's Ballet Russe and works of national choreographers like *Fiesta negra, Sóngoro cosongo, Concierto y sombras* and others.

In the mid-1950s, the government of Fulgencio **Batista** withdrew its support of the company amid great protests and it ceased performing in Cuba until the triumph of the revolution in 1959 (see **revolutions**), when it acquired its current name and became part of the new government's cultural initiatives. Through the 1960s and to the present, the school and company have enriched their repertoire, developed a most impressive roster of dancers, and stimulated significant work in other areas associated with ballet such as choreography, music and scenography. The company has travelled widely internationally and received innumerable awards, among them the prestigious Grand Prix de la Ville de Paris. Dramatic, intense, more old-fashioned and more round-armed than the current, linear American ballet style, the company has surprisingly preserved a classic style of ballet since the revolution.

Through the efforts and status of the Ballet Nacional, ballet in Cuba is a popular source of entertainment rather than an elite pastime. Its prima ballerinas – like Josefina Méndez, Mirta Plá and Rosario 'Charín' **Suárez** – have become household names and all performances typically sell out quickly. However, in recent years, especially given the limitations imposed upon the Cuban economy since the dissolution of the Soviet Union, ballet, like the other arts, has suffered. Currently directed by Laura Alonso, Alicia's daughter, and beset by hard times, it is not unusual for the company's dancers to defect while on international tours.

ANA M. LÓPEZ

Balmes, José

b. 1927, Barcelona, Spain

Painter

Balmes emigrated to Chile in 1939 aboard the *Winnipeg*, the ship famous for bringing refugees from the Spanish Civil War to Chile. He is a leader of the informalist style, following Antoni Tapiès and the Barcelona informalist group. In contrast to Spanish informalism, Balmes's paintings refer explicitly to contemporary reality, taking inspiration from political conflicts in Chile after the 1973 military *coup*, Vietnam and Santo Domingo. His paintings often incorporate objects and documents onto the canvas. In 1995, the Museum of Fine Arts in Santiago, Chile presented a major fifty-year retrospective of Balmes's works.

AMALIA PEREIRA

Balza, José

b. 1939, San Rafael, Delta Amacuro, Venezuela

Writer

Author of fiction, essayist, teacher and scholar, Balza is one of Venezuela's foremost writers. His first works were published in the 1960s; their experimental and psychological concerns explain why they represented a profound revision of the Latin American and Venezuelan narrative traditions. He founded and contributed to a number of important journals in the 1960s and 1970s – *En Haa*, *CAL*, *Cultura universitaria*, *El falso cuaderno*. His novel *Marzo anterior* (The Previous March) won the 1966 Municipal Fiction Prize, and in 1978 his novel *D* earned him **CONAC**'s Literary Prize. In

1991 he was awarded the National Prize for Literature.

JORGE ROMERO LEON

Banana Bottom

Written by the Jamaican Claude **McKay** and published in 1933, the novel *Banana Bottom* is set in a village deep in the hill country of Jamaica, and tells the story of Bita Plant, an intelligent black girl adopted by the zealous English missionaries Malcolm and Priscilla Craig. When, at thirteen, she is 'seduced' by the simple village musician, Crazy Bow, the Craigs send her to be educated in England. On her return, she is destined to marry their protégé Herald Newton Day, a smug theological student, but he is disgraced when found fornicating with a sheep and Bita settles for a traditional life on a smallholding, marrying Jubban, a local carter. McKay does not disguise the cultural differences the couple will have to face, but indicates that mutual respect will make the marriage work. It was a wedding of education and folk culture that McKay himself saw as the future of Jamaica.

The novel's title refers not to a person but a fictional place. The estate of Banana Bottom and its local village Jubilee were created in the 1930s by Adair, a Scots emigré who liberated the slaves and sold them the land in smallholdings, marrying the blackest of them. This multi-racial beginning gave rise to a distinctively Jamaican popular culture maintaining the best of African and European traditions, and evolving its own customs and rituals. Music is at the centre of village life. The Craigs teach Bita Western music, and on her return her first act is to play the piano for the Black Choristers in the chapel. But McKay also portrays the alternative tradition of the village 'tea-meetings', with their folk-based dance music, and an African-based possession ritual. Bita learns from Squire Gensir, a white folklorist closely modelled on Walter **Jekyll**, McKay's own mentor, that art transcends cultural boundaries.

Written towards the end of McKay's life of exile, lived mainly in the United States, *Banana Bottom* is a loving recreation of his childhood rural island community, and a statement of his hopes for an independent Jamaica. Both for its vivid portrayal of a black heroine and its detailed account of Jamaican village life in the late nineteenth century, the novel was ahead of its time, and can be claimed as the first major novel in the English-speaking Caribbean.

Further reading

Ramchand, K.(1970) 'Claude McKay and *Banana Bottom*', *Southern Review* 4(1): 53–66.

LOUIS JAMES

bananas

The banana grows in tropical and subtropical regions and, though it varies by botanical category, produces a delicious fruit between fifteen and twenty five centimetres long which may be eaten raw (called banana in Spanish) or a less sweet fruit which may be cooked (called *plátano* in some countries). This second variety is generally consumed in the areas where it is produced, while the sweet variety began to be exported in increasing numbers to countries in the temperate zone from the end of the nineteenth century. Belonging to the musa family, the fruit produced a most brutal form of economic exploitation, carried out by a number of USA-based multinational companies in the Caribbean region. The United Fruit Company (UFCO) was at the heart of a vast network of enterprises that included *latifundia* (see **latifundio**), railways, ports, maritime transport, electricity, telephone and telegraphic communications and even armed forces and puppet dictatorships. In Guatemala alone, the UFCO supported over forty attempted military *coups*, especially during the government of Jacobo **Arbenz**. One result was the creation (by the short story writer O. Henry) of the term 'banana republic'; it referred specifically to Honduras, where UFCO had its greatest influence, but came to signify (with deeply negative implications) a small, poor country run by governments, often military ones, who yielded to the dictates of the banana companies and opened their ports to the companies' ships and armies. The phrase 'banana curtain' referred to a kind of backyard fence around zones of US influence in Central America. A range of shops selling fashionable clothing called itself 'Banana Republic', with very obvious phallic overtones; in Argentina, the penis itself is often called 'la banana'. The name appears elsewhere too; in **calypso**, in the name of a pillow that became highly fashionable in the 1920s, and in the songs of Raúl **González Tuñón**. It became symbolic of a kind of Latin American horn of plenty, especially when it appeared on the hats of Carmen **Miranda** ('la Chiquita Bacana') and eventually came to represent the third world as a whole.

Further reading

Burbach R. and Flynn, P. (1980) *Agribusiness in the Americas*, New York: Monthly Review Press.

Schlesinger, S. and Kinzer, S. (1971) *Bitter Fruit*, New York.

Toriello Garrido, G. (1976) *Tras la cortina de banano*, México: Fondo de Cultura Económica.

Various authors (1976) *United Fruit Company: un caso del dominio imperialista en Cuba*, Havana: Editorial de Ciencias.

JULIO SCHVARTZMAN

Banco de Londres

Constructed between 1962–6 on the corner of Reconquista and Mitre off the **Plaza de Mayo** in Buenos Aires, this building is one of the most innovative structures in the city. Architects Clorindo **Testa** and the **SEPRA** studio (Sánchez Elia, Peralta Ramos and Agostini) rejected the neoclassical ostentation of nearby buildings in favour of a modern design open to street life. Designed as a type of covered plaza, its exterior facade of glass walls with a punctured concrete shell does not separate the interior space from the streets, but rather floods the open, tiered floors with light and offers clear vistas of the surrounding buildings. It symbolized the continuing economic and cultural ties between British and Argentine societies.

LAURA PODALSKY

Bandeira, Manuel

b. 1886, Recife, Brazil; d. 1968, Rio de Janeiro, Brazil

Poet

A central figure in Brazilian literature, Bandeira marks the aesthetic transition from late nineteenth-century to modern Brazilian poetry. In 1913, he was sent to a sanatorium in Switzerland for his tuberculosis and there came into contact with French symbolism, whose influence is obvious in his early work.

His first volumes *A Cinza das Horas* (Ashes of Time) (1917) and *Carnaval* (1919) represent a new kind of Brazilian poetry – simple, almost colloquial in style, it began to break with the Parnassian Symbolism which had prevailed until then. His famous 'Os Sapos' (The Toads), a satire of Parnassian formalism, belongs to that period and earned him the title of the 'John the Baptist of Brazilian Modernism' from the young organizers of the **Modern Art Week** of 1922, even though he had not participated directly in those events. In *Ritmo Dissoluto* (Dissolute Rhythm) (1924) he explores the possibilities of free verse and incorporates prosaic themes into the lyric, establishing a new diction in modernist poetry. *Libertinagem* (Libertinage) (1930) is a work of maturity, marked by great aesthetic freedom and a varied style. His intimate, sometimes melancholic lyrics reflect his nostalgia; they are markedly humorous, rebellious and ironic, employ colloquial forms, explore Brazilian themes and reveal a great technical skill in free verse and rhyme.

After *Libertinagem*, Bandeira continued to purify his expression and his style, exploring themes of childhood and folklore, as in *Estrela da Manhã* (Morning Star) (1936), *Mafuá do Malungo* (1948) and *Opus 10* (1952). *Estrela da Tarde* (Evening Star) (1958) confirmed his versatility as he ventured into the realm of **concrete poetry**. *Estrela da Vida Inteira* (Star of a Whole Life) (1966) gathered all his work into a single volume.

The musical quality of his work led composers like **Villa-Lobos** to set them to music; its simplicity guaranteed for him a special place in Brazil, influencing many other poets. It is still read and recited by every subsequent generation.

Further reading

Bandeira, M. (1966) *Estrela da Vida Inteira*, Rio de Janeiro: José Olympio.

Bandeira, M. (1989) *This Earth, That Sky: Poems by Manuel Bandeira*, trans. C. Slater, Berkeley: University of California Press.

VIVALDO A. SANTOS

banks

Bank buildings dominated the cities of Latin America at the beginning of the twentieth century, signalling the arrival of (largely European) finance capital anxious to invest in the region's raw materials, export agriculture and new infrastructural developments – particularly railways and ports. The scale and modernity of the buildings reflect their sponsors' confidence – as in the art nouveau styles that prevail in the centre of Mexico City, Montevideo, Buenos Aires and Santiago, Chile.

As the twentieth century drew to its end, banks once again dominated the urban skylines of Mexico – although this time their eclectic design reflected a postmodern movement that had found some of its most willing clients among the new financial institutions. As a result of the 'liberalization' of the national economies and the '**structural adjustment**' that threw them open to multinational capital, the private international banks once again came to prevail – this time dominated by the USA-based Rockefeller, Chase Manhattan, Citicorp and Morgan Guaranty among others; European banks like the Banco de Bilbao and Banco de Santander; British institutions like Barclays and Lloyds, etc. Their first forays were into the Chile of **Pinochet** after 1973 – the earliest 'neoliberal' experiment in Latin America. In this reorientation of the national economies to the global market, the privatization policies inaugurated in Chile became a characteristic of government policies throughout the region. In Mexico, for example, most State-owned banks were privatized under López Portillo in 1981–2. The second Mexican debt crisis of 1985 precipitated a reorganization of international finance so that cartels of multinational banks dominated economic policy-making process, in co-ordination with the World Bank and the International Monetary Fund. The various plans and proposals for resolving Latin America's **debt crisis** brought the inevitable conditions against loans – openness to private foreign investment, severe cuts in all social service and public sector spending and a reorientation of the economy towards the global market – even if that entailed large-scale structural unemployment. Brazil in 1987 was the first to experience this new hard-line policy. This finally and definitively undermined the role of the national banks, and hastened the privatization process, creating the conditions for domination by multinational finance capital.

The interior of the buildings thrown up during the region's growth period in financial activities reflect the desire of the banks to represent their activities as, in some sense, philanthropic, particularly as far as cultural patronage is concerned. The banks have become dedicated collectors of contemporary art – though it is hard to avoid the feeling that in the unstable market conditions of the 1980s and early 1990s, works of art were a reliable hedge against inflation. Private banks sponsored prizes and sustained cultural institutions in several countries, as well as assuming a conservation role by taking over and refurbishing historic buildings – as is the case of Banamex in central Mexico City and the Bank of London and South America (BOLSA) building in Buenos Aires, redesigned by Clorindo **Testa**.

There is another, less official form of banking that is symbolized by the 'offshore' financial centres in the Cayman Islands, the Bahamas, etc. Since the largest single source of wealth in Latin America in the 1990s was almost certainly the trade in drugs, it is to be assumed that these centres provided a convenient method of money-laundering, as did some of the Miami financial institutions, as recent trials of individuals like **Bouterse** and **Noriega** have made clear.

Further reading

George, S. and Sabelli, F. (1994) *Faith and Credit: The World Bank's Secular Empire*, London: Penguin.
Green, D. (1995) *The Silent Revolution*, London: Latin America Bureau.
Grosse, R. (1989) *Multinationals in Latin America*, London: Routledge.
Roddick, J. (1988) *The Dance of the Millions: Latin America and the Debt Crisis*, London: Latin America Bureau.

DANIEL BALDERSTON AND MIKE GONZALEZ

Banyan

Formed in 1974 by Christopher Laird, Bruce Paddington, and Tony Hall, Banyan produces videos on Caribbean history, art, and culture. Deriving its impetus from the artistic traditions of Trinidad and Tobago and collaborating with local cultural organizations and trade unions, Banyan's quality videos introduce the region's complex and rich culture to itself and to the world. Banyan's catalogue includes music videos, interviews with Caribbean opinion leaders, writers, cultural activists, and documentaries on secular and religious festivals. Banyan's award-winning *The Dish Ran Away With The Spoon* examines the influence of US television on Caribbean culture.

FUNSO AIYEJINA

Baptists

Baptists were among the first US-based Protestant denominations to begin mission work in Latin America in the nineteenth century. Most Latin American Baptist churches have belonged to the Southern Baptist Convention. Although Southern Baptists are considered more conservative than the American Baptist Churches, in Latin America they have historically aligned themselves more closely with liberals than with traditional conservatives. The number of Baptists in Latin America is almost one million, but during recent decades the Baptists, like other older historical Protestant denominations, have lost ground due to the rise of Pentecostalism (see **Pentecostals**).

JOUNI PIRTTIJÄRVI

Baquero, Gastón

b. 1918, Banes, Cuba; d. 1997, Madrid, Spain

Writer and journalist

Baquero's was a unique poetic voice. Many of his key poems, such as 'Testamento del pez' (The Fish's Testament) and 'Palabras escritas en la arena por un inocente' (Words Written in the Sand by an Innocent) appeared in **Orígenes**. His columns for the **Diario de la Marina** in the 1940s were influential. In 1959 he went into exile in Spain, where he published several volumes of poetry and the essay collection *Indios, blancos y negros en el caldero de América* (Indians, Whites and Blacks in the American Melting Pot) (1991), expressing his belief in the **mestizo** character of Latin America.

WILFREDO CANCIO ISLA

Barba-Jacob, Porfirio

b. 1883, Santa Rosa de Osos, Colombia; d. 1942, Mexico City

Poet

Miguel Ángel Osorio Benítez adopted the pseudonym Barba-Jacob and travelled widely through Mexico and Central America and in Guatemala. Barba-Jacob is remembered in **Lezama Lima**'s novel **Paradiso** as an early 'propagandist' for homosexuality. His friend, the Guatemalan Rafael **Arévalo Martínez**, based his short story *El hombre que parecía un caballo* (The Man Who Resembled a Horse) (1914) on Barba-Jacob's personality. Among his collections of poems are: *Rosas negras* (Black Roses, 1932), *Canciones y elegías* (Songs and Elegies, 1933), *La canción de la vida profunda* (Song of the deep life) (1937). His *Poemas intemporales* (Timeless Poems, 1944) were published posthumously.

MIGUEL A. CARDINALE

Barbachano Ponce, Manuel

b. 1924, Mérida, Yucatan; d. 1994, Mexico City

Film producer

A promotor of independent films like *Raices* (Roots) (1953), Velo's *Torero* and *Los bienamados* (The beloved) (1965) (Juan José **Gurrola** and Juan Ibáñez) and, later, producer of pathbreaking films like **Buñuel**'s *Nazarín*, Bardem's *Sonatas*, **Gavaldón**'s *El gallo de oro* (The Golden Cock) and Carlos Velo's **Pedro Páramo**. In the 1960s he formed Telecadena Mexicana, to provide alternative programmes for Mexican viewers, and acquired **CLASA** Films. CLASA promoted independent film-makers like Paul **Leduc** and Jaime Humberto **Hermosillo** and became the most important producer of films for television and video for Mexico and the Hispanic market in the USA.

PATRICIA TORRES SAN MARTÍN

Barbados

Except for the Scotland district, this coral island has no mountains or large rivers. Lack of fertile soil and major mineral deposits made first **sugar** and later **tourism** major income earners. The island's topography impeded slave revolts. Ninety-eight per cent of the people are of African descent. The culture is British and African; the language of the people is Bajan, an English creole (see **English-based creoles**). Becoming independent in 1966 after British colonization, Barbados has produced three major anti-colonial writers: George **Lamming**, Kamau **Brathwaite** and Paule **Marshall**. Theatre and music thrive on the island.

Further reading

Beckles, Hilary (1990) *A History of Barbados*, Cambridge: Cambridge University Press.

ELAINE SAVORY

Barbieri, Gato (Leandro J.)

b. 1934, Rosario, Argentina

Musician

Barbieri is a tenor saxophonist and jazz composer who became internationally renowned after his performances at festivals in Bologna, Montreux and the Newport Jazz Festival in New York. He studied with Lalo Schifrin in Buenos Aires and was influenced by John Coltrane and Charlie Parker. In 1962 he moved to Rome. His music incorporated Latin American motifs, developing his own style and playing sax along with autochthonous folk instruments as in *Chapter One: Latin America* (1973). He scored films such as *Last Tango in Paris* (1972) and Leopoldo **Torre Nilsson**'s *La guerra del cerdo* (Diary of the War of Pigs) (1975).

ALVARO FERNÁNDEZ-BRAVO

Bo Bardi, Lina

b. 1914, Rome, Italy; d. 1992, São Paulo, Brazil

Interior designer

Bo Bardi not only introduced the design methods pioneered by the Bauhaus and the new Italian and Swiss designers to Brazil, where until then France had been the only reference point; she also helped develop a genuine Brazilian design based on its popular arts and crafts. In 1946 she emigrated to Rio de Janeiro, taking Brazilian nationality in 1951. As co-ordinator of the study programmes at the São Paulo Contemporary Art Institute, established in 1951 on the initiative of P.M. Bardi, director of the **Museu de Arte Moderna**, she helped to create a design profession in Brazil, redefining the ideas of the European rationalist avant-garde in the context of and in relation to Brazil. Bo Bardi designed public buildings, stage sets, jewellery, furniture and was involved in the restoration of historic buildings.

GUILLERMO GREGORIO

Bardi, Pietro Maria

b. 1900, La Spezia, Italy

Art critic

In 1947 Bardi became the Technical Director of the **Museu de Arte de São Paulo**, the collection which he had guided the founder, **Assis Chateaubriand**, in acquiring. He travelled extensively in Europe and Latin America, and was a friend of Le Corbusier and Leger. A tireless entrepreneur, Bardi showed MASP works in Europe and the United States in the 1950s and organized several major exhibitions in the museum. He wrote extensively on Brazilian and foreign art, including a book on the landscape architect Burle **Marx**, and founded the architectural review *Habitat* in 1973.

M.A. GUIMARÃES LOPES

Barea, Batato

b. 1961, Junín, Argentina; d. 1991, Buenos Aires, Argentina

Actor

An uncompromising and iconoclastic artist, Barea became the king of the Buenos Aires underground in the flowering of democracy of the 1980s. His popularity was such that audiences applauded him even before his performances. Alongside **Urdapilleta and Tortonese**, Barea revitalized the alternative theatre scene with surrealistic circus techniques, for example his street 'reading' of Alfonsina **Storni**'s poetry dressed in women's clothes, waving handkerchiefs in the air and moving in circles as if bewitched. He died of AIDS.

RODRIGO PEIRETTI

Barenboim, Daniel

b. 1942, Buenos Aires, Argentina

Pianist and conductor

One of the most important musicians of his generation, and internationally acclaimed as both conductor and pianist, Barenboim's parents were both piano teachers. Between the ages of five and seventeen, Barenboim studied with his father, who gave him a solid aesthetic and musical grounding. He was a prodigy, playing his first solo concert at the age of seven and with an orchestra at nine. The family left for Europe in 1951 and went to Israel in 1952. He studied conducting with Igor Markevich in Salzburg and later at the Santa Cecilia Academy in Rome, and piano with Nadia Boulanger in Paris. He played in London for the first time in 1955 and two years later in New York under the direction of Stokowski. In 1962 he conducted his first orchestra in Israel, and from there went to Australia. His international career as a conductor began in London in 1964 with the English Chamber Orchestra, with which he toured Latin America and Asia. In 1968 he conducted the London Symphony in New York, the Berlin Philharmonic the following year, and the New York Philharmonic in 1970. Since then he has conducted the major orchestras of Japan, the USA, Europe and the Middle East. He was director of the Orchestre de Paris from 1975 until the late 1980s, and in 1991 was appointed Director of the Chicago Symphony. Barenboim has also directed opera, first at the Edinburgh Festival and later at Bayreuth from 1981 onwards, directing the Ring cycle in 1988. Since then he has worked in the world's most important opera houses. In the late 1980s he was appointed Director of the new Bastille Opera House in Paris, but resigned after a series of disagreements with the administration.

As a pianist, Barenboim's repertoire has been basically classical–romantic. He has recorded over 100 albums, including the complete piano works of Mozart and Beethoven. He has played chamber music with the world's best soloists, and accompanied the finest *lieder* singers. As a conductor, his repertoire has grown from Bach to twentieth-century classics such as Schonberg, Berg, Webern and Stravinsky, and moderns like Lutoslawski and Boulez. He has also branched out into television films, and has recorded an album of **tango**.

Further reading

Barenboim, D. (1991) *A Life in Music*, ed. Michael Lewin, London: Weidenfeld & Nicholson.

ALFONSO PADILLA

Barnet, Miguel

b. 1940, Havana, Cuba

Writer

Barnet is probably best known for *Biografía de un cimarrón* (Autobiography of a Runaway Slave) (1966), based on the life of Esteban Montejo. Barnet originally interviewed him for ethnographic purposes, but the resulting first person narrative proved an ideal medium for giving voice to and empowering those individuals from marginalized social groups who could not write their own stories. The success of the **testimonio** in Latin America has produced some debate over whether the editing of oral narrative may counter the authority of the informant. Barnet currently holds an extremely influential position as director of the Casa Fernando **Ortiz**.

JAMES BUCKWALTER-ARIAS

Barradas, Rafael

b. 1890, Montevideo, Uruguay; d. 1929, Montevideo

Visual artist

One of the most important figures in Uruguayan art, alongside Joaquín **Torres García** and Pedro **Figari**, Barradas worked in every area of the visual arts: drawing, painting, illustration, cartoons and set design. He spent most of his life in Europe, studying in Paris and Milan and exhibiting for the first time (in 1920) in Barcelona. He was linked to many avant-garde (see **avant-garde in Latin America**) movements, including cubism and futurism, and produced his most significant works in Spain. He evolved a number of personal styles based on an extraordinary skill in drawing, including *vibracionismo*, clownism and *pintura mística* (mystic painting).

MARCO MAGGI

Barragán, Luis

b. 1902, Guadalajara, Mexico; d. 1988, Mexico City

Architect

Barragán is now acknowledged as a central figure in the field of architecture, nationally and internationally. Although he produced only a few works, he has had considerable influence on subsequent generations. Trained as an engineer, he also studied architecture, but the turning point of his training was a journey to France and Spain in 1925–6 when he encountered Mediterranean and Arab architecture as well as the work of the artist Ferdinand Le Bac and the ideas of Le Corbusier, whose lectures he attended in 1931–2.

His first works were a series of private houses in Guadalajara expressing the spirit of colonial vernacular architecture, like the Casa Cristo, built between 1927 and 1936. Moving to Mexico City, he continued to build houses and apartment blocks, but this time influenced by Le Corbusier. Designed for sale, these houses were built with cheap materials. His love for nature was manifest in the series of gardens he designed in the 1940s, culminating with the volcanic lava fields of Mexico City's Pedregal de San Angel district where he realized his master plan for access roads, squares and three model gardens (1945–50). Years later, his planning acumen was applied in Las Arboledas (1959) and Los Clubes (1963–4) in Mexico City, with their remarkable fountains and gardens.

The construction of his own house in Francisco Ramírez Street in the district of Tacubaya bore his individual imprint within the style he called 'emotional', which integrated childhood and travel memories and the influence of artists Jesús Reyes Ferreira and Mathias **Goeritz**. The result is a richly expressive construction, imbued with religious mysticism, intensely coloured in the vernacular mode, with thick walls and small apertures,

muted light, natural forms and the repeated use of water as an expressive device. In addition to his own house, he built outstanding works for the Prieto López (1950), Gálvez (1955) and Egestrom (1968) families and in 1976, with Raúl Ferrara, a house for Francisco Gilardi. Significant too was his Capuchin Chapel in Tlalpan (1953–6) and his work with Goeritz on the towers of Ciudad Satélite outside the capital (1957). He was awarded the Pritzker Architecture Prize in 1980 and recognized in an exhibition at the New York Museum of Modern Art in 1976.

Further reading

Noelle, L. (1996) *Luis Barragán: bosquejo y creatividad:*, Mexico City: Coordinación de Humanidades, Universidad Nacional Autónoma de México.

LOURDES CRUZ GONZÁLEZ FRANCO

Barrán, José Pedro

b. 1934, Río Negro, Uruguay

Historian

One of Latin America's most distinguished historians, Barrán's writings on Uruguayan history have achieved wide readership and academic recognition and are fundamental interpretations of Uruguayan social and economic history. He was also a regular contributor to the periodical **Marcha**. Banned from university teaching in 1978 by the dictatorship, he nevertheless returned to the university in 1985. Some of his most notable works include *El Uruguay del Novecientos* (Nineteenth-Century Uruguay) (1979), and, with Benjamín Nahum, *Bases económicas de la revolución artiguista* (Economic Roots of the Artigas Revolution) (1964) and *Historia rural del Uruguay moderno* (Rural History of Modern Uruguay) (1967), and co-authorship with Gerardo Caetano and Teresa Porzecanski of *Historias de la vida privada en el Uruguay* (Stories of Private Life in Uruguay) (1996). He is a professor of the Universidad de la República (Montevideo) and of the Instituto de Profesores Artigas.

GWEN KIRKPATRICK

Barrenechea, Ana María

b.1913, Buenos Aires, Argentina

Literary critic

A disciple of Amado Alonso and Pedro **Henríquez Ureña**, Barrenechea has produced key texts in linguistics and literary criticism. *La expresión de la irrealidad en la obra de Jorge Luis Borges* (The Expression of Unreality in the Work of Borges) (1957) is one of the first systematic explorations of **Borges**'s work. She introduced structuralism into the University of Buenos Aires, which she left when Onganía took power. She is director of the Instituto de Filología and a member of the Spanish Academy; no Argentine critic can fail to acknowledge a debt to her.

DANIEL LINK

Barreto, Bruno

b. 1953, Rio de Janeiro, Brazil

Film-maker

Barreto's early success ***Dona Flor e seus dois maridos*** (Dona Flor and Her Two Husbands) (1976), combined the appeal of Sonia **Braga** and the fiction of Jorge **Amado**. His unpretentious, highly popular films include film versions of Nelson **Rodrigues**'s *O beijo no asfalto* (A Kiss on the Asphalt) (1980), and Amado's ***Gabriela****, cravo e canela* (Gabriela, Clove and Cinnamon) (1982). In the 1980s he married Amy Irving and moved to the USA. His *O que é isso, companheiro?* (Four Days in September) (1997) based on Fernando **Gabeira**'s account of the 1968 kidnapping of the US ambassador by urban guerrillas, was nominated for the Best Foreign Film Oscar. In early 2000, he released *Bossa Nova* starring his wife Amy Irving and described by a critic as a 'filmic *caipuinha* or frothy ***cachaça*** cocktail'.

ISMAIL XAVIER AND THE USP GROUP

Barreto, Fábio

b.1957, Rio de Janeiro

Film-maker

Son of producers Lucy and Luiz Carlos **Barreto**, he learned his craft by assisting directors like Antônio **Calmon**, Carlos **Diegues**, and Eduardo **Escorel**, directing short films, and producing his brother Bruno **Barreto**'s *O beijo no asfalto* (The Kiss on the Asphalt) (1980). His own feature-length films include *Índia, a Filha do Sol* (Daughter of the Sun) (1981), *O Rei do Rio* (The King of Rio) (1984), and *Bela Donna* (1998). In 1996 *O Quatrilho*, based on a novel by José Clemente Pozenato, became the second Brazilian film ever to be nominated for an Academy Award in the Foreign Film category.

RANDAL JOHNSON

Barreto, Lima

b. 1906, Casa Branca, São Paulo, Brazil; d. 1982, São Paulo

Film-maker and writer

A brilliant intellectual, Lima directed *O Cangaceiro* (The Bandit) (1952) for the **Vera Cruz Studios**; winner of Brazil's first Cannes award, it remains one of the best known Brazilian films of all time. Also a press and radio journalist, he wrote prolifically, but his novels and stories have never been published. Anselmo **Duarte** and Walter **Lima** Jr succesfully brought his screenplays to the screen, but Lima was only able to direct one other feature, *A Primeira missa* (The First Mass) (1960), which was not well received.

ISMAIL XAVIER AND THE USP GROUP

Barreto, Luiz Carlos

b. 1928, Sobral, Brazil

Film producer

Baretto is considered the 'father' of **Cinema Novo**. Originally a photojournalist, he was cinematographer for Nelson Pereira dos **Santos** and Glauber **Rocha**, and producer of many key Cinema Novo films, including dos Santos's *Vidas Secas* (Barren Lives) (1963), Joaquim Pedro de **Andrade**'s *O Padre e a Moça* (The Priest and the Girl) (1965), and Carlos **Diegues**'s *A Grande Cidade* (The Great City) (1965). He was one of the founders of Difilm, the Cinema Novo distributor. He continues to produce films, among them his sons Fábio and Bruno **Barreto**'s very successful *Dona Flor e seus dois maridos* (Dona Flor and Her Two Husbands) (1976).

ISMAIL XAVIER AND THE USP GROUP

Barreto Burgos, Chiquita

b. 1947, Colonia Dr. Cecilio Báez, Paraguay

Writer

Chiquita (Amelia) Barreto Burgos is a prolific short story writer whose publications include three collections: *Con pena y sin gloria* (With Sorrow and Without Glory) (1990), *Con el alma en la piel: 9 relatos eróticos* (With the Soul on the Skin: 9 Erotic Tales) (1994) and *Delirios y certezas* (Delusions and Certainties) (1995). She is also a professor in the Universidad del Norte and collaborates with the Unión de Mujeres para Ayuda Mutua or UMPAM (Union of Women for Mutual Help) in Coronel Oviedo.

TERESA MÉNDEZ-FAITH

Barricada

The official **FSLN** newspaper, *Barricada* was first published on 25 July 1979. By 1980, *Barricada* was one of three daily Managua newspapers, all directed by relatives of Pedro Joaquín **Chamorro** Cardenal, the *La Prensa* editor assassinated in 1978. His youngest son, Carlos Fernando Chamorro Barrios, was *Barricada*'s editor-in-chief. At first, *Barricada* was distributed only in Managua and eight other cities. However, readership spread with literacy campaigns, and labour unions and army soldiers distributed the paper in rural areas. After

1990, the splits within the FSLN produced debates over the paper's role and, in 1994, Carlos Fernando Chamorro resigned the editorship. The paper closed briefly and is now owned by Tomás Borge, ex-Interior Minister of the Sandinista government.

ESTEBAN E. LOUSTAUNAU AND
ILEANA RODRÍGUEZ

Barrios de Chungara, Domitila

b. 1937, Siglo Veinte, Bolivia

Political campaigner

Barrios de Chungara is a working-class woman of the tin mines, known for her 1977 testimony *Si me permiten hablar: Testimonio de Domitila, una mujer de las minas de Bolivia* (Let me Speak! Testimony of Domitila, a Woman of the Bolivian Mines). The testimony denounces the climate of violence and the repression imposed upon the Bolivian **mining** class throughout the 1960s and 1970s under several military and authoritarian governments. Domitila's testimony is important because rather than a product of a literary culture it is written from the perspective of a woman of the oppressed and exploited classes.

The daughter of a family of miners and married to a miner, in 1963 she joined a housewives group in her hometown (Comité de Amas de Casa de Siglo XX) whose goal was to support the miners' union in its demands for better living conditions. Barrios became its director between 1965–77, and was invited by the United Nations to a women's conference in Mexico in 1975 where she denounced the human rights violations of the dictatorial regime of General Hugo Banzer. The international attention that her statement received weakened the dictatorship. Her controversial performance shook the foundations of the universalistic **feminism** of the industrialized countries and allowed the incorporation into feminist theory of issues emanating from Third World women's experiences.

With the collaboration of Brazilian anthropologist Moema Viezzer, Domitila's testimony was published in Mexico, covering not only Banzer's violations but also the repression suffered in the mines in the 1960s. In 1977, Barrios and other women of the mines initiated a crucial hunger strike that set in motion a process leading to the overthrow of Banzer's regime.

Barrios was in Copenhagen at a women's conference at the time of the 1980 military *coup*. As an exile, she campaigned through Europe denouncing the new dictatorship. A second testimony portraying her experience in the hunger strike and in exile was published in 1984, *Aquí también Domitila* (Domitila is also here), with the collaboration of Bolivian journalist, David Acebey. Barrios continued as an active human rights fighter into the 1990s. She appears in Jorge **Sanjinés**'s film *El coraje del pueblo* (Courage of the People) (1971).

Further reading

Barrios de Chungara, D. with Viezzer, M. (1978) *Let Me Speak: Testimony of Domitila, a Woman of the Bolivian Mines*, trans. Victoria Ortiz, New York: Monthly Review Press.

Logan, K. (1997) 'Personal Testimony: Latin American Women Telling Their Lives', *Latin American Research Review* 32(1).

Sanjinés, C.J. (1996) 'Beyond Testimonial Discourse: New Popular Trends in Bolivia', in Georg M. Gugelberger (ed.), *The Real Thing: Testimonial Discourse and Latin America*, Durham, NC: Duke University Press.

Viezzer, M. (1977) *Si me permiten hablar: testimonio de Domitila, una mujer de las minas de Bolivia*, Mexico City: Siglo XXI.

MARIA ELVA ECHENIQUE

Barrios Mangoré, Agustín

b. 1885, San Bautista de las Misiones, Paraguay; d. 1944, San Salvador, El Salvador

Composer and guitarist

One of the twentieth century's most important composers for the guitar, Barrios studied the instrument with Gustavo Sosa, but was a self-taught composer. In 1914 he embarked on a concert tour of Argentina and continued for fourteen years, touring Brazil, Chile and Uruguay, where he remained to study with Antonio Giménez Manjón. Apart from one European tour (1934–6), Barrios played only in Latin America. His concerts were spectacles that combined the delicacy of his compositions and his playing with elements of exotic exhibitionism; he called himself 'Mangoré' after a legendary Guarani chief. In 1939 he was appointed Professor of Guitar at the Conservatory in San Salvador (El Salvador), where he remained until his death. He was the first guitarist to make a record (in 1909) and the first to perform a complete Bach suite for lute on guitar. Barrios composed more than 100 guitar pieces, many of which are now part of the permanent classical repertoire. His musical language was very different from the prevailing tendencies in the twentieth century elsewhere in the world, for part of his work is clearly baroque in style, another romantic in the manner of Chopin and a third owes much to various Latin American folk traditions. His most celebrated pieces include *La Catedral* (the Cathedral) (1918), *Sueño en la floresta* (Dream in the Forest) (1919–23), *Madrigal, Danzas paraguayas* (Paraguayan Dances) and several studies and preludes. His last composition was *Una limosna por amor de Dios* (Alms for the Love of God).

Further reading

Sensier, P. (1974) 'Agustín Barrios' in *Guitar*, 2, 12.

Williams, J. (1977) Notes to the record *John Williams Plays the Music of Barrios*, Holland: CBS Records, LCO149.

ALFONSO PADILLA

Barroco Andino

The military dictatorship that took power in Chile in 1973 banned cultural manifestations associated with **Popular Unity**. Included in this 'cultural blackout' was the music of the Chilean *nueva canción*, which had combined Chilean folkloric styles with socially conscious lyrics. Also prohibited were the Andean indigenous musical instruments (see **Andean music**) featured in *nueva canción*.

This prohibition was first publicly circumvented by the Barroco Andino ('Andean Baroque') group, conservatory-trained musicians who played the music of Bach and other classical composers on the banned instruments. Barroco Andino opened the way for the reappearance of Andean music in Chile that spearheaded *nueva canción*'s successor, **Canto Nuevo**.

NANCY MORRIS

Barros, José Benito

b. 1916, El Banco, Colombia

Composer

Prolific composer of popular songs in a variety of traditional Colombian rhythms such as **pasillo**, porro and **cumbia**, as well as **merengue**, **tango** and bolero. Among his more than 600 compositions are: *Navidad negra* (Black Christmas), *La piragua* (The Canoe), and *Momposina* (The Girl from Mompox).

MIGUEL A. CARDINALE

Barros, Luiz de

b. 1893, Rio de Janeiro, Brazil; d. 1981, Rio de Janeiro

Theatre and film director

A pioneer of Brazilian cinema, Barros began his career in theatre. In the twenties he directed shows in Rio de Janeiro's casinos and began to make short films and documentaries which he designed, edited, photographed and scripted. In 1929 his highly successful comedy *Acabaram-se os otários* (No More Suckers) established him as an early pioneer of sound cinema. Through his career he directed erotic films, dramas and literary adaptations, and parodies of foreign films. He was a founder of **chanchadas**, the musical comedies that dominated Brazilian cinema through the 1940s and 1950s.

ISMAIL XAVIER AND THE USP GROUP

Barros, Pía

b. 1956, Santiago, Chile

Writer

Barros's prose is centrally concerned with feminine identity, eroticism, cultural policy and politics. She also played an important role facilitating others: the writers of the Generation of 1980 were formed in her writers' workshops, and her publishing house 'Ergo Sum' published literary texts and book-objects containing narratives and graphic work by her pupils. Her works include short stories – *Miedos transitorios* (Transitory Fears) (1986), *A horcajadas* (Astride) (1995) and *Signos bajo la piel* (Signs under the Skin) (1995) – and a novel *El tono menor del deseo* (Desire in a Minor Key) (1991).

ELIANA ORTEGA

Barroso, Ary

b. 1903, Ubá, Minas Gerais, Brazil; d. 1964, Rio de Janeiro, Brazil

Composer

Hailed as the 'most Brazilian of the Brazilian composers', Ary Barroso gained international fame and recognition for his catchy stylized sambas which exalted his nation's beauty and exuberance. He was the most acclaimed composer of the 'Golden Age' of Brazilian song during the 1930s and 1940s. His compositions were recorded by top artists such as Carmen **Miranda**, Francisco **Alves**, Mário Reis, and Aracy Cortes. Born into a family of regional political élites, Barroso lost both his parents in 1911 and was raised by two great-aunts who initiated his musical education. In 1922, having received an inheritance from a wealthy uncle, he moved to Rio de Janeiro to study law. Soon after he arrived, his money ran out and he went to work as the house pianist for the Cinema Iris while playing gigs with several local jazz bands. In 1929, Barroso began to compose for musical theatre and produced more than sixty scores over the next thirty years.

In 1939 he composed his most famous song, 'Aquarela do Brasil' ('Brazil'), which was first recorded by Francisco Alves. This ultra-patriotic paean to Brazilian culture set the standard for an emerging subgenre, the *samba exaltação* (exultant samba), which was encouraged by the nationalist-authoritarian regime of Getulio **Vargas**. 'Aquarela do Brasil' became the unofficial national anthem and was later used in Walt Disney's animated film *Saludos, Amigos*, featuring the famous *malandro* parrot, Zé Carioca. Disney's subsequent 'Good Neighbour' cartoon of the war years, *The Three Caballeros*, featured Barroso's 'Os Quidins de Iaiá' (Iaiá's Cococut Candies) and his exquisite 'Na baixa do sapateiro' (Shoemaker's Row), both sung by Carmen Miranda's sister, Aurora. In 1944, his song 'Rio de Janeiro', the theme for the Hollywood film, *Brazil*, was nominated for an Oscar.

In 1946 Barroso was elected councilman of Rio de Janeiro as a candidate of the União Democrá-tica Nacional, a centre-right party. During his tenure, he was active in the movement to secure authorial rights for musicians. In 1955, he shared the prestigious National Order of Merit with classical composer Heitor **Villa-Lobos**. By this time, Barroso had become frustrated with new directions in Brazilian popular music, heralded by **bossa nova**, which he regarded as 'overly Americanized.' News of his death came on **Carnival** Sunday of 1964, just as the **samba** school Império Serrano prepared to hit the avenue with their musical homage to him entitled 'Aqua-rela brasileira' (Brazilian Watercolour).

Further reading

Cabral S (1993) *No tempo de Ary Barroso*, Rio de Janeiro: Lumiar.

CHRISTOPHER DUNN

Barrow, Dame Nita

b. 1916, St Lucy, Barbados; d. 1995, Bridgetown, Barbados

Politician

Her long career of public service has been devoted to improving the position of women; a practising nurse for many years, she pioneered the develop-ment of nursing education in the English Car-ibbean. World President of the YWCA and President of the International Council of Adult Education, Dame Nita presided over the NGO forum at the Third Assembly of Women in Kenya in 1985. She was Barbados' Resident Representa-tive to the United Nations and became its Governor General in 1990. A person of singular dedication and integrity, she has contributed greatly to the improvement of Barbados and the Caribbean Community.

JOHN H. PATTON

Bartra, Roger

b. 1942, Mexico City

Anthropologist

Bartra studies the modern capitalist state and is an important critic of those symbolic and discursive constructs, like Latin American nationalism or the concept of barbarism in Europe, which have tended to deny the diversity of subjects. A graduate of the Mexican National School of History and Anthropology (**INAH**), he earned his doctorate at the Sorbonne and is a researcher at the Institute of Social Research at the Mexican National Uni-versity (**UNAM**). He has edited the journals *El Machete* and *La Jornada Semanal*. His best known work is a study of Mexican culture, *La jaula de la melancolía* (The Cage of Melancholy) (1987).

CARLOS OLIVA MENDOZA

Bascom, Harold

b. 1951, Vergnoegen, Guyana

Writer

Bascom's acerbic, early novel, *Apata* (1986), con-fronts the effects of social and racial discrimination, documenting the life and death of the young fugitive Michael Rayburn Apata in 1959, which coincided with the Queen's visit to Guyana. Focusing on popular cultural and national themes, his plays at the National Cultural Centre in Georgetown were widely praised and awarded. In the 1990s several were presented again to considerable public acclaim. Bascom has also researched local mythical figures, and his illustrations about Indian immigration appear in the 1972 children's textbook, *Bound for Guyana* (Ministry of Education).

JILL E. ALBADA-JELGERSMA

baseball

Baseball is the national sport of Cuba, the Dominican Republic and Puerto Rico, and is a highly popular pastime in other Caribbean countries. Although the complex bat-and-ball game is usually associated with US culture, it has a rich and distinct history in the Caribbean that rivals its North American tradition. The Caribbean's first professional baseball league was founded in Cuba in 1878, only seven years after the beginning of professional play in the USA, and the annual Caribbean Series involving teams from four Latin American nations rivals the US World Series in terms of cultural significance.

Baseball was first played in the Caribbean in the late 1860s. Imported from New York by students returning to Cuba, it became firmly established in Cuba in the 1870s, thanks largely to the organizational efforts of Esteban Enrique Bellán and Emilio Sabourín. Its introduction into the island coincided with the war for independence from Spain, and the game quickly became a symbol of Cuban insurgence. Sabourín, a rebel sympathizer, channelled the proceeds from professional baseball tournaments to guerrilla groups operating against Cuba's Spanish overseers. Sabourín was imprisoned in 1895 and died two years later, and Spain banned baseball from large parts of the island, thereby ensuring the game's enduring popularity among the Cuban people. By the end of the nineteenth century, Cuban migrants had introduced baseball into the Dominican Republic, Puerto Rico, Venezuela and Mexico, and the game spread to other parts of the region.

The first half of the twentieth century witnessed the golden age of Caribbean baseball, a consequence, paradoxically, of the segregationist policies of the professional leagues in the United States.

Near the end of the nineteenth century, the owners of teams in the major US professional leagues had forged an unwritten 'gentleman's agreement' that 'coloured' players would not be employed, a policy that persisted until 1947. Occasionally fair-skinned, or even darker-skinned, Latin Americans (such as Hiram **Bithorn** and Luis **Olmo** Rodríguez) were allowed to play after signing forms attesting that their ancestry was entirely Hispanic. Generally, however, Latin Americans – including the extraordinary Martín **Dihigo**, José Méndez, Cristóbal Torriente and Luis **Tiant** – were barred from pursuing careers in the US major leagues.

The US segregationist policy, however, had a positive effect on the quality of Latin American baseball. While the colour line existed, many Latin American players excelled in the underground US Negro Leagues during the summer and returned to play in the Caribbean during the winter. They were accompanied by US blacks, who could perform in Latin America without fear of racial harassment and earn salaries that were competitive with those paid to US major leaguers. These players were often joined by players from the white US leagues, who wished to earn extra money in the age before high athletic salaries. Between the World Wars particularly, the world's highest quality baseball was probably in the racially integrated games played in Latin America over the winter months.

Immediately after the Second World War, Jorge Pascual attempted to take full advantage of the weaknesses of segregated baseball in the USA by making the Mexican League a direct rival of the established North American leagues. The Mexican League had already attracted many of the best players from Cuba and the US Negro Leagues, and in 1946 Pascual raided the white US leagues, offering players higher salaries. Pascual's efforts ultimately failed, but they hastened the demise of the 'gentleman's agreement' in the USA. The integration of the US leagues following 1947 allowed Latin Americans such as Roberto **Clemente**, Juan **Marichal**, Luis **Aparicio**, Orlando **Cepeda** and Juan González to perform impressively against top competition.

By the end of the twentieth century, Cuba regularly fielded the best amateur baseball teams in international competitions, and Puerto Rico and the Dominican Republic produced more elite professional baseball players per capita than anywhere else in the world. Nonetheless, the quality of baseball played in Latin America itself declined from the levels attained in mid-century. The integration of US leagues drew players away from the Caribbean, and dramatically escalating US salaries removed the incentive for players to return to the Caribbean leagues in the winter. None the less, baseball remains highly popular both as a spectator and participatory sport in Latin America, supplying new generations with heroes to idolize.

Further reading

Bjarkman, P.C. (1994) *Baseball with a Latin Beat*, Jefferson, NC: McFarland.

Krich, J. (1990) *El Béisbol: Travels Through the Pan-American Pastime*, New York: Doubleday.

Ruck, R. (1993) *The Tropic of Baseball: Baseball in the Dominican Republic*, New York: Carroll & Graf.

Winegardner, M. (1996) *The Veracruz Blues*, New York: Viking.

DOUGLAS W. VICK

Basilica of the Virgin of Guadalupe

According to official apparition history, the Virgin Mary appeared on 9 December 1531 before an Indian named Juan Diego as he walked on Tepeyac Hill, four miles north of downtown Mexico City. The Virgin instructed Juan to visit the bishop, Juan de Zumárraga, requesting that he build a church on the apparition site. The bishop could not be convinced. Three days later, the Virgin again appeared before Juan and told him to pick some roses and place them in his cloak. Juan carried these flowers to Zumárraga with a second request regarding the construction of a hill church. Juan Diego opened the cloak before Zumárraga to reveal an image of the virgin where the roses had been. This sacred image became the focus of veneration, and a small church was constructed on the site of the apparition in 1533. In 1556, a larger, more ornate structure was built due to the efforts of Archbishop Montúfar. By 1622, the shrine was relocated to the bottom of the hill and subsequent construction, begun in 1695, took place at the new location. Additions to the 1695 shrine occurred in 1893 and the 1930s. The shrine was officially named a basilica in 1968. However, it was decided that a new structure was necessary as the old shrine was unsafe and irreparable. A new basilica, dedicated in 1976, was designed by architect José Luis Benlliure with interior liturgical decoration by Fray Gabriel Chávez de la Mora. In 1988, a park called La Ofrenda (The Offering) was inaugurated to the east of the hill, containing 12,000 square metres of gardens, waterfalls, and sixteen bronze statues, sculpted by Antonio del Valle Talavera, of various individuals important to the apparition's history including the Virgin, Bishop Zumárraga and Juan Diego. In 1991 a carillon, an electronic system of bells and four coordinating clocks, capable of playing hundreds of songs, was installed. Unfortunately, it only worked on its inauguration day.

The shrine and the surrounding villa are the centre of large-scale pilgrimages from all over Mexico and Latin America. Pilgrims and local believers celebrate the feast day of Guadalupe (on 12 December since 1754) by joining the procession and by walking upon their knees some seven miles up the Calzada de los Misterios (Way of Mysteries). During the festival, boys dress as *dieguitos* in serapes and sandals and sport painted moustaches and Native Americans perform traditional dances wearing full regalia. **Rius** has published a book debunking the Guadalupe story as legend.

Further reading

Poole, S. and Stafford, C.M. (1995) *Our Lady of Guadalupe. The Origins and Sources of a Mexican National Symbol, 1531–1797*, Tucson, AZ: University of Arizona Press.

Rius (1996) *El mito guadalupano*, Mexico City: Grijalbo.

LINDA A. CURCIO-NAGY

basketball

Basketball only began to thrive in Latin America in the 1950s, although before this there had been regional championships and a few club tours to Europe; Mexico had won a bronze medal in the sport at the 1936 Olympics. The YMCA is credited with introducing the sport to many South American countries. The first world championship was held in Argentina in 1950 and the home team, thanks to greats such as Oscar Furlong (who had played for his US university) and Ricardo González, won the title, beating the USA (represented by the Chevrolet team) in the final. Nine years later, Brazil, which had already gained Olympic bronze in 1948 and the world vice-championship in 1954, won the first of its two world titles in Chile; the second came on home ground in 1963 with a team including stars such as Amaury Passos, Ubiratan and Vlamir. Brazil's successes continued with Olympic bronze medals in 1960 and 1964.

Uruguay also gained Olympic successes in basketball. They took the bronze medal in two successive Olympics – 1952 and 1956 – while Chile was third in the world championships of 1950 and 1959. In the 1960s, Brazil was to be the most powerful team in Latin America, taking third place in the world championships of 1967 and 1978 and second in 1970, while Cuba also appeared with a bronze medal in the 1972 Olympics.

Later, clubs were more successful than national teams, admittedly many with the help of some imported US players. In 1979, Brazil's Sirio won the William Jones Cup, considered to be the world club championship; Obras Sanitarias, of Argentina, won the same title four years later. Strong club leagues (with some US players) began to be formed in various countries in the 1980s, which led to the establishment of a Pan-American League in 1993 with Brazil's All Star becoming the first champions. Brazil also has the most outstanding contemporary player, Oscar **Schmidt**, the only player to have played in five successive Olympic Games (from 1980 to 1996) and scored over 1,000 points in Olympic competitions.

Brazil has also shown its dominance of the women's game. After taking second place in the world championships of 1967 and 1971 – something Chile had already done in 1953 – Brazil won the title in 1995 and a year later took the silver medal at the 1996 Olympics.

ERIC WEIL

Batalla de Chile, La

The tripartite documentary *La batalla de Chile: la lucha de un pueblo sin armas* (The Battle of Chile; the Struggle of a People without Arms) is considered one of Chile's most significant films. Filmed by the 'Equipo Tercer Año' (Third Year Group), headed by Patricio **Guzmán**, between the elections of February 1973 and the *coup* of September, the films use disruptive strategies to provide a dialectical account of the escalating class struggle during the last year of **Popular Unity**. One of the most dramatic moments is footage where a cameraman filmed his own death during the attempted *coup* of June 1973. Smuggled out of the country and edited in Cuba by Guzmán and Pedro **Chaskel**, the films were completed by 1979 and have won prizes at several international festivals. Guzmán's recent *Chile, la memoria obstinada* (Chile, Obstinate Memory) (1997) updates the lives of many of the participants in the earlier film, and shows reactions to it in the first showings in Chile after redemocratization.

DOLORES TIERNEY

Batista y Zaldivar, Fulgencio

b. 1901, Banes, Cuba; d. 1973, Guadalmina,Spain

Politician

An army clerk, Batista was a sergeant when he joined the ABC secret conspiracy against then president and dictator Gerardo **Machado**. He became one of the three leaders of the 'Government of the 100 Days' installed on 4 September 1933. Promoted to colonel, he was elected President of the Republic (1940–4). On 10 March 1952 he led a *coup d'état* against President Carlos **Prío Socarrás**, and installed a dictatorial regime which lasted until the early hours of 1 January 1959, when he fled on a plane together with his closest aides after the success of the rebellion led by Fidel **Castro**.

JOSÉ ANTONIO EVORA

Bauer, Tristán

b. 1959, Mar del Plata, Argentina

Film-maker

Working in the margins of the official discourses of the Argentine dictatorship, Bauer began working among independent and semi-clandestine film and photography circles, specializing in documentaries (he worked with Miguel **Littín**, Jorge Denti and Estela Bravo in Nicaragua, Chile and other countries). His first fictional feature, *Después de la tormenta* (After the Storm), in 1990 was a great popular and critical success; a non-sentimental tale of a working-class family that perseveres despite many hardships. Since then, Bauer has also taught documentary film-making and worked in video for television, most notably with the well-received *Evita, la tumba sin paz* (Evita, the Tomb without Peace) (1996), a British–Argentine TV co-production on Eva **Perón**.

ANA M. LÓPEZ

Baugh, Edward Alston

b. 1936, Port Antonio, Jamaica

Poet and critic

A leading critic of Caribbean literature, Baugh edited the seminal *Critics of Caribbean Literature* (1978); equally important was his insightful and pioneering study of Derek **Walcott**, *Derek Walcott: Memory as Vision* (1978). He is also a well-known poet whose volume of poetry, *A Tale from the Rainforest*, was published in 1988. His writing uses varieties of language to explore the consequences of a colonial history. He is Professor of English at the **University of the West Indies** Mona Campus in Jamaica.

MIKE GONZALEZ

Bauhaus architecture

The impact of the avant-garde (see **avant-garde in Latin America**) Bauhaus school in Latin America had three stages. The first, contempora-neous with its activities as a school of art, architecture and design in Germany, was a response to the dissemination of its ideas through translations of its documents in journals like the *Revista de la Sociedad Central de Arquitectos de Argentina*. In March 1932 (no.109), for example, the journal published a presentation of architect Walter Gropius by the engineer Franc Moller, together with pictures and drawings of the work of the school. The differences between the work of the Bauhaus and the dominant, classical, neocolonial styles of the time meant that Bauhaus had a dramatic impact on architectural modernizers like the Austral Group and the School of Architecture at the University of Tucumán under Bibanco and Molina. The second phase extends from the closure of the Bauhaus in 1933 to the mid-1950s, when many of its members emigrated to other countries, principally the USA. Some went to Latin America, like Hannes Meyer (one of the most politically radical members) who lived in Mexico from 1939 to 1949. The influence of Bauhaus, while less than that of Le Corbusier, is nevertheless visible in the work of architects like the Argentine Mario Roberto **Alvarez** (clearly influenced by Mies van der Rohe) or the Chilean Emilio **Duhart**, a follower of both Gropius and Le Corbusier. The third phase ocurred when Bauhaus was internationally recognized. In Latin America, 1953 was a key year, when the Grand Prix International d'Architecture of the São Paulo Bienal (see **Bienale de São Paulo**) was awarded to Walter Gropius. This prize, and the award to Max Bill in 1951, expressed a growing interest in Bauhaus, not only in architecture but also in the visual arts, design and even in poetry, as the manifestos of the Brazilian **concrete poetry** movement referred frequently to its postulates. This rediscovery had a direct impact on daily life, particularly through furniture and poster design, reflecting the dominant developmentalist ideology. That influence was echoed in the work of architectural theorists and critics like Tomás **Maldonado**. The 1970 exhibition in Buenos Aires closed the cycle which marked the definitive recognition of Bauhaus as providing the language and educational principles of modern architecture. This continues to be the case, as the reforms in

Buenos Aires University's Faculty of Architecture and City Planning in the 1980s clearly showed.

Further reading

(1970) *Bauhaus 50 años*, Buenos Aires: Museo Nacional de Bellas Artes.

Maldonado, T. (1977) *Vanguardia y racionalidad (Artículos, ensayos y otros escritos 1946–74)*, Barcelona: Gustavo Gili.

GONZALO AGUILAR

Bay, Juan

b.1892, Trenque Lauquén, Argentina; d.1978

Painter

A contributor to the **Arte Madí** movement, Bay moved to Milan in 1908 and studied art there until 1914. He exhibited in the Futurist Free Exhibition of Art in 1911, returned to Argentina in 1925 and then moved back to Italy in 1929. In 1949 he moved to Buenos Aires and exhibited from 1952 with the Arte Madí movement led by **Gyula Kosice**. His Madí works are characterized by their primary colours and irregular frames.

GABRIEL PEREZ-BARREIRO

Bayley, Edgar

b. 1919, Buenos Aires, Argentina; d. 1990, Buenos Aires

Writer

A member of the so-called 'Generation of 1940', Bayley rejected the prevailing neo-romantic and testimonial modes of his time. His very personal style, akin to **concrete poetry**, accorded poetry autonomy relative to other discourses and material reality. More than a genre, poetry for him was a category of the real. He wrote for poetry journals, as well as translating and writing occasional narrative and drama. His writings have a pure and disenchanted air, simple yet also aggressive,

even brutal. The author of over twelve volumes, Bayley died poor and unrecognized.

SERGIO CHEJFEC

Bayly, Jaime

b. 1965, Lima, Peru

Writer

Bayly's three published novels reflect contemporary Peruvian society. *No se lo digas a nadie* (Don't Tell Anybody) (1994) – transferred to the cinema by Francisco **Lombardi** in 1998 – and *Fue ayer y no me acuerdo* (It was Yesterday, and I don't Remember) (1995) include several episodes of homosexual and bisexual love. *Los últimos días de La Prensa* (The Last Days of La Prensa) (1996) narrate the final days of the newspaper, *La Prensa*, in the aftermath of a sociopolitical crisis in the Peru of the 1980s. His most recent book, *Yo amo a mi mamá* (I Love My Mummy) (1999), returns to themes of sexual repression among the Peruvian bourgeoisie. Bayly lives in Miami where he currently fronts a TV talk show.

MIGUEL A. CARDINALE

Bayón, Damián

b. 1915, Buenos Aires, Argentina; d. 1995, Buenos Aires

Art historian, critic and poet

Damián Bayón's writing is known for its methodological rigour, conceptual clarity and elegance of style. This includes *Construcción de lo visual* (Construction of the Visual) (1965), *Arte de ruptura* (Art of Rupture) (1973) and *Aventura plástica de Hispanoamérica* (Plastic Adventure of Spanish America) (1974). His *Historia del arte Hispanoamericano, Siglos XIX y XX* (Spanish American Art. Nineteenth and Twentieth Centuries) (1988) is the culmination of years of collecting information on the history of Latin American art, particularly for the twentieth century.

MAGDALENA GARCÍA PINTO

beans

The kidney bean is produced by a leguminous climbing plant (*Phaseolus vulgaris*) native to the Americas; it was first cultivated in Mexico over 7,000 years ago. There are 470 distinct varieties, growing between sea level and 2,500 metres. Basic to the Mexican diet, the *frijol* (called *poroto* in Chile) was grown in the *milpa* (corn patch) and provided the proteins, carbohydrates, vitamins and minerals necessary for a balanced diet. There are seven varieties of bean graded by colour, size, appearance and harvesting season; they include the red kidney bean, the white variety (*alubia*), the broad bean (*haba*), etc. The name of the haricot bean derives from the Náhuatl word, *ayocote*. Cooked in a number of ways – boiled and sometimes mashed and refried – it is also used in *tamales* and as a pastry filling. The flowers of the plant are used in some dishes and the pods added to salads or cooked dishes as a green vegetable.

CRISTINA BARROS AND MARCO BUENROSTRO

beauty pageants

As nations are faced with significant social and economic changes, they engage in the elaboration of an ideal citizen, often a person of a specific ethnic group or social class who embodies new values that are put forward as right or true. Although 'citizen' is usually understood to be male, nations also construct an ideal of womanhood in response to the needs of the time.

While many countries had celebrated young womanhood in traditional festivities, the commercial beauty pageant came to Latin Americans through Hollywood films and newsreels through the 1920s and 1930s. Enthusiastic participation by most nations in the Miss Universe and Miss World Pageants by the early 1950s, suggests that the pageants may have been seen as a sign of international modern status. Certainly if Gabriel **García Márquez**'s gentle satire in his story 'Los funerales de la Mamá Grande' (The Funeral of Mamá Grande) is to be believed, the pageants' popularity spread quickly and they were soon moulded to appeal to and reveal distinctly national

tastes. Today Venezuela, which has won more international beauty contests than any other country, proclaims itself the 'world centre of beauty'.

Because beauty contests are sites where femininity is created and confirmed, they are also the places where gender and other values are challenged. As Rosario **Ferré** shows in 'El regalo' (The Gift), where economic power and racial domination compete to determine who is to wear a crown, the selection of a queen uncovers many an alliance or conflict among social groups. Indeed, contests pose questions about how race and ethnicity are valued, which social classes are in ascendancy as well as what kind of woman is needed at a given historical moment. Female beauty, it seems, involves not only a highly debated physical ideal, but also intellectual and even political qualities. A 1996 pageant for the Queen of Sololá (Guatemala) makes this clear, as it was based on which contestant could best explain the newly signed Peace Accords between the government and guerrilla rebels. For all their spectacle of royalty and blatant commercialization, beauty pageants play out social struggles in a feminine world of ball gowns and bathing suits as is vividly documented in Grupo Chaski's film *Miss Universe in Peru* (1982).

See also: Martinez, Rogelia; Sáez, Irene

MARY JANE TREACY

beaux-arts

Originating at the Ecole des Beaux Arts, Paris, its Latin American success developed as countries were successively incorporated into a world economy dominated by the nineteenth-century United Kingdom. Effective bureaucracies, administrations, and foreign resources created an infrastructure of significant buildings. Concurrently, an ideological break with Spain generated a desire to identify culturally with the ideas of the French Enlightenment. Since most architects were either French or French-educated, many regional architecture schools were conceived around the *beaux-arts* model, the most significant of them in Argentina, Chile, Mexico and Uruguay.

The combination of economic prosperity and a

well educated, status-seeking aristocracy resulted in the construction of luxurious private palaces. The Petit Trianon by Gabriel (1762–64) and the new Petit-Hotel are exemplary of the French Bourbon style, marked by the French neoclassical orders, and integrated principles of symmetry, rules of composition, and mansard roof forms with new building programmes and technology. It offered the aristocracy and government a classical vocabulary with which to regain a traditional hierarchy of values amidst a stylistic crisis of historic revival and the presence of other competing styles such us **art nouveau**.

Its popularity in Argentina began around 1880 as part of the broader cultural struggle between civilization and barbarism. Here, *beaux-arts* reached its hegemony in the early decades of the twentieth century. French architect René Sergent, who had never been to Argentina, and landscape architect Achile Duchesne, designed the Errázuriz Palace (1911), currently the Museum of Decorative Arts, the Bosh Alvea residence which was converted into the present US Embassy, and the Ferreira Palace in Córdoba (1913). Paris-educated architect Alejandro Christophersen designed the Anchorena Palace (1909) which today serves as the Ministry of Foreign Affairs in Argentina. By 1910, the Parisian *beaux-arts* image of boulevards, avenues and buildings in Buenos Aires prompted French politician Clemenceau to declare it 'a great European city'.

In Chile, significant examples of *beaux-arts* architecture following the neoclassical French Bourbon style include: the Justice Palace by Emilio Doyère in collaboration with Emilio Jecquier; the University of Chile (1863–74) by Henault which contains a magnificent Salon d'Honneur; the Beaux Arts Museum by Emilio Jecquier which incorporated technological advances in iron; residences such as the Cousiño Palace (1871), with crystals and mirrors by Paul Lathoud; the September Palace (1887–99) by Stauden or Ferhman; and the El Mercurio building (1872) by Henault.

Further reading

Bayón, D. (ed.) (1974) *América latina en sus artes*, Paris: UNESCO.

Fernández, J. (1967) *El arte del siglo XIX en México*, Mexico City: Universitaria.

JOSÉ BERNARDI

Becerra-Schmidt, Gustavo

b. 1925, Temuco, Chile

Composer and musicologist

Recognized as the most influential Chilean twentieth-century composer, Becerra-Schmidt studied in Europe (1953–6) and introduced European musical currents into Chile. He taught at the National Conservatory until he was appointed Cultural Attaché in Bonn by Salvador **Allende** in 1971. Since 1974 he has been Professor of Composition and Musicology at the University of Oldenburg.

After a brief neoclassical phase, Becerra adopted post-Weberian serialism, employing a series of random techniques including graphic notation. His most recent work includes a Concerto for guitar and percussion, *Überwindung* (Overcoming) (based on a biblical text) for soprano and orchestra, *Black hole* for chamber ensemble, and his Concerto no. 2 for piano and string orchestra.

ALFONSO PADILLA

Becker (Yáconis), Cacilda

b.1921, Piraçununga, São Paulo, Brazil; d.1969, São Paulo

Actress and theatre impresario

Reigning actress of the Brazilian stage during the 1950s and 1960s, Becker played major roles in the companies that modernized Brazilian theatre in the 1940s, founding her own company with her husband, actor Walmor Chagas, and sister, actress Cleyde Yáconis, in 1958. During the 1960s, Becker was also a prominent force in the theatre class's opposition to the dictatorship. Known principally as a dramatic actress whose repertoire ranged from Greek tragedy to Beckett, she was interpreting the role of the tramp, Estragon, in Beckett's *Waiting for Godot*, at the time of her sudden and early death.

LESLIE H. DAMASCENO

Becker, Germán

b. Chile

Propagandist and film-maker

Organizer of political rallies and sporting events, Becker became known during the 1960s for the '**clásicos universitarios**', a spectacular sporting and cultural event held in the National Stadium in Santiago. He organized electoral rallies for the Christian-Democratic Party of President Eduardo **Frei** (1963–70). After 1973, he became a propagandist for the **Pinochet** regime. His successful populist films included *Ayúdeme usted, compadre* (Help Me, My Friend) (1968) which mixed patriotism, melodrama, humour, and Chilean country music, *Volver* (To Return) (1969) and *Con el santo y la limosna* (With the Saint and the Alms) (1971).

LUIS E. CÁRCAMO-HUECHANTE

Bedia, José

b.1959, Havana

Painter and installation artist

Bedia is considered the leading artist of the so-called '80s' generation in Cuba. He graduated from the influential Havana Instituto Superior de Arte in 1981. Also in 1981 he participated in the seminal group exhibition *Volumen 1*. His installations, using elements of Afro-Cuban culture such as the **Santería** religion (of which he is an initiate) launched him on a successful international career in the mid-1980s. In the late 1980s he left Cuba and in the 1990s lived in several countries, including Mexico and the USA.

GABRIEL PEREZ-BARREIRO

Bedregal, Yolanda

b.1916, La Paz, Bolivia

Writer

Intimate feelings and everyday experience dominate the poetry of this Bolivian writer. Bedregal writes about a familiar urban world, the poor districts that produced the 'unknown soldier' (who probably fought in the **Chaco War**) described in her first book, *Naufragio* (Shipwreck) (1936). Her poems for children, like *El cántaro del angelito* (The Little Angel's Pitcher) (1979), express her sympathy for the 'disabled heroes', the street children. Her novel *Bajo el oscuro solo* (Alone in the Darkness) (1971) won first prize in a Los **Amigos del Libro** competition.

J. M. DE LA VEGA RODRIGUEZ

beer

Beer has been brewed in Mexico since pre-Hispanic times for ritual purposes; today beer is brewed in most Latin American countries, although the hops are entirely imported. In Mexico, three basic types are produced – Pilsen, Vienna and Munich. Some 47 million litres are produced annually, of which 10 per cent is exported. Mexico's main breweries include the Cervecería Cuauhtémoc (1890) and the Cervecería Modelo (1925). Brazil and Argentina are the other major producers in the region, though Jamaica and Bolivia brew their own excellent local varieties.

CRISTINA BARROS AND MARCO BUENROSTRO

béguine (biguine)

A couple dance in Martinique and St Lucia related to Haitian **méringue**. There are two styles: the drum béguine and the orchestral béguine. Drum béguine, related to **bele**, danced since the times of slavery, has a more nasal vocal style, call and response singing, and relies more on drums than on brass and wind instruments. Orchestral béguine became popular after the success of Martinican bands in Paris after the Second World War, and evolved into a style that sounds somewhat like Dixieland jazz. The lyrics are usually sung in French creole (see **French-based creoles**). Ensembles includes trumpets, saxophones, guitar, bass and percussion. The most famous musician of orchestral béguine was Alexandre **Stellio**; others include Ernest Léardée, Eugène Delouche, Roger Fanfant and Léona Gabriel.

DANIEL BALDERSTON

Behrhorst, Carroll

b. 1922, Kansas, USA; d. 1990, Chimaltenango, Guatemala

Physician

Behrhorst left a Kansas medical practice for Chimaltenango, Guatemala in 1962 to undertake a Lutheran medical mission. From a single room in the departmental capital, Behrhorst's eventually independent mission evolved into a much emulated health and development programme. A network of rural 'health promoters' trained in basic medicine, vaccinations, tuberculosis control, potable water development (see **water resources in Latin America**), family planning, **literacy** training, and agronomic development functioned until 1980. Civil war in the 1980s and early 1990s severely disrupted the programme and led to the deaths of many health workers. The programme continues under the auspices of a Guatemalan foundation and the patronage of a US fund-raising organization.

CHRISTOPHER VON NAGY

Belaúnde Terry, Fernando

b. 1912, Lima, Peru

Politician

An architect by profession, Belaúnde Terry entered the Peruvian Congress in 1945. He founded the Acción Popular party and was its presidential candidate twice before being elected to the post in 1963. As president he attempted to carry through a series of reforms, but was blocked by the parliamentary opposition. In 1968 he was deposed by a military *coup* led by General Juan **Velasco**. He became President again in 1980, but during his second term of office (1980–5) he faced a profound economic crisis and the emergence of the **Sendero Luminoso** (Shining Path) guerrilla movement.

CESAR SALAS

Belaval, Emilio S.

b. 1903, Fajardo, Puerto Rico; d. 1973, San Juan, Puerto Rico

Writer

A lawyer who became a Supreme Court judge, Belaval is best known as a writer of plays and essays, but is particularly known for his three collections of short stories – *Los cuentos de la universidad* (Stories of the University) (1935), *Los cuentos para fomentar el turismo* (Stories to Promote Tourism) (1946) and *Los cuentos de la Plaza Fuerte* (Stories of the Old Fort) (1967) – in which he uses popular culture and language to create a neo-baroque text that can be seen as the direct precedent of some more recent Puerto Rican fiction, especially the works of Ana Lydia **Vega** and Luis Rafael **Sánchez**.

EFRAÍN BARRADAS

bele

Dance form found in Trinidad and other Caribbean islands with a French slave-owning past, derived from courtly dances copied by the slaves and adapted to West African styles. The slaves parodied the ceremonious bows, elegant sweeping motions and grand entrances of dances like the minuet and added three drums. It is a couples dance, although the women are central. Using their full, layered skirts in a continual wrapping and unwrapping motion, they communicate with their partners and to signal instructions to the drummers. Bele is still performed in the **Best Village competitions**, but otherwise is no longer widespread in the rural communities where it once thrived.

LORRAINE LEU

Belfiore, Liliana

b. 1949, Buenos Aires, Argentina

Dancer

An outstanding soloist and prima ballerina, Belfiore joined the London Festival Ballet in 1975, becoming one of its principal dancers in 1979. Upon returning to Argentina, she rejoined the **Teatro Colón** (where she had begun her career) and debuted as a choreographer with *La bella durmiente del bosque* (Sleeping Beauty), based on the original. By 1982 she was choreographer and artistic director of the ballet company of the Teatro. In the late 1980s she opened her own dance studio.

RODRIGO PEIRETTI

Belize

Located in the right angle between the Yucatan peninsula and the Central American isthmus, this small Caribbean–Central American country covers 22,965 square kilometres and has 210,000 inhabitants. Its population density, 9.1 per square kilometre, is one of the lowest in the world. The great diversity of the population is the consequence of a long history of migrations dating back to the sixteenth- and seventeenth-century European outposts. In the eighteenth century, English colonists brought African slaves to cut mahogany and other precious woods. A century later, workers for the **sugar** plantations were also brought from India and China; the indigenous Maya population increased with Maya migrants from Mexico and Guatemala; and Garifuna (see **Garinagu**) refugees came from the Caribbean coast of Central America. The twentieth century brought Mennonite agricultural communities from northern Mexico, Central American immigrants to rural areas, and traders from India, Southwest Asia and China who settled in Belize City, **Belmopan** (the capital)

and Orange Walk. Each of the country's six districts has a distinct ethnic composition as a result of these migratory movements. But the dominant group has always been the creoles, of African origin and English colonial cultural background, who live mainly in the cities. They are currently becoming a minority, as a new **mestizo** population arises out of migrations. In 1991, 54 per cent of the people spoke English and 44 per cent Spanish, both official languages; Garinagu and Maya are also spoken.

In the face of territorial disputes with Guatemala, independence from Britain came as late as 1981. Since then, the challenge for this young nation has been to establish its national identity. New voices have arisen beside urban creole culture, arguing for the reaffirmation of minority identities, especially the Garinagu and Maya. In literature this may be seen in the work of Zee **Edgell**, Zoila **Ellis** and Cathy Esquivel in fiction and poetry. The work of the first generation of Belizean artists shares a common concern for the conservation of the country's natural and archaeological heritage. In popular music, **punta rock**, a Belizean rhythm with lyrics in English, Garinagu and Spanish, is gaining a national and continental audience.

Further reading

Barry, T. (1995) *Inside Belize*, Albuquerque, NM: Interhemispheric Press.

Bollard, O.N. (1986) *Belize: A New Nation in Central America*, Boulder, CO: Westview Press.

Sutherland, A. (1998) *The Making of Belize: Globalization in the Margins*, Westport, CN: Bergin & Garvey.

Zammit, J.A. (1978) *The Belize Issue*, London: Latin America Bureau.

LUIS ESPARZA

Bellegarde, Dantès

b. 1877, Port-au-Prince, Haiti; d. 1966, Port-au-Prince

Writer, diplomat and historian

A Haitian intellectual giant, Bellegarde, as a senior

government official, oversaw important reforms of the state education system and also had a distinguished career in the diplomatic service representing Haiti at the League of Nations and the United Nations, and as ambassador to France, the Vatican and the United States. A prolific writer for more than sixty years, he produced twenty-one books and hundreds of articles about Haitian history, politics and social issues. An antagonist of Jean **Price-Mars**, he favored closer intellectual and economic bonds with France.

CHARLES ARTHUR

Bellessi, Diana

b. 1946, Zavalla, Santa Fe Province, Argentina

Poet, essayist and translator

Bellessi has been important in articulating a space for the emergence of the female poetic voice. Her explorations of eroticism and her intense lyricism (she is often grouped with the **neo-baroque** poets) have earned her a distinctive position. Her poetry includes *Destino y propagaciones* (Destiny and Propagations) (1970), *Crucero ecuatorial* (Cruiser on the Equator) (1981), *Tributo del mudo* (Tribute of the Speechless) (1982), *Danzante de doblemáscara* (Double-Masked Dancer) (1985), *Eroica* (1988), *El jardín* (The Garden) (1992), *Sur* (South) (1998) and with Ursula LeGuin a bilingual coedition *The Twins, the Dream: Two Voices* (1996). She has translated US female poets in *Contéstame, baila mi danza* (Answer and Dance my Dance) (1984). Her cultural criticism (editorial board of *Feminaria*, **Diario de Poesía**, *Ultimo Reino*) and feminist cultural activism have resulted in publications such as *Paloma de contrabando* (Smuggled Dove) (1988), produced by prison workshops.

GWEN KIRKPATRICK

Belli, Gioconda

b. 1948, Managua, Nicaragua

Writer

Known both for her political commitment and her erotic poetry, Belli has supported both national liberation and the struggle for women's rights in Sandinista (see **Sandinista Revolution**) and post-Sandinista Nicaragua. Her first book of poetry *Sobre la grama* (On the Grass) (1974) won a literary prize. In exile in Costa Rica from 1975, she returned with the 1979 Revolution to work in the Press and Propaganda Section of the government. She headed Daniel **Ortega**'s successful election campaign in 1984. Her poetry, collected in *El ojo de la mujer* (Woman's Eye) (1991) and three novels, all show her concern with women, the poor and the oppressed.

DEREK PETREY AND ILEANA RODRÍGUEZ

Belmopan

The capital of Belize. In 1961, after Hurricane Hattie tore into Belize City, then the capital of colonial British Honduras, the British colonial office recommended that a new city be created. By 1965 an uninhabited site fifty miles inland was selected. Soon British architects were designing a new capital from scratch. It was to be the focal point of Belizean nationalism just as the colony attained self-governing status.

The name chosen for this clearing in the bush was 'Belmopan', combining the Afro-creole name 'Bel(ize)' with 'Mopan', the Maya who were the area's pre-conquest inhabitants and still live in the region. And, although the Mayan people are among the nation's poorest (even today battling logging contracts signed in Belmopan without their consent), the ruins of their ancient empire have been useful as symbols of national patrimony. Belmopan's governmental office complex was designed to suggest indigenous temples lining a plaza, constructed from sturdy grey concrete. Concrete was seen as the epitome of modernism and development, cheap and indestructible. To this day, no wooden homes are allowed. Concrete ditches line the roads, bridged by concrete walkways that wind through the city.

While this modern approach brought clean water and a sewage system, it gave Belmopan a character different from the rest of Belize. Many homes are fenced in, American style, with guard dogs. It remains a town of about 6,000, unable to attract many beyond the requirements of government employment. Initial dreams that the capital would spark development from Guatemala's Petén to the coast never materialized, and Belize City has remained the *de facto* centre of commerce. Nevertheless, there is now some light manufacturing, a University College of Belize branch, and some tourism, as Belmopan is the chief hub of buses running east, west and south. A small market area jumps to life as each bus pulls in.

Like the remnants of the ancient Maya, the government offices are now darkened with mildew, and the town is dotted with the unintentional ruins of half-built buildings from previous administrations' plans: a fractured nationalism. A few foreign embassies, with their members-only compounds, draw a tiny cosmopolitan élite. Meanwhile, landless Belizeans and refugees from Guatemala and El Salvador have created precarious settlements on the town's periphery, regularly threatened with relocation. But new concrete 'suburbs' have also appeared on the town's edge: some in Belmopan are content with its small town atmosphere and consequent lack of crime.

Further reading

Davis, S.E. (1991) 'Designing nationalism: Belmopan, Belize', *Landscape* 31(1): 36–48.
Stone, M. (1990) *Backabush: Settlement on the Belmopan Periphery and the Challenge to Rural Development in Belize*, SPEAR Reports 6, Belize City: Society for the Promotion of Education and Research (SPEAR).

ALEX GREENE

Beltrán, Lola

b. 1932, El Rosario, Sinaloa, Mexico;
d. 1996, Mexico City

Singer

In the era of television and the recording industry, Lola Beltrán (born Lucía Beltrán Ruiz) continues the tradition of Lucha **Reyes**, creator of the modern style of ranchera music (see **canción ranchera**)

whose origins lay in provincial fairs and theatrical revue. Unlike Reyes, Beltrán had no operatic training; her voice flowed out of her temperament and her instincts – powerful, sometimes poignant, clear and sharp. From 1954 onwards, Beltrán was the principal performer of the songs of two great popular composers – José Alfredo **Jiménez** and Tomás Méndez (1920–92). She recorded Jiménez's first great hits – 'El rey' (The King), Ella (Her), 'La noche de mi mal' (My Painful Night), 'Paloma querida' (Dear Dove), 'Cuatro caminos' (When Four Roads Meet) and dozens more. Her version of songs by Méndez included 'Cucurrucú, paloma' (Coo, coo, dove) and 'Gorrioncito pecho amarillo' (Yellow-breasted Sparrow). As the genre demands, Beltrán normally sings to a sometimes treacherous and always beloved woman from the male point of view ('Dear dove, since you entered my life / I have raised my glass daily'), not because of any particular sexual orientation but because until recently women were not considered worthy to address men directly in song. If they spoke in public, it was to give voice to masculine feelings.

Beltrán's exceptional qualities were recognized early; the quality of her voice is maintained across some hundred albums, even if the songs themselves are more uneven. She appeared in about forty *comedia ranchera* (see **rancheras, comedias**) or 'Western-*enchilada*' films – all of them dreadful. (Lola may be no actress but her directors were not worthy of the name either.) The first popular singer to give a concert at the Palacio de Bellas Artes, Lola's repertoire is still closely linked to the Mexican fiesta with its colours, rockets, love duels, bullfights, cockfights and **mariachi** singers, as well as the fiesta's 'guttural nationalism'. But in her later songs she also sings of gutsy women, happy in their misfortune, whose painful solitude finds expression in her solo voice accompanied by a single guitar.

CARLOS MONSIVÁIS

Beltrán García, Alberto

b. 1923, Mexico City

Artist and illustrator

Many important studies of Mexican culture

published in Mexico or the USA during the 1940s, 1950s and 1960s, were illustrated with the woodblock prints, metal prints and lithographs by Alberto Beltrán. His illustrations are marked by a powerful nationalism and a deep-seated affection for the common folk. From 1944–60, as a key member of the **Taller de Gráfica Popular** (Popular Graphics Workshop), Beltrán participated in an outpouring of collective political art: posters, leaflets, and engravings. He also painted murals and produced many educational texts for schoolchildren. He was awarded a National Journalism Prize for his political cartoons in 1976.

CYNTHIA STEELE

Bemberg, María Luisa

b. 1922, Buenos Aires, Argentina; d. 1995, Buenos Aires

Film and theatre director, screenwriter

The most prolific female Latin American film director, Bemberg's films and screenplays focused on women's lives, particularly on the difficulties women face in asserting independent thought and action within patriarchal society. Born into a wealthy Argentine family, she at first lived the patriarchally prescribed life she later criticized. She married at twenty-three and raised four children. Her professional career began when she separated from her husband and began working in theatre, helping to found the Teatro del Globo.

Bemberg's first screenplay, *Crónica de una señora* (Chronicle of a Lady) (1971), was directed by her friend and mentor Raúl de la Torre. There then followed a collaboration with Fernando **Ayala**, *Triángulo de cuatro* (Triangle of Four) (1974). She made two well-received short films before her 1980 feature directorial debut, *Momentos* (Moments), which began a career-long collaboration with producer Lita **Stantic**. Though Bemberg rarely called herself a feminist, themes of women's empowerment pervade her work. *Momentos* and *Señora de nadie* (Nobody's Wife) (1982) narrate stories of discontented housewives who break the mould of society's expectations.

Bemberg's third feature, **Camila** (1984), won an Oscar nomination for Best Foreign Picture. Seen by two million Argentines and internationally distributed, *Camila* marked the birth of a new Argentine cinema. Her next film, *Miss Mary* (1986), was an international co-production starring British actress Julie Christie. A period drama shot in Spanish and English, it told the story of a British governess raising the children of an upper-class Argentine family in the pre-Perón 1940s. Though less popular than *Camila*, *Miss Mary* was also commercially successful in Argentina.

Bemberg's later work, *Yo, la peor de todas* (I, the Worst of All) (1990) and the comedy *De eso no se habla* (I Don't Want to Talk About It) (1993) in some ways departed from her earlier films, addressing less intimate stories and exploring the repercussions of women's independence within larger communities. A biopic about a seventeenth-century Mexican nun and poet, *Yo, la peor de todas* chronicles Sor Juana Inés de la Cruz's rise and fall from favour with the colonial Roman Catholic Church, as she chooses to defy the *machista* expectations for women in her age. During her final illness, Bemberg wrote a screenplay which will be filmed by her colleague and friend, Alejandro Maci.

ILENE S. GOLDMAN

Ben, Jorge   *see* Jorge Ben

Benacerraf, Baruj

b. 1920, Caracas, Venezuela

Scientist and medical researcher

Banacceraf is best known for his research on the genetic basis of immunology, which won him the Nobel Prize in Physiology and Medicine in 1980 (see **Nobel Prizes**). After a childhood spent in France, Benacerraf studied medicine in the USA in the 1940s. He became an American citizen in 1943, and at the end of that decade embarked on a career in medical research. He soon established an outstanding reputation in the field, especially through collaborative research carried out as an academic at New York University. In 1970 he became Professor of Pathology at the Harvard Medical School.

MARK DINNEEN

Benacerraf, Margot

b. 1926, Caracas, Venezuela

Film-maker

Benacerraf's first film, in 1951, was an acclaimed documentary about the painter Armando **Reverón**. As a Europeanized Latin American (she settled in France in 1950) Benacerraf turned to avant-garde techniques for her first full length feature, *Araya* (1959) which brought her fame in her own country (where the main cinema is named after her) as well as a critics prize at Cannes in that year. Her style is more neorealist than experimental, describing in an almost documentary manner, and in deep black and white, the history of the nitrate mines of the Araya peninsula and the wretched conditions in which the workers and their families live.

G. MONTALDO

Benavente, David

b. 1941, Santiago, Chile

Playwright

Although his later work has been largely for TV and video production, he began writing for the theatre in the early 1960s in the framework of a new and dynamic Chilean theatre scene. His first play, *La ganzúa* (The Hook) premièred in 1962, and was followed by *Tengo ganas de dejarme la barba* (I Feel Like Growing a Beard) (1964), both influenced by the theatre of the absurd. *Pedro, Juan y Diego* (published in 1989), written for the **ICTUS** company in the very different circumstances of Chile under **Pinochet**, is representative of a new kind of testimonial theatre. A graduate in sociology and consultant to PREALC (the Regional Employment Programme of the International Labour Organization) Benavente was commissioned to

produce two books of *testimonios* – *A medio morir cantando* (Half Dead Singing) (1985) and *Homo faber: Once casos sobre el trabajo y otras cosas* (Homo Faber: Eleven Cases about Work and Other Things) (1988) – which provide in **testimonio** form a human account of the experience of work and unemployment in Latin America.

MARINA PIANCA

Bendayán, Amador

b. 1920, Villa de Cura, Aragua, Venezuela; d. 1989, Caracas, Venezuela

Radio and television personality

Bendayán began his broadcasting career in 1937 on the recently founded radio station Ondas Populares, and went on to present a series of successful shows on different stations. One of his most popular programmes, *La bodeguita de la esquina* (The Little Shop on the Corner), was adapted for television, and Bendayán soon became one of Venezuela's best-known television presenters. He also acted in a number of films, but is best remembered for his television work, especially the Saturday show *Sábado sensacional*, which he presented from 1957 until shortly before his death.

MARK DINNEEN

Benedetti, Mario

b. 1920, Paso de los Toros, Uruguay

Writer, essayist and critic

Since his first attempts as a poet and short-story writer in the late 1940s, Mario Benedetti has successfully cultivated a wide range of literary genres, a fact that has contributed to his status as one of the most versatile writers of contemporary Latin America. The author of more than 70 titles, he is also one of the most prolific writers of his generation.

With his early poems, short stories and novels, like *Poemas de la oficina* (Office Poems) (1956), *Montevideanos* (1959 and 1962), and *La tregua* (The Truce) (1960), Benedetti became the national **bestseller** and gained a reputation as a great humorist and shrewd analyst of the Uruguayan lower middle-class, depicting the existential dilemmas and moral feebleness of the many civil servants in the bureaucracy of a stagnant and decaying welfare state.

Together with some of the most influential contributors to the weekly *Marcha*, Benedetti became progressively more radical in the 1960s. His greater political involvement, his anti-imperialist attitude and a broader continental preoccupation can also be detected in his literary work from this period, in particular in his poetry and in a curious novel in verse form, *El cumpleaños de Juan Angel* (Juan Angel's Birthday) (1971), a work that twenty years later inspired the 'subcomandante' of Chiapas to adopt the name Marcos (see **Subcomandante Marcos**), the enigmatic guerrilla-leader of the novel.

From 1973 until the mid-1980s, Benedetti lived in exile in Argentina, Peru, Cuba and Spain, and became the literary spokesman of Latin-Americans who suffered political ostracism during the harsh dictatorships in the Southern Cone. Being a 'communicative writer', he also collaborated closely with composers and performers like Alberto Favero, Nacha Guevara and Joan Manuel Serrat, who made his songs and poems even more familiar to Latin audiences.

The Uruguayan's literary work of the last two decades emphasizes the problems of exile and return from exile (for which he coined the term 'desexilio'). Although more reflective in tone, he is still capable of humorous invention and of denouncing social injustice and moral corruption. Some of his best books from this period, the novel *La primavera con una esquina rota* (Spring with a Broken Corner) (1982), and the collection of short stories *Geografías* (Geographies) (1984) also show a writer dedicated to formal experimentation, unusual combinations of prose and poetry, defamiliarization and play on words.

Further reading

Paoletti, M. (1995) *El aguafiestas. Mario Benedetti, la biografía*, Buenos Aires: Seix Barral.

JON ASKELAND

Benedit, Luis

b. 1937, Buenos Aires, Argentina

Artist and architect

Benedit's body of work seems like a vast metaphor of the relationship between art and science. Architect and artist, Benedit started painting in the 1950s, working within the supposedly naive world inhabited by animals, children and fantasy figures. In the 1970s, he became part of the Conceptualist movement that spanned the arts. His pictures grew in scale, and came to accommodate paintings by his son Tomás, or constructed, three-dimensional additions in wood or resin, decorated in oils and enamels. By the 1980s, Benedit concluded that his technique consisted of 'three stages: the original, the one-dimensional drawing, and the object'.

AMANDA HOPKINSON

Bengell, Norma

b. 1935, Rio de Janeiro, Brazil

Actress and film-maker

A key figure in Brazilian cinema, Bengell made her debut in Carlos **Manga**'s *O homem do Sputnik* (Sputnik Man) (1958), parodying Brigitte Bardot. A spectacularly beautiful blonde and a very talented actress, she went on to appear in films by Brazil's most important directors: Anselmo Duarte's *O pagador de promessas* (The Given Word) (1964) Ruy **Guerra**'s *Os cafajestes* (The Hustlers) (1961), Julio Bressane's *O anjo nasceu* (The Angel Was Born) (1969), Ana Carolina **Teixeira Soares**'s *Mar de rosas* (Sea of Roses) (1977) and Rogério **Sganzerla**'s *Abismu* (1977), which she also produced. She also directed documentaries and feature films (*Eternamente Pagu* (Always Pagu) (1987) and *O Guarani* (1996)).

ISMAIL XAVIER AND THE USP GROUP

Benítez, Fernando

b. 1912, Mexico City

Writer

Benítez's distinguished journalistic career began in 1934. In the 1950s and 1960s he spearheaded the creation of weekly cultural magazines like *La Cultura en México* (*¡Siempre!*), *La **Jornada** Semanal*, characterized by a new journalistic style combining in-depth interviews with chronicles and incisive criticism. Benítez's work on colonial history includes *La ruta de Hernán Cortés* (In the Footsteps of Cortes) (1950). His five-volume series of chronicles on *Los indios de México* (1967–81) combines travel narrative with anthropological and journalistic observations on the Indian tribes in various regions of the country. He was also Mexican ambassador to the Dominican Republic.

CYNTHIA STEELE

Benítez, Jaime

b. 1908, Vieques, Puerto Rico

Educator and politician

One of the most influential figures of contemporary Puerto Rico, he began his association with the University of Puerto Rico as a professor in 1931, and was appointed chancellor in 1942 and president in 1966. Under his leadership the university expanded, academically and numerically, though it also experienced dramatic clashes such as the 1948 student strike. Benítez was instrumental in recruiting international intellectuals and scholars, promoting the arts and transforming the university into a prestigious institution. He served as Resident Commissioner of Puerto Rico in the US Congress from 1972 to 1976.

VíCTOR FEDERICO TORRES

Benítez, Lucecita

b. 1942, Bayamón, Puerto Rico

Singer

Benítez came to prominence in the 1960s, as part of the musical Nueva Ola (New wave). In January 1965, together with Chucho Avellanet and Alfred D. Herger, she presented the television programme which brought the movement to public attention – 'Canta la juventud' (Youth Sings) – itself part of the television variety programme 'El show de las 12', produced by Paquito Cordero. By 1964 her songs, clearly influenced by rock, broke all existing sales records; the success of her album *¡Lucecita en escena!* (Lucecita on Stage) earned her the title 'queen of youth'.

In 1969, Benítez's spectacular success at the First World Festival of Canción Latina, held in Mexico, with her song 'Génesis' (written by Guillermo Venegas Lloveras) placed her unequivocally on an international stage. From then on she aspired to more artistic songs; her work was no longer directed exclusively at a youth audience, and her records began to include the work of poets and composers from Latin America and Europe. Through the 1970s and 1980s she became known as 'the national voice of Puerto Rico', famous for the strength and dramatic power of her voice and for its interpretative versatility. She has, with great success, recorded songs in many popular genres, including the peasant songs or **décima**, **bolero**, **guaracha**, **salsa**, *nueva canción*, **tango** and the romantic ballad. At the same time, Benítez has always stressed the political aspect of her cultural work, both as an advocate of Puerto Rican independence and through her questioning and parodies of the so-called 'essential' nature of sexual identities. Through the early 1970s, she often appeared on stage dressed as a man. She has toured widely in Latin America, Europe and the USA, and has often filled Puerto Rico's premier musical venue, the Centro de Bellas Artes (Fine Arts Centre), to capacity.

Further reading

Santiago, J. (1994) *Nueva ola portoricensis*, San Juan: Editorial del Patio.

JUAN CARLOS QUINTERO HERENCIA

Benítez Rojo, Antonio

b. 1931, Havana, Cuba

Writer

Benítez Rojo's first impact on Cuban literary circles came with the publication of his volume of short stories *Tute de Reyes* (A Trick of Kings) which won the 1967 **Casa de las Américas** prize. His next collection, *El escudo de hojas secas* (The Shield of Dry Leaves) (1968) won an award in the **UNEAC** literary competition. He edited (with Mario **Benedetti**) the anthology *Quince relatos de América Latina* (Fifteen Stories from Latin America) (1970) and is author of the important essay *La isla que se repite* (The Repeating Island) (1989). He currently lives in the United States.

WILFREDO CANCIO ISLA

Benmayor, Samy

b. 1956, Santiago, Chile

Painter

A participant in the neo-expressionist movement of the 1980s, Benmayor combines in his watercolours and acrylics a rich iconography drawn from classical mythology, daily life and memories of childhood. The result is an uninhibited, playful and ironic juxtaposition of elements formally disrupted by lines, spills and spots. Benmayor's world is one in which television cowboys, tigers and centaurs conspire to subvert the logic of everyday life.

CELIA LANGDEAU CUSSEN

Bennett, Louise

b. 1919, Kingston, Jamaica

Writer, performer and broadcaster

One of the most respected poets working in the Jamaican dialect, Bennett has lectured in Africa, Europe and North America. Her collections of poems include: *Jamaica Labrish* (1966) and *Selected Poems* (1982). Her work is also available on records and cassettes. She began writing as a teenager, and has performed her work since 1938. She wrote for the *Gleaner* in Jamaica, and collected folklore material throughout the island. In 1945, she won a scholarship to the Royal Academy of Dramatic Art in London. She later worked for the BBC. She is a recipient of an MBE and many other awards.

KEITH JARDIM

Benoit, Rigaud

b. 1911, Port-au-Prince, Haiti; d. 1987, Port-au-Prince

Visual artist

Benoit was chauffeur to DeWitt Peters, founder of the Centre d'Art in Port-au-Prince, Haiti, in 1943. Before the Centre's opening, he brought Peters several extraordinary paintings, fictitiously signed; Benoit only later revealed himself to be the artist. A close friend of Hector **Hyppolite**, they decorated the Centre's jeep and helped to decorate its walls. His masterly representations of village markets and family gatherings capture the country's grace, cleanliness, grotesquerie and humour. He specializes in complex interiors and church services, usually in grey and stone white. 'The Interrupted Marriage' (1972) and 'Fighting with Sticks' (1966) are good illustrations of his work.

MARY BOLEY

Berenguer, Carmen

b. 1942, Santiago, Chile

Poet

Berenguer is an active cultural figure and a poet of **neo-baroque** complexity. Her poetry begins as an allegorical depiction of the suffering of political minorities, and then moves on to elaborate a stark landscape of Santiago's life under military rule in *Huellas de Siglo* (Century Traces) (1986). The stress on wordplay in her next book unleashes the struggle of the female subaltern's voice toward cultural empowerment, and in *Sayal de pieles* (Skin Tunic) (1994) it highlights the excruciating pain which **AIDS** inflicts upon the human body.

OSCAR D. SARMIENTO

Bergnes, Gustavo Arcos

b. 1928, Caibarién, Cuba

Human rights activist

A leader of civic resistance to the government of Fidel **Castro** and a proponent of peaceful disobedience, Arcos Bergnes is General Secretary of the Cuban Committee for Human Rights. On 26 July 1953 he participated with Castro in the assault on the Moncada barracks – the first attack in the struggle against the dictatorship of Fulgencio **Batista**. After the victory of the Cuban Revolution in 1959 (see **revolutions**) he was named ambassador to Belgium but resigned from his post in 1964 because of political disagreements with the government. His opposition to the Castro regime earned him a ten-year jail sentence in 1966. In 1981 he joined the Cuban Committee for Human Rights and was again imprisoned. Since his release in 1988, he has been the Committee's president. He has twice been nominated for the Nobel Peace Prize.

JOSÉ ANTONIO EVORA

berimbau

A pitched percussion instrument of *bantu* African origin, the berimbau is found mainly in the Brazilian state of Bahia, and is used to accompany **capoeira**. A wooden bow with a metal or rubber string, whose tension is varied by means of a coin or wedge at one end, it produces a limited range of oscillating tones. The string is struck rhythmically with a thin wooden stick, and the sound amplified by means of a gourd resonator attached to the lower end of the bow. The berimbau's rhythmic and tonal qualities and ritualistic connotations formed the basis for Baden **Powell**'s highly successful afro-samba, 'Berimbau', of 1963, and have since been explored by percussionists such as Naná Vasconcelos and Dinho Nascimento.

DAVID TREECE

Berman, Sabina

b. 1952, Mexico City

Playwright, novelist and poet

One of the Mexico's most prominent contemporary playwrights, Berman is the first to have won the Premio Nacional de Teatro four times. Her plays are complex and provocative, with subject matter ranging from the conumdrum of Trotsky's assassination in Mexico in 1942 in *Rompecabezas* (Puzzle) (1981), to the conquest of Tenochtitlán in *Aguila o sol* (Heads or Tails) (1985), to politics and machismo in contemporary Mexico in *Entre Villa y la mujer desnuda* (Between **Villa** and the Naked Woman) (1993). All of Berman's plays are prismatically structured, producing a multifaceted view of a central subject. Plays like *Yanqui* (Yankee) (1979), *Rompecabezas*, *Herejía* (Heresy) (1983), and *El suplicio del placer* (The Agony of Ecstasy) (1985) are open-ended. They provide for a variety of different intepretations. This, of course, is not new. Any play with lasting power eschews the dogmatic and draws in its audience. The difference here is that Berman locates this confluence of possible interpretations within the characterizations themselves. In a Berman play, character is never fixed, but always fluid. The final effect of a Berman play is to produce a new found awareness of our own sense of identity. We are shown just how fragile that identity can be, how provisional the sense of self can become. In *Yanqui* the most prominent character is Bill, the US citizen who suddenly appears to offer his services as handyman to a young couple living on the outskirts of Puerta Vallarta. Obviously undergoing some ill-defined turmoil, Bill provides a series of explanations about himself and why he is in Mexico. Each successive scene cancels out the identity previously established until we are left with a man who has so many identities that he has no identity. The only constant is his desire to establish a sense of self, to quiet the confusion raging within him. *Herejía* continues this exploration of identity with its depiction of a family of *conversos* who secretly continue to practice Judaism. Journeying to New Spain they establish a new life in Mexico only to be denounced to the Holy Inquisition by the spurned suitor of one of the female members of the family. The play's focus is the interplay between the family's exterior mask of Christian respectability and its internal commitment to Judaism. Berman has also refused to confine her own identity to the theatre. She has written for television, adapted *Entre Villa y la mujer desnuda* for film (directed by Berman herself and Isabelle Tardán in 1995), and directed a Mayan village of 250 inhabitants in her play *Arux*, about the Mayan dwarf-god. Her play, *Krisis* (1996), is a blatant attack upon the political corruption and cronyism of the **PRI**, Mexico's ruling party from the Mexican Revolution until 2000.

Further reading

Burgess, R.D. (1991) *The New Dramatists of Mexico, 1967–1985*, Lexington: University of Kentucky Press.

Cypess, S.M. (1993) 'Ethnic Identity in the Plays of Sabina Berman', in R. DiAntonio and N. Glickman (eds) *Tradition and Innovation. Reflections on Latin American Jewish Writing*, New York: State University of New York Press.

Eyring Bixler, J. (Spring 1997) 'The Postmodernization of History in the Theatre of Sabina Berman', *Latin American Theatre Review*, 30(2).

ADAM VERSÉNYI

Bermuda

This island territory is located in the Atlantic Ocean roughly 550 miles east of Cape Hatteras, North Carolina on the North American mainland. Officially called 'the Bermuda Islands', the territory consists of seven larger islands linked by bridges and causeways and almost 200 other small islands and islets. Although quite distant from the geographic Caribbean basin, Bermuda has often been considered a part of the Caribbean because of cultural, demographic and historical similarities with that region. Settled by the English in the seventeenth century, Bermuda never became a sugar colony like more southerly islands but did turn to African slavery for the performance of most agricultural and other manual labour, such as in the colony's salt-raking industry. After the abolition of slavery in 1838, Bermuda remained only a minor economic player in the British colonial Caribbean. However, as with many Caribbean territories, the second half of the twentieth century brought the growth and development of a modern, large-scale tourist industry that became the mainstay of Bermuda's economy. At the end of the twentieth century Bermuda remained a British territory but had been given internal self-government in 1968. In its total population of about 60,000 Bermuda has a proportionally larger white population than most other parts of the Caribbean – approximately 30 per cent. Most of the remaining 70 per cent is made up of black descendants of enslaved Africans.

ROSANNE ADDERLEY

Bermúdez, Cundo

b. 1914, Havana, Cuba

Painter

A member of the second Cuban modernist generation of the 1940s, Bermúdez's stylish forms and bright colours suggest the influence of Amelia **Peláez**. He became associated with the **Orígenes** group. In 1967 he emigrated to Puerto Rico where, without abandoning his Cuban subjects, his work became increasingly enigmatic and fantastic, interweaving geometrical forms and symbolic objects with dream images.

WILFREDO CANCIO ISLA

Bermúdez, Lucho

b. 1904, Carmen de Bolívar, Colombia; d. 1994

Musician

When the **cumbia**, the music of Colombia's northern coast, was taken to the cities by migrants and rapidly became the most popular dance music among urban youth in the 1940s, Lucho Bermúdez and his band were among the first to create this new 'big-city' sound. Bermúdez, a clarinettist, evolved a new version of cumbia – less complex in its rhythms, more regular in its pace and therefore more appropriate for the dance clubs in the capital. This was big-band music, influenced in its turn by the rise of **mambo** and the brassy sound of **Pérez Prado**. The lyrics, however, stayed closer to the folk songs of the original cumbia.

MIKE GONZALEZ

Bernal, Ignacio

b. 1910, Paris, France; d. 1992, Mexico City

Archaeologist and ethnographer

Educated in law, Ignacio Bernal became one of this century's foremost scholars of Mesoamerica, in particular ancient Oaxaca. A student of Alfonso **Caso**, Bernal followed his lead, powerfully integrating archaeological, ethnographic and historical sources on ancient Mixtec and Zapotec kingdoms. Bernal wrote on the ancient Olmec, positioning them as the 'Mother Culture' of Mesoamerica and the wellspring of Mexican culture. Bernal played pivotal roles in the development of institutional archaeology in Mexico serving as director of **INAH** (1968–71), the National Museum of Anthropology and History (1962–8 and 1970–7), and of the massive project at Teotihuacan, turning it into the instance of national grandeur it is today. Bernal

participated in the education of scores of Mexican archaeologists in his role as professor at both the Colegio de México and **UNAM** and is a well-known author of many of the guides to Mexico's national archaeological monuments.

CHRISTOPHER VON NAGY

Bernal Jiménez, Miguel

b. 1910, Morelia, Michoacan; d. 1956

Composer, musicologist and organist

Bernal Jiménez taught, composed and played the organ at Morelia's cathedral and became director of the Escuela Superior de Música Sagrada (Higher School of Sacred Music) and of its choir (1936), as well as Dean of Music at Loyola University in New Orleans (1954–6). He toured widely as an organist, choir director and lecturer. His own works were often inspired by the historic context of his native region, like his symphonic drama *Tata Vasco* (1941) which concerned Vasco de Quiroga, the first bishop of Michoacán. His best-known work is the *Cuarteto virreinal* (Colonial Quartet). He also wrote extensively about music.

JUAN PELLICER

Bernardes, Sergio

b. 1919, Rio de Janeiro, Brazil

Architect

A taste for simplicity and an emphasis on daring forms make Bernardes heir both to neoclassical purity and innovative engineering. Driven by the constructivist ideal of social transformation through form (see **constructivism**), Bernardes understood architecture as a place from which to intervene in culture. He proposed everything from the reconstruction of the traditional instruments of daily life, as in his design for a new bicycle, to radical changes in geography, as in his proposal to link the two bays that frame Rio de Janeiro by a navigable canal, a creative use of technology which culminated in urban projects for **Amazonia** and Alaska.

ROBERTO CONDURU

Berni, Antonio

b. 1905, Rosario, Argentina; d.1981, Buenos Aires

Painter

In 1925, Berni won a travel grant to Europe and went to Paris where he studied under the Cubists André Lhote and Othon Friesz. In Paris he became interested in left-wing ideas and came under the influence of **Surrealism**. By the late 1920s, he was painting in a Surrealist style. In 1931 he returned to Argentina, and in 1932 controversially exhibited Surrealist paintings in Buenos Aires. In the same year he co-founded the *Nuevo Realismo* (New Realism) group and his style changed towards **socialist realism**. In 1933, the Mexican muralist David Alfaro **Siqueiros** visited Buenos Aires, and Berni helped him to paint his only mural in Argentina: the 'Ejercicio plástico' (Plastic Exercise) in the house of newspaper editor Natalio **Botana** near Buenos Aires. In 1939, he worked with Lino Eneas **Spilimbergo** on the murals for the New York Universal Exhibition. In 1941, he travelled along the Pacific Coast of the Americas and produced a series of works based on Indian cultures. Berni's interest in the working-class and urban poverty was to remain with him even when he abandoned the Socialist Realist style in the 1950s. In 1958, he created a famous series of collages and assemblages based on a fictional street urchin, Juanito Laguna. In 1963, he invented another character: the prostitute Ramona Montiel. These works, using rubbish and materials found in the streets, combine the collage techniques of Surrealism with the social concern of his realist period. In 1962, he won the Grand Prize at the Venice Biennial, confirming his leading role in Argentine art.

Further reading

Elliott, D. (1994) 'Antonio Berni: Art and Politics in the Avant-Garde' in D. Elliott (ed.) *Art from Argentina 1920–1994*, Oxford: Museum of Modern Art.

Glusberg, J. (1997) *Antonio Berni*, Buenos Aires: Museo Nacional de Bellas Artes.

Nanni, M.(1984) *Antonio Berni: obra pictórica*, Buenos Aires: Museo Nacional de Bellas Artes.

Ravera, R.M. (1980) *Berni*, Buenos Aires: Centro Editor de América Latina.

Squirru, R. (1975) *Berni: estudio crítico-biográfico*, Buenos Aires: Losada.

GABRIEL PEREZ-BARREIRO

Berry, James

b. 1924, Jamaica

Writer

A writer of poetry, short stories and children's fiction, Berry has lived in England since 1948. His *A Thief in the Village and Other Stories* (1988) is a collection of stories about life in contemporary Jamaica. *Ajeemah and His Son* (1992), recounts the story of Ajeemah and his son Atu, who in 1807 are kidnapped by slave traders and transported to neighbouring plantations in Jamaica, never to see each other again. The poems of *Everywhere Faces Everywhere* (1997) explore themes of growing up, nature, change, the magic of myths, and a society unwilling to embrace diversity. In 1990, Berry received the Order of the British Empire in recognition of his writing achievements.

KEITH JARDIM

Bertoni, A.F.

b. 18??, Italy; d. Costa Rica

Film-maker

Credited with making the first feature film in Costa Rica, Bertoni was residing in Costa Rica when he proposed the idea of making a film to his friend, the cinematographer and inventor Walter Bolandi. In 1930 they completed *El retorno* (The Homecoming), a ninety-minute melodrama. The film was removed from circulation shortly after its première in the Cine Variedades. More than six decades later, in 1995, *El retorno* returned to the screen, thanks to the restoration efforts of Costa Rica's national film institute, the **Centro Costarricense de Producción Cinematográfica** (CCPC).

ANN MARIE STOCK

Bésame mucho

Bésame mucho is a bolero composed in 1941 by Consuelo **Velásquez**. It was one of the first romantic ballads to move beyond provincialism, adapting to a new international music market. The lyrics express the desire of two lovers to remain together forever and their fear of separation, themes common to the majority of romantic songs. Eduardo Ugarte's film *Bésame mucho* (1944), starring Blanquita Amaro, launched the 'bolero-gangster movie'. So successful was the song that many artists have recorded it, among them the Beatles.

ALEJANDRA LAERA

beso de la mujer araña, El

El beso de la mujer araña, (Kiss of the Spider Woman) (1976) is Manuel **Puig**'s fourth novel which was circulated secretly in Argentina until the return of democracy (in 1984). It was adapted for theatre as a musical as well as a play and filmed by Héctor **Babenco** with William Hurt's brilliant performance as Molina. This ensured Puig's international recognition and ended his realist period.

Imprisoned in the same cell, two men converse. One is a left-wing activist, the other a homosexual; or, in terms of the current language, one is a 'guerrillero' (a guerrilla) the other a 'loca' (a queen). Each expresses to the other his fascination with his own worlds, governed by quite opposite values. Molina narrates and interprets to Valentin a series of classic films. Presumably their incarceration in one cell was part of a strategy to undermine Valentin's will and lead him to inform on his comrades – the 'loca' is part of the machinery of torture. But Molina and Valentin possess a similar

integrity, and in the end Molina protects his cellmate. Under threat, he dissembles before the prison authorities, but he cannot and will not betray him. At some point, the worlds of the two men touch; when their bodies encounter each other, it is an act that goes beyond copulation. Molina is freed, and Valentin presses him to take a message to his comrades. At the end of the novel, both are dead.

Puig works with powerfully drawn social types – but he cuts into the comfortable and fluid narrative with profuse footnotes which document current discourses on the relations between sexuality and politics. In some sense the novel functions like a kind of television 'docudrama' with fictional segments illustrating ideas presented elsewhere by various 'talking heads', or a fictional programme with expert commentary.

If, in the context of contemporary literature, the novel was read as a folkloric representation of two typically Latin American social types, within Argentina, Puig's text was one of the first literary representations of the repression of the 1970s. It took to its limit the use of dialogue to present plot and reclaimed a narrative method first employed by Roberto **Arlt** in his *El juguete rabioso* (The Angry Toy).

The subject matter of the novel would seem to exclude humour, but Manuel Puig's view of his characters is heavily ironic – for they rush to occupy stereotypical aesthetic compartments which Puig subjects to a constant critique in all his work.

Further reading

Amícola, J. (1992) *Manuel Puig y la tela que atrapa al lector: Estudio sobre El beso de la mujer araña en su relación con los procesos receptivos y con una continuidad literaria contestaria*, Buenos Aires: Grupo Editor Latinoamericano.

Bacarisse, P. (1988) *The Necessary Dream: A Study of the Novels of Manuel Puig*, Cardiff: University of Wales Press.

Dabove, J. (1994) *La forma del Destino: Sobre El beso de la mujer araña de Manuel Puig*, Rosario: Beatriz Viterbo Editora.

Kerr, L. (1987) *Suspended Fictions: Reading Novels by Manuel Puig*, Urbana: University of Illinois Press.

Muñoz, E. (1987) *El discurso utópico de la sexualidad en Manuel Puig*, Madrid: Editorial Pliegos.

Puig, M. (2000) *El beso de la mujer araña*, ed. J. Amícola, Paris: Colección Archivo (with essays by J. Romero, G. Goldchluk, D. Balderston and others).

DANIEL LINK

Best, Lloyd

b. 1934, Tunapuna, Trinidad

Economist and politician

A publisher and politician, Lloyd Best has had one of the most distinguished careers in the Caribbean. In 1962 he began working for the United Nations and other multilateral agencies, most of them also connected with the United Nations. In 1976 in Trinidad, he led the Tapia House Movement (of which he is the founder) in elections to the House of Representatives. Since 1978 he has been director of the Trinidad and Tobago Institute of the West Indies, and managing editor of *Trinidad and Tobago Review*. He was Opposition Leader in the Senate on two occasions – 1974–6 and 1981–2 – and founded the New World Movement. He was also the founding editor of *New World Quarterly*.

KEITH JARDIM

best-sellers

The phenomenon of 'best-sellers' in Latin America is strongly related to the '**Boom**' of the late 1960s. Before that, Latin American literature had a limited circulation, and books were not articles of mass consumption; the *folletines* (serials) were an exception in the 1920s and 1930s, but they belonged strictly to popular culture. The book becomes a commodity for the first time with the 'Boom'; indeed, for some critics the Boom itself is essentially a market phenomenon, rather than a genuine literary–cultural advance.

The 1960s brought new types of magazine like *Primera plana*, *La opinión* and *Marcha*, among others. They were the Latin American versions of *Life* or *Le Monde*, and signalled a modernization of cultural representation and criticism; their progressive, centre-left vision of society and culture radically changed the relationship between literature and public, in part by redefining the position of the writer within society. Writers became objects of new marketing strategies imported from the cultural industries of the USA and Europe. Interviews, mass-media visibility and best-seller lists began to attend the act of writing; writers became the new superstars.

The first edition of *Rayuela* (Hopscotch), by Julio **Cortázar**, published in 1965, had a print run of 4,000 copies; the book was reprinted in 1968, and half-a-million copies had been sold by 1973. The case of Gabriel **García Márquez**'s *Cien años de soledad* (One Hundred Years of Solitude) is even more revealing: the first edition of 25,000 copies in 1967 was followed by editions of 100,000 copies in subsequent years, with several reprints during a single year. Moreover, the success of one book guaranteed a market for the author's other work. Mass-media coverage of a book guaranteed success, as with the sexual scandal provoked in Argentina by *La traición de Rita Hayworth* (Betrayed by Rita Hayworth) by Manuel **Puig** and *Nanina* by Germán **García**, in 1968, both first novels by young novelists.

The 'Boom' formula still remains a guarantee of best-seller status – thus García Márquez's '**magical realism**' has become the model for success, especially since it opened a new international market for Latin American writers and publishers. 'Magical realism' became Latin America's principal cultural export. The best-sellers of the 1980s and 1990s, like Isabel **Allende** and Laura **Esquivel**, recycled the 'magical realism' formula and combined it with feminine issues to win an expanding international audience. In this new context, the relationship with cinema is decisive: the success of *Como agua para chocolate* (Like Water for Chocolate) by Laura Esquivel was due, at least in part, to the film adaptation. This new articulation of literature and cinema has created new audiences and new possibilities for literary success.

Further reading

Fernández Moreno, C. (1972) *América Latina en su literatura*, México: UNESCO-SXXI.

Viñas, D. (ed.) (1981) *Más allá del boom: Literatura y mercado*, Mexico City: Marcha.

GABRIEL GIORGI

Best Village Competition

This is an annual competition initiated by Trinidad and Tobago's first prime minister, Dr Eric **Williams**, in 1963. During a 'meet the people' tour of the islands shortly after independence in August 1962. The communication difficulties of villages isolated by poor roads and the lack of electricity, led to the idea of a government-organized event which would bring villages together to compete in various fields of community activity, including Environmental Awareness, Village Olympics and the La Reine Rivé or Best Village Queen Competition. In 1967 the Festival of Folklore was introduced to celebrate five years of independence; it has become a key feature of the competition.

LORRAINE LEU

Betancourt, Rómulo

b. 1908, Guatire, Venezuela; d. 1981, New York, USA

Politician

Founder of the Acción Democrática party and twice President of his country, he is seen by many as the father of Venezuelan democracy. Exiled for the first time (1928–36) for leading a student movement in opposition to the dictator Juan Vicente Gómez, he headed the revolutionary junta which brought down the presidency of Isaías Medina Angarita in 1945. The first democratically elected president of the modern era (1959–64), his term was marked by a sustained struggle against the **guerrillas**.

ALICIA RÍOS

Bethel, E. Clement

b. 1938, Nassau, Bahamas; d. 1987, Nassau

Ethnomusicologist

Bethel is perhaps best known for his folk opera/ballet *The Legend of Sammy Swain* (1968), which has been performed both in the Bahamas and abroad. Bethel served as chief cultural affairs officer in the Bahamian Ministry of Education and Culture; he oversaw the development of public support for indigenous culture and the work of local artists and also directed a choir, the Nassau Renaissance Singers. Bethel's *Junkanoo*: *Festival of the Bahamas*, a monograph based on his M.A. thesis for the University of California, was edited and expanded by his daughter Nicolette Bethel and published posthumously in 1991.

ROSANNE ADDERLEY

Beto Rockefeller

A *telenovela* (see **telenovelas**), Beto Rockefeller was written by Braulio Pedroso with Eloy Araujo and transmitted on Brazil's Tupy TV in 1968–9. Breaking the cycle of period series, it revolutionized the genre, recounting the adventures of a lower middle-class young man who penetrates the bourgeois circles of São Paulo by calling himself Rockefeller and claiming to be the child of millionaires. It was innovative in form, as when the protagonist looks straight to camera and speaks to the audience. It ran for 298 episodes; Luis Gustavo, playing Beto, was its undisputed star, supported by Plínio Marcos, Débora Duarte and Irene Ravache among others.

ANTONIO CARLOS MARTINS VAZ

Bianchi, Soledad

b. 1948, Antofagasta, Chile

Critic

An important literary critic whose studies reflect a concern with literary theory and the historical context of literature positioned as cultural memory. After receiving her doctorate at the University of Paris, she taught in Chile and France, returning to the Universidad de Chile after a period in exile following the 1973 military *coup*. Her most important works include *Poesía chilena (Miradas-Enfoques-Apuntes)* (Chilean Poetry (Glances, Perspectives, Notes)) (1990) and her volume of interviews with members of the literary groups of the 1960s, *La memoria: modelo para armar* (Memory: An Assembly Kit) (1995).

ELIANA ORTEGA

Bianco, José

b. 1908, Buenos Aires, Argentina; d. 1986, Buenos Aires

Writer

Editor of **Sur** from 1938 to 1961, author of two extraordinary novellas, a novel and an important body of essays, and a distinguished translator, Bianco was one of the foremost men of letters of Argentina. Though his output of narrative fiction is modest, the two novellas, *Sombras suele vestir* (Shadow Play) (1941) and *Las ratas* (The Rats) (1943) are important examples of the fantastic (see **fantastic literature**) and of **crime fiction**, respectively. *Sombras suele vestir* was written for the famous **Antología de la literatura fantástica** but was not finished in time for the 1940 edition; it was, however, incorporated in the second edition (1965). His later novel, *La pérdida del reino* (The Loss of the Kingdom) (1972), on which he worked intermittently for decades, is a fascinating portrait of post-war Paris and Buenos Aires, and something of a *roman à clef*. As an essayist, Bianco wrote delightful pieces on **Borges**, **Bombal**, Victoria **Ocampo**, **Piñera**, Sarmiento, Bierce, Camus, and above all on Proust. His work with *Sur* over a period of more than twenty years was vital in establishing that journal as the foremost organ of imaginative literature in Spanish; before Bianco began as editor, the journal was largely given over to serious (and sometimes rather solemn) essays, but during his period it came to welcome the extraordinary new work of Borges, of Jean Genet

and countless others. When Bianco went to Cuba in 1961 at the invitation of **Casa de las Américas**, Victoria Ocampo published an angry note in the magazine saying that Bianco had gone on his own and not as a representative of *Sur*; when he returned to Buenos Aires, he resigned. He then worked for several years at **EUDEBA**, the press of the University of Buenos Aires, where he directed the *Genio y figura* series of biographies (see **biography**). An extraordinary translator, his versions of Henry James, Giraudoux, Sartre, Stoppard, James Kirkwood, Genet and others are justly celebrated. A phrase from *Las ratas* exemplifies his life-long fascination with the ambiguities of human experience:

> Perhaps we never really lie. Perhaps the truth is so rich, so ambiguous, and presides from such a distance over our modest human endeavours, that all interpretations can be interchanged, and that the best we can do to honor truth is to desist from the innocuous goal of knowing it.

Further reading

Bianco, J. (1988) *Ficción y reflexión*, Mexico City: Fondo de Cultura Económica.

—— (1983) *Shadow Play and The Rats: Two Novellas*, trans. D. Balderston, Pittsburgh: Latin American Literary Review Press.

DANIEL BALDERSTON

Biblioteca Ayacucho

The Biblioteca Ayacucho, publishing arm of the Ayacucho Foundation, was established in 1974 by Presidential decree, under the government of Carlos Andrés **Pérez**, to commemorate the Battle of Ayacucho. Its object was to launch a collection of 500 titles to represent the civilizing, cultural and literary traditions of Latin America from pre-Hispanic times to the present. The list was drawn up in the light of discussions at the Seminario de Cultura Latinoamericana in 1976 and publication began the following year.

The Biblioteca's volumes include a prologue by a specialist critic and a detailed biographical, historical and cultural chronology as well as a bibliography at the end. In addition to the original collection, published in both hardback and paper, the Biblioteca has also produced complementary collections in different formats, like 'La Expresión Americana' (Expression of America) and 'Claves de América' (Keys to America).

Biblioteca Ayacucho was created by a group of internationally recognized Venezuelan and Latin American intellectuals, among them the Uruguayan critic Angel **Rama**, and Jose Ramón Medina and Oscar **Sambrano Urdaneta**, both members of its Governing Council, together with Oswaldo **Trejo**, Ramón J. Velásquez and Pascual Venegas Filardo.

JORGE ROMERO LEÓN

Biblioteca Nacional (Argentina)

Designed by Clorindo **Testa** in the early 1960s, the Biblioteca's four huge rectangular columns support the main body of the library several storeys above street-level, where reading rooms overlook the surrounding plazas and Avenida del Libertador. The library houses its book collections below ground, allowing expansion of its holdings without additions to the exterior. The Biblioteca replaced the older library on Calle México and ignited controversy for its unconventional design, the difficulties involved in accessing materials and the length of its construction, beginning in 1971 but not completed until the late 1980s. Like the **Banco de Londres**, it signalled a new anti-rationalist orientation in Argentine architecture. It was built on the site of the Palacio Unzué, the presidential palace that was demolished after the overthrow of **Perón** in 1955.

LAURA PODALSKY

Bicicleta, La

A magazine of counterculture, politics and popular arts, *La Bicicleta* (The Bicycle) provided an alternative to the censored media under the Chilean military dictatorship. The magazine was published sporadically after its founding in 1978, and then monthly as its circulation grew to 45,000. Its music

section featured articles on Chilean *nueva canción* and **Canto Nuevo** and Cuban *nueva trova*, as well as other Latin American and Anglo-American rock, folk and pop music. Its slogans, 'intrinsically round, pluralistic and democratic' and 'for a humane world', suggest the magazine's irreverent and oppositional approach. *La Bicicleta* ceased publication in 1988.

NANCY MORRIS

Bidó, Cándido

b. 1936, Bonao, Dominican Republic

Painter

Bidó's expressionist–primitivist paintings portray popular characters such as flower vendors and peasants as huge naive figures. His use of dark colours such as blue, orange and yellow make his paintings some of the most appealing and original in the Dominican Republic. He studied Fine Arts at the Escuela Nacional de Bellas Artes (Fine Arts National School) in Santo Domingo, and has participated in many national and international exhibitions.

FERNANDO VALERIO-HOLGUÍN

Bienale de São Paulo

Ever since the Second World War, São Paulo has prided itself on being among the fastest growing cities in the world, and on matching that growth with an industrial and cultural explosion. Its expansion has partly occurred as a result of the inversion of population distribution in the country over the past generation, with over 80 per cent now urban rather than rural dwellers. Partly this has occurred as a consequence of overseas immigration, and São Paulo now has the largest Japanese community outside Tokyo or Osaka. São Paulo itself has some 16 million residents, with an enormously uneven distribution of wealth and almost a third of its children categorised as streetdwellers.

Even before the first Bienale in 1951, a variety of different sources were committed to celebrating the riches rather than focusing in on the poverty of the massively modern city. Even with the relocation of the seat of government to **Brasília**, São Paulo's municipality retained immense determining powers. Its ethnic diversity, its rapid growth and its overall modernity (a pioneering architecture accompanying widespread vandalism of historical sites) made it a national metropolis. Its two new major art institutions – MASP (**Museu de Arte de São Paulo**) and MAM (**Museu de Arte Moderna**) (Museum of Modern Art) – were created by private foundations, effectively removing control from such autonomous artists' organizations as the SPAM (Modern Art Society), the CAM (Modern Artists' Club) and the artists' union. It was the union which traditionally organized regular public showings, ever since its recognition by the Labour Ministry in 1937. Its last showing was in 1949, when the MASP first opened and preparations for the first Bienale were under way.

The first Bienale was a polemical explosion. Called *From Figurative to Abstract Art*, it caused a furore by supposedly favouring the latter and for being mounted by the French critic, Léon Degand. Max Bill won the first prize for a sculpture called *Unidade Tripartida*, which put concrete art firmly on the Brazilian map.

Not to be outdone, the MAM launched itself into bienale-fever with an international showing of new plastic artists. Despite his opposition, MAM director Lourival Gomes Machado wrote in his introduction to the first catalogue (1951): 'By definition, this Bienale has set itself the hardest task: not only by putting modern Brazilian art in active contact with the art of the rest of the world...but also earning its place as a global art centre'. This spirit of internationalism was perhaps the salient characteristic of the Bienale that soon rivaled Venice in transnational prizes and auction rooms.

From the 1970s onwards art markets expanded enormously, allowing some Brazilian artists to actually live from their art for the first time. These included **Portinari**, di **Cavalcanti**, **Segall**, Burle **Marx**, **Brecheret**, Maria Martins and Bruno **Giorgi** (several of whom had already represented Brazil at Venice) and, among a younger generation of prizewinners, Ivan Serpa (painting), Geraldo de Barros (engraving) and Abraham Palatnik (winner of the 'special' prize).

In 1993 São Paulo added a photography bienal (called NaFoto, organized by curator Eduardo Castanho and photographer Nair Benedit). Held in May in the Bienale building in the central city park (designed by Oscar **Niemeyer**), it has been very successful. No further proof of the Bienale's overall performance should be needed than that afforded by the commemoration of its twenty-fifth anniversary with a hundred shows in a London festival.

AMANDA HOPKINSON

Bigaud, Wilson

b. 1929, Port-au-Prince, Haiti

Artist

Bigaud was one of the first Haitian painters to achieve success. Unable to manage the conflict between **Vodun** and Christianity portrayed in his work, he suffered repeated breakdowns. His finest work, like *Ra Ra in a Far Out Village* (1952), predates the breakdown. At twenty-two, he undertook *The Marriage at Cana* (1951), taking six weeks to cover the 528-square-foot mural expanse in the Episcopalian Cathedral in Port-au-Prince. His portrayal of *The Last Judgment* precipitated a personal crisis; he lived in the United States until his lack of legal documents forced his return to Haiti, where he still lives and works.

MARY BOLEY

bilingual education

The term refers to the use of two languages for instruction in schools. The teaching of a language as a second or foreign language, not for use as an instructional medium, does not 'count' as bilingual education.

There are various types of bilingual education: integrational, transitional, maintenance and promotional. Integrational bilingual education programmes are those offered to sub-groups of a single school's population to allow that group to receive instruction, while acquiring enough competence in the dominant code of the school to be able to move into 'normal school' classrooms. Such programmes are often seen as remedial. The language of the dominant society is seen as a tool they are deprived of by lack of fluency in that language and thus such students are treated as disadvantaged until they master the dominant code.

Transitional programmes are typical of areas with student populations who arrive in pre-school or first-grade monolingual in an autochthonous language. They receive their first classes completely in their mother tongue; as their schooling progresses through the first three years, more and more instruction is given in the dominant language of the country. Usually by the end of grade three almost all instruction is given in the official language of the country. The 'mother' tongue typically falls out of the curriculum or is given as a 'subject' and is no longer a medium of instruction.

Maintenance programmes, like transitional ones, greet incoming students in their mother tongue, gradually introducing the official language of the country. However, rather than replace the indigenous language, once fluency has been established, the national language shares the curriculum as an instructional medium across all subject matter (except language) and across the grades.

Promotional programmes, like maintenance programmes, teach across the curriculum and throughout the grade levels in the indigenous languages as well as in the official language of the country. They differ most in the amount of cultural content provided, and in that they are potentially open to members of the dominant society as well as to those who speak autochthonous languages by virtue of their ethnic affiliation.

Further reading

Cifuentes, H.E. (1988) *Educación bilingüe en Guatemala*, Guatemala: Programa de Educación Bilingüe.

JUDITH MAXWELL

bilingualism and biculturalism

Latin American nations are pluricultural and pluriethnic, some with larger proportions of indigenous peoples, some with greater mixes of European stock. In all, however, a European language is the official language, though Peru and Bolivia have made **Quechua** co-official and the Guatemala Peace Accords provide for the officialization of indigenous languages. Despite the minoritization of indigenous languages, many countries provide bilingual/bicultural educational services, to promote literacy in indigenous languages and in Spanish, and to adapt autochthonous concepts, values, and practices to classroom activities. Some programmes are transitional, aimed at promoting assimilation into the dominant culture. Others seek maintenance of indigenous cultural norms, standardization and unification of the oral code, and revitalization and dissemination of the language and the culture it embodies.

See also: language policy

JUDITH MAXWELL

Billiken

Billiken is a children's magazine published continuously by Atlántida in Buenos Aires since 1919. Founded by Constancio C. Vigil, it was widely distributed throughout Latin America, and for decades was the only magazine of its kind. In its early period it used very modern graphics and presented a wide variety of material (including notes on current affairs, stories, serials, games and hobbies). Later on, however, it emphasized its educational content by including colour plates and illustrations relating to historical events or nature, and by following the school calendar.

MIRTA VARELA

Bim

Bim is a literary magazine launched in Barbados in 1942 by E.L. (Jimmy) Cozier. The word 'Bim' is thought to be a derivative of Byam, a Royalist major whose followers were known as Bims; for a time, Barbados was referred to as Bimshire. The magazine had as significant a role as *Kyk-Over-Al* in promoting Caribbean literature. Cozier claims the first issue of *Bim* was 'hatched' in St Kitts. Eventually it contained enough advertising to permit the editors to actually pay its writers. Frank A. **Collymore** was its editor from 1942 to 1975; he was succeeded by John **Wickham**. Due to funding problems, it now appears infrequently.

KEITH JARDIM

Biografía de un cimarrón

Biografía de un cimarrón (Autobiography of a Runaway Slave) is a novel by the poet and ethnologist Miguel **Barnet**, published in 1966. Described by its author as a 'testimonial novel' (**testimonio**), it combines valuable anthropological insights and literary qualities, and goes well beyond a simple documentary transposition of reality. Its protagonist, Esteban Montejo, is a slave who became a freedom fighter (*mambí*) in the wars against Spanish colonialism. Through his peculiar vision of the world, he tells his own life story and recreates the world of the time. Widely translated, parts of the book were recorded in France by Jean Villard; it also inspired German composer Hans Werner Henze's opera *Cimarrón*.

WILFREDO CANCIO ISLA

biography

Borges, in his eccentric 1930 book on the Buenos Aires poet Evaristo Carriego, notes: 'For an individual to want to have another individual discover memories that belonged only to a third person is an evident paradox. To resolve that paradox smoothly is the innocent desire of every biography.' Although many of the works of Domingo Faustino Sarmiento in the nineteenth century could be called biographies, and Ezequiel **Martínez Estrada** devoted himself in large measure to biographies of Horacio **Quiroga**, W.H. Hudson and José Martí, the genre is not one that has been much cultivated until recently in Latin America. In contrast to the English-speaking world, where important canonical works from Boswell and Carlyle to Lytton Strachey are biographical, there are few similar monuments in the Spanish and Portuguese tradition. Instead of the secular tradition of biography, the closest available model for centuries in the Iberian and Ibero-American world was the saint's life, hardly a promising model for the modern biography (however productive it might be for imaginative literature). In recent years, though, the market for biographies of celebrities, perhaps piqued by the successes of the genre in the English-speaking world, has expanded.

In the 1960s, after being removed by Victoria **Ocampo** as editor of *Sur* for having visited revolutionary Cuba, José **Bianco** was invited by Boris Spivakow to work at **EUDEBA**, the press of the University of Buenos Aires, where he set up the series *Genio y Figura* (Character and Figure), which began publication in 1964 with a book on Rubén Darío, the *modernista* (see **modernismo, Spanish American**) poet. These compact volumes, less than two hundred pages in length, included illustrations (photographs of the author, of first editions and manuscripts, and of places important in the work) and an anthology of works, as well as a chronology. The main part of the book consisted of a biographical essay. The series included early biographies of **Borges**, **Neruda**, Alfonsina **Storni** and many others. Interestingly, though, the works are not packaged as biographies *per se* (any more than Borges's book on Carriego was fully a biography): though material was drawn together about the featured writer, the purpose was not to write a life of that person, or as Borges had mischievously pointed out in 1930, to evoke memories that belong neither to the biographer nor to the reader.

In contrast, recent years have seen an explosion of biographies, with Editorial **Sudamericana** and others publishing whole series of works of this kind. Volodia **Teitelboim**, former social realist novelist and political figure in Chile, has devoted much of the last twenty years to biographies of Neruda, Gabriela **Mistral**, **Huidobro** and Borges. Similarly, Jorge **Edwards** had great success with his biography of Neruda. There are biographies on the market of Glauber **Rocha**, **Onetti**, **García**

Márquez, Alejandra **Pizarnik** and countless others (though many major figures still have not been the subject of a biography). There are whole biographical industries around certain iconic figures: biographies of Eva **Perón**, Che **Guevara** and Frida **Kahlo**, to mention the three most obvious figures, have proliferated.

At the same time, novels that are almost biographies, or biographies that are almost novels, have also come into fashion. One of the more curious examples is Félix **Luna**'s 'autobiography' of President Julio Argentino Roca, the figure who dominated Argentine politics from 1880 to 1904: Luna insists that his *Soy Roca* (I am Roca) (1989) is not a novel, yet the narration in the first person singular is clearly a novelistic device. (Silviano **Santiago** explored a similar device in his first person continuation of Graciliano **Ramos**'s prison memoirs.) Tomás Eloy **Martínez** has written novels that come close to being biographies of Juan Domingo **Perón** and of his second wife Eva. Sergio **Ramírez**, in *Margarita, está linda la mar* (Margarita, The Sea is Beautiful) (1998), has written a novel that is at least in part a biography of Rubén Darío.

Also of interest is the literary memoir. Margo **Glantz**'s *Las genealogías* (The Family Tree) (1981) is largely a memoir of the author's father, Jacobo Glantz, a Mexican Yiddish poet and president of the Mexican Jewish Committee. José **Donoso**'s *Conjeturas sobre la memoria de mi tribu* (Conjectures About the Memories of My Tribe) (1996) is a biographical study of generations of ancestors.

Finally, it should be noted that there are elements of biography in the genre of the *crónica* (see for instance Carlos **Monsiváis**'s profiles of famous Mexican icons), which by virtue of its relative brevity escapes the trap of having to tell the whole of a life (and to base that telling on the documentary evidence), and that the *testimonio* is to a large extent a displacement of the biographical impulse from the telling of elite or famous lives to the telling of less known ones (though *testimonio* also plays with the conventions of **autobiography**): see for instance Miguel **Barnet**'s *Biografía de un cimarrón* (oddly translated as *Autobiography of a Runaway Slave*) (1966).

Further reading

Borges, J.L. (1955) *Evaristo Carriego*, Buenos Aires: Emecé.

Bromwich, D. (1984) 'The uses of biography', *Yale Review*, winter: 161–76.

Cockshut, A.D.J. (1974) *Truth to Life: The Art of Biography in the Nineteenth Century*, New York: Harcourt Brace.

DANIEL BALDERSTON

biology   *see* science

Bioy Casares, Adolfo

b. 1914, Buenos Aires, Argentina; d. 1999, Buenos Aires

Writer

Bioy Casares is best known as the writer of carefully constructed fantastic narratives (see **fantastic literature**), particularly the novels *La invención de Morel* (The Invention of Morel) (1940) and *El sueño de los héroes* (The Dream of Heroes) (1954) and the short stories of *La trama celeste* (The Celestial Plot) (1948). His friend **Borges** called the plot of *La invención de Morel* 'perfect'; its **science fiction** quality and mathematical rigor owe a great deal to one of Bioy's favourite writers, H.G. Wells. Bioy was also the author of an extensive body of other work, including diaries, **crime fiction** and screenplays. Most critics find his writing of the 1940s and 1950s, when he was working most closely with Borges, to be his most interesting.

Born into a wealthy and conservative landowning family, Bioy began to publish very young: he published four works of fiction before *La invención de Morel*. His first collaboration with Borges was on an advertising campaign for the yoghurt produced by his mother's family's dairy; for this campaign they invented an imaginary, and exceedingly long-lived, family. They would later collaborate on numerous works of crime fiction, most notably *Seis problemas para don Isidro Parodi* (Six Problems for Don Isidro Parodi) (1942), featuring an imprisoned amateur detective who is visited in his prison cell by all sorts of outlandish Buenos Aires characters. (This collaboration, under the pseudonyms H. Bustos Domecq and B. Suárez Lynch, also resulted in later parodies of modernist and avant-garde pretension.) They also co-edited two anthologies of detective stories, a very successful series of detective novels for Emecé that ran to hundreds of titles, and an anthology of gauchesque poetry for the **Fondo de Cultura Económica**. With Bioy's wife, the extraordinary Silvina **Ocampo**, Borges and Bioy edited the famous *Antología de la literatura fantástica* (Anthology of Fantastic Literature) (1940) and the *Antología poética argentina* (Anthology of Argentine Poetry) (1941); Bioy and Ocampo co-authored a detective novel, *Los que aman, odian* (Those Who Love, Hate) (1946). Late in his life Bioy published excerpts from his diaries and commonplace books.

Bioy had a strong interest in the cinema, and his legacy in that medium is strong. Leopoldo **Torre Nilsson** and Hugo Santiago made films based on several of his works. In Eliseo **Subiela**'s *Hombre mirando el sudeste* (Man Looking Southeast) (1986) the protagonist quotes from *La invención de Morel*, an acknowledgement that the film is an adaptation of Bioy's novel.

One of the interesting questions is what Bioy would have been as a writer had it not been for his long association with Borges. Perhaps he would have been a light, humorous writer whose theme was the complications of love and sex. Instead, he tried his hand at a great variety of forms and weighty themes, was rewarded with many prizes, including the top prize in the Spanish-speaking world, the Cervantes Prize (1990), and yet somehow, oddly, seemed always a shadow of Borges, but also of the Bioy he might have been.

Further reading

Bioy Casares, A. (1964) *The Invention of Morel, and Other Stories*, trans. R.L. Simms, Austin: University of Texas Press.

—— (1988) *La invención y la trampa: una antología*, Mexico City: Fondo de Cultura Económica.

—— (1994) *Selected Stories*, trans. S.J. Levine, New York: New Directions.

Camurati, M. (1990) *Bioy Casares y el alegre trabajo de la inteligencia*, Buenos Aires: Corregidor.

DANIEL BALDERSTON

Bird, Vere C.

b. 1910, St John's, Antigua; d. 1999, St John's

Politician

First Prime Minister of the Eastern Caribbean nation of Antigua and Barbuda, Bird was born into poverty. He helped organize the Antigua Trades and Labour Union and became its President in 1943, enrolling labour leaders to run for office as candidates of the Antigua Labour Party. He became Chief Minister of Antigua in 1960 and worked to eliminate discrimination, particularly in education. As leader of the Antigua Labour Party, Bird conducted the negotiations with the British that led to full independence on 1 November 1981 and retained his position as Prime Minister, with one brief interruption, until 1994.

JOHN H. PATTON

Birri, Fernando

b. 1925, Santa Fe, Argentina

Film-maker

Returning to Argentina in 1956 after studying at the Centro Sperimentale in Rome with Italian neorealist film-makers and fellow students like Julio **García Espinosa**, Tomás **Gutiérrez Alea** and Gabriel **García Márquez**, Birri founded the documentary film school **Escuela de Cine Documental de Santa Fe** at the University of the Litoral in his home town, the first of its kind in Latin America and an important precursor of the **New Latin American Cinema**.

Originally a travelling puppeteer who crisscrossed Argentina with touring companies, Birri fully absorbed the ideals of Italian neo-realism and argued that the Argentine cinema needed to become a 'realist critical popular cinema' addressing the needs and problems of all sectors of the population. Despite scarce resources and limited equipment, Birri and his students produced a series of photo-montage documentary shorts, among them *Tire Dié* (Throw Me a Dime) (1958–60), later claimed as one of the first Latin American social documentaries (see **documentary**). It exposed the marginality and poverty of a shanty town near Santa Fe and, particularly, the plight of children who chased trains over a high bridge begging the passengers for dimes. Two other shorts followed, *La primera fundación de Buenos Aires* (The First Foundation of Buenos Aires) (1959) and *Buenos Aires, Buenos Aires* (1960). Finally, in 1961 they made their first feature, *Los inundados* (Flooded Out). Shot on a shoestring budget with a few local actors and non-actors, the film shows the clear influence of Birri's neo-realist mentors and was quite unlike other contemporary Argentine productions. Although largely ignored commercially, it won prestigious international awards (Venice, Karlovy Vary). In 1964 Birri published a summary of his experiences at the Escuela Documental and a manifesto for a 'new' Argentine cinema entitled *La Escuela de Cine de Santa Fe*.

Meanwhile, however, the new Onganía regime looked unfavourably on the social critical orientation and methods of the Santa Fe school and Birri left Argentina, spending some time in São Paulo working with Thomas Farkas and eventually settling in Italy, where he made political documentaries, portraits of artists, and the highly experimental *Org* (1968), signed under the pseudonym FERMAGHORG.

In 1986 Birri was named director of the newly formed International Film and Television School near Havana (**Escuela de Tres Mundos**), where he remained until 1992. In Cuba he was able to make his second feature film, *Un señor muy viejo con unas alas enormes* (A Very Old Man with Enormous Wings) (1988), adapted from a **García Márquez** tale, which transformed his previous neo-realist affiliations into an odd kind of **magical realism**. Other attempts to put productions together have failed. He now lives once more in Italy.

Further reading

Birri, F. (1986) 'The Roots of Documentary Realism', in J. Burton (ed.) *Cinema and Social Change in Latin America*, Austin, TX: University of Texas Press, 1–12.

Chanan, M. (1983) *Twenty-Five Years of the New Latin American Cinema*, London: BFI/Channel 4.

DIANA PALADINO

Bishop, Maurice Rupert

b. 1944, Aruba, Netherlands Antilles;
d. 1983, Saint Georges, Grenada

Political leader

Bishop's parents left Grenada at the end of the 1930s and moved to Aruba where his father worked in the petroleum industry. In 1951 the family returned to Grenada. Bishop excelled in secondary school and went on to earn a law degree in London. He worked for several years in England before returning to Grenada, where he became involved in the growing opposition to the repressive government of Prime Minister Eric **Gairy** and the Grenada United Labour Party. The charismatic Bishop emerged in 1973 as the most prominent leader of the **New Jewel Movement** (NJM), a coalition of anti-Gairy groups. In 1979 the New Jewel Movement led a successful *coup* against the Gairy government and established a basically socialist regime that they called the People's Revolutionary Government (PRG) with Bishop as Prime Minister. Bishop and the PRG enjoyed popularity and success, based heavily upon government policies related to social welfare. However, they also faced predictable criticism from the USA and some Caribbean neighbours for their socialist beliefs and for their close relationship with Fidel **Castro** and the Cuban government. Bishop was executed in 1983 during an internal *coup* within the PRG. The 1983 *coup* leaders were quickly overthrown by a military invasion led by the USA, ending Grenada's socialist experiment. In Grenada and elsewhere, people of diverse political beliefs continue to revere Maurice Bishop because of his **populism**, progressivism and charisma; and also because of the manner of his death – widely viewed as one of the most shocking and tragic events in modern Caribbean history.

ROSANNE ADDERLEY

Bishop, Pat

b. 1939, Port-of-Spain, Trinidad

Musician, artist

Pat Bishop is internationally known for her work as one of the first women **steelband** arrangers, with Birdsong, Pandemonium, Phase II and Desperadoes. She has had several art exhibitions at home and abroad and is director of the Lydian Singers. Bishop was awarded the Hummingbird Gold Medal in Trinidad, 1986. In 1995 her achievements in art and culture in Trinidad and Tobago were further recognized with an Honorary Doctorate from the **University of the West Indies**. Then, in 1996, she received the nation's highest honour, the Trinity Cross.

KEITH JARDIM

Bissoondath, Neil

b. 1955, Arima, Trinidad

Writer

A well-established writer of refreshingly sober and elegant prose, Bissoondath left Trinidad when he was eighteen to study in Toronto and later became a teacher in Canada. His first novel, *A Casual Brutality* (1988), is a profoundly disturbing and prophetic portrait of Trinidad's corruption, racism and violence. The book of short stories *On the Eve of Uncertain Tomorrows* 1990) continues his examination of the consequences of the continuing flight of Trinidadians from social disintegration. He departed from fiction with *Selling Ilusions: The Cult of Multiculturalism in Canada* (1993), a controversial and often courageous review of Canadian policies.

KEITH JARDIM

Bithorn, Hiram

b. 1916, Santurce, Puerto Rico; d. 1952, Mexico City

Baseball player

Professional **baseball** in the USA remained officially segregated until Jackie Robinson broke baseball's 'color line' in 1947, but a few blacks from Latin America competed in the 'white' major leagues before Robinson's debut, including Jack Calvo and José Acosta in the 1920s, and Bithorn and Luis **Olmo** Rodríguez in the 1940s. The skin colour of Latin players disconcerted the segregationists, and Latinos were often required to attest that their heritage was entirely Hispanic. Bithorn was killed on New Year's Day 1952 by a Mexico City police officer under mysterious circumstances.

DOUGLAS W. VICK

Bizzio, Sergio

b. 1956, Villa Ramallo, Argentina

Writer

Bizzio has written for Argentine cinema and television, and has published four novels, including *El divino convertible* (The Convertible Divine) (1990) and three volumes of poetry, *Paraguay* outstanding among them. But he is best known to the general public for his theatrical pieces, written with Daniel **Guebel**, which are considered exemplary in the new Argentine theatre. *La china* (The Girl) is a mixture of Argentine **gaucho** traditions, the theatre of the absurd and the colloquial (and obscene) language of television.

DANIEL LINK

BKF Furniture

In 1939–40 the BKF chair was designed by two Argentinians, Jorge Ferrari-Hardoy (1914–77) and Juan Kurchan (1913–75), and a Catalonian, Antonio Bonet (1913–75) – architects who in 1937 worked in the office of Le Corbusier. The BKF chair, referred to as the Butterfly or AA chair, consists of two welded-rod triangles that have two points at the back of the seat, over which a leather or canvas cover is attached. The BKF is an example of appropriation and recovery from the past. Joseph Fenbey, an English inventor who arrived in Buenos Aires in 1938, invented the folding chair that was later transformed by the architects, and which established the canon of Argentine design.

ISABEL BARBUZZA

Blaaker, Carlos

b. 1961, Paramaribo, Suriname

Painter

Blaaker studied art at the **Nola Hatterman Institute** in Suriname and, with a grant from the Art Students' League, in New York. He worked as a painter and teacher at the Institute from 1987 until 1990, after which he left for the Netherlands. Painting being his dominant passion, he experimented with different styles, and sought to develop a Suriname pop art combining a variety of images and texts. He has had exhibitions in New York, in various European countries, in Curaçao, Netherlands Antilles and, of course, in Suriname.

NEL CASIMIRI

black cultures

Blackness, like any ethnic or racial categorization, is an arbitrary social construct nuanced by geography, language and history. What North Americans call *black* may in Latin America and the Caribbean be translated in a variety of ways, including *negro*, *mulato*, *cafuso*, *moreno*, *trigueño*, *antillano*, *prieto*, Afro-Latin American, creole, light-skinned and so on. Furthermore, social and personal relations, education, economic opportunities and other variables make it possible to change one's racial classification. These distinctions notwithstanding, blackness in Latin America is inextricably connected to the trans-Atlantic slave trade which brought the majority of blacks to the Americas.

Slaves came to the Americas from a number of African ethnic groups, although the most influential groups (the Yoruba, Dahomey, Ashanti, Hausa and Ibo) were from West Africa. Despite slavery, Africans preserved many of their cultural traits, although not always in their purest form. Indeed, African culture has been transformed through

centuries of *mestizaje* (mixture) and assimilation, the pillars of all Latin American national cultures. As Peter Wade so aptly explains, in many cases black culture may have clear European roots and only traceable African elements.

While blacks exist in almost every Latin American country, accurate data on black culture in some nations is difficult to find. This paucity of information stems in part from the lack of demographic data on blacks (and ethnicity in general) in many countries. While scholars have conducted much research on black culture in the Caribbean and Brazil, other countries such as Uruguay and Bolivia are only now being examined. Black culture of course is not a monolithic entity. Each country has its own values and patterns of classification which determine how different black cultures are defined. None the less, it is helpful to examine regional black cultures through five major geopolitical divisions: the Caribbean Basin, Mexico and Central America, the Andes, the Southern Cone and Brazil. Within these five regions, Africans and their descendants may fall into one of three categories: majority or near majorities, minority populations and/or immigrant populations.

In many countries of the Caribbean Basin such as Haiti, the Dominican Republic and the English-speaking islands, blacks have historically constituted a majority or near majority. The manifestation and national discourse of blackness varies from state to state, vacillating between the two major nationalist ideologies of racial culture: *mestizaje* and **négritude**. The former celebrates racial intermingling while the latter exalts the positive features of blackness. Before the 1920s, Haiti was one of the few nations that celebrated its African roots. Almost all Haitians are either black or mulatto. Rich cultural traditions – from local rhythms such as **méringue** to the Dahomean religion **Vodun** – attest to Haiti's African roots. Writers such as Jean **Price-Mars**, Jacques **Roumain** and René **Depestre** were renowned orators in the vanguard of Haitian *négritude*.

The English-speaking Caribbean, much like the French and creole-speaking islands of Guadeloupe and Martinique, remained politically tied to their former colonizers late into the twentieth century. Black culture remains implicit in the preparation of foods, national celebrations such as **junkanoo** in the Bahamas, **carnival** in Trinidad and a myriad of musical forms in Jamaica. Black liberation ideologies coincided with the independence movements of the 1960s, but most nations retained the Westminister parliamentary system. Owing to the popularity of some Caribbean music, and the personal charisma of the Jamaican Bob **Marley**, in the 1970s **Rastafarianism** and **reggae** became synonymous with black cultural celebration.

The Hispanic Caribbean shows another cultural pattern. In the 1920s and 1930s, nationalist writers such as Fernando **Ortiz**, Elías Entralgo, Nicolás **Guillén** (Cuba), Luis **Palés Matos** (Puerto Rico) and Manuel del **Cabral** (Dominican Republic) promoted black culture through *mestizaje*. For them, African influences were as important as Spanish. In all three countries, blacks and whites participate in black culture. In Cuba, for example, **Santería**, an Afro-Latin American religion derived from Yoruba beliefs, remains vital. In addition, the vast majority of Cuban popular music is African-derived: for example, the **rumba** the **son** and the guajiro. Puerto Rico and the Dominican Republic illustrate similar dynamics.

National communities from the Dutch-speaking islands of Aruba, Bonaire and Curaçao, or local groups such as the Bush Negroes of Suriname and other maroon cultures (see **maroons**), and the settlers on the Atlantic coasts of Venezuela and Colombia, retain strong black or African identities. Religion represents another rich area of importance for the exploration of black culture. In addition to Santería and Vodun, religious practices such as **Obeah** in Barbados and Jamaica and **Shango** in Trinidad are all African-based.

While the African presence in Mexico and Central America is undeniable, it is not always recognized. In colonial times, blacks in Mexico made up a large percentage of the populations of Mexico City and the Atlantic coast, particularly near Vera Cruz, and along the Costa Chica in the provinces of Guerrero and Oaxaca. Even though people who identify themselves as Afro-Mexican today are a small minority, many people have African ancestry. Moreover, the African presence

prevails in regional celebrations such as the carnival in Vera Cruz, and in the names of towns including La Mandinga, El Monzongo, Cimarrón and Palenque.

In the Central American republics, black culture is strongest on the eastern seaboard as well. In general, the black and Afro-Latin American populations on the isthmus can be divided into four major groups: *Negros nativos*, who came to the isthmus with the original settlers in the sixteenth century and are largely hispanicized; creoles, English-speakers of predominantly African or mixed ancestry; the Garifuna (see **Garinagu**), descendants of escaped African slaves and Carib Indians from the island of St Vincent; and West Indian immigrants who began to travel to the isthmus for the construction of railroads in the late nineteenth century.

Belize and Nicaragua have significant creole populations. In Belize, where black culture permeates all aspects of national life, creoles make up the overwhelming majority. Although English is the official language of Belize, the local vernacular, creole, is rich with Africanisms. In Nicaragua, creoles represent less than 1 per cent of the national population, although they are the third largest ethnic group in the Atlantic coast region. Unlike the creoles, the Garifuna were originally exiled to Roatán off the Honduran coast by the British in the late eighteenth century, and later made their way to the isthmus. Today they constitute approximately 1 per cent of the Atlantic coastal population in Nicaragua, and between 2–3 per cent of the entire population in Honduras. While the Honduran Garifuna recognize themselves as a black people, they have retained many customs and traits from their indigenous ancestors. They are also Catholic, and speak both Garifuna and Spanish.

The Garifuna in Nicaragua have attempted to preserve their lifestyle while negotiating a place in society between the creoles and the **Miskutu**, who also share African and indigenous ancestry but identify themselves as indigenous. They were a close-knit community with their own religion, language and celebrations. Since the 1950s, however, many have moved away from the Caribbean coast, assimilated into Nicaraguan society and adopted Spanish.

The only modern immigrants to the area are the black West Indians, mostly from Jamaica, Barbados and other English-speaking islands. West Indian blacks began to travel to areas such as Costa Rica and Panama at the end of the nineteenth century to work on the railroads. The building of the Panama Canal, however, was responsible for the arrival of more than 60 per cent of the immigrants. After the building of the canal many stayed on, and others went to work on the fruit plantations in northern Panama and Costa Rica. They are largely English-speaking Protestants who are responsible for the creation and crossover of West Indian music such as **calypso** and reggae into Spanish.

Of the countries of South America, Brazil is the only one with a significant body of information on black culture. Indeed, there is a dearth of information on the African impact on countries traversed by the Andes (Colombia, Ecuador, Peru, Bolivia and Chile). In Colombia, for example, the African presence is prominent on the Atlantic coast (particularly in San Andrés, Providencia and Santa Catarina, and in Palenque de San Basilio, near Cartagena). Less known are the blacks of the Pacific coast, particularly in the Tumaco and the Chocó regions and in Ecuador. As in other areas, however, *mestizaje* and miscegenation were responsible for absorbing African cultural traits. In Ecuador, blacks can be found in rural and urban areas, although Esmeraldas is considered the cradle of black culture.

The provinces of Nor and Sud Yungas in the department of La Paz are home to the only visible black population in Bolivia. Many argue that blacks are only distinguishable from their indigenous counterparts by their ethnic features. Indeed, most blacks are peasants who have been assimilated into local *altiplano* culture, speaking both **Aymara** and Spanish. Their dress is typical of Andean culture, particularly the women who wear the indigenous *pollera* and bowler hat. In recent years black consciousness has begun to emerge, particularly in Nor Yungas. Many blacks speak a local dialect of Spanish quite distinct from their indigenous counterparts, and have begun to call themselves Afro-Bolivian. Public presentations of Afro-Bolivian music and dances such as the *saya* have become forums for the celebration of cultural pride.

In the River Plate region, the nineteenth-century wars took a toll on the Afro-Latin American populations. European migration from the turn of the century to the early 1930s further displaced Afro-Argentines and Afro-Uruguayans. Afro-Argentines today represent such a small percentage of the population that any visible cultural icons are difficult to discern. Much of their cultural influence has been absorbed into mainstream culture. In Uruguay, black culture is much more visible, although its impact on national life is unfortunately still denied by many Uruguayans. The majority of the black population is disproportionately represented in the lower economic classes. This has not prohibited the celebration of the African-based cultural practices of carnival and *candombe*, and Afro-Uruguayan writers such as Beatriz Santos enjoy national prominence.

Black culture in Brazil is most salient due to the number of African slaves that came from the African continent, and the long duration of slavery (not abolished until 1888). These conditions ensured that Africans would have a steady, continual and profound effect on Brazilian society. In the 1930s, Gilberto **Freyre** claimed that the African influence on Brazil was so important that Africans should be considered co-colonizers of Brazil. While Freyre privileged miscegenation over *négritude*, he effectively illustrated the extent to which African cultures contributed to the creation of modern Brazil.

While the black presence in Brazilian national culture is irrefutable in the country's language, music and dance forms, Bahia in the northeast is considered the African Mecca. Unfortunately black culture is still too often portrayed stereotypically, or presented as folklore in the national media. Moreover, blacks continue to face commercial exploitation, while relying on white producers and directors for limited artistic work. Afro-Brazilian culture nonetheless continues to survive and change on its own terms. Black and mulatto writers had already made their impression on the Brazilian landscape when the century opened, although many mulattoes, such as Machado de

Assis (1857–1913), had, as Abdias do **Nascimento** reports, 'acculturated to the norms and standards of the European language'. Well-established in Brazilian letters are black writers such as Solano **Trinidade** and the contemporary poets Eduardo de Oliviera and Oswaldo de Camargo.

As elsewhere, the most visual materialization of black culture occurs in popular forums. Indeed, black music and dance are virtually synonymous with Brazilian popular music and dance. Africans brought a myriad of musical instruments to Brazil, and many – from the ganzá and the **berimbau** to the surdo – are essential to popular rhythms such as the **forro** or the **samba**. African influence is evident in cultural celebrations such as ***Bumba-meu-boi***, and in all of the Afro-Brazilian religions still practised in Brazil. **Candomblé**, the Afro-Brazilian religion derived from Yoruba practices, continues to be a source of religious strength for Brazilians of all ethnicities. Other religious and spiritist practices such as **Umbanda** and **Macumba** have combined diverse African customs with European and Native American ones.

National, socioeconomic and political conditions determine the manifestation of black culture. Afro-Latin Americans are found in all strata of society, although due to the legacy of slavery, many are disproportionately represented in the lower classes. It cannot be overemphasized, however, that black culture is not a monolith within any particular nation, much less in the region. In many cases black culture remains marginalized and shunned by the mainstream, while in others it is celebrated with passion.

Further reading

Bastide, R. (1972) *African Civilizations in the New World*, trans. Peter Green, New York: Harper & Row.

Minority Rights Group (1995) *No Longer Invisible: Afro-Latin Americans Today*, London: Minority Rights Group.

Nascimento, A. (1979) *Mixture or Massacre?*, Buffalo, NY: State University of New York.

Wade, P. (1993) *Blackness and Race Mixture: The Dynamics of Racial Identity in Colombia*, Baltimore, MD: Johns Hopkins University Press.

DARIÉN J. DAVIS

Black Jacobins, The

The Black Jacobins is C.L.R **James**'s brilliant and moving account of the slaves' revolt in Haiti, the first revolution on the Latin American continent. Published in 1938, its central achievement was to begin the rewriting of the history of slavery and its abolition. *The Black Jacobins* shows that the slaves *won* their liberation in a revolutionary war in Haiti in 1797; it was not the gift of Europe. The tragedy of their leader Toussaint Louverture was that the enormity of the post-revolutionary tasks led him back into the arms of the old colonial powers – who betrayed him. James draws from history contemporary lessons regarding the relationship between race and class, and between the leader and the mass of the revolutionary army.

MIKE GONZALEZ

black movements

Since the establishment of black slavery in the Americas, Africans and their progeny have always challenged the system of domination in a variety of ways including sabotage, maroonage and rebellion. Despite the abolition of slavery in the nineteenth century and the integration of blacks into national life, many continued to face discrimination, prejudice and lack of economic and political power in the twentieth century. Black men and women have thus continued to organize themselves to resist oppression and assert their social and civil rights. The twentieth century has witnessed three types of black movements in the region: mobilizations calling for racial consciousness or pride, political organizations aiming to safeguard civil rights, and, in a few cases, rebellions.

Shaped by historical and national circumstances, black movements have been more numerous and better documented in Brazil and the Caribbean Basin where people of African descent represent a large percentage of the population. In Central America and other parts of South America, black political movements have been less significant, particularly before the 1980s. Twentieth-century nationalist struggles encouraged the people of Latin America and the Caribbean to join forces against colonialism and neocolonial attacks. Leftist revolutions in the second half of the century (particularly in Cuba and Nicaragua) received the support of blacks largely by focusing on class differences rather than racial ones. The inability of these revolutions to adequately address issues of prejudice and discrimination became evident at the end of the Cold War in 1989.

Black movements in the Caribbean have ranged from cultural rejuvenation to rebellion. In many cases, such as in the British and French Caribbean where blacks are the absolute majority, black movements were closely related to nationalist struggles against colonialism. In the Spanish-speaking Caribbean, Afro-Hispanic activists such as the Cuban Juan Gualberto Gómez (1854–1933) were instrumental in the abolitionist movement in their countries. After 1900, however, many blacks and mulattoe saw that they continued to be marginalized from local political and economic activities. The century saw its first black rebellion in Cuba in 1912, led by the Partido Independientes de Color (Independents of Colour Party) who were protesting a law that prohibited the political association of people of one class or colour. Evaristo Estenoz, the party's leader, wanted to create a separate political party since he felt that blacks and mulattoe were being marginalized from the political process. As a result of the confrontation, a majority of the party members were killed and other Afro-Cubans harassed for suspicion of collaboration. This remains the only major race war in Latin America this century.

The 1920s marked a new era of black power and consciousness raising. The Jamaican-born Marcus **Garvey** spoke of decolonization by going back to Africa, but more importantly he encouraged blacks to call for a freedom without boundaries. Meanwhile, black women such as the Dominicans Petrolina Gómez, Artagracia Domínguez and Evelina Rodríguez called for gender equality. A decade later, intellectual activists throughout the region, including the Cuban Nicolás **Guillén** and the Martinican Aimé **Césaire** demanded respect and appreciation of the African heritage in the region's cultural patrimony, promoting two distinct but related cultural movements known as ***negrismo*** and ***négritude***.

Intent on emphasizing the contribution of blacks to Western Civilization, *négritude* also opposed European colonization and its racist ideology in a pugnacious manner. While Césaire and other defiant French-speaking blacks often relied on essentialist language to promote the natural poetic gifts of blacks, they were the first generation to celebrate their blackness in the face of colonialism. In the Spanish-speaking Caribbean, black consciousness took a slightly different figuration. As early as 1927, the Puerto Rican Luis **Palés Matos** had published the magazine *Paliedro* in which he criticized the aesthetic values of white Eurocentric culture. *Negrismo* in the Spanish-speaking Caribbean, however, was not as defiant as *négritude*, as it emphasized cooperation and recognition of the mulatto nature of the Caribbean. Nicolás Guillén, in particular, maintained a balance between *mestizaje* and black power. He recognized Cuba's mulatto nature while condemning discrimination against blacks.

Guillén, like many Afro-Cubans, ardently supported the Cuban Revolution of 1959, yielding to a discourse of national solidarity, rather than one of racial struggle. At the same time, Cubans supported many racial, ethnic and grassroots struggles around the world, including those in the USA. In the Dominican Republic, which is predominantly black, no black movement emerged although individual Afro-Dominicans such as Maximiliano Gómez defied the state's official policy which favored *hispanidad*, a celebration of the Hispanic tradition. Puerto Rico represents an interesting example, since it is a Spanish-speaking Caribbean nation and a territory of the USA. Blacks in Puerto Rico have traditionally been torn between the struggle for recognition of their Hispanic language and culture, and issues of racial pride and justice which they hold in common with blacks in the USA. Many black men and women have participated enthusiastically in forums and movements for racial affirmation, among them the organizers of Unión de Mujeres Puertorriqueñas Negras (The Union of Black Puerto Rican Women).

Black political movements played key roles in the intensified nationalism of the 1960s which led to the independence of most of the English-speaking Caribbean islands. The coronation of

Ras Tafari as King Haile Selassie of Ethiopia led to the creation of the first Rastafarians (see **Rasta-farianism**) who had, by the 1960s, increased racial consciousness in the poor sectors of Jamaican society. Jamaica at the time was still a colony of Great Britain, and Rastafarians, who were fervently anti-colonialist and Afrocentric, later supported Jamaica's independence in 1962. In Trinidad, black intellectuals such as C.L.R. **James** and Eric **Williams** were instrumental in promoting Caribbean liberation, while Bahamian Lyndon **Pindling** defied the predominantly white government leading to independence in 1973. Since the 1960s, black movements have been closely associated with national celebration.

Major national movements in Brazil did not begin until the rise of Getúlio **Vargas** to national prominence in 1930. The 1930s and 1940s, which began a period of political, economic and cultural reorganization, also signalled the rise of popular social movements that began to seriously challenge the status quo. Founded in September 1931, the Frente Negra Brasileira represented the first major mobilization of blacks that called for the right to work and freedom from discrimination. By 1936, the Frente had attained enough support to register as a political party and to establish a special military unit. Although this movement ended when President Vargas created the **Estado Novo** in 1937 and abolished all political parties, the Frente had succeeded in creating a defiant black consciousness among many black men and women. Frente women in particular, known as *frentenegrinas*, gained the reputation of being good hard workers who would not tolerate discrimination or insults.

In the 1940s, under the banner of the Teatro Experimental do Negro (TEN), Afro-Brazilians were determined to raise consciousness among all Brazilians by condemning racism and prejudice as well as by stressing the African contribution to Brazilian culture. TEN also forged an Afrocentric aesthetic through art, poetry and beauty competitions. Ruth de Souza, a cofounder of TEN, became one of Brazil's first black actresses to gain popularity. The other cofounder, Abdias do **Nascimento**, became one of Brazil's renowned black militants. In addition to theatre, TEN also published literature on blacks in Brazil and carried

out literacy campaigns. Although TEN's activities ended after the military *coup* of 1964, many of its members continued to speak out throughout the 1970s and 1980s.

With *abertura*, the political opening in the late 1970s, several black organizations emerged, including the Black Women's Collective which focused on the care and education of children as well as on legal assistance to women in a variety of matters. On 2 July 1975, a group of women signed the 'Manifesto of Black Brazilian Women' that declared opposition to the exploitation of women of colour. In 1978, black activists established the Unified Black Movement (MNU), the first contemporary movement which attempted to form national associations and networks. Leila de Almeida Gonzales later founded the Unified Black Movement Against Racial Discrimination, which protested about racial discrimination in São Paulo on 13 May 1979 (the anniversary of Brazilian abolition).

Throughout the 1980s, individual voices and organizations continued to emerge. According to Paulo dos Santos, researcher for the Centro dos Estudos Afro-Asiáticos, the end of the 1970s signified a watershed in civil rights in Brazil. Much of the consciousness-raising and activism was related to the emergence of the national liberation of Luso-African republics such as Angola and Mozambique. Also affected by the women's and civil rights movements in North America, Brazilians had created more than four hundred civil rights groups in different regions throughout the country by 1985.

The revision of the Brazilian Constitution that began in 1986 presented a major national forum for civil rights advocates to influence national law and attitudes concomitantly. Afro-Brazilian civil rights activists participated enthusiastically during the constitutional reform, encouraging dialogue and participation in debates throughout Brazil. In subsequent elections, the MNU also began to endorse and encourage Afro-Brazilian candidates such as Otelino da Silva to run for political office. Today, Afro-Brazilians continue to bring more issues to the public's attention. Many prominent blacks associated with grassroots movements have gained public notoriety. Frei Davi, former leader of the Commission of Black Religious, Seminarians and Priests, and Benedita Souza da **Silva**, who has held several important political positions including that of national Vice President of the Worker's Party (**PT**), are only two examples.

In Central and South America (with the exception of Belize, which is a majority black state, and Panama, which has a very large black West Indian population), mass organization and protest among blacks is a relatively new phenomenon. In Panama, West Indian organization dates back to the Marcus **Garvey** Association for Negro Betterment of the 1920s. Throughout the 1940s, protest continued against West Indian discrimination and exclusion from citizenship. In other areas of Central America, black movements have focused on cultural preservation and political visibility. This is the case of the Garifuna (see **Garinagu**) people of Honduras and the creoles in Nicaragua. Although black culture has always been celebrated by Afro-Costa Rican writers such as Quince **Duncan**, mass political organization is also a phenomenon of the 1990s.

In Spanish South America, the impact of black mobilization has been most profound in Colombia. In 1990, Colombians voted to replace the antiquated 1886 constitution with a new document that would lay the foundations for specific ethnic representation in the country's Constituent Assembly. Unfortunately, respected academics such as Víctor Daniel Bonilla, who promoted the rights of indigenous people, rallied to deny territorial rights for blacks on the Pacific coast under the same law. Nonetheless, the umbrella organization UNO AFRO (The National Union of African Colombian Organizations) has attempted to coordinate black mobilization all over the country. Pacific coast groups such as the Asociación Campesina Integral del Atrato (the Atrato Integral Peasant Association), the Movimiento Nacional Cimarrón (National Maroon Movement) and the Organización de Barrios Populares y Comunidades Negras de la Costa Pacífica del Chocó (OPABO) are determined to fight for black rights. In Ecuador, the Association of Ecuadorian Blacks (ASONE), founded in 1988, has pursued similar goals on the Pacific coast.

Uruguay, at the other end of South America, has experienced an explosion in black mobilization since 1990. MUNDO AFRO, Uruguay's largest black umbrella organization, has become increasingly militant in its demands, calling for official recognition and for education and employment opportunities free from discrimination. Other South American countries have not experienced major movements, although organizations such as Peru's Movimiento Pro Derechos Humanos del Negro en Perú (the Peruvian Movement Pro Human Rights for Blacks) provide legal assistance to blacks, and battle similar obstacles.

To gain support, many national groups turn to international forums such as the United Nations, the **Organization of American States** (OAS) and international conferences. Beginning in the late 1970s, the Congresses on Black Culture in the Americas encouraged international cooperation among black activists and scholars, although the first few conferences were not explicitly political. The Third Congress, held in São Paulo, Brazil in 1982 under the directorship of Abdias do Nascimento began a new political phase with the theme, 'The African Diaspora: Political Consciousness and African Culture'. Since then, increased black consciousness and politicization of black movements has led to a more acute condemnation of racist policies throughout the region. Afro-Latin Americans have attempted to organize extra-national activities to forge bonds across borders. In 1994, for example, Uruguay's MUNDO AFRO hosted 'The First Seminar on Racism and Xenophobia' in Montevideo, Uruguay in December 1994, with the participation of blacks from throughout the Americas. In 1996, Costa Ricans hosted 'The Second Annual Reunion of the Black Family', with activists from throughout the region.

Black people from Latin America and the Caribbean have participated in major movements throughout the twentieth century. The politics of racial identity, however, continue to pose an obstacle to mass support. Unfortunately, *mestizaje* very often constitutes a national ideology which denigrates blacks in favor of mestizos. In addition, since the vast majority of self-identified blacks are poor, there are significant barriers to mobilization of any kind. Difficulties notwithstanding, many Afro-Latin Americans have courageously opposed oppression and discrimination for centuries.

Further reading

Conniff, M.L. and Davis, T.J. (1994) *Africans in the Americas: A History of the Black Diaspora*.

Graham, R. (ed.) (1990) *The Idea of Race in Latin America*.

Knight, F. (1974) *The African Dimension of Latin American Societies*.

Minority Rights Group (1995) *Invisible No Longer: Afro-Latin Americans Today*, London: Minority Rights Group.

DARIÉN J. DAVIS

Blades, Rubén

b. 1948, Panama City

Salsa composer, singer and film star

An internationally known exponent of salsa music, throughout his prolific career Rubén Blades has constantly produced cultural artefacts addressing contemporary transnational contradictions. Blades gravitated to music while studying law at the local university, when he formed a small rock-and-roll band known for its juxtaposition of Anglo rock rhythms with the beat of Cuban **son**. After passing his bar examination, Blades moved to New York City, then emerging as the capital of **salsa**.

In 1977, he collaborated with trombone player Willie **Colón** on the highly successful album *Metiendo Mano* (Helping Hand). These early songs show Blades's predilection for experimenting with traditional salsa form and content and depict a crude urban reality. His fame was consolidated the following year with their best-selling album *Siembra* (Seed). In songs such as '**Pedro Navaja**' (Peter Blade), Blades turns mass commercial lyrics about barrio gangsters into a symbol of desperation for all American inner cities. After co-producing four more albums with Colón, Blades produced a series of records with a new group, which culminated in the superlative album *Agua Luna* (Moon Water) (1984) with lyrics inspired by the Gabriel **García Márquez**. Blades not only rewrites García Márquez's narratives, but also replaces traditional instruments with synthesizers and electric guitars.

After releasing *Buscando América* (Searching for America) (1984), Blades interrupted his music career to pursue a degree in international law at Harvard University. Then he turned his sights on Hollywood, and starred in Leon Ichaso's *Crossover Dreams* (1985). He had made his film debut earlier in Fred Williamson's *La Última Pelea* (The Last Fight) (1982), released by his first record producer, Fania, to promote his albums. A series of movies including *The Milagro Beanfield War* (1988), *The Super* (1991) and *The Two Jakes* (1990) came next. In 1990, he returned to the recording world with two superhit albums.

Yet another career shift came when Blades returned to Panama to become a presidential candidate for the first military-free elections in twenty-six years. He came in third, with about one-fifth of the vote. A year later, in 1995, he released a new album with former partner Willie Colón, *Tras la Tormenta* (After the Storm). In 1996, Blades rearticulated the interplay between the local and global with a totally Panamanian production *La Rosa de los Vientos* (Wind Rose). Creating new conditions for his music by having the percussion performed with Panamanian folkloric instruments by his new band Salara, in tone and form, this album lays the basis for a new body of work.

NORMAN S. HOLLAND

Blanco, Hugo

b. 1935, Paruro, Peru

Politician

One of Peru's most charismatic political leaders, Hugo Blanco is the leader of the Partido Revolucionario de los Trabajadores/Revolutionary Workers' Party (PRT). While a student of agronomy at the University of La Plata in Argentina, Blanco became a Trotskyist (see **Trotskyism**). He returned to Peru in 1958 and began to organize peasant unions in the southern Peruvian valleys of La Convención and Lares (Cusco), promoting land occupation as a strategy. In 1963, he was accused of murdering policemen and sentenced to death. His sentence was later commuted to 25 years imprisonment and in 1970 he was granted amnesty by the **Velasco** government and deported. Blanco was elected to the Constituent Assembly of Peru in 1978 and to Congress in 1980 and 1985.

CESAR SALAS

Blanco, José Joaquín

b. 1951, Mexico City

Writer

Known primarily as a journalist and essayist who comments broadly and incisively on the contemporary Mexican scene, particularly that of Mexico City, Blanco is a prolific writer whose articles have appeared regularly in some of Mexico's leading newspapers and journals, including La *Jornada*, El **Nacional**, *Unomásuno*, *Nexos* and *Siempre*. His contemporary chronicles and commentaries on Mexican culture are similar to the work of Carlos **Monsiváis**. They have been collected in several volumes, including *Cuando todas las chamacas se pusieron medias nylon* (When All Girls Wore Nylons) (1987) and *Se visten novias* (Specialists in Bridal Wear) (1993). He includes the gay community in his writings, as in his essay 'Ojos que da pánico soñar' (Eyes That Could Terrify Dreams) (1979), one of the earliest Mexican texts on homosexual identity, and *Las púberes canéforas* (The Pubescent Canephoros) (1983), one of five novels he has published to date. Blanco's writings also include poetry and several volumes of literary criticism on both Mexican and foreign writers. His highly acclaimed screenplay, *Frida, naturaleza viva* (Frida Still Life), on Frida **Kahlo**, written in collaboration with Paul **Leduc**, was awarded an Ariel in 1985 (see **Arieles**).

EDUARDO GUÍZAR-ALVAREZ

Blanco, Juan

b. 1919, El Mariel, Cuba

Composer

Blanco's first compositions, like 'Elegía' (Elegy) and 'Cantata de Paz' (Peace Cantata) belong within the 'nationalist' current in Cuban music. He later formed the group Vanguardia Musical, with Leo

Brouwer and Carlos Farinas, the first to promote the use of electronic instruments in Cuban symphonic music. He was a pioneer in the field of concrete and aleatory music with pieces like 'Música de danza' (Music for Dance), 'Ensamble V', 'Texturas', 'Episodio' , 'Contrapunto espacial' (Spatial Counterpoint) and 'Erotofonías' (Erotophonies), usually performed in the open air. He has also composed music for ballet and for the cinema.

JOSÉ ANTONIO EVORA

Blanco, Roberto

b. 1936, Havana, Cuba

Actor and theatre director

Blanco's unique dramatic language combined a sense of visual spectacle with a highly expressive style. A great success as an actor in the 1950s, he joined **Teatro Estudio** in 1959 and directed several of its milestone productions including an epoch-making production of Hernández Espinosa's *María Antonia* in 1967 with the Taller Dramático and Conjunto Folklórico Nacional. At the end of the decade he formed the Ocuje group, which became a fruitful laboratory for his artistic ideas. Marginalized from all artistic activity for more than a decade, he returned in 1982 with his group Teatro Irrumpe, where his work once again had a major creative impact.

WILFREDO CANCIO ISLA

Blanco Fombona, Rufino

b. 1874, Caracas, Venezuela; d. 1944, Buenos Aires, Argentina

Novelist, short-story writer, essayist and poet

One of Venezuela's most prolific writers, Blanco Fombona also occupied a number of diplomatic posts under various governments. His opposition to and criticism of the governments of Cipriano Castro and Juan Vicente **Gómez** earned him a prison sentence and a long exile until Gómez's death in 1935. Under the influence of modernism at first, and later of Nietzsche and naturalism, his work constitutes a fierce critique of the society of Caracas during the period of modernization at the end of the nineteenth century and the beginning of the twentieth.

JORGE ROMERO LEÓN

Blest Riffo, Clotario

b. 1899, Santiago, Chile; d. 1990, Santiago

Labour leader

In his trademark blue overalls, Blest was present on trade union demonstrations and political protests through much of Chile's twentieth-century history. A militant Christian socialist from his teenage years, in the 1930s he founded several radical Christian groups, chief among them Germen, seen by many as a precursor to **liberation theology**. In the late 1940s Blest established the national trade union organization JUNECH and led the non-violent campaigns that in 1950 led to the fall of the military government and in 1951 mobilized against price rises and speculation. In 1953 he created the CUT, the Chilean National Trade Union Congress, which he headed for the next eight years. Through the 1960s he worked with several revolutionary organizations; in 1968 he created the Iglesia Joven (Young Church) to propagate the new radicalism of the Church. Under the **Frei Montalva** government (1964–70) Blest agitated for human rights, and under **Allende** repeatedly warned of the conflict to come. After the **Pinochet** coup, the tireless campaigner continued to lead and organize non-violent protests until a long illness ended his life at the age of ninety.

MIKE GONZALEZ

Blind Blake

b. 1915, Matthew Town, Inagua, Bahamas; d. 1985, Nassau, Bahamas

Musician

One of the defining voices of Bahamian music in the twentieth century, Blake (born Alphonso Higgs) learned to play the banjo and guitar as a youth. He began to lose his sight in his late teens and became completely blind in 1934, but continued his musical career. His music mostly followed the Bahamian form known as **goombay**, similar to **calypso**. He composed over fifty songs, many of which lasted throughout the century and which figure among the most popular Bahamian compositions. Blake usually performed with a small band, mostly playing guitars or banjos. Throughout his career he entertained both Bahamian and tourist audiences in the Bahamas and made a few limited appearances in the USA. His songs addressed typical social themes such as romance, and occasionally dealt with international figures connected to the Bahamas. For example, one of his most famous tunes called 'Love Alone' commented on the story of Edward VIII who abdicated the British throne in order to marry American divorcee Wallis Simpson. (As the Duke of Windsor, Edward served as governor of the Bahamas in the 1940s.) In the later years of his life 'Blind Blake' enjoyed some renewed fame among both Bahamians and tourists when he was hired by the Bahamas Ministry of Tourism as one of the musicians who entertained arriving passengers at Nassau International Airport.

ROSANNE ADDERLEY

Blinder, Oda

b. 1918, Curaçao, Netherlands Antilles; d. 1969, Curaçao

Poet

Oda Blinder (Yolanda Corsen) published only one small collection of poetry, *Brieven van een Curaçaose blinde en andere gedichten* (Letters from a Blind Curaçaoan and Other Poems) (1968), during her lifetime. She published her first work in the literary magazine *De **Stoep*** in 1944 and continued to contribute until its demise in 1951. Her writings, preoccupied with unrequited love and often of a strong erotic nature, were generally written in Dutch and published posthumously in the

Netherlands under the title *Verzamelde stilte* (Collected Silence).

AART G. BROEK

Blinder, Olga

b. 1921, Asunción, Paraguay

Painter, engraver and sketch artist

In 1954, along with Josefina **Plá** and others, she founded the Arte Nuevo group and organized the Primera Semana de Arte Moderna, which challenged the traditional academicism of Paraguayan art. Blinder's works evolved from still lifes and landscapes to critical paintings and wood engravings in the 1960s, depicting pathetic human conditions. During the Re-figuración movement of the 1970s, her engravings emphasized existential and social preoccupations. She returned to painting in the 1980s, always portraying the deceived and embittered through geometric forms and arbitrary colours. After 1989 she directed the Instituto del Desarrollo Harmónico de la Personalidad (Institute for the Harmonious Development of the Personality) (IDAP).

BETSY PARTYKA

Block de Behar, Lisa

b. 1937, Montevideo, Uruguay

Literary critic

Block de Behar is Professor of Semiotics and Interpretative Theory at the Universidad de la República and, since 1996, head of its School of Communication Sciences. Her *El lenguaje de la publicidad* (The Language of Advertising) (1973) and *Una retórica del silencio* (A Rhetoric of Silence) (1984) are key texts, while her work on poetics includes *Una palabra propiamente dicha* (A Word Properly Speaking) (1994), in which she proposes a poetics of translation from a comparative perspective and addresses aspects of film theory. Her *Al margen de Borges* (**Borges** at the Margins) (1987) attests to the

Argentine writer's key aesthetic and epistemological role in her work.

CELINA MANZONI

blocos afro

A type of carnival organization which emerged in Salvador, Bahia, in the mid-1970s, the blocos afro use loud percussive instruments like surdos (large bass drums) and repiques (tenor drums) to create a variety of hybrid rhythms based on **samba**, ijexá, **reggae**, and Jamaican **dancehall**. Notable blocos afro include **Ilê Aiyê** and **Olodum**. Profoundly influenced by black pride movements in the USA, the decolonization of Lusophone Africa, and the liberatory ethos of roots reggae, the blocos afro denounced racial inequality while celebrating the cultural heritage of Africa. Several blocos afro have emerged as important centres of grassroots organization and advocacy on behalf of their neighbourhood communities.

CHRISTOPHER DUNN

Blood of the Condor   *see* Yawar malku

Blyden, Edward Wilmot

b. 1832, Saint Thomas, Virgin Islands; d. 1912, Freetown, Sierra Leone

Pan-Africanist leader

Blyden emigrated to Liberia in 1850, where he became a teacher; there he began his long career as a lecturer and author on African history and culture, and the relationship between the African diaspora and the African continent. Ordained as a Presbyterian minister in 1858, he resigned from his ministry in 1886. He held various posts in Liberian governments, including twice serving as the Liberian ambassador to Great Britain. He made several visits to the USA, where he advocated the emigration of African-Americans to Africa to escape American discrimination and assist in African development. His numerous writings on pan-African themes, including *Christianity, Islam and the Negro Race* (1887), influenced many pan-Africanist leaders and thinkers of the twentieth century including Marcus **Garvey** and C.L.R. **James**.

ROSANNE ADDERLEY

Bo, Armando

b. 1915, Buenos Aires, Argentina; d. 1981

Film-maker

The ambitious young Bo began as a leading actor, founded the production company SIFA in 1948 to concentrate on socially conscious films (which produced several **Torres Ríos** films) and began directing in 1954. *El trueno entre las hojas* (Thunder among the Leaves) (1956) was his first great directorial success and introduced the legendary duo of Bo and Isabel **Sarli**. However, at the end of the 1950s he turned away from social commentary and began to work in a genre hitherto unknown in Argentina – explicit erotic cinema. Persecuted by the censors and attacked by the critics, Bo nevertheless won a growing audience and remained highly productive. Today some of his films – *Carne* (Flesh) (1968), *Fiebre* (Fever) (1970) and *Insaciable* (Insatiable) (1976) – have achieved cult status.

DIANA PALADINO

Boal, Augusto

b. 1931, São Paulo, Brazil

Drama theoretician and playwright

Boal's fundamental aim, shared by other contemporary Brazilian dramatists, is to develop a popular theatre to serve as a vehicle for radical social change, a commitment clearly demonstrated in the plays about political struggle which he wrote from 1960 onwards, such as *Revolução na América do Sul* (Revolution in South America) (1960). Having studied drama in the USA, Boal returned to Brazil in 1956 and worked with the **Arena Theatre Group** in São Paulo, which he later directed.

His most important work, however, has taken place at the level of theory and method. With Arena, he experimented with new techniques that sought to break with the conventions of the bourgeois drama that he saw as sterile and reactionary, and created a theatre of popular participation. He continued this work in exile between 1971 and 1985, when radical drama became impossible during Brazil's military dictatorship. His highly influential *Teatro do oprimido* (Theatre of the Oppressed) (1974) summarizes those experiences and shows how spectators can be turned into actors. The techniques employed encourage participants to think critically about their society and prepare them to become active agents in its transformation. Drawing inspiration from the theories of educator Paulo **Freire**, the work explains methods for breaking down the barrier between actors and passive audience, so that the spectators participate in the dramatic action, take control of it and change its course as they see fit. Each course of action can then be critically evaluated to assess its consequences, as in 'forum theatre', where group members are invited to act out a particular problem and attempt to resolve it by trying a series of different solutions, each of which is then analysed. The aim is to empower the marginalized and oppressed, giving them the means to find their own solutions to social and personal problems. Boal believes that a truly popular theatre can function as a rehearsal for social action which can lead to real political change.

Since returning to Brazil in 1985, Boal has developed these techniques further. He has also written essays and novels, and has entered politics as a prominent member of the **PT** and Rio de Janeiro city councillor (1992–6). His international recognition, however, rests on the theories and techniques of the Theatre of the Oppressed, which have been controversial but have had considerable international impact.

Further reading

Boal, A. (1995) *The Rainbow of Desire: The Boal Method of Theatre and Therapy*, London: Routledge.
—— (1979) *Theatre of the Oppressed*, London: Pluto Press.
Schutzman, M. and Cohen-Cruz, J. (eds) (1994)

Playing Boal: Theatre, Therapy, Activism, London: Routledge.

MARK DINNEEN

Bobadilla, José Antonio

b. 1955, Santo Domingo, Dominican Republic

Writer

Poet, novelist and short story writer, Bobadilla belongs to the Generation of the 1980s. In 1984, he won Third Prize at **Casa de Teatro** (House of Theatre) with his novel *Ay, Janet, así no se puede* (Ay, Janet, It Cannot Be This Way). He has published the novels *Abalorios* (Beads) (1982) and *El jardín de Onan: navajas y coronas de una solitaria historia de amor* (Onan's Garden: Blades and Crowns for a Lonely Love Story) (1988). In his books, Bobadilla recovers Alejo **Carpentier**'s **neo-baroque** style to elaborate erotic plots.

FERNANDO VALERIO-HOLGUÍN

Bobbitt, Lorena

b. 1969, Quevedo, Ecuador

Manicurist and rape victim

In 1993, while living in Manassas, Virginia, Bobbitt severed her husband's penis after he allegedly raped her. The case attracted international media attention when she testified that she had been the victim of sexual abuse throughout their five-year marriage. Her husband John, a 26-year-old former US Marine, was acquitted of marital sexual assault; she was acquitted of malicious wounding. The case came to symbolize an assault on male power and became a rallying point both for rape victim advocates and for men hostile to radical feminism. When she returned to Ecuador, Bobbitt was acclaimed by women from all social classes.

MERCEDES ROBLES

Boca, La

The Boca is a neighbourhood in southeastern Buenos Aires by the mouth of the Riachuelo. For many years, it was a centre of Italian immigrants in Buenos Aires, with brightly painted corrugated metal houses and shacks, artists, singing waiters and nightlife. Located near Parque Lezama, which marks the likely place of the foundation of the city, the neighbourhood was a centre of proletarian culture, along with Avellaneda, a city in the province of Buenos Aires on the other side of the Riachuelo. The painter **Quinquela Martín** produced beautiful paintings of longshoremen, many of which are now found in a small museum devoted to his work and life. La Boca, and its imposing steel bridge over the Riachuelo, were important in Peronist mythology (see **Peronism**) because of their association with the events of 17 October 1945 that led to the rise to power of Juan Domingo **Perón**. Boca was also important in the mythology of the **tango**; 'Caminito' (Little Street) celebrates a corner of the neighbourhood, now a rather garish tourist attraction known for its hawkers of terrible paintings. Boca is also the name of one of the most important Buenos Aires **football** teams, and its stadium dominates the neighbourhood. These days Italians have been largely replaced in the Boca by more recent immigrants.

DANIEL BALDERSTON

Bocca, Julio

b. 1967, Munro, Province of Buenos Aires, Argentina

Ballet dancer

Argentina's greatest dancer, Bocca has had a brilliant international career since winning a Moscow ballet competition in 1985. He studied with his mother before entering the ballet school of the **Teatro Colón**. His performances in classical works like Don Quixote and Swan Lake, and in modern works with the American Ballet Theater, combine grace and strength. He is currently artistic director of the New York City Ballet and the ballet of the Teatro Colón. In 1995, he published a sort of autobiography (with the help of the journalist Rodolfo Braceli), *Bocca: Yo, príncipe y mendigo* (Bocca: I, Prince and Beggar).

DANIEL BALDERSTON

Bodeguita del medio

Famous for its intellectual founders and its famous patrons in the revolutionary Old Havana, this eating establishment in Old Havana gets its name from its unusual position in the middle of the block on the corner of *Empedrado* (cobblestone) Street. Nicolás **Guillén** dedicated a sonnet to the *Bodeguita*, also frequented by Ernest Hemingway, who maintained: 'For a daiquiri, the *Floridita*, a *mojito*, *La Bodeguita*'. A symbol of the *Bodeguita*'s roots in Cuban tradition, the *mojito* – a mixture of rum, mineral water, lemon juice, sugar, and mint leaves that dates back to colonial times – is still enjoyed by the many who pass through and leave their mark on the nostalgic bar/museum's walls.

BARBARA D. RIESS

Boedo vs Florida

A literary polemic which began in Buenos Aires in 1924 and lasted little more than a year, it came to public notice through its publication in the review **Martín Fierro** (1924–7). At that time Florida was the city's most elegant street where the offices of the magazine promoting the avant-garde were to be found; Boedo was in a lower middle class and working class immigrant area where the magazine *Claridad*, representing the cultural left, had its offices. They became the social, cultural and ethnic symbol of two aesthetic positions (the avant-garde and the realist school), but also the emblem of the problems that divided the cultural life of Argentina in the 1920s.

GRACIELA MONTALDO

Boff, Leonardo

b. 1938, Concórdia, Santa Catarina, Brazil

Theologian

One of the most published and controversial representatives of Latin American **liberation theology**, Boff left the Catholic priesthood and the Franciscan order in 1992 after his continuous conflicts with the church hierarchy. Of Italian descent, he studied philosophy and theology first in Brazil before going on to receive his doctorate in theology from the University of Munich in Germany. Ordained a Franciscan priest, he was professor of systematic theology in Petrópolis, Brazil, from 1970 to 1992, also working for several years in a slum. He was member of the board of directors of the publishing house Vozes (1971–92) and of the editorial board of *Revista Eclesiástica Brasileira* (1971–92).

There is practically no area of classical theology left untouched by Boff. His principal contribution has been in the development of a Latin American Christology which understands Jesus to be the radical liberator of the human condition, responsible for establishing a new humanity. Nevertheless, his most controversial book *Igreja: carisma e poder* (Church: Charisma and Power) (1985) is on ecclesiology and presents an alternative vision of the church. This book and its challenge to the hierarchical and authoritarian model of the contemporary Catholic Church was the primary reason he was silenced in 1985 by the Vatican: he was not allowed to teach, write or make public appearances for one year.

Due to this censorship, he left the priesthood in 1992, and has since married and started an active resistance to obligatory celibacy for Catholic priests. He continues opposing 'the clerical dictatorship' in other fields as well. His theological production has moved in a more mystical direction, including ecological and planetary issues, (eco) spirituality and depth psychology, with remarkable influence from Eastern religious traditions. He is among the few male liberation theologians who write on gender questions, even though he has also been criticized by his female colleagues for his image of women. Today, Boff is a professor of ethics at the Rio de Janeiro University.

Further reading

Boff, L. (1985) *Church: Charism and Power. Liberation Theology and the Institutional Church*, New York: Crossroad.

—— (1978) *Jesus Christ Liberator: A Critical Christology for Our Time*, New York: Orbis Books.

Boff, L. and Boff, C. (1987) *Introducing Liberation Theology*, New York: Orbis Books.

Cox, H. (1988) *The Silencing of Leonardo Boff: The Vatican and the Future of World Christianity*, New York: Meyerstone.

ELINA VUOLA

Bofill, Ricardo

b. 1943, Havana, Cuba

Human rights activist

Arrested in 1967 for involvement in a dissident group within the Cuban Communist Party known as the *microfracción*, Bofill was sentenced to twelve years in prison for 'making propaganda for the enemy'. In 1976 he formed the Comité pro Derechos Humanos (Human Rights Committee), the embryo of a dissident civilian organization. He was in prison again between 1980 and 1985, and then went into exile in 1988, creating an international campaign for the recognition and support of dissidents within Cuba. He is President of the Human Rights Committee which is headed within Cuba by Gustavo Arcos Begnes.

WILFREDO CANCIO ISLA

Bogotazo, El   *see*   Violencia, La

Bohemia

Bohemia is an illustrated weekly magazine founded in Havana in 1908 by Miguel Angel Quevedo Pérez. It evolved from a concern with social life into a modern news weekly widely read in Cuba and Latin America; in the 1950s, it printed 250,000 copies weekly. Its section 'En Cuba', beginning in 1943, represented a major advance in investigative journalism. From 1953 onwards it defended Fidel **Castro**'s revolutionary movement, drawing sustained government censure. Nationalized in 1960, it became an official journal of the new Cuban state. With the economic crisis of the 1990s, it reduced its size, number of pages and national circulation.

WILFREDO CANCIO ISLA

Bohr, José

b. 1901, Bonn, Germany

Film-maker

Brought up in Chile, Bohr began film-making as a teenager in Argentina. He reached Mexico in 1931 having first tried his luck in the US as a radio singer and composer, nightclub entertainer and actor (including *Sombras de Gloria* (Shadows of Glory) (1929), one of the first Spanish-language US productions). He directed fourteen feature films during the 1930s, most of which he also produced and scripted with his wife Eva Limiñana, known as 'Duchess Olga'. Returning to Chile, he made more than fifteen films before 1969. His Mexican work, particularly *Luponini de Chicago* (Luponini from Chicago) (1935) and *Mariguana* (1936), has won recognition for their relaxed manner and crazy humour.

PATRICIA TORRES SAN MARTÍN

Bola de Nieve

b. 1911, Guanabacoa, Cuba; d. 1971, Mexico City

Musician

Bola de Nieve's extremely personal singing style owed much to the French cabaret tradition, yet was also profoundly Cuban. Real name Ignacio Villa, he was a cultured man with a solid musical formation, who travelled the world and sang in many languages. He was given his nickname (which means 'snowball') by Rita **Montaner**, with whom he was always linked. His musical arrangements popularized the poetry of Nicolás **Guillén** and inspired new poetry and the exploration of Afro-Cuban rhythms. His compositions include classics like 'Si mi pudieras querer' (If You Could Only Love Me), 'Ay amor' and 'Tú me has de querer' (You Must Love Me).

WILFREDO CANCIO ISLA

Bolaño, Roberto

b. 1953, Santiago, Chile

Writer

Emerging as one of Chile's most significant younger writers, Bolaño has lived in **exile**, first in Mexico and later in Spain, since the 1973 *coup*. Many of his works are largely set in Spain, though often with Latin American exiles as their central characters. His best known works include *La literatura nazi en América* (Nazi Literature in the Americas) (1996), *Estrella distante* (Distant Star) (1996) and *Llamadas telefónicas* (Telephone Calls) (1997). He has also published several books of poetry, and contributes regularly to the Spanish and Chilean press. He is a recent winner of the Rómulo Gallegos Prize.

DANIEL BALDERSTON

bolero

The origins of bolero lie in the first cultural contacts and fusions between Spaniards, Africans and Indians occurring in the Caribbean from the sixteenth century onwards. It is here that its oldest and most secret roots are to be found. But, as its name suggests, the Latin American bolero in its recognisably modern form derives from Hispanic melodic forms developed and popularized during the nineteenth century. While the exact moment of the birth of its modern form is impossible to determine, some specialists point to the 1865 piece *Tristezas* (Sadness) composed in Cuba as the first example of the musical form that later became one of the most representative components of Latin American popular culture, particularly in Mexico and the Caribbean.

If its roots lie in a distant past, the modern bolero owes much to the growth of the mass media, whose influence in Latin America began to extend from the 1930s onwards and whose most representative figure was Agustín **Lara**. A key symbolic date is 1906, when the revue *El triunfo del bolero* (The Triumph of Bolero) was presented in the **Alhambra Theatre** in Havana, Cuba. That was the starting point for the growing success of a genre which, particularly between 1930 and 1960, won massive popularity thanks to the growth of the **radio** and record industries and the bolero reached every corner of the continent. Bolero lyrics, invariably about love, form part of the symbolic baggage through which every Latin American, and particularly the inhabitants of the Caribbean, has learned to express his or her own feelings of love. In this sense, bolero provides a kind of natural erotic and emotional language spoken by every level of Latin American society, where every Latin American can see himself or herself reflected in imagery which synthesizes the collective experience of love. Thus, one of the most emblematic of boleros, *Ese bolero es mío* (This is My Bolero), faithfully registers the sense that each listener finds in the bolero the echo of his or her own particular experience of love: 'That bolero is mine/because its words are my own/its tragedies are mine/as God alone knows.'

Further reading

Castillo Zapata, R. (1990) *Fenomenología del bolero*, Caracas: Monte Avila.

Monsiváis, C. (1988) *Amor perdido*, Mexico: ERA.

Rico Salazar, J. (1988) *Cien años de bolero*, Bogotá: CEEM.

Zavala, I. (1991) *El bolero; historia de un amor*, Madrid: Alianza Editorial.

RAFAEL CASTILLO ZAPATA

bolita

Bolita is a game of chance, illegal in Cuba, in which the players bet on a two-digit number to coincide with the last two numbers of the winning national lottery ticket. The *apuntadores* (runners) collected the bets and dealt with the punters directly; the *banquero* (banker) held the money and paid out the prizes through the *apuntador*. When the official lottery ended in Cuba in the late 1960s the game declined, but was revived in the 1980s, this time using the results of official lotteries in other countries, like the United States, whose draws were broadcast via the shortwave radios widely listened to in Cuba.

JOSÉ ANTONIO EVORA

Bolivia

Bolivia, a land-locked nation in the centre of Latin America, has an estimated population of seven million concentrated in the three most inhabited and developed cities, La Paz, Santa Cruz and Cochabamba. It is one of the few countries in Latin America with a large Indian population, mostly of **Aymara**, **Quechua** and **Guarani**-speaking people who predominantly inhabit the countryside. However, in the last three decades Bolivia has witnessed a large Aymara migration to La Paz. Another important shift in population was from the Andes to the Chaparé region in Cochabamba, making this region the dominant centre for **coca** leaf production used for illegal cocaine exports. In 1984, it was roughly estimated that cocaine exports were worth over twice the $724 million of legal exports.

Since the **Bolivian Revolution** of 1952, the nation has had a period of economic growth and development as well as one of the highest inflation rates in the world. The National Revolutionary Movement (MNR), the political party instrumental in the 1952 revolution, has been one of the most important political forces. During its twelve years in power, it implemented an Agrarian Reform (1953), nationalized the tin mining industry and controlled the Bolivian Workers Union (**COB**), the main labour force in the country, headed by the legendary leader Juan **Lechín Oquendo** (1952–86). From 1964 to 1982, Bolivia had a series of military regimes with varying political ideologies. Among the most successful was that of General Barrientos, known for his strong peasant support and for his opposition to labour and leftist groups. In 1966, Che **Guevara** arrived in Bolivia; in October of the following year, he was captured and executed by Barrientos with the help of his Chief of Staff, General Ovando, and with massive support from the USA. After Barrientos's death in an aeroplane accident, Bolivian politics was in the hands of one military regime after another, their politics ranging from extreme left through reformist to reactionary right. Among them, General Juan José Torres (1970–1) stands out as the most radical and left-leaning general ever to govern Bolivia. He was overthrown by a bloody *coup* led by Colonel Hugo Banzer, who remained in power from 1971 to 1982 and who, ironically, was re-elected in 1997. The MNR came back to power in 1985, remaining the principal political force until the presidency of Gonzalo Sanchez de Losada (1992–6) and the vice-presidency of Victor Hugo Cárdenas, the Aymara leader of the Tupak Katari Revolutionay Movement of Liberation (MRTKL).

In spite of political instablility, dictatorships and economic hardships, Bolivia's achievement in the arts is outstanding. Ironically, much of the literature of the early twentieth century by dominant thinkers and writers, such as Alcides **Arguedas**, Franz **Tamayo** and Tristan Marof, is related to the social and political instability of the country. These three writers, from three very different points of view, interpreted and assessed Indian reality as a main concern of the nation's politics, economy, society and pedagogy, making the 'regeneration' of the Indian a national objective.

Even though Bolivian elite culture had its eyes focused on Europe, the twentieth century is marked by a strong effort to recognize the rich Indian histories and cultures which are being studied only now by Aymara historians of the **Taller de Historia Oral Andina** (THOA), together with national and foreign historians and anthropologists such as Silvia **Rivera**, Xavier Albó, Josep Barnadas, Olivia Harris, Brooke Larson, Thérèse Bouyesse de Casagne and Tristan Platt.

Not only has Indian culture survived and been revived to an amazing extent in the countryside, but it has grown in the cities as well. Its musical traditions in the form of songs and dances have been adopted and adapted by the growing middle class, especially university students in their annual participation in the Festival of Nuestro Señor Jesús del Gran Poder (Our Lord Jesus) held in La Paz. However, most Indian culture is still identified with rural celebrations of the village's patron saint. While these celebrations show the most visible apects of Indian traditions, its music has infiltrated Bolivian society as a whole in many different forms. These include contemporary musical groups which express deep national feelings of identity and solidarity with the people following the *nueva canción* (new song) movements in Latin America. Los **Kjarkas**, Savia Andina, Rumillajta, Los Quipus and Los Masis are some of the groups which exemplify this type of music.

From the standpoint of the elite culture, *indigenismo* became a strong current in literature and the visual arts. As a literary movement, it was very much influenced by Alcides Arguedas's novel *Raza de bronce* (Bronze Race) (1919), though each individual writer interpreted it differently. Among the novelists and short story writers were Jesús **Lara**, Raúl Botelho Gonsálvez, Néstor Taboada Terán and Carlos Medinaceli. Franz **Tamayo**, Tristán Marof, Augusto **Guzmán**, Alfredo Guillén Pinto and Alipio Valencia Vega were some of the essayists. In the visual arts, *indigenismo* was a main characteristic of painters such as Cecilio Guzmán de Rojas, muralists Alejandro Mario Illanes and Miguel Alandia Pantoja, viewed as the muralist of the Revolution, as well as sculptor Marina **Nuñez del Prado**.

By the 1960s and 1970s, writers who had emerged from the Chaco War such as Oscar **Cerruto** were at the forefront of a new trend in literature. Their work was concerned with national issues such as the military dictatorships, **guerrilla warfare** and the new urban social context as well as more universal and metaphysical issues. Among the most representative are Renato **Prada**, Pedro **Shimose**, Jaime **Sáenz**, Blanca Wietuchter, Julio de la Vega, Jesús **Urzagasti** and Gaby Vallejo.

In film, some of the leading film-makers of today came from the state-controlled Bolivian Cinematographic Institute, created in 1953, and are exemplified by Jorge **Sanjinés** and Antonio Eguino. From 1968 to 1971 both Sanjinés and Eguino, together with scriptwriter Oscar Soria, formed the Ukamau Group (see **Grupo Uka-mau**) promoting alternative cinema. Among the more recent film-makers are Paolo Agazzi, Raquel Romero and Danielle Caillet.

In mass media communications, Bolivia witnessed the arrival of **television** in 1968, broadcasting only one state-controlled channel (Channel 7) until 1976, when university channels were allowed to operate if, and only if, they broadcast educational and informative programmes. By 1984, private enterprise had been allowed into the television industry. Notwithstanding the popularity of television, **radio** remained the greater means of mass communication. There are a total of 207 radio stations, some controlled by religious institutions; for example, Radio San Gabriel, which broadcasts in Aymara. Others are run by private enterprise, unions, universities or the state. Some union and university radio stations played a major role in student and miners' strikes against several dictatorial regimes.

Further reading

Dunkerley, J. (1984) *Rebellion in the Veins*, London: Verso.

Klein, H. (1982) *Bolivia: The Evolution of a Multi-Ethnic Society*, New York: Oxford University Press.

Malloy, J. (1970) *Bolivia: The Sad and Corrupt End of the Revolution*, Hanover: Universities Field Staff International.

Mesa-Gisbert, C. (1985) *Aventura del cine boliviano 1952–1985*, La Paz: Editorial Gisbert & Cia.

Rivadeneira-Prada, R. (1994) *El cine alternativo en Bolivia*, La Paz: Ediciones Signo.

Salazar Mostajo, C (1989) *La pintura contemporánea de Bolivia*, La Paz: Librería Editorial Juventud.

JOSEFA SALMÓN

Bolivian Revolution

The Bolivian Revolution began as a *coup d'état* organized by the Movimiento Nacionalista Revolucionario (Nationalist Revolutionary Movement), or MNR, against the oligarchy. This became a popular insurrection, which won a victory against the army on 9 April 1952. Between 1952 and 1956 the MNR governed jointly with the *Congreso Obrero*

Boliviano (Bolivian Workers Congress), or **COB**. The first 'national-revolutionary' government, led by Víctor **Paz Estenssoro**, nationalized the tin mines (1952), carried through an agrarian reform (1953), implemented workers' control of the nationalized mines, reorganized the army and introduced universal suffrage and other reforms such as education which were of major significance for Bolivia.

MAGDALENA CAJÍAS DE LA VEGA

Bologna, Francisco

b. 1922, Belem do Pará, Brazil

Architect

Bologna's work expressed his conception of architecture as language, exploring its lexicon and semantics, but above all its syntax. He took on various elements of Le Corbusier's rationalism, sometimes holding to them rigorously, sometimes attempting to connect them with Brazilian architectural traditions or emphasizing the plasticity of reinforced concrete. In the 1960s, he restrained that luxuriant plasticity in favour of an architecture seen as science. Later, influenced by Mies van der Rohe's purified, sober and refined rationalism, he emphasized constructive aspects and classical and contemporary architectural principles.

ROBERTO CONDURU

Bolt, Alan

b. 1951, León, Nicaragua

Playwright

Founder of the agricultural/theatre collective *La Praga* in the mountains around Matagalpa, in the early 1970s Bolt created the street theatre company *Subtiava* and was jailed and tortured twice by the Somoza (see **Somoza dynasty**) National Guard. When the Sandinista **FSLN**, of which he was a member, split into three factions after 1974, Bolt went into exile in Costa Rica. A **mestizo** whose Náhuatl ancestry was an important element of his writing, he returned to Nicaragua in the early

1980s to become National Theatre Director within the Ministry of Culture. He became disillusioned with the Sandinista government and resigned, later setting up the Nixtayolero theatre company in 1984 (see **Nixtayoleros**).

ESTEBAN E. LOUSTAUNAU AND
ILEANA RODRÍGUEZ

Bomarzo

Bomarzo (1966–7) is an opera in two acts by Alberto **Ginastera** to a libretto by Manuel **Mujica Láinez**, based on the latter's 1962 novel. The sixteenth-century Italian Duke of Bomarzo dies at the hand of his avenging nephew; the opera presents scenes from his debauched and repressed life as 'flashbacks' during his final fifteen seconds. Portrayals of sex and cruelty prompted a ban on the scheduled Buenos Aires première, despite the previously successful world début in Washington (1967). The opera, once dubbed 'Porno in Belcanto', is organised into fifteen microstructures, displaying virtuoso use of aleatoric serial technique, microtonality and renaissance forms.

SIMON WRIGHT

Bombal, María Luisa

b. 1910, Viña del Mar, Chile; d. 1980, Santiago, Chile

Writer

Bombal's fiction addresses two areas: experimentation with time, language and point of view, and the extent to which women's experiences transgress the cultural codes assigned to the 'feminine'. Within an ambiguous reality where the borders between life and death, imagined experiences and tangible reality, are obscured, Bombal denounces the imbalances created by patriarchy. Using poetic imagery, in her novels *La última niebla* (The Final Mist) (1934) and *La amortajada* (The Shrouded Woman) (1939), she presents female characters who search for their own identity through intense eroticism and sensual contact with nature.

LUCÍA GUERRA

Bonafini, Hebe de

b. 1928, La Plata, Argentina

Human rights activist

Hebe de Bonafini is a founder and leader of *Asociación Madres de Plaza de Mayo* (Mothers of Plaza de Mayo Association), the symbol of the struggle for human rights in Argentina. She is known as an impassioned speaker in her white scarf and thick glasses. Her organization continues to bring to justice those responsible for the thousands of disappearances during the 1976–83 Argentine dictatorship. Of working-class origin and a housewife until her children's disappearances, Bonafini and the other pioneer *Madres* developed a new form of activism outside the party system, which survived military repression.

See also: disappeared, the

SILVANA DASZUK

Bonevardi, Marcelo

b. 1929, Buenos Aires, Argentina; d. 1994, Córdoba, Argentina

Painter

Bonevardi's remarkable draftsmanship and formal innovations are the basis of his famous and widely exhibited 'construction-paintings'. Bonevardi lived and worked in Córdoba for most of his life. His first trip abroad was to Italy in 1950, where he admired the sense of order and measure of the masters of the Italian Renaissance. After visiting New York in 1958, he divided his time between Córdoba, where he maintained his contact with the land and nature, and New York, where he absorbed the creativity of contemporary art.

MAGDALENA GARCÍA PINTO

Bonfim

The eighteenth-century Igreja de Nosso Senhor do Bonfim (Church of Christ on the Cross) was built on a hill overlooking All Saints Bay in Salvador. Famous for its huge collection of votive objects deposited by grateful beneficiaries of divine intervention, on the second Sunday after the Epiphany, thousands of devotees and revellers dress in white to honour *Oxalá*, the *orixá* (see **orixás**) that corresponds to Christ in the **Candomblé** religion. The procession to Bonfim is led by Bahian women carrying white porcelain vessels filled with water and flowers, usually followed by percussion groups. The church doors remain closed during the ritual since local Roman Catholic ecclesiastic authorities disdain such displays of popular religious syncretism.

CHRISTOPHER DUNN

Boodhoo, Isiah James

b. 1932, Trinidad

Painter

Boodhoo started his career as a teacher and his Doctorate in Art Education led him to divide his time chiefly between painting and a position as school supervisor attached to the Ministry of Education in Trinidad. Educated in England and the USA, Boodhoo's early style is largely expressionistic and his work is known for its play with colours, which he sees as particular to Trinidadian landscapes. Recently his paintings have become more figurative in style and draw increasingly on the island's East Indian culture.

LORRAINE LEU

Boom

Although they are unavoidable, literary labels tend today to have a bad press. So-called literary 'movements' or 'styles', the best-known Latin American example being the concept of '**magical realism**', are especially deprecated. Close behind magical realism as a critical bugbear – and equally difficult to exorcize – is the 'Boom', the name neither of a movement nor a style but of a particular literary moment, the one that saw the astonishing rise of the Latin American novel to world attention in the 1960s. Many critics have argued that the use of an economic – indeed commercial – term (and in English at that) was demeaning and alienating; some added that in any case the term was also misleading, that the Latin American novel in the 1960s was not noticeably different from what it had been in the 1940s and 1950s, and that any change was more in the mode of perception, so to speak, than in the object of study. To put it more crudely, the Boom was as much a marketing and public relations exercise as a literary phenomenon.

But this, of course, was precisely the point. There was in fact an explosion of interest in the Latin American novel from the early 1960s, which did indeed lead to an increased demand for the product, a demand which in its turn led to an expanded supply and a further spiral of interest. Moreover, four product leaders emerged to dominate the new market: Carlos **Fuentes**, Julio **Cortázar**, Mario **Vargas Llosa** and Gabriel **García Márquez**. Cortázar died in 1983, but the others are all still alive and remain indisputably the three leading novelists – the most prestigious literary brand names – of the continent almost forty years after the birth of the Boom. All are well-known beyond the frontiers of Latin America, and all are in a position to live from their writing. Not even Jorge Luis **Borges**, Alejo **Carpentier** or Miguel Angel **Asturias**, giants from an earlier generation, could have dreamed of such favourable terms of trade when they first came to prominence in the 1940s and 1950s.

Critics differ in their explanation of the phenomenon. Clearly, the development of Latin American societies in the 1950s, with the generalized economic policy of import substitution (see **import substitution industrialization**), had led to the formation of a new, broader, university-educated continental middle class which was simultaneously nationalist and cosmopolitan in its tastes and ready for home-grown equivalents of international artistic commodities. The Boom novels were tailor-made to meet this demand. Politically, in the Cold War context, a wave of

populist (see **populism**) (**Perón**, **Vargas**) and quasi-revolutionary (Guatemala, Bolivia) regimes had paved the way for the most radical upheaval of all, that caused by the Cuban Revolution of 1959 (see **revolutions**). This event put Latin America at the centre of world attention for the first time and gave writers and artists a choice of commitments, whether to Cuban-style revolutionary Marxism, US-style freedom and progress, or other points in between. There is no doubt that this temporary openness of horizons – to be negated almost absolutely by the 1970s – created an aesthetic moment of extraordinary fertility. This openness, this choice between alternatives, is clearly visible in both the subject matter and the structures of the canonical texts of the era. All are about the historical formation of Latin America, the relation between that history and other mythical versions, and the contribution of both to contemporary Latin American identity: the grand themes or – as later critics would say, with pejorative intent – 'master narratives' of the great **mestizo** continent.

The Mexican Carlos Fuentes probably deserves credit as the inaugurator of what would come to be called the Boom. His *La región más transparente* (Where the Air is Clear) (1958), modelled on Dos Passos, may fairly be considered the first great novel of the new era, followed perhaps by Cortázar's *Los premios* (The Prizes) (1960). In 1962, Fuentes followed up with possibly his most important novel, *La muerte de Artemio Cruz* (The Death of Artemio Cruz), an existentialist (see **existentialism**) interpretation of the entire history of Mexico against the critical background of the recent Cuban Revolution. A year later, Cortázar published ***Rayuela*** (Hopscotch) (1963) which was not, as some have argued, the novel that began the Boom but undoubtedly the novel that confirmed, crystallized and characterized it; or, to put it another way, the novel that showed that there was a phenomenon in need of a name.

The name duly arrived. Critics argue as to who coined it, but regardless of who did, there is no doubt that the Boom's great publicist and propagandist was the Uruguayan critic Emir **Rodríguez Monegal**, who is inseparable from its trajectory, whether in the literary press or the halls of academe. Rodríguez Monegal went on to found the literary–cultural journal ***Mundo nuevo***

(1966–71), based initially in Paris, which had an extraordinary influence on Latin American literature in general and the Boom in particular until it collapsed in controversy, due in part to accusations of CIA funding. Meanwhile in Cuba, *Mundo nuevo*'s intellectual antagonist, **Casa de las Américas**, founded in the first year of the Revolution, began its less ambiguous revolutionary mission which continues, somewhat precariously, to the present time. *Casa* had its own scandal during the same period with the so-called '**Padilla** affair', and the two cases give a good insight into the pressures brought upon writers and, more specifically, the extent to which it was impossible to avoid making political choices – whether inside or outside fiction – in the tempestuous Latin American situation after *circa* 1967. In due course the writers of the Boom who, as well as being colleagues, were close friends in the 1960s, found themselves drifting apart in the 1970s. A comparison with their contemporaries the Beatles – another four-man group – proves to be more illuminating than would seem likely at first sight.

The youngest of the Boom writers was Mario Vargas Llosa, whose *La **ciudad y los perros*** (The City and the Dogs) appeared in 1962 and won a key literary prize in Spain (the influence of Spanish – particularly Catalan – publishers on the course of the Boom is a fascinating chapter in itself). He was then twenty-six. Under immense pressure to repeat his remarkable achievement, he wrote the even more extraordinary *La casa verde* (The Green House) in 1966, and the monumental *Conversación en la Catedral* (Conversation in the Cathedral) in 1969. The influence of William Faulkner on Vargas Llosa is unmistakable, but the Peruvian takes Faulkner's techniques to lengths that even Faulkner never envisaged with an audacity and a lucidity that astonished Latin America's new readers.

The central period of the brief moment that was the Boom was the intense stretch of time from 1963, when *Rayuela* appeared, to 1967, when García Márquez's ***Cien años de soledad*** (One Hundred Years of Solitude) – the Boom novel *par excellence* – appeared. Everyone agreed that *Rayuela* was something like 'Latin America's *Ulysses*'; appropriately enough, because the Boom is best understood as the crystallization and culmination of Latin America's modernist movement dating back to the 1920s. But *Cien años de soledad* changed the entire perspective, making it clear at once that something much more far-reaching had occurred for which a quite different time-frame was required; as almost everyone again agreed, *Cien años de soledad* was 'Latin America's *Don Quixote*'. Clearly, a brief literary moment which somehow conjoins a *Ulysses* with a *Quixote* is more than just a historical flash in the pan.

Many other writers and other literary phenomena were also active at the time. The Cuban exile Guillermo **Cabrera Infante** wrote the scintillating *Tres tristes tigres* (Three Trapped Tigers) (1965), which somehow became a novel of the Boom even though its politically incorrect author did not become a writer of the Boom. Some critics argue that there was a fifth Boom writer, the Chilean José **Donoso**, whose *El **obsceno pájaro de la noche*** (Obscene Bird of Night) appeared in 1970, as the moment began to fade in the face of a changing aesthetic horizon beneath a darkening political sky. Curiously enough, a more convincing candidate as fifth Boom writer, though taxonomically more problematical, would be the Spaniard Juan Goytisolo, whose own radical departures in the late 1960s had much in common with his leading Latin American contemporaries. He remained Spain's most important novelist at home and abroad in the 1990s, thirty years after the Boom.

Most intriguing perhaps for the historian, and less often noticed, is the fact that although the unparalleled success of the Boom writers sparked an explosion of literary activity, it evinced few direct imitations. If the Boom was, as we are arguing, the high point of modernism, the so-called **post-Boom**, which began in the late 1960s, was clearly postmodernist (see **postmodernism**). The best-known example is the constellation of Mexican writers of the late 1960s (José **Agustín**, Gustavo **Sainz**, Parménides García Saldaña and others) known as the **Onda** or 'New Wave', inspired less by traditional questions of politics and national identity than by rock music, drugs and urban alienation. However, individual writers like the Argentinian Manuel **Puig** were already opening new avenues in the late 1960s with works like *La traición de Rita Hayworth* (Betrayed by Rita Hayworth) (1968), based on his fascination with the movies and the mass media generally. In that sense the end of the Boom, which some would put as early as 1970, marked by Donoso's *El obsceno pájaro*, and others as late as 1975, signalled by Fuentes's mammoth *Terra nostra*, was also the end of a monolithic belief in the novel as high art.

Ironically enough, and this too is rarely understood, the Boom writers all had not one but two careers, since they all became post-Boom writers as well. Indeed, Fuentes's *Cambio de piel* (A Change of Skin) (1967) and Cortázar's *62: modelo para armar* (62: A Model Kit) (1968), both obviously 'post-Boom' and postmodernist in style, were in fact published at the height of the Boom itself. Vargas Llosa's *Pantaleón y las visitadoras* (Sergeant Pantoja's Special Service) (1973) and García Márquez's *El otoño del patriarca* (Autumn of the Patriarch) (1975) followed shortly behind and equally clearly represented new points of departure for their respective authors. No one since has achieved anything like the same authority as this quartet; and although many critics assert that loss of 'authority' is precisely what the postmodern era is all about and this is the reason no other writer has approached their unique combination of critical and commercial success, there is something rather hollow about the argument. Interestingly enough, however, the only writers who have managed since the 1960s to write convincingly 'decentred' works – in contrast with the original four's famously 'finished' works – are women, writers like the Brazilian Clarice **Lispector** (the greatest Latin American novelist of the 1960s outside the Boom's boys' club) or the Chilean Diamela **Eltit**. Another woman, Isabel **Allende**, is the only writer to have achieved a best-seller status (see **best-sellers**) comparable with the famous four.

Was the phenomenon known as the Boom an optical illusion, or did it indeed exist? The answer seems clear. The Boom was a uniquely charged moment, at what seemed at the time to be the confirmation of Latin America's passage from clinging underdevelopment to beckoning modernity, a transition we now see differently as the transition between modernity and postmodernity; with Latin America as 'hybrid' and 'heterogeneous' as ever, still unjust and uneven, still stranded between so-called development and so-called underdevelopment. When the historians look back in the twenty-first century, they may well conclude

that the novelists of the Boom brought a more critical and productive gaze to bear upon this problematic than their successors, despite their market success and the controversial label which was accordingly attached to them.

Further reading

Donoso, J. (1977) *The Boom in Spanish American Literature: A Personal Account*, New York, Columbia University Press.

Martin, G. (1989) *Journeys through the Labyrinth: Latin American Fiction in the Twentieth Century*, London: Verso.

Mudrovcic, M.E. (1997) *Mundo Nuevo: cultura y Guerra Fría en la década del 60*, Rosario: Beatriz Viterbo.

Rama, A. (ed.) (1981) *Más allá del boom: literatura y mercado*, Mexico City: Marcha.

Rodríguez Monegal, E. (1972) *El boom de la novela latinoamericana*, Caracas: Tiempo Nuevo.

GERALD MARTIN

Boquitas pintadas

Manuel **Puig**'s second novel *Boquitas pintadas*, published in 1969, was subtitled 'a serial'; in fact, Puig did consider publishing it in instalments in a magazine. He also wrote the screenplay for Leopoldo **Torre Nilsson**'s 1973 film adaptation. The story, told through a series of letters, concerns the (amorous) life of Juan Carlos, a small town Don Juan, whose excesses end in a mountain sanatorium where he is sent after contracting tuberculosis. There were three women in his life: Nené, now living in Buenos Aires with her husband and two children, who begins to write letters when she hears of his death; Mabel, whose provincial savoir-faire is set against the chaste Nené; and Raba, the servant. In her letters, Nené seeks information about her 'eternal love' Juan Carlos, whose sexual excesses, we learn in the end, were practised with Mabel. Her letters to Juan Carlos' mother are full of complaints about her husband and her peculiarly dull family life. But it is Celina, the dead lover's sister, who replies to the letters; she blames Nené for her brother's death, and her revenge is to send

Nené's letter to her husband, who does absolutely nothing when faced with proof of his wife's lack of love.

The story does not evolve so straightforwardly in the letters that compose the book, of course. Narrated entirely through the words of its characters, Puig's novel is faithful to the conventions of the serial novel, but it is also an adaptation of Thomas Mann's *Der Zauberberg*, just as his first novel *La traición de Rita Hayworth* (Betrayed by Rita Hayworth) (1970) was based on Joyce's *Ulysses*. The relationship between realism and illusion, barely hinted at in the first novel, here appears crudely exposed through the more or less perverted 'quotation' of one of the features of that relation. Puig's narrative moves resolutely towards experimental, non-representational models which he deploys with great skill. *Boquitas pintadas* was a bestseller, like some of Puig's subsequent work.

However, behind the apparently sentimental plot there is a whole theory of social relations cloaked behind relations of knowledge. Raba, the most oppressed and ignorant of the three, is the one who gains most (socially) by the novel's end. In the mysterious mix of knowledge and power proposed in *Boquitas pintadas* lie many of the keys for understanding Puig's work.

Further reading

Muñoz, E.M. (1988) *Boquitas pintadas: una zona de resistencia en el discurso novelístico de Manuel Puig*, Sacramento, CA: Department of Foreign Languages, California State University.

DANIEL LINK

Borda, Arturo

b. 1883, La Paz, Bolivia; d. 1953, La Paz

Visual artist

An outstanding painter who described himself in a posthumously published autobiography as *El loco* (The Madman) (1966), Borda's early portraits, several of members of his own family, are slightly eccentric and intricately detailed. *Yatiri* (1918) marks the start of an *indigenista* (see ***indigenismo***)

phase, often socially critical works whose subjects are the hitherto neglected indigenous people and the mountain landscapes of Bolivia. *Crítica de los ismos y el triunfo del arte clásico* (Critique of Isms and the Triumph of Classical Art) (1948) seems to be self-critical in its rejection of folkloric modes and its curious eclecticism. Towards the end of his life Borda had begun to experiment with abstraction.

MIKE GONZALEZ

borders

Of all the Latin American borders, that with Anglo-Saxon America has received the most attention and earned the greatest significance and dramatic impact in the collective imagination of successive generations of Latin Americans. A recurring theme in the **corrido** and tex-mex music heard on either side of the border, represented differently in the cinema of Mexico and Hollywood, this northern frontier (*la frontera*) is now a distinct socio-economic space, home to a number of research institutions, and a site of exchange generating and reaffirming bilingual and bicultural genres like the cross-border **performance art** of Guillermo **Gómez-Peña** and other artists. In the 1990s, the theme of the border has arisen in Mexican literature and film, as in Carlos **Fuentes**'s volume of stories *Frontera de cristal* (Glass Frontier) (1997) and Maria **Novaro**'s film *El jardín de Edén* (The Garden of Eden) (1995).

The other cultural borders to the south have been less sharply defined, and the animosity that they generate has been no greater than general border disputes in this continent, once imagined as free of all borders.

The borders of Latin American states have their antecedents in colonial administration entities. In the first quarter of the nineteenth century, the local ***criollo*** élites proclaimed themselves legitimate inheritors of distinct sections of the Spanish colonial empire. By the mid-nineteenth century, after a series of failed attempts at federation, sixteen countries had been established. Brazil's independence dates from the same era. The continuing border conflicts between Latin American nations are due to the imprecision of the original lines of division, to the ambitions of local oligarchies, and foreign intervention and neocolonialism. The instability of South America, partly due to the expansionism of states like Brazil and Chile, has led to the redrawing of borders with consequences as dramatic as the encirclement of Bolivia. In the last two decades of the twentieth century, fishing disputes renewed conflicts that had lain dormant for some time in areas like the Caribbean, while conflicts over oil (see **oil in Latin America**) and other resources led to brief wars between Ecuador and Peru. Another serious border conflict is that between Guyana and Venezuela.

See also: Chaco War

Further reading

Dwyer, A. (1994) *On the Line*, London: Latin America Bureau.

Fuentes, C. (1997) *The Glass Frontier*, New York: Farrar, Strauss and Giroux.

Martinez, O.J. (1988) *Troublesome Border*, Tucson: University of Arizona Press.

LUIS L. ESPARZA

Bordón, Luis

b. 1926, Guarambaré, Paraguay

Harpist

From childhood Luis Bordón showed an interest in music which was encouraged by his harpist father. In 1950 he formed part of a Paraguayan folk group which toured various Paraguayan cities bringing him fame for his personal and inimitable harp style. He later performed for radio and television in São Paulo as a soloist, and produced his first record *Arpa paraguaya en hi-fi* (Parguayan Harp in Hi Fi) in 1958. He now has thirty-two volumes on compact disc, not counting 78s and 45s. Bordón is also well-known outside Paraguay and has won eight gold records. His repertoire includes Paraguayan guaranias (see **guarania**) and polkas, as well as **tango** and other styles of music.

BETSY PARTYKA

Borge Martínez, Tomás

b. 1930, Matagalpa, Nicaragua

Politician

Of the three original founding members of the **FSLN**, Carlos **Fonseca**, Silvio Mayorga and Tomás Borge, only Borge survives. During the Sandinista (see **Sandinista Revolution**) administration (1979–90), he was part of the National Directorate, Minister of Interior, and headed the National Commission for the Autonomy of the Atlantic Coasts. After 1990 he became a promoter of the arts and also founded La Verde Sonrisa (The Green Smile), an organization for working-class children. Adored by many, he has been the object of controversy particularly with regard to the *piñata* of 1990, and his decision to write an authorized biography of Mexican President Carlos **Salinas**.

ESTEBAN E. LOUSTAUNAU AND
ILEANA RODRÍGUEZ

Borges, Graciela

b. 1942, Buenos Aires, Argentina

Actress

One of the most beautiful faces of the Argentine cinema, Borges (born Graciela Noemí Zabala) worked in theatre from the age of fourteen before appearing on radio, film and television. Her first major success was in Lucas **Demare**'s *Zafra* (Harvest) (1958). She was Leopoldo **Torre Nilsson**'s favourite actress, but she worked with all the best Argentine directors. She won an award at the San Sebastian festival for her role in Raúl de la Torre's *Crónica de una señora* (Chronicle of a Lady) (1971).

RODRIGO PEIRETTI

Borges, Jacobo

b. 1931, Caracas, Venezuela

Visual artist

A well-known muralist as well as one of Latin

America's outstanding artists and engravers, Borges was, in 1959, one of the five painters chosen to represent Venezuela at an exhibition in Mexico; since then his reputation has steadily grown (although he stopped painting for five years, between 1965 and 1970). Borges's breakthrough, according to one critic, came with his enormous canvas, *Ha comenzado el espectáculo* (The Show has Started) (1964). His other great achievement was the huge series *La comunión* (The Communion) of 1981. In 1976 he returned to Mexico, this time to the Museum of Modern Art, with his '*Magia de un realismo crítico*' (the magic of a critical realism) exhibition. The Argentine writer Julio **Cortázar** dedicated one of his stories, 'Reunión en círculo rojo' (Meeting in a Red Circle), to the work of Borges, and the critic Marta **Traba** wrote several articles about him.

He has always been involved with the socio-political reality in which he lived; his images represent archetypal figures charged with an intense violence. He has also produced short films and has been involved with a number of artistic and literary groups. After the experience of working for three years on the group project, *Imagen de Caracas* (Image of Caracas) (since 1965), which presented a critical reading of the country's official history through various kilometres of filmed scenes, in black and white as well as colour, – which the public observed from the centre of a large octagonal space – Borges began to produce pictures whose themes and purposes explicitly invited the spectator to take a critical view of the surrounding reality. *Esperando a...* (Waiting for...) is the first of a series of representations of the realities of power, in which a series of figures sit in hierarchical order in an official drawing room.

In recent years Borges has been involved in very important work in the prisons of Caracas, where he has organized cultural activities and prisoners' support groups. There is now a Jacobo Borges Museum in the west of Caracas (since 1995).

Further reading

Esteva-Grillet, R. (1984) *Siete artistas venezolanos del siglo XX*, Mérida: Museo de Arte Moderno.

ALICIA RÍOS

Borges, Jorge Luis

b. 1899, Buenos Aires, Argentina; d. 1986, Geneva, Switzerland

Writer

The most influential Latin American writer of the twentieth century, Borges revolutionized the practice of the essay and the short story. His family (his parents and sister, the painter Norah **Borges**) spent the years of the First World War in Geneva, where he mastered German, French and Latin; English was the first language of his father and paternal grandmother, and the language of his first readings. His early work, in the *ultraísta* avant-garde movement that began in Spain in the early 1920s, was an urban poetry much influenced by German expressionism that sought intense and bare feeling. By the time some of these poems were collected in his first book, *Fervor de Buenos Aires* (Fervor for Buenos Aires) (1923), Borges was distancing himself from the European avant-garde. His initial book of essays, *Inquisiciones* (Inquisitions) (1925), explored philosophical themes and metaphor; it was followed by two more books of essays, *El tamaño de mi esperanza* (The Extent of My Hope) (1926) and *El idioma de los argentinos* (The Argentine Language) (1928), which were largely concerned with **criollismo** and **cultural nationalism**. Two other books of poetry, *Luna de enfrente* (Moon Across the Way) (1926) and *Cuaderno San Martín* (San Martín Copybook) (1929), expressed Borges's search for a philosophical poetry, and one that included a reflection on Argentine national culture and the urban space. These concerns also animated his biography of the Buenos Aires poet Evaristo Carriego (1930).

Apart from a few minor experiments in the 1920s, he began exploring short narrative in an audacious cultural supplement he edited with Ulises Petit de Murat in 1933–4, the *Revista Multicolor de los Sábados*, for Natalio **Botana**'s newspaper **Crítica**. These portraits of murderers, gangsters, impostors and pirates were collected in 1935 as *Historia universal de la infamia* (Universal History of Infamy), a book that also includes his first person narrative of a Buenos Aires thug, the famous 'Hombre de la esquina rosada' (Man on Pink Corner). In 1936, he published a review of an apocryphal detective novel (supposedly published in Bombay); this text, 'El acercamiento a Almotásim' (The Approach to Al-Mu'tasim) inaugurated his experiments with **crime fiction** and with a new hybrid genre, somewhere between the essay and the short story (the *ficción*). The latter exploration led to two stories that have fascinated readers since their first publication: 'Pierre Menard, autor del Quijote' (Pierre Menard, Author of Don Quixote) (1939) and 'Tlön, Uqbar, Orbis Tertius' (1940). Startling examples of a new way of reading and writing, these texts were eventually collected in *Ficciones* (Fictions) (1944), along with several famous detective stories. The following collection of stories, *El Aleph* (The Aleph) (1949), continued Borges's exploration of imaginary worlds, labyrinths, time, and the aventures of reading.

Besides his work in *Crítica*, Borges also published hundreds of reviews in the popular family magazine *El Hogar*, mostly between 1936 and 1939, and thousands of articles, book reviews and film reviews in magazines like *Sur* and in newspapers like *La Nación* and *La Prensa*. Always concerned with popular culture and with political questions, he expressed himself on many aspects of Argentine and Latin American culture, as well as on a bewildering variety of literary and philosophical figures from around the world. The quintessential book of Borges's learned essays is *Otras inquisiciones* (Other Inquisitions) (1952): playful, paradoxical, these essays range widely in their references, culminating in epigrammatic, often ironic, finales. If the stories of *Ficciones* and *El Aleph* explore erudite philosophical or literary problems, so the essays of *Otras inquisiciones* often have a narrative turn, telling fascinating and tantalizing stories.

Borges's work of the 1940s and 1950s was complemented by a number of important polemical anthologies. The ***Antología de la literatura fantástica*** (Anthology of Fantastic Literature) (1940), edited with Adolfo **Bioy Casares** and Silvina **Ocampo**, was an oblique attack on the social realist tradition in Latin American writing (see **socialist realism**), suggesting that the writer's first obligation was to tell interesting and challenging stories. The same three collaborators also produced an *Antología poética argentina* (Argen-

tine Poetic Anthology) (1941), while Borges and Bioy edited several anthologies of **crime fiction** and gauchesque poetry (see **gaucho**), and directed a very successful series of detective novels (mostly translated from English) for the Buenos Aires publisher Emecé.

In 1955, about the time of the fall of Juan Domingo **Perón**, whose government Borges had vociferously opposed, Borges lost most of his eyesight and was no longer able to read; ironically, as he was to comment in his 'Poema de los dones' (Poem of the Gifts), it was at this moment that he was named director of the National Library, a post he held until 1969. The need to dictate produced a series of changes in Borges's writing: he returned to poetry, particularly to traditional forms like the sonnet and to traditional meters, as they were easier to remember and then to dictate. Similarly, the stories he was to write in the latter part of his career had a less dense and bookish character, often aspiring to the direct quality that he admired in Kipling's early *Plain Tales from the Hills*. The most significant books of his later career are *El hacedor* (The Maker) (short prose and poems, 1960), *Elogio de la sombra* (In Praise of Darkness) (short prose and poems, 1969), *El informe de Brodie* (Brodie's Report) (stories, 1970), and *El libro de arena* (The Book of Sand) (stories, 1975). His numerous later publications also include an unusual book of travel writing by a blind traveller, *Atlas* (1984).

Borges's impact on the world of letters has been significant, though often resisted (particularly by younger Latin American writers). The work of **Cortázar**, **Piglia**, **Saer** and numerous others is in constant dialogue with Borges, as has also been the case outside of Latin America in the writings of Robbe-Grillet (France), Pynchon (USA), Ben Jelloun (Morocco), Rushdie (India and the UK), Shammas (Israel) and many more. Borges has also been a favourite reading for literary theorists from Gérard Genette to John Frow, particularly for his ideas that undermine a romantic notion of authorship and originality. The critical bibliography on Borges is by far the most extensive that exists on any Latin American writer, and continues to grow in an almost alarming way. He has been translated into countless languages; for the centenary of his birth, new English translations of his stories, selected poems and selected non-fiction were published.

Further reading

Borges, J.L. (1998) *Collected Fictions*, New York: Viking.

—— (1999) *Selected Non-Fictions*, New York: Viking.

—— (1999) *Selected Poems*, New York: Viking.

Balderston, D. (1993) *Out of Context: Historical Reference and the Representation of Reality in Borges*, Durham: Duke University Press.

Dunham, L. and Ivask, I. (eds) (1971) *The Cardinal Points of Borges*, Norman: University of Oklahoma Press.

Fishburn, E. (ed.) (1998) *Borges and Europe Revisited*, London: University of London/Institute of Latin American Studies.

Molloy, S. (1994) *Signs of Borges*, Durham: Duke University Press.

Sarlo, B. (1993) *Jorge Luis Borges: A Writer on the Edge*, London: Verso.

DANIEL BALDERSTON

Borges, Norah

b. 1901, Buenos Aires, Argentina; d. 1998, Buenos Aires

Artist

Norah Borges was a painter and illustrator best known for her illustrations in important Argentine avant-garde magazines such as *Prisma* (1921–2), *Proa* (1922) and *Martín Fierro* (1924–7). Her work was exhibited several times in the late 1920s, along with that of the better-known **Xul Solar**, in the salons of Buenos Aires. She and Solar are the only visual artists associated with the Argentine literary avant-garde of this period. Borges was the sister of writer Jorge Luis **Borges** (she illustrated the cover of his first book, *Fervor de Buenos Aires* (Buenos Aires Fervour) (1925)) and wife of author and critic Guillermo de Torre.

GABRIEL PEREZ-BARREIRO

Borghetti, Renato

b. 1965, Porto Alegre, Rio Grande do Sul, Brazil

Singer

With a reputation as something of a rebel within the world of gaúcho traditionalist music (see **gaúcho culture**), Borghetti is a master of the gaita ponto or accordion. His style, which breaks radically with traditional accordion styles in southern Brazil, is marked by the bandoneón (see **accordion and bandoneón**) style of the late Argentine master Astor **Piazzola**, himself an innovator within his tradition who incorporated some of the spirit of **jazz** improvisation. Borghetti's repertoire includes songs he wrote himself (as in the case of much of the *Borghetti* album of 1991) but also songs by leading composers of the gaúcho traditionalists like Antonio Augusto Fagundes. His album covers (and titles like *Gauderiando* and *Gaúcho*) show him in traditionalist gaúcho garb, sometimes on horseback, which suggests an attempted *rapprochement* with the gaúcho traditionalists.

DANIEL BALDERSTON

Bortnik, Aída

b. 1938, Buenos Aires, Argentina

Screenwriter

Her first film, *La Tregua* (The Truce) (Sergio **Renan**, 1974), was based on a novel by Mario **Benedetti**. She later wrote the script for *La historia oficial* (The Official Version), Luis **Puenzo**'s 1985 film about the children of those who disappeared during the military regimes, and the only Argentine film to have won an Oscar. Her script for Puenzo's production *The Old Gringo* (1989) was based on a novel by Carlos **Fuentes**. In the 1990s she wrote the script for two very commercially successful films: *Tango feroz* (Fierce Tango) (1993) and *Caballos salvajes* (Wild Horses) (1995), both directed by Marcelo Piñeyro.

PAULA RODRÍGUEZ MARINO

Boscana, Lucy

b. 1915, Mayagüez, Puerto Rico

Actress

In spite of her numerous appearances on television, Lucy Boscana is first and foremost a stage actress, often regarded as the first lady of the Puerto Rican theatre. Her career has spanned several decades, beginning with radio plays in the 1930s. Boscana has excelled in playing strong-willed characters, most memorably as Doña Gabriela in René **Marqués**'s *La carreta* (The Oxcart), a role she has played repeatedly since its first production in 1953. Other critically acclaimed performances include Martha in *Who's Afraid of Virginia Woolf* and Eleonor in *The Lion in Winter*. She also founded the theatre company Tablado Puertorriqueño.

VíCTOR F. TORRES

Bosch, Juan

b. 1909, La Vega, Dominican Republic

Writer and politician

An acknowledged master of the Latin American short story, Juan Bosch published his first collection, *Camino real* (Royal Highway), in 1933. The stories describe the life of the peasants of the Cibao region of the Dominican Republic, among whom he had spent his childhood. *Dos pesos de agua* (Two Pesos-Worth of Water) (1941), by contrast, addressed other themes and introduced an element of fantasy, though the writer's social concerns were always present. *Ocho cuentos* (Eight Stories) (1947) includes 'Luis Pié', which tells the tragic story of a Haitian immigrant worker in a sugar mill in the Dominican Republic. His *Cuentos escritos en el exilio* (Stories Written in Exile) (1962) and *Más cuentos escritos en el exilio* (More Stories) (1964) included some hitherto unpublished writings as well as other stories rewritten in a standard Spanish accessible to readers not familiar with the accents of Cibao. There were also two novels, one published in 1936, *La mañosa* (The Trickster), the other in 1975, *El oro y la paz* (Gold and Peace).

In addition to his literary work, Juan Bosch published several volumes of essays on politics, history and sociology – they included *Composición social dominicana* (Social Structure of the Dominican Republic) (1974), *De Cristóbal Colón a Fidel Castro: El Caribe frontera imperial* (From Columbus to Castro: The Caribbean as the Frontier of Empire) (1970), *Judas Iscariote, el calumniado* (Judas Iscariot: A Man Much Maligned) (1955) and *Trujillo: Causas de una tiranía sin ejemplo* (Trujillo: Causes of an Unparalleled Tyranny) (1961).

While recognized as a fine writer, Juan Bosch also played an extraordinarily significant role in Dominican political life. Exiled in Cuba during the **Trujillo** dictatorship, Bosch was one of the founders of the Partido Revolucionario Dominicano (PRD – Dominican Revolutionary Party) in 1941. He helped to prepare the Luperón invasion to overthrow the dictatorship in 1949; returning to the country in 1962, he was elected president in the first free elections since 1930. Seven months later, overthrown in a military *coup*, he was driven into exile once again.

On 24 April 1965, a civil war broke out over the demand for a return to the constitution approved under the Bosch government; the result of the war was the second US invasion of the Dominican Republic this century. Bosch stood again as a presidential candidate in the elections that took place under the gaze of the US Marines in 1966, but failed to win a majority; since then, he has repeatedly presented his candidature again in a series of elections beset by fraud and won in each case by Dr Joaquín **Balaguer**. In 1973 he left the PRD and founded the Partido de la Liberación Dominicana (Dominican Liberation Party), which entered government (1996–2000) under the presidency of Dr Leonel Fernández.

Further reading

Fernández Olmos, M. (1992) *La cuentística de Juan Bosch*, Santo Domingo: Alfa y Omega.

Montero, J. (1986) *La cuentística dominicana*, Santo Domingo: Biblioteca Nacional.

FERNANDO VALERIO-HOLGUÍN

Bosco, João

b. 1946, Ponte Nova, Minas Gerais, Brazil

Singer–songwriter

A leading **MPB** artist, most of Bosco's early work (1972–85) was written with Aldir Blanc, a lyricist noted for social satire. They reworked sentimental popular song forms from the 1940s–1950s and developed a modern brand of **samba** focused on life in working-class neighbourhoods in Rio de Janeiro. Their most memorable composition was 'O bêbado e a equilibrista' (The Drunkard and the Tightrope Walker), which became the hymn of the 1979 pro-amnesty movement. Bosco established himself as a solo performer in the 1980s.

CHARLES A. PERRONE

Bosi, Alfredo

b. 1936, São Paulo, Brazil

Critic

Bosi is Professor of Brazilian Literature at the University of São Paulo, and is considered one of Brazil's major literary critics. His writings seek out the humanist sense of art and the connections between poetry and philosophy. His best known work, the *História concisa da literatura brasileira* (Concise History of Brazilian Literature) (1970), traces the course of Brazilian writing from its origins to the 1990s. *Dialéctica da colonização* (Dialectics of Colonization) (1992) is an encyclopedic study of Brazilian culture and colonization.

MILTON HATOUM

Boskaljon, Rudolf Frederik Willen (Shon Dòdò)

b. 1887, Curaçao, Netherlands Antilles; d. 1970, Curaçao

Composer and conductor

In 1939, Boskaljon founded the Curaçaosch Philharmonisch Orkest (Curaçao Philharmonic Orchestra), which he was to conduct for more than twenty-five years. On Latin American tours, numerous internationally renowned conductors and musicians stopped in Curaçao to perform with Boskaljon's orchestra. As a composer, he is especially known for the symphony *Curaçao*, for which he adopted folk songs and tunes. He is also the author of study of the history of musical life in Curaçao, *Honderd jaar muziekleven op Curaçao* (One Hundred Years of Musical Life in Curaçao) (1958).

AART G. BROEK

bossa nova

The 'new way' in Brazilian popular music was invented in the mid-1950s by a young generation of white middle-class musicians based in Rio de Janeiro's affluent **Copacabana** quarter. Associated initially and most famously with songwriter Tom **Jobim**, singer/guitarist João **Gilberto** and lyricist Vinicius de **Moraes**, it was one of many avant-garde (see **avant-garde in Latin America**) innovations which expressed the postwar optimism of Juscelino **Kubitschek**'s modernising administration.

Bossa nova's classicism gave a voice to this spirit of cosmopolitan sophistication by combining several elements in a deceptively simple but highly crafted form: a 'cool', minimalist style of performance and instrumentation typified by João Gilberto, alone with his guitar and his unaffected vocal delivery; an intimate, colloquial lyricism full of elegance, irony and a kind of erotic wisdom; and a seamless integration of subtle, unpredictable melodic phrasing, enriched dissonant harmonies and extended, syncopated rhythmic patterns. As such, bossa nova broke completely with the loudly vulgar sentimentalism and nationalism of the tangos (see **tango**), boleros (see **bolero**) and sambas (see **samba**) which were the postwar musical legacy of **populism**.

But bossa nova did not appear out of a vacuum. Some have recognised its unpredictable rhythmic syncopation as a refinement of certain percussive patterns 'hidden' beneath the strong binary pulse of traditional samba drumming. Meanwhile, the style's innovative instrumental techniques, altered harmonies and chromatic melodies were prefigured in the modernist compositions of **Villa-Lobos** and in the work of guitarists Garoto and Luiz Bonfá and composer-pianists Johnny Alf and João Donato, as well as finding echoes in contemporary US West Coast jazz.

Such precedents and affinities could not have prepared Brazilian audiences, though, for the startling impact of João Gilberto's 1958 single release of 'Desafinado' (Off-key) and '**Chega de saudade**' (Can't Take this Longing). By 1962, when the world famous '**Garota de Ipanema**' (The Girl from Ipanema) was composed, bossa nova had captured 50 per cent of the local recording market from the recently imported rock and roll. After a 1962 concert at New York's Carnegie Hall, the style was enthusiastically taken up by North American jazz musicians like Stan Getz, Charlie Byrd and Gary Burton, and thereafter became one of Latin America's most successful musical exports.

At the same time, a new generation of left-wing musicians, such as Nara **Leão**, Carlos Lyra, Baden **Powell** and Edu **Lobo**, sought to inject a sense of social criticism and political protest into the style by combining it with local elements from shanty town samba and Northeastern Brazilian–African traditions. Despite this shift away from its classical origins, though, Tom Jobim, Vinicius de Moraes and a succession of other composers continued to add to a rich repertoire of popular and jazz standards, assuring the permanence of the bossa nova idiom internationally and laying the foundations for the fertile tradition of Brazilian songwriting that would become known as **MPB**.

See also: Gilberto, Astrud; Latin American music, export of; Regina, Elis;

Further reading:

Castro, R. (1990) *Chega de saudade: a história e as histórias da Bossa Nova*, São Paulo: Companhia das Letras.

McGowan, C. and Pessanha, R. (1998) *The Brazilian Sound: Samba, Bossa Nova and the Popular Music of Brazil*, Temple University Press, ch.3.

Treece, D. (1997) 'Guns and roses: bossa nova and Brazil's music of popular protest, 1958–68', *Popular Music* 16(1): 1–29.

DAVID TREECE

Botana, Natalio

b. 1937, Buenos Aires, Argentina

Historian and political scientist

Botana, nephew of the publisher and journalist of the same name, has written from a conservative point of view on republicanism in mid-nineteenth century Argentina, political freedom in history, and Argentine politics between 1880 and 1916. Affiliated to the **Instituto Di Tella** of Buenos Aires as a researcher and faculty member, Botana received his doctorate in Political Science in Belgium in 1967. He also served on the editorial board of the conservative Catholic magazine *Criterio*. His numerous awards include a Guggenheim scholarship (1979) and the First Prize for National History for his work produced between 1982 and 1985.

THOMAS EDSALL

Botana, Natalio

b. 1888, Sarandí de Yi, Uruguay; d. 1941, Buenos Aires, Argentina

Publisher and journalist

An editor and journalist with a sharp instinct for the popular mood, Botana founded and directed the mass circulation daily *Crítica* from 1913 until his death. He first moved to Buenos Aires to work on the magazine *PBT* and the dailies *Última Hora* and *La Razón*. His ability to sense the spirit of the times, such as interest in new technology and the development of mass readership, made *Crítica* the most widely circulated paper of its day.

THOMAS EDSALL

botanical gardens

The oldest and most beautiful botanical garden in Latin America is the one in Rio de Janeiro, founded in 1808 and developed by Emperor Pedro II. With its dramatic rows of royal palms and over 5,000 varieties of plants, including an extensive collection of aquatic plants, Rio de Janeiro's botanical garden is a beautiful spot much frequented by birds and people. Buenos Aires has a beloved but rather neglected botanical garden inhabited by hundreds of cats; it features beautiful trees. Caracas has a fine tropical botanical garden next to the **Ciudad Universitaria**, with dramatic views of the city and interesting sculpture. Other cities with botanical gardens of note include Port of Spain (Trinidad), Belém do Pará (Brazil) and Medellín (Colombia).

DANIEL BALDERSTON

Botero, Fernando

b. 1932, Medellín, Colombia

Artist

Botero's hallmarks are the squat, dumpy figures reflecting a small-town Colombian bourgeoisie, satirizing those with power or at least with pomposity: politicians, military men, clerics and ladies of leisure. The compositions often refer back to Old Masters and more recent artists, like Cézanne.

At the age of twelve an uncle enrolled Botero in a toreadors' school, and he began to sketch bulls and horses in the ring. In 1948, he submitted two watercolours to an Exposición de Pintores Antioqueños (Exhibition of the Artists of Antioquia), began illustrating the magazine section of the daily *El Colombiano*, and was expelled from school for publishing an article on the nonconformity of Picasso's art. He cited the quattrocento as his inspiration.

In 1951 Botero moved to Bogotá and had his first solo show at the Leo Matiz gallery. In 1952 he won the second prize in the Ninth Colombian Artists' Salon (for *Frente al mar* (Facing the Sea)), travelled to Europe and enrolled at the San Fernando Royal Fine Arts Academy in Madrid, and went then to the Academia San Marcos in Florence. The former gave him Goya and Velázquez at the Prado; the latter Roberto Longhi's classes on the Renaissance. In 1953 he was stating his preference for the Louvre over the Musée d'Art Moderne; Piero della Francesca's frescoes in Arezzo revealed to him 'the equal importance awarded to colour and form'.

In 1955 he showed his new work at the Bogotá National Library, where it was very poorly received. He moved on to Mexico, forming friendships with the similarly cosmopolitan artists José Luis **Cuevas** and Rufino **Tamayo**. Botero painted his first *Still Life with Mandolin*, after Braque, playing with perspective by shrinking the instrument's sound hole and inflating its bulk. In 1957 he held a one-man show at the Pan American Union in Washington, and encountered abstract expressionism during his first stay in New York. In 1958 he returned to live in Colombia, teaching at the Fine Arts school at the National University in Bogotá until 1960, and finding a place in the fourth prestigious Bienale in São Paulo in 1959 (see **Bienale de São Paulo**). He painted *Mona Lisa Aged 12* and then, in New York in 1960, obtained a Guggenheim award with *The Battle of the Arch-Devil*. He mingled with de Kooning, Franz Kline, Mark Rothko and Red Grooms, and developed what became his characteristic and most recognizable subjects from among the bourgeoisie of his own country.

After a period of experimentation mixing oils with collage, in 1964 Botero won first prize in the first Colombian Salon for Young Artists organized by the Museum of Modern Art for *Apples*. He then began his series on *Rubens and his Wife*, also adding to his repertoire of seductive still lifes – with a brilliance and sensuality worthy of **Kahlo** – which were to recur as erotic elements in later paintings of brothels and odalisques. In 1966 he had solo shows in the Staatliche Kunsthalle at Baden-Baden, and at the Milwaukee Art Museum and in the New York Center for Inter-American Relations in 1969.

In 1973 he moved from the USA to Paris and started working in sculpture, particularly bronze, marble and cast resin figures of animals, humans and still lifes. Beginning in the 1970s, retrospectives of his work (paintings and sculptures) have been held throughout the world, including in 1995 with an exhibition down the avenue past Madrid's Retiro Gardens, and in 1996 in the garden walkways of the Israel Museum, Jerusalem.

Despite winning prestigious medals including the Order of Andrés Bello from the President of Venezuela (1976) and the Boyacá Cross from the Colombian government of Antioquia for services to his homeland, Botero's work has become increasingly personal. In 1974 he created a memorial to his young son, who died in an accident in 1972, with a donation of sixteen works of art to hang in a Sala Pedro Botero. In 1978 he acquired the building of the former Académie Julian in Paris, splitting it into two studios, one for his painting and the other for his sculpture. In 1983 he was nominated roving ambassador for UNESCO by Colombian President Belisario Betancur, and began dividing his working year between Paris, New York, Tuscany and Bogotá. This post was a strange and impressive accolade for a national artist whose most famous (and arguably quintessential) portrait is that of *The Presidential Family*, showing archetypes of the Colombian oligarchy, including a cardinal, a general, a president plus plump wife, child, mother-in-law and pet cat (and a fox fur glowering vehemently over the wife's arm), set against the threateningly smoking peaks of Andean volcanoes, with a snake flickering inauspiciously in the foreground. The characters do not drift into caricature, although their swollen state indicates voracity, pretentiousness and decadence; a reference to Botero's earliest formative influences in Goya and Velásquez.

Further reading

Paquet, M. (1983) *Botero*, Paris: L'Autre Musée.
Gabriel, G.J. (1962) *La pintura en Colombia*, Mexico and Buenos Aires.

AMANDA HOPKINSON

boto

A kind of freshwater dolphin, the *boto* is part of the oral tradition of Brazil's **Amazonia** region. The *boto* transforms himself into a beautiful, tall, white,

well-dressed young man who appears at night and seduces women, then returns to the river (and his original form) before dawn. In its female version, the *boto* is one of a myriad of Brazilian water myths like Iara, Mãe D'água and Iemanjá. It inspired the modernist poem *Cobra Norato* by Raúl Bopp, the 1980s political satire *A Resistível Ascensão do Boto Tucuxi* (The Resistible Rise of the Boto Tucuxi) by Márcio **Souza**, and the film *Ele, o Boto* (1991) by Walter **Lima** Jr.

VIVALDO SANTOS

Boulton, Alfredo

b. 1908, Caracas, Venezuela; d. 1995, Caracas

Historian, art critic, photographer

It is as a pioneer of photography as an art form in Venezuela that Boulton made his most original contribution. His work was an important source of inspiration for subsequent generations of Venezuelan photographers. Born of a wealthy family, Boulton built up a vast art collection, and his extensive research in the field resulted in his three volume *Historia de la pintura venezolana* (History of Venezuelan Painting) (1964–72) and many works on individual painters, the best known being his study of Armando **Reverón**. Boulton was a major participant in many cultural organizations, and, from 1962 to 1977, was editor of the *Boletín histórico*, a major journal of Latin American history.

MARK DINNEEN

Bouterse, Desi

b. 1945, Suriname

Military strongman

In 1980 a military *coup* against the government of newly (1974) independent Suriname brought Desi Bouterse to power; his regime ruled by decree and systematically murdered political opponents and critics. In 1982 it put down the first of a series of rebellions by **maroons** (or Bush Negroes) with extreme brutality. When the USA and the Netherlands reacted by suspending economic and military co-operation, Bouterse flirted briefly with Cuba. Economic crisis followed, coupled with a new maroon rising in 1986. Free elections called in 1987 brought in a civilian government, but Bouterse and the military retained much of their power. In 1990 he staged another *coup*, holding power for a year until an elected coalition government was returned under Ronal Venetiaan, who signed peace accords with the maroon and Amerindian insurgents. Bouterse left the army in 1993. Yet Venetiaan's economic policies were deemed too favourable to the multinationals and Bouterse's NDP party won the 1996 elections; his nominees then occupied key military and political posts. US drug agencies have called for Bouterse's extradition on the grounds of his involvement in cocaine trafficking, for which Suriname is a convenient transit point.

MIKE GONZALEZ

boxing

Latin American boxing entered the world scene on 14 September 1923, when Argentine heavyweight Luis Alberto **Firpo** was knocked out in the second round of a title fight with Jack Dempsey of the USA, in what has often been called 'the fight of the century' because the Argentine was knocked so hard he flew out of the ring. But in 1929, bantamweight Al 'Panama' Brown from Panama became the first world champion of the region. This gave other Latin American boxers the courage to go to the USA to fight for world titles, and several met with success: Cuba's **Kid Chocolate** (featherweight and junior lightweight) in 1931, Mexico's Battling Shaw (junior welterweight) in 1933, and Puerto Rico's Sixto **Escobar** (bantam) in 1936. After the Second World War, the outstanding fighters and world champions were Cuba's **Kid Gavilán** (welterweight), Argentina's Pascual Pérez (flyweight) and Mexican Raúl **Macías** (bantamweight).

The region continued to stand out in lower weight divisions, and in the 1960s there were more world champions in Panama's Ismael Laguna (lightweight), Cuba's José Nápoles and Luis Manuel Rodríguez (welterweight), Argentina's Nicolino Loche (junior welterweight), Puerto Rico's

José Torres (light heavyweight) and Carlos Ortiz (lightweight), Mexico's Vicente Saldívar (featherweight) and Rubén Olivares (featherweight and bantamweight), Brazil's Eder Jofre (bantamweight and featherweight) and Venezuela's Carlos Hernández (junior welterweight). On most occasions, however, these boxers had to fight for their titles and defend them abroad, as the general economic situation in the region resulted in few title fights being staged there.

The 1970s were the best years, led by Argentina's Carlos **Monzón** with a record number of defences of his middleweight title, Panama's Roberto **Durán**, the only Latin American to hold titles in four divisions, Nicaragua's Alexis **Argüello** and Puerto Rico's Wilfredo Gomez, who both held titles in three divisions, and Colombia's Antonio 'Kid Pambele' **Cervantes** (junior welterweight), perhaps the best ever in his category. Other title holders were Puerto Rico's Wilfred Benítez (in three categories), Mexico's Miguel Cano (flyweight), Panama's Eusebio Pedroza (featherweight), Venezuela's Luis Estaba (mini-flyweight), Mexico's Carlos Zárate (bantamweight), Alfonso Zamora (bantamweight), Pipino Cuevas (welterweight) and Lupe Pintor (bantamweight), Venezuela's Bertulio González (flyweight) and, the only weight exception, Argentina's Víctor Galindez (light heavyweight).

More recently Mexico has been prominent with world champions Salvador Sánchez (featherweight), Julio César **Chávez** (three divisions), Gilberto Román (super-flyweight), Humberto González (mini-flyweight) and Daniel Zaragoza (bantamweight). Others include Puerto Rico's Wilfredo Vázquez (three divisions), Argentine Santos Laciar (flyweight), Panama's Hilario Zapata (flyweight) and Colombia's Miguel Lora (bantamweight).

See also: Gatica

ERIC WEIL

Boytler Rososky, Arcady

b. 1895, Moscow, Russia; d. 1965, Mexico City

Film-maker, actor

A comic actor, Boytler directed several short films

starring himself before 1917. After the fall of the Tsar, he emigrated to Germany where he made two more silent shorts. His first full length feature, *El buscador de fortuna* (The Gold Digger) (1927) was made in Chile, before moving to New York and then to Mexico, where his career began in earnest. He made eight feature films between 1932 and 1944. His third, *La mujer del puerto* (The Woman of the Port) (1933) is a classic of early Mexican cinema.

PATRICIA TORRES SAN MARTÍN

Bracho, Julio

b. 1909, Durango, Mexico; d. 1987, Mexico City

Actor, film-maker

Bracho made his film debut in the 1941 comedy *Ay qué tiempos Don Simon* (Those Were the Days...). With its critical and commercial success he became the highest paid Mexican director, making super-productions like *Historia de un gran amor* (Story of a Great Love) (1942) and urban dramas like *Distinto amanecer* (A Different Dawn) (1943). In 1960 Bracho made *La sombra del caudillo* (Shadow of a Tyrant) based on the novel by Martín Luis **Guzmán**, which remains banned and has become legendary. His last films included melodramas and a filmed biography of muralist José Clemente **Orozco** (see **muralism**).

PATRICIA TORRES SAN MARTÍN

Braga, Sonia

b. 1951, Maringá, Paraná, Brazil

Actress

Perhaps the best-recognized Brazilian actress, nationally identified with the sensual character of Jorge **Amado**'s *Gabriela* (she starred in both *telenovela* (see **telenovelas**) (1975) and film (Bruno **Barreto**, 1983) versions), her career began with a small part on a local children's television show at age fourteen. By eighteen, Braga was working in the theatre and created a sensation by taking off her clothes in a Rio de Janeiro production of *Hair*.

She was also working for TV **Globo**, and her roles in *telenovelas* such as *Dancin' Days* (1978) made her into the national sex symbol of the 1970s, a position later augmented by her sensual roles in films like Neville d'Almeida's *A dama da lotação* (The Lady in the Carriage) (1978) and Arnaldo **Jabor**'s *Eu te amo* (I Love You) (1980). Her sensuality and subtle comedic talent came to the attention of international audiences with the title role of Bruno Barreto's extraordinarily successful *Doña Flor e seus dois maridos* (Doña Flor and Her Two Husbands) (1976) and her English-language debut in Héctor **Babenco**'s much-awarded *Kiss of the Spider Woman* (1985) (see *El **beso de la mujer araña***). She moved to the USA, but *The Milagro Beanfield War* (1988) and *Moon over Parador* (1988) – as well as a failed romance with Robert Redford – seemed to paralyse her career. In the 1990s she returned to Brazil, working again in television and starring in Carlos **Diegues**'s *Tieta* (1996), another Amado adaptation. As described by a critic, 'she has a silver nitrate soul that suffuses films with a brilliance that few stars besides Marilyn [Monroe] have ever had'.

ILENE GOLDMAN

brain drain

The term 'brain drain' refers to the massive movement abroad, often for long periods, of **intellectuals**, scientists and professionals in particular historical contexts. In Latin America, this flight of talent had two different causes: on the one hand, migrations impelled by the political persecution of intellectuals and scientists by authoritarian governments; on the other, so-called 'economic migration' caused by the lack of job prospects or the absence of satisfactory conditions for the development of professional practices. Political migrations have always occurred in Latin America, but during the 1960s and 1970s the phenomenon became more significant because of its scale, as a majority of intellectuals and scientists (as well as members of political organizations, trade union activists and popular leaders) were forced to leave their respective countries when military governments took power. Many of these exiles returned when democracy was restored, but many more, having established themselves in their new home, remained abroad.

Economic migrations are harder to measure over time, but the numbers involved increased from the 1960s onwards, and grew particularly during the 1980s, in the framework of a crisis that affected all the countries of Latin America, and which CEPAL has called the 'lost decade'. In the particular case of scientists, these migrations tended to take the form of a study trip (for postgraduate or research purposes), after which the researchers stayed on for an indefinite period in the 'host country' instead of returning home. There could be several reasons for this – the explicit policy of many developed countries of retaining highly qualified professionals, for example, or the migrant's own conviction that conditions in the home country would be difficult, that resources would be scarce, that centres of excellence were more accessible from the developed country and that it also offered the best conditions for personal development.

In general, economic migrants have travelled to Western Europe or the USA. Political migrants, on the other hand, have also moved to other countries within the region, some of which, like Mexico, have welcomed many Latin American exiles.

See also: exile

Further reading

Oteiza E. (1971) *El drenaje de talentos*, Buenos Aires: Paidos.

—— (1996) 'Drenaje de cerebros. Marco histórico y conceptual', *Redes* 3(7): 101–20.

Oszlak O. and Caputo D. (1973) *La emigración del personal médico de América Latina a Estados Unidos. Una interpretación alternativa*, Buenos Aires, Organización Mundial de Salud (WHO).

PABLO KREIMER

Brand, Dionne

b. 1953, Guayaguayare, Trinidad

Poet

Brand was one of the Caribbean intellectuals and artists who went to Grenada to contribute their talents to the revolution led by Maurice **Bishop**'s **New Jewel Movement**. As a poet, she is fascinated by history and its implications and often counters dominant male perspectives with feminist/black woman/neo-colonial perspectives. Her publications include *Chronicles of the Hostile Sun* (1984), *Winter Epigrams and Epigrams to Ernesto Cardenal in Defense of Claudia* (1983), *Primitive Offensive* (1982), *Earth Magic* (1980) and *'Fore Day Morning* (1978).

FUNSO AIYEJINA

Brandão, Ignácio de Loyola

b. 1936, Araraquara, Brazil

Writer

As a journalist in the late 1950s, Brandão wrote on political movements and social issues in Brazil for newspapers and magazines. His first novel, *Bebel que a cidade comeu* (The Bebel the City Ate), appeared in 1968 at the height of the military dictatorship. *Zero*, an experimental novel denouncing military repression, appeared first in Italy; when published in Brazil in 1974, it was immediately banned by the military. Brandão's fiction portrays Brazil's social and political reality with slang and journalistic language, different narrative genres, and the disruption of chronological time.

CRISTINA FERREIRA-PINTO

Brasília

From its inauguration in 1960, the new capital city of Brazil gave dramatic expression to various political regimes. The old Federal District located in Rio de Janeiro could no longer accommodate the institutional demands of a national public power. Built as a monument, Brasília was to be the symbol of a nation. Internationally, it became representative of Brazil's modern architecture and design.

Projects for a new capital were not unheard of in Brazil; Belo Horizonte, founded in 1897, and Goiânia, built in 1933, arose in the same way. The first was designed to replace Ouro Preto, in Minas Gerais, the second to take the place of Goias Velho in Goias. Each responded to the demand for a work that would be worthy of a modern, geographically centralized state.

In Brasília's case, the demand was a long-standing one. The search for gold by the 'bandeirantes' had led to attempts to colonize the interior of the country since the seventeenth century. In the 1920s, Le Corbusier heard about the idea of building a new capital, but although he visited Brazil in 1929 and again in 1936 as a consultant for the project for the **Ministério da Educacão e Saúde** (Ministry of Education and Health) building, it was still too early to discuss the plan.

The idea became reality through the efforts of President Juscelino **Kubitschek**, elected in 1955, who had earlier sponsored the **Pampulha** project. In 1956 he created the Companhia Urbanizadora da Nova Capital (New Capital Construction Company), or NOVACAP, to organize the public competition open to all Brazilian architects called later that same year. The jury included representatives of the Brazilian Institute of Architects and the Engineers Association, as well as town planners from the USA, France and Britain. Oscar **Niemeyer** represented NOVACAP.

The project envisaged a population of 600,000. The site chosen was near the Lake Paranoá, a virtually flat area some 200 kilometres from Goiânia. Lake Paranoá is an artificial lake, just like the Pampultta Lake, which was built for the purspose of offering living conditions to the surroundings. An expanded network of interstate highways, a rail system and an airport would link Brasília to other centres.

The project chosen was simple. Lúcio **Costa** won with a simple sketch in the form of a cross which seemed to bless the city monument at the geographical centre of the national territory. The lines he drew barely went beyond marking the main roads and the sectoral division of the various activities set out in the original project, but it was a unified monument with a diversity of functions.

Four other prizes were awarded. The second went to the team of Ney Gonçalves, Milman e Rocha; third and fourth prizes went to the Rino Levi group and the **Roberto** brothers respectively.

Fifth place was shared by several groups. All the plans shared modernist assumptions such as the separation of functions, a hierarchical organization of transport and uniformity in the construction of living units. All envisaged the construction of a pilot project followed by satellite cities that would contain indiscriminate urban growth.

The new Brazilian capital, officially inaugurated on 21 April 1960, was ready to receive its new population, made up largely of civil servants. However, people came from every part of the country in search of a new life. By 1980, the city's population was double what had been envisioned. As the year 2000 approached, the city had 1,600,000 inhabitants and the original plan is now in urgent need of adaptation.

Brasília was declared a World Heritage Site (see **World Heritage Sites**) by UNESCO in 1987. Works by Niemeyer and others were added to Lúcio Costa's original plan. The network of super-blocks was soon occupied; however, the proposal to prevent segregation by socioeconomic class did not survive. The workers who helped build this great monument could not live in it, and the city-monument became an exclusive area. The satellite cities proliferated and quickly became dormitory suburbs. The Free City, now called Núcleo Bandeirantes, was the encampment of the workers who first occupied Brasília. The demographic explosion produced a mixed population from every part of the country and of varied cultural origin. Just as modern architecture has tended towards internationalization, so local culture began to develop similar characteristics.

The audacious plan bent to the needs of various regimes and movements. The repression that followed the military *coup* of 1964 did not inhibit the plan; the military found it an appropriate space for parades. In the 1980s, the transition from an authoritarian regime to democracy happened smoothly. The Diretas-Já Movement (Direct Elections Now) held rallies for the first time opposite the Square of the Three Powers, which had been built precisely with popular demonstrations in mind. Ironically, one of the mentors of the democratic process, President Tancredo Neves, died on the city's anniversary, 21 April 1985. His funeral procession brought multitudes into the streets who filled the urban spaces of Brasília to capacity, and was watched by all Brazilians on live television. As if by magic, the empty urban scenario of the planned city was finally filled with people. The impeachment of President **Collor** de Mello in 1992 once again brought crowds into the square. The Cara-Pintadas (Painted Faces) occupied the space in their struggle against political corruption, and through the 1990s the Movimento dos Sem-Terra (Landless People's Movement) used the space to demand rights to occupy unused land. Democracy seemed to have taken control of the city.

Further reading

Bruand, Y. (1981) *Arquitetura contemporânea no Brasil*, São Paulo: Perspectiva.

Evenson, N. (1973) *Two Brazilian Capitals: Architecture and Urbanism in Rio de Janeiro and Brasília*, New Haven, CN: Yale University Press.

Holston, J. (1989) *The Modernist City: An Anthropological Critique of Brasília*, Chicago: Chicago University Press.

Vale, L.J. (1992) *Architecture, Power and National Identity*, New Haven, CN: Yale University Press.

MARIA MARTA CAMISASSA

Brathwaite, Kamau

b. 1930, Bridgetown, Barbados

Writer

Born at the height of the British colonial period, (Edward) Kamau Brathwaite studied history at Cambridge, then worked in Ghana as an education officer. African diaspora culture strongly informs his three-volume poem cycle *The Arrivants* (1973), first published as **Rights of Passage** (1967), *Masks* (1968) and *Islands* (1969). After early poems and plays (*Odale's Choice* (1967)), his poetic voice was already evident in the brilliant *Rights of Passage*.

Brathwaite's second trilogy, *Mother poem* (1977), *Sun Poem* (1982) and *X/Self* (1987) explored Barbados's significance as maternal and then as paternal source. In *X/Self*, an individual whose name registers the loss of his ancestral name is imaged as the complex confluence of West Indian history and culture. Brathwaite's historical and cultural writing and poetry speak closely to one another (*X/Self* has historical footnotes). With *The Folk Culture of Jamaican Slaves* (1969), *The Development of Creole Society in Jamaica* (1971), *Contradictory Omens* (1974) and *History of the Voice* (1984), Brathwaite has contributed immensely to Caribbean revisioning of history.

African-centred music, from ritual drum chants to the blues and **jazz** (*Black and Blues* (1995)), **reggae**, **calypso** and dub (see **dub poetry**) from the Americas, centrally informs Brathwaite's aesthetic which explores the relation of scribal and oral culture. His autobiographical *Barabajan Poems* (1994) uses 'video style', a computer-generated visual language. His reworking of Caliban and his mother Sycorax, from Shakespeare's *The Tempest*, offers the computer, icon of Western technology, as a trope of anti-colonial resistance and post-colonial creativity. Brathwaite's 'proems', most recently the major *Dreamstories* (1994), *Zea Mexican Diary* (1994) and *Trench Town Rock* (1994), combine the compression of the poem with the narrative of prose.

Brathwaite has published nineteen collections of poems, four major 'proems', two volumes of plays and eight volumes of cultural criticism, as well as academic books and many articles and essays. He won the Neustadt International Prize for Literature in 1994.

See also: nation language

Further reading

Brathwaite, D.M. (1986) *EKB: His Published Prose and Poetry 1948–1986*, Kingston: Savacou Co-operative.

Brown, S. (ed.) (1995) *The Art of Kamau Brathwaite*, Bridgend: Poetry Wales Press.

Rohlehr, G. (1981) *Pathfinder: Black Awakening in the Arrivants of Edward Kamau Brathwaite*, Tunapuna: Gordon Rohlehr.

World Literature Today (1994) 68(4): special issue, 'Kamau Brathwaite 1994: Neustadt International Prize for Literature'.

ELAINE SAVORY

Bratke, Oswaldo Arthur

b. 1907, Botucatu, Brazil; d. 1997, São
Paulo, Brazil

Architect

Twentieth-century Brazilian architecture owes a
great debt to Bratke, and above all the city of São
Paulo, where he implemented modernist ideas in a
series of residential projects. His architectural style
varied, passing through several phases until he
established his own style which incorporated
Brazilian elements and integrated residential
buildings into garden complexes combining ma-
sonry walls and stone pavements with concrete
structures. His pragmatism was fundamental; he
responded to whatever contemporary technology
had to offer with an eye to reducing construction
costs.

VIVALDO SANTOS

Bravo, Soledad

b. 1943, Logroño, La Rioja, Spain

Singer

Her versatile voice and skilful interpretations have
allowed Bravo to develop a broad repertoire going
from contemporary Spanish music (compositions
by Federico García Lorca, Joan Manuel Serrat and
Rafael Alberti), folk music of Venezuela and Latin
America (including songs by Alfredo **Zitarrosa**
and Atahualpa **Yupanqui**), to songs of the Cuban
nueva trova, Sephardic songs, Caribbean
rhythms with Willie **Colón** and contemporary
Brazilian songs by Chico **Buarque** and Caetano
Veloso as well as versions of **bossa nova** classics
like Vinicius de **Moraes**'s *Apelo*. Famous for her
performances of protest songs at the Central
University of Caracas in the 1960s, by the
beginning of the 1980s, she had turned her
attention to performing traditional boleros (see
bolero).

JORGE ROMERO LEÓN

Brazil

The largest, most populous and most geographically, ethnically and culturally diverse country of
Latin America. Eight and one-half million square
kilometres in size, it occupies the central eastern
half of the South American continent, between the
Amazon basin, the Atlantic coast and the cattle-
ranching plains of the River Plate. Its population of
some 160 million is now more than three-quarters
urbanized, with 43 per cent concentrated in the
more heavily industrialized southeast.

Brazil's unofficial code of racism makes census
statistics unreliable, but they suggest a distribution
of some 54 per cent white Brazilians, 6 per cent
'blacks', 0.6 per cent 'yellow-skinned' and 38.8 per
cent mixed race. This does not account for the
260,000 indigenous people speaking 170 different
languages and living in some 200 distinct tribes
whose lands, whether officially recognized or not,
represent something like one-tenth of the national
territory. Three and one-half million immigrants
arrived in the country this century, bringing with
them a whole range of cultural traditions from
Europe, the Middle East and Far East. Indeed,
arguably the single most important formative
influence on the country's cultural developments
has been the painful experience of physical and
social dislocation and the creative responses it has
produced, through new forms of community and
self-identification.

As the language of Brazil, Portuguese was
consolidated relatively late on in the colonial period,
and by the nineteenth century it had already, in
popular local usage, been shaped by the indigenous
and African vocabulary and inflections of its mainly
rural speakers. By the 1920s, the oral distinct-
iveness of **Brazilian Portuguese** had become a
touchstone for the artistic polemics within the
modernist movement (see **Brazilian modernism**)
in defence of an 'authentic' national-popular
culture. Its literary possibilities were explored first
by writers such as Mário de **Andrade** and Oswald
de **Andrade** and later, following the Second World
War, by João Guimarães **Rosa**. These and other
authors have drawn extensively on the rich
traditions of oral story-telling which, like the *cordel*
ballads and the improvised *desafios* or 'duels'
between the *cantadores* of the rural Northeast, are

the legacy of a culture in which literacy has been the privilege of a minority. This is a legacy which can be keenly felt within urban popular culture, too, in a uniquely sophisticated tradition of song-writing, from the **samba** composers of the 1930s, such as Noel **Rosa**, to the post-1960 musicians of **MPB**.

The black slave population, which was actively denied access to the social and political advantages that **literacy** might have brought, developed other forms of cultural expression through which, often under semi-clandestine conditions of repression, they not only preserved African traditions but also constructed a new, Afro-Brazilian post-slavery culture which has overflowed its own ethnic boundaries. **Capoeira**, originally derived from the illicit foot-fighting of the slaves, is now widely enjoyed as a skilfully choreographed gymnastic art. **Candomblé**, **Macumba** and **Umbanda**, religious practices today engaged in by a broad cross-section of society, operating in parallel with institutionalized Catholicism, resulted from the appropriation of elements of Christian theology and ritual as a legitimate framework for the continued practice of tribal traditions. In the last three decades, meanwhile, official Catholicism has faced another powerful rival for the loyalties of its mass congregations in the form of charismatic Pentecostalism (see **Pentecostals**) and, most recently, the new Japanese religions of São Paulo's expatriate Japanese community. At the same time, ritual has given way to spectacle on a mass scale, as **television** has become the predominant medium by which the country experiences the fictional dramas of the *telenovela* (see *telenovelas*) or the real-life soap operas of political scandal, religious rivalry and sport (see **sport in Latin America**).

The religious antecedents of **carnival** are no longer recognizable in today's ecumenical, national-popular spectacle. Other local and national festivities, however, such as the Catholic *festa do Bonfim* in Salvador, Bahia, the *Bumba-meu-boi* celebration of the ox, or the homage to Iemanjá, goddess of the sea, retain closer links with their sacred or secular origins.

This rich fount of dramatic traditions has been taken up, if belatedly, within Brazilian theatre, the art form that was the slowest to assimilate the innovations of the modernist movement. Dias **Gomes**'s *O*

pagador de promessas (Payment as Pledged), Ariano **Suassuna**'s *Auto da Compadecida* (The Rogue's Trial) and the stage version of João Cabral de Melo Neto's *Morte e vida severina* (Death and Life of a Severino) successfully drew upon these popular themes and forms in the 1950s and 1960s, coinciding with the consolidation of the Brazilian Theatre of Comedy and the National Theatre Service, and the work of Nelson **Rodrigues** and Jorge de Andrade. The turn to popular thematic concerns was further combined with efforts to promote a more participative and collective approach to production in projects such as **Arena Theatre Group**, Teatro Oficina (see **Oficina Theatre Group**) and, following the 1964 military *coup*, the protest theatre of **Opinião**, involving directors and playwrights such as Augusto **Boal**, Gianfrancesco **Guarnieri**, José Celso Martínez Correa and Oduvaldo **Vianna Filho**.

If the wealth of popular celebrations and performance arts is one symptom of a powerful non-literate tradition within Brazilian culture, another is music which, closely allied to dance, provides the organizational structure for so many other artistic expressions. Whereas samba and **frevo**, amongst other forms, have performed this role for carnival, newer rhythms such as **samba-reggae** are the unifying musical focus for the multidisciplinary activities of Afro-Brazilian cultural organizations of the 1980s such as Salvador's **Olodum** project and **Ilê Aiyê**.

As that hybrid name samba-reggae suggests, the history of Brazilian popular music has been one of endless fusions of diverse local and international traditions: the strangely archaic modal melodies of the fiddle and fife-and-drum bands of the rural northeast, the polyrhythmic drumming and call-and-response patterns of African origin, the song and dance forms of nineteenth-century European popular and erudite music, to name but a few. These musical migrations have spawned the jazz-like, semi-improvised **choro** from the turn of the century, the Northeastern urbanized folk-dance the *baião* from the 1940s, and the 'cool' harmonic and melodic dissonances of **bossa nova** from the late 1950s. The latter's affinities with developments in North American popular music, like the connections between 1930s samba and Hollywood in the shape of singer Carmen **Miranda** and composer Ary **Barroso**, internationalized musical production on a new scale against the background of an emergent mass media industry (to which Brazil contributed a unique genre, the *chanchada*). To the objections of nationalists and traditionalists, Anglo-American rock and pop styles found a new youth audience via the Jovem Guarda and its leading representative, Roberto **Carlos**, competing with the songwriters and performers of the MPB tradition on the televised shows and song festivals which extended through the 1960s. This new convergence of cultural forces was the focus for a shortlived movement of experimentation, *tropicalismo*, which paved the way for the diversity and eclecticism of the 1970s, 1980s and 1990s.

Just as carnival and samba were beginning to conquer the city streets and the gramophone industry in the first quarter of the century, a young generation of artists and intellectuals from São Paulo was proposing a cultural revolution informed by the avant-garde experimentation many of them had encountered first-hand on their visits to Europe. This modernist movement was first brought together in defence of a controversial exhibition of 1917 by the young painter Anita **Malfatti**, and the visual arts remained one of its strongest manifestations following the inaugural **Modern Art Week** in 1922: the sculptor Víctor **Brecheret**, the Cubist-Expressionist Lasar **Segall**, the muralist and canvas painter Cândido **Portinari** and the primitivist Antônio Di Cavalcânti were among its most prominent representatives.

The language, form and subject matter of poetry were also revolutionized in response to the inflections, rhythms and sensations of a society in flux, in the work of Mário de **Andrade**, Manuel **Bandeira**, Carlos **Drummond de Andrade** and Oswald de Andrade, with his *Manifesto da Poesia Pau Brasil* (Brazil-Wood Poetry Manifesto). In the pages of the *Revista de antropofagia*, one of the movement's many literary journals, its most radical wing, led by Oswald de Andrade, defended a theory of cultural 'cannibalism' (*Antropofagia*) whose appeal would extend to later artistic generations such as *tropicalismo*. As well as provoking comparison with Mário de Andrade's prose fable of the Brazilian cultural dilemma, *Macunaíma*, the hegemony enjoyed by the cannibalist movement was disputed by an alternative, more

xenophobic current of Indianist cultural nationalism, *verdeamarelismo* (Greenyellowism). The composer Heitor **Villa-Lobos**, a major participant in the Modern Art Week, also explored the potential of hybrid combinations of popular and classical European forms and themes, leading a new nationalist current in the art-music field which would be carried forward by Francisco **Mignone**, Camargo **Guarnieri** and, in the postwar years, by Marlos **Nobre**.

A second wave of avant-garde movements, underpinned by the nationalist-developmentalist ideas of the **ISEB** institute, was spawned by the so-called golden years of economic growth and optimism under the presidency of Juscelino **Kubitschek** (1956–61). The boundaries between literature, sculpture, painting, performance, urban design and the mass media began to be broken down by the 'verbi-voco-visual' poetry of the concretists (see **concrete poetry**), the *poema-processo*, the performance-art of Lygia **Clark** and Hélio **Oiticica**, the work of architectural designer Lina **Bo Bardi** and the pop art canvasses of Rubens **Gerchman**. With the inauguration of the new capital city of **Brasília** in 1960, modernism made its definitive mark in the arena of public works under the direction of the architects and urban designers Oscar **Niemeyer** and Lúcio **Costa**. They, together with muralist Cândido Portinari and landscape-artist Roberto Burle **Marx**, had begun the revolution in Brazilian architecture in 1936 with the construction of the **Ministério da Educacão e Saúde** building in Rio de Janeiro and in 1942 with Belo Horizonte's **Pampulha** complex.

Projects such as these were made possible through a tradition of highly interventionist, populist regimes (see **populism**), beginning with the 1930–45 administration of Getulio **Vargas**, whose developmentalist programmes seemed to many artists to offer the political and economic means to achieve their own aims of social reform. Two crucial moments of defeat for the left-popular movement, in the mid-1930s and the mid-1960s, exposed the contradiction between these aims and the priorities of Brazil's ruling classes. Amongst the casualties of the first of these were some of those writers, such as Jorge **Amado** and Graciliano **Ramos**, who had contributed to the current of social-realist fiction, known as regionalism (see *regionalismo*), which documented the hitherto forgotten lives of the country's poor as they were violently transformed or marginalized by the process of modernization.

The cultural politics of poverty and under-development returned to the arts under a more self-consciously political leadership from the late 1950s, in a global context of anti-imperialist revolutionary movements. Underlying all the projects of the period – **Cinema Novo** film-maker Glauber **Rocha**'s **aesthetics of hunger**, the Marxist-influenced manifestos of the **CPC**s (Popular Culture Centres), Augusto **Boal**'s Theatre of the Oppressed, Paulo **Freire**'s popular literacy campaigns and the grassroots Catholicism of **liberation theology** – was the belief that cultural intervention was the key to mobilizing and revolutionizing the consciousness of the country's rural and urban masses in a broad, popular alliance with the left-wing intelligentsia.

However, with the installation of a military dictatorship in 1964, and especially from 1968 onwards, direct physical repression and censorship atomized and drove much cultural activity under-ground. The songwriting of Chico **Buarque** and Caetano **Veloso**, the satirical magazine *O pas-quim*, the Mimeograph poets (see **marginal poets**), the fiction of Antonio **Callado** and the theatre of Oduvaldo **Vianna Filho**, for example, used a variety of means to both resist and circumvent the sense of social alienation and isolation imposed by the regime. Meanwhile, investment in a state-sponsored mass culture industry aimed to demobilize opposition at a different level, by promoting the passive consump-tion of nationalist and developmentalist values and the celebration of the so-called **economic mira-cle**. These aims were served both by the expansion of the **Globo** media network and by specific financial structures, such as **FUNARTE** and **Embrafilme**, intended to guarantee a market reserve for national artistic production.

The slow transition to democracy from the late 1970s, driven from below by a new trade union and popular movement and its political expression, the Partido dos Trabalhadores (**PT**), initiated the public discussion of hitherto forbidden issues, such as torture, in cinema and literature. The 1990s saw

a progressive withdrawal of state subsidies for the arts, which were still struggling to recover from the generalized economic crisis of the previous two decades. After the impeachment of Brazil's first democratically elected President, Fernando **Collor** de Mello, a new set of questions occupied the political and cultural agenda: public morality and corruption, the persistence of violence as a mediating force between the interests of the state, private property and the poor, and the true meaning of citizenship in a post-authoritarian Brazil whose social and economic inequalities still await reform.

Further reading

González Echeverría, R. and Pupo-Walker, E. (eds) (1996) *The Cambridge History of Latin American Literature*, vol. 3, *Brazilian Literature*, Cambridge: Cambridge University Press.

Johnson. R. and Stam, R. (1995) *Brazilian Cinema*, New York: Columbia University Press.

McGowan, C. and Pessanha, R. (1991) *The Billboard Book of Brazilian Music*, New York: Billboard Books.

Rowe, W. and Schelling, V. (1991) *Memory and Modernity: Popular Culture in Latin America*, London: Verso.

Schwarz, R. (1992) *Misplaced Ideas: Essays on Brazilian Culture*, London: Verso.

The Journal of Decorative and Propaganda Arts (1995) 21, Brazil Theme Issue.

DAVID TREECE

Brazilian modernism

Brazilian modernism (1922–45) represents a sharp awareness of the modern which, in a lesser sense, refers back to Machado de Assis. In fact, in Rio de Janeiro in the late nineteenth century there were already identifiable elements of modernization: authoritarian centralization imposed by the em-pire, the reconstruction of the federal capital in the style of Haussman, migration to the cities generat-ing the first *favelas* (whose name derives from the huts the army found in the Northeast in the course of repressing a movement of anti-republican religious fanaticism), and the internationalization of investments in a society devoted to leisure and consumption. But in São Paulo, to coincide with the Independence Centenary, a kind of Armory Show, the Semana de Arte Moderna (**Modern Art Week**), opened in February 1922 in the Municipal Theatre. It brought together artists from different fields around a project which Mário de **Andrade**, one of its initiators, was to describe as the stabilization of a creative national consciousness. That was the essential question for the movement; the universal tenaciously pursued by modern enlightenment thought in its democratizing urge now had to give way to the multiple, creating in this way a tension between the singular and the general. The singular arose from a heroic moment for the avant-garde of São Paulo: the division of a cultured bourgeois public which, faced with this radical proposal, vacillated between paranoia and mystification. At the same time, through the estrangement of representations, a new public was to be created capable of accepting the free lyricism of Manuel **Bandeira**, the rhapsodic constructions of **Villa-Lobos** (*Bachianas brasileiras*) and Mário de Andrade (*Macunaíma*) (1928) or the cubist syntheses of João Miramar and Serafim Ponte Grande, the infamous heroes of Oswald de **Andrade**.

The general aspect, on the other hand, points to the cynical, mercantile aspect of every avant-garde movement and brought institutionalization, that is, official capitalization of a radical historicist effort to produce a new version of the Brazilian past (for example, with the rescue of the baroque style of Minas Gerais) which led to a reappraisal of the cultural diversity of the country. This stimulated an alliance between modernism and regionalism (see *regionalismo*), but levelled out disharmonies and cacophonies at the local level. Within this tendency are included the work of **Portinari** (oscillating between committed 'muralism' and a flattering portraiture), di **Cavalcanti**'s frescoes depicting typical scenes of Bahia life, the search for less strident tones by composers like Camargo **Guarnieri** and Erico **Veríssimo**. From this effort at modernist institutionalization there emerged a number of official institutions linked to the State under Getulio **Vargas** (National Book Institute, National Historic and Artistic Heritage Service,

Embrafilme; institutions which more or less disappeared with the end of national-populist hegemony and the globalization of the 1990s) and there developed in São Paulo a strong internationalist current whose outstanding manifestations were, from the 1930s onwards, the University of São Paulo, and from the 1950s on, the São Paulo Bienale (see **Bienale de São Paulo**).

Attracted in its singular phase by the promises of futurist simultaneism and efforts at expressionist action, but marked too by orphic practices and corroded by integralista vertigo, Brazilian modernism turned in its general phase to a benevolent and euphoric reconstruction of itself through memoirs, which ensured its decline. The debate about its exhaustion (beginning prematurely in the 1930s) produced two currents of response: the 'Baudelairean' culturalism, not modernist but modern, of Murilo Mendes and **liberation theology**, and the 'Mallarmé-an' constructivism of the Utopian and the post-Utopian recognizable in the work of the concrete poets (see **concrete poetry**) (Haroldo and Augusto de **Campos**) or the musical *tropicalismo* of Caetano **Veloso**. The discontinuous memoirs of Milton **Hatoum** or the self-consciously fake memoirs of Silviano **Santiago**, as well as the stories of Rubem **Fonseca**, simulating forgetfulness, indicated a line of escape from the movement, a current of pre-individual singularities and impersonal individualities.

Further reading

Burns, E. B. (1980) *A History of Brazil*, New York: Columbia University Press.

Nist, J. (1967) *The Modernist Movement in Brazil: A Literary Study*, Austin: University of Texas Press.

Santiago, S. (1996) *Uma literatura nos trópicos?*, Durham, NC: Duke University Press.

Schwartz, R. (1993) *Misplaced Ideas*, London: Verso.

Sevcenko, N. (1992) *Orfeu extático na metrópole*, São Paulo: Companhia das Letras.

RAUL ANTELO

Brazilian Portuguese

Speakers of Brazilian Portuguese number over 150 million. The Portuguese language itself is eighth in the world (after Mandarin, English, Hindi, Spanish, Russian, Arabic, and Bengali). In addition to Brazil, it is the national language of Portugal and the official language of Angola, Mozambique, Cape Verde, Guiné, São Tomé and Príncipe. Over fourteen Portuguese-based creoles are spoken in various parts of the world today, including one variety in the Americas, **Papiamentu**. In recent decades Brazilian Portuguese has been exported to many parts of the world through artistic endeavours in literature, popular music, film, and television.

Portuguese, an Indo-European language derived from Latin, blossomed in the northwest part of the Iberian Peninsula. The first texts in Portuguese date from the early thirteenth century. During the maritime explorations of the sixteenth century a form of Portuguese was spoken in many ports of Asia, Africa, and the Americas.

Beginning in 1500, when the Portuguese arrived in Brazil, **Tupi**, an indigenous language, and Portuguese coexisted. Jesuit priests proselytized in Tupi until 1759 when the Portuguese crown expelled them from Brazil and prohibited Tupi. By the middle of the seventeenth century, use of Tupi was in rapid decline. Today Brazilian Portuguese displays a sizeable Tupi lexicon of flora and fauna, for example, *abacaxi* (pineapple), *tatu* (armadillo) and *piranha* (pirana). After the prohibition of Tupi, the **Yoruba** language brought to Brazil by the African slaves was the next to perish, but not before leaving everyday vocabulary such as *cacula* (youngest child), *moleque* (young boy), and **samba**. Contact of Yoruba and Portuguese may have brought about morphosyntactic changes such as nós vamos > nús vai (we go), as coisas > as coisa (the things), chamei-a > chamei ela (I called her), não fala > não fala, não (don't speak) (double negative) and phonological changes: folha > foia and chegar > chegá.

As a consequence of five centuries of separation and influences from indigenous, African, and European languages, Brazilian Portuguese has become a distinct variety from Continental Portuguese. Differences along the dichotomy of vernacular versus standard as evidenced in the above examples seem to be more significant than differences among regional varieties. Nonetheless, the colonization pattern from Portugal reflects in the dialects of Brazil. The northern vernacular variety which includes the Amazon and northeast exhibits similarity to Northern Continental dialects, for example epenthesis in verbs amar > amare. The southern variety (Bahia, Rio de Janeiro, Minas, São Paulo, and the South) has received influence from Southern Continental Portuguese, for example, the palatal fricative [s] in syllable final position commonly used in Rio de Janeiro. A salient property of Rio Grande do Sul and surrounding areas is use of the familiar subject pronoun tu.

Further reading

Azevedo, M. (1989). 'Vernacular Features in Educated Speech in Brazilian Portuguese', *Hispania*, 72: 862–72.

Guy, G. (1981). 'Linguistic Variation in Brazilian Portuguese: Aspects of the Phonology, Syntax, and Language History', dissertation: University of Pennsylvania.

Thomas, E.W. (1969) *Syntax of Spoken Brazilian Portuguese*, Nashville: Vanderbitt University Press.

IRENE WHERRITT

Brecha

Uruguayan weekly magazine founded in 1985 by Hugo Alfaro and other journalists who had suffered imprisonment or exile under the Uruguayan military dictatorship (1971–84). Its founders also included Mario **Benedetti**, Eduardo **Galeano**, Carlos María Gutiérrez, Ernesto González Bermejo and Carlos Amorim. In the tradition of *Marcha*, its writers take independent positions within the Latin American left. Its central topics and concerns include human rights and the development of socialist ideas world-wide. The journal also addresses cultural matters and current national and international questions. Like *Marcha*, it has won a reputation for fine investigative reporting and now includes several influential columnists. By 1995 it had become Uruguay's first medium of communication with its own website – www.brecha.com.uy.

WILFREDO CANCIO ISLA

Brecheret, Vítor

b. 1894, São Paulo, Brazil; d. 1955, São Paulo

Sculptor

Brecheret's fluid avant-garde sculptures formed part of the *Semana de Arte Moderna* (**Modern Art Week**) of 1922. He studied in Italy, receiving first prize at the 1916 Rome International Exposition of Fine Arts in Rome and in 1920 was commissioned to create the great (and controversial) ***Monumento aos Bandeirantes*** (Monument to Colonial Explorers) in São Paulo. After a successful career in Europe, he settled in São Paulo in 1932. The final phase of his work reflected a growing interest in Brazilian indigenous art. An important collection of his work is housed in the Museum of the State of São Paulo.

MARIA JOSÉ SOMERLATE BARBOSA

Brechtian theatre

Bertolt Brecht (1898–1956) is the contemporary dramatist whose influence has been most pervasive in Latin American theatrical circles during the second half of the twentieth century. His plays and theoretical writings offered an innovative model shaped by *Marxism* that allowed for the representation of socio-cultural situations. Attracted by its political implications, several generations of playwrights enthusiastically adopted his well known doctrine of the *Verfremdungseffekt* (alienation effect). Nonetheless, the results of Brecht's influence are neither a slavish imitation nor an acritical appropriation of successful devices prevailing in foreign theatre. On the contrary, his techniques underwent significant transformations and adjustments to fit the cultural history of Latin America.

From the theoretical point of view, a prominent place belongs to the Brazilian director Augusto **Boal**, who authored the influential *Teatro do oprimido* (Theatre of the Oppressed) (1975) and other texts internationally recognized as models for revolutionary theatre. In the Spanish-speaking world, the Colombian Enrique **Buenaventura** occupies a similar place. Founder in 1955 of what became the **Teatro Experimental de Cali** (TEC), he wrote several plays combining Brecht with popular culture: the many versions of *A la diestra de Dios Padre* (On the Right Hand of God the Father) (1960), *Los papeles del infierno* (Documents from Hell) (1966) and the more distinctively Brechtian *La denuncia* (The Accusation) (1973), dealing with the exploitation and massacre of workers in 1928 by the United Fruit Company and the local government.

In the 1950s, plays written under the aegis of Brecht's didactic dramatology could be found everywhere in Latin America. *El tren amarillo* (The Yellow Train) (1954), by Guatemalan Manuel **Galich**, *Ida y vuelta* (Round Trip) (1955) by Uruguayan Mario **Benedetti** and *Historias para ser contadas* (Stories to be Told) (1957) by Argentine Osvaldo **Dragún** are celebrated examples of the use of theatre to achieve a deeper understanding of social reality. From this point on, Brechtian techniques – including the use of narrators, plot fragmentation, experimentation with masks, music and other expressive resources, and acting styles designed to avoid empathy with the public – have become staples for all major playwrights. Among many examples are *La paz ficticia* (The Fictitious Peace) (1960) by Luisa Josefina **Hernández**; *Un pequeño día de ira* (A Short Day of Anger) (1962) and *Yo también hablo de la rosa* (I Also Speak of the Rose) (1966) by Emilio **Carballido**; *El atentado* (The Assault) by Jorge Ibargüengoitia; *Yo, Bertolt Brecht* (I, Bertolt Brecht) (1966) and *Pirámide 179* (1969) by Máximo Avilés Blonda; *La pasión según Antígona Pérez* (The Passion According to Antigone Perez) (1968) by Luis Rafael **Sánchez**; *Santa Juana de América* (Saint Joan of America) (1975) by Andrés Lizárraga; and *Mil años, un día* (A Thousand Years, A Single Day) (1993) by Ricardo **Halac**.

Further reading

De Toro, F. (1987) *Brecht en el teatro hispanoamericano contemporáneo*, Buenos Aires: Galerna.

Pellettieri, O. (ed.) (1994) *De Bertolt Brecht a Ricardo*

Monti. *Teatro en lengua alemana y teatro argentino*, Buenos Aires: Galerna.

Taylor, D. (1991) *Theatre of Crisis: Drama and politics in Latin America*, Lexington, KY: University Press of Kentucky.

DANIEL ALTAMIRANDA

Breeze, Jean 'Binta'

b. 1956, Hanover, Jamaica

Poet and dub performer

A scribal poet and a formidable 'dub' (see **dub poetry**) performer in a field dominated by men, Jean 'Binta' Breeze was briefly associated with **Rastafarianism** until she became disillusioned with Rastafarian gender politics. She migrated to England, where she performed with Linton Kwesi Johnson on the BBC's 'Poetry in Dub and Otherwise', wrote stage and screen plays, appeared in a film about her life, produced records (including *Riddym Ravings*, *Tracks*, and *Riding on De Riddym*) and three collections of poetry. She has toured widely. *On the Edge of an Island* (1997) interweaves poems and short stories.

PAT DUNN AND PAMELA MORDECAI

Bressane, Júlio

b. 1946, Rio de Janeiro, Brazil

Film-maker

The principal figure in Brazil's underground (*udigrudi*) film movement of the late 1960s and 1970s. After an inauspicious début with *Cara a cara* (Face to Face) (1967) – much too influenced by Glauber **Rocha** – Bressane (and Rogerio **Sganzerla**) publicly broke with the aesthetic parameters of **Cinema Novo**; his *O anjo nasceu* (The Angel was Born) (1969) and especially *Matou a família e foi ao cinema* (Killed the Family and Went to the Movies) (1969) revealed his irreverent and iconoclastic spirit. The latter is a brilliant example of meta-cinema, structured by a conceit implicit in its title: Oedipal violence carelessly linked to mindless entertainment. Upon his return from exile, he

directed *O rei do baralho* (The King of Gaiety) (1973), an incisive critique of the **chanchadas** starring **Grande Otelo**. Among his other notable films are *Tabu* (Taboo) (1982), an experimental meditation on a hypothetical encounter between composer Lamartine **Babo** and Oswald de **Andrade** (starring Caetano **Veloso**) and *O mandarim* (The Mandarin) (1995), with Gal **Costa** and Gilberto **Gil**.

ANA M. LÓPEZ

Briceño Guerrero, José Manuel

b. 1929, Valera, Venezuela

Writer and philosopher

Briceño Guerrero is best known for his deliberations on Latin American cultural identity, exemplified by *El laberinto de los tres minotauros* (The Labyrinth of Three Minotaurs) (1996), which brought together his three major studies on the subject. Philosophy and philology, which he studied as a student, have remained central concerns of his work. He has also written several novels under the pseudonym of Jonuel Brique, such as *Triandáfila* (1967) and *Holadios* (1984), characterized by a poetic narrative style, and has had a distinguished academic career. Original in his thinking and in his style of writing, Briceño Guerrero was awarded Venezuela's national prize for literature in 1996.

MARK DINNEEN

Brierre, Jean Fernand

b. 1909, Jeremie, Haiti; d. 1992, Port-au-Prince, Halti

Poet, dramatist

Brierre played an active role in the nationalist backlash against the US Occupation, at which time he established a reputation as a gifted poet of Haitian *indigenisme*. He later served as Haiti's ambassador to Argentina but spent twenty five years in exile in Dakar, Senegal, because of his opposition to the Duvaliers. He was noted for his dramatic verse celebrating the heroes of Haitian

Independence, the black diaspora and later such African-American artists as Langston Hughes, Paul Robeson and Marian Anderson. He is frequently anthologized as the poet of Haitian **négritude** because of *Black Soul* (1947) and *La Source* (The Source) (1956).

J. MICHAEL DASH

Brigada Ramona Parra

The Brigada Ramona Parra, often referred to simply as BRP emerged during the 1970 election campaign in support of Salvador **Allende** in Chile. The group would paint murals illegally, often by night, travelling around in a truck. The style of the murals was dramatic, using simplified forms and bright colours and usually incorporating political slogans into the design. The design of the murals owed something to the art of the Cuban Revolution (see **revolutions**) and would reappear again in Central America in the 1980s, again in support of left-wing political movements, such as the Sandinistas in Nicaragua (see **Sandinista Revolution**). During the presidency of Allende from 1970 to 1973, this style of mural became a semi-official art form.

GABRIEL PEREZ-BARREIRO

British West Indies *see* Caribbean

Brito, María Eugenia

b. 1950, Santiago, Chile

Writer

The topics of Brito's poetry are language itself, the inner dimensions of subjectivity, and female desire that trangresses the limits of static gender identity. They are the themes of her books *Vía Pública* (Public Highway) (1984), *Filiaciones* (Affiliations) (1986) and *Emplazamientos* (Defiances) (1993). Like other contemporary Chilean women writers, artists and critics (Diamela **Eltit**, Nelly **Richard** and Raquel **Olea** among them), Brito treats questions and issues raised by contemporary feminist and

poststructuralist theories, as well as by the Latin American condition of her own writing.

LUIS E. CÁRCAMO-HUECHANTE

Britto García, Luis

b. 1940, Caracas, Venezuela

Writer

One of the most acclaimed Venezuelan writers of his generation, García Britto is best known for his fiction. He published his first works in the 1960s, but rose to prominence in 1970 with *Rajatabla*, a collection of brief stories, characterized by humour and irony, which refer to political repression and violence. The narratives show the inclination for linguistic experiment which is central to his writing. His major work of fiction to date is his 1979 novel, *Abrapalabra*, which explores the cultural and political development of Venezuela through the present century. In 2000 he published a historical novel, *Pirates* (Pirates). A man of wide interests, García Britto has also written plays, film scripts and several notable works of political analysis.

MARK DINNEEN

Brodber, Erna

b. 1940, St. Mary, Jamaica

Novelist and social scientist

A meticulous scholar, Brodber also writes prose that is often highly poetic, like Kamau **Brathwaite**. Her first two novels, *Jane and Louisa Will Soon Come Home* (1980) and *Myal* (1988), both set out young women's self-healing and maturation within the context of a Caribbean society wounded by colonialism. Her third novel, *Louisiana* (1984), is a Jamaican-American woman's cultural journey into the collective history of black women.

Further reading

Webb, Barbara (1996) 'Erna Brodber', in B. Lindfors and R. Sander (eds) *Twentieth Century*

Caribbean and African Writers, Third Series, Vol. 157, Detroit: Gale Research, pp. 17–36.

ELAINE SAVORY

Brouard, Carl

b. 1902, Port-au-Prince, Haiti; d. 1965, Port-au-Prince

Poet

Perhaps the most notoriously bohemian and mystical of the Haitian *indigemisme* poets, Brouard established his reputation with early verse published in *La revue indigène* and from the outset, in the French tradition of the *poète maudit*, was obsessed by life in the slums of Port-au-Prince and **Vodun** religion. His most productive period was the 1930s and 1940s before he drifted off into early senility. He became known as an ardent apologist for Haitian *noirisme* and was director of *Les Griots*, the journal of the ethnological movement.

J. MICHAEL DASH

Brouwer, Leo

b. 1939, Havana, Cuba

Musician

An outstanding guitarist, composer, conductor and teacher, Brouwer has continued a fine Cuban tradition of experimental **art music**. He studied with Isaac **Nicola** and other guitar virtuosi before completing his musical education at Juillard in New York and at Hartford. Returning to Cuba he taught composition and harmony while working with Cuban radio and television, as well as with the Cuban Film Institute (**ICAIC**). He became the director of the Experimental Department of the ICAIC, where as composer, conductor and performer he explored a wide variety of musical styles – from serialism to variations on the Cuban **son** tradition, setting to music texts by Nicolás **Guillén** among others, and writing for the cinema. He has been particularly innovative in composition for the guitar. His symphony for orchestra, *La región más*

transparente (Where the Air is Clearest), was composed and performed in 1976.

MIKE GONZALEZ

Brown, Carlinhos

b. 1962, Bairo de Brotas, Salvador, Brazil

Composer, musician

Brown emerged in the 1990s as a preeminent celebrity of new Afro-Bahian music, **MPB**, and 'world music'. He first gained attention as the founder and director of the Bahian carnival group, **Timbalada**, and as the composer of several pop hits like 'Meia-lua inteira' and Fricote da Teresinha. He composed popular songs for Marisa **Monte**. In 1996, he released his first CD, *Alfagamabetizado*, a potent mix of Afro-Bahian percussion, northeastern folk, and international pop. This effort was followed in 1998 by his album *Omelete Man* from 1998. Brown has continued to organize and direct grassroots music groups in Salvador.

CHRISTOPHER DUNN

Brown, Roy

b. 1945, Orlando, Florida

Singer and composer

The son of a US army colonel and a Puerto Rican teacher, Brown moved to Puerto Rico at an early age. In 1964 he entered college in Ohio, and as a student became involved in the protests against the Vietnam War and in the folk rock that would mark his own musical development. In 1969 he graduated in Social Sciences from the University of Puerto Rico. His album *Yo protesto* (I protest) (1970) is a classic of the Puerto Rican *nueva canción*.

JUAN CARLOS QUINTERO HERENCIA

Brown, Wayne

b. 1944, Woodbrook, Trinidad

Writer

Brown is an exceptionally talented and controversial critic, journalist, short story writer and teacher. He worked for the *Trinidad Guardian* between 1964 and 1995, but now writes for *The Independent*, which was founded in 1996. Brown distinguished himself early as a poet, winning the poetry prize at the Jamaica Independence Festival (1968), and the Commonwealth Poetry Prize (1972) for the collection *On the Coast*. Other books are: *Edna Manley: The Private Years, 1900–38* (1976) (see **Manley, Edna**); *21 Years of 'Poetry and Audience'*, as co-editor (1976); *Voyages* (1989); and *The Child of the Sea* (1990). He has edited a selection of Derek **Walcott**'s poetry.

KEITH JARDIM

Brugnoli, Francisco

b. 1935, Santiago, Chile

Visual artist

Brugnoli began his controversial exploration of the boundaries between art and cultural production in the 1960s. Believing that the traditional forms of artistic expression, particularly painting, were inadequate for describing Chile's new social and political realities, Brugnoli composed collages and installations combining household objects, photographs and his own texts. His work is deliberately precarious, ephemeral and marginal to commercial networks. Its primary objective is to engage the viewer directly in the artist's critical commentary on an unjust consumer society.

CELIA LANGDEAU CUSSEN

Bruma, Eddy

b. 1925, Suriname

Politician, poet and playwright

Bruma studied law in the Netherlands, became a politician and was an outspoken defender of the 1980 *coup d'état* in Suriname. As a leading member of the cultural movement **Wie eegie sanie**, he was a fervent advocate of the use of the native creole Sranan Tongo, in which he published some poetry. His play *De geboorte van Boni* (The Birth of Boni) (1952), a eulogy of maroon life (see **maroons**), contributed to Wie eegie sanie's goal of reassesing Surinamese history from a local point of view.

AART G. BROEK

Brumana, Herminia

b. 1904, Pigüé, Argentina; d. 1954, Buenos Aires, Argentina

Writer and educator

Brumana dedicated her life to education, social activism and a prolific literary career. She married the militant socialist and writer Juan Antonio Solari in 1921, having already published her first book and founded a magazine in her hometown. A popular contributor to newspapers and magazines, Brumana published works about **feminism**, contemporary social issues and questions of national identity as well as educational materials and textbooks. A lifelong educator, author and journalist, she died while teaching in an adult education institution.

THOMAS EDSALL

Brunet, Marta

b. 1901, Chillán, Chile; d. 1967, Montevideo, Uruguay

Writer

Brunet introduced the feminine experience into **criollismo**. *Montaña adentro* (In the Heart of the Mountain) and *Bestia dañina* (Harmful Beast), both published in 1929, and *Humo hacia el sur* (Smoke in the South) (1946) placed in the landscape the discontent and rebellion of women. In Brunet's narratives, women see their hopes and expectations disappear because of social restrictions. Her work also renewed a nationalistic discourse, and looked at the effects of modernization on Chilean culture, particularly that of the rural areas.

SANDRA GARABANO

Brunner, José Joaquín

b. 1945, Santiago, Chile

Sociologist

A researcher at the Facultad Latinomericana de Ciencias Sociales (**FLACSO**), which he headed from 1981–8, Brunner has published widely on the relationship between education, culture and politics in Latin America. His work focuses specifically on the transformations undergone during the transition from authoritarianism to democracy, particularly in Chile during the 1980s. The central preoccupations of his work are the internationalization of culture, the incorporation of modernity as a basic vector of organization and development in Chilean culture, and the dependency of countries on the periphery.

In the book *Los intelectuales y los problemas de la cultura* (Intellectuals and Problems of Culture) (1989), Brunner analyses the structuring and operative rules of the cultural field. For Brunner, cultural production is concentrated in certain institutions that promote a complex and professionalized division of labour. Those who are responsible for the production of knowledge hold an increasingly important place in the formation of the state. Thus, culture in its organized dimension of production and transmission of symbolic goods acquires renewed economic value and becomes an integral part of the basic processes of social organization. He also discusses proposals by Chilean **intellectuals** for the democratization of Chile.

Un espejo trizado. Ensayos sobre cultura y políticas culturales (A Shattered Mirror: Essays on Culture and Cultural Politics) (1988) is another Brunner work crucial to understanding the possibilities and limits of democracy in Chile. Here he analyses the Chilean democratization process and the political events that led to the ousting of **Pinochet**'s military regime and the elections of December 1989.

Brunner addresses the question of national origins, postcolonialism and the debate on modernism vs **postmodernism** in *Chile, Transformaciones culturales y modernidad* (Chile, Cultural Transformations and Modernity) (1989). He attempts to explain modernity in its Latin American specificity. A crucial question in these writings is how to incorporate modernity in countries on the periphery.

Brunner's work poses questions of crucial importance for late twentieth-century Latin American intellectuals. The incorporation of modernity into Latin American culture, Chilean culture under the authoritarian-military regime and post-dictatorial Chilean culture constitute only some examples of a debate that is far from settled. In the 1990s Brunner served the government of Eduardo **Frei Ruiz Tagle** as foreign minister.

Further reading

Brunner, J.J. (1994) *Bienvenidos a la modernidad*, Santiago: Editorial Planeta Chilena.

Gomariz, E. (1991) *Modernidad y cultura en América Latina: una discusión con José Joaquín Brunner*, Santiago: FLASCO-Programa Chile.

SANDRA GARABANO

Bryce Echenique, Alfredo

b. 1939, Lima, Peru

Writer

A respected and well-known Peruvian narrator since the 1970s, his first published short-story volume, *Huerto cerrado* (Closed Orchard) was finalist for the 1968 **Casa de las Américas** prize. However, his great trans-Atlantic success was his 1970 novel *Un mundo para Julius* (A World for Julius). Later came other humorous novels about the adventures of Latin American intellectuals in European exile, such as *La vida exagerada de Martín Romaña* (The Exaggerated Life of Martin Romaña) (1981) and *No me esperen en abril* (Don't Expect Me in April) (1995).

JOSÉ ANTONIO MAZZOTTI

Buarque, Chico

b. 1944, Rio de Janeiro, Brazil

Songwriter, writer

Buarque (born Francisco Buarque de Holanda) has been a key figure in Brazilian arts since the military dictatorship (1964–85). His contribution has been in popular music, but also in drama and fiction. Son of historian Sérgio **Buarque de Holanda**, he briefly studied architecture. One of the originators of **MPB**, he is noted for social criticism, thoughtful romantic songs and for his appeal across class lines. 'Pedro Pedreiro' (Peter the Bricklayer) (1965) illustrates a characteristic linguistic agility in a narrative about the frustrating life of a common labourer and foreshadows the intricate 'Construção' (Building Site) (1970). Buarque became well known during the historic MPB festivals of the late 1960s and was involved in several controversies. In 1969, he chose exile to avoid persecution by the military. Upon his return, he was subject to close scrutiny, and his struggles with the government in the 1970s comprise an important chapter in the history of censorship. The **samba** 'Apesar de você' (In Spite of You) (1970) expressed distaste for the regime; it was banned but became a hymn of the movement for re-democratization. When Buarque returned from a 1978 cultural mission to Cuba, his books and records were confiscated, but he did manage to introduce some new Cuban music (***nueva trova***) to Brazil.

Sociohistorical criticism and adaptations are the main thrust of Buarque's dramatic work. He began by staging João Cabral's ***Morte e vida severina*** (Death and Life of a Severino) (1966) and the explosive ***Roda viva*** (Spinning Wheel) (1967). *Calabar: O elogio da traição* (Calabar: In Praise of Treason) (1973), with Ruy **Guerra**, reconsidered a notorious colonist accused of collaboration with the Dutch occupation. *Gota d'água: uma tragédia carioca* (The Last Straw, a Rio Tragedy) (1975), with Paulo Pontes, was based on a classical Greek model. The later ***Ópera do malandro*** (Hustler's Opera) (1978) had a tremendous impact and became a film. Much of Buarque's varied musical output since the 1970s has been designed for the stage or screen (e.g. ***Bye Bye Brasil***). His first novel, *Fazenda Modelo: Novela Pecuária* (Model Farm: A Bovine Novel) (1974), an Orwellian allegory, was followed by works of children's literature and the novellas *Estorvo* (Turbulence) (1991) and *Benjamin* (1995).

Further reading

Buarque, C. (1989) *Letra e música*, 2 vols, São Paulo: Companhia das Letras.
Perrone, C. (1989) *Masters of Contemporary Brazilian Song: MPB 1965–1985*, Austin: University of Texas Press.

CHARLES A. PERRONE

Buarque de Holanda Ferreira, Aurélio

b. 1910, Passo de Camarajibe, Brazil;
   d. 1989, Passo de Camarajibe

Writer and lexicographer

Part of the group around Graciliano **Ramos**, Hollanda's most important work was editing the *Novo Dicionário da língua portuguesa* (New Dictionary of the Portuguese Language) (1975, republished 1986), popularly known as the 'Aurélio,' which includes not only literary language but also the language of the mass media and popular songs. He published a book of stories, *Dois mundos* (Two Worlds) (1942), edited (with Paulo Rónai) an anthology of international short stories, *Mar de Histórias* (Sea of Stories) (1945–63), and (with Alvaro Lins) *Roteiro Literário do Brasil e de Portugal* (Literary Guide to Brazil and Portugal) (1956).

ADRIANA AMANTE

Buarque de Holanda, Heloisa (Helena Oliveira)

b. 1939, Ribeirao Preto, Brazil

Cultural critic

The 'marginal' poets of *26 poetas hoje* (26 Poets Today) were the subject of Holanda's 1979 doctoral thesis *Impressões de viagem* (Impressions on a Journey), which analysed the relationship between poetic language and politics in the 1960s and 1970s. She continued to explore the relations between culture and politics in other texts, while developing her own interests in newspaper and radio journalism and film production. She has played a key role in disseminating the cultural production of Brazilian women, organizing volumes on women film directors and silent screen actresses as well as *Ensaístas brasileiras* (Brazilian Women Essayists) (1993), in which she links them to the French and Anglo-American feminist theory which she introduced into Brazil.

ADRIANA AMANTE

Buarque de Holanda, Sérgio

b. 1902, São Paulo, Brazil; d. 1982, São Paulo

Historian and literary critic

A key figure in the dissemination of modernist ideas in Brazil, Buarque was regarded, despite his youth, as the most sophisticated thinker of those associated with **Brazilian modernism**. In 1921 he moved from São Paulo to study law in Rio de Janeiro, and there became involved in artistic circles. However, he retained links with his native city and returned to attend the seminal **Modern Art Week** of 1922. He contributed to the São Paulo modernist journal *Klaxon* and was founding editor of the journal *Estética*, published in Rio de Janeiro from 1924. In 1929 he went to Germany as a correspondent for a São Paulo magazine and there attended Meinecke's courses at the University of Berlin and studied the work of the German historical school, writing critical essays on Kantorowicz, Sombart and Weber.

Returning to Brazil he published, in 1936, his best known work – *Raízes do Brasil* (Roots of Brazil), a critical study of the Iberian origins of the authoritarian traditions of the Brazilian elite, their adaptation to the colonial context and to the Republic and their institutionalization in the state. In that same year he began to work with French historian Henri Hauser. A volume of essays, *Cobra de Vidro* (Glass Cobra) appeared in 1944, and in 1945 his classic historical study *Monções* analyzed

the riverborne expeditions out of São Paulo in the colonial period which led to the incorporation of the *sertões* (plains) of the interior into Brazilian territory, as well as the discovery of rich deposits of gold and gemstones. His *Caminhos e Fronteiras* (Roads and Frontiers) (1957) continued the same theme. In the same year he produced another definitive work, *Visões do Paraíso* (Visions of Paradise), on the projection on to America of European myths of the Garden of Eden. Between 1960 and 1972 he directed the collection *História Geral da Civilização Brasileira* (General History of Brazilian Civilization). In 1969 he resigned from the University of São Paulo, where he had worked since 1956, in protest against the military government's incursion into the university. An original member of the Socialist Party in 1946, he was also a co-founder, in 1980, of **PT**, the Workers Party. His erudition, fine writing and analytical insights make Sérgio Buarque de Holanda a key point of reference for all contemporary Brazilian historiography.

Further reading

(1988) *Sérgio Buarque de Holanda: vida e obra*, São Paulo: Secretaria de Estado da Cultura, Universidade de São Paulo.

NICOLAU SEVCENKO

Buenaventura, Enrique

b. 1925, Cali, Colombia

Playwright and theatre director

Buenventura is a true renaissance man in the midst of the tensions of the twentieth century: playwright, director, actor, poet, theoretician, professor, artist, revolutionary and maestro. He is one of the pivotal figures of the New Popular Theatre movement in Latin America. In the 1950s he participated in the Independent Theatre movement of the **Southern Cone**. Shortly after, in 1955, he returned to Colombia to teach in the newly formed Theatre School within the Escuela de Bellas Artes in Cali. They recruited students for the school by placing an advertisement in the local newspaper. An eclectic group of twenty responded, among them workers, peasants and an elderly lady who could neither read nor write.

They would eventually become the **Teatro Experimental de Cali** (TEC) under Buenaventura's direction. This was during Rojas Pinilla's dictatorship, a time in which Buenaventura was blacklisted by the military, which meant that he could not officially direct the Theatre School, even though he was its *de facto* director. He built the school and the group by going deeply into popular theatre, and by researching local folklore, dances, storytellers, popular literature, songs and music.

One of the first productions of the group was a 'nationalized' popular Nativity play in which the Massacre of the Innocents was closely tied to 'La **Violencia**' in Colombia, with Herod represented as a tropical dictator. This 'nationalization' and re-elaboration of folktales, plays, novels and short stories into a TEC style and vision would become trademark characteristics of the group. Later, they adapted Tomás Carrasquilla's *En la diestra de Dios Padre* (On God's Right Hand) for the theatre in a version that was widely acclaimed and won many prizes at the 1958 Bogotá Second Theatre Festival. Another of Buenaventura's and TEC's characteristics is the performing of a multiplicity of versions of the same play, as the interaction with the audience changes it and as the group and the author untiringly search for a new popular theatre language.

The second version of *En la diestra de Dios Padre* was marked by Buenaventura's discovery of Brecht (see **Brechtian theatre**). Buenaventura admits that Brecht's influence was one of the causes of the failure of this second version of the play. However, he realized that this happened because they were applying Brecht in a way that Brecht himself would have hated: as a recipe, a formula. Freed from those formulaic constraints they were able to incorporate Brecht in a much more dynamic, 'nationalized' manner. Together with maestri such as Atahualpa del **Cioppo** from El **Galpón** in Uruguay, Buenaventura became an authority on Brecht in Latin America. Brecht was more than a simple influence; in a profoundly confluent quest, Buenaventura reinvented Brecht as he created a fiercely unique Latin American theatrical expression. The '*método de creación colectiva*' devised with

TEC is a testament to this 'going beyond' of Brecht's original principles. The third version of *En la diestra de Dios Padre* incorporated the Mojiganga of the Antioquia peasants, a carnivalesque revision with on-stage musicians, masks and an 'abanderado' – a version that took the play away from realism. By going away from Brecht he had in fact come closer to Brecht's theories.

With the period of 'nationalization of the classics' well underway, TEC would become known for producing its own versions of *Oedipus Rex*, *La Celestina*, *Ubu Roi* and the work of Molière, Lope de Vega, etc. In 1960 they were invited to the Theatre of Nations in Paris where they presented the second version of *En la diestra de Dios Padre* and Osvaldo **Dragún**'s *Historias para ser contadas* (Stories for Telling). This was their first international success – a success that consolidated their position in Colombia. Buenaventura did not return to Colombia for a while, instead staying in Paris for two years where he wrote *El requiem* (1961) and *La tragedia del Rey Christophe* (1962). There he married Jacqueline Vidal, his lifelong companion and collaborator. Upon his return to Colombia, he began to write *La trampa* (The Trap) (1964) with TEC. This was the beginning of his questioning of the role of the individual author writing in isolation. Ethical and consequential, he attempted to relinquish his individual role as a playwright to create a new collective methodology, an actor's dramaturgy: '*El método de creación colectiva del TEC*'. This method circulated throughout Latin America, creating a veritable explosion of groups inspired by its empowering principles.

Rather than the hierarchical structure of traditional theatre, TEC advocated equality and a participatory ethics where the group's voice and viewpoint was present in each play created together. Given their ongoing militant criticism of the government, TEC and Buenaventura were expelled from the school in 1969. They had finally become an independent, non-official theatre: the now renamed Teatro Experimental de Cali. This is when he and they dived even further into the history of their country, in particular, and of Latin America, in general. This was a true expropriation of history from the '*historiotenientes*', as he called them, to rescue history for a people's perspective and to accompany that history in the making through theatre. Plays such as his *Los papeles del infierno* (Documents from Hell), five sketches that include *La orgía* (The Orgy), were continued contributions in that direction. Others followed: **Soldados** (Soldiers), *La denuncia* (Denunciation), *Opera bufa*, *El encierro* (Round-Up) and *La estación* (The Station), among so many others.

Ever present in festivals and meetings throughout Latin America and the world, Enrique Buenaventura and TEC are true incarnations of a people's theatre where what is depicted on stage is inseparable from the way of life of its members, with all of its successes, pains and contradictions. Among his theoretical works are *El 'arte nuevo de hacer comedias' y el nuevo teatro latinoamericano* (The 'New Art of Making Plays' and New Latin American Theatre), *La dramaturgia del actor* (Dramaturgy and the Actor), *Metáfora y puesta en escena* (Metaphor and *Mise-en-Scène*), *El enunciado verbal y la puesta en escena* (The Verbal Utterance and *Mise-en-Scène*) and *Notas sobre dramaturgia: tema, mitema y contexto*' (Notes on Dramaturgy: Theme, Mytheme and Context).

In 1990 (the year that TEC was disbanded) Buenaventura wrote *Proyecto piloto* (Pilot Project), a dark, heartfelt look at a world running amuck in a process of *'ratificación'* (becoming rats), a true dystopian view that seems to painfully disarticulate his previous position of Utopian revolutionary attachment. Nevertheless, this did not last, and in spite of the difficult process that groups such as TEC have had to endure in these postmodern, post-corporate times, Buenaventura continues to write and direct in his unfailing, profoundly ethical love affair with history and theatre.

Further reading

Buenaventura, E. (1990) *Teatro*, Mexico City: Siglo XXI.
Watson, M. (1976). 'Enrique Buenaventura's theory of committed theatre', *Latin American Theatre Review* 9(2): 43–8.

MARINA PIANCA

Bufanda del Sol, La

La Bufanda del Sol (The Sun's Scarf) is a significant magazine published in Quito, Ecuador. During its first period (1965–66), it disseminated the work of Ecuador's **intellectuals** through Latin America and Europe. During its second period (1975–), *La Bufanda del Sol* became the voice of the group Frente Cultural (Cultural Front). Aiming to connect with Latin American and global intellectual movements, it published articles on international literary groups and reviewed books and magazines from abroad. This advanced the journal's cultural mission to undermine the established order, probe into the inauthentic character of Ecuadorean culture, and promote a new cultural order in Ecuador and Latin America.

HUMBERTO E. ROBLES

Buitrago, Fanny

b. 1943, Barranquilla, Colombia

Writer

Novelist and playwright Fanny Buitrago is best known for her novel *Señora de la miel* (Mrs Honeycomb) (1993), an ironic story of the liberation of feminine desire, often compared to Laura **Esquivel**'s ***Como agua para chocolate*** (Like Water for Chocolate) for its sensual portrayal of food. Buitrago published her first novel, *El hostigante verano de los dioses* (The Tormenting Summer of the Gods), in 1963 and in 1964 was awarded the National Theatre Prize for her play *El hombre de paja* (The Straw Man). Buitrago portrays characters situated in the sociocultural environment of the Caribbean; some of her novels are set in Colombia during the period of La **Violencia**.

MIGUEL A. CARDINALE

Bulletin of Latin American Research

The journal of the Society for Latin American Studies is published in Oxford three times annually, in January, May and September. It was first published in 1981. It includes articles and reviews of wide interest in the social sciences and humanities. In addition to extensive research articles, the journal includes review articles, research in progress, book reviews and notes. Most articles are written by British scholars. It is indexed in *Hispanic American Periodicals Index* and *Public Affairs Information Service*. The journal's website includes a table of contents service for current issues.

PAUL BARY

bullfighting

A sport or spectacle associated with Spain (though a less violent version exists in Portugal), bullfighting involves the ritualized fight between trained fighters (almost always male) and bulls. Introduced early into Spanish America, it caught on in certain areas. In contemporary Latin America, it is fought only in Mexico, Colombia, Venezuela, Ecuador and Peru, where there is a famous Museum of Bullfighting. A bullring was constructed in Uruguay in the early part of the century but the sport was soon banned. Internationally famous matadors include Rodolfo **Gaona**, Carlos Arruza and Fermín Espinosa (Mexico), César Girón (Venezuela) and César Rincón (Colombia). A very different form of bullfighting is the Andean version involving a bull and a condor; this is the subject of José María **Arguedas**'s early novel *Yawar Fiesta* (1941).

DANIEL BALDERSTON

Bullrich, Francisco

b. 1929, Buenos Aires, Argentina

Architectural historian

As a postgraduate at the prestigious Hochschule für Gestaltung in Ulm, Germany, Bullrich studied with architect, painter and sculptor Max Bill. Bullrich designed the Argentine Embassy in **Brasília** (a city about which he wrote several essays) and the **Biblioteca Nacional** (National Library) in Buenos Aires (with Clorindo **Testa** and Alicia Ganizzaga). His most important achievements, however, are his critical writings on architecture

and town planning published in two now classic texts – *Arquitectura argentina contemporánea (Panorama de la arquitectura argentina 1950–63)* (Contemporary Argentine Architecture: Panorama of Argentine Architecture: 1950–63) (1963) and *Arquitectura latinoamericana (1950–70)* (Latin American Architecture 1950–70) (1969).

GONZALO AGUILAR

Bullrich, Silvina

b. 1915, Buenos Aires, Argentina; d. 1989, Punta del Este, Uruguay

Writer

Bullrich explored the 'small human comedy' by weaving the psychological with the social in her narratives. Few Latin American 1950s writers were able to achieve a similar degree of popularity and financial success. In 1971 she received second prize in the National Award for *Los pasajeros del jardín* (The Travellers of the Garden); she resented this secondary accolade and described it in 'The Woman Writer in Latin America' as representative of the injustices against which women writers struggle. In addition to her short stories, novels and articles she also wrote *crónicas* (see **crónica**), a biography and a television programme.

FERNANDA ANALIA ZULLO

Bumba-meu-boi

Bumba-meu-boi is popular entertainment from the northeast of Brazil, originating in the eighteenth century and normally presented between Christmas and Twelfth Night (6 January) or during the Festas Juninas (13–29 June). Including dances and comic scenes, its principal theme is the death and resurrection of an Ox (*boi*) played by one or two men carrying a cane structure; Cavalo Marinho, the owner of the ox; two Cowboys and Catirina, partner to one of them, the farm Foreman, the Vicar and the Doctor. The Ox is killed to satisfy Catirina's desires, and then resurrected via an enema. This entertainment has inspired work by **Suassuna** and Dias **Gomes**, among many others.

VIVALDO SANTOS

Bunge family

The Bunge family were a prominent German-Argentine family active at all levels of economic, political, judicial and intellectual life. Alejandro Bunge (1880–1943) led the Social Catholic movement, rejecting classical liberalism in favour of protectionism. Augusto Bunge (1877–1948) served five terms in Congress for the Independent Socialist Party which he helped found. The positivist and racialist educator Carlos Octavio Bunge (1875–1918) advocated European immigration as a means of diluting the influence of 'inferior races'. Delfina Bunge de Gálvez (1881–1952), wife of novelist Manuel **Gálvez**, was herself an important poet and writer. The Bunge & Born agricultural and industrial conglomerate paid a huge ransom to free family members kidnapped by the **Montoneros** guerrilla army in the 1970s.

THOMAS EDSALL

Buñuel, Luis

b. 1900, Calanda, Spain; d. 1983, Mexico City

Film-maker

Associated with the surrealists (see **surrealism in Latin American art**), Buñuel first worked in Paris with Salvador Dalí to make *Un chien andalou* (An Andalusian Dog) (1928). He moved on to Hollywood and New York (1938–45) before settling in Mexico in 1946. His first feature *Gran Casino* (1946) was a *ranchera* film (see *rancheras, comedias*). From then on he preferred the melodrama, though always expressed through his own 'surrealist' world view and filmic imagery. The major talents of Mexican cinema – Luis **Alcoriza** (scriptwriter), Gabriel **Figueroa** (cinematographer), Arturo de Córdova, Miroslava and Silvia **Pinal** (actors) – collaborated with him in the most intense and representative films of the period: *Los*

olvidados (The Forgotten) (1950), *Ensayo de un crimen* (Rehearsal for a Crime) (1955), *Nazarín* (1958) , *El ángel exterminador* (The Exterminating Angel) (1962) and *Simón del desierto* (Simon of the Desert) (1964). These are the films in which Buñuel reaches the highest level of creative achievement, combining intelligent irony and great tenderness.

PATRICIA TORRES SAN MARTÍN

Burgos García, Julia Constanze

b. 1914, Carolina, Puerto Rico; d. 1953, New York, USA

Poet

Although she published only two volumes of verse in her lifetime, Burgos is recognized as one of Puerto Rica's finest poets. Born in a small village, into a large, impoverished family, her poems 'Río Grande de Loíza' and 'A Julia de Burgos' express a profound appreciation for the Puerto Rican landscape and a sense of herself as a strong, passionate woman. Despite her nationalism, she lived in New York from 1942 until her death. Her bicultural life and the intensity of her verse have made her a cultural icon of Puerto Rican identity, and an inspiring figure for later women writers such as Rosario **Ferré**.

BEN A. HELLER

Burke, Elena

b. 1928, Havana, Cuba

Singer

Known as 'La Señora Sentimiento' (Lady Emotion), Burke's is one of the most popular of Cuban voices. She began her radio and cabaret career in the early forties, and was the first woman singer to develop the musical style **feeling**. She travelled to Mexico and Jamaica with the group 'Las mulatas del fuego' (Mulattas of Fire) and joined the Facundo Rivero and Orlando de la Rosa quartets on her return. Between 1952 and 1958 she was a member of the Cuarteto D'Aida. From 1960 onwards she sang solo, working with leading pianists and guitarists in Cuba and abroad, and cut her first records. On her seventy-first birthday, the Cuban artistic community paid homage to her musical achievements at a joyous gathering at the appropriately retro cabaret of the Hotel Meliá in Havana.

WILFREDO CANCIO ISLA

Burle, José Carlos

b. 1910, Recife, Pernambuco, Brazil; d. 1984, Rio de Janeiro, Brazil

Film-maker

Co-founder of the **Atlântida** production company, he directed its first film *Moleque Tião* (1943). Its combination of music and social concern brought fame to its star **Grande Otelo** and success to both Burle and the studios. He went on to make *chanchadas* and films about **football** (*Gol da vitória* (Winning Goal) (1945)) and **carnival** (*Barnabé tu és meu* (Barnabé You're Mine) (1951)). He later left Atlântida to make more football films, the comedy *O cantor e o milionário* (The Singer and the Millionaire) (1957) and his last feature *Terra sem Deus* (Land without God) (1963), filmed in his native region.

ISMAIL XAVIER AND THE USP GROUP

Burnham, Forbes

b. 1923, Kitty, British Guiana; d. 1985, Guyana

Lawyer and politician

Installed in power in the early 1960s by the CIA and the British Colonial Office in opposition to Cheddi **Jagan**, whose Marxist views they could not accept, Burnham was Prime Minister of Guyana until October 1980, when he named himself President and Commander-in-Chief of the Armed Forces. Burnham was prepared to employ any means to remain in power, including electoral fraud, bribery, control of the press and even assassination of opponents like Walter **Rodney**,

whose political project was to unify Guyana's African and East Indian populations.

KEITH JARDIM

buses

Buses are the principal means of both urban and inter-urban transport throughout Latin America, since the railways were largely built by foreign concerns with strictly commercial purposes – like those built by Henry Meggs in Peru's Central Valley to link the mines with the port of Callao, or by Victor Canning to Veracruz, or the banana companies in Central America to carry their product to the sea. Notoriously overcrowded and often mechanically unsound, the urban *camión camello*, *micro* or *guagua* – as buses are called in various Latin American countries – is often individually owned and precariously financed. Their fixed, usually low fares reflect the poor wages of those who must use these means of transport, since the middle class will tend to use one of several forms of **taxis**; they also explain the huge number of people that are crammed in during rush hours. More modern British or Eastern European buses were introduced in Mexico and Peru respectively; the Ruta 100 in Mexico City became the focus of a sustained strike in the mid-1990s against privatization.

MIKE GONZALEZ

Bustamante, Sir William Alexander

b. 1884, Blenheim, Hanover, Jamaica; d. 1977, Kingston, Jamaica

Politician

Founder of the Jamaican Labour Party (JLP) and the first prime Minister of an independent Jamaica (1962–7), Bustamante established himself as a vocal critic of British colonial governance and its failure to benefit Jamaica's working class majority when he returned to the island in 1934 after almost thirty years of working and travelling in Europe and the USA. His family name was Clarke, but during his travels he began to use the name 'Bustamante' and eventually legally changed his name. He became a labour organizer and founded the Bustamante International Trade Union in 1938. He also joined the People's National Party (PNP), founded by his cousin Norman **Manley**, though he later broke with it and formed his own Jamaica Labour Party. Bustamante had initially supported Jamaican membership in the British West Indies Federation, formed in 1958, but later changed his position to favour Jamaica's individual independence. He has been honoured with a British knighthood and also named a Jamaican national hero.

ROSANNE ADDERLEY

Bustillo, Alejandro

b. 1889, Buenos Aires, Argentina; d. 1982, Buenos Aires

Architect

Bustillo introduced the 'modern French style' at the height of modernism; he used different styles according to surroundings and clients' demands. His Buenos Aires neo-classical works include the Banco Tornquist (1925), the re-modelling of the ex-Palais de Glace and the portico of the National Fine Arts Museum (1931), and the Banco de la Nación (1944). Victoria **Ocampo**'s house was inspired by Le Corbusier, while his grand hotels of Mar del Plata and the Llao-llao in Bariloche (both completed 1937–9) were notable for their integration with the landscape.

GONZALO AGUILAR

Bustillo Oro, Juan

b. 1904, Mexico City; d. 1989, Mexico City

Film-maker and writer

Beginning as a scriptwriter for early Mexican directors like Ramón Peón and Fernando de **Fuentes**, Bustillo Oro's first sound feature, *Dos monjes* (Two Monks) (1934) revealed both expressionist and Pirandellian influences. From 1938 to 1941 he directed the most successful commercial films of the period – *En tiempos de don Porfirio* (In Don Porfirio's Time) (1939), *Ahí está el detalle* (That's the Point) (1940) – which introduced **Cantinflas** and the melodrama *Cuando los hijos se van* (When the Children Leave Home) (1941). He made fifty-eight films and left a body of journalism and literary work, some still unpublished.

PATRICIA TORRES SAN MARTíN

Butantan Institute

The Butantan Institute is a centre of scientific and technological research in São Paulo, Brazil, whose origins lie in the bubonic plague that hit the port of Santos in 1898. The city's Bacteriological Institute responded to the emergency by establishing a special unit for the production of vaccines on the Butantan plantation outside the city. On 3 February 1901 the unit became the autonomous Butantan Institute. Under its first director, Dr **Vital Brazil**, a mine-owner who became a public health authority, the Butantan began research into venomous creatures including snakes, scorpions and spiders. The antidotes it produced won the Institute the recognition of the international scientific community.

ANTONIO CARLOS MARTINS VAZ

Butler, Horacio

b. 1897, Buenos Aires, Argentina; d. 1983, Buenos Aires

Visual artist

A member of the Paris Group together with **Berni**, Basaldúa, **Badii** and **Spilimbergo**, Butler stood within the European currents of the return to order. He returned to Buenos Aires from France in 1933, where his painting focused on the landscape of the delta of the River Plate. He also became known for his illustrations, and for his set designs and costumes for a number of theatrical presentations in Argentina and outside. He published his autobiography, *La pintura y mi tiempo* (Painting and My Time), in 1966.

CECILIA RABOSSI

Butler, Uriah ('Buzz')

b. 1895, St George's, Grenada; d. 1977, Point Fortin, Trinidad

Politician

Having moved to Trinidad in 1921 in search of work, in 1935, Butler led a sixty mile hunger march of oilworkers from Fyzabad to Port-of-Spain, protesting against poor working conditions. On 19 June 1937, Butler's own political party, the British Empire Workers' and Citizens' Home Rule Party (BEWCHRP), orchestrated a massive strike and revolt, known as the Butler Riots, which led to the formation, on 26 July 1937, of the Oilworkers Trade Union (OWTU). This earned Butler the title of Father of Trade Unionism, not only in Trinidad and Tobago, but throughout the British West Indies.

JILL E. ALBADA-JELGERSMA

Bye Bye Brasil

Named after a Chico **Buarque** song, Carlos **Diegues**'s *Bye Bye Brasil* (1979) represents the attempts by the **Cinema Novo** generation to reconcile the demands of a national cinema with the desire to attract wider audiences. It tells the story of the Caravana Rolidei ('Holiday' misspelled), a travelling troupe that, having lost its audiences to television, sets off into the expanding Amazon frontier region and ends up in **Brasília**. The result is a kind of Brazilian road movie which adheres to the rules of classical cinema yet manages to be an allegory of the process of modernization in Brazil and the role of cinema within it.

ISMAIL XAVIER AND THE USP GROUP

C

Caamaño Deñó, Francisco Alberto

b. 1932, Santo Domingo, Dominican Republic; d. 1973, San José de Ocoa, Dominican Republic

Soldier and politician

An opponent of the *coup d'état* that overthrew President Juan **Bosch** in 1963, Colonel Caamaño Deñó took part in a military insurrection against the incumbent President Donald Reid Cabral in 1965, and fought the American troops that invaded the country shortly afterwards. As Constitutional President of the Revolutionary Government, Caamaño demanded the return of Bosch from exile and the application of the 1963 Constitution. After signing the peace treaty, he took up a diplomatic post in London but soon abandoned it. On 3 February 1973 he led a group of *guerrilleros* from Cuba who disembarked on Dominican soil with the aim of overthrowing the **Balaguer** regime. He was captured alive, and was executed by firing squad in the mountains.

FERNANDO VALERIO-HOLGUÍN

Caballero Calderón, Eduardo

b. 1910, Bogotá, Colombia; d. 1990, Bogotá

Writer

Author of over ten novels and eleven volumes of essays, Caballero Calderón was a major Colombian writer. His essay on *Don Quijote* demonstrates his knowledge of the Hispanic literary heritage from the *Poema de mío Cid* through the twentieth century. His novels *El cristo de espaldas* (Christ on his Back) (1952), *Siervo sin tierra* (Landless Servant) (1953), and *Manuel Pacho* (1962) are related to the civil war identified as 'La **Violencia**' and have received substantial critical attention. *El buen salvaje* (The Good Savage) (1965), which received Spain's Nadal Prize in 1965, is a self-conscious novel about a struggling novelist in Paris.

RAYMOND L. WILLIAMS

Caballero Holguín, Luis

b. 1943, Santafé de Bogotá, Colombia; d. 1995

Painter

Caballero's predominantly figurative paintings very often represent nudes. From 1970 onwards, his work was influenced by the representation of the human body during the Renaissance. The subject of his paintings are almost exclusively athletic young men, whose bodies appear in postures that suggest the experience of violence, torment or sexual ecstasy. A homoerotic sensibility is evident in Caballero's work. He studied art in Bogotá, at the Universidad de los Andes (1961–2), and later at the Académie de la Grand Chaumière, in Paris (1963–4).

MIGUEL A. CARDINALE

Caballo viejo

'Caballo viejo' (Old horse) is the title of a popular song composed by Simón **Díaz**, originating in Venezuela, and made into numerous **salsa**, **cumbia**, **canción ranchera**, **vallenato** and **son** versions throughout Latin America. Its lyrics suggest that love fortuitously revitalizes even the oldest of horses. No strong bridle can refrain him when it arrives, for with his years, experience has taught him that these things are never 'scheduled'. The song represents the stereotypical *viejo verde*, or 'dirty old man', who, unlike a colt who gives it time to grow, *caballo viejo* cannot pass up the flower before him, because after this life there will not be another opportunity.

BARBARA D. RIESS

Cabaretera films

Mexican film genre from the 1940s, set primarily in cabarets and nightclubs, and prominently featuring their female denizens and typical popular rhythms (**danzón**, **rumba** and **samba**). Incorporating aspects of the earlier 'seduced and abandoned' melodramas like **Santa** (1931) and with a clear predecessor in Arcady **Boytler**'s brilliantly iconoclastic early sound film (see **sound film, early**), *La mujer del puerto* (The Woman of the Port) (1933), the *cabareteras* emerged as a response to social changes, especially the modernizing and developmentalist ideology of the Miguel Alemán presidency (1946–52). In these films, the female protagonists were typically struggling to support their families or tricked into prostitution; what is most remarkable, however, is the free rein given to the representation (and pleasures) of female sexuality. Key examples of the genre are Julio **Bracho**'s *Distinto amanecer* (A Different Dawn) (1943) and Emilio **Fernández**'s *Salón Mexico* (1948). However, its most successful – and over-the-top – practitioner was Alberto **Gout**: in a series of films with Ninón **Sevilla** – like *Aventurera* (Adventuress) (1949) – he explored the very limits of the possibilities for representing female desire. The genre was revived in the 1970s, another period of great social uncertainty, and renamed the '*fichera*' genre.

ANA M. LÓPEZ

cabarets and nightclubs

The words that describe places of late night entertainment vary greatly among different Latin American countries. In the last thirty years, cabaret as a place for live entertainment and dancing has yielded to the nightclub, where the dance music is provided electronically. The industrialization and commercialization of leisure, the regulation of work, the crisis of public representation, the strength of consumer culture, the privatization of technology and the mechanization of art have produced an important nocturnal market sustained by the relative liberalization of heterosexual customs. In such a market the traditional cabaret, with its costly live shows and its dubious morality, found less and less favour. Cabaret modernized into huge venues for live popular music, local and international, performed by less well-known artists. The nightclub thus became a part of a mass culture with direct access to the global market and to technology. If cabaret was once associated with Bohemians and the underworld, existing at the centre or on the margins of an urban world, its modern version connects it to marginal areas within the highly fragmented space and time of medium and large Latin American cities. This night life, linked to a leisure produced by higher wage levels and longer periods of professional training in the young, created a more elitist night life, often in areas ill-served by public transport or in tourist districts.

The representation of the nightclub or cabaret has ceased to respond solely to the suspension of social hierarchies. The postulation of its intensely sexual atmosphere in film and television, its strangeness in literature, its disfunctional role analysed positively or negatively by sociologists or anthropologists, were overtaken by the ritualization and commercialization of an image of festive, hedonistic sociability in the mass media. In the joys of the little dramas of a night life increasingly confined to the bar or the dance hall, we can see the reflection of that increasingly mediated representation. In the diversification and refinement of the codes of participation in these dramas powerful conflicts emerge, linked to the meanings attributed to class, race, gender, sexuality, age and tribes. The discriminations implicit in the selection of what are considered appropriate fashions and atmospheres in different clubs, or the frisking of clients before they are admitted, have their interior projections too, through a demanding exhibition of the latest look or the deployment of an aggressive virility.

See also: PM

Further reading

Elbaum, J. (1997) *Que siga el baile. Discriminación y racismo en la diversión nocturna*, Buenos Aires: Oficina de Publicaciones del CBC.

Jiménez, A. (1992) *Cabarets de antes y de ahora en la ciudad de México*, Mexico: Plaza y Valdés Editores.

ROBERTO MADERO

Cabeza de Vaca

Directed by Nicolas **Echevarría** in 1991, the film's script, co-written by Echevarría and Guillermo Sheridan, is freely adapted from *Naufragios y Comentarios* (1527) by Alvar Nuñez Cabeza de Vaca. Alvar, a royal treasurer who joined Pánfilo Narváez's expedition to Florida, survives a shipwreck but is captured by a dwarf sorcerer called Malacosa. After many humiliations, Alvar learns the sorcerer's arts. Once freed, he is reunited with some of his companions and they undertake a journey of several years through what is now Texas, Arizona, Sonora and Sinaloa. Echevarría recreates in elliptical and minimal form the physical and spiritual journey undertaken by this far from ordinary conquistador.

PATRICIA TORRES SAN MARTÍN

Cabichu'í 2

Cabichu'í 2 is a literary journal co-founded by Moncho **Azuaga**, Emilio Lugo and Ricardo de la Vega in 1989. Published semi-annually, *Cabichu'í 2* began as the platform for the poets of the Taller de Poesía Manuel Ortiz Guerrero (Manuel Ortiz Guerrero Poetry Workshop), who became known in the last stages of the **Stroessner** dictatorship (1955–89). It continued the work begun by Editora Taller (Workshop Publishing), which published some ten titles by Paraguayan poets.

TERESA MÉNDEZ-FAITH

Cabral, Manuel del

b. 1907, Santiago de los Caballeros, Dominican Republic; d. 1999, Santo Domingo, Dominican Republic

Poet

One of the initiators of black poetry in the Caribbean, Del Cabral lived in Argentina, where in the 1940s he published *Trópico negro* (Black Tropics) (1941), *Compadre Mon* (Godfather Mon) (1943) and *Chinchina busca el tiempo* (Chinchina's Search for Time) (1945). In *Doce poemas negros* (Twelve Black Poems) (1935) and *Trópico negro*, he explored Afro-Caribbean culture and social problems. *Compadre Mon* is an extensive poem in which humanity sings to the earth in search of its origins. In *Chinchina busca el tiempo*, Del Cabral expressed his metaphysical concerns.

FERNANDO VALERIO-HOLGUÍN

Cabrera, Lydia

b. 1899, Havana, Cuba; d. 1991, Miami, USA

Writer, ethnologist

A central figure in Afro-Cuban studies, her study of Cuban folklore began under Fernando **Ortiz** before moving to Paris, where she continued her studies of the religion, myths and customs of black Cubans. At the same time she studied painting and became absorbed by Eastern religion. In Spain, she formed a close relationship with García Lorca.

Her first book, *Cuentos negros de Cuba* (Black Stories from Cuba) (1936), published in Cuba in 1940, recreated in twenty-two poetic prose pieces the experiences of a marginal population that nevertheless played a central role in the formation of Cuba's national culture. Her writing went beyond the transient interest in Afro-Cuban culture to capture the deeper sprituality of black Cubans, locating Caribbean mythology in a category of universal values.

Returning to Paris from Spain in 1938, she resumed her explorations of the surviving traditions of a population whose origins were in Africa and developed a careful and detailed study of the linguistic and anthropological aspects of black Cuban culture. The result was her most important work, *El monte* (1954), a Bible of Cuba's black culture. Its sub-title 'Notes on the religions, music, beliefs and folklore of Afro-Cubans and the people of Cuba' indicate how thoroughly documented it was, and explains why it has become the definitive work on **Santería**.

Other works in the same vein followed: *Anagó, vocabulario Lucumí* (Anagó, Lucumí Vocabulary) (1957) and *La sociedad secreta abakuá narrada por viejos adeptos* (The **Abakua** Secret Society Narrated by Aged Members) (1959).

She went into exile in 1960, but continued to work on the material collected in previous years, producing a number of works including *Cuentos para adultos niños y retrasados mentales* (Stories for Childish Adults and Mentally Handicapped People) (1983) and *La medicina popular en Cuba* (Popular Medicine in Cuba) (1984).

Further reading

Castellanos, I. and Inclán, J. (1987) *En torno a Lydia Cabrera (Cincuentenario de 'Cuentos Negros de Cuba') 1936–86*, Miami: Universal.

Hiriart, R. (1978) *Lydia Cabrera: Vida hecha arte*, New York: Eliseo Torres.

Sánchez, R. (ed.) (1977) *Homenaje a Lydia Cabrera*, Miami: Universal.

WILFREDO CANCIO ISLA

Cabrera, Pablo

b. 1933, Vega Alta, Puerto Rico

Television and theatre director

Pedro Cabrera is considered one of Puerto Rico's most accomplished directors, with a string of successful dramas, musicals and operas both on the island and abroad. After studying in Italy, Cabrera returned to Puerto Rico in the early 1960s, making his directorial debut with Luis Rafael **Sánchez**'s *La farsa del amor compradito* (Farce of Little Bought Loves) (1961). A professor at Hostos Community College since 1972, Cabrera has been consultant and director for the Puerto Rican Travelling Theatre. In 1994, he founded the CUNY-affiliated theatre ensemble Compañía de Repertorio Hostos.

VÍCTOR F. TORRES

Cabrera, Sergio

b. 1950, Medellín, Colombia

Film-maker

Cabrera has earned distinction as the only Colombian director to complete a feature film nearly every year since 1992. Moreover, his second feature, *Estrategia de caracol* (Strategy of the Snail) (1993), was the highest grossing film in Colombian history. Like Cabrera's other feature films, *Técnicas de duelo* (Techniques of the Duel) (1988) and *Aguilas no cazan moscas* (Eagles Do Not Hunt Flies) (1995), *Estrategia* is an ensemble film whose stories reveal the battles with uncertainty, memory and history which are integral components of Colombian life.

ILENE GOLDMAN

Cabrera Infante, Guillermo

b. 1929, Gibara, Cuba

Writer

One of the leading contemporary writers of Latin America, Cabrera Infante has lived in self-imposed exile in Britain since the mid-1960s and is a vocal critic of Fidel Castro. His career began as a journalist with the popular magazine *Bohemia*. In 1954, under the pseudonym G. Cain, he became the film critic for the journal *Carteles* and continued until the magazine ceased publication. He founded the Cinemateca de Cuba and was its president from 1951 to 1956; he was also editor of the literary magazine *Lunes de revolución* throughout its existence. His disenchantment with the Cuban Revolution began with the conflict over the film *PM* (1961), an experimental journey through Havana nightlife which was censored by the Castro government. After three years as a cultural attaché in Belgium, Cabrera Infante resigned his diplomatic post in 1965 and left Cuba to become resident in Europe.

Although he had won the occasional literary prize, early recognition of his work came with his *Así en la paz como en la guerra* (Rites of Passage) (1960), a volume of short stories set in pre-revolutionary Cuba. It was his novel *Tres tristes tigres* (Three Trapped Tigers) (1967) that brought him international recognition. This fabulous re-creation of Havana at night revolves around the obsessive themes of his writing – nostalgia for the city, music, the cinema and joyful games with language. It offers a broad fresco of Cuban life and manners in the 1950s, evoked with irreverence, satirical wit and a narrative certainty which gives his work its great power.

Critics agree that *Tres tristes tigres* (its title taken from a children's tongue twister) is a key work of the Latin American literary **Boom** and a landmark in Cuban literature. His subsequent work has embraced several genres. *Vista del amanecer en el trópico* (View of Dawn in the Tropics) (1974) narrates the history of Cuba from the Discovery to the present through a series of vignettes. *O* (1975) is a collection of essays and articles on contemporary issues; *Ejercicios de esti(l)o* (Style Trials) (1976) is a series of experimental writings while *La Habana para una infanta difunta* (Infante's Inferno) (1979) is a novel.

Mea Cuba (My Cuba), published in 1992, brings together his political and critical writings; *Delito por bailar el chachachá* (1995), a volume of stories, and *Ella cantaba boleros* (She Sang Boleros) (1996) a narrative based on his earlier novels followed. His passion for film is reflected in critical essays collected in *Un oficio del siglo veinte* (A Twentieth-Century Job) (1963) and *Cine y sardina* (Film and Sardines) (1997). He has also explored the history of the Cuban cigar in *Holy Smoke*, published in English in 1985.

In 1997, he won the Cervantes Prize for Literature.

Further reading

Cabrera Infante, G. (1999) *Assays, essays and other arts*, New York: Twayne Publishers.

Machover, J. (1996) *El heraldo de las malas noticias: Guillermo Cabrera Infante: ensayo a dos voces*, Miami, Fla.: Ediciones Universal.

Pereda, Rosa M. (1979) *Guillermo Cabrera Infante*, Madrid: Edaf.

Souza, R.D.(1996) *Guillermo Cabrera Infante: two islands, many worlds*, Austin, TX: University of Texas Press.

WILFREDO CANCIO ISLA

Cabrujas, José Ignacio

b. 1937, Caracas, Venezuela; d. 1995, Margarita, Venezuela

Playwright, actor, screenwriter and essayist

Together with Román **Chalbaud** and Isaac **Chocrón**, Cabrujas founded El Nuevo Grupo, one of the most important theatre companies of the sixties. His dramatic works have been frequently performed and some adapted for the cinema. It was on television, however, where Cabrujas made his particular mark, introducing major innovations into the genre of the television soap opera (**culebrón** or *telenovela* – see **telenovelas**). Among his best known plays are *Acto cultural* (A Cultural Act) and *El día que me quieras* (The Day You Love Me). His *telenovelas La señora de Cárdenas* (Mrs Cardenas) (1977) and *La dueña* (The Landlady) (1985) are classics of the genre.

JORGE ROMERO LEÓN

cacao

First discovered by Europeans in the Mayan regions of Mexico, there cocoa (*cacao*) was probably used from about AD 600. It then passed to the Aztecs, who carried chocolate with them on long military campaigns. The Spanish conquerors did not care for the drink at first, until sugar was added; it then spread through Spain and beyond as a luxury for the consumption of the wealthy. In the late twentieth century, its distribution world-wide is dominated by four or five multinational companies, many of which began as Quaker companies (Fry's and Cadbury's are examples) looking for alternatives to alcohol. In Mexico, chocolate is often added to corn (maize) in the preparation of drinks like *pinole* or *pozol*, or mixed with chilli or other spices to make cooking sauces like *mole*. The water needs to be boiling hot to dissolve the heavy tablets, hence the expression *como agua para chocolate* (like water for chocolate) immortalized in Laura **Esquivel**'s best-selling novel of that name. The pure bitter chocolate of Mexico and Central America is now largely marketed as a specialized organic product.

CRISTINA BARROS AND MARCO BUENROSTRO

cachaça

Popular alcoholic beverage, akin to **rum**, produced in Brazil from sugar-cane molasses. Like rums, *cachaças* vary in quality and strength, ranging from rare, aged and silky vintages, to the quite harsh and inexpensive varieties commonly available in large, often unlabelled bottles or produced in home stills, which can be more potent and damaging than white lightning. *Cachaça* is the base for the popular refreshing drink *caipirinha*, in which it is mixed with a tiny amount of lemon juice and lots of sugar. It is also the base for innumerable shaken drinks called *batidas*, in which it is mixed with fruit juices, coconut milk, coffee or other spirits. Although it can be quite refined and sampled like vintage scotches in fancy bars, like the 'Academia da Cachaça' in Rio de Janeiro, it is also extraordinarily popular among all classes; drunks are often referred to simply as *cachaceiros*, regardless of their beverage of choice.

ANA M. LÓPEZ

Cachafaz, El
b. 1885, Buenos Aires, Argentina; d. 1942, Mar del Plata, Argentina

Dancer

El Cachafaz (José Ovidio Bianquet) was considered the greatest of all **tango** dancers. His special moves and steps were legendary; his patent leather shoes with grey suede insets and military heels shone in the arabesques and figures that cut spontaneously in the course of the dance. As a young man, he won a dance contest which gave him free access to all the clubs of Buenos Aires, and his fame peaked when he danced in the 1933 film *Tango!* with his most famous partner, Carmencita Calderón. He died at age fifty-seven, while dancing in a theatre in Mar del Plata.

LUIS GUSMAN

Cachao   *see*   López, Israel

cachullapi

Cachullapi is the music of the mestizos of Ecuador. A **Quichua** term, translated as 'squeezed' or 'crushed', it was used early in the twentieth century to designate a bright and sociable genre of popular music. In a strict sense, cachullapi is not a musical genre, but it could be seen as a version of the typical air, the 'albazo', the 'amorfino' or the 'capishca'. It is a free, relaxed dance like all the mestizo dances of Ecuador, written in 6/8 and 3/4 time in a minor key.

ALICIA ORTEGA

CADA

CADA (Colectivo de Acciones de Arte) was an inter-disciplinary group formed in Chile around 1977 in opposition to the **Pinochet** regime. Its most important members were Lotty **Rosenfeld**, Juan Castillo (visual artist), Fernando Barcells (sociologist), Raúl **Zurita**, Diamela **Eltit** and Alfredo Jaar. Although stopping short of direct political statements, they explored the possibilities of an avant-garde expression of dissent, charged with difficult symbolism and complex critical discourse (see also **escena de avanzada**).

GABRIEL PEREZ-BARREIRO

Cadenas, Rafael

b. 1930, Barquisemeto, Venezuela

Poet

One of Venezuela's most representative and widely read poets, Cadenas was associated with the post-**Pérez Jiménez** intellectual movements. His lyrical testimony, *Los cuadernos del destierro* (Notebooks from Exile) (1960) celebrates the world as seen by a patient and obsessive observer and offers an ironic self-representation through sensual and reflective imagery. Since then his poetry has become increasingly concentrated and aphoristic, as in *Memorial* (1977) or *Gestiones* (Operations) (1992) which won him the Pérez Bonalde Poetry Prize. Cadenas has also published works straddling the line between poetry and aphorism, and volumes of essays.

RAFAEL CASTILLO ZAPATA

Cafajestes, Os

One of the classic films of Brazilian **Cinema Novo**, Ruy **Guerra**'s *Os Cafajestes* (The Hustlers) (1962) turns on the sexual games played by two young **Copacabana** hustler/playboys who seduce women and then blackmail them. Using a hand-held camera and a fragmented narrative, the film offers a startlingly innovative vision of youths caught between tedium and situations of violence and cruelty. In that sense, the film was close in spirit and style to the French New Wave. As one of the women, Norma **Bengell**'s performance was especially notable, and her frontal nudity captured in dizzying 360° pans scandalized audiences and censors.

ISMAIL XAVIER AND THE USP GROUP

café culture

The café culture inherited from the late nineteenth century was centred upon the very Spanish idea of the *tertulia*, a conversation among friends sustained over time, often on a daily or weekly basis, by a stable group of people who rarely admitted casual attendees. These groups were usually led by a charismatic intellectual or artistic figure, although both the leader and the led were invariably male. There was and remains a very strong element of male bonding in the ritual of the *tertulia*. Some important moments in literary and political history in the Spanish-speaking world are associated with rival *tertulia* groups, organized in different cafés by different leaders. For example, Spanish *ultraísmo* in the early 1920s was divided into two groups, both meeting in Madrid cafés: Ramón Gómez de la Serna's group, and Rafael Cansinos Assens's. **Borges** was an assiduous member of the latter group, and wrote a brief memoir of its meetings at the Café Pombo in one of his early books. Grand early coffee shops include the **art nouveau** Gran Café Tortoni in Buenos Aires, the site of poetic and musical recitals since the time of the *modernistas* (see **modernismo, Spanish American**) and currently the meeting place of the Academia Argentina del **Lunfardo** (Argentine Academy of Lunfardo).

Witold Gombrowicz and his friends translated *Ferdydurke* from Polish to Spanish in 1947 in the chess hall of a Buenos Aires pool parlour. The leader of that group was the Cuban Virgilio **Piñera**, but other members included Macedonio **Fernández**'s son, Adolfo de Obieta, and numerous others. This episode is replayed in the all-night café scene in Ricardo **Piglia**'s **Respiración artificial** (1980).

By contrast, many of the controversies of political and intellectual life in Mexico City through the 1960s were played out in the Café Habana, conveniently located close to the offices of the main protagonists of the magazine *Política*, the newspaper *Excélsior*, etc. In Veracruz, most disputes found their way to the Café Parroquia. Similarly important sites of intellectual encounter, exchange and debate were the two branches of Café Haití in Lima, the Café de la Paz in Buenos Aires and Café Tacuba in Mexico City. This last is the location of much of the action of an important story by Elena **Garro**, 'La culpa de los tlaxcaltecas' (Blame the Tlaxcalans) (1960), and gave its name to the contemporary Mexican rock group **Café Tacuba**.

Although these cafés have almost all survived, in many cases they show evidence of wear and tear, and the younger generation will tend to meet in other places, for example in **fast food** restaurants, galleries, book shops with cafés – like Librería Gandhi in Mexico City and Buenos Aires – or alternative bars. One curious development is the appearance, largely in the 1980s, in central Santiago, Chile, of so-called coffee shops frequented by businessmen during lunch hours and at the close of the business day, where they are served by scantily clad young women, who at regular intervals briefly remove their bras to entice passing potential customers to come in for a *café cortado* (since only coffee is served there).

MIKE GONZALEZ AND DANIEL BALDERSTON

Café Tacuba

Café Tacuba is a Mexican rock band whose members, Joselo and Enrique Rangel, Emmanuel del Real and Juan Cosme, named their band after a well-known coffee house in the heart of Mexico City. Their recognition in Latin America, Europe and the USA by the mid-1990s is due to their very eclectic repertoire, mixing Mexican, and Latin American rhythms (from **son** and **mariachi** to cumbias (see **cumbia**) and sambas (see **samba**)) along with a variety of American sounds (rock and punk to heavy metal or funk grooves) and use of urban jargon. Unlike Latin American groups that poorly imitate American or British rock groups, Café Tacuba is a truly progressive band.

EDUARDO SANTA CRUZ

CAFRA

CAFRA (Caribbean Association for Feminist Research and Action) is a regional network of feminists, individual researchers, activists and women's organizations representing Caribbean women at home and abroad, as well as women with 'Caribbean roots' living elsewhere. Formed in 1985 in Barbados and incorporated in Trinidad and Tobago in 1990, the organization has fourteen representatives, elected by membership at the national level. CAFRA's mission is to celebrate and channel the collective power of Caribbean women for individual and societal transformation, through educational programmes, institutional development, and networking projects such as the CAFRA News and the *Creation Fire* literary anthology (1990). CAFRA serves as facilitator to strengthen regionalism (see **regionalismo**) and establish proper links between research and action programmes for women.

GAY WILENTZ

Cafrune, Jorge

b. 1937, El Carmen, Jujuy, Argentina;
d. 1969, Buenos Aires, Argentina

Singer

A highly successful folk singer, Cafrune joined the Salta group Las Voces del Huayra at the age of twenty, and in 1959 joined Los Cantores del Alba, with whom he recorded folk songs in Buenos Aires. As folk music grew in popularity, Cafrune returned to Salta to form a duo with Alberto Sauad. After participating in several musical festivals in Latin America, he began recording his memorable solo interpretations of popular zambas (see **zamba**). Later his songs increasingly turned to protest. He died as he embarked on a journey throughout Argentina on horseback, when he was hit by a car outside Buenos Aires.

MAGDALENA GARCÍA PINTO

Cahier d'un retour au pays natal

Aimé **Césaire** began work on his lengthy lyric poem *Cahier d'un retour au pays natal* (Notes on a Return to the Homeland), a politically engaged meditation on a return to his native island of Martinique and a founding text of **négritude**, in 1936 while still a student in Paris. Published for the first time in the review *Volontés* in 1939, the poem underwent numerous revisions and publications, of which the 1956 **Présence Africaine** edition is considered definitive. Despite Césaire's surrealist techniques, the poem includes autobiographical detail and vehemently denounces the historical problems of colonialism, slavery, and poverty in Africa and the Antilles.

SCOTT COOPER

Cahiers des Amériques Latines

This semi-annual journal, founded in Paris in 1968, focuses on the social sciences and emphasizes the social, demographic, political and economic problems of Latin America. Each issue contains a group of articles on a particular geographical or thematic topic. It includes research and conference reports, reviews and bibliographies. The journal is published in French with summaries in English, Portuguese and Spanish, and is indexed in *Hispanic American Periodicals Index*.

PAUL BARY

Caignet, Félix B.

b. 1892, San Luis, Cuba; d. 1976, Havana, Cuba

Writer and composer

Known worldwide for his successful radio soap operas (*radionovelas*) in the 1930s, one of his scripts was adapted for Cuba's first sound feature film, *La serpiente roja* (The Red Serpent) (1937). His most famous radio serial *El **derecho de nacer*** (The Right to be Born) (1948) broke every audience record in its time and was adapted to film and *telenovela* (see ***telenovelas***). Among his popular musical compositions are the bolero 'Te odio' (I Hate You), first performed by Rita **Montaner** and the song Frutas del Caney, immortalized by the **Trío Matamoros**.

WILFREDO CANCIO ISLA

caimán barbudo, El

Founded in 1966 as a monthly supplement to *Juventud rebelde*, edited by Jesús **Díaz**, *El caimán barbudo* (The Bearded Alligator) provided a platform for young writers and a space for cultural and intellectual debates during the first phase of the Cuban Revolution (see **revolutions**). In 1971 it became independent under a new more dogmatic and exclusive editorial board. In the late 1980s, under new editors, it experienced a revival and once again began to attract young writers and artists and provide space for cultural debates. It ceased publication in August 1990 as a result of severe economic conditions, and reappeared in late 1996 as a quarterly.

WILFREDO CANCIO ISLA

Caiozzi, Silvio

b. 1944, Santiago, Chile

Film-maker

Caiozzi studied film in the USA in the mid-1960s, returning to Chile to work as a cinematographer in the new cinema movement of 1967–73. After the 1973 military *coup*, Caiozzi was one of the few film-makers to remain. His first feature, *Julio comienza en julio* (Julio Begins in July) (1979), an allegory of Chile under **Pinochet**, is about a feudal landlord struggling to maintain power. *La luna en el espejo* (The Moon in the Mirror) (1990) employs stylistic devices like mirrors to create a disorienting world. Co-written with José **Donoso**, it is an allegory of post-dictatorship Chile.

DOLORES TIERNEY

Cairo, Edgar E.

b. 1948, Suriname

Writer and playwright

Cairo grew up in Suriname. His first publication was in Sranan Tongo, a Surinamese creole, but he later turned to Dutch and the local Surinamese variant of Dutch. In the 1970s and 1980s he was a very prolific writer with over twenty-five publications of prose, poetry and drama, including the lengthy novels *Dat vuur der grote drama's* (That Fire of Great Dramas) (1982) and *Jeje Disi: Karakter's krachten* (A Character's Powers) (1980). He also became known for his lively reading sessions. Resident in the Netherlands, he was forced to stop writing due to psychological problems.

AART G. BROEK

Calamaro, Andrés

b. 1961, Buenos Aires, Argentina

Musician

Singer and keyboard player Calamaro is probably the most prolific composer of **rock nacional** in recent years. From the age of seventeen he was a member of several groups, until he joined Los Abuelos de la Nada (Grandparents of Nothingness), one of the dominant bands in 1980s Argentina; along with Miguel Abuelo, Calamaro became, at barely twenty years of age, its most famous figure. Leaving the band in 1986, he went to Spain where he formed Los Rodríguez, a group comprising Argentine and Spanish musicians which caused a sensation on the somewhat drab Iberian rock scene.

DIEGO BENTIVEGNA

calaveras

The word *calaveras* means, literally, skulls. In Mexican popular culture, the word has slang associations with a man deemed a 'madcap, rake, rouse, cad' and even with car brakelights (presumably a reflection on driving habits). Sugar skulls sold for the **Day of the Dead** bear the name of the recipient or endearments and are intricately painted and ubiquitously sold and exchanged. The skulls also feature widely in popular imagery, from the photographs of Manuel **Alvarez Bravo**, Mariana **Yampolsky** and Francisco Mata to the engravings of José Guadalupe **Posada**, Leopoldo **Méndez**, Francisco Luna and others. Originating in the Aztec death cult, their popularity has increased with the spread of Catholic iconography (see **Catholicism**) and the mass-production of the sugar skulls.

AMANDA HOPKINSON

Calcanhoto, Adriana

b. 1965, Porto Alegre, Brazil

Singer and composer

With her distinctive voice and lyrics, Calcanhoto represents, with Zélia Duncan and Cassia Eller, a new generation of 1990s Brazilian women composers and singers. In addition to her own compositions, exploring the materiality of words, love and identity, Calcanhoto has recorded songs by composers as diverse as Erasmo and Roberto Carlos, **Cazuza**, and the ex-member of **Titãs**, Arnaldo Antunes. Her 1994 album *A Fábrica do Poema* (The Factory of the Poem) is her most experimental work, including lyrics by poet Augusto de **Campos** and a montage with the voice of US avant-garde writer Gertrude Stein.

CÉSAR BRAGA-PINTO

Caldas, Waltércio

b. 1946, Rio de Janeiro, Brazil

Artist

A conceptual artist (see **conceptual art**), Caldas seeks to stimulate thought and raise questions through his work, rather than to produce aesthetically pleasing finished pieces of art. He has exhibited his drawings, but his stark, striking sculptures have attracted more attention. Though often elegant in form, they are far removed from traditional sculpture, aiming to undermine the viewers' assumptions and expectations about art and obliging them to observe objects in a new way. Since Caldas's early exhibitions in Brazil in the 1970s, he has exhibited in several countries.

MARK DINNEEN

Calderón, Teresa

b. 1955, La Serena, Chile

Poet

In the constrained conditions of the **Pinochet** regime (1973–90), Calderón's work addresses women's day-to-day experience, and their dealings with masculine culture. Her language is colloquial and direct and charged with irony. Her first book, *Causas perdidas* (Lost Causes) was published in 1983. *Género femenino* (Feminine Gender/Genre) (1989) highlights her sense of identity as a woman. In the post-1990 Chilean democracy, however, her generation saw its spaces of promotion and recognition expand. She won the prestigious Pablo Neruda Prize for Poetry in 1992.

LUIS E. CÁRCAMO-HUECHANTE

Caliban

Caliban, a rebellious island native enslaved by a colonizing Milanese Duke named Prospero in William Shakespeare's *The Tempest*, became a favorite symbol of revolutionary, anti-imperialist culture for Caribbean writers in the 1960s and early 1970s. The character's name is an anagram for 'cannibal,' a word introduced to English shortly after Christopher Columbus dubbed the natives of the West Indies *caníbales*, mishearing the name *Caribes* (**Caribs**), and saddled them with a reputation for eating human flesh. In *The Tempest*, Caliban is similarly characterized as a half-human savage. When the protagonist of the play, Prospero, tries to remind Caliban of all the latter owes him, including the use of language, Caliban responds with his most famous lines: 'You taught me language, and my profit on't/Is, I know how to curse. The red plague rid you/For learning me your language!' (I.ii.362–4).

The Tempest and Caliban were the subject of commentary for centuries, with Prospero cast in the role of civilizing force and Caliban as the barbarous savage in need of cultivation. But it was not until the Martinican psychoanalyst Frantz **Fanon**, in the midst of post-Second World War decolonization, critically reversed the traditional associations and values assigned to Prospero and Caliban that the latter began his late career as a poster boy for anti-imperialist revolutionary culture in the Caribbean. After Fanon's **Peau noire, masques blancs** (*Black Skin, White Masks*) (1968), the Barbadian author George **Lamming** devoted two chapters of his *Pleasures of Exile* (1992) to the play. Lamming, though clearly sympathetic to the plight of the colonized Caliban, nevertheless was unable to transform the figure into a symbol of defiant cultural appropriation. However, by the late 1960s, with the Cuban Revolution (see **revolutions**) in full swing and several West Indian island nations savouring newly won independence, Lamming's compatriot Edward Kamau **Brathwaite**, in his poetry volume *Islands*, and the Martinican playwright and poet Aimé **Césaire**, in his *A Tempest: Adaptation of Shakespeare's 'The Tempest' by a Negro Theater*, decisively identified Caribbean culture with Caliban and stamped it with a revolutionary and anti-imperialist character.

Just a few years later, the Cuban poet and scholar Roberto **Fernández Retamar** inflected the imagery of Caliban with a Latin American tone in his 1971 essay *Caliban*. Retamar argued that Caliban, and the ferocious island Caribs he represented, were the true ancestors and symbols for the long tradition, only then finally victorious, of Latin American revolutionary anti-imperialism. He also challenged the long-prevailing view of José Enrique Rodó, the Uruguayan writer who in his 1900 essay *Ariel*, in the wake of US intervention in the War for Cuban Independence, associated the United States with what he saw as a brutish Caliban and Latin America with Ariel, the fairy spirit of *The Tempest*. Against this view, Retamar pointed out that Ariel, like Caliban, is the slave of the imperialist Prospero, but that unlike Caliban, Ariel faithfully obeys the master. More particularly, Retamar polemicized against some of the famous novelists of the so-called **Boom** for hitching their political wagons to the horse of US-sponsored, anti-Cuban propaganda (see **Mundo Nuevo**). With this polemic, Retamar ushered in his ringing final call for the Ariels, or **intellectuals**, of Latin America to humbly seek 'from Caliban the honour of a place in his rebellious and glorious ranks'.

See also: arielismo

Further reading

Césaire, A. (1992) *A Tempest*, trans. R. Miller, New York: Ubu Repertory Theater Publications.

Fanon, F. (1968) *Black Skin, White Masks*, trans. C.L. Markmann, New York: Grove.

Fernández Retamar, R. (1989) *Caliban and Other Essays*, trans. E. Baker, Minneapolis, MN: University of Minnesota Press.

Hulme, P. (1992) *Colonial Encounters: Europe and the Native Caribbean, 1492–1797*, New York: Routledge.

Lamming, G. (1992) *The Pleasures of Exile*, Ann Arbor, MI: University of Michigan Press.

SANTIAGO COLÁS

Caliste, Canute

b, 1916, Carriacou, Grenada

Painter

Caliste has lived his entire life in L'Esterre village on Carriacou, Grenada's largest dependency. A boat-builder by trade, he is a documentarian in paint of the rich cultural heritage of his island. Working spontaneously, he fills small (typically 12 × 16') panels with childlike images of Carriacou life. His dominant themes – Afro-Caribbean ritual, Christian ceremony, myth – are rendered with unschooled directness in intricate detail usually accompanied by idiosyncratically spelled explanations. Grenada considers Caliste as a national treasure for prolifically recording a vanishing culture. He is among the last of a vanishing breed, the truly naive artist.

See also: primitive painting

TRISH BETHANY

Callado, Antonio

b. 1917, Niterói, Brazil; d. 1997, Rio de Janeiro, Brazil

Writer

A career journalist, Callado distinguished himself with nine novels, though he also published eight volumes of plays, several of journalistic essays and one of short stories. Callado always displayed a deep historical and social consciousness, and was concerned with understanding and defining Brazilian identity. His novels address the question, 'What does it mean to be Brazilian?', dealing with elements constitutive of Brazilian society such as religion, education, politics and ethnicity. After his novel *Quarup* (filmed by Ruy **Guerra**) (1967), the military dictatorship (1964–85) and subsequent political problems were central to Callado's fiction.

CRISTINA FERREIRA-PINTO

callaloo

A key feature of Sunday lunch in Trinidad, callaloo is an exquisite dish of West African origin. Callaloo's dark green colour comes from the dasheen leaves, a kind of local spinach, which are carefully stripped of their stringy spines then stewed down in fresh coconut milk with peppers and seasonings, okra, crabs, or salted pigs' tails. Callaloo's blending of ingredients has made it a metaphor for Trinidad's ethnic mix. The concept of callaloo gained its most prominent artistic expression in Peter **Minshall**'s 1983–5 carnival band trilogy, one of whose characters, 'Callaloo', shatters the harmony of his river community, betraying them in order to embrace modernization.

LORRAINE LEU

Calmon, Antônio

b. 1945, Manaus, Brazil

Cinematographer and playwright

Calmon worked as assistant director and editor on several **Cinema Novo** films, including Glauber **Rocha**'s *Terra em transe* (Land in Anguish) (1967). His first film, *O Capitão Bandeira contra o Dr. Moura Brasil* (Captain Flag against Dr Moura Brasil) (1971), was a satire that translated the montage techniques of *tropicalismo* into the genre of popular comedy. Adopting more traditional narrative techniques, he made several films through the seventies, exploring the experience of the young in *Nos embalos de Ipanema* (In the Wild Parties of Ipanema) (1978), *Garota dourada* (Golden Girl) (1981) and *Menino do Rio* (Kid from Rio) (1983). He later moved into television, directing soap operas and series for TV **Globo**.

ISMAIL XAVIER AND THE USP GROUP

calypso

The origins of calypso lie in several call-and-response song forms, such as lavway, belair, calinda and bongo, usually sung extemporaneously by slave singers, or chantwells (from the French *chantuelles*) on topical subjects, or in order to trade insults among singers. Chantwells often led bands of stick-fighters during **canboulay**, a festival that was added to **carnival** celebrations around 1843 and became associated with the masquerade bands that paraded the streets at carnival time. Prior to the carnival, a tent of bamboo and palm fronds was erected on the site of the '*mas camp*', so that the chantwells and musicians could rehearse. These tents attracted increasing interest, separating from the *mas camps* shortly after the turn of the century and consolidated during the 1920s as an independent carnival activity. A key role in this process was played by chantwell Railway ('Chieftain') Douglas, who opened his Railroad Millionaires tent in 1921. Douglas formalized the performance of calypsos sung in major keys – not the minor keys of stick-fighting or calinda songs – favouring flute, cuatro, guitar and violin over calinda instrumentation. The language of the tent also began to change from the widely spoken French patois, to English, the language of government and officialdom. Since 1868, singers could be prosecuted for the performance of obscene songs; the 1934 Theatre and Dance Hall Ordinance required calypsonians to request police permission before a performance. Censorship by the British colonial authorities increased during the Second World War, alongside the repression of political activity. Money flowed into the tents, and many were relocated to the more 'respectable' western Port-of-Spain. After the war, the audience remained mainly white, as **tourism** discovered calypso. However, in the

years leading up to independence, the tent was reclaimed as a space for incisive criticism and social commentary, a period strongly associated with the rise of The **Mighty Sparrow**. In the 1930s and 1940s, calypsonians were still adding lyrics on to a stock range of basic rhythms, but Sparrow combined masterful melodies with sophisticated lyrics and an exceptional voice. Calypsos also became more complex and varied due to increased recordings in the 1950s, and new sub-genres such as calypso-rhumba and calypso twist were created under the influence of international music. The search for variety and the use of arrangers led to what is currently calypso's dominant form, **soca**. For around a decade soca represented more of a change in rhythm than in lyrical content; more recently, both its subject matter and language have diverged from calypso and its earlier form.

Further reading

Behague, G. (ed.) (1994) *Music and Black Ethnicity: The Caribbean and South America*, Miami: North–South Center, University of Miami.

Cowley, J. (1996) *Carnival, Canboulay and Calypso: Traditions in the Making*, Cambridge: Cambridge University Press.

Hill, D.R. (1993) *Calypso Callaloo: Early Carnival Music in Trinidad*, Gainesville: University Press of Florida.

LORRAINE LEU

Câmara Cascudo, Luis da

b. 1898, Natal, Brazil; d. 1986, Natal

Folklorist

Câmara Cascudo dedicated most of his life to the study of Brazilian folkloric traditions, especially those of the north east. Nobody has produced a more thorough and detailed body of research on the subject. Of his numerous publications, many are still regarded as seminal works on folklore: *Vaqueiros e cantadores* (Cowhands and Singers) (1939), *Literatura oral* (Oral Literature) (1952) and *Cinco livros do povo* (Five Books of the People) (1953). His

Dicionário do folclore brasileiro remains an indispensable reference work.

MARK DINNEEN

Câmara, Dom Helder

b. 1909, Fortaleza, Brazil; d. 1999, Olinda, Brazil

Archbishop

As auxiliary bishop of Rio de Janeiro from 1952 to 1964 and then archbishop of Olinda and Recife, Brazil until his retirement in 1985, Helder Câmara became the most internationally renowned promoter of Latin American **liberation theology**. He was an outspoken advocate of **human rights** and socioeconomic justice, as well as an influential backer of progressive sectors of the Church. A charismatic and skilled leader, he largely organized the establishment of the **CNBB** (National Conference of Brazilian Bishops) and served as its secretary general for many years. He was also instrumental in the founding of **CELAM** (Conference of Latin American Bishops) in 1955. Under his influence, for a time these organizations directed their resources and attention to social justice issues and supported liberation theology early in its development. Along with his close friend Bishop Manuel Larraín of Chile, Helder Câmara, then first vice-president of CELAM, played a central role in orchestrating the CELAM meeting at Medellín in 1968 and in focusing its attention on the poor in Latin America.

As a champion of many of the goals of liberation theology before the theology itself was articulated, he greatly advanced the Church's engagement with social issues and was one of the first Latin American Catholic bishops to denounce capitalism in favour of **socialism**. He supported the spread of *comunidades eclesiaies de base* (CEBs – **Christian Base Organizations**) as a means of revitalizing the Church. From 1961–7, he was influential in the Basic Education Movement (MEB), an educational programme based on the pedagogy of *conscientização* (**conscientization**) developed by Paulo **Freire**.

During the dictatorship in Brazil, his publicizing of abuses and ardent defence of human rights resulted in numerous assassination attempts. As archbishop of the poorest region of the country, he endorsed land reform and was referred to by his critics as the 'Red Bishop'. He has received honorary degrees from numerous universities around the world and was nominated for the Nobel Peace Prize in 1970. Although known more for his role as an organizer and spokesperson, he has also published extensively.

See also: Catholicism; religion and politics

Further reading

Câmara, D.H. (1971) *Revolution through Peace*, trans. A. McLean, San Francisco: Harper & Row.
—— (1979) *The Conversions of a Bishop: An Interview with José de Broucker*, trans. H. Davies, London: Collins.

THOMAS A. LEWIS

Camargo, Sérgio

b. 1930, Rio de Janeiro, Brazil; d. 1990, Rio de Janeiro

Sculptor

Sérgio Camargo (sometimes called Sérgio De Camargo) was born into an Argentine–Brazilian family. He studied at the Altamira Academy in Buenos Aires in 1946 under Lucio **Fontana** and Emilio **Pettoruti**. In 1948 he travelled to Paris and studied philosophy at the Sorbonne. He lived in Paris from 1961 to 1974. Camargo's constructions are characterized by the purity of their means and materials. His most famous works are the white painted wood reliefs of the 1970s. The subtlety of optical effects in his reliefs, sculptures and murals relates him to the **kinetic art** movement.

GABRIEL PEREZ-BARREIRO

Cameron, Norman Eustace

b. 1903, New Amsterdam, Guyana;
d. 1983

Writer and historian

Cameron's broad intellectual curiosity was stimulated by boyhood travels throughout Guyana accompanying his father, a sanitary inspector. Although he studied and later lectured in mathematics, Cameron's early interest in hybrid Guyanese cultural practices informs his mature work, especially his two-volume *The Evolution of the Negro*, written in 1929 and 1934, the poetry anthology *Guianese Poetry* (1931), *Thoughts on Life and Literature* (1950) and *150 years of Education in Guyana* (1968). His play *The Price of Victory* (1965), written one year before Guyanese independence from Britain, recognizes the function of **Yoruba** culture and mythology in Afro-Guyanese syncretism.

JILL E. ALBADA-JELGERSMA

Camila

Directed by María Luisa **Bemberg** and produced by Lita **Stantic** in 1984, *Camila* can be considered the first film of the democratic era in Argentina. Produced as Argentina's military dictatorship gave way to democracy, *Camila* announced the country's need to explore the inequities of its past as part of a healing process. The film's nomination for a Best Foreign Picture Oscar gave Bemberg international recognition as well as success at home. Bemberg was fond of noting the increased number of baby girls named Camila after the film's release.

Camila recounts the love story of Camila O'Gorman, a legendary national figure whose story had already been filmed by Mario Gallo in 1910. In 1847 O'Gorman's ill-fated love affair with her confessor priest resulted in the execution of both for treason against the State. In the late 1840s and 1850s, the lovers' fate epitomized the repression and violence of the Rosas dictatorship. In 1984, *Camila* served as a historical parallel for the atrocities of the contemporary dictatorship.

Bemberg's *Camila*, played by Susú **Pecoraro**, is a strong, independent woman. She crosses her

father by refusing to marry a man she does not love, and blasphemes by running away with a priest to live as his wife. In their absence, Rosas declares her actions treasonable and sentences her to death, foregrounding the repressive morality imposed by Church, State and Father.

A travelling priest discovers Camila and Ladislao living as poor teachers in another province, where they have been accepted by the authorities of the small town and won respect for their dedication to teaching children. They are awaiting the birth of their own child. In a culture where family is so important and motherhood valued, even Camila's pregnancy is not redemptive; Camila and Ladislao are executed, side by side. Camila dies because she dishonoured her family, blasphemed the church and embarrassed the state.

Bemberg's film gave substance to Camila's legend. For many years Argentine film-makers had been prohibited from depicting it, but Bemberg took advantage of the weakening of the military government and opted not to ask permission to shoot the film. The film was made at a key moment; in 1983 – the year *Camila* began shooting – Argentina's repressive military regime was replaced by a democratic government. Perhaps Bemberg's finest film, *Camila* paved the way for films like *La historia oficial* (The Official Story), 1986 winner of the Best Foreign Picture Oscar, which explored recent atrocities, helping Argentina come to terms with its part in an effort to recreate itself.

Further reading

España, C. (ed.) (1993) *Diez años de cine argentino en democracia*, Buenos Aires: Instituto Nacional de Cinematografía.

ILENE S GOLDMAN

Camnitzer, Luis

b. 1937, Lübeck, Germany

Visual artist, art historian and critic

Of Jewish origin, Camnitzer emigrated to Uruguay with his parents in 1939. He studied art and architecture in Montevideo, then art and print-making in Munich and New York. In 1964 he co-founded the New York Graphic Workshop. He developed FANDSO (Free Assemblage, Nonfunctional, Disposable, Serial Object) and became a protagonist of the **conceptual art** movement. Late 1960s work on repression in Latin America led him to call for more active forms of artistic spectatorship. From the 1980s onward, Camnitzer's work has become more explicitly political once more and addressed issues like colonialism, torture and environmental destruction. He is author of *The New Art of Cuba* (1994).

RUDI BLEYS

Campaneris, Bert

b. 1942, Pueblo Nuevo, Cuba

Baseball player

With a nineteen-year career as a player in US professional **baseball**'s major leagues, Campaneris was best known as the offensive sparkplug for the 1972–4 Oakland As, one of the greatest teams in baseball history. He had a distinctive and oft-imitated batting stance, standing in an exaggerated crouch that reduced the 'strike zone', the area into which the opposing pitcher tries to throw the ball. In September 1965, Campaneris became the first player to play all nine defensive positions in a North American major league game.

DOUGLAS W. VICK

Campbell, Jeannette

b. 1916, Bayonne, France

Swimmer

Anglo-Argentine swimming champion in the 100, 200, and 400 metre free-style in the late 1930s and early 1940s, Campbell was the first woman to represent Argentina in the Olympic Games after becoming a naturalized Argentine citizen in 1936. An active international competitor, she won a silver medal in the Berlin Olympics (1936) and broke the South American record in the 100 metre free-style.

Her decision to become an Argentine citizen, despite her English background and education, reinforced Argentine nationalism, while her ground-breaking performance led to greater acceptance of female athletes in Argentina.

THOMAS EDSALL

campesino

The term *campesino* strictly speaking refers to small or subsistence farmers, or peasants. It has come to be used in a less precise way, however, to refer to rural populations in general. In those Latin American countries with a large indigenous presence, it may be used to refer to indigenous people. It has been absorbed into English to describe Latin Americans living in the countryside, but in the process has lost its precision – and its implicit distinction between those who own and work land (peasants) and those who work in agriculture, but are themselves landless.

MIKE GONZALEZ

Campos, Augusto de

b. 1931, São Paulo, Brazil

Poet, critic and translator

One of the original Noigandres poets of the 1950s (see **Noigandres group**), this key figure has stayed closest to the minimalist aesthetics of **concrete poetry**. He is known for experimental varieties of poetry involving colour, visual images, and electronic media, as in *Viva Vaia Poesia 1949–1979* and *Despoesia* (1993). His criticism and translations have focused on innovations in Western lyric. In other writings he was the first to recognize the poetry of **MPB** songs. His suggestive poem 'pós-tudo' (post-everything) (1984) sparked a polemic with Roberto **Schwarz** about **postmodernism** in Brazil. In the 1990s, he also began performing poetry with musical and video accompaniment.

CHARLES A. PERRONE

Campos, Haroldo de

b. 1929, São Paulo

Poet, critic and translator

One of the key figures of Brazilian poetry and literary criticism in the second half of the twentieth century, Campos first achieved distinction as co-founder and theorist of the *Noigandres* journal (see **Noigandres group**) and of **concrete poetry**. He has pursued inventive impulses in lyric and sought the expansion of borders between literary genres. In addition to exploring new writing directions, he developed a creative method of translation called 'transcreation' (renderings of ancient Chinese poetry, the Book of Genesis, Dante, Goethe, Mayakovsky, Pound and Joyce). He broadened the horizons of criticism and literary theory in Brazil through rethinkings of salient unconventional works of national or European literature. His visits to the USA and Europe helped to establish a new presence for Brazilian literature in international circles.

In early concrete poems, Campos integrated verbal and visual effects through such techniques as fragmentation and the employment of white type on black backgrounds. He was the principal theorist of the rational 'orthodox' phase of concrete poetry (cf. the provocation of **neo-concretism**), as well as of the nationalist characer of concretist experiments when they were assailed as alienated and foreign. His work on the poetry of Oswald de **Andrade** in the 1960s was essential for the re-evaluation of **Brazilian modernism**, as was his doctoral thesis, which diversified discussions of *Macunaíma*. With this and other studies, Campos helped advance aspects of literary structuralism in the 1970s. Perhaps his most significant later contribution was the essay 'The Rule of Anthropophagy: Europe under the Sign of Devoration', which affirms an uncompromising, self-assertive role for Brazilian letters. In the 1980s, Campos also completed *Galáxias*, a decades-long experimental prose-poetry project. His rethinking of lyric produced the notion of the 'post-Utopian poem', informed by the implications of historical transformations, and the classically-tinged long poem *Finismundo*.

Further reading

Campos, H. de (1976) *Xadrez de estrelas*, São Paulo: Perspectiva.

—— (1985) *A educação dos cinco sentido*, São Paulo: Brasiliense.

—— (1992) *Os melhores poemas de Haroldo de Campos*, São Paulo: Global.

—— (1992) *Metalinguagem e outras metas*.

—— (1986) 'The Rule of Anthropophagy: Europe Under the Sign of Devoration', *Latin American Literary Review* 14(27): 42–60.

Perrone, C. (1996) *Seven Faces: Brazilian Poetry since Modernism*. Durham, NC: Duke University Press.

CHARLES A. PERRONE

Campos, Roberto

b. 1917, Cuiabá, Mato Grosso, Brazil

Economist

A major influence in Brazilian economic life since 1944, Campos became economic adviser to Getúlio **Vargas** in 1952, establishing the National Development Bank (BNDE) and preparing the government's economic programme. Named ambassador to Washington, he resigned when the government of João **Goulart** nationalized foreign enterprises. Campos became the Minister of Planning in the military government that overthrew Goulart in 1964, promising to fight inflation and create a Land Statute. There followed the period known as the 'economic miracle'. With the ending of military rule, Campos became ambassador to London. He was elected federal deputy for Rio de Janeiro in 1991 and 1994.

ANTONIO CARLOS VAZ

Campos Menéndez, Enrique

b. 1914, Punta Arenas, Chile

Writer and statesman

Campos Menéndez is a prolific writer of fiction, biographies and essays. Born into one of the most prominent families of southern Chile, he has taken an active role in the political affairs of Chile, favouring the country's guidance by an enlightened minority or intellectual elite. Campos was an ardent critic of the government of Salvador **Allende** and held several positions within the regime of Augusto **Pinochet**. In 1986, while acting as Chile's Ambassador to Spain, he was awarded Chile's National Prize for Literature. Notable among his publications are the story collection *Sólo el viento* (Only the Wind) (1974) and the biography *Vida fuera la vida* (Life from Life) (1996).

ROBERTO CARLOS ORTIZ

Canal Zone

Through the Taft Agreement of 1904, the USA gained sovereignty over a ten-mile-wide strip of land on both sides of the future Panama Canal for an absurdly low rent. Until 1977, the US government operated virtually all commercial enterprises and maintained legal jurisdiction over this territory. After the 1964 riots, when Panamanian students tried to fly their flag beside to the US flag, the USA entered negotiations over the status of the Canal Zone. The 1977 Treaty transferred legal jurisdiction over the Canal Zone to Panama and created a joint commission to operate and maintain the canal until noon, 31 December 1999, when Panama secured ownership of the canal and the remaining US military installations.

NORMAN S. HOLLAND

Canaro, Francisco

b. 1888, Montevideo, Uruguay; d. 1964, Buenos Aires, Argentina

Musician

An outstanding **tango** musician and composer, the young Francisco Canaro (nickname 'Pirincho') first appeared in the tango bars of the **Boca** district of Buenos Aires in the early 1900s. Having learned his trade on a violin with one string attached to a can, he became the leader of the Orquesta Típica, with Roberto Firpo, which played for fifty years.

His conducting style, with its particular emphasis on the 'canyengue' rhythm, was particularly suited (unlike **De Caro**'s) to the accompaniment of tango dancers. 'Madreselva', 'Pampa mía' and 'La última copa' stand out among his many fine compositions.

LUIS GUSMAN

canboulay

Canboulay developed from celebrations associated with the burning of cane stubble; it consisted chiefly of stickfighting, accompanied by drumming and the singing of calindas, songs of challenge. Stickfighting was a means of settling scores between slaves; after emancipation it emerged in the urban centres. Rumours of a ban by the colonial government resulted in **carnival**'s most violent clash, the Canboulay Riots of 1881, when stickfighters fought police in protest against a threatened ban; it came in 1884, paving the way for the appropriation of Carnival by the island's emergent creole middle class. Stickfighting competitions still take place in some villages and are dramatized as part of the **Best Village Competition**.

LORRAINE LEU

Canción mixteca

'Canción mixteca' is a composition by the Mexican José López Alavés (1889–1974), inspired by nostalgia for his native state of Oaxaca, home of the Mixteca people. The song begins 'Qué lejos estoy del suelo donde he nacido...' (How far I am from the land where I was born...). It won a competition organized by the Mexico City newspaper *El Universal* in 1918 and has remained popular ever since, particularly among emigrants and all who miss their homeland. It has been recorded many times, the earlier version known by the Trío Garnica-Asencio in 1928 and famously by Lola **Beltrán**.

EDUARDO CONTRERAS SOTO

canción ranchera

The ranchera song has two powerful antecedents. The first is the **corrido**, a form that arose in the nineteenth century, stimulated by the Spanish ballad tradition, and which reached its most significant historic moment with the Mexican Revolution (1910–17) (see **revolutions**); it faded for a few years and returned under the impulse of the profound social changes that drugs and drug trafficking are producing from the 1970s onwards. The other ancestor of ranchera is the so-called '*canción mexicana*' (Mexican song), which peaked between 1929 and 1936–7. The characteristics of '*canción mexicana*' are simple enough – an idyllic vision of country life, tender sentiments, pain as others migrate, religiosity and a slightly updated traditional melody. The last successful '*canciones mexicanas*' were probably Adiós mi chaparrita (Goodbye My Little One) and Allá en el rancho grande (Out There on the Big Ranch). In 1935–7 there was an attempt to create popular songs that were urban in context but retained the sincerity and manliness associated with rural life. The first great ranchera singer was Lucha **Reyes**, who first sang corridos before joining the mariachis as they moved from the provincial towns into the city, adding trumpets to the traditional strings. In her version of Ay Jalisco no te rajes (Jalisco don't Give in), Lucha Reyes imbues the song with all the power and expression that the new genre demanded. At this early stage, the other famous singers were men – Jorge **Negrete**, Pedro **Infante**, Luis Aguilar, Miguel Aceves Mejía and Francisco Avitia. After its high point, the canción ranchera continues in a series of songs celebrating provincial life, like 'Ay qué rechula es Puebla' (Nowhere More Beautiful than Puebla). Cinema, radio and the juke-box were the favoured places for canción ranchera. The work of composers like Chucho Monge, Felipe Valdés Leal, Manuel Esperín, Tomás Méndez and Rubén Fuentes was important, but the outstanding figure in the genre was certainly José Alfredo **Jiménez**, whose first great hit Ella (Her) was in 1947.

CARLOS MONSIVÁIS

Candela, Félix

b. 1910, Madrid, Spain; d. 1997, Raleigh, North Carolina, USA

Architect

Candela's principal contribution has been the design, and construction of light roofs, covers and concrete shells based on parabolic and hyperbolic shapes, and influenced by Spanish architects Gaudí and Torroja. The 1,000 structures he created embrace every kind of solution from simple 'umbrellas' to the most sophisticated forms. He studied in Madrid, before joining the exodus of professionals who left Spain for Mexico after the Spanish Civil War. There he was consultant and draughtsman for a number of projects, founding with his brother Antonio and sister Julia the design consultancy *Cubiertas Alas* (Covered Wings) specializing in the design and construction of laminated structures and concrete shells (1950–69). He taught in Mexico and the USA, and was adviser and consultant to a number of projects throughout the Americas; he received a variety of prizes and honours including the Gold Medal of the Consejo Superior de Colegios de Arquitectos de España in 1981. Among his individual constructions in Mexico, the church of the Virgen de la Medalla Milagrosa (1953) is outstanding; columns are distributed across a rectangular floor in such a way that they become arches formed into a hyperbolic parabola as they rise and merge into an integral concrete roof only four centimetres thick. His containing structures for the Bacardí factory were also outstanding. But he is important above all for his joint work as consultant and constructor working with other Mexican architects on high quality buildings like the Chapel of Nuestra Señora de la Soledad (1955), with Enrique de la Moral; the Xochimilco restaurant (1958) with Joaquín Alvarez Ordoñez, and the open chapel at Cuernavaca, Morelos (1959) with Guillermo Rosell and Manuel Larrosa.

Further reading

Buschiazzo, F. (1960) *Félix Candela*, Buenos Aires.

Faber, C. (1970) *Las estructuras de Candela*, Mexico City: Continental.

LOURDES CRUZ GONZÁLEZ FRANCO

Candelaria, La

Theatre group founded in 1966 by a group of Colombian artists and independent intellectuals. It began by producing avant-garde plays by Peter Weiss, Arnold Wesker, Fernando Arrabal and others, and aimed to provide access to the theatre for the masses, as well as to strengthen national theatre. By the end of the 1960s, the company developed methods of *creación colectiva* (collective creation), with the intention of encouraging the production of original pieces. After 1982, some of the group's members wrote and directed their own plays, among them *La trifulca* (The Rumpus) by Santiago **García** and *El viento y la ceniza* (The Wind and the Ashes) by Patricia Ariza.

ALEJANDRA JARAMILLO

Candido, Antonio

b. 1918, Rio de Janeiro, Brazil

Literary critic

The most distinguished critic of his generation in Brazil, Antonio Candido de Mello e Souza began his career as a sociologist, and his approach to literature has always balanced the social context and the formal characteristics of the text. He studied at the Universidade de São Paulo in the 1930s with famous teachers such as Claude Lévi-Strauss and Roger Bastide, and in 1941 founded the review *Clima*. A long-time member of the Brazilian Socialist Party, he was courageous in his opposition to the military regime in the 1960s and 1970s. He has had an enormous influence on successive generations of pupils: he is the mentor of such critics as Roberto **Schwarz**, Jorge **Schwartz** and Davi **Arrigucci**. These virtues are also apparent in his prose, which is always clear and easy to read. He has worked hard to maintain links between Brazil and Spanish America, notably

through his friendship with the Uruguayan critic Angel **Rama**.

He began his career in the press, writing reviews, and the great majority of his criticism consists of essays, by no means limited to Brazilian literature. His only major long work, the two-volume *Formação da literatura brasileira* (Formation of Brazilian Literature) (1959) is an account of the development of Brazilian national consciousness through literature, in the eighteenth and nineteenth centuries. He is notably free of nationalist bias, and willing to see how Brazil has been influenced by European literature.

His essays vary in nature from academic articles to memoirs of friends and ancestors, and surveys of general topics. There is an excellent essay on Carlos **Drummond de Andrade**, for example, a powerful synthesis of the development of culture in Brazil in the 1930s, and an essay on literature and underdevelopment which ranges with enviable ease throughout Latin America. Some, notably 'Dialética da malandragem' (The Dialectics of Roguery), which traces the figure of the *malandro* in a mid-nineteenth-century novel and identifies a whole tradition of work-shy pranksters in Brazilian literature, have had a pervasive influence.

Further reading

Candido, A. (1995) *On Literature and Society*, trans. H. Becker, Princeton, NJ: Princeton University Press.
—— (1995) *Ensayos y comentarios*, trans. R. Mata Sandoval and M. Celada, Mexico City: Fondo de Cultura Económica.

JOHN GLEDSON

Candomblé

An Afro-Brazilian religion similar to Cuban **Santería** and Haitian **Vodun** that involves spirit possession, divination and ritual healing. It is practised throughout Brazil, but Salvador, Bahia is widely regarded by practitioners and scholars as its spiritual centre. Officially prohibited from practising African religions, slaves and free people of colour coalesced around Roman Catholic brotherhoods and urban work groups, or *cantos*, in the eighteenth and nineteenth centuries. These associations were identified with specific 'nations' – broadly and imprecisely defined transatlantic ethnicities such as *Nagô* (Yoruba), *Jeje* (Ewe-Fon) and *Angola* (Kongo-Kimbundu). By the early twentieth century, the Nagô nation had become dominant in Bahia due to the massive influx of **Yoruba** slaves during the previous century and the subsequent transatlantic travel of free African and Afro-Brazilian traders, professionals and religious leaders. Nagô hegemony was further solidified through deft alliance-building with patrons and scholars of the local bourgeoisie.

The oldest surviving Candomblé temple, Ilê Iyá Nassó – known as Casa Branca – was founded in the early 1830s by the free African woman and Nagô priestess Nassó. By the turn of the century, internal disputes over priestly succession led to two major splits, which would give rise to the two most prominent Candomblé houses of the twentieth century: Ilê Iyá Omin Axé Iyamassé (the temple popularly known as Gantois), led by Mãe **Meninha** until 1986; and Ilê Axé Opô Afonjá, currently led by Stella de Oxóssi. These three historic houses and their offshoots have based much of their prestige and renown on claims to 'Nagô purity' as opposed to the 'mixed' heterodoxy of the Angolan nation. The defenders of Nagô orthodoxy only worship African deities called *orixás*, while most Candomblé houses worship *orixás* as well as Amerindian spirits known as *caboclos*, which are associated with Brazilian nationality. There are over 2,000 Candomblé sacred compounds, or *terreiros*, of various sizes in metropolitan Salvador, Bahia. The Candomblé community is typically led by a head priestess, called a *mãe-de-santo*, or priest, a *pai-de santo*, or, in Yoruba, *iyálorixá* and *babálorixá*. Beneath the chief religious leader are the *mãe pequena* or *iyá kêkêrê* (little mother), her assistant, the *iyá morô*, and the *iyá basé*, who is responsible for preparing sacred foods for the *orixás*. Junior initiates called *iaôs* must complete seven years in the house before becoming senior members, or *ebomins*. The *ogans*, male dignitaries who do not manifest the *orixás*, are responsible for animal sacrifices, drumming, chanting and the material well-being of the house. Far from constituting the vestigial remains of a distant African past, Candomblé communities continue to grow in number and influence throughout Brazil.

Further reading

Harding, R. (2000) *A Refuge in Thunder: Candoblé and the Alternative Spaces of Blackness*, Indiana University Press.

Kraay, H. (ed.) (1998) *Afro-Brazilian Culture and Politics*, Armonk, NY/London: M.E. Sharpe.

Voeks, R.A.(1997) *Sacred Leaves of Candomble: African Magic, Medicine, and Religion in Brazil*, Austin: University of Texas Press.

Wafer, Jim (1991) *The Taste of Blood: Spirit Possession in Brazilian Candoblé*, University of Pennsylvania Press.

CHRISTOPHER DUNN

Canese, Jorge

b. 1947, Asunción, Paraguay

Poet and narrator

A medical doctor and professor, Canese is part of the 'generation of 70'. Among his numerous published books of poetry, *Paloma blanca, paloma negra* (White Dove, Black Dove) was one of the few books censored during the **Stroessner** dictatorship. He is also the author of the novel *Stroessner roto* (Stroessner Broken), and two collections of short stories. In 1995 he published *Apología a una silla de ruedas* (Apology to a Wheelchair), four brief satirical essays about the nation's problems.

TERESA MÉNDEZ-FAITH

Cangaceiro, O

Lima **Barreto**'s first feature, *O Cangaceiro* (The Bandit) (1952), made for **Vera Cruz Studios**, was the latter's attempt to move into popular cinema. *O Cangaceiro* was a pathbreaking film in transforming the social bandit of the Brazilian northeast **sertão** into an action hero within an emotional triangle comprising the cangaceiro, the reformed bandit and the girl. The film, with its effective portrayal of violence, was enthusiastically received by both critics and public, winning the 1953 Adventure Film Prize at Cannes and spawned a new genre, the 'nordestern'. But it was Columbia Pictures that benefitted most, having received the distribution rights from Vera Cruz.

ISMAIL XAVIER AND THE USP GROUP

cantautor

Roughly equivalent to the term 'singer-songwriter' in English, the *cantautores* were emblematic of a very particular period (the 1960s and after), style of performance and range of thematic concerns. Authors and performers of their own songs, the *cantautor(a)s* will normally be alone on stage with only an acoustic guitar as accompaniment. This allows for an intimate and direct relationship with the audience that is essential to the art of the *cantautor*, quite consciously a kind of modern troubadour – a bearer of news and a commentator on the world. Where a troubadour tradition already exists, the modern *cantautor(a)* will often set themselves in that mould – thus Atahualpa **Yupanqui**, the Argentine singer, adopted folk styles and rhythms. So too did the great Violeta **Parra**, collector, lyricist, singer and inspiration behind the Chilean *nueva canción* movement whose best known younger *cantautor* was undoubtedly Víctor **Jara**, though Patricio **Manns**, with his intense poetic song lyrics, belongs firmly within the same tradition. In Mexico Oscar **Chávez** was both collector and a commentator in song on the events of contemporary society. However, all of these remained within a folk or traditional music frame.

A quite different current arose out of the Cuban *nueva trova* movement that flowered after 1967, and particularly from the reflective songs of Silvio **Rodríguez** and Pablo **Milanés**. Daniel **Viglietti** of Uruguay wrote many of the key songs of the movement, including 'Dale tu mano al indio' (Give the Indian your Hand). Others included: León **Gieco** and Mercedes **Sosa** of Argentina; Alfredo **Zitarrosa** from Uruguay; Roy **Brown** of Puerto Rico; Luis Enrique **Mejía Godoy** from Nicaragua; and Susana **Baca** from Peru.

More than simply 'protest singers' (though their debt to Bob Dylan was often acknowledged), they provided a shared narrative of an epoch.

MIKE GONZALEZ

Cantinflas

b. 1911, Mexico City; d. 1993, Mexico City

Actor

Born in the Santa María la Redonda district of Mexico City, in the context of a new urban culture that both adored and feared modernity, Mario Moreno Reyes was a boxer (el Chato Moreno), a messenger boy, a postman, an apprentice matador and a professional Charleston dancer.

Approaching the technological age, the old city still enjoyed itself at local celebrations, civic and religious festivals, sports events and bullfights, watched the political circus with great hilarity and attended the cinema, the variety theatre and the *carpa*. This was the poor relation to music hall, where the backdrops were badly painted, the chairs barely merited the name, the clowns were exhausted, the singers skilled only in fending off what was thrown at them, and the magicians amazed when a trick worked out. The comics acted out the familiar stereotypes: the *payo* (the country cousin come to town), the cop, the little old drunk, the judge and, of course, the *peladito*, another name for the lumpenproletariat, who has nothing and holds nothing, whose skin is hardly enough to keep him warm; the urban pariah whose diminutive ending – 'ito' – reduces him to insignificance.

In 1930 Mario Moreno got his first break at a *carpa* in Atzcapotzalco, and by 1933, when he played at the Valentino *carpa*, he had perfected the appearance that would make him a myth. Here was the *peladito*, born of the dandies of the bars and the circus, his face whitened with rice flour or painted with white lead, his trousers patched and falling below the waist, an old tie to hold them up, the cap, the flannel shorts exposed at the slightest excuse, the shoes full of holes, the torn T-shirt and the rag (rechristened 'gabardine') over his left shoulder, the emblem of the market porter. As soon as he entered, the laughter began; the public loved this figure who symbolized the absence of a future.

According to legend, confirmed by Cantinflas, one memorable day at the Ofelia *carpa*, Moreno forgot his words and just said whatever came into his head, in a cascade of incoherent words and phrases. The public begin to cheer this body blow to syntax and Mario understood that chance had given him his mark, his sign: that style that was a kind of verbal incest with chaos. Not long after, the name appeared just as unexpectedly. Someone in the audience, carried along by the flow, shouts '*¿Cuánto inflas? ¿Cuánto bebes?*' (How much do you eat? How much do you drink?) or '*¿En la cantina inflas?*' (Do you eat in the bar?). The contraction is the christening name; and it doesn't matter if it happened – it's the stuff that legends are made from.

In the capital, *el desmadre* (going crazy) is the route for exploring the city; you survive if you can hold the balance between partying (the love of improvisation) and *cursilería* (ridicule) – because this is a city that is, and is not, a provincial town writ large.

Cantinflas's image certainly originated in the newspaper cartoons – caricatures, parodies, sentimental figures. And the image persisted even though Cantinflas changed his dress, distanced himself from the neighbourhood where he grew up, renounced the lumpen style. The public, whether or not it followed his transformations, held fast to the myths of origin. There was just one Cantinflas – the frozen dancer of the poor districts, the creator of a speech that takes in everything except meaning – what comes later is absorbed, but no one takes it very seriously.

The new (and changing) public recognizes how amusing it is to watch a pariah pursued by language – but that is a sociological observation. What is remarkable about Cantinflas in his early period is the leap from social marginality to front stage. Laughing aloud, it turns out that language can be plundered, that everyone can get from it what they want, and then go on with the dance. Cantinflas can give no meaning to what he says without saying it, or what he does not say when he speaks. So, in my view, the determining context of that first period is the prevailing illiteracy – in 1930 70 per cent of the population cannot read or write.

Cantinflas is the illiterate who somehow or another captures language.

What is that people so admire in him? It is his manner: the speed with which he finds common ground with strangers; his speech that starts nowhere and goes everywhere; and his triumph over the next man. In the struggle for expression, Cantinflas launches himself into facial and verbal twists and turns (an autobiography in flashes): his eyebrows enquire; his arms rise into the air; his body arches and bucks before the independent movements of words. Shout my friends, my words. A feat without sense, the word (the endless wordiness) of Cantinflas reveals a double tactic – partying can be an auditory trap, and the unexpected nonsense word can free us from language itself.

In 1936, after a series of **short films**, Cantinflas had a small role in his first full-length feature, *No te engañes corazón* (Don't be Fooled my Heart). *Aguila o sol* (Heads or Tails) (1937) explored life in the *carpas*. *Ahí está el detalle* (That's the Thing) (1940), made by Posa Films, his own company, won him an audience throughout Latin America. The films that followed brought him such fame in the Spanish-speaking world that he came to be regarded as a philosopher of Mexicanness. In *Ni sangre ni arena* (Neither Blood nor Sand) (1941), *El gendarme desconocido* (The Unknown Policeman) (1941), *Los tres mosqueteros* (The Three Musketeers) (1942), *Romeo y Julieta* (Romeo and Juliet) (1943), *Gran hotel* (1944) and *Un día con el diablo* (One Day with the Devil) (1945), Cantinflas preserved his wit and his skill in mimicry. He made one film a year and such was his popularity that he won a large number of votes in every federal election. So profound was his symbolic power that, in his 1953 mural at Mexico City's Teatro de los Insurgentes, Diego **Rivera** placed on the rag that Cantinflas drapes across his shoulder an image of the Virgin of Guadalupe (see **Virgins, miraculous**). The clergy protested and Rivera painted it out.

The cinematic Cantinflas became increasingly self-important and solemn – but public loyalty never wavered. In 1956 he played Passepartout, butler to Phineas Fogg, in Michael Todd's *Around the World in Eighty Days* – but the film was disappointing, as was his next Hollywood film, George

Sidney's *Pepe* (1977). His last film was *El patrullero 777* (Patrolman 777) in 1977.

Further reading

Monsiváis, C. (1997) 'That's the point', in *Mexican Postcards*, London: Verso, pp. 88–105.

Morales, M.A. (1996) *Cantinflas: Amo de las carpas, vol. I–III*, Mexico City: Clio.

Pérez, I.D. (1954) *Cantinflas: Genio del humor y del absurdo*, Mexico City: Indo-Hispana.

Reachi, S. (1982) *La revolución, Cantinflas y jolopo*, Mexico City: Edamex.

CARLOS MONSIVÁIS

Canto general

Canto general is the title of a 1950 book of epic poetry by the Nobel Prize-winner Pablo **Neruda**, whose core is the retelling of the history of Chile and the Americas. Throughout its 500 hundred pages, 320 poems and over 20,000 verses, *Canto general* (General Song) demystifies the dominant clichés of continental historiography to explore pre-Columbian civilizations and the social struggles of oppressed groups during periods of conquest, colonization, independence and modernization. In this sense, this monumental work offers a historical, social and political account of a collective and continental fate. His poetic discourse oscillates between moments of intense lyrical vibrancy like '**Alturas de Macchu Picchu**' (Heights of Macchu Picchu) and texts strongly marked by the narration of concrete events.

As critic René de Costa has affirmed, both Octavio **Paz**'s *El laberinto de la soledad* (Labyrinth of Solitude) (1950) and Neruda's *Canto general* reflect the quest for cultural identity in modern Latin America after the periods of independence and nation-state building. Thus, Neruda's collection embodies a poetics of political alignment and prophecy by constructing a new historical vision of the Americas, denouncing the agents of oppression and praising the collective struggles for freedom and justice, the symbols of the popular culture, the heroes of the past and the possibility of an Utopian future for the continent. The poet becomes the voice of those who have been subjugated, namely indigenous groups, the working class and Third World nations.

Neruda began to write *Canto general* in 1940 while he was in Mexico; he completed it on 5 February 1949 in Chile. At that time he had to leave Chile secretly, escaping from the anti-communist repression of Gabriel González Videla's government. For this reason, the publication of *Canto general* was prohibited in Chile and the work was published in Mexico. The first Mexican edition (1950) was limited, but its successful reception led to a second edition of five thousand copies and many more editions since.

Further reading

Costa, R. (1979) *The poetry of Pablo Neruda*, Cambridge, MA: Harvard University Press.

Neruda, P. (1991) *Canto general*, trans. J. Schmitt, Berkeley, CA: University of California Press.

Santi, E. (1982) *Pablo Neruda: The Poetics of Prophecy*, Ithaca, NY: Cornell University Press.

LUIS E. CÁRCAMO-HUECHANTE

Canto Nuevo

Canto Nuevo is a popular music movement that continued the Chilean *nueva canción* movement after the **Pinochet** *coup* of September 1973. Its first manifestation was a concert by the group **Barroco Andino** in late 1973. Ricardo **García** and the **Alerce Records** label, Miguel Davagnino and his radio programe 'Nuestro Canto' (Our Song), the Javiera folk club (*peña*) and the Agrupación Cultural Universitaria group were its most important expressions through the 1970s. Its outstanding exponents included soloists Nano Acevedo, Eduardo Peralta, Osvaldo Torres and Isabel Aldunate, and groups like **Illapu**, Ortiga, Aquelarre and Santiago del Nuevo Extremo.

ALFONSO PADILLA

Capablanca, José Raúl

b. 1888, Havana, Cuba; d. 1942, New
York, USA

Chess master

The architect of modern chess, Capablanca's
genius was manifest in his intuitive play, intense
concentration and precise positional analysis.
Learning to play at age four, he became Cuban
champion at twelve and champion of the United
States (where he then lived) in 1909. His
international career began when he won the
1911 San Sebastian tournament. His challenge to
reigning world champion Emmanuel Lasker was
accepted only in 1921, and Capablanca won. In
1927 he lost the world title to Alexander
Alekhine, who for years refused him the opportunity of a return.

WILFREDO CANCIO ISLA

Capécia, Mayotte

b. 1916?, Carbet, Martinique; d. 1955,
Paris, France

Writer

Firmly located within the landscape, culture and
the religion of the island, between Catholicism
and **Vodun**, Capécia's novels are innovative
representations of the linguistic features of
Martinican speech. Probably born as Lucette
Ceranus, Capécia's two novels – *Je suis martini-
quaise* (I am a Martinican Woman) (1948) and *La
Négresse blanche* (The White Negress) (1950) – are
narrated by mulatto Martinican women, who
seek social mobility through relationships with
French or 'béké', French creole men, and mixed
blood offspring who can pass for white. Ironically,
they confront the new affirmation of blackness in
the French Caribbean, which led Capécia to
further isolation and eventually a move to Paris.

JILL E. ALBADA-JELGERSMA

Capinam, José Carlos

b. 1941, Esplanada, Bahia, Brazil

Poet and lyricist

In the early 1960s, Capinam studied at the Federal
University of Bahia while composing politically
engaged songs for local productions of the **CPC**. At
this time he began collaborating with fellow
Bahians, Caetano **Veloso**, Gilberto **Gil** and Tom
Zé. In 1965, he published the poem 'Inquisitorial',
which expressed the existential dilemmas of those
who would confront the 'Third Reich', an allusion
to the authoritarian regime then in power. He later
composed lyrics for key *tropicalista* songs such as
'Clarice', 'Miserere Nobis' and 'Soy loco por ti,
America' (Crazy for You, America). He continues
to write poems, music lyrics and plays in Salvador.

CHRISTOPHER DUNN

capital punishment

Though common throughout Latin America and
the Caribbean into the twentieth century, it has
been banned in most countries in the region in
recent years. That is not to say that criminal
suspects or political rivals are not killed; only that
they are often killed by the police or by **death
squads** or **paramilitary organizations** rather
than through the court system. A notorious recent
phenomenon, which has grown out of frustration
with the inadequacies of the judicial and prison
systems, is that of lynch mobs, often instigated by
agents provocateurs, who take justice into their own
hands and kill suspects, including children, in the
streets; poor sections of the large Brazilian cities
have been the scene of a number of such episodes.
Cuba is one of the few countries in the region that
still carries out capital punishment.

DANIEL BALDERSTON

Capitalism and Slavery

This 1944 study by Trinidadian historian and
politician Eric **Williams** challenged the then
widely held belief that the end of slavery in the

British Caribbean came about largely as a result of the success of humanitarian arguments made by heroic British abolitionists. Williams argued that profits generated by the Atlantic slave trade were critical in financing Britain's industrial revolution and that emancipation occurred only when the system of Caribbean slavery became economically less viable and ideologically incompatible with free market ideas. Responding to Williams, some writers have argued that profits from slavery only partially financed Europe's industrial revolution and that, in fact, slave economies were still quite profitable after emancipation. These issues continue to be widely debated.

ROSANNE ADDERLEY

capoeira

Capoeira is a game or sport practised in Brazil. Its origins are unknown, but it arose during the colonial period among slaves brought from Africa in the sixteenth century. A means of self-defence and resistance, capoeira developed principally among the Afro-Brazilian community, and was marginalized because of its association with the lower social classes, criminals and vagrants until the early twentieth century. It is a combination of martial art and dance with extraordinarily graceful fluid moves and almost choreographed sequences; music is a fundamental component, whether in the form of songs, clapping or the instruments that typically accompany the sport – **berimbau**, pandeiro, agogo, reco-reco and atabaque. Capoeira began to gain in popularity in the 1930s and spread through the country and internationally, moving from the street into special academies. Part of a group of manifestations of Afro-Brazilian culture like *afoxé* and **Candomblé** that have survived through generations they represent what is most authentic in national culture, principally in the state of Bahia, where **samba** is also said to have originated. Brazilian cinema, in its project to rediscover national culture, represented the sport in Anselmo Duarte's *O pagador de promessas* (The Given Word) (1962) and Glauber **Rocha**'s *Barravento* (1961), where it earned perhaps its most poetic visual representation. Capoeira has also contributed to Brazilian popular music; its rhythms can be heard in **bossa nova**, in compositions like Vinicius de **Moraes**'s and Baden **Powell**'s 'Berimbau' and in Gilberto **Gil**'s 'Domingo no parque' (Sunday in the Park).

See also: Pastinha, Vincente

Further reading

Evleshin C. (1986) 'Capoeira at the Crossroads', Portland, Oregon, Instruction Television Services.

Lewis, J.L. (1992) *Ring of Liberation: a Deceptive Discourse in Brazilian Capoeira*, Chicago: University of Chicago Press.

Micallef, G. (1986) 'Danca da Cultura: Capoeira de Salvador da Bahia', Portland, Oregon: Filmsound.

VIVALDO SANTOS

Capricorne, José Maria

b. 1932, Curaçao

Visual artist

Returning to Curaçao in 1968 from Brazil, where he had made a living decorating porcelain, Capricorne co-founded the local Academy of Visual Arts. His own colourful oil paintings are characterized by inconspicuous but obtrusive 'eyes', that search and enjoy the world. His pleasure in life is also evident in his animals, flowers and dancing people. In 1985 he received the Cola Debrot Prize, Curaçao's most important cultural award.

NEL CASIMIRI

Caracol

The First Colombian Radio Network (Primera Cadena Radial Colombiana), known as Caracol, was founded in 1948. It is one of three radio networks in Colombia, together with RCN (Radio Cadena Nacional, or National Radio Network) and Todelar (Circuito Todelar de Colombia, or Todelar Circuit of Colombia). Caracol is a commercial network which broadcasts nationally and internationally through self-owned stations and affliates, and its programmes can also be heard through the Internet.

MIGUEL A CARDINALE

Caravelle

Caravelle is a journal founded to bring together specialists at the Institut d'Etudes Hispaniques, Hispano-Américaines et Luso-brésiliennes, which opened at the University of Toulouse, France in 1959, and provides a means of exchange between researchers in Europe and Latin America. According to the presentation by Paul Mérimée, in its first issue in 1963, its name 'is an invitation to action, discovery and exploration'. The magazine continues a tradition begun at Toulouse University in 1886, when the first Chair of Hispanic Studies was established. It is published once per year, sometimes as a monograph devoted to a single country, historical period or genre.

CELINA MANZONI

Carballido, Emilio

b. 1925, Córdoba, Mexico

Playwright and novelist

The most prolific and effective of Mexico's living dramatists, Carballido made his debut with *Rosalba y los llaveros* (Rosalba and the Key Rings) (1950), directed by Salvador **Novo** at the Theatre of Bellas Artes. His courses and workshops have produced a number of new writers for the Mexican stage, but he has also written **opera** and **ballet** librettos and film scripts. In 1970 he became director of the School of Theatre Arts in Mexico and assistant director of the University of Veracruz Theatre Department (1974–6). In 1975 he founded the theatre journal *Tramoya*, specializing in works by new authors. He has received innumerable prizes and awards, but perhaps the most important recognition is that his works continue to be presented by amateur and professional companies. In addition he has written short stories, essays and novels, including *El Norte* (The North) (1958), *Los*

zapatos de fierro (The Iron Shoes) (1976) and *Querétaro imperial* (Imperial Queretaro) (1994). His many plays range from *La zona intermedia* (The Intermediate Zone) (1950), one of his earliest, to *Un pequeño día de ira* (One Small Day of Rage) (1960–1), *Yo también hablo de la rosa* (I also Speak of Roses) (1966), *Acapulco los lunes* (Acapulco on Mondays) (1970), *Tiempo de ladrones* (Time of thieves) (1984), *Los esclavos de Estambul* (Slaves of Istanbul) (1991) and *Escrito en el cuerpo de la noche* (Written on the Body of Night) (1996).

Further reading

Bixler, J.E. (1997) *Convention and Transgression: The Theatre of Emilio Carballido*, London: AUP.

Pedeu, M.S. (1980) *Emilio Carballido*, Boston: Twayne.

TITO VASCONCELOS

Carballo, Celeste

b. 1959, Coronel Pringles, Argentina

Singer

One of the most representative figures of Argentine rock music, Carballo began her career in 1975 as a blues singer. Writing her own songs, she recorded her first album, *Me vuelvo cada día más loca* (I Get Crazier Every Day) in 1982 and *Mi voz renacerá* (My Voice Will Be Reborn) a year later. Now at the peak of her career, she launched *Celeste y la generación* (Celeste and the Generation), produced by Charly **García**, which included punk pieces. With Sandra **Mihanovich** she recorded the militantly gay *Somos mucho más que dos* (We are Many More than Two) (1988) and *Mujer contra mujer* (Woman against Woman) (1990).

RODRIGO PEIRETTI

Cardei, Luis

b. 1944, Buenos Aires, Argentina

Singer

The new voice of **tango**, Cardei reached the peak

of his career at age fifty, after a life singing in Buenos Aires clubs. Because a physical deficiency requires him to sit while he sings, his style is more dramatic monologue. In his repertoire of songs from the 1940s, his voice evokes the urban districts of low houses and wild women weeping as **carnival** passes by. Cardei sang with his friend, bandoneón (see **accordion and bandoneón**) player Antonio Pisano, with whom he graduated to Café Gandhi in Corrientes and the Club del Vino in Old Palermo, where he shared billings with the greatest tango performers. He appears in Fernando Solanas's film *La nube* (The Cloud) (1998).

LUIS GUSMAN

Cardenal, Ernesto

b. 1925, Granada, Nicaragua

Poet, political activist and priest

Cardenal's poetic work opened a new direction in Latin American poetry that he himself described as *exteriorismo*, a poetry rooted in the rhetoric of speech – renouncing metaphor in favour of rhythm and the 'things of the world'. The witty imitations of his early collection, *Epigramas* (1961), linked love and politics with his own marginal involvement in the plot to overthrow the dictator Somoza (see **Somoza dynasty**) in the failed April conspiracy of 1954. His *Hora cero* (Zero Hour) (1960) is what Steven White calls 'the quintessential Latin American political poem' – a narrative of Nicaraguan history interwoven with a visionary hope. In the intervening years, Cardenal had spent a key period in his life at the community of Gethsemani in Kentucky under the tutelage of Thomas Merton, the outstanding poet whose death would later move Cardenal to produce some of his finest writing. Although writing on secular themes was forbidden in the religious community, the spiritual commentaries written there and published as *Vida en el amor* (A Life in Love) (1970) give an insight into Cardenal's understanding of the relationship between religion and social revolution, later expressed in the principles of **liberation theology**. *Hora cero* and Cardenal's subsequent writings seek out the foundations of this new community of

loving equals in history in *Homenaje a los indios Americanos* (Homage to the Indians of the Americas) (1969), in the example of Cuba (*En Cuba* (In Cuba) (1972)) and in the apocalyptic religious visions of *Salmos* (Psalms) (1964).

But Cardenal set out to create this community in practice, on the island of **Solentiname** on the Lake of Nicaragua. At the same time, he gave his support to the **FSLN** in its struggle against the Somoza dictatorship, though he remained uneasy about the use of armed violence. None the less, he allowed Solentiname to be used for the preparation of a Sandinista assault on a barracks at San Carlos; the dictator's revenge, in 1977, was to destroy Solentiname from the air. Cardenal then moved to Costa Rica and became an active advocate of the Sandinista cause, returning to Nicaragua after the Sandinista Revolution of 1979 (see **revolutions**) to become Minister of Culture. From his new post he continued the work of Solentiname, creating **poetry** and art workshops for ordinary Nicaraguans. Some felt that Cardenal's adherence to a 'primitive' style pre-empted a more authentic creativity, but the materials gathered in the volumes called *El evangelio en Solentiname* (1976–8) leave little doubt as to the quality of both words and paintings. Cardenal's own perceptions of the Solentiname experience are gathered in *Nostalgia del futuro* (Nostalgia for the Future) (1984). His major but flawed poetic work of this era was *Cántico cósmico* (Cosmic Canticle) (1990), a sprawling volume whose eclecticism and embrace of all forms of knowledge may have been intended as a kind of *summum* but fails to achieve coherence. Coinciding as it does with the Sandinista electoral defeat, it may more significantly indicate a momentary loss of direction in the pursuit of the liberated community. The first volume of his memoirs, *Vida perdida* (A Lost Life), appeared in 1998. By this time, Cardenal had publicly split with the leadership of the FSLN and joined a new social-democratic grouping around Sergio **Ramírez**.

Further reading

Borgeson, P.W. (1984) *Hacia el hombre nuevo: Poesía y pensamiento de Ernesto Cardenal*, London: Támesis.

González-Balado, J.L. (1978) *Ernesto Cardenal, poeta,*

revolucionario, monje, Salamanca: Ediciones Sígueme.

Zimmerman, M. (1985) *Ernesto Cardenal: Flights of Victory / Vuelos de Victoria*, Maryknoll, NY: Orbis Books.

MIKE GONZALEZ

Cárdenas, Agustín

b. 1927, Matanzas, Cuba

Sculptor

Cárdenas' vast production is equally influenced by African spirituality and symbols as well as the work of Hans Arp and Henry Moore. He has worked in stone, wood, marble and (since 1970) in bronze. A member of the Los Once group he won the National Sculpture Prize in 1954 and held his first exhibition in Havana a year later. Moving to Paris, Cárdenas was enthusiastically taken up by the surrealists; his first personal exhibition in Paris in 1959 brought him international recognition and a growing reputation as one of the major figures of modern sculpture.

VIOLETA CASAL

Cárdenas, Cuauhtémoc

b. 1934, Mexico City

Politician

A former governor of Michoacán and son of one of Mexico's most beloved Presidents, Lázaro **Cárdenas** (1934–40), Cárdenas left the **PRI** (Party of the Institutional Revolution) to lead a left-of-centre reform movement that has evolved into the PRD (Party of the Democratic Revolution). Many Mexicans believe that he defeated Carlos **Salinas de Gortari** in the 1992 Presidential elections but that his victory was stolen through fraud. In July 1997 he became the first elected Mayor of Mexico City, which includes one-third of the Mexican population and all of its centres of power. He was in fact the first mayor to be elected from any opposition party.

CYNTHIA STEELE

Cárdenas, Eliécer

b. 1950, Cañar, Ecuador

Writer

Cárdenas has rapidly, and justifiably, become one of Ecuador's most highly regarded novelists. He has produced a number of works and maintained a consistent standard. His main concerns have been to recuperate popular culture and address issues of personal and collective identity and transculturation (see **cultural theory**). His clear command of narrative technique and lyrical expression are evident in *Juego de mártires* (Martyrs Game) (1977), *Polvo y Ceniza* (Dust and Ashes) (1979), *Háblanos, Bolívar* (Speak to Us, Bolívar) (1983), *Las humanas certezas* (Human Certainties) (1985), *Diario de un idólatra* (Diary of an Idolater) (1990), and *Que te perdone el viento* (May the Wind Forgive You) (1993).

MERCEDES ROBLES

Cárdenas, Guty

b. 1905, Mérida, Yucatan; d. 1932, Mexico City

Composer

Born Augusto Cárdenas Pinelo, Cárdenas was the foremost composer of the **trova yucateca**, the romantic trio music of the Yucatan peninsula from the 1920s and 1930s. His most famous song was 'El Caminante del Mayab' (The Pilgrim of the Mayan Road), a nostalgic evocation of his 'patria chica', or region, with lyrics by the well-known Yucatecan writer Antonio Mediz Bolio. Cárdenas migrated to Mexico City to pursue his career, where he was shot dead in a bar-room brawl.

CYNTHIA STEELE

Cárdenas, Lázaro

b. 1895, Michoacan, Mexico; d. 1970, Michoacan

Politician

President of Mexico from 1934 to 1940, his presidency represented the moment of consolidation of the Mexican State through the incorporation of the major sectors of Mexican society. The PRM (Party of the Mexican Revolution) was the direct predecessor of the **PRI** as the political expression of the new political arrangements. He implemented many of the Mexican Revolution's (see **revolutions**) unfulfilled promises, redistributing more land (49 million acres) than in any six-year presidency before or since, launching a system of secular State education that provoked the wrath of the Roman Catholic Church, acknowledging the rights of **trade unions** and imposing obligatory arbitration on both workers and employers, and expropriating the foreign **oil** companies in 1938. His populist policies laid the foundations of a modern Mexican economy; and his radical reputation was reaffirmed when he headed a campaign of solidarity with the Cuban Revolution of 1959 – a reputation that was transferred to his son Cuauhtémoc **Cárdenas**, who became an important political figure in Mexico from the 1980s.

LINDA A. CURCIO-NAGY AND MIKE GONZALEZ

Cardoso, Elisete

b. 1920, Rio de Janeiro, Brazil; d. 1990, Rio de Janeiro

Singer

Known as 'A Divina', Elisete Cardoso helped define the mellifluous **samba**–canção style and became the most celebrated female vocalist in Brazil during the 1950s and 1960s. Like most popular singers of her time, she began her career performing on live radio broadcasts in Rio de Janeiro and São Paulo. In 1958, Cardoso was the first to record '**Chega de saudade**' on her album *Canção do amor demais* (Song of Too Much Love), which initiated the **bossa nova** movement. In the 1960s, she hosted several televised musical showcases including *Nossa Elisete* and *Bossaudade*.

CHRISTOPHER DUNN

Cardoso, Fernando Henrique

b. 1931, Rio de Janeiro, Brazil

Sociologist and politician

Cardoso studied with Florestan **Fernandes** and Roger Bastide at the University of São Paulo prior to pursuing graduate studies at the University of Paris. While exiled in Chile, Cardoso made important contributions to the theoretical analysis of dependency (see **dependency theory**). He returned to Brazil in 1968, where he taught at the University of São Paulo prior to Institutional Act Number 5 (AI-5), a decree by which the military regime established strict control over Brazilian intellectual (see **intellectuals**) and political life.

Like Celso **Furtado**, Cardoso and his collaborator Enzo Faletto approached economic phenomena and dependency as historical problems. Cardoso's plan of 'associated dependent' development for economies controlled by local bourgeoisies treated development and underdevelopment as part of a complex international system in which the bourgeoisies of centre and periphery were important political actors. He believed authoritarian regimes could secure political demobilization of the masses in Latin America.

Cardoso ran for the Senate in 1978. In 1983, when Franco Montoro was elected governor of the state of São Paulo, he replaced Montoro in the Senate. He ran for mayor of São Paulo in 1985 but lost the election to Jânio Quadros. He was re-elected to the Senate and in 1986 helped found the PSDB (Partido da Social Democrácia Brasileira) (Brazilian Social Democratic Party). In 1992, Cardoso was named Minister of Foreign Relations by Itamar Franco, Fernando **Collor** de Mello's successor. As Minister of Finance in 1993, he developed the Plan Real to curb Brazil's hyperinflation and restructure the monetary exchange. The success of this economic plan led to Cardoso's election as President in 1994 through a coalition of the PSDB and the PFL (Partido da Frente Liberal)

(Liberal Front Party), and he assumed the Presidency in January 1995. He was re-elected for a second term in 1998 with an overwhelming majority. Described as a Marxist throughout his previous academic career, his economic policies as president were said by some to represent a pragmatic acceptance of the realities of the global market and of Brazil's role within it.

Further reading

Cardoso F.H. and Faletto, E. (1979) *Dependency and Underdevelopment in Latin America*, Berkeley, CA: University of California Press (originally published in 1969 in Mexico).

Goertich, T.G. (1999) *Fernando Henrique Cardoso: Reinventing Democracy in Brazil*, Boulder, CO: Lynne Rienner.

Goto, R. (1998) *Para ler Fernando Henrique Cardoso*, São Paulo: Geração.

Roett, R. and Purcell, S.K. (1997) *Brazil Under Cardoso*, Boulder, CO: Lynne Rienner.

PEGGY SHARPE

Cardoza y Aragón, Luis

b. 1904, Antigua, Guatemala; d. 1992, Mexico City

Writer and art critic

The great vanguard poet of the Generation of 1920 along with **Asturias**, Cardoza was a key figure during the October Revolution (1944–54) editing *Revista de Guatemala*. Mixing lyricism, colloquialism, erudite symbolism and prosaic discourse, Cardoza distanced himself from poetic norms, becoming increasingly concerned with national identity and *indigenismo* as sources of spiritual revitalization. Cardoza also wrote political articles, essay books, and art criticism. His principal prose works are *Guatemala, las líneas de su mano* (Guatemala, The Lines of its Hands) (1955) an essay on Guatemalan culture and history, and his memoirs, *El río: Novelas de caballería* (The River: Chivalry Novels) (1986). Following the 1954 *coup*,

Cardoza lived in Mexico, where he was renowned as an art critic and essayist.

MARC ZIMMERMAN

Careaga, Enrique

b. 1944, Asunción, Paraguay

Painter

Careaga was co-founder of Los Novísimos (1964), a group concerned with revitalizing Paraguayan art by introducing a more cosmopolitan style. In 1965 he helped to set up the Museo de Arte Moderno in Asunción. In 1966 he won a scholarship to study in Paris with Victor Vasarely and Groupe de Recherche d'Art Visuel, who were interested in using optical effects to generate images; he remained there until 1978. Careaga's career consists of two phases. In the first he used two-dimensional fields to study the effects of vibration and instability created by the interreaction of strongly contrasting colours. In the early 1970s, he introduced three-dimensionality in spatial projects.

BETSY PARTYKA

Caretas

Caretas is a current affairs magazine founded in 1950 by Doris Gibson and Francisco Igartua. It has since become one of Peru's most important and prestigious journals. The journal and its writers have received numerous awards for their defence of human rights and press freedom. Its political position has exposed *Caretas* to persecution; it was repeatedly closed down by both the **Velasco** and the Morales Bermúdez governments, and its director Enrique Zileri was deported. It has varied in frequency over the years, but since 1979 it has remained a weekly.

CÉSAR SALAS

Carew, Jan

b. 1925, Agricola, Guyana

Novelist and cultural historian

Carew's first novels, *Black Midas* (1958) and *The Wild Coast* (1958), dealt with the racial politics of Guyana and were heavily influenced by the **Marxism** of Frantz **Fanon**. Having travelled and lived in many parts of the world, Carew's work is not limited to Caribbean themes. Russia is the setting for two 1964 novels: *Green Winter*, about an African student who travels there, and *Moscow Is Not My Mecca*, while Harlem is the setting for *The Last Barbarian* (1960). He has published poems, plays and several children's stories, such as *The Third Gift* (1974). Much of his scholarly writing— such as *Fulcrums of Change: Origins of Racism in the Americas and Other Essays* (1988), *Rape of Paradise: Columbus and the Birth of Racism in the Americas* (1994), and *Ghosts in Our Blood: With Malcolm X in Africa, England, and the Caribbean* (1994) – deals with issues of **race** in post-colonial societies. He is Professor Emeritus of African American Studies at Northwestern University.

CAROL J. WALLACE

Carew, Rodney Cline

b. 1945, Gatún, Panama Canal Zone

Baseball player

Among the greatest offensive players of his generation, Rod Carew won seven major league batting titles and was named to seventeen All-Star teams in a nineteen-year playing career in US professional **baseball**. Carew registered a batting average that exceeded .300 in fifteen consecutive seasons, a performance of offensive prowess bettered by only three men in US baseball history. In 1991, he became the fifth Latin American to be elected to the baseball Hall of Fame.

DOUGLAS W. VICK

Caribbean

'Caribbean' is a geographic term describing the island territories of the Caribbean Sea and also some parts of the Central and South American mainland bordering that sea. Guyana, Suriname and French Guiana in South America and Belize in Central America are usually included as 'Caribbean' on the basis of historical experiences such as European colonization, widespread African enslavement and staple commodity production, which these areas shared with the Caribbean islands. Similarly, the Bahamas and Bermuda, located in the Atlantic Ocean between the Caribbean Basin and North America are also often included; as are parts of some Central and South American countries, such as Nicaragua or Colombia, which border the Caribbean Sea and also share cultural or historical similarities with the Caribbean islands. Some scholars use phrases such as 'circum Caribbean' or 'greater Caribbean' to denote these more expansive definitions. The word 'Caribbean' originates with the name Carib given to one group of the native inhabitants encountered by European explorers in the Caribbean area at the end of the fifteenth century. The term 'Caribbean' is often used in the UK to refer only to the English-speaking islands, but actually signifies the entire region, which includes English, French, Spanish, Dutch and Papiamentu-speaking areas.

See also: Greater Antilles; Lesser Antilles

ROSANNE ADDERLEY

Caribbean Artists Movement

Active from 1966 to 1972, mainly in London, the Caribbean Artists Movement (CAM) proved to be a significant and far-reaching force in British and Caribbean cultural life. Its programme of meetings – private and public – conferences, exhibitions and newsletters sought to define a Caribbean aesthetic, to explore new directions and extend the audience for Caribbean arts. It was interdisciplinary in practice and regional in focus; its members included the writers Edward Kamau **Brathwaite**, Wilson **Harris** and C.L.R. **James**, the artists

Ronald Moody and Aubrey **Williams**, and the critic Gordon Rohlehr.

ANNE WALMSLEY

Caribbean Broadcasting Union

Founded in 1970, the goal of the Caribbean Broadcasting Union (CBU) is to to improve the overall quality of regional programming and to increase the flow of radio and television programming and services between the countries of the English-speaking Caribbean, fostering regional cooperation and unity. The organization provides programmes such as the CBU Annual Merit Awards for outstanding work in radio and television, seminars addressing issues such as developments in global copyright regulations, and workshops on news direction, marketing, engineering or other topics of concern. Among the challenges facing the union has been gaining the cooperation of non-member broadcasting systems in honouring exclusive rights agreements for programming such as the Olympic Games.

CAROL J. WALLACE

Caribbean Communications Network

Caribbean Communications Network (CCN) is a media group which operates a newspaper, *Trinidad Express*, a television station, TV6, and Prime Radio 106FM. Created out of a need to educate and inform the general public of Trinidad and Tobago and the region, CCN was established as a public company in May 1991. Prime Radio 106FM and TV6 were launched in 1991. After four years in operation, TV6 emerged as the leader in prime time television in Trinidad and Tobago. Located in Port-of-Spain, Trinidad, the company's chairman and chief executive officer is Ken Gordon. The directors include Sidney Knox, Arthur Lok Jack, Gordon Butch Stewart, Thomas Gatcliffe and Lawrence Duprey.

KEITH JARDIM

Caribbean English

English settlements in the Caribbean make the English language the oldest exportation of that language from Britain. Anglophone creoles were the first distinct overseas byproducts and joint ancestors of today's Caribbean English spoken by about 6 million people. In the last three decades of the twentieth century twelve independent nations have emerged each with a national standard language. While these individual varieties may differ tremendously, their common English base makes them part of Caribbean English, a subvariety of English distributed over a large number of non-contiguous territories.

Differences in settlement history have made for the present-day varieties. In Guyana, aboriginal groups – Arawak, Wapishana, Akawaio, etc. – have each contributed to everyday words that are known to Guayanese but not to other Caribbeans, for example, *curri-curri* 'red, or a red bird', *mora* 'a large timber tree'. In the same way in Belize come words from Kekchi, Mopan, Yucatecan, Miskito, and Garifuna – *craboo* 'cherry-like fruit', *gibnut* 'guinea pig-like animal' – as well as Spanish loan words such as *relleno* and *tamales*.

Although Jamaican, Barbadian, Trinidadian and Guyanese intonations are noticeably different, all have a reduction in the number of dipthongal glides and a unique phrasal intonation e.g. teach.er /1'2/ /versus /2'1/ in Standard English. Likewise, in word formation, final consonant clusters are often reduced – *he beg for* 'he begs' and parts of speech are converted, e.g. *good* = well. Pronominal forms allow for a number of functions hence I, me, my, my own, mine(s), meself/myself are headwords in idiomatic phrases. Intensification is obtained by reduplification – *stupid-stupid* – and by introducing the main verb of a short utterance at the beginning of the sentence, *Is borrow she borrow it*: 'She actually borrowed it.' Idiomatic expressions which defy individual word-for-word translation are also very common: *cut your eye at somebody* 'contempt', *suck your teeth* 'disgust', and *be behind somebody like a slave-driver* 'annoyance'. The lexicon of Caribbean English comprises an active core vocabulary of World English together with all Caribbean regionalisms produced by the ecology, history, and culture of the area.

Caribbean English has always felt pressure to change from the colonial forces as well as from the persistence of the stigmatized **creole languages** of the working classes. In 1971, the Caribbean Lexicography Project initiated a survey of usage in West Indian speech communities to create a dictionary which is the definitive work today on Caribbean English.

Further reading

Allsop, R. (ed.) (1996) *Dictionary of Caribbean English Usage*, Oxford: Oxford University Press.

Gorlach, M. and Holm, J. (eds) (1986) *Focus on the Caribbean: Varieties of English around the World*, Amsterdam: Benjamins.

IRENE WHERRITT

Caribbean Quarterly

Published by the **University of the West Indies** since 1949, each issue of *Caribbean Quarterly* includes a group of scholarly articles on one theme in Caribbean studies, focusing on the social sciences. Themes of recent issues have been Cuba, the Indian presence and the Grenada Revolution. The journal includes book reviews. It is indexed in *Hispanic American Periodicals Index*.

PAUL BARY

Caribbean Review

This quarterly journal, published in Miami from 1969 to 1980, includes articles on the political and cultural affairs of the Caribbean islands and the Central and South American countries surrounding the Caribbean. It includes general interest articles, illustrations, and book reviews. It is indexed in *Hispanic American Periodicals Index*.

PAUL BARY

Caribbean Studies

The quarterly publication *Caribbean Studies*, published at the University of Puerto Rico in Río Piedras since 1961, is multidisciplinary and includes scholarly articles on a wide range of topics covering all islands, as well as occasional book reviews, documents and bibliographies. Each issue includes 'Caribeña', a regular feature listing current books, pamphlets, articles and essays on the Caribbean. Articles are predominantly in English but are also in Spanish and French, and are written by Caribbeanists and other persons interested in keeping up with research and writing in Caribbean Studies. The journal is indexed in *Hispanic American Periodicals Index*.

PAUL BARY

Caribbean Voices

The importance of this BBC radio programme, which was broadcast between 1945 and 1958, would be hard to overestimate. The series provided an opportunity for Anglophone writers from the Caribbean to present their work on an international network. In many cases it provided a first platform for writers who would later develop an international reputation, like Nobel Prize winner Derek **Walcott**, George **Lamming** or John **Figueroa**. Its first producer, Jamaican Una Marson, was succeeded in 1946 by Henry Swanzy and later by others as distinguished as V.S. **Naipaul** and Andrew **Salkey**. It did provoke controversy, as its adventurous programming included new varieties of Caribbean speech performance as well as more 'conventional' poetic and fictional texts. Some of the broadcast verse, edited by John Figueroa, was later published as *Caribbean Voices: An Anthology of West Indian Poetry* in two volumes (1966, 1970)

MIKE GONZALEZ

Caribs

The Caribs loom large in the colonial and national histories of northern South America, for they were the savage counterpoint to the civilizing mission of the conquistadors to make a 'New World'. Their identification with 'cannibalism' and their socio-political history of alliance with French, English and Dutch has created an enduring image of the Carib as fierce, warlike and intractable. This image was, of course, partly correct, for the manner of Spanish colonial warfare against the *caribes* did much to engender precisely that savagery and bellicosity that was the justification for their conquest in the first place. So it is also the case today that the Karinya (Venezuela), Carib (Guyana, Surinam) and Galibi (French Guiana) still retain an antipathy to outsiders and proud memory of their struggles to remain autonomous from the colonial and national states of the region.

The Carib language is part of the Cariban family, one of the largest language families in northern South America. For example, the Ye'cuana, Panare, and Pemon in Venezuela, the Akawaio, Patamona, Macuxi and Wai-Wai in Guyana, the Macuxi and Kalapalo in Brazil, and the Trio and Wayana in Suriname and French Guiana all share a common language and cultural history with the Caribs, although these languages are not necessarily mutually intelligible. Because Carib peoples were so widely dispersed over the northern part of the continent and played such a prominent role in the unfolding of colonial occupation and national establishment, many of their terms have been adopted into other languages. Examples include *arepa* (Venezuelan Spanish 'cassava cake') *kanawa* (English 'canoe'), *hamaca* (English 'hammock'), *ouragan* (English 'hurricane'), *mapoya* (Caribbean English 'obeah') and of course their own name in various forms such as '*caribal*' (English 'cannibal'), or '*caribe*' (Spanish 'wild, fierce').

The current situation of these peoples may be broadly related to the manner of their interactions with the surrounding state societies whose progressive encroachments have been carefully evaluated and often violently resisted by Carib peoples. For example, the Karinya in Venezuela have had to negotiate with various oil companies over the past forty years as their ancestral lands lie directly over the Orinoco oil shale deposits. Similarly, the upland Pemon, Ye'cuana, Akawaio, Patamona and Macuxi have been in the front line of recent contacts with *criollo* gold-prospectors in the gold fields on the borders of Brazil, Guyana and Venezuela. The Caribs sustain that tradition of autonomy from external encroachment that has notably defined their cultures and identities for the last five hundred years.

Further reading

Henley, P. (1982) *The Panare: Tradition and Change on the Amazonian Frontier*, New Haven, CN: Yale University Press.

Kloos, P. (1971) *The Maroni River Caribs*, Assen: Van Gorcum.

Rivière, P.G. (1985) *Individual and Society in Guiana*, Cambridge: Cambridge University Press.

Thomas, D. (1982) *Order Without Government: The Society of the Pemon Indians of Venezuela*, Urbana, IL: Illinois Studies in Anthropology.

Whitehead, N.L. (1988) *Lords of the Tiger Spirit: A History of the Caribs in Venezuela and Guyana*, KITLV Caribbean Studies Series, Dordrecht: Foris Publications.

NEIL L. WHITEHEAD

Caribscope

A thirty-minute television programme produced by the **Caribbean Broadcasting Union** (CBU) beginning in 1990 and broadcast in nineteen different Caribbean territories. The programme features segments on regional culture as well as relatively non-controversial social issues such as environmental protection or strategies for economic development. For example, *Caribscope* segments during the late 1990s addressed subjects as diverse as the restoration of a zoo in Jamaica, traditional New Year's Eve celebrations in Suriname and the discovery of a wrecked vessel believed to be an eighteenth-century slave ship off the island of Saint Vincent. Although somewhat dominated by the more numerous members from the English-speaking Caribbean, the CBU and its

Caribscope programme attempt to cover the whole region. Indeed, the CBU was founded with the specific aim of 'stimulating the flow of broadcast material between radio and television systems in the Caribbean'. In 1999 the CBU described *Caribscope* as 'the most durable programme' that it had created in fulfilment of this mission.

ROSANNE ADDERLEY

CARICOM

Acronym describing the Caribbean Community, an organization formed in 1973 to promote economic, social and foreign policy cooperation between countries of the Commonwealth Caribbean; that is territories formerly colonized by Great Britain. This was a successor organization to the Caribbean Free Trade Association (**CARIFTA**) founded in 1968. While some cooperative trade and tariff arrangements were made and significant joint endeavours established in areas such as education and research, at the end of the twentieth century the community remained far from economic integration. From its earliest years, non-Commonwealth countries from the Caribbean and Latin America sent observers to CARICOM meetings. From among these observer nations Haiti and Suriname eventually became full members.

ROSANNE ADDERLEY

CARIFESTA

CARIFESTA (The Caribbean Festival of Creative Arts) is one of the practical outcomes of the attempts to foster unity, co-operation and a sense of personal and collective identity through culture in a Caribbean which, in spite of a shared history, is fragmented along linguistic, economic and ideological lines dictated by its former colonial masters. With the exception of the short-lived Federation of West Indian Nations (1958–62), Caribbean political unity has remained an illusion. In spite or because of the failure of political unity, West Indian artists and intellectuals have always articulated the need for, and possibility of, cultural

unity on the understanding that the commonality of Caribbean historical and contemporary experiences is best demonstrated in the region's complex cultural traditions. Such thinking informed the 1952 Caribbean Festival of the Arts held in San Juan, Puerto Rico. The birth of the Federation in 1958 was also marked with a similar festival. But with the collapse of the Federation, the hope that the festival would become a regular one fizzled out.

In May 1966, a Caribbean Writers and Artists' Conference held as part of Guyana's independence celebrations resolved to petition for the establishment of a Pan-Caribbean festival and, in the summer of 1967, the **Caribbean Artists Movement** (Britain) held a conference at the University of Kent and resolved to establish a festival based in the region, designed to encourage the growth and development of Caribbean culture, and financed with the support of regional institutions. A similar resolution resulted from another conference held in Guyana (February 1970) during that country's attainment of republican status, and was reaffirmed by a Cultural and Conservation Conference held July–August 1970 at the **University of the West Indies**, Mona, Jamaica. Forbes **Burnham** subsequently accepted these recommendations on behalf of the Government and peoples of Guyana and hosted the first Carifesta from 25 August–15 September 1972.

At the first Carifesta, a petition was submitted to the Secretary-General of the Caribbean Regional Secretariat requesting that Carifesta be established as a periodic, mobile, cultural festival embracing the whole of the Caribbean, without prejudice to language, colonial history and ideology, under the auspices of the Secretariat. This has remained Carifesta's distinctive characteristic as it continues to draw participants from French, Spanish, English and Dutch Caribbean nations and to define the Caribbean as all the countries that are in or touched by the Caribbean Sea as well as the Caribbean diasporas in Britain and America.

Six Carifestas have taken place to date: Guyana (1972), Jamaica (1976), Cuba (1979), Barbados (1981), and twice in Trinidad and Tobago (1992 and 1995).

Further reading

Carifesta '76, the Literature of a People: A Select List of Books on the Creative Writings of the Participating Countries in the Second Caribbean Festival of Arts (1976) Kingston, Jamaica: Jamaica Library Service.

Carifesta Forum: An Anthology of 20 Caribbean Voices (1976) Produced for Carifesta by the Institute of Jamaica and *Jamaica Journal*.

Martínez, R.V. (1981) *Carifesta (3rd: 1979: Havana, Cuba) Carifesta 79 Cuba*, Havana: ORBE.

The New Aesthetic and the Meaning of Culture in the Caribbean 'The Dream Coming in with the Rain': Proceedings of the CARIFESTA V Symposia Port of Spain 1992 (1995) Port of Spain, Trinidad: National Carnival Commission CARIFESTA VI Secretariat.

Republic of Guyana: Contemporary Art: Carifesta 76, Jamaica (1976) Georgetown: Bovell's Printery.

FUNSO AIYEJINA

CARIFTA

Acronym for the Caribbean Free Trade Association. Formed in 1968 in the wake of the collapse of the Federation of the West Indies more than five years earlier, CARIFTA sought to promote economic co-operation among former British colonies despite the failure of the plan for a single federal nation. The organization formally began with the signing of the Treaty of Antigua by Antigua, Barbados, Guyana, and Trinidad and Tobago. CARIFTA grew to a total of thirteen members by 1971. In addition to economic matters, CARIFTA members also pursued co-operation in other areas related to social and economic development. It also sponsored some regional events such as the CARIFTA athletic games. CARIFTA was succeeded by the Caribbean Community (**CARICOM**) formed by the Treaty of Chaguaramas in 1973.

ROSANNE ADDERLEY

Carlos, Roberto

b. 1941, Itapemirim do Cachoeira, Espírito Santo, Brazil

Singer–songwriter

Since the mid-1960s, Roberto Carlos has been the top selling music performer in Brazil and abroad. In the massive international market for romantic music, he is second only to the Spanish crooner Júlio Iglesias. Roberto Carlos Braga was born into a working class family from a small, provincial city, he then moved to the North Zone of Rio de Janeiro in 1952. Five years later, he first appeared on TV Tupí singing a Portuguese version of Tutti Frutti. Around this time, he met Erasmo Carlos, who would become his everlasting musical partner.

Roberto Carlos's first recording in 1959 was an unsuccessful attempt to reinvent himself as a **bossa nova** singer. Alienated from the sophisticated, upper-middle class world of Rio de Janeiro's South Zone, where this new genre was being developed, he returned to the televised rock programmes hosted by Carlos Imperial on TV Continental. In the early 1960s, he recorded several successful albums targeted at the emerging urban middle class 'youth market'. By 1964, when a right-wing military regime took power, bossa nova had entered a second, more politicized phase which emphasized nationalist and populist themes. Meanwhile, Roberto Carlos emerged as the undisputed 'rei do iê-iê-iê' (king of rock and roll) with his weekly programme on TV Record, *Jovem Guarda* (Young Guard) named after the Brazilian rock movement. His 1965 album, *Jovem Guarda* featured the movement's manifesto 'Quero que vá tudo pro inferno' (To hell with all of the rest), which was resolutely apolitical. Framed from the perspective of the urban 'playboy', most Young Guard songs dealt with romance, fast cars, fancy clothes, and wild dance parties. Like teen idols elsewhere, he starred in several musical comedy films such as *Roberto Carlos em ritmo de aventura* (Roberto Carlos in Adventurous Rhythm) of 1967.

With the emergence of the **Tropicália** movement in 1968, the naive, largely derivative rock of the Young Guard suddenly seemed passé. By the end of the decade, Roberto Carlos reinvented himself again; this time as a more sensitive and vulnerable balladeer. In 1971, he composed and recorded 'Debaixo dos caracóis dos seus cabelos' (Beneath the Curls of your Hair), a poignant homage to Caetano **Veloso**, who had been exiled to London. He is most famous for his love songs and sentimental ballads sung in a soft, breathy voice like 'Detalhes' (Details), 'Emoções' (Emotions), and 'Fera Ferida' (Wounded Beast). In 1989, Roberto Carlos won a Grammy as the Best Performer in the Latin Pop Music category.

Further reading

Carvalho, M (1995) 'Tupi or not Tupi MPB: Popular Music and Identity in Brazil', in D. Hess and R. DaMatta (eds) *The Brazilian Puzzle*, New York: Columbia University Press.

Medeiros, P (1984) *A aventura da jovem guarda*, São Paulo: Brasiliense.

CHRISTOPHER DUNN

Carmagnola, Gladys

b. 1939, Guarambaré, Paraguay

Writer

Carmagnola's early work is considered 'children's poetry', but her poetry for adults includes *Lazo esencial* (Essential Bond) (1982), *A la intemperie* (Outdoors) (1984), *Igual que en las capueras* (Same As in the Farms) (1989), *Depositaria infiel* (Unfaithful Trustee) (1992) and *Un sorbo de agua fresca* (A Sip of Fresh Water) (1995). She has published eight books of poetry and various commemorative poetry collections. In 1996, she and Jacobo A. **Rauskin** shared the Premio Municipal de Literatura (Municipal Prize in Literature), the highest literary award in Paraguay.

TERESA MÉNDEZ-FAITH

Carneiro, Édison de Sousa

b. 1912, Salvador da Bahia, Brazil;
d. 1972, Rio de Janeiro, Brazil

Lawyer, journalist and folklorist

Along with Jorge **Amado** and Artur **Ramos**, Carneiro was a member of a group of left-wing Bahian modernists (see **Brazilian modernism**) founded in 1928. Carneiro wrote for Bahian newspapers, worked in Rio de Janeiro for the British News Service and, after 1941, served as editor-in-chief for Associated News. A proponent of the creation of the *escolas de samba* (see **samba schools**), he published extensively on Afro-Brazilian slavery, popular culture, religion, folklore and the *quilombos* (run-away slave communities) in works such as *Religiões negras* (Afro-Brazilian Religions), *O Quilombo de Palmares* (The Palmares Slave Community), *Negros Bantus* (The Bantu Negroes) and *Dinâmica do folclore* (The Dynamics of Folklore).

PEGGY SHARPE

carnival

Carnivals in the Americas are elaborate annual festivities that embrace large segments of urban populations as they gather in historically-designated public spaces to watch and/or participate in a variety of traditional and innovative activities. Commonly staged during the pre-Lenten period of the Catholic religious calendar (February–March), these carnivals receive support from competing state, political, commercial and grassroots interests. For what are at stake in the successful orchestration of these events are the ways in which collective identities are celebrated or contentiously represented via theatrical street performances, music, song lyrics, dance and costuming for national as well as international consumption. Such debates about cultural identities and the degree to which artistic and musical representations appropriately express them emerge, for instance, around carnival activities in Oruro (Bolivia), Rio de Janeiro (Brazil) and Port-of-Spain (Trinidad and Tobago).

Because they draw upon three or more centuries of diverse indigenous, European and African traditions and practices, carnivals in the western hemisphere are historically verifiable. These carnivals began as and still constitute visual archives and interpretive frameworks for rival histories and mythologies, Biblical episodes and contemporary issues. Under colonial rule, sanctioned religious feasts and processions initially provided a mostly illiterate spectatorship with visual and performed displays of imposed European doctrines, customs and codes. It was in the midst of this temporary freedom from the routine and hardships of daily economic life and against colonial hierarchies that certain members of the public would create their artistic and musical forms of celebration and/or subterfuge. Central to these festivities were the evolving status and styles that masquerading and its allied carnival arts assumed for a wide spectatorship. In short, these carnivals became the time and place in which the marginalized, illicit, vilified and dispossessed could take centre stage by dominating public thoroughfares and arenas.

These carnival arts and activities cannot be considered mere vestiges of a pre-modern era, however. They are contemporary, resilient and open to innovations, because they provide both traditional and new spectators and participants with opportunities to enjoy, critique and, to a limited extent, intervene in the open exhibition of national and foreign customs and issues. In keeping with their development during colonialism, carnival arts and practices continue to please or appal the public by symbolically interrogating, mocking, or inverting social hierarchies. At the same time, these arts and practices are not completely reducible to relentless displays of parody, satire, caricature and mimicry. The serious competitiveness with which individuals, local groups and communities prepare for and celebrate carnival illustrates the degree to which they foster and affirm this annual occasion to fashion collective identities and self-recognition in spite of historical and current forms of oppression. It is this briefly staged coincidence of the traditional and the contemporary and of the oppressive and the Utopian that gives carnivals their social complexity, imaginative scale and mass appeal.

The following descriptions of carnivals in Oruro, Rio de Janeiro and Port-of-Spain offer some contextualized facts about aspects of carnival which can be found in varying degrees in other parts of Latin America and the Caribbean.

Oruro's carnival manifests obvious pre-Columbian origins. In an apocalyptic contest, a legendary **Quechua** and Uru-speaking princess (*la Ñusta*) singlehandedly saved the Uru people from the semi-god of strength, Huari, and his scourges: an enormous snake from the south, a giant toad from the north, an immense lizard from the northeast and an invasion of ants from the east. This contest subsequently evolved into the struggle between the Virgen de la Candelaria or Virgen del Socavón, the patron saint of Bolivian miners, and the Devil. During the colonial period, until roughly the end of the eighteenth century, there was widespread reverence for the Devil, that is, for pre-Columbian deities and spirits that the figure and significance of the Devil came closest to symbolizing. From the end of this period until about 1944, the Virgen del Socavón gained greater influence. However, from 1944 onwards, that is, by the time Oruro was officially declared the capital of Bolivian folkloric traditions, various dance groups of fastidiously costumed devils (see **diablada**) had begun to assume greater visibility in the festivities, even though it is widely understood that the carnival pays homage to the Virgen del Socavón.

One of Oruro's first pre-Carnival events is the traditional invitation (*rodeo*) through which influential members of the community are encouraged to contribute to the festivities. Additional preparations for Oruro's carnival begin as early as November with auditions for dancers. Apart from the scrupulous attention that costumes receive, the choreographical and performative aspects of the celebrations are also of great importance. The *diabladas* re-enact the struggle between good and evil through dance and popular theatre. These performances are usually allegorical plays that recall their baroque Spanish counterparts as well as their pre-Columbian origins. Other costumes and dances may be categorized by genre. The *morenos* and *caporales*, for example, depict African slaves and the slave trade; the *wacatokoris* is a dance that satirizes Spanish bullfighting; and the *chutas* or *paceños* commemorate a variety of historical periods and events. These performative and choreographical practices are the means by which local communities appreciate the representations of their history and the transformations of their culture.

Originating in the Portuguese mock battles with buckets of water thrown about indiscriminately (*entrudos*) and in diverse rituals and practices that African slaves and their descendants introduced, carnival in Rio de Janeiro is the largest parade of masqueraders in the Americas today. However, it was not until the middle of the nineteenth century that associations called 'great societies' (*grandes sociedades*) began to arrange masked balls and other activities and thereby promote organized masquerading. Despite initial attempts by members of the bourgeoisie and upper classes to prohibit or control such activities, these associations represented the first of many simultaneous and subsequent efforts to coordinate celebrations according to multiple alliances based on neighbourhood, place of origin in Brazil, economic class, skin colour and so on. During the first two decades of the twentieth century, *cordões*, bands of masqueraders led by a standard bearer, began to appear. No longer as ubiquitous today, groups of strollers (*ranchos*), with a musical band and chorus, also circulated, performing their brand of sentimental songs. Around that time, groups of loosely organized masqueraders accompanied by music (**blocos**) emerged and today form one of the city's major carnival institutions. The development of carnival in Rio de Janeiro during this century, therefore, took place along two organizational axes. The first was the gradual arrangement of masqueraders in guilds which, despite the external coherence of their parading, still facilitated annual differences in themes, music, choreography and costumes. The second axis was the intense competitiveness that arose and presently characterizes the relations between guilds.

These axes are most notable in two of the carnival's most important institutions: the *bloco* and the *escola de samba* (see **samba schools**). Complex constitutions and by-laws and democratically elected officials run these bodies. The *bloco* is more traditional and porous that the *escola*. There are hundreds of *blocos* in Rio de Janeiro, which include, for example, the 'dirty ones' (*blocos de sujos*) and guilds (*blocos de arrastão*) that invite the public's participation with their infectious music, drumming

sections (*bateria*), and dancing. Emerging around 1928 from the *blocos*, the *escolas*, by contrast, are well drilled in their respective neighbourhoods for competition against guilds from the same category. Loosely derived from original samba performances of African heritage, the *escolas* today concentrate on elaborate choreography, costuming and song. With their large floats, the *escolas* are among the most visible features of Rio de Janeiro's carnival.

The French creole plantocracy of the late eighteenth and early nineteenth centuries initiated Port-of-Spain's first public carnivals. While families from this class indulged in masked balls and costume parades on drawn carriages, slaves practised their own forms of mimicry and African masking rituals and performances in backyards at night. The first post-emancipation carnival (1838) saw a radical transformation of the public celebration with former slaves and the free coloured taking to the streets and the upper classes retreating and lamenting the new scenario. What had previously been the disruptive nocturnal activity (*canboulay*) of putting out fires on plantations accompanied by sticks and torches became, with the addition of drums, one of the original forms of collective celebration. *J'ouvert*, Carnival Monday's pre-dawn revelries, harkens back to plantation life with the annual appearance of the molasses devils (*jab molassi*), masqueraders covered in coloured oil, mud or molasses. Members of the *jamette* society, that is, those who came from 'beyond the diameter' or fringes of polite bourgeois society, were also prevalent at this early stage of the revelries. Some of the most parodic and satirical figures usually emerged at this juncture as well. As carnival grew larger and more elaborate, theme bands began to parade. By the beginning of the twentieth century, a few of their genres included Pierrots, devils, dragons, costumed stilt dancers (*moko jumbies*), red Indians and bats. Over the years, themes and some costumed figures faded in and out of the parades, so that carnival may be said to retain a flexibility and resilience of form while its thematic content varies annually. It is this accretive capacity that accounts for the celebration's dynamism and longevity.

Carnival is assimilative, which is a quality that explains why calypsos (see **calypso**) and music from steel drums (see **steelband**) have accompanied the parade of bands even though these musical expressions have somewhat separate origins and lines of development within a common colonial history. In keeping with this quality, the expansion of East Indian cultural influences in the 1980s and 1990s has also manifested itself in some of the festivity's musical accompaniment and innovations. Currently, aspects of Trinidad's carnival are also being officially promoted in other Caribbean islands as well as in West Indian immigrant communities in Brooklyn (New York), Miami, Toronto and London. Trinidad Parliamentary Act No. 9 of 1991 created a National Carnival Commission in order to make carnival a national, cultural and commercial enterprise.

The legislative and restrictive policies that nineteenth-century, colonial and post-colonial regimes in the Americas assumed with respect to carnival have given way in contemporary life to state support for the celebration's arts and activities. National cultural organizations have become some of the most prominent caretakers and promoters of carnival as both an emblem of national patrimony and a resource for cultural **tourism**. The extent to which these dual aims represent an internal contradiction varies according to the specific historical and cultural contexts of the carnival in question. The degree of contradiction also depends on the freedom and potential that non-governmental organizations (NGOs) enjoy as they contribute to celebrations of national culture.

See also: Afro-Latin American arts; folk; folklore festivals; indigenista art; Minshall, Peter; street art; syncretism; tourism and the sacred; tourist art

Further reading:

Cowley, J. (1996) *Carnival, Canboulay and Calypso: Traditions in the Making*, London: Cambridge University Press.

da Matta, R. (1991) *Carnivals, Rogues, and Heroes: An Interpretation of the Brazilian Dilemma*, trans. J. Drury, Notre Dame, IN: University of Notre Dame Press.

García Canclini, N. (1995) *Hybrid Cultures: Strategies for Entering and Leaving Modernity*, trans. C.L. Chiappari and S.L. López, Minneapolis, MN: University of Minnesota Press.

Gardel, L. (1967) *Escolas de Samba: An Affectionate Descriptive Account of the Carnival Guilds of Rio de Janeiro*, Rio de Janeiro: Livraria Kosmos Editôra.

Trinidad Carnival: A Republication of the Caribbean Quarterly Trinidad Carnival Issue (Vol. 4; Nos 3–4, 1956) (1988) Port-of-Spain, Trinidad: Paria Publishing Company.

GERARD ACHING

carpa

Carpa is an itinerant, working-class entertainment that appeared in central Mexico around the turn of the century. Among its influences are vaudeville, *teatro de revista* (variety shows) and especially circus, under whose tents or *carpas* these hybrid spectacles took place after the circuses lost their horses and other animals to the Mexican Revolution (see **revolutions**). In the new socio-political climate, the clowns modified their appearance and discourse to personify the urban *pelado* (underdog figure who mocks and defies authority), and developed a scathing political satire based on witty language twists. Among the most famous were Roberto Soto 'Panzón', 'Clavillazo', 'Resortes' and '**Cantinflas**'. *Carpa* shows also included cabaret, tango and rumba numbers. The troupes travelled around the country, reaching the US southwest. Its influence lives on in theatre, cinema, radio and television.

ANTONIO PRIETO-STAMBAUGH

Carpentier, Alejo

b. 1904, Lausanne, Switzerland; d. 1980, Paris, France

Writer

A founding figure in the new novel movement in both Cuba and Latin America, Carpentier also wrote journalism and essays on a wide range of topics. The son of a French father and a Russian mother, there is some doubt as to whether he was born in Cuba or at Lausanne in Switzerland. As a young man his education was largely in the hands of his father, who encouraged him to read the great works of French literature. In 1921 he entered the school of architecture of Havana University, but was obliged to abandon his studies to maintain his mother after his father's departure from the family home.

He began as a columnist and reporter for the newspaper *La discusión* in 1922. Through the 1920s, Carpentier was linked to the **Grupo Minorista** and several avant-garde (see **avant-garde in Latin America**) groups; his writings appeared regularly in magazines like *Social* and *Carteles* as well as the review he helped to found, the *Revista de avance*. He also published poetry and ballets with Afro-Cuban themes.

In 1928 Carpentier left for Paris, where he lived for the next eleven years, writing regular *crónicas* (see *crónica*) which took journalism from reportage into new areas of creative expression. From 1933 he also worked for radio and was a director of the Foniric studios, which produced state-of-the-art recordings. Carpentier's time in Paris was central in defining his ideas about both art and society. He wrote prolifically about his contacts with surrealism (see **surrealism in Latin American art**) and other European artistic currents, which allowed him to see the American experience in a more profound way. 'Suddenly, like an obsession, I became absorbed by the idea of America', he wrote, describing this period of his life. He travelled across Europe, participating in the Congress in Defence of Culture which took place in Madrid in 1937, during the Spanish Civil War (see **Spanish Civil War, impact of**).

On his return to Cuba in 1939, Carpentier continued his journalism and produced radio programmes, beginning too the research that would culminate in his study of *La música en Cuba* (Music in Cuba) (1946). He moved to Venezuela in 1945 and remained there, working in advertising, until his return to Cuba in 1959 after the Cuban Revolution (see **revolutions**). It was during this period that his reputation as a writer began to grow and his work become known more widely.

Carpentier had published his first novel, *Ecue Yamba O* in 1933; it owed much to the novel of rural manners and, as its author later acknowledged, represented a failed attempt to capture the syncretic world of black Cubans. It was his story 'Viaje a la semilla' (Journey to the Seed) (1944) that

marked a definitive change in his narrative conceptions; its culmination was the novel *El reino de este mundo* (The Kingdom of this World) (1943) and the formulation of his theory of '*lo real maravilloso*' (marvellous realism).

If his excursion into the magical world of Haitian **Vodun** in 1943 was a determining factor in this evolution, his travels around the remoter corners of the Venezuelan savannah and the Upper Orinoco through 1947 and 1948 would complete his American worldview; out of that experience was born *Los pasos perdidos* (The Lost Steps) (1953), which earned him a central place in Latin American literature. The cycle of novels of this period ends with *El acoso* (The Siege) (1956), a text structured like a sonata and set in the political context of Cuba in the 1930s, and the volume of stories called *Guerra del tiempo* (Time War) (1958) and the novel *El siglo de las luces* (Explosion in a Cathedral) (1963), the result of another series of journeys.

When he returned to Cuba, Carpentier immersed himself in the profound changes the country was undergoing. He produced less in the 1960s, having assumed several public posts and taken a leading role in the cultural institutions created by the new revolutionary government. In 1961 he was elected vice-president of **UNEAC**, and a year later appointed director of the Editora Nacional (the national publishing house). He travelled widely on official delegations while continuing to write for newspapers in Cuba, among them *El mundo*, until his appointment as Cuban ambassador to Paris, where he lived and worked during his final years.

His late writings reaffirm the permanence, through time and changing circumstances, of an essentially baroque spirit in Latin American art, ideas expressed in the essays of *Tientos y diferencias* (Essays and Differences) (1964), *Razón de ser* (Reason for Being) (1976) and the posthumously published *La novela latinoamericana en vísperas de un nuevo siglo y otros ensayos* (The Latin American Novel on the Eve of a New Century and Other Essays) (1981). He also published the novels *Concierto barroco* (Baroque Concert) and *El recurso del método* (For Reasons of State) (both 1974), the epic novel *La consagración de la primavera* (The Consecration of Spring) (1978) and *El arpa y la sombra* (The Harp and the Shadow) (1979). In 1977 he was awarded the Cervantes Literature Prize.

Further reading

González Echevarría, R. (1990) *The Pilgrim at Home*, Austin, TX: University of Texas Press.

López Lemus, V. (ed.) (1985) *Entrevistas*, Havana: Letras Cubanas.

Muller-Bergh, K. (1972) *Alejo Carpentier. Estudio biográfico-crítico*, New York: Las Americas.

Padura, L. (1994) *Un camino de medio siglo: Carpentier y la narrativa de lo real maravilloso*, Havana: Letras Cubanas.

WILFREDO CANCIO ISLA

Carranza, María Mercedes

b. 1945, Santafé de Bogotá, Colombia

Poet and journalist

Carranzas' first book of poetry, *Vainas y otros poemas* (Things and Other Poems) (1972), communicates her disappointment with traditional poetry, and proposes instead to speak about contemporary issues in an irreverent manner. Her collections of poems include *Tengo miedo* (I Am Afraid) (1983) and *Hola, Soledad* (Hello, Loneliness) (1987). Carranza's journalistic writing has been published in the newspaper *El Siglo* and the journal *Semana*.

MIGUEL A. CARDINALE

Carrasco, Ted

b. 1933, La Paz, Bolivia

Sculptor

One of Bolivia's few working sculptors, Carrasco works in monumental dimensions which in size and scale reflect the mountainous landscapes of his country. Though not representational, they achieve a mythic quality by evoking the powerful geometric forms of pre-Hispanic Andean civilizations. His earlier work owed much to indigenous figures and implements. Having worked abroad for some years, Carrasco returned to Bolivia in 1970 and began to

incorporate into his work the symbolic figure of the condor, which some of his contemporaries had already used to represent the Andes. His 1988 *Andes*, for example, depicts a massive earth-mother figure, her body opened wide and fertile.

MIKE GONZALEZ

Carrasquel, Chico

b. 1928, Caracas, Venezuela

Baseball player

Carrasquel (full name Alfonso Carrasquel Colón) was the first Venezuelan to play in a major league baseball All-Star game (1951, 1953–55). He played with the Chicago White Sox (1950–55; he was replaced by another Venezuelan shortstop, Luis **Aparicio** in 1956), Cleveland Indians (1956–58), Kansas City Athletics (1958) and Baltimore Orioles (1959). He was especially known for his fielding and base-stealing. He managed the Leones de Caracas when they won the Caribbean World Series in 1982. In Venezuela, Puerto La Cruz's baseball stadium is named after him.

RICHARD V. MCGEHEE

Carreño, Mario

b. 1913, Havana, Cuba; d. 1999, Santiago, Chile

Visual artist

Carreño's canvases cover a range of styles from figurative to abstract, but all are distinguished by his great technical skill and painstaking craftsmanship. The variety of his work and his technical achievement make him an outstanding figure in contemporary Cuban art. Largely self-taught, he exhibited his work in Mexico between 1930 and 1935, and was profoundly affected by the work of the muralists (see **muralism**), particularly **Rivera** and **Orozco**. Later he studied and exhibited in Paris. In 1957 he became permanently resident in Santiago, Chile; he helped to established the Art School at the Catholic University, where he was a professor for twenty years. He was also art critic for the newspaper *El Mercurio*. Carreño's *El ciclón* (The Cyclone) is part of the permanent collection of the New York Museum of Modern Art.

WILFREDO CANCIO ISLA

Carrera, Arturo

b. 1948, Coronel Pringles, Argentina

Poet

Carrera has published more than fifteen volumes of poetry. *La partera canta* (The Midwife Sings) (1982) and *Mi padre* (My Father) (1985) are intensely baroque in style, reminiscent of Mallarmé. *Arturo y yo* (Arthur and I) (1984), an absolutely fundamental work in the poetic panorama of twentieth-century Argentina, marks a move towards a 'neosimplicity' that is precise and anything but naive. *Children's Corner* (1989), *La banda oscura de Alejandro* (Alexander's Obscure Band) (1994), *El vespertilio de las parcas* (1997) have confirmed his reputation as a major poet. The recurrent themes of his work are rural life, children, the passing of time, desire and modernity.

DANIEL LINK

Carrera, Carlos

b. 1962, Mexico City

Film-maker

One of the most promising Mexican filmmakers of the 1990s, Carlos Carrera's films are remarkably varied in genre, mood and style, but all plumb the depths of human solitude. His most acclaimed films include *La mujer de Benjamín* (Benjamin's Wife) (1991), a bittersweet portrait of a mentally retarded man who kidnaps the object of his love; *La vida conyugal* (Married Life) (1993), which lampoons the murderous impulses inspired by middle-class marriage; and *Sin remitente* (No Return Address) (1994), a sombre study of a bitter old misanthrope cruelly

tricked into believing he has caught the eye of an attractive younger woman.

CYNTHIA STEELE

Carrera, Margarita

b. 1929, Guatemala City

Writer, critic and professor

Carrera is known for her broad philosophical and psychological interests and has written poetry, essays, and literary criticism. In *Del noveno círculo* (Of the Ninth Circle), written after the 1976 earthquake, she created a powerful image of Guatemalan reality modelled on Dante's *Inferno*, in which the personal and the national meet, anticipating 1980s Guatemalan **feminism**. In *Signo XX* (1986), a volume written before the emergence of Vinicio Cerezo, her Freudian tendencies transform specific forms of Guatemalan class domination and military oppression into characteristics of a modern civilization governed by a 'mindless malignity'.

MARC ZIMMERMAN

Carrera Andrade, Jorge

b. 1903, Quito, Ecuador; d. 1978, Quito

Writer

Carrera began his poetic career during the transition between *modernismo* (see **modernismo, Spanish American**) and the avant-garde. An endless traveller, his poetry registered the world imagistically in 'micrograms', a poetic form reminiscent of the epigram and the haiku. His early delight in the metaphorical and sensual yielded to the pre-eminence of the 'secret country' of the soul of contemporary man: anguish, solitude, death. His principal books of poetry are *Boletines de mar y tierra* (Bulletins from Land and Sea) (1930), *La hora de las ventanas iluminadas* (The Time of Lit Windows) (1937), *Lugar de origen*

(Native Country) (1945) and *Hombre planetario* (Planetary Man) (1959).

HUMBERTO E. ROBLES

Carrilho, Nelson

b. 1953, Curaçao, Netherlands Antilles

Sculptor

Three of Carrilho's massive sculptures stand in Amsterdam, where he had been a student. *Dragers van verre* (Carriers from Afar) in the Westerpark is at the centre of a multicultural neighbourhood. Though he started with massive human figures, in the last decade his figures have grown slender and open. In the 1990s Carrilho has also had important exhibitions in Curaçao.

NEL CASIMIRI

Carrillo, Álvaro

b. 1920, Cacahuatepec, Mexico; d. 1969, near Mexico City

Musician

A frequent performer in theatre, radio and television, his songs won him an international reputation. They included 'Sabor a mí' (A Taste of Me) and 'La mentira (Se te olvida)' (The Lie – You Are Forgotten), which became the theme of a film and a *telenovela* (see **telenovelas**). His songs are dramatic, and strongly influenced by the music of his native Oaxaca; they include 'Luz de luna' (Moonlight), 'Seguiré mi viaje' (I'll Continue My Journey) and 'Sabrá Dios' (God Knows). Also active in artists trade unions, he was killed in a car accident.

EDUARDO CONTRERAS SOTO

Carrillo, Isolina

b. 1907, Havana, Cuba; d. 1996, Havana

Musician

A pianist and composer, Carrillo's Dos gardenias (Two Gardenias) is one of the most popular boleros ever written (see **bolero**). Her compositions were widely played and sung through the 1940s, including Miedo de ti (Fear of You), Castillo de ensueño (Castle of Dreams), Increíble (Incredible) among others; at that time she was a member of the singing group Siboney. She was a founder member of one of the first female septets, Las Trovadoras del Cayo, in which she played trumpet, *güiro* (scraper), bongo and double bass. After the Cuban Revolution (see **revolutions**), she worked as an accompanist, conducting choirs and teaching singing. Towards the end of her life, she hosted the club that bore the name of the song which made her famous.

WILFREDO CANCIO ISLA

Carrillo, Julián

b. 1875, San Luis Potosí, Mexico; d. 1965, Mexico City

Composer

Carillo is one of the most important figures in the field of experimental music in the first half of the century. He studied at the National Conservatory, at Leipzig, and at the Ghent Conservatoire. Returning to Mexico, he became Director of the National Conservatory in 1913 and founded the Beethoven Orchestra and String Quartet. In 1915–18 he established the American Symphony Orchestra in New York. From 1920–4 he returned to Mexico as Director of the Conservatory and of the National Symphony Orchestra. In the 1920s, Leopold Stokowski conducted his orchestral works in various countries, and Carrillo himself travelled with Stokowski's orchestra through Europe and America and recorded most of his own work.

Carrillo was an important innovator. On the one hand, using the traditional chromatic scale as his starting point, he conceived a number of new and unusual scales as the basis of his 'atonal' works. On the other, he developed scales employing fractional intervals, which in many cases required specially built instruments and a new type of musical notation. He called this type of microtonality *sonido 13*.

Carrillo's extensive musical work, written in a style very different from the prevailing Mexican musical nationalism, includes both pieces for 'normal' musical training and temperament and works that employ microtonality. The first group includes the **opera** *México en 1810*, three symphonies, the triple concerto for flute, violin and cello, a *Requiem*, four string quartets and many other chamber works and concertos. His hundreds of microtonal works include the opera *La mujer blanca* (The White Woman), three symphonies, two concertos for violin and one for cello, *Horizontes* (Horizons) for violin, cello, harp and orchestra, the *Misa para Pope John XXIII* for male voice choir, the *Preludio a Colón* (Prelude to Columbus) for soprano, flute, guitar, harp and piccolo, and eight string quartets.

Further reading

Béhague, G. (1979) *Music in Latin America: An Introduction*, Englewood Cliffs, NJ: Prentice-Hall.
Benjamin, G. (1967) 'Julian Carrillo and sonido trece', in *Yearbook of the Interamerican Institute for Musical Research*, III: 33–68
—— (1980) 'Julian Carrillo', in S. Sadie (ed.), *The New Grove Dictionary of Music and Musicians*, Hong Kong: Macmillan, III: 826–9.

ALFONSO PADILLA

Carrington, Leonora

b. 1917, Clayton Green, Lancashire, England

Painter

An English-born surrealist painter (see **surrealism in Latin American art**), book illustrator and stage designer, Carrington has carved a singular niche in the Mexican art world. Following her studies in Florence, Paris and London, she settled in Mexico City in 1942, adopted Mexican citizenship and married the photographer Chiqui Weiz. Carrington was a close friend of the surrealist painter Remedios **Varo**, has illustrated books by leading Mexican writers, and has published two

original works of fiction, *The Hearing Trumpet* (1976) and *The House of Fear: Notes from Down Below* (1988).

CYNTHIA STEELE

Carrión, Benjamín

b. 1898, Loja, Ecuador; d. 1979, Quito, Ecuador

Critic and writer

Carrión's contributions to the sociology of culture and literary tastes of twentieth-century Ecuador are inestimable. Founder of the **Casa de la Cultura Ecuatoriana** (Ecuador's House of Culture) in 1944, he set out to make accessible the national experience, from history and literature to music and folklore, with a particular emphasis on indigenous contributions to the creation of a collective identity. Some of his essays are collected in *Obras* (Works) (1981), while his polemical commitment to social justice is expressed in his *García Moreno: El Santo del Patíbulo* (García Moreno: The Gallows' Saint) (1959).

HUMBERTO E. ROBLES

cartel

A cartel is an agreement among producers to control the supply and price of a specific commodity. The term is applied specifically to collaborating groups based in Colombia engaged in large-scale drug smuggling, particularly cocaine (see **drugs in Latin America**; **coca and its derivatives**). Dating from the mid-1970s, these trafficking enterprises, although technically not cartels, evolved from cottage industries into corporate-like structures able to efficiently dominate the production and distribution of cocaine. By pooling expertise and resources and integrating specialized domains, individuals such as Pablo **Escobar**, the Ochoa Vásquez brothers and José Rodríguez Gacha (Medellín) and José Santa Cruz Londoño and the Rodríguez Orejuela brothers (Cali) achieved economies of scale, opened new markets and money laundering outlets, diminished their own vulnerability and linked up with other international crime syndicates.

KAREN BRACKEN

Carteles

Carteles is a monthly sports and entertainment magazine founded in Havana in 1919 by Oscar H. Massaguer. In 1924, it increased its size and became a richly illustrated mass circulation weekly. It reported national and international news, invited prominent **intellectuals** to explore educational, historical and artistic themes, and became one of Cuba's most popular publications. From the late 1920s onwards it published crime and fantasy stories, and from 1954 included a regular Latin American short story section with many pieces by Cuban writers. It was taken over by the *Bohemia* group in 1953, and ceased publication when it was nationalized in 1960.

WILFREDO CANCIO ISLA

Carter, Anthony

b. Barbados

Calypsonian

Anthony Carter (The Mighty Gabby) is a pioneering **calypso** king and cultural artist in Barbados, active from the 1960s to the present. Gabby has provided distinctive leadership and creativity for the development of calypso in Barbados. He founded Battleground Calypso Tent in 1979 and won the annual Cropover calypso competition in 1968, 1976, 1977 and 1985. His songs focus on specific problems encountered in daily life, and on crucial political issues. They are delivered with driving rhythms and frequently with biting satire. Among his most famous calypsos are 'Jack', which affirms the rights of local Barbadians to use the beaches without restriction, and 'Boots', written to critique his own government's role in aiding the US invasion of Grenada. Gabby has also written and composed countless calypsos for many leading performers throughout the Caribbean. He has a wide musical range from up-tempo calypsos to

haunting ballads. The latter are best represented by 'Bridgetown', in which Gabby brings the listener into the streets and markets of the city in a memorably personal way. His music allows audiences to participate and see the experiences he relates, giving him a distinctive quality among Caribbean artists. He has currently formed a partnership with Eddy Grant for the preservation and restoration of Caribbean music, and works at Blue Wave Studio at historic Bayley's Plantation in Barbados.

JOHN H. PATTON

Carter, Martin (Wylde)

b. 1927, Georgetown, British Guiana

Poet and historian

Carter is one of the Caribbean's most important poets. His collection *Poems of Resistance* (1954) is about his experience in the anti-colonial struggle in British Guiana. He was imprisoned by the British for some months in 1953 because of his involvement with the early nationalist movement. Eventually he became Minister of Culture in a post-independence government (1967–70). Since then he has been writer in residence at several universities. A regular contributor to the journal *Kyk-Over-Al*, his work develops a distinctive voice of rebellion and resistance and a strong sense of landscape and geography, as in *Poems of Shape and Motion* (1955).

KEITH JARDIM

Cartey, Wilfred

b. 1931, Laventille, Trinidad; d. 1992, New York, USA

Teacher, critic, editor, poet and novelist

Cartey's critical and creative visions are informed by a commitment to the dignity of the African spirit. He published five critical works including *Whisper from a Continent* (1969), twelve volumes of poetry including *The House of Blue Lightning* (1973), one novel (*Oakman*, 1989) and edited several journals. He attended the **University of the West Indies**, Jamaica, and was Fulbright-Hays scholar at Columbia University, where he also taught (1957–77) before becoming the first Martin Luther King, Jr. Distinguished Professor at Brooklyn College, City University of New York, a post he held until his death.

FUNSO AIYEJINA

Cartola

b. 1908, Rio de Janeiro, Brazil; d. 1980, Rio de Janeiro

Singer, songwriter and actor

From the age of eleven, Cartola (real name, Angenor de Oliveira) lived in Rio de Janeiro's Mangueira *favela* or shanty town where, in 1929, he co-founded the city's most traditional *escola de samba* (see **samba schools**), Estação Primeira. In this first phase of his career he produced, with others, a number of hit songs. With the re-emergence of the classical grassroots 'samba de morro' in the late 1950s, Cartola was rediscovered, appearing in the 1957 Marcel Camus film, ***Orfeu negro*** (Black Orpheus). The Zicartola restaurant, which he ran with his wife Zica, became an important meeting point for sambistas and the new **bossa nova** artists.

DAVID TREECE

carurú

One of the best liked Afro-Brazilian dishes set on colonial tables, *carurú* has become synonymous with the cookery of the state of Bahia. It is traditionally served in honour of the twin saints Cosme and Damian, an interesting custom also celebrated in the month of September in households where there are twins. The dish is prepared with okra, *taioba* (a leafy green vegetable), onions, shrimp, *malagueta* peppers, ***dendé*** **oil** and fish. While preparing the dish, it is customary for the cook to see that seven okra pods remain whole. Each person served a whole okra pod is required to duplicate the party the following year.

ANA M. LÓPEZ

Carvalho, Flávio de

b. 1899, Barra Mansa, Rio de Janeiro, Brazil; d. 1973, Valinhos, São Paulo, Brazil

Artist

A civil engineer, Carvalho returned to Brazil in 1922, and became caught up in primitivist trends inspired by Nietzsche and Freud. He wrote experimental theatre *A origem animal de Deus o O bailado do Deus morto* (Dead God's Dance) (1933), a volume of travel writing *Os ossos do mundo* (The World's Bones) (1936), and an analysis of his own anthrophagic performance against a Catholic procession in São Paulo (*Experimento número 2*) (1931). The nationalist aesthetics of **Brazilian modernism** failed to acknowledge the value of Carvalho's work and simply categorized him along with less expressive artists.

RAUL ANTELO

Carvalho Neto, Paulo de

b. 1923, Simão Dias, Brazil

Folklorist

Carvalho Neto is a distinguished figure in his field, and is recognized throughout Latin America. His all-inclusive, scientific and pioneering *Diccionario del folklore ecuatoriano* (Dictionary of Ecuadorian Folklore) (1964) has been a lasting influence on cultural life in Ecuador and is an indispensable tool for students of culture, history, literature and language. He is also the author of a novel in Portuguese, *Meu tio Atahualpa* (My Uncle Atahualpa) (1972).

HUMBERTO E. ROBLES

Carybé

b. 1911, Lanús, Buenos Aires Province,
  Argentina; d. 1997, Salvador, Brazil

Painter, sculptor and illustrator

Together with his contemporaries Jorge **Amado**
and Pierre **Verger**, Carybé (Hector Júlio Páride
Barnabó) was a celebrated chronicler of the
daily lives and sacred practices of Afro-Brazilians. He established residence in Salvador,
Bahia in 1950. Over the next half century the
city's most prominent public spaces – most
notably the foyer of the Teatro Castro Alves –
were adorned with his multimedia murals and
sculptures. His most ambitious project, a set of
sculpted wooden panels of the Yoruba *orishás*,
is on permanent display at the Museu Afro-
Baiano in Salvador.

CHRISTOPHER DUNN

Casa de América

An institution founded by the Spanish government
in 1991 to promote understanding with Latin
America. In 1992, as part of the **Columbian
quincentenary**, a nineteenth-century palace, the
Palacio Linares, located in the Plaza Cibeles in
central Madrid, was inaugurated. Facilities there
include a theatre, an art gallery and offices, with
regular activities including a film series and a
variety of lectures on Latin American culture and
society. Two important departments are the
Tribuna, which works in the area of the social
sciences, and the Ateneo, which includes researchers in the arts, literature and cinema. Unlike the
older **Instituto de Cooperación Iberoamericana**, the Casa de América does not publish a
journal or have branches in the Latin American
countries. Instead, its privileged location in central
Madrid makes it a site for a wide variety of cultural
activity, from book launches to plays and art
exhibits.

DANIEL BALDERSTON

Casa de la Cultura Ecuatoriana

Created in 1944 by Benjamín **Carrión**, during the
presidency of José María **Velasco Ibarra**, the
Casa de la Cultura Ecuatoriana (Ecuador's House
of Culture) has supported every aspect of culture.
Its publishing house and museums have sponsored
major cultural events including creative writing,
painting, theatre, archaeological recovery, folklore
and history. Centred in Quito, it had corresponding branches in various provincial cities. A key
element of its work has been the recovery of
autochthonous elements of Ecuadorean culture.

HUMBERTO E. ROBLES

Casa de las Américas

Casa de las Américas is a cultural organization
whose purpose is to develop socio-cultural contacts
between Cuba, the rest of the Caribbean and Latin
America. It was created by decree of the Revolutionary Government of Cuba on 28 April 1959.
Subsidized through most of its existence by the
Cuban state, it became self-financing in some areas
during the 1990s. Originally, it set out to spread the
message of the Cuban Revolution (see **revolutions**) and break the political, economic and
cultural siege to which Cuba was subjected during
the 1960s, when most Latin American countries
severed diplomatic relations with the government
of Fidel **Castro**. Its first director, Haydée **Santamaría**, brought in outstanding artists and intellectuals from Cuba and elsewhere, who raised
the organization's international profile and earned
it a significant reputation in the Latin American
cultural arena.

The functions of the Casa de las Américas
included the promotion of the whole range of Latin
American cultural expressions, publishing books
and recordings, organizing theoretical debates and
art exhibitions, and developing links with cultural
institutions across the world. Each area of work
had a specific department within the Casa,
outstanding among them being a library containing 140,000 volumes and 8,400 periodical titles.
The visual arts department researches the field
and organizes temporary exhibitions in its Latin

American Gallery. The resources of the collection Arte de Nuestra América (Art of our America) include 6,000 works of art donated by artists, collectors and cultural organizations; they form part of the Casa's permanent collection exhibited in its headquarters as well as in the Hadyée Santamaría gallery, specialising in graphics and photography, and the Mariano gallery devoted to popular arts. The Casa also offers the Joven Estampa prize for graphic artists under thirty-five years old, and the Ensayo Fotográfico (Photographic Essay) prize, offered for the best collection of photographs reflecting Latin American reality.

The music department organizes recitals and concerts, like the Festival de la Canción Protesta (Festival of Protest Song) in 1967, and possesses an important collection of donated sheet music, discs and tapes. It has its own record label, Música de esta América, and from 1970 onward published a monthly bulletin. Under its auspices, a biennial prize is offered in the field of Latin American and Caribbean musicology.

The theatre department promotes exchanges of directors, actors and playwrights as well as offering drama and directors workshops. It presents works by Caribbean authors, organizes the Gallo de la Habana prize and produces the quarterly drama journal, *Conjunto*.

The editorial department coordinates and designs the Casa's various collections, including the publication of the prizewinners in its annual literary contest, the Literatura Latinoamericana collection of classic works, La Honda for short stories and young writers, Nuestra América for essays and Nuestros Países (monographs), Valoración Múltiple, collections of essays on specific authors, and Colibrí for children's writers.

The Literary Research Centre produces anthologies and essay collections on specific authors and movements, organizes programmes of lectures and the Archivo de la Palabra, an archive of spoken recordings by outstanding literary, artistic and political personalities. It publishes records and cassettes and the journal *Criterios*, in collaboration with **UNEAC** (the Cuban Writers Organization), and organizes the international literary competition which is Casa de las Américas's most important activity. This was originally held in October 1959 in the categories of poetry, novel, short story and essay;

testimonial writing (see ***testimonio***), writing for children and young people and special prizes for Brazilian, Caribbean Anglophone and Francophone writers have all since been added. The participation of important Latin American writers in the judging panels was testimony to the significance of the prizes. The early competitions, held during the period of consolidation of the Cuban Revolution, brought to Havana the intellectual elite of Cuba and Latin America. Later, debates about the social responsibilities of writers and disagreements over increasing dogmatism and censorship in Cuban cultural life at the beginning of the 1970s led to a drastic reduction in the number of artists and **intellectuals** travelling to Havana for the prize competitions.

Though relatively independent, Casa de las Américas was never able to stand apart from the centralization of social and political power in Cuba, and has always served to execute official cultural strategies towards Latin America. Nonetheless, the journal *Casa de las Américas* (1960–) has had an undeniable impact on Latin American literary life, publishing important cultural and philosophical texts. Its editor since 1965 has been Roberto **Fernández Retamar**, who also took over the Presidency of the Casa in 1986 from painter Mariano **Rodríguez**. In 1979, the Caribbean Studies Centre of the Casa was created to encourage an expansion of research in that area, and to organize the publication of the journal ***Anales del Caribe***.

The Casa has also established a women's studies programme which organizes courses and conferences, publishes anthologies of women's writing and seeks to contribute to knowledge of women's cultural and historical production in the region. It has a bookshop and a screenprinting workshop which reproduces work by the key artists of the region.

Further reading

25 aniversario de Casa de las Américas 1959–1984 (1984), Havana: Casa de las Américas.

Campuzano, L. (1996) 'La revista *Casa de las Américas* 1960–1995', *Unión* 24: 25–34.

Escajadillo, T. (1989) 'Una sólida casa', *Quehacer* 58(2): 96–101.

Frenk, S.F. (1984) 'Two Journals of the 1960s, *Casa de las Américas* and *Mundo Nuevo*', *Bulletin of Latin American Research* 3(3): 83–93.

Lie, N. (1991) 'Casa de las Américas y el discurso sobre el intelectual (1960–71)', *Cuadernos Americanos* 5(28): 287–9.

—— (1996) *La revista cubana Casa de las Américas (1960–1976)*, Leuven: Leuven University Press.

Pogolotti, G. (1969) 'Introducción', in *Índice de la revista casa de las Américas (1960–67)*, Havana: Biblioteca Nacional José Martí.

WILFREDO CANCIO ISLA

Casa de Rui Barbosa

The Fundação Casa de Rui Barbosa is a research institution in the humanities (literature and history), located in Rio de Janeiro, Brazil, in and behind the Botafogo house of the important turn-of-the-century author and politician after whom it is named. Founded in the 1970s, and with a permanent staff, it houses important collections of books, reviews and manuscripts donated by writers and others. It supports publication of research materials, editions and so on, and has a programme of visiting scholars.

JOHN GLEDSON

Casa de Teatro

The Casa de Teatro (House of Theatre) is a non-profit cultural institution founded by Freddy Ginebra in the early 1970s in Santo Domingo. In 1974, singers such as Mercedes **Sosa**, Silvio **Rodríguez** and Noel **Nicola** performed there. Since then, Casa de Teatro has offered young and progressive artists the opportunity to make their works known, while offering interested general audiences an alternative cultural space. Casa de Teatro presents a variety of activities such as popular music concerts, plays, painting exhibits, foreign film series and film forums, photography courses, literary prizes, theatre workshops, and literary and theatre events.

FERNANDO VALERIO-HOLGUÍN

Casa del ángel, La

La casa del ángel (1957) is a key work in the career of Leopoldo **Torre Nilsson**, the film's director and co-writer together with Beatriz **Guido** and Martín Rodríguez Mentasti. Based on an original idea by Guido, *La casa del ángel* (House of the Angel) is the story of an adolescent girl repressed by a mother who inculcates in her an obsessive fear of divine retribution. The work proved to be revolutionary, opening the doors to a new intellectual generation in Argentine cinema. Its cast included Elsa Daniel, Lautaro **Murúa**, Guillermo Battaglia, Bárbara Mújica and Onofre Lovero; the music was by Juan C. **Paz**, the editing by Jorge Gárate and the camera work by Aníbal González Paz.

RODRIGO PEIRETTI

Casa grande e senzala

Published in 1933, *Casa grande e senzala* is the most important work of Brazilian sociologist Gilberto **Freyre**. It was translated into English as *The Masters and the Slaves* (1952). It had an enormous impact on the study of Brazil's social and cultural history. Discarding negative interpretations based on racist dogma, the work presents an alternative view, centred upon cultural **syncretism**. Freyre argued that a distinct Brazilian national culture had emerged which was dynamic and full of potential. However, many critics have criticized Freyre's vision of cultural unity and harmony, arguing that it conceals the deep class and racial divisions in Brazilian society.

MARK DINNEEN

Casaccia, Gabriel

b. 1907, Asunción, Paraguay; d. 1980, Buenos Aires, Argentina

Writer

The founder of contemporary Paraguayan narrative, Casaccia lived most of his life in Argentina, where he also wrote and published almost all his seven novels and two short story collections – *El*

Guajhú (The Howl) (1938) and *El pozo* (The Well) (1967) – and one play. A few days before his death, he finished the manuscript for his last novel, *Los Huertas* (The Huertas), published posthumously in 1981. His most important works are three novels: *La babosa* (The Gossiping Woman) (1952), *La llaga* (The Wound) (1964) and *Los exiliados* (The Exiles) (1966).

TERESA MÉNDEZ-FAITH

Casaldáliga, Pedro

b. 1929, Barcelona, Spain

Bishop

An influential supporter of **liberation theology**, Casaldáliga was ordained in 1952 in Barcelona and appointed bishop of São Félix do Araguaia, Brazil in 1971. He has been active in domestic political struggles, particularly on behalf of Amazonian indigenous groups, yet his impact has extended far beyond Brazil. He has written extensively, both poetry and theology; many of his writings are collected in *In Pursuit of the Kingdom: Writings 1968–1988* (1990). For his activism and theological views, he has faced repression by the military as well as repeated criticism and investigation from within the Roman Catholic Church. In 1988, he was censured by the Vatican.

THOMAS A. LEWIS

Casals Festival

Musical event established in 1957 by Spanish emigré cellist Pablo (or Pau) Casals in San Juan, Puerto Rico, and traditionally held in June. The Festival has evolved since its inception as a series of chamber music concerts to a lavish annual event that features symphonic orchestras, choirs and world renowned soloists. Its repertoire has also developed from the personal selection of Casals to encompass the widest spectrum of classical music by international composers. The Festival, one of the best of its kind, was instrumental in establishing

the Conservatory and the Puerto Rico Symphonic Orchestra.

ViCTOR F. TORRES

Casanovas, Jean François

b. 1949, Paris, France

Actor, choreographer and theatre director

Casanovas's career began with an independent theatre company formed with actor Michel Delhaye; they toured their show 'Cocktel Cie' through several European countries. In 1980 he settled in Buenos Aires, where he has produced most of his artistic work. His extravagant drag productions have won several awards, including one given by the Asociación Cronistas de Espectáculos (Theatre Reviewers Association). His work has included 'Fénix' (Phoenix), 'Noches de Caviar' (Caviar Nights), 'Bailando con caviar' (Dancing with Caviar), all influenced by music hall, and his 1997 presentation of Brecht's *Seven Deadly Sins*...

CLAUDIA TORRE

Casaravilla Lemos, Enrique

b. 1889, Montevideo, Uruguay; d. 1967, Las Piedras, Uruguay

Poet

A controversial and rather isolated figure within Uruguayan literature, Casaravilla published very little. His first volume of poetry, *Celebración de la primavera* (Celebration of Spring) (1913) was followed in 1920 by *Las fuerzas eternas* (The Eternal Forces) and ten years later by *Las formas desnudas* (Naked Forms) (1930). His unpublished work was later anthologized by Esther de Cáceres as *Partituras secretas* (Secret Scores) (1967), which, she argued, expressed his 'formal rigour'. Not all critics agreed; some felt that his work lacked literary value, while others found a unity of expression circling the conflict betwen asceticism and sensuality.

CELINA MANZONI

Casartelli, Mario

b. 1954, Asunción, Paraguay

Poet and musician

By the early 1990s Casartelli had published five books of poetry, among them *Contrapunto* (Counterpoint) (1988) and, under the pseudonym Braulio Gamarra, *Monodia del verano* (Summer Monody) (1993). A singer and composer, in 1985 he recorded *Según el color del cristal* (According to the Colour of the Glass). In 1992 he won second prize in the 'José Asunción Flores' national composition competition with his song 'A un hermano del futuro' (To a Brother of the Future). He is also a cartoonist for the afternoon newspaper *Ultima Hora*.

TERESA MÉNDEZ-FAITH

Casartelli, Victor

b. 1943, Puerto Pinasco, Paraguay

Poet

Victor Casartelli is the author of three books of poetry: *Todos los cielos* (All the Heavens) (1987), his first book; *La transparencia de los días* (The Transparency of the Days) (1990), which received the 1990 El Lector Prize; and *La vida que vivimos* (The Life We Live) (1992). He also has had poems published in national and foreign literary journals and anthologies. He is director of the municipal library and was President of the Society of Paraguayan Writers.

TERESA MÉNDEZ-FAITH

Casas, Myrna

b. 1934, San Juan, Puerto Rico

Playwright

Casas is one of a generation of writers who began to approach Puerto Rico's social problems in formally and thematically innovative ways in the 1960s. She was professor of theatre at the University of Puerto Rico, and has participated in every facet of theatrical production. Her dramas

treat the problem of Puerto Rican national and cultural identity explicitly and implicitly in early plays such as *Eugenia Victoria Herrera* and *La trampa* (The Trap), and in more recent metatheatrical works such as *El gran circo eukraniano* (The Great Ukranian Circus). Her plays are noted for their experimentalism, female protagonism and critical vision of Puerto Rican society.

CAMILLA STEVENS

Casazola, Matilde

b. 1943, Sucre, Bolivia

Composer

Casazola is a poet, composer and singer to her own guitar accompaniment. She studied the instrument with the Spanish master Pedro García Ripoll. In 1974 she began to present her own compositions (now numbering more than 100) embracing several different forms – the **cueca**, bailecito, **yaraví**, **huayno**, takirari and song – which are an authentic contribution to popular music. Many of her songs are folkloric in origin, while others are songs of social commentary. Her poetic compositions have been sung by many important artists and recognised as an important milestone in the renewal of popular song.

BEATRIZ ROSSELLS

Casey, Calvert

b. 1924, Baltimore, USA; d. 1969, Rome, Italy

Writer and critic

A member of the group of writers around *Ciclón* and later a contributor to *Lunes de revolución*, Casey moved to Havana in the late 1950s. The central themes of his fiction were displacement, frustration and the anguished search for personal identity. In Cuba he published the volume of stories *El regreso* (The Return) (1962) and brief essays in *Memorias de una isla* (Memoirs of an Island) (1964). The only surviving chapter of his unpublished novel *Piazza Margana* is regarded as a key text of

Cuban homoerotic literature. He committed suicide in 1969.

WILFREDO CANCIO ISLA

Caso, Alfonso

b. 1896, Mexico City; d. 1970, Mexico City

Archaeologist

Alfonso Caso devoted his life to the study of pre-Hispanic civilizations as a key to understanding contemporary Mexican culture. From 1931–48 he directed explorations at Monte Albán, Oaxaca, with his wife, María Lombardo Caso, resulting in the discovery of Tombs 104 and 7 (containing the greatest archaeological treasure of the Americas), and in a revised understanding of the pictographic codices and stellas as historical, rather than simply religious, documents. Caso published some 300 articles and was the founding director of both the **INAH** (National Institute of Anthropology and History) and the **INI** (National Indian Institute), introducing systems of cultural coordination designed to integrate Mexico's Indians into national culture.

CYNTHIA STEELE

Caso, Antonio

b. 1883, Mexico City; d. 1946, Mexico City

Philosopher

Caso was a founder of the intellectual circle that culminated in the formation of the Ateneo de la Juventud (1909–10) with Pedro **Henríquez Ureña**, Alfonso **Reyes**, José **Vasconcelos** and others. Caso's lectures at the Ateneo, and their critique of positivism, the official doctrine of the regime of Porfirio Díaz, were of fundamental intellectual significance in the period prior to the Mexican Revolution (1910–17) (see **revolutions**). Mexico's first professor of sociology, he was an outstanding university teacher. Caso's philosophy, rooted in Bergson's intuitionism, is summarized in

his *La existencia como economía, como desinterés y como caridad* (Existence as Economy, Disinterest and Charity) (1916). His brother, Alfonso **Caso**, was one of Mexico's most important archaeologists.

RAFAEL OLEA FRANCO

Cassá, Roberto

b. 1948, Santo Domingo, Dominican Republic

Historian

A history professor, Cassá studied in the former Soviet Union and was a visiting professor at **FLACSO**. In 1975 he published *Acerca del surgimiento de las relaciones capitalistas en la República Dominicana* (On the Origin of Capitalist Relations in the Dominican Republic). His most acclaimed book is *Historia social y económica de la República Dominicana* (Social and Economic History of the Dominican Republic) (1982), a two-volume Marxist interpretation of the history of the Dominican Republic. Since the early 1990s, Cassá has been researching **Olivorismo** (a messianic movement) and *campesino* popular culture.

FERNANDO VALERIO-HOLGUÍN

Cassano, Eleonora

b. 1964, Buenos Aires, Argentina

Dancer

Co-founder in 1990 of Ballet Argentino, with Julio **Bocca**, with whom she twice toured Europe and Latin America, she has won several international prizes and shared the stage with many of ballet's most important figures. A graduate of the Advanced Art Institute at the **Teatro Colón** in 1983, she began her career with the Fundación Teresa Carreño (Teresa Carreño Foundation) in Venezuela. Returning to Argentina, she became leading dancer at the Teatro Colón. In 1994 she moved from classical ballet to review theatre, where she now dances and sings.

RODRIGO PEIRETTI

Cassell, Alphonsus ('Arrow')

b. 1954, Montserrat

Musician

Montserrat's most famous person, Arrow is re-nowned throughout the English-speaking Carib-bean and the Caribbean diaspora as one of the outstanding musicians of **soca** (soul-calypso). His song Hot, Hot, Hot (1982) has been recorded by Buster Poindexter and others, and used in Toyota commercials. His shop in Plymouth was forced to move to Salem after the eruption that began in 1995 of Montserrat's volcano (see **volcanoes**), an event to which Arrow responded in a song entitled 'Ah You Just Can't Run Away' (1995).

DANIEL BALDERSTON

Castañeda, Jorge G.

b. 1953, Mexico City

Political historian

Castañeda's analysis of the experience of the Latin American left since the **1960**s, *La utopía desarmada* (Utopia Unarmed) (1993), offered a highly critical assessment of the political strategies that flowed from the 1959 Cuban Revolution (see **revolutions**). His writings are part of a general rethinking of the experience of revolution against the back-ground of the 1989 collapse of Stalinism. His biography of Che **Guevara**, *Compañero: The Life and Death of Che Guevara* (1998) controversially con-cluded that Guevara's symbolic significance was not matched by his largely misconceived political ideas. Currently teaching in the United States, Castañeda is a regular columnist in several news-papers and a frequent commentator on Latin American affairs.

MIKE GONZALEZ

Castellanos, Rosario

b.1925, Mexico City; d. 1974, Tel Aviv, Israel

Writer and feminist thinker

In an untitled manuscript published twenty-three years after her untimely death in 1974, which the editor titled *Declaración de fe* (Declaration of Faith) (1997) after an early poem, Rosario Castellanos traces the representation of women throughout the trajectory of Mexican cultural history, from classi-cal Aztec and Maya literature, to Sor Juana, to the heroines of the Wars of Independence, to the poets of her own generation. Her own rich body of literary work – novels, short stories, poetry, plays and essays – remains unparalleled in the history of Mexican letters, for its simultaneous interrogation of the roots of oppression in internal colonialism, under-development, and the Mexican variants of the patriarchal family.

Having grown up amid the Mayan-ladino (white) apartheid of Chiapas, in a dysfunctional colonial family, Castellanos was exposed to both the burden of privilege and the pain of margin-alization. The turning point in her life was the death of her younger brother, the only male heir and her parents' favourite; with his death, her parents withdrew from her all the more. In *Declaración de fe* she describes the Mexican family constellation that appears obsessively in her fiction: the distant, disenfranchised, and ultimately weak patriarchal father; and the masochistic mother who uses her suffering to manipulate her husband and chain her son to her for life, while teaching her daughter to drink from the fountain of obedience and self-contempt.

The author became conscious of the import of her early experiences while writing her first, autobiographical, novel, *Balún-Canán* (The Nine Guardians) (1957). Feeling an acute intellectual and moral responsibility to address the Indian problem, Castellanos worked for the next several years with the National Indian Institute, in both

Chiapas and Mexico City, helping to found a bicultural, travelling puppet theatre and a bilingual literary magazine, which would serve as important precursors to the Mayan literary movement of the 1980s and 1990s (see **Maya revitalization movement**). At the same time she began writing an unparalleled cycle of novels, short stories, and poetry about the poisoning effect of colonial relations on all sectors of society in Chiapas – after *Balún-Canán* came *Ciudad real* (City of Kings) (1960), *Oficio de tinieblas* (The Book of Lamentations) (1962); *Los convidados de agosto* (The August Guests) (1964); and *Lívida luz* (Livid Light) (1960).

After her return to Mexico City in 1957, Castellanos's writings turned away from Chiapas ethnic conflicts, to satire of gender roles among the urban middle classes and analyses of female creativity. She became a Professor of Comparative Literature at the National Autonomous University of Mexico (**UNAM**), as well as a visiting professor at several US universities. At the same time, her literary and political prominence grew. She won a series of important literary prizes for her Chiapas cycle: the Premio Chiapas in 1958, the Premio Sor Juana Inés de la Cruz in 1961, and the Premio Xavier Villaurrutia in 1962. When Castellanos died in 1974, allegedly by accidental electrocution, she was serving as Mexico's ambassador to Israel. At age forty-nine, she became the first woman to be buried in the Rotunda of Illustrious Men in Mexico City.

During these final years Castellanos continued to have a troubled personal life, as is evident in her *Cartas a Ricardo* (Letters to Ricardo), published in 1994. She was prone to depression and low self-esteem, and her marriage to the philosopher Ricardo Guerra soon went sour. However, the birth of their only child, Gabriel, following two miscarriages, seems to have brought her some measure of happiness, as did her lifelong love affair with literature.

In 1997, three years after they finally authorized the publication of her letters, Castellanos's ex-husband and son allowed the publication of both *Declaración de fé* and a long-lost novel manuscript that she had chosen not to publish, entitled *Ritos de iniciación* (Rites of Passage) (1997). The appearance of three new books by this major author, two

decades after her untimely death, provide a rare opportunity for reassessment of her *œuvre*.

Castellanos's poetic vocabulary follows a trajectory from the highly rhetorical and tragic, to the conversational and mordant. Similarly, her fiction progresses from autobiographical, lyrical and fragmented prose, to historical fiction, to urban satire. The best of her plays is the posthumously published feminist farce *El eterno femenino* (The Eternal Feminine) (1974). Much of Castellanos's writing is marked by a confessional tone, which perhaps helps to explain the ambivalence that many male critics have expressed toward her work, and the enthusiasm it tends to elicit in women readers.

Further reading

Alarcon, N. (1992) *Ninfomanía: el discurso feminista en la obra poética de Rosario Castellanos*, Madrid: Editorial Pliegos.

Castellanos, R. (1988) *A Rosario Castellanos Reader*, trans. M. Ahern, Austin: University of Texas Press.

—— (1989) *Obras. I: Narrativa*, Mexico City: Fondo de Cultura Económica.

—— (1994) *Cartas a Ricardo*, Mexico City: Consejo Nacional para la Cultura y las Artes.

—— (1997) *Declaracion de fé. Reflexiones sobre la situación de la mujer en México*, Mexico City: Alfaguara.

—— (1998) *The Book of Lamentations*, trans. E. Allen, New York: Penguin.

—— (1998) *Obras. II: Poesía, teatro y ensayo*, Mexico City: Fondo de Cultura Económica.

Castillo, D. (1992) *Talking Back: Toward a Latin American Feminist Literary Criticism*, Ithaca: Cornell University Press.

Franco, J. (1989) *Plotting Women: Gender and Representation in Mexico*, New York: Columbia University Press.

López González, A. (1991) *La espiral parece un círculo*, Mexico City: Universidad Autónoma Metropolitana, Unidad Ixtapalapa.

O'Connell, J. (1995) *Prospero's Daughter. The Prose of Rosario Castellanos*, Austin: University of Texas Press.

CYNTHIA STEELE

Castello Branco, Humberto de Alencar

b. 1897, Fortaleza, Brazil; d. 1967, Fortaleza

Marshal and president

Castello Branco joined the army in 1918, studied at the Brazilian Superior War College and served in Italy with the Brazilian Expeditionary Force during the Second World War. After the Brazilian military *coup d'état* (31 March 1964), the controlling right-wing officers selected him for the presidency of Brazil (11 April 1964–15 March 1967), trusting him to eradicate communism and corruption. He promulgated the Second and the Third Atos Institucionais (Institutional Acts) which ensured centralization of power in the president, dissolved political parties and established military courts to judge civilians.

MARIA JOSE SOMERLATE BARBOSA

Castilla, Manuel J.

b. 1918, Salta, Argentina; d. 1980, Salta

Poet

One of the exceptional lyric poets of northern Argentina, Castilla's poetry examines the indigenous world from within. The people, culture and nature of Salta and Chaco Provinces and the Bolivian mining regions are the central themes of his poetry. Castilla, together with his predecessor Juan Carlos Dávalos, is one of the few voices of the interior to earn the admiration of Buenos Aires and to have received important regional awards. Two of his most memorable books of poems are *Copajira* (Corrosive Mining Water) (1964) and *Triste de la lluvia* (Sad of Rain) (1977).

MAGDALENA GARCÍA PINTO

Castillo, Abelardo

b. 1935, San Pedro, Buenos Aires, Argentina

Writer

An important contemporary writer whose stories appear alongside **Borges**, **Quiroga** and **Cortázar** on standard secondary school booklists. He won the **Casa de las Américas** prize in 1961, and in 1965 a jury that included Ionesco rewarded his play *Israfel*. Founder and editor of the literary journal *El escarabajo de oro* (The Golden Scarab), he has written two novels *El que tiene sed* (He Who is Thirsty) (1985) and *Crónica de un iniciado* (Chronicle of an Initiate) (1991). His essays are collected in *Las palabras y los días* (Words and Days) (1988).

ENRIQUE FOFFANI

Castillo, Julio

b. 1944, Mexico City; d. 1988, Mexico City

Theatre director

Acclaimed Mexican theatre director Julio Castillo began his career as an actor in Fernando Arrabal's play *Fando y Lis*, directed by Alejandro **Jodorowsky** in 1961. His directorial debut was with Arrabal's *Cementario de automóviles* (Auto Graveyard) in 1968, which opened to critical praise and placed Castillo as a key director of avant-garde theatre in Mexico. He directed plays by Sergio **Magaña**, Héctor **Mendoza**, and Carlos **Olmos**, as well as his own plays *El evangelio* (The Gospel) (1972) and *Los insectos* (The Insects) (1973). Shortly before his untimely death, he directed two very successful productions: *De película* (Like a Film) (1985) authored by his wife Blanca Peña, and Jesús **González Dávila**'s *De la Calle* (From the Street) (1988).

ANTONIO PRIETO-STAMBAUGH

Castillo, Oscar

b. 1941, Costa Rica

Film-maker, producer and actor

The premiere of Oscar Castillo's feature film *Eulalia* (1987) led critics to herald the birth of Costa Rican cinema, though Castillo and associates had produced over a dozen films through their Central American Istmofilm company including the award-winning *Nicaragua patria libre o morir* (Nicaragua, Free Country or Death) (1979), *El Salvador vencerá* (El Salvador Shall Overcome) (1980) and *Alsino y el Cóndor* (Alsino and the Condor) (1982). The versatile Castillo also starred in *La Insurrección* (The Uprising) (1979–80) and *La Segua* (The Enchanted Horsewoman) (1984). He directs the popular television series, *El barrio* (The Neighbourhood), and is the founder of the production company, Producciones Paraíso.

ANN MARIE STOCK

Castillo, Otto René

b. 1937, Quetzaltenango, Guatemala; d. 1967, Zacapa, Guatemala

Writer

Founder and best-known poet of the group Generación Comprometida (the Committed Generation), Castillo belonged to the Guatemala Workers' Party (PGT) and was frequently exiled. In El Salvador, he collaborated with Roque **Dalton** and others in a new 1960s revolutionary poetry. When he returned to the armed struggle in Guatemala, he and his *compañera* Nora Paíz were killed by army operatives. Castillo's poems, simple and lyrical, are filled with an idealism in which romantic love and death are treated in function of revolutionary hope and sacrifice. He became an icon of revolutionary poetry, influencing Dalton, Leonel Rugama and many others.

MARC ZIMMERMAN

Castillo de la pureza, El

El castillo de la pureza (The Castle of Purity) (1972) was director Arturo **Ripstein**'s third feature length film and his first to attract a wide international audience. It revisits this auteur's earlier concerns: intolerance, male heterosexual socialization, enclosed spaces. A contemporary family melodrama, based on a notorious 'true crime', the film focuses on Gabriel, an authoritarian and paranoid Mexico City patriarch, a manufacturer of rat poison, who locks his wife and three children in their home to prevent their contamination by external social forces. The film's sadomasochistic black humour rewrites the conventional Mexican family melodrama, directly quoting Alejandro **Galindo**'s classic exploration of the clash between modern values and patriarchal traditions in *Cuando los hijos se van* (When the Children Leave) (1948).

SERGIO DE LA MORA

Castor, Suzy

b. 1936, Port-au-Prince, Haiti

Historian and social researcher

An opponent of the **Duvalier** dictatorship, Castor lived in exile in Mexico until she returned to Haiti in 1986, where, together with her husband Gérard **Pierre-Charles**, she founded the non-governmental organisation, Centre de Recherche et de Formation Economique et Sociale pour le Développement (CRESFED – Centre for Research and Economic and Social Education for Development). She is a specialist in the development of Haiti's grassroots organisations. She has written numerous books and articles in French and Spanish, in particular concerning the US occupation of Haiti (1915–34), Haiti's relations with the Dominican Republic, and the women's movement in Haiti.

CHARLES ARTHUR

Castro, Bélgica

b. 1920?, Concepción, Chile

Actress

A founding member of the important Teatro Experimental of the Universidad de Chile, Bélgica Castro has been one of Chile's most outstanding actors for almost six decades. Awarded Chile's National Arts Prize in 1995, she has been a professor of theatre, founder of theatre companies in Chile and Costa Rica, film and television actress, and has developed a vast range of roles in plays by international and Chilean dramatists including many works by her second husband, Alejandro **Sieveking**. After retirement from the University of Chile she founded with Sieveking her own company *El Teatro del Angel*.

GWEN KIRKPATRICK

Castro, Juan José

b. 1895, Buenos Aires, Argentina; d. 1968, Buenos Aires

Composer

Castro helped to create the Renovación group (1929) and the Argentine Composers' League (1948), both dedicated to the defence of artistic independence against academic formalisms. Manager of Buenos Aires's **Teatro Colón**, he was elected to the Academy of Fine Arts in 1945. He taught in the National Conservatory (1939–43) and was appointed Dean (1959–64) at the Conservatory of Puerto Rico upon Pablo Casals's recommendation. He composed operas, ballets, choral symphonies, orchestral and chamber pieces and works for voice, piano and bandoneón. He wrote the film score for Edmundo Guibourg's *Bodas de sangre* (Blood Weddings) (1938).

CLAUDIA TORRE

Castro, Tomás

b. 1959, Santo Domingo, Dominican Republic

Poet

Like other members of the literary group *Taller Literario César Vallejo*, Castro started publishing his poetry in magazines and journals in the early 1980s. He has won the Samuel Santana National Prize for Poetry and the University Poetry Prize . His most acclaimed book *Amor a quemarropa* (Pointblank Love) (1985), reprinted four times, is concerned with everyday life images about love and despair and is reminiscent of Pablo **Neruda**'s *Veinte poemas de amor* (1924).

FERNANDO VALERIO-HOLGUÍN

Castro, Verónica

b. 1953, Mexico City, Mexico

Actress

The award of the annual 'El Rostro' prize by the newspaper *El Heraldo de Mexico* as the most beautiful and promising young 'face' of 1970 effectively determined Castro's career. She went on to study international relations at the National University (**UNAM**), but ended up accepting the acting offers that came her way and becoming one of Mexico's best-known and most powerful female television personalities.

At first she was only a 'pretty face'. Her first film appearance in *El arte de engañar* (The Art of Deceit) (1970) – including a famous nude scene – and a popular theatre piece (*Coqueluche*) led to a leading role in the film *Chiquita pero picosa* (Small But Spicy) (1986). But Castro's breakthrough was the early 1980s telenovela (see **telenovelas**) *Los ricos también lloran* (The Rich Also Cry), in which she played the first of her many humble young women roles. With this and other successful *telenovelas* – including *El* **derecho de nacer** (The Right to be Born), a remake of the oft-adapted *radionovela* by Cuban Felix B. **Caignet**, in which she played a much-too-young mother, *Rosa salvaje* (Wild Rose) and *Mi pequeña Soledad* (My Little Soledad), which were widely exported throughout Latin America, the USA, Europe, Asia and the Soviet Union – Castro became an international star. Capitalizing on this popularity, she went into the pop music business where she was a critical failure (her singing is not of the highest quality, and even in her TV performances always uses playback) but a modest commercial success; her most popular releases have been the theme songs for her own *telenovelas*.

After working in Italy and Argentina, she returned to Mexico in the 1990s, starred in a popular theatrical revue (*La mujer del año*, Woman of the Year) and hosted a series of television talk and entertainment shows for **Televisa**, among them *Mala noche no* (Not a Bad Night), *Aquí está* (Here It Is), *La movida* (What's Going On) and *¡Vero América!* Perhaps the best moment of this phase of her career was her three-night interview with and homage to the great Mexican diva María **Félix**. *Valentina* (1993) was her comeback to *telenovelas* with a twist: besides playing the too-youthful protagonist she also was producer of the series. However, this *telenovela* was not as commercially successful as her previous endeavours and a critical failure. Her son, Cristian Castro, became a successful pop singer in the mid-1990s.

EDUARDO SANTA CRUZ

Castro Leiva, Luis

b. 1943, Caracas, Venezuela; d. 1999, Chicago, USA

Academic and lawyer

Castro Leiva had an outstanding academic career, teaching political science and philosophy at universities in Caracas. His lucid analyses of Venezuela's political and cultural reality became well known through regular newspaper articles. His main interest was the history of ideas. Though his books were relatively few, they were polemical and influential. The best known, *La Gran Colombia, una ilusión ilustrada* (An Enlightened Illusion) (1984) and *De la patria boba a teología bolivariana* (From the Foolish Nation to Bolivarian Theology) (1991),

were particularly controversial in Venezuela, for they presented a highly critical view of the thought and influence of Bolívar.

MARK DINNEEN

Castro Ruz, Fidel

b. 1926, Biran, Cuba

Politician

Cuban leader since 1959, Castro would certainly not have survived until then had the then-President Fulgencio **Batista** employed the same level of repression against his opponents as Fidel Castro has against those who have opposed him. Officially the world's longest-standing political leader, Fidel Castro is the only survivor of what was once called 'actually existing socialism'. Although his power at the century's end was clearly unchallenged, and his political opponents subject still to repression and vilification, the Cuban model seems to have traced a circle. The declared purposes of his regime – to end dependency, diversify the economy and provide a focus and an example for Latin American revolutionary movements – have manifestly not been fulfilled. Through the 1990s, Cuba has, in fact if not in name, become reintegrated into a world market on which it once again depends – though to what extent the process is under any kind of control from Cuba remains a matter of debate.

In the same period Castro has embarked on a kind of charm offensive to facilitate reintegration – welcoming the Pope and the King of the **Yoruba** to Havana, and speaking very publicly to a number of Western European leaders. The US embargo, however, remains in place after forty years – and the US conservative right still regards Cuba as a touchstone of American power. The experience of the 'special period in time of peace' that followed the effective withdrawal of Soviet aid in 1986 ravaged the Cuban population and exposed the tensions and contradictions at the heart of Cuban society. With his usual pragmatic skill, Castro rode the storm with a combination of charismatic declarations and repression of dissent.

Indeed Castro has displayed throughout his tenancy extraordinary skill and cunning in maintaining himself in power. A fierce revolutionary in the mid-1960s, he abandoned the revolutionary road by 1968 and sought *rapprochement* with regimes as different as that of **Allende** in Chile, **Torrijos** in Panama and **Velasco Alvarado** in Peru. While insisting on Cuban independence, he was arguing the Soviet case unequivocally at the 1970 Non-Aligned Conference at Algiers and through most of the decade Cuban troops were present in Africa supporting Russian interests in the Horn and Southern Africa.

The third of five children, Castro's father came from Galicia in Spain, and had made his fortune in Biran in what was then Oriente province. Fidel went to school in Santiago de Cuba and in 1945 entered the Law Faculty at Havana University. He is remembered by fellow students for his prodigious memory and for the pistol he always carried in his belt.

When in 1952, Fulgencio **Batista** organized a *coup* to overthrow President Carlos Prío Socarrás, Castro took the government to court for violating the Constitution – the case did not prosper. On 26 July 1953, he led a group of 165 young people in an assault on the Moncada Barracks in Santiago; many were killed during or after the battle. Castro himself was sentenced to fifteen years in prison but was released in 1955 under an amnesty. Moving to Mexico, he set up the 26th July Movement and organized an armed expedition of eighty-one men, which would land on the coast of Oriente from the motor yacht 'Granma' late in 1956. The expedition was met and decimated by Batista's troops; the few survivors (including Castro's brother Raúl, Camilo Cienfuegos, Che **Guevara** and others) reorganized themselves in the Sierra Maestra with the aid of local peasants including one Crescencio Pérez, a local man of less than pure reputation. They launched a successful guerrilla war (see **guerrillas**) against Batista, who fled Cuba on 1 January 1959.

Designated Prime Minister in February, Castro used his undoubted charisma and his persuasive power to gather power to himself. The US refusal to engage with Castro and the subsequent imposition of a total economic siege moved Castro to react by expropriating foreign property and accelerating the process of agrarian and economic reform. By the end of 1960 some half-a-million Cubans, mainly the wealthier classes and the professionals, had left the island to swell the Cuban population of Miami. Thereafter, Castro would turn again from time to time to the tactic of mass expulsion as a way of generating internal cohesion and support. The failed Bay of Pigs invasion in 1961 reinforced the general hostility to the USA, while the October Missile Crisis of 1962 led Castro to distance himself for a time from the Soviets.

The US embargo and its mounting hostility created a justification for an increasingly centralized control of Cuban society and a concentration of power in the small circle around Fidel himself. While it was argued by supporters that this reflected the extraordinary popularity of the *comandante en jefe*, there was little possibility of ever testing that assertion, since by the end of the 1960s there were no forms of democratic control left. The trade unions, committees for the defence of the revolution, and communist youth were little more than conduits from the leadership to the base – and the expressions of dissent that occurred in the late 1960s were met with increasingly draconian forms of social control through the identity card system, the so-called 'voluntary' labour schemes, the Advanced Worker Code that rewarded loyalty and penalized absenteeism and so on.

The 1976 Constitution was passed unanimously in every particular by a nominated assembly; its clauses resonate with the kind of expressions more familiar in the dictatorial regimes of Eastern Europe – 'the nation was founded by José Martí and now progresses under the wise leadership of Fidel'. By then Castro was Commander-in-Chief of the army, President of the Council of State and First Secretary of the Cuban Communist Party – which was according to the same Constitution 'the leading force in society and the State'.

The mid-1980s was another period of crisis, and one whose effects were visible in the deepening social differentiation within Cuba, and the dominance of a tourist industry that transforms every relationship into one of exploitation and dependence. It is noticeable that Fidel's portrait is not very much in evidence in the streets of Cuba – as opposed to Guevara's, which is everywhere – and that his public appearances are fewer now. The popular names for him are not particularly flattering; his macho image in a country with an appalling history of homophobia is profoundly double-edged. And there remains the paradox of a leader who is proclaimed a popular hero by adherents abroad, yet who runs a ferociously repressive, impenetrable power apparatus that is accountable to no one but Castro himself.

Further reading

Balfour, S. (1990) *Fidel Castro*, New York/London: Longman.

Eckstein, S.E. (1994) *Back from the Future*, Princeton, NJ: Princeton University Press.

Franqui, C. (1984) *Family Portrait with Fidel: A Memoir*, New York, Random House.

Szulc, T. (1986) *Fidel: A Critical Portrait*, New York, Morrow.

Thomas, H. (1977) *The Cuban Revolution*, New York: Harper & Row.

MIKE GONZALEZ

Catholicism

Catholicism in Latin America is the dominant religious culture, yet it is not precisely or ubiquitously the culture of domination. If it had been exclusively the culture of the rich and powerful and for the rich and powerful, it would never have attained or preserved the hegemonic position which it enjoyed throughout the continent for 500 years until, in the late twentieth century, finally, its position began to be seriously undermined by charismatic movements emerging from the Protestant tradition (see **Protestantism**), Pentecostalism in particular. As in Italy and Spain, the Church as an institution managed to preserve an extraordinary stability in an environment characterized by extreme political and economic instability – and it was only with the social transformation brought about by first industrialization and then – in short order – deindustrialization, and by the contemporaneous building and subsequent dismantling of the corporate state in the twentieth century, that the Church's influence began to wane. The influence of Catholic culture goes beyond that of the Church itself, and can be observed in

Catholicism's pervasive presence in language and urban scenery, and at public state celebrations. In the 1980s and 1990s, priests and bishops were called upon to act in a relatively new role as disinterested intermediaries in delicate political situations – during transitions to democracy or in negotiations with armed **guerrillas** – in recognition of the Church less as a religious and more as a national institution.

As throughout the Latin countries of Southern Europe, Latin American Catholicism is a culture marked by a continuous, ancient and creative tension between the formulae, symbols, rituals, personnel, organization and doctrine of the Popes and the official Church apparatus which they head, and a vast and varied array of local cults, brotherhoods and rituals which deal with the day-to-day issues of religion – namely ill health, death and misfortune, rites of passage and the legitimation of authority. These practices draw on both indigenous rituals and early modern Southern European popular religion.

The two-way relationship between popular Catholicism and the official Church is most famously illustrated by the cult of the Virgin of Guadalupe (see **Virgins, miraculous**). Launched in the mid-seventeenth century, one hundred years after her apparition to the humble Juan Diego, the Virgin gradually evolved into a symbol of Mexican nationhood, which has endured through countless revolutions, both liberal and nationalist. At the core of the cult lies the story of how an Indio eventually, after much difficulty, and only with the help of a miraculous event in the presence of the Archbishop of Mexico, persuaded the Church to build a shrine on the spot where there are now two churches and the sanctuary itself – the Villa or ensemble at Tepeyac on what was once the edge of the Mexican capital. Thus the cult is at once a reaffirmation of the authority of both the Church and the state – even the ferociously anti-clerical post-revolutionary state – and also a champion of the poor and the indigenous population.

'La Guadalupana' is but the most prominent of thousands of local cults of saints and Virgins who are petitioned for personal favours of all kinds, and which also provide the focus for annual village celebrations. These fiestas are an occasion for conspicuous consumption and also a degree of accumulation by local élites, and in the Andes and Mexico especially, attract urban migrants back to their places of origin and encourage them to do good works for those places. If popular Catholicism provides the ritual life of the poor, especially in rural areas, in urban areas the institutional Church services the ritual needs of the middle classes. The Church finds it difficult to attend adequately to the urban popular classes in cities that have multiplied in population many times over in the period after 1940, and it is among these strata that Protestant churches have found the most readily available market.

Thus the role of the Church as an institution is not congruent with the role of Catholicism as a culture. Even when 15–20 per cent of the population professes to be Protestant or evangelical, and when large numbers openly deny any religious affiliation at all, the statements of bishops retain prestige and influence – so that for example in Chile, a highly secularized society, abortion continues to be illegal under any circumstances whatsoever, and divorce has no existence in law.

Despite the violence which accompanied its introduction in the Americas, Catholicism has neither always nor everywhere been moulded to suit the interest of the oppressor. Indeed, although for a time the notion that an entire culture could be instrumentalized in this way did gain some currency, recent writing has become altogether more sensitive and sophisticated on the subject. Even in the sixteenth century, voices of fierce dissent made themselves heard against the atrocities committed by the conquerors – the Dominican Bishop Bartolomé de las Casas, seen as a precursor and emblematic hero by modern liberation theologians (see **liberation theology**, turned the claims that this was an extirpation of diabolic forces of paganism against the conquerors themselves, describing their own acts as marked by sin and greed and defending indigenous religion as the native peoples' own distinctive way of worshipping God. In the seventeenth century, chroniclers claimed that St Thomas the Apostle had gone as far as Mexico and Paraguay and that Christianity had been preserved pure and untouched by the corruption of the intervening centuries in Europe. To be sure, the Church as upholder of an oppressive social order has also been much in evidence, but especially in the post-colonial era: Bartolomé de las Casas had many clerical opponents, and recently we have witnessed the Church's role in condoning fascistic sympathies in Argentina in the 1930s, in sanctioning ultra-montane fanaticism in Colombia's **Violencia** between 1945 and 1958, in promoting the military *coup* in Brazil in 1964 (a gesture which the Bishops soon came to regret) and in offering succour (again) to the Argentine military regime of 1976–83, whose barbarism that country's bishops have never properly condemned, let alone repented for their own complicity and their refusal of help to those who suffered in one of the most systematic campaigns of political persecution and victimization in the region during that period. The influences here have been of modern European and Spanish rather than American heritage.

By the second half of the twentieth century, here as elsewhere, the Church lost its grip on the upbringing of the young, on sexual mores, on marriage, and on public decorum. Yet the institution has succeeded in shifting its sphere of influence from the private to the public, from the confessional to the political arena, and within the political from ceremonial legitimation to direct involvement and active lobbying. The Church may not be able to persuade individuals to change their behaviour, but it can attempt to influence legislation in pursuit of the same outcome. Beginning with pronouncements of the Vatican in the last decade of the nineteenth century, it became more closely involved in social issues and eventually in sponsoring secular political movements. A strong movement developed within the institutional Church and among lay intellectuals who had been educated by the Church in favour of a more worker-oriented corporatism, known broadly as the 'social doctrine of the Church', which was particularly influential in Chile, as a formally established political Christian Democratic party, but was influential as a current of thought in Argentina, Brazil, Peru, Venezuela (the COPEI – Social Christian Party) and even Mexico, where the PAN (Partido Acción Nacional) was inspired by the more traditionalist and free market-oriented variety of this broad school of thought.

These social and eventually political

involvements, in a confluence with the Second Vatican Council (Vatican II – 1962–5), created severe theological and political divisions within Catholicism, and were a prelude to the retrenchment which has marked the Papacy of John Paul II (1979–). When social and political conflict became most acute (in Brazil, 1964, Argentina 1968–76, and Chile 1970–3) **Christian Democracy** itself tended to polarize between those who leaned towards socialist, even marxist solutions in deeply divided societies, and those who, when faced with such dramatic choices, leaned the other way. The former found a theological banner in Liberation Theology and a political expression in social movements operating under the umbrella of the Church especially those known as *comunidades de base* (**Christian Base Organizations**). These developments, together with the postconciliar atmosphere of open debate, were accompanied by and often blamed for a haemorrhage of priests from Holy Orders, a decline in vocations and a consequent ageing of the clergy – the Brazilian Church lost eight per cent of its priests between 1965 and 1970 alone. There was also ferocious infighting within the Church as different currents of opinion struggled for position, resources and appointments. Middle class church worshippers not infrequently became alienated by the 'preferential option for the poor' and the more radical commitment to that option espoused by some clergy, and which figured so prominently in the pronouncements of influential bodies such as Episcopal Conferences in Brazil or Chile and of prominent figures such as Dom Helder **Cámara**, even when a closer inspection on the ground might reveal the relatively limited audience which that message was reaching among the poor (who by now were migrating in droves to the Pentecostal churches). There is some doubt as to whether the prophetic message of figures such as Dom Helder **Cámara** truly resonated with the popular culture of Catholicism or with the culture of the people more generally. Indeed, a distinction should be drawn between an audience which might listen to the message about the preferential option for the poor as a religious message, as one which they felt drawn to on account of their loyalty to the Church or their Catholic sense of identity, and another more secularized audience which has seen in the

Church and the institutions operating under its aegis, useful and trustworthy allies in struggles for land, for civil and human rights, for the democratic transition and so on.

The period since the early 1960s has seen the emergence of two different responses to modernity within Catholic culture in the region. On the one hand, the postconciliar school reduced emphasis on personal piety and the regulation of daily life of the faithful and sought to emphasize what the Church as an institution stood for in society. For this tendency – for it is a tendency rather than a coherent school of thought, being defined more by a sensibility and set of alliances – the forms and rituals of religious observance counted for less than the substance of doctrine and the translation of doctrine into action; for them too the pursuit of salvation in the Kingdom of God could be interpreted as the empowerment of the People of God in this life. This commitment was underpinned by an identification of the beliefs and utterings of the people mobilized in social movements with an untainted inspiration from which the intelligentsia could learn and with which they could overcome the burdens of their privileged background. This project extended the Vatican II project of rationality and modernity to the point where any ritual might be considered a relic of superstition. On the other side a more straightforward project of modernization, developed with great energy by John Paul II, consisted in further centralization, in the encouragement of the use of modern methods of communication, and in the application of these methods to personal expressions of piety and commitment. Thus the **Opus Dei** can be seen as what St Ignatius, the founder of the Company of Jesus, might have founded had he lived not in the sixteenth, but in the twentieth century.

The internal politics of the Church can also be traced through the meetings of **CELAM**, the Latin American Bishops' Conference, in Medellín (1968), Puebla (1979) and Santo Domingo (1992). Medellín was undoubtedly the high point of commitment to the advocacy of social justice even at the expense of evangelization, but although Puebla enshrined the preferential option for the poor, it was there also that Pope John Paul II imposed a much stronger emphasis on the evangelization of culture, much to the disappointment of the Liberation Theology school and their followers in the *comunidades de base* and social movements. By the time of Santo Domingo, what was expected to be a triumphal celebration of 500 years of evangelization in the Americas turned out to be a somewhat low-key affair because the grassroots activists and their theological and clerical counterparts had been marginalized or even silenced, and also because there was a closing of the ranks in the face of the Protestant 'explosion'.

Less noted until recently has been the movement of Charismatic Renewal which has gained many more followers than the grassroots, or *basista* social movements which received most attention from intellectuals and the international media. Although on the surface they resemble Pentecostal movements in their espousal of gifts of the spirit, of healing and glossolalia, the charismatics remain within the Church, tend to be of more middle class composition than Pentecostals, and do not transmit the message of social dissent that is so central to Pentecostal image and identity. Their large-scale meetings nevertheless do break with traditional forms of both official and popular Catholicism on account of the type of music, of the orchestration of the occasions and their mediatic qualities, and of the exhibitionism attached to the descent of the Holy Spirit and 'speaking in tongues'. The future of the Catholic Church in terms of numbers of active followers will be heavily influenced by the development – or stagnation – of the Charismatic movement, and the Vatican, after initial reluctance, has come to look with favour upon it, especially because Charismatics do not raise sensitive political issues and because they bring in large numbers who otherwise would stay away from church. Yet there is absolutely no sign of the Church accepting or adopting charismatic beliefs in such things as the descent of the Holy Spirit, or the acquisition by individuals of the gift of healing.

See also: Religion and politics; new social movements

Further reading

De Kadt, E. (1970) *Catholic radicals in Brazil*, Oxford: Oxford University Press.

Gheerbrant, A. (1970) *La iglesia rebelde de América Latina*, Mexico City: Siglo Veintiuno.

Gruzinski, S. (1993) *The Conquest of Mexico: the Incorporation of Indian Societies into the Western World, 16th–18th Centuries*, Cambridge: Polity Press.

Gutierrez, G. (1988) *A Theology of Liberation: History, Politics, and Salvation*, London: Student Christian Movement.

Rowland, C. (ed) (1999) *The Cambridge Companion to Liberation Theology*, Cambridge and New York: Cambridge University Press.

Turner F.C. (1971) *Catholicism and Political Development in Latin America*, Chapel Hill, University of North Carolina Press.

DAVID LEHMANN

Cavalcanti, Alberto

b.1897, Rio de Janeiro, Brazil; d.1982, Paris, France

Film-maker

Cavalcanti learned his trade with Renoir and others in the French avant garde and with John Grierson, with whom he worked after moving to Britain in 1934, directing and producing documentaries like *Night Mail* (1936) and fictional features like *Went the Day Well?* (1942). Invited back to Brazil by **Assis Chateaubriand**, in 1949 he became executive director of the **Vera Cruz Studios**: he supervised the establishment of the company, imported a cadre of technicians from Europe, and produced its first two films. Personality and managerial differences led to his resignation in 1951. After directing a parody of the **Vargas** government, *Simão, o caolho* (1952) for São Paulo producer Maristela, he formed the Kino company and directed the lyrical paean to Recife, *O canto do mar* (The song of the sea) (1953), and *Mulher de verdade* (Real woman) (1954) before returning to Europe. Although not well-received at the time, all three films evidence Cavalcanti's talent and sensitivity.

ISMAIL XAVIER

Cavalcanti, Emiliano di

b. 1897, Rio de Janeiro, Brazil; d. 1976,
Rio de Janeiro

Artist

One of the first modernists, Emiliano di Cavalcanti
(full name Emiliano Augusto Cavalcanti de Albuquerque e Melo) both exhibited in and promoted
the historic Semana de Arte Moderna (**Modern
Art Week**) of 1922. Starting very young as a
cartoonist and magazine illustrator in Rio, he had
his first shows in 1916 and 1917. A ludic spirit
informed his caricatures and as a painter he was
sensitive to Rio's luxuriant landscape. Multi-
talented, this draftsman, etcher, designer and
muralist (see **muralism**) was also a poet and
memoirist. Early in his career, he followed fashion
in depicting unreal female figures and landscapes
in pastel tones. Subsequently his style evolved as he
observed the objective world and learned to
express human life through its more despicable
but real aspects. Di Cavalcanti was not waylaid by
excessive modernist technical research. Cubist and
futurist theories did not disorient him but enriched
his technique, allowing him to express a unique
worldview.

In 1923 he studied in Europe and fell under its
cultural spell, especially that of Paris. He lived
there between 1923–5 and 1935–40. He returned
to Rio, of which he said, 'I could not live without
Rio de Janeiro because everything I see as a painter
is part and parcel of the *carioca* landscape.' His
understanding of Brazilian culture guided his work,
which was lyrical, romantic and grotesque. Like
other modernists, di Cavalcanti was preoccupied
with the Brazilian essence and the country's social
problems. The former he often represented
through humble mulatto and black figures, especially of women. The latter, expressionistically
portrayed as grotesques (illumined however by
tenderness and compassion) are prostitutes and
other social outcasts.

Together with first and second-phase modernists
(Anita **Malfatti**, Tarsila do **Amaral** and Cândido
Portinari) di Cavalcanti's painting created a
territory of Brazilian imagery. Moreover, he also
situated his art in a broader Latin American
context, in relation to the great Pacific American

civilizations and particularly to Mexican painting.
At the 1953 São Paulo Bienale (see **Bienale de
São Paulo**), di Cavalcanti shared the best
Brazilian painter award with Alfredo **Volpi**. He
also won a gold medal at the Inter-American
Biennial in Mexico, 1960.

Further reading

di Cavalcanti, E. (1987) *Emiliano di Cavalcanti 1897–
1976: Works on Paper*, New York: The Americas
Society.

M.A. GUIMARÃES LOPES

Cavour, Ernesto

b. 1940, La Paz, Bolivia

Musician

Self-taught, Cavour is a master of the **charango**, the principal instrument of **mestizo** music.
He was a dancer with the national ballet and co-
founder of the group Los **Jairas**. He has travelled
widely, as a charango soloist, winning a growing
audience for the instrument. Composer of more
than 200 popular songs and of film music, he has
recorded some ten CDs and fifty LPs. Inventor of
instruments (for example the chromatic zampoña)
he was a founder of Bolivia's Museum of Musical
Instruments and invented various methods for
learning the traditional instruments of Bolivia.

BEATRIZ ROSSELLS

Cayetano Carpio, Salvador

b. ?; d. 1983, Managua, Nicaragua

Revolutionary

Veteran revolutionary leader of El Salvador's FPL
(Fuerzas Populares de Liberación – Popular
Liberation Forces), Carpio (called 'Marcial') had
a long and distinguished trajectory as a trade
unionist (he led the Bakers' Union) and member of
the Salvadoran Communist Party, before he split
from it to form the FPL in 1972. Carpio's political
position was unequivocal – that power would be

won only by armed struggle. At the same time he was deeply critical of the **foco** theory of guerrilla war, arguing instead that only an armed peasant and workers' movement with a programme for economic transformation could bring about revolutionary change. The intensification of the struggle in 1979–80 led to the formation of a united front organization, the **FMLN**, in 1980. United in action, the FMLN remained politically divided between the Guevarist ERP (see Roque **Dalton**) and the Resistencia Nacional (RN – National Resistance), which argued for a broader, cross-class resistance front. Eventually, in 1983, the argument penetrated the FPL and Carpio's policies were defeated internally by a faction led by vice-president 'Ana María'. Shortly afterwards Ana María was murdered by pro-Carpio militants and a little later Carpio himself apparently committed suicide. The truth of these events remains obscure – but in the wake of both deaths the FPL moved closer to the positions that Carpio had opposed.

MIKE GONZALEZ

Cayman Islands

South of Cuba and east of Jamaica, in the path of hurricanes, lies the small Cayman archipelago, comprising Grand Cayman, Little Cayman and Cayman Brac. These three islands, 259 square kilometres in all, are one of the United Kingdom's remaining Caribbean possessions. Its 25,000 mainly English-speaking inhabitants (mestizos, and people of European and African origin) are concentrated on Grand Cayman. Since 1959, when Jamaica relinquished the administration of the islands to Britain, thousands of international financial institutions have established themselves there, attracted by liberal fiscal policies. **Tourism** is the major industry, with an average of 620,000 visitors annually; other industries include construction and the manufacture of pharmaceuticals for export.

LUIS ESPARZA

Caymmi, Dorival

b. 1914, Salvador, Bahia

Composer and singer

An autodidact of extraordinary musical sensibility, Dorival Caymmi composed many standards of the modern Brazilian songbook including 'O que é que a baiana tem' (What is it the Bahian Woman has?), recorded by Carmen **Miranda** in 1939, and 'Marina'. His songs, which often invoke the folklife of coastal Bahia, had a profound impact on subsequent generations of Brazilian artists. In the late 1950s, the leading innovator of **bossa nova**, João **Gilberto**, popularized 'Rosa Morena', 'Doralice' and 'Samba da minha terra'. Gal **Costa** dedicated an entire album to his compositions (*Gal canta Caymmi*) (1973). His children are also important in contemporary Brazilian music.

CHRISTOPHER DUNN

Cazals, Felipe

b. 1937, Guéthary, France

Film-maker

He made short films for Mexican state television before directing the first of twenty feature films, *La manzana de la discordia* (The Apple of Discord) in 1968. After the dissolution of the **Grupo Cine Independiente** in 1970, Cazals produced three major commercial films: *Emiliano Zapata* (1970), *El jardín de la Tía Isabel* (Aunt Isabel's Garden) (1971) and *Aquellos años* (Those Years) (1972). His creative period began with a documentary on the Seri Indians and continued with a trilogy on the theme of violence – *Canoa* (Canoe) (1975), *El apando* (The Cell) (1975) and *Los poquianchis* (1976) – which confirmed Cazals's prominent place within auteur cinema.

PATRICIA TORRES SAN MARTÍN

Cazuza

b. 1958, Rio de Janeiro, Brazil; d. 1990, Rio de Janeiro

Singer and composer

Cazuza was a key figure in Brazilian rock in the 1980s and was for three years lead singer of the popular rock band Barão Vermelho, with whom he recorded three albums and a number of hits. He later concentrated on solo work, incorporating elements from Brazilian popular music from **bossa nova** to Caetano **Veloso**. He was one of the first Brazilians to be publicly identified with **AIDS** after the magazine *Veja* published a controversial report about his illness. The lyrics in his last and most powerful albums express his struggle against the disease as well as his anger at the Brazilian bourgeoisie.

CÉSAR BRAGA-PINTO

CDR

The CDR (Comités de Defensa de la Revolución) (Committees for the Defence of the Revolution) were founded in September 1960, at Fidel **Castro**'s suggestion, to provide each district of Havana with a system of vigilance whereby local residents would inform the police of any oppositional activities; activities which from then on were generically labelled 'counter-revolutionary' and forced underground. CDRs were subsequently set up throughout the country, and by 1997 had a nominal membership of seven million, representing all Cubans over fourteen. Their original purposes were also extended and they were charged with the organization of voluntary labour, mass vaccinations, census taking, blood donation and recycling. One commentator has described them as 'the institution that made informing into an act of heroism'.

See also: Isla 70

JOSÉ ANTONIO EVORA

CEDIM

The Center of Maya Documentation and Research (Centro de Documentación e Investigación Maya) (CEDIM) is a scientific research institute in Guatemala, founded by the Maya for the study and promotion of Mayan cultural values within a pluralistic society. CEDIM maintains library holdings on the Maya and other nations native to the Americas. CEDIM carries out and publishes studies, provides resource support for educators, organizes conferences, seminars and exhibitions, and fosters scholarly collaboration at all stages in the production of knowledge, from collection to synthesis and dissemination.

JUDITH MAXWELL

Cedrón, Jorge

b. 1946, Buenos Aires, Argentina; d. 1980, Paris, France

Film-maker

A militant filmmaker, Cedrón studied film at the University of La Plata and worked with the filmmakers of the Brazilian **Cinema Novo**. Returning to Argentina, he made two shorts and directed *El habilitado* (The Paymaster) (1971), and a year later, in a similar register of social criticism and denunciation, *Operación Masacre*, a militant film based on the Rodolfo **Walsh** documentary novel depicting the shooting of Peronist workers in 1956. After the 1976 military *coup* he went into exile in Paris where he died. Although officially a suicide, the circumstances of his death remain unclear.

DIANA PALADINO

CELAM

CELAM (Consejo Episcopal Latinoamericano – the Conference of Latin American Bishops), brings together Catholic bishops of Latin America and the Caribbean to coordinate the Church's activities throughout the region. Prior to its formation at a conference in Rio de Janeiro in 1955, each bishop or national bishops' conference related directly to

Rome, without intervening institutions. The new structure enabled international networks and communication essential to the development of the consciousness of a 'Latin American Church' as well as to the rapid dissemination of ideas throughout the region.

The second general conference, held in Medellín, Colombia in 1968, was a watershed for Latin American **Catholicism**. Convened to examine the significance of Vatican II for Latin America, the meeting's conclusions were strongly influenced by and supportive of the **liberation theology** then emerging. The resulting document, published in English as *The Church in the Present-Day Transformation of Latin America in the Light of the Council* (1979), emphasized social justice concerns and encouraged the spread of *comunidades eclesiaes de base* (CEBs, **Christian Base Organizations**). CELAM's endorsement was seen as official approval of central aspects of liberation theology. During this period, CELAM-sponsored research centres and retreats provided institutional support for liberation theologians.

At the 1972 meeting in Sucre, Bolivia, conservatives organized to elect Alfonso López Trujillo secretary general. Under his leadership, progressives were largely removed from CELAM institutions, and the organization's resources were mobilized to oppose liberation theology. The third general meeting, in Puebla, Mexico in 1979, came as a showdown between conservatives and liberationists. Through careful selection of delegates as well as the exclusion of theologians from the conference itself, conservatives sought to repudiate certain stances taken in the Medellín documents. Support for liberation theology had a broad base, however, and its supporters were well organized. As a result, the Puebla document reaffirmed certain liberationist themes, such as the 'preferential option for the poor', yet was less prophetic than the Medellín conclusions. The fourth major meeting, in Santo Domingo, Dominican Republic, in 1992, was also characterized by strong disagreement – with the Vatican playing an important role in supporting the conservatives – and the resulting document was a heterogeneous compromise.

Further reading

Hennelly, A. (ed.) (1993) *Santo Domingo and Beyond: Documents and Commentaries from the Historic Meeting of the Latin American Bishops Conference*, Maryknoll: Orbis Books.

Smith, C. (1991) *The Emergence of Liberation Theology: Radical Religion and Social Movement Theory*, Chicago: University of Chicago Press.

THOMAS A. LEWIS

CELARG

The Centro de Estudios Latinoamericanos Rómulo **Gallegos** (CELARG) (Rómulo Gallegos Centre for Latin American Studies) was established in 1974 to encourage social, cultural and literary research on Latin America. In the past it has hosted some of the continent's best-known scholars, though its current research is limited to Venezuela. It produced a critical review, *Actualidades*, and its literary seminars were important for a generation of Venezuelan writers. In 1967 it set up the prestigious and economically valuable Rómulo Gallegos Prize (see **Gallegos, Rómulo**) for the best novel written in Spanish. Winners have included Mario **Vargas Llosa** (1967), Gabriel **García Márquez** (1972), Carlos **Fuentes** (1977), Fernando **del Paso** (1982), Abel **Posse** (1987), Mempo **Giardinelli** (1993) and Javier Marías (1995).

VERONICA JAFFÉ

CELCIRP

CELCIRP (Centro para el Estudio de las Literaturas y la Civilización Rioplatense) (Centre for the Study of the Literatures and Civilizations of the River Plate region) is an international centre based in France, which draws together specialists in the study of the cultural production of the countries of the River Plate region: Argentina, Paraguay and Uruguay. Founded in 1982 by Paul Verdevoye, Claude Cymerman and Nilda Díaz, CELCIRP organizes various academic and cultural activities, and in particular a biennial congress. Between 1985 and 1997, CELCIRP published eighteen issues of its journal *Río de la Plata*.

JULIO PREMAT

cemeteries

In colonial times, cemeteries were adjacent to neighbourhood churches. Important community members were buried inside and ordinary people buried outside in the *camposanto* or sacred land. Population growth, the need to control the theocracy, sanitary conditions and the epidemics of the nineteenth century created an urgent need for new locations. The concept of a city within the city, surrounded by walls, was repeated throughout Latin America. The combination of grid planning, large mausoleums, tombs, communal niches and landscaping embody urban characteristics.

La **Recoleta** in Buenos Aires, Argentina, is such an example. It was created in 1822 by the Government Minister Rivadavia. As a result of an 1875 epidemic, the aristocracy moved to the northern part of the city and the area earned renewed attention. The neo-classical entrance was remodelled in 1881 by Juan Buschiazzo. Its development followed the precedent of the Père Lachaise Cemetery in Paris by including an area for Protestant 'dissidents'. La Recoleta is marked by grand mausoleums and sculptures depicting allegorical themes such as time, death, angels, pity and sorrow. Between 1880 and 1930 a series of revivals using imported materials and designs from Paris were executed. After the 1930s, ornamentation became more austere. In 1946, a presidential decree declared many mausoleums national monuments; among them, the tomb of a former president and writer, Domingo F. Sarmiento.

La **Chacarita**, the popular grand cemetery of Buenos Aires, located south of the city, was created after the epidemics of the 1880s. The mausoleum of Carlos **Gardel**, author and singer of tangos (see **tango**) and milongas is located there. The repetition of communal tombs, the arrangement of cypress trees, and countless crucifixes and ornamentation create a more subdued, monotonous vision. The contrast between these cemeteries

has been celebrated by Jorge Luis **Borges** in his book *Fervor de Buenos Aires* (Buenos Aires' Fervour) and in the poem 'Death of Buenos Aires'.

The Colón (Columbus) Cemetery is in Havana, Cuba. Located in the centre of the city, it was designed by Calixto de Loira in 1869. The cemetery has a Romanesque style portal with bas-relief by José Villalba de Saavedra, who also designed other pieces, such as the statue *Miraculous*. The faded magnificence of the Colón Cemetery depicts an extraordinary array of tombs and mausoleums.

In the late 1980s, Latin American countries have seen a change in the design of cemeteries. The cemetery city concept has been discontinued in favour of the cemetery garden, which emphasizes landscape architecture and concentrates less on individual objects.

JOSÉ BERNARDI

censorship

Restrictions on freedom of expression were endemic to Latin America throughout the twentieth century, but there is no single discernible pattern to censorship, other than its recurrence. Thus the issue of censorship can only be addressed in the context of each individual country.

Paraguay stands apart. General Alfredo **Stroessner**, who ruled the country from 1954 until his overthrow in 1989, corresponded most closely to the image of the military dictator who orders every evening what he wants to read in the next morning's papers.

In *Cuba*, the most curious case of direct censorship involved the poet Heberto **Padilla**. He was arrested on 20 March 1971, then released on 25 April after protests from fifty-four Latin American and European writers. Two days after his release, his 'confession', delivered at a meeting of the Cuban Writers Union (**UNEAC**), was broadcast throughout the country. Though the Cuban press had been severely restricted since Fidel **Castro**'s victory in 1959, the affair produced a general protest, although Latin American **intellectuals** were divided over the degree of commitment that a revolution could demand. Some, like Eduardo

Galeano, Julio **Cortázar** and Gabriel **García Márquez**, argued that the revolution had a right to defend itself from attack; others, including Mario **Vargas Llosa**, Carlos **Fuentes** and Juan **Rulfo**, were vociferously critical.

In *Brazil*, military rule began on 1 April 1964 under Marshal **Castello Branco**, who immediately imposed *de facto* press censorship. Law 5250, dated 9 February 1967, 'regulated freedom of thought and expression'. In fact it was his successor, Marshal Costa e Silva, who launched an unprecedented crackdown on individual freedom. Act No. 5, of 13 December 1968, modified the Constitution to allow the President to suspend the rights of any citizen; one of its articles threatened with arrest any commentator whose writings contravened the 1967 Press Law. An additional clause, dated 7 June 1969 and relating to the visit of Nelson Rockefeller, instructed the press 'not to publish or divulge in any form whatsoever news of acts hostile to our illustrious visitor'. On 26 January 1970 preventive censorship was imposed, requiring the submission of publications to the federal police prior to distribution. Twelve composers of popular music were also banned. Some newspapers, including the conservative *O Estado de São Paulo* attempted a rebellion of sorts; they would leave a blank space where pre-censored material should have appeared. When ordered not to embarrass the military in this way, they filled the space with a hymn or a poem, until they were ordered to replace the offending piece with a new article. The satirical weekly *O Pasquim* was regularly required to change its cover, until its entire staff was arrested in December 1970. The main target, of course, was the left-wing press, especially during the phase of urban guerrilla actions led by Carlos **Marighela** in the 1970s. Towards the end of the 1970s censorship was slightly relaxed, but was not lifted until the return to elected civilian rule in 1985.

In *Peru*, on 3 October 1968, General Juan **Velasco Alvarado** led a nationalist *coup* against the elected President Fernando **Belaúnde Terry**. The new government closed down two radio stations as well as the liberal weekly *Caretas*, whose editor Enrique Zileri Gibson was obliged to leave the country for nearly two months, despite the cautious protests of *El Comercio*, *La Prensa* and

Correo. Subsequently, all newspapers with more than 20,000 circulation were reallocated to 'organized sections of society'. The first Freedom of the Press Statute (December 1969), ordered the *peruanization* of the press; only native-born citizens could hold shares. Next day several papers were fined for not printing the name of the proprietor, as required by the Statute. *Caretas* led a critical campaign against the new rules. In July 1974, a new Press Law ruled that newspapers had to have a social function. Thus *El Comercio*'s new editor represented the farming or *campesino* sector, for example; *Ultima hora* was allocated to the cooperative sector, *Correo* went to the professions, *Ojo* to musicians and artists, *Expreso* and *Extra* to the teaching profession. *Caretas* was closed down and its editor and publisher exiled to Buenos Aires. The ruling represented a unique experiment linked to the concept of 'development journalism' launched in 1967 by the Press Foundation of Asia, and to the UNESCO-inspired New World Information Order, which met sustained criticism in the West. By the end of 1978, most of the 'socialized' press was near bankruptcy; a year later, the military government advised former owners that they could have their papers back.

Chile's experience was as blatant as Peru's, but much more brutal. The *coup* of September 1973 led by Augusto **Pinochet**, which overthrew the constitutional government of Salvador **Allende**, unleashed a savage repression against all the opposition press; though it was prepared to ignore the occasional and timid criticisms coming from the conservative, establishment press. That repression was best symbolized by the decision to round up and detain all its opponents in the National Stadium. Those arrested included journalists like Manuel Cabieses, Jorge Pacull and Oscar Waiss, radio and television broadcasters, and the personnel of the **Quimantú** publishing house, which was immediately closed. The regime's propaganda claimed to have discovered '13,000 foreign extremists in Chile'. The home of the Nobel Prize-winning poet Pablo **Neruda**, who died shortly after the *coup*, was raided and many of his possessions destroyed. Newspapers which had supported Allende, like *Clarín*, *Puro Chile*, *La Nación* and others were closed down. A newly appointed official censor ordered an immediate ban on thirty-seven books, mainly economics and political science texts; books seized from private homes and libraries were burned. The regime claimed it was destroying Marxist texts, because **Marxism** was banned, but its criteria extended to the work of most of the leading Latin American writers of the time. Despite later attempts by Pinochet to blur the memory of those days, it was the burning of books and the savage torture of individuals which will remain the remembered hallmarks of the Pinochet regime.

Uruguay would not have appeared in this survey until June 1973, when President Juan María Bordaberry oversaw the military takeover of the country, ostensibly in order to defeat the **Tupamaros** guerrillas. Until then, it was known as the 'Switzerland of Latin America'; yet it soon became, in the words of US Senator Frank Church, 'the biggest torture chamber on the continent'. Yet neither torture nor the battle against the urban guerrillas gained as much notoriety as the arrest of the leading writer Juan Carlos **Onetti**. He had been a judge on a literary panel assembled by the left-wing magazine *Marcha*, which awarded its annual prize to Nelson Marra for his short story 'El guardaespaldas' (The Bodyguard), a detailed description of a familiar political character of the time. *Marcha* (which had already been banned in Argentina in 1966) was closed on 9 February 1974 and Carlos Quijano and Hugo Alfaro, its co-editors, and Marra and Onetti were arrested. The detainees were later released into exile. The accounts of torture and repression grew in horror from then on. Leading literary critics like the brothers Carlos and Angel **Rama** were forced into exile, as were writers like Eduardo **Galeano** and Mario **Benedetti**. Censorship reached absurd proportions; the conservative poet Juan Zorrilla de San Martín (1855–1931) was banned from local libraries, as were some of the writings of national hero José Artigas concerning freedom. The regime even pursued its detractors into Argentina with the help of local paramilitaries; the capture of journalist Enrique Rodríguez Larreta in July 1976 and his clandestine return to Uruguay was a case in point. Although press and radio began to recover some freedoms in the late 1970s, it was only with the restoration of constitutional rule in the mid-1980s that full freedoms were restored.

Argentina has its own place in the history of terror in Latin America; it gave the language the term '**disappeared**' to describe what happened to enemies of governments even before the beginning of military rule in 1976. The exact number of the disappeared will probably never be known, but it ranges from the 9,000 cases investigated by Amnesty International to the 30,000 claimed by the relatives of the missing. It is estimated that ninety-seven journalists and writers, from well known names like Haroldo **Conti** and Francisco **Urondo** to unknown newsroom staff 'disappeared' during the regime of General Jorge **Videla** (1976–80). Censorship was seldom open and direct; critical voices were simply 'disappeared' or murdered and self-censorship increasingly ensured a tame press. A whole generation of intellectuals grew up in exile. There is some dispute as to the date of Argentina's decline into terror; the crisis expressed in the terror and counter-terror of the mid-1970s had its origins in the *coup* of June 1966, led by General Onganía, which ended the period of civilian rule cautiously set in train after the overthrow of **Perón** in 1955. Now aged and infirm, Perón returned from exile in June 1973 and died a year later, having been re-elected to the Presidency. The ensuing violence marked the battle for Perón's political inheritance among his own followers; the military then stepped in and claimed power in what rapidly became a virtual civil war.

Argentina's tragic descent into terror could be foreseen. When Perón was elected President in 1946 and expropriated much of the press, the society became deeply divided. The ideological differences that resulted from the Cold War served merely to exacerbate the split between pro- and anti-Perónistas. The defeat of the military governments came indirectly, and as the result of a combination of economic crisis and the failure to reclaim possession of the British-occupied Falkland islands (see **Malvinas**) in April 1982. The defeat at Port Stanley paved the way for elections in 1983, constitutional rule and a cultural renaissance.

Speaking at a meeting of writers called by Nobel Prize-winner Octavio **Paz** in 1992, Mario **Vargas Llosa** called *Mexico* the perfect dictatorship. This was refuted by Paz, who argued that, at worst, it was a case of one-party rule. Freedom of expression and of religious belief are enshrined in Mexico's 1917 Constitution; yet censorship exists in many forms. Some Mexican intellectuals argue that it is neither institutional nor systematic; nevertheless, there clearly are restrictions, largely corresponding to the needs of the dominant Institutional Revolutionary Party (**PRI**) whose six-year President is a virtual dictator for the duration of their regime. The Mexican economy, including the press, publishing and the arts, is dominated by thirty-three family groups integrated in various ways into the ruling party. But the PRI also includes the local civil servants, policemen or party bosses who set the rules, and the State monopoly of newsprint has provided a useful additional weapon. In that atmosphere, self-censorship has been preferred over official restrictions, and official patronage of individual writers and artists has provided another means of dealing with protest. In addition to the PRI, the Roman Catholic Church (see **Catholicism**) remains strong in the poorest areas, where dissident groups might emerge to challenge the PRI. In the mid-1990s, however, small voices of defiance began to be heard; the newspapers *La Reforma* in Mexico City, *El Norte* in Monterrey and *Zeta* in Tijuana, the dailies *La Jornada* and *El Financiero* and the magazine *Crisis*, all published in the capital, decided to defy the political class and appeared to win public support and approval.

In *Central America*, three particular cases are significant. In *Nicaragua*, the murder of Pedro Joaquín **Chamorro**, owner-editor of *La Prensa*, in 1978 by the Somoza dictatorship (see **Somoza dynasty**) set in motion a train of events that led to the Sandinista revolutionary victory in July 1979 (see **Sandinista Revolution**). In 1990 Chamorro's widow Violeta was elected to the presidency, with the defeat of the Sandinistas at the polls. In *El Salvador* it was another murder, that of Archbishop Oscar **Romero**, archbishop of San Salvador, that focused world attention on the repression of human rights in that country, where civil war claimed tens of thousands of lives through the 1980s. In *Guatemala*, the '**death squads**' ruled the press and broadcasting, threatening journalists in national and local media. As the regime of terror

grew under a series of military rulers through the 1970s and 1980s, the free press was an early casualty, as the intellectual community was subjected to terror, murder and exile. It remains to be seen how a free press can be built in the fragile peace initiated in 1996.

Further reading

Annual Reports of *Reporters sans frontières* (Paris) and *Attacks on the Press*, New York: Annual Report of the Committee to Protect Journalists.

Article 19, an annual publication concerned with censorship and containing individual country entries, London: Article 19.

Graham-Yooll, A. (1984) *The Press in Argentina*, London: Writers and Scholars Educational Trust.

Index on Censorship, particularly issues (1972) I/2 (On the Padilla case), I/3–4 (on Brazil), (1977) VI/5 (on Argentina) VI/6 (on Guatemala).

Press Freedom in the Americas: Unpunished Crimes Against Journalists (1977), Interamerican Press Association.

ANDREW GRAHAM-YOOLL

Centraal Historisch Archief van de Nederlandse Antillen

The Centraal Historisch Archief van de Nederlandse Antillen (Central Historical Archives of the Netherlands Antilles), or CHA, was founded in 1969 in Willemstad, Curaçao and houses nineteenth- and twentieth-century documents of the government of the Netherlands Antilles. Those over forty years old can be consulted freely. Since the 1980s, with a new building and modern facilities, many private collections have also been entrusted to the CHA. Older government documents were shipped to the Netherlands before the Second World War, and were placed in the national archives in The Hague to prevent them from further decay.

AART G. BROEK

Central American and Caribbean Games

Mexico, Cuba and Guatemala competed in the Central American Games in Mexico City in 1926. These were the first regional games in the Western Hemisphere recognized by the International Olympic Committee. Interrupted only by the Second World War, the festival has been held each four years since. Its name changed in 1938 to Central American and Caribbean Games. Around thirty countries, all but El Salvador touching the Caribbean Sea, are eligible to participate in this event, whose eighteenth repetition was held in Maracaibo in 1998 with a programme of thirty-one sports. Cuba, Mexico and Puerto Rico have won the most Central American and Caribbean medals.

RICHARD V. MCGEHEE

Central American Common Market

The Central American Common Market (CACM) was founded in December 1960. The original plan, formulated by ECLA, was designed to encourage a gradual process of regional planning and development in which the stronger economies of the region would aid the weaker ones. The final agreement, by contrast, emphasized free trade and therefore open access for North American capital; this combined well with the perspectives of the **Alliance for Progress** in encouraging controlled growth. Central America had not undergone the **import substitution industrialization** of other Latin American economies; the CACM, therefore, prompted a development of manufacturing that absorbed some 60 per cent of the foreign investment, which multiplied ten times in the course of the 1960s. In those ten years industries like fertilizers, cosmetics, plastic and pharmaceuticals grew alongside more traditional ones like tobacco and textiles. The share of industry in regional GDP grew from 13 per cent to 18 per cent in that period. Yet by the end of the decade, it was clear that most of that industry was controlled by US interests and that the social structure of the region ensured that the elite alone would consume its products. The

new class of businessmen and the modernizing military were as dependent on US capital as their predecessors in agriculture had been – and certainly had no interest in the independent regional development that ECLA, for all its extreme caution, had proposed in the early 1950s. US investment (which was the bulk of foreign capital present in the area) began to dwindle. The regional market was too small to merit further investment, and the majority of Central Americans benefitted little from the CACM experience. Indeed the weaker regional economies, like Honduras, found themselves in increasing debt to their stronger neighbours – one of the direct causes of the 1969 '**football** war' with El Salvador that initiated the definitive crisis in the CACM. As it gradually declined, US capital found a different method of investment in Central America; on the one hand, this involved the 'modernization' of its traditional corporate interests in the region, with the giant banana companies, for example, moving into processing and distribution. On the other, the assembly industries moved in to take advantage of the low-wage Central American economies to produce goods for re-export to Europe and the USA. Twenty years after the creation of the CACM, Central America was more, not less, in thrall to corporate US capital.

Further reading

Dunkerley, J. (1988) *Power in the Isthmus: A Political History of Modern Central America*, London: Verso.
Pearce, J. (1981) *Under the Eagle: US Intervention in Central America and the Caribbean*, London: Latin America Bureau.

MIKE GONZALEZ

Central Trinidad Potters

The craft of clay pottery was brought to Trinidad in the nineteenth century by indentured plantation labourers from the Indian subcontinent, and has been passed on through families since. The clay is extracted from land surrounding the town of Chaguanas, where the potteries are concentrated, mixed with sand, soaked and trampled upon until the colour, consistency and even the sound of the moist clay indicate that it is ready for working. The potters are particularly relied upon for the Divali Nagar festival, the Hindu festival of lights, to supply the *deyahs*, tiny oil-filled lamps, which light the way for Maha Lakshmi, goddess of light and spiritual wealth.

LORRAINE LEU

Centro Costarricense de Producción Cinematográfica

Costa Rica's national film institute, Centro Costarricense de Producción Cinematográfica (Costa Rican Centre for Cinema Production) a branch of the Ministry of Culture, was founded in 1973 by Kitico Moreno. The early emphasis on documentary production in the 1970s gave way to efforts to educate audiences and disseminate local films on video in the 1980s. Thereafter, the CCPC has focused on coproduction ventures while still supporting local film-makers. In 1995, to commemorate the centenary of cinema in Latin America, CCPC Director Rogelio Chacón effected the restoration of the country's first feature film, *El Retorno* (The Homecoming) (1930), directed by A.F. **Bertoni**. The 90-minute melodrama was projected onto the screen of the Variedades cinema, where it had premiered decades earlier.

Centro Cultural Banco do Brasil

The Centro Cultural Banco do Brasil was built between 1880 and 1906, to a design in the historicist style by Francisco Bethencourt da Silva, to house the Public Stock Exchange. The building was later adapted for different administrative and commercial purposes. In 1923 it became the headquarters of the Banco do Brasil, and remained so until 1989 when the financial function was replaced by the promotion and diffusion of cultural values. The bank offices were converted into a cultural centre with specific areas for theatre, film, plastic arts, literature and social sciences, contributing to the revitalization of Rio de Janeiro's historic centre.

See also: banks

ROBERTO CONDURU

Centro Cultural Borges

Centro Cultural Borges is a cultural centre in the Galerías Pacífico in downtown Buenos Aires. It was inaugurated in October 1995 after an irregular public bidding process for the Galerías in 1989, which brought protests from Fernando **Solanas**. In its vast space, the Centro has an auditorium, exhibition spaces and classrooms, and other facilities; it has a permanent exhibition honouring **Borges**, including some first editions and manuscripts. The Centro has staged national and international painting and sculpture exhibitions, as well as concerts and other cultural activities. Since 1997, dancer Julio **Bocca** and painter Guillermo **Kuitca**, among others, have given lectures and classes there.

FERNANDO RABOSSI

Centro Cultural Recoleta

An important cultural centre located in a wealthy Buenos Aires neighbourhood, the Centro Cultural Recoleta was designed by Clorindo **Testa**, Luis **Benedit** and Jacques Bedel, using some of the existing structures of the former Recoleta monastery. The multi-purpose site includes exhibition halls, film-screening facilities and an auditorium. Its eclectic mixture of architectural styles makes it one of the most visited postmodern structures in Buenos Aires. In the late 1990s, the opening of the adjacent Centro de Diseño, a commercial centre filled with design outlets and restaurants, increased the lively street culture in the area.

LAURA PODALSKY

Centro Editor de América Latina

Centro Editor de América Latina (CEAL) was founded by José Boris Spivakow on 21 September 1966 after his forced departure from the University of Buenos Aires publishing house (**EU-DEBA**) in the wake of the Onganía military *coup* of June that year. Beatriz **Sarlo** described CEAL as 'a publishing company in a hurry', the best description of the business of an intellectual anxious to record Argentina's literary and historic heritage in popular editions before devastation by military censorship.

The CEAL publishing venture began under Spivakow's overall control with editor Horacio Achaval's *Serie del Encuentro* (Encounter Series), which in 1966 included forty-three titles by new and established authors. This was followed by popular, low cost newsstand editions that included children's books like *Cuentos de Polidoro* (Polidoro's Tales) (1967), and by a variety of general information books, the *Biblioteca de Economía* (Economic Library) series (1967–9) on the economy, *Los hombres de la historia* (The Men of History) (1968) about the men and women who shaped world history, and an account of Argentine history under the general title of *Polémica* (Polemics) which ran over 146 weekly issues. Other series covered Latin American history and a history of the working class in the River Plate region (1972). Its most popular series was *Capítulo* (Chapter) (1979), a weekly chronicle of Argentine writers which ran excerpts and comments from the earliest writers under Spanish colonial rule to the most recent and best-known Argentine writers. Each week readers would queue for their weekly copy, which also included a cheap paperback.

Siglomundo (1968) was the company's most popular as well as best-selling collection, edited by Jorge Lafforgue and covering twentieth-century history. The series that followed, *Narradores de hoy,* (Contemporary Writers) edited by Luis Gregorich, embraced the best of contemporary Argentine writing, including among others Isidoro Blaisten, Jorge **Asís** and Liliana Hecker. The company was always a ground-breaker, but was branded as left wing and dangerous by the military. With the restoration of constitutional rule in 1983 the company tried to keep going, but it was under-capitalized and its important, indeed great work was over. The company was wound up by the heirs of Spivakow in 1995.

Further reading

Spivakow, B. (1995) *Memoria de un sueño argentino. Entrevistas de Delia Maunás*, Buenos Aires: Colihue.

ANDREW GRAHAM-YOOLL

Centro Nacional de las Artes

Mexico City's Centro Nacional de las Artes (CENART) is a subdivision of Mexico's **Consejo Nacional para la Cultura y las Artes** charged with education and research in the arts. Since its creation in 1994, it has become an important instrument of cultural dissemination. CENART sponsors a wide range of programmes designed to provide Mexico's future artists with a combination of formal education coupled with practice/apprenticeship. Five schools have been formed, in which students receive the education and training needed to exercise the disciplines of theatre, cinema, dance, music and the visual arts, as well as four research centres, a library and a physical infrastructure consisting of museums, galleries, indoor and outdoor theatres, movie houses, auditoriums in which students present their productions.

EDUARDO GUÍZAR-ALVAREZ

Cepeda, Orlando

b. 1937, Ponce, Puerto Rico

Baseball player

Cepeda played professional **baseball** in the US major leagues from 1958 until 1974. Speaking little English, he began his career in the USA playing for a racist field manager who tried to ruin Cepeda's standing. Cepeda's career was plagued by controversy (usually not of his own making), but he hit the most home runs of any Latin American in major league baseball (tying Tony **Pérez**). After his playing career ended, Cepeda was imprisoned in Puerto Rico for smuggling marijuana, but his selfless community work upon his release restored his reputation.

DOUGLAS W. VICK

ceramics

The ceramic tradition (*alfarería*) in Latin America dates from pre-Columbian times. Ceramic objects, ranging from musical instruments, household implements like the *comal* (a flat griddle) and the mortar and pestle (*molcajete*), figures, religious artefacts such as incense burners (*sahumarios*), funeral urns and representations of deities, are crucial archaeological evidence. Pottery was not merely functional but embodied a high level of design and decoration. Each region had distinctive designs, but many of the geometric themes still feature in contemporary pottery.

With the Conquest, the Spaniards brought to America their ceramic tradition known as Talavera. Hernán Cortés' house, which survives in Puebla, Mexico, is decorated with original Talavera glazed tiles, and the city has many other examples decorating houses and churches. Local potters continue to make highly decorative glazed ceramics.

Since the Conquest a fusion between pre-Columbian and Colonial styles, techniques and imagery has taken place. Though ceramic art is still regarded as a craft (see **crafts**), ceramics has progressed from the purely functional – or a vehicle to generate tourist revenue – to an increasingly well-respected art form in its own right. Metepec, State of Mexico, for example, has grown from the manufacture of everyday household objects and *cuadrillas*, figures and animals made for the curing ceremonies of local medicine men (*curanderos*), to become a flourishing centre of production of Trees of Life (*árboles de la vida*) – ranging from miniatures to gigantic clay sculptures. The trees can be vibrantly painted with a mixture of aniline and acrylic paints, glazed or simply left as fired terracotta; imagery can range from themes such as Bible stories and the history of Mexico to the interpretation of dreams and contemporary literature.

The ceramic industry, like many other Latin American popular arts, involves the entire family and women often have an important role, as can be seen in the Tarascan Indian village of Ocumichu, Michoacán in western Mexico; well known for its humorous, erotic clay devils, mermaids and religious scenes, painted with strong colours. These have developed to supplement rural incomes and are aimed at popular art collectors and tourists alike. Whilst families work collectively, competition is fierce between different families.

Further reading

Gori, I. (1975) *Arte popular latinoamericano: Brasil, Chile, Peru*, Buenos Aires: Centro Editor de America Latina.

Magrassi, G.E. (1977) *Arte popular latinoamericano: Ecuador, Guatemala, Colombia*, Buenos Aires: Centro Editor de America Latina.

Sayer, C. (1990) *Arts and Crafts of Mexico*, London: Thames & Hudson.

JAN NIMMO

Cerruto, Oscar

b. 1912, La Paz, Bolivia; d. 1981, La Paz

Writer

Cerruto was one of the most important figures in contemporary Bolivian literature. A poet, short story writer and novelist, he introduced many innovations that superseded traditional notions about literature. Part of the Chaco Generation, a term referring to an ideological current emerging after the **Chaco War** (1932–5) which focused on a nationalist vision, his novel *Aluvión de fuego* (Fireflood) (1935) is representative of the period. His poetry and short stories are also important. Cerruto was a career diplomat.

MARÍA DORA VILLA GÓMEZ

Cerutti Guldberg, Horacio

b. 1950, Mendoza, Argentina

Philosopher

One of Latin America's most important historians of ideas and a key figure in the philosophy of liberation, Cerutti also specializes in political philosophy and epistemology. Now a naturalized Mexican, his contributions to the discussion about Utopian thought have been of fundamental significance throughout Latin America. He is a researcher at the Latin American Studies Coordinating Centre and a professor of Philosophy at the Mexican National University (**UNAM**).

CARLOS OLIVA MENDOZA

Cervantes, Antonio ('Kid Pambele')

b. 1945, San Basilio de Palenque, Colombia

Boxer

One of the best ever junior welterweights, Cervantes made his professional debut in January, 1964 and won the World Boxing Association title in December 1972, knocking out Panama's Alfonso Fraser. He successfully defended the title ten times, losing on points to Puerto Rico's Wilfred Benítez in March 1976 and winning it back in June 1977 against Argentine Carlos Giménez. After six more successful defences he lost it to Aaron Pryor of the USA in August 1980 and retired in 1983 with a record of 66 wins (36 by knockout), 12 defeats and one draw. He later became addicted to drugs.

ERIC WEIL

Césaire, Aimé

b. 1913, Basse-Pointe, Martinique

Poet and playwright

One of the founders of the **négritude** movement in Francophone literature, Césaire was also an important politician in his native Martinique. His poetry stands out as a culminating example of French modernism, while also occupying a pre-eminent place among twentieth century texts of the African diaspora.

Césaire was born in Basse-Pointe in the north of Martinique, then a French colony, to a family of moderate means which valued formal education and high French culture. He attended the prestigious Lycée Schoelcher in Martinique's capital, Fort-de-France, where he met Léon Gontran **Damas**, from the French colony of Guyane,

whose later collection of poetry, *Pigments* (1937), occupied an important place in the *négritude* movement. In 1932, Césaire was awarded a scholarship to study in France, where he met Léopold Senghor, poet and future president of Senegal, with whom he formed a lasting friendship; these two were the main forces behind the *négritude* movement. Césaire entered the Ecole Normale Supérieure in Paris in 1935 and obtained his diploma in 1939, with a thesis on the theme of the South in African-American literature. That same year he published his first and most influential book of poetry, **Cahier d'un retour au pays natal** (Notebook of a Return to The Native Land) in a small magazine in Paris.

Césaire's meeting with Senghor was a psycholgical seismic shock. In Senghor, he found a representative of an African culture untainted by the negative images propagated by the French colonial system. It made possible Césaire's discovery of his own African-ness. Paris in the 1930s was in intellectual ferment. In vogue at this time were African and African-American art forms ranging from African sculpture to US blues and jazz. The writers of the Harlem Renaissance, particularly Claude **McKay** and Langston Hughes, enjoyed great success; they, along with young Haitian poets such as Jacques **Roumain**, were the proximate models for these young black Francophone poets. (Césaire was relatively untouched by the Afro-Cuban movement until after the war.) Senghor and Césaire read widely on African culture, particularly the anthropological works of Frobenius; they were also steeped in the poetic tradition of late nineteenth-century France – Rimbaud, Verlaine, Mallarmé – and the burgeoning modernist movements that capitalized on these predecessors. Part of the attraction of French modernism – particularly of surrealism – was its revolutionary stance, its will to contest the values of Western civilization. This also brought Césaire to Marxism, which had the added attraction of addressing the colonial question and of associating capitalist society with imperialism.

These intellectual avenues converge in the *Cahier*, written between 1936 and 1939 and revised numerous times thereafter. A long, impassioned, semi-autobiographical poem, it tells of the narrator's return to the island of his birth. The poem is a journey at the end of which the narrator accepts his people's history of suffering, his island geography, his body, his blackness. Hence the term *négritude*, by which Césaire meant the recognition of being black, and the acceptance of black history and culture.

Shortly before the Second World War, Césaire returned to Martinique and a post at the Lycée Schoelcher, teaching such future writers as Frantz **Fanon**, Edouard **Glissant** and Joseph **Zobel**. He also published the literary journal *Tropiques* from 1941–5, a key surrealist magazine of the time.

The end of the war in 1945 marked Césaire's entrance into politics, representing Martinique to the Constituent Assembly as a member of the Communist Party. Shortly thereafter he successfully introduced to the French Parliament legislation to turn the colonies of Martinique, Guadeloupe, Guyane and Réunion into departments of France, with full rights of citizenship. This move, prompted by a general postwar optimism, had sparked criticism from those advocating Martinican independence. Césaire himself quickly grew disillusioned with departmental status, especially given the French Parliament's turn towards the right during the Cold War. Césaire also later broke with the Communist Party and formed his own party, the Parti Progressiste Martiniquais, which continues to play an important role in Martinican politics.

Césaire's reputation as a major surrealist poet was confirmed by the publication in 1946 of *Les armes miraculeuses* (The Miraculous Weapons), and by the subsequent publication of *Soleil cou coupé* (Solar Throat Slashed) (1948) and *Corps perdu* (Lost Body) (1950), this last illustrated by Picasso. Césaire also published in 1950 his influential essay, *Discours sur le colonialisme* (Discourse on Colonialism), a ringing condemnation of European colonialism and racism from a rather orthodox Marxist position. *Ferrements* (Ferraments) (1960) initiated a mature poetic phase, more accessible and moving, especially in the elegiac pieces devoted to Louis Delgres, Paul Eluard and others; this tone is also present in the later volume, *moi, laminaire* (i, laminaria) (1982).

Césaire was also a distinguished playwright, an activity allowing him a more direct communication with his public. His *La Tragédie du roi Christophe* (The Tragedy of King Christophe) (1961–3) treats a historical figure from post-independence Haiti, while his last play, *Une Tempête* (A Tempest) (1969), is a reworking of Shakespeare's *The Tempest*, which has provided much material for Caribbean writers interested in colonialism.

See also: Caliban

Further reading

Arnold, A.J. (1981) *Modernism and Negritude: The Poetry and Poetics of Aimé Césaire*, Cambridge, MA: Harvard University Press.

Césaire, A. (1976) *Oeuvres complètes*, Fort-de-France: Désormeaux.

—— (1983) *The Collected Poetry*, trans. C. Eshleman and A. Smith, Berkeley, CA: University of California Press.

Irele, A. (ed.) (1994) *Cahier d'un retour au pays natal*, Ibadan, New Horn.

Pallister, J.L. (1991) *Aimé Césaire*, New York: Twayne.

BEN A. HELLER

César, Ana Cristina

b. 1952, Rio de Janeiro, Brazil; d. 1983, Rio de Janeiro

Writer

In the early 1980s César published her most important works: *Literatura não é documentação* (Literature is not Documentation), on the political ramifications of documentary film; and two volumes of poetry that contained powerful, political metaphors for lesbian voices – *Luvas de pelica* (Kid Gloves) (1980), and *A teus pés* (At Your Feet) (1982). César was an integral part of the 'Mimeograph Generation' (see **marginal poets**). She committed suicide after returning to Rio de Janeiro from studying abroad.

SUSAN CANTY QUINLAN

Céspedes, Augusto

b. 1903, Cochabamba, Bolivia

Writer

One of Bolivia's best-known writers, Céspedes is identified with Bolivian **populism** and with the intellectual currents that led to the **Bolivian Revolution** of 1952. *Sangre de mestizos* (Blood of Mestizos) (1936) is a group of eight linked stories about the suffering of the common soldiers in the desert **Chaco War** between Bolivia and Paraguay (1932–5). *Metal del diablo* (The Devil's Metal) (1946) is a fictive biography of the Bolivian tin baron Simón I. Patiño, and is thought to have contributed to the nationalization of the tin mines in the revolution of 1952. Céspedes served in the Bolivian congress in 1938 and 1944, and also worked in the diplomatic service, most notably as Bolivian ambassador to UNESCO in 1978.

DANIEL BALDERSTON

Céspedes, Diógenes

b. 1941, Santo Domingo, Dominican
   Republic

Critic

Professor Céspedes is one of the few Dominican critics with a solid academic formation in literature. He studied with the famous semotician A.J. Greimas and with Henri Meschonnic, and obtained his Ph.D. from the University of Paris VIII. Among his most important books are *Seis ensayos sobre poética latinoamericana* (Six Essays on Latin American Poetics) (1983), *Estudios sobre literatura, cultura e ideologías* (Studies on Literature, Culture and Ideologies) (1983) and *Lenguaje y poesía en Santo Domingo en el siglo XX* (Language and Poetry in Santo Domingo during the Twentieth Century) (1985). Since 1982 he has been the director of *Cuadernos de Poética* (Poetry Notebooks).

FERNANDO VALERIO-HOLGUÍN

Céspedes García Menocal, Carlos Manuel de

b. 1929, Havana, Cuba

Priest

Recognized as one of the intellectual leaders of the Cuban Catholic church, he is a direct descendant of Carlos Manuel de Céspedes, leader of Cuba's nineteenth-century independence struggles. He studied theology in Havana before attending the Gregorian University in Rome, and was ordained in 1961. He was Vicar-General of the Havana archdiocese. He founded and continued to edit the journal *Vivarium*, regarded as the most important Catholic cultural journal to be published since the Cuban Revolution (see **revolutions**). In 1994 he published *Recuento* (Anthology), a collection of his articles from the 'Catholic World' section of *El mundo*.

WILFREDO CANCIO ISLA

ceviche

Ceviche (also spelled with 's' and 'b') is a typical dish made of raw shrimp or fish, marinated in lime or lemon juice and tomato, onions and green pepper. Usually served as a first course, it is popular in the coastal areas, but is eaten throughout Ecuador as well as parts of Mexico, Peru and Colombia.

MERCEDES ROBLES

cha cha cha

The cha cha cha is Cuban musical form derived from the **danzón** which emerged at the end of the 1940s. Its structure is similar to danzón, but it is the core rhythm that gives it its distinct character. Cha cha cha is an onomatopeia, describing two rapid beats followed by one longer beat which represents the movements of the dancer. Enrique Jorrín (Cuba, 1926–87) is regarded as its creator, since it was his song 'La engañadora' (Cheating Woman)

(1951) which made the rhythm internationally famous.

JUAN CARLOS QUINTERO HERENCIA

chacal de Nahueltoro, El

Based on a shocking real event in the early 1960s in Chile, *El chacal de Nahueltoro* (The Jackal of Nahueltoro) is one of the most significant works of **New Latin American Cinema**. Directed by Miguel **Littín** in 1970, the film tells the story of José (played by the wonderful actor Nelson Villagra), an illiterate peasant who had murdered his girlfriend and her five children in a drunken stupor. Narratively complex and stylistically eclectic, the film proceeds non-chronologically, beginning with José's arrest in an almost *cinéma vérité* **documentary** mode and, through flashbacks, leads us to understand the background to the crimes. Littín brilliantly analyses the forces surrounding the killer and, in the end, indicts the Chilean system: when José is finally 'educated' in prison – learning to read and write, smile, play soccer, make friends – he is executed. *El Chacal* was exhibited during Salvador **Allende**'s successful election campaign in trade unions and schools; later it was released in theatres and eventually seen by an estimated 500,000 people.

ANA M. LÓPEZ

Chacarita, La

Though the Recoleta is more frequented by tourists, the Chacarita holds a special place in the mythology of the city. It is considered the middle-class cemetery, in contradistinction to the aristocratic **Recoleta**. Some of the tombs are prone to the same extravagance that marks the ornate tombs in the Recoleta, they are largely those of popular heroes: Juan Domingo **Perón**, Carlos **Gardel** (often with a lighted cigarette in his bronze hand), the aviator Jorge Newbery. **Borges** wrote a famous poem about the Chacarita in *Cuaderno San Martín* (San Martín Copybook) (1929), and in the note on the poem he tells a fascinating story about an experience he had during the night of the

electoral triumph of Hipólito Yrigoyen when – in a neighbourhood centre of the **Unión Cívica Radical** just outside the cemetery wall – he and a friend joined the local *compadritos* in saluting the image of the once and future president.

DANIEL BALDERSTON

Chacha, Armando

b. 1956, Veracruz, Mexico

Composer and singer

Mexican composer and singer of trova music, with themes centred principally around Mexican social and cultural issues. An anthropologist by profession and a musician by vocation, Chacha's (born Armando Chacha Antele) strong interest in and support of popular culture is reflected in his position as General Co-ordinator of CONACUL-TA's Programa de Apoyo a las Culturas Municipales y Comunitarias (Programme for Cultural Support of Municipalities and Communities). His compositions have been recorded on three disks to date, *Biografía rota* (Broken Biography) (1985), *Litorales* (Coastlines) (1991) and *Matamba* (1999), a word of African origin that is the name of a town in Veracruz with African heritage. The latter recording features rhythms typical of Veracruz, in particular, those with indigenous and African influences, such as the **son jarocho**, the **danzón**, the **bolero** and the son montuno.

EDUARDO GUÍZAR-ALVAREZ

Chaco War

A long-standing border dispute between Paraguay and Bolivia over the Chaco region erupted into war on 15 June 1932; the specific motive was a rumour (unfounded as it transpired) that there were oil deposits in this inhospitable region. The three-year war left an enormous toll of dead on both sides – many of them dead of thirst or hunger. From the Paraguayan side, **Roa Bastos** described its raw horror in his novel *Hijo de hombre* (Son of Man) (1960); from the Bolivian perspective, Augusto **Céspedes**'s *Sangre de mestizos* (Mestizo blood) (1983) told a similar story. On 12 June 1935, the belligerents agreed to submit to arbitration. Peace was finally signed in July 1938, granting most of the region to Paraguay but guaranteeing Bolivia an outlet to the sea along the Paraguay River.

PABLO JAVIER ANSOLABEHERE

Chacón, Iris

b. 1950, Santurce, Puerto Rico

Singer

Chacón's physical appearance and moves have made her 'the showgirl (*la vedette*) of America and the world'. Her rapid rise to fame in the 1970s and early 1980s transformed her into a symbol of Caribbean sensuality. Successes like 'Caramelo y chocolate' (Candy and Chocolate) and 'Me gusta, me gusta' (I Like It), and her choreographies made the 'Iris Chacón Show' the most popular show on Puerto Rican **television**. She has been the subject of work by writers like Luis Rafael **Sánchez** and Edgardo **Rodríguez Juliá**.

JUAN CARLOS QUINTERO HERENCIA

Chacrinha

b. 1916, Surubim, Pernambuco; d. 1988, Rio de Janeiro, Brazil

Television entertainer

Born José Abelardo Barbosa de Medeiros, the 'Old Warrior' Chacrinha dominated Brazilian television for nearly thirty years with several irreverent, carnivalesque comedy hours, including 'A Hora da Buzina' and 'A Discoteca do Chacrinha'. In the late 1960s, he helped to popularize rising stars of **MPB**, including Caetano **Veloso** and Gilberto **Gil**, the leaders of a cultural movement called *tropicalismo*. Resolutely low-brow and often grotesque, Chacrinha was generally adored by the Brazilian masses and detested by the left-wing intelligentsia, who regarded his programmes as politically alienated, if not reactionary.

CHRISTOPHER DUNN

Chagas' disease

Discovered in 1909, Chagas' disease, also called American trypanosomiasis, is an infectious disease caused by the protozoan parasite Trypanosoma cruzi, that travels to humans mainly through the bite of triatomine bugs, a particular order of sucking insects. Characterized by the invasion and deterioration of cardiac, gastrointestinal, and nervous tissue, it affects some 18 million people in Central and South America. One of Latin America's major public health problems, it debilitates and kills adults in the prime of life. Infection rates are higher in Bolivia than in any other Latin American country. Currently, there is no cure for the chronic stage of Chagas' disease, but it can be controlled through improved housing and hygiene.

EDUARDO GUÍZAR-ALVAREZ

Chahín, Plinio

b. 1959, Santo Domingo, Dominican Republic

Poet

With José **Mármol**, Dionisio de **Jesús**, Tomás **Castro** and Adrián **Javier**, Chahín belongs to the generation of the 1980s which originated around the *Taller Literario César Vallejo*, sponsored by the Department of Culture of the Universidad Autónoma de Santo Domingo. Chahín's first two books are *Consumación de la carne* (Consummation of the Flesh) and *Solemnidades de la muerte* (Solemnities of Death). Informed by Octavio **Paz**'s aesthetics, his poetry explores the metaphysics of everyday life and the power of words.

FERNANDO VALERIO-HOLGUÍN

Chalbaud, Román

b. 1931, Mérida, Venezuela

Playwright, theatre and film director

Co-founder, with José Ignacio **Cabrujas** and Isaac **Chocrón**, of the Nuevo Grupo theatre group, he entered Venezuelan theatre in the 1960s and changed its face for ever. Probing the grotesque sides of the individual and set in the poor quarters of the city, Chalbaud's work represents a new critical realist exploration of contemporary democratic and urban Venezuela. His works have become classics of Venezuelan theatre, but his major impact has been in cinema, with key works like *Sagrado y obsceno* (Sacred and Obscene), *Carmen la que contaba dieciseis años* (Carmen who was Sixteen) and *La oveja negra* (The Black Sheep).

JORGE ROMERO LEÓN

chamamé

Chamamé is a form of popular music and dance from northeastern Argentina. The origin of the word is obscure, but the genre replaced the older polka of Corrientes, whose roots were American and European. Written in a major mode and in 6/8 time, its lyrics are usually in couplets and jocular in tone; traditionally, the accordion and the guitar provide the accompaniment. The dance, danced in couples in the rural areas, is central to popular celebrations in the region. Three musicians in particular made it popular in the late twentieth century: Ernesto Montiel, Tránsito Cocomarola and Isaco Abipbol.

See also: Galarza, Ramona; Parodi, Teresa

CRISTINA IGLESIA

Chambi, Martín

b. 1891, Coaza, Peru; d. 1973, Cuzco, Peru

Photographer

Martin Chambi is, in the words of Sara **Facio**, the first indigenous Latin American photographer 'who looked without any taint of colonialism upon his people'. He came from an Andean region whose majority population was, like himself, Inca. From a humble rural family, he belonged to the first generation to leave the land, and came to photography as an adjunct to his work in the gold

mines, almost the only source of employment in those mountains.

Nicknamed 'the Nadar of Cuzco', Chambi established himself in Cuzco, capital of the former Inca empire and base of the 'Cuzco School' of photography. From 1910, it was significant also as the home of the first university studies into **indigenismo** under the directorship of Albert Giesecke, which involved field trips into the Andes. In 1924, when Chambi arrived there, Cuzco was the centre of *indigenista* revivalism. Luis **Valcárcel** was directing a Peruvian Mission of Incaic Art with a touring programme of Inca music, dance and theatre through Latin America.

Chambi had already spent nine years (1908–17) apprenticed to the photo studio of Max Vargas in the colonial city of Arequipa. Hints that he felt undervalued and the victim of racial discrimination combined with the need for change, and he went freelance, opening a studio in the small town of Sicuani. From there he worked as a peripatetic, documenting the villages of the Canchis and effectively pioneering ethnographic work that echoed the broader anthropological interests of the new *indigenista* movement. His black- and white-family portraits, taken on a large plate wooden camera, often out of doors at communal reunions, were a unique document of what he called 'the cradle of Inca civilization, my eternal paradise'.

The people he photographed crossed social divides, as did he himself, from a rural peasantry deeply attached to its lands and customs to a new bourgeoisie that despised indigenous roots and traditions. His work was effectively cut short by the 1950 earthquake, which devastated Cuzco and left 35,000 victims. Having been an official photographer at the excavations of Macchu Picchu in 1913, he took to the ruins of his beloved adoptive home, taking pride in throwing into relief the Inca origins of the Baroque viceroyalty.

In 1948, the North American photographer Irving Penn rented this studio and the international recognition of Chambi's gift and the importance of his life's work began. In the 1950s, Edward Rannery harnessed an *Earthwatch* expedition to recover and catalogue the 14,000 glass negatives in his archive, now under the protection of his daughter, Julia Chambi. Ranney's research culminated in a major retrospective exhibition at New

York's Museum of Modern Art, which later toured Paris, London, Zurich and Buenos Aires. He is now as much a subject for those concerned with photography and fine art as with anthropology and ethnology.

Further reading

Antrobus, P. (1940) *Peruvian Photography*, Colchester: University of Essex.

Martín Chambi, Paris: Livres de Poche.

Martin Chambi 1920–1950 (1990), texts by Mario Vargas Llosa and Publio López Mondejar, Barcelona/Madrid: Círculo de Bellas Artes/ Lunwerg Editores.

Ponce de León, C. (1988) *Martín Chambi, Fotografías de Perú*, Lima: Banco de la República.

AMANDA HOPKINSON

Chamoiseau, Patrick

b. 1953, Fort-de-France, Martinique

Dramatist and novelist

A prominent contemporary French-Caribbean novelist inspired by Edouard **Glissant**, Chamoiseau wrote the *créoliste* manifesto *Eloge de la créolité* (In Praise of Créolité) with Jean Bernabé and Raphael **Confiant** in 1989 (see **Créolité**). His novels reveal a preoccupation with Fort-de-France's sub-culture of hustlers or *djobeurs* and are written in an interlect combining French and creole. His first successful novel *Chronique des sept misères* (Chronicle of Seven Miseries) (1986) dealt with the decline of Fort-de-France's vegetable market. After *Solibo Magnifique* (Solibo the Magnificent) (1988), he won the Prix Goncourt in 1992 for the novel *Texaco*.

J. MICHAEL DASH

Chamorro, Pedro Joaquín

b. 1924, Granada, Nicaragua; d. 1978, Managua, Nicaragua

Newspaper editor

Though he came from a conservative family,

Chamorro was a consistent opponent of the Somoza regime (see **Somoza dynasty**). In 1952 he succeeded his father as editor of *La Prensa*. In 1959 he was involved in an attempted armed overthrow of Somoza. In the late 1970s, Chamorro organized a coalition of political opponents of the Somozas (UDEL, the Democratic Union for Liberation) and his newspaper consistently exposed the activities of the dictatorship, including the Somozas' involvement in the sale of blood and plasma in Miami. He was assassinated in January 1978. His funeral became a mass demonstration of opposition to Somoza, setting in motion a movement culminating in July 1979 in the overthrow of the Somoza regime. His wife Violeta **Chamorro** embarked on a political career after his death and became President of Nicaragua in 1990.

ESTEBAN LOUSTAUNAU AND ILEANA RODRÍGUEZ

Chamorro, Violeta Barrios de

b. 1930, Rivas, Nicaragua

Politician

The assassination by Somoza (see **Somoza dynasty**) of her husband Pedro Joaquín **Chamorro**, editor of *La Prensa*, transformed Violeta Chamorro into a public figure. She became the first female member of the Sandinista junta in 1979 (see **Sandinista Revolution**), though she resigned soon after to become co-director of *La Prensa*, which became the internal mouthpiece for opposition to the Sandinistas. In 1990 she ran for President as the consensus candidate of the fourteen party coalition **UNO** (United National Opposition); the US government contributed $1.8 million to her campaign. The unconditional support of the USA and the promise to end the contra war (see **contras**) ensured her victory. She was Nicaragua's President from 1990–6, overseeing a period of **structural adjustment** in the Nicaraguan economy.

ESTEBAN E. LOUSTAUNAU AND
ILEANA RODRÍGUEZ

chanchada

Chanchada is a prolific Brazilian film genre, heir to the long tradition of parody of the silent cinema (see **silent film**) and to the **carnival** revue films produced in the 1930s to take advantage of new sound technologies. Combining music, dance, humour and melodrama, it was perfected by the Rio de Janeiro **Atlântida** studios in the 1940s and 1950s. Reasonably well-capitalized and with guaranteed access to Rio movie theatres, Atlântida's success was based on the creativity of well-seasoned directors and energetic apprentices like Carlos **Manga**. Its *chanchadas* catapulted popular comedians (especially the 'couple' **Grande Otelo** and **Oscarito**) and actors (Anselmo **Duarte**, Tonia Carrero, Cyll Farney, José Lewgoy, Eliana and others) into stardom. Among the best examples of the genre are *Carnaval Atlântida* (José Carlos **Burle**, 1952), *Nem Sansão nem Dalila* (Neither Samson nor Delilah) and *Matar ou Correr* (Kill or Run) (both by Carlos Manga, 1954).

Of contested etymology, the word '*chanchada*' can be literally translated as 'pig slop', pointing to the genre's always contested status. Adored by audiences, it sustained Brazilian film production on a quasi-industrial scale for two decades. Despised by critics and intellectuals until the late 1960s (Glauber **Rocha** argued that it was a 'conformist cancer of underdevelopment'), the genre's irreverent combination of parody and music began to be reassessed in 1973 by Paulo Emílio Salles **Gomes**, who argued that, after all, the *chanchada* was Brazilian and that it had allowed for a privileged, positive relationship between the cinema and national audiences: parody emerged as the only possibility within underdevelopment for a cinema attempting to imitate Hollywood standards that ends up laughing at itself in happy complicity with its audiences.

Despite infusions of new talent in the 1950s and 1960s – especially the work of the comedian **Mazzaropi** and the group Os **Trapalhões** (The Morons) – the genre began to run out of steam in the 1960s. On the one hand, it veered into the explicit sexuality of the ***pornochanchada***; on the other, its popular audiences increasingly turned to **television** for the pleasures previously derived from the genre.

Further reading

Augusto, S. (1989) *Este mundo é um pandeiro*, São Paulo: Companhia das Letras.

Dias, R. de Oliveira (1993) *O mundo como chanchada*, Rio de Janeiro: Pelume.

Gomes, P.E.S. (1997) 'Cinema, a Trajectory Within Underdevelopment', in R. Johnson and R. Stam (eds) *Brazilian Cinema: Expanded Edition*, New York: Columbia University Press, 244–55.

Viera, J.L. (1997) 'From High Noon to Jaws: Carnival in Parody in Brazilian Cinema', in R. Johnson and R. Stam (eds) *Brazilian Cinema: Expanded Edition*, New York: Columbia University Press, 256–70.

ISMAIL XAVIER AND THE USP GROUP

Chang, Carlisle

b. 1921, San Juan, Trinidad

Painter

One of Trinidad's most diverse artists in the consciousness-raising years before independence, Chang's paintings sought symbols of a nascent national identity to transcend ethnic categorizations. During the 1960s Chang was a leading designer of **carnival** costumes, with creations such as 'China, The Forbidden City' (Band of the Year, 1967). In the 1970s Chang abstracted his carnival designs on to canvas and murals in public and private buildings around Trinidad. In 1990, bandleader and artist Peter **Minshall** asked Chang to contribute a work on appliquéd cloth for the band 'Tantana', which Chang then wore as a 'dancing painting' in that year's carnival parade.

LORRAINE LEU

Chapotín, Félix

b. 1909, Havana, Cuba; d. 1983, Havana

Musician

A renowned trumpet player, Chapotin joined the youth band of Guanajay at eleven; he later became director of La Chambelona, a band which roamed the streets at election times campaigning to music. In 1927 he joined the Sexteto Colin in Havana, and a year later joined the famous Sexteto Habanero. In 1940 he was a founder member of Arsenio **Rodríguez**'s band, and took over as its director in 1950 when Rodríguez went to New York. Now known as the Estrellas de Chapotín, the orchestra made a number of recordings inside and outside Cuba, often accompanying the great **son** singer Miguelito **Cuni**.

JOSÉ ANTONIO EVORA

Chapuseaux, Manuel

b. 1954, Puerto Plata, Dominican Republic

Actor

Chapuseaux studied theatre at the Escuela Nacional de Arte Escénico with the famous Venezuelan actor Rómulo Rivas. He founded the Teatro Gayumba and became its director in 1978. Chapuseaux has also participated in many international theatre festivals throughout Latin America, the United States and Europe. His book *Manual del teatrero* (Theatre Manual) (1987) won the *Premio Nacional de Didáctica* (National Didactic Prize). Chapuseaux and his company Gayumba Theatre have taught many workshops at the **Casa de Teatro**.

FERNANDO VALERIO-HOLGUÍN

charango

Originating in the Andean region in the early eighteenth century, the charango is a small guitar-style stringed instrument with a rounded back made of armadillo shell or wood. Traditionally strummed to accompany dancers or singers, often in combination with percussion, zampoñas and quenas (see **quena**), the slightly harsh tones of the traditional charango were sweetened when Andean music became popular among a wider audience; this occurred during the 1930s and then, more enduringly, with the emergence of the *nueva canción latinoamericana* in the late 1960s, which revived the

traditional instruments and expanded both the audience for traditional playing and the range of music available. Ernesto **Cavour**, who played with Los **Jairas** in Bolivia, is an acknowledged master of the instrument.

MIKE GONZALEZ

Charín   *see*   Suárez, Charín

Charlemagne, Manno

b. 1948, Port-au-Prince, Haiti

Singer and songwriter

Charlemagne gained popularity among Haiti's urban poor and disenfranchised in the 1970s and 1980s. His bitingly satirical lyrics, sung in creole, castigated corrupt politicians and made fun of the country's social and economic elite.

Born Emmanuel Charlemagne, he grew up in the sprawling new suburb of Carrefour, to the south of the capital, where he was influenced as much by the songs of the peasants who moved into the area in search of a livelihood, as by his Catholic school choir. In the 1970s, he was part of the *kilti libete* or freedom culture movement that promoted popular culture, including acoustic, folk music. Charlemagne's writing drew on the *twoubadou* (troubadour) tradition, a guitar-based music that can trace its roots to the rural songs of the Haitian peasantry and to the Cuban influences brought to Haiti by returning migrant sugar-cane cutters in the early decades of the twentieth century.

The Jean Claude **Duvalier** regime renewed the repression of political and cultural dissent in 1980, and Charlemagne was forced into exile. With the fall of the Duvaliers in 1986, he returned home, and was active in both political organizing and the burgeoning roots or *racines* music scene. He formed a live group, Koral Konbit Kafou, which included drummers from a **Vodun** temple, and played concerts that provided a soundtrack for the popular mobilization for political change in the late 1980s. Some of these songs can be heard on *Nou nan male ak Oganizasyon Mondyal* (The New World Order is our Misfortune) (1988).

His support for the grassroots, popular movement frequently landed him in trouble with the Haitian military, and, after receiving death threats, he spent several years in semi-clandestinity. Charlemagne was a supporter of the Lavalas political movement of President Jean-Bertrand **Aristide**, against whom the military launched a brutal *coup d'état* in September 1991. Charlemagne took refuge in the Argentine embassy and then went into exile once again. During 1991–4, he played concerts in Miami, New York and Montreal, where he rallied the expatriate Haitian communities in support of Haitian democracy. He released a recording, *La fimen* (The Smoker) in 1994.

Following the United Nations intervention to restore the constitutional government in September 1994, Charlemagne returned to Haiti. In June 1995 he was elected mayor of the capital city, Port-au-Prince, defeating the incumbent, Evans **Paul**, but his term of office, which expired in early 1999, was beset with difficulties and controversy, and is not regarded as a success. His administrative responsibilities overshadowed his musical career, and one of his few public performances in recent years was with the Haitian–American rap group, The Fugees, in Port-au-Prince in April 1997.

Further reading

Averill, G. (1997) *A Day for the Hunter, A Day for the Prey: Popular Music and Power in Haiti*, Chicago: University of Chicago Press.

Arthur, C. and Dash, M. (eds) (1999) *Libete: A Haiti Anthology*, London: Latin America Bureau.

CHARLES ARTHUR

Charles, Dame Mary Eugenia

b. 1919, Pointe Michel, Dominica

Politician

Best known for her anti-communism and leading the invitation to the USA to invade Grenada in 1983, Charles studied law at the University of Toronto and was called to the bar at Inner Temple, London, in 1949. She founded the Dominica Freedom Party in 1968, entered the House of Assembly as Nominated Member in 1970, and was elected and became Leader of the Opposition in 1975. She became the first Caribbean woman prime minister when DFP won the 1980 general elections, was elected again in 1985 and 1990, and was made a dame in 1991.

LENNOX HONYCHURCH

charro

The Mexican cowboy, or *charro*, emerged on the cattle ranches of the north where his skills in cattle droving and horsemanship were honed. In the twentieth century, however, those skills had become the province of the weekend horsemen, often members of the wealthy classes, who rehearse their equestrian and droving skills at weekend rodeo-style gatherings called *charreadas*. Their characteristic dress – silver-studded suits with broad-brimmed decorated hats – is echoed by the **mariachi** musicians whose sentimental ranchera ballads (see **canción ranchera**) are the preferred music of the *charro*. The term '*charro*' has acquired an additional meaning in Mexico – referring to the leaders of the 'official' trade unions whose loyalty is usually to the government party rather than to their members. The term derives from the custom of one such leader in the 1940s of arriving at union meetings in *charro* dress.

MIKE GONZALEZ

charros, Cine de

Cine de charros was a subgenre of Mexican cinema fashionable in the 1940s, set in the state of Jalisco. A form of melodrama, its most famous exponent was the singer Jorge **Negrete**, star of the Golden Age of Mexican cinema, whose career was launched by José Rodríguez's 1941 film *¡Ay Jalisco no te rajes!* (Jalisco Don't Give Up). The prototypical betting, drinking and womanizing Mexican macho (see **machismo, Mexican**), the mythical **charro** was the protagonist of a series of film comedies and dramas. Raúl de Anda appeared in five such films as the legendary 'black *charro*', a character created in 1936 by Muriño Ruiz for his best-selling comic strip (see **comic strips**).

PATRICIA TORRES SAN MARTÍN

Charry Lara, Fernando

b. 1920, Bogotá, Colombia

Poet

Charry is best known as a member of the Cántico and *Mito* groups, which greatly influenced the Colombian cultural scene during the 1940s and the 1950s. His poetry, lyrical and erotic, includes the 1949 *Nocturnos y otros sueños* (Nocturnes and other Dreams), and *Pensamientos del amante* (A Lover's Thoughts) (1981). His prose centres on the work of poet José Asunción Silva. Charry studied law and political science at the Universidad Nacional in Bogotá, where he later served as director of Cultural Affairs; he was also director of the Radiodifusora Nacional de Colombia, a member of the Academia Colombiana de la Lengua and honorary member of the prestigious **Instituto Caro y Cuervo**.

HÉCTOR D. FERNÁNDEZ L'HOESTE

Chaskel, Pedro

b. 1932, Germany

Film-maker

An important figure of the new Chilean cinema of the 1960s, Chaskel lived in Chile from 1939 and became involved with the cinema through the university. He founded a cine club and, with Sergio Bravo, the Centro de Cine Experimental in 1957, a production centre where he began making **documentary** shorts (see **cine clubs**). In the 1960s he was director of the film department at the University of Chile and collaborated with Miguel **Littín**, editing his *El chacal de Nahueltoro* (The Jackal of Nahueltoro) (1970). He headed the Union of Latin American **cinematheques** between 1972 and 1980. He lived in Cuba following the 1973 **Pinochet** *coup*; there he continued editing, including Patricio **Guzmán**'s *La batalla de Chile* (The Battle of Chile) (1973–9), and made

documentaries, among them *Una foto recorre el mundo* (A Photograph Travels the World) (1981), about **Korda**'s famous photograph of Che **Guevara**. After living for a while in Germany, he returned to Chile in the mid-1980s and once again began making documentary shorts.

ANA M. LÓPEZ

Chasqui

Chasqui is a journal of Latin American literature published since 1972 at Brigham Young University. Its title is a **Quechua** word used to designate the messengers of the Inca empire, but the journal is not particularly focused on the Andes or on indigenous questions. Edited for many years by Ted Lyon, it is currently directed by David William Foster. It publishes creative writing as well as articles and book reviews.

DANIEL BALDERSTON

Chaves, Raquel

b. 1938, Asunción, Paraguay

Writer

The author of social poetry in *La tierra sin males* (The World Without Evil) and of a series of mini-poems with a mythical-philosophical content – true Paraguayan haikus – in *Espacio Sagrado* (Sacred Space) (1988), Chaves has also published *Todo es del viento: Siete viajes* (Everything Belongs to the Wind: Seven Trips) (1984) and received the 1977 Segundo Premio Municipal (Second Municipal Prize) for 'Ciudadalma' (City-Soul), an ecological text co-authored with Nila López.

TERESA MÉNDEZ-FAITH

Chaves, Ricardo

b. 1951, Porto Alegre, Brazil

Journalist and photographer

Beginning as a freelancer, Chaves later became

assistant editor of *IstoÉ* (1986–91) while coordinating photography projects for the first São Paulo photography biennial in 1994. In 1991, he became editor of *O Estado do Brasil*; later he was the photography coordinator of the Brazilian news agency, Agencia Estado. In 1999 he was the photography editor of the Porto Alegre newspaper *Zero Hora*. His photographs are heterogeneous, often trans-Latin American in scope as in his solo show *Images of Recent History* (1987). Unlike most photo-journalists, Chaves prefers to work in brilliant colour, framing subjects at angles and from below, and using the flash sparingly and unexpectedly.

AMANDA HOPKINSON

Chávez, Carlos

b. 1899, Popotla, Mexico; d. 1978, Mexico City

Composer

One of Mexico's foremost composers, during the 1920s and 1930s Chávez developed a nationalist musical language that was wholly identified with the cultural transformation led by José **Vasconcelos** in the aftermath of the Mexican Revolution (see **revolutions**). A student of Manuel M. **Ponce**, a key member of an earlier nationalist generation who fused traditional melodies with a Romantic style, Chávez abandoned the Romantic legacy and developed a musical idiom directly inspired by indigenous rhythms, instruments and melodies, as in *El fuego nuevo* (New Fire) (1921) and his famous *Sinfonía India* (Indian Symphony) (1936). But Chávez's work spread wider than his better known *indigenista* works (see **indigenous literature**). After visits to Europe and the USA in the 1920s, Chávez became enthusiastic about some of the newer modernist currents in music, particularly the abstract compositions that employed mathematical and scientific formulae as the foundation of musical form. *Polígonos* (Polygons) (1923) for piano and *Energía* (Energy) (1931) for nine instruments belong to this period. His ballet *H.P.* (1926–31) developed the geometric patterns but in conjunction with the rhythms of Mexican folk dance, on

the one hand, and a soundscape reproducing the cacophony of the modern city, on the other. In 1928, though only 29 years old, he was made director of the Mexican National Conservatory, where his pupils included such distinguished names as Daniel **Ayala** and Blas **Galindo**, among others. In the same year he founded the Orquesta Sinfónica de México. His political convictions also informed his music – the series of concerts for workers, *Conciertos para Trabajadores*, which were launched in 1930 was one expression of them, his *Sinfonía Proletaria* (Proletarian Symphony) (1934) another. But at the same time he was enthused by the variety of contemporary music and the potentiality of electronic reproduction – which he explored in his book, *Hacia una nueva música: música y electricidad* (Towards a New Music: Music and Electricity) (1937). In the late 1930s he turned back to composing for piano and an almost classical purity and discipline of style. For a time director of music at the Instituto Nacional de Bellas Artes (INBA), Chávez devoted the latter part of his life to composing, producing among his many works a Violin Concerto (1948–50), the ballet *La hija de Cólquide* (1943–4), written for Martha Graham, four further symphonies and the opera *The Visitors*.

Further reading

García Morillo, R. (1960) *Carlos Chávez: Vida y obra*, Mexico City: Fondo de Cultura Económica.
Stevenson, R. (1952) *Music in Mexico: A Historical Survey*, New York: Crowell.

MIKE GONZALEZ

Chávez, Hugo

b. 1957, Barinas, Venezuela

Military leader and politician

Chávez first came to prominence in 1992 in a failed military *coup* against Venezuelan president Carlos Andrés **Pérez**, after which he spent several years in prison. Upon release he devoted himself to building a populist movement (see **populism**) that was independent of the traditional political parties.

Elected president in 1998 by a huge margin (greater than 80 per cent), he spearheaded a reform of the Venezuelan Constitution (see **Constitutions**) and dubbed himself leader of a 'Bolivarian' revolution, though the immediate model seems not to be Simón Bolívar but Fidel **Castro**. He won the first presidential elections in July 2000 under the new constitution, but by a slimmer margin than in 1998. It is too soon to know whether his talk of a twenty- or thirty-year revolutionary process is premature.

DANIEL BALDERSTON

Chávez, Julio César

b. 1962, Ciudad Obregón, Mexico

Boxer

Julio Cesar Chávez started boxing at age sixteen and turned professional in 1980. A remarkable fighter, his impressive record (97–1–1, 79 KOs) by 1996 had made him a legend. Six times world champion, he had already defended his titles successfully between April 1985 and August 1987. He has been awarded more honours from the major boxing organizations than any other fighter. A protégé of Don King, the celebrated boxing entrepreneur, his boxing matches were frequented through the 1990s by celebrities and politicians from Mike Tyson to former president Carlos **Salinas de Gortari**.

EDUARDO SANTA CRUZ

Chávez, Oscar

b. 1935, Mexico City

Musician

A balladeer and guitarist with a seductive baritone voice, for three decades Oscar Chávez has been among the leading Mexican singers and promoters of the '**Canto Nuevo**' or 'New Song' Movement, which reworks traditional music for contemporary audiences. Along with Chava Flores, Los **Folkloristas**, Amparo **Ochoa**, Tehua and other Mexican singers of the 1970s and 1980s, Chávez has

recorded hundreds of folk songs from an extraordinary variety of regions and historical periods (notably the Mexican Revolution (see **revolutions**) and the Student Movement of 1968), as well as contemporary poetry and scathing political satire.

CYNTHIA STEELE

Chávez Alfaro, Lizandro

b. 1929, Bluefields, Nicaragua

Writer

An important Nicaraguan novelist, Chávez Alfaro was born on the Atlantic coast of Nicaragua. In his literary production he discusses the ambivalence between the Atlantic and Pacific regions by reference to *mestizaje* and *creolité*. His most important work, *Trágame Tierra* (Swallow Me Earth) (1969) is a profound reflection upon land divided across ethnic lines and cultural traditions. He lived in Mexico and Costa Rica during the Somoza (see **Somoza dynasty**) era, and during the Sandinista (see **Sandinista Revolution**) administration he was the National Librarian and the Nicaraguan ambassador to Hungary. He currently works at Managua National University.

DEREK PETREY AND ILEANA RODRÍGUEZ

Chega de saudade

Composed by Antônio Carlos **Jobim** and Vinícius de **Moraes** and first recorded in 1958 by João **Gilberto**, 'Chega de saudade' (No More Blues) defined the emerging **bossa nova** sound of Rio de Janeiro's south zone. Several Brazilian musicians have remarked that this song, which was so unlike any popular music of the time, inspired them to learn to play the guitar and pursue a musical career. Initially, however, critics and the general public responded negatively to João Gilberto's version, which they considered 'off-key' and 'strange'. Yet by the time his first LP (also called

Chega de saudade) appeared in 1959, the bossa nova craze was in full swing.

CHRISTOPHER DUNN

Chejfec, Sergio

b. 1956, Buenos Aires, Argentina

Novelist

While distanced from the explicitly experimental, the texture of Chejfec's fiction addresses the limits of language, the minimalist events of daily life and the personal and generational tales that weave the underside of history. Chejfec is as much at ease in recovering his Jewish roots as in reconstructing disquietingly fragmentary urban routines. His writings include *Lenta biografía* (Slow Biography) (1990), *Moral* (1990), *El aire* (Air) (1992), *El llamado de la especie* (The Call of the Species) (1997) and *Cinco* (Five) (1996). Chejfec has lived in Caracas since 1990, where he is currently managing editor of the leading journal **Nueva sociedad**.

SAÚL SOSNOWSKI

chemistry

The development of chemical research in Latin America in the second half of the twentieth century is more closely tied than any other to the production sector. An example is the expansion of petrochemical as well as pure chemical research in Venezuela, closely linked to the oil boom; in Brazil, research developed in relation to the paint and varnish industries. Since the Second World War, many national governments have actively promoted such research, particularly in its multiple applications to production, in the context of the development plans set in motion throughout the region in the fifties and sixties.

See also: science

PABLO KREIMER

Chen, Willi

b. 1934, Coura, Trinidad

Artist and writer

A prolific and multi-faceted artist, Chen began publishing his stories of Trinidad life in the 1980s in journals and newspapers. His only collection to date, *King of the Carnival and Other Stories*, was published in 1982. Traditional in his literary style, his central theme is the encounter between cultures in the often harsh context of his native island; strangely, the Chinese community, into which he was born, rarely appears in his work. A painter and sculptor, he designed the Christ the Lord Roman Catholic Church in Marabella, Trinidad. He was awarded the National Hummingbird Medal for Art and Culture in 1989.

KEITH JARDIM

Chester, Ilán

b. 1954, Israel

Musician

One of a group of young pop musicians who came to fame in the 1980s (including **Yordano**, Franco de Vita and Ricardo Montaner), Chester is known as 'the Venezuelan musician'. A composer, arranger and singer, he accompanies himself on the piano. One of his most popular songs concerns the mountain above Caracas called El Avila, the lungs of the city. Son of the city's chief rabbi, he himself is an active member of the Hare Krishna community. In 1996, having achieved considerable success, he decided to retire from public life to the interior of the country, where he continues to write songs on commission.

ALICIA RÍOS

chewing gum

An incision into the chicozapote plant, which abounds in Central America, produces a resinous gum which, with the addition of sweeteners and flavouring, produces chicle (from the Náhuatl 'tzitctli', to stick) or chewing gum. A habit typical of urban neurotics, the automatic mastication of gum serves no useful purpose in the feeding process. The gum chewer consumes his/her own saliva, sometimes blowing bubbles with it and sometimes keeping it on the underside of a table from which it can be recovered and chewing resumed. Thrown on to the public highway, the gum will contrive to continue its journey on some passing sole. In a market dominated by the Chicago-based Wrigley Company, chewing gum is sold everywhere in the streets of Latin America, mainly by small children. In some countries it has even become a minor currency.

JULIO SCHVARTZMAN

Chibas, Eduardo

b. 1907, Santiago de Cuba; d. 1951, Havana, Cuba

Politician

Founder of the Partido del Pueblo Cubano (*Ortodoxos*), Chibas campaigned to end corruption in Cuba; his party's symbol was a broom. One of the country's most popular political figures at the time, he attracted supporters like the young lawyer Fidel **Castro**. When he publicly accused the Education Minister of corruption, the official demanded that he prove it. Chibas announced that he would produce the evidence during his regular Sunday night programme on radio station CMQ on 5 April 1951. On that day he shot himself in the stomach while on air. He died eleven days later, and his funeral attracted unprecedented crowds.

JOSÉ ANTONIO EVORA

Chicago Boys

The 'Chicago Boys' is an expression coined to refer to a group of economists in Chile who formulated and implemented a neoliberal (see **neoliberalism**) economic model during the **Pinochet** dictatorship. Most of them had studied at the University of Chicago, the hotbed of monetarism

and neoliberal economics in the USA. They formed a cohesive team and captured the 'commanding heights' of the economic policy-making bureaucracy. They were anti-Marxist, relatively autonomous from Chile's traditional business interests and pressure groups, and organic technocrats of a military regime which radically transformed the Chilean economy by privatizing state enterprises, health care and social security and opened it up to foreign capital and world markets.

CRISTÓBAL KAY

chicha

An alcoholic drink made from fermented maize or masticated **manioc**, it was originally the preferred drink of the Incas though is still very popular today especially among the heavily populated indigenous communities of the Andean and Amazonian regions of Ecuador, Peru and Bolivia and drunk at '*chicheras*' or *chicha* parties. The word *chicha* is also used as a name for several other alcoholic beverages made from pineapple, grapes, apples or naranjilla, a small orange-coloured Andean fruit. So much was *chicha* a part of Andean identity that in the late 1960s a genre of popular music emerged in Peru and took its name – **chicha music** – from the drink.

PETER WATT

chicha music

A meeting point between traditional folk and modern rock, *chicha* began to emerge in late 1960s Peru, drawing from a wide range of styles such as Cuban **guaracha**, **cumbia** from Colombia and North American rock and roll. Its pentatonic melodies and **huayno** rhythms are deeply rooted in Andean music though these are played on electric guitars and kept in rhythm with drums originally associated with British and American bands of the early 1960s. It is no coincidence that the music appropriated its name from an alcoholic beverage drunk in the Andes and the Amazon rainforest made from fermented corn or **manioc**, as much *chicha* would be consumed while listening and dancing to the music at *chicheras* (*chicha* parties) and also because *chicha* was a symbol of a distinctly Andean identity. First exponents of the style (Los Destellos, Los Ecos, Los Diablos Rojos, Los Pakines, Los Mirlos, Chacaln, Los Shapis) made the music danceable, and thus attractive to a young audience and offered an opportunity for Peru to create its own identity in the world of popular music though *chicha*'s influence was later enjoyed from Colombia to Argentina.

PETER WATT

chicle *see* chewing gum

Chico Science

b. 1967, Recife, Pernambuco, Brazil; d. 1997, Recife

Composer and musician

Born Francisco de Assis França, Chico Science and his band revolutionized Brazilian pop music in the 1990s, mixing funky bass lines, heavy metal guitars, and Afro-Brazilian rhythms such as **maracatú**. The group's 1994 debut, *Da lama ao caos* (From Mud to Chaos), became the album-manifesto of *mangue beat*, a musical movement which juxtaposes an on-the-ground perspective of urban under-development from Recife's muddy slums with global postmodern sensibilities; a cultural strategy which is akin to the **Tropicália** experience of the late 1960s. Shortly after the group's second recording, *Afroceberdélia*, Chico Science died in a car accident.

CHRISTOPHER DUNN

Chihuailaf, Elicura

b. 1952, Temuco, Chile

Writer

Chihuailaf is a poet and thinker of the Mapuche people (see **Mapuches**), Chile's largest indigenous group, who live primarily in the south-central regions of Chile. He has translated the poetry of Pablo **Neruda** into Mapudungún, the Mapuche language, and published a bilingual edition of Neruda's work. For Chihuailaf, the power and richness of language are the most valuable legacy of his Mapuche ancestors. Chihuailaf's recent collection of poetry, *Azul* (Blue) (1996), touches upon the contradictions and hypocrisy of modernity in Latin America, which has not overcome **race** and class discrimination. He organized the Workshop for South American Writers of Indigenous Languages, held in Temuco, Chile, in 1996.

See also: indigenous writing

AMALIA PEREIRA

child labour

Clear definitions of what constitutes child labour are impossible when there is no clear dividing line between chores in the home and work contributing to family income. Even so, UN figures suggest the extent of child labour in Latin America, with one in five 10–14 year olds working in Brazil, Honduras and Haiti, and more than one in ten in most other countries. The International Labour Organisation (ILO) claims 17.5 million working children in Latin America and the Caribbean between five and fourteen years old. The numbers are much higher among boys, underlining the statistical under-representation of girls' labour in the home.

Most child labourers work in the informal economy. Girls are more likely to do domestic work as maids (see **domestic labour**), many starting work at the ages of six or seven. Boys are more likely to work in public, for example as street vendors. The growth of the informal sector in recent years has increased the number of child workers in the region.

The reasons why children work are complex, including poverty, gender, the quality of schooling, the availability of paid jobs, and the need to care for younger children, animals or the house. Important cultural issues are also involved; many children want to go out to work, while many parents think work is at least as valuable for their children as Latin America's decrepit **education** system.

For any child, going out to work brings both benefits and costs. By working, children gain self-esteem, skills and respect from their elders. On the other hand, working long hours can rob them of the chance of a decent education, since even if they manage to go to school, they are often too tired to concentrate in class. There are also more direct costs, in jobs where children run serious health risks from poisonous chemicals, dust or workplace accidents, or simply by placing too much strain on growing bodies.

Adults concerned about the impact of children's work, however, often fail to weigh the pros and cons of child labour. This can lead to counter-productive attempts to ban child labour through legislation, often making matters worse for the children involved, whose labour is then driven underground where conditions are often worse.

Further reading

Green, D. (1998) *Hidden Lives: Voices of Children in Latin America and the Caribbean*, London: Cassell.

Marcus, R. and Harper, C. (1996) *Small Hands: Children in the Working World*, London: Save the Children Fund.

DUNCAN GREEN

childhood

Family structures in Latin America are increasingly fluid. Yet for all its diversity, the family remains the basic social unit, taking the crucial decisions over a child's early life in terms of work, schooling and even whether they should be given away to another family. Children grow up knowing that they may have to move between homes and be raised by a range of adults. For a child, any family structure brings a combination of benefits and risks. A large household full of different generations of adults can provide more stimulus, companionship and love than the harassed parents in a nuclear family, or it can leave a child feeling utterly lost, passed from uncaring adult to uncaring adult; a grandmother no longer in work can make a wonderful full-time parent or become an exhausted and irritable tyrant; *regalitos* (little presents), as

Colombian children given away by their parents are known, may be just as loved as any other child, or may end up as little more than child slaves in their new homes.

Most children grow up in urban areas, which are home to well over half of Latin America's population and an even higher proportion of its children. A large percentage of urban children grow up in the shanty towns (see **shanty towns and slums**) which surround the major cities. Shanty town children have hard lives, but find more time for play than in rural areas, although the environment is often more dangerous. Homes are small and overcrowded, and there is little or nothing in the way of **parks** or playgrounds. As a result, children are forced to play on the streets, with the consequent dangers of pollution, traffic accidents and the street culture of drugs, gangs and petty crime. Boys especially are lured away by the exhilaration of street life (see **street children**).

According to UNICEF, 'most of the region's children are poor, and most of the poor are children'. Nevertheless, a significant proportion (though much smaller than in Europe or North America) are middle class. Based on fieldwork in Brazil, one US anthropologist concluded that middle-class and poor families have a fundamentally different relationship with their children. Among the families of the better-off, children are *nurtured*, pampered by parents and maids who shower them with attention, toys and encouragement and expect little in return. In the families of the poor, children are seen as *nurturing*, expected to help their mothers by taking part in the domestic chores and, especially with boys, by bringing in income from an early age. Poor children share this world view, eagerly awaiting the day when they can go out to work and fulfil their expected role.

Family life, especially among the urban poor, can be violent and abusive (see **domestic violence**). In the fluid world of the Latin American home, the worst beatings are often handed out by stepfathers and stepmothers rather than parents. Battering by stepfathers is the commonest reason given by street children for leaving home. Power and conflict within the family mirror broader power relations, with adult men at the top of the pecking order and girls at the bottom. Disabled children, especially those that cannot speak, are particularly at risk, both because they can add enormously to the family's workload and because they cannot bear witness to their suffering. Poverty both increases the likelihood of abuse, and makes it harder for the mother to leave the father once the truth emerges. The majority of children suffering sexual abuse are girls (over 80 per cent, according to statistics from Honduras). Mothers often find this so hard to accept that they blame their daughters for 'egging on' the father, and the child may be the one who is punished or expelled from the home as a result.

Virtually all Latin American children start school, but drop-out and repetition rates are among the highest in the world. As a result, many teenagers leave school able to write little more than their name. Children, especially from poor families, usually combine study and work, often alternating long stints on market stalls or working in the home, with one of the relatively brief shifts in the school system; schools frequently run a system of morning, afternoon and evening shifts.

Children in Latin America are expected to grow up faster than in the North. Early on, girls take on the tasks of running the home and caring for younger siblings, while boys are often expected to contribute to the family income by the time they are ten years old. Although commentators frequently portray this as children being 'robbed of their childhood', child historians such as Philippe Ariès point out that the notion of a separate period of protected, dependent 'childhood' is a recent concept, and that the lives of children in Latin America are, in historical terms, far less anomalous than those of children in Europe or North America.

The 1989 UN Convention on the Rights of the Child led to a wave of child-centred legislative reform across Latin America. In many cases the new legislation, while rarely fully implemented, greatly strengthens notions of children's rights in areas such as the criminal justice system and access to health and education, as well as more controversial areas such as children's rights to participate in policy formulation. One of the most far-reaching reforms has been in Brazil, where the new 'Code of the Child and Adolescent' (ECA) created a network of children's rights councils (*conselhos de direitos*) and guardianship councils

(*conselhos tutelares*) in all of the country's nearly 5,000 municipalities. The rights councils, made up of representatives from NGOs and government institutions, are responsible for implementing the ECA, by monitoring policy-making and law enforcement. The guardianship councils function as local advocates for children, intervening when abuses occur and acting rather like child-specific social workers.

Further reading

Ariès, P. (1962) *Centuries of Childhood*, London: Pimlico.

Green, D. (1998) *Hidden Lives: Voices of Children in Latin America and the Caribbean*, London: Cassell.

UNICEF (1996) *State of the World's Children 1996*, New York: UNICEF.

DUNCAN GREEN

children's literature

Latin American writers who have written important works of children's literature include Horacio **Quiroga**, Silvina **Ocampo**, Rosario **Ferré** and Monteiro **Lobato**. The poet, singer and writer Maria Elena **Walsh** is perhaps most famous for her children's literature and music. (One of her songs is sung – hauntingly – by the little girl in **Puenzo**'s film, *La historia oficial* (The Official Story) (1985)). Until recently, there was no children's publishing market *per se*, except perhaps for magazines like *Billiken*, but that has changed with the huge expansion in the field world-wide. There are nearly four hundred publishers specializing in children's literature today, including more than a hundred in Brazil. In contemporary Chile, half of the books published are for the children and youth market (compared to 20 per cent in Brazil, 9 per cent in Venezuela and 5 per cent in Argentina). Two prominent authors who specialize in children's literature today are Ana Maria Machado of Brazil and Graciela Montes of Argentina.

DANIEL BALDERSTON

Chile

The first conquerors discovered how isolated the country that is now Chile was: to reach the central valley where Santiago, the capital, now sits huddled against the Andes, they had to cross the Atacama Desert, one of the driest places on earth, with the forbidding Andean *cordillera* rising as high as 7,000 metres close to their left shoulder. Had they continued along its 4,300 kilometre length they would have passed a region of lakes and volcanoes, fertile valleys, the fjords and islands south of Chiloé, and skirted an impassable glacier before reaching Punta Arenas and the sheep farms of Chilean **Patagonia**. Beyond that lies Antarctica.

In the late twentieth century, Chile felt far less remote and separate from the northern world. Its name had become synonymous with military dictatorship, on the one hand, and neoliberal economics (see **neoliberalism**), on the other – both in some sense symbolized by the elderly ex-general who had set both in motion. But Augusto **Pinochet** began the new millennium under house arrest in Britain while a Spanish court tried to extradite him for crimes against humanity.

For most of its independent history as a republic, Chile has depended on a single export product for its prosperity. In the latter part of the nineteenth century it was the naturally occurring nitrates in the northern desert regions that financed Chilean expansion; this motivated the annexation of the ports of Antofagasta, once belonging to Bolivia, and Tacna, long disputed with Peru, from which its products could be exported. With the First World War, the development of artificial nitrates undermined this profitable commerce, but another took its place – copper – also mined in the harsh Atacama regions that housed the huge mines of Chuquicamata and El Teniente. The majority of these resources were foreign-owned; and the working conditions in the mining sector were as brutal as the surrounding landscape. Small wonder, then, that this area should have given birth to the strong trade union movement in which Luis Emilio **Recabarren** was such a moving force. And it was those same workers who provided the solid base for the creation of Chile's socialist and communist parties. The decline of the nitrate industry created

rising unemployment and deepening social conflict. The Ibáñez *coup* of 1928 was a populist (see **populism**) response that failed in the face of the world-wide economic depression; so too did the brief (hundred-day) socialist republic led by Marmaduke **Grove**. The government of Aguirre Cerda, a radical, came to power in 1938 with the active support of the communists and socialists, then pursuing the popular front policies adopted by all Latin American **communist parties** at the time. The early 1940s was a period of recovery and the growth of a State sector; but in 1947 Aguirre's successor, González Videla, outlawed his erstwhile communist allies. It was while fleeing persecution that Pablo **Neruda** began to write his great epic poem of Latin American history, the *Canto general* (1950). And it was during the same period, beginning in the late 1930s, that Chile's most internationally acclaimed painter, the surrealist **Matta**, began to develop his unmistakable ironic style, mainly set on large canvases.

Baldomero Lillo's socialist realist writing was often set among the miners in the early part of the century; Francisco **Coloane**'s short stories reflected the life of the coastal fishing communities. But the dominant cultural figures of the 1920s and 1930s were poets. Gabriela **Mistral** wrote powerful verses that arose from her own experience in rural Chile, though her work also clearly reflected the marginalization and limitations set upon women in a country where women only achieved the vote in 1949 – four years after Mistral was awarded the Nobel Prize for Literature (see **Nobel Prizes**). Pablo **Neruda** published his first volume of poetry in 1919, and in the following year produced the best loved and most frequently quoted of his early writings, *Veinte poemas de amor y una canción desesperada* (Twenty Love Poems and a Desperate Song). He then left Chile on a series of diplomatic missions during which he wrote the first two parts of his *Residencia en la tierra* (Residence on Earth) (1932–4), avant-garde and self-absorbed poetry very different from the public poetry for which he is best known. Neruda had his enemies, including the irascible and eccentric Pablo de **Rokha**. And it could be argued that Nicanor **Parra** conceived his **antipoetry** as a prosaic antidote to Neruda's flights of rhetoric; but his poet as antihero had already made an earlier appearance as ***Altazor*** in the long poem of that name by Vicente **Huidobro** – one of Latin America's most important avant-garde poets of the 1920s. There was little of the withering irony of *Altazor* in the *poesía pura* of Pedro Prado. Parra defined a new school of Chilean poetry, whose achievements were beyond question – the searching philosophical doubt of Gonzalo **Rojas**, and the ironies and paradoxes of the writing of Enrique **Lihn** were key examples.

Chile had traditionally absorbed the music of its neighbours – particularly the songs and dances of Argentina and, in the 1930s and 1940s, the **cumbia** from Colombia. But it also had its own strong folk traditions. The *tonada* traditionally sung by women accompanied the rural migrants to the cities in the 1920s and after, and created a new urban music of rural nostalgia sung by *huasos* (see ***huaso***), the rural cowboys who became a symbol for a kind of lost rural community. Groups like Los Cuatro Huasos and Los Huasos Quincheros typified these close-harmony quartets. The **cueca** is largely regarded as the national dance, while the tradition of *cantaores* or *poetas populares* (people's troubadours), with their improvised verses – *cantos a lo divino y a lo humano* (songs to the divine and the human) – remained vital but neglected until the towering figure of Violeta **Parra** began to collect and sing them in a one-person crusade to rediscover Chile's popular culture. It would be impossible to overestimate her contribution to Chilean cultural life.

Through the 1940s and 1950s Chile's copper-dependent economy had brought considerable prosperity to a small, Europeanized elite; at each election from 1952 onwards, a coalition of socialists and communists under various names had presented their own candidate. It was in 1964 that Salvador **Allende** ran for the first time. But the atmosphere that year was coloured by the impact of the Cuban Revolution (see **revolutions**) on a new generation that had already made clear its hostility to the USA's imperialist role in the region. The response of the US government was twofold: to isolate Cuba by tying Latin America into a joint-security treaty for the hemisphere, on the one hand, and by offering a programme of guided reform, on the other. The favoured instrument for this latter policy was **Christian Democracy**, and

the Chilean party was an ideal vehicle. It won the 1964 elections under Eduardo **Frei Montalva** and with a promise of reforms in land tenure, social policy and in the ownership of Chile's major resources, principally copper.

The promises produced an atmosphere of expectation, fuelled by the optimism that Cuba generated; when by 1967–8 it became clear that Frei would not carry through the promised reforms, the result was a radicalization of those who expected to benefit – peasants, students, workers, squatters and so on. The ambience was powerfully expressed in the songs of the new ***nueva canción*** movement. Violeta Parra's famous venue, la Peña de los Parra, became a meeting point for artists and musicians bent on rediscovering the national culture and for those for whom art, in its various forms, was a weapon in the struggle for change. Víctor **Jara**, Horacio **Salinas** and those who would later make up **Inti-Illimani** and **Quilapayún** – many of them students – performed there for the first time. It was also evident in the experimentation and political engagement of new film-makers, participating in the **Viña del Mar Festival** and producing critical, socialist realist films like Aldo **Francia**'s *Valparaíso mi amor* (Valparaiso, my Love) (1969) and Raúl **Ruiz**'s *Tres tristes tigres* (Three Trapped Tigers) (1966). Between 1968 and 1970 a rising movement of public protest, strikes, occupations and demands for education reform created the conditions under which Salvador Allende, now heading the Unidad Popular (see **Popular Unity**) coalition of six parties, could finally win the presidential elections of 1970. A range of new cultural expressions were associated with the campaign – the Brigadas Ramona Parra were anonymous groups of young artists who painted public surfaces with monumental representative figures (see **Brigada Ramona Parra**), and drama students were beginning to create new forms of street theatre and **agitprop**.

Allende's programme was essentially one of economic reform and social development. He was enthusiastically encouraged in this by those who had carried him to power, while the Christian Democrats and the more conservative forces worked hard to block change. As events quickened in pace, Allende seemed less and less in control of events. A dramatic record of those events is provided by the work of **Chile Films**, whose outstanding young directors included Miguel **Littín** and Patricio **Guzmán**. Guzmán recorded these years in a two-part documentary (later extended to three) called *La **batalla de Chile*** (The Battle of Chile) (1973–9). **DICAP**, the newly formed record label, provided an opportunity for the new generation of musicians to record and disseminate their music.

The military *coup* of 11 September 1973 transformed the country. Its much-vaunted (if not entirely accurate) reputation for democracy now lay in ruins; Allende himself was killed in the Moneda Palace in the course of the *coup* and thousands of Unidad Popular supporters and activists were arrested, killed or tortured – the extent of the repression would continue to be a subject of controversy, though the 1991 **Rettig Report** began the long process of truth-seeking. In the meantime Chilean cultural life underwent a deep split. Within Chile itself, severe censorship affected every branch – even Andean musical instruments were banned for a time. Those who continued to write and work – and many did – found oblique ways to address the contemporary reality, like Marco Antonio **de la Parra**'s intensely psychological plays, Diamela **Eltit**'s allusive and difficult prose works, and Raúl **Zurita**'s extraordinary poetry, so suggestive and full of silences. Theatre was permitted to continue under restricting conditions – **ICTUS** found imaginative ways to maintain the critical theatrical tradition, including improvisations and the creative use of video, while the **Teatro del Silencio** developed a drama of gesture that was not amenable to censorship and Las **Yeguas del Apocalipsis** turned performance art into a powerful challenge to both the institutions and the morality of the new regime. The times also produced unexpected new creative forms – the ***arpilleras*** or patchworks used traditional craft skills to make poignant and dramatic representations of life in the dictatorship. One of the most powerful new forms of resistance was women's centres and groups evolving from several different directions, like the La **Morada** centres, on the one hand, and the women's organizations among the poor and marginal, on the other.

There was also a Chilean culture of **exile**: the film-makers continued their work abroad – Valeria **Sarmiento** was one of those whose work explored the experience of Chileans abroad. The musicians of the Unidad Popular period won a new audience outside Chile – while, ironically, their music was banned inside the country, the new younger musicians like Santiago del Nuevo Extremo and Los **Prisioneros** evolved a music of their own but acknowledged their predecessors. The reception that welcomed Inti Illimani on their return to Chile in 1989 testified to their continuing importance.

José **Donoso** had begun to publish in the late 1950s and was a participant in the **Boom** generation, writing an idiosyncratic personal history of the time. Indeed his works, like *El **lugar sin límite*** (Hell has no Limits) (1966) and *El **obsceno pájaro de la noche*** (Obscene Bird of Night) (1970), include some of the most innovative and challenging of these personal histories. Antonio **Skármeta**'s writing was a reflection on his own country's recent history. His novella *Ardiente paciencia* (Burning Patience), based on Neruda's relationship with the postman at Isla Negra, was twice filmed, the second time as *Il postino*, with great commercial success. Patricio **Manns**, a singer and lyricist as well as a writer was also in exile – his beautiful Cuando me acuerdo de mi país (When I Remember my Country) became almost an anthem of exile.

The economic boom of the 1980s benefitted few, but did produce a new architecture, like **Santiago Airport, International Terminal**. But the end of the economic experiment began to be seen in the late 1980s, when the Pinochet regime was rejected in a huge plebiscite in 1988. A year later, Chile enjoyed its first elections for nearly two decades – and the transition to democracy, painful and incomplete, began with the election of Patricio Aylwin to the presidency with the support of many of the parties who had once comprised Unidad Popular.

Since the return of democracy, cinema has undergone a new resurgence, with many film-makers returning from exile, the reinstitution of the Viña del Mar Film Festival, and new governmental initiatives in support of the national cinema. A new generation of film-makers, many of whom grew up with the dictatorship, has re-established the viability of Chilean cinema, especially Gonzalo **Justiniano**, Silvio **Caiozzi**, Pablo **Perelman** and Gustavo **Graef-Marino**.

Women writers and critics have dominated the last decade of the century: Nelly **Richard**'s journal, *Revista de crítica cultural*, helped to reshape the cultural debate around issues of feminism, postmodernism and the discourses of desire – issues explored powerfully by Diamela Eltit, Ana María **Del Río**, Lucía **Guerra** and Pía **Barros** among others.

Further reading

Allende, S. (1973) *Chile's Road to Socialism*, Harmondsworth: Penguin.

Aman, K. and Parker, C. (1991) *Popular Culture in Chile: Resistance and Survival*, Boulder/Oxford: Westview.

Collins, J. and Lear, J. (1995) *Chile's Free Market Miracle: A Second Look*, Oakland, CA: Food First.

Constable, P. and Valenzuela, A. (1991) *A Nation of Enemies: Chile under Pinochet*, New York: W.W. Norton.

Goic, C. (1991) *La novela chilena: Los mitos degradados*, Santiago: Editorial Universitaria.

Jara, R. (1988) *El revés de la arpillera: Perfil literario de Chile*, Madrid: Hiperión.

O'Brien, P, Roxborough, I. and Roddick, J. (1975) *State and Revolution in Chile*, London: Macmillan.

Richard, N. (1998) *Residuos y metáforas: ensayos de crítica cultural sobre el Chile de la transición*, Santiago: Ed. Cuarto Propio.

—— (1994) *Margins and Institutions: Art in Chile since 1973*, Melbourne: Art & Text.

MIKE GONZALEZ

Chile Films

State agency for the cinema in Chile, founded in 1942 as part of the Popular Front government's efforts to invest in the country's industrial infrastructure. Boasting modern new studios, it attracted Argentine technical assistance and directors such as Carlos Hugo **Christensen** (from Argentina) and Pierre Chenal and Jacques Rémy (from France). However, its efforts to establish Chilean films in the domestic market and to create export markets through its 'international' films had essentially failed by 1947. The agency was 'reinvented' in 1970, when **Allende**'s **Popular Unity** (UP) government came to power and put the agency in the hands of a group of film-makers who had supported UP during the electoral process. Miguel **Littín** was named its first director. Although crippled by an unwieldy bureaucratic structure and beset by the political differences that also undermined UP itself, Chile Films embarked on **documentary**/newsreel (see **newsreels**) production and organized film-making workshops and seminars. However, it was not able to produce any feature length films before Pinochet's September 1973 *coup* closed its doors forever.

ANA M. LÓPEZ

Chircales

Made by Colombian film-makers Marta **Rodríguez** and Jorge **Silva**, *Chircales* (The Brickmakers) (1976) documents the lives of a family of brickmakers in the outskirts of Bogotá, using the personal experience of the Castañeda family to expose the exploitation of manual laborers. Rodríguez's doctoral work at the National University, *Chircales* examines the social structures and class relations which feed the oppression of Bogotá's slums. Rodríguez and her photographer husband Silva worked on *Chircales* from 1966 to 1972, establishing a relationship with the family which allows the viewer an intimate look at their hardships. For the first six months, Rodríguez and Silva worked at getting to know the community, assuring the families' active participation and gaining the community's trust. The resulting film combines modes of critical inquiry (anthropology, sociology) with a variety of **documentary** approaches (direct address, observational sequences and re-enactments).

Without preaching, Rodríguez and Silva denounce the treatment of these people, showing how the family works as a team, right down to the smallest child who contributes by helping to fill brick moulds and to carry hard bricks up a steep hill to the kiln. The film's texture and pace emphasize the poverty which traps the family. Voiceover narration by the children explains the difficulty of having to provide for a large family and the ironic necessity of a large family in order to do the work. Images of a first communion and talks of dreams for a better life remind us that faith and hope are all the brickmakers have.

A political and ideological exercise, *Chircales* was the first Colombian film to criticize the social structures that created an impoverished subclass. The production of *Chircales* made the brickmakers themselves aware of oppressive class structures which perpetuated their poverty. The completed film appealed to a middle-class audience, leaving the resolution of the situation to the viewer. Union and labour groups used *Chircales* to initiate dialogue among themselves. Students viewing the film in the mid-1960s may have had their social consciousness awakened. As Zuzana Pick notes, 'The film-makers realized that the making of a film, rather than an end itself, constitutes only a starting point, that the political work of the film begins with its audiences' (p. 44).

With *Chircales*, Rodríguez and Silva joined the ranks of the **New Latin American Cinema**, using an ethnographic approach to depict the social reality of Colombia. The influence of this documentary can be seen in the work of other Colombians, most notably Gabriela **Samper**, Gloria Triana, **Cine Mujer**, Carlos **Mayolo** and Luis **Ospina**. Furthermore, as one of the earlier New Latin American documentaries, *Chircales* influenced film-makers across Latin America and around the world.

Further reading

Burton, J.(1976) '*The Brickmakers*', *Cinéaste* 7(3): 38–9.

—— (1986) 'Cine-Sociology and Social Change: Jorge Silva and Marta Rodríguez', in J. Burton (ed.), *Cinema and Social Change in Latin America: Conversations with Filmmakers*, Austin, TX: University of Texas Press.

Pick, Z. (1993) *The New Latin American Cinema: A Continental Project*, Austin, TX: University of Texas Press.

ILENE S. GOLDMAN

Chocrón, Isaac

b. 1930, Maracay, Venezuela

Playwright, essayist and novelist

Although he studied economics and international relations in the United States, Chocrón's major contribution to the culture of his country has been in the theatre and in prose fiction. His theatre pieces transcend the simple references to the national reality to present conflicts and passions of universal significance. In the 1960s he co-founded, with José Ignacio **Cabrujas** and Román **Chalbaud**, the Nuevo Grupo theatre company, and at the end of the 1980s formed the Compañía Nacional de Teatro. In 1963 he was awarded the Ateneo de Caracas prize for his *Animales feroces* (Fierce Animals), and in 1979 won the National Theatre Prize.

JORGE ROMERO LEÓN

cholera

A gastrointestinal infection caused by the micro-organism *vibrio cholerae*, cholera causes a sudden and violent diarrhoea leading to dehydration which, if untreated, may be fatal. Like typhoid fever and hepatitis, it is communicated by faecal contamination of water and food. Contagion is easily prevented by maintaining toilet and kitchen hygiene, washing hands before meals, sterilizing drinking water and avoiding uncooked food. Cholera tends to affect poor people living in unsanitary conditions.

The disease had not been diagnosed in Latin America since the late nineteenth century until January 1991, when a cholera epidemic started in Chimbote, Peru. This spread quickly to other parts of Peru and, despite border controls, intense hygiene education and sanitation campaigns, to neighbouring Ecuador, Chile and Bolivia. Cases of cholera were subsequently diagnosed throughout Latin America and the Caribbean, and the disease has become endemic, causing regular minor epidemics during the warmer months of the year and during religious and traditional festivities. From its appearance in January 1991 until

November 1995, cholera affected 1.1 million people and killed 9,000 victims in Latin America, 5,000 of whom died in Peru during the first eighteen months.

The variety of *vibrio cholerae* responsible for the epidemic is *El Tor*, a mild form of the disease. Mortality rates were low relative to several other causes; compare the outcome of the 1.5 million HIV-positive cases estimated to exist in Latin America. However, cholera had a greater impact on society and culture than any other disease in the 1990s, in part due to extensive media coverage.

Cholera appeared in Peru when municipal infrastructure was decaying after the hyperinflation years of the 1980s (see **inflation and hyperinflation**) and as a result of the reductions in public sector funding typical of **neoliberalism**. Street vending of food proliferated as unemployment rose, and hygiene and sanitation regulations were generally neglected. President **Fujimori** signed a decree legalizing street vending shortly before the 1991 outbreak. Crucial in the spread of the epidemic was *ceviche*, the Peruvian national dish of uncooked fish marinated in lime juice. The fishing industry resisted warnings against eating raw fish, and contagion levels increased.

The cholera epidemic reinforced Latin America's third world image; there was talk of the 'Calcuttaization' of Latin America. The positive effect has been an increased awareness of the dangers of intestinal infections, often considered normal in children, like diarrhoea and gastrointestinal diseases.

Further reading

Reyna, C. (1991) *Crónica sobre el cólera en el Perú*, Lima: Desco.

MAARIA SEPPÄNEN

cholo

A *cholo* is a person of mixed race, the offspring of Indian and white parents but with a preponderance of indigenous features. In general, *cholo* refers to a social climber who follows western cultural practices. He is a despised person in the Andean highlands because he exploits the Indians. Likewise, whites reject him because the *cholo*'s social condition and manners are still improvised and unrefined. The perceived increase in the number of *cholos* in the twentieth century led (in the 1940s) to the revalorization of *cholo* culture, including the creation of *cholista* poetry.

JUAN ZEVALLOS-AGUILAR

choro

Also known as *chorinho*, choro is a primarily instrumental tradition of music which is comparable to, but predates, early North American jazz. Typically played by a small ensemble of string and wind instruments with light percussion, it combines rhythmic syncopation, contrapuntal, virtuoso melodic improvisation and unexpected harmonic modulations.

The uncertain etymology of the name reflects the style's ambiguity: it may derive from the Portuguese word for 'weeping' or from the Afro-Brazilian *xolo*, meaning 'party'. Its musical origins, meanwhile, are found in the inflected interpretations which amateur instrumentalists of Rio de Janeiro gave to popular European dance forms, such as the polka, waltz and mazurka, from the 1870s onwards. These musicians, such as the virtuoso flautist Joaquim Antônio da Silva Calado, were often petty functionaries and ex-military bandsmen whose access to a degree of formal education and training brought a classical musical culture to bear on the popular traditions of the city's black, ex-slave communities. The same musical hybridity was reflected in many of the genre's classically-trained composers, such as the pianists Chiquinha **Gonzaga**, Ernesto **Nazaré** and Zequinha de Abreu, whose 1917 composition 'Tico-Tico no Fubá' was performed by Carmen **Miranda** in the 1947 film *Copacabana*. The early choro ensembles occupied an intermediate position, performing both in the city's working-class suburbs and the households of its bourgeois elite.

Until the second decade of the century, the choro band typically had comprised three instruments: the cavaquinho, a four-stringed, miniature guitar similar to the ukulele; the violão, a conventional six-string guitar sometimes supplemented with an additional bass-string; and the flute, which leads the improvisation and carries the melodic theme.

This instrumentation was enriched by the legendary flautist **Pixinguinha** and his group Oito Batutas, who first added percussion instruments such as the ganzá (a metal shaker), the pandeiro (a tambourine) and the reco-reco (a scraper). Then, following a hugely successful six-month period in Paris, Pixinguinha and the Oito Batutas incorporated the trumpet, clarinet and saxophone they had encountered in the European foxtrot orchestras, as well as bringing back a new repertoire of dance styles, such as ragtime, shimmies and the foxtrot itself. Their stay in Paris also initiated a musical dialogue with modernist composer Darius Milhaud, which was taken up in Brazil by Heitor **Villa-Lobos**, whose 'Suite Populaire Brésilienne' for guitar, the orchestral 'Choros' and the 'Bachiana Brasileira No.5', recombined this already hybrid tradition with classical European structures.

Since the 1920s, the commercial success of this essentially small-scale, bar-room genre has ebbed and flowed in competition with other musical traditions enjoying greater mass appeal, such as **samba**. But the latter has also been coloured and shaped by its stylistic idiom, whose technical demands have influenced the development of successive generations of instrumentalists. The revivals of the 1940s and 1970s produced new string virtuosos such as Jacó do Bandolim and Waldir Azevedo, and reeds players Abel Ferreira and Paulo **Moura**, as well as experimental fusions with rock and jazz in the work of Novos Baianos and Hermeto **Paschoal**.

Further reading

Vasconcelos, A. (1984) *Carinhoso etc: história e inventário do choro*, Rio de Janeiro: Gráfica Editora do Livro.

DAVID TREECE

Christensen, Carlos Hugo

b. 1916, Buenos Aires, Argentina

Film-maker

At age twenty-two, Christensen entered the **Lumitón** Studios, and a year later (1939) he directed his first feature. He went on to become the principal Lumitón director of the 1940s and set the studio's style, especially after his *Safo, historia de una pasión* (Sappho, Story of a Passion) (1943) and *El ángel desnudo* (The Naked Angel) (1946) introduced explicit eroticism into the melodrama. He made over two dozen films in Argentina, Chile and Venezuela before emigrating to Brazil in 1954, where he worked for the mainstream industry. His films are notable for their visual style, exotic ambiences and skilful performances.

DIANA PALADINO

Christian Base Organizations

In the socio-ecclesial context of Latin America and the Caribbean, the three words that make up the terms Christian Base Organizations (CBOs) have a specific significance. 'Organizations' refers to the voluntary and conscious association of people pursuing common objectives, usually linked to an agenda of social justice, by means of collective, continuous and often conflictive activities. 'Christian' refers to the concepts, symbols and ethical-religious principles rooted in the Christian tradition, from which many of these organizations take their inspiration. 'Base' refers to those social groups who make up the membership of the CBOs, the poor and oppressed majority. In this sense, the CBOs constitute a central space for the education, participation and transforming activity of oppressed groups seeking to intervene in their society and for the churches who seek greater social justice in accordance with the central message of Christian Scripture. The CBOs have to be understood in the current context of reality as social subjects contributing to the social and religious life of Latin America and the Caribbean.

The decade of the 1990s has been marked by the collapse of the historic socialist regimes, the end of the cold war and the imposition of a capitalist economy as the sole model on a world scale. This model comes endowed with a totalitarian neoliberal (see **neoliberalism**) ideology, which affirms that capitalism is the best guarantee of human progress, that the sustained development of humanity is impossible outside that framework and that capitalism's ethical foundations are the guarantee of the welfare of society as a whole. In fact, the current capitalist model is based on the disproportionate accumulation of capital, an unrestrained competition where only the strongest survive, the growing concentration of social power in the hands of powerful groups (usually) of men, the abuse of the environment and the protection of the interests of the powerful nations of the North. In reality, the model places the weaker nations of the South, the non-white peoples, women, the poor and the earth itself at a structural disadvantage. The actual functioning of the model has produced growing social discontent among the victims of injustice, has universalized the suffering of the oppressed, has created a culture of institutional violence and has provoked a series of social explosions against these abuses and this violence. These explosions of resistance to the prevailing social model have been expressed in the growth of networks, organizations and social movements working for social justice, democracy, participation, resistance, self-determination and the survival of the poor and oppressed of the earth. Many of these movements have been inspired by the liberating message of the Christian faith; it is these which constitute the main body of Christian Base Organizations.

Although the CBOs emerged towards the end of the 1960s with the support of the **Medellín Conference**, **liberation theology** and the Ecclesial Base Communities, it was in the 1990s that they acquired their main significance. Unlike the past, the social force capable of transforming society is no longer the traditional working class but the diverse and plural social movements that have come to intervene directly in the life of society and the churches in the struggle for their own rights. These movements are considered new social subjects because they have generated continuous,

organized and self-conscious activity directed at the transformation of social life. Although there is a great variety of social subjects, together they constitute a key social force for the establishment of a new social model free of violence, racism and patriarchal domination. The most dynamic social movements in the Latin America and Caribbean of the 1990s are the feminist (see **feminism**), indigenous (see **indigenous movements**), black (see **black movements**), green (see **green activism**) and youth movements.

The CBOs must be set in the context of this dynamic process of composition, participation and articulation of new social subjects. Given Christianity's enormous .influence in Latin America, the CBOs not only add a deep religious content to social life, but also contribute to the definition of a social subject which is growing in power and increasing its transforming impact on church and society. These organizations advocate the communal activities of the victims of injustice: to build a new social power 'from below' based on justice, liberty and the well-being of the whole of creation; to seek collective means to support solidarity and respect for human rights; to strengthen every action that favours the survival, resistance and self-determination of people and peoples; to develop social and religious models that value and encourage the participation of the poor, women, indigenous peoples, non-white races and all other groups excluded from the exercise of social power; to encourage the development of new cultural models free from violence, alienation and oppression; to support every initiative that seeks to eliminate violence against women; and to build alliances with the variety of actors and socio-religious subjects who express an authentically ecumenical and culturally plural Christianity. Finally, the Christian Base Organizations bring a message of hope for the victims of injustice in two senses: on the one hand they are the incarnation of the idea of Christianity as 'good news' for the poor and oppressed, and on the other they give a glimpse of what the future could be like in a society and a church genuinely devoted to human liberation.

Further reading

Fornet-Betancourt, R. (1994) 'El cristianismo:

perspectivas de futuro en el umbral del tercer milenio a partir de la experiencia de América Latina', *Pasos* 51: 1–8.

Gallardo, H. (1995) 'América Latina en la década de los noventa', *Pasos* 59: 11–25.

Rauber, I. (1995) 'Actores sociales, luchas reivindicativas y política popular', *Pasos* 62: 15–31.

Richard, P. (1991): 'La teología de la liberación en la nueva coyuntura: temas y desafíos para la década de los 90', *Pasos* 34: 1–8.

MARÍA PILAR AQUINO

Christian Democracy

Christian Democracy is a political movement based initially on the Catholic social doctrines which emphasised improving the living standards of the poor. It reached Latin America from western Europe in the 1940s and 1950s, claiming to represent a 'third way' between capitalism and communism. Christian Democrat parties were established in Chile (1957), Bolivia (1964), Paraguay (1965), Peru (1955) and Venezuela (1946). Latin American Christian Democrats have their own regional organization and labour federation (CLAT). They have received major funding from Germany's Konrad Adenauer Foundation as well as from the USA, which regards them as a useful bulwark against the more radical parties of the left.

Christian Democrat candidates have won the presidency in three countries. In 1964, Eduardo **Frei** came to power in Chile with a programme of major reforms in health and education as well as an ambitious agrarian reform. But few of the promises were fulfilled. The radical and youth sections split from the party, while by 1973 many Christian Democrats supported the military *coup* against the **Allende** government. When it became clear that General **Pinochet** had no intention of relinquishing power to them, as some had hoped, Christian Democracy moved into opposition, becoming the chief organising force behind the successful 'No' campaign in the 1988 plebiscite. The 1989 elections were won by Christian Democrat Patricio Aylwin, and the party retained the presidency in 1994 under Eduardo **Frei Ruiz**

Tagle. His party remains the single largest group in Chile.

In Venezuela, the Social Christians (COPEI) became the second largest political party and won presidential elections in 1968 under Rafael Caldera and in 1978 under Luis Herrera Campins. In the turmoil following President Carlos Andrés **Pérez**'s impeachment and two attempted military *coups* in 1992 and 1993, Caldera was again elected president, this time as the candidate of Convergencia Nacional, an electoral alliance of sixteen small parties.

El Salvador's Christian Democratic Party was founded by José Napoleón Duarte, a US-trained civil engineer who became mayor of San Salvador in 1964. Duarte appeared to win the presidential elections of 1972, but the military refused to recognise the victory and forced him into exile. He returned to El Salvador with US backing to head a civilian–military coalition, and in 1984 was elected president. He proved unable to end repression or achieve peace, however, and after his death in 1992 his party lost much ground to the right wing **ARENA**.

Christian Democracy has been, and remains, a major political movement in Latin America, whose explicitly Catholic character has helped it to cut across class, regional, ethnic and gender divisions and whose ideology of the 'third way' has offered an alternative to the traditional organizations of the right and left.

Further reading

Fleet, M. (1985), *The Rise and Fall of Chilean Christian Democracy*, New York: Praeger.

Martz, J. and Myers, D. (eds) (1986) *Venezuela: The Democratic Experience*, Princeton, NJ: Princeton University Press.

Webre, S. (1982) *José Napoleón Duarte and the Christian Democratic Party in Salvadorean Politics 1960–1972*, Baton Rouge, LA: Louisana State University Press.

Williams, E. (1967) *Latin American Christian Democrat Parties*, Knoxville: University of Tennessee Press.

PHILIP O'BRIEN

Christmas

The present-day celebration of Christmas in Latin America is characterized by changes in traditional customs brought about by secularization and commercialization. Some Christmas customs, formerly considered indispensable, have been done away with – for example, in some places the display of a manger or crèche scene, and, in Mexico, the presentation of a *pastorela*, or Christmas skit, depicting scenes of or related to the Nativity. Christmas trees, both artificial and natural, in cities and towns, contribute to the holiday atmosphere, created in large part by television and radio Christmas programmes, movies and visits to shopping malls. Pop or rock music versions of Christmas carols are played, while the more traditional *pastorela* is presented in theatres, schools and public squares.

Christmas celebrations and parties with neighbours and friends, which provide an opportunity to eat and drink, and to dance **salsa**, **merengue** or rock, also include such traditions as breaking the *piñata* or seeking *posada*, or lodging, for the Christ Child. Fireworks fill the skies at midnight on Christmas Eve and, again, on New Year's Eve. The Christmas holidays provide an opportunity to display newly acquired clothing and to exchange gifts. Children traditionally receive their gifts from the Christ Child on Christmas Day and from the Magi on 6 January, although Santa Claus and his reindeers are also very much in evidence now. Attendance at *Misa de Gallo*, or Midnight Mass, on Christmas Eve is still *de rigueur*. This follows Christmas dinner with the family, at which roast turkey is now served in place of or alongside more traditional meals of mole and fish in Mexico, *ajiaco* (corn, pork, eggs, olives, capers and raisins) in Venezuela, sweet breads and cider in Argentina and Brazil, or suckling pig, and chicken and rice in Colombia. Families gather on Christmas Day to eat the *recalentado*, or leftovers, either at home or at the beach, and frequent gatherings and parties are held throughout the week. This is until New Year's Eve, which is greeted with another large family meal, by the customary eating of twelve grapes at the stroke of midnight, and with attendance at another Midnight Mass, which once again provides the opportunity to display newly acquired clothing.

Further reading

Brady, A.M. and Márquez de Moats, Margarita (1986) *La Navidad: Christmas in Spain and Latin America*, Lincolnwood: National Textbook.

Foley, D. (1967) *Christmas the World Over*, Philadelphia: Chilton Book.

EDUARDO GUÍZAR-ALVAREZ

Chumpitaz, Héctor

b. 1944, Cañate, Peru

Soccer player

An outstanding defender with a strong left foot shot, he is the only Peruvian player with over 100 international matches to his credit; between 1965 and 1981 he played 111 times for his country in A internationals alone. He defended Peru in two World Cup final rounds (1970, 1978) and two South American championships (1975, 1979), winning the title on the earlier occasion. His career spanned from 1963 to 1983 and, with the exception of two years in Mexico, he played all his football in Peru, mostly with two big clubs, Universitario and Sporting Cristal.

ERIC WEIL

Churata, Gamaliel (Arturo Peralta)

b. 1897, Puno, Peru; d. 1969, Lima, Peru

Writer

Churata was the leading figure of the avant-garde movement in Puno, the provincial centre of 1920s vanguard activity in Peru, and editor of its journal *Boletín Titikaka*. Central to his agenda was the reconciliation of the indigenous Andean cultural tradition with the liberating forces of modernity. That project underlies *El pez de oro* (The Golden Fish) (1957), a long, hermetic book that employs surrealist techniques (see **surrealism in Latin American art**), generic mixing, and a hybrid language combining Spanish with **Quechua** and

Aymara in an attempt to fuse conflicting traditions into a cohesive whole.

JAMES HIGGINS

Churubusco Studios

The film studio Churubusco Studios was founded in 1944, in the heyday of Mexican cinema, under the direction of Emilio Azcárraga, Mauricio de la Serna and others and RKO's financial backing. It offered up-to-date technology and a sophisticated infrastructure. Starting with Emilio 'El Indio' **Fernández**'s *La perla* (The Pearl) (1945), the best Mexican films were made at Churubusco, providing the main source of work for the members of the Cinema Workers Trade Union (**STPC**). By the 1990s, despite occasional financial crises which threatened to lead to its reprivatization, the studio continued to offer the best facilities to both Mexican and foreign film-makers.

PATRICIA TORRES SAN MARTÍN

chutney

Chutney's up-tempo beat and often irreverent lyrics have always made it a favourite among East Indians in Trinidad and Guyana, but recently it has started to win a wider audience. By taking Indian film music, East Indian folk songs and *bhajans* (devotional songs), and infusing them with a **calypso** or **soca** beat, chutney musicians rearticulate their cultural heritage as Trinidadian Guyanese Indians. Chutney songs traditionally relied on the harmonium for melody and the dholak (a goatskin drum, just over two feet long) and the dhantal (a metal rod) for percussion. In the studios, keyboards and drum machines are now added, as well as tassa drumming, a feature of the Muslim *hosay* festival.

LORRAINE LEU

CIA

If popular mythology were to be believed, the CIA (Central Intelligence Agency) would be responsible for the majority of invasions, interventions and plots in Latin America. It has become a metaphor for US meddling in Latin America's internal affairs and an emblem of international conspiracy. It would be foolish to deny the constant attention given to Latin American internal politics by the CIA, formed in 1947 out of the Office of Strategic Services, which had been created during the Second World War to organize covert operations. It was one of a network of institutions and agencies whose brief was to ensure the ideological and political 'stability' of the Western bloc in the Cold War arena. In 1954, for example, its involvement in the overthrow of the progressive **Arbenz** government was quite explicit, as the United Fruit Company – an exemplar of free-market capitalism – defended its Guatemalan territories through the good offices of the Dulles brothers, one the Secretary of State and the other head of the CIA, and both owned stock in the company. Its active involvement with anti-**Castro** Cuban exiles was demonstrated in its training and preparation of the disastrous Bay of Pigs invasion of 1961. Rumours of its continuing attempts to kill Castro by increasingly exotic means (exploding cigars for one) belonged to the realm of folklore. However, its direct involvement in disinformation, corruption and support of covert operations was never in doubt. A CIA operative was present at the death of Che **Guevara** in Bolivia in 1967, for example; and CIA involvement in the attempted sabotage of the 1964 Chilean elections was well proven. More significant than these isolated acts, however, were the financing of anti-communist **trade unions** throughout the region, and the marshalling of newspapers and other information media in the anti-communist cause. And culture was not alien territory, as the ***Mundo nuevo*** affair revealed the extent of CIA involvement in the Congress for Cultural Freedom. The Chilean *coup* of 1973 was frequently attributed to the CIA – in fact, it now seems undeniable that US involvement implicated the military directly, on the one hand, and ideological and financial support for local forces and groups, on the other. In Central America in the 1980s, the CIA played a significant part in a massive US operation to contain and destroy the 1979 Nicaraguan Revolution (see **revolutions**), its growing role reflecting the difficulty for the US government in using direct military involvement in the wake of the Vietnam debacle – though the involvement of Oliver North in arms dealing in the 1980s showed that the lines between direct and indirect involvement were often very hazy. After the fall of the Berlin Wall, there was some evidence of confusion as to the future role of the CIA – though since then it seems to have turned its activities towards other international 'agents of subversion', like Islamic fundamentalism or cocaine traders.

Further reading

Agee, P. (1975) *Inside the Company: CIA Diary*, New York: Stonehill Communications.

Woodward, B. (1987) *Veil: The Secret Wars of the CIA 1981–1987*, New York: Simon & Shuster.

MIKE GONZALEZ

Ciclón

The magazine *Ciclón* (1955–7, 1959) signalled a moment of rupture with the writers and aesthetics of **Orígenes** and José **Lezama Lima** (both magazines were financed by José Rodríguez Feo). *Ciclón's* publication coincided with the waning days of the **Batista** dictatorship in Cuba. Editor Virgilio **Piñera** risked the ire of his compatriots by outing Emilio **Ballagas** as homosexual and publishing translations of texts such as Sade's *120 Days of Sodom* in 1955, in a section titled 'Textos futuros'. After the 1959 Cuban Revolution (see **revolutions**), most of its members worked in the even more anarchic ***Lunes de revolución***, until it was shut down by the revolutionary government and its members went into exile or settled into an uneasy accommodation with the government.

JOSÉ QUIROGA

Cien años de soledad

Probably the most successful novel to come out of Latin America, Gabriel **García Márquez**'s *Cien años de soledad* (One Hundred Years of Solitude) was published in 1967. The novel is set, like most of his writing, in the fictional community of Macondo. Macondo has several narrative functions: it stands for Colombia's particular experience and for Latin America's colonial history. The town is isolated and enclosed, and yet is subject to forces and changes that lie beyond its imprisoning frontiers that shape and determine its destiny. In precisely that sense, Macondo echoes the experience of a colonized world imagined and structured by a distant and unreachable metropolis. The 'hundred years' of the title is not exact time, but a metaphorical 'century' that embraces all of the key experiences of the region from Conquest through the military authoritarianism of the post-independence republics to the neo-colonialism practised by US capital; it chronicles, too, the acts of resistance (strikes and rebellions), the natural and man-made catastrophes, and the ultimate abandonment by those very colonial powers leaving a Latin America that will ultimately be consumed in a final cataclysm.

Yet it is also an immensely funny book, its humour sustained by the exaggerated mythical actions of some of its key characters, the distortions and disturbances of time, the mockery of life and death. It is as if there were twin narratives at work – the first historical and linear, the second rooted in myth and legend, a kind of popular alternative history in which the inescapable truths of one world were reversed in another. It is this conjunction of narrative modes, this mutual reflection of history upon myth and vice versa, that is encapsulated in García Márquez's own description of his method of writing as '**magical realism**'.

The encounter of opposites continues in other ways too: José Arcadio Buendía, patriarch of the family/clan whose family history evolves through the novel, spends most of his life bent on a search for the philosopher's stone, the scientific solution to the transformation of lead into gold and thus of nature into culture. His lifelong companion, Ursula, is profoundly sceptical about the enterprise, trusting instead to a different but equally present knowledge – the collective understanding of folk wisdom and collective experience sometimes described as 'magic' or even 'superstition'. It gives her gifts of prophecy, of healing and a capacity to move effortlessly between the two. That conflictive relationship between nature and science, popular wisdom and science, is replayed in one way or another with each generation of the Buendías. But the problem seems to be that the secrets of scientific knowledge are held elsewhere and introduced piecemeal into the community, often by the travelling gypsy Melquíades, who brings ice and false teeth to the village.

Yet at the same time another power seems to govern the lives of this community and its members, a destiny symbolized by the pig's tail that Ursula knows will one day appear on the body of a Buendía child and mark the fulfilment of a curse; a judgement on some original sin, a fall from Eden that preceded the creation of Macondo. This, of course, is another (religious) narrative – and a prediction fulfilled in the final moments of the novel when knowledge immediately precedes destruction, in an uncanny echo of some of the fictions of Jorge Luis **Borges**. Yet, in the end, the narrative – the tale told – does remain as evidence of a history already lived and of a history to come, which will add its own account to the sum of myth and history that is Latin America.

Further reading

Bell, M. (1993) *Gabriel García Márquez: Solitude and Solidarity*, London: Macmillan.

Ludmer, J. (1975) *Cien años de soledad: Una interpretación*, Buenos Aires: Editorial Sudamericana.

Martin, G. (1987) 'On magical and social realism in García Márquez', in B McGuirk and R. Cardwell (eds) *Gabriel García Márquez: New Readings*, Cambridge: Cambridge University Press.

Wood, M. (1990) *García Márquez: One Hundred Years of Solitude*, Cambridge: Cambridge University Press.

MIKE GONZALEZ

Cienfuegos, Camilo

b. 1932, Havana, Cuba; d. 1959, Camagüey, Cuba

Political leader

Cienfuegos was a popular hero of the Cuban Revolution (see **revolutions**). He joined the 26th of July movement in Mexico and was a member of the 1956 Granma expedition led by Fidel **Castro**. His courage in action in the Sierra Maestra earned him the rank of Comandante of the Rebel Army; in the final assault, in late 1958, he led one of the military columns marching from the east. Appointed Chief of Staff of the Rebel Army after the revolution, he was killed in an air crash, the causes of which remain unknown.

WILFREDO CANCIO ISLA

cigars

No accessory complements the Latin American man as well as the phallic symbol *par excellence* of a smouldering cigar. Most Latin American strongmen have relished them publicly; it is hard to imagine Fidel **Castro** without one clenched tightly between his teeth (despite his recent public renunciation of the habit). Many consider a fine Cuban cigar one of life's great luxuries; its intensely rich and multidimensional flavours can give as much pleasure as the most majestic of European wines or the finest of world-class cuisine. In the 1980s and 1990s, cigar smoking became *de rigueur* for the rich and famous everywhere.

Columbus and the explorers who followed him in Cuba, Mexico, Central America and Brazil found that the Indians smoked a long, thick bundle of twisted tobacco leaves wrapped in a dried palm leaf or corn (maize) husk. By 1600 the cigar had been introduced into Spain, where it was a symbol of conspicuous wealth for two centuries before it was widely used in other European countries. Columbus may have been disappointed when he discovered tobacco instead of gold in Cuba, but the value of his discovery has turned out to be a treasure in its own right.

Cigars consist of three basic types of tobacco

leaves. The filler leaves are the heart or centre of the cigar; most cigars use two to four different types of tobacco to create the filler blend. Once put together, it is known as the bunch. The bunch is bound with a separate tobacco leaf known as a binder. Finally, a delicate tobacco leaf, known as the wrapper, is placed around the outside of the bunch. A painstaking process, cigar rolling is a skill that can take years to master. Rollers typically work together in large rooms or *galerías*, where a reader – usually paid for by the rollers themselves – reads the daily news or literary works.

The cigar became the national symbol of Cuba in the 1850s when it became a fully fledged industry with over 9,000 plantations and factories. It was in the rolling *galerías* that the first words of revolution against Spain were spoken in the late 1800s; Jose Martí is said to have sent orders from Key West, Florida, to Cuba hidden inside a cigar.

Cuba has five key tobacco-growing districts; of these, Vuelta Abajo in Pinar del Río province (about 100 miles west of Havana) is to tobacco what Bordeaux and Burgundy are to wines: it produces the very best. Tobacco is an extremely important product to Cuba, its fourth biggest export behind sugar, nickel and citrus fruits; annual sales, primarily to Europe, total about $150 million. Cuban cigars have been banned from the USA since 1962, although many millions find their way into US humidors illicitly. Before the Cuban Revolution (see **revolutions**), the cigar industry was in private hands with large US corporations controlling a significant amount of the business. Since 1960, when the government took control of the industry, the Cuban cigar trade has had its ups and downs, which has led to periodic quality control problems, although the Cubans always say that they save the best for export.

At one time Cuba sold hundreds of different cigar brands, with distinctive bands in each cigar and in wooden boxes adorned with exquisite lithographs (these have now become collector's items). Today Cuba produces about two-dozen different brands, with Montecristo accounting for about 40 per cent of all exports. Some of these brands are also produced in the Dominican Republic, Honduras and other countries (H. Upmann, Partagas, Punch, and Romeo & Julieta, for example), a practice that began when the

original brand owners fled from the revolution with their trademarks and set up shops in other countries. Until recently, Cuba also continued to produce and sell these brands, but recent court decisions in Spain and France have questioned Cuba's ownership of various brands.

It is ironic, of course, that at a time when Castro continues to argue that Cuba remains a beacon of socialist values in a world heading for ruin because of rampant capitalism, the island's most successful export should have become the greatest symbol of capitalist success.

Further reading

Cabrera Infante, G. (1985) *Holy Smoke*, London: Faber & Faber.

Ortiz, Fernando (1940) *Contrapunteo del tabaco y el azúcar*, Havana, J. Montero.

ANA M. LÓPEZ

Cine Argentino

Cine Argentino was an Argentine journal devoted to national cinema. Its memorable cover photos (outstanding among them the work of Annemarie Heinrich and Rosa Marie) launched many young actors and marked a career highlight for many famous actresses. Its various sections covered three areas: interviews with actors, news on future programming and reviews of new and coming films. It was published between 1938 and the mid-1940s, and was an invaluable chronicler of the 'golden age' of Argentine cinema.

DIANA PALADINO

cine clubs

Cine clubs were groups organized by film enthusiasts, often aspiring film-makers, to study the art of cinema through screenings, discussions, or actual filmmaking. Originating in France in the 1920s, alongside the general effervescence of the arts and avant-garde, cine clubs were the motors for the development of the cinema as an art form and of film culture (specialized cinemas, film criticism (see **film criticism and scholarship**), dedicated magazines, **cinematheques**, ´**film festivals**, etc.). Marked by the 'classics' of the period – the Surrealist and Soviet cinematic avant-garde – **Buñuel** and Eisenstein, for example – cine clubs soon became hotbeds of radical intellectual and political culture.

In Latin America, cine clubs appeared and followed a similar trajectory some years later; in the early years of film, until the coming of sound, the principal concern of those interested in the cinema was the viability of national film making. 1928 was the crucial year for Latin American cine clubs: in Brazil, a group gathered in Rio de Janeiro under the name 'Chaplin Club' and published its own journal (*O Fan*), while, in Cuba, film studies pioneer José Manuel Valdés Rodríguez, began gathering friends (including Fernando **Ortiz**, Raul Roa, and Juan **Marinello**) at his house to screen and debate international films.

Cine-clubism reached its apogee in the 1940s and 1950s. In Argentina, for example, the Cine Club Gente de Cine, established in 1942, evolved the model – hosting a radio show, screenings, publications, debates and conferences – followed by other clubs in Buenos Aires and throughout the provinces. Most notable was the impact of Cine Club Núcleo, headed by Salvador Sammaritano, Jose Agustín Mahieu, Héctor Vena and others. In Brazil, São Paulo's first cine club was organized by Paulo Emílio Salles **Gomes** in 1940, closed by the police in 1941, and not reopened until 1946. Subsequently, cine clubs and film associations mushroomed in the cities and provinces (Porto Alegre, Santos, Fortaleza, Minas Gerais) and film culture thrived through the 1950s with debates, conferences, and publications. They were the springboard for many of the innovations of **Cinema Novo** film-makers.

Meanwhile, in Cuba, following the example of the 'Cine de Arte' group created within the university in 1949 by Valdés Rodríguez, the Sociedad Nuestro Tiempo was created in 1951 with a film section which organized screenings and debates and published its own magazines. Other cine clubs were organized throughout the 1950s in the city – Cine Club Estudiantil, Cine-club Nocturno, Grupo Lumiere, Cine Club Visión – and in the provinces, most notably the group Cine

Local de Aficionados, in San Antonio de los Baños, future site of the Escuela Internacional de Cine y Televisión, which also dabbled in production. Nuestro Tiempo was instrumental in introducing Italian neorealism into Cuba and its members were the core group that, after the triumph of the Cuban Revolution in 1959 (see **revolutions**), created and were the spiritual and creative leaders of **ICAIC**, the Cuban film institute.

In the 1960s and 1970s, cine-clubism continued to grow and evolve in Cuba, under the sponsorship of schools, universities and various ministries. Elsewhere, however, cine clubism came under pressure from politics, especially in the 1970s. In Brazil, although a national congress had gathered representatives from more than 300 clubs in 1963, by 1969 the weight of repression from the military government had essentially liquidated the movement. In Argentina, the cine clubs became, in a sense, film-making collectives, most notably, the **Grupo Cine Liberación**. In Montevideo, the Cine Club Marcha, evolved into the more politized Cinemateca del Tercer Mundo under the leadership of Walter **Achugar**; it was closed down by the military in 1972.

By the 1980s, the inroads of television and new video technologies obviated the function of cine clubs and film associations. Most notably, however, in Cuba, the creation of the Film Workshop of the Asociación Hermanos Saez in 1987, as an outlet for would-be film-makers unable to gain access to the ICAIC, renovated the spirit of cine-clubism, although turned toward production rather than film appreciation and/or criticism.

ANA M. LÓPEZ

Cine cubano

A film magazine founded in Havana in 1960 by Alfredo **Guevara**, *Cine cubano* was also edited by Julio **García Espinosa** (1981–91). Initially a monthly, it moved to publication four times a year and since the 1980s it has appeared irregularly. Mainly devoted to promoting Cuban and Latin American cinema, it has also published numerous articles and interviews concerned with film in the socialist countries and other currents that offered aesthetic alternatives to Hollywood. Its contributors have included recognized Cuban and foreign film critics, and from the 1960s onwards it provided an open space for the Cuban graphic artists who developed the Cuban film poster. It has also published policy documents relating to cinema and broader cultural issues, as well as political articles in support of official policy.

WILFREDO CANCIO ISLA

Cine de la Base *see* Grupo Cine de la Base

cine imperfecto

This term was coined by Julio **García Espinosa** in an essay entitled 'Por un cine imperfecto' (For an Imperfect Cinema), which was first published in **Cine cubano** no. 42/3/4 in 1967 and widely translated and reprinted. This powerful reflection on the practices of revolutionary film-making became a credo for the **ICAIC** cinema and one of the principal theoretical statements of the **New Latin American Cinema**. Much misunderstood and debated, the essay warned against seeking cinematic technical and artistic 'perfection' as an end in and of itself. Arguing that attempting to match the production values of Hollywood and European cinemas was wasteful of resources and resulted in works with beautiful surfaces that could only be passively consumed, the essay called for films that actively engaged with audiences by inserting themselves and the audiences into their social reality. Thus the films would remain 'incomplete' or imperfect without audience participation. For García Espinosa, an authentic revolutionary film culture must draw on popular art forms and use as its raw materials the struggles and problems of ordinary people, with film-makers and spectators functioning as co-authors.

ANA M. LÓPEZ

Cine Independiente *see* Grupo Cine Independiente

cine móvil

The 'mobile cinemas' were based on the experience of early Soviet film-makers, who took equipment for projecting films to the most remote parts of the country where there were no cinemas. Beginning in 1961 under the auspices of the Cuban Film Institute **ICAIC**, these cinemas continued in some rural areas into the 1990s. Their original purpose was to inform and entertain the population while raising their general cultural level. Octavio **Cortázar**'s documentary *Por primera vez* (For the First Time) (1967) records the first visit of a 'mobile cinema' to a rural community and the emotions of a community encountering film for the first time.

WILFREDO CANCIO ISLA

Cine Mujer

Cine Mujer is a women's film and video production collective, founded in 1978 in Bogotá, Colombia by Sarah Bright and Eulalia Carrizosa. In twenty years, the Cine Mujer team became the longest surviving independent production and distribution entity in Latin America, its work transcending boundaries of national culture through themes of social change and feminism. Their award-winning fiction and documentary work includes *¿Y su mamá qué hace?* (And What Does Your Mother Do?) (1982), *Lucero* (1988), *Carmen Carrascal* (1982) and *A la salud de la mujer* (To Women's Health) (1992), a thirteen-part series on women's health care issues in Colombia.

ILENE S. GOLDMAN

Cinearte

Cinearte was a journal founded in 1926 by a group of journalists led by Adhemar **Gonzaga**, committed to inserting cinema into the range of cultural activities legitimated by the Brazilian bourgeoisie. It published articles by young idealists, advocated a Brazilian cinema aspiring to the level of Hollywood and tried to persuade government and local entrepreneurs to finance Brazilian productions which would follow strictly both the techniques and the plots of the dominant cinema. In practice, these ideas informed the work of **Cinédia**. The magazine's principle function was to make foreign and particularly North American films more widely known among Brazilian audiences, a role it played with great success from 1926 to 1942.

ISMAIL XAVIER AND THE USP GROUP

Cinédia

Cinédia was a film production company established in 1930. Its founder, Adhemar **Gonzaga**, assembled the best Brazilian film professionals to create the kind of film studio advocated by the journal *Cinearte*, closely modelled on Hollywood's big studios and star system. When it turned to comedy, the studios became successful with local stars like Carmen **Miranda** and the comic **Oscarito**, and helped establish the *chanchada* as the first Brazilian film genre. *Chanchadas* continued even when Cinédia lost its key role in Rio's film scene and turned over its studios to foreign directors and, later, to Brazilian television. Cinédia produced many important films, including Humberto **Mauro**'s *Ganga bruta* (Brutal Gang) (1933).

ISMAIL XAVIER AND THE USP GROUP

Cinelândia

Created in 1952 in Rio de Janeiro, the magazine *Cinelândia* (like its predecessor *Cinearte*) transformed a group of young actors (Anselmo **Duarte**, Cyll Farney) and actresses (Tonia Carrera, Eliana) from Rio de Janeiro's musical comedy scene into stars like their Hollywood equivalents. Even though it ultimately served to disseminate news about US cinema rather than to promote Brazilian film, the magazine did play its part in ensuring that some successful *chanchada* films by Brazilian producers like **Atlântida** became nationally known. This contributed to the popularization of this genre

which dominated the national film industry through the 1950s.

ISMAIL XAVIER AND THE USP GROUP

cinema

The history of the cinema in Latin America began with the importation of the equipment from Europe less than six months after its commercial introduction in 1895. Its status as a foreign import marked the cinema's early history as primarily a history of exhibition: foreign films arrived along with the equipment and awed audiences with their display of cosmopolitan modernity (see **cultural theory**). Nevertheless, throughout the silent cinema (see **silent film**) period, Latin Americans used the medium to document national reality (the events of the Mexican Revolution, for example) and experimented with various narrative formats, most notably the historical epic (which highlighted national history) and the melodrama. For the most part, however, these early films were for local consumption and rarely travelled beyond national/regional borders; production was sporadic, artisanal and nomadic.

By the First World War, when the Hollywood industry consolidated its hold over international distribution and the Latin American market, indigenous production became even more difficult, yet the **film exhibition** sector prospered as a result of the increased presence of foreign films. It continued to prosper throughout the transition to sound, circa 1927–30, as movie palaces were built – often financed by Hollywood firms – in all major cities, and specialized **film magazines** mushroomed. With sound, the cinema – alongside the also booming new medium of **radio** – became an important business and a significant social force. As audiences and critics rejected Hollywood's efforts to produce Spanish-language films – the so-called Hispanic cinema (see **Hispanic cinema in Hollywood**), with its typical mixture of accents and personnel – Latin American producers saw a window of opportunity based on their potential ability to be linguistically and musically authentic. Comparatively, it took much longer for the new technology to establish itself than it had for the silent cinema to appear, but the results were arguably much more profound.

Early sound film (see **sound film, early**) throughout the continent was characterized by technological and aesthetic experimentation, the former marked by a lack of a solid technological infrastructure, the latter by a search for new narrative forms. The most accomplished film-makers of this period – José Agustín **Ferreyra** in Argentina, Humberto **Mauro** in Brazil, Fernando de **Fuentes** and Arcady **Boytler** in Mexico, for example – reflected both a national consciousness and musical national culture, often within the parameters of melodrama.

The 'Golden Age'

From the mid-1930s through the 1940s, the cinema in Latin America developed following an industrial model of production: entrepreneurs saw the cinema as a business opportunity and developed it according to the then-triumphant Hollywood example. Lacking the Hollywood studios' ample economic resources, however, this film-making bourgeoisie would often also seek assistance from the State in an attempt to overcome its limitations. In Argentina, the first studio-based production companies appeared in 1933: **Argentina Sono Film** and Lumiton. Both amply exploited the popularity of the **tango** in, for example, Mario **Soffici**'s *El alma del bandoneón* (The Soul of the Bandoneón) (1935), starring Libertad **Lamarque**. Sono Films was especially lavish and well-funded. Other important directors were Luis Savslasky, Luis César **Amadori**, Lucas **Demare**, Manuel **Romero** and Leopoldo **Torres Ríos**. Under **Perón**, the industry was regulated by the Ministry of Information headed by Raul Apold – who apparently received direct orders from Evita **Perón** and forced many in the industry (like Lamarque) into exile. However, beyond a screen quota established in 1944, **Peronism** did not intervene directly in distribution and exhibition. In Mexico, the unprecedented success of the *comedia ranchera* (see **rancheras, comedias**), *Allá en el rancho grande* (Over There in the Big Ranch) (Fernando de Fuentes, 1936), stimulated production and international distribution: from twenty-five features films in 1936 to fifty-seven in 1938.

The politics of the Second World War also favoured the Mexican industry: backed by the USA, the Mexican industry was able to unhinge Argentina's popularity in the Spanish-language market and to establish its own hegemony. Between 1943 and 1950, the Mexican industry enjoyed a 'golden age', featuring the studios **CLASA**, Azteca, **Churubusco Studios** and a half-dozen others, and growing levels of protection from the State, beginning with the **Cárdenas** government's support of the CLASA studios and leading to the establishment of a Banco Nacional Cinematográfico (1947) and the creation of an important State agency for international distribution (Pelmex, 1945).

Without the experimentation of early sound cinema, this period is marked by its adherence to generic models, especially the melodrama and comedy. Already well-exploited in the silent period, the sound melodrama was 'nationalized' in Mexico and Argentina, and developed its own singular characteristics and frames of reference. It absorbed and featured popular music (the tango, **bolero**, etc.) and performers, and articulated a certain moral and sexual ambiguity that undeniably contributed to its appeal. In Mexico in particular, the genre was predominant and permeated all others, attracting ambitious directors like Luis **Buñuel**, Emilio **Fernández** and Roberto **Gavaldón**, as well as their more commercial counterparts like José **Bohr** and Juan **Orol**. It also made unique contributions to the **star system**. Among the women, the divas Dolores **Del Río** and María **Félix** coexisted alongside the idiosyncratic *cabareteras* Ninón **Sevilla** and María Antonieta **Pons**, and the all-suffering prototypical mother figure of Sara **García**. Especially in its revolutionary variants, the melodrama also consolidated the stardom of Pedro **Armendáriz**, Arturo de Córdova, Pedro **Infante** and Jorge **Negrete**.

Comedy, although less respected critically than the melodrama, was no less significant, and also had popular and more sophisticated variants. No other figure in the history of Latin America cinema ever matched the popularity and, in his earliest films, the critical ingenuity of Mario Moreno **Cantinflas**. Other important comedians were Luis **Sandrini** and Niní **Marshall** in

Argentina, and **Tin Tan** and Joaquín **Pardavé** in Mexico. Among the more sophisticated comedies of the period were Julio **Bracho**'s *¡Ay qué tiempos Señor Don Simón!* (Oh, What Times Don Simon) (Mexico, 1941) and Francisco **Múgica**'s *Los martes orquídeas* (Orchid Tuesdays) (Argentina, 1941).

The Brazilian industry developed less effusively than the Argentine and Mexican, and was dominated by carnivalesque musical comedies (***chanchadas***), popularized after the commercial success of *Alô, Alô, carnaval* (Hello, Hello, Carnival) (1936) by Adhemar **Gonzaga**, the founder of the **Cinédia** studios. The genre blossomed after the foundation of the **Atlântida** studios and the introduction of the great comic duo of **Grande Otelo** and **Oscarito**. Melodramas were also significant, but never acquired the currency of the Mexican and Argentine modes. Most notable was, perhaps, Gilda de Abreu's *O ebrio* (The Drunk) (1946), another Cinédia production. Carmen **Santos**, an almost *sui generis* example in this period of a female film entrepreneur was an actress, director and founder of the studio Brasil Vita Films. She worked with two of the most creative personalities of the period, Mário **Peixoto** and Humberto **Mauro**, and starred in and produced the latter's *Favela dos meus amores* (Favela of My Love) (1935) and *Argila* (Clay) (1940).

The other nations of the continent had to struggle both with the hegemonic presence of Hollywood and with the not-insignificant regional success of the Mexican and Argentine industries. Cuba, for example, became the supplier of Caribbean exoticism for the Mexican cinema, the source of rhythms and curvaceous rumberas, while local producer/directors like Félix B. **Caignet** strove to tropicalize the Mexican models. For the smaller nations of the continent, **co-productions** with either Mexico or Argentina were perceived as a way into international distribution and greater production resources: Cuba had a series of co-productions with Mexico in the 1940s and 1950s; **Chile Films**, the State institute for the cinema, with Argentina in the 1940s; Bolívar Films, a new Venezuelan producer, also reached out to Argentina and Carlos Hugo **Christensen**.

Searching for alternative models

The 1950s were decisive for Latin American cinema, a decade of increased expectations, renovation and expansion, marked, on the one hand, by the introduction of **television** (premièred in Mexico, Brazil and Cuba in 1950) and quantitative growth in production (Mexico had 136 features in 1958 and Argentina fifty-seven in 1950) and, on the other, a transformation of the expectations of audiences. A crucial factor was the development of film culture, exemplified by the growth of **cine clubs** and alternative cinema circuits, the rise of specialized film publications (see **film magazines**) and serious film criticism, and the entrance of film into universities (see **film criticism and scholarship**). The crisis of the studio mode of production – already being felt in Hollywood – was confirmed by the resounding failure of the Companhia Cinematográfica Vera Cruz (see **Vera Cruz Studios**) (1949–54) in Brazil, an ambitious, albeit tardy, attempt to create a quality, studio-based cinema. In the 1950s, Latin American audiences begin to turn towards other cinemas, especially Italian Neorealism, which presented an attractive non-industrial alternative. Neorealism had a marked impact on many of the new approaches to the medium in the 1950s, ranging from Margot **Benacerraf**'s *Araya* (Venezuela, 1959) and Fernando **Birri**'s *Tire Dié* (Throw me a Dime) (Argentina, 1958) to Ugo **Ulive**'s *Un vintén p'al Judas* (Twenty Cents for Judas) (Uruguay, 1959) and Nelson Pereira dos **Santos**'s *Rio 40 graus* (Rio, 40 Degrees) (Brazil, 1955). Another, albeit less visible influence, was the work of the British documentary school and John Grierson; its social preoccupations were very attractive to this new generation of 'cultured' audiences and Grierson was the guest of honour at one of the first **film festivals** sponsored by the **SODRE** in Montevideo.

Many would-be film-makers flocked to Europe to study film rather than learning via industry apprenticeships. They went to the Centro Sperimentale in Rome, the birthplace of Neorealism, as well as to the IDHEC in Paris and schools in London, Madrid, Germany, Moscow and Łódź. But within the industry itself, new figures emerged with a different consciousness, most notably

Mexico's first independent producer (see **independent film producers**), Manuel **Barbachano Ponce**, and the intellectual film-maker exemplified by Leopoldo **Torre Nilsson** in Argentina, who was the first to undertake the challenges of an *auteur* cinema.

The new cinemas

The 1960s witnessed not only the triumph of the Cuban Revolution (1959) (see **revolutions**) and the establishment of the **ICAIC**, but a definitive change in Latin American film production. The cinema became an art of personal expression and film-makers undertook a search for new cinematic languages more closely aligned to national (and continental) cultural and political realities. Perhaps the first evidence of this change is to be found in Cuba, in the work of Santiago **Alvarez**, whose first newsreel (see **newsreels**) for ICAIC premièred in 1960, and who transformed the **documentary** via collage and complex sound–image relations. ICAIC used the documentary as a school, both to train its young film-makers and to bring to the screen heretofore unprecedented materials. A similar project was proposed by Fernando **Birri** in Argentina, while other variants followed: **agitprop** and militancy (Mario **Handler** in Uruguay, Carlos **Alvarez** in Colombia), the lyrical or ironic (Nicolás **Guillén** Landrián and Sara **Gómez** in Cuba), the anthropological (Marta **Rodríguez** and Jorge **Silva** in Colombia) or the sociological (Thomas Farkas, and Geraldo **Sarno** in Brazil).

In Brazil, the **Cinema Novo** movement was the first of several 'new' cinema movements in the continent. With 'an idea in the head and a camera in hand', Glauber **Rocha** and others proposed a cultural revolution, elaborating a new cinematic language through which to bring to the screen, and reflect upon, national problems. In Cuba, ICAIC film-makers like Tomás **Gutiérrez Alea**, Julio **García Espinosa**, Manuel Octavio **Gómez** and Humberto **Solas** experimented with mixed documentary and fictional modes, and new popular narrative forms. In Argentina, a generation of young urban film-makers – la **Generación del 60** – elaborated an introspective but profoundly political practice that became increasingly radicalized after the military *coup d'état* of 1966, and was capped by the Brechtian/Fanonian critique of Fernando **Solanas**, Octavio Getino and the collective **Grupo Cine Liberación**'s *La hora de los hornos* (The Hour of the Furnaces) (1968). These new cinema movements eventually cohered as the **New Latin American Cinema** (including others like Jorge **Sanjinés** and the Ukamau Group (see **Grupo Ukamau**) in Bolivia), a unique pan-national cinematic movement of great resonance and aesthetic innovation.

After the 'new' cinemas

In the 1970s and 1980s, Latin American film-makers faced three central interrelated issues. The first had to do with a concern with audiences – which the New Latin American Cinema, as a radical deconstructive practice, had essentially ignored – and resulted in a general return to more straightforward narrative and stylistic approaches of greater popular appeal. Resulting from the first, the second issue evolved out of a growing consciousness of the commercial nature of the medium and its marketing viability. Throughout the continent film-makers demanded increased State protectionism and financial support, resulting in the creation of **Embrafilme** in Brazil, an almost complete statization in Mexico under **Echeverría** (**Conacine uno, dos**) and the inauguration of State film institutions in Colombia (FOCINE), Peru and Venezuela. The third issue was political. In the wake of military dictatorships, film-makers were forced to contend with censorship and repression, exile, and/or torture and imprisonment. Among the many exiles, the Chileans who fled from **Pinochet** in 1973 were incredibly productive, producing a vibrant diasporic cinema unparalleled in film history (Raúl **Ruiz**, Miguel **Littín**, Patricio **Guzmán**, Valeria **Sarmiento**, etc.). As democracy returned and repression eased, film-makers began to address contemporary history: in Argentina, for example, Adolfo **Aristaraín**'s *Tiempo de revancha* (Time of Revenge) (1981) and the inventive Eliseo **Subiela**'s *Hombre mirando al sudeste* (Man Looking Southeast) (1985).

In Brazil, the cinema thrived in the early years of Embrafilme with popular films like Bruno

Barreto's *Dona Flor e seus dois maridos* (Dona Flor and Her Two Husbands) (1976), Héctor **Babenco**'s *Pixote a lei do mais fraco* (1981) and Suzana **Amaral**'s *A hora da estrela* (The Hour of the Star) (1985), which obtained international distribution and won awards. At the other extreme, a healthy underground – Júlio **Bressane**, Rogério **Sganzerla** and Arthur **Omar** – continued with aesthetic experimentation. In Venezuela, Peru and Colombia, the films of Román **Chalbaud**, Francisco **Lombardi** and Sergio **Cabrera** found great popular acclaim, while other nations with even less film-making traditions appeared in international circuits. In Uruguay, Pablo Dota directed *El dirigible* (The Dirigible) (1994), a sophisticated comedy; Jacobo **Morales** directed four significant films in Puerto Rico; the Dominican cinema began with Agliberto **Meléndez**'s *Un pasaje de ida* (One Way Ticket) (1988); and in Curaçao, Felix **De Rooy** directed the well-received *Ava and Gabriel* (1990).

In post-Echeverría Mexico, as the State began to abandon the film business, commercial production wallowed in sex comedies, but a few film-makers managed to overcome their financial constraints. Most notable among them are Arturo **Ripstein**, Jaime Humberto **Hermosillo** and Paul **Leduc**, who in the 1990s were joined by a younger generation including Guillermo **del Toro**, María **Novaro**, Carlos **Carrera** and Dana Rotberg.

At the end of its first century, the cinema in Latin America is financially beleaguered yet vibrant. Despite the indisputable competition of television (especially from the popular **telenovelas**), declining theatrical attendance, reduced direct State support (like the closing of Embrafilme in 1990) and the potentially encroaching effects of globalization in the industry (epitomized by **NAFTA**), film-makers continued to figure out ways to exercise their craft. Some have moved away from Latin America (Barreto, **Arau** and Del Toro to Hollywood, for example), others, primarily as a result of contacts established at the **Festival Internacional del Nuevo Cine Latinoamericano** in Havana, or elsewhere, have been able set up co-production deals with European producers like Television Española, Great Britain's Channel 4 or the ZDF in Germany. The effects of this late-1990s globalization are still to be fully felt. It will undoubtedly bring Latin American films forward in international art cinema circles (like the Oscar nomination for Walter Salles Jr's *Central do Brasil* (Central Station) in 1999 or the unprecedented box-office success of Arau's *Como agua para chocolate* (Like Water for Chocolate) in 1991), but it may also mean the final disappearance of the concept of national cinemas in the continent.

Further reading

Barnard, T. and Rist, P. (1996) *South American Cinema: A Critical Filmography*, Austin: University of Texas Press.

King, J. (1990) *Magical Reels: A History of Cinema in Latin America*, London: Verso.

Paranaguá, P.A. (1995) *Mexican Cinema*, London: BFI.

—— (1996) 'América Latina busca su imagén', in *Historia General del Cine*, vol. X, Madrid: Cátedra.

Stock, A.M. (1997) *Framing Latin American Cinema*, Minneapolis: University of Minnesota Press.

ANA MARÍA LÓPEZ

cinema as a gun

This is a concept that emerges in alignment with the politicized new cinema movements comprising the **New Latin American Cinema** of the 1960s and 1970s. Stemming from the experiments in political film-making in the Soviet Union, young film-makers throughout Latin America took on the medium for explicit political activism, taking their cameras to the streets and documenting the poverty and underdevelopment plaguing the continent. Central was the belief that the cinema could function as a detonator for direct political action. Key practitioners were Fernando **Solanas**, Octavio Getino and the collective **Grupo Cine Liberación**, whose *La hora de los hornos* (Hour of the Furnaces) (1968) is a prime example. Also important were Mario **Handler**'s scathingly effective short, *Me gustan los estudiantes* (I Like Students) (1969); after the film's first screening, the audience staged an impromptu demonstration in the streets of Montevideo. Also of significance is the work of Santiago **Alvarez** in Cuba, especially his renowned condemnation of racism in *Now* (1965).

ANA M. LÓPEZ

cinema laws in Brazil

Demands for legal measures to protect the Brazilian film industry from its powerful northern neighbour began in the 1930s. In 1937, the National Institute for Educational Cinema (INCE) was set up and two years later the **Vargas** dictatorship established **DIP** (the Press and Propaganda Department), to censor and control the national cinema, including the compulsory showing of government-produced newsreels. The industry was won over by screen quotas for national early sound feature films and tax exemptions on locally-copied foreign films. The National Film Council, established in 1942, fixed a national film screen quota and an allocation of income.

With the return of democracy in 1945, the national screen quota rose to three features per year and in 1951 the formula 'one (national film) for every eight (foreign films)' was set down. Exemption from duties for imported film equipment encouraged the creation of national studios in São Paulo like **Vera Cruz Studios**, Maristela and Multifilmes. The failure of these enterprises was ascribed to the artifically low ticket prices established by the government; the response was a demand for greater state intervention. With subsidies, the proportion of Brazilian films exhibited domestically rose through the 1950s and early 1960s.

The demand for a National Film Institute was not answered until 1966, when the Instituto Nacional do Cinema (INC) was set up by the military government to provide prizes and subsidies. In 1969, the government set up **Embrafilme**, a mixed public–private enterprise, to finance and export Brazilian products. Its principal source of income was state subsidies and income taxes on foreign films. The demise of the INC in 1975 strengthened the position of Embrafilme which extended its activities into distribution; by the early 1980s its income equalled that of the subsidiaries of the US majors, largely due to

protective measures which included the compulsory exhibition of shorts and the establishment of a national quota in the home video market. There were limits to this protectionism, however; it was impossible to regulate television production and any serious challenge to US interests brought threats of retaliation against Brazilian exports.

Protective legislation had run its course by the late 1980s, and was removed by a simple Presidential decree in 1990. Initially, municipal and provincial subsidies replaced national subsidies until 1992–3, when new laws laid down a national quota as well as tax incentives for national productions. Yet Brazilian films are typically now shown only in art cinemas. The popular audiences that Brazilian cinema had traditionally enjoyed had transferred their allegiance to television, and only the quota ensured a continuing Brazilian presence on cinema screens. In the late 1980s, Brazilian films occupied 140 screen days per year; by 1998 the figure had fallen to forty nine.

Further reading

Johnson, R. (1987) *The Film Industry in Brazil*, Pittsburgh: University of Pittsburgh Press.
Simis, A. (1996) *Estado e Cinema no Brasil*, São Paulo: Annablume.
Pereira, G. (1973) *Plano geral do cinema brasileiro*, Rio de Janeiro: Borsoi.

ISMAIL XAVIER AND THE USP GROUP

Cinema Marginal

Cinema Marginal were a group of Brazilian directors – including Júlio **Bressane**, Rogério **Sganzerla** and Andrea **Tonacci** – who between 1969 and 1973 opposed **Cinema Novo**'s compromises with the market. They rejected its universalizing narrative for more radical forms. The term 'marginal' referred both to their distance from the market and to the socially dysfunctional people who populated their films in a kind of 'garbage aesthetics'; the detritus of an underdeveloped country composed into an apocalyptic mosaic which replaced the revolutionary fervour of Cinema Novo with scatological hysteria and dead-end despair. The group's work reflected an increasingly desperate time; it also questioned narrative in the deconstructionist spirit of the time.

ISMAIL XAVIER AND THE USP GROUP

Cinema Novo

Cinema Novo was the Brazilian film movement of the 1960s and 70s which addressed the country's social crisis and underdevelopment in an aesthetically original way, transforming film into a medium of great political and cultural significance. The movement brought to the fore new young directors like Joaquim Pedro de **Andrade**, Leon **Hirszman**, Carlos **Diegues**, Ruy **Guerra**, Paulo César **Saraceni** and David **Neves**, under the leadership of the talented Glauber **Rocha**. These young film-makers opened a dialogue with corresponding movements of renewal in other areas of Brazilian culture like popular music, plastic arts and theatre.

Although there had been several frustrated attempts to establish a film industry in Brazil with private capital, the most successful of which was the **Vera Cruz Studios** (1949–55), Brazilian cinema later developed in the direction of *auteur* cinema: making low budget films inspired by Italian neo-realism and closely associated with the contemporary French new wave, and resolved to revolutionize cinematic language and reject commercial modes. Cinema Novo's watchword was 'a camera in the hand and an idea in the head'; its political concerns led it towards a mixture of the styles traditionally associated with fiction and documentary. The strategic objective was to diagnose the Brazilian crisis in the context of increasing tensions between imperialism and the peripheral countries through the 1960s. It was a period when Brazilian expectations were rising in response to the modernization policies of Juscelino **Kubitschek** (1956–60) and sectors of progressive intellectuals were fighting to defend structural reforms. In cinema there was a confluence between an earlier generation of directors – Alex Vianny, Nelson Pereira dos **Santos**, Roberto **Santos** – and a group of younger film-makers emerging from the universities and student movements.

The first feature films made by the group were very successful at international festivals and earned a favourable critical response. Outstanding in 1962 were Rocha's *Barravento* and Guerra's *Os Cafajestes* (The Hustlers); in 1963 Diegues' *Ganga Zumba*, de Andrade's *Garrincha, Alegria do Povo* (Garrincha, the People's Joy), Saraceni's *Porto das Caixas*. Pereira dos Santos's *Vidas secas* (Barren Lives) (1963) and Rocha's *Deus e o diabo na terra do sol* (Black God, White Devil) (1964) made a considerable impact at Cannes in 1964, and Guerra's *Os Fuzis* (The Guns) won critical acclaim at Berlin in the same year, consolidating the international reputation of a movement whose aesthetic principles were later set out in Rocha's 'Por uma estética da fome' (An Aesthetic of Hunger) (1965). (See **aesthetics of hunger**.)

In its first phase (1960–64), Cinema Novo discovered Brazilian social reality, filming in different regions and focusing on the many forms of domination and exploitation. Its objective was to precisely describe social reality and provoke a revolutionary consciousness among the popular classes, but the movement's films were often too complex for their pedagogical purpose. In 1964, the military *coup* created a political climate hostile to cultural activities designed to expose the darker side of Brazilian modernization. Censorship was introduced, but despite these difficulties, the film-makers found ways of rethinking the national reality, exploring the failure of left-wing projects associated with populism and alliances with the so-called national bourgeoisie. **Jabor**'s *A Opinião Pública* (Public Opinion) (1967) and Saraceni's *O Desafio* (The Challenge) (1965) focused the debate on the conduct of the middle classes. Rocha's *Terra em transe* (Land in Anguish) (1967) was the key work of this phase, expressing the film-maker's disillusionment and brilliantly depicting the different nuances of the political debate.

During this second phase, Cinema Novo also turned to the problem of its shrinking audiences. Gustavo **Dahl**, one of the movement's ideologues, insisted in 1965 that the movement must make a decisive turn towards the market, and that adaptations of literary classics would reopen a dialogue with traditional genres. With Andrade's *O Padre e a Moça* (The Father and the Girl) (1966), Hirszman's *A Falecida* (The Dead Woman) (1965) and Santos's *A Hora e A Vez de Augusto Matraga* (The Hour and Time of Augusto Matraga) (1965), and within the limits of a domestic market dominated by foreign films, Cinema Novo succeeded in winning a wider audience. Andrade's **Macunaíma** (1969) was Cinema Novo's greatest success, working within the **chanchada** genre to create a political allegory designed to promote discussion about the Brazilian national character. The debate had reopened in 1968, with *tropicalismo*, a cultural movement characterized by irony and a critical response to the euphoria over modernization. Cinema Novo became involved in the polemic and incorporated elements of *tropicalismo* in films like Walter Lima Jr's *Brasil Ano 2000* (Brazil Year 2000) (1969), Rocha's *Antonio das Mortes* (1968), dos Santos's *Azyllo Muito Loco* (Very Crazy Asylum) (1969), Guerra's *Os Deuses e os Mortos* (The Gods and the Dead) (1970) and Jabor's *Pindorama* (1971).

After the December 1968 *coup* and the consolidation of the military regime, Cinema Novo attempted to finance its films through co-productions with European television companies. Aesthetically, the films moved towards political allegories that permitted double readings of powerful narratives capable of internalizing the complex historical and political forces in conflict within the country. The allegory could rest on adaptations from the classics – Hirszman's **São Bernardo** (1972) – migratory movements – Bodansky and Senna's *Iracema* (1974) – and family dramas like Jabor's *Tudo Bem* (All's Well) (1978).

In 1974 the state film company **Embrafilme** began to finance productions, assuring the continuity of Cinema Novo and its dominance within Brazilian cinema; with Geisel's government, its members trained directors in Embrafilme's own school. Its new commercial direction and collaboration with official institutions generated opposition movements like **Cinema Marginal**, which advocated radical forms and experimental language against what they regarded as political compromising.

Between the 1970s and the end of the military regime in the late 1980s, commercial and experimental film coexisted with new projects for popular cinema, such as the direction proposed by Nelson Pereira dos Santos on the occasion of the premiere of his *O Amuleto de Ogum* (Ogum's Amulet) (1974).

The Cinema Novo group of directors continued to dominate production through Embrafilme, and represented Brazilian cinema abroad until 1984, when its last two great films were produced – Eduardo **Coutinho**'s *Cabra marcado para morrer* (Man Marked for Death) and dos Santos's *Memórias do cárcere* (Prison Memoirs) based on the eponymous novel by Graciliano **Ramos**.

See also: New Latin American Cinema

Further reading

Johnson, R. and Stam, R. (1997) *Brazilian Cinema: Expanded Edition*, New York: Colombia University Press.

Rocha, G. (1981) *Revolução do Cinema Novo*, Rio de Janeiro: Alhambra/Embrafilme.

Xavier, I. (1997) *Allegories of Underdevelopment*, Minneapolis: University of Minnesota Press.

ISMAIL XAVIER AND THE USP GROUP

cinema ownership *see* film exhibition

cinematheques

An outgrowth of the earlier cine club movement (see **cine clubs**), film archives or *cinematecas* appeared in Latin America throughout the 1950s and 1960s with the mission to promote less-commercial films shunned by the **film exhibition** sector, preserve the national film heritage and promote the study of the cinema. An important mission of *cinematecas* is to promote film restoration efforts, especially the highly volatile material on nitrate-based film stock (all films pre-1951), most of which has disappeared or has already been destroyed. They also often sponsor publication series and magazines, and organize travelling film series highlighting the national cinema.

Although an organization called Cinemateca de Cuba was organized in 1951 by a group including Néstor **Almendros** and Guillermo **Cabrera Infante**, the group lacked a permanent film archive or documentation centre and never achieved the status of a real cinematheque (the current Cinemateca de Cuba was created in 1960 as a cultural department of **ICAIC**). According to the existing evidence, the first – and longest in continuous operation – Latin American cinematheque was the Cinemateca Uruguaya, established in 1952 in Montevideo. During the dictatorship, the Cinemateca Uruguaya was able to compensate for the conservatism of the film exhibition sector by distributing foreign films and even stepped into production in 1982 with *Mataron a Venancio Flores* (They Killed Venancio Flores) (directed by Juan Carlos Rodríguez Castro).

The Cinemateca Brasileira was founded in São Paulo in 1956 with federal and State support. To date it continues to be one of the principal film repositories in the continent and its new facility since 1997 is the best equipped for film restoration. In Rio de Janeiro, the Museo da Arte Moderna, a private institution, inaugurated its Cinemateca in 1957. It still operates and has an important collection, but lacks the resources of its counterpart in São Paulo. In Mexico, **UNAM** created the Filmoteca in 1960, later followed by the Cineteca Nacional. Both were very active in preserving the national film heritage; unfortunately a disastrous fire in the Filmoteca in 1982 destroyed a great part of its archives and materials. To date, Argentina lacks a national, federally funded *cinemateca*. However, the Fundación Cinemateca Argentina, a private foundation based in Buenos Aires since 1954, holds an important collection of films and documents, and has undertaken significant publication initiatives.

Through membership of FIAF (Federation Internacional del Archives Filmiques), the international organization of film archives, these and other Latin American cinematheques in Colombia, Chile, Peru, Bolivia and elsewhere struggle against their perennial shortage of funds to preserve their national film heritages.

ANA M. LÓPEZ

Cioppo, Atahualpa del

b. 1904, Montevideo, Uruguay; d. 1993, Montevideo

Theatre director

Perhaps the most influential director in modern Uruguay, Cioppo began his career in the 1930s with the children's theatre company La Isla de los Niños, which later merged with Teatro del Pueblo. The merger of the two groups was the genesis of one of Uruguay's most important theatre companies, El **Galpón**. Del Cioppo's work with El Galpón until his death in 1993 was instrumental in creating a style of Uruguayan theatre that was politically committed, integrated with its community and theatrically rich. In his writing, teaching and theatre practice, Del Cioppo emphasised that Latin American theatre had a social responsibility.

See also: Brechtian theatre

ADAM VERSÉNYI

Círculo de Bellas Artes

Founded in 1905, the Círculo de Bellas Artes was the pioneering institution in the field of visual arts in Uruguay. Many of the country's most important artists participated in its exhibitions and courses, including Pedro Blanes Viale, Rafael **Barradas**, Alfredo de Simone, José Cuneo, Carmelo de Arzadum, Luis Alberto Solari, Washington Barcala, María Freire, Amalia Nieto, Vicente Martin, Jorge Damiani and sculptors like José Belloni, José Luis Zorrilla de San Martín, Bernabé **Michelena** and Germán Cabrera.

MARCO MAGGI

circus

The initial division between popular and elite theatres was established through the distribution of cultural spaces, the former being housed outdoors and the latter finding its locales indoors. Nevertheless, these spaces did not remain closed within themselves but rather experienced a great deal of mutual interconnection. By the early nineteenth century, the colonial *corrales* had either become marginal spaces or had been replaced by tent shows (see **carpa**). The playhouses and opera houses soon found themselves hosting touring companies, many of which had originated in the marginal spaces of the *carpas* and circus. Since then, the circus and derived spaces such as the Mexican tent shows have provided the arena for genuine popular theatre, where not only whole families learned and practised their art but where theatrical representations of melodramas and comic sketches also found a popular locale. They also provided a participatory space that could not be reproduced in the more traditional theatrical venues, which relied on a more distant physical relationship to the audience. In spite of the vulnerability of the physical space inherent to circus and tent shows – a space often temporarily appropriated and converted – they none the less were able to establish a cultural permanence due to an organizational structure which relied on specific 'acts' rather than individuals, all tightly centred around a family unit with a single director. In such a structure, *commedia dell'arte*-type comic characters were able to reproduce themselves into myriad clowns that sometimes evolved into important figures of commercial theatre., A 'transgressive mirroring' of society, as Bouissac has called it, often involved political commentary in which current events and key figures of the time were viewed through a subverting lens. The steps from marginalized outdoor circus and tent show acts of all kinds to indoor music hall and vaudeville can also be traced.

The history of the circus in Argentina, seen through the Podestá brothers, is particularly illuminating, since many consider the play *Juan Moreira*, born of their circus, as the dawning of Argentine theatre. In the 1870s the Podestá brothers, children of Italians, learned their trade from a travelling circus from Uruguay. Having formed their own circus, they performed all the traditional circus acts plus various pantomimes. One of the brothers created a very important popular character, 'Peppino el 88'. Having read Gutiérrez's novel, *Juan Moreira*, as it was published in ongoing *folletines*, the Podestá brothers decided to recreate this gaucho tragedy in pantomime. Nevertheless, Moreira was a character who did not speak in spite of the rather complex staging of the pantomime, which included live animals, battles, etc. Some believe that an audience member asked that Moreira speak, thus inaugurating Argentine theatre. Others document that, in the spirit of the times where foreign touring companies dominated the stage, a travelling Italian company led by the Carlo brothers was asked to perform 'Juan Moreira'. Realizing that they were ill equipped in both language and tradition to incarnate such a popular gaucho figure, they sought out the Podestá brothers for the task, thus creating *Juan Moreira*, the play from the original *folletín* novel, and thus leading an outdoor popular performance into an indoor space.

By the end of the century, the Podestá brothers had become the owners of several commercial theatre houses in Buenos Aires, becoming the promoters of a national theatre where once foreign companies had commanded the stage. Their circus is also responsible for the creation of the '**cocoliche**', a comic character widely imitated in comedies and dramas well into the twentieth century; a character who embodies the speech and the demeanour of the new immigrant. Cocoliche was the surname of two Calabrian circus hands who were comically impersonated by one of the Podestá's circus staff. Jerónimo Podestá caught a glimpse of the impersonation and urged his staff member to develop the character; thus was born 'cocoliche' as both a character and as a new vocabulary word signifying both immigrant ways and immigrant speech.

The Podestá Brothers' circus incarnates both the permanence and specificity of an artistic form as well as the fluidity of its influences on culture and theatrical practices in general. The continuity of the circus in its original form, particularly outside major metropolises, and its spectacular new incarnations such as that present in the Cirque du Soleil as well as the ongoing resurgence of the circus among young theatre groups such as the Argentine Club del Clan speak of the continuity of this venue and its role in society from the earliest times.

Further reading

Pianca, M. (ed.) (1987–9) *Diógenes: Anuario crítico del teatro latinoamericano*, 3 vols, Otttawa: Nuevo Teatro/Girol Books.

MARINA PIANCA

Cisneros, Antonio

b. 1942, Lima, Peru

Poet

Cisneros is the leading representative of the 1960s generation which renovated poetry in Peru through the use of more open forms, intertextual dialogue and an irreverent conversational manner, for example in *Canto ceremonial contra un oso hormiguero* (Ceremonial Song against an Ant-eater) (1968). Reflecting the spirit of the 1960s, his work deploys a devastating irony to subvert the conservative ethos of Peru's middle classes. At the same time, he seeks to establish a modern Peruvian and Third World identity by rewriting national history and defining himself in relation to the forces which have shaped his country.

JAMES HIGGINS

city

The city has been central to Latin American material and cultural life. In some cases housing one-quarter or more of their country's total population, capital cities like Buenos Aires, Montevideo, Havana, Lima, Mexico City, and San José have long monopolized their nation's economic wealth, political power, and cultural institutions (**museums**, **publishing** houses, theatres). Traditionally much less powerful, provincial cities have experienced remarkable growth in the last half of the twentieth century. Aside from its material importance, the city occupies a privileged place in the Latin American cultural imagination as a sign of civilization and progress and has been the celebrated subject of innumerable novels, films, paintings, and songs. In the early part of the twentieth century, the city symbolized modernization of Latin American society while after the 1950s it often became a metaphor for the region's lost promise.

Many capital cities experienced immense material changes in the first decades of the twentieth century through urban renovation projects designed to accommodate society's changing economic and social needs; the widening of streets, the establishment of public parks, the installation of electric lights on public streets, and the growth of public transportation (trains, trolley lines, and **subways**). Cities like Buenos Aires and Mexico City served as showcases for the economic prosperity and political might of certain elites. The modernizing city was an important influence on the work of many visual artists, writers, filmmakers, and musicians who found inspiration there for their formal experimentations. Uruguayan painter Rafael Pérez Barradas captured the fast-paced vibrancy of street life in his colourful, kaleidoscopic work. His compatriot Joaquín **Torres García** painted numerous cityscapes of the port of Montevideo along with his more abstract works. In his first books of poetry (*Fervor de Buenos Aires* (Buenos Aires Fervour) (1923), *La luna de enfrente* (The Moon Across the Street) (1925) and *Cuaderno San Martín* (San Martin's Notebook) (1929)), Argentine Jorge Luis **Borges** also relied on modernist principles to write whimsical elegies to Buenos Aires neighbourhoods. **Brazilian modernism** was crystallized in 1922 in a decidedly urban event, the **Modern Art Week** in São Paulo, although its practitioners often found more inspiration in rural folklore. Urban life also filtered into early Latin American film-making serving as the backdrop of early documentaries and the topic of experimental films like Brazil's *São Paulo: Sinfonia de uma Metrópole* (São Paulo: Symphony of a Metropolis, dir. Adalberto Kedemy and Rudolf Lustig) (1929).

Other cultural texts were in conflict with this modernist celebration of city life. While Buenos Aires experienced a massive European immigration beginning at the end of the nineteenth century, other cities were transformed by internal immigrants who moved to the cities from the provinces starting in the 1930s. As many Latin American countries facing falling agricultural exports began to institute **import substitution industrialization**, the shrinking demand for rural labour encouraged the lower classes to look for work in the city. From these new sectors emerged new types of popular urban culture like **tango** in Argentina, **samba** in Brazil, and *bufo* or variety comic theatre in Mexico and elsewhere. Often incorporating rural traditions, these new cultural forms responded to the consolidation of working-class districts and the reformulation of popular memory.

Films and literature also registered the harsher aspects of the modernizing city. Film-makers in several countries carved out the genre of the urban crime film (often based on famous real-life crime) like Brazil's *Os Estranguladores* (The Stranglers, dir. Francisco Marzullo) (1908) or Mexico's *El automóvil gris* (The Grey Car, dir. Enrique Rosas) (1919). Other films focused on working-class neighbourhoods as did the works of Argentine José Agustín (El Negro) **Ferreyra** and a number of early Mexican films about brothels and port life like *Santa* (dir. Antonio Moreno) (1931) and *La mujer del puerto* (Woman of the Port, dir. Arcady Baytler) (1933) that contrasted the decadence of the city to the purity of rural life. Although official discourse of the Mexican Revolution favoured the countryside as the site of its new nation-building project, Diego **Rivera** at times included machines and other signs of urban life in the murals he painted on the walls of government buildings in Mexico City. Meanwhile, writers in many countries like Argentina's Roberto **Arlt** penned tales about the gritty life of the underclass.

Provincial immigration continued during the 1940s and 1950s spurred on by industrialization during and after the Second World War. Latin American cities became increasingly heterogeneous and, at times, were the site of political and social conflicts. Known as the Bogotazo, the April 1948 rioting in Colombia's capital city set off by the assassination of liberal leader Jorge Eliécer Gaitán marked the initiation of decades of violence between liberals and conservatives (see La **Violencia**). Economic disparities were the subject of Luis **Buñuel**'s *Los olvidados* (The Young and the Damned) (1958) and the backdrop for *Cabaretera* **films** set in Mexico City while authors like Peru's José María **Arguedas** wrote about ethnic tensions in capital and provincial cities. The scarcity and expense of existing housing forced many recent immigrants to build make-shift housing on the outskirts of major cities. Often ignored by politicians, the shanty towns (see **shanty towns and slums**) were the focus of a series of collages by Argentine Antonio **Berni** in the early 1960s. Imitating the patchwork quality of the dwellings through the incorporation of card-

board, metal sheets, and pieces of cloth, the collages expressed both the shanty towns' poverty and the inventiveness of their residents,who created homes out of cast-off materials.

Although the mushrooming shanty towns disturbed many elites, they also had reasons to rejoice as architects in many cities introduced the so-called International Style and other design innovations. Buoyed by developmentalism (see **development**), many sectors felt that Latin America would soon achieve the modernized status it had pursued for so long. Built between 1956–60, Brazil's new capital incarnated that optimism through Oscar **Niemeyer**'s provocative designs. If **Brasília** symbolized the promise of the era, Cuba's Havana demonstrated its contradictions. Celebrated for its scintillating night life and tourist trade (as captured in Guillermo **Cabrera Infante**'s *Tres Tristes Tigres* (Three Trapped Tigers), Havana was also awash with **prostitution**, crime, and corruption that would ebb only after the 1959 Revolution.

Some of the twentieth century's most exciting new literature emerged from these urban paradoxes. Rejecting the conventions of social realism, Juan Carlos **Onetti**'s *La vida breve* (A Brief Life) (1950) plumbed the psychological depths of a man whose fantasies allow him to escape his confining life in Buenos Aires. Carlos **Fuentes**'s *La región más transparente* (Where the Air is Clear) (1958) brilliantly captured the quick pace of urban living in 1950s Mexico City and the anomie of its residents. Ernesto **Sabato**'s *Sobre héroes y tumbas* (On Heroes and Tombs) (1961), Mario **Vargas Llosa**'s *La ciudad y los perros* (The Time of the Hero) (1962) and *Conversación en la catedral* (Conversation in the Cathedral) (1969), and Julio **Cortázar**'s *Rayuela* (Hopscotch) (1963) similarly explored the alienating cityscapes of Buenos Aires and Lima. Although these authors shared an interest in formal experimentation with the early modernists, the novels from the 1950s and 1960s figured the city in more pessimistic terms as a chaotic and isolating terrain. If Jorge **Amado**'s novels took a more light-hearted look at life in provincial cities in northeastern Brazil, Sebastián Salazar Bondy's extended essay *Lima, la horrible* (Lima the Horrible) (1964) directly attacked the mythic status of the city.

The 1950s and 1960s also witnessed the emergence of a new type of film culture in many

Latin American cities. Middle-class *aficionados* established cine clubs to screen alternative films and published **film magazines** in which they developed their own theories about cinema. Argentine film culture gave birth to the **Generación del 60** (Simón Feldman, David José **Kohón**, Rodolfo **Kuhn**, José Martínez Suárez) who used on-location shooting and inventive camerawork to examine the alienation of young, middle-class adults in Buenos Aires. A more politicized response to the region's so-called underdevelopment, the **New Latin American Cinema**, focused on the socially marginalized. While highlighting rural areas, Brazil's **Cinema Novo** also examined the urban poor in films like Nelson Pereira dos **Santos**'s *Rio 40 Graus* (Rio 40 Degrees) (1955) and *Rio Zona Norte* (Rio Northern Zone) (1957) and the alienated urban middle class in Luís Sergio Puson's *São Paulo, S.A.* (1964), *A Falecida* (The Deceased), and Paulo César Saraceni's *O Desafio* (The Challenge) (1965). Cuban film-maker Tomás **Gutiérrez Alea**'s early comedies and later films *Memorias del subdesarrollo* (Memories of Underdevelopment) (1965) and *Fresa y chocolate* (Strawberry and Chocolate) (1993) cleverly employed urban scenery to critique revolutionary bureaucracy (ever visible in jingoistic posters) as well as to celebrate Havana's architecture and the vitality of its streets.

More radical urban films like **Solanas**'s *La hora de los hornos* (The Hour of the Furnaces) (1968) and **Guzmán**'s *La batalla de Chile* (The Battle of Chile) (1973–9) responded to the city's role in the rise of armed combat between repressive government forces and leftist groups. In 1968, popular protests erupted in Córdoba, Argentina and Mexico City but were quickly and violently put down by the government. Known respectively as the Cordobazo and the massacre at **Tlatelolco** (the square in which the protest took place), the two events became important symbols of governmental repression. Many artists responded by reasserting popular voices and memories. Elena **Poniatowska**'s *La noche de Tlatelolco* (Massacre in Mexico) (1971) juxtaposed the testimonies of numerous witnesses to simulate the collective voice of the people. In Argentina, Pablo **Suárez** and other artists put together the multi-media exposition *Tucumán arde* (Tucuman in Flames) in conjunction

with a workers' union to criticize the military government's industrialization projects and their disastrous effects on provincial cities. Popular voices and social protest were also present in new types of music. The New Song (*nueva canción*, **Canto Nuevo** and *nueva trova* movements recuperated rural musical traditions and disseminated them in the city. Created by the children of rural immigrants, Peruvian *música chicha* (see **chicha music** was less socially conscious but offered an exciting mix of indigenous musical traditions, the Colombian **cumbia**, and electric instrumentation.

The armed conflict between right- and left-wing groups intensified in the 1970s. Although guerrilla warfare was largely isolated to rural areas in countries like Bolivia and Colombia (see **guerrillas**), rebels carried out urban attacks (bombings and kidnappings) in Argentina, Brazil, and Uruguay. The retaliatory practices of military governments in many countries focused on controlling urban space. In Chile, the armed forces bombed the presidential palace in Santiago to remove leftist President Salvador **Allende** in September 1973. In all **Southern Cone** countries, military juntas placed soldiers on the streets, declared curfews, and raided private homes in search of so-called subversives, many of whom were never seen again. In Argentina, the military carried out a parallel campaign of urban beautification in Buenos Aires to expand public parks and to eliminate shanty towns.

By the 1980s and 1990s, when many South American countries returned to democracy, urban culture had irrevocably changed not only as a result of political events but also through the proliferation of new technologies (**television**, videocassette players, and, in some countries, cable television and computers) that kept people off the city streets and in the home. Exclusive residential communities for the upper classes popped up in many cities as did postmodern skyscrapers. At the same time, factories moved out of capital cities in countries like Mexico where assembly plants (*maquiladoras*) began to dot its northern border with the USA. These recent transformations of some Latin American cities reflect globalizing trends as well as neoliberal economic policies that favour free trade (see **neoliberalism**). Even while clinging to socialism, the Cuban government gave its capital a face-lift to stimulate tourism by renovating nineteenth-century colonial structures in Old Havana and building new hotels and a huge commercial mall.

Further reading

García Canclini, N. (1990) *Culturas híbridas*, Mexico City.

Monsivais, C. (1995) *Los rituales del caos*, Mexico City: Ediciones Era.

Rama, A. (1984) *La ciudad letrada*, Hanover: Ediciones del Norte.

Romero, J.L. (1976) *Latinoamérica: las ciudades y las ideas*, Buenos Aires: Siglo Veintiuno.

Sarlo, B. (1988) *Una modernidad periférica: Buenos Aires, 1920 y 1930*, Buenos Aires: Ediciones Nueva Visión.

LAURA PODALSKY

Ciudad Darío

A typical Nicaraguan rural town, small, with narrow streets and white painted walls, Ciudad Darío is famous for being the birthplace of the Nicaraguan poet laureate, Rubén Darío. During the Sandinista (see **Sandinista Revolution**) administration, his house was repaired and transformed into the Darío Museum. In the open theatre behind the house, cultural activities were staged annually on Darío's anniversary, during which the Ministry of Culture invited several notable poets to Ciudad Darío to celebrate the poet's birthday, and asked them to read parts of their work at a public day-long outdoor recital.

SILVIA CHAVES AND ILEANA RODRÍGUEZ

Ciudad Satélite

Already part of the metropolitan area to the northwest of Mexico City, this upper middle-class residential area developed during the demographic growth of the 1950s and 1960s on land appropriated by *permuta* or exchange of *ejidos* (see **ejido**) (community lands) in the 'public interest'. Of

modern design and surrounded by important industries, Ciudad Satélite has an immense mall, Plaza Satélite, of functional design and outstanding architecture. The five brightly coloured towers of Torres sin Función (Functionless Towers) by Mathias **Goeritz** and Luis **Barragán** which symbolize the union with the cosmos were described by the latter as 'huge modern torches' and are the first visible sign when approaching this area.

EDUARDO SANTA CRUZ

Ciudad Universitaria

The construction of Caracas's university city began during the 1940s, at a time when a number of Latin American governments financed the building of large-scale public works (such as ministries, hospitals, universities and working-class housing complexes) in order to demonstrate the State's involvement in the process of modernization. At this time the State presented itself in the role of mediator between the dominant economic interests and the new, emerging classes, acknowledging new needs in the cultural, educational and health fields as a consequence of the incipient process of industrialization. The design for the Ciudad Universitaria by Carlos Raúl **Villanueva** was completed in 1944. The first stage of construction began a year later with the clinical hospital, the medical faculty and the nursing school. The Olympic stadium was built in 1952; the Aula Magna (main hall), library, Plaza Cubierta (covered square), covered corridors and botanical institute in 1953. The following two years marked the completion of humanities, science and physics, biology faculties, the school of dentistry and the schools of chemistry, hydraulics and oil technology. From 1957–9, the project was completed with the building of the faculty of architecture and town planning, the school of pharmacology and the Olympic swimming pool.

This vast complex exhibits three fundamental characteristics. First, the redefinition of an architecture originating in rationalism and the **International Style**; second, the fusion of architecture and art, particularly in the Aula Magna, where

Villanueva worked in collaboration with sculptor Alexander Calder and acoustic engineer Robert Newman to achieve a synthesis of art, technology and architecture. Other internationally recognized artists also contributed to the project – among them Hans Arp, Fernand Leger, Victor Vasarely, Mateo Manaure and Henri Laurens. The third feature was the control of sunlight; contrasting light and shadow were used in the covered square to highlight the works of art that hung there. Similarly the light of the tropical sun, filtered through various screens, was used in the Aula Magna to modulate space. This is also a key feature of the facades of the architecture faculty, which is also notable for the interplay between a relatively conventional high-rise block and a free-form ground floor.

Further reading

Bullrich, F. (1969) *New Directions in Latin American Architecture*, New York: George Braziller.
'Caracas University City' (1954) *Arts and Architecture*, Los Angeles: November.

GUILLERMO GREGORIO

ciudad y los perros, La

Mario **Vargas Llosa**'s first novel, *La ciudad y los perros* (The Time of the Hero) was published in 1963 and won a prize from Seix Barral. The novel paints a harsh picture of a military school in Lima, presented as a microcosm of the fractious society of Peru. The Leoncio Prado military school establishes military discipline, but that discipline is the source of tension, violations of the rules, and all sorts of intrigue among the school's students and staff. The all-male world of the school is riven by sexual tension as well as by authoritarianism, which operates in terms of masters and slaves. The novel is a *Bildungsroman* or novel of education, with the shifting narrators and fragmented narration that Vargas Llosa would use (perhaps to better effect) in his subsequent novels. The novel was adapted to the cinema by Francisco **Lombardi** in 1986.

DANIEL BALDERSTON

CLACSO

CLACSO, or the Consejo Latinoamericano de Ciencias Sociales (The Latin American Council of Social Sciences), is an international, non-governmental, non-profit network dedicated to promoting academic research, discussion and the dissemination of information in the social sciences. Founded by Latin American social scientists in 1967, it has some ninety affiliated centres with 5,000 full-time researchers from Latin America and the Caribbean. The council's activities include research, education and consultancy as well as publication and dissemination of discussions on economy, politics and culture. Its headquarters are in Buenos Aires.

SANDRA GARABANO

Clair, Janet

b. 1925, Conquista, Minas Gerais, Brazil; d. 1983, Rio de Janeiro, Brazil

Television writer

One of the most innovative writers to have used her considerable talents in the service of the Brazilian *telenovela* (see **telenovelas**), dubbed by Carlos **Drummond de Andrade**, 'a usineira de sonhos' (the weaver of dreams). Born Janette Emmer, Clair began as a radio actress in São Paulo, where she met and worked with her future husband, the playwright Alfredo Dias **Gomes**. After achieving considerable success writing **radionovelas**, she transferred her skills to the newly booming medium of television. She innovated upon the staid historical formats of TV **Globo**'s *telenovelas* by setting her extraordinary romantic stories in 'real' modern locations and featuring popular songs in the soundtrack in series like *Veu de noiva* (Bridal Veil) in 1969. One of her greatest successes was *Os Irmãos Coragem* (The Brothers Courage) (1970), which aired for almost an entire year. Throughout the difficult 1970s, she created dreams for a country receiving daily doses of dictatorship.

ANA M. LÓPEZ

Claridad

Claridad began in 1959 as the newsletter of the Puerto Rican Pro-Independence Movement (MPI). When the MPI became the Socialist Party, *Claridad* became its official newspaper. Published weekly, *Claridad* actively promotes Puerto Rican independence (see **Puerto Rican independence groups**) and other Socialist Party goals and is read by Puerto Rican intellectuals, politicians and activists of all ideological positions. Its cultural section *En rojo* regularly features Puerto Rico's best-known writers and poets.

See also: *El Mundo*; *El Nuevo Día*; *San Juan Star*

NANCY MORRIS

Clarín

Argentina's, and indeed the Spanish-speaking world's, highest-circulation daily, *Clarín* was founded in 1945 by Roberto **Noble**, and has been the leading force in Argentine journalism ever since. Moderate in opinion, and independent of any political group, it has seventy-two tabloid pages and a print run of over half a million; its 250-page Sunday edition sells around one million copies.

Innovative and flexible in design, it actively seeks new readers in the market – with the result that it dominates 50 per cent of the print advertising market in the country. Its promotional methods include competitions and sponsorship of media events. It was the first Argentine newspaper to include specialist supplements – including *Deportes* (sport), *Arquitectura*, *Olla y sartenes* (cookery), *Lo nuevo* (ecology and tourism), *Cultura y nación* (culture and nation), *Para todos* (beauty and entertainment), *Sí* (youth interest), *Suplemento rural*, *Viajes y turismo* (travel), *Business*, and a Sunday supplement called *Viva*. In 1996, it launched *Olé*, the country's first daily sports newspaper.

More than a newspaper, *Clarín* is an institution. For over twelve years, it has offered education workshops for teachers and journalism students, to whom it also offers grants. It publishes between six and eighteen pages of international news and has correspondents in many of the world's major cities

as well as in all the Argentine provinces. It also publishes two daily editorial and opinion pages.

One of *Clarín*'s most important scoops was the discovery that Argentine arms were being sent to Ecuador during the 1994 border conflict with Peru. Its powerful position in the market, allowed *Clarín* to buy Radio Mitre and TV Channel 13; it is the co-owner of the Multicanal cable system and of a printing plant, Clarín-Aguila, all of which comprise the *Clarín* corporation. Its Internet website is www.clarin.com.ar, which offers thirty minutes of radio news, special reports and the text of the newspapers (but not the supplements) daily.

WILFREDO CANCIO ISLA

Clark, Lygia

b. 1920, Belo Horizonte, Brazil; d. 1988, Rio de Janeiro, Brazil

Painter, sculptor and multi-media artist

Lygia Clark was one of the most influential artists of the Brazilian neo-concrete movement (see **neo-concretism**). Clark began studying landscape architecture with Robert Burle **Marx**. From 1950–2 she lived and studied in Paris. In 1954 she joined the Grupo Frente in Rio (see also **constructivism**). Her early works are monochrome paintings of great simplicity of means which often generate a tense relationship between the wall and the picture plane. In 1959 she supported Ferreira Gullar's manifesto of neo-concretism, together with Hélio **Oiticica**. At this time she abandoned painting and began to make articulated aluminum sculptures with the generic name of *Bichos* (Animals). These works are designed to be manipulated by the viewer, thus showing an early interest in finding a more dynamic relationship between the artist and the audience. The *Bichos* developed into two new series called *Trepantes* (Climbing Grubs) and *Borrachas* (Rubber Grubs) in the 1960s. These 'grubs' were made of poorer materials than the 'animals', and physically deny a pedestal-type base by having to be hung or wrapped around an object. By the late 1960s, her burning interest in the active relationship with the spectator led her into a series of aesthetic experiments with psychotherapy and tactile experience. Some objects of this period are made of the simplest 'throwaway' materials such as carrier bags or old bits of string. These works are activated by the individual experience of handling the object and do not claim to contain any special 'aesthetic' value beyond their use. She also made a series of collective experiences, in which people were encouraged to interact with each other through tactile or sensorial experience. From 1970 to 1975 Clark taught at the Sorbonne in Paris, where most of her collective experiences took place. In 1978 she abandoned artistic production to dedicate herself to therapy using unconventional techniques.

Further reading

Ades, D. (ed.) (1989) *Art in Latin America*, London: Yale University Press.

Brett, G. (1993) 'Lygia Clark and Hélio Oiticica', *Latin American Artists of the 20th Century*, New York: Museum of Modern Art.

—— (1994) 'Lygia Clark: In Search of the Body', *Art in America* 82, 7: 56–63.

GABRIEL PEREZ-BARREIRO

Clarke, Austin M.

b. 1934, St. Matthias, Barbados

Novelist

Clarke's work addresses the problem of being Caribbean in Canada. He studied economics at the University of Toronto and has taught at several universities in the USA. For a time he worked as a broadcaster. He has lived in Toronto since 1955. Author of six novels, a trilogy beginning with *The Meeting Point* (1967); an autobiography, *Growing Up Stupid Under the Union Jack* (1980); and the story collections *When He Was Free and Young and He Used to Wear Silks* (1971), about Anancy, the mythical Caribbean trickster, *When Women Rule* (1985), and *Nine Men Who Laughed* (1986). His essay, 'Exile', appears in the anthology *Altogether Elsewhere* (1994), edited by Marc Robinson.

KEITH JARDIM

Clarke, Leroy

b. 1938, Gonzalez, Trinidad

Visual artist

Clarke's work consistently addresses the question of diasporization and Afro-Caribbean identity. At his studio on El Tucuche, Trinidad's highest mountain peak, Clarke has recently explored his vision of the Afro-Caribbean odyssey, from dispossession to regeneration, in a series of paintings. Clarke's iconography relies on the spirit underworld of local folklore, the forces and fertility of nature and the spirituality drawn from his practice of Orisha (see **orishas**). In *Under All I Alright* (1987), an apocalyptic, subterranean vision of the internal machinery of the body suggests a chaotic consciousness, withstanding attack from multiple and masked totemic figures who threaten self-knowledge.

LORRAINE LEU

CLASA

Mexican film studio built in 1934 in Mexico City with the financial assistance of the state (during the government of Lázaro **Cárdenas**). Its first film was Mexico's first 'super production', Fernando de Fuentes's controversial *¡Vámonos con Pancho Villa* (Let's Go With Pancho Villa!) (1935). Considered the MGM of Mexico because of the excellence of its facilities, CLASA was expensive but much in demand through the 1940s; the best films of the period were shot there. CLASA shut down on June 1957, after twenty-two years contributing to the Mexican cinema, due to the intervention of interests connected with the exhibition and distribution monopoly headed by US businessman William **Jenkins**.

ANA M. LÓPEZ

Clásicos universitarios

Clásicos universitarios were events which transformed the classic soccer games between the professional teams University of Chile (the 'U') and Catholic

University of Chile (the 'Cato') into imaginative mass spectacles. Traditionally held in Chile's National Stadium from the late 1930s to the early 1970s, the *clásicos* provided an opportunity for players and fans to be actively creative and included fireworks, dances, songs, stilt puppets and brief representations of classical Greek and Golden Age plays, transforming the field into a spectacular site. Producers included Aurelio Vega, Alejandro Gálvez, Germán **Becker** and Rodolfo Soto.

LUIS E. CÁRCAMO-HUECHANTE

class

Class is defined by the relationship between groups within a socioeconomic formation; it arises in its classic Marxist (see **Marxism in Latin America**) formulation from the social division of labour produced and sustained by a particular form of economic organization. The two major classes, in Marxist terms, are those thrown into direct conflict by the development of capitalist society – those owning the means of production – the bourgeoisie – on the one hand, and those whose productive labour is mobilized to generate wealth – the proletariat – on the other. These are the two major classes – but they are not the only ones. The petit-bourgeoisie, for example, owns its own means of production but does not control or direct the labour of others. This can include shopkeepers, small businessmen or peasant farmers. At the other end of the scale are workers who are excluded from the labour market and who do not form part of the proletariat. There are also a number of social groups or layers whose role is more ambivalent – professionals, scientists, managers and supervisors, etc. – who may act on behalf of the ruling classes while not members of it by dint of property ownership or actual control of resources.

The criticism often made of these Marxist categories is that they were born out of a narrow European experience of an industrial society. Latin America, still predominantly agricultural at the beginning of the twentieth century, does not fit the Marxist model.

The important issue, especially in the light of current arguments, is to underline the objective character of class – that it arises from a location within the social organization of production. There are many contemporary theorists, however, who follow Max Weber in seeing class as an attribute of behaviour or consciousness. This may help to understand changing attitudes – but it cannot deny that people are located within society independently of their will or attitudes.

The confusion arises when, particularly in agrarian communities, individuals or families may own small plots of land on which they depend; clearly they do not share the fundamental characteristic of all proletarians – that they are propertyless and have only their labour to sell. On the other hand, it is equally clear that these small peasants or *minifundistas* are normally unable to survive on the product of their land alone and will often work for wages in cash or kind for a more powerful landowner. In so far as their labour is bought and paid for at less than the value it produces, that peasant is exploited in the classic sense.

The earliest class-based organizations, the **trade unions** of miners and railwaymen in Chile, Bolivia or Mexico, for example, were founded by workers in exactly that position. And industrialization in the region has produced the very phenomena that Marx described – the concentration of labourers in larger and larger units of production, and the increasing severance of these labourers from their land, on the one hand, and the proletarianization of agricultural labour, on the other. The last two decades of the twentieth century, the era of globalization, demonstrated that relationship in an increasingly unmediated way.

As the century unfolded, more and more Latin Americans moved into the working class as such – employed for wages and depending on that income for their whole sustenance. Trade union organization – the banana workers' unions in Central America, the sugar refinery workers in Cuba and the meat-packing plants in Argentina are some examples – reflected that changing picture. **Import substitution industrialization** drew new layers of workers from the countryside, to the engineering factories of Buenos Aires and Córdoba in Argentina, around São Paulo in Brazil and in the Toluca valley in Mexico, for example. By the 1980s, the urban working population was larger than the rural. The *maquiladora* (see ***maquiladoras***) assembly plants on the Mexican border, for example, employed some 200,000 Mexicans by the end of the decade, and most of the world's car producers were represented by major factories in the region, as were pharmaceutical companies and electronics giants like Phillips (in Chile). In agriculture, too, the expansion of export agriculture led to the absorption of more and more land, and a consequent loss in land occupied by *minifundia* or other small farms and devoted to the production of food crops. Those who continued to work the land were as often as not wage-labourers employed by major corporations – though there was some successful resistance to this development, for example among the well-organized **coffee** producers of Costa Rica.

In the 1940s, it had been argued with some force by dependency theorists, often employing Marxist categories, that the interests of the Latin American bourgeoisies lay in independent economic development and that they could therefore be convinced of the need to adopt a nationalist position. The debate highlighted what has been the most important and the most conflictive issue in Latin American political debate over recent decades – the relationship between nation and class. If indeed the interests of the population as a whole were served by nationalism, then divisions of class could be seen as disruptive or divisive. Another version, adopted by most of the region's **communist parties** in the same period, argued that national independence and class struggle were distinct *stages* in the revolution; for dissenting revolutionary leftists, for example those in the Trotskyist tradition (see **Trotskyism**), however, this staged development in reality signified the abandonment of an internationalism based on the common interests of workers across the world, and its replacement by the bourgeois project of the construction of a strong Nation-State. This did not necessarily mean that workers should withdraw from a struggle for national independence, only that they should recognize the transient nature of these class alliances and organize themselves accordingly. In the event,

the fate of the Bolivian and Nicaraguan Revolutions (see **revolutions**), and Cuba's inability to escape the influence of the world market, provide their own evidence of the limitations of the 'national project'. By the 1990s, **neoliberalism** represented the reintegration of Latin American capitalists into a global system in which they had both some degree of autonomy but also to whose laws they were inescapably subject.

The fall of the Berlin Wall in 1989 had profound repercussions in the region, especially when it was linked to the concurrent failure of the Nicaraguan and other nationalist projects, and the apparent ease with which even powerful economies like Mexico were absorbed (through free-trade associations like **NAFTA**) into the global economy. The Stalinist tradition embodied in the region's communist parties largely collapsed with the Wall – the more so because it had so closely identified itself with the failed 'nationalist' project. The Maoist organizations, the most important of which was **Sendero Luminoso** in Peru, offered a similar project, though one accompanied by armed struggle – but by the late 1990s Sendero was no longer an alternative. The Zapatista movement (see **Zapatistas**) in Chiapas, on the other hand, seemed to belong in the company of a range of **new social movements** that were carrying forward the struggle for social justice and redistribution across the continent in the name of a new, specifically *non*-class-based (but based on ethnicity or gender, for example) politics. New protagonists seemed to occupy the centre of Latin American political life in the 1990s – **indigenous movements**, women's organizations, **gay and lesbian movements**, environmental groups (see **environmental issues** and so on.

The objective reality of a society divided along class lines, between the owners of the means of production and those who sell their labour power and have no other source of income seems clearer now than at the century's beginning. The perception and understanding of class as a prevailing reality, and thus as the basis for common organization and struggle, on the other hand, is less clear.

Further reading

Anderson, C. (1967) *Politics and Economic Change in Latin America*, Princeton, NJ: Van Nostrand.

MIKE GONZALEZ

Claudia de Colombia

b. 1952, Santafé de Bogotá, Colombia

Popular singer

Born Blanca Gladys Caldas, Claudia de Colombia became popular during the 1970s and 1980s. Among her song hits are: Tú me haces falta (I Need You), Te dejo la ciudad sin mí (I Leave You the City without Me) and Río Badillo (Badillo River).

MIGUEL A. CARDINALE

Clemente, Roberto

b. 1934, Carolina, Puerto Rico; d. 1972, Puerto Rico (offshore)

Baseball player

Clemente began his career at the age of eighteen with the Santurce team, Cangrejeros. From 1954 until his tragic death in an aviation accident, while helping to take supplies to the victims of the Nicaraguan earthquake, he played in the US major leagues, principally with the Pittsburgh Pirates. He won the batting championship on four occasions, made 3,000 hits and had a lifetime average of .318. On nine occasions he received the 'golden glove', and in 1973 was inducted posthumously into the Baseball Hall of Fame.

JUAN CARLOS QUINTERO HERENCIA

Cliff, Jimmy

b. 1948, Somerton, Jamaica

Musician

One of the first internationally recognised **reggae** artists, Cliff (born James Chambers) worked as a singer and songwriter in the 1960s and became a backup vocalist in London. In 1962 his 'Daisy Got Me Crazy' became a hit song; his landmark album, *Wonderful World, Beautiful People*, released in 1969, included some of his most notable songs such as 'Many Rivers to Cross' and 'Vietnam'. His music built on the earlier foundations of **ska** in Jamaica, and also captured the energy of reggae as the religion of black liberation in Jamaica and the African diaspora. Cliff is especially well known for his role in the 1970 Jamaican film *The **Harder They Come***.

JOHN H. PATTON

Cliff, Michelle

b. 1946, Kingston, Jamaica

Writer

Born in Jamaica, Cliff grew up in New York. The prose poem *Claiming an Identity They Taught Me to Despise* (1980) and the novels *Abeng* (1984) and *No Telephone to Heaven* (1987) establish Cliff's central autobiographical theme of a light-skinned Jamaican's desire to claim her African heritage. Her *Land of Look Behind* (1985), prose poetry, and the powerful short stories of *Bodies of Water* (1990) explore issues of migration and fractured identity. The novel *Free Enterprise* (1993) mixes historical and fictional characters and deals with slavery in the USA and its aftermath.

Further reading

Brice-Finch, J. (1996) 'Michelle Finch', in B. Lindfors and R. Sander (eds) *Twentieth Century Caribbean and African Writers*, Third Series, Vol. 157, Detroit: Gale Research, pp. 49–58.

ELAINE SAVORY

clothing and dress

While ethnic and indigenous clothing has often symbolized membership of a community, it has also been the case historically that the wearing of indigenous dress has brought discrimination and exclusion in its wake. Rural migrants reaching

Latin America's major cities – Lima, Mexico, La Paz – may still be seen wearing ponchos, headgear and sandals or home-made footwear, like the Mexican *huaraches* with soles carrying names like 'Goodyear' or 'Dunlop'. But the treatment they are likely to receive once they depart from their customary behaviour as market or street traders, beggars or travelling musicians, etc. will almost certainly lead their children to abandon ethnic dress in favour of 'Western' clothing – the ubiquitous jeans, check shirts, boots or sport shoes that might enable them to merge more easily with a modern urban crowd.

By the same token, the resumption of ethnic dress may be in itself an act of defiance or resistance – as the protagonist's brother does, for example, at the end of **Sanjinés**'s 1971 Bolivian film *Yawar Malku* (Blood of the Condor). In Guatemala, Rigoberta **Menchú**'s mode of dress – poncho, wide skirt (*pollera*), brightly coloured woven or cotton blouses (*huipiles*) – are emblematic of a combative indigenous movement of Mayan resistance, whose clothing defiantly distinguishes that community from the Westernizing *ladinos*. In Brazil, membership of the gaúcho traditionalist movement (see **gaúcho culture**) is largely signalled by dress, and the distinctive dress of the northeastern **sertão** is a marker of identity familiar in Brazilian cinema, and particularly **Cinema Novo**, and among northeastern musicians. The flowing, usually white, skirts of black women street vendors, known as *baianas*, during Brazil's **carnival** mark connections through popular religions like **Candomblé** to a more distant, African past. It is a powerful mark of rebellion and difference that the 1994 (and continuing) Zapatista resistance (see **Zapatistas**) in Chiapas, southern Mexico, assumed as its symbolic dress the indigenous dress of the southern ethnicities, the red scarf of the Central American revolutionaries and the balaclava of countless anonymous armed-resistance groups. The **Madres de Plaza de Mayo** in Argentina, for their part, have transformed the white headscarf into a potent symbol of protest against the abuse of human rights.

In a similar way, artistic and cultural movements like the *indigenistas* of the 1930s and 1940s, the Bolivian cultural movements following the 1952 Revolution (see **revolutions**), the *nueva canción*

movements of the 1960s or the Nicaraguan Revolution of 1979 have often adopted emblematic dress. The Bolivian musical group Los **Jairas**, the Chilean groups **Quilapayún** and **Inti-Illimani**, and the Mexican Los **Folkloristas** all adopted local clothing for their stage performances. The omnipresent embroidered shirt of the Caribbean, the **guayabera**, however, is one of the few traditional pieces of apparel that remain in common and natural use.

There have also been periodic attempts to create a uniform clothing code as a symbol of a new equality. In Nicaragua, the Minister of Culture, poet Ernesto **Cardenal**, tried (largely unsuccessfully) to encourage the general use of the simple peasant *cotona*, which he himself wore. In Cuba, after the 1959 Revolution, the new regime tried to impose a Chinese-style system of uniforms for many social groups and professions. Students had grey uniforms (topped by an obligatory red scarf identifying them as 'pioneers'), hotel workers wore orange shifts, etc. Even as late as the founding of the Escuela Internacional de Cine y Televisión (1986), the first batch of students were still assigned tasteless uniforms to wear to the opening ceremonies.

In a different sense dress can also reflect both the prevalent moral codes and the aspirations of a society. In post-revolutionary Cuba again, there was a moralistic conservatism about the dress code that meant women rarely wore shorts or bermudas in the streets, mini-skirts were counter-revolutionary and jeans or trousers of some kind *de rigueur* even in sweltering summer temperatures. Since the late 1980s, of course the *jineteras* (see **jinetera**) are publicly identified by their provocative dress, and young girls are warned not to dress in mini-skirts or revealing outfits so as not to be 'confused' with them on the streets.

In a quite different context, Buenos Aires has taken great pride in its European style and elegance; for many years it was a feature of Argentine life that women would dress with great elegance simply to go out into the street. Those who remember those times may be heard to lament the decline of elegance as casual wear has become increasingly the norm. At the other end of the spectrum, Brazil – and particularly Rio de Janeiro – has become synonymous with an open display and overt sensuality; a brief 'tanga' bikini barely concealed by an artfully wrapped *pareo* scarf around the waist is common street wear for women throughout the Zona Sul. Men walk around shirtless and in micro-bikini briefs on their way to and from beaches like Copacabana.

Sometimes, of course, the most characteristic ethnic dress is itself not necessarily 'traditional'; the ubiquitous and defining bowler hats worn by Bolivian indigenous women, for example, began to be manufactured in the nineteenth century by a German businessman. The elaborate and highly decorated dress of Mexico's weekend cowboys, the *charros* (see **charro**), in turn, are recreations or artistic elaborations of the festive uniforms traditionally worn by rural cowhands who would have been very unlikely to be able to afford the proliferation of silver the modern costumes display.

Headgear is often functional as well as symbolic; from the woollen helmets with earflaps (*chuyos*), highly functional in the harsh Andean night, to the ever present straw hats (often called panamas and mostly made in Ecuador – see **panama hat**) worn by agricultural workers, to the adopted Stetsons of northern Mexico. The varieties of woven blankets that served as daytime dress and night-time covering are still used in the countryside – the poncho, *serape*, *ruana* and so on often bear distinctive regional patterns.

The paradox, of course, is that one effect of globalization has been the increasingly wide distribution of ethnic cultural products, from musical instruments and decorative arts to clothing. Very few European or US cities are without their ethnic clothing store – adopted in more basic form by a New Age culture and in more refined and elaborate expressions by a fashion industry that has often imitated the poncho or the *chuyo*, albeit in unusual materials and colours. Alpaca ponchos have become high fashion items, and sweaters, skirts and scarves in alpaca or llama wool are sold in enormous quantities to tourists from the north in tandem with the growing taste for the music of the high Andes. Straw headgear made in damp and difficult conditions in Mexico and Ecuador travel the world easily. The irony is that, by and large, these items are eschewed by people of rural or peasant origin in Latin America itself. They largely prefer the jeans that proliferated from the USA after the Second World War and which are now found in multiple varieties with labels that indicate that they are made in Taiwan, the Philippines or Korea. These have supplanted, by the even more profound exploitation of their labour, many of the sweatshop industries that produced cheap clothing in Latin America through the 1960s and 1970s.

While Latin America exports much of its craft work (see **crafts**) to Europe and the USA, its imports of jeans and shorts from the Far East are often supplemented by bundles of used clothing, compressed and resold to Latin America's poorest peoples.

MIKE GONZALEZ

Clube da Esquina

The Clube da Esquina (Corner Club) refers to a group of composer-musicians, mostly from the mountainous state of Minas Gerais, which coalesced in the early 1970s around the celebrated vocalist Milton **Nascimento**. The Clube was noted for creative fusions of Brazilian genres, Anglo-American rock and Chilean *nueva canción*. The group's first double album of 1972 featured Wagner Tiso, Eumir Deodato, Lô Borges, Márcio Borges, Beto Guedes and lyricists Fernando Brant and Ronaldo Bastos. Nascimento reunited the group in 1978 to record a sequel, *Clube da Esquina 2*, a homage to Brazilian and Spanish American popular music.

CHRISTOPHER DUNN

CMQ-TV

CMQ, a powerful radio network belonging to the brothers Abel and Goar **Mestre**, began television transmission in December 1950. Television was officially inaugurated in Cuba in October 1950 when Channel 4, Unión Radio Televisión, owned by Gaspar **Pumarejo**, went on air. The two networks then entered into an intense competitive race for control of the medium. CMQ-TV gained ground, launching CMBF-TV Channel 7 and consolidating a chain which became one of the most influential in the western hemisphere. In

1960, under the revolutionary government's new nationalization decree, the Mestre brothers' property was expropriated and passed to the state.

WILFREDO CANCIO ISLA

CNBB

Established in 1952 under the leadership of Dom Helder **Câmara**, the CNBB (Conferencia Nacional dos Bispos do Brasil – National Conference of Brazilian Bishops), constitutes a mediating institution between individual bishops and Rome. By enabling bishops to speak with a common voice, it facilitated taking controversial yet influential stands on public issues. Initially, the CNBB was dominated by some of the more radical bishops of Latin America and strongly supported **liberation theology**. Appointments in the 1980s and 1990s have included more conservative bishops. The CNBB was highly significant as a model for larger international organizations of bishops, such as **CELAM**.

THOMAS A. LEWIS

co-productions

Beginning in the 1940s, the deals between film producers in different countries (known in the film business as co-productions) have proven to be of extraordinary significant for the development – and survival – of national cinemas in Latin America.

The earliest source of co-production financing was Mexican producers who reached out eagerly to nations without a national cinema infrastructure, especially those with exotic auras like Cuba and Guatemala. For producers in these nations, the Mexican industry's financing, technical expertise and distribution networks were desirable allies. The trend began with director Juan **Orol**'s *Embrujo Antillano* (Antillean Spell) (1945), a co-production with Cuba. The most important years for co-productions with Cuba were 1953 and 1954 (with six and eight films, respectively); films like *Mulata* (Gilberto **Martínez Solares**, 1953) and *Sandra: La mujer de fuego* (Sandra: The Woman of Fire) (Orol,

1952) relativized the Mexican cinema's typically nationalistic fervour via exotic, racially differentiated 'others'. The first film produced in post-revolutionary Cuba was also a Mexican co-production (through independent producer (see **independent film producers**) Manuel **Barbachano Ponce**), but under very different circumstances: Julio **García Espinosa**'s *Cuba baila* (Cuba Dances) (1960).

The Argentine industry also extended its reach beyond national borders to Uruguay (*Los tres mosqueteros* (The Three Musketeers) (Julio Saraceni, 1946) and Venezuela (*La balandra Isabel llegó esta tarde* (The 'Isabel' Arrived this Afternoon) (Carlos Hugo **Christensen**, 1949). **Argentina Sono Film** also struck a co-production agreement with the struggling **Chile Films** to provide technical assistance and co-produce a series of films to jump-start their activities. None of the eight films produced were particularly successful, however.

By the late 1960s and 1970s, with the established industrial sectors in crisis and the rise of the **New Latin American Cinema**, the flow of co-productions shifted and they acquired a different politicized function. **ICAIC** in Cuba, already a solid institution, opened its arms to exiled filmmakers and productions from the rest of the continent. Its co-productions with Chilean exiles like Patricio **Guzmán** and Miguel **Littín** were especially important, as was its co-operative agreement with the Nicaragua's Sandinista (see **Sandinista Revolution**) film institute, **INCINE**.

In the 1980s and through the 1990s, however, although ICAIC continued to seek out co-production possibilities with other Latin American producers, European producers entered the equation, injecting capital – especially from television companies like Spain's TVE – and increased international marketing possibilities. Even the most established directors have had to seek co-productions, as did Tomás **Gutiérrez Alea** for his last two films: *Fresa y chocolate* (Strawberry and Chocolate) (1993) was co-produced with Mexico; *Guantanamera* (1995) with Spain. As states have increasingly withdrawn their direct support of the national cinema – as with the dismantling of **Embrafilme** in Brazil – international co-production deals have become even more important. Many are concerned with the potentially denationalizing and homogenizing effects of these practices – transforming all Latin American national cinemas into art cinemas for international consumption – but, given contemporary financial constraints on film-making (ranging from devalued currencies to soaring production costs), it is unlikely that the trend will be reversed in the near future.

Further reading

Podalsky, L. (1994) 'Negotiating differences: National cinemas and co-productions in pre-revolutionary Cuba', *The Velvet Light Trap* 34: 59–70.

Stock, A.M. (1997) *Framing Latin American Cinema*, Minneapolis: University of Minnesota Press.

ANA M. LÓPEZ

COB

COB (Central Obrera Boliviana) (Bolivian Workers Central) was founded in 1952, one week after the National Revolution, by the worker ministers Germán Butrón and Juan **Lechín**. Inspired by the Trotskyist thesis of permanent revolution, the COB came to be considered one of the most militant **trade union** organizations in the world. It briefly ran the country with the Nationalist Revolutionary Movement (MNR) in a *co-gobierno* (formal worker representation in the government) where workers and armed militias pressed for the nationalization of the tin mines, implementation of an agrarian reform and abolition of the armed forces.

The COB became increasingly anti-MNR in 1957, following the introduction of a US-inspired monetary stabilization plan. It backed the formation of the Popular Assembly in 1971 during the left-wing government of General Juan José **Torres**, and went underground throughout the 1971–8 dictatorship. The COB's power base has been declining ever since the mass 'relocalization' of over 20,000 miners in the mid-1980s, following the collapse of the international price of tin. Many of the former miners migrated to the lowlands to become coca leaf farmers.

Miners or salaried workers no longer hold sway in the COB, an organization formally led by them, but where the most militant rank and file members are the urban and rural school teachers and the coca leaf farmers. The COB argue the organization must be led by proletarians, thus resisting calls for reform to allow greater participation and leadership positions for new social movements such as peasants, regional ethnic groups and women.

WINSTON MOORE

Cobo Borda, Juan Gustavo

b. 1948, Santafé de Bogotá, Colombia

Poet, essayist and literary critic

In *La tradición de la pobreza* (Tradition of Poverty) (1980), Cobo Borda affirms that in the history of Colombian literature there are very few who really deserve to be called poets. His own poetry is often hilarious or sarcastic, or celebrates popular culture. Among his collections of poems are: *Consejos para sobrevivir* (Advice on Survival) (1974), *Ofrenda en el altar del bolero* (Offering on the Altar of Bolero) (1981) and *Todos los poetas son santos e irán al cielo* (All Poets are Saints and Will Go to Heaven) (1983).

MIGUEL A. CARDINALE

cockfights

'In the cockfight, man and beast, good and evil, ego and id, the creative power of aroused masculinity and the destructive power of loosened animality fuse in a bloody drama of hatred, cruelty, violence, and death.' Clifford Geertz's synthesis, based on his work in Bali, has universal application. It applies too, of course, to other forms of fighting, even between humans. In Spain and Latin America, aggressive men with a tendency to fight are called *gallos* (cocks), and by contrast cowards are called, in an alarmingly obvious way, *gallinas* (chickens). But the terminology is also self-critical, and *gallo* can also mean an overbearing and self-important ('cocky') person. Brought to

Latin America by the conquistador Hernán Cortés, fighting cocks soon spread across the continent; the *palenque* (ring) where the fight took place was also the name given to the fortified communities of runaway slaves. The Spanish birds were interbred with local birds to produce a range of hybrids. Some experts have seen in these Latin American variants specific modes of fighting, like the *papilla* (pulp) attack, where the bird evades the enemy and itself attacks in a rapid turn, from behind.

Whether clandestine or legal, cockfights take place from Mexico to Argentina, but the tradition is particularly important in Cuba, Colombia, Puerto Rico and Peru. The practice leads to exchanges of money (in bets) and passionate confrontations; there are fierce rituals of triumph and defeat, from cannibalistic joy to suicidal grief – and this for both men and animals, for there is a strong identification between them. Proverbs and sayings, breeding customs and rules of combat, enshrine elements of ideology. Purebred fighting cocks, according to one manual, are 'true battle machines, aggressive, cruel, vengeful and full of malice from the moment they enter the ring'. The first rule states that: 'If a cock dies before the count of ten is completed, the battle will be awarded to the survivor; if both die, the battle is awarded to the last animal to die.' Desmond Morris has suggested that contrary to what devotees may believe, the racehorse does not know that he has won; that is certainly not true of the victorious cock. There are moving representations of cockfights in **García Márquez**'s *El coronel no tiene quien le escriba* (Nobody Writes to the Colonel) (1961) and Leonardo **Favio**'s fine film *El romance del Aniceto y la Francisca* (The Ballad of Aniceto and Francisca) (1961).

Further reading

Geertz, C. (1973) 'Notes on the Balinese Cockfight', in C. Geertz, *The Interpretation of Culture*, New York: Harper Collins.

Mañas Perdomo, R. (1991), *Manual básico de gallos de riña*, Buenos Aires: Albatros.

JULIO SCHVARTZMAN

cocoliche

'Cocoliche' was initially a caricature of the Italian immigrant in Argentine literature. Argentina underwent a transformative process at the turn of the century, during which large numbers of European immigrants arrived in the country. The largest single group, from Italy, were viewed with hostility by the local population. **Gaucho** literature, in works such as *Martín Fierro* (1872, 1879) and *Juan Moreira* (1876), included representations of Italian immigrants; the dramatization of *Moreira* gave birth to the cocoliche character. Later the word came to refer to the language attributed to Italian immigrants, a mixture of Spanish and Italian.

A. FERNÁNDEZ-BRAVO

Codallo, Alfred Antonio

b. 1913, Trinidad; d. 1970, New York City, USA

Graphic artist

While working at a local newspaper as an illustrator, photographer and lithographer, Codallo began to produce his famous series of pen and ink drawings of Trinidadian festivals, dance forms and key characters of folk tales. These tales combine symbols of European colonial rule with residual memories of West African culture. Codallo's human figures are frequently at the mercy of an ongoing battle between good and evil, played out in natural settings. His best-known work is the watercolour *Trinidad Folklore* (1970), which hangs in the National Museum. His work has influenced LeRoy **Clarke**, who has reinscribed elements of the spirit world into his portrayal of the contemporary Caribbean struggle.

LORRAINE LEU

CODEFF

Founded in 1968, CODEFF (Comité Nacional por la Defensa de la Fauna y Flora) (National Committee for the Defence of Fauna and Flora) is the oldest private environmental organization in Chile. It promotes the defence of the environment, focusing on citizen involvement and emphasizing legal intervention. Additional functions include research, education and administering a Wildlife Rehabilitation Centre. CODEFF's successes include ending whaling activity in Chile, gaining legal protection for native alerce and araucaria trees, protecting national parks considered biospheric reserves, and defending communities affected by mining, industrial or logging activity.

AMALIA PEREIRA

Coelho, Paulo

b. 1947, Rio de Janeiro, Brazil

Writer

Latin America's best-selling **New Age** author, Coelho became known around the world for *O alquimista* (The Alchemist) (1988), which has been translated into numerous languages. In his youth, he was committed several times to mental hospitals and subjected to electroshock treatments; he has used this experience as a vehicle to talk about the need for human beings to look for their destiny within. His first career was as a writer of rock lyrics for artists like Elis **Regina** and others; some of his songs were considered subversive and he was imprisoned and tortured by the Brazilian military regime in 1974. His first book *O peregrino* (The Pilgrimage) (1987) was an account of his experience walking to the great medieval pilgrimage church of Santiago de Compostela in Galicia, Spain. He has published seven more books since then, selling over 23 million copies to date. He was invited to speak at the World Economic Forum in 1998 and 1999, and spoke on the need to respect spirituality and culture. In an interview on BBC with Tim Sebastian, broadcast in early 2000, he stated that 'When you want something the whole world conspires to help you get it'; his optimistic message has obviously been well received by many readers, though his writing has yet to be taken seriously by literary critics.

DANIEL BALDERSTON

coffee

From its humble beginnings as a drink for Ethiopian goatherds, coffee evolved into an extravagant global phenomenon, both culturally and economically. Coffee ranks second only to petroleum in dollar value among natural commodities traded internationally. It is a major source of foreign exchange in Latin America and more than 20 million people depend upon it for their livelihood. In most of Latin America, a day without coffee is unthinkable: coffee is typically imbibed first thing in the morning with milk, as in *café con leche*; throughout the day in small, very sweetened portions (the Brazilian *cafezinho* (little coffee) or the Cuban *buchito* (little gulp)); and after all meals, still very sweet but in medium-sized cups. It is brewed in homes and workplaces (with a filter-drip apparatus or a fancy espresso machine), but is also frequently enjoyed in bars, luncheonettes, coffee-only stands and, of course, the ubiquitous cafés (see **café culture**), which in addition to serving coffee have served as centres of political, social and literary influence.

Latin America produces about two-thirds of the world's coffee. The crop was introduced in the 1700s via a single Java plant smuggled by a French soldier into Martinique. It is said that the Brazilian emperor Dom Pedro II loved coffee so much that he charged an agent to obtain seeds abroad, no matter the cost. As legend has it, this sly fellow seduced the wife of the governor of French Guiana and returned with the seedlings that were the foundation for the world's greatest coffee empire. Brazil's fertile soil and copious harvests transformed coffee from an elite indulgence to an everyday elixir for the people. And it also produced tremendously wealthy and powerful *barões de café* – coffee barons – who at one time controlled national life. In Central America, also, coffee growers created not only plantations (*fincas*), but also the infrastructure of the region (railroads, ports, banking systems) in order to get the beans to markets; they were and continue to be the political elite of the isthmus.

Since early in the twentieth century, Brazil has been the world's largest producer – and consumer – of coffee; it produces a third of the world's supply and drinks a good third of that domestically. The Central American nations (especially Costa Rica,

El Salvador and Guatemala) and Colombia each produce about a tenth of the world's total. Because of the economic importance of coffee exports, several Latin American countries made arrangements before the Second World War to allocate export quotas and apportion the US coffee market. The idea of regulating the market was developed internationally in 1962, via an International Coffee Agreement, negotiated through the United Nations, which called for a quota system limiting the outflow of beans from producing nations in times of over-supply. The agreement was renegotiated several times, but the participating nations failed to sign a new pact in 1989 and, since then, world coffee prices have varied wildly.

Further reading

Calvert, C. (1994) *Coffee: The Essential Guide to the Essential Bean*, New York: Hearst.

Paige, Jeffery M. (1998) *Coffee and Power: Revolution and the Rise of Democracy in Central America*, Cambridge, MA: Harvard University Press.

ANA M. LÓPEZ

cofradía

A *cofradía* is a society or organization composed of Catholic (usually) male laity united for religious and charitable purposes. *Cofradía* members are devoted to a particular saint, although some *cofradías* maintain devotions to the Holy Eucharist, a manifestation of Mary or Christ Crucified. Members pay annual dues, attend services at specific chapels housed in larger churches, maintain the upkeep of their chapels, and celebrate the feast day of their saint. *Cofradías* also provide for the families of deceased members and do charitable works; today, they donate food to poor families, offer scholarships to needy students, and host fundraising events for worthy causes.

LINDA A. CURCIO-NAGY

Cohen, Gregory

b. 1953, Santiago, Chile

Playwright

Cohen's work gained a reputation in the 1980s. His plays from that decade include *La pieza que falta* (The Missing Piece), *Lily yo te quiero* (Lily, I Love You) and *A fuego lento* (On Low Heat). A notable success of the 1990s was *Reality Show* in 1997. Cohen was active in the ACU (Asociación Cultural Universitaria) movement at the Universidad de Chile, one of the most creative and active non-professional theatres during the **Pinochet** regime. He formed the theatre group Teniente Bello (Beautiful Deputy) and participated in many of the theatre festivals that struggled against the regime's censorship. In 1998 he scripted and starred in Claudio Sapiaía's film *El hombre que imaginaba* (The Man I Imagined).

RUTH DOMINGUEZ

COICA

COICA (Coordinadora Indígena de la Cuenca Amazónica) (Indigenous Coordinator of the Amazon Basin) was founded in Lima in 1984 by indigenous organizations of Bolivia, Brazil, Colombia, Ecuador and Peru. Its goals are to provide representation of indigenous peoples to governmental and non-governmental agencies, to defend indigenous lands, to promote solidarity among indigenous groups and to value Indian cultures and traditions. The 'Declaration of Iquitos', a document written by five South American national indigenous federations, sixteen environmental/conservation organizations and fifteen non-governmental organizations in 1990, outlines an alliance in the management and conservation of the Amazonian biosphere.

REGINA HARRISON

Cojtí, Demetrio

b. 1948, Iximché, Guatemala

Indigenous leader

A K'akchikel Maya, Cojtí was one of the first indigenous figures to benefit from a higher education, having migrated to the city and worked in a factory by day to finance his studies at night. Active in the Maya movement from the mid-1970s onwards, he returned permanently in 1980 and became a university professor and his country's leading Maya intellectual. A leading consultant for international bodies dealing with ethnic issues, his writings include *Configuración del pensamiento maya* (Configuration of Maya Thought) (1994–5) and *El movimiento maya* (The Maya Movement) (1997). He holds a doctorate from the University of Louvain, in Belgium.

ARTURO ARIAS

Cold War, impact of

Winston Churchill's 1947 speech at Fulton, Missouri officially divided the world into two warring superpowers on either side of an 'iron curtain'. Thus was the Cold War announced. The idea that Latin America 'belonged' to an American hemisphere dominated by the USA, however, was a determining feature of its twentieth-century history – as the periodic occupation of Cuba, Haiti, Puerto Rico and Nicaragua among others had shown. The free movement of USA-based multinational corporations like United Fruit or Standard Oil with Washington's explicit support expressed that relationship in economic terms. Latin American governments not approved by Washington found themselves under pressure well before the onset of the Cold War. **Cárdenas** in Mexico and **Perón** in Argentina, for example, were the objects of vigorous opposition orchestrated from the US embassies.

The Cold War gave this hemispheric control legitimacy and ideological cohesion. In Guatemala in 1954, the attempt at reform by the **Arbenz** government was undermined by a military *coup* supported by a US State Department whose incumbent, John Foster Dulles, was a director of the United Fruit Company, which owned so much of Guatemala's land. Here and elsewhere the defence of US interests was justified as a war against communism.

With the Cuban Revolution of 1959 (see **revolutions**), such crude anti-communism was criticized by several commentators in the USA who argued vehemently that the impulse to independent national development should not be tarred with the communist brush. The Eisenhower government ignored them and within a year imposed a fierce economic embargo. The irony was that Fidel **Castro** himself was bitterly hostile to a Cuban Communist Party riddled with corruption and hopelessly compromised by the Batista dictatorship. Indeed the general line of the **communist parties** of the region since the early 1950s had been one of collaboration with 'progressive' regimes rather than the fomenting of revolution.

In fact the embargo drove Cuba into the Soviet embrace – providing the most virulent anti-communism with an emblematic enemy that has survived *détente* and even the fall of the Berlin Wall in 1989. In reality, the Soviets were reluctant to become involved with Cuba; its geo-political interests embraced Africa rather than a Latin America it recognized as lying within a US ambit. The USA responded to Cuba, in any event, by tightening its control over the hemisphere, through the Tratado Interamericano de Asistencia Recíproca (Inter American Defence Treaty) (TIAR) formed at Punta del Este in 1961, which co-ordinated the region's military structures with the dual purpose of isolating Cuba militarily and strengthening the internal mechanisms of control against any possible revolutionary upsurge. The creation of the **Alliance for Progress** was designed to pre-empt more radical reform proposals by offering support for guided development programmes in the context of a continuing relationship with US capital. The creation of a series of Christian Democratic organizations across the continent was a clear attempt to repeat the experience of post-war Europe and provide alternative political leadership.

Culture was not exempt from the same high-level intervention, as the *Mundo nuevo* affair clearly showed; this journal along with others was shown to have been financed through a **CIA**-organized body called the Congress for Cultural Freedom, whose task it was to continue the Cold War into the field of culture and the arts. There was also a more indirect cultural intervention that Mattelart and **Dorfman**'s timely study, ***How to Read Donald Duck*** (1971) brilliantly addressed – the proliferation of American cultural commodities, from music to Disney products to cinema and comic books and patterns of consumption.

Further reading

Gerassi, J. (1965) *The Great Fear in Latin America*, New York: Collier Books.

Lieuwen, E. (1961) *Arms and Politics in Latin America*, London/New York: Praeger.

Mattelart, A. (1971) *Agresión desde el espacio: Cultura y napalm en la era de los satélites*, Mexico City: Siglo XXI.

Melville, T. and M. (1971) *Guatemala: Another Vietnam?*, Harmondsworth: Penguin.

MIKE GONZALEZ

Collar, Enrique

b. 1964, Itaugua Guazú, Paraguay

Artist and engraver

Collar's work, part of the postmodern era (see **postmodernism**), is characterized by the use of 'mythopoesía' in which the myth of fertility dominates. The metamorphosis of human beings from animal conditions to a supernatural state is also a common element of his painting. Collar lived and studied art in Buenos Aires from 1971–94, graduating in fine arts in 1988. He has presented individual shows since 1987 in Argentina, Paraguay and the USA, and has participated in collective exhibitions since 1983. Collar won awards for his painting in Asunción and Buenos Aires in 1992, 1993 and 1995. He returned to Buenos Aires in 1996.

BETSY PARTYKA

Collins, Merle

b. 1950, Aruba, Netherlands Antilles

Poet, novelist and scholar

Collins's work addresses the Caribbean populations' diasporic foundations and experiences, which are representatively embodied by his life and career in the Caribbean, USA and UK. She explores these themes in works like the 1992 poetry collection, *Rotten Pomerack*, and the 1995 novel, *The Colour of Forgetting*. Collins weaves the stories or sings the emotion of personal memories, which are narrated against the grain of official history by voices ranging freely over and on the back of oral traditions, myth, education, family and nation.

JOHN D. PERIVOLARIS

Collor, Fernando

b. 1949, Rio de Janeiro, Brazil

Politician

In 1989, Collor became the youngest president in the history of Brazil. He was President of the family media empire when he was elected federal deputy for the state of Alagoas in 1982, and Governor in 1987. His attack on the salaries of public officials was popular and set the tone for his successful Presidential campaign. In September 1992, the legality of his economic reforms was called into question and his mandate was ended (by 441 votes to 38) when he was accused of corruption. The senate found him guilty by 76 votes to 3 and he was banned from public office for eight years.

DANIEL BALDERSTON

Collor Riti *see* Qoyllur Rit'i

Collyer, Jaime

b. 1955, Santiago, Chile

Writer

Collyer has published novels and short stories,

including the novels *Infiltrado* (The Infiltrator) (1989), *Cien pájaros volando* (100 Birds Flying) (1995) and the collection of short stories *Gente al acecho* (People on the Prowl) (1992). He lived in Madrid, Spain from 1981 to 1991, when he returned to Chile. Once in Chile he contributed to the post-dictatorship renewal of writing and publishing, working as an editor at the publishing company **Planeta Chilena** and as a regular contributor to the leftist magazine *Apsi* and the newspaper *La **Epoca***. The ironic and humorous stories included in *Gente al acecho* have won literary prizes in Spain, Cuba and Chile.

AMALIA PEREIRA

Collymore, Frank

b. 1893, Woodville, Barbados; d. 1980

Writer

As editor of the magazine ***Bim***, Collymore played a central role in the growth and development of Caribbean literature from the 1940s onwards, publishing the work of George **Lamming** and Austin **Clarke** among many others. His acknowledged importance in that role, however, has unfortunately led to a neglect of his own writing; his five volumes of poetry, gathered in the *Collected Poems* (1971) and his short stories which, while set in the Caribbean, address issues of wider resonance – madness (in 'Shadows') (1942), loneliness ('Rewards and chrysanthemum') (1961) and the power of atavistic forces (in his poem 'Hymn to the sea', 1959) for example.

MIKE GONZALEZ

Coloane, Francisco

b. 1910, Chiloe, Chile

Writer

Coloane's writing returns to the traditional themes of the struggle between man and nature in the southernmost part of Chile, in **Patagonia**, the southern seas and Tierra del Fuego, where he grew up. Moving to Santiago, he worked as a journalist

and published his collections of stories *El último grumete de La Baquedano* (La Baquedano's Last Cabin Boy) and *Cabo de Hornos* (Cape Horn) (both 1941). The novel *Los conquistadores de la Antártida* (Conquerors of the Antarctic) (1945) and the collection of short stories *Tierra del fuego* (1956), among others, followed. In 1964 he was awarded the National Literature Prize.

CELINA MANZONI

Colombia

Located on the northern part of the South American continent, Colombia has coasts on both the Pacific and Atlantic sides of Panama. The nation is one of the world's major **coffee** producers, birthplace of world-class painters and sculptors, as well as popular music composers, and homeland of Nobel Laureate Gabriel **García Márquez**. Yet its impressive and productive economic and cultural history has often been overshadowed in the past two decades by its drug trafficking (see **drugs in Latin America**).

Despite its violent first century, Colombia is the only Latin American nation in which the traditional nineteenth-century political parties – the Liberal and the Conservative Parties – have survived. Party rivalries led to some outbreaks of violence in the 1930s and 1940s, culminating in an undeclared civil war identified as La **Violencia** during the 1950s, which resulted in approximately 300,000 deaths. This war was ignited on 9 April, 1948, when a populist candidate representing the Liberal Party, Jorge Eliecer Gaitán, was assassinated in Bogotá. Most of the conflicts between the two traditional parties were resolved with the peace accords of 1958, creating a systematic sharing of power between the Liberals and Conservatives called the National Front. Since the 1960s, a variety of leftist guerrilla groups have been active in Colombia, some of which have been integrated into the institutional political system in recent years. (This is the case of the **M-19**, which was founded as an urban guerrilla movement in 1970.) The phenomenal rise of drug trafficking since the late 1970s has further destabilized political and social life, particularly since the active campaign of

President Virgilio Barco (1986–90) against the drug cartels.

Two cartels have been most responsible for the illicit international drug trade. The Medellín group had humble origins as small-time importers of contraband and exporters of marijuana in the late 1960s and 1970s. By the late 1970s, however, they had organized massive and elaborate international networks to export cocaine. In the late 1980s and early 1990s, they were responsible for widespread bombings and kidnappings in Colombia. The Cali cartel was created by individuals with business and banking backgrounds and has not employed the violence associated with the Medellín group (see **Rodríguez Orejuela**, Gilberto). Both cartels were weakened in the 1990s with the arrest and death of many of their leaders, including Pablo **Escobar** from Medellín. Despite these defeats, the cocaine and heroin trade remain multi-milliion dollar operations.

The intense conflicts and ongoing political crises have affected all sectors of social and economic life; nevertheless, several spheres of Colombian culture have flourished, particularly since the 1960s. Traditional and conservative forces tended to dominate Colombian cultural life until a generation born in the 1920s, and including García Márquez, began to successfully modernize cultural expression in the 1950s and 1960s. Many of them were associated with the cultural journal *Mito* in the 1950s. From 1955 to 1967, García Márquez published his famous novels set in mythical Macondo, incorporating the oral culture of the Caribbean coast where he spent his childhood. This fiction, which always questioned traditional values and society in Colombia and Latin America, culminated in his magisterial novel *Cien años de soledad* (One Hundred Years of Solitude) (1967). Of his later novels, *El otoño del patriarca* (Autumn of the Patriarch) (1975) and *El amor en los tiempos de cólera* (Love in the Time of Cholera) (1985) have won the most critical acclaim and the largest readership. García Márquez has remained an active journalist throughout his career, as well as writing short stories and film scripts. Other writers of this generation, such as Manuel **Mejía Vallejo**, Héctor Rojas Herazo, and Alvaro **Mutis**, have created a significant body of fiction. Mutis is also one of Colombia's premier poets. This generation

modernized writing in Colombia and brought the Colombian novel into the international literary arena.

Since the 1970s, a new generation of writers has arisen, including Gustavo **Alvarez Gardeazábal**, R.H. **Moreno-Durán**, Darío **Jaramillo Agudelo**, Albalucía **Angel**, and Fanny **Buitrago**. Alvarez Gardeazábal's early work dealt with La Violencia, and his later work satirized the local elite in the Cauca region. Moreno-Durán and Jaramillo have taken more innovative, postmodern approaches to fiction set in urban spaces. Angel's work has evolved from an early concern with La Violencia to later feminist themes (see **feminism**). Fanny Buitrago has been more interested in conventional and popular forms.

The **essay** has been a historically vital genre in Colombia, and remains so today. Germán **Arciniegas** and Otto **Morales Benítez** have been the most productive essayists, writing in the tradition of the 'man of letters' rather than the specialist. Their essays cover a broad range of topics, from the cultural to the historical and political. The Colombian poet and literary critic Juan Gustavo **Cobo Borda** is the most recent intellectual to join this venerable tradition, publishing several wide-ranging volumes of essays.

Colombia has also been a leader in other arts. Three contemporary painters of the same generation have become recognized as world-class artists since the 1950s: Alejandro Obregón, Fernando **Botero**, and Enrique **Grau**. Obregón's pioneer work portrays much of the Caribbean physical world that García Márquez recreates in his fiction. Botero's irreverent and satirical work always carries the trademark of oversized human figures. His paintings satirize a variety of sectors of the Colombian oligarchy, from the politicians to the socialites and church hierarchy. Grau is just as accomplished a master technician and modernizing force in Colombian painting as Obregón and Botero. In sculpture, Rodrigo Arenas Betancur is the major figure of the century and most prominent in creating enormous public statues with allegorical content. His sculpture of Simón Bolívar in the nude riding a horse, located in the centre of the town of Pereira, is one of his most famous works.

Colombia has been a leader in Latin America in musical production. The **cumbia**, one of Latin America's most popular dance rhythms, has its origins in the Caribbean coast of Colombia. Likewise, the **vallenato** was developed as a popular Caribbean music from early in the century and was used in the 1920s and 1930s as a means of communicating regional news (and local gossip) from one rural town to the next. Since the 1940s, traditional accordion music has evolved with new technology, and has become increasingly popular in Colombia and Latin America. García Márquez's admiration for the vallenato has had considerable impact in Colombia.

Throughout its history, Colombia has been one of the most markedly regionalist nations in Latin America. In the nineteenth century, Colombia was a loose coalition of four semi-autonomous regions: the interior highland, greater Antioquia, the Caribbean coast, and greater Cauca. The interior highland has been a predominantly white and Spanish culture. Greater Antioquia has had significant Basque and Jewish immigration, and its local indigenous population has also contributed to the cultural and racial make-up of the people of the region. The Caribbean coast has been a tricultural region, with strong influences of African culture, and the presence of indigenous and Spanish culture. The greater Cauca region has had a notable presence of indigenous and Spanish cultures.

Colombia's regionalism has affected many aspects of political, economic, and social life for centuries, and has only abated slightly since the introduction of national newspapers in the 1930s, national television in the 1950s, and new mass media technologies in recent decades.

Further reading

Blutstein, H.I. *et al.* (1984) *Colombia: A Country Study*, Washington: United States Government.

Dix, R.H. (1967) *Colombia: the Political Dimensions of Change*, New York: Yale University Press.

Williams, R.L. (1991) *The Colombian Novel: 1844– 1987*, Austin: University of Texas Press.

RAYMOND LESLIE WILLIAMS

Colombino, Carlos

b. 1937, Concepción, Paraguay

Artist, architect and poet

Colombino is probably Paraguay's most notable artist both nationally and internationally. He has produced innovative creations over five decades and is associated with the Neofiguración movement of the late 1960s, the Refiguración of the mid-1970s and with the postmodern era (see **postmodernism**). Trained in architecture, Colombino briefly studied art in Madrid from 1964–5 and in Paris from 1969–70, but is essentially self-taught. In the late 1960s, as well as building a number of houses reminiscent of traditional adobe buildings, Colombino found a stable personalized artistic style that, through ferocious caricatures, depicted the deplorable abuse of human rights experienced not only in Paraguay but under other Latin American dictators. It was during this period of experimentation with new art forms and social criticism (Neofiguración) that he began using xylopintura, which he continued to use through the 1980s. He experimented with colours by employing wood-engraving tools on plywood, which he then stained so that the image would appear through the layers as the cross-grains absorbed the dyes. Colombino, like **Careaga**, also experimented with geometric and constructivist works during the 1960s. In the 1970s Colombino composed large wood engravings that superimposed contrasting colours and tones to introduce new concepts of graphic space. He was also influenced by the Refiguración movement, which revived traditional forms and methods. Into the 1980s he created important sculptures and continued the use of xylopinturas. More recently his interests have turned to neo-geometry with realist elements.

In addition to his prolific artistic production, Colombino is responsible for the directorship and promotion of many of the museums in Asunción. In 1972 he and Olga **Blinder** organized a circulating collection of forty-two (later sixty-five) Paraguayan and Latin American drawings and engravings. In 1976 the 'Permanent Collection', which includes paintings, sculpture and ceramics, was developed under his direction, so that larger, more cumbersome paintings could go on public display. Both collections constitute the Museo Paraguayo de Arte Contemporáneo with 500 works. The Museo de Arte Indígena (or Museo del Barro) is directed by Colombino, whose own collections formed an important part of its holdings together with donations or exchanges of work by Paraguayan, Latin American and other artists. Paraguayan painters represented include Blinder, Colombino, **Careaga** and **Migliorisi**.

Colombino is also the author of various collections of poems under the pseudonym of Esteban Cabañas.

Further reading

Escobar, T. (1982) *Una interpretación de las artes visuales en Paraguay*, Asunción: Centro Cultural Paraguayo de las Artes.

BETSY PARTYKA

Colón, Miriam

b. 1933, Ponce, Puerto Rico

Actress

A key figure in New York's Hispanic theatre, she trained at the University of Puerto Rico and the Actor's Studio. She co-founded the Nuevo Círculo Dramático, New York's first Spanish arena theatre (1954) and founded the Puerto Rican Traveling Theatre (1967), a non-profit theater organization vital in promoting bilingual productions among the Latin community. For her endeavours, including her work as an actress and director, she has received numerous awards from the city and state of New York and has held prominent positions in cultural and civic organizations.

VíCTOR F. TORRES

Colón, Willie

b. 1950, New York, USA

Composer, arranger and singer

Born in the Bronx to Puerto Rican immigrants, 'El malo' (Bad Boy) Colón is inextricably linked to the rise of **salsa**. At sixteen years of age, Colón joined the record company which created the salsa phenomenon, the Fania All Stars.

Colon has often said that it was the stories told by his grandmother Antonia and his childhood trips to the island that first established for him the connection between his artistic concerns and Puerto Rico. By age eleven he could play the flute and the bugle, and he assembled his first band at fourteen. It was the music of the Puerto Rican Mon Rivera and the American Barry Rogers that inspired his lifelong interest in the trombone; Colón's introduction of the trombone into salsa arrangements would later become one of the defining national characteristics of salsa.

Colon began his career playing in an American Legion hall in the Bronx. He was recommended to the Fania label by Irving Greenbaum, the sound engineer, and signed by them for $800 a disc. His 1967 album *El malo* launched a new era in the salsa genre and a new stage in his professional career. Together with the extraordinary Puerto Rican vocalist Héctor Lavoe, he developed a new aggressive and experimental sound which took the salsa form far beyond the rhythms and orchestrations that were characteristic of it until then. His work is invariably a rhythmic mix that has produced a string of hits like 'Abuelita' (Grandma), 'Ah-ah/O-No', 'Ghana-e', 'El día de mi suerte' (My Lucky Day), 'Barrunto' and 'Calle Luna, Calle Sol' (Moon Street, Sun Street), in which the Colón–Lavoe combo tell the story of the daily life of Puerto Ricans both on the island and in New York. Later, Colón joined Rubén **Blades** to produce a series of recordings regarded as fundamental to the international recognition of salsa, among them *Siembra* (Planting) (1979), which includes the famous numbers '**Pedro Navaja**' and 'Plástico' and is the best-selling salsa album in the world.

Further reading

Rondón, C.M. (1980) *El libro de la salsa*, Caracas: Ed. Arte; translated as *Salsa*, London: Latin America Bureau, 1993.

JUAN CARLOS QUINTERO HERENCIA

Colón Cemetery

Located in the Vedado district of Havana, Cuba, between Zapata and 12th streets, the Colón Cemetery (see **cemeteries**), and especially its main portal, are outstanding examples of the nineteenth-century Cuban Romantic-Byzantine genre. Nearly 22 metres high and 35 metres wide, the gate is crowned by José Villalta de Saavedra's sculptured group *Fe, Esperanza y Caridad* (Faith, Hope and Charity). Its most famous graves include the monument to the firemen who perished in the Havana fire of May 1890, the statue commemorating the medical students killed in 1871 and the old ossary, as well as several twentieth-century family mausoleums. Construction of the Cemetery began in 1871 and was completed in 1886. Its design was offered in open competition in 1870, and the winning project came from the architect Calixto de Loira; Eugenio Rayneri y Sorrentino, who took over the building of the cemetery after Loira's death in 1872, modified the design. Its overall structure reflected the contemporary custom of building around two intersecting avenues forming a cross; the resulting four 'districts' or *cuarteles* were each divided into four in their turn in the same way. The central chapel was built by Francisco Marcotegui.

JOSÉ ANTONIO EVORA

Columbian quincentenary

The 500th anniversary of the first Columbus voyage to the New World was commemorated in the Americas in 1992 in very different ways. While the celebrations organized in Spain included a world's fair in Seville, a banknote featuring portraits of the conquerors of indigenous Mexico and Peru, Hernán Cortés and Fernando Pizarro, and a blizzard of publications with the seal and economic support from the Fundación Quinto Centenario, commemorations in Latin America were decidedly more muted. There were numerous polemical essays which argued against 'celebration' of the kind that was emanating from Spain, some collected in advance in *Nuestra América frente al V Centenario* (Our America Responds to the Quincen-

tenary) (1989), with essays by Fidel **Castro**, Augusto **Roa Bastos**, Mario **Benedetti**, Miguel **León-Portilla**, Noam Chomsky and others. Leopoldo **Zea** compiled three volumes of reflections on 500 years of history in Latin America, responding to an initiative by the Mexican government for a reflection on what was neutrally called the 'Encuentro de Dos Mundos' (Encounter of Two Worlds). Carlos **Fuentes** starred in a television documentary on Latin American history, *El espejo enterrado* (The Buried Mirror), and authored a spin-off book based on that series. Guillermo **Gómez-Peña** and Coco Fusco dressed as latter-day savages, the last Indians of Guanahani, and had themselves put on display in a large cage in various art museums around the world (an event captured in a fascinating documentary film). The Catholic Church in Guatemala erected crosses all over the country to celebrate 500 years of Christianity in the New World. The Ecuadoran indigenous coalition **CONAIE** held a series of marches across Ecuador to protest 500 years of exploitation of the indigenous population. A large monument of an indigenous head, fractured by violence, was erected in a corner of the Plaza de Armas of Santiago, Chile. And the Guatemalan indigenous woman Rigoberta **Menchú** was awarded the Nobel Peace Prize.

These contradictory images serve to show that the Columbian voyages, which inaugurated an important and brutal phase of world history, are still unsettling in many ways. The Spanish banknote commemorating Pizarro and Cortés was unthinkable in the Americas. The church, the state, and diverse public **intellectuals** were prompted to respond to the anniversary and the diverse ways in which it was commemorated, and many spoke of it as an open wound. The long-term significance of the debate around the 'Encounter' and the ways to commemorate it may lie not only in significant new editions of early accounts of the Spanish conquest but in the fact that the **indigenous movements** were emboldened to press for their rights. Numerous changes in legislation, including clauses in new **Constitutions** recognizing indigenous sovereignty, land rights, and cultural rights, were direct or indirect consequences of the sustained reflection on the legacy of the Columbian voyages.

If one of the key products of the 1892 Chicago Exposition, a commemoration of 400 years since the Columbian voyages, was Frederick Jackson Turner's reflection on the significance of the frontier in US history, which was taken up by those who saw the US as invested with a 'manifest destiny', so undoubtedly the 1992 commemorations of the 'Encounter of Two Worlds' will be remembered for the battles between a cultural establishment in Spain that was striving to prove its importance in the new Europe and the voices of numerous Latin Americans who protested against that celebration, and who sought to channel their protest into a new recognition of indigenous rights.

Further reading

Greenblatt, S. (ed.) (1993) *New World Encounters*, Berkeley: University of California Press.

Small, D. and Jaffe, M. (1991) *1492: What Is It Like To Be Discovered?* New York: Monthly Review Press.

Steffan, H.D. (ed.) (1989) *Nuestra América frente al V Centenario: Emancipación e identidad de América Latina*, Mexico City: Joaquín Mortiz.

Zea, L. (ed.) (1989) *El descubrimiento de América y su sentido actual*, Mexico City: Fondo de Cultura Económica.

—— (1991) *Ideas y presagios del descubrimiento de América*, Mexico City: Fondo de Cultura Económica.

—— (1991) *Quinientos años de historia, sentido y proyección*, Mexico City: Fondo de Cultura Económica.

DANIEL BALDERSTON

Columbus Lighthouse *see* Faro a Colón

Combinado del Este

A high-security prison on the outskirts of Havana, Cuba, Combinado del Este was built by prison labour and opened in 1974. The largest prison in the country, it houses both political and common prisoners. It consists of three four-storey blocks in a U shape which contain the prisoners' rooms and isolation cells, a hospital and a section for special prisoners known as Outpost 47 or 'the rectangle of death'. The precinct also contains prisoners' housing, visiting areas and a sports field. It is estimated that the prison population reached its highest levels in the mid-1980s, when it held more than 11,000 people.

WILFREDO CANCIO ISLA

Comedia Nacional, La

The Comedia Nacional emerged from the presentation of *El León Ciego* (The Blind Lion) at Montevideo's Teatro Solís in 1947 to become one of Uruguay's most important cultural institutions. Its first president, Justino Zavala Muniz, with the support of the Municipality of Montevideo, created a high level professional company presenting a programme which included the best of world theatre. It presents ten new shows every year, eight shows every week, and enjoys enormous popularity. For fifty years it has provided a foundation for Uruguayan theatre as a whole.

MARCO MAGGI

Comedia Puertorriqueña

Comedia Puertorriqueña is a theatre company established in Puerto Rico by actress Sandra Rivera, stage director Rafael Acevedo and set designer Carlos Marichal. After staging Shaffer's *Five Finger Exercise* and Lorca's *Yerma* in 1965, they were invited to participate regularly at the annual International Theater Festival sponsored by the **Instituto de Cultura Puertorriqueña** (Institute of Puerto Rican Culture) since its inception in 1966. In addition to presenting plays by major contemporary dramatists (O'Neill, Pirandello, Williams), the Comedia was a frontrunner in promoting theatre throughout the island, staging scenes from Puerto Rican plays such as **Marqués**' *Los soles truncos* (Cut-down Suns) and Francisco **Arriví**'s *Sirena* (Siren) in the 1970s.

VÍCTOR F. TORRES

comic strips

In the predominantly illiterate societies of Latin America, visual communication has occupied a key place, from the wood engravings of the Jesuit catechisms to the leaflets of the anti-colonial struggle. Visual humour, inherited from the European cartoon, played an important role in nationalist propaganda. The comic strips produced in the USA, therefore, were rapidly translated and imitated. The first comic magazine, *Tico-Tico*, was produced in Brazil in 1905. In Argentina, *Tit-bits* began publication in the 1910s. And in Mexico, the newspapers *El Heraldo de México* and *El Universal* began to produce comic strips in 1920.

But it was in the 1930s that the comic itself was born. *Paquín* began publication in Mexico in 1934. It was followed in 1936 with the first in the series by G.O. Butze, *Los supersabios* (The Superwise), and in 1937 by **Vargas**'s *Familia Burrón*. In Argentina D. Quinterno created the comic character **Patoruzú**, who gave his name to an enormously successful magazine in 1935. In the same year, Lino Palacio created another very popular character, Don Fulgencio. And in 1937 *Pif-Paf* made its first appearance. In Brazil, the decisive moments were the publication of the magazines *Suplemento juvenil* (1934) and *Gibi* (1939).

In the 1950s comic strips grew up and began to play an important political role in denouncing and exposing the mechanisms of colonialism and cultural dependency. In this respect the creations of **Rius** in Mexico, *Los agachados* and *Los super-machos*, were decisive; significant too were the adventures of El Payo by Vigil and of El Torbellino, created by J.O. Ortiz. In Argentina the outstanding figure is **Quino**'s girl-prodigy **Mafalda** and **Fontanarrosa**'s proto-fascist backwoodsman Boogie. In Peru Acevedo made an impact with his Andean rodent Cuy, a Latin American *alter ego* to Disney's more famous mouse. In Cuba, cartoons and comic strips played a subversive part during the revolution, especially through R. Nuez's satirical figure El Loquito, and continued after 1959 through the magazines *El sable* and *Dedeté*. Under **Allende**, the government of Chile used the **Quimantú** publishing house to disseminate its ideas. In Brazil, Ziraldo's Pererê cartoons, beginning in 1959, focused on national culture. And in

the 1960s, the political humour of Jaguar and **Millor** made their mark, though it was **Henfil**'s mordant criticism through the Fradinhos that created the largest resonance.

In the 1980s and 1990s new generations developed a vigorous critical language that went beyond political satire or liberal conscience and moved in the direction of artistic experimentation, intellectual concern and a confrontation with the conventions that defined Latin American identity. In that iconoclastic current the anarchic humour of the Mexicans Giz and Trino can only be compared with the tragicomic adventures of *Los Tres Amigos* (The Three Friends), written in an extravagant Hispano-Portuguese dialect, created by the Brazilians Laerte/Laetón, Angeli/Angel-Villa and Glauco/Glauquito.

Further reading

http://www.mythoseditora.com/elink.htm
Rubinstein, A. (1998) *Bad Language, Naked Ladies, and Other Threats to the Nation: A Political History of Comic Books in Mexico*, Durham: Duke University Press.

NICOLAU SEVCENKO

comics

A lively and contested field, in addition to the constant presence of Disney and other US characters (like Snoopy, for example), comic books and strips have also had important indigenous creators. Throughout the continent, comics are aimed primarily at children, but many have had significant crossover impact into the adult market and some have been developed exclusively for adults.

Mafalda, drawn by **Quino** (Joaquín Salvador Lavado), is the most famous comic strip to come out of Latin America. First appearing in Argentina in 1963, *Mafalda* used the language of Buenos Aires to represent the Argentine bourgeoisie's daily life. It humorously engaged with topics as diverse as politics, gender roles, ecology, medicine, nuclear war, death and religion. His first comic book, *El mundo Quino*, appeared in 1963. Although Quino ceased to publish *Mafalda* in 1973, he has continued to draw single-panel and narrative strips to this day. In 1982 and again in 1992, Quino was chosen as 'Cartoonist of the Year' and awarded the KONEX Platinum Award for Visual Arts and Graphic Humour. Quino's cartoons were made into a short film series called *Quinoscopios* (1984) by **ICAIC animation** director Juan **Padrón**, after he travelled to Cuba to participate on the jury of the Festival Internacional del Nuevo Cine Latinoamericano (see **film festivals**) in Havana.

Brazil's most famous cartoonist is Maurício de **Sousa**, especially for his *Turma da Mônica* (1970) series, which is translated into nine languages and exported to seventeen countries, with international sales of 25 million books per month. In the 1980s, de Sousa opened an animation studio to compete against the increasingly popular Japanese animation. His studio produced a fifty-two episode *Mônica* cartoon series as well as nine feature-length *Mônica* cartoon films. De Sousa's animation company, Maurício de Sousa Productions, is the fourth largest animation company in the world and earns US$300 million per year in revenues generated from products licensed with the Mônica trademark. De Sousa even built two Mônica amusement parks, one in São Paulo's Eldorado shopping centre and the other in Curitiba. Plans for a Mônicaland are pending.

Rius, pen-name of the Mexican comic book artist Eduardo del Río, gained international recognition for the comic book series, *Los supermachos* (The Supermales), *Los agachados* (The Crouching Ones) and *Para principiantes* (For Beginners); the last a series that includes *Cuba para principiantes* (Cuba for Beginners) and *Marx para principiantes* (Marx for Beginners). Known for his witty political satire, Rius uses the comic book medium to force his primarily adult readers to consider the problems facing Mexican society, such as foreign domination, dependency and US imperialism.

Other important Latin American cartoons include: the counter-culture comic strip from Brazil's late 1960s, *Jeremías, o bom* (Jeremías, the Good); *Boogie, el aceitoso* and *Inodoro Pereyra* by Argentine Roberto **Fontanarrosa**; *Cuy*, a guinea pig character drawn by Peruvian Juan Acevedo; and the Chilean series *Condorito*.

Further reading

Foster, D. (1989) *From Mafalda to Los Supermachos: Latin American Graphic Humor as Popular Culture*, Boulder: L. Rienner.

Rubenstein, A. (1998) *Bad Language, Naked Ladies, and Other Threats to the Nation: A Political History of Comic Books in Mexico*, Durham: Duke University Press.

Zeledón Cambronero, M. (1995) *La historieta crítica latinoamericana*, San José, Costa Rica: INADECC, Editorial Fernández-Arce.

MARCIE D. RINKA

communist parties

In the wake of the Russian Revolution of 1917, communist parties were established throughout the world. In Latin America, the new parties were formed by ex-members of socialist and social-democratic parties in Argentina (1918), Uruguay (1920) and under the leadership of **Recabarren** in Chile (1922); elsewhere they emerged from breaks within the anarchist tradition (see **anarchism**), as in Mexico (1919) and Brazil (1922). In Peru, a new revolutionary organization was formed by **Mariátegui**, one of Latin America's most creative Marxist thinkers, while in Cuba, **Mella** was a leading actor in the formation of the communist party in 1925. These new parties were linked by their internationalism and their commitment to working class revolution – though the uneven development of Latin America, and its small working class relative to the peasantry, required some adaptation of those ideas.

The 1920s were, in some senses, the heroic days of the communist parties. Stalin's domination of Russia brought more direct control of communist parties around the world, as they increasingly became agents of Soviet foreign policy. This became clear at the first meeting of Latin American Communist Parties in Montevideo (1929), where Mariátegui's formulations were rejected and the conference used to attack

Trotskyism. The new communist leaders, like Vittorio Codovilla (1894–1970), general secretary of the Argentine party, did Stalin's bidding, first mechanically applying 'third period' sectarianism against reformist and populist parties and leaders (like **Cárdenas** in Mexico), then switching to a line of collaboration with those very parties ('the popular front') on the basis of a common anti-fascism – once again reflecting Russia's foreign policy needs. The Cuban party in fact dissolved itself early in 1940 to facilitate an alliance with the US government.

There were exceptions, like the Communist Party of El Salvador, which organized the mass insurrection of 1932 under its outstanding leader, Farabundo **Martí**. Communists also supported the failed 1935 military insurrection in Brazil led by **Prestes**.

By the 1940s, the communist parties were interwoven with the trade union bureaucracy and discredited by the compromises of the popular front period, as exemplified by the Mexican party under **Lombardo Toledano**. Only in Chile did the communist party retain any degree of influence, playing a leading part in the **Popular Unity** government of 1970–3.

The Sino-Soviet split of 1962 produced in Latin America a number of new Marxist-Leninist communist parties, the name assumed by those organizations supporting the Chinese line, the most influential of which was the Peruvian Party, **Sendero Luminoso**. By and large, Maoist groups made only a limited impact. The revolutionary banner was taken up in the 1960s (see **1960s, the**) by groups influenced by the guerrilla warfare strategies identified with the Cuban Revolution (see **guerrillas**), and deeply critical of the role of the communist parties.

Further reading

Lowy, M. (1992) *Marxism in Latin America from 1909 to the Present*, New Jersey and London: Humanities Press.

Castañeda, J. (1993) *La utopía desarmada*, Mexico City: Joaquín Mortiz.

Alexander, R. (1957) *Communism in Latin America*, New Brunswick: Rutgers University Press.

MIKE GONZALEZ

Como agua para chocolate

Laura **Esquivel**'s *Como agua para chocolate* (Like Water for Chocolate) (1989) was an international phenomenon as both novel and film, and forms part of a best-selling boom in Latin American women's writing. This woman-centred narrative focuses on three generations of land-holding female members of the de la Garza family, who reside on the Mexican side of the USA–Mexico border. A core section of this historical melodrama, largely set between 1895 and 1934, focuses on the period of the 1910 Mexican Revolution (see **revolutions**), the event that marks Mexico's entry into modernity. Unlike the traditional novel of the revolution, in *Como agua para chocolate* the revolution is of secondary importance; the focus is on how Tita breaks from the family tradition that the youngest daughter is obligated to remain unwed in order to care for her mother during her old age. The privileged site for social change in this film is within the domestic sphere. Tita's role as caretaker and carrier of tradition proves to be a vantage point in her quest to wed Pedro who, given Tita's unavailability, marries her older sister to be near his loved one. With the kitchen as centre of Tita's universe, her culinary skills give her power over family members and friends. Through food Esquivel employs magical realist techniques (see **magical realism**) to underscore the ritual function of food as a spiritual code for communication. Mexico, in this narrative, is associated with exotic and sensual food, given the narrative's structural organization around the cookbook genre; each chapter is preceded by a recipe. National gastronomic delights stand in for eminently consumable and exportable images of Mexico. The spatial focus on the kitchen underscores the maternal-feminine space *par excellence*. The revolution provides the moment for representing shifting gender power relations and generational tensions. As of 1992, Esquivel's novel had been translated into over twenty-four languages. Its US publisher, Doubleday, issued the novel in both Spanish and English editions; both sold phenomenally well. *Like Water for Chocolate* was in the top ten *New York Times* best-seller list for thirty-nine weeks, making it the only Latin American novel to have remained among the top ten best-sellers for such an uninterrupted period.

Director Alfonso **Arau**'s 1991 film adaptation is the Mexican film industry's biggest international commercial success to date. The film broke international box-office records and became one of the highest earning foreign language films in the USA, having grossed, as of 1996, $22 million in its theatrical release.

Further reading

Noriega, C. and Ricci, S. *The Mexican Cinema Project*, Los Angeles: UCLA Film and Television Archives.

Wu, H. (2000) 'Consuming tacos and enchiladas: Gender and nation in *Como agua para chocolate*', in C. Noriega (ed.) *Visible Nations*, Minneapolis: University of Minnesota Press, pp. 174–92.

SERGIO DE LA MORA

Como era gostoso o meu francês

Filmed at a time when **Cinema Novo** was privileging allegory, Nelson Pereira dos **Santos**'s *Como era gostoso o meu francês* (How Tasty was My Little Frenchman) (1971) is one of the most interesting films of its third phrase. With brilliant anthropophagic irony, its narrative represents the imaginary of a tropical indigenous society, idyllic but condemned, but inverting and parodying colonial travel literature (see **travel writing**). The film (spoken mostly in **Tupi**) is linked to the idea of anthropophagy as a metaphor for the resistance of the oppressed, rescuing the perspectives of the defeated in the colonization process.

ISMAIL XAVIER AND THE USP GROUP

compadrazgo and comadrazgo

Compadrazgo reflects the Latin American emphasis on **kinship** affiliations by giving importance to ritual or pseudo-kinship ties through the mechanism of godparenthood. *Compadre*, literally co-father, and *comadre*, co-mother, are the terms used between the godparents and parents of a child. *Compadrazgo*

relations are set up through the ritual sponsorship of the Catholic system by appointing godparents for children at baptism, and in many areas on a number of other ritual occasions, such as confirmation, first communion and marriage. Many communities also have their own individual ceremonies, such as the Peruvian *padrinos* of the first hair-cutting of a male child, revealing a strong syncretic element in the ritual.

Compadrazgo establishes permanent relationships between parents, godparents and child/godchild, in which the most important social relationship excludes the child. The godparents may have a ritual role towards the child such as participating in her/his wedding ceremony, but the strongest relationship under the obligation to help at all times is between parents and *compadres*.

In the insecurity of daily life in Latin America, *compadrazgo* imbues friendship relationships with the lasting and obligatory character of kinship, thus establishing strong personal ties on which they can lean in difficult times. Because of the prominence of large families and availability of a variety of ceremonies, *compadrazgo* offers extensive opportunities to fortify oneself with supportive personal relationships. In the early years of married life a couple may try to establish as wide a network as possible but, in later life they may ask relatives to serve as godparents, thus reaffirming the existing kinship network ties rather than extending them further. At the level of village life this pattern provides stability and cohesion, for villagers are interlinked by the criss-crossing relationships of *compadrazgo*. It also serves to elicit the support of patronage by inviting those of superior status, such as the local landowner, to become a godparent.

In urban areas, *compadrazgo* is more informal, though in some areas just as effective. There is considerable regional variation. In Mexico, Peru and Bolivia, especially in rural areas, it operates as a principle of social organization, while in Chile it has lost much of its formal and obligatory nature.

Further reading

Cubitt, T. (1995) *Latin American Society*, New York: Longman.

Foster, G. (1967) *Tzintzuntzan: Mexican Peasants in a Changing World*, Boston: Little, Brown & Co.

Nutini, H. (1976) *Ritual Kinship: the Structure and Historical Development of the Compadrazgo System in Santa María Belén and Rural Tlaxcala and its Comparative and Ideological Implication for Latin America*, Austin, TX: University of Texas Press.

TESSA CUBITT

Companhia das Letras

Companhia das Letras is an important São Paulo publishing house, founded by Luís Schwarz in the late 1980s, which has set new standards for books with a broad-based academic appeal and has continually expanded in the 1990s. Its success is largely due to an intelligent choice of best-selling and 'prestige' titles, and (an innovation in this type of publishing) an efficient and reliable system of payment to authors. Companhia das Letras has also taken initiatives such as paying authors of possible best-sellers stipends while they write, and promoting Brazilian literature abroad.

JOHN GLEDSON

Comparato, Doc

b. 1949, Rio de Janeiro, Brazil

Scriptwriter

Comparato practised medicine before moving into television to write *telenovelas* and mini-series for TV **Globo**, including the groundbreaking feminist *Malu Mulher* (1979) and ***Lampião e Maria Bonita*** (1982), awarded a gold medal at the New York Film International. He has also scripted films, most notably Bruno **Barreto**'s *O Beijo no asfalto* (Kiss on the Asphalt) (1980) and published a short-story collection, *Sangue, papéis e lágrimas* (Blood, Papers and Tears) (1979) and books and essays on dramaturgy. He also collaborated with Gabriel **García Márquez** on the mini-series *Me alquilo para soñar* (Dreamer for Hire) (1994).

ANTONIO CARLOS VAZ

Compère Général Soleil

Compère Général Soleil (Comrade General Sun) (1955) was Jacques Stephen **Alexis**'s first novel, dealing with a 1937 massacre of Haitian cane-cutters in the Dominican Republic. Alexis practises a form of social realism in the detailed depiction of the misery of the protagonist, Hilarius Hilarion, and in his biting satire of the Haitian elite. The novel's views of Haitian culture are not dissimilar from those found in Jacques **Roumain**'s *Gouverneur de la rosée* (Masters of the Dew) (1944), but Alexis's work is marked by a dense, episodic style that draws on Alejo **Carpentier**'s theory of *lo **real maravilloso*** (marvellous realism). In the story, the epileptic hero, ostracized because of his illness, becomes politicized in prison but pays with his life for his involvement in the cane-cutters' strike.

J. MICHAEL DASH

Comunidad Homosexual Argentina

Born out of anarchist gay groups, CHA (Comunidad Homosexual Argentina – Argentine Homosexual Community) is a non-profit organization created in 1984 to defend the rights of homosexuals in Argentina. Its founding president was Carlos Jáuregui. By the end of the 1990s it was active in five areas: civil rights and providing legal aid; the **AIDS** campaign 'Stop Sida'; the campaign against discrimination; Convocatoria, a self-awareness group promoting workshops on AIDS prevention, sexuality and human rights; and the Proyecto Nombres, in remembrance of those who died of AIDS. All its services are free.

RODRIGO PEIRETTI

CONAC

CONAC, the National Council for Culture, was created by the Venezuelan government of President Carlos Andrés **Pérez** in 1975, as an agency for coordinating and promoting state support for cultural projects and the arts. It has had considerable autonomy in planning its activities. It grants subsidies to artists and organizations; organizes events in Venezuela and abroad; and is responsible for a wide range of workshops, courses, exhibitions, conferences and national prizes. Numerous groups and foundations, representing virtually all the arts, are linked to it, formally or informally. It has, however, often generated controversy, facing criticism over both its organization and its effectiveness.

MARK DINNEEN

Conacine uno, dos

The Conacines were film production companies created in Mexico in 1974–5, when the State (during the **Echeverría** *sexenio*) purchased the long-standing Studio América and took over the bulk of Mexican film production. This was done to combat steady annual declines and was also part of a larger project to revive Third-Worldist discourses in the wake of **Tlatelolco**. Through the Conacines, the State took over production, funding thirty-six out of the fifty-six feature films produced in 1976, and forty-five out of the seventy-seven in 1977. However, Conacine uno was short lived: it closed down in 1977 when Margarita López Portillo, sister of the new president elected in 1976, took charge of the new Directorate of Radio, Television and Cinema (RTC), and reversed the policies of the previous administration. Conacine dos lasted only a little longer, till 1979.

ANA M. LÓPEZ

CONAIE

The process of unification of the indigenous communities of Ecuador reached a crowning moment with the founding of CONAIE (Confederación de Nacionalidades Indígenas del Ecuador, or Confederation of Indigenous Nationalities of Ecuador). Having freed itself from the domination of the Marxist parties on the one hand and the Catholic and Protestant churches on the other, the indigenous movement formulated its own political project, representing the **Quichua**, Awa, Tsáchila, Chachi, Siona, Secoya, Huaorani, Cofán, Shuar and Achuar nations, which together constitute

some 25 per cent of the total population of Ecuador. CONAIE's principal activity has been to achieve constitutional recognition of the multi-national character of the country. Its objectives also embrace the resolution of land disputes and the strengthening of indigenous education and natural medicine.

In June 1990, CONAIE organized an uprising that led to the placement of pluri- or multi-nationality on the nation's political agenda and to the recognition of the Indians as an autonomous social force. In June 1994 CONAIE organized another uprising in opposition to a law that eliminated communal land ownership and privatized the water supply. Two weeks later the government conceded, decreeing that communal lands could not be sold and water would remain in the public sector.

During the 1996 elections, CONAIE supported the Presidential candidacy of Freddy **Ehlers** and participated directly through the Pachakutik movement, which won eight seats in the Congress. Its unity was threatened, however, when the populist government of Abdalá Bucaram created an Ethnic Ministry, corrupting some indigenous leaders and using conflicts within the leaderhsip to divide the organization. After Bucaram's fall from power, the movement began to reconstitute itself. Its presence in the political arena helped to modify democratic practices as well as create a new vision of the diversity of Ecuadorean society. It was once a central actor in the events of late 1999, when a mass movement resisting the dollarization of the economy led to the collapse of the Mahud regime.

Further reading

CONAIE (1988) *Las nacionalidades indígenas en el Ecuador. Nuestro proceso organizativo*, Quito: ILDIS/ Tincui-CONAIE.

Selverston, M. (1994) 'The Politics of Culture: Indigenous Peoples and the State in Ecuador', in D.L. Van Cott (ed.), *Indigenous People and Democracy in Latin America*, New York: St Martin's Press.

Vallejo, R. (1996) *Crónica mestiza del nuevo Pachacutik*, College Park, MD: Latin American Studies Center, University of Maryland at College Park.

RAÚL VALLEJO

Concepción, David

b. 1948, Aragua, Venezuela

Baseball player

Davy Concepción enjoyed a nineteen-year career playing professional **baseball** in the USA between 1970 and 1988. He was the greatest player of his era at shortstop, the game's most important defensive position. He was honoured as a baseball All-Star nine times and five times awarded the 'Golden Glove' (conferred upon the best defensive player at each position in a given year). Concepción was the captain of the legendary Cincinnati Reds team of 1975–6, considered by many the greatest baseball team in the post-Second World War era.

DOUGLAS W. VICK

conceptual art

Conceptual art in Latin America is linked to the international avant-garde movements which stress the concept over the finished object. Since the 1960s, conceptual art has had diverse manifestations, including **happenings**, body art, mail art, installation art and **performance art**. Unlike Euro-American trends, Latin American conceptual art is more politically engaged and often traces its sources to popular and indigenous cultures. Common themes are socio-political oppression, exile, Euro-American imperialism, gender roles, ecology, national identities and technology's impact on traditional cultures. The majority of conceptual artists come from Argentina, Brazil, Chile and Mexico. Artists from the first three countries often addressed the oppressive and violent conditions lived under military regimes, while the Mexicans were inspired by the 1968 student movement. Outstanding examples are Argentine Marta **Minujín**, a pioneer in interactive environments and performance art. Her compatriot, Víctor **Grippo**, is famous for his installations using potatoes and technology to comment on ecological issues and natural energy sources. Brazilians include installation artist Cildo **Meireles**, who denounces US cultural imperialism; Hélio **Oiticica**, who began the **Tropicália** movement in 1966; Roberto Evangelista and Regina Vater, who created a group of installations on the fate of the Brazilian rainforest. From Chile are Eugenio **Dittborn**, who denounces exile and imprisonment through his 'airmail art'; Diamela **Eltit**, who works in marginal spaces such as brothels and jails; Lotty **Rosenfeld**, whose 1979 painted crosses on the pavement were aimed at awakening an impulse of civil disobedience; Alfredo Jaar, who uses installation and photography to work on exile and dictatorship, and Catalina Parra, whose installations evoke the slaughters of the 1973 *coup*. Another key South American conceptual artist and critic is Uruguayan Luis **Camnitzer**, who focuses on issues of torture.

In the wake of the 1968–71 student movement, the first generation of Mexico City-based conceptual (or 'non-objectual') artists formed a number of groups to a great extent guided by critic Juan Acha. In 1977, for example, Proceso Pentágono created a politically charged installation for the 10th Paris Biennial that reproduced a police headquarters after a torture session. These groups dissolved in the mid-1980s, but some of the artists are still productive, including Felipe Ehrenberg, Maris Bustamante and Melquiades Herrera. The new generation of conceptual artists includes Eloy Tarcisio, Sylvia Gruner, Rubén Ortiz, Ana Casas and César Martínez. Most of them avoid explicit political themes, focusing on mass media, aesthetic challenges to social norms, gender and popular culture.

Important conceptual artists from the Caribbean include Cubans José **Bedia**, with installations based on Cuba's Afro-Caribbean roots, and Ana **Mendieta**, who appropriated **Santería** and other popular religions to create images linking her body to the earth. Puerto Rican Pepón Osorio, now based in the USA, creates installations of baroque kitsch that link domestic spaces to the collective memories of diasporic Latinos.

Further reading

Edwards, R. (1996) *Painted Bodies: By Forty-Five Chilean Artists*, first English-language ed., New York: Abbeville Press.

Lindsay, A. (ed.) (1996) *Santeria Aesthetics in*

Contemporary Latin American Art, Washington, DC: Smithsonian Institution Press.

ANTONIO PRIETO-STAMBAUGH

concheros

The popular name given to the members of the diverse sects or groupings of the Movimientos de la Mexicanidad, who dance in white indigenous clothing to the accompaniment of pseudo-indigenous music in the **Zócalo** in central Mexico City. The *concheros* are usually urban youth who are seeking to rediscover indigenous roots; the groups offer Náhuatl (see **Náhuatl and Aztecan languages**) classes and instruction in aspects of pre-Columbian culture. The place where they dance, near the Templo Mayor excavation and museum, is at the centre of Aztec Tenochtitlan. Though there are aspects of their movement that suggest a neo-Aztec fascism (*à la* D.H. Lawrence's *The Plumed Serpent*), they could also be viewed as part of the panoply of **New Age** groups in Mexico and elsewhere.

DANIEL BALDERSTON

concrete poetry

Concrete poetry was an organized international avant-garde (see **avant-garde in Latin America**) movement in the 1950s and 1960s. The prime exponents of these experiments in lyric and spatial minimalism were the co-founders, Swiss-Bolivian poet Eugen Gomringer (b. 1924) and the **Noigandres group** of Brazil. The cosmopolitan movement owes much to productions and conceptualizations in Brazil, where *poesia concreta* evolved in three phases. In its initial years (1952–6), prime procedures included desentimentalization and visual shaping, including colourizing. 'Classical' or 'orthodox' material emerged in a second period (1956–61) that involved ultra-rational principles of composition and extensive theorization, including the manifesto 'pilot plan for concrete poetry' (see **manifestos**). In a third stage, from 1962 on, open notions of 'invention' led to different practices, from semantic variations to word collages and abstract designs with lexical keys. Several splinter-groups appeared: *neo-concretismo* (see **neo-concretism**) (1957), the politically-charged *poesia praxis* (1962), and the graphically-oriented *poema processo* (1967). Of the original Noigandres trio, the later work of Augusto de **Campos** is the most influenced by the movement itself, which was over by the early 1970s. Non-denominational mixtures of words and text in the 1970s and 1980s which show the influence of concrete poetry, whether by original concrete poets or the next generation, can be placed under the rubric of 'intersemiotic creation'.

Since the 1960s, the term 'concrete poetry' has been used to refer to various kinds of alphabetic, verbal and semi-verbal experiments on the printed page, many of which fall short of the profoundly poetic and conceptual 'high' concretism of Brazil, which tried to reconcile social realities, formal research and advances in communication media, incorporating and anticipating technological progress in poetry.

The contributions of Spanish America to concrete poetry were limited. Gomringer wrote a few texts in Spanish, and Solt includes one Mexican artist. As Espinoza *et al.* show, later related production in the River Plate region (for example, Clemente Padín) tends more often more towards visual poetry and other modes of experimentation.

Further reading

Espinosa, C. (ed.) (1990) *Corrosive Signs: Essays on Experimental Poetry (Visual, Concrete, Alternative)*, Washington DC: Maisonneuve Press.

Perrone, C. (1996) *Seven Faces: Brazilian Poetry since Modernism*, Durham, NC: Duke University Press.

Poetics Today (1982) 3(3), special issue (feature articles and translations of theoretical pieces).

Solt, M. (ed.) (1970) *Concrete Poetry: A World View*, Bloomington: Indiana University Press (fundamental historical essay and international anthology).

Williams, E. (1967). *An Anthology of Concrete Poetry*, New York: Something Else Press (key examples of Brazilian work).

CHARLES A. PERRONE

Condarco Morales, Ramiro

b. 1927, Oruro, Bolivia

Historian

Condarco's works are an important contribution to Bolivian historiography, particularly in relation to indigenous history and Bolivian historical geography. His work on complementary ecological levels within the indigenous system of the Andes (*La teoria de la complementareidad ecosimbiótica* (Theory of Ecosymbiotic Complementarity) (1971)) presents the same hypotheses on the vertical control of ecological levels as were suggested by John Murra in his famous work. Condarco's best-known work, first published in 1966 and in several editions since, is *Zárate el temible Vilca* (Zarate the fearsome Vilca), a study of the articulation of an indigenous rising in 1899 with the Bolivian federalist movement.

XIMENA MEDINACELI

Condé, Maryse

b. 1937, Pointe-à-Pitre, Guadeloupe

Writer

A novelist whose writing career began in 1976 with the publication of *Heremakhonon*, Condé has become one of the pre-eminent writers of the French Caribbean. Her work spans the African diaspora from West Africa to the Caribbean to the North American continent. In 1959, she married Mamadou Condé, an actor from Africa, and moved to the Ivory Coast. Her second novel, *Une saison à Rihata* (A Season at Rihata) (1981), is the story of an unhappy marriage between Marie-Hélène, far from her native home in Guadeloupe, and her African husband, Zek.

Condé's reputation was established with the publication of *Ségou* in 1984, which narrates the history of Africa on the eve of the slave trade. Her next novel, *Moi, Tituba, sorcière noire de Salem* (I, Tituba, Black Witch of Salem) (1986), creates a fictional narrative of the slave from Barbados who became the only black victim of the Salem witch trials. *Traversée de la mangrove* (Crossing the Mangrove Swamp) (1989), is a story of the mystery surrounding the death of a young outsider found face down in the mud near a small village in Guadeloupe. Whether they loved him, hated him or feared him, every villager has an opinion and each holds a piece of the puzzle of his death. *Les derniers rois mages* (The Last Magi) (1993), is a story of exile and lost origins which tells of an African king, Behanzin, exiled to Martinique for his opposition to French colonialism. As the novel follows the lives of his offspring in the Caribbean and the USA, it paints a picture of the diversity of the African diaspora. *La migration des coeurs* (The Migration of Hearts) (1995), retells the Emily Brontë novel *Wuthering Heights*, setting the tale of obsessive love in nineteenth-century Guadeloupe and Cuba.

Condé received her doctorate in Comparative Literature at the Université de Paris in 1975, her research focusing on black stereotypes in Caribbean literature. She spent many years teaching French in Guinea, Ghana and Senegal. Since 1995, she has taught French Caribbean Literature at Columbia University and divides her time between New York City and Guadeloupe. Her husband, Richard Philcox, is the English translator of the majority of her novels.

Further reading

Kadir, D. (ed.) (1993) 'Focus on Maryse Condé', special issue of *World Literature Today* 67.4.

Perret, D. and Shelton, M-D. (eds) (1995) 'Maryse Condé', special issue of *Callaloo* 18(3): 535–711.

CAROL J. WALLACE

Cóndores no entierran todos los días

Cóndores no entierran todos los días (Condors Are Not Buried Every Day) (1972), a novel by the Colombian writer Gustavo **Alvarez Gardeazábal**, exemplifies the literature of La **Violencia** (Violence), the brutal period following the assassination of Liberal leader Jorge Eliecer Gaitán on 9 April 1948. Amidst a fast-paced recollection of events, it narrates the story of León María Lozano, the head of the death squads of the Conservative party in the author's home town, Tulua, a city near Cali in western Colombia. Its 1984 film version, directed by Francisco Norden and starring Frank Ramírez, represents the first major international success of Colombian cinema, receiving awards at the Chicago, Huelva, Havana and Biarritz **film festivals**.

HÉCTOR D. FERNÁNDEZ L'HOESTE

Condori Mamani, Gregorio

b. 1908, Acopía, Peru; d. 1979, Cuzco, Peru

Cargador (a 'strapper' carries purchased goods on his back from the market to home or to a store)

Gregorio Condori Mamani, with his wife Asunta Quispe Huamán, dictated the story of their lives to their neighbours, anthropologists Ricardo Valderrama Fernández and Carmen Escalante Gutiérrez, in Cuzco in 1975. *Autobiografía* (Autobiography) was originally published in Quechua and Spanish in 1977; an English version, titled *Andean Lives*, was printed in 1996. Rich in detail, the autobiographies provide narratives of indigenous communal survival patterns (*ayllu*, *ayni*); workplace conditions in markets, the streets, and the factory; an Indian slant on politics in Peru and the nature of history (the first airplane arrives, workers on strike). Andean rituals (**Qoyllor Rit'i**, **Inti Raymi**) and customs (marriage of the sheep, burials, foodways, male/female relationships) are highlighted. An Andean reverence for the craft of storyteller permeates the pages.

REGINA HARRISON

Condorito

Condorito is a comic-strip character created by René Ríos Bottiger ('Pepo') in 1949 in the Chilean magazine *Okey*, as 'Condorito the Adventurer'. The condorito, diminutive of Chile's national bird, was first a migrant *campesino* struggling to make a living in the city. Every time he was rejected, expelled or mistreated, he reacted with a trademark expres-

sion: 'I demand an explanation!' When published in his own magazine distributed throughout Latin America, Spain and Portugal, he abandoned his underdog image and began to represent a wide array of characters, including cowboys, troglodytes, Roman soldiers and astronauts. Devoid of social criticism, his adventures now always end well.

JUAN ARMANDO EPPLE

Confiant, Raphael

b. 1951, Fort-de-France, Martinique

Novelist and essayist

The most outspoken member of the **Créolité** movement, to whose manifesto, *L'éloge de la créolité* (In Praise of Creolity) he also contributed, Confiant wrote his first novels entirely in creole (see **creole languages**). International success came, however, with a stream of novels written in a creative combination of French and creole, of which the best known are *Le Nègre et l'Amiral* (The Black Guy and the Admiral) in 1988, *L'allée des soupirs* (The Walkway of Sighs) in 1994 and *La vierge du grand retour* (The Virgin's Great Comeback) in 1996. His novels are as outrageously ribald as his essays are provocative, the most important of these latter being his critique of **Césaire**, *Aimé Césaire, une traversée paradoxale du siècle* (Aimé Césaire, a Paradoxical Journey Across the Century), in 1993.

J. MICHAEL DASH

Congress Building (Chile)

As part of a controversial plan to relocate Chile's legislative powers away from Santiago, in 1988 the **Pinochet** government announced a competition to design a new Congress Building for the port city of Valparaíso. The monumental, big-shouldered building, designed by the firm of Cárdenas, Covacevic and Farrú, stands in stark contrast to the classical architecture of the rest of the city's central district and the decaying Victorian houses which crowd the surrounding hills. The project failed to create a geographic and political counterweight to Santiago or a renewal of urban Valparaíso.

CELIA LANGDEAU CUSSEN

CONICET

The Argentine National Council for Scientific and Technical Research (CONICET) was established in 1958. It was initially charged with the general planning and coordination of **science** in the country and the promotion of scientific research and technological development. Its first elected President, Bernardo **Houssay**, held the post until his death in 1970. In practice, the organization promoted primary scientific research; SECyT, the Secretariat of the National Council of Science and Technology, was formed in 1968 to fulfil the political and coordinating functions. Under the military governments (1976–83), CONICET allocated grants and subventions and carried out direct research. The result was the creation of almost 200 new institutes.

PABLO KREIMER

Conjetural

Conjetural is a psychoanalytic journal first published in Buenos Aires in 1983, edited by Jorge Jinkis. The journal's goal was to dismantle the 'Lacanian system' by 'conjecturing' a style which, decentred from the traditional themes of Lacanian psychoanalysis would return it to the intellectual camp, including topics as different as the discursive value a language may possess within another (Joyce and Borges), the subject of law, and state terror, among others.

See also: Lacan in Latin America

BEATRIZ CASTILLO

conscientization

'Conscientization' (concientización/concientização) refers to an educational experience in which the poor 'awaken' to discover that poverty is not a natural condition but a consequence of political and economic oppression. In stimulating alternative visions of social organization, it is often argued that 'conscientization' will lead to action for social change. The word was popularized in the early 1970s by the educationalist Paulo **Freire**. It became fashionable to present 'conscientization' as a panacea for all social ills, however, and Freire himself stopped using the word, claiming its meaning had been distorted.

LIAM KANE

Consejo Nacional para la Cultura y las Artes

The Consejo Nacional para la Cultura y las Artes (CONACULTA) is a branch of the Mexican government that is charged with studying and preserving the national cultural patrimony by fomenting the work of artists and intellectuals, and by disseminating national and international culture. It coordinates the work of a large number of national offices that direct much of Mexico's cultural infrastructure and services, made up of museums and galleries, archaeological areas, historical and artistic monuments, theatres, cultural centres, auditoriums, libraries, archives, and research and education centres, as well as programmes that support intellectual and artistic creative efforts, many of which are carried out in cooperation with state and municipal governments, organizations, and with individual members of the intellectual and artistic community of Mexico. In the international arena, CONACULTA works to foment and strengthen a cultural dialogue and exchange with other nations in an attempt to increase the presence of Mexican culture abroad and of foreign cultures in Mexico.

EDUARDO GUÍZAR-ALVAREZ

Conselho Nacional de Pesquisa

The Conselho Nacional de Pesquisa (Brazilian Research Council), or CNPq, was created in 1951, during the government of Eurico Gaspar Dutra, to promote scientific and technological development and support scientific research. Under its auspices, numerous other agencies and institutes have been established, including the Institute of Pure and Applied Mathematics, the Institute of Amazonian Research, the Brazilian Institute of Information in Science and Technology and the National Institute of Space Research. The Council's responsibilities include formulating national scientific and technological policy and funding graduate and postgraduate education for Brazilian scholars both at home and abroad.

RANDAL JOHNSON

Constantine, Learie

b. 1901, Tunapuna, Trinidad; d. 1971

Cricketer and politician

Constantine made his early reputation as an outstanding international cricketer, representing the West Indies in tours of England, India and Australia (1923–39). At the outbreak of the Second World War he worked in England as a Welfare Officer in the Ministry of Labour, and then read law, becoming a barrister in 1954. Returning to Trinidad, he practiced law and became Chairman of the People's National Movement (PNM) and Minister of Works and Transport (1956–61). Constantine returned to England as High Commissioner to prepare for the Independence of Trinidad and Tobago in 1962. His dedication to the well-being of West Indians in the face of racial discrimination earned him a knighthood in 1962 and a life peerage in 1969.

JILL E. ALBADA-JELGERSMA

Constitutions

Constitutions are the legal expression of the structure of government and the relationship between the State and the society. In Latin America, there has often been a gap between the ideal embodied in the constitution and political reality. Constitutions often reflect liberal democratic values, but participation has usually been limited. Despite constitutional guarantees of checks and balances, in practice the executive branch has dominated the legislature and judiciary in most cases. Mexico's government, for example, has been unable to fully implement much of the progressive social legislation and nationalistic policy embodied in its Constitution of 1917.

The transition to democratic government in South America in the 1970s and 1980s involved important constitutional questions that had to be negotiated between the military and pro-democracy actors. Constitutional arrangements, whether they entailed the return to previous constitutions (Argentina and Uruguay), the construction of a new constitution (Ecuador, Peru and Paraguay) or remained with a version of the military-imposed constitution (Brazil until 1988 and Chile), typically assured that the military retained substantial influence in government. Chile's President Eduardo **Frei Montalva** made limiting the constitutional role for the military, a legacy of the government of General Augusto **Pinochet**, a major issue in the 1993 Presidential campaign.

While the constitutions of the new democracies grant substantial powers to the executive, including the ability to declare states of emergency and to rule by decree, many Constitutions prohibit immediate re-election or impose a one term limit. President Carlos Saúl **Menem** of Argentina, who attempted to impose economic reforms over the objection of a hostile legislature, created a constitutional crisis in 1993 when he proposed that reforms allow for his re-election. As part of the settlement, he accepted limits on the president's power of decree and increased judicial power. Brazilians chose a presidential system over a parliamentary system in a plebiscite held in 1993. In Peru, President Alberto **Fujimori** dismissed the Congress and the Judiciary in 1992, claiming both to be corrupt. A new Constitution, introduced in 1993, paved the way for Fujimori's re-election and also increased the powers of the president, introduced the death penalty and limited labour's right to organize.

Constitutional reforms also entailed the expansion of the franchise in Latin America. The Constitutions of 1978 in Ecuador and 1979 in Peru allowed illiterates to vote for the first time. Indigenous groups were guaranteed seats in the Colombian legislature in 1991. The efficacy of such expansions of popular participation will be shaped in part, however, by the long-term resolution of the powers of executives, legislatures, courts and the military.

Further reading

Alcántara, M. and Crespo, I. (1995) *Los límites de la consolidación democrática en América Latina*, Salamanca: Ediciones Universidad de Salamanca.

Domínguez, J.I. and Lowenthal, A. (1996) *Constructing Democratic Governance in Mexico, Central America and the Caribbean in the 1990s*, Baltimore: Johns Hopkins University Press.

—— (1996) *Constructing Democratic Governance in South America in the 1990s*, Baltimore: Johns Hopkins University Press.

Loveman, B. (1993) *The Constitution of Tyranny: Regimes of Exception in Spanish America*, Pittsburgh/London: University of Pittsburgh Press.

E. BROOKE HARLOWE

constructivism

Originally developed in Revolutionary Russia and then in Central Europe, the term 'constructivism' in Latin America tends to encompass a broad range of abstract and non-figurative art movements across the region. The first significant artist to use to the term was Joaquín **Torres García** in Uruguay. In the 1930s, Torres García had been involved with pioneering constructivists in Europe. In 1934 he returned to Uruguay with the ambition of creating a 'School of the South', adapting European constructivist ideas which he saw as too materialist and 'northern'. Torres García proposed a 'universal constructivism' which would be a synthesis of primitive and modern art. Across the River Plate in Argentina, a group of young artists and writers were developing their own ideas about constructivism, often using information provided by Torres García, which they used to attack his proposed new art in favour of a more radical and hard-edge abstraction. These artists founded **Arte Madí** and the Asociación Arte Concreto-Invención, which both professed an attachment to materialism, Marxism and the social functions of

constructivism against the 'idealism' of Torres García, although some artists such as Carmelo **Arden Quin** and Alfredo **Hlito** were personal admirers of Torres García. In the 1950s there was a revolt against Torres García's legacy in Uruguay itself, with the Arte No-Figurativo group which rejected Torres-García's mix of figurative and abstract art in favor of pure abstraction.

In the early 1950s Brazilian artists began to admire constructivism, especially after an exhibition of the Swiss artist Max Bill in São Paulo in 1950. The launch of the **Bienale de São Paulo** in 1951 also encouraged abstract artists. Two groups inspired by this Swiss 'concrete' art were formed in 1952, one in São Paulo called 'Ruptura' and the other in Rio de Janeiro, called 'Frente'. Both these groups followed Max Bill's pure mathematical art, but the Rio group gradually became more interested in the Utopian and transformative possibilities of constructivism, and moved towards a new expression: **neo-concretism** (exemplified in the work of Brazilian painters Lygia **Clark** and Hélio **Oiticica**). During the later 1950s in Venezuela, Carlos **Cruz-Diez**, Jesús **Soto** and Alejandro **Otero** developed the languages of constructivism into **kinetic art**. In the 1970s and 1980s, artists such as Edgar **Negret** and César Paternosto postulated a certain link between modern constructivist languages and the monuments of Amerindian cultures. Constructivism in Latin America has flourished in those regions most open to European influence, particularly the Southern Cone and the Atlantic coast.

Further reading

Amaral, A. (1993) 'Abstract Constructivist Trends in Argentina, Brazil, Venezuela and Colombia', in *Latin American Artists of the 20th Century*, New York: Museum of Modern Art.

GABRIEL PEREZ-BARREIRO

Contemporáneos

The Contemporáneos were a group of young writers who in the 1920s rallied round the literary journal *Contemporáneos*, published in Mexico City from 1928 to 1931. They played an important role in the intense discussions that followed the 1910 revolution, arguing for a cosmopolitan Mexican literature aware of its own roots but in touch with innovative international developments. Jaime **Torres Bodet**, Bernardo Ortiz de Montellano, José **Gorostiza**, Carlos **Pellicer** and Enrique González Rojo were the nucleus of the group; later members were Salvador **Novo**, Xavier **Villaurrutia**, Jorge Cuesta and Gilberto **Owen**. The group is considered one of the most distinguished in twentieth-century Mexican letters.

MERLIN H. FORSTER

Conti, Haroldo

b. 1925, Chacabuco, Argentina; d. 1976, place unknown

Writer

Conti's early work was largely descriptive; journeys and wanderings set in motion long, melancholy meditations on reality in his novels *Sudeste* (Southeast) (1962) and *En vida* (In My Lifetime) (1971). His later work brought changes in literary style which corresponded to the writer's growing political involvement; they increasingly embraced the exhilaration and richness of **magical realism**, as in his 1975 novel *Mascaró, el cazador americano* (Mascaró the Latin American Hunter), for example. One year after its publication, he joined the list of Argentine writers '**disappeared**' during the **Videla** dictatorship.

JULIO PREMAT

Contorno

A combative journal associated with a group of angry young men that Emir **Rodríguez Monegal** called the *generación de los parricidas* (the generation of parricides), who were drawn to the Sartrean idea of *littérature engagée*. The names associated with the journal were David **Viñas** and his brother Ismael, Tulio **Halperin Donghi**, Adolfo Prieto, Noé **Jitrik**, Ramón Alcalde, Leon **Rozitchner**, Rodolfo **Kusch** and Juan José

Sebreli, though eventually the Viñas brothers were the most directly involved. At the time of the founding of the journal, they felt alienated in a society dominated by **Peronism**, and after the fall of Perón in 1955, Halperin Donghi published an article in the journal that traced continuities from fascism to Peronism; later, several of those who had been associated with *Contorno*, particularly the Viñas brothers, were drawn into the Peronist left. The ten issues of the journal (which have been studied in a useful book by William Katra, *Contorno: Literary Engagement in Post-Peronist Argentina*, 1988) appeared at irregular intervals; *Contorno* also published a few books and pamphlets. The idea of the responsibilities of the intellectual to society evolved over time from 'engaged' literary criticism to political analysis and theory, and then to political action. In the final issues, Rozitchner and Ismael Viñas called on the middle-class intellectual (see **intellectuals**) to take a vanguard position in the coming proletarian revolution.

DANIEL BALDERSTON

Contrapunteo cubano del tabaco y el azúcar

A lengthy historical, sociological, ethnographic and anthropological essay by Fernando **Ortiz**, published in 1940, *Contrapunteo cubano del tabaco y el azúcar* (Cuban Counterpoint of Tobacco and Sugar) establishes an interesting parallel between the two planks of the national economy. It explores the way in which the two crops are reflected in the history of the Cuban people, their ethnicity and even their political experiences. Ortiz introduced in this work the concept of transculturation, designating the interactive phenomenon that results when two cultures come into contact and begin to influence one another, even where one culture dominates the other.

See also: critical theory

WILFREDO CANCIO ISLA

contras

In the United States, the fear of a Communist Nicaragua after the fall of the **Somoza dynasty** in 1979 generated a multifaceted programme to overthrow the Sandinistas (see **Sandinista Revolution**). Under President Ronald Reagan, the US government launched a 'destabilization program' to destroy Nicaragua's fragile economy by ending US financial aid and multilateral bank loans. Between 1981 and 1988 more than $20 million was spent to mobilize and train three contra (counter-revolutionary) groups. One operated along the Honduran–Nicaraguan border, another along the Costa Rican–Nicaraguan border, and the third along Nicaragua's Atlantic Coast. They were later unified into the Nicaraguan Democratic Force (FDN). The price of US intervention was appalling. Between 1980 and 1989, the official death toll was 30,865, damage to property amounted to $221.6 million, and losses due to the trade embargo were calculated at $254 million.

The Reagan administration's campaign to build the contras was accompanied by a parallel political campaign to force the Sandinistas to negotiate with their domestic opposition and regional neighbours. In 1984 the Sandinistas signed the Contadora Act, which called for the withdrawal of foreign military advisers, reduction in US military aid and other measures. However, the United States and some Central American countries withdrew from the Contadora Group on the grounds that the Sandinistas could not be trusted.

Further meetings at Esquipulas, Guatemala, produced a new draft, called the **Arias** Plan. Meanwhile, the contra war continued. The elections of 1990 provided the USA with a further opportunity for clandestine intervention. It spent millions of dollars to weld a united opposition (**UNO**) out of fourteen disparate microparties, and to promote the electoral success of its candidates. It endorsed UNO's conservative presidential candidate, Violeta Barrios de **Chamorro**, and indicated that the economic blockade and US support for the contras would end if she won. In the event, UNO won 55 per cent of the presidential votes, and Chamorro was elected president. In the aftermath of the elections, the contras were encouraged to

return and promised help if they did so. When the anticipated economic aid did not materialize, many returned to armed banditry, calling themselves the *recontra*.

Further readings

Dickey, C. (1985) *With the Contras: A Reporter in the Wilds of Nicaragua*, New York: Simon & Schuster.

Pardo-Maurer, R. (1990) *The Contras, 1980–1989: A Special Kind of Politics*, New York: Praeger.

Walker, T. (1991) *Revolution and Counterrevolution in Nicaragua*, Boulder, CO: Westview.

ANUPAMA MANDE AND ILEANA RODRÍGUEZ

Contreras, Gonzalo

b. 1958, Santiago, Chile

Writer

Contreras's first novel *La ciudad anterior* (The City Before) (1991) was one of the best-selling novels published in Chile after the country's return to democracy. The novel, about a small-time arms dealer who travels to a mysterious town in the northern desert, alludes to Chile's politically repressive and violent recent past. It won *El Mercurio*'s literary competition in 1991. His *El Nadador* (The Swimmer) (1995) is set in Santiago and deals with the upheavals experienced by a family living in a rapidly changing and modernizing country. Contreras's third novel, *El Gran Mal* (The Great Evil), was published in 1998.

AMALIA PEREIRA

Contreras, Salvador

b. 1912, Cuerámaro, Guanajuato, Mexico; d. 1982, Mexico City

Musician

An outstanding violinist and composer, Contreras studied with Silvestre **Revueltas** and Candelario **Huízar** before joining Carlos **Chávez**'s Orquesta Sinfónica de México in 1931. In succeeding years, he was professor of violin at the Centros

Populares para Obreros (1933) and organizer of musical and choral groups at the Centros Nocturnos para Trabajadores (Workers' Evening Institutes) (1935), as well as professor of Orchestral Direction at the Conservatorio Nacional (1935). Founder and Director of the Orquesta de la Opera, he retired in 1964 to devote himself to composition. His seventy four compositions include **Corridos Para Coro Y Orquesta** (Ballads for Chorus and Orchestra) (1941), **Cantata a Juárez** (1967) and his **Sinfonía No. 3** (1963) for strings.

EDUARDO GUÍZAR-ALVAREZ

Contreras Torres, Miguel

b. 1899, Morelia, Michoacán, Mexico;
   d. 1981, Mexico City

Film-maker

Contreras's early silent films included *El hombre sin patria* (Man Without a Country) (1921), the first to address the issue of migration. In 1929 he made two of the first Mexican sound films, *El águila y el nopal* (The Eagle and the Cactus) and *Soñadores de gloria* (Dreamers of Glory). His subsequent historical films were conservative, but critical recognition came with his version of J. Rubén Romero's *La vida inútil de Pito Pérez* (Pito Pérez's Futile Life) (1943). Thereafter he worked closely with comic actor Manuel Medel.

PATRICIA TORRES SAN MARTÍN

Convite *see* Grupo Convite

Cony, Carlos Heitor

b. 1926, Rio de Janeiro, Brazil

Writer

A leading figure in the left-wing opposition to military rule in Brazil, Cony distinguished himself as a prolific novelist and essayist. He has written several regular columns in major national newspapers, including *Correio da Manhã* and *Folha de*

São Paulo. His most acclaimed novel, *Pessach: a travessia* (Passover: The Crossing), from 1967, narrates the story of a novelist who joins the urban guerrilla movement on his fortieth birthday, a radical life change which parallels the gradual acceptance of his Jewish heritage.

CHRISTOPHER DUNN

Copacabana

In its hundred-year history, Copacabana has evolved from a peripheral beach resort to becoming the synthetic image of Rio de Janeiro. Between sea and mountains, it shelters a population that includes every class, creed, political position, race, gender and age among those who live, work and enjoy themselves there. To the original bungalows were added historicist and art deco buildings, the first modernist buildings in the city, speculative apartment blocks and some examples of postmodern dilution. The result is a tropical Babel. Natural beauty, urbanity and bohemia give this 'princess of the sea' a unique place in the national and international imaginary.

ROBERTO CONDURU

Copan

The Copan is a building designed in 1952 by Oscar **Niemeyer** in São Paulo, Brazil, and representative of his style. As opposed to the principles of orthodox functionalism, Copan is designed around free forms and curved surfaces that differ greatly from simple rectangular walls. It is characterized by the exposed piles on the first floors, interspersed common areas and the S-shaped main facade. Thirty-eight floors high, it comprises garages, a shopping gallery, interspersed office space and 1,160 living units. Its reinforced concrete structure is 150 metres long and 115 metres high. It was completed in 1971.

ANA CECILIA OLMOS

Copes, Juan Carlos

b.1931, Buenos Aires, Argentina

Dancer and choreographer

Copes synthesised the figures and moves of traditional **tango** with ballet. Born in a Buenos Aires district where the tango was popular, it is said that at 16 he already knew that tango dancing would be his future. There he learned the code of the **milonga**, which included the recognition of tango's boundaries; dancing with improvised steps, for example, was forbidden on the grounds that tango could not become part of popular culture because of its origins. For Copes the essence of tango was dance, so he became a professional dancer; it was sensual rather than erotic. Two people come together, enjoy dancing and share only the obligation to create new dance movements. Copes insisted that a tango could either 'tell a story in three minutes' or be transformed into 'a two hour musical comedy'. Thus he created 'tango shows' like *Malena*, *Percal* and *El día que me quieras*, referring to the precedents set by **Canaro**, who included saxophone, timbales, black light, and tango dancing couples in his orchestra. Until then, tango dancers had been restricted to burlesque theatres; Copes' most original contribution was to have challenged the orthodoxy that tango could only be danced by individual couples by creating collective choreographies embracing many couples. He was inspired by tango figures, from **Troilo** to **Piazzola**, and by his dance idols Gene Kelly and Fred Astaire, but without compromising his own style. He understood that the subordination of singers and orchestras to dancers was changing since the 1950s *café concert* brought in paying customers who did not dance and listened to the singer, violinist or **bandoneón** player. The dance was increasingly restricted to clubs where live orchestras were replaced by recordings. To incorporate the work of innovative musicians like Piazzola, and to restore dance to its central place, Copes formed dance companies like the *Conjunto Coreográfico de Tango* in the 1950s. His efforts culminated in the *Tango Ballet* which toured the United States in 1959 under Piazzola's musical direction, appearing on the Ed Sullivan Show. He also starred in the touring show *Tango argentino* in the 1980s, in which he danced with his ex-wife, María Nieves.

Further reading

Ferrer, H. (1977) *El libro del tango*, Buenos Aires.

Salas, H. (1996) *El tango una guía definitiva*, Buenos Aires.

Vilariño, I. (1995) *El Tango*, Montevideo: Ed Cal y Canto.

LUIS GUSMAN

Copi

b. 1937, Buenos Aires, Argentina; d. 1987, Paris, France

Writer and actor

Copi (Raúl Damonte) was a member of an important Uruguayan–Argentine family (his grandfather was Natalio **Botana**, founder of the journal *Crítica*). His father was a diplomat, whose itinerant lifestyle meant that Copi spent most of his childhood in Europe. When Copi was twenty-two his father sought political asylum in the Uruguayan embassy in Paris, and Copi himself remained in France as well. Most of his writing, including theatre, short stories and several comics, the best known of which is *La mujer sentada* (Seated Woman), is in French. Copi's work, which used stereotypes of Argentine and gay culture (see **gay and lesbian cultures**), initiated a kind of Argentine minimalism as well as a new form of non-representational realism.

GRACIELA MONTALDO

Coppola, Horacio

b. 1906, Buenos Aires, Argentina

Artist, photographer and film-maker

Coppola's largely abstract images (often homages to painters) are quite different from his black and white portraits of artists, musicians and sculptures. After founding the first Cine Club in Buenos Aires (1929) and illustrating Jorge Luis **Borges**'s *Evaristo*

Carriego (1930), Coppola went to Europe and studied photography in Walter Peterhans's Bauhaus studio and made his first 16mm film *Traum* (Dream) (1932). He accompanied his future wife, Grete **Stern**, to England and then back to Argentina, where they held their first joint photographic exhibition at *Sur*, the legendary magazine edited by Victoria **Ocampo**. His most recent touring retrospective was commissioned in 1996 by the national archives of Valencia, Spain.

AMANDA HOPKINSON

coraje del pueblo, El

Produced by the **Grupo Ukamau** (with Jorge **Sanjinés**) collective in Bolivia in 1971, *El coraje del pueblo* (The Courage of the People) is a brilliant demonstration of an approach to film-making that privileges the voices and experiences of the Andean indigenous population and is a key film of the **New Latin American Cinema**. The film tells the story of a massacre of miners that took place at the Siglo XX mines in 1967. Featuring as its protagonists some of the survivors of the massacre, including activist-leader Domitila **Barrios de Chungara**, the film functions both as a historical reconstruction of a crucial event in the history of the Bolivian class struggle and as a **documentary** of one community's collective remembering and recreation of that event.

The film was co-financed by the Italian television company RAI (in a deal put together by Walter **Achugar**); Ukamau finished shooting only days before a military *coup d'état*, which forced most of them into exile and post-production work in Europe. It was banned in Bolivia until 1979, although the group did self-exhibit it among indigenous communities in the Andean region. When shown in La Paz for the first time in 1979, it triggered intense debates that led to it being banned by direct orders of the Bolivian army.

ANA M. LÓPEZ

Corales

Corales are awards distributed at the annual **Festival Internacional del Nuevo Cine Latinoamericano**, held in Havana since 1979. Fashioned by local artisans from sprigs of natural black coral, a species unique to reefs in Cuba's warm waters, and mounted on marble, each award is unique and a beautiful artefact. The Corales are awarded by international juries in various categories, ranging from typical film festival (see **film festivals**) categories like best fiction film, best documentary film and best director, to *sui generis* categories like 'Best documentary film about Latin America by a non-Latin American director' and 'Best film poster' (both since 1981).

ANA M. LÓPEZ

Cordero, Roque

b. 1917, Panama City

Musician

A former director of the National Institute of Music, Cordero is Panama's most celebrated classical composer, conductor and teacher. He began his musical studies in Panama and then went to the United States, studying with Mitropoulos and Krenek in Minneapolis and with Chapple at Tanglewood. Although his mostly instrumental compositions have had a very limited reception in Panama, they have been performed throughout the Western hemisphere and Europe. The Symphony No. 2 (1956), structured as a compound sonata–allegro form, won the 1957 Interamerican Music Festival prize. Continental acclaim followed. Several of his works have been recorded by US symphony orchestras.

NORMAN S. HOLLAND

Cordobazo

The Cordobazo was a popular rebellion which began on 29 May 1969 out of a car workers strike in the Argentine city of Córdoba, in response to the political methods, economic policies and repressive measures of the military dictatorship of Juan Carlos Onganía. After five days of street battles between the police and the people, the army took control of the city. The mass mobilization sparked further risings and demonstrations in the other Argentine towns and cities. Its result was the fall of Onganía in June 1970, the take-over of the presidency by General Alejandro Lanusse and the eventual decision to hold elections in 1973.

JORGE ELBAUM

Córdova, Arnaldo

b. 1937, Mexico City

Scholar and politician

Córdova's work has centred on research into the historical construction of the networks and apparatuses of power in Mexico. In his *La ideología de la Revolución Mexicana* (The Ideology of the Mexican Revolution) (1973), he demonstrated how a powerful, new state emerged from the Mexican Revolution of 1910 (see **revolutions**) and was consolidated in the 1940s. Córdova studied law, history and political science. He has been involved in a number of important left-wing political organizations and has been a member of the country's Congress.

EDITH NEGRÍN

corn and corncakes

Corn or maize (*zea mays*) is native to Mexico – and there is evidence of its cultivation some seven centuries BC. Even in pre-Hispanic times it was an important source of nutrition for millions of people from southern Canada to Colombia and Peru. Its central significance in the lives of the pre-Hispanic community is signalled in the Aztec belief that the fifth age was the age of the men of maize – the *hombres de maíz* of Miguel Angel **Asturias**'s great novel, *Hombres de maíz* (The Men of Maize) (1949). In Mexico it represents half the food eaten

annually – some 12 million tonnes are produced or imported each year.

There are thirty-five varieties of maize grown between sea level and 2,500 metres. The whole plant is used: the stalks produce honey and once dried can be used for the construction of rural housing or as animal fodder. The leaves serve to wrap tamales and even the flower is edible. The grains of the plant produce oil, apart from the six-hundred or more dishes that can be made with it – sweet and salted *tamales*, gruels, soups and other cooked dishes – or they can be transformed into popcorn. Even the gluten and the germ have industrial and medicinal uses. The dried grains are boiled with calcium, the skin removed and then crushed; this dough or *nixtamal* can be made into *tortillas*, the daily bread of all Mexicans.

The machines for making *tortillas* are largely of Mexican invention and are capable of producing 10,000 *tortillas* per hour, which may be bought warm at the *tortillerías* or cold in plastic bags at the supermarket. In Mexico, it is the soft, white, well-cooked *tortillas* that are most popular, eaten direct from the flat metal or ceramic griddle where they are toasted. They are made by taking a ball of dough and then patting it flat with the hands to about 16 centimetres diameter (though there are larger ones). If it is to last longer, it may be toasted hard, when it is called *totopo*. However, it is mainly eaten soft in a variety of guises; rolled, filled with meat, chicken or vegetables, garnished with hot sauces and metamorphosed into a *taco*, *flauta*, *enchilada* or myriad other incarnations.

Further reading

Casatelló T. (1996) *Prenencia de la cocina prehispánica*, Mexico: Fundación Cultural Banamex.
'El maíz' (1997) special issue of *Arqueología Mexicana*, Mexico, May–June.
Kennedy, D. (1991) *The Tortilla Book*, New York: Harper Perennial.
Quintana, P. (1986) *The Taste of Mexico*, New York: Stewart, Tabori & Chang.

CRISTINA BARROS AND MARCO BUENROSTRO

Cornejo Polar, Antonio

b. 1936, Lima, Peru; d. 1997, Lima

Literary critic

A dominant figure in Andean studies, professor and rector of the Universidad Mayor de San Marcos, founder (1975) and editor of ***Revista de crítica literaria latinoamericana***, Cornejo Polar also wrote one of the earliest (1973) and best studies of José María **Arguedas**. While his sustained emphasis was on Peruvian authors, notably on *indigenista* writers, through several collections of essays he also built a systematic cultural approach to literary studies by focusing on 'heterogeneity' as a defining term for Latin American literatures. Literature as a social act, and literary systems as historical categories, link him to critics such as Angel **Rama**, Antonio **Candido** and Agustín **Cueva**. After leaving Peru, he taught at the University of Pittsburgh and at the University of California-Berkeley.

SAÚL SOSNOWSKI

Coronel Urtecho, José

b. 1906, Granada, Nicaragua; d. 1994, San Juan, Nicaragua

Writer

Known as the founding father of Nicaraguan poetry, in the early 1920s, together with Luis Alberto Cabrales, Coronel founded the Vanguardista movement which also included Pablo Antonio **Cuadra** and Joaquín **Pasos**. He had a profound influence on several generations of poets, from the first avant-garde (see **avant-garde in Latin America**) writers to Gioconda **Belli** and Daisy **Zamora**. His works include translations, poems and short stories that use avant-garde and surrealist (see **surrealism in Latin American art**) techniques to explore the effects of urban living, though he spent much of his life living in relative isolation near the Costa Rican border. His political positions, before and after 1979, were always ambiguous.

DEREK PETREY AND ILEANA RODRÍGUEZ

coronelismo

The term *coronelismo* refers to the almost dictatorial power exercised by large landowners and rich merchants in the small communities of the Brazilian northeast (***sertão***). In the nineteenth century, such individuals were given the honorary title of colonel (*coronel*), commanding local regiments of the auxiliary force, the National Guard. The force disappeared but the name became fixed in the northeastern mentality as a way of describing local political bosses. The influence of the *coronel*, once used to win elections, is now exerted more indirectly through allies in the liberal professions. A favourite theme of regionalist writers in the 1930s, *coronelismo* was later immortalized in the television soap opera (see ***telenovelas***) *O Bem-Amado* (Well Loved) (1971).

VIVALDO SANTOS

Corradi, Pedro

b. 1942, Montevideo, Uruguay

Actor

A graduate in acting and scenography from the Uruguayan School of Dramatic Art (in 1971), Corradi continued his training at the Actors Studio, La MaMa and the Studio Theatre in New York and the Teatro Campesino in California. He studied in Paris with Jean Louis Barrault, Peter Brook and Gisela May. He was secretary of the Uruguayan Society of Actors and at time of writing is vice-president of the International Actors' Federation.

MARCO MAGGI

Corrales, Antonio

b. 1942, Bogotá, Colombia

Actor and director

Beginning his performing career in 1959, Corrales worked with several important Colombian theatre groups, including the Teatro Popular de Bogotá. He co-founded **Teatro La Barranda** in 1985, which he directed until his death. Among other works he directed Juan **Rulfo**'s *Anacleto Morones* (1974) and Robert Lamoreux's *The Soup Dish* (1977), and won several awards, including Best Actor at Cartagena's 1967 National Theatre Festival.

ALEJANDRA JARAMILLO

Corrales, Raúl

b. 1925, Ciego de Avila, Cuba

Photographer

Poetic and humanistic images distinguish the work of Corrales (born Raúl Corral Valera), one of which – 'El sueño' (The Dream) – is often cited as one of the hundred best photographs in the history of the craft. His career began in 1944, when he photographed Cuban peasants for the Cuban Sono Films Agency; he went on to work for the magazines *Hoy* and *Carteles*. From 1959 to 1964, he devoted himself to photo-reportage of the Cuban Revolution, documenting transcendental moments like the **literacy** campaign, the Bay of Pigs invasion and the Missile Crisis of October 1962. He later occupied important posts in the Academy of Sciences and the State Council. His work has been widely exhibited, and in 1996 he won the Cuban National Prize for the Visual Arts, the first time it had ever been awarded to a photographer.

WILFREDO CANCIO ISLA

Correa, Djalma

b. 1942, Ouro Preto, Minas Gerais, Brazil

Composer and percussionist

Djalma Novaes Correa helped to redefine the role of percussion in Brazilian music from rhythmic accompaniment to a highly sophisticated solo form. In the early 1960s he studied percussion and composition in the Seminários de Música at the Federal University of Bahia. During this time, he secured a workshop space where he began experiments with electronic music and Afro-

Brazilian percussion. In the 1970s Correa led the percussion group Baiafro, which recorded with several **jazz** fusion artists. In 1988 he recorded the highly acclaimed album *Quarteto Negro*, with vocalist Zezé **Motta** and clarinetist Paulo **Moura**.

CHRISTOPHER DUNN

Correia, Carlos Alberto Prates

b. 1941, Montes Claros, Brazil

Film-maker

Correia's central concern is the conflict between the culture of his home state of Minas Gerais and the conservative modernizing process in Brazil in the 1970s and 1980s. He worked with **Cinema Novo** directors, assisting Joaquim Pedro de **Andrade** on *Macunaíma* (1969) and *Guerra conjugal* (War of the Sexes) (1974) before going on to make his own mythic, ironic films replete with the culture of Minas. His other feature length films include *Perdida* (Lost) (1975), *Noites de sertão* (Nights in the Backlands) (1984), based on a novel by Guimarães **Rosa**, and *Minas-Texas* (1989).

ISMAIL XAVIER AND THE USP GROUP

Correia, José Celso Martinez *see* Zé Celso

Correio da Manhã

Correio da Manhã was a daily newspaper founded in 1901 in Rio de Janeiro by Edmundo Bitencourt. From the outset it took an oppositional stance. During the **Vargas** regime, under the editorship of Costa Rego, it defied the censors and published an interview with José Américo de Almeida by Carlos Lacerda. Years later it supported Juscelino **Kubitschek** (elected in 1955) against a military *coup* led by the same Lacerda. After Bitencourt's death the newspaper passed to his son Paulo, who invited many of Brazil's most important **intellectuals** to contribute to it. He died in 1963. In 1969 the paper was sold to a real estate group; it ceased publication in June 1974.

ANTONIO CARLOS VAZ

Corretjer, Juan Antonio

b. 1908, Ciales, Puerto Rico; d. 1985, San Juan, Puerto Rico

Writer

A member of the Nationalist Party and a friend of Pedro **Albizu Campos**, he was also imprisoned in the USA and accused of being involved in political violence in Puerto Rico. He founded the Socialist League to secure independence for Puerto Rico by any means. His poetry addresses Puerto Rico's Amerindian and African roots, the history of the peasants and workers, the struggle for independence, his love for his companion Consuelo Lee, his people and his nation. His poem 'Oubao Moin' was put to music and has become an unofficial national anthem.

MARÍA CRISTINA RODRÍGUEZ

corrido

Usually of anonymous authorship, a corrido is a popular song of northern Mexico that narrates a memorable event, often based on romantic, fatalistic or humorous topics. Said to be derived from the *romance*, the traditional ballad, of Castile in Spain, it was transferred to Mexico where it became a vehicle for conveying information and news. In the nineteenth century, they were printed and sold – much like the broadside ballads of Britain – often with accompanying illustrations. It was with the Mexican Revolution (1910–17) (see **revolutions**) that the corrido was in some sense formalized and became the standard means of creating mythic figures and exploits, and transferring news and accounts of the revolution across the national territory. Words came to prevail over musical form, as the corrido created a new gallery of heroes in Pancho **Villa**, Emiliano **Zapata** and Francisco Madero to add to the criminals, bandits and jilted lovers of the nineteenth-century tradi-

tion. The corrido's role in popular culture continued long after the revolution, providing a mnemonic vehicle for the relation of political events, ranging from the Cristero War to the 1968 student movement in Mexico. It would frequently provide the narrative structure for films of Mexican cinema's 'Golden Age'. Among the Spanish-speaking population of the United States, the corrido is a vital and popular form, often accompanied by the music known as Tex-Mex. The corrido of Gregorio Cortez, for example, provided the basis of an important film by Robert Young, *The Ballad of Gregorio Cortez* (1983).

The corrido is also found in Venezuela, Nicaragua and in other Latin American countries.

Further reading

Avitia Hernández, A. (1998) *Corrido histórico mexicano: Voy a cantarles la historia*, Mexico City: Porrua.

Castañeda, D. (1943) *El corrido mexicano, su técnica literaria y musical*, Mexico: Editorial Surco.

Contreras Islas, I. (1989) *Dos realidades en el corrido mexicano*, Mexico: Universidad Nacional Autónoma de México.

Mendoza, V.T. (1997) *El romance español y el corrido mexicano: Estudio comparativo*, second edn, Mexico: Universidad Nacional Autónoma de México.

—— (1974) *El corrido mexicano. Antología*, second edn, Mexico: Fondo de Cultura Económica.

Serrano Martínez, C. (1963) *El corrido mexicano no deriva del romance español*, Mexico: Centro Cultural Guerrerense.

EDUARDO GUÍZAR-ALVAREZ

Corrieri, Sergio

b. 1938, Havana, Cuba

Writer

A founder member of the **Teatro Estudio** in 1958, Corrieri taught at the National School of Art before founding **Teatro Escambray** in 1968, which he directed for twenty years. His most important roles were in the films *Memorias del subdesarrollo* (Memories of Underdevelopment)

(1968) and *El hombre de Maisinicú* (The Man from Maisinicú) (1973) and in the television series *En silencio ha tenido que ser* (It Had To Be in Silence) (1980). He was vice-president of Cuba's Radio Corporation (**ICRT**) and is currently President of the Instituto Cubano de Amistad con los Pueblos (Cuban Institute of International Friendship). More recently, political responsibilities have taken him away from his artistic career.

WILFREDO CANCIO ISLA

corruption

The self-enrichment of powerful politicians and the petty corruption of lower-level officials is an often caricatured feature of Latin American societies. But it is not because there is venality somehow built into the Latin American character; the history of the region is full of endless examples of self-denial, sacrifice and solidarity among the majority of people. But corruption is an inevitable consequence of the combination of two factors – scarcity of goods and resources, and the absence of democracy. For much of the present century, Latin America has been dominated by foreign capital, which ensured that power within each state lay with 'amenable' politicians – whose co-operation was well rewarded. The arbitrary exercise of power would then be reflected at every level of a State machine, which functioned as a means of distributing patronage in exchange for loyalty – and which rested on the threat and regular use of violence.

In some cases, like Mexico's **PRI**, that system of patronage was the State – and reached into the furthest corners of civil society, embracing trade union leaders and political figures alike. By contrast, while democratic systems are never exempt from power-broking or influence-peddling, they do at least make the authoritarian distribution of power more visible and less easy. In the period of economic growth in the 1960s and 1970s, corruption was a less central feature of everyday life – at least in those societies where growth was accompanied by some level of democratization. The imposition of military governments during the period, however, invariably brought with it nepotism and the arbitrary use of power and their attendant corruption. By the 1980s, the reintegration of the Latin American economies into the global market – coupled with the vagaries of a high-inflation period – created conditions where corruption was once again rife; surrogates were placed at the heart of states and the direct control of local economies by multinational capital enabled them to profit from that relationship. The most notorious cases occurred in Mexico, where the manipulation of the market by President Carlos **Salinas de Gortari** and his cohorts netted uncounted millions. The growth of a clandestine but immense trade in drugs, particularly cocaine (see **drugs in Latin America**), provided new opportunities for corruption, as revelations of the virtual control of every branch of the Colombian government by the drug cartels so clearly revealed. There were unexpected examples too; in Nicaragua, the end of the Sandinista (see **Sandinista Revolution**) regime led to a pillaging of the public sector by outgoing functionaries known as *la piñata* that, however elaborate the justifications, rated as corruption of the highest order. And in Cuba, as it became increasingly reliant on tourism, an authoritarian political system lent itself to many cases of self-enrichment by government officials as the market, and the dollar, increasingly came to control the national economy. As the century drew to a close, the mix of globalization, the growing power of the drug trade and neoliberal economic projects within each state created the ideal conditions for corruption – deepening scarcity and declining control of the State over domestic political life.

Further reading

Castañeda, J. (1994) *Utopia Unarmed: The Latin American Left after the Cold War*, New York: Vintage Books.

Galeano, E. (1989) *Century of the Wind*, trans. Cedric Belfrage, London: Minerva.

—— (1973) *The Open Veins of Latin America*, New York: Monthly Review Press.

Green, D. (1995) *Silent Revolution: The Rise of Market Economics in Latin America*, London: Latin America Bureau.

MIKE GONZALEZ

Cortázar, Julio

b. 1914, Brussels, Belgium; d. 1984, Paris, France

Writer

Born in Brussels to Argentine parents, Cortázar was educated in Buenos Aires. His earliest works (essays, stories and two novels) were only published after his death. Cortázar's search for a distinctly personal voice and a world of his own was conducted in solitude, until he moved to France in 1951. His *Bestiario* (Bestiary) was published in that year, and was followed five years later by *Final del juego* (End of the Game). These two collections of stories contained many of his best known pieces – such as 'La noche boca arriba' (The Night Upside Down), 'Axolotl' and 'La casa tomada' (The Occupied House) – and signalled an original form of fiction in which our perceptions of time, space and identity are systematically destabilized. His constant questioning of reality led to increasingly sharp and fantastic representations of the world, as in the perfect stories that comprise the 1966 volume, *Todos los fuegos el fuego* (Fire is Every Fire). With **Rayuela** (Hopscotch), in 1963, Cortázar embarked on a body of writing that exasperated all formal enquiry and moved instead into metafiction and the rituals of initiation. As with so many avant-garde artists, Cortázar's aesthetic questioning led him towards the left in politics. His involvement with the Cuban Revolution (see **revolutions**) began in 1962; in the 1970s he was active in solidarity work with the **Sandinista Revolution** and with the victims of repression in the Southern Cone. In *El libro de Manuel* (Manuel's Book), published in 1973, his political commitment became explicit for the first time, though still in the context of the author's customary concerns, characters and situations. In the volumes of stories published between 1977 and 1983 – *Alguien que anda por ahí* (There's Someone Walking Around out There), *Queremos tanto a Glenda* (We Love Glenda so) and *Deshoras* (Out of time) – Cortázar set aside some of his aesthetic concerns in order to place the representation of historical violence at the centre of his fiction. When he died in Paris, in 1984, Cortázar was one of Latin America's most widely read writers.

Cortázar's work could be defined as an attempt to express duplicity – two versions of reality, two identities (formed of mirror images and arising from the discovery of an intimate Other), two sets of moral values and often two spatio-temporal systems (or two mutually contradictory diegeses that mysteriously combine). That duplicity is expressed in fantastic tales like 'La noche boca arriba', where a traffic accident in a modern city coincides with an incident during a War of Flowers in pre-Columbian Mexico. This duplicity provokes an often quasi-mystical search for synthesis (as in his novels, *Los premios* (Prizes) (1960) and *62 modelo para armar* (62: A Model Kit) (1968)), which, as so often, induces his hero to magically slip from one space–time to another through the syntagmatic flow of language. As the familiar readings are transformed into a self-reflective discourse, it becomes clear that Cortázar yearns for a lost Eden (called 'the island at mid-day', 'the kibbutz of desire' or the 'artificial sky' in some texts); for values long since lost. This explains his interest in primitive societies, infantile perception, surrealism (see **surrealism in Latin American art**), Jungian archetypes, music (as the expression of a meaning both before and beyond meaning) and in a magical thought rooted in a pre- or alogical terrain. This search for Utopia explains the writer's ideological evolution from the kibbutz of desire to a commitment to socialist ideals. At the same time, the dialectics of rebellion and legality, of desire and frustration, operate in all of Cortázar's work through humour and game-playing, particularly in the short texts collected in *Historias de cronopios y famas* (1961). Following on from the absurd humour of Macedonio **Fernández** and the speculations of Jorge Luis **Borges**, Cortázar's work gave new impetus to fantastic literature, multiplying the doubts, fables, invasions and the terrors that desire can evoke, yet sustaining throughout a stylistic and formal rigour.

In the 1960s Cortázar's work found a passionate readership among a younger generation of Latin Americans who identified with the irreverence, the valorization of the imaginary, the rebellion and the yearning for (social, sexual and discursive) liberation expressed in these texts. Of the writers of his generation only Gabriel **García Márquez** enjoyed a similar reputation in both Latin America and Europe. The wealth of translations, the success of Antonioni's film *Blow-Up*, based on a story from the 1959 volume *Las armas secretas* (The Secret Weapons) and the inclusion of his writings on countless student reading lists have contributed to the growing interest in his work. And yet Cortázar did not influence subsequent generations of writers, perhaps because his political development provoked public criticism of him by both the nationalist left and the conservative right. The recent publication of his complete works, however, including a number of unpublished texts, variations and drafts, have generated an affectionate complicity and a general agreement that, despite their occasional ideological naïvety, his texts are still extraordinary.

Further reading

Alazraki, J. (1994) *Hacia Cortázar: Aproximaciones a su obra*, Barcelona: Anthropos.

Cortázar, J. (1994) *Obra crítica*, eds S. Yurkievich, J. Alazraki and S. Sosnowski, 3 vols, Madrid: Alfaguara.

—— (1976) *Los relatos*, 3 vols, Madrid: Alianza.

Ivask, I. and Alazraki, J. (eds) (1978) *The Final Island: The Fiction of Cortázar*, Norman: University of Oklahoma Press.

Ortiz, Carmen (1994) *Julio Cortázar: Una estética de la búsqueda*, Buenos Aires: Almageste.

Yurkievich, S. (1994) *Julio Cortázar: Mundos y modos*, Madrid: Muchnik.

JULIO PREMAT

Cortázar, Octavio

b. 1935, Havana, Cuba

Film-maker

An important **documentary** film-maker, Cortázar joined the newly created **ICAIC** (Cuban Institute of Cinematic Art and Industry) in 1959 as a production assistant. In 1960 he directed a series of educational documentaries called *La Enciclopedia Popular* (People's Encyclopedia). He studied at Prague's Charles University (1963–7) before returning to Cuba to make a number of documentary films including *Por primera vez* (For the First Time) (1967) and *Acerca de un personaje que algunos llaman San Lázaro y otros llaman Babalú* (Concerning a Person that Some Call St Lazarus and Others Call Babalú) (1968) and the feature films *El brigadista* (The Literacy Campaigner) (1977) and *Guardafronteras* (Border Guard) (1980).

JOSÉ ANTONIO EVORA

Cortés, Alfonso

b. 1893, León, Nicaragua; d. 1969, Managua, Nicaragua

Poet

One of Nicaragua's most important poets, Alfonso Cortés suffered from schizophrenic episodes and was committed to the Managua Asylum for the Insane where he spent over twenty-five years. He was discovered by José **Coronel Urtecho** and Ernesto **Cardenal**, who published one of his books. Works he wrote during and in between his mental episodes are extremely varied in quality, ranging from works derivative of modernism and Parnassianism to bizarre, highly creative poems that incorporate philosophical and metaphysical inquiries into space, time and self-knowledge that question the principles of Catholic beliefs. His intellectual rebellion prefigures the attitudes of subsequent generations of Vanguardist and revolutionary poets.

DEREK PETREY AND ILEANA RODRÍGUEZ

Cortijo, Rafael

b. 1928, Santurce, Puerto Rico; d. 1982, Santurce

Musician

Cortijo was percussionist and leader during the 1950s of one of the legendary Caribbean musical ensembles, *Cortijo y su combo*. The group brought to international attention the Puerto Rican rhythms of the bomba and plena drums. His hits, like 'Quítate de la vía Perico' (Out of the way Perico), 'Maquinolandera' and 'El negro Bombón', were heard everywhere in Latin America. The group included among its members Ismael Rivera, Rafael Ithier (director of the *Gran Combo de Puerto Rico*) and Roberto Roena.

JUAN CARLOS QUINTERO HERENCIA

Cossa, Roberto

b. 1934, Buenos Aires, Argentina

Playwright

In the context of the 1976–83 military dictatorships in Argentina, Cossa's work accepted the challenge of producing a critical theatre. In 1977, his *La nona* (Granny), opened, playing for two years. Its central figure, a senile Italian immigrant grandmother, is the grotesque embodiment of the promise to immigrants to 'make it in America'. Cossa participated in the **Teatro Abierto** 1981 movement, defying government repression of the arts, with a play about Italo-Argentine exiles in Italy, *Gris de ausencia* (The Greyness of Absence). Both plays depict the destruction of the family by a dictatorship that touted the family as a sacred national institution.

DAVID WILLIAM FOSTER

Costa, Gal

b. 1945, Salvador, Bahia, Brazil

Singer

Gal Costa (Maria da Graça Costa Pena Burgos) is among the most popular female interpreters of **MPB**, together with fellow Bahians Caetano **Veloso**, Gilberto **Gil** and Maria Bethânia. Her early demure **bossa nova** vocal style changed abruptly in the late 1960s during her participation in the rock-inspired *tropicalista* movement. During the most repressive phase of military rule in the early 1970s she became the 'muse' of the Brazilian counterculture, as exemplified by her live recording *Gal a todo vapor* (Gal Full Steam Ahead). She recorded beautifully updated versions of classic compositions by Ary **Barroso** and Dorival **Caymmi**, and in the 1990s recorded hits of the

blocos afro of Salvador and compositions by Chico **Buarque** and Caetano Veloso.

CHRISTOPHER DUNN

Costa, João Cruz

b. 1904, São Paulo, Brazil; d. ?

Philosopher

Cruz Costa, who taught for many years at the University of São Paulo, was a student there in its early years and colleague of such intellectuals as Antonio **Candido**. He is best known as the author of *Contribuição à história das idéias no Brasil* (A History of Ideas in Brazil) (1956). It is a historicist work, 'a history of ideas in the context in which they were thought', which links the development of ideas in Brazil, especially the advent of positivism in the late nineteenth century, to the development of the country.

JOHN GLEDSON

Costa, Lúcio

b. 1902, Toulon, France; d. 1998, Rio de Janeiro, Brazil

Architect

Graduating in 1924 from the Escola Nacional de Belas Artes (National School of Fine Arts) in Rio de Janeiro, where an eclectic *fin-de-siècle* atmosphere prevailed, Costa leaned towards the neo-colonial movement. His involvement with modernism began only after his term as Director of ENBA between 1931 and 1933. His contributions to the design for the **Ministério da Educação e Saúde** (Education and Health Ministry) building give evidence of his new direction. His project (or 'Plan Piloto') won the competition for the design of the new capital, **Brasília**, which he later built together with **Niemeyer** and others.

MARIA MARTA CAMISASSA

Costa Rica

The modern history of the Central American republic of Costa Rica has been dominated by two products – bananas and coffee. It has a reputation for democratic stability that is both more complex and less encouraging than might at first appear.

Unlike the other Central American republics, much of Costa Rica's coffee is grown on small and medium farms, though the processing and distribution of the product has always been concentrated in the hands of a small and powerful agrarian elite. The result has been a consensual politics reflecting the paternalistic relations dominant within the sector. Bananas, by contrast, have been controlled by foreign corporations whose relations with their workers have been conflictive and exploitative. The great strike of 1934 against the United Fruit Company was the most bitter in the country's history. Its leader Carlos Luis **Fallas** produced a famous novel about the life of banana workers, *Mamita Yunai* (1941).

The result of these conflicts, however, was not a revolutionary movement but a politics of democratic consensus built on an alliance between the Communist Party under Manuel Mora (its general secretary from 1931 to 1983) and a reformist current within the coffee elite. One consequence (a highly unusual one in Latin America) was the creation of a welfare system during the Calderón presidency of the 1940s. Resistance to this collaboration crystallized, however, around a coalition of conservative forces led by José Figueres, whose seizure of power in the so-called 'revolution' of 1948 placed him at the heart of Costa Rican politics for the remainder of the century.

Anti-communist in ideology, the Figueres period was an attempt at economic modernization. The banks were nationalized and the national army abolished. The longer-term intention to industrialize was realized to some extent; yet the manufacturing of the 1970s remained largely in traditional areas like textiles and food processing. In 1985, 56 per cent of export earnings still came from coffee and bananas.

Figueres and his PLN dominated Costa Rican political life throughout the period; but by the late 1970s events in neighbouring Nicaragua began to influence Costa Rica's internal affairs. In the late 1970s, Costa Rica's government allowed the Sandinistas (see **Sandinista Revolution**) to use the country as a base in their struggle against the Somoza dictatorship. After the Nicaraguan Revolution of 1979 (see **revolutions**), however, Costa Rica came under increasing pressure from Washington to change its position. Under Monge (1982–6) Costa Rica became a launching pad for anti-Sandinista operations; in exchange it received significant US direct aid as a buffer against the effects of falling coffee prices and the recession of the late 1970s. At the same time, its security forces grew dramatically (to nearly 20,000) under US pressure, and were often used against strikes and labour protests.

Oscar **Arias**, president from 1986, became a mediator in the Central American conflict. A member of Figueres's PLN party and closely connected with both the old coffee oligarchy and the new industrial elite, his key role in the Central American process also indicated how far Costa Rica had become absorbed into the US ambit.

During the 1980s, Costa Rica did not suffer the violent conflicts that affected its neighbours in Nicaragua and El Salvador, and its social welfare provisions remained in advance of any other country in the region. Yet its distribution of income was among the most uneven in Latin America and the small political elite that still dominated the country pushed through neoliberal (see **neoliberalism**) policies in the 1980s and 1990s whose effect was to raise unemployment levels and depress living standards.

Costa Rican writing in the 1930s and 1940s was dominated by the socialist realism inaugurated by Fallas, Joaquín Gutiérrez and Carmen **Lyra**, among others; the work of Yolanda **Oreamuno**, however, represented an urban writing of psychological depth. Eunice **Odio** and Ana Istarú explored the relations between men and women in their poetry.

Although most often Costa Rica has served as an exotic backdrop for international **co-productions** (like Carlos Saura's *Eldorado*, 1988), the national cinema dates back to A.F. **Bertoni**'s *El retorno* (The Return) (1930). An important documentary movement emerged in the 1970s from a government-sponsored film institute, while independent production through Oscar **Castillo**'s

Istmo Films also took off. His *telenovela*-inspired (see **telenovelas**) feature *Eulalia* (1987) was very successful. Also notable is the work of two women film-makers – Patricia **Howell** and María Ramírez, especially the latter's *La libélula del Guaraní* (The Dragonfly of the Guaraní) (1984) – and the work of the collective **Audiovisuales Chirripó**.

Music has occupied a central role in the school curriculum in Costa Rica; but the music of Mexico and South America remain the most popular. The black population around Limón, however, whose culture Quince **Duncan** has collected and written about, has a vital musical tradition and its annual carnival testifies to the continuity of an African-based musical culture. The presence of many migrant workers from the Caribbean also explains the popularity of **calypso**; visiting calypsonians like **Lord Kitchener** and the **Mighty Sparrow** in the 1950s and 1960s encouraged the emergence of local calypsonians like Edgar 'Pitún' Hutchinson. The cultural contribution of indigenous communities, like the Guaymí and the Maleku, has also been recognized in recent years.

Further reading

Duncan, Q. and Meléndez, C. (1974) *El negro en Costa Rica*, San José: Editorial Costa Rica.

Dunkerley, J. (1988) *Power in the Isthmus: A Political History of Modern Central America*, London: Verso.

Paige, J.M. (1998) *Coffee and Power: Revolution and the Rise of Democracy in Central America*, Cambridge, MA: Harvard University Press

MIKE GONZALEZ

costumbrismo

The description of ordinary life in a particular milieu, especially of provincial, regional or rural life, *costumbrismo* was a favourite genre in nineteenth-century Spanish literature (with such authors as Larra, Mesonero Romanos, Pereda and Fernán Caballero), and spread early in Spanish America. The 'cuadro de costumbres' (sketch of manners and customs) influenced classic nineteenth-century works like Esteban Echeverría's *El matadero* (The Slaughterhouse) (published post-

humously in 1871), often claimed as the first Spanish American **short story**, Sarmiento's *Facundo* (translated as *Life in the Argentine Republic in the Days of the Tyrants*) (1845) with its descriptions of life on the *pampas* (see **pampa**), and Jorge Isaacs' *María* (1867), with its descriptions of life on a Colombian plantation. The genre survived at least until the middle of the twentieth century in areas whose national culture depended to some extent on the idealization of a rural past, such as Uruguay (the 'nativist' tradition) and especially Costa Rica, where large anthologies of *costumbrista* writing have been compiled, and where the genre forms an important component of the literary canon.

DANIEL BALDERSTON

Cote Lamus, Eduardo

b. 1928, Cucuta, Colombia; d. 1964, Cucuta

Poet

Although he attended law school in Bogotá, Cote Lamus later studied Spanish philology in Salamanca, thanks to a Spanish government scholarship. During his time in Spain, he established himself as poet and befriended many intellectuals, including writer Vicente Aleixandre. He then served in diplomatic positions in Glasgow and Frankfurt. In 1957 he returned to Colombia and pursued an expeditious political career, serving as secretary of education, congressman, senator and governor for his province. He was one of the founding members of the magazine *Mito* (Myth), marking an important moment in Colombia's cultural scene in the 1950s. His most mature work reflects the influence of T.S. Eliot.

HÉCTOR D. FERNÁNDEZ L'HOESTE

Coutinho, Afrânio

b. 1911, Salvador, Bahia, Brazil

Critic

Afrânio Coutinho introduced literary historiography and aesthetic analyses to Brazilian audiences more familiar with impressionistic criticism. A staunch New Critic, Coutinho did much to anthologize and republish literature and literary criticism throughout Brazil. Many of his anthologies are used as textbooks, including the *Enciclopédia de literatura brasileira* (Encyclopedia of Brazilian literature) (1971). Coutinho offered his personal library to students and scholars via the Oficina Literária Afrânio Coutinho (OLAC) in Rio de Janeiro, a tradition continued by his daughter Graça Coutinho de Goes. Gregory Rabassa's 1969 translation of *Introdução à literatura brasileira* (An Introduction to Brazilian Literature) introduced Coutinho's work to English-speaking audiences.

SUSAN CANTY QUINLAN

Coutinho, Eduardo

b. 1933, São Paulo, Brazil

Film-maker

Coutinho was cinematographer for several **Cinema Novo** films, including **Hirszman**'s *Garota de Ipanema* (Girl from Ipanema) (1967) and Bruno **Barreto**'s *Dona Flor e seus dois maridos* (Dona Flor and Her Two Husbands) (1976). From the 1970s he devoted himself to making documentaries for the television programme 'O **Globo** Repórter' (1976–83). His magnificent *Cabra marcado para morrer* (Goat for the Slaughter) (1984) resumed a collaboration with a group of militant peasants begun in the 1960s, to produce an analysis of both the social and cinematic development of Brazil through the intervening years. In 1993 he completed *O fio da memoria* (Thread of History), exploring the conditions of Afro-Brazilians.

ISMAIL XAVIER AND THE USP GROUP

Covarrubias, Miguel

b. 1904, Mexico City; d. 1957, Mexico City

Artist

In the 1920s and 1930s, Covarrubias drew celebrated satirical cartoons for several leading Mexican and US magazines, including *Vanity Fair, The New Yorker* and *Vogue*. Subsequently he painted important murals, illustrated thirty-two books, and wrote and illustrated two books on Mesoamerican art and two travel books. The second of these, *Mexico South: The Isthmus of Tehuantepec* (1946), helped to forge the national mystique of the Isthmus Zapotecs as elegant, spirited, independent, sensual and creative.

CYNTHIA STEELE

Cox, Robert John

b. 1933, Ealing, England

Journalist

Editor of the *Buenos Aires Herald* from 1968 to 1979, Cox gave the small (17,000 circulation) English-language daily (founded in 1876) an international reputation as a defender of **human rights**. After the 1976 military *coup*, Cox confronted the dictatorship's practice of making its opponents 'disappear'. Although his arrest had been ordered since 1976, a direct threat against his ten-year old son in 1979 forced him into exile. He was given an Order of the British Empire in 1979, the US Mergenthaler Prize, the Interamerican Press Association's top award in 1977 and the Maria Moors-Cabot Prize in 1978.

ANDREW GRAHAM-YOOLL

Cozarinsky, Edgardo

b. 1943, Buenos Aires

Film-maker, writer

Through the 1950s, Cozarinsky wrote journalism for *Tiempo de cine, Primera plana* and *Panorama*. After publishing his first literary essay, he completed his highly experimental first film ...*Puntos suspensivos* (Line of Dots...) (1970), born he says, 'out of my desire to speak about Argentina, the Onganía regime, and the rhetoric of film'. He published *Borges y el cine* (Borges and Film) (1974) before emigrating to France, where he made *Les apprentis sorciers* (The Sorcerer's Apprentices) (1977) and the documentary *Guerre d'un seul homme* (One Man's War) (1980). The 1987 co-production *Guerreros y cautivas* (Warriors and Slaves) marked his return to film-making in Argentina.

DIANA PALADINO

CPC

CPC (Centro Popular de Cultura) was a shortlived but crucial focus of left-wing cultural initiatives in the years immediately preceding and following Brazil's military *coup* of 1964. The first of several CPCs was established under the leadership of film-maker Leon **Hirszman**, dramatist Oduvaldo **Vianna Filho** and Carlos Estevam Martins in December 1961, during the reformist administration of João **Goulart** (1961–4). Goulart's promised concessions to rural and urban demands for grassroots reforms stimulated the growth of a mass-based movement with broadly socialist and anti-imperialist aspirations. Associated with the Brazilian Communist Party, the CPC represented one means by which the left's new, university-educated intelligentsia sought to win the ideological and organisational leadership of this movement.

The CPC's theoretical analysis of the relationship between culture and popular mobilisation, in its pre-Manifesto of 1962, displays the strong influence of the Stalinist Marxism (see **Marxism in Latin America**) which dominated left-wing thinking. It drew a clear dividing line between two conceptions of popular artistic practice: on the one hand, the 'Revolutionary Popular Culture' which carried to the people an enlightened understanding of the nature of capitalist and imperialist oppression; on the other, the people's own artistic traditions, which either crudely reproduced the dominant ideology's description of their world or offered them a passive, consumerist escapism. To bridge the gap between 'revolutionary' and 'false' consciousness, the CPC artist was required to 'opt to be an integral part of the people', familiarising himself with their 'primitive' aesthetic resources, language and forms, whilst inserting into them a revolutionary 'content'.

Some of the CPC's, however, preferred more openly democratic projects; erstwhile **bossa nova** songwriter Carlos Lyra and poet Ferreira **Gullar** won an argument to change the organisation's original name (Centre of Popular Culture) to Popular Centre of Culture. Gullar moved beyond its founders' simplistic, anti-modernist theoretical analysis in *A Cultura posta em questão* (1965) (Culture Under Question) and *Vanguarda e Subdesenvolvimento* (1969) (Avant-Garde and Underdevelopment). Augusto **Boal**'s Theatre of the Oppressed and Paulo **Freire**'s popular **literacy** methodology implicitly challenged the CPC's top-down approach to popular consciousness-raising, prioritising the people's own experience and creativity in their self-transformation as active subjects. Arguably the severest critique, from within the left, of the messianic voluntarism and manichaeism to which the orthodox CPC ideologues were prone was Glauber **Rocha**'s 1967 film *Terra em transe* (Land in Anguish).

While the CPC's grassroots work was cut short by the repression which followed the 1964 *coup*, there can be no doubt of the impetus it gave to a whole range of cultural initiatives in poetry, popular music, cinema and education. Its legacy can still be felt today: it is an unavoidable reference point for any debate on the relationship between culture and politics.

Further reading

Hollanda, H.B. de (1981) *Impressões de viagem: CPC, Vanguarda e Desbunde: 1960/1970*, São Paulo: Brasiliense.

Martins, C.E. (1979) 'Anteprojeto do Manifesto do CPC', *Arte em Revista: Anos 60*, I(1): 67–79.

Schwarz, R. (1992) 'Culture and politics in Brazil, 1964–68', in *Misplaced Ideas: Essays on Brazilian Culture*, London: Verso.

DAVID TREECE

craft export, international market for

While the transporting of archaeological remains and anthropological artefacts from Latin America to Western museums and collections may be seen as its precursor, the export of **crafts** proper did not begin until the 1960s, spurred by the **Alliance for Progress**, which saw an expansion in the production and commercialization of crafts as one means towards economic and social development in the region. The same decade witnessed a rapid growth in **tourism** to Latin America, raising awareness of local products which were sought as exotic souvenirs. Subsequent (and previous) portrayals of the region and its inhabitants in film, literature and music for audiences likely to be in a position to purchase craft imports have overwhelmingly tended to highlight the exotic and the 'other' in Latin America, its inhabitants and their actions, with attendant consequences on the type of crafts accepted as 'authentic' by buyers in non-Latin American countries. At the same time, however, the export market can be very profitable, particularly in Europe, North America and Japan. The programme run in the mid-1990s by the US Agency for International Development and Asociación de Exportadores (ADEX) in Peru is an interesting extension of this idea: technology (for improving handmade production) is brought from the US, as are the current season's designs and preferences for materials. Peruvian export companies place orders with local workshops, have displays at the New York International Gift Show and hope to gain access to the US market for products such as plates and wooden furniture with designs and decoration which have lost their qualities as markers of something distinctly Peruvian, being taken instead from a modern Western tradition. At this point, rather than a single market for craft export, there are a series of markets for specific export lines.

A 1978 study by the Sistema Económico Latinoamericano (**SELA**) determined that in the late 1970s Latin American countries were supplying 10 per cent of all craft exports to industrialized nations, worth at the time some $100 million. Mexico and the Central American countries accounted for 57 per cent of this figure, with the remainder exported by the Andean nations (in particular Peru, Colombia, Bolivia and Ecuador). Mexico's domination of the region's craft exports may be explained by its high proportion of producers (28 per cent of the economically active population, more than twice the figure for any other country of the region), its geographical location (in addition to exports proper almost as much is raised through sales at state craft shops on the US border) and, since 1994, membership of **NAFTA**. Despite such a privileged position, craft exports in Mexico accounted for only 0.1 per cent of GNP and some 3 per cent of all exports at the end of the 1980s. Similarly, in Peru through the 1970s (when crafts enjoyed strong state support), craft exports averaged only some 3 per cent of non-traditional exports.

Figures for the early 1990s from Peru's Ministry of Industry show a situation with regard to destination of craft exports which is representative of the region: slightly over half of all craft exports go to the USA, with the European Union accounting for a fifth. Other Latin American nations receive 10 per cent (for resale as exports or to the tourist market), while Canada and Japan account for 4 per cent each. Apart from the obvious relative wealth of these industrialized nations as export destinations, preferential import tariffs for handmade crafts also offer a significant advantage to exporters wishing to target them. Ecuador and Peru – two of the countries, after Mexico, in which state involvement in craft export has been greatest – have departments in the Ministry of Industry devoted to crafts, their focus being primarily commercial and promotional, organizing delegations of producers for international craft fairs in Latin America and beyond, and apprising producers and exporters of regulations and practices for exports.

Despite the low export figures generated by crafts as percentage of GNP across the countries of the region, a number of governments have recognized the sociopolitical and socioeconomic importance of craft exports. Whatever the outcome of increased state interest, the social and political value of craft exports will continue to outweigh the economic benefit, on a national scale at least, while the objects exported will carry on making a significant contribution to an awareness and appreciation of the various cultures of the region of origin.

See also: clothing exports; crafts; fairs and markets; panama hat

Further reading

Lauer, M. (1989) *La producción artesanal en América Latina*, Lima: Mosca Azul Editores.

DAVID WOOD

crafts

Crafts or arts and crafts, folk art and **popular art** are terms commonly used in English, but none conveys satisfactorily the specific traditions, symbolic values and social structures carried by the Spanish *artesanía* (or Portuguese *artesanato*). Crafts, arts and crafts and folk art suggest a preciousness lacking in the original objects and their conditions of production, while folk art and popular art are problematic as a result of the tension between the elite and non-elite inherent therein, as the two are rarely so happily conjoined as these terms might suggest. *Artesanía* is the preferred term, and will be used here throughout.

Ceramics, **weaving**, **gourds**, jewellery and basketry have all been produced in Latin America since pre-Columbian times for ceremonial, functional and ornamental purposes, and while some kinds of *artesanía* are found across the region, factors such as cultural differences, climate, altitude and the raw materials at the producers' disposal have led to a considerable variety of form and design between areas.

In the first decades of the present century *indigenismo* brought peasant and rural culture, including *artesanía*, to the attention of an urban public, and since the late 1960s the rapid growth of **tourism** has had a significant impact on the production methods and designs of many forms of *artesanía*, as producers have sought to satisfy growing demand at the same time as meeting the expectations and preconceptions of Western tourists about the exotic and the traditional. The result has been a shift away from production for ceremonial and functional purposes towards objects that are mass produced for commercial ends, to be sold for their aesthetic appeal alone.

It is estimated that by the late 1980s some fifteen million people across the region were involved in the production of *artesanía*, with Peru, Mexico, Ecuador and Guatemala having the greatest and most varied output. It is no coincidence that these countries are areas in which the pre-Columbian cultures were highly developed, for twentieth-century producers continue to draw significantly on ancient tradition in terms of form, design and, to a lesser extent, technique. While the aforementioned growth of the tourist market has undoubtedly contributed to an increase in the number of producers, other factors such as the failure of the agricultural sector to provide a secure existence, the relative loss in value of agricultural produce, widespread migration to the cities and high urban unemployment and underemployment have also played their part. A survey carried out by the Sistema Económico Latinoamericano (**SELA**) in fourteen countries of the region found that *artesanía* was produced by 6 per cent of the population, and by 18 per cent of the economically active population, underlining not only the traditional and symbolic worth of this form but also its modern value in socioeconomic terms. Under such conditions, *artesanía* becomes an important point of encounter between traditional rural and modern urban cultures.

The differences across time and space referred to above can be appreciated in a brief examination of the situation in Peru with regard to textiles which, together with ceramics, represent the most widely found form of *artesanía* in Latin America. Textiles had been produced, predominantly on backstrap looms, for centuries before the arrival of the Spanish on the Peruvian coastal desert, in the Andes and in the high jungle, for both religious and functional purposes. Although small-scale production of textiles for the use of the producer's family may continue on the backstrap loom, most commercial weaving takes place on the treadle looms introduced by the Spanish and, more recently, on electric looms. The heavy weaves of the highlands, using the wool of sheep and native cameloids, offer protection against the harsh Andean climate, while cloth made from soft cotton in the high jungle provides relief from mosquitoes and seasonal cool breezes. Urban migration, particularly to Lima, has meant that these types of textiles are now produced in the coastal cities as well as their areas of origin, often using electric looms for the supply of high-quality rugs, sweaters and other garments to tourist shops and markets.

Also, as is the case with many other raw materials, llama and alpaca wool is bought up for export to Europe, the United States and Japan.

Two other forms of Peruvian *artesanía* which have undergone processes of change in the second half of the twentieth century are *retablos* (see **retablos and ex votos**) or St Mark's boxes and the pottery of Chulucanas. The *retablos* were introduced by the Spanish in the sixteenth century as portable altars, but were subsequently also given a syncretic function in traditional ceremonies such as the branding of livestock. An expanding road network meant that by the 1940s the muleteers who had traditionally transported the *retablos* to other regions were being replaced by trucks, but at the same time the roads facilitated access to such areas for Lima-based *indigenistas*, whose interest revived the tradition and started a process whereby scenes depicted respond to the often romanticizing demands and expectations of the buyer. Travel has not only been in one direction, however: accelerated migration to the cities in the 1980s and early 1990s as a result of the war between **Sendero Luminoso** and the armed forces brought production to the cities and images of the conflict into the *retablos*, which thus contributed to a familiarization of urban dwellers with the rural and peasant reality of their own country.

The potters of Chulucanas had traditionally produced terracotta pots for everyday use, but the discovery of the nearby pre-Columbian Vicus tombs in 1960 encouraged attempts to recapture ancient forms and techniques, leading to more stylized pieces that enjoy great commercial success both in Peru and further afield. The potters of Chulucanas are an outstanding example not only of a group reflecting upon their cultural past and cultural identity through their *artesanía*, but also of producers whose pieces cross the boundaries between elite and non-elite art with an ease which renders such distinctions highly questionable.

The situation in neighbouring Ecuador is similar to that in Peru with regard to cultural traditions, raw materials and types of products, although the range is not as extensive. An important difference, however, is the outstanding success of one community in adapting to the modern market economy and in commercializing their products. The indigenous inhabitants of Otovalo, a medium-sized town north of Quito, show that mainstream reproduction of traditional items and acceptance of the modern can represent not only economic wealth but the reaffirmation of those same traditions. As the renown of the high quality and ingenuity of design of Otovaleño textiles has grown, the Saturday market in particular has become a national tourist focus, attracting in turn a wide range of other forms of *artesanía* produced in the area, and the Otovaleños themselves, with their instantly recognisable traditional dress, sell their products with great success in markets across Ecuador and far beyond. Interestingly, for a community which has achieved such success in a market economy, the producers of Otovalo are organized into cooperatives, a factor which has helped to maintain the cohesive force of their traditional values while adapting to the demands of modern urban society.

A large Indian population (*circa* twelve million or 15 per cent of the total), a rich and diverse cultural heritage, a varied geography providing a wide range of raw materials, and the Mexican Revolution of 1910–20 (see **revolutions**) have combined to ensure that Mexican *artesanía* is not only produced in greater quantity than in any other country of the region, but also that it continues to have practical uses and religious associations, as well as offering pieces appreciated purely for their aesthetic appeal. It is perhaps the wealth of imagery taken from **Catholicism**, especially the Virgin of Guadalupe (see **Virgins, miraculous**), that sets much Mexican *artesanía* apart from that of other countries of the region, although pre-Hispanic concerns are also well represented, particularly in imagery revolving around death and the national symbol of an eagle perched on a prickly pear with a serpent in its talons. The modern is equally evident in items such as the *diablitos* produced since the 1960s in Ocumicho, placing the traditional figure of the devil in a wide variety of modern situations such as riding motorbikes or taking a bus to the USA. This juxtaposition of the modern and the traditional articulates the position in which many inhabitants of rural Mexico now find themselves, maintaining traditions from decades and even centuries past while at the same time moving in a material culture of the late twentieth century.

Support from the state and other institutions, particularly in the cases of Peru and Mexico, has recognized the socioeconomic importance of *artesanía*, and has played an important role in its development in these two countries. In Peru, encouragement through *ferias artesanales* (fairs of *artesanía*), organized by urban collectors, and *Talleres artesanales* (workshops for producers), sponsored by the Ministry of Education, coincided with the implementation of the **Alliance for Progress** programme. The ensuing rise of the first commercial production and export companies received further stimulation under the military government of **Velasco Alvarado** and other members of the armed forces (1968–78), which undertook the first serious steps to improve the lot of the rural peasant since colonial times. As well as establishing new fairs and festivals for indigenous producers, the regime took the highly symbolic and polemical decision to award the 1975 National Prize for Culture to Joaquín **López Antay**, a renowned maker of *retablos*.

The involvement of the Mexican state in the promotion of *artesanía* dates back to the 1920s, and it is no surprise that Mexico has the greatest number of state-run and independent museums and organizations which support or are entirely devoted to *artesanía*. The setting-up of Fondo Nacional de las Artesanías (FONART) in the 1970s and inauguration in 1982 of the National Museum for Popular Cultures, which often features *artesanía*, can be seen as governmental acknowledgement of its increasingly important role in the life of the nation, occupying – as it did in 1989 – 28 per cent of the economically active population. Economic reasons alone, however, are not enough to explain the level of state support enjoyed by an activity which accounted for only 0.1 per cent of GNP and some 3 per cent of exports at the end of the 1980s. While state support of *artesanía* in Mexico and Peru may have improved conditions for rural peasant populations, it has also served political ends, engendering a sense of nationhood among sectors of the population traditionally excluded from the process of nation-building, slowing peasant migration to the cities, alleviating unemployment and providing symbols of common cultural heritage and identity across various levels of society.

Ready access to materials and, increasingly, to large markets, both domestic and foreign, means that as well as providing an important source of income for many, *artesanía* offers groups excluded from other channels of expression (**television**, **radio**, the printed media) a means of expressing and communicating their values to a broad public that would otherwise be denied them.

See also: Andean culture; Day of the Dead; fairs and markets; craft exports; patchwork; woodcuts

Further reading

Braun, B. (1995) *Arts of the Amazon*, London: Thames & Hudson.

Davies, L. and Fini, M. (1994) *Arts and Crafts of South America*, London: Thames & Hudson.

De la Fuente, M.C., Nolte, M.J., Nuñez Rebaza, L. and Villegas Robles, R. (eds) (1992) *Artesanía peruana*, Lima: Allpa.

Sayer, C. (1990) *Arts and Crafts of Mexico*, London: Thames & Hudson.

Walter, L. (1981) 'Otovaleño development, ethnicity and national integration', *América Indígena* XLI(2): 319–38.

DAVID WOOD

Craig, Christine

b. 1943, Kingston, Jamaica

Writer

Craig is a poet, short story writer and writer of children's books as well as a working journalist. Her first volume of poems, *Quadrille for Tigers* (1984) was very strong, with very assured poems articulating social, political, racial and gender tensions in subtle and original ways, such as her well-known 'Crow Poem' and 'All Things Bright ...'. She has said that her poetry is most realistic when it is most obscure; her gift is for unusual images of complex feeling. Her story collection *Mint Tea* (1993) is of uneven quality but contains some vivid portraits of Jamaican women.

ELAINE SAVORY

Cravo Jr, Mario

b. 1923, Salvador, Bahia, Brazil

Sculptor and printmaker

After a brief stint in New York in the late 1940s, Mario Cravo Jr returned to Salvador where he participated in an emerging modern art scene inspired by Afro-Brazilian culture together with **Carybé** and Rubens Valentin. Since participating in the First **Bienale de São Paulo** in 1955, he has exhibited extensively throughout Latin America, the United States and Europe. He has worked with several mediums including metals, wood, soap stone, plastics and synthetic resins. In 1994, he mounted a sculpture park in Salvador featuring stabiles, mobiles and sound sculptures.

CHRISTOPHER DUNN

Cravo Neto, Mario

b. 1947, Salvador, Bahia, Brazil

Photographer

A photographer of international renown, Cravo Neto combines ethnographic references to the Afro-Brazilian **Candomblé** religion with formal experimentation. In the early 1960s, he travelled to Berlin with his father, Mario **Cravo** Jr, where he came into contact with several European photographers. In 1968, he moved to New York, where he studied black-and-white photography with the Art Student League. After returning to Brazil in 1970, his work was regularly featured at the prestigious **Bienale de São Paulo**. Cravo Neto was profoundly inspired by the documentary field work of Pierre **Verger**, yet has produced most of his photography in the studio.

CHRISTOPHER DUNN

creole

One of the key terms to describe New World cultures, this word is also famously ambiguous. Derived from the Latin verb *creare* (to create), its various forms (**criollo** in Spanish, *crioulo* in Portuguese, *créole* in French, *creole* in English) refer first of all to persons born in the New World. The term *criollos* is often used to describe the white and **mestizo** elites (primarily though not exclusively of Spanish stock) who led the independence wars against Spain. The same word is often used in nineteenth-century Portuguese, however, to designate blacks born in Brazil (as opposed to those who were born in Africa); it is used in this sense in Adolfo Caminha's famous gay-themed novel *Bom Crioulo* (1895). In contemporary Louisiana, 'creole' is used as a self-identifying word by both blacks and whites, with both groups claiming ownership of the term. The word creole is also used in linguistics to designate **creole languages** (see **English-based creoles**; **Dutch-based creoles**; **French-based creoles**; **Papiamentu**); 'creoles and pidgins' is a term used to refer to a hybrid, often radically simplified, language born as a lingua franca by native speakers of different languages. The various forms of the word are also used to describe cuisine, customs, even culture itself.

DANIEL BALDERSTON

creole languages

A term thought to be of Portuguese origin, creole was originally used to distinguish between persons of European ancestry born in the colonies and those born in Europe. Subsequently it was applied to slaves born in the colonies, and then to the languages they used to communicate outside their own linguistic group.

The creole languages of the Caribbean are a set of new languages emerging from the patterns of social interaction in plantation societies in which a small, relatively linguistically homogenous European population dominated a large and often linguistically heterogenous group of slaves of West African origin. The creole languages are normally described by reference to their European lexical donor language (English-based, French-based, Dutch-based) though this practice masks the seminal West African linguistic input. In each case in the Caribbean, the grammar and semantics of these creole languages display enough significant differences from the European parent to justify their classification as new or separate languages. The most significant morphological characteristic of these languages is their highly reduced (by comparison with the input languages) use of inflections.

The creoles show remarkable structural similarity across lexical boundaries, and thus all theories of their origin and development find it necessary to account for this similarity. The most popular current theories of the origin of these languages propose a strong influence from the substrate West African languages or argue for a set of universal principles of language formation operating in the peculiar sociolinguistic contexts. This input is usually demonstrated through examination of the grammatical and semantic structures underlying the creoles. The lexicon of these languages is derived, in the main, from the European language which was dominant in the territory in which each developed.

In Caribbean territories, creole languages are the first language of the majority of the population. In territories such as Haiti and Curaçao, the creole languages have been accorded the status of national and even official languages. In most Caribbean societies, however, these languages are stigmatised because of their particular sociolinguistic history, although they are the main vehicle for expressing the folk culture.

See also: Dutch-based creoles; English-based creoles; French-based creoles; Haitian creole; Papiamentu

Further reading

Balutanus, K.M. (ed.) *Caribbean Creolization: Reflections on the Cultural Dynamics of Language, Literature and Identity*, Gainesville, FL: University of Florida Press.

Holm, J.A. (1988) *Pidgins and Creoles*, 2 vols, Cambridge: Cambridge University Press.

Taylor, D.M. (1977) *Languages of the West Indies*, Baltimore, MD: Johns Hopkins University Press.

Wekker, H. (ed.) (1995) *Creole Languages and Language Acquisition*, Amsterdam: Mouton de Gruyter.

IAN ROBERTSON

Créolité

A literary and cultural movement begun in Martinique in the 1900s, Créolité was shaped by Edouard **Glissant**'s theories. It is as much a reaction against the Europeanization of France's Overseas Departments as a reaction against *négritude*. Its ideas are expressed in the 1989 manifesto *Eloge de la créolité* (In Praise of Créolité) by Jean Bernabé, Patrick **Chamoiseau** and Raphael **Confiant**, the polemical articles in the weekly magazine *Antilla* and in the novels of Chamoiseau, Confiant and the Guadeloupeans Ernest Pepin and Gisele **Pineau**. Créolité advocates the use of creole and is centred on the diverse, multi-ethnic identity of Martinique.

J. MICHAEL DASH

Crespi, Carlos

b. 1891, Milan, Italy; d. 1982, Cuenca, Ecuador

Priest

Crespi was a Catholic priest whose pastoral dedication earned him a legendary reputation. He arrived in Ecuador in 1923 as a missionary for the Italian Salesian order, and worked in agriculture, the education of the poor and children, the organization of Eucharistic congresses, and the training of aspirants to the Salesian mission. His ability to raise funds for his multiple projects was admirable; his work to conserve the historic character of his adopted city of Cuenca is an example. He was also the founder of an eccentric museum dedicated to proving Egyptian and Phoenician influence on Amazonian Indian culture.

MERCEDES M. ROBLES

Crespo, Luis Alberto

b. 1941, Carora, Venezuela

Poet

Crespo's first book, *Si el verano es dilatado* (If Summer

is Late) (1968) revealed a very particular poetic voice full of the resonances of provincial speech and populated by images of the arid and luminous landscapes of his native region. His poetry has kept faith with that diction, at once archaic and despairing and employing a symbolic vocabulary determined by experiences of distance, solitude, desert and the emptiness of space. In 1991, he published his first anthology, *Como una orilla* (Like a Shore) and he has published tirelessly ever since: *Duro* (Hard) (1995), *Más afuera* (Further Out) (1995), *Solamente* (Only) (1996).

RAFAEL CASTILLO ZAPATA

Crespo Rodas, Alberto

b. 1917, La Paz, Bolivia

Historian

University Librarian, founder of the La Paz Historical Archive and member of the Bolivian Academy, he has held various diplomatic posts. In his youth he was a journalist active in the PIR (Partido de Izquierda Revolucionaria – Party of the Revolutionary Left); after the **1952 Revolution**, he spent several years in exile. He was the first professional historian in Bolivia, and for many years edited the journal *Historia y Cultura*. His sensitive writings embrace, among others, the colonial period (like *Reclutamiento y mita de Potosí* (Recruitment and Forced Labour in Potosí – 1970) and *Esclavos negros en Bolivia* (Black Slaves in Bolivia – 1977)), and the wars of independence (*La vida cotidiana en La Paz durante la guerra de Independencia* (Daily life in La Paz during the Independence Wars – 1975)).

XIMENA MEDINACELI

cri-cri   *see*   Gabilondo Soler, Francisco

Crichlow, Kenwyn

b. 1957, Trinidad

Arts administrator

The Creative Arts Centre of the **University of the West Indies** was established by the English Department in 1987 to encourage the study of Caribbean-oriented creative arts, including the theory and practice of art and design. Crichlow is Director of the Creative Arts Department at the St Augustine campus, where the teaching programmes emphasize how historical and cultural processes influence contemporary artistic practice. In 1997 he supervised the introduction of the Visual Arts Special, a six-semester programme that combines artistic practices as diverse as drawing, textiles, video and ceramics, with cultural studies and research.

LORRAINE LEU

cricket

A famous English commentator (E.W. Swanton) once asserted that 'in the West Indies cricket is not a sport, it is life itself'. Hyperbole apart, cricket has certainly served as a metaphor for the changing relationship between the colonial power (Britain) and its erstwhile West Indian subjects. From another point of view, cricket (like boxing and athletics in the USA) has provided one of the few routes available for youngsters from the poorest classes of society to find success and economic security.

Cricket was introduced by the colonists, and was very largely played by them through the nineteenth century. The first club (St Anns) was founded in Barbados in 1806 – and that island has ever since provided a number of cricket 'greats' disproportionate to its tiny size. While English teams visited the Caribbean in the intervening years, the first West Indian team visited the UK only in 1900 – it included L.S. Constantine, father of Learie **Constantine**, the first authentic legend of the game. L.S. scored the first ever century by a West Indian in Britain – though had it not been for a last-minute public collection he would never have been able to afford the trip.

The first serious West Indian challenge to a visiting MCC team (though not a strong one) came in 1923 under George Challenor. Five years later, West Indies was admitted to the test circuit but played a very disappointing series – with the luminous exception of Learie Constantine, who was immediately recruited into the Northern Leagues in Britain. Something of a hero, he was nevertheless refused admission to a central London hotel in 1941 because he was black; he was later awarded damages – but he remained an exception to a racist rule.

The war suspended cricket tours, but the game continued in the British Caribbean colonies – and in that hothouse atmosphere a group of new stars emerged who created a sensation when they beat a visiting MCC team in 1950 and toured England with similar results later that year. Here the three Ws (Walcott, Weeks and **Worrell** – three magnificent young batsmen from Barbados) hit runs in enormous quantities, while two young spin bowlers – Ramadhin and Valentine – virtually won the tests by themselves and were lionized in a famous **calypso** of the time as 'those two little pals of mine/Ramadhin and Valentine'. In 1955 West Indies beat the Australians and the great Gary **Sobers** made his first international appearance. Two years later, his massive 365 beat Len Hutton's record, which had stood since 1938.

It cannot be mere accident that the pinnacle of West Indies cricket was reached under the first black captain of a West Indies team – Frank Worrell – on the eve of decolonization (see **decolonization and independence**). As C.L.R. **James** had suggested in his epoch-making collection of cricket commentaries, *Beyond a Boundary* (1963), the rise of the West Indies team marked the developing resistance to colonial domination – and the raucous celebrations that accompanied each win at home and in Britain can have left little doubt of that. The racial confrontations at test matches between West Indies and England, in England in the early 1960s, gave additional testimony.

Half a million Australians acclaimed the departing West Indians after the 1960–1 tour; and the 1964–5 Australia–West Indies series fielded probably the two strongest ever elevens in the game. By now West Indian professionals were playing in Australia and the UK, and their dominance of the game was everywhere acknowledged. The arrival of Kerry Packer and the final collapse of the myth of amateurism, together with the unashamed commercialization of the game in its form and its

organization, wrought havoc in the West Indies and elsewhere. And yet Clive Lloyd's test team of the early 1980s was one of the most successful West Indian teams ever. He was succeeded by Viv **Richards**, whose contribution to the game would be hard to overestimate and who in his first (1985) series achieved a 5–0 defeat of England – evidence if such were needed of the decline of a once powerful imperialism.

In the 1990s the balance has shifted; West Indies has ceased to be the power it once was, even though it has also produced Brian **Lara**, widely acknowledged as the greatest batsman of all time. But it is hard to imagine that even now in Barbados, in the suburbs of Kingston, Jamaica or on one of the smaller islands some new Richards or Lara is not already hitting a ball with his eyes on the prize.

Further reading

Birbalsingh, F. (1988) *The Rise of West Indian Cricket: From Colony to Nation*, St John's, Antigua: Hansib.

James, C.L.R. (1963) *Beyond a Boundary*, London: Serpent's Tail.

Manley, M. (1988) *A History of West Indian Cricket*, London: André Deutsch Ltd.

Nicole, C. (1957) *West Indies Cricket*, London: Phoenix Sports Books.

MIKE GONZALEZ

crime fiction

The dominant paradigms of the crime fiction genre are embedded in British and US literary history and bear the ideological imprint of their respective social contexts. The puzzle-solving British whodunit developed in the nineteenth century as a formula that displays aberrant criminal behavior against the framework of a basically stable and secure society. The hard-boiled model which surfaced in the 1920s in the United States works, in contrast, to expose a violent and corrupt society in which crime is all-pervasive and institutions are distrusted. Works of both types were translated and widely distributed in Latin America, where writers also began to appropriate the genre as early as the late nineteenth century. The centres of crime fiction writing in Latin America are Argentina, Brazil, Cuba and Mexico, although important examples have been produced elsewhere including Colombia, Peru and Chile.

Latin American crime fiction writers often produce works that deliberately undermine the conventions of the genre in order to raise fundamental questions about truth, political order and economic justice. One of the best-known detective tales from Latin America, 'La muerte y la brújula' (Death and the Compass) (1942) by Argentine author Jorge Luis **Borges**, is a metaphysical reflection on time and space. The solution-oriented aim of the genre breaks down in this anti-detective story that locates the coordinates of the puzzle in a universe characterized by paradox and limitlessness. Another challenge to the ordering principle of conventional crime fiction was developed by Argentine authors of the 1970s such as Ricardo **Piglia**, who adopted the hard-boiled model to comment on institutionalized violence and injustice. A satirical mode is also common throughout Latin American crime fiction, where examples can be found even in the otherwise generally didactic works that have flourished in post-revolutionary Cuba.

The association of crime fiction with popular or 'low' culture is apparent in the ambivalence with which the Latin American literary elite has regarded the genre, especially the hard-boiled school of detective fiction. Crime fiction has consequently developed in some contexts, especially Argentina, as a site where the territories of high and low culture, and the social identities attached to them, are explored and negotiated. Recent decades have seen a shift in the way in which the genre marks boundaries between elite and popular culture, in part because of a developing market abroad for crime fiction by Latin American authors. Mexico's Paco Ignacio **Taibo** II and Brazil's Rubem **Fonseca** are two writers whose works have been translated and distributed abroad, thus reversing the pattern of virtually exclusive importation of texts.

Further reading

Lafforgue, J. and Rivera, J.B. (eds) (1977) *Asesinos de papel*, Buenos Aires: Calicanto.

Medeiros e Albuquerque, P. de (1979) *O mundo emocionante do romance policial*, Rio de Janeiro: Francisco Alves.

Nogueras, L. (1982) *Por la novela policial*, Havana: Ediciones Unión.

Simpson, A. (1990) *Detective Fiction from Latin America*, Rutherford, NJ: Fairleigh Dickinson University Press.

AMELIA SIMPSON

criollismo

A term derived from *criollo* (**creole**), it is used to refer to a regionalist tendency in Spanish American writing in the first decades of the twentieth century (see **regionalismo**), often associated with certain currents of *modernismo* (see **modernismo, Spanish American**) (though some claim that the gauchesque poem *Martín Fierro* of 1872–9 and the serial novels of Eduardo Gutiérrez as earlier examples of the tendency, because of their affirmation of local culture). Used in 1902 by Ernesto Quesada in the polemical essay *El criollismo en la literatura argentina* (*Criollismo* in Argentine Literature), it was used in the following decades as a term to designate literature that represented the local or national culture (as opposed to that of the immigrant masses); it is employed in that way by **Borges** in his essays of the 1920s, particularly in those of *El tamaño de mi esperanza* (The Shape of My Hope) (1926). In Uruguay and southern Brazil, the same tendency is often called *nativismo*. *Criollismo* was also a dominant tendency in Colombian and Venezuelan literature in the same period. The term is notable for its ambiguities, however, since it is often used interchangeably with **arielismo** and **mundonovismo**, and to designate the so-called novela de la tierra (see **novel**).

DANIEL BALDERSTON

criollo

The name *criollo* describes people descended from those who moved from the Old World to the New World. In colonial Brazil, locally born black people were called *crioulo*; in the Spanish colonies the term *criollo* distinguished Spaniards from those born in the American continent. In the French and English Caribbean *créole* referred to anyone of European ancestry, and was later applied to those groups who had become the majority (usually of African origin) and who had assimilated the colonial language and culture. Today, *créole* is freely used as a synonym of Caribbean. Historically, *criollos* and *créoles* retained colonial privileges in the newly independent nations, and today these groups usually enjoy cultural and economic monopoly.

See also: Creole

LUIS ESPARZA

Crisis

Crisis is a ground-breaking literary magazine noted for its breadth and unique wealth of contributors. Subtitled 'Arts and Literature in the Crisis', and with a strong interest in the visual arts, *Crisis* was launched in Buenos Aires in May 1973, during Argentina's short-lived revolutionary, constitutional Peronist government. Well-funded by industrialist Federico Manuel Vogelius and his wife Ana Amalia Ruccio, its first editor was Uruguayan writer Eduardo **Galeano**. In May 1975, editor Carlos Villar Araujo was abducted by the police for two days. A subsequent wave of anonymous threats after the 1976 military *coup* prompted the publishers to cease publication after the fortieth issue.

ANDREW GRAHAM-YOOLL

Cristero War

The War for Christ – the Cristiada – erupted in Mexico in 1927 over the anticlerical Articles 3 and 130 of the Constitution of 1917. The fiercely anticlerical President Calles closed church schools and expelled foreign priests. Tension rose with the passing of the Calles Law (1926), requiring the registration of all priests. When the Church suspended masses, bands of poor and unorganized peasants armed themselves at the rallying cry of *¡Viva Cristo Rey!* ('Long Live Christ the King!'). The brutal war ended in 1929 with a compromise negotiated by US Ambassador Morrow. The Cristero War forms the background of Juan **Rulfo**'s *Pedro Páramo* and Elena **Garro**'s *Los recuerdos del porvenir*.

SOFÍA DE LA CALLE

Cristi, Carla

b. *c.* 1935, Chile

Actress

Cristi joined the **ICTUS** group from the Teatro de la Universidad Católica. Her most important roles were in *El cepillo de dientes* (The Toothbrush) (1961), *El velero en la botella* (The Ship in the Bottle) (1962) and *Réquiem para un girasol* (Requiem for a Sunflower) (1961), all by Jorge **Díaz**, and Egon **Wolff**'s *Flores de papel* (Paper Flowers) (1971). In 1973 she went into exile in France, where she worked in cinema with Raúl **Ruiz** and Valeria **Sarmiento**, before settling in Spain and returning to theatre and television work. She returned to Chile in 1982 and formed her own company, the Teatro del Alma, which presented a range of new works.

CAROLA OYARZÚN

Criterio

The Catholic literary journal *Criterio* first appeared in 1928, when literature was an area of growing cultural activity around the debates between Boedo and Florida (see **Boedo vs Florida**), and the publication of serial novels and magazines like **Nosotros**. *Criterio*'s most important period was between 1928 and 1930, when it was edited by Atilio Dell'Oro Maini; after that its influence in Argentine literary life declined. Its last issue, number 1535, appeared in November 1967.

SERGIO WOLF

Crítica

Crítica is an Argentine newspaper founded in 1913 by Natalio **Botana**. It was the first paper to print various editions and to use rotogravure; it introduced cinema criticism, innovative headlines, a crime section and a colour supplement. By 1930 it had achieved the highest circulation of any Spanish-language newspaper, at 350,000 copies. Although it was destined for a mass audience, it included among its collaborators some of the outstanding figures in Argentine literature, including Jorge Luis **Borges**, Roberto **Arlt**, the brothers Enrique and Raúl **González Tuñón** and Homero **Manzi**. It interrupted publication during **Peronism**, then ceased in September 1963.

LIBERTAD BORDA

crónica (genre)

This term is used today to refer to a genre that emerged in the late 1960s throughout Latin America as an intermediate form between journalism and literature, and which explores the everyday life of the people, their culture and social conventions in the urban context. Its texts are characteristically short, designed to be published in newspapers and magazines, although they are later usually collected in book form. The term *crónica* also identifies a historiographic tradition that flourished in antiquity and the Middle Ages, in which historical events are narrated in chronological order. The historical element is still significant in the *crónica*, which not only registers the avatars of everyday life, but also manifests an explicit inclination to uncover the origins of the present and to rescue its forgotten memories. Today's *crónica* has its antecedents in the nineteenth-century *cuadro de costumbres* (see **costumbrismo**), a vignette in which urban characters and the everyday life of the nation are represented in their typicality, and in the *crónica modernista* from the turn of the century, where the *cronistas* – often poets such as Martí, Darío and Gutiérrez Nájera – mapped with literary sophistication the landscapes of the city and guided their readers through the good manners and taste defined by foreign, modern standards. The *crónica* –

influenced by the 'New Journalism' of the USA – can be characterized by the central position of its writer as the source who narrates the facts, often appearing as a character in the text as well; by the narrativization and fictionalization of the events it portrays, thus creating a certain ambiguity between reality and fiction; by its descriptive intention (it recreates the atmosphere in which particular events have taken place); and by the significant presence of orality, both in the writer's language, which is close to spoken language, and in the direct speech of its characters. It is moreover a stylised text through which the *cronistas* address their readers in an individual and recognizable voice. The *crónica* assumes its purpose to be to express the contemporary culture of the city in its manifold manifestations. It often draws its imagery from popular and mass culture, which it incorporates in its language and form, and from emerging social movements. This is why it can be considered, in its widest sense, a report from the unofficial culture, appropriating and revealing the energy and creativity of the social forces from below and deriding and exposing, at the same time, the hypocrisy of political life and the social conventions of the elite and the middle classes. The *crónica* has developed strongly in Mexico, thanks in part to the efforts of its most renowned *cronista*, Carlos **Monsiváis**, who as well as producing a contemporary history of Mexican life in his several volumes of *crónicas*, has critically analysed the genre and anthologized it. Other *cronistas* include Pedro **Lemebel** in Chile and Jorge Martillo Montserrate in Ecuador. There is a related journalistic genre in Brazil, the *crónica*. Famous practitioners in recent decades include Carlos Drummond de Andrade and Clarice **Lispector**.

Further reading

Martillo Monserrate, J. (1999) *La bohemia en Guayaquil y otras historias crónicas*, Guayaquil: Archivo Histórico del Guayas.

Monsiváis, C. (1997) *Mexican Postcards*, ed. and trans. J. Kraniauskas, London: Verso

—— (1978) *A ustedes les consta. Antología de la crónica en México*, México D.F.: Era.

—— (1976) *Amor perdido*, México D.F.: Era.

Moser, G.M. (1971). '"The crônica": A new genre

in Brazilian literature', *Studies in Short Fiction* 8(1): 217–29.

(1980 and 1981) *O melhor da crônica Brasileira*, 2 vols, Rio de Janeiro: José Olympio Editora.

ESPERANZA BIELSA

Crónica (newspaper)

Crónica is a newspaper founded in Argentina in 1963 by Héctor Ricardo García. With an average sale of 500,000 across its three editions (its circulation occasionally reached a million) this tabloid is characterized by its unconventional headlines, its direct language, the importance it gives to crime reporting and its extensive use of photography. *Crónica* boasted that it never editorialized, though its detractors accuse it of 'sensationalism'. García, a newspaper proprietor who began his career as a photojournalist, was also at different times the owner of the journal *Así*, television channels 11 and 2 and the Uruguayan radio station *Radio Colonia*. In 1994 he created the cable news channel *Crónica TV*.

LIBERTAD BORDA

cross-dressing

The practice of cross-dressing (mainly of men dressed as women) spans a wide variety of contexts in Latin America, and is not necessarily linked with homosexual activity. In Mexico, it can be traced to pre-Hispanic ritual dances, and is to be found today in some indigenous communities of Oaxaca, especially in Juchitán, where female-identified men are known as *mushes*. The practice is widespread during carnivals (see **carnival**) across the continent, when role-reversals of many kinds take place.

During the late nineteenth and early twentieth centuries, cross-dressing as a cabaret-like spectacle became popular through European influences. Cross-dressing for the sake of parody was also common in *carpa* performances. The practice was known at first as *transformismo* until the 1960s, when the word *travesti* appeared. Some popular transvestites in the Mexican night-club scene have been

'Shalimar', during the 1950s, and 'Francis' (who is also transsexual) from the 1970s onwards. Typically, *travestis* impersonate and lip-synch to Mexican, Spanish and US singers, but may also have their own personas.

Throughout Latin America, many working-class transvestites practise prostitution, which has made them targets of systematic repression and violence. In Brazil and Mexico, waves of murders have periodically swept the transvestite communities. For example, in the early 1990s over twenty murders were reported in Chiapas, Mexico. To defend their rights, Mexican transvestites have begun to organize in groups such as EON Inteligencia Transgenérica.

In literature and film, transvestism was famously addressed in José **Donoso**'s 1966 novel *El **lugar sin límites*** (Hell Has No Limits) and its 1977 celluloid version by Arturo **Ripstein**. In the film, actor Roberto Cobo, himself a sometime drag performer, did a splendid rendering of the character of La Manuela. Chilean essayist Pedro **Lemebel** has written eloquently about transvestite prostitutes. In theatre, cross-dressing permeates Carlos **Fuentes**'s 1985 *Orquídeas a la luz de la luna* (Orchids by the Light of the Moon), where two men impersonate María **Félix** and Dolores **Del Rio**. Jesús **González Dávila**'s 1985 play *De la calle* (From the Street) features a climactic scene where a woman in drag is revealed to be the protagonist's father. Performers Tito **Vasconcelos** and Jesusa **Rodríguez** have prominently featured cross-dressing in their shows since the 1980s. Rodríguez, for example, is best known for her impersonation of former Mexican president Carlos **Salinas de Gortari**. Mexican television has likewise had its share of cross-dressing with performers like Manuel 'Loco' Valdés, Los Polivoces and 'Bibi' Gaytán.

ANTONIO PRIETO-STAMBAUGH

Crusoob

The Crusoob of Quintana Roo state, Mexico, are descendants of insurgent Maya who carried out a briefly successful attempt to reestablish ethnic autonomy against Yucatecans of European descent and the Federal Government during the Caste War

(1847–1901). Driven to war, the Crusoob united under a new folk-catholic synthesis in which a 'speaking cross' representative of the True God played a preeminent role. The Crusoob lost their autonomy under concerted attack by the Díaz regime and were gradually integrated into the nation during the twentieth century through the construction of schools and roads, regularization of land tenure, and insertion into the global market system. This process has accelerated during the 1980s and 1990s, although conservatives remain faithful to the speaking cross and to cultural autonomy.

CHRISTOPHER VON NAGY

Cruz, Celia

b. 1921, Havana, Cuba

Singer

Generally considered the foremost female exponent of Afro-Caribbean music, Celia Cruz's career is a long series of successes. She was already recognized when, as a young singer, she recorded with the important group **Sonora Matancera** an impressive list of hits like 'Caramelo' (Candy), 'Mi cocodrilo verde' (My Green Crocodile),'Luna sobre Matanzas' (Moon over Matanzas), 'Yemayá' and others. After the triumph of the Cuban Revolution in 1959 (see **revolutions**) she went into exile and recorded albums with the major figures in the world of Latin **jazz** and **salsa** such as Tito **Puente**, Johnny **Pacheco**, Willie **Colón** and La Sonora Ponceña. She joined the legendary Fania All Stars, who presented her at each performance as 'the goddess of Latin music'; and indeed among her peers she is acknowledged as an unequalled singer and performer. In 1990, she was awarded an honorary doctorate by Yale University.

Cruz moved easily into the world of salsa, and the great power and extraordinary range of her voice allowed her to move effortlessly between the different salsa genres. In fact, many of her pre-1959 Cuban hits were rerecorded with salsa groups with great success. With Johnny Pacheco she made *Celia y Johnny* (1974) and *Tremendo Caché* (1975), with Willie Colón *Only They Could Have Made This Album*

(1977) and with Sonora Ponceña *Celia Cruz y la Sonora Ponceña* (1979). All are testimony to her vitality and intepretative skills. Only a woman as exceptional as Celia Cruz could have opened a path for herself in the male-dominated world of salsa.

Cruz's recordings cover the whole spectrum of Caribbean music. She was a pioneer in working with the materials and the imaginary of the different Afro-Caribbean belief systems, particularly La Regla de Ocha or **Santería**. Her album with La Sonora Matancera *Homenaje a los Santos* (Homage to the Saints) (1955) is exemplary in this sense. On the other hand, many of the songs she has recorded over the years speak of the specific experience of women and offer interesting anecdotes on the relations between the sexes. In the late 1990s she also began acting for television, appearing in **Televisa**'s *telenovela* (see **telenovelas**) *Valentina* (1994).

Further reading

Quintero Herencia, J.C. (1995) 'Notas para la salsa', *Nómada* 1 (April): 16–34.
Rondón, C.M. (1993) *Salsa*, London: Latin America Bureau.

JUAN CARLOS QUINTERO HERENCIA

Cruz-Diez, Carlos

b. 1923, Caracas, Venezuela

Painter and multimedia artist

Cruz-Diez is one of the most famous international exponents of **kinetic art**. Together with Jesús **Soto** and Alejandro **Otero**, he is seen to represent Venezuela's boom in kinetic art from the 1960s. Cruz-Diez trained in manual and applied arts in Caracas, and his first job was as artistic director for McCann-Ericson from 1946 to 1951. During this period he also worked as an illustrator for the *El Nacional* newspaper. In 1957 he set up his own industrial design workshop before moving to the Universidad Central of Venezuela. In 1960 he left for Paris, where he became one of the most successful artists associated with the famous Galerie

Denise René. Since then he has stayed in Paris, with regular visits to Venezuela. Cruz-Diez's first works from the mid-1950s are wall reliefs which are architectural projects for external walls. These works, in the visual language of **constructivism**, show an early interest in movement (many of the shapes can be moved), colour and geometry. In some of these early works, the surfaces are painted different colours on each side, so that they show different colours depending on the angle at which they are seen.

In 1959 he made the first of his *Physichromie* works, a generic title which was to apply to many of his subsequent paintings, with an elaborate numbering system to distinguish them. The *Physichromies* (a neologism from 'physical' and 'chromatic') are constructed in such a way that a slight protrusion of the serial forms creates an effect of optical and chromatic movement as the spectator walks past. Cruz-Diez's principal interest is in colour and in how reflected and refracted light can generate virtual colours and volumes. The same general principles apply to his other series called *Color aditivo* (Additive Colour) and *Inducción cromática* (Chromatic Induction). He has made many large-scale public works in the open air, electricity stations and airports. The theoretical basis for his works is explained in his 1989 book *Reflexión sobre el color*.

Further reading

Boulton, A. (1975) *Cruz-Diez*, Caracas: Ernesto Armitano.
Brett, G. (1968) *Kinetic Art*, London: Studio Vista.
Cruz-Diez, C. (1989) *Reflexión sobre el color*, Caracas: FabriArt.

GABRIEL PEREZ-BARREIRO

Cruz Martínez, Rogelia

b. 1942, Guatemala City; d. 1968, Guatemala City

Beauty queen

Rogelia Cruz Martínez was crowned Miss Guatemala of 1959–60 and Guatemalan representative at the Miss Universe pageant that year. She either joined the Fuerzas Armadas Rebeldes (FAR) or had a lover in the guerrilla organization. After death squad threats (see **death squads**), she was taken by force and found dead, naked and mutilated in a riverbed.

For Guatemalan writers, the sadism of Rogelia's murder is an example of the cruelty unleashed during the repression of the 1960s. Manuel José Arce dedicated his play *Delito, condena y ejecución de una gallina* (Crime, Punishment and Execution of a Hen) (1969) to her, and she is a character in Edwin Cifuentes' *Carnaval de sangre en mi ciudad* (Carnival of Blood in My City) (1968) and Arturo **Arias'** *Después de las bombas* (After the Bombs) (1990).

MARY JANE TREACY

CTC

The Confederación de Trabajadores de Cuba (Cuban Workers Confederation) was created at a national congress of workers organizations in January 1939. It drew together all sectoral interests and became an important ally of workers in struggle. In 1961, the second Congress of the 'revolutionary CTC' adopted a new name, the Central de Trabajadores de Cuba (CTC). Communist trade union leader Lázaro Peña was its general secretary. The CTC now organizes all unionized workers behind its central principle: to support, strengthen and defend the revolutionary State. In practice, the organization is subordinated to government decisions, and has no autonomous decision-making powers.

WILFREDO CANCIO ISLA

CTG (Centros de Tradicão Gaúcha) *see* gaúcho culture

Cuadernos Americanos

Cuadernos Americanos is one of the most prestigious of the cultural journals devoted to the the study of Latin America from a multidisciplinary perspective. Founded in Mexico in 1942, it has continued to appear ever since, maintaining its high circulation through the period of Cold War and globalization. Its first series (1942–86) was directed by Mexican economist Jesús Silva Herzog; from 1987 the editorship passed to philosopher Leopoldo **Zea** under the auspices of **UNAM**, Mexico's National University. The journal includes essays and critical studies of a broad range of Latin American issues – economic, political, cultural, social, philosophical, historical and critical, as well as some creative writing.

LILIANA WEINBERG

Cuadra, José de la

b. 1903, Guayaquil, Ecuador; d. 1941, Guayaquil

Writer

Cuadra was a distinguished writer of the **Guayaquil Group**. His 'montuvian novel' *Los Sangurimas* (The Sangurimas) (1934) is a ground-breaking work, an early example of **magical realism**. His early work focused on the loves, nostalgia and yearnings of the petit bourgeoisie of his native city. Later his writings concentrated on the urban marginal, the Indians and, principally, the inhabitants of the coast, the *montuvios*, a mixed race group about whom he wrote in *El montuvio ecuatoriano* (1937). He also wrote literary and sociological essays and biography. His major works are *Los monos enloquecidos* (Wild Monkeys) (1931), *Repisas* (Drawers) (1931) and *Horno* (Kiln) (1932).

HUMBERTO E. ROBLES

Cuadra, Pablo Antonio

b. 1912, Managua, Nicaragua

Writer

Director of several literary magazines, Cuadra began the review *Vanguardia* in 1930 with fellow Nicaraguan poet Octavio Rocha. He worked with José **Coronel Urtecho** on the post-Vanguardist review *La Reacción*. Although he was internationally educated and strongly influenced by French literature, his poetry stimulated modern Nicaraguan poets to search for that which is native to their own country, in a complementary stance to Rubén Darío's internationalism. Cuadra's Vanguardist poetry, especially that of *Poemas nicaragüenses* (Nicaraguan Poems) (1934), paints Nicaragua as a mythical birthplace of heroes (most notably the mariner Cifar) in danger of destruction due to outside invasion. The characterization of the pre-Columbian indigenous societies of his homeland as primitive, idyllic, pre-capitalist and pre-Fall paradises prefigured the imagery used by Ernesto **Cardenal** in his works at **Solentiname**. Aside from the obvious invasion of the Spanish conquerors, the occupation of the country by US Marines between 1926 and 1933 also figures prominently in his early work. He spent much time in the Nicaraguan countryside, and his knowledge of it is well used in his rich portrayals of the paradisical landscape.

Cuadra became a respected and established member of the Nicaraguan literary elite, and his service as longtime director of *La Prensa Literaria*, a literary supplement to the newspaper **La Prensa**, enabled several new poets to be introduced to the Nicaraguan reading public. He is considered the major influence in modern Nicaraguan poetry before Ernesto Cardenal. During the Somoza regime he was the *de facto* Minister of Culture. His opposition to the Sandinistas (see **Sandinista Revolution**) distanced him from his friends, particularly from Cardenal and Coronel Urtecho. In the post-Sandinista era, he was asked to run as a presidential candidate for the 1996 election, but declined the offer.

Further reading

Balladares, J. (1986) *Pablo Antonio Cuadra: La palabra y el tiempo, secuencia y estructura en su creación poética*, San José: Editorial Libro Libre.

White, S. (1993) *Modern Nicaraguan Poetry: Dialogues with France and the United States*, London and Toronto: Associated University Press.

DEREK PETREY AND ILEANA RODRÍGUEZ

Cuarón, Alfonso

b. 1962, Mexico City

Film-maker

One of a new generation of Mexican film talent (along with director Guillermo **del Toro** and actress Selma Hayek) who have made their début films in Mexico but have chosen to emigrate to Hollywood in pursuit of fame and glory (and bigger budgets), Cuarón became known with his first film, *Sólo con tu pareja* (Only with Your Partner) (1991), an edgy comedy about a Lothario who is misdiagnosed with **AIDS**. Although not released in the USA, it gained him entry into Hollywood, where he has subsequently directed two films, *A Little Princess* (1995) and *Great Expectations* (1998).

ANA M. LÓPEZ

Cuarteto Cedrón

Cuarteto Cedrón is a modern **tango** group formed in Buenos Aires in 1964 by composer and guitarist Juan Cedrón, viola player Miguel Praino and bandoneonist César Stroscio. It began performing in student halls and clubs. The group later became a quartet in the late sixties, and recorded five albums in Argentina, where they were based until 1974. Between 1974 and the group's disbanding in 1988, they recorded twelve discs in Paris. They were distinguished by their tango settings of a variety of poetic texts by, among others, Juan **Gelman**, Bertolt Brecht, Raúl **González Tuñón** and Julio Huaso.

ALFONSO PADILLA

Cuarteto Latinoamericano

A balance between contemporary Latin American music and traditional string quartet fare characterizes the repertoire of the Cuarteto Latinoamericano: recordings of music by Ravel and Dvořák sit alongside those of the complete quartet works of Silvestre **Revueltas**, and recordings of works by **Ginastera** and **Villa-Lobos**. The Quartet was founded in Mexico in 1981 by the three Bitrán brothers, Saúl (violin), Arón (violin) and Alvaro (cello), with violist Javier Montiel. It has toured worldwide, and taken up residences at Carnegie-Mellon University (USA), San Miguel de Allende Chamber Music Festival (Mexico) and the Pittsburgh Summerfest (USA).

SIMON WRIGHT

Cuarto Propio

Cuarto Propio Press was founded in 1984, during the **Pinochet** dictatorship in Chile, by women **intellectuals** opposed to the military government. Its name recalls Virginia Woolf's famous essay, 'A Room of One's Own'. Cuarto Propio created a channel for women from any social and economic class to write and publish, but it has also published a wide variety of poetry, fiction and criticism by male and female authors from Chile and other countries that question dominant ideologies and discourses. Cuarto Propio's stated purpose is to broaden cultural horizons in Chile by maintaining a non-commercial focus and publishing a multitude of viewpoints.

AMALIA PEREIRA

Cuatro Tablas

Cuatro Tablas is a Peruvian theatre group directed by Mario Delgado. The group began, in 1971, by presenting simple political theatre, but soon moved towards experimental work in the current of European innovators like Jerzy Grotowski and Eugenio Barba. Their later work maintained its social critique, but placed increasing emphasis on theatricality; sound, silence, new body movements, different uses of space and so on. Their successful appearance at international festivals in 1988 and 1989 facilitated contacts with major foreign directors as well as the renovation of Peruvian theatre. In 1986 Cuatro Tablas created a new centre. They have since visited the East in search of new directions, and have recently acquired new theatrical facilities.

ROSALINA PERALES

Cuba

The 'Pearl of the Antilles', Cuba – at 40,519 square miles – is the largest island of the archipelago of 1,600 islets and keys that constitutes the Republic of Cuba. Strategically positioned at the entrance to the Gulf of Mexico (forty-eight miles from Haiti, eighty-seven miles from Jamaica and ninety miles from the US), its strategic location and natural resources (fertile soil, rich mineral deposits, mild tropical climate and spectacular beaches) have awoken the envy of more than one foreign power. Its capital and largest city, Havana, sits on a broad bay flanked by the historic Morro castle and bordered by the sparkling Malecón seawall, traditionally a gathering spot for its citizens.

Discovered by Columbus in 1492, the colonizing Spaniards left a lasting imprint, decimating the indigenous Taino population and importing large numbers of African slaves to create a rich ethnic and cultural *mestizaje*. The contemporary population, estimated at 11,096,395 (1999) is 51 per cent mulatto, 37 per cent white, 11 per cent black and 1 per cent other. Spain also developed a spectacular **sugar** industry on the island, once the most mechanized in the world and producing more than two-thirds of the world's supply.

US interest in Cuba led it to attempt to purchase the island from Spain and, when that failed, to gain control by intervening in its war of independence. When Cuba was granted its independence from Spain in 1899, it was under US occupation. The Platt Amendment of 1901 gave the USA the right to oversee Cuba's international commitments, economy and internal affairs, and to establish a naval station at **Guantánamo** Bay.

The first governments of the Republic of Cuba set a pattern of graft, corruption, mis-administration, fiscal irresponsibility and social insensitivity – especially toward Afro-Cubans – that characterized Cuban politics until 1959. Indeed dictator Fulgencio **Batista**'s overthrow by a guerrilla army led by Fidel **Castro** in that year was as much the result of internal decay as the challenges of Castro's 26th of July Movement. Castro himself had been jailed after a failed attempt to take the Moncada barracks in 1953; his speech from the dock at his trial, *La historia me absolverá* (History Will Absolve Me), became a manifesto for the small group that landed on the island from Mexico (where Castro had gone after an amnesty) in December 1956 to initiate guerrilla war against Batista. When they took control on 1 January 1959, the group still numbered less than 1,000.

The 26th of July Movement had vague political plans, relatively insignificant support and totally untested governing skills, but they quickly forged a following among poor peasants, urban workers, the young and idealists of all classes and groups. The first stage of the new regime, between 1959 and 1963, was dominated by the progressive dissolution of capitalism, an erratic drift toward socialism and a growing economic dependence on the Soviet Union, especially after Castro proclaimed the Marxist–Leninist nature of the new revolutionary State. Hundreds of thousands of Cubans, especially the professionals and the wealthy, emigrated to the USA, Spain and other countries. The nationalization of US property and businesses provoked a retaliatory trade embargo by the US government, which continues in force in 2000, and an unsuccessful invasion by Cuban exiles at the Bay of Pigs in April 1961. The Soviet Union quickly became Cuba's major trading partner and its main source of funds and military supplies. From 1960 until 1991 the Soviet Union bought the major portion of the Cuban sugar crop, generally at a price above that of the free-world market and Soviet aid – loans, petroleum, armaments and technical advice – amounted to several billions of dollars annually.

It is tempting to separate Cuba's history and cultural life into pre- and post-revolutionary periods, for no other event in contemporary history has had a greater impact than the Cuban Revolution (see **revolutions**). In the 1960s and 1970s, this small nation was the epicentre of Latin American politics, as the example of Castro's guerrilla war echoed throughout the continent's revolutionary movements. The revolution also redefined the Cuban cultural sphere. However, the dividing line is not quite as clear as it may seem.

Cuba's location at the mouth of the Caribbean and its ethnic and racial mixing made Cuba a fertile musical melting pot, creating distinctive rhythms that have travelled world-wide. Perhaps the first autochthonous Cuban rhythm was the habanera; later came the **danzón**. The **son** and **bolero** arrived in Havana from the eastern province of Santiago de Cuba in the early 1900s via the great composers, Alberto Villalon and Sindo **Garay**, influenced by Pepe Sánchez who wrote the famous Tristezas (Sadnesses) in 1883. Among the best Cuban son-bolero composers were Orlando de la Rosa and Isolina Carrillo, authors of the sublime Dos gardenias. The typical sextets first arrived in Havana's high-society salons in the 1920s. The **Trío Matamoros** started their enduring career in 1925 in Santiago de Cuba, composing classics like Son de la loma (Song from the Hill) and Lágrimas negras (Black Tears). In the golden era of son, orchestras like Arcaño y sus Maravillas and La Sensación enlivened Havana parties playing danzones and charangas through the 1940s and 1950s. Enrique Jorrín composed the first **cha cha cha**, La engañadora, in 1950; Dámaso **Pérez Prado** the first mambo in 1952; and Beny **Moré** later innovated by combining the traditional son montumo with jazz. Los **Van Van**, the popular orchestra created by Juan **Formell** in 1970, is, in a sense, a direct descendant of the achievements of this great era, together with contemporary groups like **Irakere**, **NG La Banda** and El Médico de la Salsa.

Since the revolution, Cuba's many music schools have produced new generations of musicians and composers who have adapted Cuba's musical traditions into innovative forms like the Mozambique, developed by composer-singer Pello 'el *Afrokan*' to displace the popularity of rock and roll, then banned from Cuba. The *nueva trova*, which also emerged in the 1960s, modernized the troubadour style through *cantautores* (see **cantautor** like Silvio **Rodríguez** and Pablo **Milanés**, who incorporated political and popular messages into songs that reverberated within and outside Cuba.

Cuban Art Music composers and performers have also been important. In the 1920s Amadeo **Roldán** and Alejandro **García Caturla** – both members of the **Grupo de Renovación Musical** – were among the first to introduce Afro-Cuban rhythms and instruments into symphonic compositions. Ernesto **Lecuona**, the pianist-composer who founded the Havana Symphony Orchestra also made an outstanding contribution, as did, a generation later, composers Juan **Blanco**

and Leo **Brouwer** (who has done innovative film scoring).

The Cuban **avant-garde** awakening of the 1920s, including the notable work of Carlos **Enríquez**, complemented anthropologist Fernando **Ortiz**'s thesis that Afro-Cuban culture was the central aspect of Cuban culture. Their work evolved into an important modern movement in the 1940s, dubbed the Havana School, and comprising painters like René **Portocarrero**, Amelia **Peláez** and Mariano **Rodríguez**, whose work often featured abstract variations of typical Cuban architectural features like stained-glass windows and church façades. Wifredo **Lam** incorporated elements of **Santería** into his generally surrealist work (see **surrealism in Latin American art**), like his most famous painting, *La jungla* (1943). The triumph of the revolution strengthened the fine arts, with the foundation in 1962 of the National Art Schools. The faculty of the Sculpture and Painting School (brilliantly designed in what has been called an exotic 'pre-postmodern' style by Ricardo Porro) included important figures like Raúl **Martínez** and Antonia **Eiriz**. Among the most notable contemporary Cuban artists are Tomás **Sánchez**, Manuel **Mendive** and Nelson Domínguez. Young artists like José **Bedia**, Kicho and Flavio Garciandia have also forged a new avant-garde path.

Cuba's many galleries, art museums and community cultural centres include the National Museum of Fine Arts and the Haydée Santamaría Gallery at the **Casa de las Américas**. Until the 1990s, the Ministry of Culture provided most of the materials and also guaranteed jobs to graduates of the Instituto Superior de Arte. Contemporary Cuban painters work in many genres, designing fabrics (called by the trade name Telarte), and movie and theatre sets. Cuban posters for films, books, cultural events and community campaigns have become a major cultural export (see **poster art**). Economic difficulties since the 1990s, however, have led many artists to seek other means of survival, including the creation of non-governmental co-operatives to promote their work to tourists and abroad.

Before the revolution, photography was associated more with news and social reporting than with art: the archives of the newsweekly *Bohemia* and of **Diario de la marina** contain a magnificent visual catalogue of Cuban life captured by photographers like Constantino **Arias**. With the revolution came a new group of photographers, among them Alberto Díaz (**Korda**), whose photograph of Che, '*Guerrillero heróico*' (Heroic Guerrilla), is one of the most reprinted in the history of world photography. Other notable contemporary photographers are 'Marucha', 'Mayito' and Roberto Salas.

In literature, Cuba's achievements have been great, yet this was one of the cultural spheres most affected by the revolution. A modern avant-garde movement began with the formation of the **Grupo Minorista** in 1923 and their journal, **Revista de avance**. Two decades later, the poet José **Lezama Lima** founded the enormously important journal **Orígenes**. The novelist Alejo **Carpentier** is noted not only for his fiction but also for coining the critical term '*lo* **real maravilloso**', while Nicolás **Guillén**, doyen of the **négritude** movement, and José **Tallet** were both activist poets. After the revolution, **Lunes de revolución**, a newspaper cultural supplement, specialized in publishing writing that reflected social issues while simultaneously rejecting any explicit political affiliation; its sponsorship of the short film *PM* in 1960 produced a famous confrontation with the government over the relationship between artists and the State. The result was Castro's famous definition in **Palabras a los intelectuales** (Words to Intellectuals) (1961) – 'Within the Revolution everything; against it, nothing.' Although ambivalent, in practice this generated a series of direct and implicit acts of censorship; *Lunes* was permanently closed and writers began to face government intolerance of potentially non-revolutionary ideas in literature. Although the works of many notable writers span the pre- and post-revolutionary periods – Emilio **Ballagas**, Antón **Arrufat**, Eliseo **Diego** (awarded the Juan Rulfo prize for his life's work), Cintio **Vitier** – many either left Cuba – Guillermo **Cabrera Infante**, Severo **Sarduy**, Jesús **Díaz**, Reinaldo **Arenas** – or have been silenced internally (Virgilio **Piñera**, for example). Many new literary magazines were established by the revolution and the National Union of Cuban Writers and Artists (**UNEAC**), but literature remains one of the most scrutinized

cultural activities as the 1971 **Padilla** affair clearly showed. Others, however, have continued to write prolifically, including Roberto **Fernández Retamar**, Gastón **Baquero**, Nancy **Morejón**, Miguel **Barnet** and Senel **Paz**.

Although there had been some eighty or so films produced before the revolution, no stable industry had developed and movie audiences primarily watched Hollywood imports. The national cinema began to emerge in 1960 after the establishment of the film institute **ICAIC**, controlled by young filmmakers like Tomás **Gutiérrez Alea** and Julio **García Espinosa**. In addition to producing key films like **Memorias del subdesarrollo** (Memories of Underdevelopment) (Gutiérrez Alea, 1968), **Lucía** (Humberto **Solas**, 1968) and the innovative **documentary** work of Santiago **Alvarez**, ICAIC also published the magazine **Cine cubano**, established a cinematheque (see **cinematheques**) and established innovative distribution and exhibition practices like the **cine móvil** programme. The aesthetic innovations and stability of Cuban cinema made it an important cornerstone of the **New Latin American Cinema** of the 1960s and 1970s. Other important figures of Cuban cinema are Sergio **Giral**, Pastor **Vega**, Sara **Gómez**, Manuel Octavio **Gómez**, Fernando **Pérez** and Juan Carlos **Tabio** (who collaborated with the already ailing Gutiérrez Alea for the internationally successful **Fresa y chocolate** (Strawberry and Chocolate) (1993)).

Although dormant in the early twentieth century, Cuban theatre boomed from the 1940s; many small theatres were opened and new writers like Piñera, Arrufat, Abelardo **Estorino** and José **Triana** appeared. The revolution also stimulated a lively popular theatre movement, which produced peripatetic theatrical troupes like the **Grupo Escambray**. The Cuban National Ballet, directed by prima ballerina and choreographer Alicia **Alonso**, incorporated Afro-Cuban folklore, rhythms and movements into its repertoire and trained a generation of dancers. In sport, the revolutionary period has produced world-class sportspeople like Teófilo **Stevenson**, Alberto **Juantorena** and Ana Fidelia **Quirot**.

Old Havana, declared a World Heritage Site by UNESCO (see **World Heritage Sites**), houses Spanish Colonial buildings (castles, churches, houses and fortresses) as well as world-class art deco structures. Beyond them, however, sit the now widely discredited Soviet prefab housing of the 1970s. By the 1990s, much of Cuba's infrastructure was crumbling, and many historic buildings were collapsing through neglect; renovation has centred on Old Havana, under the guidance of city historian Eusebio **Leal**. The area is, of course, a major attraction for tourists and many of Old Havana's best houses are being converted into hotels and offices.

With aid from the Soviet Union being cut by $3.1 billion a year since 1990, Cuba has had to rely heavily on tourists (see **tourism**) attracted by Old Havana, beach resorts like Varadero and Cayo Largo, **sex tourism** and Cuba's famous hedonistic pleasures like **cigars** and fancy **rum** cocktails (daiquiris, and *mojitos*). In 1999, Cuba attracted about 1.4 million tourists, mostly from Europe and Canada. When – and if – the embargo ends for Americans, the Cubans expect tourism to increase tenfold. Cuba has authorized residents to open family-run restaurants – *paladares* – and to rent out rooms in their homes. The *jineteras* (see **jinetera**) who prostitute themselves only in dollars are also another local innovation resulting from the emphasis on tourism.

Tourism and the circulation of dollars are producing profound changes in Cuban life in the late 1990s. Hotels are multiplying and advertising billboards – absent since the early 1960s – are beginning to appear. Government-run fast-food restaurants like El Rápido are starting to appear and Cuba's first American-style indoor mall has just opened, together with the first Benetton's.

Further reading

Chanan, M. (1985) *The Cuban Image: Cinema and Cultural Politics in Cuba*, London: BFI.
Pérez, L.A. (1999) *On Becoming Cuban: Identity, Nationality and Culture*, Durham: Duke University Press.
Schwartz, R. (1997). *Pleasure Island: Tourism and Temptation in Cuba*, University of Nebraska Press.

Simons, G.L. (1996) *Cuba from Conquistador to Castro*, New York: St Martin's Press.
Szulc, T. (1986) *Fidel: A Critical Portrait*, New York: Morrow.

ANA M. LÓPEZ

Cubillas Arizaga, Teófilo Juan

b. 1949, Puente de Piedra, Peru

Soccer player

A player of outstanding technique and a great play organizer, Cubillas was nicknamed 'El Nene' (the Kid) because of his childlike face. During his professional career (1964 to 1987) he played for clubs in Switzerland, Portugal and the USA, but is most closely associated with Alianza Lima, the only Peruvian club he played for and with which he finished his career. He played eighty times for his country between 1968 and 1982, taking part in three World Cup final rounds (1970, 1978, 1982) and scoring twenty-six international goals. Although a midfielder, he netted 268 goals in 469 career league games and was voted South American Player of the Year in 1972.

ERIC WEIL

cueca

Cueca is a musical genre and dance of the Andean region. It is assumed to derive from the zamacueca, originating in Peru at the beginning of the nineteenth century. The zamacueca was also the source of the **marinera** (Peru), the cueca (Chile but also Argentina and Bolivia) and the **zamba** (Argentina, Uruguay). The choreography of the dance rehearses the man's attempt to seduce his partner. The texts are festive or picaresque, but they sometimes also address historical and social themes. In Chile it is considered to be the national dance; there are at least ten different versions.

ALFONSO PADILLA

Cuentos fríos

Cuentos fríos (Cold Tales) (1956) is Virgilio **Piñera**'s most important collection of short stories, but was reprinted only once in Cuba (1964), undoubtedly because of the marginalization suffered by Piñera after the Cuban Revolution (see **revolutions**). The stories are set in a no-man's land, an ill-disguised mirror of society with systems of regimentation and repression imposed by self and others. In Piñera's world there is no meat in the city, so its inhabitants cut fillets from their own flesh; a woman's wedding album becomes an event dislocating notions of time and space. In Piñera's universe, the absurd collides with absolute logic.

JOSÉ QUIROGA

Cuestionario

A political monthly with strong cultural content, *Cuestionario*'s first issue appeared in May 1973. Published in Buenos Aires by Rodolfo **Terragno**, a lawyer, *Cuestionario* achieved a circulation of 30,000 and came under pressure from all quarters. Its last issue came out in July 1976 and was then closed by Terragno, who did not wish to submit to censorship by the military dictatorship and refused to soften his criticism of the military authorities. Terragno went into exile in Venezuela in August 1976, where he co-founded *El Diario de Caracas*.

ANDREW GRAHAM-YOOLL

Cueva, Agustín

b. 1937, Ibarra, Ecuador; d. 1995, Quito, Ecuador

Sociologist and critic

The most important Ecuadorean sociologist of his generation, Cueva's writings transcended the borders of his country. Trained in France, he held distinguished academic posts in Ecuador, Chile and Mexico. A Marxist, his historical view of the world can be discerned in *Entre la ira y la esperanza* (Between Wrath and Hope) (1967) and *El proceso de dominación política en Ecuador* (The Exercise of Political Power in Ecuador) (1972). Cueva wrote important essays on José de la **Cuadra**, Gabriel **García Márquez**, Jorge **Icaza** and Pablo **Palacio**, and on the cultural activities of the members of his generation.

HUMBERTO E. ROBLES

Cuevas, José Luis

b. 1934, Mexico City

Draughtsman, printmaker and painter

Cuevas was born in Mexico City and began to draw from a very young age. He is self-taught, and his first lessons were improvised by copying scenes seen from his window. In his autobiography, Cuevas describes being impressed by some of the most sordid scenes he saw, such as the blood and pus seeping from a man's open wound. His development as an artist was incredibly fast, and his first exhibition in Mexico City was at the age of fourteen. At this time, the art scene was completely dominated by Mexican **muralism** and by the 'tres grandes' (three greats), Diego **Rivera**, José Clemente **Orozco** and David Alfaro **Siqueiros**. Cuevas reacted strongly against this type of heroic and assertive art, preferring to concentrate on the more sardonic and critical aspects of contemporary Mexico. In 1953 he entered into open debate with the muralists by publishing an article called 'La cortina del nopal' (The Cactus Curtain) in which he attacked the oppressive domination of muralism. Inspired by this stand, a group was founded in 1960 called Nueva Presencia (New Presence) to support the claim for greater individual freedom in art. Cuevas's visual style draws on a long tradition of satirical and humorous art, taking in caricature, cartoons, Goya, Daumier and Picasso. Cuevas has continued to write throughout his life, often using the same sharp humour and irreverent wit which characterizes his graphic work. His art was influential on several generations of Latin American artists looking for a way to portray their reality. In 1965, the influential Argentinian critic Marta **Traba** placed Cuevas alongside Francis Bacon, Willem de Kooning and Dubuffet in her book *Los cuatro monstruos cardinales* (The Four Cardinal Monsters).

Further reading

Cuevas, J.L. (1965) *Cuevas por Cuevas*, Mexico City: Ediciones Era.

—— (1982) *Les obsessions noires de José Luis Cuevas*, Paris: Galilée.

Gómez Sicre, J. (1978), *José Luis Cuevas*, Washington, DC: Museum of Modern Art of Latin America.

GABRIEL PEREZ-BARREIRO

Cuffy (Kofi) Statue

Kofi, a cooper of Akan origin, and Guyanese hero, led the bloody Berbice Slave Revolt against the Dutch colonists in the Berbice region of Guyana during the mid-1760s. Ethnic rivalry between the slaves almost undermined the success of the rebellion. After negotiating with the Dutch and losing the confidence of his fellow leaders, Kofi killed himself; shortly thereafter, the leaders of free Berbice were overcome by the Dutch.

The dictatorship of Forbes **Burnham** erected in the early 1980s a well-known statue of the hero (by Phillip Moore), which, from a particular angle, shows an act of standing, almost euphoric, masturbation. This was unintentional, but it has become for many Guyanese a symbol of Burnham's murderous rule.

KEITH JARDIM

culebrón

Meaning 'a long snake', *culebrón* is the name popularly given to television soap operas in Venezuela because of their length and the conflictive nature of their plots. From the late 1950s they became the focus of every evening's television. Despite the impact of the cinema and other mass media, the *culebrón* remained locked in a style and narrative form derived from its origins in radio serials (***radionovelas***), to which it continued to owe a great deal. Among the most famous

culebrones of the 1960s were *Lucecita* and *Esmeralda*. In the mid-1970s the genre underwent radical changes under the pen of new writers and directors like José Ignacio **Cabrujas**, Salvador **Garmendia** and Román **Chalbaud**; *La señora de Cárdenas* (Mrs Cardenas), *La hija de Juan Crespo* (Juan Crespo's daughter) and *La dueña* (The Landlady) belong to the new era.

JORGE ROMERO LEÓN

Cultura *see* Revista Cultura

cultural imperialism *see* cultural theory

cultural nationalism

Cultural nationalism refers to those aspects of nation-building not directly identified with the official apparatus of the state or which originate more autochtonously from below. However, official state nationalism has always used these social practices in the construction of national identity. Thus, cultural nationalism can be found in classical music or in popular rock songs, in visual arts or in national sports. It is always present when the national element is associated with cultural phenomena, those social and cultural practices that are more than local, but not universal.

In general, nationalism as theory and practice has taken quite specific forms in Latin America. Using concepts and sentiments normally identified as the basis of nationalism – cultural traditions, language, common descent, territory, historical memory, and so on – is perhaps even more problematic in Latin America than in other regions. Herder's definitions of nationalism, for example, which rest on the uniqueness and intrinsic historical value of each national culture, never applied in the region. Thus the modern model for political community, the nation, had to be invented from almost nothing in the new republics of Latin America during the nineteenth century. The basic problem for Latin American nation-building was the vast cultural and ethnic heterogeneity of each independent and, in many cases, artificial state. Finding the common descent or original national language was impossible, not least because the leading **creole** elites in power after independence never accepted or appreciated the existing pre-Columbian cultural heritage, or any other non-European cultural presence, as important actors in national culture.

Cultural nationalism has always been used as an auxiliary force for political patriotism. The existing state had to be justified by the national culture; the basic problem was to find it. One of the most famous examples of Latin American cultural 'proto-nationalism' is the cult of the Virgin of Guadalupe (see **Virgins, miraculous**) in Mexico, a religious tradition that has become a central unifying factor of Mexicanness. Later indigenous folklore was used in cultural nation-building all over the continent. The most famous case comes again from Mexico, where the post-revolutionary cultural politics of the 1920s strongly emphasized the role of regional indigenous cultures, as for example in Diego **Rivera**'s murals. Although this aspect of cultural nationalism was obvious in most Latin American countries, it was more significant in those nations that were able to identify with great civilizations or 'states' of the pre-Columbian past. Today, many Peruvians or Mexicans proudly recognize that they are Inca or Aztec descendants.

Most Latin American countries, however, do not have such a historically glorified ancient past. They have found their cultural particularity in different syncretized traditions (see **syncretism**). Afro-Caribbean music is without doubt one basic element of cultural and national identity for all the Caribbean states: to think of Jamaica without **reggae** or Cuba without **son** is almost impossible. We can easily add to this musical list Brazilian **samba**, Argentine **tango**, Mexican rancheras (see **canción ranchera**), Colombian cumbias (see **cumbia**) and so on. Thus, popular culture is always clearly linked to cultural nationalism.

A more precise description of the evolution of cultural nationalism in Latin America requires an examination of different historical phases. The official nationalism of the end of the nineteenth century was perhaps the first conscious effort to develop cultural nationalism. In most countries, this meant the Eurocentric nationalism of the upper (white) classes. Many states sent their official historians to find 'national documents' in European archives, each state produced its national dictionary, based on regional Spanish vocabulary ('diccionario de costarriqueñismos', 'diccionario de colombianismos', and so on), and the state founded national libraries, archives, museums and national theatres, and even discovered national historical heroes. Even such literary styles as *costumbrismo*, describing local customs and beliefs, served this kind of purpose.

At the beginning of this century the attack against positivism, started by Arielist intellectuals, led to a new kind of nationalism in which Hispanic spiritual values were presented as the real strength of Latin American culture. Later, these quite Eurocentric ideas turned into more political interpretations in the form of so-called anti-imperialist nationalism. Locating anti-imperialism in the category of nationalism is problematic because, from the beginning, that kind of nationalism argued for continental Latin American unity. Nevertheless, concepts like José **Vasconcelos**'s 'Raza cósmica' (Cosmic Race), which emphasized the importance of Latin American cultural mixture and *mestizaje*, were important also for national cultural identity and self-consciousness in most countries of the continent.

From the 1920s on, nationalism's cultural aspects became more diversified because of the growing influence of the mass media and expanding literacy. The role of national press (see **press and mass media**), movies, **radio** and so on created new national symbols. These were also used by populist movements like **Peronism** in Argentina or Aprismo in Peru. After the Cuban Revolution (see **revolutions**), cultural nationalism acquired yet more new dimensions, when culture was seen as an important ideological factor in developing an emancipatory national identity. Different liberation movements adopted these ideas and, as in Cuba, the new cultural nationalism was also part of the official state culture in Sandinista Nicaragua (see **Sandinista Revolution**).

To be able to define cultural nationalism in Latin America today, it is necessary to look not only at the narrow interpretations of 'high' culture (national art, literature, architecture, theatre, cinema and so on), but also a wide range of different phenomena in a popular culture. In Brazil, for example, national **football** or local television soap operas (*telenovelas*) are certainly more important generators of cultural nationalism than Jorge **Amado**'s novels or the modern architecture of the country's capital, **Brasília**.

Further reading

Beverley, J. and Oviedo, J. (eds) (1993) *The Postmodernism Debate in Latin America*, Durham, NC: Duke University Press.

García Canclini, N. (1995) *Hybrid Cultures: Strategies for Entering and Leaving Modernity*, Minneapolis, MN: University of Minnesota Press.

Molina Jiménez, I. and Palmer, S. (1992), *Héroes al gusto y libros de moda: Sociedad y cambio cultural en Costa Rica,1750–1900*, San José: Porvenir-Plumsock Mesoamerican Studies.

JUSSI PAKKASVIRTA

cultural survival

Minority peoples strive for cultural survival as they try to maintain their ways of life in the face of modernization and the pressures of the state. Indigenous minorities are particularly at risk since they have been conquered by alien states that marginalize them and treat them as second class citizens. For them, cultural survival does not imply secession but rather an arrangement with the state that permits them to keep their traditions and exercise local control over their own affairs and resources. Cultural Survival is also the name of an organization in Cambridge, Massachusetts founded by professors from Harvard University in 1972 that assists indigenous peoples to defend their rights.

DAVID MAYBURY-LEWIS

cultural theory

The analysis of Latin American culture in the twentieth century has unfolded in the context of broader theoretical approaches to society and economy. In each of them, however, the central issue has been the dynamics of the historic colonial relationship, its continuities and transformations,

and the conflictive and contradictory relationship between local and regional cultural expressions and metropolitan – and later global – cultural forms. By the end of the twentieth century, that debate was transformed by a process of globalization that seemed to undermine the notion that the terrain of struggle was the encounter between peripheral nation and metropolitan power. For that relationship, in the view of Néstor **García Canclini**, Jesús **Martín-Barbero**, J.J. **Brunner** and Norbert Lechner, for example, was now transmuted into an *internal* contradiction expressed in **hybrid cultures** which were at once fields of conflict and forms of resolution.

But the significance of that concept only becomes clear by first reflecting back on the evolution through the century of the theory of culture. At the heart of the debate that runs from the mid-nineteenth century to the early twentieth is the formula 'civilization–barbarism'. Derived from the Argentina writer and politician Sarmiento's *Facundo* (1846), it returns in the early part of the twentieth century in works like **Gallegos**'s *Doña Bárbara*, where the question of cultural development is posed as a struggle between atavistic and instinctual forces on the one hand and the civilizational impulse enshrined in European culture in the other. What is absent here is any sense of the organic relationship between the two factors. But the conclusion drawn from this simplistic characterization was that Latin America should find its way into the civilizational circle (there was only one) and control the instinct to barbarism.

This represents, quite clearly, a cultural theory legitimating conquest and colonization, whether the Spanish or the European variant, as a 'civilizational project'. As the twentieth century dawned, and the US claimed hegemony in the region, the theory of 'manifest destiny' would come to occupy the same terrain. Resistance to the presence of the newest imperialism expressed itself in the struggle to create nation-states – the truncated project begun with independence a century earlier – with the economic capacity to endure. In the process – and it is the Mexican Revolution that marks the watershed – a new theory of culture emerges that can provide the cohesion required by the nation-building project. Its distinctness – its specificity – is derived from the long buried indigenous or subordinated cultures, from national traditions and popular expression, fused with the modernizing impulse. The result is a theory of **mestizaje**, in one of several variants. In Mexico it is articulated by José **Vasconcelos**'s notion of 'la raza cósmica'; in Cuba by the recuperation of black culture expressed in the pages of Havana's ***Diario de la Marina*** which are headed 'Ideales de una raza', where Nicolás **Guillén**, among others, published his first poetry of **negritude**. This notion of mestizaje or syncretism became a matter for long theoretical argument in the writing of Edourd **Glissant** and Aimé **Césaire** in the Francophone Caribbean and in the discussion of Fernando **Ortiz**'s notion of 'transculturation' later developed by Angel **Rama**. In Brazil the **antropofagia** movement embraced every area of art and culture in reversing the order of civilization – exoticizing the Brazilian interior as in the work of Sergio Buarque de **Holanda**. For the Andean countries, indigenismo fulfilled a similar function, though more radical in its identification with the oppressed and hitherto invisible **Quechua** and **Aymara** speaking communities of the sierra. How radical it was as a project was the issue of fierce polemic between José Carlos **Mariátegui**, for whom its implication was a form of socialist organization based on Inca collectivism, and **Haya de la Torre**, whose **APRA** organization claimed Indian heritage but represented a broader populism in its political strategies. In Argentina and the river Plate region, and to some extent in Chile, that emblematic role was filled by the disputed figure of the **gaucho** or the urban immigrant whose realities and desires were expressed in the **tango**. Yet by the 1930s, when Latin America was suffering the effects of the Depression, more radical identifications with the oppressed were current – and the identities of ethnicity or tradition were replaced by the experiences of class addressed in the **social realism** of Ecuador's **Guayaquil** school and the work of the Mexican **Muralists**, and in particular of Diego **Rivera**.

In the late 1930s the culture of nationhood arose again in a project for state-led development expressed by the **Estado Novo** in Brazil or the **Cárdenas** regime in Mexico. In both cases a resurgent national culture provided a symbolic language in which to legitimate the political project and represent it credibly to every section of the society. The unity of nation was expressed in an imagery transmitted in music – the **ranchera** in Mexico, the officialized **samba** of Brazil, the **trova** of Cuba – through the newly popular **radio** networks, and in the filmic spectacles of national unity exemplified by the Golden Age of Mexican cinema and the musical extravaganzas of Carmen **Miranda**. It was the peculiar power of Evita **Perón** that she brought the spectacle to politics, and the **radionovela** to reality before the rapt gaze of a newly arrived and disorientated layer of migrant workers who would become, at least in rhetorical terms, the very heart of the national dream.

After the Second World War the unified nation aspired to economic and political independence – the economic surge occasioned by the war and its aftermath produced a new economic theory exemplified by **SELA**. Led and organized from the state, and in the context of a continental market, the new nation-states could reach modernity. The failure of the industrialization project was manifestly the result of the exercise of hegemonic economic and political power by the USA – particularly in the wake of the **Cuban Revolution** of 1959 which had announced its project for independence precisely in those terms. The US domination of the world market, of the key commodities, and of patterns of consumption was mirrored in the proliferation of its cultural instruments – the growth of the commercial music industry, the birth of a **television** system dominated completely by US capital and technology, a film industry whose **Hollywood** production values made it impossible for an impoverished regional film industry to compete. The continental penetration of **Disney** products, for example, ensured the dissemination both of a fundamental anti-communism on the one hand, and a model of growth and success based on the American way, on the other.

The reintegration of Latin America into the US ambit politically, economically and ideologically was addressed and theorized by a new layer of intellectuals for whom the problem was not 'underdevelopment' – a failure of states to develop – but an international system of inequality whose mechanisms maintained and deepened the imbalance. This dependency theory – in the writings of Gunder **Frank**, **Furtado**, **Cardoso** – acknowledged that culture and ideology were key modes of control and discipline. As Armand Mattelart, co-author with Ariel **Dorfman**, of the seminal study ***Para leer al Pato Donald*** (How to read Donald Duck) (1971), revealed in his researches, 'culture is not a light industry'. Control of news, of the new mass culture of pop music, television, and Hollywood cinema, and the ability to define the aspirations and values of a whole society were potent and key weapons of domination. The fruit of that insight was the theory of *cultural imperialism*.

In the early 1970s, the concept of cultural imperialism both responded to what, descriptively, seemed an obvious truth – television was still dominated by US programmes, although **Globo** and **Televisa** were growing into the conglomerates they would become in the next decade. International news distribution was overwhelmingly controlled by United Press and Reuters; the cinemas, despite attempts to impose a quota of national films in Brazil, for example, were full of American products, particularly the progeny of the Disney stable. US capital remained powerful, though venture capital and private financial institutions seemed increasingly central – particularly in Mexico and Chile – a high profile reinforced by the overpowering architecture of foreign-owned **banks** in most of the region's major cities. **Salsa**, a US-generated dance rhythm, was sweeping the Latin American music market before it.

Underpinning the argument, however, was a late version of the dependency thesis. The aspiration to independent development of the 1960s had clearly failed, the construction of the national state had arrested or begun to assume the distorted forms of a military authoritarianism whose national projects involved new forms of combination with foreign investors. The explanation offered by the cultural imperialism thesis was that the US used its economic, political and ideological power to subvert national independence; the analyses of the Chilean coup of 1973, for example, insisted on US involvement and curiously underplayed the leading role played by the Chilean bourgeoisie itself. The call for a New International Information Order, first mooted in 1976, was one response to the theory – and the result was the McBride Commission, set up a year later. But it did permit the reinvention of nationalism, despite its many failures, and the assertion that the central cultural contradiction was on the border between nation and imperialism, and that these were the protagonists of the cultural struggle. Roberto **Schwarz**'s concept of 'misplaced ideas', first proposed in 1977, developed a more sophisticated conception of the same conflict. The rediscovery of tradition and the excavation of the past for the foundations of national culture followed, though this often developed in **exile**, where the national intellectuals found themselves more often than not as the new military regimes expelled its critics. The political consequence, however, was a series of national coalitions created in exile and emerging in the early to mid-eighties in Central America, Chile, Argentina and Uruguay.

At the same time, however, changes in both the external reality and the theoretical explanation of it were laying the foundations of a transformation as profound as any in the century. A new *modernity*, officially designated **post-modernism**, signalled a new economic globalization and a cultural metamorphosis. As John Beverley affirms, the thesis of modernity reflcts a crisis of the national project in the face of the global reorganization of capital. **Neo-liberal** economic strategies increasingly subordinate the national state to administrative functions as international agencies impose the priorities of the world market. Most loans and aid programmes to the countries of the region in the eighties carry conditions which directly involve cuts in public spending. The Caribbean Basin initiative promoted by President Ronald Reagan, for example, like most aid packages in the period, were joint public-private initiatives. In Mexico the government of Miguel de la Madrid (1982-88) embarked on a massive privatization of state enterprises as a precondition for the closer integration of the regional economy eventually consolidated through the **NAFTA** agreement. The cultural industry was no different in that respect from any other branch of the economy; but privatization/marketization implied the simultaneous undermining of state-subsidized broadcasting and its public service ethos and the massive growth of the Latin American conglomerates like Globo, Televisa, **Manchete** and **Venevisión**.

As Renato **Ortiz** argues throughout his work, this is a function of economic and market integration and of a new phase of economic growth – but not now in the context of a protected national market but rather in an alliance of powerful economic actors in a global context. Thus Televisa moves into the US context, serving a growing Hispanic audience, Globo beams across Latin America but also into Europe and Venezuela conquers a large part of the niche market in **telenovelas**. The simple confrontation of imperialism and nation is swept away and replaced by a notion of an interconnected and interdependent system dominated by global patterns of consumption and production (symbolized perhaps by Ford's 'world car' whose components were produced in a number of different countries and assembled in yet another, or the '**maquiladora**' phenomenon, in which regional assembly plants produce goods for often distant markets – the Japanese factories on the Mexican–US border are a key example). The fall of the Berlin Wall in 1989 simply serves to reinforce the sense of a single and universal environment.

The cultural effects are undoubtedly extraordinarily far-reaching. Post-modernism enunciates the eclecticism of the new cultures, which merge high and low, the canon and the consumer good; the **city** as the favoured locus of the new culture no longer has a rural past to yearn for as it did in the 1950s, since the countryside itself is now a place of production for the market – paradoxically signified in the growth of the **cocaine** trade, an international commodity par excellence! In the urban space tradition and modernity mingle in an undifferentiated way – indigenous market traders wear Discmen, television reaches into the furthest corners, as witness the forest of aerials over the region's **shanty towns**, the globalization and reselling of Latin American music. The mass media provide the model for the new culture. More significant still is the appropriation by the market of the very language of liberation – 'empowerment', for example, now refers not to the emancipatory strategies for social classes or groups but to subjectivities and the freedom of choice.

Jesús **Martín Barbero** and Néstor **García Canclini** theorize and interrogate this new reality from the perspective of Latin America – and it is significant that they do not share the cultural pessimism of some of their contemporaries in the old metropolitan centres. The post-modern space does not allow national redefinitions perhaps – the national territorial frontiers (**borders**) are now shifting spaces. The primary advocates of the nation-state, the bourgeois beneficiaries of the old populist projects, are now partners with multinational financial institutions. But the new 'hybrid cultures' of which Canclini speaks are not simply new products, but spaces of conflict and contestation. Popular culture is not simply overwhelmed and domesticated – it also resists, reshapes and remakes even the products of the global market – the new technology serves to create a vast industry in pirated music, new identities replace the nation – youth culture, for example, which according to Barbero crosses frontiers and links resistances in constant merging and remaking of music in **rap** and **roots samba** and **reggae**. Local community radio reconnects with oral cultures as the technology for transmission becomes more simply available. It is a phenomenon that **Canclini** desribes as 'decollection' – the reordering of cultural products. The video permits the reconstruction of film, the rapid remote control reconstructs the TV image, and the new age of internet music will presumably permit new mosaics.

The dilemma is that in the crisis of representation and of politics that has marked the end of the twentieth century such resistances are by their nature fragmentary, local, sometimes transient – the **Zapatista** rebellion in Mexico is emblematic. The liberation of the majority of the region's population from want and despair, however, remains an urgent and ever-present need. The rediscovery of the common experience and the joint action is still a precondition for that emancipatory project – and the categories that underpin such a strategy must find a language of common experience.

Further reading

Franco, J. (1999) *Critical passions* edited by Kathleen

Newman and Mary Louise Pratt, Durham and London: Duke University Press.

García Canclini, N. (1989) *Culturas híbridas: estrategias para entrar y salir de la modernidad*, Mexico: ERA.

Martin Barbero, J (1987) *De los medios a las mediaciones* Barcelona: Ed Gili Rama Angel, (1982) *Transculturación narrativa en América Latina* Mexico: Siglo XXI.

Rowe W and Vivian Schelling (1991) *Memory and modernity in Latin America*, London: Verso.

Schwarz R (1992) *Misplaced Ideas: Essays on Brazilian culture*, trans. J. Gledson, London: Verso.

MIKE GONZALEZ

cumbia

Of the many rhythms of Colombia, the best known internationally is cumbia. Its origin is unclear, and the subject of some debate among scholars; some trace the term back to the word *cumbe* or *koombe*, a popular dance in the Bata region of Guinea, while others see it as an abbreviation of *cumbancha*, an Afro-Cuban word meaning a great fiesta with music and dance. Some scholars, like José **Barros**, suggest that cumbia originated as a lamentation among the Pocabuy Indian tribe, inhabitants of the Atlantic coast of Colombia, when they mourned their dead warriors killed in the struggle against the Spaniards. Others trace its origin to the contacts between black slaves of African descent and the coastal indigenous populations. There is general agreement, however, that cumbia is essentially **mestizo**, a product of the encounter between native Indians, African slaves and Spaniards.

The music for cumbia, slow and fast, is provided by the Indian cane flute, together with several percussion instruments: two small drums – the *llamador* (caller) and *alegre* (happy) – and a tall conga drum called the *tambora*, a *guache* (a metal cylindrical shaker filled with tiny stones) and *maracas* or rattles. The drums are the African contribution, while the dress of the dancers suggests a Spanish origin. Women wear the *pollera* (a long, broad skirt), a blouse, and flowers in their hair; men dress like peasants with white shirt and pants, a red kerchief around their neck and a straw hat – they also carry a small backpack and a machete, suggesting that they have come from work in the fields.

A typical cumbia choreography might begin with the men on stage (who are chatting and drinking as the women enter the stage in groups of two or three). Usually, the women are smoking and the drums are playing. Since the dance usually happens at night, men approach women and offer them lighted candles. That is the sign for the musicians to strike up, as the men seek a partner and begin the circle dance, and the women flirt and play with the candle in their hand. The dance ends and the men and women leave the stage embracing.

MIGUEL A. CARDINALE

Cumparsita, La

Considered the most successful **tango** composition, 'La Cumparsita' was composed by a Uruguayan, Gerardo Mattos Rodríguez, in 1917. It was inspired by a 'joyful march' played by student musical groups called 'comparsas' or murgas (see **murga**) as they walked through the streets of Montevideo. Despite its origin, 'La Cumparsita' came to symbolise the Buenos Aires of tango, stemming from the arrangement and lyrics added by Pascual Contursi and later performed by Carlos **Gardel**. Its reputation was enhanced when Gardel sang it on Corrientes Street for the visiting Prince of Wales.

LUIS GUSMAN

Cumper, Patricia

b. 1954, Kingston, Jamaica

Writer

A novelist and short story writer, Cumper is best known as a dramatist; she has written extensively for radio, stage and screen in the Caribbean and Britain. Author of three series and a children's play for Jamaican radio, her widely toured 1987 black comedy, *The Fallen Angel and the Devil Concubine* was followed by a play with **Sistren** Theatre based on a Claude **McKay** story exploring nineteenth-century class prejudice, as well as a UNICEF-commissioned piece on ghetto violence. Since her move to England in 1993, she has written for theatre, radio and television.

SITA DICKSON LITTLEWOOD

Cuni, Miguelito

b. 1920, Pinar del Río, Cuba; d. 1984, Havana, Cuba

Singer

A singer with some of the most famous bands of Cuban **son**, Cuni began his career with the Yamile orchestra, led by Rolando Luis, in his home town. In 1938 he went to Havana and sang with Arcano y sus Maravillas before joining Arsenio **Rodrí-guez** in 1940. In 1956 he sang with Beny **Moré**'s big band and in 1959 with Bebo Valdés's orchestra. Most of his recordings were made in the 1960s with the Conjunto Chapotin. His compositions include 'Todos bailan con la guajira' (Everyone Dances with the Country Girl), a son, and the **bolero** 'Las ansias mías' (My Desires).

JOSÉ ANTONIO EVORA

Curacas

Curacas was a musical group, part of the Chilean *nueva canción* movement, formed in 1966 as 'Los de la Peña'. Its founder and first leader was Angel **Parra**, though he never played with the group. Specializing in **Andean music**, Curacas cut two albums of its own and others acompanying Parra. When several of its members were arrested during the 1973 Chilean military *coup* and others sent into exile, the group disbanded. Its key figures included Carlos Necochea who, with Ricardo **García**, set up the **Alerce Records** label in 1974; this became the main distributor of the music of **Canto Nuevo**.

ALFONSO PADILLA

Curatella Manes, Pablo

b. 1891, La Plata, Buenos Aires, Argentina; d. 1962, Buenos Aires

Sculptor

One of the pioneers of modern sculpture in Latin America (see **sculpture, contemporary Latin American**), Curatella's sculpture is fluid and full of concave and convex surfaces which produce sharp contrasts of lights and shade. In 1921, he initiated the cubist period of his work with *El guitarrista* (The Guitarist); during this period he associated with Léger and Brancusi, among others. In 1930 he began a series of abstract torsos, an exploration of abstract form that culminated in the series *Derivaciones de una estructura* (Derivations from a Structure) (1945). He studied in Europe from 1911, and after 1926 returned to Argentina where he occupied a number of diplomatic posts.

CECILIA RABOSSI

Curi, Jorge

b. 1931, Montevideo, Uruguay

Theatre director

Curi's nomination as director of the newly restored Teatro Victoria in 1998 confirmed his central place in Uruguayan theatre. He worked with Atahualpa del **Cioppo** in the 1950s before becoming head of El **Galpón** through the 1960s and Teatro Circular into the 1990s. His adaptations for the stage include Rodolfo **Walsh**'s *Operación masacre* (1973) and, with Mercedes **Rein**, *Del pobre B.B.* (On poor BB) (1983), based on texts by Brecht, as well as the extremely popular *El herrero y la muerte* (Death and the Blacksmith) (1982), whose ironies and critical vision marked the beginning of the end of military dictatorship.

See also: Brechtian theatre

NORAH GIRALDI DEI CAS

Curiel, Gonzalo

b. 1904, Guadalajara, Mexico; d. 1958,
   Mexico City

Composer and conductor

An internationally successful composer of popular
songs, Curiel also composed scores for over 140
films as well as three piano concertos. A student of
medicine, he abandoned his studies to become a
pianist and conductor of the orchestra of radio
station XEW in Mexico City. The fine melodic
quality of his songs led many artists to record them.
Among the best known are 'Caminos de ayer'
(Yesterday's Roads), 'Incertidumbre' (Uncertainty),
'Dime' (Tell Me), 'Mañanita fría' (Cold Morning)
and the international hit **bolero** 'Vereda tropical'
(A Tropical Path).

EDUARDO CONTRERAS SOTO

currulao

Currulao is a rhythm and dance of African origin,
typical of the Pacific coast of Colombia. The word
currulao derives from *cununo* (a **Quechua** word), a
type of drum. The adjective *cununado* suffered a
transformation: the first n became a rolling r, and
the second n became l. Besides several types of
drums, the **marimba** (a type of xylophone) is
another important instrument in the currulao.
Recently, cymbals and clarinet have also been
incorporated. In the currulao dance, the dancers
carry handkerchiefs which they flap to mark the
rhythm.

MIGUEL A. CARDINALE

Cuzzani, Agustín

b. 1924, Buenos Aires, Argentina; d. 1987,
   Buenos Aires

Playwright, novelist and lawyer

Agustín Cuzzani's long and distinguished career in
Argentine arts included work in film, television and
adaptations of foreign plays such as *Hair* and
Marat/Sade. Cuzzani is best known for his 'farce-
satires', *Una libra de carne* (A Pound of Flesh) (1954),
El centroforward murió al amanecer (The Centerforward
Died at Dawn) (1955), *Los indios estaban cabreros* (The
Indians Were Angry) (1957) and *Sempronio* (1957).
All four plays mix highly farcical elements with
biting satire relating to humanity's condition.

ADAM VERSÉNYI

cycling

Colombia and Argentina have monopolized honours in cycling. Colombian Martín 'Cochise'
Rodríguez is the continent's only world champion
in 4-kilometre pursuit, (1971), while another
Colombian, Luis Herrera, is the only South
American winner of one of the world's three classic
road races – the Tour of Spain (1981). Argentina,
on the other hand, has also had some outstanding
speed racers, such as Jorge Batiz, a world vice-
champion in 1955 and 1956. Currently the best
Latin American cyclists are Argentina's Curuchet
brothers, Juan and Gabriel, winners of various
world championship medals in the 1990s.

ERIC WEIL

D

D'Abuisson, Roberto

b. 1944; d. 1992, San Salvador, El
Salvador

Soldier and politician

A retired major in the Salvadoran Army and the
founder of the ultra right wing political party
ARENA, D'Abuisson was a leader of the extreme
right in El Salvador. He was accused of participating and promoting death squad activity in the
country throughout the 1970s and 1980s (see
death squads). In 1992, when the United
Nations released the Truth Commission Report,
D'Abuisson was singled out as the intellectual
perpetrator of Cardinal Oscar **Romero**'s assassination on 24 March 1980, and linked to a series of
other crimes and death squad kidnappings and
murders perpetrated during the Salvadoran Civil
War (1979–92).

BEATRIZ CORTEZ

Dabydeen, Cyril

b. 1945, Berbice, Guyana

Writer

Dabydeen became a poet in Guyana, where he
won several prestigious prizes in the 1960s. Much
of his work addresses the problems of exile in
Canada. Recent poetry collections are *Islands
Lovelier than a Vision* (1986), *Selected Poems* (1990),
Poems in Recession (1972), *Goatsong* (1977) and
Distances (1979). His fiction includes *Dark Swirl*
(1989) and *The Wizard Swami* (1990). He moved to
Canada in 1970 and now teaches at Algonquin
College and the University of Ottawa. He is Poet
Laureate of the city of Ottawa, and the only West
Indian member of the League of Canadian Poets.

KEITH JARDIM

Dabydeen, David

b. 1955, Berbice, Guyana

Writer

Obtaining his Ph.D. in eighteenth-century literature and art, Dabydeen sees the tension between
insider and outsider (immigrant) as an impetus to
exciting creativity in language, as suggested in the
critical notes to his 1984 book of poetry, *Slave Song*,
and in the play between Standard English and
creole (see **English-based creoles**) in his 1991
novel, *The Intended*. Born of Indo-Guyanese parents,
he moved to England in 1969 and, despite
adolescence difficulties, excelled academically at
Cambridge and London University. As editor of
the *Handbook for Teaching Caribbean Literature* (1988)
and of *Across the Dark Waters: Indian Identity in the
Caribbean* (1996), Dabydeen has promoted an
appreciation of Caribbean literature and culture.

JILL E. ALBADA-JELGERSMA

Dahl, Gustavo

b. 1938, Buenos Aires

Critic and film-maker

In the **Cinema Novo** debates of the late 1960s and 1970s, Dahl advocated 'culture in the market', a turn towards industrial production in line with the desires of audiences. Originally a critic, Dahl began working in São Paulo at the Cinemateca Brasiliera with Paulo Emílio Salles **Gomes**. After editing films (by Paulo César **Saraceni**, Carlos **Diegues**, and others) and making several documentary shorts, he joined Cinema Novo in its second phase with the brilliant feature *O Bravo guerreiro* (The Brave Warrior) (1968), exemplary of the movement's turn towards self-analysis. He was director of distribution of **Embrafilme** from 1975 to 1979, its most productive period.

ISMAIL XAVIER AND THE USP GROUP

Daily Gleaner, The

Founded in September of 1834 by the Jamaican Jewish De Cordova family, *The Daily Gleaner* is Jamaica's oldest existing newspaper. Beginning as a weekly, it moved to daily publication and by the second half of the twentieth century, the Gleaner Publishing Company also produced the *Sunday Gleaner*, a tabloid called *The Star* as well as overseas Gleaner editions. In the 1990s it became available on the Internet. Partly because Jamaica is the most populous country in the English-speaking Caribbean, and partly because of the quality of its journalism, the *Gleaner* is often considered the premier English-language newspaper of the Caribbean.

ROSANNE ADDERLEY

Dalton, Roque

b. 1935, San Salvador, El Salvador; d. 1975, unknown location, El Salvador

Poet

Though he wrote historical and critical essays, and a famous biography of the old communist, *Miguel Mármol* (1972), Dalton's literary reputation rests on his poetry. It is a poetry defined by its wit and humour, on the one hand, and its absolute commitment to human freedom, on the other.

From an early age Dalton was a political activist – he described his early experience in a wonderfully self-deprecating little poem 'Buscándome líos' (Looking for Trouble) in which his over-earnest responses at his first political meeting are gently parodied by his comrades – and his mother rebukes him when he is late for tea. But these sardonic poems directed at himself are not mere iconoclasm – Dalton's poetry humanizes the revolutionary left to which he belonged, exposing its pomposities and its sectarianism, and in a sense rescuing the project for human liberation at its core.

In that sense, the poetry has a didactic purpose specific to time and place. 'La segura mano de Dios' (God's Sure Hand) is spoken by the assassin of ex-dictator Hernández Martínez of El Salvador. And his *Historias secretas de Pulgarcito* (Secret Lives of Tom Thumb) (1974) is a brilliant eclectic narrative of the history of his country.

The poet Dalton also lived the life of Dalton the militant; the years of organization and the prison terms, the torture, the death sentence from which he escaped when an earthquake broke open the walls of his cell, the subsequent exile in eastern Europe, recalled frequently in his poetry with a mixture of sadness and nostalgia.

Dalton spent most of the late 1960s and early 1970s in Cuba, preparing a guerrilla force for El Salvador (the ERP – the People's Revolutionary Army). Yet an armed-resistance organization, the FPL (People's Liberation Front) already existed under the leadership of a legendary political figure, Salvador **Cayetano Carpio**. It had mass support, based on Carpio's long years in the trade union movement. The ERP, on the other hand, was a collection of radical Christians and Guevarists, with little in the way of a base, dedicated to building a guerrilla cell or *foco* – which Dalton himself had criticized (in 'Maneras de morir' (Ways of Dying), for example) for its elitism and its contempt for popular organization.

When he did return to El Salvador in 1973, Dalton was stopped from assuming the leadership and, in the ensuing internal battles, Dalton was killed by his own comrades in 1975. The *Poemas clandestinos* (Clandestine Poems) were written during this period, though not published until 1980, while Dalton was living and working with the **guerrillas**. Written in a variety of voices, and through several personae, Dalton explores the nature of commitment and idealism. Why these pseudonyms? It was an offence punished by torture or even death to carry the poetry of Roque Dalton; he was after all a leader of the armed opposition. Multiplying his words through a group of students, Dalton's voice remains unmistakable. These are not alternative personalities; nor are they mere entertainments. As 'Vilma Flores' put it in 'Sobre nuestra moral poética' (On Our Poetic Morality), 'Let's be clear, we are poets writing from underground – we're not comfortably and safely anonymous, but face to face with the enemy, attacking the system from our poetry.' In some ways they are Dalton at his least ironic and subtle – yet placed back within the body of his work they are just one (or several) of the faces of a poet, revolutionary, historian, organizer and thinker – and a key figure in enriching the general understanding of what is meant by a poetry of transformation.

Further reading

Dalton, R. (1994) *En la humedad del secreto: Antología poética*, ed. Rafael Lara Martínez, San Salvador: Concultura.

—— (1980) *Poemas clandestinos*, San José, Costa Rica: EDUCA.

Beverley, J. and Zimmermann, M. (1990) *Literature and Politics in the Central American Revolutions*, Austin: University of Texas Press.

MIKE GONZALEZ

Damas, Léon Gontran

b. 1912, Cayenne, French Guyana; d. 1978, Washington, DC, USA

Poet and essayist

A contemporary of Aimé **Césaire** and Leopold Senghor, Léon Damas was one of the founders of the **négritude** movement. He was one of the rare writers from French Guyana to achieve international success, as his first book of poems *Pigments* (1937) articulated the themes of cultural **exile** and racial dispossession that were characteristic of *négritude*. This reputation for political militancy was further enhanced with his sharp critique of French colonialism, *Retour de Guyane* (Return from Guyana), in 1938. His deep interest in oral culture and folk retentions, stimulated by the Harlem Renaissance, was later manifested in a volume of folktales translated into French *Veillées noires* (Black Wakes) in 1943. After spending two years as Deputy for the Department of French Guyana, he travelled widely and spent his last years at Howard University in the USA.

J. MICHAEL DASH

Damián Huamani, Máximo

b. *c.* 1945, San Diego de Ishua, Peru

Violinist

Recognized while still a young man by José María **Arguedas** for his superb playing of the violin in a traditional Andean style, Damián played at Arguedas's funeral in 1969. His testimony of his friendship with Arguedas, published in *Recopilación de textos sobre José María Arguedas* (Gathering of Texts on José María Arguedas) (1976) is a moving assertion of his feeling of being bereft and alone after losing his finest listener. A French recording by ASPIC, *Máximo Damián, le violon d'Ishua*, gives beautiful examples of his art.

DANIEL BALDERSTON

D'Amico, Alicia

b. 1933, Buenos Aires, Argentina

Photographer

Having studied painting with her father, the photographer Luís D'Amico, in 1960 D'Amico opened a studio in Buenos Aires with her colleague Sara **Facio**. They collaborated on many projects, including columns in the newspapers ***Clarín***, ***La***

Nación and even the magazine *Autoclub*. With the Guatemalan photographer María Cristina Orive, in 1973 she founded La Azotea publishing house, the only one dedicated to photography in all Latin America. Outstanding among her publications are *Buenos Aires, Buenos Aires* (1968) and *Fotografía Argentina 1960/85* (1985). In 1979, with five colleagues, she established the Argentine Photographic Council to promote and study national photography, and, in 1997, a National Collection and annual photography prize.

AMANDA HOPKINSON

dancehall

A contemporary successor of **reggae** developed in the 1980s, dancehall music, also known as raggamuffin or ragga, is a hybrid form that combines recorded music with the rapping/singing performance of a DJ. Its rhythms can be traced to reggae, although generally much faster, while the performance style traces its roots to the sound-system dances of the 1950s and 1960s where DJs used verbal theatrics to increase crowd excitement. This performance developed into an art form all its own, known as 'toasting'. Dancehall music is seen by many as a degradation of reggae, because it discards the social justice themes of reggae in favour of 'slack' lyrics of sexual boasting, violent posturing and drug references. Major dancehall figures include Yellowman (born Winston Foster) and Shabba Ranks (born Rexton Rawlston Fernando Gordon).

CAROL J. WALLACE

dancing

Probably the most popular form of entertainment throughout the continent, dancing has long been considered almost an essential characteristic of Latin Americans, who are popularly portrayed in the international media as suave masters of elegant ballroom moves and/or fiery movers and shakers of body parts unknown in more puritan societies. Despite the hegemony of these mass-mediated stereotypes, the prevalence of dancing varies

regionally, being much stronger in those areas where the indigenous populations were either weak or overwhelmed by colonization.

Thus we can trace the popularity of dancing in certain areas to the cultural **syncretism** produced by slavery and the importation of hundreds of thousands of Africans who brought little but their rhythms (and beliefs) into the New World. As a sign of the cultural resistance of enslaved peoples, these roots have been well studied in the work of, for example, Fernando **Ortiz** and Lydia **Cabrera**. Certainly, the Caribbean – and Cuba in particular – have been the epicentre of Latin American social dancing, generating not only the lion's share of popular musical forms, but also the bodily movements to accompany them: the **danzón**, **rumba**, **mambo**, conga, **merengue**, plena, **salsa**, etc.

Evolving from the circle dances of African-based rituals, led by percussion and in contrast to the stiffer movements of European dances, modern Latin American social dancing was tinged with the spectre of sexuality and the expression of forbidden desires. The Argentine **tango**, for example, emerged from the Buenos Aires underworld at the turn of the century as a dance of desire, marked by syncopated music and lyrics drawing from the **Lunfardo** tradition. As it travelled into the middle classes and respectability, it was 'sanitized', yet retained its aura of dangerous sexuality. Similarly, the Brazilian **samba** has been described by Rowe and Schelling as 'one of the means by which resistance to the reduction of the body to a productive machine was expressed', while José Piedra has argued that the movements of a female rumba dancer constitute a 'poetics of the hip' via its complex parrying of seduction, display, compliance and defiance.

Latin American dances have been commercialized and fetishized as embodiments of national cultures. Following the lead of the tango in the 1920s, for example, an international samba craze was set off by its success in the USA after Carmen **Miranda**'s sojourn at the 1939 World's Fair and her subsequent movie career. The merengue is considered the 'national' rhythm of the Dominican Republic. However, Latin social dancing – the pleasure of the dance – eludes usefulness and exchange value through constant improvisation and through its emphasis on the human body as the site for the production and reproduction of cultural memories. Like the protagonist of the film **Danzón**, most dancing Latin Americans would agree that no amount of fetishization or commercialization can take away the pleasure of the dance or the memories it produces.

Further reading

Fraser Delgado, C. and Muñoz, J.E. (eds) (1997) *Everynight Life: Culture and Dance in Latin America*, Durham: Duke University Press.

Rowe, W. and Schelling, V. (1991) *Memory and Modernity: Popular Culture in Latin America*, London: Verso.

Piedra, J. (1997) 'Hip Poetics', in C. Fraser Delgado and J.E. Muñoz (eds) *Everynight Life*, pp. 93–140.

ANA M. LÓPEZ

Dania, Winfred

b. 1950, Aruba

Painter

A self-taught naive painter, Dania moved to Bonaire in 1977 where, although deaf, he was influenced by Bonairian storyteller and painter, Frans Booi. The mythology and legends of Bonaire became his favourite themes. In all his paintings, the first people came from the darkness but climbed into the light and the sweet sunny colours of the island. Some of his paintings now form part of the collection of the Amsterdam Municipal Museum.

NEL CASIMIRI

Danzahoy

Danzahoy was a contemporary dance company founded in Caracas by Venezuelan dancers and choreographers Adriana and Luz Urdaneta and the Franco-Mexican Jacques Broquet, all of whom studied at the London School of Contemporary Dance. Of their repertoire of almost fifty pieces, most written by the founder members of the company, many explore issues of Latin American identity. They include *Selva* (Jungle) and *Travesía*

(Crossing). Danzahoy was later absorbed into the Centro Latinoamericano de Danza, which includes a dance school and organizes the Latin American Dance Congresses.

TERESA ALVARENGA

danzón

A Cuban dance rhythm, the first danzón was composed and played by Miguel Failde, on 1 January 1879, at the Liceo in Matanzas. It was called 'Las alturas de Simpson' (Simpson Heights) after the town's wealthy district. The new rhythm became popular because it was slower than the contradanza. Composed in 2/4 time, the central section introduces the flute, which provides the defining sound of the danzón, and it is the flautist who is usually given the opportunity to improvise and decorate the basic tune. A third part brings in violins before a final closing section introduces the faster rhythm of the **son**. Although its popularity has waned in Cuba, it remains vibrant throughout parts of the Caribbean and Mexico, as evidenced in the film **Danzón** (directed by María **Novaro**) (1990).

JOSÉ ANTONIO EVORA

Danzón (film)

Danzón was the second feature film by Mexican director María **Novaro**. Her first, *Lola* (1989), had already broken with all the conventions of Mexican melodrama and its female stereotypes. With the support of several institutions, Novaro immediately went on to make *Danzón* in 1990. It became one of the key Mexican films of the 1990s and won many national and international awards. The script, researched and written by the director and her sister Beatriz, was written especially for actress María **Rojo**, who plays Julia Solórzano, a lower middle-class woman with a passion for **danzón**, the popular dance immortalised in the 1940s in the 'arrabalero' films about life in the city slums.

When Julia's dance partner Carmelo disappears suddenly, she sets out to look for him, leaving behind her daughter, work and friends. On her journey, she discovers an inner world and a capacity for joy through her friendships with a hotel owner, a prostitute, a friendly transvestite (played by Tito **Vasconcelos**) and a young man with whom she has a love affair.

In Novaro's film, the dance has a ritual and symbolic character. The camera captures discontinuous images: a heel, a hat, a skirt and finally the feet only. The dancers are presented in a fragmentary way, their lives and bodies concentrated in their sinuous moving feet. For Julia Solórzano, the dance is also a journey. In Veracruz she fails to find Carmelo, but she does find love and reappropriates her body sexually. When she returns to Mexico City, the enigmatic Carmelo returns, but is different now, and as they dance the code of the danzón – that the dancers never look at each other – is broken. Almost all the clichés of Mexican cinema are present in *Danzón*, yet all the moulds are broken. The constants of all Novaro's films are present here; her construction of a feminine universe, her musicality, and the sea as representative of the inner life of a character.

Further reading

López, A. (1997) 'Of Rhythms and Borders', in C.F. Delgado and J.E. Muñoz (eds), *Everynight Life: Culture and Dance in Latin America*, Durham, NC: Duke University Press, 310–44.

Tierney, D. (1997) 'Silver Sling-Backs and Mexican Melodrama: *Salón México* and *Danzón*', *Screen* 38(4): 360–71.

PATRICIA TORRES SAN MARTÍN

Dathorne, Oscar Roland

b. 1934, Georgetown, Guyana

Writer, Scholar, Critic

Dalthorne is one of the most influential figures in the development of a Caribbean ethic and identity in the postcolonial literary world, explored through fiction, poetry, and literary criticism.

Dathorne received a prestigious scholarship to Guyana's Queen's College and studied there, hoping to become a teacher. But his life changed when his father lost his job and the family emigrated to England. This disruptive but fruitful transition is reinvented in his first novel, *Dumplings in the Soup* (1963), which details the lives of colonials trying to make it in the metropole.

Dathorne's subsequent life experiences continued to inform his creative and critical work. After earning a certificate of education from the University of London, Dathorne travelled to Nigeria to teach at Amadou Bello University, where he began the interrogation with his heritage that frames his entire corpus. His second novel, *The Scholar Man* (1964), is an early manifestation of the literary subgenre that explores the dilemmas of Afro-Caribbeans writers who attempt to come to terms with their African heritage, For Dathorne, as for others of his generation, the fit is not comfortable. Neither European nor African, the West Indian writer, according to Dathorne, must carve out a place for his/her Caribbean self.

Dathorne's inquiry into his African heritage has also led him to be one of the major critics of the Caribbean. With his edited collections of Caribbean and African literatures and his critical anthologies, Dathorne has helped develop the corpus of African and Diasporan literature. His most significant critical work to date is *The Dark Ancestor: The Literature of the Black Man in the Caribbean* (1981), an exhaustive study of the growing body of Caribbean literature.

Dathorne is a Professor of English at the University of Kentucky and still remains an active scholar and writer. He is editor of *The Journal of Caribbean Studies*, and, reflecting upon his experiences at an American university, he has published a critical anthology, *In Europe's Image: The Need for American Multiculturalism* (1994). Dathorne is presently finishing a new volume of poetry, *Text and Territory*, and working on a novel based on the mutiny on the slave-ship Amistad.

Further readings

Dathorne, O.R. (1969) *African poetry for schools and colleges*, London: Macmillan.

—— (1994) *Imagining the world: mythical belief versus reality in global encounters*, Westport, CT: Bergin & Garvey.

——(1996) *Asian voyages: two thousand years of*

constructing the other, Westport, CT: Bergin & Garvey.

GAY WILENTZ

David, Juan

b. 1911, Sagua la Grande, Cuba; d. 1981, Havana, Cuba

Caricaturist

One of the world's best cartoonists, David's spare lines revealed not only an individual's most salient features but also aspects of their personality captured by the artist in gestures, looks and postures – evidence of his powerful psychological insight. Educated at art school in Cienfuegos, David held his first exhibition there in 1931. In 1936, he began to draw for the magazines *Isla*, *Resumen*, *Mediodía* and *Social*, and a year later mounted his first solo exhibition in Havana. From 1938 to 1949 he was political cartoonist for the Havana newspaper *Información*, publishing a daily drawing for all of those eleven years, and in 1953 he began his 'Davidcaturas' section in the journal **Bohemia**. From 1960–7 he held diplomatic posts in Uruguay and France.

JOSÉ ANTONIO EVORA

Dávila, Juan

b. 1946, Santiago Chile

Painter and installation artist

Dávila left Chile in 1974, after **Pinochet** came to power, and moved to Australia. Most of his works of the 1980s and 1990s are sardonic and witty parodies of the Western art tradition, which he sees as being narrow and parochial. He uses a variety of pictorial techniques, such as three-dimensional painting, and often uses pornographic or obscene images. He is particularly concerned with cultural issues of post-colonialism.

GABRIEL PEREZ-BARREIRO

Dávila Andrade, César

b. 1918, Cuenca, Ecuador; d. 1967, Caracas, Venezuela

Writer

Dávila Andrade's works figure among the most important in the literature of Ecuador, particularly his *Boletín y elegía de las mitas* (Report and Elegy for the Mitas) (1967), with its adventurous use of language and its creation of new epic forms. His early poetic works include *Canción a Teresita* (A Song to Teresita) (1946). He went on to publish more poetry and three volumes of stories including *Abandonados en la tierra* (Abandoned on Earth) (1952) and *Cabeza de gallo* (Cock's Head) (1966). He taught university in Caracas, where he committed suicide.

CELINA MANZONI

Davison, Tito

b. 1912, Chillán, Chile; d. 1986, Mexico City

Film director

One of the most skilled melodramatists of the Mexican cinema, Davison had a roving life before settling in Mexico. He worked as a journalist in Chile, acted in Hollywood, assisted Luis César **Amadori**, made his directorial debut in Argentina, and returned to Hollywood as Latin American Affairs Adviser for the Fox studios. In Mexico from 1944, he honed his melodramatic skills, working in **Cabaretera films** and bringing bolero composer Agustín **Lara**'s life to film in *La mujer que yo amé* (The Woman I Loved) (1950). In the 1950s, he embarked upon a long and productive association, becoming the favourite director of Argentine émigrée, Libertad **Lamarque** after her debut with Arturo de Córdova in *Te sigo esperando* (I Am Still Waiting For You) (1950). Davidson's melodramatic talent fitted Lamarque's lachrymose style to perfection.

ANA M. LÓPEZ

Day of the Dead

Day of the Dead (Día de los Muertos) is a particularly Mexican indigenous and **mestizo** festival which combines pre-Hispanic and catholic traditions to remember dead relatives and ancestors. It coincides with the Catholic Festival of All Saints on 2 November. It combines celebration with mourning, though each community creates a different mix; accentuating the importance of altars at home or of visits to the cemetery, of mourning or joy, abstinence or excess. Certain Mexican communities, like Pátzcuaro and Mixquic, or regions like the Huasteca or Altos de Chiapas, are noted for their unique ceremonies. But every household makes some kind of offering – cakes, bread, drinks, together with flowers, fruit, toys and candles – often in the form of a skeleton (*calavera*) symbolizing death. The *calavera* became a central motif in the satirical drawings of Guadalupe **Posada**.

VICTOR MARTÍNEZ ESCAMILLA

D'Costa, Jean

b. 1937, St Andrew, Jamaica

Writer

A linguistic scholar specializing in Caribbean language, literary critic and writer of fiction for young people, D'Costa is the author of the highly successful 1975 adventure story, *Escape to Last Man Peak*, which has gone through thirteen reprintings. Her novels and short stories for children draw on a highly skilled and sensitive use of Jamaican lore and language varieties, with imaginative plots set in closely observed, realistic settings. D'Costa has also published lucid essays on Roger **Mais** and Jean **Rhys**, some poems and substantial contributions to the historical linguistics of Caribbean creole (see **creole languages**). She taught English language and literature at the **University of the West Indies** for fifteen years before moving to Hamilton College, New York.

BRIDGET JONES

de Boissiere, Ralph A.C.

b. 1907, Trinidad

Novelist

Ralph de Boissiere's first novel, *Crown Jewel* (1952), is considered one of the most important novels of the Caribbean region. It tells the story of the Butler riots in the oilfields of southern Trinidad in the 1930s. Other novels include *Rum and Coca-Cola* (1956), about the US occupation of Trinidad during the Second World War, which de Boissiere has called 'the first real blow to British prestige'; and *No Saddles for Kangaroos* (1964), based on his experiences in Australia working for General Motors during a period of strong anti-communist sentiment. De Boissiere left Trinidad and Tobago in 1947 and has lived in Melbourne, Australia since that time. His novels have been translated into eight languages, including Chinese.

KEITH JARDIM

De Caro, Julio

b. 1899, Buenos Aires, Argentina; d. 1985, Buenos Aires

Musician

In his thirty years as director of a tango orchestra, De Caro founded an 'interpretative' school of **tango**. Tango was originally played by intuitive musicians, but De Caro, first violin in the Arolas orchestra at the age of eighteen, introduced the idea of 'arrangements' and 'interpretations'. When he formed his sextet, tango became organized: each musician had sheet music, the instruments played in counterpoint and new elements, like the double bass, were introduced into the musical line-up.

LUIS GUSMAN

De cierta manera

Shot by Cuban director Sara **Gómez** but not completed until 1977, *De cierta manera* (One Way or Another) addresses an issue never previously explored in Cuban cinema; the incorporation of the marginal population into the new revolutionary institutions. It combines documentary footage with fiction and includes a live debate held in the Miraflores district of Havana. The director died of cancer soon after the completion of filming, and it was Tomás **Gutiérrez Alea** who edited the final cut. The cast included Mario Balmaseda, Yolanda Cuéllar, Mario Limonta, Isaura Mendoza, Bobby Carcases and Sarita Reyes.

JOSÉ ANTONIO EVORA

De Corpo e Alma

De Corpo e Alma (Body and Soul) is a *telenovela* (see *telenovelas*) written by Glória Pérez and broadcast by TV **Globo** in 1992–3. It tells the story of a judge whose jilted lover dies in a road accident. Her heart is transplanted into another woman; the judge seeks her out and she falls in love with him without knowing of his involvement with the heart donor. Reality added impact to the fiction; the actress Daniela Pérez, daughter of the writer, who played Yasmin, was murdered on 28 December 1992 in Rio de Janeiro by the actor Guilhermo de Padúa, who played Bita in the programme.

ANTONIO CARLOS MARTINS VAZ

De Greiff, León

b. 1895, Medellín, Colombia; d. 1976, Santafé de Bogotá, Colombia

Poet

De Greiff developed a very personal style without attaching himself to any particular literary tendency. His poetry concentrates on four major themes: nature, love, the mysteries of life (death, loneliness, madness), and poetry and art itself. His major work is collected in eight volumes, each one identified subsequently with a subtitle indicating the numerical order from *Tergiversaciones. Primer mamotreto* (Distortions: First Big Book) (1925) to *Nova et Vetera. Octavo Mamotreto* (Nova et Vetera: Eighth Big Book) (1973). De Greiff never became

involved directly in politics, but he would identify himself as a left-wing liberal.

MIGUEL A. CARDINALE

De Groote, Christian

b. 1931, Valdivia, Chile

Architect

De Groote stands out for his rejection of the shallow eclecticism of Chilean suburban architecture. His work, primarily single-family residences, has a formal economy of simple lines, geometric volumes, and spacious and luminous interiors. A student and associate of Emilio **Duhart** in the 1970s, de Groote began a search for a synthesis between local forms and materials and contemporary concepts of space. Constructed of stone, concrete and glass, de Groote's designs convey a sense of weight and serenity, punctuated with the richness of light and shadow characteristic of classical and baroque architecture.

CELIA LANGDEAU CUSSEN

de la Parra, Marco Antonio

b. 1952, Santiago, Chile

Playwright and novelist

A practising psychiatrist, de la Parra's debut as a dramatist was in 1978, with the plays *Matatangos* and *Lo crudo, lo cocido, lo podrido* (The Raw, the Cooked and the Rotten). Other plays such as *La secreta obscenidad de cada día* (The Secret Obscenity of Every Day) (1984), *King Kong Palace* (1990) and *Dostoyevski va a la playa* (Dostoyevsky on the Beach) (1990) won several drama awards in Chile and Spain. He has published the short story collection *Sueños eroticos/Amores imposibles* (Erotic Dreams/ Impossible Loves) (1986), and the novels *El deseo de toda ciudadana* (Every Citizen's Desire) (1987), *La Secreta Guerra Santa de Santiago de Chile* (The Secret Holy War of Santiago, Chile) (1989) and *Cuerpos prohibidos* (Forbidden Bodies) (1991).

AMALIA PEREIRA

de la Parra, Teresa

b. 1889, Paris, France; d. 1936, Madrid, Spain

Writer and essayist

Teresa de la Parra's 1924 novel *Ifigenia*, like her letters and essays, are texts out of their time. Her story of 'a young lady who writes because she is bored' in the patriarchal Caracas of the late nineteenth century is as eccentric as her relationships (her impossible loves, her ambiguous friendships with women). She developed an autobiographical register as the key strategy for delineating the strong feminine voice that emerges in her second novel *Memorias de Mamá Blanca* (1929). Her intellectual activity was intense; she was involved in a number of political and cultural movements in her country. In the context of the aesthetic experiments of the **avant-garde**, de la Parra attempted a different kind of break with tradition; the creation of an anomalous voice. In the 1990s, feminist (see **feminism**) readings have taken her out of the '*costumbrista*' (see *costumbrismo*) context in which she was always read and explored her interrogation of gender. She died of tuberculosis in Spain.

GRACIELA MONTALDO

De Palm, Norman

b. Aruba, Netherlands Antilles

Film-maker and artist

Working with Curaçao-born artist Felix **De Rooy**, whom he met in the Netherlands, de Palm runs the multicultural arts foundation 'Cosmic Illusion', which originated in Curaçao and has since then been re-established in Amsterdam. De Palm also wrote the script for and produced De Rooy's groundbreaking film *Ava and Gabriel* (1990). His theatrical and artistic work all revolve around issues of multiculturalism and the representation of ethnic minorities. In 1999 he directed Papa's Song, which was premiered at the Kwakoe festival in Amsterdam.

ANA M. LÓPEZ

De Rooy, Felix

b. 194?, Willemstad, Curaçao

Film-maker

His well-known *Ava and Gabriel* (1990) is the first film from or about Curaçao to hit international art circuits. With this film, De Rooy addressed the lack of cinematic representations of the Dutch Antilles via the passionate romance between Gabriel, a black Surinamese artist, and Ava, a teacher of mixed origin. Resettled in Holland, Gabriel travels to Curaçao to paint a mural commissioned by the local church, and falls in love with Ava. When Gabriel chooses Ava as his model for the Virgin Mary, their union sparks intense racial and cultural clashes. De Rooy lived and worked in Mexico and New York before moving to the Netherlands and settling in Amsterdam. Besides directing films (*Almacita* in 1986), he also directs theatre, organizes exhibitions, paints and co-founded and manages with Norman **de Palm** an arts centre called 'Cosmic Illusion'. *Ava and Gabriel*, although set in the 1940s, portrays his daily life, which he characterizes as a 'carefully constructed chaos'.

ANA M. LÓPEZ

De Soto, Hernando

b. 1941, Arequipa, Peru

Economist

The best-selling author of *El otro sendero* (The Other Path) (1989), De Soto was a champion of free-market neoliberalism who attracted the attention of a number of right-wing figures at the end of the 1980s. Among them was Mario **Vargas Llosa**, the Peruvian novelist who drew on many of De Soto's ideas in his unsuccessful 1990 campaign for the Peruvian presidency. De Soto's idiosyncratic argument suggests that government interference is the source of all economic ills and that a market free of any institutional controls will produce the greatest good – his examples are culled from the informal sector of the economy, where, he argued, the purest free-market principles applied. The title of his book, a specific allusion to the Maoist

Sendero Luminoso (Shining Path) organization, then at the height of its war with the Peruvian State, made him a target for a series of assassination attempts.

MIKE GONZALEZ

De Vicenzo, Roberto

b. 1923, Chilavert, Argentina

Golfer

Argentina's most famous golfer, as a boy De Vicenzo searched for lost balls on golf courses, then became a caddie and turned pro at fifteen.He won over 250 tournaments in his long career, including the 1967 British Open. But he is almost as famous for one that got away. In the 1968 US Masters he signed his scorecard which had been wrongly filled in by his playing partner and owned up, losing his chance of a playoff for the title. In 1979 he was elected to the US PGA Hall of Fame and still plays and teaches golf at the Rarelegh Club in Buenos Aires where he first became a professional golfer.

ERIC WEIL

death squads

Repressive governments throughout Latin America have used paramilitary organizations to sow terror and quell the resistance of citizens defined as 'subversives' or 'communists'. Often comprising off-duty and retired police and military personnel, the death squads, using obscure sinister names like Mano Blanca (White Hand) or AAA (Argentine Anticommunist Alliance), abduct, torture and kill their victims. The Guatemalan squads in the 1960s flaunted their actions, publishing broadsheets containing the names and photos of future victims. In 1980s El Salvador they left mutilated bodies in public areas. Those that flourished in the Southern Cone in the 1970s preferred to 'disappear' citizens to clandestine jails or kill or bury them in mass graves or waterways (see **disappeared, the**).

MARY JANE TREACY

Debate feminista

Debate feminista (Feminist Debate) is a feminist (see **feminism**) scholarly journal, appearing quarterly, founded in Mexico City in 1992 and directed by Marta **Lamas**. Along with *Fem* it is the most important feminist journal in Mexico.

CYNTHIA STEELE

Debroise, Olivier

b. 1952, Jerusalem, Israel

Art critic and writer

One of Mexico's leading art historians, Debroise's focus has been on twentieth-century painting and photography. He has also curated major exhibitions of contemporary art in Mexico and the United States. His first book, *Diego de Montparnasse* (1979), examines Diego **Rivera**'s cubist period. Other texts include *Figuras en el trópico* (Figures in the Tropics) (1982), a survey of Mexican art from 1920–40; *Fuga mexicana* (Mexican Fugue) (1995), a survey of Mexican photography; and numerous monographs. Novels include *En todas partes, ninguna* (Everywhere, No One) (1984) and *Lo peor sucede al atardecer* (The Worst Happens at Dusk) (1990).

JAMES OLES

Debrot, Nicolaas

b. 1902, Bonaire, Netherlands Antilles;
  d. 1981, Laren, Netherlands

Politician, writer and critic

Nicolaas (Cola) Debrot studied medicine and law before turning to politics in the 1950s. In the 1960s, he became the first Governor-General of the Netherlands Antilles to have an Antillean background. He was a poet, novelist, short story writer, literary critic and essayist, who generally wrote in Dutch. Hardly anyone leaves secondary school in the Netherlands Antilles without having read his short first novel *Mijn zuster de negerin* (My Sister the Negro) (1935), in which he focuses on inter-ethnic relations, a topic which remained a central preoccupation in his work.

AART G. BROEK

debt crisis

The debt crisis broke in Latin America in August 1982, when Mexico threatened to default on its foreign bank loans. In the years that followed, nearly every Latin American country (and much of the rest of the Third World) followed suit, precipitating a 'lost decade' of recession and growing poverty, as governments cut spending on areas such as social services and food subsidies in order to meet crippling interest payments on their debts.

These debts had been contracted during the previous decade. When OPEC producers raised their oil prices in 1973, oil producers invested their newfound wealth in European and US banks, who in turn lent at low interest rates to Third World governments. From 1975–82, US $60 billion entered Latin America in foreign loans. These were considered risk-free investments since, as one bank official said 'governments do not go bankrupt'. Unfortunately, they did. In 1979, a second oil price rise prompted the new generation of neoliberal politicians such as Margaret Thatcher and (later) Ronald Reagan to raise interest rates as part of austerity programmes designed to control inflation. Latin America, which had contracted its loans at floating interest rates, saw its interest repayments rocket just as its export markets shrivelled in recession-hit Europe and Latin America. In 1982 Mexico ran out of foreign reserves and declared itself in default.

The debt crisis forced Latin America into a constant round of debt negotiations, providing the Reagan government, the International Monetary Fund (IMF) and other international financial institutions with the opportunity to exercise their clout. The IMF and banks pressured governments to crack down on inflation by cutting spending and to keep up their debt repayments. At the same time, commercial banks decided Latin America had become a bad risk and stopped lending. Throughout the 1980s, capital flowed out of Latin America to the north. This flow squeezed out US $218.6 billion, over US $500 for every man, woman and child in the region.

By 1991, foreign investors had regained their interest in Latin America and capital started to flow back into the region. However, debt service payments remained a burden on many smaller economies, while the Mexican peso crisis in December 1994 showed that even the larger economies have not yet achieved lasting economic stability. The prevalence of austerity programmes throughout the region has sharply reduced government subsidies to cultural activities, notably cinema. Film production has slumped as a result.

Further reading

Green, D. (1995) *Silent Revolution: The Rise of Market Economics in Latin America*, London: Latin America Bureau.

George, S. (1988) *A Fate Worse than Debt*, London: Latin America Bureau.

DUNCAN GREEN

décima

A décima is an eight-syllable line of verse, following a structural model first presented in Spain by Vicente Espinel in his *Diversas rimas* (Various Rhymes) (1591). The verses consist of two four-line verses linked by a two line verse: the rhyme scheme is abba:ac:cddc. Although originally a high literary form, it was later widely used in Latin American popular culture, especially in Puerto Rico and the Caribbean region. It remains the form favoured by popular singers and balladeers in Cuba and Puerto Rico.

JUAN CARLOS QUINTERO HERENCIA

déco art and architecture

Déco art characterizes a broad shift in taste that originated with the 1925 international exhibition of decorative art and industry in Paris. Its fluid expressiveness marked an early twentieth-century search for new expressive forms, and affirmed the transition from academic styles to the modernist tradition. Its style is evidenced by an ornamental and decorative synthesis of nature and primitive references: Egyptian, Assyrian and Indo-American styles combine rectilinear lines with circles and juxtapose geometric patterns. Many incorporated pre-Hispanic forms to convey the use of natural decorative elements. Déco art and architecture was preferred by clients who could not identify with an academic or neo-colonial language. It stylistically defined building types such as bars, cinemas, shops and hotels, and is prevalent in cities subjected to rapid growth such as: Córdoba and Rosario in Argentina; São Paulo and Porto Alegre in Brazil; Montevideo in Uruguay; and Bogotá, Colombia. Art déco influenced typography, furniture and the decorative arts, and reflected the new technologies of iron, concrete, glass, chrome and stainless steel. Magazines such as *Caras y caretas* (Faces and Masks) popularized art déco in Argentina.

Examples in Buenos Aires include: the Kavanath skyscraper (1936) by Sánchez, Lagos y de la Torre and Alejandro Virasoro's Capitol Cinema and House of the Theatre (1927), which include sculptures by Juan Passani; in Córdoba: the Feigin Building and car dealership (1931) by engineer Angel T. Lo Celso. French-born architect Alfred Hubert Donat Agache was invited to Brazil to design a plan for Rio de Janeiro in 1927; although his ideas were only partially implemented, his influence can be seen in magnificent art déco buildings along the Esplande of Castelo. French interior designer Michel Dufet and art critic Leandre Vaillet had a successful collaborative office in Rio de Janeiro, the atelier Red Star, which stylistically combined new industrial and luxury materials. There are presently 110 art déco buildings and monuments remaining in Rio de Janeiro. The El Mastil building in El Pocito Beach, Montevideo, Uruguay, offers one of the most noteworthy art déco façades in Latin America.

Although the use of art déco in Mexico lacks a theoretical basis, it reflects a commercial strategy intended to combine various styles. Mexican architect Carlos Obregón Santacilia employed the art déco style in shifting his vocabulary to a modernist language. His works include: the Ministry of Public Health Building with murals by Diego **Rivera**; the **Monumento a la**

Revolutión; and the Bank of Mexico. Carlos Obregón collaborated on the interiors.

Further reading

Ramos de Dios, J. (1991) *El sistema del Art Déco: Centro y periferia. Un caso de apropiación en la arquitectura Latinoamericana*, Santa Fé de Bogotá: Escala.

Roca, M.A. (1995) *The Architecture of Latin America*, London: Academy.

Segre, R. (ed.) (1981) *Latin America in its Architecture*, trans. E. Grossman, New York: Holmes & Meier.

JOSÉ BERNARDI

decolonization and independence

This phrase is most often used to describe the period between approximately 1960 and 1980 when most British colonies in the **Caribbean** gained independence, all through negotiation. In the same period, the British colonies that did not become independent gained various forms of self-government. Somewhat earlier in the 1940s and 1950s, the less numerous Dutch and French territories had also received versions of self-government, although only **Suriname** (Dutch Guiana) became fully independent. This mid-twentieth-century period thus saw the transformation of the Caribbean from a region dominated by European colonies to one consisting mostly of independent or quasi-independent states. Cuba, the Dominican Republic and Haiti had become independent in the nineteenth century. Puerto Rico and the US Virgin Islands remained territories of the USA, although they too acquired degrees of self-rule. This political transformation of the Caribbean basin in the mid-twentieth century paralleled similar decolonization processes occurring among former European colonies in Africa and Asia during the same period. With respect to Latin America, this phrase might also reasonably be used to describe the mid-nineteenth-century era in which nationalist wars brought independence to most of mainland Latin

America. However, the phrase is not usually employed in this way.

ROSANNE ADDERLEY

Defilippis Novoa, Francisco

b. 1890, Paraná, Entre Riós, Argentina; d. 1930, Buenos Aires, Argentina

Playwright

In some of his works, like *Tu honra y la mía* (Your Honour and Mine) (1925) or *El alma del hombre honrado* (Soul of an Honourable Man) (1926), he addresses the relationship between real life and fiction, and the conflict between passion and social convention in a Pirandellian form. His later works – *Despertáte Cipriano* (Wake Up Cipriano) (1929) and *He visto a Dios* (I Have Seen God) (1930) belong to the **grotesco criollo** genre and explore the construction of false values and the problems of immigrant identity.

NORA MAZZIOTTI

Del buen salvaje al buen revolucionario

Carlos Rangel's interpretation of Latin American civilization, *Del buen salvaje al buen revolucionario* (From the Noble Savage to the Noble Revolutionary) (1976), attributed Latin America's inadequate response to the challenges of modernity to a collective neurosis inhibiting reflection and generating instead various justifying myths; the 'noble savage' to explain the break with Spain, 'guerrillaism' (a condition afflicting university students) to justify rejection of the United States. These myths of 'noble savages' incapable of recognizing the advantages of belonging to the Western world supplant a logical and rational response to imperialist expansion in the nineteenth and twentieth century. Rangel denounced most of Latin America's **intellectuals** for their collusion in propagating these myths.

CELINA MANZONI

Del Carril, Delia

b. 1895, Saladillo, Buenos Aires Province, Argentina; d. 1999, Santiago, Chile

Painter and engraver

Like many of her contemporaries, Del Carril studied painting in Paris with André Lhote and Fernand Léger. When engraving became her main artistic medium, she worked with W. Stanley Hayter and later with architect and painter Nemesio **Antúnez**. Her first exhibition (1960) took place in Santiago, Chile, where she lived after 1963. Her work, which mainly depicts horses, has been widely exhibited internationally. She was married to Pablo **Neruda** from 1943 to 1955.

MAGDALENA GARCÍA PINTO

Del Carril, Hugo

b. 1912, Buenos Aires, Argentina; d. 1989, Buenos Aires

Singer, actor and film-maker

A popular radio singer in the 1930s, Hugo Del Carril (Piero Hugo Bruno Fontana) made his acting debut as a tango singer in a Manuel **Romero** film and was contracted by **Lumitón**. He developed successful singing and acting careers simultaneously, and made his directorial debut with the *costumbrista* (see **costumbrismo**) *Historia del 900* (Story of 1900) (1949). Known as 'the voice of **Peronism**' for his recording of 'the Peronist march,' he directed social dramas focused on workers' rebellions against oligarchical exploitation, most famously, *Las aguas bajan turbias* (Troubled Waters) (1951).

RODRIGO PEIRETTI

Del Moral, Enrique

b. 1906, Irapuato, Mexico; d. 1987, Mexico City

Architect

From his earliest works, Del Moral gave expression

to what was specifically Mexican in an international context. He studied at Mexico's National University (**UNAM**) and directed the School of Architecture from 1944 to 1949. He worked with José **Villagrán**, from whom he learned the principles of functionalism. Convinced that architecture was an art, he used local materials together with the latest technologies. He worked with several architects, including Mario **Pani**, with whom he collaborated on the master plan and the Rectory Tower of Mexico's **Ciudad Universitaria** (1950–52). His hospital architecture was outstanding.

LOURDES CRUZ GONZÁLEZ FRANCO

Del Paso, Fernando

b. 1935, Mexico City

Novelist

Fernando Del Paso is one of the leading Mexican novelists of the past thirty years. He is the author of three monumental, linguistically experimental novels exploring national history, including the railroad workers' movement of 1958–9, the 1968 student movement and the French occupation of Mexico by the Austrian Archduke Maximilian and the Empress Carlota. His first novel, *José Trigo* (1970), was followed by *Palinuro de México* (1977) and *Noticias del imperio* (News of the Empire) (1987). Most recently Del Paso has experimented with a modern detective novel, with *Linda 67, Historia de un crimen* (Linda 67, Story of a Crime) (1995).

CYNTHIA STEELE

Del Río, Ana María

b. 1948, Santiago, Chile

Writer

Del Río has published two short story collections and four novels including *Oxido de Carmen* (Carmen's Oxide) (1986) and *Tango Abierto* (Open Tango) (1995). An admirer of Chilean writer José **Donoso**, she is interested in writing about 'what is unspoken' in the lives of Chilean women of all ages.

She lived in the USA from 1987–91 and afterwards taught literature and writing in universities in the northern Chilean cities of Arica and Iquique.

AMALIA PEREIRA

Del Rio, Dolores

b. 1904, Durango, Mexico; d. 1983, Newport Beach, California, USA

Actor

Dolores Del Rio (Dolores Asúnsulo López Negrete), the most beautiful face in Mexican cinema, enjoyed her greatest success between 1941 and 1949 in the films of Emilio 'El Indio' **Fernández**: *Flor silvestre* (Wild Flower) (1943), *María Candelaria* (1943), *Bugambilia* (Bougainvillea) (1944), *Las abandonadas* (Abandoned Women) (1944), *La malquerida* (A Woman Spurned) (1949) and *Doña Perfecta* (1950). She worked with US directors like Edwin Carewe (*Resurrection*) (1926), Raoul Walsh (*Red Dancer from Moscow*) (1928), King Vidor (*Bird of Paradise*) (1932) and John Ford (*The Fugitive*, 1947) and in Mexico made films with Roberto **Gavaldón**, Alejandro **Galindo**, Julio **Bracho** and Ismael **Rodríguez**.

Del Rio showed a talent for the theatre from an early age, making her debut at Mexico City's Teatro Iris in 1920. Having married Jaime Martínez Del Rio, she signed a contract with Edwin Carewe, who described her as 'the female Valentino'. In Hollywood, make-up artists and cinematographers created a sensual face, and she achieved fame and fortune in both silent and talking films. She made twenty-eight films between 1925 and 1942, including Raoul Walsh's 1926 *What Price Glory?* By 1930, Dolores del Rio was one of the great new Hollywood stars, surrounded by luxury, wealth and prizes. Her grace and presence captivated audiences and she was both a fine actress and a *grande dame*, a very different figure from the ethnic characters she later portrayed alongside Pedro **Armendáriz**. When she returned to her country in 1943, the great diva's image underwent a radical change. In *Flor silvestre*, the first film she made in Mexico, she found an ideal partner in Pedro Armendáriz; both became emblematic of Mexican beauty. The actress herself explained that when she began to play 'self-sacrificing Mexican women' in the Mexican films of the 1940s, 'I had to exchange my furs and diamonds, pearl necklaces and high heeled shoes for a shawl and bare feet.' The Palme d'Or she won at Cannes in 1946 for her performance in *María Candelaria* confirmed her as the archetypal indigenous beauty that Mexican cinema needed to go beyond its national frontiers. With Roberto Gavaldón's *El niño y la niebla* (Child in the Fog) (1953), however, her career began to decline and she devoted herself to the theatre. Hal Bartlett's *Los hijos de Sánchez* (The Children of Sanchez) (1977) was her last screen appearance.

Further reading

De los Reyes, A. (1997) *Dolores Del Rio*, Mexico: Ed. Condumex.

Monsiváis, C. (1997) *Mexican Postcards*, London: Verso.

PATRICIA TORRES SAN MARTÍN

del Toro, Guillermo

b. 1964, Guadalajara, Mexico

Film-maker

Before making his first feature film, *Cronos* (1992), del Toro worked in television and became an expert in special effects; his company, Necropia, did the effects for Nicolas **Echevarría**'s *Cabeza de Vaca* (1990) and many other films. He also taught at the University of Guadalajara and published a monograph on Hitchcock. Distilled from his expertise in horror and special effects, *Cronos* is a science fiction tale, mixing the history of the conquest with vampiric and diabolical motifs; its international success (and Cannes award) allowed del Toro to move to Hollywood, where he directed *Mimic* in 1997, another fantastic tale this time set in the New York City subways. In 1999 he was working on another US production, *Mephisto's Bridge*.

ANA M. LÓPEZ

Delgado, Susy

b. 1949, San Lorenzo, Paraguay

Poet

An important bilingual poet, Susy Delgado has been published in Spanish – *Algún extraviado temblor* (Some Misplaced Tremor) (1986), *El patio de los duendes* (The Fairies' Patio) (1991) and *Sobre el beso del viento* (On the Kiss of the Wind) (1995) – and **Guarani** – *Tesarái mboyvé* (Spanish translation *Antes del olvido* (Before Oblivion)) (1987). With degrees in media and sociology, Delgado is also a journalist for the newspaper *La Nación*. She has received a number of national and international literary prizes.

TERESA MÉNDEZ-FAITH

Demare, Lucas

b. 1910, Buenos Aires, Argentina; d. 1981, Buenos Aires

Film-maker

Demare learned film-making in Spain, debuted with *Dos amigos y un amor* (Two Friends and One Love) (1937) and became famous with *La guerra gaucha* (The Gaucho War) (1942), an intense epic drama scripted by Homero **Manzi** and Ulises Petit de Murat and for decades the highest-grossing Argentine film. Although best at historical epics – *Pampa Bárbara* (1945) – his filmography of over thirty-three films also includes important social realist films, especially *La calle grita* (The Street Screams) (1948) and *Detrás de un largo muro* (Behind a Long Wall) (1958) about the shanty towns (see **shanty towns and slums**) or *villas miseria*.

RODRIGO PEIRETTI

democracy

Democracy has never been as widespread in Latin America and the Caribbean as it is today. By the mid-1990s, all countries in the region, except for Cuba, chose their leaders through democratic elections.

In the 1960s, the **Alliance for Progress**, sponsored by the USA to improve socioeconomic conditions and prevent the spread of Communism in the region, included a commitment to democratization. However, military *coups* were often condoned or even encouraged by the US government. By the mid-1970s, only a few Latin American countries were democratic (Colombia, Costa Rica and Venezuela, as well as the recently independent English-speaking Caribbean islands).

In the 1980s, a wave of democratization swept the region. Starting with Bolivia, then followed by Argentina, Uruguay, Brazil and Chile, elected civilian governments replaced often brutal military regimes. In Grenada and Panama, democracy was restored through US military invasion. In the late 1980s and early 1990s, Central America saw the end of several civil wars and the return to civilian rule. In the 1990s, the Mexican political system increasingly allowed more competition.

A new threat to democracy appeared in the 1990s, known as the *autogolpe* or self-*coup*. The term was coined when democratically elected President Alberto **Fujimori** of Peru closed down Congress in 1992, suspended the constitution and centralized power in his hands. Yet when Guatemalan President Jorge Serrano attempted to do the same in 1993, international pressure and opposition from the military high command forced him to resign.

To many people in Latin America and the Caribbean, democracy is not determined solely by holding periodic free and fair elections; it also entails greater social justice, human and civil rights, government transparency and accountability, and the rule of law. Despite its apparent strengths, democracy in the region remains under threat from a variety of actors and conditions, including discontented soldiers, extreme poverty and inequality, destabilizing neoliberal economic reforms, the concentration of power in the presidency, and the drug trade.

Further reading

Lowenthal, A.F. (ed.) (1991) *Exporting Democracy: The United States and Latin America*, Baltimore, MD: Johns Hopkins University Press.

O'Donnell, G., Schmitter, P.C. and Whitehead, L. (eds) (1986) *Transitions from Authoritarian Rule*, 4 vols, Baltimore, MD: Johns Hopkins University Press.

Stepan, A. and Linz, J.J. (1996) *Problems of Democratic Transition and Consolidation: Southern Europe, South America and Postcommunist Europe*, Baltimore, MD: Johns Hopkins University Press.

STEPHEN BROWN

dendé oil

Dendé oil, distinctive of northern Brazilian cookery is extracted from the palm *Elaesis guineensis* (an African palm grown in Brazil) that is responsible for the flavour and gusto of such well-known Bahian dishes as ***vatapá***, ***acarajá***, ***moqueca*** and others. Although it is a rich source of vitamin A, it is a highly saturated fat and very high in cholesterol; its use has been the source of much controversy among contemporary nutritionists. A yellowish, very dense liquid, *dendé*, has a unique exotic flavour that takes some getting used to and for which there is no substitute. It was introduced into Brazilian cookery by African slaves, who used it as a substitute for the olive oil favoured by the Portuguese settlers.

ANA M. LÓPEZ

dengue fever

An acute, contagious virus in the tropics, dengue fever is characterized by fever, severe pain and fatigue. Transmitted by the *Aedes aegypti* mosquito, the same mosquito that spreads yellow fever, in the last three decades this disease has spread to nearly every corner of Latin America; outbreaks in the 1980s in Bolivia, Brazil, Colombia, Cuba, Ecuador, El Salvador, Paraguay, and Peru resulted in thousands of severe cases and hundreds of deaths. In 1991, PAHO (see **Pan American Health Organization**) called together a team of experts in an attempt to control and prevent the disease. By 1993, the only tropical Latin American countries to have remained free of dengue, Costa Rica and Panama, reported indigenous transmission of it. Attempts to eradicate the mosquito have met with limited success; there is no effective vaccine, but research is continuing.

EDUARDO GUÍZAR-ALVAREZ

Denis Molina, Carlos

b. 1918, San José, Uruguay; d. 1983, Montevideo, Uruguay

Writer

Poet and novelist best known for his work in theatre, Denis Molina was an actor in, and artistic director of, the Teatro Solís. *Orfeo* (Orpheus) (1949), with Margarita Xirgu in the leading role, brought him early success. His absurd and poetic vision was expressed in several plays, including *Soñar con Ceci trae cola* (Dreaming of Ceci has After-Effects) (1983); performed at the Comedia Nacional while he was gravely ill, this play satirized the situation under Uruguay's military dictatorship and imagined a different future. His magical realist novel, *Lloverá siempre* (It Will Always Rain) (1950), occupied a central place in Uruguayan fiction.

NORAH GIRALDI DEI CAS

dependency theory

The concept of dependency appears in the social sciences and throughout Latin American social thought from the mid-1960s onwards, though it rests on earlier discussions and concepts. Figures associated with it include André Gunder **Frank** and Fernando Henrique **Cardoso**, who was to become Brazilian president in the 1990s. It is not a single theory, but rather a body of theories and systems of political analysis interwoven with two other factors: first, the advance of the metropolitan powers into the underdeveloped countries after the Second World War with their financial–economic strategies (Bretton Woods) and cultural policies (neocolonialism); and second, the political development of the countries of the Third World out of the Bandung Conference and various attempts at autonomous development. These theories argued that since the Industrial Revolution, development was founded upon underdevelopment; they re-

jected the postulates of functionalism in sociology, the neoclassical school in economics, and the linear and biological view of progress. According to these theories, dependency implied a deterioration in the terms of trade, the appropriation of the surplus product in the metropolis through an increasing control over decisions relating to technology, finance, trade and distribution and, directly or indirectly, politics. The proof of the concentration and centralization of capital and of new capital exports was focused at that time on the multinationals, just as today it centres on the global conglomerates; it was argued at the time that underdevelopment could only be overcome outside the framework of capitalism and its various versions of developmentalism.

On the cultural level, dependency theories transformed the concept of culture by introducing anthropological, semiotic, historico-social readings, connecting the work of Third World and Latin American thinkers like **Fanon** and **Mariátegui** with the ideas of Gramsci and Althusser, and linking them to contemporary struggles for liberation (see *How to Read Donald Duck*). This implied distinct types of cultural analysis that focused on material production and the production of texts, on systems of distribution, forms of consumption and recognition. The question of national identity arose in the analysis of cultural and communicative inequality, the contrast between national and international cultural industries, and the defence of independent scientific and technological developments. The discussion continued as the world economic and financial map began to change, now embracing issues of globalization and the notion of interdependence. Nevertheless, the gaps – economic as well as cultural and communicative – keep widening, both between North and South and within the so-called Third World countries. The centre–periphery model seems increasingly less relevant, but the gulf between rich and poor still remains.

See also: FLACSO

Further reading

Chilcote, H. (ed.) (1982) *Dependency and Marxism:*

Toward a Resolution of the Debate, Boulder, CO: Westview.

Chilcote, H. and Edelstein, C. (1986) *Latin America: Capitalist and Socialist Perspectives on Development and Underdevelopment*, Boulder, CO: Westview.

Frank, A.G. (1967) *Capitalism and Underdevelopment in Latin America*, New York: Monthly Review Press.

ANÍBAL FORD AND ALEJANDRO GRIMSON

Depestre, René

b. 1926, Jacmel, Haiti

Writer

Like his contemporary Jacques Stephen **Alexis**, Depestre was born during the US occupation of Haiti and was influenced by the Marxism of Jacques **Roumain**. He was one of the student leaders of *La Ruche* who, inspired by the visit of Andre Bréton, helped overthrow the government in 1946. While in Paris as a student in the 1950s, he was drawn to the ideas of the Communist poet Louis Aragon. This meant the beginning of a nomadic life for Depestre, who eventually returned home in 1957 after spending three years in Latin America where he became close friends with writers like Nicolás **Guillén**, Pablo **Neruda** and Jorge **Amado**. Threatened by **Duvalier**'s regime, he left for Cuba just after Fidel **Castro**'s takeover of the country and stayed for twenty years. Eventually, at odds with the Cuban government, he left in 1979 to work for UNESCO in Paris, and has lived in the south of France since his retirement in 1986.

Depestre's first collections of poems *Etincelles* (Sparks) (1945) and *Gerbe de Sang* (Spray of Blood) (1946) were exuberant celebrations of youthful revolt influenced by the lyricism of Paul Eluard. While most of his 1950s poems were little more than Marxist tracts, the later poems, especially *Mineral noir* (Black Ore) (1956) and *Journal d'un animal marin* (Diary of a Sea Creature) (1964) reveal a fuller range of themes, from lyrical love to wry evocations of exile. Anti-US politics become apparent in his Cuban writing with the publication of the dramatic poem *Un arc en ciel pour l'occident chretién* (A Rainbow for the Christian west) (1967)

and *Poète à Cuba* (Poet in Cuba) (1976). These years also represent an explicit critique of Haitian *noirisme* and a shift in interest to fiction. The short stories in *Alleluia pour une femme jardin* (Alleluia for a Garden Woman) in 1973 celebrate the theme of erotic adventure, not favourably viewed by Depestre's Cuban hosts. Similarly, the anti-Duvalierist *roman à clef, Le mat de cocagne* (Festival of the Greasy Pole) (1979) associates political dictatorship with sexual repression and imagines **Vodun** as a salutary source of sexual and political liberation. Eroticism has become more pronounced in his fiction since his move to Paris. *Hadriana dans tous mes rêves* (Hadriana in My Every Dream) is written in the tradition of lo **real maravilloso** (marvellous realism) and was awarded the Prix Renaudot in 1988. It is the first of an erotic trilogy, the second of which is a collection of tales, *Eros dans un train chinois* (Eros in a Chinese train) (1990).

Further reading

Couffon, C. (1986) *René Depestre*, Paris: Seghers.
Dayan, J. (1977) *A Rainbow for the Christian West*, Amherst, MA: University of Massachusetts Press.

J. MICHAEL DASH

Derecho de nacer, El

A radio soap opera (see **radionovelas**) written by Félix B. **Caignet**, *El derecho de nacer* (The Right to be Born) began transmission on 1 April 1948 on Goar **Mestre**'s **CMQ-TV** network. It soon won over the entire Cuban audience, who followed its 314 episodes addressing risqué topics such as abortion, incest and miscegenation in the context of tempestuous and misguided love and familial relations. It has become the most famous of all radio serials, and has been broadcast worldwide; it is considered the classic model for radio soaps and a foundational example of the genre. It was filmed twice, in 1951 by Zacarías Gómez and in 1996 by Tito **Davison**.

WILFREDO CANCIO ISLA

Desanzo, Juan Carlos

b. 1939, Buenos Aires

Cinematographer and film director

Originally in advertising and cinematography (he did the lighting for *La **hora de los hornos*** (The Hour of the Furnaces) (1968) and many other films in the 1970s, and is considered one of the best Argentine cinematographers), Desanzo broke into direction immediately after the return to democracy with a trilogy of thriller films that explored the paranoia of violence and such bizarre contemporary figures as unemployed torturers – the cruel legacy of the dictatorship. His *Eva Perón* in 1996 was timely and much debated in the context of Alan Parker's Hollywood version, *Evita* (also 1996); his Evita was quite different from the Madonna incarnation, a politically engaged woman whose strength even overshadowed **Perón**'s. His 1997 *Hasta la victoria siempre* (Always until Victory) was also a historical film, although not as successful.

ANA M. LÓPEZ

D'Escoto, Miguel

b. 1933, Hollywood, California, USA

Priest and politician

D'Escoto was one of the three Catholic priests in the Sandinista (see **Sandinista Revolution**) government of Nicaragua, all of whom were ordered by their superiors to choose between the priesthood and a government position. He thus became one of the symbols of the conflict between the Sandinistas and the Catholic Church. A proponent of non-violence and pacifism, in 1985, he launched an 'evangelical insurrection' including a one-month fast for peace. He saw it as a Christian response to the violence and 'the theological war' levelled against the Sandinista revolution. Currently he is director of FUNDECI, a non-governmental organization working with local community development projects in Nicaragua.

ELINA VUOLA

Desideria

A character created by Ana González Olea (1915–), Desideria is a familiar figure of the peasant woman working as a maid in the city. Interpreted at first through a series of delicate and funny radio monologues by Ana Gonzalez herself in the 1940s, Desideria later joined the programme 'La familia chilena' (The Chilean Family), where her witty comments and sharp retorts won her enormous popularity. Ana González herself is an actress of great versatility, winner of numerous prizes and awards, among them the Premio Nacional de Arte 1969.

EUGENIA NEVES

Desnoes, Edmundo

b. 1930, Havana, Cuba

Writer

Desnoes is the author of novels including *No hay problema* (No Problem) (1961) and ***Memorias del subdesarrollo*** (Memories of Underdevelopment) (1965) and critical essays collected in *Lam: azul y negro* (**Lam**: Blue and Black) (1963) and *Punto de vista* (Point of View) (1967). He studied and worked in New York before returning to Cuba after the victory of the Cuban Revolution in 1959 (see **revolutions**). He contributed to the newspaper ***Revolución*** and its cultural supplement ***Lunes de revolución***. From 1965 to 1970 he was a member of the editorial board of the journal ***Casa de las Américas***. He currently lives in the United States.

WILFREDO CANCIO ISLA

Deus e o diabo na terra do sol

Deus e o diabo na terra do sol, Glauber **Rocha**'s second feature film from 1964, together with Ruy **Guerra**'s *Os fuzis* (The Guns) (1964) and Pereira dos **Santos**'s *Vidas secas* (Barren Lives) (1963), forms the nucleus of the first phase of Brazilian **Cinema Novo**.

Characteristically, *Deus e o diabo na terra do sol* (Black God, White Devil) works with allegorical forms, projecting onto the universe of the north-eastern **sertão** forces that represent the collective experience of a nation in process of formation. The film tells the story of a cowboy, Manuel, and his wife Rosa who, after a violent break with a domineering local landowner, join first the messianic leader Sebastião and then the bandit Corisco, the last *cangaceiro* or bandit. The two protagonists, around whom the film's two sections are organized, are inspired by the historical reality of messianic movements (like that of Antonio Conselheiro) in the late nineteenth century and of the bandits, whose archetypal representative was Lampião (see **Lampião e Maria Bonita**). Both Sebastião and Corisco are killed by Antonio das Mortes, an assassin who represents the necessity of overcoming those earlier ways of thinking. The film rejects all realist conventions; the highly theatrical 'God' and 'The Devil' sections represent a search for a synthetic representation of historical experience, advancing through successive rupture with forms of alienation – messianism and banditry – which prefigure the Revolution and the prophesied hope of redemption for the characters who represent the People in their struggle for liberation.

The narrative of the film combines erudite and popular sources. On the one hand, the double unfolding which goes beyond the consciousness of the characters and is informed by a dialectical philosophy of history; on the other, the explicit narrative vehicle is the **literatura de cordel**, which organizes the representation of social experience around a concept of Destiny. With these figurative strategies, Rocha incorporated into his work the central social and political question of this period immediately prior to the military *coup*: what was the relationship between intellectual critical thought and cultural forms embedded in the historical experience of the popular classes?

The incorporation into the film of contemporary issues gave it an original and aggressive style. Breaking with balanced plot development and temporal and spatial continuity, the narrative undergoes violent leaps. The accumulation of tension at the dramatic level drew on the use of hand-held cameras, vertical editing, composing with scarce resources what Rocha called an 'aesthetics of hunger', an artistic expression of the condition of underdevelopment and an instrument in the struggle to overcome that condition.

Further reading

Xavier, I. (1998) *Allegories of Underdevelopment*, Minneapolis, MN: University of Minnesota Press.

ISMAIL XAVIER AND THE USP GROUP

development

Development was initially defined as the attainment of economic growth over time. It is measured in terms of the gross national product (GNP) or national income which is the monetary value of the total output of goods and services produced by a country's economy. Furthermore, GNP had to grow faster than the population growth rate if the standard of living per person was to be improved. In the 1970s, increasing dissatisfaction was expressed with this way of defining and measuring development. While many Latin American countries had achieved relatively high rates of growth in the 1950s and 1960s, a large proportion of their population continued to live in poverty. If a country had experienced economic growth but poverty, unemployment and income inequality had not diminished, then it was argued that development had not taken place. Thus development was no longer defined exclusively in terms of economic growth, a change which is often referred to in the development discourse of the 1970s as 'the dethronement of growth' in favour of the pursuit of 'basic human needs' and 'redistribution with growth'.

However, income per capita continued to be the main indicator used to measure development, as it is difficult to construct a credible alternative index. One such alternative, however, is the human development index (HDI) developed by the United Nations Development Programme (UNDP) in 1990. The HDI consists of three components: longevity, measured by life-expectancy; knowledge, calculated by adult literacy and years of schooling; and standard of living, valued by real per capita income adjusted for the local cost of living. This composite indicator aims to reflect well-being and development more accurately than the single indicator of income. More recently, there have been attempts to incorporate gender, political freedom and human security into the HDI, but this has been controversial and more difficult to measure. The consideration of environmental concerns, as in the term 'sustainable development', has also proved problematic.

In addition to debates on the meaning of development, there are also contending theories on the origins and continuance of underdevelopment and on how to achieve development. Writers from a neo-Marxist dependency perspective (see **dependency theory**) argue that Latin America and other less-developed countries (LDCs) cannot achieve development within the capitalist system. It is only by delinking from the world capitalist system and pursuing a socialist development strategy that they can achieve development. Gunder **Frank** is a key exponent of this view as seen in his thesis of 'the development of underdevelopment', which states that the underdevelopment of the LDCs (or periphery) is due to the development of the developed countries (or centre). By contrast, neoliberal (see **neoliberalism**) development theory and modernization theory (see **cultural theory**) argue that LDCs should follow in the footsteps of the capitalist developed countries. According to this perspective, the best and quickest way for LDCs to develop is to weave even closer economic, social, political and cultural links with the advanced capitalist countries.

Writing within dependency theory, Fernando H. **Cardoso** in *Dependencia e desenvolvimento na América Latina* (Dependency and Development in Latin America) (1970) rejects the notion of the development of underdevelopment as this implies that the capitalist development of LDCs is unviable. He argues that rapid economic growth has taken place in most of Latin America and that the forces of production have been developed, particularly since the new phase of dependence associated with Latin America's industrialization under the aegis of multinational corporations. Cardoso does not deny that capitalist development in dependent countries is highly uneven, unequal and full of contradictions, but this does not mean that no develop-

ment takes place at all or that it is unviable. In place of what he sees as Frank's mistaken notion of the development of underdevelopment, Cardoso proposes the term 'dependent development' as a more accurate representation of the processes of development *and* dependency in Latin America.

Many structuralist and dependency writers are concerned with the achievement of autonomous development. Contrary to common sense thinking, this does not imply a lack of economic links with other countries; rather, it refers to the ability of a country to control its own development without undue interference from or dependence on outside economic forces. An autonomous development strategy is concerned with inner-directed development or development from within. By this is meant that the network of external linkages are determined from within the LDC itself. With autonomous development, the aim is to subordinate external relations to the needs of internal accumulation, production and interests. Autonomous development implies relative independence of decision making, and invokes a certain degree of introversion and a self-generated development which caters for external markets only insofar as internal needs and interests require it.

With the decline of socialism and the rise of capitalist globalization, autonomous development may appear Utopian. However, while the world economy has become increasingly interdependent, this is a highly unequal and uneven interdependence. Furthermore, while levels of income, nutrition, health and life expectancy have increased in Latin America since the 1950s, more than one-third of the population were still living in absolute poverty at the end of the 1990s. Thus many of the problems relating to underdevelopment and development which were raised by dependency theory have not yet been resolved.

Further reading

Cardoso, F.H. (1971) *Política e desenvolvimento em sociedades dependentes*, Rio de Janeiro: Zahar Editores.

Cardoso, F.H. and Faletto, E. (1982) *En torno al estado y al desarrollo*, Mexico D.F: Centro de Estudios Económicos y Sociales del Tercer Mundo.

—— (eds) (1979) *Dependency and Development in Latin America*, Berkeley, CA: University of California Press.

Inter-American Development Bank (1999) *Economic and Social Progress in Latin America*, Baltimore, MD: Johns Hopkins University Press.

Jameson, K.P. and Wilber, C.K. (eds) (1996) *The Political Economy of Development and Underdevelopment*, 6th edn, New York: McGraw-Hill.

Kay, C. (1989) *Latin American Theories of Development and Underdevelopment*, London: Routledge.

CRISTÓBAL KAY

D'Halmar, Augusto

b. 1882, Santiago, Chile; d. 1950, Santiago

Writer

D'Halmar was a Utopian writer who wrote of the yearning for a new social order. In 1904 he and other writers tried to form a 'Tolstoyan colony' in southern Chile, but the attempt failed and he returned to Santiago to form a similar group in San Bernardo. At the core of this project was a return to nature which reflected the naturalist aesthetics of D'Halmar and many of his Latin American contemporaries (like José Eustacio **Rivera** or Ricardo **Güiraldes**). He was the first recipient of the National Prize of Literature for Chile, in 1942. His novel *La pasión y muerte del cura Deusto* (The Passion and Death of Father Deusto) (1924) is one of the first Latin American novels of homosexual love.

LUIS E. CÁRCAMO-HUECHANTE

Di Benedetto, Antonio

b. 1922, Mendoza, Argentina; d. 1986, Buenos Aires, Argentina

Writer

Di Benedetto stands at the opposite extreme from regionalist writing (see *regionalismo*). His novels and short stories are characteristically anti-naturalist and laconic, speculating on questions of logic

and identity within a framework of fantastic writing influenced by **Borges**. His **avant-garde** concerns led him to techniques close to the French *nouveau roman*, as in the stories of *El juicio de Dios* (God's Judgment) (1975). His novel *El hacedor de silencio* (The Silence Maker) (1964) uses noise as the starting point for a metaphysical exploration, while a historical novel set in colonial Paraguay (*Zama* (1956)) employs the distance in time as an opportunity to explore **existential** issues.

JULIO PREMAT

Di Tella, Guido

b. 1931, Buenos Aires, Argentina

Economist and politician

A member of a prominent family of industrialists and philanthropists, Di Tella is the author and co-editor of eighteen books on economics and international studies such as *Las etapas del desarrollo económico argentino* and *Argentina, Australia and Canada*. He served in the Economics Ministry in 1975, and returned with **Menem** as Minister of Economics (1991) and subsequently as Foreign Minister. He has held the position of Foreign Policy Minister since 1991. He received a degree in industrial engineering at the University of Buenos Aires and a Ph.D. in Economics at MIT (1959). He has taught at the University of Buenos Aires, the Catholic University of Buenos Aires and St Anthony's College, Oxford.

See also: Instituto Di Tella

ALVARO FERNÁNDEZ-BRAVO

Día de los Muertos   *see*   Day of the Dead

diablada

The diablada is a dance performed in religious festivals in Bolivia. Diablo dancers, with brilliant costumes and acrobatic leaps, recreate the revolt of Lucifer and his submission to the Virgin Mary. Despite its ostensibly Christian characters, the dance originates from Andean ideas about reciprocity with the Tío (uncle) or Supay, whom miners must compensate for riches extracted from his veins. Andean ideas about fertility and reciprocity are inherent in this contract with Supay and homage to the Virgin. The diablada appeared in Oruro in the seventeenth century, and has spread to La Paz and also to Peru and Chile.

BRET GUSTAFSON

Diario de la Marina

Founded in 1844 as a limited company, *Diario de la Marina* became the leading Cuban newspaper. A successor to the island's first newspaper, *El noticioso y lucero de la Habana* (1832), it was linked to colonial interests of the nineteenth century and established its influence in the early twentieth century. In 1926 it began publishing the *Suplemento literario* (Literary Supplement), a platform for the avant-garde and one of the most influential journals in Cuban cultural life. It came into conflict with the revolutionary government after 1959, and ceased publication in May 1960.

WILFREDO CANCIO ISLA

Diario de Poesía

Diario de Poesía is a poetry journal in tabloid form appearing four times a year. Founded in 1986 and edited in Buenos Aires by poet Daniel Samoilovich, it is divided into 'Information', 'Creative Writing' and 'Essay' sections, all three embracing poetry written in languages other than Spanish. Its translations of poetry and critical essays are a major contribution. Its newspaper format suggests an effort to popularize poetry, underlining the fact that a poem can be a news event; it also dates, documents and preserves poetry in the collective memory. Issue 38, published in 1996, provides a full index of its first ten years.

ENRIQUE FOFFANI

Diario Noticias

The independent Paraguayan daily *Diario Noticias* was founded in April 1984 and at first distributed as a pro-government successor to **ABC Color** (closed down in March 1984). It is a morning paper of national coverage and general interest with no party-specific political orientation, directed at the middle and upper socioeconomic classes. It is distributed throughout Paraguay and abroad. Under its director, Néstor López Moreira, it has reached a circulation of 80,000 and employs about 400 people.

BETSY PARTYKA

Dias, Cicero

b. 1908, Recife, Brazil

Painter

Together with Tarsila do **Amaral** and Ismael **Nery**, Dias was instrumental in linking surrealism (see **surrealism in Latin American art**) and modernism (see **Brazilian modernism**). An architect, he studied painting in Rio de Janeiro and Paris, where he settled in 1937, visiting Picasso's studio and joining the surrealists. He exhibited in several Brazilian and European cities, including the Revolutionary Salon, Rio (1931) and the São Paulo Modern Art Museum show (1949). At first figurative, his paintings represent northeast colours and topics with formal rhythms and chromatic harmony. Turning to abstractionism in 1948, he painted the first abstract mural in South America, in Recife. In the 1960s he reverted to figurativism.

M.A. GUIMARÃES LOPES

Días, Luis

b. 1951, Bonao, Dominican Republic

Musician

Días (born Díaz) began as singer and guitarist of **Grupo Convite** in 1976, interpreting folkloric and popular Dominican songs, influenced by the *nueva canción* latinoamericana. In the late 1970s Días experimented with fusions of rock, jazz and **bachata** with the group Transporte Urbano. In 1985 he wrote techno-bachatas, salsas (see **salsa**) and boleros (see **bolero**) for Sonia **Silvestre**'s album *Quiero andar* (I Want to Keep Moving). Among his greatest hits are 'La perdida' (Loose Woman), 'Andresito Reina', and 'The wachimán' (The Watchman). His songs tell the story of downtrodden Dominican people and have influenced younger musicians such as Juan Luis **Guerra**.

FERNANDO VALERIO-HOLGUÍN

Díaz, Jesús *see* Díaz Rodríguez, Jesús

Díaz, Jorge

b. 1930, Rosario, Argentina

Playwright

In 1959, Díaz began to work with **ICTUS** in Chile, the group that would stage many of his plays. With them, he would also work as an actor and stage designer. Originally located within the theatre of the absurd movement, his plays have branched in many directions He has written several children's plays and many scripts for radio and television. Twice winner of the coveted Tirso de Molina prize, his plays include *Introducción al elefante y otras zoologías* (Introduction to the Elephant and other Zoologies) (1968), *Mata a tu prójimo como a ti mismo* (Kill Thy Neighbour as Thyself) (1977) and *Ayer sin ir más lejos* (Yesterday to Go no Further) (1986).

MARINA PIANCA

Díaz, Rolando

b. 1947, Havana, Cuba

Film-maker

With mordant wit, Díaz (alongside Juan Carlos **Tabio**) was responsible for the renaissance of Cuban film comedy in the 1980s. The younger brother of Jesús **Díaz**, Rolando entered **ICAIC** in

1969 to work in the sound department (he had previously worked in radio), but soon moved over to production. He was a war correspondent in Angola in 1976 and, between 1977 and 1981, worked for *Noticiero ICAIC Latinoamericano* – his name appears in more than fifty weekly editions – and directed short documentaries. His first feature was *Los pájaros tirándole a la escopeta* (Tables Turned) (1984), a gentle satire of contemporary Cuban life, gender relations and generational conflicts. After several rather uninspired comedies in the 1980s, his *Melodrama* (1994) was a lovely surprise, as he used humour once again to critically portray Cuban social issues. His most recent film, *Si tú me comprendieras* (If Only You Understood Me) (1998), follows a self-reflexive mode, as a film-maker looking for an Afro Cuban actress for a musical comedy takes to the streets with a video camera in search of the perfect face and gesture.

ANA M. LÓPEZ

Díaz, Simón

b. 1928, Barbacoas, Aragua State, Venezuela

Musician

Díaz is a key figure in the history of Venezuelan and Latin American popular music, particularly as a collector of the folk music of central Venezuela, the tonada llanera. His songs have been performed by a range of artists including Celia **Cruz**, Caetano **Veloso** and Plácido Domingo; they include 'Caballo viejo' (Old Horse) and 'El becerrito' (Little Calf). From a poor rural family, with little schooling, his humour and passion for music opened a path into television. He still presents a children's programme on state **television**, where he is known as Tío Simón (Uncle Simon), but his greatest successes were in the 1960s.

ALICIA RIOS

Díaz Quiñones, Arcadio

b. 1940, Mayagüez, Puerto Rico

Literary critic

Díaz Quiñones has devoted many articles to the writing of history and to the role of intellectuals in Hispanic-Caribbean society in the nineteenth and twentieth centuries. His publications include *Conversación con José Luis González* (A Conversation with José Luis **González**) (1976) and *La memoria rota: ensayos de cultura y política* (Broken Memory: Essays on Culture and Politics) (1993). He directs the series 'La Nave y el Puerto' for Ediciones Huracán in San Juan, which has published work by Tomás Blanco, Cintio **Vitier** and Mario **Vargas Llosa** among others. He taught at the University of Puerto Rico before taking a position as Professor of Spanish at Princeton University in 1983.

JUAN CARLOS QUINTERO HERENCIA

Díaz Rodríguez, Jesús

b. 1941, Havana, Cuba

Writer and film-maker

Exiled from Cuba since 1990, his articles, critical of the Cuban regime, provoked the wrath of Armando Hart, Cuban Minister of Culture, who denounced him for treason. Díaz participated in the student movement against Fulgencio **Batista** in the mid-1950s. In 1966 he won the **Casa de las Américas** short-story prize for his collection, *Los años duros* (The Hard Years). In 1967 he founded, and later edited, seventeen issues of the journal, *El caimán barbudo*. In 1971 he joined the Cuban Film Institute (**ICAIC**), becoming a feature director in 1977. His novel, *Las inciales de la tierra* (Origins of Earth), written in the mid-1970s, was not published in Cuba until a decade later. He directed the feature films, *55 hermanos* (55 brothers) (1981) and *Lejanía* (Distance) (1985), both groundbreaking for their focus on the exile experience. He is editor of the review, *Encuentros de la cultura cubana*, published in Spain.

JOSÉ ANTONIO EVORA

Díaz Solís, Gustavo

b. 1920, Guiria, Sucre, Venezuela

Writer

Although he published little, Díaz Solís was undoubtedly a major influence on generations of short story writers. A lawyer and university professor, he occupied a number of important university posts. Having studied English and US literature in Washington and Chicago, he published his first writings in the journal *Contapunto* as well as *Elite*, *Revista nacional de cultura*, *Fantoches* and others. His brief stories are built around strong and often subconscious emotions such as death, desire and conflict. He also has an important body of translations of Romantic and modern poetry from English. In 1996 he won the National Literature Prize.

JORGE ROMERO LEÓN

Díaz Torres, Daniel

b. 1948, Havana, Cuba

Film-maker

A key member of the second generation of the Cuban film institute's (**ICAIC**) film-makers, Díaz Torres began at the **Noticiero ICAIC Latinoamericano** making documentaries; his first fictional works were directly indebted to his documentary experiences. *Jíbaro* (The Wild One) (1985) was a fictionalization of the subjects of two of his earlier documentaries. Although not his best work, *Alicia en el pueblo de maravillas* (Alice in Wonder Town) (1991), based on a Jesús **Díaz** script, certainly became his most controversial. Its parodic allusions to contemporary social problems were widely criticized by party bureaucrats. The film was quickly pulled from distribution and, in the context of the **Festival Internacional del Nuevo Cine Latinoamericano** (see **film festivals**), shown only once to foreign delegates. Simultaneously, Julio **García Espinosa** resigned as head of ICAIC and Alfredo **Guevara** returned from his diplomatic post in Europe to take over. After teaching at the Escuela Internacional de Cine y Televisión for some time, Díaz Torres returned to direction with *Quiéreme y verás* (Love Me and See) (1995) and, most notably, *Kleines Tropikana* (Tropicana Nights) (1997), the latter a Cuban–German co-production (see **co-productions**).

ANA M. LÓPEZ

DICAP

DICAP is the record label most closely associated with the Chilean *nueva canción* movement. Formed in 1968 as Jota Jota, it became the Discoteca del Cantar Popular (Popular Song Collection) in 1969. It produced over one hundred records before the 1973 military *coup*. Thereafter it produced one hundred more from exile in Paris (1973–8) and Madrid (1978–87). Within Chile, its work was continued through the **Alerce Records** label. The artists who recorded for DICAP included the Parras (Isabel and Angel), Víctor **Jara**, Margot Loyola, Tito Fernández, **Quilapayún**, **Inti-Illimani**, **Curacas**, Aparcoa, **Illapu**, Patricio **Manns** and Los Jaivas.

ALFONSO PADILLA

Didi

b. 1917, Salvador, Brazil

Candomblé dignitary and artist

A leading figure in the Afro-Brazilian cultural life, Mestre Didi (Deoscóredes Maximiliano dos Santos) is *assobá* (minister of the *orixá* Omolú) in one of the most prestigious **Candomblé** temples in Salvador, Ilê Axê Opô Afonjá, and *alapini* (high priest) of Ilê Axipá, a temple dedicated to the worship of the *eguns* (spirits of the ancestors) on the Island of Itaparica. An acclaimed artist who works with natural materials to create sacred objects and vestments used in Candomblé rituals, Didi is also author of several books, including the first Yoruba–Portuguese dictionary, a history of Ilê Axé Opô Afonjá, and many volumes of short stories and legends relating to Afro-Brazilian religion. In the late 1990s, a multimedia CD, *Ancestralidade africana*

do Brasil (African Ancestry in Brazil) was produced to commemorate his eightieth birthday.

CHRISTOPHER DUNN

Diego, Eliseo

b. 1920, Havana, Cuba; d. 1994, Mexico City

Writer

Originally a member of the **Orígenes** literary group, Diego was more influenced by his readings of the Spanish Golden Age lyric and English poetry and prose (especially the fantastic) than he was by his early association with Juan Ramón Jiménez or José **Lezama Lima**. His poetry and stories were always superbly crafted and luminously simple, combining affection for everyday things with a profound reverence for the (frustrated) promise of the Republican era of Cuban history. After the 1959 Revolution, Diego stayed in Cuba, working at the National Library, and later at the Union of Writers and Artists of Cuba (**UNEAC**).

BEN A. HELLER

Diegues, Carlos

b. 1940, Maceió, Brazil

Film-maker

Diegues was the director of one episode of the collective film *Cinco vezes favela* (Five Times Shanty Town) (1961), produced by the Centre of Popular Culture (**CPC**) in Rio, many of whose film-makers became prominent in **Cinema Novo**. He made several films with a national-popular perspective, and argued for a technically poor, socially engaged cinema. In the 1970s Diegues became a principal advocate of the 'turn to the market', directing successes like **Xica da Silva** (1976) and **Bye Bye Brasil** (1979). In the 1980s, he penetrated the market further through co-productions with television. In 1996 he directed *Tieta*, based on a novel by Jorge **Amado**.

ISMAIL XAVIER AND THE USP GROUP

Dieste, Eladio

b. 1917, Artigas, Uruguay

Engineer

For fifty years Dieste has studied the uses of tiles as building materials. His designs in reinforced ceramics have been adopted for warehouses, gymnasia and shopping centres and in the arched roofs of churches – the Iglesia de Atlántida (1957) and the Iglesia de Durazno (1967), both in Uruguay. Professor of Mechanical and Structural Engineering at the University of Montevideo, he has taught throughout Latin America. He is a member of the Academy of Sciences and of Fine Arts of Argentina and of the Academy of Engineering of Uruguay.

MARCO MAGGI

Diez, Barbarito

b. 1909, Bolondrón, Cuba; d. 1995, Havana, Cuba

Singer

An outstanding singer of **danzones**, Diez's reputation as a performer was already well established in his home province of Oriente by the age of fourteen. In 1930 he moved to Havana, and a year later formed a trio with Graciano Gómez and Isaac Oviedo. The pianist and composer Antonio María Romeu invited him to join his orchestra in 1935, and he continued thereafter as its main soloist. When Romeu died twenty years later, the orchestra adopted Barbarito Diez's name. His eleven recorded albums are testimony to the range of his repertoire.

JOSÉ ANTONIO EVORA

Díez de Medina, Fernando

b. 1908, La Paz, Bolivia; d. 1990, La Paz

Writer

One of the most prolific writers in twentieth-century Bolivian literature, Diez de Medina often used literature for political purposes. He wrote poetry, essays such as *La teogonía andina* (Andean Theogony) (1973), drama, a novel *El guerrillero y la luna* (The Guerrillero and the Moon) (1972), biographies and a history of Bolivian literature. Despite his vast output, current criticism does not consider him to be of theoretical significance as a philosopher or a sociologist. He was famous for his polemical newspaper articles, and played a prominent political role, filling government and diplomatic posts. He investigated and idealized the mythology of the **Aymara**.

MARÍA DORA VILLA GÓMEZ

Dihigo, Martín

b. 1906, Matanzas, Cuba; d. 1971, Cienfuegos, Cuba

Baseball player

One of the most versatile Cuban baseball players of all time, 'El Inmortal' (The Immortal) Dihigo's career began in the Cuban professional leagues. He played in Mexico and then in the segregated black US league with the Cuban Stars, as well as in Venezuela, Puerto Rico and the Dominican Republic. In Cuba he registered the highest number of victories as pitcher (between 1923 and his retirement in 1947) and was also leading batter on several occasions. He is the only Cuban player to appear in three halls of fame: Cuba, Mexico and Cooperstown, USA.

WILFREDO CANCIO ISLA

Dios se lo pague

A classic of Argentine cinema, *Dios se lo pague* (May God Reward You) (1948) stands midway between doctrinaire social discourse and the conservatism of melodrama. Based on a play by Brazilian playwright Joracy Camargo, and directed by Luis César **Amadori**, it centres on the interplay of appearance and reality. Poverty and wealth, love and money, honesty and hypocrisy come together in the characters of a beggar (played by Arturo de Córdova) who philosophizes about social justice from a church doorway, yet turns out to be a millionaire businessman, and a woman (Zully **Moreno**) who seems wealthy and distinguished yet every night risks all in a gambling house in exchange for a few pesos. At root, it is a story of contempt and vengeance; his against an industrialist who, years earlier had robbed him, patented his invention as the latter's own and had him sent to prison; hers against an aristocracy to which she aspires but cannot enter. Finally when each achieves their objective the truth is revealed and, when everything seems to have reached its conclusion, the couple seek redemption by offering jewels to the Virgin in the very church where they first met. These elements, with the sure direction of Amadori, a high level of technical accomplishment and the grand sets and costumes provided by **Argentina Sono Film**, made *Dios se lo pague* one of the greatest box office successes in the history of Argentine cinema. For Zully Moreno, it opened up the whole Spanish-speaking world; for de Córdova, it meant a return to his earlier prominence. The same actors took the leading roles in *Nacha Regules* (based on the novel by Manuel **Gálvez**) (1950) and *María Montecristo* (1951), both by Amadori.

The film won the highest awards of the Argentine Academy of Film Arts and Sciences and of the Argentine Association of Film Critics, as well as first prize in the Latin American Film Section in Madrid 1948 and the Montecristo Award in Italy. It was also nominated for an Oscar for the best foreign film. Although the statistical evidence does not exist, many claim it was the highest-grossing Latin American film of the classical period.

DIANA PALADINO

DIP

The Brazilian Departamento de Imprensa e Propaganda (DIP, Department of Press and Propaganda) was created in 1939 as an institutional organ of the proto-fascist **Estado Novo**, established after a political *coup* headed by then President Getulio **Vargas**. Its objective was to construct and preserve the good image of the regime and the dictator, both internally and externally; to consolidate and disseminate the legitimating doctrines of the new political order; and to counter any criticisms or resistance. The department answered directly to the President and consisted of six sections: propaganda, **radio** broadcasting, cinema, theatre, tourism and print.

NICOLAU SEVCENKO

disappeared, the

As repressive regimes flourished throughout Latin America from the 1960s through the 1980s, **death squads** and secret police created an atmosphere of terror and eliminated real, potential or imagined enemies of the state. *Testimonios* (see **testimonio**) from these years explain how Ford Falcon automobiles roamed the streets, occasionally plucking people off as they walked to work; at other times the military surrounded whole neighbourhoods, plundering houses and dragging their occupants into waiting vehicles. Although many of the individuals carrying out these kidnappings were part of national institutions, such as the armed forces and police, their actions were extralegal and neither traced nor held up for judgement. The victims' loved ones at first fled to police stations seeking help, then to the courts and other authorities, unaware that they would be ignored, mocked or piteously deceived.

Most of the disappeared met with death and were never found. Argentines Jacobo **Timerman** and Alicia Portnoy survived their disappearances to give testimonial accounts to bring a military junta to account in *Preso sin nombre, celda sin número* (Prisoner Without a Name, Cell Without a Number) (1981) and *The Little School: Tales of Disappearance and Survival* (1986), respectively. They tell of those taken to clandestine jails, tortured and interrogated for considerable lengths of time. Some were later 'released' to official jails, while others were killed and buried in mass graves, pushed into rivers and the sea or, in a macabre performance by the military, dressed up and left on streets as evidence of shootouts with **guerrilla fighters**. Pregnant female prisoners were frequently allowed to live until they gave birth and their child could be taken for adoption. Argentine film-maker Luis **Puenzo**'s *La historia oficial* (The Official Story) (1985) reveals the webs of complicity and willed ignorance that allowed disappearances to remain unremarked and the appearances of these babies to be unquestioned.

Eventually, groups were formed to confront the official silence. Mothers in Argentina began to demonstrate in the **Plaza de Mayo** every week to demand accountability of the government, just as today the Grandmothers of the Plaza de Mayo continue to ask about the infants who were taken from the disappeared. Marta **Traba**'s *Conversación al sur* (Mothers and Shadows) (1981) tells a particularly vivid story of how women from various social classes felt as they joined forces to cry out for their children's return. Women and men from all over Latin America now take to the streets with placards and silhouettes with the names and photos of remembered ones as an act of love and political resistance.

This kind of terror which penetrates into everyday life and intimate relationships overwhelms a society and requires many decades to be explored and absorbed as a personal and social loss. Psychotherapists such as the Chileans Elizabeth Lira and Eugenia Weinstein have searched for ways to help the circles of people affected by even one disappearance, while other social scientists have looked for evidence in the documentation, the testimonies and the bodies that are now being unearthed, and artists express the feelings of loss and hope that this terror will not happen again.

Further reading

Amnesty International (1993) *Getting Away With Murder: Political Killings and 'Disappearances' in the 1990s*, New York: Amnesty International.

Anderson, M.E. (1993) *Dossier Secreto: Argentina's Desaparecidos and the Myth of the 'Dirty War'*, Boulder, CO: Westview.

Corradi, J. *et al.* (eds) (1992) *Fear at the Edge: State Terror and Resistance in Latin America*, Berkeley, CA: University of California Press.

MARY JANE TREACY

Discépolo, Armando

b. 1887, Buenos Aires, Argentina; d. 1971, Buenos Aires

Playwright

Discépolo is one of the founding figures of contemporary Argentine drama. The son of Italian immigrants, Discépolo devoted most of his works to the abyss between the promised prosperity of the New World and the reality of immigrant life. He developed a theatrical language called the ***grotesco criollo*** in which details of plot, character and interpersonal relations are marked by profound contradictions and a strident despair, providing audiences with a sense of the monstrous underbelly of vaunted national prosperity.

DAVID WILLIAM FOSTER

Discépolo, Enrique Santos

b. 1901, Buenos Aires, Argentina; d. 1951, Buenos Aires

Musician, actor and director

The name of Discépolo is synonymous with the high points of tango song – 'Uno' (One), 'Cambalache' (Thrift Shop) or 'Cafetín de Buenos Aires' (Buenos Aires Cafe) – yet he was a multi-talented artist, lyricist, intuitive musician, playwright and actor. His tango lyrics are characteristically reflective and intellectual, exploring life at its most unhappy and critical. His lyrics grew increasingly sceptical and despairing, expressed in the mocking, cynical words of songs like 'Yira, yira' or 'Cambalache' and the mordant ironies of 'Chorra', 'Justo el 31' or 'Fangal'. If **Manzi** is the poet of tango, Discépolo is its philosopher. His portrayal of the characters and personalities of Buenos Aires, isolated and despairing, achieves a level of literary insight comparable to that of Roberto **Arlt**.

An actor since 1917, appearing in plays by his brother Armando **Discépolo**, he was also growing as a composer. In the mid-1920s, his composition 'Quevachaché', with its expressionist aesthetic and its powerful caricature, was initially rejected by a public accustomed to very different lyrics: in the song the woman calls her husband *un otario* (a fool) because of his ethical misgivings: 'Give me food, and keep your moral sense/give me money, money, money – I want to live!'

In 1931 his theatrical and musical interests came together in a show called *Caramelos surtidos* (Assorted Sweets). In 1934 he met the actress and singer Tania, with whom he shared the rest of his life. After a failed attempt to become an orchestra director, he turned to the cinema, writing music for films like *El alma del bandoneón* (Soul of the Bandoneon) (1935), appearing as an actor in *Mateo* (1937) and acting as both scriptwriter and director for *Fantasmas de Buenos Aires* (Ghosts of Buenos Aires) (1942). In 1951, while directing *Blum* for the theatre, his tuberculosis worsened; he disappeared from the late night tango clubs and became a silent recluse. According to Tania, his weight dropped to 37 kilos, yet he never lost his sense of irony: 'They'll soon have to inject me in my overcoat'. He lives on in the words and music of his tangos and in Homero Manzi's homage, the tango 'Discepolín', with music by **Troilo**.

Further reading

Collier, S. *et al.* (1993) *Tango: The Dance, the Song, the Story*, London: Thames and Hudson.

Discépolo, E.S. (1977) *Cancionero*, Buenos Aires: Torres Agüero.

Romano, E. (1995) *Las letras del tango (Antologia cronológica 1900–1980)*, Rosario: Fundación Ross.

LUIS GUSMAN

Discours Antillais, Le

Published in 1981, *Le Discours Antillais* (Caribbean Discourse) is a monumental essay collection which established Edouard **Glissant**'s reputation as the major Caribbean theorist of the postwar, post-**négritude** period. As the title suggests, the book is both a discourse on the **Caribbean** and a study of Caribbean discursive practices. In dense and wide-ranging essays, Glissant addresses Caribbean history, cultural resistance, a poetics of landscape and his theory of *antillanité*. He theorizes that the Caribbean islands are typified by an irreducible **creole** diversity, threatened in Martinique because of departmentalization. The region, he argues, possesses an exemplary indeterminacy in a world increasingly dominated by cultural archipelagos.

J. MICHAEL DASH

Discurso Literario

Discurso Literario appeared initially in 1983. It was published semi-annually at Oklahoma State University and directed by exiled Paraguayan writer Juan Manuel **Marcos**, whose personal energy was decisive in its success. The journal undertook to represent the broad sweep of Hispanic and Latin American literature, particularly the **Boom** and **post-Boom**. In 1984 it added sections devoted to creative writing, interviews and reviews. Its unadorned pages included such notable contributors as Augusto **Roa Bastos**, Mempo **Giardinelli**, Elvio **Romero** and Isaac Goldemberg. When Marcos's exile was lifted in 1989, he transplanted *Discurso* to Paraguay but relinquished the directorship in 1992. Since then *Discurso Literario* has continued to publish, but without the renown of its heyday.

TRACY K. LEWIS

Disla, Reynaldo

b. 1956, Cotuí, Dominican Republic

Playwright

Disla belongs to the generation of the 1980s. His 1985 play *Bolo Francisco* won the **Casa de las Américas** Prize. He was also recognized at **Casa de Teatro** (House of Theatre) for his play *La muerte aplaudida* (The Applauded Death). He has acted in forty-two plays, pioneered **puppet theatre** for children, and founded several theatre groups, such as Texpo and Los Teatreros. In his plays, Disla uses new experimental techniques to express social conflicts. Influenced by Bertolt Brecht's aesthetics (see **Brechtian theatre**), Disla is always looking for interaction between audiences and actors.

FERNANDO VALERIO-HOLGUÍN

Distéfano, Juan Carlos

b. 1933, Villa Celina, Buenos Aires, Argentina

Sculptor, draughtsman and graphic designer

Distéfano trained as a graphic designer before specializing in drawing. From 1960 he worked in the graphic design department of the influential **Instituto Di Tella** in Buenos Aires. His first solo exhibition was in 1964. In 1977, following the banning of a play by his wife Griselda **Gambaro**, they moved to Barcelona, returning to Buenos Aires in 1980. His sculptures are often graphic or metaphorical comments on torture and violence, based on the human figure.

GABRIEL PEREZ-BARREIRO

Dittborn, Eugenio

b. 1943, Santiago, Chile

Artist

Dittborn is best known for the work called the *Airmail Paintings*, which he circulated from 1983 to 1989. This coincided with the latter half of General **Pinochet**'s military dictatorship, when the repression of artists and **intellectuals** was most intense and when many (if not most) of Dittborn's colleagues had fled the country. Sending artwork overseas where consciousness-raising and solidarity was most needed was a brilliant ruse to circumvent censorship. Dittborn described these packages of subversive images of repression – often drawn from other historical moments (such as that of earlier colonization and genocide in Chile) or artists (such as **Posada**'s famous portrait of a hanged peasant) – as 'pregnant mothers [who] contain their *unborn* children in amniotic fluid; like tombs contain *white bones*' and 'love letters painted in some place of confinement'. Approximately seventy-five *Airmail Paintings* were mailed out.

Dittborn received a formal art education in Chile and then pursued studies in graphic arts and painting in Paris, Madrid and Berlin until 1970. He became professor of both the latter disciplines in Santiago. Following the putsch against the **Popular Unity** President **Allende**, Dittborn decided to remain and combat militarism not with conventional dialectical Marxism but with unorthodox and often impromptu street art and **happenings**. This involved collaboration with fellow artists Juan **Dávila**, Catalina Parra and Lotty **Rosenfeld**, and writers Diamela **Eltit**, Enrique **Lihn**, Nelly **Richard** and Raúl **Zurita**, in a variety of dramatic, poetic, dance and visual events.

In the latter 1970s Dittborn experimented with compound materials, combining oils, fabric, feathers with backing of jute, perspex, card and chipboard. These early *Impinturas* developed into the *Airmail Paintings* shown in Colombia and Australia in 1984, then circulated to seventeen cities. In the early 1980s he also commented on the despoliation of his homeland by pouring 400 litres of burnt car oil on the Tarapaca Desert, the culmination of a series of controlled/uncontrolled spillages exploring the properties of such fluids as acids, and thinning or cleaning agents. Much of the work was documented on video or on national television.

In the 1990s, Dittborn received major international showings in *The Interrupted Life* (The New Museum of Contemporary Art, New York), the Fourth Bienal (Havana, Cuba), *The Absent Body* (ICA, Boston), *America, Bride of the Sun* (Koninlijk Museum, Antwerp), *Documenta 9* (Kassel), and *La Cita Transcultural* (Museum of Contemporary Art, Sydney). His work has been widely written about by critics in both Latin America and the West, where a major exhibition (*Mapa*) at the ICA in London (1992) included commentaries from Nelly **Richard**, Adriana Valdés, Guy Brett, Sean Cubitt and Roberto Merino.

Further reading

Dittborn, E. (1985) *Another Periphery: 17 Airmail Paintings from Chile*, Melbourne.

—— (1987) *Chile Vive*, Madrid: Círculo de Bellas Artes.

—— (1994) *MAPA. Airmail Paintings/Pinturas Aero-postales*, London: ICA/Arts Council catalogue

—— (1991) *Camino/Way*, texts by Sean Cubitt and Guy Brett, Santiago de Chile: Morgan-Marinetti.

AMANDA HOPKINSON

D'León, Oscar

b. 1943, Antímano, Caracas, Venezuela

Musician

Named 'the king of **salsa**' after a successful US tour, Oscar D'León is one of Latin America's most important popular musicians and one of its outstanding bass players. In 1975 D'León and his orchestra, La Dimensión Latina, achieved the highest sales of any Venezuelan salsa band. He has shared the stage with major figures like Celia **Cruz** and Tito **Puente**. From a poor background, his personal life has tended to be chaotic and prone to scandal; on the other hand, he has given generous help to the needy. Like all the great salseros, D'León wears flamboyant colours in performance and possesses a tireless energy.

ALICIA RiOS

Dobru, R.

b. 1935, Suriname; d. 1983, Suriname

Writer and politician

Dobru (real name Robin Raveles) was a political activist, politician and literary author from the 1960s until his death. He is the author of one the best-known poems in Sranan Tongo, 'Wan bon' (One Tree), which appeared in his 1965 debut poetry collection *Matapi: poewema*. His poetry and prose writing was greatly influenced by Cuban and Chinese communist ideology and his strong nationalist feelings. A selection of his poetry, *Boodschappen uit de zon* (Messages from under the Sun) was published by a Dutch publishing house in 1982.

AART G. BROEK

Doces Bárbaros

The Doces Bárbaros (Sweet Barbarians) was a musical project for the 'Age of Aquarius' which reunited Caetano **Veloso**, Gilberto **Gil**, Gal **Costa**, and **Maria Bethânia**, a cohort of artists from Bahia who first performed together in 1964. The 1976 project yielded a double album, a documentary film, and a major national tour conceived as a countercultural parallel to the third century barbarian invasions of Rome. The theme song announced: 'With love in our hearts/ We prepare to invade/ Filled with joy/ We enter the beloved city'. The tour ended abruptly in Florianopolis when Gil and the band's drummer were arrested for marijuana possession.

CHRISTOPHER DUNN

documentary

A mode of film-making distinguished by its attempts to present actual people, places and activities, and to deal with facts rather than fiction, it is a direct descendant of the films of current events of the early silent cinema (see **silent film**) and cousin to the newsreel (see **newsreels**). Its status in Latin American is long and prestigious: Latin America has often been the subject of documentary interest to the USA and Europe (beginning with the Spanish–American War of 1898, already amply documented in film), but it has also generated significant indigenous movements. The first documentary impulse of significance was a series of films chronicling the events of the Mexican Revolution (1910–20) (see **revolutions**) that, according to historian Aurelio de los Reyes, constitute the real 'golden age' of the Mexican cinema.

However, with few exceptions, the documentary did not thrive in the 1930s and 1940s, when the main preoccupation of producers was the viability of national cinema industries. Only in nations where the State had begun to exhibit an interest in the cinema is there evidence of imaginative documentary production, as in Brazil, for example, where the **Vargas** regime created the Instituto Nacional do Cinema Educativo (1937–66) to produce didactic and informational documentaries. There, Humberto **Mauro** produced dozens of documentaries on diverse topics, most notably the extraordinary seven-film series, *Brasilianas* (1945–56), which has been described as 'small masterpieces of magical and poetic images'.

A renaissance in documentary production occurred alongside the development of film culture in the late 1940s and 1950s mostly as a result of the growth of **cine clubs**, which often screened landmark social documentaries by the likes of Robert Flaherty, Joris Ivens and John Grierson (guest of honour at a **SODRE**-sponsored festival in Montevideo in 1958), and stimulated interest in using film for social documentation among amateur film-makers. Almost simultaneously, in the late 1950s, a series of remarkable documentaries appeared in several countries: *Tire dié* (Throw Me a Dime) (1958–60) by Fernando **Birri** and his students at the **Escuela de Cine Documental de Santa Fe** in Argentina; Margot **Benacerraf**'s *Araya* (1958) in Venezuela; Alberto Miller's *Cantegriles* (Shanty Towns) (1958) and Ugo **Ulive**'s *Como el Uruguay no hay* (There's no Place like Uruguay) (1960) in Uruguay; Linduarte Noronha's *Aruanda* (1959) in Brazil; Julio **García Espinosa** and Tomás **Gutiérrez Alea**'s *El mégano* (The Charcoal Workers) (1954) in Cuba and Sergio Bravo's *La marcha del carbón* (The March of Coal) (1960) in Chile.

Although many of the film-makers of this first explosion of the documentary worked in relative isolation and lacked the supporting context necessary to continue producing (Benacerraf in Venezuela, for example), their experience set the stage for important work in the 1960s, especially among film-makers constituting the new national cinemas of the era and the **New Latin American Cinema** movement, which was at first identified precisely by documentary work like Jorge **Sanjinés**'s *Revolución* (Bolivia, 1963), Mario **Handler**'s *Carlos* (Uruguay, 1965), and Geraldo **Sarno**'s *Viramundo* (Brazil, 1964–5), all screened at the first **Viña del Mar Festival** in 1967. The documen-

tary was not only a privileged mode for social protest; its alleged immediacy and authenticity also made it attractive to fictional film-makers who consistently began to mix both modes: Sanjinés in *El **coraje del pueblo*** (The Courage of the People) (Bolivia, 1971); Sara **Gómez**'s *De cierta manera* (Cuba, One Way or Another) (1974–7); Jorge Bodansky and Orlando Senna's *Iracema* (Brazil, 1974).

Santiago **Alvarez**, in Cuba, was one of the most important documentarists of this period and director not only of the newsreel *Noticiero ICAIC Latinoamerica* but of a series of brilliantly innovative films through the 1970s. Following a militant agitprop model, Alvarez transformed the scarcity of resources at ICAIC into the departure point of a search for new aesthetic possibilities based on collage. Alvarez was a brilliant editor, not only of images but of sound/image relations and graphics, which in his films often replaced the voice-over typically overused in the genre: thus *Now* (1965) was 'narrated' by Lena Horne's radical rendering of Hava Nagila, while *Hanoi, Martes 13* (Hanoi, Tueday 13th) (1967) used verses by José Martí. Alvarez's work influenced an entire generation of militant film-makers, including Handler in Uruguay, Carlos **Alvarez** in Colombia, and, perhaps most famously, Fernando **Solanas**, Octavio Getino in Argentina and **Grupo Cine Liberación**, whose *La **hora de los hornos*** (The Hour of the Furnaces) (1968) remains the genre's greatest achievement.

Considered crucially important for training film-makers as well as a very accessible informational resource, the documentary thrived in Cuba's **ICAIC**, expanding beyond the militant agitprop genre. Among the most important documentarists of the 1960s and 1970s were Nicolás **Guillén** Landrián, whose *Coffea arábiga* (Coffee Seed) (1968) was an important deconstruction of the didactic subgenre; Octavio **Cortázar**, who tackled cultural and religious themes with great subtlety in *Por primera vez* (For the First Time) (1967) or *Hablando de un personaje que unos llaman San Lázaro y otros Babalú* (Speaking of a Character Some Call St Lazarus and others Babalu) (1968); and Sara **Gómez**, who began to develop her unique first-person mode of address in films like *Iré a Santiago* (I'll go to Santiago) (1964). Later, film-makers like Luis Felipe

Bernaza, Rolando **Díaz**, and Enrique Colina developed a witty, personal style that made them very popular with national audiences.

In Brazil, **Cinema Novo** included an important documentary component. Many directors better known for their fictional work began with social documentaries: Arnaldo **Jabor**'s *Opinião pública* (Public Opinion) (1967) and Leon **Hirszman**'s *Maioria absoluta* (Absolute Majority) (1964), for example. In São Paulo, producer Thomas Farkas inaugurated an ambitious documentary project, first focusing on urban issues – as in *Nossa escola de samba* (Our Samba School) (Manuel Horacio Giménez, 1962) – and later turned to the problems of the northeastern *sertão*.

An important strain in documentary filmmaking in this period was a now politicized ethnographic or anthropological variant (see **ethnographic film**), especially in the work of Marta **Rodríguez** and Jorge **Silva** in Colombia, like *Chircales* (Brickmakers) (1968–72). In Mexico, the work of Nicolas **Echevarría** was an important, albeit solitary, example (*María Sabina, mujer espíritu* (Maria Sabina, Spirit Woman) (1978)). Following a different model, another important Mexican documentarist was Paul **Leduc**, whose *Reed: Mexico insurgente* (Reed, Insurgent Mexico) (1970) was inspired by Casasola's photographs of the revolution and presented a different, more human face of that often representationally overblown historical process.

Political changes and military governments had a direct impact upon documentary production in the 1970s and 1980s: militant documentarists like Raymundo Gleyzer in Argentina were tortured and/or disappeared; others went into exile, like Chilean Patricio **Guzmán**, who finished the monumental trilogy, *La batalla de Chile* (The Battle of Chile) (1973–9), in Cuba. An important commentary upon this period was produced by Eduardo **Coutinho**'s *Cabra marcado para morrer: Vinte anos depois* (Man Marked to Die: Twenty Years Later) (1984), in which he takes up a documentary project aborted by the 1964 *coup* and documents what has occurred to the family and town that he had begun filming twenty years earlier.

The militant documentary was again revived in Central America in the 1980s in El Salvador and Nicaragua. In the former, the **FMLN** sponsored several militant works, like *Carta de Morazán* (Letter from Morazan) (1983) by the collective Cero a la Izquierda. In the latter, the Sandinistas followed the ICAIC model, focusing on newsreels and, somewhat later, documentaries like *Bananeras* (Ramiro Lacayo, 1982). However, by this time, technological change had made video the medium of choice for militant and interventionist filmmaking.

Since the 1980s the independent documentary on film has languished, although it has not disappeared; individual practitioners continue to make films, although it is difficult to discern the existence of movements or schools. Some notable examples are Jorge Zanayda's *Tango, bayle nuestro* [*sic*] (Tango, Our Dance) (Argentina, 1986), a contemplation of the social space of the dance; the idiosyncratic series, *Imagens do inconsciente* (Images from the Unconscious) (1983–6), by Leon Hirszman in Brazil; Miguel **Littín**'s chronicle of his clandestine return to Chile, *Acta general de Chile* (Letter from Chile) (1985); Patricio Guzmán's nostalgic *La memoria obstinada* (The Obstinate Memory) (1996); Leandro Katz's *El día que me quieras* (The Day You Will Love Me) (1998), about the last pictures of Che **Guevara**.

Further reading

Aray, E. (1983) *Santiago Alvarez: Cronista del Tercer Mundo*, Caracas: Cinemateca Nacional.

Burton, J. (1990) *The Social Documentary in Latin America*, Pittsburgh: University of Pittsburgh Press.

Johnson, R. (1999) 'Documentary discourses and national identity', *Nuevo Texto Crítico* 21(22): 193–206.

ANA M. LÓPEZ

domestic labour

An important but undervalued part of the labour force of Latin American and Caribbean countries, women who are household workers face long hours, low pay, few days off, disrespectful treatment, low self-esteem and, often, sexual advances or assault by male members of the household.

Statistics show that about 20 per cent of the female labour force of these countries consists of household workers. Generally young (as young as twelve years old and mostly in the fifteen to thirty-five years age group), poor, uneducated and of a different racial origin than their employers, these women are easily exploited. Many are single mothers who have sole responsibility for the care of their own children. Often considered too old to do a good day's work by the age of forty, they face an insecure future with no pension and few alternatives.

Several factors have made it difficult for domestic workers to organize for better conditions: the lack of a common workplace, a lack of free time for organizing, the demands of family responsibilities and the threat of being fired if employers become aware of their union activities. The availability of a nearly endless supply of poor women needing work gives employers little incentive to improve conditions for the women who work in their households.

Despite these difficulties, there have been efforts to unionize on the part of household workers. In Mexico and Chile, unions of household workers appeared as early as the 1920s. Several countries now have national federations and in 1988 workers from twelve countries met in Bogotá, where they founded the first continent-wide women's labour organization, the Confederación Latinoamericana y del Caribe de Trabajadoras del Hogar (Latin American and Caribbean Confederation of Household Workers). This organization has begun to work with other groups throughout the world to address the common problems of domestic workers. Many of these groups met in Beijing in 1995 at the United Nations World Conference on Women, and, in 1996, the United Nations Commission on Human Rights for the first time mentioned household workers in its discussion of violence against women.

Further reading

Chaney, E.M. and García Castro, M. (eds) (1989) *Muchachas No More: Household Workers in Latin American and the Caribbean*, Philadelphia: Temple University Press.

Goldsmith, M. and Chaney, E. (1996) 'From Bolivia to Beijing: Household workers organize at the local, national, and international levels', in V.E. Rodriguez *et al.*, *Memoria of the Bi-National Conference: Women in Contemporary Mexican Politics II*, Austin: The Mexican Center of ILAS, University of Texas at Austin, 12–13 April (http://lanic.utexas.edu/ilas/mexcenter/women2).

CAROL WALLACE

domestic violence

'Mujer, No Estás Sola' (Woman, You are Not Alone) is the name of a programme for battered women in Costa Rica; the phrase represents the growing recognition that domestic violence is a widespread social, not individual, problem in Latin America. Statistics starkly illustrate this point. A study in Columbia suggests that one out of every five women have been beaten by a partner (Heise 1994). In Mexico, one in three women had been victims of family violence; twenty per cent reported blows to the stomach during pregnancy (Valdez and Shrader Cox 1991). In Costa Rica, 37 per cent of a randomly selected sample of 169 women reported receiving blows to the face or body; 7 per cent had been threatened with a firearm during an argument (Noonan 1998).

These seemingly inevitable results of *machista* culture mean that men feel entitled to beat 'their' women when they challenge male authority. Indeed, until recently, domestic violence was considered a logical, legitimate expression of *machismo* across Latin America. However, **women's movements** in various countries have challenged not only the cultural (e.g. *machismo*), but also the economic, and social relationships that produce domestic violence.

Women's movements in South America became vocal opponents of military authoritarianism, demanding democracy in the nation and the home. As they critiqued male violence at the state level, they became more aware of undemocratic tendencies in their own homes (e.g., see Jaquette 1989). Women in Brazil, for example, organized to establish women's police stations (*delegacias da mulher*) to record crimes against women and to offer support to victims (Eluf 1992). In Costa Rica, women's organizations have fought to provide women with greater economic independence and titles to homes in an effort to liberate them from abusive men (Carcedo 1997).

Even in countries with well-defined laws against domestic violence (e.g., Brazil, Costa Rica, Chile) significant extra-legal problems persist. First, women and men are still socialized to accept a certain degree of male violence as 'normal'. As a result, few cases go to court, and even fewer result in prosecution. In Brazil, courts continue to acquit men for beating or killing their female partners even though its highest court rejected the 'honour defence' in 1991 (a plea used to justify 'crimes of passion' as a defence of male honour) (Corral 1993). Second, women are usually economically dependent upon the men who beat them. In Chile, women are reluctant to prosecute because it may disrupt the family unit, an important source of cultural legitimacy and economic stability (González 1992). Despite significant gains, women's movements continue to face an up-hill battle.

Further reading

Carcedo, A. (1997) 'Never To Cry Alone Again: Women and Violence in Costa Rica', in I. Abshagen Leitinger (ed.) *The Costa Rican Women's Movement*, Pittsburgh, PA: University of Pittsburgh Press, pp. 160–68.

Corral, T. (1993) 'Brazil's women-run police station fights the odds', *MS*, November/December: 18.

Eluf, L.N. (1992) 'A New Approach to Law Enforcement: The Special Women's Police Stations in Brazil', in M. Schuler (ed.), *Freedom From Violence: Women's Strategies From Around the World*, New York: United Nations Development Fund for Women, pp. 199–212.

Gonzalez, N. (1992) 'A New Concept of Mediation: An Interdisciplinary Approach to Domestic Violence in Chile', in M. Schuler (ed.) *Freedom From Violence: Women's Strategies From Around the World*, New York: United Nations Development Fund for Women, pp. 227–53

Heise, L.L. (1994) *Violence Against Women: The Hidden Health Burden*, Washington DC: The World Bank, Discussion Paper No. 255.

Jaquette, J. (ed.) (1989) *The Women's Movement in Latin America: Feminism and the Transition to Democracy*, Boston: Unwin Hyman.

Noonan, R. (1998) 'Health Hierarchies and Heresies: Domestic Violence and Physical Quality of Life in Costa Rica', San Francisco, CA: Paper presented at the American Sociological Association Meetings.

Valdez S.R. and Shrader Cox, E. (1991) *Estudio Sobre la Incidencia de Violencia Doméstica en una Microregión de Ciudad Nezahualcóyotl, 1989*, Mexico City: Centro de Investigación y Lucha Contra la Violencia Doméstica.

RITA K. NOONAN AND CYNTHIA ESTEP

Domínguez, Franklin

b. 1931, Santo Domingo

Playwright

Domínguez is one of the most prolific playwrights of the Dominican Republic and the Director of the National School of Scenic Arts. His play *La extraña presencia* (The Strange Presence) won the Annual Prize of Literature in 1991. Among his most acclaimed plays are *Se busca un hombre honesto* (In Search of an Honest Man), *Lisístrata odia la política* (Lysistrata Hates Politics) and *La broma del senador* (The Senator's Joke). Domínguez has also written comedies and musical comedies. In his plays, Domínguez uses satire and humour to critique the Dominican society.

FERNANDO VALERIO-HOLGUÍN

Domínguez Caballero, Diego

b. 1915, Panama City

Philosopher

After receiving his doctorate in philosophy from the Universidad Central de Madrid, Diego Domínguez Caballero returned to his homeland to teach and promote the teaching of philosophy. He has published numerous pedagogical essays and books, including the aptly titled *Filosofía y Pedagogía* (Philosophy and Pedagogy) (1952).

NORMAN S. HOLLAND

Dominica

Situated in the Lesser Antilles, Dominica is a volcanic island forty kilometres long and nineteen kilometres wide. First settled by Amerindians around 6000 BC and called by them Wai'tukubuli, it was renamed in 1493 by Columbus. The object of great rivalry between the French and the British after it was relinquished by Spain, it was finally occupied by Britain in 1805. Its population of 83,000 (1990) is of mainly **Carib** and African descent, speaking a French-based creole (see **French-based creoles**). Dominica achieved independence in 1978. The next decade was dominated by Prime Minister Eugenia **Charles**, who made several unsuccessful attempts to link Dominica politically with other small Eastern Caribbean island states.

LENNOX HONEYCHURCH

Dominican Republic

The Dominican Republic shares with Haiti the island of Santo Domingo or Hispaniola, the second largest island in the Greater Antilles. It is 48,730 square kilometres in size, with a population of 7,826,075 (1994). Its capital is Santo Domingo.

Until the 1980s and the collapse of the world market price, **sugar** was the island's principal industry. Now, much of the land previously devoted to sugar has been diverted to citrus production. The experience of life on the plantations and in the shacks (*bateyes*) where the workers lived have been recorded in the cycle of 'sugar novels', among them Ramón Marrero Aristy's *Over*.

The country's principal source of income in the 1990s is tourism; one and a half million visitors used its 23,000 hotel rooms in 1992. Another source of income are the 'free zones' (*zonas francas*) where foreign plants are established within the country with special tax incentives. The dollars sent back by the one million Dominicans working abroad are also an important source of foreign currency.

From 1980 onwards, the economic crisis forced many Dominicans to emigrate, principally to the United States. Every year, thousands risk their lives attempting to cross the Mona Channel to reach Puerto Rico. The film *Pasaje de ida* (One Way Ticket), directed by Agliberto **Meléndez**, tells the story of a group of Dominicans who died by suffocation under an avalanche of sugar in the hold of the ship *Regina Express* where they had stowed away. In 1995, Angel Muñiz's *Nueba Yol* depicted the ups and downs in the life of one of the million Dominicans living in New York.

The island of Santo Domingo was discovered and colonized by Christopher Columbus, who landed on its north coast on 5 December 1492. On his second journey, in the following year, he founded Isabela, the first European town in the New World. In the city of Santo Domingo de Guzmán, founded on 4 August 1496 by the Admiral's brother Bartolomé, the Alcazar (or Fort) was built for the first Viceroy, Diego Colón, and the Real Audiencia (the Royal Tribunal) was set up there in 1511; it was the site for the first hospital (San Nicolás de Bari) and the first cathedral (Santa María la Menor) in the Americas, and in 1538, the first University (Santo Tomás de Aquino) was established. Manuel de Jesús Galván's historical novel *Enriquillo* described life in sixteenth-century colonial Santo Domingo.

Popular culture has it that Columbus's name contained a *fucú*, a curse that will bring disaster to anyone who utters it; for some Dominicans this is an expression of the catastrophe that the Admiral's arrival represented for the Taino population of the island. Nonetheless, the **Columbian quincentenary** Anniversary of the Encounter of Two Worlds was marked in Santo Domingo by the inauguration of the controversial **Faro a Colón** (Columbus Lighthouse), built by the octogenarian President Joaquín **Balaguer** whose passion for public works projects drained the public purse. The monument, 800 feet long and 150 feet high, projects a cross of light into the sky. Its cost was estimated at $250 million.

Between 1916 and 1924, the country experienced its first invasion by the United States. In 1930 Rafael Leonidas **Trujillo** came to power, and he ruled with an iron hand for the next thirty-one years. His assassination in 1961 threw the country into chaos, culminating in the first democratic elections, which brought Juan **Bosch** to the Presidency. He was overthrown by a military *coup* seven months later. In 1965 the April Revolution broke out, led by Colonel Francisco Alberto **Caamaño**; as a consequence, the United States invaded for the second time. For the next twenty years, a series of repressive governments headed by Balaguer have dominated the country's political life, with brief democratic interludes of government under the PRD (Dominican Revolutionary Party) and the PLD (Party of Dominican Liberation).

The two US invasions, the Trujillo dictatorship and the April rising have provided thematic material for many artists since 1960. Pedro **Mir**'s novel *Cuando amaban las tierras comuneras* (When They Loved the Common Lands) (1978) is set in the period between the two invasions. René **Fortunato** produced two documentaries, *Abril, la trinchera de honor* (April, the Trench of Honour) (1988) and *El poder del jefe* (The Power of the Chief) (1991). Marcio **Veloz Maggiolo**, who wrote several novels about Trujillo including *La biografía difusa de Sombra Castañeda* (The Diffuse Biography of Sombra Castañeda) (1980), is also the author of *De abril en adelante* (From April Onwards) (1975), the best-known novel about the second invasion. The 1965 American invasion produced an important generation of writers including René del **Risco Bermúdez**, Tony **Raful**, Andrés L. **Mateo** and Norberto James.

Dominican literature and painting have followed the same course as the other artistic movements of Europe and Latin America. The early twentieth century saw the formation of several **avant-garde** movements, including Vedrinismo, Postumismo and Los Nuevos. During the 1940s new writers' movements and groups again emerged, among them **Poesía Sorprendida**, the Independientes del 40 and the Generación del 48. In the fine arts, an important group of painters arose who employed abstraction, symbolism and 'tenebrismo' as a means of avoiding dictatorial censorship; Silvano **Lora**, Guillo **Pérez**, Eligio Pichardo, Ada Balcácer and Domingo Liz belong to this generation. The artists emerging in the 1960s took Dominican art in a different direction; Ramón **Oviedo**, Iván **Tovar**, Cándido **Bidó**, José Félix Moya, Alberto **Ulloa** and Soucy de **Pellerano** turned to new forms, from figurative expressionism to chromatic drama, embracing surrealism and sometimes developing social and political themes.

Dominican music is strongly influenced by Africa. The **merengue**, which Trujillo used for propaganda purposes, has become the national music. Johnny **Ventura**, Wilfrido **Vargas** and Juan Luis **Guerra** are among the artists and composers who have made this musical form known across the world. The traditional instruments used in merengue are the guira (scratch gourd), the tambora (drum) and the button accordion of German origin (see **accordion and bandoneón**). The Dominican tradition embraces other less well known rhythms too, like the **bachata**, the mangulina, the carabiné and the 'palos' or 'atabales', hollow sticks played in religious festivals. Traditional groups like **Grupo Convite** have researched and interpreted the national folk traditions.

Dominican culture is a melting pot, fusing different aspects of African, Spanish, indigenous, Oriental and Arab cultures. The Dominican population consists of 73 per cent mulattoes, 16 per cent white and 11 per cent black. The official language is Spanish, with strongly Andalusian features reinforced by a substratum derived from African languages. **Catholicism** is the majority religion, though others, like evangelical **Protestantism**, are also practised; in some parts of the country a form of **Vodun** is also practised. The basic diet is rice, beans, beef, bananas and root vegetables like potatoes and sweet potatoes. One typical dish is *sancocho*, a soup of meat and root vegetables; indeed, *sancocho* probably serves as the most appropriate representation of Dominican culture itself.

Further reading

Alcántara Almánzar, J. (1990) *Los escritores dominicanos y la cultura*, Santo Domingo: Amigo del Hogar.

Cassá, R. (1985) *Historia social y económica de la*

República Dominicana, vols 1 and 2, Santo Domingo: Ed. Alfa y Omega.

Ferguson, J. (1992) *Dominican Republic: Beyond the Lighthouse*, London: Russell Press.

Luzón Benedicto, J. (1988) *República Dominicana*, Madrid: Ediciones Anaya.

Miller, J. (1983) *Historia de la pintura dominicana*, Santo Domingo: Amigo del Hogar.

FERNANDO VALERIO-HOLGUÍN

Don Francisco

b. 1940, Talca, Chile

TV show host

Born Mario Kreutzberger, he was barely out of university when in 1962 he began to work in television in the studios of the station of the Universidad Católica in Santiago de Chile and created a new programme, *Sábado gigante* (Giant Saturday). A *show de auditorium*, or variety show, taped in front of a live audience, the programme incorporates contests, comedic skits, musical performances, interviews and even mini-documentary segments. In 1986 Don Francisco moved the show to the USA, where it is distributed to all Spanish-speaking counties. Each Saturday the programme is watched by more than 100 million viewers in more than thirty countries; this has made Don Francisco a much loved figure throughout the continent. His fundraising efforts via telethons earned him the title of Unicef Ambassador to the Americas.

ANA M. LÓPEZ

Doña Bárbara

Doña Bárbara is Rómulo **Gallegos**'s best-known and most emblematic novel, published in Spain in 1929 for fear of government censorship, and for years regarded as a comprehensive image of a rural Venezuela facing modernization. The novel's principal figure was regarded by Venezuela's 'civilizers' as the fascinating and fearsome symbol of a savage and hostile region, which rejected the benefits of progress – the dark interior clinging to its old barbaric habits. The book became, and remains, a canonical text. The film adaptation, directed by Mexican Fernando de **Fuentes** with María **Félix** in the title role, added little to the novel but did project Félix into the limelight.

VERONICA JAFFÉ

Dona Flor e seus dois maridos

Adapted from a novel by Jorge **Amado**, *Dona Flor e seus dois maridos* (Dona Flor and her Two Husbands) (1976) is a highly successful film directed by Bruno **Barreto**, which combined good production values, a classic story, the sex appeal of Sonia **Braga** (already a star for her role in the *telenovela* (see *telenovelas*) **Gabriela** (1975)), a brilliant soundtrack by Chico **Buarque** and a story with popular appeal, full of national cultural elements like sensuality and food. The most successful Brazilian film in history, it was an outstanding example of a new Brazilian cinema which set out to attract a wide public and win a place in foreign markets.

ISMAIL XAVIER AND THE USP GROUP

Doña Herlinda y su hijo

Made in 1984 by Jaime Humberto **Hermosillo**, *Doña Herlinda y su hijo* (Doña Herlinda and Her Son) was one of the first Latin American films to take a sympathetic look at a homosexual relationship, and one of the first gay films to place the relationship in a positive family setting. The relationship between a doctor, Rodolfo, and his musician boyfriend, Ramón, is watched over anxiously by Rodolfo's mother, Doña Herlinda. Once she has found the solution to the anomaly or problem of her son's sexuality by getting him to marry Olga and father a child, she then happily has additions made to her house so that Rodolfo, Ramón, Olga and the baby will all be under one – her own – roof. The film is based on a short story by Jorge López Páez, who was involved in writing the screenplay; the actors are largely unknown.

At the same time that Hermosillo tells of the complex extended family, he relentlessly links their story with that of Mexico, filling the screen with colourful images of Mexican food (see **food and drink**) and **crafts**, and the soundtrack with old chestnuts of Mexican music, including an on-screen performance by Lucha Villa. The film implicitly argues that these unorthodox arrangements can be incorporated into the larger Mexican (national) family, just as the **PRI** has adopted a strategy of cooptation and accommodation for a half century. At the same time, the director's own comments in an interview with Robin Wood suggest that he sees Doña Herlinda as the perfect dictator, the very words that Mario **Vargas Llosa** used (famously – and controversially – at a conference organized by Octavio **Paz**) to describe Mexico under the PRI.

The positive, indeed almost treacly, presentation of Ramón and Rodolfo's relationship leaves some important questions unanswered. Is Rodolfo bisexual, and what does he really want apart from to keep his mother happy? How much does she know consciously? Is Olga lesbian, or at least bisexual? The 1873 poem that Rodolfo recites in the closing scene, 'Nocturno' (Nocturne) by the Mexican romantic poet Manuel Acuña, ends with the idyllic portrayal of the two lovers always united, always satisfied, 'y en medio de nosotros, mi madre como un dios!' (and between us, my mother like a god!). An ironic reading of the mother's intrusion in Rodolfo's life is inevitable, and yet Hermosillo also presents this ending as the best possible one, certainly preferable to Rodolfo's breaking with his mother and being expelled from the house.

Further reading

Balderston, D. (1997) 'Excluded Middle? Bisexuality in Doña Herlinda y su hijo', in D. Balderston and D.J. Guy (eds) *Sex and Sexuality in Latin America*, New York: New York University Press, pp.190–9.

Jacobowitz, F., Lippe, R. and Wood, R. (1993) 'An Interview with Jaime Humberto Hermosillo: The Necessity of Telling a Story', *Cineaction* 31: 33–43.

DANIEL BALDERSTON

Donga, Ernesto Joaquim Maria Dos Santos

b. 1889, Rio de Janeiro, Brazil; d. 1974, Rio de Janeiro

Musician

Donga learnt to play the *cavaquinho* and guitar when still a child. He became one of the *batutas* or master-musicians and founders of modern **samba** who met at the famous home of Tia Ciata. In 1916 he registered, under his own name, the group composition 'Pelo Telefone' (On the Phone), the first official 'samba'. He then began a long association with **Pixinguinha**, his touring ensemble Oito Batutas and the studio bands Guarda Velha and Diabos do Céu. In 1940 Donga and some of his compositions were included in a series of recordings for the US market under the direction of Leopold Stokowski.

DAVID TREECE

Donn, Jorge

b. 1947, Buenos Aires, Argentina; d. 1992, Lausanne, Switzerland

Ballet dancer

Donn was renowned for his work with the choreographer Maurice Béjart, for whom he created roles of great intensity. His youthful portrayal of Romeo, a role he began to dance in 1966, was followed by starring roles in Béjart's *Messe pour le temps présent* (Mass For The Present Time) (1967) and *Le Voyage* (The Voyage) (1968). Other famous roles included a recreation of a famous earlier dancer, *Nijinsky, Clown de Dieu* (Nijinsky, Clown of God) (1971) and roles in Béjart's versions of several Stravinsky ballets. He appeared in several ballet films including *Le Danseur* (The Dancer) (1968). In 1963 he returned triumphantly to Buenos Aires (where he had studied at the **Teatro Colón**'s ballet school from 1952 to 1962) with Béjart's Ballet du XXe Siècle, and he appeared with the New York City Ballet in

1977; the important moments of his career took place, however, in Europe.

DANIEL BALDERSTON

Donoso, José

b. 1924, Santiago, Chile; d. 1996, Santiago

Writer

One of Latin America's most important novelists and a key figure in the emergence of a 'new' Latin American novel that moves beyond realism. Born into an upper-middle class family, Donoso from childhood rejected the rituals and aspirations of the Chilean bourgeoisie. In 1943 he dropped out of school, and two years later, unable to hold a job for more than a few months, he travelled to Magallanes, the southern tip of Chile, and then through Patagonia to Buenos Aires working as a shiphand and a dockhand. In 1947 he returned to Chile, finished high school and studied English at university. Two years later he received a scholarship to study at Princeton University under Allen Tate. This was when Donoso developed his fascination with the works of Henry James. His first short stories, 'The Poisoned Pastries' and 'The Blue Woman', were published in *MMS*, a Princeton literary review.

At first sight, *Coronación* (Coronation) (1965) offers a traditional realistic depiction of urban society and an existentialist hero in Andrés Abalos. Yet, the novel's final scene is the threshold of his future fiction. The grotesque figure of the old and feeble Elisa Abalos, dressed in rags as a queen by her old drunken maids, creates the atmosphere of a bizarre carnival which transgresses the realist mode.

In Donoso's subsequent novels, all centres of power enter into conflict and are displaced by the margins. Thus, in *El **lugar sin límites*** (Hell Has No Limits) (1972), the homosexual Manuela is the destabilizing axis, erasing the official borders delimiting the 'masculine' and the 'feminine'. Dressed as a woman, old Manuela's grotesque body sensually performs a Spanish dance and seduces his/her 'manly' audience in the whore-

house: a carnivalized version of the bourgeois family. Arturo **Ripstein** later brilliantly adapted it for the screen.

In his account of the Latin American **Boom**, Donoso describes how national regionalisms were left behind and became cosmopolitan under the influence of **Asturias**, **Bioy Casares**, **Borges** and particularly **Carpentier**, whose writings on the baroque suggested to him that the distorted and excessive considerably increased the possibilities of the novel.

In *El **obsceno pájaro de la noche*** (The Obscene Bird of Night) (1973), he elaborates the baroque through the opposition of order and chaos, through a proliferation of masks, multiple identities, and deforming mirror reflections and stories which annul the possibility of a centre or unity. Significantly, both houses in the work are unconventional spaces: the House of Spiritual Exercises is a maze of closed corridors and patios filled with the surplus possessions of wealthy families, not only objects but old women who were former servants; La Rinconada, on the other hand, has been converted into a monstrous asylum to protect and imprison Boy, a deformed child whose parents could also be any of the characters. Boy's body is described as chaos and disorder, as a different but worse form of death and, in his monstrosity, he is the other who threatens any power exerted upon society, artistic forms or language. Therefore, he must be silenced and suppressed like the female characters who represent waste, witchcraft and the irrational. Symbolically, Humberto's writing, attempting an orderly biography of Jerónimo, becomes a chaotic polyphony of displaced voices; the narrator as centre of consciousness and unity is reduced to zero, to a confined body wrapped up in burlap and consumed by fire.

Games in Donoso's novels are always a source of transgression. In *Este domingo* (This Sunday) (1967), children's games momentarily subvert bourgeois prescriptions; in *Casa de campo* (A House in the Country) (1978), they lead to torture and evil, to the removal of all fences and invasion by the natives and the primitive forces of nature. To some extent an allegory of dictatorial power in Chile, the novel also ironically dismantles the rules of fiction. Between order and insurrection, the narrator playfully tears away the veils of orderly configurations to show their deceitful nature.

In 1981, after seventeen years of voluntary exile, Donoso returned to Chile. His experiences abroad constitute an underlying motif in *La misteriosa desaparición de la marquesita de Loria* (The Mysterious Disappearance of the Little Marquise of Loria) (1980) whose Nicaraguan protagonist is viewed by Spaniards as a primitive symbol of Latin America. The Marquise, like the mysterious dog, is the indomitable force which surpasses even the transgressive quality of the erotic and can only be re-encased in rumour and legend. Exile in *El jardín de al lado* (The Garden Next Door) (1981) represents identity as a split self, both in terms of a national territory and a mythical lost paradise. *La desesperanza* (Curfew) (1988) shows the return to one's own land, now under military dictatorship. Swaying between the present and the past, the protagonist and Chile itself, in spite of the abuse of power, maintain a multiple reality submerged in dreams and magic within a landscape of natural wonders which remain impervious to the horrors of military rule.

Further reading

Adelstein, M. (1990) *Studies on the Works of José Donoso: An Anthology of Critical Essays*, Lewiston, NY: Edwin Mellen.

Cerda, C. (1988) *José Donoso: originales y metáforas*, Santiago: Planeta.

Donoso, J. (1977) *Personal History of the Boom*. New York: Columbia University Press.

Mandri, F. (1995) *José Donoso's House of Fiction: A Dramatic Construction of Time and Place*, Detroit: Wayne State University.

McMurray, G. (1979) *José Donoso*, Boston: Twayne.

Swanson, P. (1988) *José Donoso: The 'Boom' and Beyond*, Liverpool: Francis Cairns.

LUCÍA GUERRA

Donoso Pareja, Miguel

b. 1931, Guayaquil, Ecuador

Writer

A truly 'postmodern' writer who has broken new paths for Ecuadorean letters, Donoso Pareja's works masterfully address exile and the search for identity, the complexities of memory and forgetfulness, the essence of invention and the creative process, eroticism and the demystification of sexual norms. Donoso Pareja is also a cultural activist – director of writers' workshops, editor of magazines and classics, journalist and literary critic. His principal works include *Nunca más el mar* (Never Again the Sea) (1981), *Todo lo que inventamos es cierto* (Everything We Invent is True) (1990), *Ultima canción del exiliado* (The Exile's Latest Song) (1994), and *Hoy empiezo a acordarme* (Today I Begin to Remember) (1995).

HUMBERTO E. ROBLES

Dorfman, Ariel

b. 1942, Buenos Aires, Argentina

Writer and critic

Born in Buenos Aires and Chilean by choice, after the electoral triumph of Salvador **Allende** in 1970 Dorfman participated actively in the **Popular Unity** administration. The construction of a peaceful road to socialism in Chile marked his life in a definitive way. The *coup* by Augusto **Pinochet** forced him to leave the country and become an exile in France, Holland and eventually the USA where he works as a professor, literary critic and journalist.

Imaginación y violencia en América Latina (Imagination and Violence in Latin America) (1970), a volume of critical essays, was followed by the publication of ***Para leer el Pato Donald*** (How to Read Donald Duck: Imperialist Ideology in the Disney Comic) (1971), written with Arnold Mattelart, which was an important contribution to the intellectual debate on the mass media. In the context of the 1970s, the book was a challenge for those critics who felt that the importance of critical work is directly proportional to its object. In that sense, the work dismantled not only the axioms of the Disney industry but certain presumptions about high culture, and presented a project for the creation of a new national and popular culture.

His first novel, *Moros en la costa* (Hard Rain) (1973), stands in the tradition of the search for the new initiated by the vanguard of the 1920s and followed by the **Boom** of the Latin American novel. It is an attempt to deepen the debates about the possibility of a revolutionary literature and in that sense is reminiscent of *Rayuela* by Julio **Cortázar**. If *Moros en la costa* is the novel about the revolutionary process, *Viudas* (Widows) (1981) narrates the experience of a military *coup* and of exile. A year later, Dorfman published his third novel, *La última canción de Manuel Sendero* (The Last Song of Manuel Sendero) (1982). Two voices resonate in the novel, that of Manuel Sendero and that of his grandfather, voices that interweave to the point of becoming one single voice. Grandson and grandfather refuse to be born, given the political circumstances that await them. This work presents a radical departure in the novelistic style of Dorfman, as it presents a new way of understanding political commitment, calling into question ideas of representation, partisan ethics and even the notion of exile and homeland.

Máscaras (Masks) (1988) explores the subject of State violence, continuing and further exploring the trend begun in *La última canción de Manuel Sendero* and with sly humour delivers a work open to diverse readings and interpretations. His play, *La muerte y la doncella* (Death and the Maiden), has been successful in several languages, and was made into a film in 1995 with Ben Kingsley and Sigourney Weaver, directed by Roman Polanski. Subsequent works include the novel, *Konfidenz* (1995), and an autobiography, *Looking South, Heading North* (1998).

Further reading

Oropesa, S. (1992) *La obra de Ariel Dorfman*, Madrid: Pliegos.

Vidal, H. (1989) *Cultura nacional chilena, crítica literaria y derechos humanos*, Minneapolis: Ideology and Literature.

SANDRA GARABANO

dos Santos, Descoredes M. *see* Didi

doubles

Doubles are an Indo-Trinidadian savoury snack made of curried *channa* between two *bara*. The *channa*, or chickpeas, are soaked overnight, boiled in salt and curry powder, then fried in seasonings, before being used to fill the *bara*, circles of fluffy, fried dough made from ground split peas. Doubles are usually eaten with pepper sauce or mango chutney, applied 'slight' or 'heavy' by the roadside vendors from whose bicycle panniers they are sold. The best doubles vendors are known nationally; doubles are a favourite with partygoers on their way home at dawn, and a favoured vendor can be the centre of a hubbub of social activity.

LORRAINE LEU

Dragún, Osvaldo

b. 1929, Entre Ríos, Argentina

Playwright

Beginning with the **teatro independiente**, Dragún later co-founded the **Teatro Abierto**. In *La peste viene de Melos* (The Plague Comes from Melos) (1956), he sought the origins of a conflictive present in the past. The bulk of his work – ranging from *Historias para ser contadas* (Stories to be Read Aloud) (1956), to *¡Arriba corazón!* (Lift Up, My Heart) (1987) – explores individual alienation in everyday life. His theatre, realist in intent, employs a metaphorical discourse and a reflective estrangement.

STELLA MARTINI

Drayton, Geoffrey

b. 1924, Christchurch, Barbados

Writer

Drayton is the author of two novels. *Christopher* (1959), grounded in his Caribbean childhood, is the story of an imaginative child, a white son of the planter class of Barbados, whose father resents his dependence on his wife's money. The male adult world of the father, along with the resentment he extends to his son, taints the joys of childhood, especially the relationship between Christopher and his black nanny, Gip. *Zohara* (1961), is the story of a Spanish village where superstition and fear lead to the murder of the fourteen-year-old protagonist. Drayton has also written poetry. He has a degree in Economics from Cambridge University, England and lived for many years in England and Canada before retiring to live in Spain.

CAROL J. WALLACE

dreadlocks

Dreadlocks generally refers to the style of hair worn by adherents of the Rastafari religion (see **Rastafarianism**). This style originated in native cultures in Asia and Africa as a sign of spiritual election, renunciation of the world or ostracism from the community. Mau Mau warriors in the 1950s revived locked hair as a sign of their repudiation of the West and their commitment to victory against colonialism, as did Ethiopian freedom fighters resisting Mussolini in 1935. The Rastamen of the Pinnacle community in St Catherine, Jamaica, also adopted locked hair as a sign of their uncompromising stance against colonialism. Rastas believe locking the hair is ordained in the Bible in the Book of Numbers.

JUNE ROBERTS

D'Rivera, Paquito

b. 1948, Havana, Cuba

Musician

Jazz saxophonist and clarinettist D'Rivera has incorporated a wide range of Latin American rhythms into his jazz playing. In 1963 he led the Orquesta Cubana de Música Moderna and was a founder member of the group **Irakere**. In 1980 he left Cuba for New York, where he set up the Havana/New York Ensemble, the testing ground for a number of musicians. In 1989 he brought together several generations of Cuban musicians for the album, *40 Years of Cuban Jam Session* (1993). Since moving to New York, he has recorded with

Astor **Piazzola**, Tito **Puente**, Dizzy Gillespie and others. Oustanding among his albums are *Blowin'* (1981), *Manhattan Burn* (1986) and *Portraits of Cuba* (1996), which won a Grammy award. In 1998 he published his memoirs – *Mi vida saxual*.

WILFREDO CANCIO ISLA

drug traffic   *see*   drugs in Latin America

drugs in Latin America

The 1980s and 1990s witnessed an extraordinary boom in the drug trade generally, and in the international traffic in cocaine particularly. Regarded as almost certainly the world's most heavily traded commodity after oil, its use proliferated dramatically through the developed areas of the world, particularly in the USA, in the last two decades of the twentieth century. Its production and commerce produced a generation of hugely wealthy people who did not, by and large, come from any traditionally powerful elites; yet they, in their turn, acquired power not only in the economic arena but also in politics. Throughout the 1990s in Colombia, for example, cocaine money financed political campaigns, arranged for the disappearance of opponents, bought judges and generals or arranged irrefusable contracts for any public official who resisted their blandishments. Northern Mexico was in some ways transformed by the cross-border drug traffic, and there seems very little doubt that leading figures in Mexican political life have been, and continue to be, financed by its profits. Luis Donaldo Colosio, Mexican presidential candidate in 1994, and several other prominent officials were murdered by drug interests, while the scale of corruption can only be imagined. Central America, which until the 1980s lay outside the usual drug-smuggling routes, was becoming a point of exchange and redistribution, by the end of that decade, for cocaine exported from the south. Post-Sandinista Nicaragua (see **Sandinista Revolution**), like its neighbour Honduras, had the rising profile of cocaine commerce as the sole legacy of the decade-long USA-backed contra war (see **contras**) waged against the Nicaraguan revolution out of Honduran territory. In Surinam, the looming presence of the corrupt ex-dictator Desi **Bouterse** persists because he too has become an agent for myriad cocaine smuggling interests in the region. The US trial of Panamanian strongman **Noriega** was preceded by direct US intervention in December 1990 that left thousands dead and injured, and tens of thousands homeless – although just a few years earlier his involvement in drug smuggling was known but ignored.

At the other end of the distribution chain, until the end of the century coca was largely grown on small plots by peasant farmers, for whom the income from coca growing – itself not illegal in the countries of the Andean region for example – was more reliable and a slight improvement on other agricultural exports. Their product would be bought by middlemen who would take the semi-processed leaf (transformed into a paste by combining with kerosene) to one of the innumerable processing laboratories in the Amazon region or the Colombia–Ecuador border. Thence the drug would be transported by air or sea, sometimes hidden in human carriers, to the centres of consumption. The apparently unstoppable trade was greatly assisted by the drug cartels' ability to purchase any and every form of equipment, from planes to submarines, and from the enormously complex web of corruption, collusion and self-interest that enabled the cartels, while warring amongst themselves, to buy co-operation at every level.

The reaction of the USA, particularly in the 1990s, was to launch a War against Drugs that took US military personnel into Latin America directly, or gave them licence to train local military forces in anti-drug operations. And yet the worldwide commerce increased exponentially, and only rarely was the weight of repression directed against anyone other than the first-level peasant growers. The eventual murder of Pablo **Escobar**, leader of the Medellín Cartel and a man of extraordinary power, came only after years of collusion with governments, and the construction of a private army almost as well-armed as the national armed forces – as Gabriel **García Márquez** records in his *Noticia de un secuestro* (News of a Kidnapping) (1996). Escobar and his cartel were rapidly

replaced by the rival Cali cartel, whose leader **Rodríguez Orejuela** lacked nothing in ruthlessness and manipulative power.

The continuing cultivation of coca was clearly an economic decision made by small farmers with little alternative, or, in the case of Bolivia, by unemployed miners from an altiplano that could offer no employment opportunities, in receipt of a government land grant. Yet the War against Drugs envisaged no economic approaches to the problem, only a militarization of the entire region, which reinforced the power of the military in each country. The result of this, for example, was the virtual militarization of the Colombian State by the late 1990s and the sinister (but as yet unrealized) threat of direct US military intervention there. And at the point of consumption, particularly the cities of the USA, the economic strategies that might transform the alienated lives of inner-city youth were discussed at the token level only, and there too ever more aggressive policing became the only consistent response.

The trade in cocaine was worth $20 billion by the late 1980s, with some 80 per cent of it controlled from Colombia. Because cocaine is illegal, it could not be controlled by the multinational corporations who have established global control in the case of all other commodities – the global organization of the cocaine trade, therefore, is conducted by a massive and equally multinational criminal apparatus. While the profits from the trade declined somewhat in the early 1990s, mainly as a result of internal rivalries, the value of the trade began to rise again by the end of the decade, and there seemed some evidence to suggest that cocaine was beginning to undergo the rationalization and reorganization – production combined into larger base units who would also process the drug before delivering it to the distribution machine – that had characterized the history of all previous commodities. And like them, the accumulated income from the trade would not find its way to the economies from which it came, but into the vast financial laundering machine that took those profits and invested them in the economies of Europe and the USA.

The moral issues are easily fogged. No moral opprobrium can fall on the small producers, who benefit only marginally and who are in no way responsible for creating the consumer need; and the shock and outrage quite rightly expressed at the impact of cocaine – its connection with a culture of violence; its reinforcement of cultural and social estrangement, particularly among youth; its corruption of all those embroiled in its immense income-generating potential – have produced little except more sophisticated forms of policing at one end, and some limited, token mechanisms of care at the other.

Further reading

Clawson, P. *et al.* (1998) *The Andean Cocaine Industry,* Basingstoke: Macmillan.

Cockburn, A. and St Clair, J. (eds) (1998) *Whiteout: The CIA, Drugs and the Press,* London: Verso.

Leons, M.N. and Sanabria, H. (1997) *Coca, Cocaine and the Bolivian Reality,* New York: State University of New York.

Webb, G. and Waters, M. (1998) *Dark Alliance: The CIA, the Contras, and the Crack Cocaine Explosion,* New York: Seven Stories Press.

MIKE GONZALEZ

Drummond de Andrade, Carlos

b. 1902, Itabira do Mato Dentro, Minas Gerais, Brazil; d. 1987, Rio de Janeiro, Brazil

Poet and journalist

Born in a small agricultural and iron-mining town some 300 miles inland from Rio de Janeiro, Drummond was the youngest son of a landowning family. After a surprise expulsion from a Jesuit boarding school when seventeen ('I lost the faith: I lost time'), he moved with his family to Belo Horizonte, capital of Minas Gerais. There, he became the unofficial leader of the group of poets who adhered to the modernist movement (see **Brazilian modernism**) led by Mário de **Andrade** and others from São Paulo. In 1930 he published his first collection, *Alguma poesia* (Some Poetry). The poems are short and prosaic, with an offhand humor. Some of them have achieved considerable fame (or notoriety), including 'In the

middle of the road', in which this phrase, with the addition of 'there was a stone' is repeated some six times, making up almost the whole poem. As Drummond said, for years this poem served to divide Brazilians into two categories (roughly, those who had some notion of what modern life was about and those who did not). He is regarded as the greatest Brazilian poet of the century, and he continued to produce good poetry until almost the moment of his death. The variety of his work gives something for everybody. Underlying it, there is an honesty and ability to question his own motives ('Set fire to everything, including myself') which brings him level with his reader in experience, if not in finding the words to express it.

He married in 1925, and had one daughter. In 1934 he moved to Rio as secretary to the Minister of Education in the **Vargas** government, Gustavo Capanema. Drummond kept this job until 1944, in spite of the dictatorial nature of the regime: this was more a matter of personal loyalty to Capanema than of political conviction. His poetry, especially the three collections published in the 1940s, *Sentimento do mundo* (The Feeling of the World) (1940), *José* and *A rosa do povo* (The People's Rose) (1945) shows that he was moving left during this period, and in 1945 he all but joined the Communist Party. There is, however, little that is directly political about his poetry, which is concerned above all with the place of the alienated individual in mass urban society ('I have only two hands/and the feeling of the world'). Within this alienation, the poet has the duty to bring new life to words and so allow people to communicate, with themselves, with each other and with society at large. This central period ends on a high note of optimism, with the long, six-page 'Song to the man of the people Charlie Chaplin'. Chaplin as a silent film-maker emerges from the blackness of the cinema to make us laugh and vicariously kick the backsides of the rich and powerful. Yet at the end, he can also give a verbal message for the whole of humanity (as Chaplin had done in *The Great Dictator*), which transcends political rhetoric.

This moment did not last. In the collections of the 1950s, beginning with *Claro enigma* (Clear Enigma) (1951), there is a new sense of disgust and disenchantment with the public world, and a turn to formalism and traditional 'poetic' topics:

love, or nostalgia for his provincial past, for instance. Much of this reaction is more apparent than real. Just as the poet of *A rosa do povo* was rarely if ever a truly political animal, the 'older and wiser' man remains surprisingly subversive. His sonnets are not quite conventional in form, and his love poetry is about a doting fifty-year old poet who has fallen for a much younger woman: the facts of the case, which are plain enough in the poetry, became public after his death. These poems, some of them long (a page or two) and very ingenious in the formal sense, are among many readers' favourites: in them, the shapes and patterns we make of our lives seem to appear and disappear, in the poetry as in life.

His imaginary return to Itabira is not new in this poetry either. His identification with his home town, though it makes him one of the generation who lived in urban 'exile' from the countryside, defined by Roberto **Schwarz** as 'farmers of the air' (*fazendeiros do ar*) has a larger context, for Itabira has since the 1940s become the centre of a huge open-pit iron mine. From the 1942 'Viagem na família' (Travelling in the Family), he maintained a dialogue with his extended family, beginning with his father (who had died in 1931) but prolonged into a more distant past also. In every collection he returned to this theme, and finally in the 1968 *Boitempo* (Oxtime) dedicated a whole book to recalling life in Itabira early in the century.

Drummond's influence is hard to estimate, but it is huge. Along with Manuel **Bandeira**, he did more than anyone to bring erudite poetry close to everyday life and speech. He is very widely read, and posthumous collections, including some erotic verse, have sold very well. But he is difficult to imitate, because of his simplicity and technical skill. A civil servant for most of his life, he was also a prolific and popular journalist, mostly of the weekly columns known as *crônicas* (see **crónica**), published in the *Correio da Manhã* and the *Jornal do Brasil*.

Further reading

Drummond de Andrade, C. (1985) *Nova reunião*, Rio de Janeiro: Aguilar.
—— (1986) *Traveling in the Family: Selected Poems*, ed. T. Colchie and M. Strand, New York: Random House.
—— (1994) 'Song to the man of the people Charlie Chaplin', trans. D. Treece in *Modern Poetry in Translation* 6: 43–9.
Gledson, J. (1981) *Poesia e poética de Carlos Drummond de Andrade*, São Paulo: Duas Cidades.
Gonzalez, M. and Treece, D. (1992) *The Gathering of Voices*, London: Verso.
Sternberg, R. (1986) *The Unquiet Self: Self and Society in the Poetry of Carlos Drummond de Andrade*, Valencia: Albatros.

JOHN GLEDSON

Duarte, Anselmo

b. 1920, Salto, Brazil

Actor and film-maker

One of Brazilian cinema's most prolific actors, Duarte won popularity with roles in **chanchada**s like Watson Macedo's *Carnaval do fogo* (Carnival of Fire) (1949) and eventually became Brazil's favourite leading man. He directed his first film in 1957, and in 1962 produced and directed *O **pagador de promessas*** (The Given Word), a religious and social drama set in the northeast and based on a work by Dias **Gomes**. He played his most daring dramatic role in Luiz Sérgio **Person**'s *O Caso dos irmãos Naves* (The Case of the Naves Brothers) (1967). He continued to work in films, never migrating to **television**.

ISMAIL XAVIER AND THE USP GROUP

dub poetry

Dub is a performance poetry, rhythmically aligned with **reggae** or **ska** bass beats. Its language is the language of the Jamaican street; its content the experience of the most oppressed members of that society – but it is also their cry of protest. In the Caribbean the dub poets are 'orators as well as poets' – like Louise **Bennett**, in an earlier generation, and later Jamaican poets like **Mutabaruka** (recorded on *Any Which Way Freedom* (1989), for example), or Mikey **Smith**, who was murdered at twenty-nine but who had already established a reputation with his album, *Mi Cyaan*

Believe it (1982) or Grenada's Paul **Keens-Douglas**. Dub was brought to Britain and adapted to the Caribbean diaspora by poets like Linton Kwesi Johnson, Benjamin Zephaniah and Pepsi Poet.

MIKE GONZALEZ

Duclos, Arturo

b. 1959, Santiago, Chile

Painter

Duclos is often considered to be one of the most representative artists of the post-dictatorship period in Chile. His distinctive use of deadpan images, painted in an almost commercial style, shows considerable humour and irony. Duclos makes particular use of political and religious symbolism, often in unexpected juxtapositions. In the 1990s, Duclos's work was often discussed in terms of **postmodernism**.

GABRIEL PEREZ-BARREIRO

Duhart, Emilio

b. 1917, Temuco, Chile

Architect

Duhart was an early advocate of breaking away from nineteenth-century formal decorative styles. Trained at Harvard with Bauhaus founder Walter Gropius (see **Bauahus architecture**), he rejected Chile's Hispanic tradition of continuous facades. In the 1950s Duhart designed steel, concrete and glass towers incorporating commercial arcades at street level and light, airy apartments above. His later designs, including the CEPAL building and the **Santiago Airport, International Terminal**, expressed the formal principles of modern architecture, but they also demonstrated a new concern for Chile's rugged geography.

CELIA LANGDEAU CUSSEN

Duncan, Quince

b. 1940, Limón, Costa Rica

Writer

Duncan was born and raised in Limón, a province with a large Afro-Caribbean population. Deeply conscious of these African roots and of his own Jamaican descent, in his short stories and anthologies Duncan explores the problems of black people both within the hostile Latin society of Costa Rica and throughout the whole of the African diaspora. In addition to his treatment of the racial and linguistic marginalization of Costa Rican blacks, Duncan's strong interest in the **syncretism** of West African and European Protestant religious traditions is of particular note.

SCOTT COOPER

Duprat, Rogério

b. 1932, Rio de Janeiro, Brazil

Arranger and composer

During the formative period of contemporary **MPB** in the 1960s, Rogério Duprat was arguably the most important link between popular and erudite music in Brazil. Throughout his career, he composed soundtracks for theatre, film, and television, and wrote many arrangements for pop artists. In the early 1960s, he participated in the **Música Nova** movement of São Paulo, which promoted trends in the international **avant-garde** and critiqued musical nationalism. Later in the decade he arranged key songs of the *tropicalista* movement (see **Tropicália**) which are among the most innovative and successful fusions of the popular and the erudite in Brazilian music.

CHRISTOPHER DUNN

Duque, Adolfo Domingo

b. 1890, Havana, Cuba; d. 1957, Havana

Baseball player

One of the greatest players of all time, Duque was

the first Latin American to pitch in the US Major Leagues, and the first to take part in a World Series. He began playing in 1912 and for twenty-three years played in the Cuban leagues, mainly for the Almendares and Habana clubs. In Cuba, his record of ninety-three victories and sixty-two defeats as a pitcher was outstanding. During his career in the Majors (1914–35), he played for Cincinnati, Boston, Brooklyn and New York, scoring 194 victories and 179 defeats in 550 games. He became legendary during the 1923 season with a record almost unrivalled in the Majors – twenty-seven victories and eight defeats, an average of 1.93. His mythic status was underlined by his explosive temperament and his longevity – he played his last game at age fifty-five. Manager of the Cuban and Mexican teams he was inducted into the Cuban Baseball Hall of Fame in 1958 and the Mexican in 1985.

WILFREDO CANCIO ISLA

Duque Naranjo, Lisandro

b. 1943, Sevilla Valle, Colombia

Film-maker and critic

Duque was part of the prolific and controversial school of the *ley de* **sobreprecio**, making his first irreverent documentary short, *Favor correrse atrás* (Please Move Back), in 1974. His first feature *El escarabajo* (The Beetle) (1982) was awarded best picture, director and screenplay at the Bogotá Film Festival of that year. His greatest films are perhaps *Visa USA* (1986) and *Milagro en Roma* (Miracle in Rome) (1988), the latter based on a **García Márquez** story. Duque's anthropological background and nostalgia for the details and colours of his provincial upbringing give him a particular eye for the quotidian in both his **documentary** and fiction films.

DOLORES TIERNEY

Durán, Ciro

b. 1937, Convención (Santander del Norte), Colombia

Film-maker

Durán garnered international awards for his hard-hitting documentary *Gamín* (1978), about Bogotá **street children** living in gangs, surviving by begging, robbery and prostitution. His wife Joyce **Ventura** produces his films, and their son Alexis leads a second generation of film-makers. Duran's third feature, *La nave de los sueños* (The Ship of Dreams) (1996), tells of stowaways on a ship bound for New York who dream of a better life in the USA and, like much contemporary Latin American film-making, was an international co-production (see **co-productions**).

ILENE S. GOLDMAN

Durán, Jorge

b. 1942, Santiago, Chile

Screenwriter and director

Like many others, Durán fled Chile after the 1973 military *coup*. In Brazil he became a well-known scriptwriter, including among his credits *Lucio Flavio* (Héctor **Babenco**, 1978); *Gaijin* (Tizuka **Yamasaki**, 1979); *Pixote a lei do mais fraco* (Hector Babenco, 1981) and *Como Nascem os Anjos* (How Angels are Born) (Murilo **Salles**, 1996) which, like *Pixote*, deals with *favela* children. *A Cor do seu destino* (Colour of Destiny) (1988), Durán's only film as a director, depicts a Chilean adolescent coming to terms with his exile in Brazil through art work. Recently he has returned to work in Chile and scripted *Mi último hombre* (My Last Man) (Tatiana Gaviola, 1996).

DOLORES TIERNEY

Durán, Roberto

b. 1951, Guarare, Panama

Boxer

Known as 'Manos de Piedra' (Stone Hands), Durán held the world championship at lightweight (1972–79), welterweight (1980), junior middleweight (1983) and middleweight (1989–90). During his early years his success was spectacular: his record was 71 wins and 2 losses between 1967 and 1980. Continuing an extremely long career for a boxer, he won his 100th bout on 15 June 1997; his final record was 100 wins and 13 losses. Moving upwards through weight classes, he won the welterweight crown from Sugar Ray Leonard, who later regained it. Several of his losses were to excellent fighters, such as Leonard, Marvin Hagler (1983) and Héctor Camacho (1996).

RICHARD V. MCGEHEE

Durant, Alberto

b. 1951, Lima, Peru

Film director

A graduate in economics, 'Chicho' Durant studied film in Britain and then returned to Peru to make a number of shorts. His productions are relatively few. In 1982 he made his first full-length feature, *Ojos de perro* (Dog's Eyes), which narrated the experience of forming a trade union on a Peruvian **hacienda** in the 1920s. Subsequently he made *Malabrigo*, a thriller following a woman's search for her missing husband. His third full length film, *Alias la Gringa*, recreated the life of a famous criminal and is the most aesthetically successful of all his films.

CÉSAR SALAS

Dussel, Enrique

b. 1934, La Paz, Mendoza, Argentina

Philosopher, theologian and historian

A founder of the Latin American **philosophy** of liberation school (*filosofía de la liberación*) which arose in Argentina in the 1970s, Dussel was an active participant in the **liberation theology** movement. He represents one current within the philosophy of liberation school. His question 'is it possible to philosophize authentically in a dependent and dominated culture?' places him among the 'ontologicists' (following **Cerutti**) for whom the starting point of philosophy is the 'ontological dependence' of Latin America. Dussel has developed a philosophical method he called *anadialectical*: a method that goes beyond (*ana-*) and not merely through (*dia-*) the 'totality' – a central term in Dussel's philosophy. Against the dominant Totality, he sets alterity or the Other, which is the Latin American 'people', the poor, the oppressed.

In his ethics, Dussel created three sets of relationships, which are also concretizations of the dominant–dominated relationship: male–female (the erotic realm), parent–child or teacher–student (the pedagogical) and brother–brother or nation–nation (the political). For example, the conquest of America was not only a political, economic and cultural enterprise, but also erotic: the *mestizaje* of the American peoples is the result of the violence of the European conquistador. The dominant Totality does not acknowledge the existence of the Other in his or her alterity or difference. Ethics and philosophy are inseparable for Dussel: 'To affirm the Other and serve him is the good act, and to dominate him is the evil act'. This is the absolute criterion for metaphysics and ethics.

Dussel has been criticized for representing an antihistoricist populist idealism, since he presupposes the existence of some essential 'Latin American rationality'. Feminists have criticized him for essentialism and dualism, which in the specific case of male–female relationship may easily lead to authoritarian and conservative views, especially on issues of sexual ethics. Among male liberation theologians, Dussel is one of the few to have written on women and feminism. He has also rewritten the history of the Church in Latin America, emphasizing the roots of liberation theology in the work of Las Casas and others. A political refugee in Mexico since 1975, Dussel became Professor of Ethics at Mexico's National University (**UNAM**) in 1976.

Further reading:

Cerutti, G.H. (1983) *Filosofía de la liberación latinoamericana*, México City: Fondo de Cultura Económica.

Dussel, E. (1981) *A History of the Church in Latin America: Colonialism to Liberation, 1492–1979*, Grand Rapids, MI: Eerdmans.

—— (1985) *Philosophy of Liberation*, New York: Orbis Books.

—— (1988) *Ethics and Community*, New York: Orbis Books.

—— (1995) *The Invention of the Americas. Eclipse of 'the Other' and the Myth of Modernity*, New York: Continuum.

ELINA VUOLA

Dutch-based creoles

Creole languages that have a predominantly Dutch-derived lexicon have only been documented in three territories of the Caribbean. Of these, only two, Berbice and Essequibo in what is now Guyana, are known to have developed in territories which were former Dutch colonies. The third creole is Negerhollands of the former Danish islands of St Thomas and St John, which are now part of the US Virgin Islands.

These three creoles are of considerable significance. Negerhollands is the first creole with a published grammar (1770), and it also boasts a translation of the New Testament. There is some evidence that there were two socially determined dialects of this language, one used primarily by the Europeans and the other by the Africans. This creole is now extinct, but there is a considerable amount of written data available for further research. Ironically, the territories in which it was formed were Danish and not Dutch, but the Dutch were the European majority population and the primary European source for lexical items.

Berbice and Skepi Dutch remain the only instances in which fully developed creole languages with a Dutch-based lexicon are known to have developed in Dutch colonies. Berbice and Essequibo were separate Dutch colonies in what is now Guyana. Essequibo (Skepi) Dutch developed in the westernmost colony, and its basic lexicon suggests a close relationship with Negerhollands. There is considerable evidence that it was the language of the majority of the population up to the end of the last century; it was used for preaching in church in the nineteenth century, a wordlist was prepared in 1792 and possibly a dictionary some fifty or sixty years later, though neither has survived. Surviving evidence of this creole is very fragmentary and there are no current speakers.

Berbice Dutch developed in the easternmost Dutch colony of Guyana. The earliest evidence of this language is a 1792 wordlist, but Berbice Dutch is moribund; indeed it may be considered dead, since it has fewer than ten remaining fluent speakers. Both these creoles were discovered in the 1970s, when several speakers of the Berbice variety were still available to provide live data. There are now two full-length descriptions of this language and a considerable collection of data recorded on audio cassettes.

Nevertheless, it is Berbice Dutch that is most significant because it is the only Caribbean creole language for which the substratum element may be clearly identified and its role analysed. It contains the highest percentage of West African lexical survivals in all the Caribbean, which strengthens the argument for tracing the genesis of **creole languages** through adult second language learning theory rather than through first language or even universal language acquisition theory.

Further reading

Holm, J.A. (1988) *Pidgins and Creoles*, 2 vols, Cambridge: Cambridge University Press.

Taylor, D.M. (1977) *Languages of the West Indies*, Baltimore: Johns Hopkins University Press.

Van Rossem, C. and van der Voorts, H. (eds) *Die Creol Taal: 250 years of Negerhollands*, Amsterdam: University of Amsterdam Press.

Wekker, H. (ed.) (1995) *Creole Languages and Language Acquisition*, Amsterdam: Mouton de Gruyter.

IAN ROBERTSON

Duvachelle, María Elena

b. 1942, Chile

Actress and director

A member of **ICTUS** from 1967 to 1973, Duvauchelle appeared in Jorge **Díaz**'s *Introducción al elefante y otras zoologías* (Introduction to the Elephant and other Zoological Phenomena) (1968) and *Cuestionemos la cuestión* (Let's Question the Question) (1969) by Nissim **Sharim** and ICTUS, as well as participating in the television programme *La manivela*. She emigrated to Venezuela (1974–84) where she won the Municipal Prize for Best Actress, the first foreigner to win it. Returning to Chile, she formed the Nuevo Grupo, and acted in and directed works such as Marco Antonio **de la Parra**'s *La secreta obscenidad de cada día* (The Secret Obscenity of Every Day) (1983).

CAROLA OYARZÚN

Duvalier, François ('Papa Doc')

b. 1907, Port-au-Prince, Haiti; d. 1971, Port-au-Prince

Politician

For over thirteen years the dictatorial ruler of Haiti, Duvalier was elected to the presidency in 1957. He soon established himself as a dictator, however, vigorously suppressing all political opposition. When first elected, Duvalier had in fact enjoyed considerable popular appeal, based on his claims of supporting workers and peasants, and the wide perception of him as a leader who embraced the culture of the black Haitian masses – an important issue in a country with a long tradition of both black and mulatto elites who favoured Western culture in general and French culture in particular. This popular appeal was strengthened by Duvalier's well known association with **Vodun**. Later, under his dictatorship, Duvalier manipulated his connections with Vodun, both implicitly and explicitly claiming supernatural support for his regime and using the threat of supernatural retribution against his opponents. He was re-elected in the corrupt election of 1961, and in

1964 declared himself '*président-à-vie*' – literally president-for-life – with power to appoint his own successor. Most notoriously, in 1958 Duvalier had established a police-like force loyal to him, popularly known as the '**tontons macoutes**'. This force led the way in the arrest, torture, murder and general persecution of anyone perceived as an opponent of the government. By design, their sinister public presence also intimidated most of the Haitian population from any thought of criticizing the Duvalier regime.

Born into a basically middle-class family – his father was a primary school teacher and his mother a bakery employee – Duvalier was educated at the respected Lycée Alexandre Pétion in Port-au-Prince where he was taught by several prominent Haitians, including ethnologist Jean **Price-Mars** and future president Dumarsais Estimé, before going on to medical school. Duvalier's years as a student coincided with the US occupation of the country (1915–34). During his medical school days he nurtured his interest in both the study and practice of Vodun, and studied other aspects of the history and culture of Haiti's black population, though he was not involved directly in nationalist politics. After qualifying as a doctor, Duvalier worked in various public health positions, becoming involved in politics during the 1940s, when he joined the MOP (Mouvement des Ouvriers et Paysans – Workers' and Peasants' Movement), an organization less united around a particular platform than around its leader, Daniel Fignolé.

When his former teacher Dumarsais Estimé became president in 1946, Duvalier was appointed Director of Public Health and eventually became Minister of Public Health and Labour in the Estimé cabinet. When Estimé was deposed in 1950, Duvalier returned to public health work with the Inter-American Co-operative Health Service. However, he was now a confirmed political actor and in the mid-1950s went into political hiding, under threat of persecution from the Magloire government that had overthrown Estimé, emerging in 1956 to announce his presidential candidacy.

In 1971 an ailing Duvalier appointed his son, Jean Claude **Duvalier**, to succeed him, and the younger Duvalier maintained another fifteen years of repressive rule before he was deposed in February 1986. The continuity of character between their two regimes was exemplified in the way that Jean-Claude inherited his father's popular nickname – he was called 'Baby Doc'. Although Haiti has a long history of political chaos and dictatorship, the Duvaliers stand out for their brutality and the length of their tenure.

ROSANNE ADDERLEY

Duvalier, Jean Claude ('Baby Doc')

b. 1952, Port-au-Prince, Haiti

Politician

Succeeding his father, François (Papa Doc) **Duva-** **lier** as dictator of Haiti in 1971, at the age of nineteen, Jean Claude (Baby Doc) Duvalier lived the life of a playboy. His rule vacillated between periods of relative 'liberalization' and periods of extreme repression. **Corruption** was rife: 70 million dollars of foreign aid were stolen or wasted on large infrastructural schemes, while US private investment in light industry was attracted by low wages. By 1985 Haitians, driven by poverty, purged the country of Duvalierism. Baby Doc went into exile in France, taking 900 million dollars of embezzled state funds with him.

MARY BOLEY

Bibliography

Ades, D. (ed.) (1989) *Art in Latin America*, New Haven, CT and London: Yale University Press.

Agosin, M. (ed.) (1995) *A Dream of Light & Shadow: portraits of Latin American women writers*, Albuquerque, NM: University of New Mexico Press.

Alexander, R.J. (1988) *Biographical dictionary of Latin American and Caribbean political leaders*, New York: Greenwood Press.

Arbena, J. (comp.) (1999) *Latin American Sport: an annotated bibliography, 1988–1998*, Westport, CT: Greenwood Press.

Arnold, A. J. (ed.) (1994-) *A History of Literature in the Caribbean*, Amsterdam and Philadelphia, PA: J. Benjamins.

Baddeley, O. and Fraser, V. (1989) *Drawing the Line: art and cultural identity in contemporary Latin America*, London and New York: Verso.

Beezley, W.H. and Curcio-Nagy, L.A. (2000) *Latin American Popular Culture*, Wilmington: Scholarly Resources.

Behague, G. (1979) *Music in Latin America. An Introduction*, Englewood Cliffs, NJ: Prentice-Hall.

Benson, E. and Conolly, L.W. (eds) (1994) *Encyclopedia of Post Colonial Literatures in English*, 2 vols, London and New York: Routledge.

Bethell, L. (1998) *A Cultural History of Latin America: literature, music, and the visual arts in the 19th and 20th centuries*, Cambridge and New York: Cambridge University Press.

—— (ed.) (1995–2000) *The Cambridge History of Latin America*, 11 vols, Cambridge: Cambridge University Press.

Blakemore, H., Collier, S. and Skidmore, T.E. (eds.) (1985) *The Cambridge Encyclopedia of Latin America and the Caribbean*, Cambridge: Cambridge University Press.

Burton, J. (1983) *The New Latin American Cinema: an annotated bibliography of sources in English, Spanish, and Portuguese, 1960–1980*, New York: Smyrna Press.

Castedo, L. (1969) *A History of Latin American Art and Architecture from Pre-Columbian Times to the Present*, New York: F.A. Praeger.

Cole, R.R., (ed.) (1996) *Communication in Latin America: journalism, mass media, and society*, Wilmington: Scholarly Resources.

Corke, B. (ed.) (1989) *Who is Who in Latin America: government, politics, banking and industry*, New York: Decade Media.

Ficher, M. (1996) *Latin American Classical Composers: a biographical dictionary*, Lanham, MD: Scarecrow Press.

Fox, E. (1997) *Latin American Broadcasting: from tango to telenovela*, Luton, Bedfordshire: John Libbey Media and University of Luton Press.

Franco, J. (1967) *The Modern Culture of Latin America. Society and the artist*, New York: F.A. Praeger.

Gonzalez, A. and Luis, W. (eds) (1994) *Modern Latin-American Fiction Writers. Second series*, Detroit, MI: Gale Research.

Gonzalez, M. and Treece, D. (1992) *The Gathering of Voices: the twentieth-century poetry of Latin America*, London and New York: Verso.

King, J. (1990) *Magical Reels: a history of cinema in Latin*, London and New York: Verso, in association with the Latin American Bureau.

Mainwaring, S. and Valenzuela, A. (1998) *Politics, Society, and Democracy. Latin America*, Boulder, CO: Westview Press.

Martin, G. (1989) *Journeys Through the Labyrinth: Latin American fiction in the twentieth century*, London and New York: Verso.

Martin, M.T. (1997) *New Latin American Cinema*, Detroit, MI: Wayne State University Press.

Molloy, M. (ed.) Internet Resources for Latin America, New Mexico State University Library. http://lib.nmsu.edu/subject/bord/laguia.

Navarro, M. and Sanchez Korrol, V. (1999) *Women in Latin America and the Caribbean: restoring women to history.* Bloomington, IN: Indiana University Press.

Olsen, D.A. and Sheehy, D.E. (eds) (1998) *The Garland Encyclopedia of World Music. Vol. 2: South America, Mexico, Central America and the Caribbean,* New York and London: Garland Publishing, Inc.

Osorio, N., (ed.) (1995) *Diccionario enciclopédico de las letras de América Latina,* 3 vols, Caracas: Monte Avila and Biblioteca Ayacucho.

Poupeye, V. (1998) *Caribbean Art,* London and New York: Thames & Hudson.

Roca, M.A. (ed.) (1995) *The Architecture of Latin America,* London: Academy Editions.

Rossi, E.E. (1992) *Latin America: a political dictionary,* Santa Barbara: ABC-CLIO.

Rubin, D. (ed.) (1995–2000) *The World Encyclopedia of Contemporary Theatre,* 6 vols, London and New York: Routledge.

Schechter, J.M. (ed.) (1999) *Music in Latin American Culture: regional traditions,* New York: Schirmer Books.

Scott, J.F. (1999) *Latin American Art: ancient to modern,* Gainesville, FL: University Press of Florida.

Smith, V. (ed.) (1997) *Encyclopedia of Latin American Literature,* London, Chicago, IL: Fitzroy Dearborn.

Standish, P. (ed.) (1995) *Hispanic Culture of South America,* Detroit, MI: Gale Research.

—— (ed.) (1996) *Hispanic Culture of Mexico, Central America, and the Caribbean,* Detroit, MI: Gale Research.

Sullivan, E. (ed.) (1996) *Latin American Art in the Twentieth Century,* London: Phaidon Press.

Tenenbaum, B.A. (ed.) (1996) *Encyclopedia of Latin American History and Culture,* 5 vols, New York: Charles Scribner's Sons; London: Simon & Schuster.

Versenyi, A. (1993) *Theatre in Latin America: religion, politics, and culture from Cortes to the 1980s,* Cambridge and New York: Cambridge University Press.

Williamson, E. (1992) *The Penguin History of Latin America,* London: Allen Lane.